hermeneia

Judith

A Commentary
on the Book of Judith

by Lawrence M. Wills

Edited by
Sidnie White Crawford

Fortress Press Minneapolis

Judith
A Commentary

Scripture quotations from the New Revised Standard
Version of the Bible are copyright © 1989 by the
Division of Christian Education of the National Council of the Churches of Christ in the U.S.A. and are
used by permission.

Cover and interior design by Kenneth Hiebert
Typesetting and page composition by
The HK Scriptorium

Print ISBN: 978-0-8006-6105-2

eISBN: : 978-1-5064-6382-7

The paper used in this publication meets the mini-
mum requirements of American National Standard
for Information Sciences—Permanence of Paper for
Printed Library Materials, ANSI Z329.48–1984.

Manufactured in the U.S.A.

Contents

Jubilees 1

Lawrence M. Wills is visiting professor of Judaic Studies and Religious Studies at Brown University. He graduated from Harvard University with a degree in social anthropology, and from Harvard Divinity School with an M.T.S. and a Th.D., both in New Testament and Hellenistic Judaism. He then taught at Harvard Divinity School, held the Ethelbert Talbot Chair in Biblical Studies at Episcopal Divinity School, and also taught at Wesleyan University. In 2019 he was the Croghan Bicentennial Visiting Professor at Williams College before returning to Brown University as visiting professor. His books include *The Jewish Novel in the Ancient World* (1995), which was named an Outstanding Academic Book of 1995 by *Choice* magazine for academic librarians, and also *The Quest of the Historical Gospel: Mark, John, and the Origins of the Gospel Genre* (1997); *Not God's People: Insiders and Outsiders in the Biblical World* (2008); and *The Jew in the Court of the Foreign King: Ancient Jewish Court Legends* (1990). He has also co-edited two books, *Conflicted Boundaries in Wisdom and Apocalypticism* (with Benjamin G. Wright, 2005), and *Jewish Annotated Apocrypha* (with Jonathan Klawans, forthcoming).

The name *Hermeneia*, Greek ἑρμενεία, has been chosen as the title of the commentary series to which this volume belongs. The word *Hermeneia* has a rich background in the history of biblical interpretation as a term used in the ancient Greek-speaking world for the detailed, systematic exposition of a scriptural work. It is hoped that the series, like its name, will carry forward this old and venerable tradition. A second, entirely practical reason for selecting the name lies in the desire to avoid a long descriptive title and its inevitable acronym, or worse, an unpronounceable abbreviation.

The series is designed to be a critical and historical commentary to the Bible without arbitrary limits in size or scope. It will utilize the full range of philological and historical tools, including textual criticism (often slighted in modern commentaries), the methods of the history of tradition (including genre and prosodic analysis), and the history of religion.

Hermeneia is designed for the serious student of the Bible. It will make full use of ancient Semitic and classical languages; at the same time, English translations of all comparative materials—Greek, Latin, Canaanite, or Akkadian—will be supplied alongside the citation of the source in its original language. Insofar as possible, the aim is to provide the student or scholar with full critical discussion of each problem of interpretation and with the primary data upon which the discussion is based.

Hermeneia is designed to be international and interconfessional in the selection of authors; its editorial boards were formed with this end in view. Occasionally the series will offer translations of distinguished commentaries which originally appeared in languages other than English. Published volumes of the series will be revised continually, and eventually, new commentaries will replace older works in order to preserve the currency of the series. Commentaries are also being assigned for important literary works in the categories of apocryphal and pseudepigraphical works relating to the Old and New Testaments, including some of Essene or Gnostic authorship.

The editors of *Hermeneia* impose no systematic-theological perspective upon the series (directly, or indirectly by selection of authors). It is expected that authors will struggle to lay bare the ancient meaning of a biblical work or pericope. In this way the text's human relevance should become transparent, as is always the case in competent historical discourse. However, the series eschews for itself homiletical translation of the Bible.

The editors are heavily indebted to Fortress Press for its energy and courage in taking up an expensive, long-term project, the rewards of which will accrue chiefly to the field of biblical scholarship.

The editor responsible for this volume is Sidnie White Crawford of the University of Nebraska–Lincoln.

Sidnie White Crawford	*Harold W. Attridge*
For the Old Testament	For the New Testament
Editorial Board	Editorial Board

Acknowledgments

So many people have aided me on my long Judith journey, and I am grateful to all of them. Here I would like to thank some of them in particular: Giovanni Bazzana, Joan Branham, Bernadette Brooten, Elena Ciletti, Nathaniel DesRosiers, David Frankfurter, Deborah Gera, Angela Kim Harkins, Thomas Christopher Hoklotubbe, Jonathan Klawans, David Konstan, Outi Lehtipuu, Mary Joan Leith, Peter Machinist, Gregory Mobley, Laura Nasrallah, Gregory Nagy, George Nickelsburg, Saul Olyan, Michael Satlow, Barbara Schmitz, Christopher Stroup, Christine Thomas, Daniel Ullucci, Annewies van den Hoek, Benjamin Wright, and Gale Yee. I am especially indebted to Sidnie White Crawford, the Hermeneia editor assigned to my volume. No one could ask for a more committed, thorough, and helpful editor. The editorial team of Hermeneia has been outstanding; I would like to thank Maurya P. Horgan, Paul Kobelski, and Chuck John. Faculty, staff, and students of Episcopal Divinity School provided a supportive and challenging community for many years. Since then, I have been a visiting professor at Brown University, where I experienced much mutual engagement and encouragement. It has been a pleasure and an honor to join the Brown community. I also spent a very productive and enjoyable semester as a visiting professor at Williams College, with the generous support of the Croghan Bicentennial Professorship in Biblical and Early Christian Studies. At home as well, my family was amazingly tolerant of my obsession with Judith and indeed became infected themselves: Shelley Rubin, Jessica Rubin-Wills, Daniel Rubin-Wills, Heloisa Nogueira, Laurie Rubin, and the newest member of my Judith team, Emma.

Reference Codes

1. Abbreviations

AB	Anchor Bible
ABD	David Noel Freedman, ed., *The Anchor Bible Dictionary* (6 vols.; New York: Doubleday, 1992).
ABRL	Anchor Bible Reference Library
AGJU	Arbeiten zur Geschichte des antiken Judentums und des Urchristentums
AIL	Ancient Israel and Its Literature
AnBib	Analecta Biblica
ANET	James B. Pritchard, ed., *The Ancient Near Eastern Texts Relating to the Old Testament* (3rd ed.; Princeton, NJ: Princeton University Press, 1969).
ANRW	Hildegard Temporini and Wolfgang Haase, eds., *Aufstieg und Niedergang der römischen Welt: Geschichte und Kultur Roms im Spiegel der neueren Forschung* (Berlin: de Gruyter, 1972–).
APOT	R. H. Charles, ed., *The Apocrypha and Pseudepigrapha of the Old Testament* (2 vols.; Oxford: Clarendon, 1913).
AYBRL	Anchor Yale Bible Reference Library
BA	*Biblical Archaeologist*
BBB	Bonner biblische Beiträge
BEATAJ	Beiträge zur Erforschung des Alten Testaments und des antiken Judentums
Bib	*Biblica*
BibInt	*Biblical Interpretation*
BIOSCS	*Bulletin of the International Organization of Septuagint and Cognate Studies*
BJS	Brown Judaic Studies
BNTC	Black's New Testament Commentaries
BR	*Biblical Research*
BTB	*Biblical Theology Bulletin*
BZ	*Biblische Zeitschrift*
BZAW	Beihefte zur Zeitschrift für die alttestamentliche Wissenschaft
BZNW	Beihefte zur Zeitschrift für die neutestamentliche Wissenschaft
CBQ	*Catholic Biblical Quarterly*
CBQMS	Catholic Biblical Quarterly Monograph Series
ClQ	*Classical Quarterly*
COS	W. W. Hallo, ed., *The Context of Scripture* (3 vols.; Leiden: Brill, 1997–2003).
CP	*Classical Philology*
CurBR	*Currents in Biblical Research*
DCLS	Deuterocanonical and Cognate Literature Studies
EJL	Early Judaism and Its Literature
EncJud	*Encyclopedia Judaica* (16 vols.; New York: Macmillan, 1971–1972).
EP	Elephantine Papyri
Eusebius	
Praep. ev.	*Praeparatio evangelica*
ExpT	*Expository Times*
FGrH	Felix Jacoby, ed., *Die Fragmente der griechischen Historiker* (Leiden: Brill, 1954–1964).
HBS	Herders biblische Studien
HCS	Hellenistic Culture and Society
HDR	Harvard Dissertations in Religion
HeyJ	*Heythrop Journal*
HR	*History of Religions*
HSCP	*Harvard Studies in Classical Philology*
HSM	Harvard Semitic Monographs
HThKAT	Herders Theologische Kommentar zum Alten Testament
HTR	*Harvard Theological Review*
HUT	Hermeneutische Untersuchungen zur Theologie
HvTSt	*Hervormde Teologiese Studies*
IEJ	*Israel Exploration Journal*
JAAR	*Journal of the American Academy of Religion*
JAJ	*Journal of Ancient Judaism*
JAJSup	Journal of Ancient Judaism Supplements
JANES	*Journal of the Ancient Near Eastern Society of Columbia University*
JAOS	*Journal of the American Oriental Society*
JBL	*Journal of Biblical Literature*
JBLMS	Journal of Biblical Literature Monograph Series
JETS	*Journal of the Evangelical Theological Society*
JHebS	*Journal of Hebrew Scriptures*
JJS	*Journal of Jewish Studies*
JNES	*Journal of Near Eastern Studies*
JQR	*Jewish Quarterly Review*
JRS	*Journal of Roman Studies*
JSem	*Journal of Semitics*
JSHRZ	Jüdische Schriften aus hellenistisch-römischer Zeit
JSJ	*Journal for the Study of Judaism*
JSOT	*Journal for the Study of the Old Testament*

TSAJ	Texte und Studien zum Antiken Judentum
TTZ	*Trierer theologische Zeitschrift*
VC	*Vigiliae Christianae*
VT	*Vetus Testamentum*
WUNT	Wissenschaftliche Untersuchungen zum Neuen Testament
ZAW	*Zeitschrift für die alttestamentliche Wissenschaft*
ZDMG	*Zeitschrift der deutschen Morgenländischen Gesellschaft*
ZDPV	*Zeitschrift des deutschen Palästina-Vereins*

2. Short Titles

Adelman, *Female Ruse*
Rachel Adelman, *The Female Ruse: Women's Deception and Divine Sanction in the Hebrew Bible* (Sheffield: Sheffield Phoenix, 2017).

Adler, "Jewish Ritual Immersion"
Yonatan Adler, "The Hellenistic Origins of Jewish Ritual Immersion," *JJS* 69 (2018) 1–21.

Adler, "Priestly Cult"
Yonatan Adler, "Between Priestly Cult and Common Culture: The Material Evidence of Ritual Purity Observance in Early Roman Jerusalem Reassessed," *JAJ* 7 (2016) 228–48.

Aharoni and Avi-Yonah, *Macmillan Bible Atlas*
Yohanan Aharoni and Michael Avi-Yonah, *Macmillan Bible Atlas* (New York: Macmillan, 1968).

Alonso Schökel, *Narrative Structures*
Luis Alonso Schökel, *Narrative Structures in the Book of Judith* (Protocol of the Colloquies, Center for Hermeneutical Studies in Hellenistic and Modern Culture 12.17, March 1974; Berkeley: Center for Hermeneutical Studies, 1975).

Anderson, *Time to Mourn*
Gary A. Anderson, *A Time to Mourn, a Time to Dance: The Expression of Grief and Joy in Israelite Religion* (University Park: Pennsylvania State University Press, 1991)

Apostolos-Cappadona, "Lord Has Struck"
Diane Apostolos-Cappadona, "'The Lord Has Struck Him Down by the Hand of a Woman!' Images of Judith," in Diane Apostolos-Cappadona and Doug Adams, eds., *Art as Religious Studies* (New York: Crossroad, 1987) 81–97.

Bach, *Women, Seduction*
Alice Bach, *Women, Seduction, and Betrayal in Biblical Narrative* (New York: Cambridge University Press, 1997).

Bailey, "Judith"
Elizabeth Bailey, "Judith, Jael, and Humilitas in the *Speculum Virginum*," in Kevin R. Brine, Elena Ciletti, and Henrike Lähnemann, eds., *The Sword of Judith: Judith Studies across the Disciplines* (Cambridge: OpenBook, 2010) 275–90.

Baker, *Jew*
Cynthia M. Baker, *Jew* (Key Words in Jewish Studies 8; New Brunswick, NJ: Rutgers University Press, 2017).

Bakhtin, *Dialogic Imagination*
Mikhail Bakhtin, *The Dialogic Imagination: Four Essays* (University of Texas Press Slavic Series 1; Austin: University of Texas Press, 1981).

Bakhtin, *Rabelais*
Mikhail Bakhtin, *Rabelais and His World* (Cambridge, MA: MIT Press, 1968).

Bal, *Artemisia Files*
Mieke Bal, ed., *The Artemisia Files: Artemisia Gentileschi for Feminists and Other Thinking People* (Chicago: University of Chicago Press, 2005).

Bal, "Head Hunting"
Mieke Bal, "Head Hunting: 'Judith' on the Cutting Edge of Knowledge," *JSOT* 63 (1994) 3–34.

Bal, *Narratology*
Mieke Bal, *Narratology: Introduction to the Theory of Narrative* (Toronto: University of Toronto Press, 1985).

Bal, *On Story-Telling*
Mieke Bal, *On Story-Telling: Essays in Narratology* (Foundations and Facets: Literary Facets; Sonoma, CA: Polebridge, 1991).

Ballentine, *Conflict Myth*
Debra Scoggins Ballentine, *The Conflict Myth and the Biblical Tradition* (New York: Oxford University Press, 2015).

Baslez, "Polémologie et histoire"
Marie-Françoise Baslez, "Polémologie et histoire dan le livre de Judith," *RB* 111 (2004) 362–76.

Beentjes, "Bethulia Crying"
Pancratius C. Beentjes, "Bethulia Crying, Judith Praying: Context and Content of Prayers in the Book of Judith," in Renate Egger-Wenzel and Jeremy Corley, eds., *Prayer from Tobit to Qumran: Inaugural Conference of the ISDCL at Salzburg, Austria, 5–9 July 2003* (Deuterocanonical and Cognate Literature Yearbook 2004; Berlin: de Gruyter, 2004) 231–54.

Belanoff, "Judith"
Patricia A. Belanoff, "Judith: Sacred and Secular Heroine," in Helen Damico and John Leyerle, eds., *Heroic Poetry in the Anglo-Saxon Period: Studies in Honor of Jess B. Bessinger Jr.* (Studies in Medieval Culture 32; Kalamazoo, MI: Medieval Institute Publications, 1993) 247–64.

Ben-Eliyahu, *Between Borders*
Eyal Ben-Eliyahu, *Between Borders: The Boundaries of Eretz-Israel in the Consciousness of the Jewish People in the Time of the Second Temple and in the Mishnah and Talmud Period* [in Hebrew] (Jerusalem: Yad Ben-Zvi, 2013).

Berlin, "Between Large Forces"
Andrea Berlin, "Between Large Forces: Palestine in the Hellenistic Period," *BA* 60 (1997) 2–57.

Berlin, "Manifest Identity"
Andrea Berlin, "Manifest Identity: From *Ioudaios* to Jew," in Rainer Albertz, ed., *Between Cooperation and Hostility: Multiple Identities in Ancient Judaism and the Interaction with Foreign Powers* (JAJSup 11; Göttingen: Vandenhoeck & Ruprecht, 2013) 151–75.

Bernardini, "Judith"
"Judith in the Italian Unification Process, 1800–1900," in Kevin R. Brine, Elena Ciletti, and Henrike Lähnemann, eds., *The Sword of Judith: Judith Studies across the Disciplines* (Cambridge: OpenBook, 2010) 397–409.

Białostocki, "Judith"
Jan Białostocki, "Judith: Story, Image, and Symbol: Giorgione's Painting in the Evolution of the Theme," in *The Message of Images: Studies in the History of Art* (Bibliotheca artibus et historiae; Vienna: Irsa, 1988).

Biolek, "Die Ansicht"
Anton Biolek, "Die Ansicht des christlichen Altertums über dem literarischen Charakter des Buches Judith," *Weidenauer Studien* 4 (1911) 335–68.

Bloch-Smith, *Israelite Ethnicity*
Elizabeth Bloch-Smith, "Israelite Ethnicity in Iron I: Archaeology Preserves What Is Remembered and What Is Forgotten in Israel's History," *JBL* 122 (2003) 401–25.

Bogaert, "Le calendrier"
Pierre-Maurice Bogaert, "Le calendrier du livre de Judith et la fête de Hanukka," *RTL* 15 (1984) 67–72.

Bogaert, *Judith*, Fascicule 1
Pierre-Maurice Bogaert, *Judith*, Fascicule 1: *Introduction* (Vetus Latina: Die Reste der altlateinischen Bibel 7.2; Freiburg: Herder, 2001).

Bogaert, "Recensions"
Pierre-Maurice Bogaert, "Recensions de la vielle version latine de Judith: I. Aux origines de la vulgate hiéronymienne. Le 'Corbeiensis'; II. Le 'Monacensis'; III. La tradition allémanique; IV. Trois manuscrits et deux recensions; V. La tradition carolingienne, *RBen* 85 (1975) 7–37, 241–65; 86 (1976) 7–37, 182–217; 88 (1978) 7–44.

Bogaert, "Version latine"
Pierre-Maurice Bogaert, "La version latine du livre de Judith dans la première Bible d'Alcala," *RBen* 78 (1968): 7–32, 181–212.

Bohn, "Death, Dispassion"
Babette Bohn, "Death, Dispassion, and the Female Hero: Artemisia Gentileschi's *Jael and Sisera*," in Mieke Bal, ed., *The Artemisia Files: Artemisia Gentileschi for Feminists and Other Thinking People* (Chicago: University of Chicago Press, 2005) 107–28.

Bolle and Llewelyn, "Intersectionality"
Helena M. Bolle and Stephen R. Llewelyn, "Intersectionality, Gender Liminality and Ben Sira's Attitude to the Eunuch," *VT* 67 (2017) 546–69.

Bowra, *Heroic Poetry*
C. M. Bowra, *Heroic Poetry* (London: Macmillan, 1952).

Boyd-Taylor, "Semantics"
Cameron Boyd-Taylor, "The Semantics of Biblical Language Redux," in Robert J. Hiebert, ed., *"Translation Is Required": The Septuagint in Retrospect and Prospect* (SCS 56; Atlanta: Society of Biblical Literature, 2010).

Bradley, *Anglo-Saxon Poetry*
S. A. J. Bradley, *Anglo-Saxon Poetry* (London: Dent, 1995).

Branham, "Penetrating the Sacred"
Joan Branham, "Penetrating the Sacred: Breaches and Barriers in the Jerusalem Temple," in Sharon E. J. Gerstel, ed., *Thresholds of the Sacred: Architectural, Art Historical, Liturgical, and Theological Perspectives on Religious Screens, East and West* (Washington, DC: Dumbarton Oaks Research Library; distributed by Harvard University Press, 2006) 6–24.

Bremmer, "Myth and Ritual"
Jan Bremmer, "Myth and Ritual in Greek Human Sacrifice: Lykaon, Polyxena and the Case of the Rhodian Criminal," in Jan Bremmer, ed., *The Strange World of Human Sacrifice* (Studies in the History and Anthropology of Religion 1; Leuven: Peeters, 2007) 55–79.

Bremmer and van den Bosch, *Between Poverty*
Jan Bremmer and Lourens van den Bosch, eds., *Between Poverty and the Pyre: Moments in the History of Widowhood* (London: Routledge, 1995).

Brenner, *Feminist Companion to Esther*
Athalya Brenner, ed., *A Feminist Companion to Esther–Judith–Susanna* (Feminist Companion to the Bible 7; Sheffield: Sheffield Academic Press, 1995).

Brenner-Idan, "Clothing Seduces"
Athalya Brenner-Idan, "Clothing Seduces: Did You Think It Was Naked Flesh That Did It?," in Athalya Brenner-Idan and Helen Efthimiadis-Keith, eds., *A Feminist Companion to Tobit and Judith* (Feminist Companion to the Bible [Second Series]; London: Bloomsbury T&T Clark, 2015) 212–25.

Brenner-Idan and van Dijk Hemmes, *On Gendering Texts*
Athalya Brenner-Idan and Fokkelien van Dijk-Hemmes, *On Gendering Texts: Female and Male Voices in the Hebrew Bible* (Biblical Interpretation Series 1; Leiden: Brill, 1993).

Brenner-Idan and Efthimiadis-Keith, *Tobit and Judith*
Athalya Brenner-Idan and Helen Efthimiadis-Keith, eds., *A Feminist Companion to Tobit and Judith* (Feminist Companion to the Bible [Second Series]; London: Bloomsbury T&T Clark, 2015).

Brine, Ciletti, and Lähnemann, *Sword of Judith*
Kevin R. Brine, Elena Ciletti, and Henrike Lähnemann, eds., *The Sword of Judith: Judith*

Studies across the Disciplines (Cambridge: OpenBook, 2010).

Brooten, *Love between Women*
Bernadette J. Brooten, *Love between Women: Early Christian Responses to Female Homoeroticism* (Chicago Series on Sexuality, History, and Society; Chicago: University of Chicago Press, 1996).

Burstein, "Cleitarchus in Jerusalem"
Stanley M. Burstein, "Cleitarchus in Jerusalem: A Note on the *Book of Judith*," in Frances B. Tichenor and Richard F. Morton Jr., eds., *The Eye Expanded: Life and the Arts in Greco-Roman Antiquity* (Berkeley: Unversity of California Press, 1999) 105–12.

Callaghan, "Ambiguity and Appropriation"
Leslie Abend Callaghan, "Ambiguity and Appropriation: The Story of Judith in Medieval Narrative and Iconographic Tradition," in Francesca Canadé Sautman, Diana Conchado, and Giuseppe di Scipio, eds., *Telling Tales: Medieval Narratives and the Folk Tradition* (New York: St. Martin's, 1998) 79–99.

Camp, *Wisdom and the Feminine*
Claudia V. Camp, *Wisdom and the Feminine in the Book of Proverbs* (Bible and Literature Series 11; Sheffield: Almond, 1985).

Caponigro, "Holding the Tale"
Mark Stephen Caponigro, "Judith, Holding the Tale of Herodotus," in James C. VanderKam, ed., *"No One Spoke Ill of Her": Essays on Judith* (EJL 2; Atlanta: Scholars Press, 1992) 47–59.

Cazelles, "Le personnage d'Achior"
Henri A. Cazelles, "Le personnage d'Achior dans le livre de Judith," *RSR* 39 (1951) 125–37, 324–27.

Chickering, "Poetic Exuberance"
Howell Chickering, "Poetic Exuberance in Old English *Judith*," *Studies in Philology* 106 (2009) 119–36.

Ciletti, "Patriarchal Ideology"
Elena Ciletti, "Patriarchal Ideology in the Renaissance Iconography of Judith," in Marilyn Migiel and Juliana Schiesari, eds., *Refiguring Woman: Perspectives on Gender and the Italian Renaissance* (Ithaca, NY: Cornell University Press, 1991) 35–70.

Ciletti and Lähnemann, "Judith in the Christian Tradition"
Elena Ciletti and Henrike Lähnemann, "Judith in the Christian Tradition," in Kevin R. Brine, Elena Ciletti, and Henrike Lähnemann, eds., *The Sword of Judith: Judith Studies across the Disciplines* (Cambridge: OpenBook, 2010) 41–65.

Clayton, "Ælfric's *Judith*"
Mary Clayton, "Ælfric's *Judith*: Manipulative or Manipulated?" *Anglo-Saxon England* 23 (1994) 215–27.

Cohen, *Beginnings of Jewishness*
Shaye J. D. Cohen, *The Beginnings of Jewishness: Boundaries, Varieties, Uncertainties* (HCS 31; Berkeley: University of California Press, 1999).

Cooper, "Judith"
Tracey-Anne Cooper, "Judith in Late Anglo-Saxon England," in Kevin R. Brine, Elena Ciletti, and Henrike Lähnemann, eds., *The Sword of Judith: Judith Studies across the Disciplines* (Cambridge: OpenBook, 2010) 169–96.

Corley, "Divine Sovereignty"
Jeremy Corley, "Divine Sovereignty and Power in the High-Priestly Prayer of 3 Macc 2:1–20," in Renate Egger-Wenzel and Jeremy Corley, eds., *Prayer from Tobit to Qumran: Inaugural Conference of the ISDCL at Salzburg, Austria, 5–9 July 2003* (Deuterocanonical and Cognate Literature Yearbook 2004; Berlin: de Gruyter, 2004) 359–86.

Corley, "Imitation"
Jeremy Corley, "Imitation of Septuagintal Narrative and Greek Historiography in the Portrait of Holofernes," in Géza Xeravits, ed., *A Pious Seductress: Studies in the Book of Judith* (DCLS 14; Berlin: de Gruyter, 2012) 27–34.

Corley, "Septuagintalisms"
Jeremy Corley, "Septuagintalisms, Semitic Interference, and the Original Language of the Book of Judith," in Jeremy Corley and Vincent Skemp, eds., *Studies in the Greek Bible: Essays in Honor of Francis T. Gignac, S.J.* (CBQMS 44; Washington, DC: Catholic Biblical Association of America, 2008) 65–96.

Corley, "Unconventional Heroine"
Jeremy Corley, "Judith: An Unconventional Heroine," *Scripture Bulletin* 31 (2001) 70–85.

Cowley, "Book of Judith"
Arthur E. Cowley, "The Book of Judith," in *APOT* 1:242–67.

Craven, *Artistry and Faith*
Toni Craven, *Artistry and Faith in the Book of Judith* (SBLDS 70; Chico, CA: Scholars Press, 1983).

Craven, "Book of Judith in Context"
Toni Carven, "The Book of Judith in the Context of Twentieth-Century Studies of the Apocryphal/Deuterocanonical Books," *CurBR* 1 (2003) 187–229.

Crawford, "4QTales of the Persian Court"
Sidnie White Crawford, "4QTales of the Persian Court (4Q550A–E) and Its Relation to Biblical Royal Courtier Tales, Especially Esther, Daniel, and Joseph," in Edward D. Herbert and Emanuel Tov, eds., *The Bible as Book: The Hebrew Bible and the Judaean Desert Discoveries* (London: Oak Knoll, 2002) 121–37.

Crawford, "Esther and Judith"
Sidnie White Crawford, "Esther and Judith: Contrasts in Character," in Sidnie White Crawford and Leonard J. Greenspoon, eds., *The Book of Esther in Modern Research* (JSOTSup 380; London: T&T Clark, 2003) 60–76.

Crawford, "In the Steps of Jael"
Sidnie White Crawford [as Sidnie Ann White], "In the Steps of Jael and Deborah: Judith as Heroine," in James C. VanderKam, ed., *"No One Spoke Ill of Her": Essays on Judith* (EJL 2; Atlanta: Scholars Press, 1992) 5–16.

Cummings, "Aestheticization"
Robert Cummings, "The Aestheticization of Tyrannicide: Du Bartas's *La Judit*," in Kevin R. Brine, Elena Ciletti, and Henrike Lähnemann, eds., *The Sword of Judith: Judith Studies across the Disciplines* (Cambridge: OpenBook, 2010) 227–38.

Dalley, *Esther's Revenge*
Stephanie Dalley, *Esther's Revenge at Susa: From Sennacherib to Ahasuerus* (Oxford: Oxford University Press, 2007).

Dancy, *Judith*
J. C. Dancy, *Judith* (The Shorter Books of the Apocrypha; Cambridge: Cambridge University Press, 1972).

Deines, *Jüdische Steingefässe*
Roland Deines, *Jüdische Steingefässe und pharisäische Frömmigkeit: Ein archäologisch-historischer Beitrag zum Verständnis von Joh 2.6 und der jüdischen Reinheitshalacha zur Zeit Jesu* (WUNT 2/52; Tübingen: Mohr, 1993).

Delcor, "Le livre de Judith"
Mathias Delcor, «Le livre de Judith et l'époque grecque,» *Klio* 49 (1967) 151–79.

Dijkstra, *Idols of Perversity*
Bram Dijkstra, *Idols of Perversity: Fantasies of Feminine Evil in Fin-de-Siècle Culture* (New York: Oxford University Press, 1986).

Di Lella, "Women in the Wisdom"
Alexander A. Di Lella, "Women in the Wisdom of Ben Sira and the Book of Judith: A Study in Contrasts and Reversals," in J. A. Emerton, ed., *Congress Volume: Paris 1992* (VTSup 61; Leiden: Brill, 1995) 39–52.

Dixon, *Women Who Ruled*
Annette Dixon, ed., *Women Who Ruled: Queens, Goddesses, Amazons in Renaissance and Baroque Art* (London: Merrell, 2002).

Dombkowski Hopkins, "Judith"
Denise Domkowski Hopkins, "Judith," in Carole A. Newsom and Sharon H. Ringe, eds., *Women's Bible Commentary* (expanded ed.; Louisville: Westminster John Knox, 1998) 279–85.

Doran, *Temple Propaganda*
Robert Doran, *Temple Propaganda: The Purpose and Character of 2 Maccabees* (CBQMS 12; Washington, DC: Catholic Biblical Association of America, 1981).

Dubarle, *Judith*
A.-M. Dubarle, *Judith: Formes et sens des diverses traditions* (2 vols.; AnBib 24; Rome: Institut biblique pontifical, 1966).

Eckhardt, "Reclaiming Tradition"
Benedikt Eckhardt, "Reclaiming Tradition: The Book of Judith and Hasmonean Politics," *JSP* 18 (2009) 243–63.

Efthimiadis-Keith, "Genealogy"
Helen Efthimiadis-Keith, "Genealogy, Retribution and Identity: Re-Interpreting the Cause of Suffering in the Book of Judith," *Old Testament Essays* 27 (2014) 860–78.

Elder, "Judith"
Linda Bennett Elder, "Judith," in Elisabeth Schüssler-Fiorenza, ed., *Searching the Scriptures*, vol. 2: *A Feminist Commentary* (New York: Crossroad, 1997) 455–69.

Elder, "Virgins, Viragos"
Linda Bennett Elder, "Virgins, Viragos and Virtuo(u)si among Judiths in Opera and Oratorio," *JSOT* 92 (2001): 91–119.

Engel, "Das Buch Judit"
Helmut Engel, "Das Buch Judit," in Erich Zenger, ed., *Einleitung in das Alte Testament* (Stuttgart: Kohlhammer, 1998) 256–66.

Engel, "Der HERR"
Helmut Engel, "'Der HERR ist ein Gott, der die Kriege zerschlächt': Zur Frage der griechischen Originalsprache und der Struktur des Buches Judit," in Klaus-Dietrich Schunk and Matthias Augustin, eds., *Goldene Äpfel in silbernen Schalen: Collected Communications to the XIIIth Congress of the International Organization for the Study of the Old Testament, Leuven 1989* (BEATAJ 20; Frankfurt am Main: Lang, 1992) 155–68.

England, "Violent Superwomen"
Emma England, "Violent Superwomen: Super Heroes or Super Villains? Judith, Wonder Woman and Lynndie England," in Athalya Brenner-Idan and Helen Efthimiadis-Keith, eds., *A Feminist Companion to Tobit and Judith* (Feminist Companion to the Bible [Second Series]; London: Bloomsbury T&T Clark, 2015) 242–58.

Enslin, *Book of Judith*
Morton S. Enslin and Solomon Zeitlin, *The Book of Judith* (Jewish Apocryphal Literature 7; Leiden: Brill, 1972).

Eskenazi, *In an Age of Prose*
Tamara Cohn Eskenazi, *In an Age of Prose: A Literary Approach to Ezra-Nehemiah* (SBLMS 36; Atlanta: Scholars Press, 1988).

Esler, "Ludic History"
Philip F. Esler, "Ludic History in the Book of Judith: The Reinvention of Israelite Identity?," *BibInt* 10 (2002) 107–43.

Esler, *Sex, Wives, and Warriors*
Philip D. Esler, *Sex, Wives, and Warriors: Reading Biblical Narrative with Its Ancient Audience* (Eugene, OR: Wipf & Stock, 2011).

van den Eynde, "Crying to God"
Sabine van den Eynde, "Crying to God: Prayer and Plot in the Book of Judith," *Bib* 85 (2004) 217–31.

Fischer and Obermayer, "Die Kriegstheologie"
Irmtraud Fischer and Bernd Obermayer, "Die Kriegstheologie des Juditbuches als Kondensat alttestamentlicher Sichtweisen des Krieges," in Ulrich Dahmen and Johannes Schnocks, eds., *Juda und Jerusalem in der Seleukidenzeit: Herrschaft, Widerstand, Identität; Festschrift für Heinz-Josef Fabry* (BBB 159; Göttingen: V&R Unipress, 2010) 227–42.

Foucault, *Care of the Self*
Michel Foucault, *The History of Sexuality*, vol. 3: *Care of the Self* (New York: Pantheon, 1986).

Fowler, *Renaissance Realism*
Alastair Fowler, *Renaissance Realism: Narrative Images in Literature and Art* (Oxford: Oxford University Press, 2003).

Friedländer and Rosenberg
Max J. Friedländer and Jakob Rosenberg, *The Paintings of Lucas Carnach* (rev. ed.; London: Southeby Parke Bernet, 1978).

Friedman, "Metamorphoses"
Mira Friedman, "Metamorphoses of Judith," *Jewish Art* 12–13 (1986–87) 225–46.

Fritzsche, *Die Bücher Tobi und Judith*
Otto Fridolin Fritzsche, *Die Bücher Tobi und Judith* (Kurzgefasstes exegetisches Handbuch zu den Apokryphen des Alten Testamentes 2; Leipzig: Hirzel, 1853).

Frye, *Anatomy of Criticism*
Northrop Frye, *Anatomy of Criticism* (Princeton, NJ: Princeton University Press, 1957).

Fusillo, "Modern Critical Theories"
Massimo Fusillo, "Modern Critical Theories and the Ancient Novel," in Gareth Schmeling, ed., *Novel in the Ancient World* (rev. ed.; Boston: Brill Academic, 2003) 277–305.

Gamberoni, *Die Auslegung des Buches Tobias*
Johann Gamberoni, *Die Auslegung des Buches Tobias in der griechisch-lateinischen Kirche der Antike und der Christenheit des Westens bis zum 1600* (Munich: Kösel, 1969).

Gardner, "Song of Praise"
Anne E. Gardner, "The Song of Praise in Judith 16:2–17 (LXX 16:1–17)," *HeyJ* 29 (1989) 413–22.

Garrard, *Artemisia Gentileschi*
Mary D. Garrard, *Artemisia Gentileschi: The Image of the Female Hero in Italian Baroque Art* (Princeton, NJ: Princeton University Press, 1989).

Garrard, "Leonardo da Vinci"
Mary Garrard, "Leonardo da Vinci: Female Portraits, Female Nature," in Mary Garrard and Norma Broude, *The Expanding Discourse: Feminism and Art History* (New York: Routledge, 1992) 58–86.

Garrard and Broude, *Expanding Discourse*
Mary Garrard and Norma Broude, *The Expanding Discourse: Feminism and Art History* (New York: Routledge, 1992).

Gaster, "Unknown Hebrew Version"
Moses Gaster, "An Unknown Hebrew Version of the History of Judith," *PSBA* 16 (1893–94) 156–63.

Gera, "Jewish Textual Traditions"
Deborah Levine Gera, "The Jewish Textual Traditions," in Kevin R. Brine, Elena Ciletti, and Henrike Lähnemann, eds., *The Sword of Judith: Judith Studies across the Disciplines* (Cambridge: OpenBook, 2010) 23–40.

Gera, "Judah and Judith"
Deborah Levine Gera, "Judah and Judith" [in Hebrew], in Joseph Geiger, Hannah M. Cotton, and Guy D. Stiebel, eds., *Israel's Land: Papers Presented to Israel Shatzman on His Jubilee* (Ra'anana, Israel: Open University, 2009) 29–38.

Gera, *Judith*
Deborah Levine Gera, *Judith* (Commentaries on Early Jewish Literature; Boston: de Gruyter, 2014).

Gera "Shorter Medieval Hebrew Tales"
Deborah Levine Gera, "Shorter Medieval Hebrew Tales of Judith," in Kevin R. Brine, Elena Ciletti, and Henrike Lähnemann, eds., *The Sword of Judith: Judith Studies across the Disciplines* (Cambridge: OpenBook, 2010) 275–90.

Gera "Speech in Judith"
Deborah Levine Gera, "Speech in Judith," in Melvin K. H. Peters, ed., *XIV Congress of the IOSCS, Helsinki, 2010* (SCS 59; Atlanta: Society of Biblical Literature, 2013) 413–23.

Gera, *Warrior Women*
Deborah Levine Gera, *Warrior Women: The Anonymous Tractate de Mulierebus* (Mnemosyne Supplement 162; Leiden: Brill, 1997).

Gera, *Xenophon's Cyropaedia*
Deborah Levine Gera, *Xenophon's Cyropaedia: Style, Genre, and Literary Technique* (Oxford Classical Monographs; Oxford: Clarendon, 1993).

Gill, *Structured Self*
Christopher Gill, *The Structured Self in Hellenistic and Roman Thought* (Oxford: Oxford University Press, 2006).

Glancy, "Mistress–Slave Dialectic"
Jennifer A. Glancy, "The Mistress–Slave Dialectic: Paradoxes of Slavery in Three LXX Narratives," *JSOT* 72 (1996) 71–87.

Goldhill, *Invention of Prose*
Simon Goldhill, *The Invention of Prose* (Oxford: Oxford University Press, 2002).

Goodblatt, "Israelites Who Reside"
David Goodblatt, "'The Israelites Who Reside in Judah' (Judith 4:1): On the Conflicted Identities of the Hasmonean State," in Lee I. Levine and Daniel R. Schwartz, eds., *Jewish Identities in Antiquity: Studies in Memory of Menahem Stern* (TSAJ 130; Tübingen: Mohr Siebeck, 2009) 74–89.

Griffith, *Judith*
Mark Griffith, *Judith* (Exeter Medieval English Texts and Studies; Exeter: University of Exeter Press, 1997).

Grintz, *Book of Judith*
Jehoshua M. Grintz, *The Book of Judith: A Reconstruction of the Original Hebrew Text with Introduction, Commentary, Appendices, and Indices* [in Hebrew with English summary] (Jerusalem: The Bialik Institute, 1957).

Gruen, *Diaspora*
Erich Gruen, *Diaspora: Jews amidst Greeks and Romans* (Cambridge, MA: Harvard University Press, 2002).

Gruen, *Heritage and Hellenism*
Erich Gruen, *Heritage and Hellenism: The Reinvention of Jewish Tradition* (HCS 30; Berkeley: University of California Press, 1998).

Guyot, *Eunuchen*
Peter Guyot, *Eunuchen als Sklaven und Freigelassene in der griechisch-römischen Antike* (Stuttgart: Klett-Cotta, 1980).

Haag, *Das Buch Judit*
Ernst Haag, *Das Buch Judit* (Geistliche Schriftlesung 15; Dusseldorf: Patmos, 1995).

Haag, *Studien*
Ernst Haag, *Studien zum Buche Judith: Seine theologische Bedeutung und literarisches Eigenart* (Trier theologische Studien 16; Trier: Paulinus-Verlag, 1963).

Hägg, *Novel in Antiquity*
Tomas Hägg, *The Novel in Antiquity* (Berkeley: University of California Press, 1991).

Hall, *Inventing the Barbarian*
Edith Hall, *Inventing the Barbarian: Greek Self-Definition through Tragedy* (Oxford Classical Monographs; Oxford: Oxford University Press, 1989).

Hanhart
Robert Hanhart, ed., *Iudith* (Septuaginta: Vetus Testamentum graecum 8.4; Göttingen: Vandenhoeck & Ruprecht, 1979).

Hanhart, *Text und Textgeschichte*
Robert Hanhart, ed., *Text und Textgeschichte des Buches Judith* (Mitteilungen des Septuaginta-Unternehmens 14; Göttingen: Vandenhoeck & Ruprecht, 1979).

Harkins, "Function of Prayers"
Angela Kim Harkins, "The Function of Prayers of Ritual Mourning in the Second Temple Period," in Mika S. Pajunen and Jeremy Penner, eds., *Functions of Psalms and Prayers in the Late Second Temple Period* (BZAW 486; Berlin: de Gruyter, 2017) 80–101.

Haynes, *Fashioning the Feminine*
Katharine Haynes, *Fashioning the Feminine in the Greek Novel* (London: Routledge, 2003).

Hellmann, *Judit*
Monika Hellmann, *Judit–eine Frau im Spanngsfeld von Autonomie und göttlicher Führung: Studie über eine Frauengestalt des Alten Testaments* (Frankfurt am Main: Lang, 1992).

Heltzer, "Eine neue Quelle"
Michael Heltzer, "Eine neue Quelle zur Bestimmung der Abfassungszeit des Judithbuches," *ZAW* 92 (1980) 437.

Hengel, *Judaism and Hellenism*
Martin Hengel, *Judaism and Hellenism: Studies in Their Encounter in Palestine during the Early Hellenistic Period* (Philadelphia: Fortress Press, 1974).

van Henten, "Female Moses"
Jan Willem van Henten, "Judith as a Female Moses: Judith 7–13 in Light of Exodus 17, Numbers 20, and Deuteronomy 33:8–11," in Fokkelien van Dijk-Hemmes and Athalya Brenner, eds., *Reflections on Theology and Gender* (Kampen: Kok Pharos, 1994) 33–48.

van Henten, "Judith as an Alternative Leader"
Jan Willem van Henten, "Judith as an Alternative Leader: A Rereading of Judith 7–13," in Athalya Brenner, ed., *A Feminist Companion to Esther–Judith–Susanna* (Feminist Companion to the Bible 7; Sheffield: Sheffield Academic Press, 1995) 224–52.

Holzberg, "Genre"
Niklas Holzberg, "Genre: Novels Proper and the Fringe," in Gareth Schmeling, ed., *The Novel in the Ancient World* (rev. ed.; Boston: Brill Academic, 2003) 11–28.

Hopkins, "Novel Evidence"
Keith Hopkins, "Novel Evidence for Roman Slavery," *Past and Present* 138 (1993) 3–27.

Ilan, *Integrating Women*
Tal Ilan, *Integrating Women into Second Temple History* (TSAJ 76; Tübingen: Mohr Siebeck, 1999).

Ilan, *Jewish Women*
Tal Ilan, *Jewish Women in Greco-Roman Palestine: An Inquiry into Image and Status* (TSAJ 44; Tübingen: Mohr Siebeck, 1995).

Jacobson, *Commentary on Pseudo-Philo*
Howard Jacobson, *A Commentary on Pseudo-Philo's Liber antiquitatum biblicarum: With Latin Text and English Translation* (2 vols.; AGJU 31; Leiden: Brill, 1996).

Jeffreys, Jeffreys, and Scott, *John Malalas*
Elizabeth Jeffreys, Michael Jeffreys, and Roger Scott, *The Chronicle of John Malalas* (Melbourne: Australian Association for Byzantine Studies, 1986).

Jensen, "Juditbogen"
Hans Jørgen Lundager Jensen, "Juditbogen," in Troels Engberg-Pedersen and Niels Peter Lemche, eds., *Tradition og nybrud. Jødedommen i hellenistik tid* (Forum for bibelsk eksegese 2; Copenhagen: Museum Tusculanum, 1990) 153–89.

Jacobus, "Judith, Holofernes"
Mary Jacobus, "Judith, Holofernes, and the Phallic Woman," in Mary Jacobus, *Reading Women: Essays in Feminist Criticism* (New York: Columbia University Press, 1986) 110–36.

Jansen, "La composition"
 H. Ludin Jansen, "La composition du chant de Judith," *Acta Orientalia* 15 (1936) 63–71.

Joannides, "Titian's *Judith*"
 Paul Joannides, "Titian's *Judith* and Its Context: The Iconography of Decapitation," *Apollo* 135, no. 361 (March 1992) 163–70.

Johnson, *Historical Fictions*
 Sara Raup Johnson, *Historical Fictions and Hellenistic Jewish Identity: Third Maccabees in Its Cultural Identity* (HCS 43; Berkeley: University of California Press, 2004).

Johnson, "Novelistic Elements"
 Sara Raup Johnson, "Novelistic Elements in Esther: Persian or Hellenistic, Jewish or Greek?," *CBQ* 67 (2005) 571–89.

Joosten, "Original Language"
 Jan Joosten, "The Original Language and Historical Milieu of the Book of Judith," in Moshe Bar-Asher and Emanuel Tov, eds., *Meghillot: Studies in the Dead Sea Scrolls V–VI: A Festschrift for Devorah Dimant* (Jerusalem: Bialik Institute; Haifa: University of Haifa, 2007) 159–76.

Jouanno, "Novelistic Lives"
 Corinne Jouanno, "Novelistic Lives and Historical Biographies: The *Life of Aesop* and the *Alexander Romance* as Fringe Novels," in Grammatiki A. Karla, ed., *Fiction on the Fringe: Novelistic Writing in the Post-Classical Age* (Mnemosyne Supplement 310; Leiden: Brill, 2009) 33–48.

Karla, *Fiction on the Fringe*
 Grammatiki A. Karla, ed., *Fiction on the Fringe: Novelistic Writing in the Post-Classical Age* (Mnemosyne Supplement 310; Leiden: Brill, 2009).

Kim "Bloody Signs"
 Susan Kim, "Bloody Signs: Circumcision and Pregnancy in the Old English Judith," *Exemplaria* 11 (1999) 285–307.

Klawans, *Impurity and Sin*
 Jonathan Klawans, *Impurity and Sin in Ancient Judaism* (Oxford: Oxford University Press, 2004).

Klawans and Wills, *Jewish Annotated Apocrypha*
 Jonathan Klawans and Lawrence M. Wills, *Jewish Annotated Apocrypha* (New York: Oxford University Press, forthcoming).

Knotts, "Judith in Florentine"
 Robert Knotts, "Judith in Florentine Renaissance Art, 1425–1512" (Ph.D. diss., Ohio State University, 1995).

Konstan, *Sexual Symmetry*
 David Konstan, *Sexual Symmetry: Love in the Ancient Novel and Related Genres* (Princeton, NJ: Princeton University Press, 1994).

Konstan, *Testament of Abraham*
 David Konstan, "The *Testament of Abraham* and Greek Romance," in Ilaria Ramelli and Judith Perkins, eds., *Early Christian and Jewish Narrative: The Role of Religion in Shaping Narrative Forms*

(WUNT 348; Tübingen: Mohr Siebeck, 2015) 45–51.

Koppelman, "Fearing the Neighbor"
 Kate Koppelman, "Fearing the Neighbor: The Intimate Other in *Beowulf* and the Old English *Judith*," *Comitatus* 35 (2004) 1–21.

Kosmin, "Hellenistic Period"
 Paul J. Kosmin, "Hellenistic Period," in Jonathan Klawans and Lawrence M. Wills, *Jewish Annotated Apocrypha* (New York: Oxford University Press, forthcoming).

Kosmin, *Land of the Elephant Kings*
 Paul J. Kosmin, *The Land of the Elephant Kings: Space, Territory, and Ideology in the Seleucid Empire* (Cambridge, MA: Harvard University Press, 2014).

Kraus, *Limits of Historiography*
 Christina Shuttleworth Kraus, *The Limits of Historiography: Genre and Narrative in Ancient Historical Texts* (Mnemosyne Supplement 191; Leiden: Brill, 1999).

Kubiak, "Iconography"
 Joseph Kubiak, "The Iconography of Judith in Italian Renaissance Art" (master's dissertation, University of Wisconsin, Madison, 1965).

Kugel, *Bible as It Was*
 James L. Kugel, *The Bible as It Was* (Cambridge, MA: Belknap Press of Harvard University Press, 1997).

Kuhrt, "Earth and Water"
 Amélie Kuhrt, "Earth and Water," in Amélie Kuhrt and Heleen Sancisi-Weerdenburg, eds., *Method and Theory: Proceedings of the London 1985 Achaemenid History Workshop* (Achaemenid History 3; Leiden: Nederlands Instituut voor het Nabije Oosten, 1988).

LaCocque, *Feminine Unconventional*
 André LaCocque, *The Feminine Unconventional: Four Subversive Figures in Israel's Tradition* (OBT; Minneapolis: Fortress, 1990).

Lähnemann, "Cunning of Judith"
 Henrike Lähnemann, "The Cunning of Judith in Late Medieval German Texts," in Kevin R. Brine, Elena Ciletti, and Henrike Lähnemann, eds., *The Sword of Judith: Judith Studies across the Disciplines* (Cambridge: OpenBook, 2010) 275–90.

Lähnemann, *Hystoria Judith*
 Henrike Lähnemann, *Hystoria Judith: Deutsche Judithdichtungen vom 12. bis zum 16. Jahrhundert* (Berlin: de Gruyter, 2006).

Lambert, "Fasting"
 David A. Lambert, "Fasting as a Penitential Rite: A Biblical Phenomenon?," *HTR* 96 (2003) 477–512.

Lambert, *Repentance*
 David A. Lambert, *How Repentance Became Biblical: Judaism, Christianity, and the Interpretation of Scripture* (Oxford: Oxford University Press, 2015).

Lang, "Lord Who Crushes"
Judith Lang, "'The Lord Who Crushes Wars': Studies on Judith 9:7, Judith 16:2, and Exodus 15:3," in Géza G. Xeravits, ed., *A Pious Seductress: Studies in the Book of Judith* (DCLS 14; Berlin: de Gruyter, 2012) 179–87.

Langdon, *Building Inscriptions*
Stephen Langdon, *Building Inscriptions of the Neo-Babylonian Empire,* part 1 (Paris: Leroux, 1905).

Lange, *Die Juditfigur*
Lydia Lange, *Die Juditfigur in der Vulgata: Eine theologische Studie zur lateinischen Bibel* (DCLS 36; Berlin: de Gruyter, 2016).

Lawrence, *Washing in Water*
Jonathan D. Lawrence, *Washing in Water: Trajectories of Ritual Bathing in the Hebrew Bible and Second Temple Literature* (Academia Biblica 23; Atlanta: Society of Biblical Literature, 2006).

Lefkovitz, *In Scripture*
Lori Hope Lefkovitz, *In Scripture: The First Stories of Jewish Sexual Identities* (Lanham, MD: Rowman & Littlefield, 2010).

Lefkowitz, *Women in Greek Myth*
Mary R. Lefkowitz, *Women in Greek Myth* (Baltimore: Johns Hopkins University Press, 1986).

Lehtipuu, "Receive the Widow"
Outi Lehtipuu, "'Receive the Widow Judith, Example of Chastity': The Figure of Judith as a Model Christian in Patristic Interpretations," in Agnethe Siquans, ed., *Biblical Women in Patristic Reception/Biblische Frauen in patristischer Rezeption* (JAJSup 25; Göttingen: Vandenhoeck & Ruprecht, 2017) 186–218.

Lemos, "They Have Become Women"
T. M. Lemos, "'They Have Become Women': Judean Diaspora and Postcolonial Theories of Gender and Migration," in Saul M. Olyan, ed., *Social Theory and the Study of Israelite Religion: Essays in Retrospect and Prospect* (Resources for Biblical Study 71; Atlanta: Society of Biblical Literature, 2012) 81–109.

Levine, "Sacrifice and Salvation"
Amy-Jill Levine, "Sacrifice and Salvation: Otherness and Domestication in the Book of Judith," in Athalya Brenner, ed., *A Feminist Companion to Esther–Judith–Susanna* (Feminist Companion to the Bible 7; Sheffield: Sheffield Academic Press, 1995) 208–33.

Lightstone, *Commerce of the Sacred*
Jack N. Lightstone, *The Commerce of the Sacred: Mediation of the Divine among Jews in the Greco-Roman World* (New York: Columbia University Press, 2006).

Llewellyn, "Example of Judith"
Kathleen M. Llewellyn, "The Example of Judith in Early Modern French Literature," in Kevin R. Brine, Elena Ciletti, and Henrike Lähnemann, eds., *The Sword of Judith: Judith Studies across the Disciplines* (Cambridge: OpenBook, 2010) 213–25.

Llewellyn-Jones, "Eunuchs"
Lloyd Llewellyn-Jones, "Eunuchs and the Royal Harem in Achaemenid Persia (559–331 B.C.)," in Shaun Tougher, ed., *Eunuchs in Antiquity and Beyond* (London: Duckworth, 2002).

Llewellyn-Jones and Robson
Lloyd Llewellyn-Jones and James Robson, *Ctesias' History of Persia: Tales of the Orient* (London: Routledge, 2010).

Loader, *Pseudepigrapha*
William R. G. Loader, *The Pseudepigrapha on Sexuality: Attitudes towards Sexuality in Apocalypses, Testaments, Legends, Wisdom, and Related Literature* (Attitudes towards Sexuality in Judaism and Christianity in the Hellenistic Greco-Roman Era; Grand Rapids: Eerdmans, 2011).

Ludlow, *Abraham Meets Death*
Jared Ludlow, *Abraham Meets Death: Narrative Humor in the Testament of Abraham* (JSPSup 41; London: Sheffield Academic Press, 2002).

Ludlow, "Weeping and Falling Down"
Jared Ludlow, "Are Weeping and Falling Down Funny? Exaggerations in Ancient Novelistic Texts" (paper presented at the Society of Biblical Literature Annual Meeting, Baltimore, Maryland, November 25, 2013).

Marsh, "Judith in Baroque Oratorio"
David Marsh, "Judith in Baroque Oratorio," in Kevin R. Brine, Elena Ciletti, and Henrike Lähnemann, eds., *The Sword of Judith: Judith Studies across the Disciplines* (Cambridge: OpenBook, 2010) 385–96.

Martin, *Syntactical Evidence*
Raymond A. Martin, *Syntactical Evidence of Semitic Sources in Greek Documents* (SCS 3; Cambridge, MA: Society of Biblical Literature, 1974).

Mastrangelo, "Typology"
Marc Mastrangelo, "Typology and Agency in Prudentius's Treatment of the Judith Story," in Kevin R. Brine, Elena Ciletti, and Henrike Lähnemann, eds., *The Sword of Judith: Judith Studies across the Disciplines* (Cambridge: OpenBook, 2010) 153–68.

Matthews, *Perfect Martyr*
Shelly Matthews, *Perfect Martyr: The Stoning of Stephen and the Construction of Christian Identity* (Oxford: Oxford University Press, 2010).

McHam, "Donatello's *Judith*"
Sarah Blake McHam, "Donatello's *Judith* as the Emblem of God's Chosen People," in Kevin R. Brine, Elena Ciletti, and Henrike Lähnemann, eds., *The Sword of Judith: Judith Studies across the Disciplines* (Cambridge: OpenBook, 2010) 275–90.

McKeon, *Origins of the English Novel*
Michael McKeon, *The Origins of the English Novel, 1600–1740* (Baltimore: Johns Hopkins University Press, 1987).

Mecky Zaragosa, *"Da befiel sie Furcht"*
Gabrijela Mecky Zaragosa, *"Da befiel sie Furcht und Angst . . .": Judith im Drama des 19. Jahrhunderts* (Munich: Iudicium, 2005).

Mendels, *Land of Israel*
Doron Mendels, *The Land of Israel as a Political Concept in Hasmonean Literature: Recourse to History in Second Century B.C. Claims to the Holy Land* (TSAJ 15; Tübingen: Mohr, 1987).

Mendels, *Rise and Fall*
Doron Mendels, *The Rise and Fall of Jewish Nationalism* (ABRL; New York: Doubleday, 1992).

Merideth, "Desire and Danger"
Betsy Merideth, "Desire and Danger: The Drama of Betrayal in Judges and Judith," in Mieke Bal, ed., *Anti-Covenant: Counter-Reading Women's Lives in the Hebrew Bible* (Sheffield: Almond Press, 1989) 63–78.

Miller, *Die Bücher Tobias*
Athanasius Miller, *Die Bücher Tobias, Judith und Esther* (3 vols. in 1; Die Heilige Schrift des Alten Testamentes 4.3; Bonn: P. Hanstein, 1940–41).

Miller, "Femme Fatale"
Geoffrey D. Miller, "A Femme Fatale of Whom 'No One Spoke Ill': Judith's Moral Muddle and Her Personification of Yahweh," *JSOT* 39 (2014) 223–45.

Milne, "What Shall We Do?"
Pamela J. Milne, "What Shall We Do with Judith? A Feminist Reassessment of a Biblical 'Heroine,'" *Semeia* 62 (1993) 37–58.

Mittmann-Richert, *Einführung in den jüdischen Schriften*
Ulrike Mittmann-Richert, *Einführung zu den jüdischen Schriften aus hellenistisch-römischer Zeit: Historische und legendarishe Erzählungen* (JSHRZ Supplement 6.1.1; Gütersloh: Gütersloher Verlagshaus, 2000) 82–96.

Mobley, *Empty Men*
Gregory Mobley, *The Empty Men: The Heroic Tradition of Ancient Israel* (ABRL; New York: Doubleday, 2005).

Mobley, *Samson*
Gregory Mobley, *Samson and the Liminal Hero in the Ancient Near East* (LHBOTS 453; New York: T&T Clark, 2006).

Montague, *Esther and Judith*
George T. Montague, *The Books of Esther and Judith* (Pamphlet Bible Series 21; New York: Paulist Press, 1973).

Moore, *Judith*
Carey A. Moore, *Judith: A New Translation with Introduction and Commentary* (AB 40B; Garden City, NY: Doubleday, 1985).

Morales, "History of Sexuality"
Helen Morales, "The History of Sexuality," in Tim Whitmarsh, ed., *The Cambridge Companion to the Greek and Roman Novel* (Cambridge: Cambridge University Press, 2008) 39–55.

Morales, *Vision and Narration*
Helen Morales, *Vision and Narrative in Achilles Tatius' Leucippe and Clitophon* (Cambridge Classical Studies; Cambridge: Cambridge University Press, 2005).

Morgan, "Representation of Philosophers"
John R. Morgan, "The Representation of Philosophers in Greek Fiction," in John R. Morgan and Meriel Jones, eds., *Philosophical Presences in the Ancient Novel* (Ancient Narrative: Supplementum 10; Eelde: Barkhuis; Groningen: Groningen University Library, 2007) 23–52.

Morgan and Stoneman, *Greek Fiction*
John R. Morgan and Richard Stoneman, eds., *Greek Fiction: The Greek Novel in Context* (London: Routledge, 1994).

Nagy, *Best of the Achaeans*
Gregory Nagy, *The Best of the Achaeans: Concepts of the Hero in Archaic Greek Poetry* (Baltimore: Johns Hopkins University Press, 1979).

Nassichuk, "Prayer of Judith"
John Nassichuk, "The Prayer of Judith in Two Late-Fifteenth-Century French Mystery Plays," in Kevin R. Brine, Elena Ciletti, and Henrike Lähnemann, eds., *The Sword of Judith: Judith Studies across the Disciplines* (Cambridge: OpenBook, 2010) 197–211.

Navarro Puerto, "Reinterpreting the Past"
Mercedes Navarro Puerto, "Reinterpreting the Past: Judith 5," in Núria Calduch-Benages and Jan Liesen, eds., *History and Identity: How Israel's Later Authors Viewed Its Earlier History* (Berlin and New York: de Gruyter, 2006) 115–39.

Newman, *Praying by the Book*
Judith H. Newman, *Praying by the Book: The Scripturalization of Prayer in Second Temple Judaism* (EJL 14; Atlanta: Society of Biblical Literature, 1999).

Newsom, *Daniel*
Carol A. Newsom, *Daniel: A Commentary* (OTL; Louisville: Westminster John Knox, 2014).

Nickelsburg, *Jewish Literature*
George W. E. Nickelsburg, *Jewish Literature between the Bible and the Mishnah: A Historical and Literary Introduction* (2nd ed.; Philadelphia: Fortress Press, 2005).

Niditch, "Eroticism and Death"
Susan Niditch, "Eroticism and Death in the Tale of Jael," in Peggy Day, ed., *Gender and Difference in Ancient Israel* (Minneapolis: Fortress Press, 1989) 43–57.

Nolte and Jordaan, "Ideology and Intertextuality"
S. Philip Nolte and Pierre J. Jordaan, "Ideology and Intertextuality: Intertextual Allusions in Judith 16," *HvTSt* 67 (2011) 1–9.

Nutu, "Framing Judith"
  Ela Nutu, "Framing Judith: Whose Text, Whose Gaze, Whose Language?," in Ela Nutu and J. Cheryl Exum, eds., *Between the Text and the Canvas: The Bible and Art in Dialogue* (Bible in the Modern World 13; Sheffield: Sheffield Phoenix, 2007) 117–44.

Olyan, *Biblical Mourning*
  Saul M. Olyan, *Biblical Mourning: Ritual and Social Dimensions* (Oxford: Oxford University Press, 2004).

Olyan, "Isaiah 40–55"
  Saul M. Olyan, "Is Isaiah 40–55 Really Monotheistic?," *JANES* 12 (2012) 199–201.

Olyan, *Ritual Violence*
  Saul M. Olyan, ed., *Ritual Violence in the Hebrew Bible: New Perspectives* (Oxford: Oxford University Press, 2015).

Orlinsky, *Essays*
  Harry M. Orlinsky, *Essays in Biblical Culture and Biblical Translation* (New York: Ktav, 1974).

Otzen, *Tobit and Judith*
  Benedikt Otzen, *Tobit and Judith* (Guides to the Apocrypha and Pseuepigrapha 11; Sheffield: Sheffield Academic Press, 2001).

Patterson, "Re-membering the Past"
  Dilys Naomi Patterson, "Re-membering the Past: The Purpose of Historical Discourse in the Book of Judith," in Patricia G. Kirkpatrick and Timothy D. Goltz, eds., *The Function of Ancient Historiography in Biblical and Cognate Studies* (New York: T&T Clark International, 2008) 111–23.

Perkins, "Lord Is a Warrior"
  Larry Perkins, "'The Lord Is a Warrior,' 'The Lord Who Crushes Wars,' Exodus 15:3 and Judith 9:7; 16:2," *BIOSCS* 40 (2007) 121–33.

Perkins, *Suffering Self*
  Judith Perkins, *The Suffering Self: Pain and Narrative Representation in the Early Christian Era* (London: Routledge, 1995).

Pfeiffer, *History*
  Robert H. Pfeiffer, *History of the New Testament Times, with an Introduction to the Apocrypha* (New York: Harper, 1949).

Poirier, *Judith: Echos*
  Jacques Poirier, *Judith: Echos d'un mythe biblique dans la littérature française* (Rennes: Presses universitaires de Rennes, 2004).

Preuss, *From Shadow to Promise*
  Samuel L. Preuss, *From Shadow to Promise: Old Testament Interpretation from Augustine to the Young Luther* (Cambridge, MA: Belknap Press of Harvard University Press, 1969).

Priebatsch, "Das Buch Judith"
  Hans J. Priebatsch, "Das Buch Judith und seine hellenistischen Quellen," *ZDPV* 90 (1974) 50–60.

Purdie, *Story of Judith*
  Edna Purdie, *The Story of Judith in German and English Literature* (Paris: Librairie Ancienne Honore Champien, 1927).

Radin, *Trickster*
  Paul Radin, *The Trickster: A Study in American Indian Mythology* (New York: Schocken, 1972).

Rahlfs
  Alfred Rahlfs, *Ioudith: Septuaginta, id est Vetus Testamentum graece iuxta LXX interpretes* (5th ed.; Stuttgart: Württembergische Bibelanstalt, 1952) 973–1002.

Rakel, "I Will Sing"
  Claudia Rakel, "'I Will Sing a New Song to My God': Some Remarks on the Intertextuality of Judith 16.1–17," in Athalya Brenner, ed., *Judges: A Feminist Companion to the Bible* (Second Series; Sheffield: Sheffield Academic Press, 1999) 27–47.

Rakel, *Judit–Über Schönheit*
  Claudia Rakel, *Judit–Über Schönheit, Macht, und Widerstand im Krieg: Eine feministisch-intertextuelle Lektüre* (Berlin and New York: de Gruyter, 2003).

Rakel, "Judith: About a Beauty"
  Claudia Rakel, "Judith: About a Beauty Who is not What She Pretends to Be," in Louise Schottroff, ed., *Feminist Biblical Interpretation: A Compendium of Critical Commentary on the Books of the Bible and Related Literature* (Grand Rapids: Eerdmans, 2012) 515–30.

Ramelli and Perkins, *Early Christian and Jewish Narrative*
  Ilaria Ramelli and Judith Perkins, eds., *Early Christian and Jewish Narrative: The Role of Religion in Shaping Narrative Forms* (WUNT 348; Tübingen: Mohr Siebeck, 2015).

Reardon, *Collected Ancient Greek Novels*
  Bryan P. Reardon, ed., *Collected Ancient Greek Novels* (Berkeley: University of California Press, 1989).

Reinhartz, "Better Homes"
  Adele Reinhartz, "Better Homes and Gardens: Women and Domestic Space in the Books of Judith and Susanna," in Stephen G. Wilson and Michel Desjardins, eds., *Text and Artifact in the Religions of Mediterranean Antiquity: Essays in Honour of Peter Richardson* (Studies in Christianity and Judaism 9; Waterloo, ON: Wilfrid Laurier University Press, 2000) 325–39.

Reiterer, "Meines Bruders Licht"
  Friedrich V. Reiterer, "Meines Bruders Licht: Untersuchung zur Rolle des Achior," in Géza Xeravits, ed., *A Pious Seductress: Studies in the Book of Judith* (DCLS 14; Berlin: de Gruyter, 2012) 111–60.

Reiterer, "Religion und hellenistische Realpolitik"
  Friedrich V. Reiterer, "Religion und hellenistische Realpolitik im Buch Judit," in Friedrich V. Reiterer, Renate Egger-Wenzel, and Thomas R. Elßner, eds., *Gesellschaft und Religion in der spätbiblischen und deuterokanonischen Literatur* (DCLS 20; Berlin: de Gruyter, 2014) 29–54.

Roddy, "Way It Wasn't"
Nicolae Roddy, "The Way It Wasn't: The Book of Judith as Anti-Hasmonean Propaganda," *Studia Hebraica* 8 (2008) 269–77.

Roitman, "Achior"
Adolfo D. Roitman, "Achior in the Book of Judith: His Role and Significance," in James C. Vander-Kam, ed., *"No One Spoke Ill of Her": Essays on Judith* (EJL 2; Atlanta: Scholars Press, 1992) 31–45.

Roitman, "This People"
Adolfo D. Roitman, "'This People Are Descendants of Chaldeans' (Judith 5,6): Its Literary Form and Historical Setting," *JBL* 113 (1994) 245–63.

Ruiz-Montero, "Rise of the Greek Novel"
Consuelo Ruiz-Montero, "Rise of the Greek Novel," in Gareth Schmeling, ed., *The Novel in the Ancient World* (rev. ed.; Boston: Brill Academic, 2003) 29–85.

Ryan, "Ancient Versions"
Stephen D. Ryan, "The Ancient Versions of Judith and the Place of the Septuagint in the Catholic Church," in Géza Xeravits, ed., *A Pious Seductress: Studies in the Book of Judith* (DCLS 14; Berlin: de Gruyter, 2012) 1–21.

Ryan, "Judith's Deed"
Stephen D. Ryan, "Judith's Deed of Hope and Hope in the Book of Judith" (unpublished paper) 10–11.

Sandy, "New Pages"
Gerald Sandy, "New Pages of Greek Fiction," in J. R. Morgan and Richard Stoneman, eds., *Greek Fiction: The Greek Novel in Context* (London: Routledge, 1994) 130–45.

Satlow, "Be a Man"
Michael Satlow, "'Try to be a Man': The Rabbinic Construction of Masculinity," *HTR* 89 (1996) 19–40.

Sawyer, "Dressing Up"
Deborah F. Sawyer, "Dressing Up/Dressing Down: Power, Performance, and Identity in the Book of Judith," *Theology and Sexuality* 8 (2001) 23–31.

Sawyer, "Gender Strategies"
Deborah F. Sawyer, "Gender Strategies in Antiquity: Judith's Performance," *Feminist Theology* 28 (2001) 9–26.

Schmeling, *Novel in the Ancient World*
Gareth Schmeling, ed., *The Novel in the Ancient World* (rev. ed.; Boston: Brill Academic, 2003).

Schmitz, "Function of the Speeches"
Barbara Schmitz, "The Function of the Speeches and Prayers in the Books [*sic*] of Judith," in Athalya Brenner-Idan and Helen Efthimiadis-Keith, eds., *A Feminist Companion to Tobit and Judith* (Feminist Companion to the Bible [Second Series]; London: Bloomsbury T&T Clark, 2015) 164–74.

Schmitz, *Gedeutete Geschichte*
Barbara Schmitz, *Gedeutete Geschichte: Die Funktion der Reden und Gebete im Buch Judit* (HBS 40; Freiburg im Breisgau: Herder, 2004).

Schmitz, "Holofernes's Canopy"
Barbara Schmitz, "Holofernes's Canopy in the Septuagint," in Kevin R. Brine, Elena Ciletti, and Henrike Lähnemann, eds., *The Sword of Judith: Judith Studies across the Disciplines* (Cambridge: OpenBook, 2010) 71–80.

Schmitz, "ΙΟΥΔΙΘ and *Iudith*"
Barbara Schmitz, "ΙΟΥΔΙΘ and *Iudith*: Überlegungen zum Verhältnis der Judit-Erzählung in der LXX und der Vulgata," in Johann Cook and Hermann-Josef Stipp, eds., *Text-Critical and Hermeneutical Studies in the Septuagint* (VTSup 157; Leiden: Brill, 2012) 359–79.

Schmitz, "Trickster"
Barbara Schmitz, "Trickster, Schriftgelehrte oder *femme fatale*? Die Juditfigur zwischen biblischer Erzählung und kunstgeschichtlicher Rezeption," *Biblisches Forum* 2004, www.bibfor.de (ISSN: 1437-9341).

Schmitz, "War, Violence and Tyrannicide"
Barbara Schmitz, "War, Violence and Tyrannicide in the Book of Judith," in Jan Lisen and Pancratius Beentjes, eds., *Visions of Peace and Tales of War* (Deuterocanonical and Cognate Literature Yearbook 2010; Berlin and New York: de Gruyter, 2010) 103–19.

Schmitz, "Zwischen Achikar"
Barbara Schmitz, "Zwischen Achikar und Demaratos—die Bedeutung Achiors in der Judit-erzählung," *BZ* 48 (2004) 19–38.

Schmitz/Engel, *Judit*
Barbara Schmitz and Helmut Engel, *Judit* (HTh-KAT; Freiburg: Herder, 2014).

Schneider, "Donatello and Caravaggio"
Laurie Schneider, "Donatello and Caravaggio: The Iconography of Decapitation," *American Imago* 33 (1976) 76–101.

Schöpflin, "Judith on Stage"
Karin Schöpflin, "Judith on Stage: The Dramatic Career of a Biblical Heroine," in Géza Xeravits, ed., *A Pious Seductress: Studies in the Book of Judith* (DCLS 14; Berlin: de Gruyter, 2012) 198–213.

Schorch, "Genderising Piety"
Stefan Schorch, "Genderising Piety: The Prayers of Mordecai and Esther in Comparison," in Géza G. Xeravits and József Zsengellér, eds., *Deuterocanonical Additions of the Old Testament Books: Selected Studies* (DCLS 5; Berlin: de Gruyter, 2010) 30–42.

Schuller, "Apocrypha"
Eileen M. Schuller, "Introduction to the Apocrypha," in Carol A. Newsom and Sharon H. Ringe, eds., *Women's Bible Commentary* (expanded ed.; Louisville: Westminster John Knox, 1998) 263–65.

Schwartz, "Un fragment grec"
  Jacques Schwartz, "Un fragment grec du Livre de Judith (sur ostracon)," *RB* 53 (1946) 534–37.
Schwartz, "Israel and the Nations"
  Seth Schwartz, "Israel and the Nations Roundabout: 1 Maccabees and the Hasmonean Expansion," *JJS* 42 (1991) 16–38.
Sheaffer, *Envisioning*
  Andrea M. Sheaffer, *Envisioning the Book of Judith: How Art Illuminates Minor Characters* (Bible in the Modern World; Sheffield: Sheffield Phoenix, 2014).
Shearman, "Christofano Allori's Judith"
  John Shearman, "Cristofano Allori's Judith," *Burlington Magazine* 121 (1979) 2–10.
Shemesh, "Stories of Women"
  Yael Shemesh, "The Stories of Women in a Man's World: The Books of Ruth, Esther, and Judith," in Susanne Scholz, ed., *Feminist Interpretation of the Hebrew Bible in Retrospect*, vol. 1, *Biblical Books* (Recent Research in Biblical Studies 5; Sheffield: Sheffield Phoneix, 2013) 248–67.
Shemesh, "Yet He Committed No Act"
  Yael Shemesh, "'Yet He Committed No Act of Sin with Me, to Defile and Shame Me' (Judith 13:16): The Narrative of Judith as a Corrective to the Narrative of Yael and Sisera" [in Hebrew], *Shnaton: An Annual for Biblical and Ancient Near Eastern Studies* 16 (2006) 159–77.
Simkovich, "Book of Judith"
  Malka Simkovich, "The Book of Judith: A Fantasy Alternative Narrative to 2 Maccabees" (unpublished paper, 2013).
Simkovich, *Jewish Universalism*
  Malka Simkovich, *The Making of Jewish Universalism: From Exile to Alexandria* (Lanham, MD: Lexington, 2017).
Skehan, "Hand of Judith"
  Patrick W. Skehan, "The Hand of Judith," *CBQ* 25 (1963) 94–110.
Skemp, *Vulgate of Tobit*
  Vincent T. M. Skemp, *The Vulgate of Tobit Compared with Other Ancient Witnesses* (SBLDS 180; Atlanta: Society of Biblical Literature, 2000).
Smith, "Domestication of Sacrifice"
  Jonathan Z. Smith, "The Domestication of Sacrifice," in Robert Hamerton-Kelly, ed., *Violent Origins: Walter Burkert, René Girard, and Jonathan Z. Smith on Ritual Killing and Cultural Formation* (Stanford, CA: Stanford University Press, 1987) 191–238.
Smither, *History of the Oratorio*
  Howard E. Smither, *A History of the Oratorio* (4 vols.; Chapel Hill: University of North Carolina Press, 1977–2000).
Soubigou, "Judith"
  Louis Soubigou, "Judith: Traduit et commenté," in Louis Pirot and Albert Clamer, *La Sainte Bible* (Paris: Letouzey et Ané, 1952) 481–575.

Steinmann, *Lecture de Judith*
  Jean Steinmann, *Lecture de Judith* (Paris: Gabalda, 1953).
Steinmetzer, *Geschichtlichkeit der Juditherzählung*
  Franz Steinmetzer, *Neue Untersuchung über die Geschichtlichkeit der Juditherzählung: Ein Beitrag zur Erklärung des Buches Judith* (Leipzig: Rudolf Haupt, 1907).
Stephens and Winkler, *Ancient Greek Novels*
  Susan A. Stephens and John J. Winkler, *Ancient Greek Novels: The Fragments; Introduction, Text, Translation, and Commentary* (Princeton, NJ: Princeton University Press, 1995).
Stetkevych, *Mute Immortals*
  Suzanne Pinckney Stetkevych, *The Mute Immortals Speak: Pre-Islamic Poetry and the Poetics of Ritual* (Myth and Poetics; Ithaca, NY: Cornell University Press, 1993).
Stiehl and Altheim, *Die aramäische Sprache*
  Ruth Stiehl and Franz Altheim, *Die aramäische Sprache unter den Achaimeniden* (Frankfurt am Main: Vittorio Klostermann, 1963).
Stocker, *Judith*
  Margarita Stocker, *Judith: Sexual Warrior Women and Power in Western Culture* (New Haven: Yale University Press, 1998).
Stoneman, *Alexander Romance*
  Richard Stoneman, *The Greek Alexander Romance* (London: Penguin, 1991).
Strait, "Wisdom of Solomon"
  Drew J. Strait, "The Wisdom of Solomon, Ruler Cults, and Paul's Polemic against Idols in the Areopagus Speech," *JBL* 106 (2017) 609–32.
Stronk, *Ctesias' Persian History*
  Jan P. Stronk, *Ctesias' Persian History*, part 1: *Introduction, Text, and Translation* (Düsseldorf: Wellem, 2010).
Stummer, *Geographie*
  Friedrich Stummer, *Geographie des Buches Judith* (Bibelwissenschaftliche Reihe 3; Stuttgart: Katholisches Bibelwerk, 1947).
Talbot, *Sacred Vocal Music*
  Michael Talbot, *The Sacred Vocal Music of Antonio Vivaldi* (Florence: Olschki, 1995).
Tan, "Judith's Embodiment"
  Nancy Tan, "Judith's Embodiment as a Reversal of the Unfaithful Wife of Yhwh in Ezekiel 16," *JSP* 21 (2011) 21–35.
Tatum, *Search for the Ancient Novel*
  James Tatum, ed., *The Search for the Ancient Novel* (Baltimore: Johns Hopkins University Press, 1994).
Thayer, "Judith and Mary"
  Anne T. Thayer, "Judith and Mary: Hélinand's Sermon for the Assumption," in Jacqueline Hamesse et al., eds., *Medieval Sermons and Society: Cloister, City, University; Proceedings of International Symposia at Kalamazoo and New York* (Textes et études du moyen âge 9; Louvain-la-Neuve:

Fédération Internationale des Instituts d'études médiévales, 1998) 63–75.

Thiessen, "Aseneth's Eight-Day Transformation"
Matthew Thiessen, "Aseneth's Eight-Day Transformation as Scriptural Justification for Conversion 1," *JSJ* 45 (2014) 229–49.

Thiessen, "Protecting the Holy Race"
Matthew Thiessen, "Protecting the Holy Race and Holy Space: Judith's Reenactment of the Slaughter of Shechem," *JAJ* 49 (2018) 165–88.

Thomas, *Acts of Peter*
Christine Thomas, *The Acts of Peter, Gospel Literature, and the Ancient Novel: Rewriting the Past* (Oxford: Oxford University Press, 2003).

Thomas, *Herodotus in Context*
Rosalind Thomas, *Herodotus in Context: Ethnography, Science, and the Art of Persuasion* (Cambridge: Cambridge University Press, 2000).

Thompson, *Motif-Index*
Stith Thompson, *Motif-Index of Folk-Literature* (rev. and enl. ed.; 6 vols.; Bloomington: Indiana University Press, 1955–58).

Tinagli, *Women*
Paola Tinagli, *Women in Italian Renaissance Art: Gender, Representation, Identity* (Manchester: Manchester University Press, 1997).

Tomes, "Heroism"
Roger Tomes, "Heroism in 1 and 2 Maccabees," *BibInt* 15 (2007) 171–99.

Torrey, *Apocryphal Literature*
Charles Cutler Torrey, *Apocryphal Literature: A Brief Introduction* (New Haven: Yale University Press, 1945).

Uppenkamp, *Judith and Holofernes*
Bettina Uppenkamp, *Judith und Holofernes in der italienischen Malerei des Barock* (Berlin: Dietrich Reimer, 2004).

VanderKam, *No One Spoke Ill*
James C. VanderKam, ed., *"No One Spoke Ill of Her": Essays on Judith* (EJL 2; Atlanta: Scholars Press, 1992).

Venter, "Function of the Ammonite"
Pieter Venter, "The Function of the Ammonite Achior in the Book of Judith," *HvTSt* 67(3) Art. #1101, 9 pages, http://dx.doi.org/10.4102/hts.v67i3.1101.

Voigt, *Latin Versions*
Edwin Edgar Voigt, *The Latin Versions of Judith* (Leipzig: Drugulin, 1925).

Voitila, "Deuteronomistic Heritage"
Anssi Voitila, "Judith and Deuteronomistic Heritage," in Hanne von Weissenberg, Juha Pakkala, and Marko Marttila, eds., *Changes in Scripture: Rewriting and Interpreting Authoritative Traditions in the Second Temple Period* (BZAW 419; Berlin: de Gruyter, 2011) 369–88.

Walbank, "Speeches"
F. W. Walbank, "Speeches in Greek Historians," in F. W. Walbank, *Selected Papers: Studies in Greek and Roman History and Historiography* (Cambridge: Cambridge University Press, 1985) 242–61.

Walker and Uysal, *Tales Alive*
Warren S. Walker and Ahmet E. Uysal, *Tales Alive in Turkey* (Cambridge, MA: Harvard University Press, 1966).

Warren, *My Flesh Is Meat*
Meredith J. C. Warren, *My Flesh Is Meat Indeed: A Non-Sacramental Reading of John 6:51–58* (Minneapolis: Fortress Press, 2015).

Watanabe-O'Kelly, *Beauty or Beast?*
Helen Watanabe-O'Kelly, *Beauty or Beast? The Woman Warrior in the German Imagination from the Renaissance to the Present* (Oxford: Oxford University Press, 2010).

Watanabe-O'Kelly, "Figure of Judith"
Helen Watanabe-O'Kelly, "The Figure of Judith in Works by German Women Writers between 1895 and 1921," in Claire Bielby and Anna Richards, eds., *Women and Death 3: Women's Representations of Death in German Culture since 1950* (Rochester, NY: Camden House, 2010) 101–16.

Wegner, *Chattel*
Judith Romney Wegner, *Chattel or Person? The Status of Women in the Mishnah* (Oxford: Oxford University Press, 1988).

Weingarten, "Food, Sex, and Redemption"
Susan Weingarten, "Food, Sex, and Redemption in *Megillat Yehudit* (the Scroll of Judith)," in Kevin R. Brine, Elena Ciletti, and Henrike Lähnemann, eds., *The Sword of Judith: Judith Studies across the Disciplines* (Cambridge: OpenBook, 2010) 97–126.

Weitzman, "Literary Approaches"
Steven Weitzman, "Literary Approaches," in Jonathan Klawans and Lawrence M. Wills, eds., *Jewish Annotated Apocrypha* (New York: Oxford University Press, forthcoming).

Weitzman, *Song and Story*
Steven Weitzman, *Song and Story in Biblical Narrative: The History of a Literary Convention in Ancient Israel* (Indiana Studies in Biblical Literature; Bloomington: Indiana University Press, 1997).

Weitzman, *Surviving Sacrilege*
Steven Weitzman, *Surviving Sacrilege: Cultural Persistence in Jewish Antiquity* (Cambridge, MA: Harvard University Press, 2005).

West, "Croesus' Second Reprieve"
Stephanie West, "Croesus' Second Reprieve and Other Tales of the Persian Court," *ClQ* n.s. 53 (2003) 416–37.

Weststeijn, "Wine, Women"
Johan Weststeijn, "Wine, Women, and Revenge in Near Eastern Historiography: The Tales of Tomyris, Judith, Zenobia, and Jalila," *JNES* 75 (2016) 91–107.

Whitmarsh, *Cambridge Companion*
Tim Whitmarsh, ed., *The Cambridge Companion to the Greek and Roman Novel* (Cambridge: Cambridge University Press, 2008).

Wills, "Ascetic Theology"
Lawrence M. Wills, "Ascetic Theology before Asceticism? Jewish Narratives and the Decentering of the Self," *JAAR* 74 (2006) 902–25.

Wills, "Death of the Hero"
Lawrence M. Wills, "The Death of the Hero and the Violent Death of Jesus," in Jonathan Klawans and David A. Bernat, eds., *Religion and Violence: The Biblical Heritage* (Recent Research in Biblical Studies 2; Sheffield: Sheffield Phoenix, 2007) 79–99.

Wills, "Depiction of Slavery"
Lawrence M. Wills, "The Depiction of Slavery in the Ancient Novel," *Semeia* 81 (2000) 113–32.

Wills, "Jew, Judean, Judaism"
Lawrence M. Wills, "Jew, Judean, Judaism in the Ancient Period: An Alternative Argument," *JAJ* 7 (2016) 169–93.

Wills, *Jew in the Court*
Lawrence M. Wills, *The Jew in the Court of the Foreign King: Ancient Jewish Court Legends* (Minneapolis: Augsburg Fortress, 1990).

Wills, *Jewish Novel*
Lawrence M. Wills, *The Jewish Novel in the Ancient World* (Myth and Poetics; Ithaca, NY: Cornell University Press, 1995).

Wills, *Not God's People*
Lawrence M. Wills, *Not God's People: Insiders and Outsiders in the Biblical World* (Religion in the Modern World; Lanham, MD: Rowman & Littlefield, 2008).

Wills, *Quest*
Lawrence M. Wills, *The Quest of the Historical Gospel: Mark, John, and the Origins of the Gospel Genre* (London: Routledge, 1997).

Wright and Edwards, "She Undid Him"
Benjamin G. Wright and Suzanne M. Edwards, "'She Undid Him with the Beauty of Her Face' (Jdt 16.6): Reading Women's Bodies in Early Jewish Literature," in Géza G. Xeravits, ed., *Religion and Female Body in Ancient Judaism and Its Environments* (DCLS 28; Berlin: de Gruyter, 2015) 73–108.

Zeitlin, *Book of Judith*
Morton S. Enslin and Solomon Zeitlin, *The Book of Judith* (Jewish Apocryphal Literature 7; Leiden: Brill, 1972).

Zenger, *Das Buch Judit*
Erich Zenger, *Das Buch Judit*, in *Historische and legendärische Erzählungen* (JSHRZ 1.6; Gütersloh: Mohn, 1981) 424–534.

Zenger, "Judith/Judithbuch"
Erich Zenger, "Judith/Judithbuch," in *TRE* 17:404–8.

Zenger, "Der Juditroman"
Erich Zenger, "Der Juditroman als Traditions- modell des Jahweglaubens," *TTZ* 83 (1974) 65–80.

Zertal, "Reality"
Adam Zertal, "The Reality of the Book of Judith," *Eretz-Israel* 29 (2009) 161–75.

Zimmermann, "Recovery"
Frank Zimmermann, "Aids for the Recovery of the Hebrew Original of Judith," *JBL* 57 (1938) 67–74.

Zsengellér, "Judith as a Female David"
József Zsengellér, "Judith as a Female David," in Géza G. Xeravits, ed., *Religion and Female Body in Ancient Judaism and Its Environment* (DCLS 28; Berlin: de Gruyter, 2015) 186–211.

Introduction

1. The Name Judith, the Title of the Book, and Its Place in the Canon

The earliest spelling of our heroine's name in the textual tradition is Ιουδειθ, *Ioudeith*, also spelled *Iudith* or *Ioudēth*, the Greek rendering of Hebrew *Yehudit*, יהודית. The Hebrew is reflected in the Syriac spelling, *Yehudit*, although the internal *h* sound of Semitic languages could not be represented in the Greek alphabet. Yehudah, for instance, the masculine equivalent of Yehudit, is spelled *Iouda*. The critical editions of the Greek text by Robert Hanhart and Alfred Rahlfs show *Ioudith*, assimilating it to the Hebrew spelling. As a result of itacism (the tendency for some Greek vowels to be pronounced like *iota*), the three spellings would have been indistinguishable in oral dictation.[1] English and other European spellings are derived from Latin *Iudith*.

The masculine *Yehudah* means "Yahweh is praised," *Ye + hōdah,* a connection played upon when Leah names Judah, saying, "I will praise the LORD" (Gen 29:35). *Yehudit* could mean a woman praiser or hymner. As an adverb, *yĕhûdît* also means "in Jewish," that is, in the Hebrew language (Neh 13:23–24), as *'ibrît* also means in Hebrew. Despite its meaning, the name also appears for the Hittite wife of Esau in Gen 26:34 (in LXX as *Ioudin*). This reference comes *before* the birth of Judah, when the etiological significance of the name is given, but this sort of anachronism is not uncommon in biblical narrative. A foreigner is named Yehudi in Jer 36:14. As a result of these instances, Carey A. Moore cautions against seeing the name as inherently Judean,[2] but a Judean name has likely been ascribed here to foreigners, or perhaps foreign names have been assimilated. (Compare the case of Bagoas in 12:11).

The feminine name was not common in ancient Judaism but is still attested. A Jewish Aramaic ostracon from Persian-era Egypt mentions Yehudit, and the name was found in texts and inscriptions from first century BCE–

second century CE, in both western and eastern diasporas.[3] In the rabbinic period we hear of Judith daughter of Dalluy, and also Judith the wife of Rabbi Hiyya (second–third century CE, b. Yeb. 65a–b, b. Qidd. 12a–b). The latter has a challenging association, on which see §8 below.

The title of our text in the early Greek manuscripts is Ιουδιθ, "Ioudith," attested in some papyri with different spellings, as well as Book of the History (*historias*) of Judith (see text-critical notes). The Old Latin versions have her name and the title of the book as *Incipit liber Iudit* or *Iudith,* and in the Vulgate, *Liber Iudith*. The books of Ruth, Esther, and Tobit also take their names from the principal character, as did many of the prophetic books and Job. One also finds the title *Biblion historias Ioudith,* "Book of the History of Judith." In addition, biblical books were numbered; appearing for Judith are *Biblion ith'*, or Book 19; *Biblion eikoston triton*, or Book 23; and even *Biblion eikoston triton ouk ekklēsiazetai*, "Book 23 Which Is Not Read in Worship." Although the Greek novels were first probably known by the neuter plural of the geographical region—*Babyloniaka, Ephesiaka, Milesiaka, Phoinikika* (similar to the historical texts *Persika, Skythica, Indika*), they were also known by the female protagonist's name.[4]

The Name Judith and Jewish Identity

Every introduction to the book of Judith notes that her name means "Jewish woman" but often without any reflection on what "Jew" would mean in this period. There is some debate on this question. Throughout Israelite and Jewish history, from the most ancient period to the modern, the term *Israel* has been the most common and consistent insider's term to identify the people as a whole, even though the term *Israel* was often associated

---

1   Barbara Schmitz and Helmut Engel, *Judit* (HThKAT; Freiburg im Breisgau: Herder, 2014) 235, 240. All of these spellings are indeclinable, but compare the accusative *Ioudin* in the LXX of Gen 26:34.

2   Carey A. Moore, *Judith: A New Translation with Introduction and Commentary* (AB 40B; Garden City, NY: Doubleday, 1985) 179.

3   Michael Heltzer, "Eine neue Quelle zur Bestimmung der Abfassungszeit des Judithbuches," *ZAW* 92 (1980) 437; Tal Ilan, *Lexicon of Jewish Names in Late Antiquity* (4 vols.; Tübingen: Mohr Siebeck, 2002–2012) 1:27–28, 241–42, s.v. Yehudit; Ilan, *Jewish Women in Greco-Roman Palestine: An Inquiry into Image and Status* (TSAJ 44; Tübingen: Mohr Siebeck, 2006) 54.

4   Susan A. Stephens and John J. Winkler, *Ancient Greek Novels: The Fragments; Introduction, Text, Translation, and Commentary* (Princeton: Princeton University Press, 1995) 318–19; see also §7 below.

with the north. The author may have been participating in a dramatic, relatively new affirmation of "Jewish identity" (see below and at commentary on 4:1–15). After the First and Second Temples had been destroyed, the term *Israel* continued to connote membership in the people constituted by God.

In contrast to *Israel*, the terms that are translated as "Jew"—Hebrew *yĕhûdî* (masculine) and *yĕhûdîyâ* (feminine) and related terms in Aramaic, and Greek *Ioudaios/ Ioudaia* and related terms in Latin—were surprisingly rare in ancient Israel. This began to change in the Second Temple period. Ezra-Nehemiah, treating the rebuilding of Jerusalem, often utilizes the *yĕhûd-* root as a strong identity term.[5] In 2 Maccabees, both *Ioudaioi* and even the new word *Ioudaismos*, or Judaism, are emphasized. We also find that the coins minted under the Hasmonean John Hyrcanus (c. 128 BCE) are inscribed on one side:[6]

Jehohanan the high priest and the council of the Jews.

יהוחנן הכהן הגדול וחבר היהודים

The sense of *Yehudi, Ioudaios*, and related terms may also shift dramatically in this period (see at 12:5b–9). An engaged scholarly debate has emerged on this issue, yet to be resolved.[7] Judith's name may be an assertion of Jewish identity, suggesting that she is an ideal Jewish woman or heroine. Corroborating this is the observation that most of the uses of the *Yehud-/Ioudai-* root in the Second Temple period are found in the Jewish novellas and court narratives: Esther often, Dan 3:8, 12, Bel 28, Susanna OG 22–23, 56–57; and the Prayer of Nabonidus and Tales of the Persian Court (4Q550d–e) from Qumran (see §7 below).

The name Judith may also suggest a personification of the people as a whole, as Britannia or Roma were personified figures. Subjugated peoples in Greek culture were often represented as women: Thracia, Aithiopia, *hē Aigyptos*. Finally, the name may call to mind a female consort to Judah the Maccabee (see §5 below). Although it is conceivable that there is no particular resonance to the name other than that of a female character, that does not seem likely. It is more likely that all three resonances— personification of the people, the subjugated people (now victorious), and a symbolic female consort of Judah the Maccabee—were heard in her name.

Canon and Placement

Judith was not canonized by Jews, although there is a medieval Jewish Judith tradition (see §8 below). It is never mentioned by Jewish authors, nor in rabbinic literature in antiquity, with one possible exception: it may have been known to the authors of Greek Esther and Pseudo-Philo, *Biblical Antiquities*.[8] The lack of canonization is often compared to the case of Esther, which was canonized in the Jewish Scriptures only with difficulty. Esther also contained challenging motifs, such as a Jewish queen of a non-Jewish king, but nothing nearly as provocative as the characterization of Judith. The popularity of Esther as the Purim reading likely brought that text into the canonical fold, and although Judith might have been associated with a holiday much like Nicanor's Day (b. Ta'an. 18b)—as Third Maccabees was also associated with a holiday in Egypt—this is speculative.

The reason that Judith was not canonized by Jews may be as simple as the language. There is no known Hebrew text, although in about 400 CE Jerome claims familiarity with Aramaic texts.[9] A number of other aspects of the Judith narrative have been proposed as possible explana-

---

5   Specifically, in Ezra 1–6 and the Nehemiah Memoir; see Lawrence M. Wills, "Jew, Judean, Judaism in the Ancient Period: An Alternative Argument," *JAJ* 7 (2016) 169–93.

6   Ya'akov Meshorer, *A Treasury of Jewish Coins: From the Persian Period to Bar Kokhba* (in Hebrew; Jerusalem: Yad Yitshak Ben-Tsevi, 1997) 35–36.

7   Wills summarizes the debate ("Jew, Judean, Judaism").

8   I use the term Greek Esther rather than LXX Esther or Add Esth because it is clearer to readers outside of biblical studies. On the influence of Judith on Greek Esther Addition D, see Moore, *Judith*, 212–16;

on the influence on Pseudo-Philo, see Howard Jacobson, *A Commentary on Pseudo-Philo's Liber Antiquitatum Biblicarum* (2 vols.; AGJU 31; Leiden: Brill, 1996) 1:226.

9   Crawford, "Esther and Judith: Contrasts in Character," in Sidnie White Crawford and Leonard J. Greenspoon, eds., *The Book of Esther in Modern Research* (JSOTSup 380; London: T&T Clark, 2003) 60–76, here 70–71. See also Jan Joosten, who argues that Judith was not canonized by Jews because it was originally written in Greek ("The Original Language and Historical Milieu of the Book of Judith," in Moshe Bar-Asher and Emanuel Tov, eds., *Meghillot:*

tions for why it was not canonized, none being definitive. Jean Steinmann was the first to suggest that the conversion of an Ammonite was viewed as a problem for the rabbis; Deut 23:4 prohibits the entry of Ammonites and Moabites to "the assembly of the Lord."[10] This argument is not conclusive, however, since Ruth was a Moabite. The book of Ruth may have been canonized *despite* its challenge to Deut 23:4. That Achior is circumcised when he converts yet does not undergo a ritual immersion was raised as a problem by Solomon Zeitlin. Shaye J. D. Cohen points out, however, that ritual immersion was probably not introduced as a necessary part of conversion until later.[11] Still, by the time canonization was actually raised as an issue, immersion might have become a required practice.

Some scholars have suggested that the problem was the general demeanor of Judith. Toni Craven concludes simply, but likely correctly, that the book presents too brazen a protagonist.[12] True, the Hebrew Bible contains many outrageous acts by Israelite women, yet Craven catalogues the activities that would presumably have challenged an ancient Jewish audience: Judith upbraids the elders; she remains unmarried and without children; and she manages an estate through a female slave. Craven grants that there is some evidence that all of these actions might have been possible for a wealthy Jewish widow, but Judith's further violations of sexual norms would present a greater challenge. Tamar had broken similar taboos (Genesis 38), but she was a foreign woman and her story is probably included as one of the ironies of patriarchal history. Moore argues that no one reason can be given as to why the book was not canonized, and there has been no further clarity on this.[13]

Early Christian authors in the West, says Moore (88–91, with a map), regarded our text as canonical, those in the East often did not. This observation will be relevant in the history of reception when we note that in about 400 CE a number of Latin fathers developed important interpretations of our text (see §8 below). Yet soon after, Judith can be found in all of the early versions of the Bible, West and East. In the earliest known versions of the Christian Bible, Judith is grouped with Esther and Tobit—all novellas, even though there is no known name for such a genre designation. It was positioned with Esther in Vaticanus, and with Tobit between them in Sinaiticus and Alexandrinus. The so-called Syriac Book of Women (sixth century CE) included Judith with Ruth, Esther, Susanna, and Thecla.[14] Judith came to be deuterocanonical in Catholic and Orthodox Bibles, evidently canonical in Ethiopic Bibles, but not included in Protestant Bibles.[15] As early as 1 Clem. 55:4–6, Judith is treated like other biblical texts, but the lack of a consistent treatment of deuterocanonical texts must be noted (see appendix below). The ambiguity of the "Apocrypha" in the early church remains unresolved.

Anton Biolek's 1911 study had already indicated that

Studies in the Dead Sea Scrolls V–VI: A Festschrift for Devorah Dimant [Jerusalem: Bialik Institute; Haifa: University of Haifa, 2007] *159–*176, here 175–76.

10 Jean Steinmann, *Lecture de Judith* (Paris: Gabalda, 1953) 61–62; see the commentary on 14:10.

11 Solomon Zeitlin, in Morton Enslin and Solomon Zeitlin, *The Book of Judith: Greek Text with an English Translation* (Jewish Apocryphal Literature 7; Leiden: Brill, 1972) 25; Harry M. Orlinsky, *Essays in Biblical Culture and Biblical Translation* (New York: Ktav, 1974) 281; Shaye J. D. Cohen, *From the Maccabees to the Mishnah* (LEC 7; Philadelphia: Westminster, 1987) 53. Note that Mathias Delcor argues that the Essenes were not interested in Judith because of its Pharisaic leanings, but it was likely for other reasons ("Le livre de Judith et l'époque grecque," *Klio* 49 [1967] 151–79, here 170).

12 Toni, Craven, *Artistry and Faith in the Book of Judith* (SBLDS 70; Chico, CA: Scholars Press, 1983) 117–18.

13 Carey A. Moore, "Why Wasn't the Book of Judith Included in the Hebrew Bible," in James C. VanderKam, ed., *No One Spoke Ill of Her: Essays on Judith* (EJL 2; Atlanta: Scholars Press, 1992) 61–71.

14 Lucas Van Rompay, "'No Evil Word about Her': The Two Syriac Versions of the Book of Judith," in W. Th. Van Peursen and R. B. Ter Haar Romeny, eds., *Text, Translation, and Tradition: Studies on the Peshitta and Its Use in the Syriac Tradition Presented to Konrad D. Jenner on the Occasion of His Sixty-Fifth Birthday* (Monographs of the Peshitta Institute, Leiden 14; Leiden: Brill, 2006) 205–302, here 205.

15 Jan Joosten, "The Origin of the Septuagint Canon," in Siegfried Kreuzer, Martin Meiser, and Marcus Sigismund, eds., *Die Septuaginta: Orte und Intentionen*, 5: *Internationale Fachtagung veranstaltet von Septuaginta Deutsch (LXX.D), Wuppertal 24.–27. Juli 2014* (WUNT 361; Tübingen: Mohr Siebeck, 2016) 688–99.

the book of Judith was not universally accepted as part of the Christian canon.[16] In the fifth century, Pope Hilarius stated that the canon of the Old Testament consisted of twenty-two books, and omitted Judith and Tobit (*Prologue on Psalms*). Some other Christian authors apparently omitted it from the canon. We must also ask what canonization meant for interpretation. Jerome was hesitant to accept Judith into the canon—there was, he insisted, no known Semitic text—but at the same time, it is often overlooked that he strongly affirms Judith as a model for both men and women.

Protestant Bibles, following the Jewish practice, do not include Judith as part of the proto-canon, but Protestants continued to use the Apocrypha, and often included these texts in their printed Bibles. In the Luther Bible and King James Version, the Apocrypha were included in a separate section, only later omitted in popular printings. The Apocrypha were routinely excluded in the Reformed Tradition, and this became the norm for most Protestant Bibles. Yet Judith lived on in art and popular culture even in Protestant countries.

---

16   Anton Biolek, "Die Ansicht des christlichen Altertums über den literarischen Charakter des Buches Judith," *Weidenauer Studien* 4 (1911) 335–68, here 361; see also André Marie Dubarle, *Judith: Formes et sens des diverses traditions* (2 vols.; AnBib 24; Rome: Institut biblique pontifical, 1966) 1:110–19, 173–79; Enslin, *Book of Judith*, 43–52.

2. Historical Context of Judith: Historicity, Date, Author, Location of Composition, Language

It is assumed in this commentary that Judith was written at the end of the second or the beginning of the first century BCE (see below). The historical context of this period should be sketched briefly. The vast empire of Alexander the Great—covering part of Europe, extending east to India and south to Egypt—was divided soon after his death into the large quadrants of the *diadochoi,* successors. Two of these successors were the Seleucids in Syria and the Ptolemies in Egypt. Under the previous rule of the Persians, Yehud or Judah had been reestablished as a province and a local temple-state, with a governor and a high priest. Under the Greeks only the high priest remained, serving at the pleasure of the Hellenistic king.

The area of Judah, or Judea, was a buffer state, first part of the Ptolemaic kingdom and then the Seleucid. It is likely that hellenization proceeded quickly and successfully as a policy precisely because it focused on changes at the public and constitutional level, while allowing native cultural life on the local and private level to continue much as it had.[1] In the Hellenistic borderland of Judea, Jews thus negotiated a relationship with empire. A creative colonial membrane resulted, the boundary at which an indigenous people could assert an identity not necessarily *in opposition* to Persians or Greeks but *in negotiation* with these empires. But such a situation was not to last. Attempts by the new Seleucid king, Antiochus IV Epiphanes, to hellenize the temple organization in Jerusalem resulted in a full-scale guerrilla insurrection by the Hasmonean family, some of whom were nicknamed Maccabees. The revolt was eventually successful, and in 165 BCE the Hasmoneans established a new political structure in Jerusalem. In Anthony Smith's cross-cultural analysis of the rise of nations, he included the Maccabean Revolt as an ancient example of "ethnicism," a colonized people's assertion of their own native identity, using the language of the colonizers.[2] This was true not only of Jews but of other ethnic groups as well.

At first the Maccabean rebels engaged in a nativist revitalization of ancient Israelite traditions, reasserting the old tribal ideal of the charismatic prophet (1 Macc 14:41–42), the Hasmonean leaders now latter-day successors to the judges (see §4 below). Soon, however, the Hasmonean leaders took on more titles. Jonathan declared himself to be high priest as early as 153 BCE, while Simon Maccabee, who ascended in 141 and declared full independence, claimed the role, but not the title, of king. He was, rather, *ethnarchēs* and *stratēgos* (1 Macc 14:47; see the discussion of "high priest" at Jdt 4:6–7). Only in 104 BCE did a Hasmonean ruler, Aristobulus I, officially claim the title of king (in addition to high priest). Depending, then, on the dating of Judith, the focus on the office of high priest and not king *may* reflect the then-current Hasmonean titles. Whenever Judith was written, it certainly affirmed the role of the high priest, and it is possible that the author lived at a time when it was considered inappropriate for the earthly rule in Judah to be associated with kingship. That would align with the policy of the Hasmoneans from 152 BCE (official independence from the Seleucids and the Hasmonean leaders' assumption of the title high priest) to 104 BCE (Aristobulus's assumption of the title king).

The attitude of the book of Judith toward outside nations is difficult to determine precisely. Erich Gruen has rightly challenged the view that Jewish authors were systematically opposed to Hellenistic influences and control, but he perhaps paints an overly consistent and positive view.[3] In his works, statements about "Jews" often refer to a tiny subset of elite, hellenized authors. He includes the Jewish novellas, which may be elite, but does not incorporate the many apocalypses in his analysis, which reflect alternative perspectives. It is not the case that "Jews" were all well disposed to their Hellenistic rulers; rather, there were very mixed, searching, deeply ambivalent engagements with Hellenism that problema-

1   Seth Schwartz, "The Hellenization of Jerusalem and Shechem," in Martin Goodman, ed., *Jews in a Graeco-Roman World* (Oxford: Clarendon, 1998) 37–46.

2   Anthony Smith, *The Ethnic Origins of Nations* (Oxford: Blackwell, 1986) 56–57; Shaye J. D. Cohen, *The Beginnings of Jewishness: Boundaries, Varieties, Uncertainties* (HCS 31; Berkeley: University of California Press, 1999) 138–39.

3   Erich Gruen, *Heritage and Hellenism: The Reinvention of Jewish Tradition* (HCS 30; Berkeley: University of California Press, 1998) 12–40; Gruen, *Diaspora: Jews Amidst Greeks and Romans* (Cambridge, MA: Harvard University Press, 2002) 219–31.

tized Jews' status at the colonial periphery, even when they claimed to be triumphant. There was in Judea, as in other provinces, a nativist revitalization movement that in some cases affirmed a separate identity in response to Hellenistic cultural forces, even while Greek intellectual trends were all the while being absorbed unconsciously. Steven Weitzman points out that Jews under colonial rule sometimes took up the "arts of the weak" as strategies: appeasement, symbiosis, flattery, mimicry, diplomacy:

> In some cases . . . what might look like assimilation to a foreign culture can be placed within an alternative narrative of cultural persistence, one in which Jews poach resources from the *other* for use in sustaining their own culture.[4]

True enough, and it was likely often subconscious as well. Both Gruen and Weitzman often stress *conscious* reactions of Jewish elites to *explicit* threats from great empires arising against a *public* and *central* aspect of Jewish identity, the temple. It is possible to stress as well *unconscious* reactions to *implicit* threats against *private* and *marginal* sectors of Jewish life. The two approaches should be quite complementary.

Although Judea now enjoyed self-rule, it was hardly cut off from Hellenistic culture; it simply functioned as another Hellenistic kingdom. The older scholarly dichotomy of "Judaism and Hellenism" often overstated the difference between the two, framing the question incorrectly as the mixing of a clear Judaism and a clear Hellenism: Do the Jewish authors have a core of Jewish values and an outer garment of Hellenism? Are Jewish authors positive about Hellenism or negative? Is Josephus more Jewish or more Hellenistic? Yet an unmixed Judaism or Hellenism never existed; the Judaism before Hellenism was a Persianized Judaism (Ezra and Nehemiah)

struggling against a Syrianized Israel (the opponents of Ezra and Nehemiah). Hellenism itself was already indigenized, Persianized, and syncretized.[5] The indigenous authors negotiated the boundary with the imperial center, on the one hand, and multiple boundaries with neighboring peoples, on the other. Earlier descriptions of Hellenistic Jewish authors in terms of a series of either/or's—either Jewish or Greek identity, Jewish core with a Greek surface, positive or negative toward Hellenism—have been largely dropped in favor of a recognition of the hybridized relation of Greek colonizers and many competing colonized peoples. Judith reflects this hybridized and ambivalent status constantly, as noted in this commentary.

The uniqueness of Judaism, indeed, has often been articulated too sharply, reflecting the interests of Jewish and Christian theology. Yet distinctive aspects of a changing Judaism can still be discerned. It is important to register that, while in some ways Jews exhibited similarities with other peoples, they simultaneously displayed strategic differences. Whereas Samarians and Phoenicians were in general more willing to allow a mixing of religious symbols with Greek culture, many Jews—or at least those Jews that we hear from—retained tighter boundary markers.[6] And other indigenous peoples, it should be noted, were sometimes as restive as Jews. Although scholars have often assumed—and 1 and 2 Maccabees and Judith would have us believe—that Jews alone developed an uncompromising religious identity, many indigenous groups mounted Maccabee-like opposition movements. Rebellions against the Hellenistic rulers occurred around Thebes in Egypt, and apocalyptic texts also appeared in that region (Oracle of the Potter, Demotic Chronicle). Not only Yahweh but other local deities inspired nationalistic resistance: Edomite Cos, Tyrian Melkart, Egyptian Osiris. Ethnic rebellion was not just "Jewish" but part

4   Steven Weitzman, *Surviving Sacrilege: Cultural Persistence in Jewish Antiquity* (Cambridge, MA: Harvard University Press, 2005) 9.

5   Lawrence M. Wills, *Not God's People: Insiders and Outsiders in the Biblical World* (Religion in the Modern World; Lanham, MD: Rowman & Littlefield, 2008) esp. 53–86.

6   Paul J. Kosmin, *The Land of the Elephant Kings: Space, Territory, and Ideology in the Seleucid Empire* (Cambridge, MA: Harvard University Press, 2014). See

also Martin Hengel, *Judaism and Hellenism: Studies in Their Encounter in Palestine during the Early Hellenistic Period* (Philadelphia: Fortress Press, 1974) 70–71, 83–87; Doron Mendels, *The Rise and Fall of Jewish Nationalism* (ABRL; New York: Doubleday, 1992) 23, 29 n. 17; but see also 66–69, 137, 356; Samuel K. Eddy, *The King Is Dead: Studies in the Near Eastern Resistance to Hellenism, 334–31 B.C.* (Lincoln: University of Nebraska Press, 1961) 133–36, 163–64, 327–31; Wills, *Not God's People*, 91.

of a broader colonial resistance. The fissures, of course, were not simply between local peoples and the empire; Judeans fought and negotiated boundaries with other indigenous ethnic groups as well.

Although the campaign of Holofernes is fictitious, it bears resemblances to campaigns by Alexander the Great and Antiochus IV Epiphanes, in addition to the earlier expedition of Artaxerxes III Ochus of Persia. These would have entered into Judean lore. Antiochus Epiphanes fought against Egypt, Judea, Media, and Ecbatana, all of which figure in Judith, crossing the Euphrates in doing so. In the same way that Judith's Nebuchadnezzar had established a principle of one world, one king, one god (3:8), 1 Macc 1:41–42 said the same in regard to Antiochus IV Epiphanes: "the king wrote to all his kingdom for all to become one people, and for each to abandon his own customs."[7] Boundary-maintaining laws in Jerusalem were thus threatened; Jews would be swallowed up by "the nations roundabout." This reflects not only the policies of Antiochus but those of the Hasmoneans as well to incorporate Idumeans and Itureans through conversion. The fictitious irony of a one-world, one-god king defeated by a one-temple, one-God God parallels the irony of a forced-conversion empire (the Seleucids) being matched by a forced-conversion local kingdom (the Hasmoneans).[8] Judith saves her people from, among

other things, colonization, but the text is also propaganda for the Hasmonean rulers: opposing the greater empire by supporting the local, expanding empire.

Many of the narrative elements and images of our novella would have found some background in Hellenistic iconography. After Alexander, the Greek Seleucids took on the mantle of the Babylonian Empire quite literally: the king's robe represented Nebuchadnezzar. The replaying of the memory of Antiochus IV Epiphanes as the Babylonian king would resonate in a similar way. There was also a great fascination in the Hellenistic world with temple miracles. The book of Judith is a "temple protection story" away from the temple, just as 2 Maccabees is a temple protection story treating the site. This is a broad Hellenistic theme, but temple-protection stories circulated in two subtypes: some recounted how the gods had saved *our* temple; others told a more satirical story of how *others'* temples were saved, not by gods but by trickster priests. Second Maccabees 1:14–17, for instance, tells the story of a group of temple tricksters, while Polybius (*Histories* 31.9) depicts *the same event* as an act of the goddess Artemis.[9]

To be sure, some scholars have argued, based on the Persian-period references, that an early stage of the book of Judith was composed before the Hellenistic period and then reworked in the Hasmonean period.[10] In addition

---

7 Moore, *Judith,* 55; Hans Jørgen Lundager Jensen, "Juditbogen," in Troels Engberg-Pedersen and Niels Peter Lemche, eds., *Tradition og nybrud: Jødedommen i hellenistisk tid* (Forum for bibelsk eksegese 2; Copenhagen: Museum Tusculanum, 1990) 153–89, as summarized in Benedikt Otzen, *Tobit and Judith* (Guides to Apocrypha and Pseudepigrapha 11; Sheffield: Sheffield Academic Press, 2001) 120–21; Seth Schwartz, "Israel and the Nations Roundabout: 1 Maccabees and the Hasmonean Expansion," *JJS* 42 (1991) 16–38; Doron Mendels, *The Land of Israel as a Political Concept in Hasmonean Literature: Recourse to History in Second Century B.C. Claims to the Holy Land* (TSAJ 15; Tübingen: Mohr, 1987) 51–56.

8 Ela Nutu, "Framing Judith: Whose Text, Whose Gaze, Whose Language?" in Ela Nutu and J. Cheryl Exum, eds., *Between the Text and the Canvas: The Bible and Art in Dialogue* (Bible in the Modern World 13; Sheffield: Sheffield Phoenix, 2007) 117–44, here 117. Some scholars have questioned the extent of

forced conversions, suggesting that it was more of a literary motif; see Aryeh Kasher, *Jews, Idumaeans, and Ancient Arabs: Relations of the Jews in Eretz-Israel with the Nations of the Frontier and the Desert during the Hellenistic and Roman Era (332 BCE–70 CE)* (TSAJ 18; Tübingen: J. C. B. Mohr, 1988) 46–77; Cohen, *Beginnings of Jewishness,* 110–19; and see also Schwartz, "Israel and the Nations," 17–21; Steven Weitzman, "Forced Circumcision and the Shifting Role of Gentiles in Hasmonean Ideology," *HTR* 92 (1999) 37–59.

9 Paul J. Kosmin, "The Persian Version: Indigenous Revolts in *2 Maccabees,*" lecture at Harvard Divinity School, May 6, 2014. Similar to 2 Maccabees 3–4 are Herodotus on Xerxes (*Histories* 8.37–38); Pausanias, *Description of Greece* 10.23.3–6; 9.25.9; Justin, *Epitome* 24.8; Lindos Chronicle, col. D 13–32; I.Stratonikeia 10, *SEG* 55:2119. On viewing others' temples as protected by tricksters, note the priests of Bel in Bel and the Dragon.

10 So Franz Steinmetzer, *Neue Untersuchung über die*

to the Persian names and the similarities to the campaign of Artaxerxes III Ochus, there are other Persian terms and phrases: *akinakēs* for dagger, "God of heaven," "king of all the earth," earth and water for surrender. But, whereas the possibility that the book may have been composed in multiple editions will be considered, this is not likely; the book of Judith was probably composed of a piece. The Persian context still breathes through our text, however. After an eastern indigenous rebellion, coins were minted that depict a Persian figure killing a Greek hoplite with an *akinakēs*.[11] This very image reminds us of Judith's central decapitation of Holofernes with a Persian *akinakēs*. It is hauntingly similar to the later European visual images of Judith. Even the humorous telescoping of Assyrian, Babylonian, Persian, and Seleucid/Hasmonean eras—along with the Medes!—can be compared with the Babylonian, Median, Persian, and Seleucid epochs placed in sequence in Daniel 2 and 7.

Archaeological evidence is now also presenting a clearer picture of the nature of the Hasmonean nativistic movement that is reflected in Judith. At the beginning of this period, the Hasmonean partisans, unlike their Jewish opponents, used Hebrew names—compare Yehudit, even if the text was written in Greek—and at the end of this period archaeological evidence indicates a rurally based revitalization movement: hewn stone vessels (which unlike pottery, were not considered susceptible to impurity), *mikvaot*, and Herodian lamps. Andrea Berlin has

summarized these changes. The population and settlement of Jerusalem increased in the second half of the second century BCE, and even more in the first half of the first century.[12] One may characterize this as a period of growth and of relative prosperity throughout Judah. It is not a situation of urbanization. New residents in Jerusalem are not simply moving in from surrounding regions, because the number of settlements increased as well, in both Judah and Benjamin. Rather, sites remain small, but there are more of them.

For the "nations roundabout," however—an important characterization in Judith and in 1 Maccabees—the situation could be characterized archaeologically in this way:

[L]ater second century BCE material remains from areas surrounding Judea reveal that people there live in a fundamentally different economic and social universe. Urbanized settlement patterns, Greek styles of house décor, Aegean wines and imported plates, figurines in Greek styles and subjects—the pervasiveness of all such goods demonstrates that at ground level, people were intimately connected to the wider Mediterranean world and its dominant Hellenizing culture.[13]

Further:

[Judea is] a largely rural society whose members live in an emphatically and deliberately simplified mode, devoid of foreign material affectations, culturally

---

Geschichtlichkeit der Juditherzählung: Ein Beitrag zur Erklärung des Buches Judith (Leipzig: Rudolf Haupt, 1907) summarized in Moore, *Judith,* 52; and Hans Yohanan Priebatsch, "Das Buch Judith und seine hellenistischen Quellen," *ZDPV* 90 (1974) 50–60; J. C. Greenfield, "The Jewish Historical Novella of the Persian Period," in H. Tadmor and I. Efal, eds., *The World History of the Jewish People: The Persian Period* (in Hebrew; Jerusalem: 'Am 'Oved, 1983) 208–9; Erich Zenger, *Das Buch Judit,* in *Historische und legendärische Erzählungen* (JSHRZ 1.6; Gütersloh: Mohn, 1981) 424–534, here 431; George W. E. Nickelsburg, *Jewish Literature between the Bible and the Mishnah: A Historical and Literary Introduction* (2nd ed.; Philadelphia: Fortress Press, 2005) 101; Heltzer, "Eine neue Quelle," 437. Moses Gaster had argued this on the assumption that the medieval Hebrew versions reflect a Persian-era Hebrew original ("An Unknown Hebrew Version of the History of Judith,"

PSBA 16 [1893–94] 156–63). Others who perceived echoes of the campaign of Artaxerxes Ochus include Delcor, "Le livre de Judith," 151–79.

11 M. Rahim Shayegan, *Arsacids and Sasanians: Political Ideology in Post-Hellenistic and Late Antique Persia* (Cambridge: Cambridge University Press, 2011) 169–72.

12 Andrea Berlin, "Manifest Identity: From *Ioudaios* to Jew," in Rainer Albertz, ed., *Between Cooperation and Hostility: Multiple Identities in Ancient Judaism and the Interaction with Foreign Powers* (JAJSup 11; Göttingen: Vandenhoeck & Ruprecht, 2013) 151–75, here 152; Yonatan Adler, "Between Priestly Cult and Common Culture: The Material Evidence of Ritual Purity Observance in Early Roman Jerusalem Reassessed," *JAJ* 7 (2016) 228–48. On revitalization movements, see Wills, *Not God's People,* 105–6.

13 Berlin, "Manifest Identity," 160.

insular, traditional and inwardly oriented. Meanwhile, people living in Idumea, along the coast, and at Samaria are intimately connected to the wider Mediterranean world and its dominant Hellenizing culture.[14]

Despite the fact that this evidence is largely from rural Judea, these developments reflect a Jerusalem-centered policy. Bethulia relates to Jerusalem as do these rural towns. And although the author of Judith knows a long literary tradition of stereotyped eastern luxury, this was not an entirely unknown experience. The riches found in Holofernes's tent may be compared to the imported luxury items of sites found just outside the borders of Judea. The broad geographical origins of the luxury goods indicate the interconnectedness of Hellenistic trade over long distances. What is striking is the "Hellenic" nature and western origin of most of these luxury items, and yet in Judith the fictitious danger arises from the East. Despite many parallels to Greek literature (see §4 below), there is no explicit reference to Greeks. This is presumably because of the idealized, pseudo-historical, biblicizing, and archaizing frame of the story. In the background of our text, then, is a nativistic movement and a rejection of foreign luxury goods. The facts that our heroine is named Yehudit, Jewish woman, and that she is a champion of Jewish identity render her a character appropriate for this ethos.

Historicity of the Narrative

The book of Judith telescopes multiple historical epics into one imaginary frame. "Nebuchadnezzar king of the Assyrians" provides a fictional setting in the Assyrian period, but also the Neo-Babylonian, while less obvious references suggest the Persian period, the Hellenistic period, and the Hasmonean period. Nebuchadnezzar in our text is "the lord of all the earth" (2:5) from India to Ethiopia, but that area is *Persia*'s extent, not Assyria's, Babylon's, or Alexander's. The geographical sweep is similar to the opening of MT Esther. The story thus exists in a "bygone" age within an eastern-looking geography.

For two millennia, scholars have struggled in vain to restore plausibility to the historical time line of Judith. Yet the list of historical and geographical inconcinnities is far too great. Here I assume that the text is a work of fiction and that the author was intentionally playing with a fanciful story line that would have been obvious to the audience. A historical setting for the *composition* of the text, however, may still be proposed, and indeed on this point there is both more consensus and a narrower window than for many biblical texts. It is, ironically, the flippant attitude toward historical verisimilitude that allows us to discern so many connections to an actual historical period, late second–early first century BCE.

In the periods telescoped together—Assyrian, Neo-Babylonian, and Persian—Jews would have seen Jerusalem threatened, destroyed, and rebuilt. In addition, conditions of a fourth period, the second century BCE, are also reflected in clear references to the reconsecration of the temple by the Maccabees.[15] The fact that the temple, altar, and vessels are said to have been polluted and *reconsecrated* (4:1–3), rather than simply *rebuilt*, suggests a post-164 date. The opening words explicitly combine the two earlier time periods, "Nebuchadnezzar, who ruled the Assyrians from Nineveh." This name and title pair

---

14 Berlin, "Manifest Identity," 164–65. See also Berlin, "Jewish Life before the Revolt: The Archaeological Evidence," *JSJ* 36 (2005) 417–70; Berlin, "Identity Politics in Roman Galilee," in Mladen Popović, ed., *The Jewish Revolt against Rome: Interdisciplinary Perspectives* (JSJSup 154; Leiden: Brill, 2012) 69–106; André LaCocque likely misconstrues the situation when he says that Judith belongs to "the polemic, subversive reaction of Jewish faithful against the Hellenization process of their society" (*The Feminine Unconventional: Four Subversive Figures in Israel's Tradition* [OBT; Minneapolis: Fortress Press, 1990] 47). He idealizes Judith and insists that this text, like the Hasidim and Daniel, is at odds with Maccabean

texts and tradition. Similarly, Jan Willem van Henten holds that Judith as an alternative leader protests against the Hasmoneans ("Judith as an Alternative Leader: A Rereading of Judith 7–13," in Athalya Brenner, ed., *A Feminist Companion to Esther, Judith and Susanna* (Feminist Companion to the Bible 7; Sheffield: Sheffield Academic Press, 1995) 224–52, here 244).

15 Otzen, *Tobit and Judith*, 95–96; see his summary at 81–87; and Ernst Haag, *Das Buch Judit* (Geistliche Schriftlesung: Erläuterungen zum Alten Testament für die geistliche Lesung 15; Düsseldorf: Patmos, 1995) 1–8; Weitzman, *Surviving Sacrilege*, 34–54; and cf. 1 Macc 4:36–61; 2 Macc 10:1–8.

the empire (Assyria) that defeated the northern half of Israel in 721 BCE and the king (Nebuchadnezzar of Babylon) who defeated the southern half, Judah, in 587 BCE.[16] Nineveh was indeed the capital of Assyria, but it was destroyed in 612 BCE, before Nebuchadnezzar ascended in Babylon. In addition, Arphaxad, who is said to reign from Ecbatana, is unknown to history. The period of return from exile is also mentioned as having already taken place (4:3; 5:18–19). Mentioned as a past event also is the renewal of the temple precincts, which the audience would perceive as the *recent* restoration at the time of the Maccabean Revolt. The easy incorporation of these last political events, even in a muddled way, allows a secure dating of the text after 165 BCE.

Despite the audacious mockery of actual historical and geographical order, the author also provides details of historical dates and long series of geographical sites. Yet, although the telescoping of history has been judged to be outrageous and playful, patently fictitious, it is not entirely unique in the ancient world. The Assyrian invasion of Egypt in the eighth century was felt in that nation for centuries, and the free-narrative national hero romances of the Egyptians often commingled the Assyrian, Babylonian, and Persian Empires.[17] In the patriarchal

narratives of the Bible, Abraham is an Aramean (Deut 26:5), but Aram, the progenitor of the Arameans, is elsewhere Abraham's grandnephew (Gen 22:21). The rabbis often connected disparate time frames by a *pia fraus* concerning the primordial period: "Adam can instruct his son Seth in the Torah, Shem and Eber establish a house of study."[18] But Judith is not primeval history, subject to its own special dispensations. It is both bolder and more fanciful, drawing together more periods, combining ancient, recent, and international settings, and was likely not taken as historical in the earliest performance context. There are two opposing tendencies in Jewish literature of this period, the historical—a strict chronologizing found in both history and apocalypses—and the novelistic—the imaginative play of epochs.[19] As in Greece and Rome, novelistic play becomes popular as the other side of the coin of new rigorous historicism (see §7 below).

Anton Biolek noted that patristic authors often discussed the canonicity of Judith and revealed their attitudes about historicity at the same time. Most early references indicate that they received it as a historical text. Examples include 1 Clem. 55:4–6 and Origen, "who, although he so dearly loved allegory, took Judith's act as a historical fact."[20] Biolek finds, for instance, that Apostolic

---

16   One could quibble about whether "Nebuchadnezzar king of Assyria" was *necessarily* absurd. Kings were sometimes referred to as rulers of the *defeated* empire. Eupolemus (mid-second century BCE) identified Nebuchadnezzar as an Assyrian king (in Eusebius, *Preparation for the Gospel* 9.39). In Ezra 6:22, Cyrus of Persia is called "the Assyrian king" because he is heir of Assyria; Neh 13:6 refers to "Artaxerxes king of Babylon." Greeks also sometimes conflated Assyria and Babylon (Herodotus, *Histories* 1.95, 106), and there was some leeway in naming nations; see Deborah Levine Gera, *Judith* (Commentaries on Early Jewish Literature; Boston: de Gruyter, 2014) 116; Priebatsch, "Das Buch Judith."

17   Kim Ryholt, "The Assyrian Invasion of Egypt," in J. G. Derckson, ed., *Assyria and Beyond: Studies Presented to Mogens Trolle Larsen* (Uitgaven van het Nederlands Instituut voor het Nabije Oosten te Leiden 100; Leiden: Nederlands Instituut voor het Nabije Oosten, 2004) 483–510.

18   Yosef Hayim Yerushalmi, *Zakhor: Jewish History and Jewish Memory* (The Samuel and Althea Stroum Lectures in Jewish Studies; New York: Schocken, 1982) 17.

19   On chronology and historicizing, see Demetrius the Chronographer; Daniel 7–12; Josephus; Ben Sira 44–50; and Seder Olam Rabbah. Yet it is not a neat separation of modes: note the telescoping of epochs even in the "history" of Ezra-Nehemiah, where in Ezra 4:6–24 an account from the earlier period of Artaxeres is inserted.

20   Biolek, "Die Ansicht," 357: "der so sehr die Allegorie liebte, die Tat Judiths für ein geschichtliches Faktum hielt." See also Origen, *Homilies on Jeremiah* 19.20; also *IX Homilies on Book of Judges; Homilies on Ezekiel* 20.7–12; and Tertullian, *Against Marcion* 1.7; *On Monogamy* 17.1–3, although the latter takes Holofernes to be Orophernes, king of Cappadocia. On the ancient comments, see §8 below, and Outi Lehtipuu, "'Receive the Widow Judith, Example of Chastity': The Figure of Judith as a Model Christian in Patristic Interpretations," in Agnethe Siquans, ed., *Biblical Women in Patristic Reception / Biblische Frauen in patristischer Rezeption* (JAJSup 25; Göttingen: Vandenhoeck & Ruprecht, 2017) 186–218.

Constitutions assumed the historicity of Judith, although the author reasoned that Nebuchadnezzar must have been Darius, and Eusebius noted that Jews referred to Cambyses as a second Nebuchadnezzar. However, after these, says Biolek, "The later Greek patristic authors do not entertain the slightest doubt about the historical deed of Judith."[21] Augustine, in a list of "histories," includes Job, Tobit, Esther, Judith, along with the books of Maccabees, Esdras, and the books of Reigns and Chronicles (*On Christian Doctrine* 2). There is some attempt to understand the history of Judith as part of secular, not "biblical," history and a new attempt to take Nebuchadnezzar of the Assyrians to be Darius or Cambyses. These very attempts indicate a concern to correct apparent misunderstandings in our text, thus assuring its ultimate historicity. From the earliest period to the Middle Ages, then, Biolek finds that all accorded Judith a historical value, despite the corrections of the kings' names.

There have been many other attempts to "discover" the true identity of the principal characters. In c. 403 CE Sulpicius Severus (*Sacred History* 2.16; *PL* 20:138) identified Nebuchadnezzar with Artaxerxes III Ochus of Persia, who ruled 358–338 BCE. Not only had Artaxerxes Ochus passed through the same region in 351 to attack Egypt, quashing rebellions in Phoenicia and Cyprus in the process, but a general in his army was named Holofernes and a powerful eunuch was named Bagoas. This campaign was quite serious for Jews. A scholarly discourse about the identity of "Nebuchadnezzar king of the Assyrians" developed, and Sulpicius responded to those who had identified this figure with Cambyses. Significant also

is the appearance of Cambyses in the textual variants; this indicates an attempt at correction. Somewhat later, Isidore and Hrabanus Maurus allegorized Nebuchadnezzar to explain him historically, and Ælfric supposed there were two Nebuchadnezzars.

Minor corrections to a narrative understood as historical were thus common for Christian commentators; it was not until Martin Luther that we encounter a more fundamental challenge. Luther, who contributed much to historical views of biblical narrative,[22] was the first to suggest that Judith was fictional. He also referred to Tobit as a "very beautiful, wholesome, and useful fiction or drama by a gifted poet." A follower of Luther, Charles Capellus, in 1689 also rejected the historicity of Judith, considering it "a most silly fable invented by a most inept, injudicious, impudent, and clownish Hellenist."[23] The latter's tirade may very well have been influenced by the battles between Protestants and Catholics over the canonical importance of the Apocrypha, although Luther also made critical statements about Esther and James as well.

Modern scholars also tried to discern actual personages behind the historically troubled characters of the novella. Many of those who sought some historical key were Catholic scholars, for whom Judith was a deuterocanonical text. Franz Steinmetzer assumed an Assyrian context for the beginning of the story, the name Nebuchadnezzar having replaced Ashurbanipal.[24] By 1949 Robert Pfeiffer had catalogued seventeen such suggestions for the identity of Nebuchadnezzar, and by 2001 Otzen had twenty.[25] Some Catholic scholars continued to seek historical referents for Nebuchadnezzar; the most

---

21 Biolek, "Die Ansicht," 360–61: "Die späteren griechischen Kirchenschriftsteller hegen nicht mehr den geringsten Zweifel an der historischen Tat Judiths."

22 Samuel L. Preuss, *From Shadow to Promise: Old Testament Interpretation from Augustine to the Young Luther* (Cambridge, MA: Belknap Press of Harvard University Press, 1969); Helen Watanabe-O'Kelly, *Beauty or Beast? The Woman Warrior in the German Imagination from the Renaissance to the Present* (Oxford: Oxford University Press, 2010) 115–16. For Luther's view, see *Luther's Works* (55 vols.; Philadelphia: Muhlenberg, 1960) 35:337–38.

23 Capellus, *Commentarii et notae criticae in Vet. Test.*, 575, quoted in Moore, *Judith,* 46.

24 Steinmetzer, *Geschichtlichkeit der Jud43erzählung*, summarized in Moore, *Judith,* 52. Note also Hugo

Winckler, "Zum Buch Judith," *Altorientalische Forschungen* (3 vols.; Leipzig: Eduard Pfeiffer, 1893–1905) 2:267, 272–75, in Moore, *Judith,* 42, and 49–56; Louis Soubigou, *Judith: Traduit et commenté* (Paris: Letouzey et Ané, 1952) 481–575, here 490.

25 Robert H. Pfeiffer, *History of the New Testament Times, with an Introduction to the Apocrypha* (New York: Harper, 1949) 292–96; Otzen, *Tobit and Judith,* 83–85. See also Haag, *Das Buch Judit,* 1–8; Gottfried Brunner, *Der Nabuchodonosor des Buches Judith: Beitrag zur Geschichte Israels nach dem Exil und des ersten Regierungsjahres Darius I* (2nd ed.; Berlin: Rudolph Pfau, 1959) 7–9, 66–102; Julius Lewy, "Enthält Judith I–IV Trümmer einer Chronik zur Geschichte Nebukadnezars und seiner Feldzüge von 591 und 597?" *ZDMG* 81 (1927) 52–54; Claus Schedl, "Nabuchodonosor, Arpaksad und Darius,"

viable candidate was Ashurbanipal of Assyria, 668–626 BCE. He engaged in campaigns similar to those in Judith and fought with the Medes. The other obvious candidate, Nebuchadnezzar II of the Babylonians, is clearly recalled by the dates in 1:1, 13; 2:1, although in our text Jerusalem is saved.[26] Still, one should note that in the novelistic fantasies of Daniel 1–4, Nebuchadnezzar is won over by Daniel's action. Another connection to this time frame is that the Manasseh who was king of Judah (seventh century BCE) was also captive for part of that time in Babylon, just as Judith's husband Manasseh was an absent husband. During King Manasseh's captivity, the high priest would have also held authority. But these considerations were rightly not viewed as compelling, and among Catholic scholars as well a postexilic dating came to be viewed as inescapable.[27]

At the turn of the twentieth century Charles James Ball made the reasonable suggestion that, as in the book of Daniel, the figures stood for leaders from the period of the Maccabean Revolt: Nebuchadnezzar the Assyrian represented Antiochus IV Epiphanes the Seleucid—or Syrian, a form sometimes used for Assyrian—while Holofernes represented Nicanor; Judith stood for Judah the Maccabee, and Joakim for Alcimus the high priest. It was not a neat theory, however; whereas Judith and Joakim in the narrative acted very much in concert, the real Judah and Alcimus were bitter enemies.[28] Still, shades of Antiochus IV can surely be seen in the character of Nebuchadnezzar.

Protestant scholars moved much earlier to a postexilic dating for the book. In the seventeenth century, Hugo Grotius perceived references here to the Maccabean Revolt: Holofernes represents Antiochus; Bethulia, Jerusalem; and Judith, the Jewish people. In the mid-nineteenth century, Otto F. Fritzsche followed Luther in declaring the book to be fiction, dating it to the post-Maccabean period.[29] He rightly noted that the campaigns of Artaxerxes III Ochus (359–336) supplied some of the names and background, the date of composition being after the Maccabean Revolt. As late as 1972, George T. Montague continued the identification of the Nebuchadnezzar of Judith with Antiochus IV Epiphanes,[30] but by the turn of the twenty-first century the more common scholarly view was that, although the characters may be amalgams of a whole range of historical figures, there is no meaningful historical scheme. This is not to suggest that the political history of the Hellenistic period is not reflected in Judith, only that the text does not narrate an actual historical episode.[31] Historical blunders indeed played quite an entertaining role in the Jewish novellas of the period; Tobit, Daniel, Esther, and Joseph and Aseneth all feature them prominently (see §7 below). The rationalizing and historicizing approaches to Judith are now viewed as practically obsolete.

The geography of the text is as muddled as the history, but in the past many scholars attempted to uncover an obscure order here as well. The story itself presumes that the only approach to Jerusalem from the north is through

ZDMG 115 (1965) 242–54, here 243–48. Jehoshua M. Grintz, "Judith, Book of," _EncJud_ (16 vols.; New York: Macmillan, 1971–1972) 10:451–59, here 452, alone argues that it refers to Artaxerxes II (404–358), known from Diodorus Siculus 15.90–92.

26 Moore (_Judith_, 54) says F. C. Movers "was alone in his support for Nebuchadnezzar II," yet Athanasius Miller (_Das Buch Judith, in Die Bücher Tobias, Judith und Esther_ [3 vols. in 1; Die Heilige Schrift des Alten Testaments 4.3; Bonn: Peter Hanstein, 1940–1941] 4–5) suggested this as well.

27 So Miller, _Das Buch Judith_, 10–13, 22–23; cf. Soubigou, _Judith_, 491–92, 496; Giuseppe Priero, _Giuditta_ (La Sacra Bibbia; Turin: Marietti, 1959) 6–8.

28 Ball's theory is summarized in Moore, _Judith_, 53, and compared in tabular form with those of Gustav Volkmar and Moses Gaster. In the latter two the victory of Judith would play strangely. Delcor also provides

details of the Antiochus IV comparison ("Le livre de Judith," 168–73).

29 Otto F. Fritzsche, _Die Bücher Tobi und Judith_ (Kurzgefasstes exegetisches Handbuch zu den Apokryphen des Alten Testamentes 2; Leipzig: Hirzel, 1853) 125–31. See also Nickelsburg, _Jewish Literature_, 50–51; Moore, _Judith_, 55.

30 George T. Montague, _The Books of Esther and Judith_ (Pamphlet Bible Series 21; New York: Paulist Press, 1972) 8.

31 Friedrich V. Reiterer, "Religion und hellenistische Realpolitik im Buch Judit," in Friedrich V. Reiterer, Renate Egger-Wenzel, and Thomas R. Elßner, eds., _Gesellschaft und Religion in der spätbiblischen und deuterokanonischen Literatur_ (DCLS 20; Berlin: de Gruyter, 2014) 29–54. On the text as a _parable_ of history, see §6 below.

a narrow mountain pass.[32] This is not only false but would have been known to be false to the first audience—unless, of course, the text was composed far from Judea (see below). Other geographical impossibilities include Holofernes's three-hundred-mile march from Nineveh to the southern coast of Asia Minor in three days, from which the army proceeds to Put and Lud, normally referring to Libya and Lydia. What follows is also muddled: they march along the Euphrates River through Mesopotamia to reach Cilicia on the Mediterranean, facing Arabia (2:21–25). Unknown geographical entities are found in Jubilees as well, a sign of the common interest in "free narrative" in both apocalypses and novellas.

In the nineteenth century, Otto Fritzsche examined textual variants in hopes of resolving geographical problems, and even recently leading works on the geography of ancient Israel have tried to assign logical places for the strange geography of Judith.[33] Exotic lands and local color, however, are a staple of ancient novels—note Ragau in Tobit and Hydaspes in Esther—and are perhaps even more entertaining if they are in the wrong place. As others had found a symbolic history, Charles Cutler Torrey read the fictitious sites as symbolic geography: Bethulia, which may mean "house of ascent" or "lofty abode," stands for Shechem; Betomesthaim (6:6), which may

mean "place of enmity" or "home of the devil," represents Samaria.[34] To be sure, Jdt 4:4 and other passages also include real sites near Jerusalem, some well known: Samaria, Beth-Horon, Jericho. The geography of Judith, similar to that of the Greek novels, mixes real, known places, ancient biblical sites, and fanciful and invented locales, the topography of mountains, borders, and rivers now serving as stagecraft and geographical storytelling.[35] And as Otzen points out, the real center of the story is Jerusalem, not the fictional mountain town of Bethulia. The Vulgate text even blurs the distinction between Jerusalem and Bethulia, and in the medieval Jewish tales Bethulia is dropped altogether and the action is transferred to Jerusalem.[36]

Because Bethulia is located in Samarian territory, some have toyed with the possibility that an originally Samarian story had been adapted in a Judean editing. However, there is no evidence in the text of separate literary layers, and, in addition, the author sees Judea as including Samaria.[37] The Davidic boundaries of Israel are thereby reconstituted, and "the entire territory of Israel" participated in the pursuit and slaughter of the Assyrians (14:4). "The author," says Gera, "imagines a Samaria without any Samaritans, erasing them as it were, and incorporating the territory into Judea."[38] In this story world, the

---

32 Moore, *Judith,* 138–39; Marc Stephen Caponigro, "Judith, Holding the Tale of Herodotus," in VanderKam, *No One Spoke Ill,* 47–59, here 53–54. Gera points out that there is no reason why a mountain pass would be the only means to attack Jerusalem; the obvious route would be along the west bank of the Jordan to Jericho, then westward to Jerusalem (*Judith,* 31). See Otzen, *Tobit and Judith,* 87–91; Ernst Haag, *Studien zum Buche Judith: Seine theologische Bedeutung und literarische Eigenart* (Trierer theologische Studien 16; Trier: Paulinus Verlag, 1963) 12–18.

33 Fritzsche, *Die Bücher Tobi und Judith,* 135–36; Friedrich Stummer, *Geographie des Buches Judith* (Bibelwissenschaftliche Reihe 3; Stuttgart: Katholisches Bibelwerk, 1947) 16; Yohanan Aharoni and Michael Avi-Yonah, *Macmillan Bible Atlas* (New York: Macmillan, 1968) 132; Marie-Françoise Baslez, "Polémologie et histoire dan le livre de Judith," *RB* 111 (2004) 362–76; Adam Zertal, "The Reality of the Book of Judith" (in Hebrew), *Eretz-Israel* 29 (2009) 161–75.

34 Charles Cutler Torrey, *Apocryphal Literature: A Brief*

Introduction (New Haven: Yale University Press, 1945) 91–92. On possible meanings and locations for Bethulia, see commentary on 6:10–21.

35 Craven, *Artistry and Faith,* 76–80; Eyal Ben-Eliyahu, *Between Borders: The Boundaries of Eretz-Israel in the Consciousness of the Jewish People in the Time of the Second Temple and in the Mishnah and Talmud Period* (in Hebrew; Jerusalem: Yad Ben-Zvi, 2012) 175–93.

36 Otzen, *Tobit and Judith,* 94–97; Moore, *Judith,* 101. On the Vulgate and Jewish tales, see §8 and the appendix below.

37 David Goodblatt, "'The Israelites Who Reside in Judah' (Judith 4:1): On the Conflicted Identities of the Hasmonean State," in Lee I. Levine and Daniel R. Schwartz, eds., *Jewish Identities in Antiquity: Studies in Memory of Menahem Stern* (TSAJ 130; Tübingen: Mohr Siebeck, 2009) 74–89, here 80–81.

38 Gera, *Judith,* 32. Cities in northern Israel are also included in 3:9–4:7; so Otzen, *Tobit and Judith,* 82; and see Ben-Eliyahu, *Between Borders,* chap. 4, esp. 88.

historical areas of all Israel are under the control of the Jerusalem temple. The geographical indicators thus support the historical indicators in placing the composition during the later period of Hasmonean rule.

Date of Composition

The free creation of a fictitious story-world revealed as much about the author's own situation as would a "history." The larger context of the book of Judith was the empire of Alexander and his successors.[39] A number of Greek motifs reflect this era: garlands (3:7), worship of a king as a god (3:8), reclining while eating (12:15), and olive wreaths (15:13). From the reference to the restoration of the temple sacrifices in 4:3, it is clear that the earliest possible date for the writing of Judith is after the Maccabean Revolt. The text's several references to Nebuchadnezzar's destruction of religious sites also does not comport with practices before Antiochus IV Epiphanes, indicating awareness of the issues before and during the Maccabean Revolt. Similarities to the death of Nicanor in 161 BCE (1 Maccabees 7; 2 Maccabees 15) also make it very likely that it was written after that event.[40]

The political and military terms are consistent with Seleucid usage: *satrapēs, stratēgos,* and *hēgoumenos.* More specifically, the use of *gerousia* (4:8; 11:14; 15:8) was introduced by Antiochus III in about 200 BCE, and *gerousia* has not been replaced in our text by *boulē* or *synedrion,* indicating that it was written before Hyrcanus II.[41] The author of Judith may be claiming, perhaps unconsciously, a Greek-style superiority over a Persian-style enemy. This has been pressed by Katell Berthelot:

In Judith, Judea's independence is at stake, and the use of Herodotus clearly (and somehow ironically) implies that the Seleucid kings (disguised in Assyrian-Babylonian dress) are not the true heirs of their Greek predecessors but rather the heirs of the Persians, the archetypal enemies of Greece. . . . The use of Herodotus is thus not so much an example of openness to "foreign wisdom" as a case of the bold and ironic use of the enemy's cultural references to show one's superiority, even according to the enemy's own standards.[42]

This phenomenon—the colonized author claiming superiority to the colonizer—also occurs in 2 Maccabees (see commentary on 8:35, and below in §7).

Other scholars have attempted to narrow the window of composition, with uncertain results. Not only does our text assume the *events* of the Maccabean Revolt, but it partakes of the literary view of 1 and especially 2 Maccabees as well (see §4 below). This suggests but does not require a composition at about the time of those texts.[43] Judea is here ruled by a high priest (4:6–8), which occurred only under Jonathan in 153 (1 Macc 10:20). Yet this is not as probative as it first appears, since the text creates an imagined past. Also expressed is an idealized view of Judah and Samaria acting in tandem (see 4:4–6), commensurate with a date after the annexation of Samaria by John Hyrcanus in 107 BCE, although this is not a necessary conclusion. The story may express an idealized reunification of Israel.

39 See most recently Reiterer, "Religion und hellenistische Realpolitik"; Paul Niskanen, *The Human and the Divine in History: Herodotus and the Book of Daniel* (JSOTSup 396; London: T&T Clark International, 2004) 23–30.

40 For a date just before the Maccabean Revolt, which seems impossible, see Leonhard Rost, *Einleitung in die alttestamentlichen Apokryphen und Pseudepigraphen einschliesslich der grossen Qumran-Handschriften* (2nd ed.; Heidelberg: Quelle & Meyer, 1979) 40–41; A. Lefèvre, "Judith," in A. Robert and A. Feuillet, eds., *Introduction à la Bible* (2 vols.; Tournai: Desclée, 1957–1959) 1:742–50, here 748; Baslez, "Polémologie."

41 Delcor, "Le livre de Judith," 153–63, 168–74. *Synedria* is used in a nonspecific sense in 6:1.

42 Katell Berthelot, "Hellenization and Jewish Identity in the Deuterocanonical Literature: A Response to Ben Wright," in Géza G. Xeravits, József Zsengellér, and Xavér Szabó, eds., *Canonicity, Setting, Wisdom in the Deuterocanonicals: Papers of the Jubilee Meeting of the International Conference on the Deuterocanonical Books* (DCLS 22; Berlin: de Gruyter, 2014) 69–88, here 75.

43 Nickelsburg, *Jewish Literature,* 108–9, Claudia Rakel, *Judit–Über Schönheit, Macht, und Widerstand im Krieg: Eine feministisch-intertextuelle Lektüre* (BZAW 334; Berlin: de Gruyter, 2003) 265–72, Gera argues that similarities to Eupolemus (passages from c. 158–157 BCE) provide a *terminus* as well (*Judith,* 43–44).

Scholars have also tried to ascertain a precise date from the political relations of cities and peoples, yet our text may recreate an image of a broader historical era rather than an exact mirror of the author's present. The expansions of the Hasmonean kingdom are likely reflected; Judea, for instance, extends up to the Jezreel Valley (Esdraelon, 3:9; 8:21; 11:19).[44] The process of discerning more precise usages has resulted in some ambiguity. Doron Mendels, for instance, notes that Moab, Ammon, and Edomites are independent, and, as a result, he argues for a date of 140–134 BCE.[45] This assumes, however, too neat a relation between narrated events and the setting; the author archaizes and invents. It is also interesting that only the area of Judah is called Israel, despite the fact that other tribes are assumed (8:18; 9:14), and Uzziah is of the tribe of Simeon (6:15). Yet Samaria is under Judean rule, and as a result many date Judith to the period after the annexation of Samaria by John Hyrcanus, 107–104 BCE.[46] The coastal cities of Jamnia and Azotus are still independent (2:28), reflecting the period *before* the taking of these cities by Alexander Jannaeus in 102–76.[47] If these were reliable indicators, that would place the composition between 104 and 76 BCE. But, alternatively, does the *omission* of Gaza indicate that the text was written after that city was taken by

Alexander Jannaeus in 96 BCE? Moore reminds us that the absence of a place-name means little here (139–41). None of these observations about Hasmonean politics pushes us to a more precise dating, although the era as a whole seems clearly reflected.

A more sociological argument for a precise date comes from Tal Ilan, who proposes a date in the reign of Queen Salome Alexandra (Shelamzion), 76–67 BCE, more precisely c. 76 BCE.[48] The texts of Susanna, Esther, and Judith, she theorizes, all appeared during or just before the reign of Queen Salome Alexandra in order to support her rule. Those scholars who have seen Pharisaic tendencies in Judith find support here, as Salome Alexandra favored that party.[49] This queen was also a widow, pious, well regarded by people, and she organized the army to defend against enemies. She also died of old age, and the rabbis credited her piety for miraculous harvests (Sifra Behuqotai 1:1, Lev. Rab. 35:10). Yet the parallels to Shelamzion, intriguing as they are, are ultimately too vague to draw a conclusion. Gera reminds us that both figures, Salome Alexandra and Judith, the historical and the fictional, could have been influenced by the strong Egyptian queens Cleopatra II and III (second century BCE).[50] The contemporary novelistic depiction of the Assyrian queen Semiramus attests a common Hellenis-

---

44 Otzen, *Tobit and Judith*, 132–35.

45 Mendels, *Land of Israel*, 51–56.

46 Goodblatt, "Israelites Who Reside," 80–81.

47 Delcor, "Le livre de Judith," 179; Avi-Yonah in Aharoni and Avi-Yonah, *Atlas*, 132; Moore, *Judith*, 67–71.

48 Tal Ilan, *Integrating Women into Second Temple History* (TSAJ 76; Tübingen: Mohr Siebeck, 1999) 127–53, esp. 150–53. She renewed the argument of Zeitlin (*Book of Judith*, 180–81) and is in turn followed by Denise Dombkowski Hopkins ("Judith," in Carole A. Newsom and Sharon H. Ringe, eds., *Women's Bible Commentary* [expanded ed.; Louisville: Westminster John Knox, 1998] 279–85, here 281). See also Jeremy Corley ("Septuagintalisms, Semitic Interference, and the Original Language of the Book of Judith," in Jeremy Corley and Vincent Skemp, eds., *Studies in the Greek Bible: Essays in Honor of Francis T. Gignac, S.J.* [CBQMS 44; Washington, DC: Catholic Biblical Association of America, 2008] 65–96, here 65–66; "Judith: An Unconventional Heroine," *Scripture Bulletin* 31 [2001] 70–85, here 79–80), and Dilys Naomi Patterson ("Re-membering the Past: The Purpose of Historical Discourse in the Book of Judith," in Patri-

cia G. Kirkpatrick and Timothy D. Goltz, eds., *The Function of Ancient Historiography in Biblical and Cognate Studies* [LHBOTS 489; New York: T&T Clark, 2008] 111–23). Gabriele Boccaccini ("Tigranes the Great as 'Nebuchadnezzar' in the Book of Judith," in Géza G. Xeravits, ed., *A Pious Seductress: Studies in the Book of Judith* [DCLS 14; Berlin: de Gruyter, 2012] 55–69) supports Ilan's argument by pointing to Tigranes the Great, who, like Holofernes, almost invaded Judea but was stopped by Shelamzion when she bribed him.

49 See commentary on 9:6. See also Janelle Peters, "A Pharisaic Reading of Esther and Judith in First Century Corinthian Churches?" (presentation at Society of Biblical Literature Annual Meeting, San Francisco, California, November 20, 2011; Jehoshua M. Grintz, *The Book of Judith: A Reconstruction of the Original Hebrew Text with Introduction, Commentary, Appendices, and Indices* (in Hebrew with English summary; Jerusalem: Bialik Institute, 1957) 47–51.

50 Gera, *Judith*, 42.

tic interest in powerful women (see §4 below). Further, Gruen notes that Judith's retirement from public life at the end of her heroism would hardly constitute support for a strong queen.[51] The results of this survey of the evidence confirm that Judith was written at the end of the second century or beginning of the first century BCE, but a more precise dating cannot be posited.

As for the latest possible date, no fragments have been found at Qumran, and it is not quoted or alluded to by Philo, Josephus, the New Testament, or early rabbinic literature. Judith may have influenced Greek Esther Additions C and D (dated between 114 and 48 BCE), and the depiction of Jael in Pseudo-Philo, *Biblical Antiquities* (first century CE) may reflect our text.[52] The earliest clear reference to Judith is in 1 Clem. 55:4–6, dated near the end of the first century CE. In 1 Clement, Judith asks permission of the elders instead of ordering them, and one could argue that this passage is evidence of a narrative tradition of Judith the heroine, not necessarily the *book* of Judith. However, the same sort of domestication of women can be seen in 1 Pet 3:6, which describes Sarah as more obedient to Abraham, and 1 Clement makes use of some of the same words as our text (see Jdt 9:11). By the turn of the first to second centuries CE, then, a textual tradition of Judith was already popular enough to be referenced.

Author and Place of Composition

The author of the text is not indicated, and there are no clues on this matter. (On the possibility of a female author, see §5 below.) Regarding the place of composition, it is often assumed that Judith was written in Jerusalem because of the book's pro-Hasmonean stance, the high regard for both the temple and the high priest—the high priest is the only Israelite figure apart from Judith who is strong—and the similarity to 1 and 2 Maccabees.[53] The preservation of the temple is paramount; Judith prays at the time of the incense offering (9:1) and declares to Holofernes, there "I will set your seat" (11:19). She later dedicates her plunder to the temple, and there the people celebrate. The date of the eighteenth year of "Nebuchadnezzar" (2:1) is also the date of the fall of the temple, an event that will be reversed in Judith. When the original language was assumed to be Hebrew or Aramaic, the Jerusalem provenance was considered a firm conclusion.

However, a Semitic original is no longer considered certain, and this has thrown open the discussion of place of origin (see below under "Language of Composition"). The motifs listed above might be found in a Jewish text written in other places. Second Maccabees, for example, based on a text by Jason of Cyrene, shares these empha-

51 Gruen, *Diaspora,* 321–22 n. 110.

52 On Esther, see Howard Jacobson, *A Commentary on Pseudo-Philo's Liber antiquitatum biblicarum: With Latin Text and English Translation* (2 vols.; AGJU 31; Leiden: Brill, 1996) 1:199–210, 226; van Henten, "Judith as an Alternative Leader," 224–52, here 246–47; Moore, *Judith,* 212–16; idem, *Daniel, Esther, and Jeremiah: The Additions; A New Translation with Introduction and Commentary* (1977; repr., AYB; New Haven: Yale University Press, 2007) 220–22; Gera, *Judith,* 12; Linda Day, *Three Faces of a Queen: Characterization in the Books of Esther* (JSOTSup 186; Sheffield: JSOT Press, 1995) 222–25. Unlikely is the suggestion of Rendel Harris that Jdt 8:14 is referenced in 1 Cor 2:10–11, 16 ("A Quotation from Judith in the Pauline Epistles," *ExpT* 27 [1916] 13–15).

53 Erich Zenger, "Der Juditroman als Traditionsmodell des Jahweglaubens," *TTZ* 83 (1974) 65–80, here 69. The motif of the rededication of the temple is the main link to Hasmonean ideology, along with the insistence that Israel has not recently sinned (8:18–20). Weitzman adds that the conversion of Achior is parallel to Hyrcanus's conversion of Idumeans and Aristobulus's conversion of Itureans (*Surviving Sacrilege,* 34–54, esp. 52). Some scholars, however, claim to find a critique of Hasmonean excesses, with "Judith" an improvement on "Judah" Maccabee; so Nicolae Roddy, "The Way It Wasn't: The Book of Judith as Anti-Hasmonean Propaganda," *Studia Hebraica* 8 (2008) 269–77, here 275–76; van Henten, "Judith as an Alternative Leader," 244–45; and Benedikt Eckhardt, "Reclaiming Tradition: The Book of Judith and Hasmonean Politics," *JSP* 18 (2009) 243–63, here 249–55. Rakel sees in Judith a more virtuous form of resistance (headed by a priest) to the Seleucids (headed by a king) (*Judit–Über Schönheit,* 271–72). However, the high priest can be a stand-in for Hasmonean kings; Hasmoneans took on the title of high priest. The text is creating a pious model with a woman at the center, not a direct reflection of the political situation.

ses on the temple. Yet, although we know that Jason was *from* Cyrene, we do not know where he wrote his history. Further, the combination of Jerusalem-oriented elements is very strong and pushes toward a Judean provenance. Many incidental aspects may also reflect a composition in Judea. Samaria (and Shechem) are problematized often, yet the text seems to assume that this region is part of the author's Israel.[54] The neighboring nations of Ammon, Moab, and Edom also figure as opponents, a focus on near-Others that would be less likely if the text were written elsewhere. The authority of the high priest could certainly be remarked on from a distance (as in Philo), but the city politics of Jerusalem, including typical political terms, are referenced as well: "The Israelites did as Joakim the high priest and the council of the entire people of Israel, in session in Jerusalem, had commanded" (Jdt 4:8).[55]

Other scholars, however, have pushed for a composition in the diaspora, especially Egypt. Jan Joosten, for example, has revived Hans Priebatsch's argument to this effect.[56] Like the Letter of Aristeas, Judith focuses not on kings, which a Hasmonean provenance would suggest, but on the twelve tribes, led by the high priest. Joosten assumes that the text was written in Greek, and the absence of our text from any Jewish canon also indicates an Egyptian provenance, where it was received as scripture by Christians. Judith's inheritance of her husband's estate may also correspond to Egyptian practice. Yet, apart from the question of the original language, these considerations are not strong. The fact that Eupolemus wrote in Greek indicates that a Judean author could compose a text in that language.[57]

Language of Composition

In 1972, Morton Enslin could aver, "That the Book of Judith . . . was originally written in Hebrew is recognized by all scholars."[58] Moore seconded this conclusion, and Hanhart was equally assured of a Semitic *Vorlage*. Some claimed to have found evidence for either a specifically Hebrew or Aramaic original. When Priebatsch suggested in 1974 that the work may have been composed in Greek in a style that intentionally mimicked the Greek Bible, few scholars considered it.[59] Their number began to grow, however, through the second half of the century, until they are now in the majority. The question, however, is complex.

Arguments for both a Semitic and a Greek original are strong. As for Semitic syntax, there is, first, the ubiquitous use of *kai* + aorist verb, a sign of the Hebrew *waw*-conversive, and in particular *kai egeneto* for Hebrew *wayhî*. The *eimi eis* construction is equivalent to the Hebrew *hāyāh lĕ* (or *lihyōt lĕ*). There is only one *men/de* construction, and absent are particles common in original Greek prose, such as *oun, te, ara,* and *ge*. Also typical of Semitizing Greek is the use of resumptive pronouns, common in Semitic languages but unnecessary and even awkward in better Greek (see 7:10; 10:2). Participles are not common in Judith and are not given the full range of syntactic functions that Greek prose would employ. There is little separation of article and noun by genitives.

---

54   Since the story is set in Bethulia in the Samarian region, some have sought to locate it there as well, but Bethulia and all of Samaria are subordinated to Jerusalem's control.

55   Isaiah Gafni notes that texts written in the diaspora might be expected to have some reference to the role of diaspora Jews (*Land, Center and Diaspora: Jewish Constructs in Late Antiquity* [JSPSup 21; Sheffield: Sheffield Academic Press, 1997] 24); although such references are lacking here, that might not be viewed as a strong indicator in an imaginative text.

56   Joosten, "Original Language," 172 n. 30; Priebatsch, "Das Buch Judit." See also Reiterer, "Religion und hellenistische Realpolitik."

57   Gera, *Judith*, 94–96.

58   Enslin, *Book of Judith*, 39–40; Moore, *Judith*, 66–67; Robert Hanhart, ed., *Text und Textgeschichte des*

Buches Judith (Mitteilungen des Septuaginta-Unternehmens 14; Göttingen: Vandenhoeck & Ruprecht, 1979) 9. Origen, *Letter to Africanus* 19, said that Jews had told him that they knew of no Judith text in Hebrew, yet he also says they knew no Semitic version of Tobit, but Semitic texts of Tobit were discovered at Qumran. Much later, Jerome utilized texts of Judith in Aramaic, but they may have been derived from the LXX textual tradition. There is no firm evidence from Jerome about an early Semitic version; see appendix below.

59   Priebatsch, "Das Buch Judit." Others who followed include Zenger, who had changed his mind ("Judith/Judithbuch," *TRE* 17: 404–8), Helmut Engel, "'Der HERR ist ein Gott, der die Kriege zerschlächt': Zur Frage der griechischen Originalsprache und der Struktur des Buches Judit," in Klaus-Dietrich Schunk

Many other markers of Semitic syntactical constructions have been noted:[60]

- cognate accusative[61]
- repetition of cognate verbal parts, equivalent to the Hebrew infinitive absolute[62]
- *hou . . . ekei* = Hebrew resumptive *šām* in the idiom *'ăšer . . . šām* (5:9; 7:10)
- *sphodra* = *mě'ōd*; *sphodra sphodra* = *mě'ōd mě'ōd*
- *pas* for *kōl*
- *kai nun* = *wě'attāh*
- *idou* = *hinnēh*
- construct state for an adjective, e.g., "words of truth" for "true words" (10:13)
- *en* for Hebrew *bě*, especially in an instrumental sense (good Greek typically uses dative without *en*)

Common idiomatic Hebrew nouns and phrases include:

- "all flesh"
- idioms with face
- idioms with eye
- oath formula, "as X lives"
- "it was without number"
- "on the left" for north
- "put to the mouth of the sword"
- "month of days"
- "image of the heart" = *yētzer* (8:29)

- "to generations of generations" (8:32)
- "from small to great" (13:4)
- "amen"
- "speak peace with her" (15:8)
- "for many days"
- *psychē* used for *nepeš*, person
- gave them over to destruction (2:7; 4:1)

Some scholars claimed to have isolated instances where the Greek reflects a misreading of Semitic words, thus indicating a Semitic original. Frank Zimmermann, for instance, argued that in Jdt 13:19 the translator misread תהלתך, "your praise," for תחלתך, "your hope." According to Moore, with this argument Zimmerman "has ended all debate on the LXX's ambiguous reading."[63] Yet Corley found good reason for dismissing this and other examples. The entire phrase, he shows, likely alludes to Prov 23:18 LXX, and in fact the surrounding verses in Proverbs include parallels in Judith. And even if that were not the case, *elpis* could be a simple scribal error for *epainos*.

A similar case occurs in 10:8, which reads "she bowed to God" (*prosekunēsen tō theō*; see text-critical notes). Moore conjectures that the translator saw אליהם in the original, "she bowed *to them*," and misread it as לאלהים, "she bowed *to God*." Corley, however, prefers the Greek text as it is: she bowed to God.[64] In yet a further example, Zimmermann even postulated a three-stage corruption in

---

and Matthias Augustin, eds., *Goldene Äpfel in silbernen Schalen: Collected Communications to the XIIIth Congress of the International Organization for the Study of the Old Testament, Leuven 1989* (BEATAJ 20; Frankfurt am Main: Lang, 1992) 155–68; Rakel, *Judit–Über Schönheit*, 33–40, 106–10; Corley, "Septuagintalisms," 65–66; and Schmitz/Engel, *Judit*, 40–43. Good summaries of the question can be found at Otzen, *Tobit and Judith*, 137–41, and in Gera, *Judith*, 79–97, who, as in the present commentary, maintains that the question is still open.

60 This and the following list are indebted to Corley, "Septuagintalisms," 75–80; Moore, *Judith*, 75–80; and Gera, *Judith*, 81. On similar issues in Ben Sira, which we know was translated from Hebrew and for which we have much of the underlying Hebrew text, see Benjamin G. Wright, "Sirach (Ecclesiasticus)," in James K. Aitken, ed., *The T&T Clark Companion to the Septuagint* (London: Bloomsbury T&T Clark, 2015) 410–24, here 413–20.

61 Gera argues that the cognate accusative can occasionally be found in Greek and so is not an indisputable marker of Semitic style (*Judith*, 84–85); however, it is rare in Greek and common in Hebrew.

62 Gera notes that the infinitives absolute are handled differently (2:13; 6:4; 7:15; 9:4), which would be less likely if the work were composed in Greek (*Judith*, 84–85).

63 Moore, *Judith*, 223, regarding Frank Zimmermann, "Aids for the Recovery of the Hebrew Original of Judith," *JBL* 57 (1938) 67–74, here 71; see also Corley, "Septuagintalisms," 90–91; Barbara Schmitz, *Gedeutete Geschichte: Die Funktion der Reden und Gebete im Buch Judit* (HBS 40; Freiburg im Breisgau: Herder, 2004) 11–12.

64 Moore, *Judith*, 201–2; Corley, "Septuagintalisms," 95; the following example is from p. 89.

the Hebrew. For *diexane,* "she combed" (10:3), Zimmermann posits an original Hebrew ותסך, "she anointed," misread as שתסדר, "she arranged," and then ותרסק, "she combed." Corley again offers a simpler solution: Sinaiticus attests the likely original reading of *diexane,* but since this is a rare word, Vaticanus and Alexandrinus replaced it with forms of *diatassō.* In general, Zimmermann *presumed* a Hebrew original and then tried to trace it by complicated retroversions. His conjecture is ultimately weak. The textual variants can often be explained within the Greek textual tradition alone. The arguments from misunderstandings of Hebrew are thus no longer considered compelling, although the Semitizing style in general is still discussed.

At the same time, there are many features that exhibit a more typical Greek style:
- eight future infinitives[65]
- complicated Greek words, some unattested in LXX or in Greek in general.[66]
- *nyktos kai hemeros,* "night and day" (11:17) in Greek order; Hebrew is more often "day and night"
- relative pronouns preceding the antecedent (5:3; 8:15; 9:1, 9)
- *legō* or *phēmi* + infinitive to express indirect discourse (13:3)
- prepositions used correctly (12:11; 13:10), often without resumptive pronouns[67]
- *hothen* (8:20; 11:16)
- correct use of imperfect (12:7–9) and pluperfect (12:7–9; 14:8)
- verb of perception with participle (7:27; 10:7; 14:5)
- *hōs* + participle (14:2; 21:11)
- precise use of prefixes (13:1)
- correctly used conditionals (8:11; 11:2; 12:12)
- wordplay on *gen-,* which cannot be reproduced easily in Hebrew (8:32)

- occasional elegant variation of word order of genitive (9:11; in Hebrew genitive must come after the noun it modifies)

Some indicators may at first seem to suggest Greek style but are actually unclear:
- *Prognōsis* (9:6; 11:19) has no exact Hebrew equivalent, although Grintz proposed *mē'ôlām.*[68]
- Participles seem "Greek," yet they always come before the verb and not in other positions.
- *Dē* immediately after an imperative seems Greek, but it could translate *nā'.*
- The word order of verbs after *heōs, henika, hopēnika, hina, mēpote, hopōs,* and *hote* follows the Hebrew tendency.[69]

Judith sometimes utilizes hypotaxis and at times attests unusual vocabulary. The combination of short sentences (by elite Greek standards) and varied vocabulary is actually typical of Greek novels, and perhaps novels cross-culturally: simple sentences combined with colorful and even pretentious vocabulary is the attraction of novels in many different times and places. Gera notes that the Hebrew-sounding threat, "I will give you over to X," is completed in a more Greek way with, at different times, a large number of terms for death or destruction: *diarpagēn, phonon, harpagēn, aphanismon, rhomphaion, pronomēn, ekdikēsin, aichmalōsian, katabrōma,* and *olethron.*[70] Alternatively, a case of the misreading of Hebrew, which above was taken to indicate a Semitic original, can in one case also indicate a Greek original. In Jdt 6:2 mercenaries of Ephraim evoke Isa 28:1 LXX. But the LXX reading comes about from an alternative pointing of Hebrew *šikkōrê,* "drunkards," as *śĕkîrê,* " hirelings" (the only difference in a consonantal text would be the *yod* in the latter, but it would also be optional). It is argued that the author of Judith knows the LXX, not the MT, version of Isaiah.[71]

---

65 See 1:12; 8:9, 11, 33; 13:3; 16:4 (3x). There are only three future infinitives in the entire Pentateuch! See Joosten, "Original Language," 161; Gera, *Judith,* 85, 129.

66 *Apegnōsmenoi* 9:11, *apēlpismenoi* 9:11, *euphrosynos* 14:9; *anyperblētos* 16:13.

67 Gera, *Judith,* 82–83; see also Soubigou, "Judith," 483–87.

68 Grintz, *Book of Judith,* 142.

69 Cf. Georg Walser, *The Greek of the Ancient Synagogue:*

An Investigation on the Greek of the Septuagint, Pseudepigrapha and the New Testament (Studia Graeca et Latina Lundensia 8; Stockholm: Almquist & Wiksell, 2001) 111–22.

70 Gera, *Judith,* 86, 143. Yet some of this variety can be found in the Hebrew Bible at times, e.g., Isa 42:24; Jer 25:31; 26:6; 30:16; Ezek 25:12; 31:14. Here they are images of exile and destruction.

71 Gera, *Judith,* 220; Schmitz, *Gedeutete Geschichte,* 126–27.

The better Greek is also largely restricted to certain sections. It is the conversations, speeches, and prayers that "are written in livelier, more colloquial Greek and seem to point to a writer who is sensitive to the nuances in Greek."[72] It is in the speeches that we encounter most of the particles, connectives, and verbal modes; optatives and almost all subjunctives; sophisticated stylistic effects of rhyme and rhythm (9:8, 11–12; 4:9–15); and alliteration and assonance (5:19; 8:32; 15:9). Although we must ask whether the narrative and speeches derive from different authors, or whether some narrative sections were composed separately, there is not enough evidence of this to raise the question seriously.[73]

What has proven to be the most compelling argument for a Greek original is the fact that, when Judith quotes or alludes to biblical verses, the text often attests the LXX rather than the Masoretic Hebrew text. True, offers Joosten, a translator might have inserted readings from the better-known Greek Bible, but much more telling is the fact that the *point* of the allusion is sometimes found only in the LXX version.[74] The example most often treated is Jdt 9:7 and 16:2: "the God who crushes wars." Although the idea here is found in various forms in the Hebrew Bible (Hos 2:18; Ps 46:9; 76:5–6), the words used in Judith are distinctive to the LXX of Exod 15:3 and Isa 42:13.[75] But even here, a Greek original is not proven. It is possible that the LXX wording may be based on variant

Hebrew readings that were known to the author, variants that did not appear in the Masoretic Text. In the context of Jubilees, Matthew Goff notes a similar phenomenon:

> Thus it is not always clear in *Jubilees* what form of a given scriptural verse is being engaged. In many cases, for example, the text presumes forms of verses closer to that of the Greek Septuagint than the Hebrew (Masoretic) text (e.g., 10.18 and 18.1). The 'scripturalesque' self-presentation of *Jubilees* also means that, while the composition not infrequently interprets a verse that corresponds to one in our Masoretic text, the composition is steeped in idioms and expressions that echo the language of scripture and do not necessarily constitute exegesis of a specific verse.[76]

Concerning the texts at Qumran Eva Mroczek also writes:

> At least one Qumran text, *4QTestimonia*, is often cited as containing quotations from Deuteronomy and Joshua with non-biblical additions; but its sources are, in fact, passages from a non-MT, proto-Samaritan version of Exodus and the non-biblical *Psalms of Joshua*, without embellishment.[77]

In the freer textual tradition of this period, we cannot be sure that the agreements with the LXX entered in through a body of Greek texts or through other, possibly Semitic texts.

---

72 Gera, *Judith,* 87–88; see also Gera, "Speech in Judith," in Melvin K. H. Peters, ed., *XIV Congress of the IOSCS, Helsinki, 2010* (SCS 59; Atlanta: Society of Biblical Literature, 2013) 413–23; Soubigou, *Judith,* 483–87. Gera notes that 2 and 3 Maccabees reflect the opposite situation: the narrative portions are written in better Greek, the stylized martyr scene in 2 Maccabees 7 and the prayer in 3 Macc 6:2–15 in more biblical Greek (*Judith,* 92–93).

73 As a comparison, we note that other texts, such as Luke-Acts, exhibit a mix of Semitizing/Greek style, and that the LXX of the Song of the Sea is more elegant; see Gera, *Judith,* 89 n. 358; Moore, *Judith,* 228–29.

74 Joosten, "Original Language," 163–67; Larry Perkins, "'The Lord Is a Warrior,' 'The Lord Who Crushes Wars,' Exodus 15:3 and Judith 9:7; 16:2," *BIOSCS* 40 (2007) 121–33; Judith Lang, "'The Lord Who Crushes Wars': Studies on Judith 9:7, Judith

16:2, and Exodus 15:3," in Xeravits, *Pious Seductress,* 179–87. These examples are treated also in Rakel, *Judit–Über Schönheit,* 265–72; and Schmitz, *Gedeutete Geschichte,* 167. Matthew Thiessen takes the misunderstanding of *kyrios* as both God and human lord as evidence for a Greek original ("Protecting the Holy Race and Holy Space: Judith's Reenactment of the Slaughter of Shechem," *JAJ* 49 [2018] 165–88, here 176 n. 28), but this double meaning occurs just as easily in Hebrew or Aramaic.

75 The two other most important examples of Judith's quotation of the LXX are Jdt 9:22/Gen 34:7 LXX and Jdt 8:16/Num 23:19 LXX.

76 Matthew Goff, "*Jubilees,*" in Lawrence M. Wills and Jonathan Klawans, eds., *Jewish Annotated Apocrypha,* forthcoming.

77 Eva Mroczek, "The Hegemony of the Biblical in the Study of Second Temple Literature," *JAJ* 6 (2015) 2–35, here 32.

Overlooked by almost all commentators on this question, however, are the statistical studies by Raymond A. Martin. He carefully catalogued the Semitizing characteristics in two groups of texts: those known to be translated from Semitic sources and those composed in Greek. The presence of translation Greek, Martin concluded, can be argued based on the "relative *frequency* or *infrequency* of an idiom, rather than its mere *occurrence* or *non-occurrence*."[78] Martin was able to tabulate seventeen indicators of translation Greek, along with—and this is more important—their *frequencies* in the two types of texts. It would be possible, Martin speculated, to mimic biblical translation Greek, but it would be difficult for an author, no matter how clever, to mimic biblical Greek style *across all of the indicators, and at the frequency that is typical of translation Greek*. Indeed, these indicators are often so subtle that they are "not the kinds of syntactical features which would be readily chosen if a writer should seek deliberately to imitate translation Greek style."[79] When applied to Judith, Martin's criteria provide a strong argument for a Semitic original.

The first eight criteria that Martin isolates involve the use of prepositions with particular cases, and are given here,[80] followed by the results as evidenced in Judith. Tendencies of Greek translated from Semitic languages include:

1. Far fewer instances of *dia* + genitive than *en* + dative. Judith is well within the range of biblical translation Greek.

2. Far fewer instances of *dia* + all cases than *en* + dative. Judith is in the middle of the range of translation Greek.

3. Fewer instances of *eis* + all cases than *en* + dative. Here Judith lies exactly in the gray area between the two categories.[81]

4. Fewer instances of *kata* + accusative than *en* + dative. Judith is well within the range of translation Greek.

5. Fewer instances of *kata* + all cases than *en* + dative. Judith is well within the range of translation Greek.

6. Fewer instances of *peri* + all cases than *en* + dative. Judith is in the middle of the range of translation Greek.

7. Fewer instances of *pros* + dative than *en* + dative. Judith is in the range of translation Greek.

8. Fewer instances of *hypo* + genitive than *en* + dative. Judith is well within the range of the translation texts.

Judith was thus in the middle of the range for texts translated from Hebrew or Aramaic in every case except for number 3, where it was exactly on the boundary line. But since many of the translated texts exhibited variation, the fact that Judith was on the boundary line for one criterion does not differentiate it from the translation texts.[82]

Martin conducted follow-up studies that isolated other criteria associated with translation Greek, but while his studies of the above criteria included Judith, in the later studies he omitted the Apocrypha. I have therefore supplemented his research by analyzing a sample of

---

78 Raymond A. Martin, *Syntactical Evidence of Semitic Sources in Greek Documents* (SCS 3; Cambridge, MA: Society of Biblical Literature, 1974) 2 (italics his); Martin, "Some Syntactical Criteria of Translation Greek," *VT* 10 (1960) 295–310; Martin, "Syntactical Evidence of Aramaic Sources in Acts I–XV," *NTS* 10 (1964) 38–59; Martin, "Syntax Criticism of Baruch," in Claude E. Cox, ed., *VII Congress of the International Organization for Septuagint and Cognate Studies (Leuven, 1989)* (SCS 31; Atlanta: Scholars Press, 1991) 361–71. One of the issues is the educational level of comparison texts; what we perceive as "biblical style" may also simply reflect uneducated Greek. Martin includes studies of papyri to get at the issue of educational level. James R. Davila ("[How] Can We Tell If a Greek Apocryphon or Pseudepigraphon Has Been Translated from Hebrew or Aramaic?," *JSP* 15 [2005] 3–61, here 36–37) takes note of Martin's

studies. Davila also helpfully distinguishes between Semitisms and Septuagintalisms; that is, Semitic influences that are common in the Septuagint might influence a Jewish or Christian author who has no firsthand knowledge of Semitic languages.

79 Martin, *Syntactical Evidence*, 2.

80 Because Hebrew and Aramaic use fewer prepositions than does Greek, and rely especially on the preposition *bĕ*, translation Greek is skewed toward dependence on *en* + dative.

81 In regard to this criterion, there are several biblical texts that are in the range of original Greek, while some original Greek, specifically the papyri and Xenophon, are on the line along with Judith. This may indicate that this criterion is not as dependable as the others.

82 It could also be argued, however, that Martin's comparison Greek texts reflect a higher educational

Judith (chaps. 1–2 and 11–12) to provide data for these criteria as well:[83]

9. As a result of the ubiquity of *wĕ* and *wayhî* in biblical prose, biblical translation Greek utilized *kai* to introduce independent clauses much more often than *de*. Judith fell well within the range of translation Greek.
10. Biblical translation Greek rarely separated the definite article from its substantive, while texts composed in Greek often did. Judith contained only one example (2:5), consistent with translation Greek.
11. Texts composed in Greek place a genitive either before the word it depends on or after about equally often, but biblical translation Greek texts rarely or never place the genitive before. The Judith sample contained one such example, in 11:22, and is thus typical of translation Greek.
12. Biblical translation Greek uses genitive personal pronouns often, while original Greek does so only about once every thirty lines. Judith used genitive personal pronouns the most often of any of the sample texts.
13. Because an article is not required in the construct state in Hebrew, biblical translation Greek often omits an article when a noun is accompanied by a genitive. Judith is in the middle of the range for translation Greek.
14. Because Hebrew and Aramaic generally place adjectives after the noun they modify, translation Greek contains more attributive adjectives placed after the noun. Judith is on the border between translation Greek and original Greek.
15. Hebrew and Aramaic utilize a construct relation more than attributive adjectives ("the table of the king" rather than "the royal table"); therefore, the total number of attributive adjectives in translation Greek is lower than in original Greek. The Judith sample was well within the range for translation Greek.
16. Hebrew and Aramaic do not depend on adverbial participles to subordinate one verbal clause to

another as Greek does. Judith was well within the range for translation Greek.
17. Hebrew and Aramaic do not have a dative case and use the preposition *bĕ*, often translated by Greek *en*, for these meanings. (Note that criteria 1–8 concerned various prepositions with substantives, while this criterion concerns the use of the dative without any preposition.) The Judith sample diverges from original Greek texts even more than do the translation Greek texts.

Martin's statistical studies thus suggest that mimicking a very long list of subtle attributes, all in a way close to the statistical center of translation Greek, would be very difficult. Judith corresponds to translation Greek in fifteen of the seventeen criteria and is on the borderline in two (numbers 3 and 14). Texts known to be translations from Semitic languages typically do not exhibit translation Greek qualities in *all* the linguistic indicators, but rather in about nine to fourteen of the seventeen criteria.[84] Thus, if Judith was translated from a Semitic language, the fact that it lies in a gray area in regard to two criteria should not surprise us.

Yet it may be significant that Judith differs from original Greek in *only* two of the criteria: *Judith appears more Semitizing than the translation texts.* Presumably, a clever author—and it is my assumption in this commentary that the author is indeed very clever—would be sensitive enough to subtle stylistic differences to re-create them. The author may even be overcompensating. The sixty-eight occurrences of idioms with face, for instance, may occur too often for Semitic languages. They are more common in Judith than in all the narrative texts of the Hebrew Bible, although they are still less common than in Jeremiah and Ezekiel. The proliferation of face idioms, however, may have occurred in a Semitic composition, resulting perhaps from an attempt to sound "biblical" or at least traditional. Alternatively, the evidence could indicate that a translator is here attempting to be as bibli-

---

level than Judith (even though his sampling includes Jewish texts in Greek, less elegant Greek authors, and papyri). It is therefore possible that Judith represents, not just a biblicizing Greek style, but a less elite biblicizing Greek.

83 Together these chapters constitute 229 lines in

Robert Hanhart's *Iudith* (Septuaginta, Vetus Testamentum Graecum 8.4; Göttingen: Vandenhoeck & Ruprecht, 1979]), which is about the average of Martin's biblical translated Greek and his samples of original Greek.

84 Martin, *Syntactical Evidence*, 38.

cal as possible, as is sometimes the case, for instance, with Theodotion. Further, the fact that the Semitizing aspects were not found evenly distributed might be explained by either hypothesis. That is, an author writing in Greek might mimic Septuagintal style for the most part, slipping into better Greek in the heightened rhetorical situations; or, conversely, a translator might utilize a biblical style for the most part, while resorting to better Greek in certain sections.[85]

Although many recent scholars, then, have concluded that our novella was composed in a Semitizing Greek, some, such as Cameron Boyd-Taylor, still maintain that it was originally written in Hebrew, and others, Gera and Corley, leave the question open.[86] In my opinion, it is somewhat more likely that Judith was written in a Semitic language, but strong evidence can be amassed on both sides of the question.

Even if it is concluded that Judith was written in Greek, there are two different processes that must be considered. Either the author is mimicking biblical style (so Joosten and many others), or a poorly educated author, whose Greek is thoroughly but not intentionally Septuagintal, is at work (so Corley).[87] But Gera counters the latter suggestion by reminding us that some sections indicate an author capable of writing passable Greek.[88] If our text was indeed written in Greek (which Gera leaves open), the Septuagintal style must have resulted from intentional mimicry for effect, carried through differently in different sections. If it was translated from a Semitic language into Greek, the translator must have varied the style by section.

---

85 Joosten posits the former ("Original Language," 163–64). The number of parallels to Greek literature may be relevant here. It is also interesting to note that in the *later* manuscript tradition we find both improvements in Greek style and also occasional examples of further Semitizing, or one might say *faux*-Semitic.

86 Cameron Boyd-Taylor, "Judith," *NETS,* 441–42; Gera, *Judith,* 79–97; Corley, "Septuagintalisms," 93–94, 97.

87 Joosten, "Original Language," 162–63; Corley, "Septuagintalisms," 67–68.

88 Gera, *Judith,* 84.

3. Literary Structure

The book of Judith is longer than the other Jewish novellas—twice as long as Esther, half again as long as Tobit. It can be easily divided into two parts, chaps. 1–7 and 8–16, the second part 42 percent longer than the first.[1] The first half relates the rise of the threat of the campaign of Nebuchadnezzar, king of the Assyrians, his huge expeditionary force bearing down on the tiny Jewish village of Bethulia. The second half recounts the appearance of the heroine Judith and her successful plan to defeat the Assyrian army and to save Bethulia and, thus, Jerusalem.

Biblical scholars in the past have criticized the book for presenting what seemed a long and rambling first half. "The historical setting," said J. C. Dancy, "has few merits. Dramatically it is spoiled by tedious descriptions and confusions, stylistically by exaggerations and empty rhetoric." Literarily sensitive critics such as Luis Alonso Schökel could also fault it.[2] Dancy seemed to be seeking a real biblical history, Alonso Schökel a better novel. Even Craven and Moore register the objection that there is a late entry for our main character.[3] More recent scholars are still less satisfied with the first half. Otzen speaks of the "somewhat dry style of the first chapters" in contrast to the "more emotional style of the descriptions of the despair of the Israelites facing disaster" and "the sophisticated style of the Judith section."[4]

I will have reasons to disagree with these judgments. Our author executes well the narrator's trick of putting off the *expected* climactic scene and building the tensions as long as possible. The musical *West Side Story* is forty minutes old before Tony and Maria even meet, and in *The Birds* Alfred Hitchcock intentionally delayed the first attack by birds, knowing that the audience had indeed come to the theater to see exactly that. The delay in the two cases, which is experienced as impatience, also builds anticipation. In the same way, the post–Maccabean Revolt audience felt keenly—more keenly than modern readers—the rising tensions of world empires amassing on the horizon to defeat their small vassal kingdom. It would actually have been quite stirring in the original performance situation. And contrary to the impressions of many, the first half is not simply a list of battles. In addition to military developments, there is also much dialogue. Gera identifies a similar process in Xenophon's *Cyropaedia*: dialogue, lively court characters, and "emotional, grandiloquent passages" are introduced to enliven "long battle-ridden stretches."[5] A central part of the talk, Achior's speech to Holofernes in chap. 5, is also about what God's covenant means.

Craven's structural study did much to instill an appreciation of the structure as a whole and to rehabilitate the first half in scholars' eyes.[6] If every element of the first half was part of the author's plan, reasoned Craven, then it must be appreciated for what it contributes. In each of the two halves a clear chiastic pattern can be discerned:

---

1 Moore, *Judith*, 56.

2 J. C. Dancy suggested a separate author for the first half (*Judith* [Shorter Books of the Apocrypha; Cambridge: Cambridge University Press, 1972] 67–68). Arthur E. Cowley had made the same judgment ("Book of Judith," *APOT* 1:242–43). See also Luis Alonso Schökel, *Narrative Structures in the Book of Judith* (Protocol of the Colloquies, Center for Hermeneutical Studies in Hellenistic and Modern Culture 12.17, March 1974; Berkeley: Center for Hermeneutical Studies, 1975) 3. Tessa Rajak notes that the slightly earlier Letter of Aristeas has a structural looseness and a delay in getting to the most important part, the translation process, told rather quickly near the end (*Translation and Survival: The Greek Bible of the Ancient Jewish Diaspora* [Oxford: Oxford University Press, 2009] 73).

3 Craven, *Artistry and Faith*, 56, 58; Moore, *Judith*, 56.

4 Otzen, *Tobit and Judith*, 126. Yet he can note that "one observes the impressive contrast between all the men, cruel or bewildered, in the first part, and the pious and determined woman in the second part" (127).

5 Deborah Levine Gera, *Xenophon's Cyropaedia: Style, Genre, and Literary Technique* (Oxford Classical Monographs; Oxford: Clarendon, 1993) 198. Our text also repeats many key words to echo and foreshadow the repeated points of concern: *kyrios, ischys, cheir, phobos* (and synonyms), *apatē, kallos, (ana)boaō,* and *dynamis;* see Craven, *Artistry and Faith*, passim; Gera, *Judith*, 86; Zenger, *Das Buch Judit*, 433–34; Rakel, *Judit–Über Schönheit*, 88, 92. An appreciation for the literary qualities of the first half can also be found in the work of the Catholic scholar George T. Montague, *Books of Esther and Judith*, 15.

6 Craven, *Artistry and Faith*, esp. 60–63. Crawford notes that both Judith and Esther use chiasm with series of reversals to resolve the plot ("Esther and Judith," 63).

First half

A   Campaign against disobedient nations;
     the people surrender (2:14–3:10)

  B   Israel is "greatly terrified";
       Joakim prepares for war (4:1–15)

    C   Holofernes talks with Achior;
         Achior is expelled (5:1–6:13)

    C′   Achior is received in Bethulia;
          Achior talks with the people (6:14–21)

  B′   Holofernes prepares for war;
        Israel is "greatly terrified" (7:1–15)

A′   Campaign against Bethulia;
     The people want to surrender (7:6–32)

Second half

A   Introduction of Judith (8:1–8)

  B   Judith plans to save Israel (8:9–10:9a)

    C   Judith and her slave leave Bethulia (10:9b–10)

      D   Judith beheads Holofernes (10:11–13:10a)

    C′   Judith and her slave return to Bethulia (13:10b–11)

  B′   Judith plans the destruction of Israel's enemy (13:12–16:20)

A′   Conclusion about Judith (16:21–25)

From her structural arrangement one can see that chap. 1 set the stage by demonstrating how one great king, Arphaxad of the Medes, was quickly destroyed and brought to nothing by the greater king, Nebuchadnezzar of the Assyrians. It is in chaps. 2–7 that Nebuchadnezzar will turn from what was simply a military conquest to a greater conquest, the control of the entire known world, both a military and a theological battle. The simple question of what happens in the first half allows for an appreciation of the dialogue, the theological and historical contextualizing, the simple building and maintaining of tension, along with the cinematic sweep from international politics to a narrowing focus on the single point of opposition. Many important plot developments and themes are established in chaps. 2–7, only to be resolved in Judith's quickly paced actions in chaps. 8–16. The brief decapitation scene in chap. 13 in particular—what the audience is waiting for—responds narratively to a host of issues that are developed in chaps. 2–7.

At the center of the chiasm of the first half is the dialogue of Holofernes and Achior, which leads to Achior's expulsion from the Assyrian camp as a punishment. Achior is then received in Bethulia, where he has a dialogue with the people. A central character in Judith, Achior becomes a sort of male heroic partner. His movements criss-cross Judith's: he moves from the Assyrian camp to Bethulia just before she moves from Bethulia to the Assyrian camp. His conversion will cement this movement (see chap. 5). His expulsion and reception per se would not seem to be the crux of the narrative arc, but the structure suggests—and the audience would probably have realized—that this is really the point at which the fortunes of the Israelites would change. That is, although they suffer greatly after this point, Achior's brave statement about the nature of Israel's history foreshadows God's victory, and the seed of their triumph is seen in Achior's movement to Bethulia. The narrative point of view has shifted from the Assyrians and the worldwide perspective, to the dialogue of Holofernes and Achior (chap. 5), to the expulsion of Achior to the village of Bethulia, where the attention will remain (the Assyrian camp is in the valley below Bethulia). Craven also reminds us that the underlying theological/national identity question of the whole work is, What god is there except Nebuchadnezzar? This question comes to a head at the point of Achior's expulsion, the center of the chiasm of the first part, and is answered at the center of the chiasm in the second part (10:11–13:10a) through the actions of a woman whose name means "Jewish woman."

The chiasm in the second half also provides thought-provoking contrasts. The second half focuses attention first on all the Bethulians, then on Judith and her slave, then in the center on Judith alone, then again on Judith and her slave, ending with Judith and all the Bethulians. Craven argued that in these patterns we find a literary artistry in the telling of the story. Although schematic patterns should not necessarily be counted as "artistry" in a literary work, her discernment of many compelling structural aspects greatly altered the perception of this literary project and they contribute to a popular literary artistry. Continuing the efforts of Alonso Schökel and his respondents from a few years earlier, Craven's analysis challenged the general sense of literary embarrassment that had clouded the text among Protestant scholars. But is the book *too rigidly* ordered in its patterns, as some have suggested?[7] This overindulgence in literary patterning simply continues the author's program of extravagance, the excess of popular artistry.

A number of other literary aspects serve to structure the text. Nebuchadnezzar has inflated himself as a would-be god, and Holofernes will represent him. Standing opposite them are God and *his* general, Judith. Holofernes and Judith will thus engage in a heroic battle, representing Nebuchadnezzar and God, respectively. The climactic scene of the novella finds the two proxies coming into close contact with each other, literally in a clutch, as Judith grabs Holofernes's head by the hair.[8] This results in an odd role for Nebuchadnezzar. Like his namesake in the book of Daniel, he is blustery and full of hubris, but in this text we do not hear what happens to him. His mighty expeditionary army is destroyed, to be sure, and Israel is not oppressed again for a long time. As God remains in the background, so Nebuchadnezzar moves to the background.

The first half of Judith is also carefully arranged in scenes that alternate between the sweep of threatening military campaigns and pauses for the audience to catch their breath: "[Nebuchadnezzar] returned with them, along with all his mixed force, a vast host of troops, and there he and his army spent a period of rest and feasting that lasted a hundred and twenty days" (1:16). A pattern of such pauses can be discerned:

action	action	action	action	dialogue	action
pause	pause	pause	pause	pause	pause
1:16	2:28	3:10	4:13–15	6:21	7:32

This is not a unique literary technique, since the Gospel of John also interjects narrative rests at 2:12; 3:22; 4:40; 10:40; and 11:54.

Craven and others have also drawn attention to other parallels in language or motif between the first and second halves:[9]

- The first half is the public zone of men at war; the second moves to the more typical novelistic zone of a woman in domestic space, a kind of contrast that is prepared for by women's stories in Herodotus and Ctesias, and found also in Esther.
- The first half opens with the introduction of an important antagonist, Nebuchadnezzar, which is immediately interrupted by a long parenthesis on a supporting character who quickly dies, Arphaxad. The second half opens with the introduction of an important protagonist, Judith, which is immediately interrupted by a long parenthesis on a supporting character who quickly dies, her husband Manasseh.
- In the first half, Achior moves from one side in the military campaign to the other. In the second, Judith and her slave move in the opposite direction from one side to the other. Achior and Judith then become paired: only they show true courage and confess God openly.
- Nebuchadnezzar called together his officers and nobles to propose a secret plan (2:2). Judith called the elders of the city, Uzziah, Chabris, and Charmis, to tell them of her plan (8:10, 34).
- Nebuchadnezzar says, "I have spoken and I will accomplish these things by my hand" (2:12). Judith says, "The Lord will deliver Israel by my hand" (8:33).
- Holofernes's preparations for his army (2:18) are balanced by Judith's preparations for herself and her maid (10:5).
- Holofernes says to Achior, "Who are you, Achior . . . to prophesy among us?" (6:2), while Judith says to the

7   Moore (*Judith*, 58 n. 34) and Otzen (*Tobit and Judith*, 129) think Craven sometimes overstates or overvalues the structural patterns, as I earlier agreed (*The Jewish Novel in the Ancient World* [Myth and Poetics; Ithaca, NY: Cornell University Press, 1995] 133–34). However, I am now more inclined to think of the patterning as another part of the author's popular literary achievement.

8   Gera, *Judith*, 7–8.

9   See also Moore, *Judith*, 57; and Gera, *Judith*, pas-

sim. According to Wayne H. Peterson (response to Alonso Schökel, in *Narrative Structures*, 34), the minor characters "mirror and heighten for the reader the changing fortunes of the plot. They are the reactors to the major characters and situations." See also Andrea M. Sheaffer, *Envisioning the Book of Judith: How Art Illuminates Minor Characters* (Bible in the Modern World 64; Sheffield: Sheffield Phoenix, 2014).

elders, "Who are you . . . to set yourself in the place of God?" (8:12).

- Holofernes demands that all peoples call upon Nebuchadnezzar as god (3:8), while Judith urges the elders to join her in calling upon God (8:17).
- The Israelites are greatly disturbed (7:4), and finally the Assyrians are greatly disturbed (14:19).
- Fear and trembling fall upon the rebellious nations (2:28), while trembling and fear fall upon the Assyrian armies (15:2).
- Holofernes enacts the plan (*boulē*) of Nebuchadnezzar (2:2), while Judith condemns the elders for interfering with the plan (*boulē*) of God (8:16).

While agreeing with Craven's structural analysis, others discern further patterns as well. Zenger, for instance, divides the book into three parts:

1. Chaps. 1–3: Nebuchadnezzar establishes himself as god.
2. Chaps. 4–7: Who is God—Nebuchadnezzar or Yahweh?
3. Chaps. 8–16: Yahweh—through Judith—demonstrates that he is God.[10]

Each of these three sections develops what Zenger asserts is the overall theme of the book: "Who is the true god, the Assyrian god or the Israelite god?" Further, within section 2 one finds two symmetrical descriptions of Israel's distress (4:1–15; 7:1–32), within which there are two pleas for God and Nebuchadnezzar (5:1–24; 6:1–21).

Barbara Schmitz also finds patterns and developing themes in the six speeches in Judith, which themselves exhibit a chiastic pattern:

A Nebuchadnezzar's public speech (chap. 2)
  B Dialogue of Holofernes and Achior (chaps. 5–6)
    C Judith and the elders, in Bethulia (chap. 8)
    C′ Judith's prayer, in Bethulia (chap. 9)
  B′ Dialogue of Holofernes and Judith (chap. 11)
A′ Judith's public song (chap. 16)

Echoes among the speeches can also be heard. They provide a theological anchor to the narrative components, standing, says Schmitz, in contrast to the misogyny of the Western art tradition, which often "de-moralizes" Judith.[11] She draws other provocative conclusions: in the *narrative* structure (not the speech structure), there is a low point at chap. 7 and an upswing at chap. 13, which confirms Zenger's structure above but highlight as well the *different* structure of the speeches.[12] The speech structure will highlight Judith's experience and de-emphasize the decapitation as the center of the story.

Schmitz's analysis raises helpful questions about how narrative and speech may operate in different arcs over the book, and how theme and structure are also developed in different passages. Further, she reminds us that the messages of the text are being communicated simultaneously on different levels. In this commentary, I will also distinguish between the narrative arc and the speech arc, in a way parallel to but also disagreeing with Schmitz. I use the metaphor of the music and libretto of opera: the

---

10 Zenger, *Das Buch Judit*, 432–34.
11 Schmitz, *Gedeutete Geschichte*, 418–81, esp. 421–36; Schmitz, "Trickster, Schriftgelehrte oder *femme fatale*? Die Juditfigur zwischen biblischer Erzählung und kunstgeschichtlicher Rezeption," *Biblisches Forum* (2004) 1–18, here 13 (www.bibfor.de). Ulrike Mittmann-Richert discusses the structure in terms of three speeches, Achior (chap. 5), Judith (chap. 8), and Judith before Holofernes (chap. 11) (*Einführung zu den jüdischen Schriften aus hellenistisch-römischer Zeit: Historische und legendarische Erzählungen* [Gütersloh: Gütersloher Verlagshaus, 2000] 82–96, here 83). The different structural arrangements are not necessarily mutually exclusive; we may simply conclude that

Judith's words *in general* mark turning points in the story.
12 Schmitz, "The Function of the Speeches and Prayers in the Books (*sic*) of Judith," in Athalya Brenner-Idan and Helen Efthimiadis-Keith, eds., *A Feminist Companion to Tobit and Judith* (Feminist Companion to the Bible [Second Series]; London: Bloomsbury T&T Clark, 2015) 164–74, here 167–68. For other notes on structure, see Rakel, *Judit–Über Schönheit*, 84–92; Adolfo D. Roitman, "Achior in the Book of Judith: His Role and Significance," in VanderKam, *No One Spoke Ill*, 31–45; Haag, *Das Buch Judit*, vii–viii; van Henten "Judith as an Alternative Leader," 225–32.

narrative is the music and the speeches the libretto. The former operates on a more suggestive level, the latter on a more cognitive level, although there are complexities to both. The narrative level, however, communicates a more satiric, transgressive message, while the speeches serve to inoculate Judith against censure. Whereas Schmitz reasserted the value of the speeches, it is also true that the speeches are in dialogue or even contrast with the narrative arc as libretto-to-music. This is a trickster novella about a woman who seduces and beheads a man, punctuated as well by her prayers.

Thus, it may be that the thematic aspect of the entire novella is found not only in the speeches, nor only in the decapitation, but in both, as well as in the excited utterance of the eunuch Bagoas when he discovers the headless corpse of Holofernes:

> These slaves have deceived us! One woman of the Hebrews has shamed the house of King Nebuchadnezzar! Look here! Holofernes is lying on the ground, and his head is missing! (14:18)

True, this utterance is in itself also a short speech, but is not usually considered together with the reflective speeches of the novella. (See also on Bagoas in 12:10–12.) Note here that Bagoas's utterance is similar in function to the denouement of Ehud's assassination of Eglon in Judges 3, and more telling: just as the book of Esther has several points at which the fortunes turn dramatically (4:16–17; 6:1–11; 7:8), there is also a point at which an opponent of Israel comments on a Jewish victory, almost as a form of unconscious prophecy:

> When Haman told his wife Zeresh and all his friends everything that had happened to him, his advisers and his wife Zeresh said to him, "If Mordecai, before whom your downfall has begun, is of the Jewish people, you will not prevail against him, but will surely fall before him. (Esth 6:13)

As a *comment* on the turn in the narrative, this statement by Zeresh is analogous to that of Bagoas.

In terms of both structure and theme, to what extent does Judith partake of an Israelite tradition of heroes? It is first necessary to consider how heroic narratives may be characterized cross-culturally. A pattern emerges of the hero *of narrative*. It is not just an ideal type but also a story pattern, a drama of challenges posed and overcome; not just as an assemblage of motifs but a *structure* of motifs within a Proppian analysis.[13]

The following general characteristics often apply to hero narratives, even though a world rich in heroes would also know exceptions. Usually male, the hero is an ideal human being who acts as a benefactor for his own people. When the people are attacked from the outside by an uncivilized monster, they become desperate, and call upon the hero to beg for deliverance. At first isolated from society and unable to integrate, the hero, when called upon, emerges from reclusiveness to save his or her people. Because the heroes are figures larger than life who are antisocial and march to their own rules, they do not feel inhibited by the constraints of culture. The hero is thus capable of crossing boundaries among peoples, or from civilized to wild places, even the boundary with the underworld. But even after saving their people, heroes cannot reintegrate into the very society they saved but must die or return to isolation.

The Greeks and Romans raised the cult of heroes to such a level that the reverence for heroes in Israel is often overlooked, yet the heroic tradition in Israel is actually quite strong. As in ancient Greece, so also in Israel the family offerings to ancestors at their tombs and the communications with dead heroes likely provided the background for the reverence for figures from "our history," such as the patriarchs and matriarchs, Moses, dead kings, prophets, and judges.[14] Says Jack N. Lightstone:

13 Vladimir Propp, *The Morphology of the Folktale* (Austin: University of Texas Press, 1968). On Israelite heroes, see Wills, "The Death of the Hero and the Violent Death of Jesus," in Jonathan Klawans and David A. Bernat, eds., *Religion and Violence: The Biblical Heritage* (Recent Research in Biblical Studies 2; Sheffield: Sheffield Phoenix, 2007) 79–99; Ronald S. Hendel, *Epic of the Patriarch: The Jacob Cycle and the Narrative Traditions of Canaan and Israel* (HSM 42; Decatur, GA: Scholars Press, 1987), and works below. On Greek heroes, see Gregory Nagy, *The Best of the Achaeans: Concepts of the Hero in Archaic Greek Poetry* (Baltimore: Johns Hopkins University Press, 1979) 251, 286, 296–97, 301–8; Todd Compton, "The Trial of the Satirist: Poetic *Vitae* (Aesop, Archilochus, Homer) as Background for Plato's *Apology*," *American Journal of Philology* 111 (1990) 330–47.

14 Wills, "Death of the Hero"; P. W. van der Horst,

the corporate welfare of the living depended in some significant manner upon the corporate unity of the bones of the elite dead in their ancestral tomb. . . . The tomb is a new altar, the dead, a new sacerdotal functionary; and some dead at least, for example, the martyrs, a new and perhaps more efficacious sacrifice.[15]

From reverence for the family ancestors there is a development toward culture-wide narratives of special heroes. In Israel, heroes transported after death include Enoch, Moses, and Elijah, a process that is similar to that of Romulus. The increasing focus on the purity of the temple forced a new policy of forbidding graves in the vicinity, a separation of the realm of God and that of the dead. (The exception was the cult of dead kings, which remained near the temple [Ezek 43:7–9].) One people, one God, one temple deconstructed older local family religion. In both Greece and Israel, however, the final chapter for the hero is a compensation in memory: the *effects* of the hero's intervention last beyond his or her days. In Wis 4:1–2 the truly righteous may have eternal life but may also reap a reward of immortal memory: "For in the memory of virtue is immortality . . . , throughout all time it marches, crowned in triumph, victor in the contest for prizes that are undefiled" (NRSV).

There are many traditions concerning the special dead in ancient Israel, which provide a surprisingly rich background for our story of Judith the heroine of Israel, even if it is a satirical or inverted version. These traditions, however, have been nearly deleted from Jewish and Christian memory. Some of the relevant examples can be listed here:

- The offspring of the *nĕpīlîm* and human women, the *'anšê šēm*, "men of renown" (Gen 6:4), and the mysterious *tĕrāpîm* (Gen 31:19; 35:4; cf. 1 Sam 19:13).
- References to the *marzēaḥ* festival for the residents of Sheol (Jer 16:5–9; Amos 6:7; Lev 19:28; 21:1–11).
- An older tradition of Abraham as heroic warrior in Genesis 14, just as in Exod 4:24–26, where God tries to kill Moses, may retain a vestigial reference to god–hero antagonism.
- The book of Judges speaks of heroes who delivered Israel; the term *šōpĕṭîm* is better translated as "heroes." The burial sites are often noted (8:32; 10:2, 5; 12:7, 10, 11, 15), probably in regard to tomb cult. These stories include the antisocial Samson and Gideon. Samson, indeed, is marginalized from good society and finally experiences not only hero–people antagonism but hero–god antagonism as well, as he is abandoned by God (Judg 16:20). In this process, he is depicted as a sacrifice for others.[16] Jephthah's daughter (Judges 11) is offered up like a sacrificial animal, an event reenacted by young women, likely as an etiology for a heroine cult for fertility. There are strong similarities here to Greek heroines (Pausanias 9.17.1), and also to a newly discovered fragment of a play by Euripides on the sacrifice of his virgin daughters by Erechtheus, an archaic king of Athens. It is likely this sacrifice that was depicted on the front frieze of the Parthenon, which may mean "of the maidens."[17]

"The Tombs of the Prophets in Early Judaism," in idem, *Japheth in the Tents of Shem: Studies on Jewish Hellenism in Antiquity* (Contributions to Biblical Exegesis and Theology 32; Leuven: Peeters, 2002) 119–38; Karel van der Toorn, *Family Religion in Babylonia, Syria, and Israel: Continuity and Change in the Forms of Religious Life* (SHCANE 7; Leiden: Brill, 1996) 138–39, 141–46; Herbert Niehr, "The Changed Status of the Dead in Yehud," in Rainer Albertz and Bob Becking, eds., *Yahwism after the Exile: Perspectives on Israelite Religion in the Persian Era* (Assen: Van Gorcum, 2003) 136–55; Jacob Wright, "Making a Name for Oneself: Martial Valor, Heroic Death, and Procreation," *JSOT* 36 (2011) 131–45; Shmuel Shepkaru, *Jewish Martyrs in the Pagan and Christian Worlds* (Cambridge: Cambridge University Press, 2006); Ra'anan Boustan, *From Martyr to Mystic: Rabbinic Martyrology and the Making of Merkavah Mysticism* (Tübingen: Mohr Siebeck, 2005).

15 Jack N. Lightstone, *The Commerce of the Sacred: Mediation of the Divine among Jews in the Greco-Roman World* (New York: Columbia University Press, 2006) 41, 45, 53–54, 62. See Isa 57:9; Pss 6:5–6; 30:10; 88:6–12, but note 1 Sam 1:21; 2:19; 20:6, 29; Isa 38:18. Later texts include Tob 4:17; Sir 17:27–28; and 30:18.

16 Gregory Mobley, *Samson and the Liminal Hero in the Ancient Near East* (LHBOTS 453; New York: T&T Clark, 2006); Mobley, *The Empty Men: The Heroic Tradition of Ancient Israel* (ABRL; New York: Doubleday, 2005).

17 Joan Breton Connelly, *The Parthenon Enigma* (New York: Knopf, 2014).

- The prophetic guilds were likely responsible for transmitting legends about Samuel, Elijah, and Elisha. Samuel has a miraculous birth and childhood, intervenes with God for his people, and speaks from the grave to Saul. Elijah achieves a kind of special immortality when he ascends to God in a chariot of fire—like Heracles or Romulus—and he is expected to return before the end. Elisha's bones even bring a dead man back to life on contact—the boons of the dead hero.[18]
- The fourth Servant Song of Isaiah 52–53 spins an image of an unnamed hero as a sacrificial animal whose death expiates sins, and the Prayer of Azariah in the Apocrypha hymns the near-death of Daniel's three friends as a sacrifice.
- Ben Sira praises the bones of the judges and the twelve prophets, which will bring new life where they lie (46:11–12; 49:10; cf. 48:11). He points to a heroic memory of the sage (39:1–11).
- More proximate to our discussion of Judith, the Maccabean literature treated the miraculous intercession of a number of recently dead heroes. In 2 Maccabees, the high priest Onias III is a "benefactor of Jerusalem" but is treacherously killed and reappears after death, along with Jeremiah, to inspire the Maccabees to defend their city and temple (2 Macc 15:11–16).

In 2 Macc 12:39–45, Judah Maccabee is said to have offered sacrifices and prayed for the dead. Fourth Maccabees goes even further: the martyr Eleazar is an expiation (*katharsion*) for his people (6:29); the other martyrs are "as though a ransom [*antipsychon*] for the sins of the people. Through the blood of these pious ones and the expiation [*hilastērion*] of their death, divine Providence saved Israel" (17:21–22).[19] The tombs of the Maccabees were highly regarded in their day, as was the second-century BCE Bnei Hazir family tomb in the Kidron Valley. Compare here the first-century CE tomb of Zechariah ben Jehoiada, a priest stoned in 2 Chr 24:20–21 (Matt 23:35).

- The Lives of the Prophets provides information on the grave sites of the prophets, along with their post-death benefits for the people.[20]
- Many Jewish healers performed their miracles in the name of Solomon,[21] and when a miracle worker, Honi the Circlemaker, suffered the effects of hero–people antagonism, God punished the perpetrators by sending a year-long drought, illustrating the post-death effects of the hero (Josephus, *Antiquities* 14.2.1–2 §§22–28).

---

18   On the bones and boons of the dead hero in Greece, see Walter Burkert, *Greek Religion* (trans. John Raffan; Cambridge, MA: Harvard University Press, 1985) 207; and Erwin Rohde, *Psyche: The Cult of Souls and Belief in Immortality Among the Greeks* (International Library of Psychology, Philosophy, and Scientific Method; London: Kegan Paul, Trench, Trübner; New York: Harcourt Brace, 1925) 122. See also Joseph Blenkinsopp, *A History of Prophecy in Israel* (Philadelphia: Westminster, 1983) 71–72.

19   In agreement, see Jan N. Bremmer, "The Atonement in the Interaction of Greeks, Jews, and Christians," in Jan N. Bremmer and Florentino García Martínez, eds., *Sacred History and Sacred Texts in Early Judaism: A Symposium in Honour of A. S. van der Woude* (Contributions to Biblical Exegesis and Theology 5; Kampen: Kok Pharos, 1992) 75–93. Sammy K. Williams makes too fine a distinction between an expiatory death and the appeal to God as a temporary sacrificial moment (*Jesus' Death as Saving Event: The Background and Origin of a Concept* [HDR 2; Missoula, MT: Scholars Press, 1975] 178–79).

20   Although David Satran has argued that the text as a whole is late (*Biblical Prophets in Byzantine Palestine: Reassessing the Lives of the Prophets* [SVTP 11; Leiden: Brill, 1995]), this is based on passages that appear to be interpolated. It is more likely a Jewish text from about the turn of the Common Era into which some later references are inserted; so Anna Maria Schwemer, *Studien zu den frühjüdischen Prophetenlegenden Vitae Prophetarum* (2 vols.; TSAJ 49, 50; Tübingen: Mohr Siebeck, 1995) 1:65–71.

21   Dennis C. Duling, "Solomon, Exorcism, and the Son of David," *HTR* 68 (1975) 235–52; Gideon Bohak, *Ancient Jewish Magic: A History* (Cambridge: Cambridge University Press, 2008) 135–42, 298–313; Josephus, *Antiquities* 8.2.5 §§45–49; Todd E. Klutz, *Rewriting the Testament of Solomon: Tradition, Conflict and Identity in a Late Antique Pseudepigraphon* (LSTS 53; London: T&T Clark, 2005) 83–87.

This is but a partial list, but the reverence for special dead in Israel does not subside. The tombs of the patriarchs and prophets merge with the tombs of the Maccabees, which merge with the tombs of the rabbis, which are cult sites to this day. Christian reverence for saints, martyrs, and their relics seems an extension of the rich tradition of Jewish heroes.

The book of Judith reveals a number of important parallels to this Israelite tradition, and this structures the entire book. From beginning to end, our text is a comic treatment of the hero narrative. The threat of a wild monster on the horizon—like Beowulf's Grendel—brings the people of Bethulia and Israel to a state of desperation, and Judith, an exceptionally wise and pious woman, emerges from her isolation to save her people. She leaves the civilized zone of her town, passing ritually through the city gates to traverse the valley and enter the dangerous zone of the enemy camp. The hero cross-culturally often has a dutiful servant, and Judith's unnamed slave fills this role. In addition, the hero often has a double, as Achilles has Patroklos and Gilgamesh has Enkidu. This twinning of heroes is even more pronounced in Israel and early Christian tradition: Moses/Aaron, David/Jonathan, Ezra/Nehemiah, Sheshbazzar/Jeshua, Mordecai/Esther, Hillel/Shammai, Jesus/John the Baptist, and Peter/Paul. Achior appears to become just such a heroic double for Judith (see at chap. 5). At last, Judith slays the beast and returns with Holofernes's head, perhaps a magical boon—again, just as Beowulf took away Grendel's head. The head inspires the Bethulians, and allows for a triumphal victory. And it is probably not a coincidence that the most important text of *Beowulf* was found in the Nowell Codex with the Old English Judith epic (see §8 below). After a celebration, Judith returns to the reclusive state in which she began.

In §4 below on biblical motifs found in Judith, we will note how many parallels to Judith are found in the book of Judges, which is actually a book of heroes. This observation may be extended: the frame narrative of Judith mimics the book of Judges, precisely because this is the language of Israelite heroes. Judith begins with a military threat similar to those in Judges and very pointedly takes up the notion of heroic memory: "I am about to do a deed," says Judith, "that will reach to generations upon generations of our people" (8:32). The end of the book is concluded with a formula very similar to those that conclude each cycle of heroes' stories: "And no one was able to strike terror among the Israelites while Judith was alive, nor for a long time afterwards" (16:25; cf. 1 Macc 9:22; Deuteronomy 34; John 20:30–31). Though the book of Judith is a comic version of the hero paradigm, she does attain a cult of memory—ironic, again, in that she was a fictitious character!

Yet, while Judith takes up the cross-cultural pattern of heroic narrative, differences remain.[22] Her quest is not far—out into the valley—but for a respected, wealthy widow this is a significant sojourn. Her quest is also limited to one goal, to slay the monster. Another major change is a shift to the novelistic: the heroic narrative is now transposed to a domestic level, much as Susanna transposes the court conflict narrative to a local level. We note especially how elements highlighted by Craven's structuring of the second half of Judith correspond to typical hero narratives:

---

22 One may compare the Proppian analysis of Moses in Exodus by William H. C. Propp (no relation), *Exodus 1–18: A New Translation with Introduction and Commentary* (AB 2; New York: Doubleday, 1999) 32–36. Pamela J. Milne ("What Shall We Do with Judith? A Feminist Reassessment of a Biblical 'Heroine,'" *Semeia* 62 [1993] 37–58, here 50–53) considers Vladimir Propp but prefers the approach of Aleksandr Skaftymov, a pre-Proppian Russian formalist, and Heda Jason's "epic struggle genre" (*Ethnopoetry:* *Form, Content, Function* [Forum theologiae linguisticae 11; Bonn: Linguistica Biblica, 1977]). Philip F. Esler compares Beowulf and Grendel (*Sex, Wives, and Warriors: Reading Biblical Narrative with Its Ancient Audience* [Eugene, OR: Wipf & Stock, 2011]); see also Deborah Levine Gera, "Judah and Judith" (in Hebrew), in Joseph Geiger, Hannah M. Cotton, and Guy D. Stiebel, eds., *Israel's Land: Papers Presented to Israel Schatzman on His Jubilee* (Ra'anana, Israel: Open University, 2009) 29–38, here 35–36.

Craven's structure of second half	Heroic quest
A Introduction of Judith (8:1–8)	Seclusion (8:1-8)
B Judith plans to save Israel (8:9–10:9a)	Response to need (8:9-36)
	Prayer (9:1–14)
	Bathing/preparation (10:1–5)
	Blessing, leave-taking (10:6–8)
C Judith and slave leave Bethulia (10:9b–10)	Departing at gate (10:9–10)
D Judith overcomes Holofernes (10:11–13:10a)	Heroic journey, slaying beast (10:11–13:10)
C′ Judith and slave return to Bethulia (13:10b–11)	Re-entry at gate (13:11)
B′ Judith plans to destroy Israel's enemy (13:12–16:20)	Battle, with boon of Holofernes's head (13:12–15:7)
A′ Conclusion about Judith (16:21–25)	Celebration (15:8–16:20)
	Heroic epitaph (16:21–25)

It seems apparent, then, that a fundamental structuring principle of Judith is the cross-cultural paradigm of the heroic quest.

4. Possible Sources of the Story

Israelite Sources

Our novella brims with biblical quotations and allusions, as well as many parallels to ancient Near Eastern and Greek traditions. Judith may very well be one of the most "intertexted" texts in the larger Bible.[1] In regard to biblical and Jewish parallels, A.-M. Dubarle's study remains foundational with many others now built upon it. Scholars have been struck by the *quantity* of allusions, but two cautions should be raised. First, while it is true that much Jewish narrative invention in this period can be attributed to an engagement with a coalescing notion of "scripture," even Dubarle admits that the parallels may not result from the direct adoption of scriptural passages, nor even from an indirect oral transmission of biblical motifs, but rather from a broader folkloristic play of motifs.[2] We may refer to these two alternative explanations of parallels as "literate intertextuality" versus the "ocean of story."[3] In literate intertextuality—which is the approach that has dominated discussion—it is assumed that biblical and noncanonical *written* texts influenced Jewish writings of the late second century BCE, even if there was an oral intermediary stage. The ocean of story refers to internationally transmitted folk and popular motifs that enter into a text simply because they are part of the raconteur's delight. Such traditions may have been orally or textually transmitted but may not be part of a developing scripturality. Where the biblicist sees a midrashic play on "scripture," the comparativist sees at work a *bricoleur* who borrows from Herodotus as readily as Genesis. There is one difference: our author *explicitly* references some biblical figures, such as Simeon, but even here the biblical version is altered. This in itself is not unknown in Jewish tradition, but it raises the issue of how *our author*—not necessarily the author of Jubilees or Qumran texts—registers scripturality. And if words of scripture are alluded to often, does this imply a sense of reverence for an authoritative text? Does our author love the classical text, or love to play literary games?

The second caution is that the listing of a long series of biblical parallels has a tendency to equalize their value. To a biblicist, they are all *equally* scriptural echoes. "It almost seems," says Claudia Rakel, "as though the book of Judith were trying to touch upon the whole biblical tradition."[4] One can posit similarities between Judith and almost all of the women of the Bible, the male characters

---

1   But why then Judith more than Esther or Tobit? They also quote and allude to biblical passages, but not as often as Judith. Yet any quantification of parallels may be subjective. According to Armin Lange and Matthias Weigold, the quotations and direct allusions here are no richer than, say, Tobit; 1, 2, and 4 Maccabees; Baruch; Psalms of Solomon; Wisdom, or the Aramaic Levi Document, and significantly fewer than Damascus Document, Hodayot, 1 Enoch, and Ben Sira (*Biblical Quotations and Allusions in Second Temple Jewish Literature* [JAJSup 5; Göttingen: Vandenhoeck & Ruprecht, 2011] 233–35). Tobit also can be divided into three parts; the shorter, framing parts at the beginning and end contain biblical allusions, and also allusions to Ahikar, but the large middle section—the main story—contains very few.

2   Dubarle, *Judith*, 1:137.

3   Among the literary studies of different kinds of intertextuality, see Manfred Pfister, "Konzepte der Intertextualität," in Manfred Pfister and Ulrich Broich, eds., *Intertextualität: Formen, Funktionen, anglistische Fallstudien* (Tübingen: Niemeyer, 1985) 1–30. Mary P. Coote and Alan Dundes compare Judith

to folktale type 888, the Faithful Wife, a woman dressing as a man to save her husband, reported in Alonso Schökel, *Narrative Structures*, 21–29. Other relevant folk motifs might include K873.1, king given sleeping potion and then beheaded in his bed by his wife; K1510.1, adulteress kills home-coming husband; Q411.2.1, undesired suitor killed asleep in his tent; T173, murderous bride; T182, death from intercourse. See Stith Thompson, *Motif-Index of Folk-Literature* (rev. and enl. ed.; 6 vols.; Bloomington: Indiana University Press, 1955–1958); Antti Aarne, *The Types of the Folktale: A Classification and Bibliography* (2nd ed.; trans. and enlarged by Stith Thompson; Helsinki: Suomalainen Tiedeakatemia, 1964); Gera, *Judith*, 57–58; Lawrence M. Wills, *The Jew in the Court of the Foreign King: Ancient Jewish Court Legends* (HDR 26; Minneapolis: Fortress Press, 1990).

4   Claudia Rakel, "'I Will Sing a New Song to My God': Some Remarks on the Intertextuality of Judith 16.1–17," in Athalya Brenner, ed., *Judges* (Feminist Companion to the Bible, 2nd series 4; Sheffield: Sheffield Academic Press, 1999) 27–47, here 38. The following discussion is indebted to Dubarle, *Judith*, 1:137–62; Haag, *Das Buch Judit*, 118–24; Zenger, *Das Buch Judit*,

in Judith and most of the men of the Bible, and even Judith and some of the men of the Bible. This is the biblicist's dilemma: any similarity can seem like an intertext. And perhaps it is! Yet we will also see below that there are close parallels to ancient Near Eastern and Greek narrative traditions.

The complex process of intertextuality can never be fully systematized, but Julia Kristeva, building on the work of Mikhail Bakhtin, has introduced a series of observations on intertextuality. A text is not a distinct and separate entity with a single meaning but an intersection of countless previous textual and cultural performances. A text is "an intersection of different texts and, because of that confluence of different texts, no text is really original, but rather a space where different voices meet."[5] This insight was articulated in regard to texts in general, yet we emphasize as well an observation of Bakhtin: the novel as a genre is more emphatically dialogical and multivocal than other genres—very true of Judith (see §7 below). Bakhtin identified as one of the defining aspects of the novel the bricolage of available materials, in terms both of content and of style.[6] The novel is a packrat genre that borrows and blends—one may almost say *mocks*—older, accepted, conservative genres. Susan A. Stephens and John J. Winkler invoke Bakhtin's name

in regard to the ancient Greek novel, claiming that this genre "fused together in its structure almost all genres of ancient literature."[7] Judith, which predates the Greek novels, could provide Bakhtin with strong evidence: it is a Bakhtinian orgy of Israelite and non-Israelite motifs, thoroughly puréed.

It is also necessary to state what Judith is *not*. Although the word *midrash* is sometimes used to describe Hellenistic Jewish literature that is biblically influenced, that term should be reserved for compositions that investigate—*dāraš*—the meaning of a biblical text for a present application. Likewise, the terms "rewritten Bible" and "rewritten scripture" have entered scholarship to describe certain works of the Hellenistic and Roman periods that retell the stories of the Bible with new narrative features. These texts include Jubilees, Genesis Apocryphon, the Temple Scroll, Pseudo-Philo's *Biblical Antiquities,* and (perhaps) the Reworked Pentateuch texts from Qumran.[8] These texts also reinterpreted the biblical history for a new age. Judith was written in the period of the rewritten scripture texts but before the known earliest dates for the targums and midrashic texts. Yet, although the book of Judith includes so many resonances with scripture, by genre it is in a separate zone from midrash or rewritten scripture.

439–46; Zenger, "Der Juditroman," 72–74; Schmitz, *Gedeutete Geschichte,* passim; Schmitz/Engel, *Judit,* passim; Patrick W. Skehan, "The Hand of Judith," *CBQ* 25 (1963) 94–110, here 96–98; Moore, *Judith,* 247–57. The book of Judith is sometimes likened to "anthological style," the tendency of Second Temple Jewish texts to collect and replay biblical styles and motifs; see LaCocque, *Feminine Unconventional,* 35. Whether the older base texts were already viewed as "scripture" need not detain us; they were increasingly authoritative as a literary tradition. For the "scripturalization of communal memory," see Judith H. Newman, *Praying by the Book: The Scripturalization of Prayer in Second Temple Judaism* (EJL 14; Atlanta: Scholars Press, 1999); József Zsengellér, "A Bible's Digest—The Book of Judith as a Hermeneutical Composition," in Renate Egger-Wenzel, Karin Schöpflin, and Johannes Friedrich Diehl, eds., *Weisheit als Lebensgrundlage: Festschrift für Friedrich V. Reiterer zum 65. Geburtstag* (DCLS 15; Berlin: de Gruyter, 2013) 451–86.

5   S. Philip Nolte and and Pierre J. Jordaan, "Ideol-

ogy and Intertextuality: Intertextual Allusions in Judith 16," *HvTSt* 67 (2011) 1–9, here 3. A critique of Kristeva ("generalized intertextuality") and Clifford Geertz can be found in George Aichele and Gary A. Phillips, "Exegesis, Eisegesis, Intergesis," *Semeia* 69/70 (1995) 7–18; and David M. Carr, "The Many Uses of Intertextuality," in Martti Nissinen, ed., *Congress Volume: Helsinki 2010* (VTSup 148; Leiden: Brill, 2012) 519–49. James L. Kugel treats this question in general in "Early Interpretation: The Common Background of the Late Forms of Biblical Exegesis," in James L. Kugel and Rowan Greer, *Early Biblical Interpretation* (LEC 3; Philadelphia: Westminster, 1986) esp. 70–78, 101.

6   Bakhtin, *The Dialogic Imagination: Four Essays* (University of Texas Press Slavic Series 1; Austin: University of Texas Press, 1981).

7   Stephens and Winkler, *Ancient Greek Novels,* 9.

8   Geza Vermes first coined the term, in *Scripture and Tradition in Judaism: Haggadic Studies* (2nd rev. ed.; SPB 4; Leiden: Brill, 1973) 95.

We turn first to the three explicit references to heroes and events of Israel's past. Many scholars have commented on the central importance of the author's use of the Song of Moses. Rakel comments:

> As a synecdoche this quotation calls to mind the entire Exodus tradition, which is for Israel not only a historical event but also a token of memory (*Erinnerungsfigur*). . . . [T]he recipients are meant both to recognize the quotation and with it the intertextual relationship to the song [of Moses], and to interpret their liberation through Judith's actions as a new experience of the Exodus.[9]

With the Song of Moses comes a proliferation of other exodus references. The weak Israelites and the arrogant Pharaoh and his army are called to mind, and the only reference in Judith to God's intervention ("The Lord heard their cry and had regard for their affliction," 4:13) is parallel to Exod 3:7. Judith rescues her people as a "female Moses," and there is a murmuring of the Bethulians over lack of water.[10]

Achior's speech in chap. 5 reprises the historical credos such as Joshua 24. The historical credos are covenant renewal texts that affirm the mighty acts of God for Israel. Judith's prayers (8:26; 9:2) refer explicitly to Abraham, and also to the slaughter of the Shechemites by Simeon and Levi. The latter becomes one of the strongest biblical themes in our text. The comments concerning many of the biblical figures sometimes go beyond the biblical versions, picking up traditions known from postbiblical texts (see notes at 8:26–27; 9:2–4; 5:6–9). Intertextual connections are created by the reader as much as by the author; later texts often do not simply reference an earlier text but remake it in the process. Such is the case with Judith's invocation of Simeon and Levi as zealous for God (9:4). Her language picks up allusions to Phinehas (Pinchas), who in his zeal struck down an Israelite who had taken a Midianite wife, and he was as a result granted a covenant of peace (Numbers 25). Whereas in Gen 49:5–7 the action of Simeon and Levi in slaughtering the Shechemites is criticized by their father Jacob, the inclusion of Phinehas here renders it a pious act.[11]

Next we turn to the many implicit or possible allusions and will analyze their functions in various ways. Granting the general statements about intertextuality by Kristeva and Bakhtin above, certain specific approaches may be distinguished, best viewed as subsets of the larger processes of intertextuality. Biblicists emphasize the literary relations of later texts to the earlier texts of scripture; scholars of folklore, sociolinguistics, and popular culture tend to emphasize the operationalism of parallels—how do they function in the new performance situation, especially in the engagement of a new genre? The former approach is generally semantic—what does this particular (and generally isolated) sign mean in relation to the earlier text?—and the latter is often syntactic—how does a motif in the new composition function in relation to other elements in the text? The first approach is associated with semiotics; the second, with structuralism. Aspects of Judith partake of both. The narrative frame of the book of Judith—its *faux*-genre, the genre that it is mimicking—is Deuteronomistic History. This can be seen in the opening lines and first historical episode. Like the openings of Joshua, Judges, and 1 and 2 Samuel, the first words set the date in the reign of the king of a great empire. The very mention of "Nebuchadnezzar king of the Assyrians" commits to a mock-genre—not history, but mock-history. The novelistic texts Ruth, Esther, and Jonah also play on a sense of *faux*-history.[12]

The book of Judges is particularly well represented in Judith. The narrative event in Judges that is most similar

---

9   Rakel, *Judit–Über Schönheit*, 40.

10   Van Henten, "Judith as an Alternative Leader," 232–38; Alonso Schökel, *Narrative Structures*, 18. Other links to the Song of the Sea are noted in the commentary.

11   Gera, *Judith*, 54, 100–101; Joosten, "Original Language," 170 n. 26. Simeon's act is also evaluated more positively in Jub. 30:1–26; Aramaic Levi Document 1.2; T. Levi 5:3, Joseph and Aseneth 23:14, although in the last text he is restrained by Levi.

12   See §7 below. On the dating formula, note also, on the historical side, 2 Chr 1:1; Ezra 1:1; 2 Esdr 1:1; 1 Macc 1:1; also the interior uses of this dating formula at the beginning of a new narrative arc: 1 Sam 15:1; 16:15, 29; 2 Sam 12:1; 13:1. On the novelistic side, note Dan 1:1; 2:1; OG 4:1; 5:1, and especially Dan Th 3:1 with a genitive of time as in Judith.

to Judith is the story of Deborah and Jael in Judges 4–5.[13] The parallels are more compelling if we note that the relevant motifs in Judges are divided between two women, Deborah and Jael.[14] Sidnie Ann White (Crawford) points out that the similarity to Judith is not limited to stories of women who gain the confidence of an enemy ruler and kill him with a blow to the head.[15] In both Judges 4–5 and Judith the female agent, whose husband is absent, is introduced late; they both deceive the man in question; the assassination is committed in a tent; the men are manipulated into taking a lulling drink; the role of

God is mentioned as part of the background yet the women act without miraculous help; in each a man of noble bearing stands to the side, serving as the assistant of a strong female character (Barak for Deborah, both Uzziah and Achior for Judith). There is in both a sexual implication to the encounter, a powerful interweaving of *Eros/Thanatos*. Both Judith and Deborah also have a song as a counterpoint to prose narrative.[16] Margarita Stocker argues that Jael is not as complex a character as Judith,[17] but the difference in period and genre between the two—patriarchal legend versus novella—may render

13 Otzen, *Tobit and Judith*, 76; Gera, *Judith*, 46; Zenger, *Das Buch Judit*, 440, 509; Alonso Shökel, *Narrative Structures*, 14; Corley, "Imitation of Septuagintal Narrative and Greek Historiography in the Portrait of Holofernes," in Xeravits, *Pious Seductress*, 27–34. After each period of peace in Judges, there is recidivism: "As soon as Gideon died, the Israelites relapsed and prostituted themselves with the Baals, making Baal-berith their god" (Judg 8:33). Judith lacks this backsliding, as she reminds the Bethulians, "We've been good" (8:18–20; cf. 16:25).

14 Monika Hellmann sees Deborah, not Jael, as the real model, because she is a prophetic savior of Israel (*Judit–eine Frau im Spannungsfeld von Autonomie und göttlicher Führung: Studie über eine Frauengestalt des Alten Testaments* [Europäische Hochschulschriften 23.444; Frankfurt am Main: Lang, 1992] 96–103). Still, does this miss the shock of the role of the foreign woman, so common in the Bible?

15 Sidnie Ann White (Crawford), "In the Steps of Jael and Deborah: Judith as Heroine," in VanderKam, *No One Spoke Ill*, 5–16; Yael Shemesh "'Yet He Committed No Act of Sin with Me, to Defile and Shame Me' (Judith 13:16): The Narrative of Judith as a Corrective to the Narrative of Yael and Sisera" (in Hebrew), *Shnaton: An Annual for Biblical and Ancient Near Eastern Studies* 16 (2006) 159–77. Other biblical women who would fit this description include the woman of Thebez (Judg 9:50–57) and the woman of Abel-beth-Maacah (2 Sam 20:14–22). This trope is found in Greece also: King Pyrrhus of Epirus attacked Argos in 272 BCE and was hit in the head by a tile thrown by a woman from her roof. But the ending of the Greek tradition demonstrates the difference: the tile was judged to have been thrown by Demeter, and the Argives were instructed by an oracle to bury Pyrrhus

on that spot and build a sanctuary to Demeter. Pyrrhus is given a hero's treatment and thereafter healed the sick (Pausanias 1.13.7–8; Pliny, *Natural History* 7.20). See also Susan Niditch, "Eroticism and Death in the Tale of Jael," in Peggy Day, ed., *Gender and Difference in Ancient Israel* (Minneapolis: Fortress Press, 1989) 43–57; Robert Alter, *Art and the Nature of Biblical Poetry* (New York: Basic Books, 1985) 43–49; Gale A. Yee, "By the Hand of a Woman: The Metaphor of the Woman Warrior in Judges 4," *Semeia* 61 (1993) 99–132, here 101–16.

Other commonplaces in Judges find an echo in Judith, for instance, the image of the staggering numbers of the enemy—like grasshoppers (Judg 6:5 and esp. 7:12 (*akris* is also used in Jdt 2:20). Achior's blessing of Judith, "Blessed are you in every tent in Judah!" is similar to Judg 5:24; see also Sheaffer, *Envisioning*, 43. In Judges 16, Delilah uses beauty and deceit to seduce a leader; see Betsy Merideth, "Desire and Danger: The Drama of Betrayal in Judges and Judith," in Mieke Bal, ed., *Anti-Covenant: Counter-Reading Women's Lives in the Hebrew Bible* (JSOTSup 81; Sheffield: Almond, 1989) 63–78.

16 Crawford ("In the Steps of Jael," 11), Rakel (*Judit–Über Schönheit*, 33, 37), and Anne E. Gardner ("The Song of Praise in Judith 16:2–17 [LXX 16:1–17]," *HeyJ* 29 [1989] 413–22, here 422) all assert that Judges 5 is a closer parallel to Judith than is Exodus 15. This may be true if we distinguish speech and narrative in Judith. Esler minimizes the literary dynamic between Judith and Jael as well as the sexual implications in the Jael story (*Sex, Wives, and Warriors*, 271–72).

17 Margarita Stocker, *Judith: Sexual Warrior Women and Power in Western Culture* (New Haven: Yale University Press, 1998) 150.

the two cases incommensurable. Is the Jael story simply shorter by genre? Does the character Jael simply lack a backstory? Because it is placed within Israelite history of the judges, rather than in a fictitious and satirical context, does the Jael story invite more complex emotions from the audience? On the other hand, is it possible that Jael *is* less complex simply because she is not an Israelite? The underlying narrative force of the Judith novella is that a wise and pious *Israelite* woman is playing the strumpet, lying, and chopping off heads. The audience is not as invested in Jael's virtue. We will also have occasion to compare Judith to the transgressive, trickster hero Ehud, who travels into the land of the enemy, connives his way into the foreign king's inner quarters and kills him with a knife. The king's servants, like Holofernes's, stand outside his chambers, assuming that he is at peace within. A similar rough humor and irony are found throughout.

In addition to the Jael and Ehud episodes, the accounts of campaigns in Judges and elsewhere clearly serve as the model for the Assyrians' campaign.[18] In Judg 6:1–10, for instance, Midian, the Amalekites, "and the peoples of the East" came up against Israel to destroy the produce of the land "as far as Gaza." They and their livestock, even their tents, are "as thick as locusts; neither they nor their camels could be counted." The heroic-historical style of Judges manages to respect the rules of plausibility, but in Judith the geographical scale is greatly expanded, once again for humorous effect, to include the Great Empires. Many of the sections in Judges chronicling the good judges also conclude with the heroic formula: "the land had rest X years" (e.g., Judg 3:30; 5:31). In Judg 8:32, a formula gives closure to the Gideon-as-hero episode: "Gideon died at a good old age, and was buried in the tomb of his father Joash at Ophrah of the Abiezrites" (cf. also Judg 10:1–2; 12:7). Judith constitutes a longer, that is, "novelistic," hero narrative, focusing on a woman in a more domestic setting but concludes like

the Judges episodes, "And no one was able to strike terror among the Israelites while Judith was alive, nor for a long time afterwards" (16:25). We also note that, while in Judges there are traditions of both a brash, independent Gideon (Judges 8) and an obedient Gideon (Judges 6–7), Judith presents mainly the former persona.

Two important differences from Judges should still be noted. First, as Judith lacks any critique of the actions of Simeon and Levi in Gen 49:5–7, it also omits the deep historical critique found in Judges, the recurrent editorial theme of apostasy. Most of the hero cycles in Judges conclude with the falling away of Israel after a period: "As soon as Gideon died, the Israelites relapsed and prostituted themselves with the Baals, making Baal-berith their god" (8:33). Judith, as noted, actually affirms that Israel has been good (8:18–20), somewhat in tension with her criticism of the elders. Second, in Judges the hero often arises because the spirit (*rûaḥ*) of God is upon him or her (3:10; 6:34; 11:29; 13:24, assumed for Deborah because she was a prophet; cf. 1 Sam 11:6). Despite the wisdom terms attributed to Judith, it is never said that the spirit of God is upon her—although in Holofernes's presence she will *claim* that God will inform her of the Bethulians' sin, all the while lying (11:17)! The omission of a prophetic spirit may be significant, conceivably arising out of reverential concern that what she does is too transgressive to be provoked by the spirit of God. In the commentary on 9:9–10 we will consider whether she is actually exercising her own agency and willfulness and is not waiting for God to act. At any rate, Judith acts without the spirit of the judges.

Much has also been made of the relation of Judith's story to that of David and Goliath (1 Samuel 17). David, like Judith, took the enemy warrior's own sword to kill him and chopped off his head with his own sword.[19] In addition, many of the details of the two stories are also similar. Judith's pouch, which serves to transport her own

---

18   Cf. also 1 Sam 4:5–9; 7:11; 11:11; 12:6–17; 14:15.

19   On parallels to David and Goliath, see József Zsengellér, "Judith as a Female David," in Geza Xeravits, ed., *Religion and Female Body in Ancient Judaism and Its Environments* (DCLS 28; Berlin: de Gruyter, 2015) 186–211. In Renaissance Florence, Judith was practically the consort of David; see §8 below. On the cross-cultural motif of hero–antagonist combat,

see S. P. Oakley, "Single Combat in the Roman Republic," *ClQ* 35 (1985) 392–410; Roland de Vaux, "Single Combat in the Old Testament," in de Vaux, *The Bible and the Ancient Near East* (Garden City, NY: Doubleday, 1971) 122–35. Many parallels to Judith can be found in ancient Near Eastern traditions; see below in this section under "Possible Sources: Ancient Near Eastern Parallels."

acceptable food to the enemy camp and Holofernes's head back to Bethulia, calls to mind David's bag with the five smooth stones. David's is a more natural fit in the story, but Judith's is both more multifunctional and more ritually suggestive. In preparation for his meeting with Goliath (1 Samuel 17), David first tries on the armor of Saul but finds that it is too heavy and that he is not accustomed to the weapons of the warrior. Like Judith, he must find an alternative, less typically martial stratagem. David, as a boy, and Judith, as a woman, are both tricksters who use the weapons more at home to them which they can manipulate—youth and beauty, respectively. The military conclusion is the same in the two stories: when the enemy forces realize that their leader is without a head, they flee in fear. The rout of the enemy in both stories is similar.

There are both positive and negative traditions about Saul, and one of the positive ones, 1 Sam 11:1–11, should also be considered. The weakness of the Israelites in the face of outside aggression is similar to the narrative of Judith, and Saul is angry with the people for being willing to surrender in seven days. As in Judges, the spirit falls upon one figure, Saul, who comes forward, calls upon the people to stand firm, and wins a military victory. Another parallel in the Deuteronomistic History is also significant. In 2 Kgs 18:13–19:37 (= Isaiah 37), Yahweh condemns Sennacherib of Assyria as an inadequate suitor for his "virgin Zion" (2 Kgs 19:21; the word for virgin is *bĕtûlâ*, similar to Betulia; see the commentary). The foreign invaders here, as in Judith, are the Assyrians, laying a siege. The Rabshakeh's court speeches are similar to Nebuchadnezzar's and Holofernes's, including the questions "Whose god is strong?" and "On whom do you rely?" (2 Kgs 18:20, 22; cf. Jdt 5:3). God intervenes in both, and the size of the armies is nearly the same (2 Kgs

19:35; Jdt 2:5; 7:2). But most important, the satirical play in 2 Kings 18–19 on *bĕtûlâ*, "virgin," may provide a key to our author's naming of the village Betulia, perhaps a play on virginity.[20] The Chronicler also contains passages that might have influenced Judith. In 2 Chronicles 20, Jehoshaphat rallies Israel in the face of a foreign invasion. It is the king's prayer that is significant here as a possible model for Judith's.[21]

There is evidence of a strong Danielic tradition in ancient Judaism, although there is also at times ambivalence about this courtier who became so close to Nebuchadnezzar. Influences are readily visible in our text. Historically speaking, most ancient empires did not require the worship of the "correct" god, but in the book of Daniel (and in other Jewish and Christian texts as well), the opposition between two divine loyalties became a central drama. It should not surprise us that the campaigns of Holofernes are vaguely similar to those of Antiochus IV Epiphanes in Daniel 11, since the Seleucid king was likely the real-world model for the Assyrian general. More relevant for the Judith story is the book of Daniel's interpretation of the hubris of the Babylonian Nebuchadnezzar and his successor, Belshazzar (see the commentary on 3:8).[22] "Who is God except Nebuchadnezzar?" says Holofernes (6:2; cf. 3:8), and in Jdt 11:7 Nebuchadnezzar protects the animals (cf. Dan 2:37–38). Nebuchadnezzar's confession of the God of Israel in Dan 2:46–47; 3:29–30; 4:2–3, 37 provides a Danielic context for Holofernes's confession of Judith's God (Jdt 11:22–23). Judith's feigned adulation of Nebuchadnezzar in 11:7 seems to borrow from passages like Dan 2:38.

Many other incidental parallels to biblical motifs can be adduced. The opening of Judith is similar to the first verses of the anomalous tradition in Genesis 14 about Abram the warrior.[23] Both Judith and Achior are

---

20   Gera, *Judith*, 46–47, 296; Zenger, *Das Buch Judit*, 441–42; Otzen, *Tobit and Judith*, 76–78; Rakel, *Judit–Über Schönheit*, 278–82. In 9:2–4 Judith also invokes her ancestor Dinah, a *bĕtûlâ*, "virgin," who was raped.

21   Cf. also 2 Chr 13:4–20; 14:7–14; and see Gera, *Judith*, 46; Haag, *Das Buch Judit*, 118–24; Zenger, *Das Buch Judit*, 444–45.

22   Delcor, "Le livre de Judith," 174–79; O. Loretz, "Roman und Kurzgeschichte in Israel," in J.

Schreiner, ed., *Wort und Botschaft: Eine theologische und kritische Einführung in die Probleme des Alten Testaments* (Würzburg: Echter-Verlag, 1967) 290–307, here 302–3; Dubarle, *Judith*, 1:155; Gera, *Judith*, 48; Otzen, *Tobit and Judith*, 100–101, 106–7; Eckhardt, "Reclaiming Tradition," 248; Jacques Poirier, *Judith: Echos d'un mythe biblique dans la littérature française* (Rennes: Presses universitaires de Rennes, 2004) 41.

23   Dubarle, *Judith*, 1:139; Otzen, *Tobit and Judith*, 75; Zenger, *Das Buch Judit*, 441; Gera, *Judith*, 408–9.

depicted in ways similar to Balaam in Numbers 22–23.[24] One of the ironic moments of the novella, Holofernes's question noted above, "Who is god except Nebuchadnezzar?" (Jdt 6:2), also plays upon the "monotheism" formula of Isa 45:21 (cf. Ps 18:32). When Judith swears by Nebuchadnezzar, king of the earth and all creatures who live (11:7), it is perhaps influenced by Jer 27:6–7, where God grants Nebuchadnezzar authority. The sackcloth placed on the livestock in Judith is reminiscent of Jonah 3:7–8, also a humorous motif. Ruth as a widow, invited to dine, bathe, and perfume (Ruth 3:3), has been likened to Judith.[25] Holofernes's confession of loyalty to Judith and her God (Jdt 11:23) is a parodic contrast to Ruth's "Your god shall be my God" (Ruth 1:16).

With all of the similarities to biblical texts that Dubarle amassed, he also noted, 160–62, that there are no clear parallels to Esther.[26] To be sure, the date of Esther is contested; it may be a contemporaneous text. Still, several scholars have explored similarities between Judith and Esther. White (Crawford), who dates Esther before Judith, points out general parallels: both feature beautiful female protagonists, one an orphan and one a widow; both use humor and irony; and both are structured with a chiasm and a series of reversals to resolve the plot. She grants as well, however, that these are likely aspects of the genre and do not reflect direct borrowing.[27] Gera introduces an interesting but ultimately vague observation on their relation.[28] She suggests that in one sense Judith "improves" upon Esther: the heroine does not sleep with a gentile nor eat prohibited food. Judith also prays and openly practices aspects of Jewish identity. Esther, however, is set in the eastern diaspora during peacetime,

Judith near Judah in a time of war. It is not clear that either the authors or the *original* audiences would have perceived Judith as improving the moral or theological message of Esther. Greek Esther, composed after Judith, is a more obvious correction of Esther (see §6 below).

Occasional parallels can be found to Psalms and Prophets (noted in the commentary), and Ben Sira— hardly "scripture" at this time—presents an interesting case. Ben Sira 1:6–7 and 42:18 mention wisdom's *panourgeumata,* "subtleties," which also appear in Judith's words to Holofernes in 11:8 "We have heard of your wisdom and *panourgeumata* . . . ." Both texts use *sophia, panourgeumata,* and *epistēmē* in the same order.[29] In addition, we may compare the image of the harlot in the Bible and cross-culturally. Ezekiel 16:28 states, "You played the whore with the Assyrians," and in Ezek 23:3–4 she sleeps only with powerful foreign men. Judith, then, takes a chance by being seen as similar.[30]

The Maccabean texts provide important comparisons to Judith, although we cannot be certain that they were written before Judith. The Bethulians' campaign in Judith against Nebuchadnezzar assumes the actual guerrilla campaign of the Maccabees against the Seleucids/Syrians—Syrian is a shortened form of Assyrian—and there are many echoes between Judith and 1, 2, and 4 Maccabees. Above all, we note the death of Nicanor in both 1 and 2 Maccabees, so similar to the death of Holofernes. The scene, in fact, concludes 2 Maccabees. Judith is sometimes seen as a female consort of Judah Maccabee. They are both pious figures who fast, pray, harangue their fellow Israelites for lack of faith, and are celebrated in song

---

24 Gera, *Judith,* 49; Craven, *Artistry and Faith,* 47–48.
25 Dubarle, *Judith,* 1.145–46.
26 Dubarle, *Judith,* 160–62.
27 Crawford, "Esther and Judith," 60–76. Note also Tales of the Persian Court from Qumran (4Q550 [4QPrEstherᵃ ar]), which contains no references to the Esther narrative but also reflects the same genre and includes a name similar to Bagoas.
28 Gera, *Judith,* 54.
29 Alexander A. Di Lella, "Women in the Wisdom of Ben Sira and the Book of Judith: A Study in Contrasts and Reversals," in J. A. Emerton, ed., *Congress Volume: Paris 1992* (VTSup 61; Leiden: Brill, 1995) 41; see also the excursus below at 8:35, "The Book of Judith and Greek Philosophy."

30 Nancy Tan helpfully compares Judith's bathing and dressing to Ezek 16:9–12 ("Judith's Embodiment as a Reversal of the Unfaithful Wife of YHWH in Ezekiel 16," *JSP* 21 [2011] 21–35, here 25–26); see also T. M. Lemos, "The Emasculation of Exile: Hypermasculinity and Feminization in the Book of Ezekiel," in Brad E. Kelle, Frank Ritchel Ames, and Jacob Wright, eds., *Interpreting Exile: Displacement and Deportation in Biblical and Modern Contexts* (AIL 10; Atlanta: Society of Biblical Literature, 2011) 377–93, here 378–79; and Phyllis Bird, "The Harlot as Heroine: Narrative Art and Social Presupposition in Three Old Testament Texts," *Semeia* 46 (1989) 119–39.

and mourned when they die. The relevant parallels to the Maccabean texts can be listed:[31]

1. The hero or heroine prays to God.
2. The arrogant foreign king sends a field commander to destroy Israel.
3. Judith and Judah first pose as friends of their arch-enemy.
4. The field commander is killed.
5. The enemy army is thrown into panic and retreats.
6. The surrounding Israelites attack.
7. They kill and plunder.
8. The enemy commander's head (and arm) is chopped off.
9. The Israelites celebrate.
10. There is peace over the land.

The theological belief behind both texts—that victory depends not on the size of the army but on the support of God—is not uncommon in the Bible but is expressed in very similar ways in 1 Macc 3:19 and Jdt 9:11. It was noted above how Judith's honors at the end of her life were similar to those of the judges, and this motif is found in regard to Judah as well, 1 Macc 9:19–21.

Judith is sometimes compared to the widow in 2 Maccabees 7, but, as noted, there is much more; the parallels between Judith and 2 Maccabees are even richer than those with 1 Maccabees. Both are favorable to the Hasmonean house. 2 Maccabees focuses on and is more reverent of Judah among the brothers, and Judith's name

suggests that she may be understood as the "female Judah."[32] Just as Renaissance Italy embraced Judith as a virtual consort of David, the first audience of this text probably saw Judith as a sort of consort of Judah the Maccabee. The Nicanor episode in 2 Maccabees serves as the climax and conclusion of the text and is thus an even closer comparandum to the conflict between Judith and Holofernes.

The death and burial of Mattathias, and the song in his honor (1 Macc 2:69–3:9; cf. 13:25–26; 14:4–15) are similar to the burial and song of Judith. That such similarities are not simply the result of Judean tradition but are literary as well can be noted in one detail: Jdt 15:5 uses the rare *hyperkeraō*, which appears in the LXX only here and in 1 Macc 7:46. "Our author," says Gera, "is using the book of 1 Maccabees just as he uses the Bible, including an explicit verbal echo taken from the scene which underlies his own."[33] To be more specific, the author is referencing 1 Maccabees in a very similar way to the referencing of biblical texts but perhaps as "history" and not "scripture." The Greek novels later also borrowed from histories, especially Herodotus.[34]

Second Maccabees is also closer to Judith than 1 Maccabees in terms of theology. Malka Simkovich tabulates the references to halakah in the two texts. In Judith, the commandments mentioned include dietary laws, tithes, circumcision, and holidays; in 2 Maccabees they are dietary laws, tithes, circumcision, holidays, as well as the sabbatical year.[35] Both Judith and 2 Maccabees are from

---

31 Gera, "Judah and Judith," 30–31; see also Gera, *Judith*, 39; van Henten, "Judith as an Alternative Leader," 243–45; Rakel, *Judit–Über Schönheit*, 260–72. Also, in both 1 Macc 3:43–54 and Jdt 4:8–12 the people gather to pray, fast, and put on sackcloth and ashes, the former passage an earnest rendition of events, the latter comic; cf. also 1 Macc 7:39–50. On "feminine" novel versus "masculine" history, see §7 below. The book of Judith may also reflect the influence of Eupolemus. The latter's account of the historical Nebuchadnezzar's campaign against Israel bears some similarities: Nebuchadnezzar first attacks Samaria, where Bethulia was supposedly located, with an army that included 120,000 cavalry, similar to the 120,000 infantry of Judith.

32 While this is more explicit in the medieval Jewish versions (on which see §8 below), it is already implied in the earliest period; so Pierre-Maurice

Bogaert, "Le calendrier du livre de Judith et la fête de Hanukka," *RTL* 15 (1984) 67–72. The feast at the defeat of Arphaxad in 1:16 is near Hanukkah, and the celebration in 16:20 ends on the same day a year later; thus, the book of Judith as a whole honors Hanukkah. On whether Judith's name evokes Judah the Maccabee or the personification of Judah the province, see §1 above and §9 below.

33 Gera, *Judith*, 55.

34 Alan J. Ross, "Syene as Face of Battle: Heliodorus as Late Antique Historiography," *Ancient Narrative* 12 (2015) 1–26.

35 Malka Simkovich, "The Book of Judith: A Fantasy Alternative Narrative to 2 Maccabees" (unpublished paper, 2013). The references are Jdt 10:5; 12:1–2, 9, 19; 14:10; 16:20; 2 Macc 1:9, 15, 18, 60–63; 2:12, 46; 3:49; 5:25; 6:6, 11, 49, 53; 8:26; 10:5–6; 12:32, 38; 15:4, 36.

beginning to end temple propaganda.[36] In Judith, the Jerusalem temple is constantly referenced and provides the timing and sacred center of the narrative world. Our story literally orients toward Jerusalem both geographically and in terms of the loyalty of the Bethulians and their obedience to the Jerusalem high priest. The author and original audience of Judith were probably both in the environs of Jerusalem. The search, for instance, for a hidden Samaritan origin, based on the fictitious location of the invented Bethulia, is misguided. To be sure, God intervenes for the temple directly only in 2 Maccabees 3–4, but this irony is noted in §7 below: miraculous interventions by God are found more in histories, especially second-register histories, than in novelistic texts. Since 2 Maccabees may have been written at about the same time as Judith or even later, it should not be assumed that the author of Judith is referencing 2 Maccabees. Yet, even if 2 Maccabees were written a few years earlier, we should not assume that the novelistic Judith author treated 2 Maccabees as somehow more authoritative as "history"; note especially the disclaimer by the author of 2 Maccabees at the beginning about the popularizing text, combined with the exhortation to "enjoy" it (2 Macc 2:19–32; 15:37–38). Simkovich also points out differences in theology that are often ignored. 2 Maccabees strongly emphasizes resurrection, immortality of the soul, and a divine justice that extends beyond death (2 Macc 7:14, 23, 29; 15:46). These are not to be found in Judith, although we should not discount the role of genre.

Finally, we note a generic similarity to the other Jewish novellas. Esther, Daniel and its Additions, Judith, and 2 Maccabees all feature a national or ethnic reaction to a threatening king, the prayer or fasting of Jews, help from God by the hand of the one whom God has sent, vengeance on the enemies, peace for Jews, and celebration. The Tales of the Persian Court and the Prayer of Nabonidus (4Q242) from Qumran are similar. Further, all of these texts give prominence to the word "Jew"—*Yehud-* in Hebrew and Aramaic, *Ioudai-* in Greek—the basis of the name Judith. This term, quite surprisingly, is rare in Israelite and Jewish literature before the first century CE (after which it fades again until the modern period) but seems to find a sharp definition in just these novelistic texts.[37]

Possible Sources: Ancient Near Eastern Parallels

Our author may very well have been influenced by ancient Near Eastern literature. Paul Kosmin outlines the Hellenistic developments that provide a context for this:

> A sense of the distinctiveness of the present world, different from a pre-Hellenistic past that had been superseded, permitted conscious anachronism and playful re-enactment in both material culture and literature. Collecting, studying, editing, and commenting on earlier writings—in short, library culture—was common to Alexandria and Pergamum, Qumran and Uruk, and even the distant Seleucid colony of Aï Khanoum, at the borders of China.[38]

Some of the details of the Judith story find Persian parallels: the sword, *akinakēs* (13:6; 16:9); turban, *kidaris* (4:15); the names Holofernes and Bagoas; and the phrase "to have earth and water available" (2:7). When Nebuchadnezzar commissions Holofernes, he also speaks in phrases found in Assyrian or Persian royal inscriptions.[39] Achior may share aspects of other biblical righteous gentiles—Jethro, Balaam, and Rahab—as well as the tragic warner from Herodotus (see below), but his character is

---

36   Robert Doran (*Temple Propaganda: The Purpose and Character of 2 Maccabees* [CBQMS 12; Washington, DC: Catholic Biblical Association of America, 1981]), van Henten ("Judith as an Alternative Leader," 244–45), Rakel (*Judit–Über Schönheit*, 271–72), Baslez ("Polémologie"), Roddy ("Way It Wasn't," 269–77), and LaCocque (*Feminine Unconventional*, 41, 43, 44–45) all find in Judith a *corrective* of 2 Maccabees, but this seems unlikely. Judith does not offer any critique of the political theology of 2 Maccabees, but rather a different sort of celebration of it.

37   Wills, "Jew, Judean, Judaism."

38   Paul Kosmin, "Hellenistic Period," in Klawans and Wills, eds., *Jewish Annotated Apocrypha*, forthcoming.

39   Athanasius Miller, *Die Bücher Tobias, Judith und Esther* (3 vols. in 1; Die Heilige Schrift des Alten Testamentes 4.3; Bonn: P. Hanstein, 1940–1941) 39; see also Otzen, *Tobit and Judith*, 100–101; Haag, *Das Buch Judit*, 18, 34; Zenger, *Das Buch Judit*, 458–60, 476; Hellmann, *Judit*, 30–31.

first and foremost derived from the Story of Ahikar (see the excursus below at 5:3, "Achior the Ammonite").

The larger narrative patterns of Judith can also be compared with Near Eastern myths of goddesses. These striking parallels are treated in the commentary on 9:1–14. Here we focus on Near Eastern narrative traditions of violent revenge committed by a woman. Among the warrior-women stories preserved in Greek sources (see below) is the story of Tomyris (Herodotus 1.204–14; Polyaenus, *Stratagems* 8.28), which Johan Weststeijn has grouped with pre-Islamic Arabic stories of Zenobia and Jalila, specifically to develop a comparison with Judith.[40] Such Near Eastern stories may have come to our author from the same Greek sources that are treated below.

These warrior-women stories all have a similar structure, quite comparable to our novella, even though interesting omissions or variations of story elements can be detected:

- A strong-willed heroine opposes a foreign tyrant.
- A wise counselor warns the tyrant not to proceed in battle.
- The tyrant, filled with hubris, ignores the advice, punishes the counselor in response, and proceeds.
- The adviser either switches allegiances or pretends to.
- The tyrant attempts to woo the heroine.
- The heroine intoxicates and either murders the tyrant or participates in the murder.[41]

Weststeijn notes the interrelated network of powerful symbolic elements in these narratives: wine, blood, women, revenge, and inverted rituals of marriage, sex, childbirth, and sacrifice. For instance, the theme of revenge is often played out here and in pre-Islamic Arabic poetry as inverted commensal meals and, as a result of the woman's role, as inverted childbirths and weddings as well.

The relationship between wine and revenge in these stories is also a case of poetic justice, in the way that intemperance leads to death. The reckless amount of alcohol drunk by the ruler is echoed in the barbaric way he is murdered and the corpse is defiled.[42]

The villains are foreign kings who are driven by hubris to conquer new kingdoms and expand their empires. Enemies at the horizon, they are also fools, reduced by their intemperance and their unwillingness to listen to the best advice of proven counselors. The stories suggest a restoration of moral order after a tyrant has become a monster.

The conclusion of the vendetta is also like a sacrifice:

An avenger concludes his status of *iḥrām* by killing his enemy: in vengeance, the murder of the enemy takes the same place and has the same function as the ritual sacrifice of an animal victim.[43]

Could this narrative type be the *closest* parallel for our story? Weststeijn continues,

All four tyrants expect a wedding [or at least sex] but get revenge. Instead of the conventional gender roles in which the groom is the active party who penetrates the passive bride, here the bride is the active party who kills the groom.[44]

The tyrant, for instance, is also blinded by Jalila's beauty. She has "made him drunk without wine"; cf. Jdt 16:9, "her beauty took his soul captive." Weststeijn summarizes the narrative action of this tale type: "Conventionally, men take revenge, and brides lose blood in their wedding night. When a bride takes revenge, the man ends up as blood lost in an inverted wedding." The Song of Judith in chap. 16 may be even closer to Zenobia and Jalila than is the narrative of Judith 1–15. But while these other

---

40   Johan Weststeijn, "Wine, Women, and Revenge in Near Eastern Historiography: The Tales of Tomyris, Judith, Zenobia, and Jalila," *JNES* 75 (2016) 91–107.

41   Tomyris intoxicates Cyrus in the Polyaenus version, but not in Herodotus.

42   Weststeijn, "Wine, Women," 97.

43   Weststeijn, "Wine, Women," 97; Suzanne Pinckney Stetkevych, *The Mute Immortals Speak: Pre-Islamic Poetry and the Poetics of Ritual* (Myth and Poetics;

Ithaca, NY: Cornell University Press, 1993) 55–83, 161–205.

44   Weststeijn, "Wine, Women," 97; see also Nicole Wilkinson Duran, "Having Men for Dinner: Deadly Banquets and Biblical Women," *BTB* 35 (2005) 117–24, here 120.

narratives take personal revenge as a main motivator, for Judith the personal becomes political: she is motivated by love of God and defense of her people. (Late-modern Judith dramas would transpose the motive to revenge; see §8 below.) Still, the similarity of Judith to ancient Near Eastern oral traditions is compelling, especially since the Herodotus versions indicate that they were current long before Judith.[45]

Like Judith, these ancient Arabic literary traditions also treat the protagonist's movements as a heroic quest and include aspects of purity and impurity. Weststeijn continues:

> In Arabic culture, pagan as well as Islamic, an avenger was compared to a pilgrim. From the moment he swears revenge until he fulfills his vow and exacts his vengeance, the vendettist assumes a self-imposed status of impurity, *ihrām*. During this period he abstains from washing, combing, shaving, using perfume, having sex, or drinking wine.[46]

Now, Judith seems to reverse all of these abstentions, but her *usual* state was asocial and uncosmetized; she undertakes these actions only as a disguise of her true nature, a cross-dressing. In Arabic culture these abstentions are related to the *hajj* to Mecca (a ritual that predates Islam). In Judith, there may be a reversal of typical pilgrimage practices, even a mockery of them.

But are all of the aspects of the Arabic vendetta present in the Judith story? Arabic vengeance includes the concept of *ghasl al-dam bi-l-dam*, washing away blood with blood. Unavenged blood pollutes the relatives of the victim, and the only liquid that can clean away the impurity is the blood of the perpetrator. In Judith, the tyrant has committed many atrocities but has not yet shed Israelite blood. To be sure, Holofernes has vowed to take revenge on the Jews until the mountains are "drunk with their blood," but more to the point—and this is another way in which Judith differs from these other texts—the tyrant (here Nebuchadnezzar) has *insulted* God. The vendetta is a response not to bloodshed but to insult. And surprisingly absent from Judith's decapitation is any mention of blood!

The stories attain their attraction and currency largely because they depict women in outrageous violations of custom. The women are sexually provocative, and the murders are heinous crimes, even regicides. Further, the villains are not even defeated in a fair fight; the avenging women gain access by deceit and sexual provocation, the men are murdered in their sleep, overtaken by wine. Further, the corpses are abused in unconscionable ways.

Possible Sources: Greek Parallels

Although there has been a strong tendency to perceive Judith as a biblically influenced composition, the large number of parallels to Greek and ancient Near Eastern traditions are almost as compelling.[47] If the prayer, the Song, and Achior's speech are set aside—that is, if one

---

45 Weststeijn argues for a written version ("Zenobia of Palmyra and the Book of Judith: Common Motifs in Greek, Jewish, and Arabic Historiography," *JSP* 22 [2013] 295–320), but this does not seem necessary. His other article proposes only a common tale type, but one localizable to the Near East.

46 Weststeijn, "Wine, Women," 97–98, where he also notes that drinking wine in these vendetta texts is a metaphor for drinking blood, but Judith also differs slightly: Holofernes's injudicious drinking of wine could be compared to his shedding of blood, but his beheading is so bloodless that the narrative action-and-response seems to be that he loses control and then loses his head.

47 On Greek parallels, see Moses Hadas, *Hellenistic Culture* (New York: Norton, 1959) 165–69; Hengel, *Judaism and Hellenism*, 110–15; Arnaldo Momigliano, "Biblical Studies and Classical Studies: Simple Reflections about Historical Method," *BA* 45 (1982) 224–28; Caponigro, "Judith, Holding the Tale"; Stanley M. Burstein, "Cleitarchus in Jerusalem: A Note on the *Book of Judith*," in Frances B. Tichenor and Richard F. Morton Jr., eds., *The Eye Expanded: Life and the Arts in Greco-Roman Antiquity* (Berkeley: University of California Press, 1999) 105–12; Stocker, *Judith*, 20–22; Otzen, *Tobit and Judith*, 79–80; Schmitz, "Zwischen Achikar und Demaratos—die Bedeutung Achiors in der Juditerzählung," *BZ* 48 (2004) 19–38; Sara Raup Johnson, *Historical Fictions and Hellenistic Jewish Identity: Third Maccabees in Its Cultural Identity* (HCS 43; Berkeley: University of California Press, 2004) 24–29, 46–48.

looks at the *narrative* sections alone—it is striking that the parallels to Greek themes may be as strong and numerous as the parallels to biblical motifs. Scholars such as Dubarle were certainly performing a scholarly service to catalogue the very high number of possible biblical intertexts, but in scholars' minds this may have have had a tendency to limit the literary world of the author.[48]

First we turn to the Greek world's own "biblical" text, Homer. The dressing scene of Judith may be modeled on Homeric dressing or arming scenes for male and female figures and will be discussed further in the commentary on 9:1–14.[49] Odysseus's stratagem of inebriating, then blinding the cyclops Polyphemus (*Odyssey* book 9) may seem a vaguer comparison, but, were it in the Bible, it would be included in every list of echoes. The later Greek novel heroines would be associated with the epic women Ariadne, Penelope, and Helen, and the author of Judith may have looked to the great women of epic as well.[50]

But it is in the Greek historians that we perceive the closest parallels, some quite specific. The surrender by presenting earth and water in Jdt 2:7 is known elsewhere only in Herodotus 6.48.[51] Indeed, the author of Judith may have known the works of Herodotus, Ctesias, and Xenophon of Athens. They were popular during this period, likely contributing to the growth of history writing among both Greeks and non-Greeks. Gera has also noted the Herodotean background of motifs that many have labeled Jewish: "Some Herodotean kings"—these would be eastern, barbarian kings in Herodotus's view—"also share with Nebuchadnezzar the belief that they are the equal of the gods."[52] In addition, even the very inquiry about another nation's makeup (Judith 5) is typical of the anthropological interest found in Herodotus and other

Greek authors. Holofernes's questions about Israelites are similar to those of Atossa, queen of Persia, in Aeschylus's *Persae* 230–45 (see the commentary on 5:3–4).

Ctesias also may have been known by our author and the author of Esther as well, along with Xenophon's *Anabasis* and *Cyropaedeia*. If Greek history was written in two different registers, a restrained, rationalistic register (Herodotus, Thucydides, Polybius), and a less-restrained, popular register that manipulated emotional responses (Hellanicus of Lesbos; see §7 below), then our author may have known a series of authors in both registers.

That our author plays on conventions of the eastern courts, even in an expeditionary camp, demonstrates the sort of common storytelling tradition of the court narratives, both Jewish and non-Jewish. This tradition may have made its influence felt through both eastern and Greek sources. As Gera again notes,

> There is an implicit formula in Greek writings about oriental courts: powerful and clever women go hand in hand with passive or ineffectual men. Strong women were often depicted by Greek authors not for their own sake, but in order to demonstrate how weak Persian kings could be undermined or out-maneuvered by mere women. . . . These Greek writers of history and pseudo-history provide dramatic stories of harsh despots, independent women, and plotting eunuchs, whose caprice and cunning seemingly dictated the course of Persian history.[53]

The theme of Holofernes's luxury and feminization within his tent matches the Greek stereotype of eastern luxury.[54] If Judith was composed in a Greek style that mimicked Septuagintal Greek, this connection would

---

48 An analogous problem, but moving in the opposite direction, is to limit the biblical influences to one or two passages. Esler focuses more exclusively on parallels to David and Goliath (*Sex, Wives, and Warriors,* 274–99). Van Henten has emphasized Moses but grants that we should not limit the discussion to one intertext ("Judith as an Alternative Leader," 224).

49 Gera, *Judith,* 57. Gera notes that 1 Macc 3:3, Judah dressing in the armor of the hero, is similar ("Judah and Judith," 34–35).

50 Meredith J. C. Warren, *My Flesh Is Meat Indeed: A Non-Sacramental Reading of John 6:51–58* (Minneapolis: Fortress Press, 2015) passim.

51 Amélie Kuhrt, "Earth and Water" in Amélie Kuhrt

and Heleen Sancisi-Weerdenburg, eds., *Method and Theory: Proceedings of the London 1985 Achaemenid History Workshop* (Achaemenid History 3; Leiden: Nederlands Instituut voor het Nabije Oosten, 1988) 87–99; Gera, *Judith,* 60–61.

52 Gera, *Judith,* 63, on Herodotus 1.204, 2.169, 7.10; see also Samuel Vollenweider, "Der 'Raub' der Gottgleichheit: Ein religionsgeschichtlicher Vorschlag zu Phil 2.6(–11) [*sic*]," *NTS* 45 (1999) 413–33, here 417–18.

53 See Gera, *Judith,* 59–78; the quotation is from Gera, *Warrior Women,* 120. See also Grintz, *Book of Judith,* 24–28.

54 Xenophon states that the softness of the Medes

be even more likely, since in that case the author was quite capable of a convincing literary conceit in Greek. Further evidence is that Judith may have been familiar with Eupolemus, and he was familiar with Ctesias and Herodotus.[55] One narrative arc within Ctesias relevant to Judith concerns the beautiful Semiramis. She joins Ninus in his campaign against the mighty Bactrians and is a Judith in reverse. She dresses in an ample garment that obscures the fact that she is a woman taking on the role of a woman warrior. Ninus demands of Semiramis's husband that he give up his wife to the king, but instead he goes mad and hangs himself. The husband has died ignominiously, as Manasseh perhaps had (see commentary on chap. 8), and Semiramis aims higher, marrying the great soldier.[56]

The motif of the narrow pass at Bethulia may have been suggested by the three hundred Spartans' defense of the narrow pass at Thermopylae during the attack of Xerxes of Persia and his huge army.[57] What confirms this connection is another passage, in this same context, concerning Xerxes: the discussion between the eastern king and his counselor Demaratus on the power of the Spartans' obedience to their law.[58] According to Demaratus,

the military strength of the Spartans is derived from their allegiance to only one master, their law, unlike the Persian soldiers, who fear only the whip of their master, the king. This is quite similar to Achior's speech in Judith 5—indeed, Achior's speech reminds one of the "tragic warner" theme in Herodotus[59]—but in addition, Demaratus has just marshaled and counted his troops, as Holofernes had done in Jdt 2:14–18. Mark Stephen Caponigro goes so far as to perceive a "Xerxizing" of Nebuchadnezzar in the book of Judith, similar but not identical to the Danielic depiction of Nebuchadnezzar noted above.[60] He also finds similarities between Nebuchadnezzar's war council in chap. 2 and Xerxes's war council in Herodotus 7.5–11.

The collocation of parallels here—marshaling and counting a huge invading foreign army, brave citizen-soldiers defending the route to the heartland at a narrow pass, the contrast of the noble obedience to law and the obedience of fear—all indicate some influence of the Herodotean passage. And as Achior is like the Herodotean tragic warners, so Judith is similar to Themistocles, who acts the part of a traitor to deceive the Persians into engaging the battle of Salamis. Like Judith, Themistocles strengthens his own citizens with insights into divine

---

had infected the Persians (*Cyropaedia* 8.15–17). The Romans continued the belief that northern climes had produced hypermasculine peoples, while the East and South (Egyptians, Phoenicians, Persians, and Jews) were "effeminate"—often understood as lacking self-mastery; see Benjamin H. Isaac, *The Invention of Racism in Classical Antiquity* (Princeton, NJ: Princeton University Press, 2004) 324–70, 411–91; but now also Robert J. Gorman and Vanessa Gorman, "The Tryphē of the Sybarites: A Historiographical Problem in Athenaeus," *Journal of Hellenic Studies* 127 (2007) 38–60.

55 Priebatsch, "Das Buch Judith."

56 Ctesias, *Persica* 2.6.1–10; see Lloyd Llewellyn-Jones and James Robson, *Ctesias' History of Persia: Tales of the Orient* (London: Routledge, 2010) 118–19.

57 Herodotus 7.101–4, 175–76, 210–34. See Schmitz, "Zwischen Achikar"; Schmitz, "'Achior aber glaubte aus ganzem Herzen an Gott' (Jdt 14,10): Der Ammoniter Achior im Buch Judit (3)," *Bibel und Liturgie* 78 (2005) 215–19; Caponigro, "Judith, Holding the Tale," 54–55; Corley, "Imitation," 27–34; Gera, *Judith*, 66–67. Carolyn Dewald argues that Herodotus describes cultures as they are encountered by the Persians, and that women often function to

defend and define cultural boundaries with Persians ("Women and Culture in Herodotus' *Histories*," in Helene P. Foley, ed., *Reflections of Women in Antiquity* [4th ed.; Philadelphia: Gordon & Breach, 1992] 91–125). Judith's role can be considered a comic version of this imperial interaction; see also Patterson, "Re-membering the Past." Judith is sometimes also likened to the traitor Ephialtes, who provides the Persians with the secret of the pass (7.213–18), or the ruse of Themistocles to lure the Persian fleet into the battle of Salamis (8.75–90); see Gera, *Judith*, 64–65; Caponigro, "Judith, Holding the Tale," 55–56.

58 Herodotus 7.101–4; Jdt 5:5–21. See Gera, *Judith*, 61–62; Momigliano, "Biblical Studies," 227–28, Schmitz, "Zwischen Achikar," 31; Steinmann, *Lecture de Judith*, 57.

59 Judith replays this motif from the colonized point of view, as Daniel and Esther had also done; see Wills, *Jew in the Court*, 55–70; and Gera, *Judith*, 62–63, on Achior as an example. As noted above, Achior combines elements of righteous gentiles in biblical tradition and the "tragic warner" from Herodotus. See also Corley, "Imitation," 34–41.

60 Caponigro, "Judith, Holding the Tale," 51–53.

will, while using persuasion and deceit with the enemy.[61] Judith's final days may be borrowed from a tradition about Aretaphilia, who freed her city from a tyrant and, rejecting pleas to join in the government, returned home to her women's quarters and spent the rest of her life weaving.[62] It is the nature of an intertext to bring with it some of the resonances of the earlier tradition, and that is likely the case here as well.

The Greek and Persian traditions influence the depiction not only of Judith but of the eunuch Bagoas as well (see the excursus below at 12:10–12: "Bagoas the Eunuch"). Eunuchs are encountered often in Herodotus, Xenophon, and especially in Ctesias's *Persica,* and in the Persian-centered book of Esther.[63] Guarding the entrance to the leader's tent is typical of their role. Holofernes turns to Bagoas to discuss his plans for Judith just as Stryngaeus in Ctesias turns to a eunuch for a similar discussion concerning Zarinaea. In Greek tradition, eunuchs were invested with stereotypical emotion and tearful exhibitions; they wailed and mourned for their dead kings, sometimes following them by killing themselves.

A further argument of Katell Berthelot must also be considered.[64] In Judith, Judea's independence is at stake, and the use of Herodotus clearly, but ironically, implies that the Seleucid kings—here an "Assyrian"—are not the true heirs of their Greek predecessors but rather the heirs of the Persians, the archetypal enemies of Greece. The use of Herodotus may thus be not so much an example of openness to "foreign wisdom" as a bold and ironic use of the colonizer's cultural references to claim superiority, *even by the colonizer's own standards.* This process may not be conscious, but it may be in evidence never-

theless. The colonized often assert that they embody the broader, imperial virtues more fully than the colonizers. This "colonial universalism" may suffuse our text (and other Jewish texts as well, such as 2 Maccabees) and may ironically indicate a sense of the triumph of Herodotus's virtues over the Greek successors. The orientation of the Greek novels may also suggest a Greek triumph over Rome (see §7 below).

Some of the novelistic precursors of the Greek novels are also similar to Judith and should be considered here. The Alexander Romance features the sweep of nations, military campaigns, and fanciful geography of Judith. Under attack, King Nectanebos of Egypt says,

> It is not just one nation that is advancing upon us but millions of people. Advancing on us are Indians, Nokimaians, Oxydrakai, Iberians, Kauchones, Lelapes, Bosporoi, Bastranoi, Azanoi, Chalybes, and all the other great nations of the East, armies of innumerable warriors advancing against Egypt. (1.2)[65]

Inscriptional evidence from this period, the Lindos Chronicle (99 BCE, based on older traditions), also provides the likely source for the pledge to surrender within five days.[66] When Lindos on Rhodes was besieged by Darius of Persia and the water supply was depleted, the citizens prayed to Athena to bring rain within five days. Rain did come to Lindos, and Darius realized that the city enjoyed divine protection and passed it by. The Lindos Chronicle, unlike Judith, betrays no reservation whatsoever about placing a time limit on the divinity's action.

The more telling Greek models for Judith, however, are not the male generals from the histories such as

61   Herodotus 7.143–44; 8.57–63, 75–90; Momigliano, "Biblical Studies," 228; Caponigro, "Judith, Holding the Tale," 55–56, Schmitz, "Zwischen Achikar," 31; Gera, *Judith,* 65.

62   Gera, "Judith and the Warrior Women of Herodotus" (paper presented at the Society of Biblical Literature Annual Meeting, Atlanta, Georgia, November 20, 2003; Gera, "Speech in Judith."

63   Gera, *Judith,* 72–73; cf. Bagoas with the role of eunuchs in Herodotus 3.130.4; Xenophon, *Cyropaedia* 6.4.11, 7.3.14–15. The Stryngaeus passage is at Ctesias, *Persica* F8c; cf. F6b.6, F13.13.

64   Bertholet, "Hellenization," 75.

65   Translation of Richard Stoneman, *The Greek Alexan-*

der Romance (London: Penguin, 1991). The invasion referred to here is that led by Artaxerxes III Ochus of Persia, the very invasion that may have influenced our author (see §2 above). The later historian Curtius Rufus (8.3.6–10) also provides a parallel from the Alexander tradition: Spitamenes's murder by his wife (see also the Metz Epitome 20–21). This tradition is not found in the Alexander Romance but may have been known from the lost *History of Alexander* by Cleitarchus; so Burstein, "Cleitarchus in Jerusalem," 105–12; see also Gera, *Judith,* 57.

66   Carolyn Higbie, *The Lindian Chronicle and the Greek Creation of the Past* (Oxford: Oxford University Press, 2003).

Themistocles, but the warrior women.[67] Judith's combination of deceit, murder, and abuse of the enemy's dead body occurs not in Israelite tradition but in Greek (see the commentary on 13:9b–10a). The Tractatus de mulieribus claris in bello, or Book of Women Renowned in Warfare, from as early as first century BCE, treats fourteen Greek and barbarian queens culled from earlier sources (Herodotus, Ctesias, Aeschines, Hellanicus, Timaeus).[68] A long tradition of warrior women thus circulated, but this particular text may have arisen in the same era as Judith. Judith and Esther may both respond to a surge of interest in women in public roles, perhaps spurred by the reigns of queens in Egypt.

The warrior women in Greek tradition are generally eastern queens and warriors; they appear to be the Greek adaptations of ancient Near Eastern warrior women. These women are associated with weak or effete men—compare the elders, Judith's dead husband, and Achior as well.[69] In addition, the beautiful warrior women sometimes arouse desire in their male opponents:

Sexual voracity is a feature often associated with warrior women: their anomalous or marginal position in society leaves them particularly liable to accusations of sexual misconduct. This is true of widows as well.[70]

The issue of Judith's widowhood has generally been analyzed by scholars in terms of Israelite widows and Jewish practice; widows are weak and vulnerable members of society and must be protected by the gôʾēl, the tribal redeemer. In the Israelite context, the active and even dangerous role of Judith reads as a transgression of typical practices, but in this hybrid Hellenistic context, her behavior is more typical of this type. If eastern women (from the Greek point of view), all widows, could be sexually provocative, strategic, and militarily violent, is Judith then "within" expectations, specifically *Greek* expectations? The author of Judith has perhaps rewritten this topos from the colonized perspective, now valuing what the western Greeks feared as dangerously barbarian.[71]

Gera focuses more closely on three of these women, all widows, for a comparison with Judith: Tomyris and Artemisia from Herodotus, and Zarinea from Ctesias.[72] In the Tomyris legend, for example, Gera highlights "different food eaten by the two sides, intoxication leading to a foe's downfall, and ironic exchanges with the enemy."[73]

---

67 Gera, *Judith*, 42, 65–72; Gera, *Warrior Women*; and cf. Plutarch, *Virtues of Women*. On Chinese examples, see Chen Fan Pen, "Female Warriors, Magic and the Supernatural in Traditional Chinese Novels," in Arvind Sharma and Katherine K. Young, eds., *The Annual Review of Women in World Religions,* vol. 2: *Heroic Women* (Albany: State University of New York Press, 1992) 91–109.

68 Schmitz also provocatively draws attention to the tyrannicide-as-hero in Greek tradition ("War, Violence and Tyrannicide in the Book of Judith," in Jan Lisen and Pancratius C. Beentjes, eds., *Visions of Peace and Tales of War* [Deuterocanonical and Cognate Literature Yearbook, 2010; Berlin: de Gruyter, 2010], 103–19; she kindly allowed me to read a version of this article revised for later publication). In the base narrative of Harmodius and Aristogeiton, however, the female figures are more tangential. Still, the combination of tyrannicide and honoring with cult is suggestive for Judith 16 (which see).

69 On Manasseh as weak, see Amy-Jill Levine, "Sacrifice and Salvation: Otherness and Domestication in the Book of Judith," in Brenner, *Feminist Companion to Esther*, 208–23. Gera reminds us (*Judith*, 258) that there are other strong women with weak husbands in the Hebrew Bible: Rebekah (Genesis 24–27), the Shunammite woman (2 Kings 4), Manoah's wife (Judges 13), Naomi (Ruth 1–4); and the story of Abigail and Nabal (1 Samuel 25) is also similar.

70 Gera, *Warrior Women,* 82; also 93. This may derive from Achilles and the Amazon queen Penthesilea; so already Eduard Schwartz, *Fünf Vorträge über den griechischen Roman* (Berlin: Reimer, 1896) 75. This is similar to the later Zarinea and Stryangaeus.

71 To be sure, the popularity of this tradition in Greece is partially explained as revenge against Persians: the texts assert that Persian kings were defeated by eastern women. Gera also notes that, in regard to biblical motifs, Judith's brazen seductiveness evoked both the negative memory and positive memory of *foreign* women—negatively, Delilah, Potiphar's wife; Cozbi the Midianite; the strange or foreign woman of Proverbs 1–9; but positively (and ironically!) Tamar and Ruth (*Judith*, 103).

72 Gera, *Judith*, 65; see also Patterson, "Re-membering the Past"; Corley, "Imitation," 35–36, 41.

73 Gera, *Judith*, 67.

Tomyris also places Cyrus's head in a bag of wine. Again, if this were in the Bible, it would appear in every list of intertexts; and indeed, in Christian art Tomyris is associated with Judith (see §8 below). But the main difference is perhaps genre: the Tomyris story is earnest and compelling, the Judith story broadly satirical, the fantasy fulfillment of the colonized.

Most of these stories contain no erotic element, but Ctesias's treatment of Zarinaea is an exception.[74] When Zarinaea leads her Scythian army against the Medes, the opposing general, Stryangaeus, gets the best of her militarily yet is undone by her beauty. Stryangaeus's eunuch is also a party to his erotic attachment. He urges him to marry Zarinaea, but when she refuses his advances, he commits suicide and Zarinaea continues as a great queen. Since Zarinaea is a Scythian, and Scythian women were accustomed to fight in battle, this is not a gender reversal for *Scythian* culture. In the *Greek* imagination, however, it is likely a gender-reversal fantasy projected onto an exotic eastern culture. Zarinaea, like Judith, remains a widow after her exploits, and both are honored to the end of their days and mourned and memorialized in death.

Another story in this grouping also contains a romance-novel element. Panthea, a beautiful Assyrian woman, is taken by Cyrus (Xenophon, *Cyropaedia* 4–7). Her husband changes sides to join her in Cyrus's retinue but dies in battle. Cloaking her intentions in ambiguous words, she asks to mourn his body in private; she pulls out a hidden dagger—as in Judith, an *akinakēs*! (*Cyropaedia* 7.3.14, Jdt 13:6)—and stabs herself to death. The melodrama here may have inspired depictions of other heroines in the Greek novels, one of which is written by Xenophon of Ephesus, likely a pen name that honors the historian Xenophon of Athens. Panthea commands not on the battlefield, as Zarinaea does, but in the bedroom.

Lori Hope Lefkovitz captures this same theme in Israel: "In the Hebrew Bible, the bedroom is the battlefield where men always lose."[75] The bedroom-battlefield is a common motif in narratives cross-culturally.

Conclusion on Possible Sources

Only the Israelite traditions are referenced in an explicit way in Judith. None of the ancient Near Eastern or Greek parallels rises to this level of clarity. Judith is also associated with the Hasmonean renewal of Israel and is resolutely protective of God's temple and its city. Israelite tradition thus provides much of the form and content of the narrative. The Deuteronomistic History is the history for which Judith is mock-history. But the narrative itself is formed, perhaps equally, from Hellenistic, Persian, and broader Near Eastern motifs. The author plays on whatever material lies at hand, restringing motifs in a new structural pattern. Harold Bloom notes how every new literary work must misread tradition, borrowing while also transforming or even reversing what the audience has known.[76] Judith is therefore a child of Judges and Exodus but spins a different, fanciful version. This same question could be investigated in regard to any genre, such as history (2 Maccabees), wisdom (Wisdom of Solomon), or apocalypse (Daniel 7–12), but it is especially vibrant in regard to the rise of the novel. The Bakhtinian impulse is discernible in the mixing of Israelite, Greek, and Near Eastern narrative in a new mock-history.

Another way of assessing this is to inquire about the audience's competence. How many of the Greek motifs would have been widely known?[77] If Judith was written in Alexandria, then the familiarity would be much stronger, but even in Judea the Greek historians might be known. Would the audience have been familiar with the Greek

74 Ctesias, *Persica* F5, 34.1–6; F7a–b, F8a–c; see Gera, *Judith*, 69–70.

75 Lori Hope Lefkovitz, *In Scripture: The First Stories of Jewish Sexual Identities* (Lanham, MD: Rowman & Littlefield, 2010) 111. Her examples include Delilah, Jael, Tamar, and Esther, in addition to Judith.

76 Harold Bloom, *A Map of Misreading* (2nd ed.; New York: Oxford University Press, 2003).

77 A similar problem is identified in regard to the Gospel of Mark by Dennis R. MacDonald, *The Homeric Epics and the Gospel of Mark* (New Haven: Yale University Press, 2000). MacDonald would place the Greek background—Homer—on an equal footing with the Israelite biblical quotations and allusions. However, they are clearly operating on different levels, in that the Israelite are both explicit and more common; so Karl Olav Sandnes, *The Challenge of Homer: School, Pagan Poets, and Early Christianity* (LNTS 400; London: T&T Clark, 2009)) 13, 43.

Lindos Chronicle? And would the audience have recognized that Ben Sira—not yet a "biblical" text—lay behind Judith's reference to *panourgeumata* in Greek? We need not posit that the audience was *competent* in regard to these traditions, only that the author was, but that the motifs would be meaningful, even powerful for the audience in a Hellenistic world.

The most interesting question remains to be answered. The entire Western tradition, both Christian and Jewish, patriarchal and feminist, has staunchly assumed that, however we evaluate Judith, what she does is unique, transgressive. But at the conclusion of our inventory of literary parallels, she seems to partake of a common type. And yet she may be unique after all. Unlike all the other women warriors, boundary crossers, tricksters, and vamps, Judith is viewed as pious, maintaining among her people an impeccable social standing. Does any other woman combine virtue and vice so closely?

5. The Feminist Interpretation of Judith in the Last Century[1]

When asked, "Can a virtuous character be interesting?," novelist Thomas Mallon responded, "Goodness has been getting on readers' nerves since the publication of *Pamela* in 1740."[2] The author of the book of Judith did all that was humanly possible to render the virtuous heroine interesting by having her violate every rule of feminine decorum. Both virtue and titillation coexisted in this heroine. The protagonist Judith is seductive and deceitful, disrespectful of her male elders, violent without any hesitation, and she crosses many dangerous boundaries. She enters the inner chamber of the tent of the Assyrian general Holofernes and, using her beauty, brains, deceit, and sexual innuendo, seduces him into drinking so much wine that he passes out. She draws his own sword and chops off his head, then contemptuously rolls his body onto the floor. Her story thus climaxes with a transgressive scene of sex and violence, indeed, the purest admixture of sex and violence in respectable world literature. It imprints on the imagination. Margarita Stocker rightly refers to this scene as the Judith "acteme."[3] The story caught on, and her persona was launched.

When we speak of the feminist interpretation of ancient texts we are often combining diachronic and synchronic aspects. A diachronic approach isolates the different time periods of a textual tradition, limiting discussion strictly to those resonances that can be attributed to each period separately. A synchronic approach collapses the original performance situation with subsequent periods of interpretation, including the present. While all ancient texts can be studied in both their diachronic and synchronic dimensions, some biblical texts have called forth this dual perspective more than others: the narrative of Adam and Eve, the Akedah or sacrifice of Isaac, Job, Song of Songs, and the passion narratives of the Gospels.

The persona of Judith also has a strange ability to transcend her original text and provoke synchronic judgments. Judith is a fictitious and imaginative work of art that presents psychological, anthropological, and cultural challenges to an audience in any age. It is too easy to suggest that diachronic and synchronic approaches can be engaged independently. If certain motifs in the Judith story were opened up in later centuries to new expressive energies—for instance, the way Judith grasps the general's head by his hair in order to behead him—does this suggest that there was a "potential energy" in that motif in the earliest version, even if it was not emphasized? The fact that Judith chides the elders and orders them about is often omitted in the modern period. Do we see here the elimination of what was *originally* a more transgressive motif? Does what later interpreters think of as obvious also resonate in the first audience's experience, even if unconsciously?

We begin with a preliminary comparison with Israelite narrative. For a text to include a woman character, or be named after a woman, was not unusual in Israel or in Greece. Why, then, should Judith's actions be a problem? Why should a woman *not* cajole, flatter, lie, seduce, murder, and defile corpses to save her people? Men in the Bible do, often for very selfish goals.[4] Helen Watanabe-O'Kelly observes that, cross-culturally, heroic men violate laws of family and society, "the son sleeping with his mother, the father sacrificing his own child"—antisocial acts in fact *typical* of the hero—"but the idea of a woman with the potential to kill causes deep unease."[5] Judith's transgressive act is not only cross-culturally like that of heroic men, who are often not condemned; it is like that of some women as well, such as Antigone or Jael. Women's spectacular acts of devotion are seen in their exposure of their own protected status, as they

---

1　The history of interpretation of Judith, especially in art, will be addressed below in §8; here we limit discussion to more recent feminist interpretation of the LXX story. Note that I refer to God as male in this commentary to reflect the particular narrative world created by the text. Our author explores many edges of the gender of Judith, but the masculinity of God is consistent.

2　Thomas Mallon, *New York Times Book Review*, August 9, 2015, 35.

3　Stocker, *Judith,* 11. On mixing diachronic and synchronic approaches, note that Stocker sometimes speaks of the original book and sometimes of later artists without distinguishing them (e.g., p. 7).

4　Geoffrey D. Miller, "A Femme Fatale of Whom 'No One Spoke Ill': Judith's Moral Muddle and Her Personification of Yahweh," *JSOT* 39 (2014) 223–45, here 226–27.

5　Watanabe-O'Kelly, *Beauty or Beast?*, 1.

violate boundaries of honor and shame. Judith, like Antigone and Jael, is willing to place herself outside humanity for a higher moral goal.[6] Yet it is significant that Antigone was the product of incest and Jael was foreign. These questions will set the context for the following discussion.

The Twentieth Century Ponders Judith as Heroine

At the turn of the twentieth century, the book of Judith was rarely studied. Comments on Judith from 1880 to 1950 are almost all confined to surveys of the Apocrypha that required comment on every text, Judith dutifully included. Very few books or articles on Judith alone can be found. For Protestant scholars, the book was almost an embarrassment: weak as history, weak as theology, weak as narrative, weak as ethics.[7] The protagonist was deceitful, sexually provocative, coolly murderous. By the latter half of the twentieth century, however, the search for female characters and women's voices in the Bible brought Judith to the fore. In the first wave of post–World War II feminism, there were several attempts to find a feminist impulse in Judith's actions. Patricia Montley follows out Judith's androgynous shifts from female to male roles and back again. "In her marvelous androgyny," Montley concludes, "Judith embodies yet somehow transcends the male/female dichotomy. To

this extent, she is a heroine who rises above the sexism of her author's culture."[8] Toni Craven's close analysis of the literary patterns in Judith rehabilitated both the narrative art of the text and the moral character of the female protagonist: "Once Judith takes the stage in chapter 8, she shares it with others but surrenders it to no one."[9] Judith's lying, which had been criticized by many previous scholars, was affirmed by Craven as a strategy; Judith even prays to God for the power of deceit (9:10, 13). In addition, "the Book of Judith may have stood as good a chance as the Book of Ruth of becoming part of the Hebrew canon had Judith been a male in this story and had Achior been a female."[10] Craven stops short of a full endorsement of Judith as a feminist model but does idealize at one point the relationship between Judith and her slave.[11]

A host of women scholars followed who presented a positive assessment of the protagonist's role. Elisabeth Schüssler Fiorenza raised the interesting possibility that in some respects Judith may in fact *not* be violating established rules of decorum for women; we do not know whether women's roles would be so severely restricted in a town in Samaria.[12] Judith lives alone and does not remarry; she has a civic role; she is a respected leader; and she does not appear veiled in public. These practices *may* have been permitted to women, or perhaps to widows, or perhaps to wealthy widows in village life as

---

6 "Put herself outside humanity" is from Renate Peters's discussion of the early twentieth-century Judith plays of Thomas Bailey Aldrich, quoted in Dan W. Clanton Jr., *Daring, Disreputable and Devout: Interpreting the Hebrew Bible's Women in the Arts and Music* (New York: T&T Clark, 2009) 148.

7 H. Maldwyn Hughes pointed out that, while Judith observed ritual laws, she prayed for and practiced deceit: "The moral standard is low" (*The Ethics of Jewish Apocryphal Literature* [London: R. Culley, 1909] 85–86).

8 Patricia Montley, "Judith in the Fine Arts: The Appeal of the Archetypal Androgyne," *Anima* 4 (1978) 37–42, quoted in Moore, *Judith*, 65.

9 Craven, *Artistry and Faith*, 62, 121–22.

10 Craven, *Artistry and Faith*, 118. If Judith was written in Greek, canonization would still have been an issue, but Craven's basic point remains.

11 Craven, *Artistry and Faith*, 121. However, since the

nameless and speechless companion is a slave with no individual choice in following Judith into danger, others have balked at valorizing the relationship; see Wills, *Jewish Novel*, 151; Jennifer A. Glancy, "The Mistress–Slave Dialectic: Paradoxes of Slavery in Three LXX Narratives," *JSOT* 72 (1996) 71–87. In later Christian tradition, the slave does receive the name Habra or Abra, a word that means "Favorite Female Slave" (see the excursus below at 8:11: "Judith's Slave, Habra/Abra"). On Judith's benevolence to her slave at the end of the story, see the commentary. On Artemisia Gentileschi's reimaging of this cooperative relationship, see §8 below.

12 Elisabeth Schüssler Fiorenza, *In Memory of Her: A Feminist Theological Reconstruction of Christian Origins* (New York: Crossroad, 1983) 115–18; Schüssler Fiorenza, *Bread Not Stone: The Challenge of Feminist Biblical Interpretation* (Boston: Beacon, 1985) 148.

opposed to life in Jerusalem. Schüssler Fiorenza then presses a conclusion that is not commonly held by other scholars: the very actions depicted in the book of Judith constitute evidence that restrictions on women's power were not as tightly drawn as people have assumed. To be sure, there is much empirical evidence that a pious Jewish woman would not be allowed to exercise such a public role, but there is evidence as well of wealthy women acting as public benefactors.[13] It is unsafe to assume that social codes were consistently imposed, or that they even existed in the same way in every era or in every area. I take the the position that, for the original audience, many of Judith's actions would have been seen as violating prevailing gender codes.

Alice Ogden Bellis also concluded that Judith was "perhaps the strongest Hebrew hero in all of biblical literature."[14] While the early biblical stories of women seem to present mixed messages, Bellis asserts that Ruth and the late stories of Esther, Susanna, and Judith are the most liberating. She notes Judith's retirement from power at the end but does not criticize this. In Bellis's defense, at the end of hero narratives, cross-culturally, the male heroic figure often either dies or withdraws from society (the biblical judges are exceptions). One might argue that, although Judith does not become a village elder, *like many male heroes* she retires at the end to a position outside of society. Eileen Schuller also noted

that the story is often retold by Latin American women in struggle,[15] and Denise Dombkowski Hopkins defended Judith's use of deceit, as did Sheila Shulman.[16] Linda Bennett Elder went so far as to suggest that negative views, even by women scholars, rob Judith of her feminist achievement.[17]

Male commentators sympathetic to feminist analysis also contributed to the discussion. John F. Craghan pointed out that Judith exhibits a female agency that is not limited by social constraints.[18] Moore suggested that Judith escapes androcentric restrictions: "clearly, Judith is a feminist kind of person!"[19] George W. E. Nickelsburg referred broadly to Judith's "feminism" and noted, still early in the awakening of feminist interest, that Judith towered above her male counterparts. She wisely used the weapons of deceit, sexuality, and treachery to save her people: "She plays [Holofernes's] game, knowing that he will lose. In so doing she makes fools out of a whole army of men."[20] Alexander A. Di Lella more specifically argued that Judith does the very things that Ben Sira condemns in a woman. In Ben Sira there is a danger of being beguiled by a woman (Sir 9:8–9); elders are to be respected (Sir 6:34; 8:9); Ben Sira praises the silent wife (26:14). Di Lella thus finds an ameliorating reform in our text's presentation of a female protagonist: "it seems reasonable to conclude that the author of Judith included many of the narrative details, including the dialogue, to

13   In both cases the evidence is later than Judith. See Ilan, *Jewish Women,* passim, but esp. 129; Bernadette J. Brooten, *Women Leaders in the Ancient Synagogue: Inscriptional Evidence and Background Issues* (BJS 36; Chico, CA: Scholars Press, 1982); see also below on m. Ketub. 7:6.

14   Alice Ogden Bellis, *Helpmates, Harlots, and Heroines: Women's Stories in the Hebrew Bible* (2nd ed.; Louisville: Westminster John Knox, 2000; 1st ed., 1994) 219; see also 205.

15   Eileen M. Schuller, "Apocrypha," in Carol A. Newsom and Sharon H. Ringe, eds., *Women's Bible Commentary* (expanded ed.; Louisville: Westminster John Knox, 1998) 243. Schuller is one of the few European or North American scholars writing before 2000 to note the reception of Judith in other global contexts.

16   Denise Dombkowski Hopkins, "Judith," in Carol A. Newsom and Sharon H. Ringe, eds., *Women's Bible*

Commentary (expanded ed.; Louisville: Westminster John Knox, 1998) 279–85, here 283; Sheila Shulman, "A Woman of Strong Purpose," in Sybil Sheridan, ed., *Hear Our Voice: Women Rabbis Tell Their Stories* (London: SCM, 1994) 71–80.

17   Linda Bennett Elder, "Judith," in Elisabeth Schüssler Fiorenza, ed., *Searching the Scriptures,* vol. 2: *A Feminist Commentary* (New York: Crossroad, 1997) 455–69.

18   John F. Craghan, "Esther, Judith, and Ruth: Paradigms for Human Liberation," *BTB* 12 (1982) 11–19, here 17.

19   Moore, *Judith,* 65.

20   This quotation is from Nickelsburg, *Jewish Literature,* 1st ed. (1981) 108. In the second edition Nickelsburg broaches the problems in the text that later feminists also perceived (2nd ed., 99–100), on which see below.

serve as a corrective to the sexist mind-set of that day."[21] Di Lella, it should be noted, is comparing Judith to the most conservative strand of wisdom tradition, but Ben Sira is not unique, as the roughly contemporaneous Letter of Aristeas 250–51 indicates:

> The female sex is bold, positively active for something which it desires, easily liable to change its mind because of poor reasoning powers, and of naturally weak constitution. It is necessary to have dealings with them in a sound way.[22]

Di Lella's analysis provided an opportunity for an important dialogue with Dombkowski Hopkins. While the former was tabulating the ways that Judith violates the rules of decorum for a wise *woman*, the latter noted that Judith is also depicted as performing the functions associated with *personified, heavenly Wisdom*, a relatively independent cosmic agent. Dombkowski Hopkins observes that Judith steps out from the shadow of God to run her own show: "Judith pushes herself forward, challenging us to confront her complexity rather than to idolize her piety."[23] There is here almost a Wisdom-against-wisdom reading, the free actions of *heavenly* Woman Wisdom transcending the rules governing the *mortal* wise woman:

> As she moves across the gender spectrum from widow to seductress to soldier, Judith subverts the presuppositions about gender that we bring to the text. . . . Perhaps Judith transcends masculine and feminine altogether as archetypal androgyne, asexual at the beginning and end and merely play-acting seductress and assassin in the middle.

The later Gnostic exploration and ambivalence about a cosmic Wisdom (Sophia) as self-willed agent should be compared at this point, although the latter is more negative.

Van Henten catalogued the ways in which Judith, playing on the memory of Moses, was also a charismatic leader leading a new exodus. Judith's agency is "superior to all male acts," that is, to all the men in Bethulia. Van Henten argues that in this regard the text reflects nearly hidden female voices and may have been written by a woman.[24] Caponigro agreed with van Henten in considering the possibility of a female author for our text.[25] By slaying Holofernes with a sword, Judith evokes David's killing of Goliath and also models herself on Moses. Judith's Song in chap. 16 references the Song of Miriam after Moses's exodus victory. In this way Judith now *leads* a new exodus and gives a new woman's voice to Miriam's lost voice.

Perceiving the narrative play of comedy in the text, André LaCocque also focused on the intertextuality between Judith and *all* biblical women.

> [She is] a panegyric of the biblical woman. . . . Something is happening with Judith that announces a new era. The numerous literary parallels established by the author of the story with so many other Bible women are not just for the sake of comparison. The book grants to them en bloc a heretofore unrealized power through the cumulative effect of synchronism.[26]

By evoking so many biblical women, Judith becomes a palimpsest, even an icon of the "biblical woman," as her

---

21 Di Lella, "Women in the Wisdom," 44–49. Judith's story is in some ways like the *'ēšet ḥayil*, "woman of substance or valor," of Proverbs 31: she is active, not passive; commands others (slaves, not elders!); and it is her mouth, hand, and palm that accomplish many things: "She girds her loins with strength, she steadies her arms." Yet the woman of valor does not transgress any boundaries. On the woman of valor, see Jacqueline Vayntrub, "Beauty, Wisdom and the Poetics of Description" (unpublished manuscript).

22 Translation of R. J. H. Shutt, "Letter of Aristeas," in James H. Charlesworth, ed., *The Old Testament Pseudepigrapha* (2 vols.; New York: Doubleday, 1983, 1985) 2:7–34, here 29.

23 Dombkowski Hopkins, "Judith," 283. The subsequent quotation is from 287 and 290.

24 Van Henten, "Judith as an Alternative Leader," 246; cf. 225. The question of a female author was taken up again by Ellen Juhl Christiansen, "Judith: Defender of Israel—Preserver of the Temple," in Xeravits, *Pious Seductress,* 70–84.

25 Caponigro, "Judith, Holding the Tale." Ilan even suggests that the stories of Judith, Susanna, and Esther provided images of female heroines that might have specifically reflected favorably on the only Judean queen in this period, Salome (Shelamzion) Alexandra (*Integrating Women,* 150–53) (see §2 above). She adds, however, that patriarchal structures in Judean society were not thereby challenged.

26 LaCocque, *Feminine Unconventional,* 35, 38.

name might suggest. Just as synchronic analysis sometimes collapses the original performance context with all of the *subsequent* ones, so also the original performance could collapse together all of the *previous* biblical heroes, especially the women. (See §4 above on Kristeva and intertextuality.) One may question, however, LaCocque's exclusively female focus at this point. Judith evokes as many biblical men—Moses, David, Simeon, in addition to Judah the Maccabee—as biblical women. She also evokes non-Israelite women. For LaCocque, the new era that Judith announces is not just a literary style but a new synthesis in theology. Five hundred years later Jerome asserted that Judith presents a pious, chaste ideal, but LaCocque insists that asceticism, chastity, and widowhood already come together in her original performance situation. Like Hans Jørgen Jensen (see below), LaCocque sees in Judith's mission a self-sacrifice: "Judith substitutes herself as a propitiatory sacrifice," evoking the servant of Isaiah 52–53.[27]

Judith is also similar to Esther in some ways. Both beautiful and courageous, these women risk their lives to save their people by venturing into the banquet-life of foreign potentates. Judith, however, is much more assertive and never runs the risk of eating unacceptable food or having sex with a foreigner. As a result, Adolfo D. Roitman and Amnon Shapira describe Judith as a "reflection story" to Esther, a corrective. Yael Shemesh also sees Judith as a corrective of Jael, since Judith is an Israelite and, by her virtue and widowhood, maintains a sexually untainted relationship with Holofernes.[28] Yet in what sense does Judith function as a "corrective" in these two cases, since they are all three simply alternative interpretations on the theme of woman and power?

Does this novella, then, encourage transgressive behavior? Would pious Jewish women be emboldened to take similar chances, as was suggested in the book of Esther regarding Vashti? Certainly, in the late twentieth century women often welcomed Judith as a courageous sister who decapitated a threatening male figure, as did Artemisia Gentileschi in the seventeenth century. But this assessment is now often questioned. Victor Turner's theories about the untethered world of the liminal state suggest that Judith can perform these outrageous deeds *because* she temporarily inhabits a liminal zone.[29] He argued that the wild and animalistic masks sometimes worn in the highly charged liminal period indicated that in this stage anything was possible. But mundane order was restored when the masks came off and those people were reaggregated into mundane society (see at 9:1–14). Something like this is expressed in the prologue of the erotic Greek romance *Daphnis and Chloe*: "To us, though, may the god grant to write what has happened to others, while we ourselves remain moderate, modest, decent, and chaste" (Prologue).[30] Sociological theories of deviance would press us to similar conclusions. Expressions of deviance do not necessarily move culture into a less bounded zone but may serve instead to mark the boundaries more clearly. The person who deviates from the norms *defines* where the line is *for others*.[31] If the normally pious behavior of an Israelite woman passes over in a liminal state into impious behavior, the clear boundary between the two is reinscribed at the end, *and should not be transgressed by other women*. True, there is an enjoyment for the audience, both women and men, who experience this sojourn, just as would later be the case for the audience of the Greek and Roman novels, but in neither case is the exhilaration allowed to become something permanent. The conservative order is restored.

---

27 LaCocque, *Feminine Unconventional*, 48. See the commentary on 13:9b–10a on the possibility that Judith is not being sacrificed but is, rather, the sacrificer.

28 Adolfo D. Roitman and Amnon Shapira, "The Book of Judith as a 'Reflection Story' of the Book of Esther" (in Hebrew), *Beit Mikra* 49 (2004) 127–43; Shemesh, "'Yet He Committed no Act,'" 159–77.

29 Victor Turner, "Betwixt and Between: The Liminal Period in *Rites de Passage*," in Turner, *The Forest of Symbols: Aspects of Ndembu Ritual* (Ithaca, NY: Cornell University Press, 1970) 93–111.

30 Translation is by Moses Hadas, *Three Greek Romances* (Indianapolis, IN: Bobbs-Merrill, 1953) 3.

31 Jack T. Sanders, *Schismatics, Sectarians, Dissidents, Deviants: The First One Hundred Years of Jewish–Christian Relations* (Valley Forge, PA: Trinity Press International, 1993) 129–51; Helmut Mödritzer, *Stigma und Charisma im Neuen Testament und seiner Umwelt: Zur Soziologie des Urchristentums* (NTOA 28; Freiburg, Schweiz: Universitätsverlag/Göttingen: Vandenhoeck & Ruprecht, 1994) 133–44.

Parallel Developments: A Negative Assessment of Judith and the Embrace of Contradictions

In addition to the positive assessment of Judith by feminist scholars, both male and female, a more negative—or at least ambivalent—trend also developed. Early on, Mary P. Coote insisted that the message of Judith is not particularly feminist: "It is often patriarchal societies, where male and female roles are sharply distinguished and women have a passive role, that in fantasy produce myths of a female savior."[32] Folklorists in other contexts as well have catalogued boundary-crossing women as favorite figures of patriarchal audiences:

Occasionally in folktales there is a toying with the notions of a female religious leader in Islam, an idea characterized by the same attraction-repulsion syndrome that informed the Pope Joan legend in the West.[33]

By the end of the twentieth century, many feminist scholars had begun to find problems with the portrayal of Judith. Betsy Merideth registered reservations in regard to Judith similar to her reservations for Delilah: both stories are anti-woman in assuming that a desire for woman is dangerous for men, as Proverbs and Ben Sira indeed say.[34] This reflects an androcentric view *of* women, *not* a feminist view *by* women. For Fokkelien van Dijk-Hemmes, "Heroines like Esther and Judith fit perfectly into a man-made gallery of ideal femininity."[35] The persona is ironically a comfortable paradigm within male-controlled institutions. To this round of more negative assessments of her role as a feminist icon, Pamela Milne added: Judith is still in servitude to a male God. She may be a female warrior or a femme fatale but is not a "woman-identified woman. . . . In Jdt 9:9–10 she, not the narrator, draws attention to the added ignominy of being defeated by a woman."[36] Alice Bach also:

The tropes of beautiful women seducing men with food or wine and killing them instead of soothing them are basically the same, and in my view represent the generalized male fear of the courtesan as killer.[37]

Two tendencies, then, can be highlighted in feminist research on Judith in the period 1985–1995. On the one hand, Judith's strong-willed agency and strategic transgression of gender codes gave rise to a notion of a heroic Judith who transcends patriarchal rules and roles. On the other hand, her temporary escape of patriarchal restrictions—and this only at a time of national threat—can be interpreted as a titillating but liminal and temporary release of *male* desire and reversals. Yet both single-level readings of Judith—the positive and the negative, the pro-feminist and the anti-feminist or un-feminist—came to be challenged, often viewed as simplistic or dualizing. The assumption of a unitary meaning was de-emphasized, whether that meaning was perceived as pro- or anti-feminist. Perhaps the real impact of her story, it was argued, was the simultaneous, contradictory levels. This corresponded as well to the next stage in the cultural or literary turn in theory: a stronger emphasis on sexuality and gender, the effects of intertextuality, and the affirmation of transgression and theatricality in texts.

Amy-Jill Levine perceived in this text the deliberate confusion and reversal of categories, from an extraordinarily, even exaggeratedly pious widow to a provocative strumpet, and back again. Judith begins hyperseparated from normal female roles (compare here Aseneth); she then speaks brashly to the elders and acts brazenly before

32 Coote quoted in Alonso Schökel, *Narrative Structures,* 26.

33 Warren S. Walker and Ahmet E. Uysal, *Tales Alive in Turkey* (Cambridge, MA: Harvard University Press, 1966) 260.

34 Merideth, "Desire and Danger," 63–78.

35 Fokkelien van Dijk-Hemmes, "Traces of Women's Texts in the Hebrew Bible," in Fokkelien van Dijk-Hemmes and Athalya Brenner-Idan, eds., *On Gendering Texts: Female and Male Voices in the Hebrew Bible* (Biblical Interpretation Series 1; Leiden: Brill, 1993) 17–109, here 31.

36 Milne, "What Shall We Do?," 45–46, 54. Milne

provided even more negative assessments of Judith's violent and dehumanizing decapitation in "Labouring with Abusive Biblical Texts: Tracing Trajectories of Misogyny," in Fiona C. Black, Roland Boer, and Erin Runions, eds., *The Labour of Reading: Desire, Alienation, and Biblical Interpretation* (Semeia Studies 36; Atlanta: Society of Biblical Literature, 1999) 267–83.

37 Alice Bach, *Women, Seduction, and Betrayal in Biblical Narrative* (New York: Cambridge University Press, 1997) 186.

Holofernes, only to retire finally to her extreme seclusion. Says Levine:

> All that remains of the intrusion of Judith's otherness into the public realm is her "fame". . . . [H]er deed becomes incorporated into public memory . . . and it is thereby controlled.[38]

Judith returns to seclusion at the end, and male power is reasserted in the town square. Levine thus entertains both sides of the question:

> [E]ach time her story is told, this woman who represented the community as well as exceeded that representation, will both reinforce and challenge Bethulia's—and the reader's—gender-determined ideology.

But because she is unique and in effect unreal, Judith can be "tolerated, domesticated, and even treasured by Israelite society."

Judith's marginal status as a woman and a widow presents an interpretive problem: although one might assume that she is marginalized, she is presented as a wealthy and powerful woman and regarded as a wise leader of the community. Schmitz notes that the position of wealthy widow allows Judith the freest status that a woman could have, even independence and a choice of lifestyle.[39] In addition, Judith is not just beautiful, but also learned. True, she lacks, as Crawford notes, family position,[40] but she is not hampered by that. Levine even states, "her status, rhetoric, wealth, beauty, and even her genealogy abort the metaphor of widowhood."[41] Yet our heroine is not totally domesticated. The book of Judith sets off a chain of surprisingly deep and complex psycho-logical reactions that defy explanation and compartmentalization. As will be noted in §7 below, the character of Judith is not "complex" in the sense usually associated with the modern novel—character development, a mixture of good and bad elements, self-doubt or uncertainty about her virtue—but her character may be complex in the question she provokes in the audience: are her character traits "good" or "bad"?

Crawford also catalogues the contradictions in the book of Judith, beginning with a positive assessment of the many strong aspects of Judith's character, especially in comparison to Esther, that would challenge the patriarchal order. While Esther finds a way to save Jews by working with the foreign king, Judith very actively *defeats* the foreign king. Esther works in the private quarters and communicates with Mordecai in the public realm, but Judith commands both the public and the private. Esther upholds ancient patriarchal codes, but Judith violates them.

> [I]t is precisely the fact that Esther does uphold the patriarchal social order that helped the book to be accepted eventually as canonical. . . . Unlike Esther, however, Judith subverts the patriarchal social order of the period.[42]

This becomes even more striking when we note what happens to the men in her life. Manasseh, Holofernes, and Achior all succumb to strange, passive ends: "Judith's assumption of the masculine role, and the consequent demasculinization of the men around her, is thus emphasized."[43] Judith's lying also stands in direct contradiction to the warnings of Prov 7:21–23 concern-

---

38 Levine, "Sacrifice and Salvation," 24. The subsequent quotations are from p. 28. Both asceticism and widowhood were later viewed as opportunities for women to exercise some independence, but often within male-ordered structures. In this story, asceticism and widowhood may provide a too-safe haven.

39 Schmitz, "Function of the Speeches," 170, 172.

40 Sidnie White Crawford, "Esther Not Judith: Why One Made It and the Other Didn't," *Bible Review* 18 (2002) 22–31, 45, here 27.

41 Levine, "Sacrifice and Salvation," 19.

42 Crawford, "Esther and Judith," 73; Crawford, "In the Steps of Jael."

43 Crawford, "Esther and Judith," 74 n. 7, a point attributed to Susan Houchins. The other quotations are from p. 75. Note also that the elders are weak and passive as well—in fact, so are all the males in the story except for the high priest in Jerusalem. Richard A. Freund also provides a diachronic analysis of lying in this period ("Lying and Deception in the Biblical and Post-Biblical Judaic Tradition," *SJOT* 5 [1991] 45–61). The LXX translation of the Bible did not filter out the deception practiced by the patriarchs, but Josephus edited out some of the examples of lying and Philo omitted most. Was it Judith's bold lying that kept her out of the Jewish Bible?

ing the strange woman: "With much seductive speech she persuades him." Holofernes's actions follow upon this as predicted in Proverbs: "Right away he follows her, and goes like an ox to the slaughter." "Judith is not subsumed back into the patriarchal order," continues Crawford, and yet Judith does concede to male power at the end by returning to widowhood. It takes Judith out of a real engagement with society: "She makes no special claims on Israel beyond saving it." Crawford still insists that it is Judith's uninhibited persona that was partially responsible for keeping the text from being canonized among Jews: "Judith as a dangerous female must be and is marginalized; this is demonstrated by her exclusion from the Jewish canon." There is a danger, however, of canonizing the Jewish canonizers. We do not know what Jews thought about the "canonical potential" of the book of Judith at the turn of the era. Among Christians, Judith was as fully canonical as the rest of the Apocrypha, and Jerome's negative view of the state of the *text* is often misinterpreted as a negative view about *Judith* (see the appendix below).

This shift toward a complex rendering of gender in Judith became common by the end of the twentieth century, influenced by contributions of scholars from an entirely different area, European art and literature: Mary Jacobus, Mieke Bal, Mary Garrard, Elena Ciletti, Diane Apostolos-Cappadona, and others.[44] They saw in the artistic representations of Judith a changing, challenging, and complex cultural icon. Elena Ciletti comments:

> To study Judith is not only to stray across disciplinary boundaries but also to address the conjunction of nothing less than our central conceptual dualities:

woman–man, virtue–vice, art–artifice, appearance–reality, life–death.[45]

This swerve in the study of European cultural history had a dramatic effect on modern biblical scholarship: the assumptions of diachronic research were temporarily disrupted as insights of a synchronic kind—developments in art and literature from a much later period—were retrojected onto the ancient narrative. One could argue that the new insights from the fine arts were also diachronic, for they were concerned with the precise changes in artistic representation from about 1450 to 1800 and later. But the net effect for both biblicists and art historians was an engagement between synchronic and diachronic, "Judith across time." By the end of the period 1985–1995 an almost universal theme in feminist Judith scholarship was the emphasis on the contradictions, multiple layers, and complexity of the text. In looking back at this period, Yael Shemesh states:

> [I]nitial enthusiasm on finding empowered women in the androcentric literature morphed into adamant criticism of women's roles in the male-dominated texts. The search for middle ground is perhaps the phrase of the day, seeking a compromise between enthusiasm and rejection, with the hope of holding on to the stories regardless.[46]

In a later review article Craven also recognized the new wave of studies at this time that affirmed the coexistence of opposite points of view in the text, ambiguities that served both to sustain and subvert, construct and deconstruct.[47]

---

44   We therefore register even more strongly the important early contributions of scholars in the biblical field like Craven and Alonso Schökel. See also Nira Stone, "Judith and Holofernes: Some Observations on the Development of the Scene in Art," inVanderKam, *No One Spoke Ill*, 73–93.

45   Elena Ciletti, "Patriarchal Ideology in the Renaissance Iconography of Judith," in Marilyn Migiel and Juliana Schiesari, eds., *Refiguring Woman: Perspectives on Gender and the Italian Renaissance* (Ithaca, NY: Cornell University Press, 1991) 35–70, here 38–39. See also §8 below.

46   Shemesh, "The Stories of Women in a Man's World: The Books of Ruth, Esther, and Judith," in Susanne

Scholz, ed., *Feminist Interpretation of the Hebrew Bible in Retrospect*, vol. 1: *Biblical Books* (Recent Research in Biblical Studies 5; Sheffield: Sheffield Phoenix, 2013) 248–67, here 248–49.

47   Craven divided modern Judith scholarship in general, not just feminist scholarship, into three periods: 1913–1949, focusing on R. H. Charles, W. O. E. Oesterley, and R. H. Pfeiffer; 1950–1985 and the new interest in the Apocrypha and Protestant/Catholic/Jewish dialogue; and 1985–2001 and the awakening of critical methods and the cultural turn ("The Book of Judith in the Context of Twentieth-Century Studies of the Apocryphal/Deuterocanonical Books," *CurBR* 1 [2003] 187–229, here 196).

The feminist scholarship that followed assumed a greater complexity of the text and placed at the center of discussion a number of challenging aspects: humor, irony, contradictions and reversals, transgression, but also a liminal escape-and-reconfinement. Bringing diachronic considerations back into the synchronic, questions were also raised about the patriarchal institutions that transmitted the text in each generation. Although at one point early on there may have been a "popular" transmission of the text, for instance, for festival or dinner performances, or simply as a popular text, the only *known* transmission of Judith was through male church figures. Stated simply, for two thousand years, hierarchical churchmen have loved Judith. Even where feminist culture historians have focused on anxiety, ambivalence, or misogyny in depictions of Judith, it must be acknowledged that many representations of Judith over the centuries remained earnest and reverential within a Christian church environment.

This relates as well to the question of the "iconic" nature of Judith, and also the observation of Dombkowski Hopkins that Judith is not so much the wise woman as Woman Wisdom herself. The iconic nature of Judith can be witnessed from an early period in Christianity, when she became identified with Virtue or Mary. Other biblical women cross boundaries, but they are generally *distant* boundaries. Ruth the Moabite crosses geographical and ethnic boundaries, as does Tamar. The most important boundaries that Judith crosses, however, are not the distance between Bethulia and Holofernes's tent—which is not very far—but the *domestic* boundaries of propriety. Most of her activity occurs as she hovers around the near boundaries of everyday Jewish life, darting back and forth across them with ease. The fact that

the story, while quite unbelievable, is given a "realistic" setting (village life in Samaria) with a "realistic" protagonist (a wealthy widow), in a somewhat "realistic" medium (the novella) only serves to accentuate the hovering back and forth over near, realistic boundaries.[48] In the commentary I will argue that there is in play here the ironic interplay between Judith's words and her actions. She *says* that she needs God's assistance, but her *actions* suggest that she does not. She is introduced as simply a pious, wise, beautiful widow, but from the moment that she upbraids the elders she controls both the events and the interpretation. It is a narrative device that suggests that she herself wields a higher perception and agency—*even if, and especially if, it is all in fun.* Toril Moi has theorized that woman can be either a boundary *or* a portal between man and chaos. This can either be a boundary that protects or one that frightens as an opening to chaos: "Women . . . share in the disconcerting properties of all frontiers."[49] By this observation Moi explains both the positive heroine of virtue and the threatening Lilith. Yet I emphasize again: before the early modern period, there is no evidence that Judith was perceived by men as frightening.

Increasingly, scholars now also recognize Judith as a trickster, her transgression turned against a foreign enemy. Indeed, along with the trickster men in the Bible, there are trickster women, such as Rebekah or Tamar, and this is one of the reasons that she can get away with what she does. The deceptive woman in the Hebrew Bible is similar to the deceptive goddesses in the ancient Near East (see §4 above). Corinne Jouanno considers novels like the Alexander Romance and Life of Aesop—roughly contemporaneous with Judith—to be trickster novels.[50] Indeed, in honor/shame cultures, lying is not a vice when defending one's people, while being tricked is a matter

48   "Realism in fiction" is an ironic oxymoron but is so taken for granted in the modern novel that it is difficult for twenty-first century readers to grasp that it had to be invented; see §7 below. On the near boundary and the near Other, see Wills, *Not God's People*, chap. 1.

49   Toril Moi, *Sexual/Textual Politics: Feminist Literary Theory* (New Accents; New York: Routledge, 1988) 167.

50   Corinne Jouanno, "Novelistic Lives and Historical Biographies: The *Life of Aesop* and the *Alexander*

Romance as Fringe Novels," in Grammatiki A. Karla, ed., *Fiction on the Fringe: Novelistic Writing in the Post-Classical Age* (Mnemosyne Supplement 310; Leiden: Brill, 2009) 42–46. Cf. Helen Efthimiadis-Keith below on Jung used in a different way. See also Paul Radin, *The Trickster: A Study in American Indian Mythology* (New York: Schocken, 1972) 202–9; Schmitz, "Trickster," 15; Philip F. Esler, "Ludic History in the Book of Judith: The Reinvention of Israelite Identity?," *BibInt* 10 (2002) 107–43, here 139.

of shame.[51] Judith also achieves a postcolonial triumph, fooling the colonial overlord. "The *menace* of mimicry," says Homi Bhabha, "is its *double* vision which in disclosing the ambivalence of colonial discourse also disrupts its authority."[52]

The trickster theme, combined with many ironic reversals, directly affects how the audience views Judith-as-woman. We begin with the most significant example of ironic reversal in the text. Holofernes intends to penetrate the narrow mountain pass that leads to Bethulia, which may mean Virgin. But "Judith penetrates Holofernes' camp rather than Holofernes penetrating [Bethulia]."[53] Since decapitation can signify castration, Holofernes is also symbolically castrated. Benedikt Otzen adds many other ironic contradictions:

> Judith is a widow, but at the same time she is celibate; Judith is a female, but she acts in all respects as a male; Judith personifies virtue, but moves out into the borderland between decency and moral laxity; Holofernes wants to seduce Judith, but it is Judith who "seduces" Holofernes to death; Holofernes has every intention to go through with the intercourse, but he ends up being impotent by excessive drinking.[54]

He draws out the larger arcs or themes of ironic contrast: good versus evil, male versus female, Israel versus enemies, God versus non-Israelite king. The identification of contradictions noted above (Levine, Crawford) has been extended to include many more, including the juxtaposition of eating and sex as symmetrical operations at the center of our text. Judith parades her sexuality while pointedly eating acceptable Jewish food but reverses this at the point of decapitation by placing the bloody head in her pouch. Food that is proper for Jews to eat is replaced by something defiling that can never be eaten. Upon her return to Bethulia, she exhibits the head and at the same time declares her sexual purity: "He never committed a sin with me" (13:16).[55] The effect of the feminist studies at the turn of the century, in fact, was to recast the discourse of Judith. It was no longer a didactic story of proper actions in a world of conflict but an iconic and symbolic comic performance of the relations of sex and gender.

The question of whether the book of Judith is feminist or not must also depend on the prior definition of feminism. This definition, and the resolution of the question, changed dramatically over the last decades. Most of the commentators since 1995 have adopted a complex view of the text's reception and assume, whether consciously or not, the approaches of Mikhail Bakhtin and Michel Foucault, respectively. A Bakhtinian reading might be defined in this way: novels and the carnivalesque both have a quality of celebrating multiplicity and indeterminacy, although even novels have ideology, as do carnivals. A Foucauldian reading concerning power might be defined in this way: in the cloud of power relations in a society, all actors participate in constructing it and maintaining it, but in different ways.[56] Judith includes a dialogue of voices that may continue to coexist without canceling each other out, and men and women may both participate in the cloud of relationships that define power. Further, men and women may both engage in

51   David A. deSilva, "Judith the Heroine? Lies, Seduction, and Murder in Cultural Perspective," *BTB* 36 (2006) 55–61, here 56–57.

52   Homi Bhabha, *Location of Culture* (London: Routledge, 1994) 88–89.

53   Alan Dundes, response in Alonso Schökel, *Narrative Structures,* 28; Wills, *Jewish Novel,* 148–51.

54   Otzen, *Tobit and Judith,* 111–12; and also Moore, *Judith,* 64–66; Levine, "Sacrifice and Salvation," 19, 25–26; Stocker, *Judith,* 6–10.

55   See Jensen, "Juditbogen," 177–78, who wrote in 1990 in Danish but was little known in English-speaking scholarship until summarized in Otzen, *Tobit and Judith,* 121–22.

56   Bakhtin, *Dialogic Imagination*; Bakhtin, *Rabelais and His World* (Cambridge, MA: MIT Press, 1968) 7–21; Michel Foucault, "Why Study Power? The Ques-

tions of the Subject," in Herbert L. Dreyfus and Paul Rabinow, eds., *Michel Foucault: Beyond Structuralism and Hermeneutics* (Chicago: University of Chicago Press, 1982) 212. On the methodological discussion, see Wills, *Jewish Novel,* esp. 31–32, 111–15, 224–32, 246–47; Wills, "Ascetic Theology before Asceticism? Jewish Narratives and the Decentering of the Self," *JAAR* 74 (2006) 902–25. Howard Eilberg-Schwartz notes that to take cosmetics, coverings, and hair as relevant only to male viewing "is to participate in the process of decapitation, of denying women agency in these practices" ("Introduction: The Spectacle of the Female Head," in Howard Eilberg-Schwartz and Wendy Doniger, eds., *Off With Her Head! The Denial of Women's Identity in Myth, Religion, and Culture* [Berkeley: University of California Press, 1995] 1–14, here 10). See also Luce Irigaray below.

the disciplines of the self that are communicated in the performance of the text. The tendency at the end of the twentieth century toward indeterminacy and multiple layers of meaning in Judith can be highlighted by reference to Mieke Bal. The multifaceted, contradictory nature of the book of Judith can be described by reference to Judith as an "ideo-story," a "narrative whose structure lends itself to be the receptacle, or projection screen, of different, often opposing ideologies which the narrative appears to emblematize."[57]

The ideo-story calls for multiple performances, reimaging, rethinking; Judith's primary function, then, is to serve as a "locus of confusion." Bal argues that indeterminacy can allow room for women's engagement: "when truth is absent women can creep in."[58]

As evidence in favor of considering Judith an ideo-story, one notes that many commentators speak of Judith *the character* as if she somehow existed, or even continues to exist, *as a real persona* outside the text, outside the restrictions placed upon her by the audience, by her patriarchal culture, or even by her author.[59] Judith is spoken of as a figure who exists apart from any (male?) creator. She is not only an agent who saves her people but also an agent who controls the interpretation of her text and confounds interpreters. This is not as illusory a notion as it first sounds. Is it possible for an artist to create something larger than he or she realizes? In twentieth-century New Criticism it was debated whether characters had any existence outside the words of the texts. And it is the audience, and not the author, who respond to the various levels of a text, who transmit or refigure a text, and it is the audience that changes over time. Imagining a supertextual protagonist, even unconsciously, is a sort of interpretive play. Do varied audiences who perceive a Bakhtinian dialogue of levels also imagine a single agent, a Judith who transcends the text and has a higher, controlling perspective? She may not really exist, but she becomes easy to imagine and difficult to silence. Indeed, any strong character in a text can be spoken of as a figure *outside* the text, but *Judith is unusual in the extent to which audiences and commentators have projected a still-existing, supertextual agent,* even though she is a "minor" biblical figure! Judith seems to be more of a supertextual character than Moses or David or Job. That is, some audiences today may find it easier to think of Judith as a continuing, "living" figure who controls the text more than Moses or David.[60]

---

57 Mieke Bal, *On Story-Telling: Essays in Narratology* (Foundations and Facets: Literary Facets; Sonoma, CA: Polebridge, 1991) 13–14; see also Bal, *Murder and Difference: Gender, Genre and Scholarship on Sisera's Death* (Indiana Studies in Biblical Literature; Bloomington: Indiana University Press, 1988) esp. 105.

58 Bal, *Lethal Love: Feminist Literary Readings of Biblical Love Stories* (Indiana Studies in Biblical Literature; Bloomington: Indiana University Press, 1987) 1. The recourse to indeterminacy would be taken up by many, but this avoids a resolution on whether there is a net effect of "more feminist" or "less feminist." Can an ideo-story, like a carnival, still have an ideological effect, a residual political message, if at the end the point is simply, "The fun is over; get back to work"? Bal however, promulgates her own reading as only one distinctive reading (*On Story-Telling*, 17–18). For her there is no final conclusion concerning the feminist message of Judith.

59 See Craven, "Book of Judith in the Context," 208; Nutu, "Framing Judith." Stocker often speaks as though Judith were a supertextual figure: "She is

an image of the autonomy that is constantly being wrested from us all, and an icon of the way to recover it" (*Judith*, 252). Some scholars of literature have spoken of characters as living outside of their texts. Vladimir Nabokov is said to have declared that, in Don Quixote, Cervantes created a character who exceeded in quality the book that made him; see Guy Davenport, "Don Quixote Restored," *New York Times Book Review,* February 13, 1983, https://www.nytimes.com/1983/02/13/books/don-quixote-restored.html. See also E. M. Forster, *Aspects of the Novel, and Related Writings* (London: Edward Arnold, 1974) 67–78. Opposed to such character realism are those who insist that characters are mere "actants," figures required by narrative functions; so Robert E. Scholes, *Elements of Fiction* (New York: Oxford University Press, 1968) 17. Shlomith Rimmon-Kenan, advocates a middle view (*Narrative Fiction: Contemporary Poetics* [New Accents; New York: Routledge & Kegan Paul, 1983] 31–36).

60 An interesting question is the cross-cultural differences in the way audiences think of the heroes of old: are they sequestered in the past, or do they still

The complex, indeterminate nature of the narrative also invited speculation about psychological complexities. Freudian motifs of castration were discerned, but other aspects of phallic reversal as well. Ancient conceptions of sexuality were related to honor and shame: it was honorable for men to penetrate but shameful to be penetrated, and it was a dangerous violation for a woman to take a dominant position with a man. Speaking of the very similar scene in Jael's killing of Sisera, Susan Niditch considers whether female power and castration may reflect a male concern, "a man's fear of both death and his own sexuality, his insecurities, a male fantasy of Eros become Thanatos."[61] So also in Judith, sex and death, Eros and Thanatos, are closely associated. To be sure, Judith is not unique in the Bible or in ancient literature in bringing sex and death into one encounter, nor in placing women in scenes of sex and intrigue.[62] In Xenophon of Ephesus's *Ephesian Tale* 3.8.5, the heroine even moans, "I am a sacrifice to two gods, Eros and Thanatos!" ($\Delta\nu o\hat{\iota}\nu$ $\dot{\alpha}\nu\alpha\kappa\epsilon\acute{\iota}\mu\alpha\iota$ $\theta\epsilon o\hat{\iota}\varsigma$, $\H{E}\rho\omega\tau\iota$ $\kappa\alpha\grave{\iota}$ $\Theta\alpha\nu\acute{\alpha}\tau\omega$). Further, the deceptive woman is common in the Hebrew Bible, although she often serves as God's ironic means of righting things. Yet the power of this narrative device consists precisely in the fact that it is deviant, that it violates normativizing restrictions. The Jael story and our text are unusual, however, in bringing sex and death, Eros and Thanatos, *so closely together* in one character and in one scene—in fact, in just a few verses (Jdt 12:16–13:10). Stocker refers to this scene

in Judith as the "acteme."[63] But in the Hebrew Bible it is mainly foreign women who seduce (Ruth) or who seduce and deceive (Tamar, Potiphar's wife, Delilah, Jael). Is such a charged text liberative of women's roles, or simply charged? Is this a feminist theme or a male fantasy of sexual domination, penetration, and violence?[64]

Even Freudian analyses of the phallic nature of the story have rarely registered that Holofernes's tent may be a vagina symbol. The inner curtain that Judith pulls down to deposit in the temple is perhaps his symbolic hymen. (If Bethulia does mean Virgin, then this irony is even more provocative.) The curtain, with Holofernes's head in it, would have taken on some of his blood, like the bloodstained cloth of the wedding chamber. His head is exhibited on the wall, but the curtain/virginity cloth is deposited in Jerusalem as a spoils offering. While these readings may at first seem to be modern, synchronic intrusions into an ancient text, we note that these resonances are suggested in medieval Near Eastern sources and some European paintings as well. In an Arabic story, evidently an alternative version of Judith, Zenobia captures a drop of the tyrant's blood in a piece of cotton and keeps it among her perfumes.[65]

To get at the feminist nature of Judith, we must also consider whether she may be a personification rather than a strictly human character, in which case her outrageous actions may be understood differently. First, Judith—Hebrew *Yehudit*–may have been understood as

---

act upon those who are audiences of the text? It is possible that in black churches, in the Hasidic Jewish tradition, in the Muslim tradition, in Pentecostal churches, or among Chinese or Latin Americans or South Sea Islanders, some biblical figures may be seen as alive and active in controlling the interpretation of the texts. By channeling Judith's continuing role, are some present-day feminists participating in an interpretive method found among other groups globally? Yet a question remains: Why Judith more than other female figures? Is it her boundary-crossing? Her perceived need for a defender?

61   Niditch, "Eroticism and Death," 51–52. On Freud's equation of decapitation and castration, see his "Medusa's Head," in Philip Rieff, ed., *Sexuality and the Psychology of Love* (New York: Collier, 1963) 202–4.

62   Also see Esther Fuchs, "Who Is Hiding the Truth? Deceptive Women and Biblical Androcentrism," in

Adela Yarbro Collins, ed., *Feminist Perspectives on Biblical Scholarship* (Biblical Scholarship in North America 10; Chico, CA: Scholars Press, 1985) 137–44. Cf. the folklore motif "Death by intercourse," T182 in Thompson, *Motif-Index*, 362.

63   Stocker, *Judith*, 11.

64   For Mary Jacobus, acting out the fear of castration can reassure the male audience members ("Judith, Holofernes, and the Phallic Woman," in Jacobus, *Reading Women: Essays in Feminist Criticism* [New York: Columbia University Press, 1986] 110–36, here 127–28).

65   See §4 above. Some of the bloody, sexual, and sacrificial aspects of the text are treated in a speculative but suggestive way by Susan Kim, "Bloody Signs: Circumcision and Pregnancy in the Old English Judith," *Exemplaria* 11 (1999) 285–307; and Heidi Estes, "Feasting with Holofernes: Digesting Judith in Anglo-Saxon England," *Exemplaria* 15 (2003) 325–50.

"ideal Jewish woman" or even "Jewish heroine." Recall as well that her name suggests a female equivalent to Judah Maccabee (see §4 above). *Yĕhûdî* and related terms, often translated "Jew," are surprisingly fairly rare in ancient Jewish literature, and so this name for the heroine may be more representative. *Yĕhûd-* terms (except for the tribe or province of Judah) are used only four times in the Mishnah, and, interestingly, those uses pertain to women—*yĕhûdît* and *yĕhûdîyâ*. Cynthia Baker notes that, apart from quoting Esther,

[T]he remaining two instances come in passages in which the prospect of a married "Jewish" woman's assertion of sexual autonomy or expression of transgressive sexual subjectivity forms the substance of the tradition. [66]

One of them, m. Ketub. 7:6, states:

These are the wives who are divorced without their *ketubbah*: a wife that transgresses the law of Moses [*dat Moshe*] and the law that pertains to the Jewish woman [*dat Yehudit*, or possibly "Jewish law"]. . . . And what is "the law that pertains to the Jewish woman"? If she goes out with her hair unbound, or spins cloth in public, or speaks with any man.

Other grounds for a woman to be divorced without a *ketubbah* include: cursing her husband's parents to his face, or being a loud or scolding woman. But most important of all, we notice that Judith—Yehudit—gleefully violates almost every aspect of the "law of the *Yehudit*." Though this passage is attested later, one cannot help but notice what it suggests for "Yehudit," Jewish Woman.

In addition, Judith may also be understood as a personification of the kingdom Judah.[67] That is, she is not *saving* her people, she *is* her people—or rather, she represents her people saving her people. An iconographic comparison can be made to other women who represent nations: in the ancient world, Roma and Britannia, and in Europe and the United States, Germania, Italia Turrita, Marianne (France), Columbia, and Liberty.[68] In propagandistic and nationalistic contexts, and especially in public art, the representative female figure can appear seminude, as if she is at that moment giving herself over sexually for her people, even sacrificing herself sexually for her people as a sort of virgin sacrifice, an androcentric reappropriation of Judith for a national agenda. Linda Bennett Elder objects to this identification of Judith as Judah: if this were the only meaning of Judith, it would rob her of any role as an independent woman. This may appear to be special pleading on behalf of a supertextual "Judith," but, be that as it may, Rakel—continuing the investigation of a complex figure—counters that Judith as an icon may operate at several levels simultaneously. "Judith" may *include* a personification as Judah or Israel, but this does not rob the *character* of independent agency.[69] It is in this context that we might also consider other cross-cultural or synchronic depictions

66 Cynthia Baker, "When Jews Were Women," *HR* 45 (2005) 114–34, here 115. See also Baker, "Imagined Households," in Douglas Edwards, ed., *Religion and Society in Roman Palestine: Old Questions, New Approaches* (New York: Routledge, 2004) 113–28. Cf. m. Ned. 11:12; Wills, "Jew, Judean, Judaism"; and Ilan, *Jewish Women*, 129, also quoting m. Ketub. 7:6. On *Yehudit*, see §1 above.

67 Hellmann, *Judit*, 126, 137–38. See also Levine, "Sacrifice and Salvation," 17; Schuller, "Apocrypha," 242; Esler, "Ludic History," 31.

68 As Lefkovitz notes, the deceptive woman in the Bible plays games, "her body a stand-in for the body politic, and her agency an extension of both corporate and divine will" (*In Scripture*, 112). The female bodies representing peoples communicate something other than what Moses's or David's or Judah's bodies do. In Eugène Delacroix's iconic *Liberty Leading the People*, Liberty or Marianne is partially nude, and— more dramatic but less well known—in the entrance of Harvard University's Widener Library there is a large painting by John Singer Sargent commemorating the U.S. soldiers who died in World War I. Above an inscription—"Happy those who with a glowing faith in one embrace clasped Death and Victory"—a U.S. soldier embraces a nude Victory in one arm and a shadowy Death in the other. His mouth is at Victory's breast, his hand holding a bloody bayonet that meets at Victory's vagina. Eros and Thanatos are here intimately and simultaneously experienced.

69 Rakel, "Judith: About a Beauty Who Is Not What She Pretends to Be," in Louise Schottroff, ed., *Feminist Biblical Interpretation: A Compendium of Critical Commentary on the Books of the Bible and Related Literature* (Grand Rapids: Eerdmans, 2012) 515–30, here 520; Elder, "Judith," 457.

that suggest iconic meanings: the Indian goddess Kali or even Wonder Woman.[70]

The examples above of nudity and permissible erotica in public art derive from modern contexts, but in ancient times as well images of military slaughter were invested with sexual overtones. Military conquest was often described in hyper-masculinized language, subjugation in passive and feminized language.[71] Judith enacts a masculinized conquest of a feminized Holofernes. The "acteme" of Judith beheading Holofernes is similar to the somewhat later statue of Claudius overpowering Britannia, though the gender roles are reversed.[72] Following upon this more complex view of the contradictory resonances of the text, many feminist scholars expressed skepticism about assigning our text to a female author, and Rakel even assumes the author is male because Judith is described from a male point of view. The acteme is a very phallic execution, even a "pornographic" mixture of sex and violence.[73] Gera also cannot perceive a female voice in this work and resorts throughout to a male pronoun for the author.

Another way that scholars now approach the depiction of the woman Judith is to reformulate the question: to what extent does Judith exhibit *agency,* especially an agency that could be held up as a model to women? In the text, it is often emphasized that deliverance will come through the hand of Judith, and in both clear and subtle ways the narrative depicts a woman who simply takes charge.[74] Our novella, indeed, depicts a riot of female agency that seems to burst the bonds of patriarchy. The reference to God working through her hand becomes an interesting test case of a multilevel reading of the text. We must distinguish three possible interpretations: (1) the "hand of a woman" is feminist because it affirms that God here works through a woman; (2) the "hand of a woman" is not feminist because it gives all agency over to a male God; or (3) the "hand of a woman" is not feminist because it is ironic; as elsewhere in the Bible, it plays on the *shame* of being killed by a woman. Milne (above) had taken up argument number 2, that Judith gives all agency over to a male God, but it must be granted that Abraham, Moses, David, and Elijah are

---

70 See §8 below; and also Emma England, "Violent Superwomen: Super Heroes or Super Villains? Judith, Wonder Woman and Lynndie England," in Brenner-Idan and Efthimiadis-Keith, *Tobit and Judith,* 242–58; Jill Lepore, *The Secret History of Wonder Woman* (New York: Knopf, 2014).

71 T. M. Lemos, "'They Have Become Women': Judean Diaspora and Postcolonial Theories of Gender and Migration," in Saul M. Olyan, ed., *Social Theory and the Study of Israelite Religion: Essays in Retrospect and Prospect* (Resources for Biblical Study 71; Atlanta: Society of Biblical Literature, 2012) 81–109, here 103–4; Lemos, "Emasculation of Exile," 377–93; S. Tamar Kamionkowski, *Gender Reversal and Cosmic Chaos: A Study on the Book of Ezechiel* (JSOTSup 368; Sheffield: Sheffield Academic Press, 2003) 85; Wills, *Jewish Novel,* 150; Niditch, "Eroticism and Death," 43; Emily Vermeule, *Aspects of Death in Early Greek Art and Poetry* (Sather Classical Lectures 46; Berkeley: University of California Press, 1979) 101–3, 145–78; Rakel, "Judith: About a Beauty."

72 Lemos even argues that Judith's reversal is matched by Daniel's feminization. Daniel does not slay the lions; he calms them by the power of his piety. He longs for a colonial reversal but sympathizes with the foreign kings in Daniel 1–6. And, unlike Judith, he is incapable of engineering reversal himself. He cannot

"conceive of carrying out the violence himself, the centuries of diasporic life have left him emasculated, impotent. . . . He can only project masculine power onto angelic beings" ("'They Have Become Women,'" 105). Rachel Adelman will argue similarly about the feminization of Joseph and the masculinization of Esther (*The Female Ruse: Women's Deception and Divine Sanction in the Hebrew Bible* [Hebrew Bible Monographs 74; Sheffield: Sheffield Phoenix, 2017] 198–230). Somewhat after Judith we encounter the pious male protagonist who suffers, who even remains a *parthenos,* a "virgin," in Philo and in the Greek novels; see Wills, "Ascetic Theology."

73 Rakel, "'I Will Sing,'" 29.

74 See Jdt 9:9–10; 12:4; 13:14–15; 15:10; 16:5; contrast the hand of Nebuchadnezzar in 2:12. See Jan Willem van Henten, "Words and Deeds: Seduction and Power in *Judith* and *Death Proof,*" in Brenner-Idan and Efthimiadis-Keith, *Tobit and Judith,* 226–41. Agency is treated in a more detailed and nuanced way in regard to Acts by Mitzi J. Smith, *The Literary Construction of the Other in the Acts of the Apostles: Charismatics, the Jews, and Women* (PTMS 154; Eugene, OR: Wipf & Stock, 2011), based on theorists such as A. J. Greimas and Michael Halliday.

also unlikely heroes who give agency over to God. In the Bible, the unlikely victor by his actions points to the role of God.[75] There is a Foucauldian sense that "feminist" or "anti-feminist" are far too simplistic, and that a cloud of power relations envelops both the text and the audience. Male and female presences are both represented, but it is a festival of reversal and annihilation of gender boundaries, like Purim, Mardi Gras, or the Indian Holi festival. And recall, Judith has been masculinized and Holofernes feminized. Who is to say that a "man" did not decapitate a "woman"?

The search for multiple layers to the story seems to know no end, with the result that a final assessment about whether the text is feminist seems out of reach. Rakel can be taken as representative: she grants that the text swings between positive and negative assertions about Judith but argues that the (present-day?) female reader should as a result move between trust and suspicion.[76] Judith is forced to play the only roles she has that are provided by patriarchy. Borrowing from Luce Irigaray on beauty and deception, Rakel argues that, by using her beauty, Judith may be feminist within a playing field devised by men: "Mimesis, the deceptive nature of beauty, turns the beautiful woman into a resistance fighter."[77] Rakel recognizes the problem of a feminist hero who uses beauty and sexuality and notes at the same time that Judith uses her brains as well, is even a leader, and tells men what to do. But while this makes her, and not God, the hero, she is not by this necessarily a *feminist* hero.[78] She does not, for instance, identify with the Shechemite women whom Simeon had doubtless raped but rather applauds his action.

Judith and Feminism in the Twenty-First Century

More recent scholars have followed in one of the three categories that have dominated since the 1980s: a single-level assessment of Judith as a moderately feminist work, a single-level reading that denies that the text is feminist, or a multidimensional reading of Judith. In this last group, diachronic and synchronic approaches continue to be merged.

We begin with a single-level interpretation that defends Judith as a feminist text. William Loader is positive about Judith's role as a female agent, albeit with reservations: "Judith is a hero but within a man's world and in service to the God of Israel."[79] Judith is a civic leader, is wise and pious, and even is a theologian. Further,

---

75 Irmtraud Fischer and Bernd Obermayer ("Die Kriegstheologie des Juditbuches als Kondensat alttestamentlicher Sichtweisen des Krieges," in Ulrich Dahmen and Johannes Schnocks, eds., *Juda und Jerusalem in der Seleukidenzeit: Herrschaft, Widerstand, Identität; Festschrift für Heinz-Josef Fabry* [BBB 159; Göttingen: V&R Unipress, 2010] 227–42) and Esler (*Sex, Wives, and Warriors,* 274–99) note the similarity to David/Goliath. Contrast here Milne, "What Shall We Do," 48–55; and van Henten, "Judith as an Alternative Leader," 246. Note also that God's listening to Judith's prayers (4:13) is the only direct action of God; so Sabine van den Eynde, "Crying to God: Prayer and Plot in the Book of Judith," *Bib* 85 (2004) 217–31.

76 Rakel, *Judit–Über Schönheit,* 516. Rakel also notes that Judith's song is in a war-critical tradition (110); God averts war and, in contrast to Nebuchadnezzar's view, does not depend on the male military power tradition. This ignores, however, the distinction between Judith's words and the narrative. The text is a martial, pro-Hasmonean work: Judith assassinates the foreign general, and the Bethulians destroy

the Assyrian army in a massacre; see also Shemesh, "Stories of Women," 266.

77 Rakel, *Judit–Über Schönheit,* 221–27, here 225: "Die Mimesis, der Täuschungscharakter der Schönheit, macht die Schöne zu einer Widerstandkämpferin." See also Luce Irigaray, *This Sex Which Is Not One* (Ithaca, NY: Cornell University Press, 1985). In agreement with van Henten ("Judith as a Female Moses: Judith 7–13 in Light of Exodus 17, Numbers 20, and Deuteronomy 33:8–11," in Fokkelien van Dijk-Hemmes and Athalya Brenner, eds., *Reflections on Theology and Gender* [Kampen: Kok Pharos, 1994] 33–48) Rakel argues (1) that Judith is in the tradition of Moses and David and thereby transcends gender boundaries, and (2) that Judith's condemnation of rape in her prayer is an example of a female voice (248–72). Some of Rakel's points were also anticipated by Levine, "Sacrifice and Salvation," 18–19, and we note as well that Judith's *ambivalence* about rape weakens her condemnation.

78 Rakel, *Judit–Über Schönheit,* 522–25.

79 William R. G. Loader, *The Pseudepigrapha on Sexuality: Attitudes towards Sexuality in Apocalypses, Testa-*

while many feminist commentators assume that Judith's return to seclusion at the end is a relinquishing of power, Loader argues that we read this into a text that does not say it. The return at the end is not necessarily a reduction of her status but merely an honorable retirement.[80] And while cross-culturally the hero often either dies or must depart again to wander alone, there is also a tradition of honored retirement and tomb cult, apparent in the book of Judges (see §3 above). Loader, like Schüssler Fiorenza, rejects the argument that Judith is transgressing established roles for women; rather, Judith's actions are not a revolution in gender roles but strategic choices within real possibilities.

Loader's unitary reading also returns to conclusions similar to those of Bellis and LaCocque. While he grants a level of male voyeurism in Judith, "Judith also owns her own sexual attractiveness, but decides herself how she will express it."[81] He often pauses to ask whether other scholars retroject a post-1500 femme fatale into the original text. In the LXX text there is no evidence of a condemnation of Judith's cosmetizing; her clothes, after all, were hers from the earlier years when she was married. The elders also do not condemn Judith's beautification, although her cosmetizing does not continue when she returns to Bethulia at the end. Loader is adamant that critics should not entertain *any* reference to levels

of meaning not expressed in the text or ascribed to the author's intentionality; the synchronic should not intrude upon the diachronic. His contribution, therefore, is both a single-level reading and methodologically uninfluenced by the cultural turn in theory.

Gera also returns to a unitary reading, but in the more negative stream of van Dijk-Hemmes, Merideth, Milne, and Bach. Even if Holofernes deserves to die, here

> women's beauty and sexuality are dangerous, even fatal to men. . . . The message that women use their beauty to deceive and harm men is not a feminist one. . . . Neither Judith's behavior nor her concerns nor her outlook are those of a flesh and blood woman.[82]

The lesson, then, that beauty and brains are dangerous in a woman, outlives the lesson that Judith used them to defeat an enemy. And if Judith utilized weapons bestowed by patriarchal culture, she is not, as above, a *feminist* hero, but simply a hero. Judith exhibits throughout a strong sense of self-control, which in the Greek philosophy of this period was considered a male trait—and a philosophically heroic male trait at that. Judith's identification with Simeon in his revenge on Shechem for the rape of Dinah (9:2-4) is expressed in the typical language of male outrage and revenge. Rape in ancient Israel was

---

ments, Legends, Wisdom, and Related Literature (Attitudes towards Sexuality in Judaism and Christianity in the Hellenistic Greco-Roman Era; Grand Rapids: Eerdmans, 2011) 211–13. Nickelsburg agrees (*Jewish Literature*, 100). Nutu ("Framing Judith," 117–18) is similar to Loader, although with more methodological sophistication: "Judith's character is more complex than Esther's and one cannot escape the fact that Judith kills, and she does so sword in hand. . . . Judith's weapon, the sword of her enemy, is both male and political." Two other positive readings of Judith's role for women are by Pierre Johan Jordaan, "Reading Judith as Therapeutic Narrative," in Johann Cook, ed., *Septuagint and Reception: Essays Prepared for the Association for the Study of the Septuagint in South Africa* (VTSup 127 (Leiden: Brill, 2009) 335–46; and Zonia C. Narito, "The Book of Judith," in Lee Oo Chung et al., eds., *Women of Courage: Asian Women Reading the Bible* (Seoul: SaDang, 1992) 53–62. Adelman would point out that Esther, like Judith, also finds her own agency in the text (*Female*

Ruse, 198–230); after telling Mordecai what to do, she works within the Persian palace to save the Jews.

80 Crawford also notes that Judith's return is not without power: she retains status and wealth, and she frees her slave to become the estate manager ("Esther and Judith," 75). A manumitted slave would normally become a client to the patroness. Yet should managing an estate through a slave or a client be considered "feminist"?

81 Loader, *Pseudepigrapha*, 193, 200–201. Loader grants that Vulgate Judith 10:4 reflects a shift on this question: her beauty proceeded from virtue.

82 Gera, *Judith*, 103, 109; see also 101. While Ilan (*Integrating Women*, 127–53) had dated Judith precisely to the reign of Alexandra Shelamzion (= Salome, 76–67 BCE) as a championing of the reign of a queen, Gera avers correctly that this is too precise. Gera does grant, however, that Judith is a proud declaimer of theological truths (104–5), rare for a woman in Jewish texts.

perceived as an offense against the father, brother, or male redeemer rather than an offense against the female victim, and Judith is no different; she simply assumes the male perspective of Simeon. Judith even celebrates the fact that Shechemite women were taken away captive by Simeon. Through copious comparisons to warrior women in Greek tradition, Gera also fleshes out the early observation of Montley that Judith is a quite typical phallic woman warrior.

Gera, then, engages a single-level reading of Judith, but, unlike Loader, draws a negative judgment on its femininsm. Also unlike Loader's work, Gera's study is not methodologically prior to the cultural turn, though she is unconvinced by the arguments of a transgressive Judith. One might counter that Gera undervalues the irony in the text and underemphasizes the distinction between Judith's words and her narrative actions, the "libretto" and "music" (although she does recognize this distinction: 102, 105–7, 311, 318). It may in fact be humorous that Judith prays to God as she coolly hacks Holofernes's neck twice and places the bloody head in her food pouch.[83] It could also be argued that, as a woman, Judith *must say* certain things that Moses or David is not required to say: she *must* invoke God, and she *must* say that she was not defiled by Holofernes.[84] Is the character

of Judith, then, less three-dimensional than that of Moses or David because of their flaws? Are they cherished more than she because of their flaws? As male heroes, do they have the privilege of flaws?

Several recent studies advocate a multilevel interpretation. Deborah F. Sawyer, like Montley, first notes the alternation of female, male, and ungendered moments in Judith's self-presentation and incorporates the theory of Irigaray and Judith Butler to address this process of gender subversion. According to Irigaray, a female agent can choose to take on male or female gender roles by a process of *mimesis*, usually translated as "imitation," but here more like parody—even theatricality or transvestism:

> The ideas of Irigaray and Butler allow us to interrogate the figure of Judith in more fluid terms, liberating us from defining the character at the polarities of a given binary gender construction. . . . [Judith], as encountered and perceived by Holofernes, enacts what woman might be expected to be, but as a *mimesis* of that category, she parodies and subverts the given boundaries. [She] performs gender across a spectrum of possibilities. . . . [T]he elusive figure of Judith offers us a subversive, even anarchic, paradigm of gender

---

83 Linda Day also posits a disjunction between Judith's attribution of power to God and her own agency ("Faith, Character and Perspective in Judith," *JSOT* 95 [2001] 71–93, here 86–90). Loader is robbing the text of irony when he insists that there is no *explicit* distinction to be found here (*Pseudepigrapha*, 205 n. 266).

G. Miller also brings a negative judgment against Judith's actions but will ultimately raise the issue of the second level of interpretation: Judith's actions need not be defended because "she serves a symbolic function in the story, speaking and acting in ways meant to recall Israel's ultimate hero: Yahweh" ("Femme Fatale," 226, 231–32). Yet Miller's negative judgment, for instance, that Judith is more interested in vengeance than in protecting her people (9:2), perhaps misses the nature of tribal structures, where the *gô'ēl* engages in honor killing to protect the kin. Two other scholars provide similar negative judgments without recourse to a second level. Michael Wojcieschowski refers to her killing as a "terrorist murder" ("Moral Teaching of the Book of

Judith," in Xeravits, *Pious Seductress*, 84–96, here 86), and Day notes that Judith bathes even though people are dying of thirst and chases fleeing Assyrians, which will endanger Bethulians ("Faith, Character," 90). Miller, Wojcieschowski, and Day, however, may be invoking too strict a doctrine of moral consistency. This text is an operetta of symbolic actions and arias; not to give chase, for instance, would miss the stage setting of ancient warfare.

84 Other feminists had noted the problem that at crucial points in the narrative—points where Judith was about to step outside of a woman's typical role—she reminds the audience that God is the source of her strength. Stocker points out that Judith's feminist defeat of the patriarch ruler Nebuchadnezzar/Holofernes could seem to challenge God's rule also (*Judith*, 8–9; but see also 23). "This is why, despite its own thematics, the Book of Judith cannot afford to be feminist. It stresses that it is not Judith, but God, who has killed Holofernes—'by the hand of a woman.'"

play evident within the patriarchal meta-narrative of biblical tradition.[85]

David Noel Freedman and Schmitz, it should be noted, also use terms like "vamp" to describe our protagonist. In addition, says Sawyer,

> Judith's actions in the narrative demonstrate how gender-games could be utilized by an ancient writer to produce his desired purpose. By creating a character that represented a counter-culture, by moving the figure to and fro across the gender spectrum, the power of the deity is made absolute.[86]

The male God allows the woman Judith to move outside of the gender codes to do *his* will. Sawyer grants that Judith attains a great deal of autonomy in her mode of life and in her actions to save Bethulia. Judith's autonomy derives from her radical piety; it allows her to command the elders, to violate gender roles; to sojourn in the wilderness; and to lie, seduce, and kill. In addition, while other biblical women were powerful in terms of their ability to produce offspring—Sarah, Rebekah, Rachel, Tamar, Naomi, and Ruth—Judith is powerful in her own agency; she is childless and makes no attempt to alter or explain this.[87]

While some—Milne, for instance—see Judith as a mere servant of a male God, Sawyer emphasizes that Judith carefully uses language to skirt God's agency and even relegate God to the status of witness to her agency: "*Look* this hour on the work of *my* hands. . . . Now indeed is the time to help *your inheritance* and to carry out *my design*" (13:4–5).[88] Judith may be depicted as executing her own plan. A challenge to Sawyer, however, may lie in the fact that Judith's ability to ignore gender restrictions, or to journey out alone, is a typical part of the hero paradigm. The motif of Achilles disguised as a woman, for instance, absent in the *Iliad* but common elsewhere, became as popular in European art, drama, and music as Judith playing the vamp. Alternatively, the text may express a typical function of the carnivalesque, the festival time in which people may temporarily explode social codes of all sorts.

The performativity of Judith, then, consists in the fact that she acts out different gender games, and, by having power to hover back and forth over the boundaries,

---

85 Deborah F. Sawyer, "Gender Strategies in Antiquity: Judith's Performance," *Feminist Theology* 28 (2001) 9–26, here 23. See Irigaray, *This Sex*; Judith Butler, *Gender Trouble: Feminism and the Subversion of Identity* (Routledge Classics 36; New York: Routledge, 2006). One thinks also of Bhabha's colonial mimicry and hybridity (above). Freedman is quoted in Moore, *Judith,* 186; and see Schmitz, "Trickster," 4–5.

86 Deborah F. Sawyer, "Dressing Up/Dressing Down: Power, Performance, and Identity in the Book of Judith," *Theology and Sexuality* 15 (2001) 23–31, here 29–30. On Judith's autonomy, see also Adele Reinhartz, "Better Homes and Gardens: Women and Domestic Space in the Books of Judith and Susanna," in Stephen G. Wilson and Michel Desjardins, eds., *Text and Artifact in the Religions of Mediterranean Antiquity: Essays in Honour of Peter Richardson* (Studies in Christianity and Judaism 9; Waterloo, ON: Wilfrid Laurier University Press, 2000) 325–39, here 327. Judith's tent is her first zone of autonomy; it is contrasted with the thick walls of Ecbatana, though ironically much stronger. It also "demonstrates her independence of male control and protection."

87 Sawyer, "Gender Strategies," 19. Cf. Wis 3:13; 4:1 on voluntary childlessness, and see Wills, "Ascetic Theology," for the context that might draw Judith and Wisdom of Solomon together on this point. Sawyer, like Schüssler Fiorenza, normalizes Judith's actions to some extent: Judith's independence as a wealthy woman is similar to new developments in Rome beginning in the third century BCE, and her freedom in regard to gender codes is mirrored by the male *galli*, the priests of Magna Mater, who castrate themselves and wear women's clothes (17–18, 23). Jeremy Corley nuances this in an interesting way: Judith *begins* by performing deeds like a typical biblical woman but *ends* by performing deeds like the women's male counterparts, "from Sarah to Abraham, from Dinah to Simeon, from Miriam to Moses, from Delilah to Samson, and from Abigail to David" ("Judith," in James K. Aitken, ed., *T&T Clark Companion to the Septuagint* [London: T&T Clark, 2015] 222–36, here 231–32).

88 Sawyer's translation ("Gender Strategies," 19–20). Sawyer references the observation of Elder ("Judith," 449): Judith's theology is similar to Job 38. Yet Sawyer also adds: while in Job 38 it is God who speaks, here Judith speaks for God. Cf. Rakel, *Judit–Über Schönheit,* 46; Rakel, "Judith: About a Beauty," 517.

she subverts them. It is a performed parody of gender constructions. But ultimately, Sawyer suggests that Judith is not that disruptive of patriarchal processes:

> Judith embodied in female form . . . presents a safe counterpart to the male God. She can be safely elevated without any risk of phallus rivalry.[89]

And elsewhere:

> The author uses the device of unconventionality to subvert the reader's expectations, but his purpose is incidentally and not ultimately anarchic. The use of the female hero allows for God to act in the most unexpected fashion. . . . Rather than an anarchic outcome, however, what eventually emerges is confirmation of the limitless power of the deity.[90]

Helen Efthimiadis-Keith authored an article that offered multidimensional readings of the feminism of Judith. She tries to hold the male and female aspects of Judith, along with other contradictions, in relation. The conscious mind in general seeks to impose a single-level evaluation of the messiness of history and morality. Patriarchal culture (at least since the Renaissance) often dismisses Judith on both historical and moral grounds, but Efthimiadis-Keith notes that many feminist scholars also impose a similarly single-level reading, arguing that Judith is either lacking a fully feminist moral position or is "a feminist triumph within the ancient literature of its time."[91] Efthimiadis-Keith counters these warring, single-level readings by recourse to Jungian concepts of dream, myth, and the unconscious. By moving to a more mythical level, our text can maintain multiple possibilities at once. Single-level assessments, asserts Efthimiadis-Keith, even feminist readings, may be patriarchal in that they force a dualistic value judgment on a text that expresses multiplicity; they close meaning and, "in closing meaning for others, we are essentially closing meaning for ourselves."

Finally, Benjamin G. Wright and Suzanne M. Edwards proffer a multidimensional interpretation, but without reference to the Jungian key.[92] They argue that earlier attempts to impose a single-level reading, whether a positive or negative assessment, are limited and fail to recognize the contradictory responses that the text elicits in the audience. Multiple levels are in play at the same time, and, as a result, *each* is unsettled. Indeed, a "higher" perspective emerges that is "associated with Judith herself": "To take Judith's interpretive scheme seriously is to open up new avenues. . . . [S]he critiques the very construction of gendered embodiment in which she appears as an exemplary figure."[93] Judith herself embraces multiplicity, overcoming even the text's own assertion of her chastity and final seclusion. Wright and Edwards thus invoke the same supertextual Judith noted above, the female agent behind the story performance who oversees the interpretation, even though they would grant that she never really existed. Practically alone in actually naming this very common interpretive trope, they assert that the supertextual Judith "herself" critiques the narrow reader who would limit her potential to a single-level reading. The character of Judith is so active and so vocal, so adept at establishing herself—in short, so self-willed—that the anonymous author rendered Judith's character as though a real person. And unlike, say, Pip, Judith not only exists as a character outside the text but even seems to have authority over the interpretation—and is still at work.

Wright and Edwards focus, for instance, on Judith's

---

89 Sawyer, "Dressing Up," 30.

90 Sawyer, "Gender Strategies," 14–15.

91 Helen Efthimiadis-Keith, "Judith, Feminist Ethics and Feminist Biblical/Old Testament Interpretation," *Journal of Theology for Southern Africa* 138 (2010) 91–111, here 93, 100; the following quotation is from 109. It is rightly noted here that Stocker also makes different sorts of judgments about the feminism of our text.

92 Benjamin G. Wright and Suzanne M. Edwards, "'She Undid Him with the Beauty of Her Face' (Jdt 16.6): Reading Women's Bodies in Early Jewish Litera-ture," in Xeravits, *Religion and Female Body*, 73–108, here 79–84.

93 Wright and Edwards, "'She Undid Him,'" 87–89, 103–5. Claude Lévi-Strauss also argued that contradictions coexist in a mythical narrative that are nevertheless reconciled in a stable but more hidden message ("The Stuctural Study of Myth," in Lévi-Strauss, *Structural Anthropology* [New York: Basic Books, 1963] 206–31). For another discussion that emphasizes the multiple natures of Judith, here in French literature, see Poirier, *Judith: Echos.*

beauty. Her beauty is first described *after* her piety is emphasized; it is a "natural" beauty that *results from* her piety.[94] But she undergoes a transformation by bathing, dressing, and applying cosmetics to achieve a *seductive* beauty. The natural or artless beauty that first arose in Bethulia is contrasted with the artificial beauty that was afterward enhanced with cosmetics and clothes (10:4). The Assyrians view her in this second state, and, unlike the Bethulians, their perception of her physical beauty comes *before* they perceive her wisdom. Different perspectives on Judith's beauty are thus presented, but which is her "real" beauty?

> In this sense, the Jews' strategies for reading Judith's body and words as manifestations of her submission to God are as flawed as the Assyrians' belief that her body and words witness her submission to Holofernes's desire.[95]

The Bethulians and the Assyrians both err in seeking a unified, stable, single-level meaning in her body.

Single-level readings are limiting not only for the audience, Wright and Edwards assert; they are also limiting for characters in the text. The Bethulians have a single-level reading of Judith; if they were left to their own devices, this would have led to their demise. The Assyrians also have a single-level reading, and this does lead to their destruction. The reader is thus alerted, *by the text,* to move to a higher perspective. The Bethulians themselves also experience a moment of recognition when they see her made up, witnessing the even greater beauty that the cosmetics bring out in her. "The leaders of the city, so accustomed to seeing a flesh that embodies faith in precisely the way they expect, see her beauty—now sexualized—as if for the first time."[96] But as Loader had asked, where did the clothes and cosmetics come from? They are not items reserved for prostitutes or foreign

women, but the clothes from her previous life as the wife of a wealthy man. But Judith's transformation is yet another of the improbabilities of the text. The reversals, double levels, and irony of the text give rise to a situation in which multiple Judiths are available to the audience at the same time. Wright and Edwards correctly note that associating Judith with trusting faith, on the one hand, or deceitful sensuality, on the other, is "equally misogynist."[97]

By adducing comparisons to other texts of the period, Wright and Edwards also provide a crucial corrective to the argument that the "cultural turn" in studies of Judith imposes modern sensibilities on an ancient text. The gender and sexual issues observed by modern scholars are identifiable in ancient texts as well. Wright and Edwards first discuss the ancient single-reading masculinist texts Ben Sira and Wiles of the Wicked Woman (4Q184) from Qumran. The woman of *Wiles*, for instance, though modeled on the "strange woman" of Proverbs 2, 5, 7, 9, exercises her wiles in a much murkier fashion. This text describes an unreservedly wicked woman *who does just the things that Judith does* (compare the "law of the Jewish woman" above in Mishnah Ketubot). In contrast to *Wiles*, the Genesis Apocryphon (1QapGen), like Judith, calls forth multiple readings.[98] It is approximately contemporaneous with Judith, probably from the same general locale, and is also a novelistic treatment of some of the characters from Genesis. It also confirms that this is precisely what ancient novels often do.

We draw this section to a close by noting that the Greek and Roman novels also play on the element of transgression, and several are fully satiric novels: Heliodorus's *Ethiopian Story* and Longus's *Daphnis and Chloe* among the Greek novels, as well as the Roman *Golden Ass* by Apuleius and *Satyricon* by Petronius.[99] In the Greek novels, the active roles of the female protagonists are matched by the passive and emotional male

---

94   Cf. Schmitz, "Trickster," 15: "Judits Schönheit ist Ausdruck ihrer Gottesfurcht und Weisheit." The beauty of Greek novel protagonists is associated with their virtue and innocence, but does not result from it. Beauty had not been a required trait of earlier biblical women, but by the time of Esther, Judith, Susanna, the matriarch Sarah in *Genesis Apocryphon*, and Aseneth, it is as essential as the beauty of Greek protagonists, both male and female.

95   Wright and Edwards, "'She Undid Him,'" 85–88.

96   Wright and Edwards, "'She Undid Him,'" 85–87.

97   Mieke Bal has a similar perspective regarding the history of art ("Head Hunting: 'Judith' on the Cutting Edge of Knowledge," *JSOT* [1994] 3–34, here 12–13).

98   Wright and Edwards, "'She Undid Him,'" 89–96. Gera also considers the strange woman of Proverbs 1–9 (*Judith,* 289). Judith, intriguingly, shares qualities of both Wisdom and the strange woman.

99   Some fragments as well play on the satirical or transgressive model. Stephens and Winkler often reference the "criminal-satiric fiction" of some of the

characters—here one thinks of Achior. Further, outlandish transgression characterizes the Life of Aesop, an important comparandum for Judith.[100] What Judith does for women, Aesop does for slaves. In both the Jewish texts and the Greek and Roman, we may wonder whether women or slaves are any better off at the end than at the beginning. In the performances of both groups of texts, however, we may also wonder whether in the audience men and women, slaves and free, *heard* different registers in the story and *stole* different moments of triumph.[101] In both cases, was the transgressive romp possible because society was *comfortable* with the status quo or *anxious* about it?

novels, the protagonists' transgression of laws and mores as humorous and outlandish (*Ancient Greek Novels*, 7). It was earlier thought to be the staple of Latin fiction, but now papyri reveal it in Greek as well.

100 For a translation, see Lawrence M. Wills, *The Quest of the Historical Gospel: Mark, John, and the Origins of the Gospel Genre* (London: Routledge, 1997) 180–215.

101 As Keith Hopkins has argued for Aesop, "Novel Evidence for Roman Slavery," *Past and Present* 138 (1993) 3–27.

In twentieth-century scholarship, the theology of the book of Judith was treated as typical of the Jewish texts of the period. Covenant theology is expressed often, and Judith is said to possess wisdom and intelligence, *sophia* and *synesis*. Like the other early Jewish novellas, it exhibited a heartfelt and conventional Jewish piety. There are few theological innovations here, and in Judith one will not find surprises on the level of explicit theology. This was at times acknowledged with disappointment. Judith's religious views, says Moore,

> while neither felicitously nor memorably expressed, are nonetheless quite clear, namely, retributive justice, God's omnipotence and omniscience, the true basis of might and power, the central importance of Jerusalem and its Temple, and God's universality. . . . If most, or at least many, of the important ideas of Judaism exist in Judith, that is all they really do, that is, they do not seem alive and vibrant.[2]

Indeed, Judith, like Esther and Tobit, may have achieved a canonical status among Christians based on its popular appeal rather than any original theological message. As a result, many of the most engaged and challenging treatments of Judith of the last fifty years have concentrated more on the narrative aspects of the text than the strictly theological. Because it has been part of the Christian canons, one also occasionally senses a duty among scholars to find the nugget of theology that would justify its inclusion as a "biblical" text.[3] The hunt for a theological theme may at times have a conservative edge, an attempt to protect Judith from being treated as "pure story" or, worse, "entertainment." The theological kernel that was

sometimes put forward was the heroine's insistence that one cannot set a deadline when praying to God for deliverance, or the assurance that God is not punishing Israel but only testing (8:11–27).

In the last half of the twentieth century, however, a number of scholars found more indirect theological themes expressed. While an explicit discipline can be found in the book of Proverbs or in Ben Sira, and biblical history provided moral models for God's plan for Israel, popular stories allowed for a freer creation of, on the one hand, symbolically coded threats to Jewish life—adultery, idolatry, foreign rule—and, on the other hand, a model for overcoming them, a "lifestyle for diaspora."[4] In addition, as studies of Israel's wisdom tradition turned to the role of wisdom in narratives, from the Joseph story in Genesis to the Daniel and Esther court narratives to the theology of the book of Ruth, this text was seen as illustrative of the Israelite wisdom tradition. Even Judith, who was brash, sexually provocative, deceitful, and ultimately cool and violent at the same time, could be considered an agent of God's wisdom, displaying her wisdom and intelligence, *sophia* and *synesis*.

Some have found important connections between Judith and wisdom narratives or wisdom heroes in Israel. Tal Ilan perceives in Joseph, the slave who dares to refuse his lady's sexual advances, the model of Judith, Susanna, and Esther; they all share a story of moral courage and reversal.[5] Here God's intervention is not in obvious miracles but in the decisive action of wise servants of God. For Susan Niditch, wisdom heroes in Jewish tradition, from Joseph to Judith and Esther, reflect

---

1   For the reception history of Judith before 1900, see §8 below.

2   Moore, *Judith,* 194–95; see also 60–61; Craven, *Artistry and Faith,* 114; Otzen, *Tobit and Judith,* 68–69, 98–99. We note, however, that resurrection of the body, central in both Daniel and 2 Maccabees, is not found in Judith (Malka Simkovich, "The Book of Judith: A Fantasy Alternative Narrative to 2 Maccabees" (paper, 2013) 11.

3   David A. deSilva, *Introducing the Apocrypha: Message, Context, and Significance* (Grand Rapids: Baker, 2002) 99–102. Ellen Juhl Christiansen argues that our text justifies all resistance to an outside force ("Judith: Defender of Israel," 70–84)—but was that view ever part of a theological dialogue?

4   W. Lee Humphreys, "A Life-Style for Diaspora: A Study of Esther and Daniel," *JBL* 92 (1973) 211–23. Judith, to be sure, is not likely a diaspora text, nor is it a court narrative, but its genre was created in the same crucible; see Wills, *Jew in the Court,* passim; and Wills, "Jew, Judean, Judaism."

5   Ilan, *Integrating Women,* 148, 150–51. Michael P. Carroll ("Myth, Methodology and Transformation in the Old Testament: The Stories of Esther, Judith, and Susanna," *SR* 12 [1983] 301–12) has applied the work of Claude Levi-Strauss to suggest that Esther, Judith, and Susanna reflect transformations of the same myth.

clever, behind-the-scenes manipulation of those of higher status to secure oneself benefits. . . . The wisdom heroes and heroines seek to become part of the system that threatens them . . . and enjoy being part of the establishment, deriving much benefit from it.[6]

There is a parallel here, but Judith's foray into foreign power is intentionally brief; she destroys the power that she infiltrates.

Linda Bennett Elder examines some of the details of the wisdom tradition and argues that Judith demonstrates in her actions and character the very education in wisdom that is reflected in the contemporary Ben Sira.[7] The wise male sage in Ben Sira searches out the wisdom of the ancients, takes a stand in the throng of the elders, returns an answer in time of need, prays, is prepared to serve before the great rulers, and travels through the lands of strange peoples to test the good and evil among them. According to Elder, Judith displays all of these traits except the first, searching out the wisdom of the ancients. Still, Elder may exaggerate the institutional wisdom of Judith and downplay the folkloristic or novelistic nature of the story. First, while Israel's wisdom texts affirmed that abiding in God's wisdom would result in long life, children, and wealth, our novella challenges this correlation: Manasseh has wealth but neither long life nor children, and Judith has wealth and long life but no children. Second, Judith violates more protocols of wisdom than she observes. When Judith stands, for instance, in the throng of elders, it is to browbeat them and shame them into changing their course of action. Like the young upstart Daniel in Susanna, she brings the feckless elders to a higher standard.

Elder also attributes to Judith a knowledge of military strategy and history, but the wellspring of our story may rather be the pluck and cleverness of the trickster, not the skilled mastery of the sage. A distinction between wisdom and cleverness in Israel applies here.[8] Novelistic works take on a certain power *precisely* from the violation of expectations, especially the transgressive actions of virtuous protagonists. Without the extraordinary, there is no story. In the two cases of Judith and Daniel, the brash protagonist breaks the normal rules of wisdom to fulfill God's higher purpose, a purpose that the protagonist alone understands. Yet in the very act of violating the norms, the brash protagonist also reinscribes them for the audience. Deviant acts may reenforce the conservative norms that they break. (See §5 above on the carnivalesque.) The didactic effect is still quite strong. There is a general association of Judith with attributes of Israelite wisdom, even though the story itself places the strong heroine at odds with conservative wisdom. Her "wisdom and intelligence," it is true, may act as a sort of inoculation, the armor that protects her from condemnation, much as Jerome's translation would later insert language about her chastity (see appendix)

Deuteronomistic theology has also been found in Judith but should not be read in the traditional way of the prophets and history books. There Israel and Judah had fallen because they had forsaken God. Efthimiadis-Keith allows that Deuteronomy 28 and Deuteronomic theology serve as the backdrop to Judith, but she argues that this is precisely what the author *counters*.[9] In Judith, the approach of an invented empire on the horizon is *not* explained as a result of Israel's sin. Although the

---

6   Niditch, "Esther: Folklore, Wisdom, Feminism and Authority," in Brenner, *Feminist Companion to Esther*, 26–46, here 41.

7   Linda Bennett Elder, "Judith's *Sophia* and *Synesis*: Educated Jewish Women in the Late Second Temple Period," in Linda Bennett Elder, David L. Barr, and Elizabeth Struthers Malbon, eds., *Biblical and Humane: A Festschrift for John F. Priest* (Scholars Press Homage Series 20; Atlanta: Scholars Press, 1996) 52–70. Di Lella also traces some interesting parallels between Ben Sira's treatment of wisdom and Judith's embodiment of it, while at the same time noting Judith's violations of Ben Sira's gender codes ("Women in the Wisdom"). In §5 above I treated the question of whether Judith is acting out the role not

of the model woman but of Woman Wisdom herself, the helpmate of God.

8   On the difference between wisdom and cleverness, the Joseph type and the Jacob type, see Wills, *Jew in the Court*, passim.

9   Helen Efthimiadis-Keith, "Genealogy, Retribution and Identity: Re-Interpreting the Cause of Suffering in the Book of Judith," *Old Testament Essays* 27 (2014) 860–78, here 875. To be sure, Anssi Voitila ("Judith and Deuteronomistic Heritage," in Hanne von Weissenberg, Juha Pakkala, and Marko Marttila, eds., *Changes in Scripture: Rewriting and Interpreting Authoritative Traditions in the Second Temple Period* [BZAW 419; Berlin: de Gruyter, 2011] 369–88, here 378–81) and Nolte and Jordaan ("Ideology and Inter-

Bethulians have jumped to the conclusion that they are being punished for their sins (7:28), Judith insists rather that Israel has not fallen (8:18). For the audience, of course, this reads as a celebration of the contemporary Hasmonean rule but in no way challenges the older Deuteronomistic theology.

Others have looked outside Deuteronomistic theology and the conservative wisdom books of Proverbs and Ben Sira. Haag was one of the first scholars to perceive in the book of Judith an extended parable, an unreal story that depicted a theological struggle between a foreign king who arrogates the role of a god and the true, living God who protects the people.[10] Nebuchadnezzar becomes a transhistorical figure who stands for all who oppose Israel. Haag discerns a well-developed theological exploration that resonates with themes from Daniel and Esther, and this parable stands within an Israelite tradition, specifically the tradition of exodus and Deuteronomistic and penitential theology. Further, the dysfunctional, blustery general is marked by foolishness, while Judith is marked by wisdom. Irony functions to mark out the two sides in what was perceived in Israel as a continuing struggle. If irony includes a perception by the audience of truths that the characters cannot see, then it can also imply the providence of God. The wisdom tradition and the Deuteronomistic tradition are thus perceived in the plot.

Haag's reading of the text as a parable also allowed him to account for the historical absurdities.[11] The author's telescoping of historical epochs and geographical regions suggests a "universal extension," a "metahistory" or mythologized history, ultimately based on Gog's attack in Ezekiel 38–39. There is no particular enemy in mind, but all enemies throughout the ages. The parable is eschatological in that at the end of the metahistory the kingdom of God arrives, as in Daniel 2 and 7. In addition, the geographical setting now encompasses the entire known world (understood as the *Persian* Empire; Greece lies in the future in this historical fantasy). Zenger followed suit. The known world history of the Judeans was "theologically transcendentalized," even though it was still emplotted in a pseudo-historical text. This is even communicated in some of the grandiose verbiage, such as the use of *pas* forty-three times in chaps. 1–3.[12]

The central theme that Haag discerned—that our text is a parable of the conflict between God and the idolatry of foreign empires—was found by other scholars in numerous individual passages. In Jdt 9:9 Holofernes relies on his army in contrast to Israel's reliance on God, and Rakel notes that here Nebuchadnezzar's *hyperēphania* ("arrogance") is contrasted with God's love for the lowly. Stephen Ryan relates the parabolic history to a developed theology of hope.[13] In Greek tradition, hope is a simple expectation and desire, but *elpis* in the LXX is influenced by Hebrew *bāṭaḥ* and means confidence and assurance, with God as the object and hope as certain and even efficacious. Judith echoes the Israelite tendency to elevate hope to a theological and metahistorical category.

---

textuality") see Judith as in line with Deuteronomic theology.

10 Haag, *Studien*, 27 n. 104.

11 Haag, *Studien*, 16–18, 71–78.

12 Zenger, *Das Buch Judit*, 438–84; embraced also by Otzen, *Tobit and Judith*, 92. See also Zenger, "Der Juditroman." Some saw here an apocalyptic scheme in Judith, while others, correctly, have demurred. Much earlier, Anton Scholz had argued that Judith was modeled on Ezekiel 38–39 and Daniel (*Das Buch Judith–eine Prophetie* [Würzburg and Vienna: Leo Woerl, 1885] 33–48, here 46). An apocalyptic reading of the text was thus embraced by Scholz and Steinmann, *Lecture de Judith*, 47–54; Delcor, "Le livre de Judith," 178–79; and André Barucq, *Judith, Esther* (2nd ed.; La Sainte Bible de Jerusalem 14; Paris: Cerf, 1959) 15–16. Rightly opposing an apocalyptic reading are Moore (*Judith*, 73–76) and Otzen (*Tobit*

and Judith, 92). Judith borrows imagery from apocalyptic texts, but in the service of a nonapocalyptic eschatology, as in the introduction of Greek Esther.

13 Rakel, *Judit–Über Schönheit*, 199; Stephen Ryan, "Judith's Deed of Hope and Hope in the Book of Judith" (unpublished paper) 10–11. A similar contrast is communicated by the pairing of *hybris* and *elpis* in Isa 28:1–5 LXX. Note 2 Cor 1:7, and see Ceslas Spicq, *Theological Lexicon of the New Testament* (trans. and ed. James D. Ernest; 3 vols.; Peabody, MA: Hendrickson, 1994) 1:485, 490–91. But Ryan cautions that this can be overinterpreted ("Judith's Deed," 14); cf. Cameron Boyd-Taylor, "The Semantics of Biblical Language Redux," in Robert J. Hiebert, ed., *"Translation Is Required": The Septuagint in Retrospect and Prospect* (SCS 56; Atlanta: Society of Biblical Literature, 2010) 41–57. The Greek novels also develop the theme of hope and rescue.

Otzen also uncovers theology behind the unreal aspects of the text but insists that they are not "just for fun." Historical telescoping and geographical telescoping

> have a common trait: both history and geography have, so to speak, been inflated or distended; history in the category of time, and geography in the category of space. This is done intentionally; history becomes universal history, and geography becomes total geography covering, more or less, the whole of the then-known world. By this artifice the book of Judith obtains a cosmic dimension, and the conflicts in the book are raised to a level where they represent the eternal struggle between God and Evil.[14]

Otzen grants that history and geography are abused in this text; this parable of good and evil is also comical. Nebuchadnezzar's plan is a de-differentiation of Israel and nations, reducing all to sameness, which must have suggested the threat of Hellenistic education and culture. The hellenization attempt in Jerusalem lay behind this, an assimilation to one "oikoumenical" culture.

As Craven had earlier emphasized, theological ideas such as these are expressed in oppositions, and they are more explicitly presented in Jdt 9:7; 16:3 with the quotation of Exod 15:3 LXX: "The Lord is a God who crushes wars" (see §4 above).[15] For Rakel and Schmitz, these quotations of Exod 15:3 bear the message of the whole book.[16] From this reprisal of Exodus in Judith's words, Schmitz develops a particularly strong thesis. The speeches, prayers, and songs of Judith, taken together, constitute about a third of the whole, and yet they are often marginalized by scholars. The extended theme of the book as a whole can be seen in Judith's words in chaps. 8–9. Not only does the work express an intertextuality with previous biblical texts, but the speeches and prayers of Judith tend to reinforce each other.

Here there is found a theory of history, developing the theme of the power of God in relation to humans. The words of Judith give theological direction to the story as a whole; without them, the book would be only "a taut and quickly recounted story" (*eine spannende und flott erzählte Geschichte*); through the framing of Judith's words the book becomes "a theologically conceived narrative" (*theologisch reflektierten Erzählung*). By this Schmitz shifts the focus from the *plot*–from which often arises a characterization of Judith as a femme fatale–to a more strictly theological expression. Schmitz's reading protects Judith from the charge of sexual taint, but ultimately the fact that the book of Judith can be *both* salacious *and* theological may indicate a hidden complexity. Like Jonah, Song of Songs, and Esther, our text may have resonated on various levels and had a mixed reception history.

The speeches have attracted the attention of scholars as well. The suffering, says Otzen, causes a crisis of understanding for the people, which is resolved in Judith's addresses. While the people think that the suffering is punishment for sins (7:28), or may cause one to think that God is forsaking them (7:30), Judith insists that God is only testing Israel (8:11–27). This speech garners for Judith the title of "the sole female theologian in the Old Testament"–so Moore and others[17]–but these judgments may reflect a Christian tendency to restrict theology to propositional statements. Is the embodied, narrative theology of Naomi, Ruth, or Tamar hereby excluded? Judith resides in a biblical tradition of women who do things, not just say things.

The theological emphases of these scholars may serve to ameliorate the unbridled revenge of the text. Otzen argues that "the Lord is a warrior" in Exod 15:3 MT was presumably changed in the LXX to "the Lord is one who crushes wars," the version that Judith quotes (Jdt 9:7; 16:2). He continues:

---

14 Otzen, *Tobit and Judith*, 90. He also paraphrases Jensen, "Juditbogen," 153–89. Esler perceives larger theological themes in the elements of play (*Sex, Wives, and Warriors*, 295–96).

15 Craven, *Artistry and Faith*, passim.

16 Rakel, *Judit–Über Schönheit*, 40; Schmitz, *Gedeutete Geschichte*, 3, 421–38, 454–62. See Christina Leisering's review of both Rakel's and Schmitz's books, *Jahrbuch der Europäischen Gesellschaft für die theologi-sche Forschung von Frauen* 13 (2005) 204–7; and cf. the commentary below on 14:18 on Bagoas's final cry as the *narrative* center of the book.

17 Moore, *Judith*, 186. See also Otzen, *Tobit and Judith*, 102–3; Haag, *Studien*, 40–43; Dubarle, *Judith*, 1:170–71; Hellmann, *Judit*, 121–26. Gera rightly insists on the theological engagement of Hagar, Rebekah, and Susanna (*Judith*, 275).

The God of the book of Judith is a *God of peace*. It is only on a superficial view that he is a violent and belligerent god, as when he, at the beginning of Israelite history, crushed the whole Egyptian army in the Red Sea. . . . [I]n his kingdom there will be peace.[18]

Otzen does acknowledge the contradiction that the "God of peace" is helping Judith decapitate someone and then wipe out his army, yet he does not sufficiently consider how much our text also finds justification in the revenge against Shechem. Even in Genesis, Jacob had condemned Simeon's actions (Gen 49:5–7). Indeed, "God of peace" does not imply pacifism. *Shalom* is not "peace" but an imposed, ordered, integrity of parts. In Judith, God maintains peace with power, even to the point of inflicting slaughter. God's chastisement is temporary for Israel (Jdt 8:24–27) but full of vengeance for those who threaten Israel (16:17).[19]

The narrative nature of theological themes in Judith is also reflected in the way that novelistic texts replay older themes and provide them with a new, very human context. The Exodus parallels condition this text; the elders and Bethulians represent the weak-willed, murmuring Israelites in the wilderness: "We will be slaves, but our lives will be spared" (7:27). This negative association of the Bethulians with the murmurers in the wilderness can be compared with the later command in the Passover haggadah, "In each generation, each person is obligated to see him or herself as having just come out of Egypt."[20]

The Discipline of the Self and the Body in Judith

Other scholars have uncovered unexpected levels of theological anthropology in Judith. LaCocque perceives a sort of proto-Christian ideal of "new woman" in the heroine; she is an icon of weakness, representing the suffering of the poor in spirit; she also sacrifices herself, evoking the Suffering Servant of Isaiah 52–53.[21] On the basis of the conversion of Achior, LaCocque develops a "subversive Judith" theme: the book of Judith is a political text that advocates not for the Hasmonean party after the Maccabean Revolt (as the text clearly indicates!) but for the opposition party, the Hasidim. The conversion of an Ammonite signals an opening to outsiders, again taking on the image of the Servant of Isaiah:

> [The] ideal was rather the figure of the Isaianic servant, and this explains why they would have a contender who seems to be weakness incarnate. Judith is a woman, a widow, a loner; in short, she is representative of the *anawim* (the humble, the poor in spirit).[22]

In addition to his anachronistic adoption of a Matthean reading here ("poor in spirit," Matt 5:3), LaCocque invests the Judith persona with a political program almost the opposite of what the text says:

> Her God is not the God of the Priestly tradition that the Chronicler reinforces. . . . The salvation of Bethulia is wrought without the help of the Temple. . . . [It

---

18 Otzen, *Tobit and Judith,* 98–99 [emphasis original]. He notes the other traditional epithets for God in Judith: Creator God (8:12–14; 16:14); *kyrios pantokratōr* (4:13; 8:13; 15:10; 16:5, 17); God of the lowly and oppressed (9:11–12), on which see commentary.

19 Cf. Isa 66:24; Ezek 38:22; 39:6–20—again, Gog and Magog. Schmitz similarly argues that Judith focuses on a justified tyrannicide, not on military conquest and revenge ("War, Violence and Tyrannicide"). However, the tyrannicide motif merely *begins* the military and revenge themes that celebrated the Hasmonean kingdom.

20 LaCocque, *Feminine Unconventional,* 41.

21 LaCocque, *Feminine Unconventional,* 43–48.

22 LaCocque, *Feminine Unconventional,* 41. Although the poor in spirit, *'ānî rûaḥ,* also exist at Qumran

(1QM 14:7), LaCocque's interpretation still reads as an imposition of Christian theology. Esler's view is somewhat different: Judith provided "the stimulus to reconsider afresh the nature of Israelite ethnicity" ("Ludic History," 132). See Pieter Venter, "The Function of the Ammonite Achior in the Book of Judith," *HTS Teologiese Studies/Theological Studies* 67(3), Art. #1101, 9 pages, http://dx.doi.org/10.4102/hts.v67i3.1101; and see also the commentary. At first, these arguments seem idealizing, yet Ruth the Moabite, in an admittedly less satirical text, may be opening a door for inclusion. Alternatively, however, Achior's conversion simply sanctions the Hasmonean policy of forced conversions.

is] an anti-establishment utopia displaying a great deal of skepticism about [the Temple's] capabilities in a time of crisis. . . . Judith does not shun rituals and exterior marks of piety, but it is clear that her existential options are determined by faith alone.[23]

One could hardly express a more typical (but now often challenged) Christian reading of Jesus-versus-the-temple, nor a less accurate summation of Judith's tricking and butchering of an enemy general—more Ehud than Jesus! LaCocque also ignores the fact that Judith times her prayer to coincide with the temple incense offerings (9:1) and the Bethulians' hope, in the hills of Samaria (part of Hasmonean Israel!), to prevent the desecration of the temple (8:24). Further, behind claims of weakness often lies a strategy of power, visible in the ascetic and martyrological tradition, and also 2 Maccabees 7.[24] Much like Jerome's translation, LaCocque's reading is a Christian *alteration* of Judith.

LaCocque was indeed correct, however, that Judith holds an important place in the development of ascetic ideas in Judaism, a development that does relate to the Christian asceticism to come. The biblical prophets had called upon Israel as a whole—a corporate personality—to repent, but, beginning with the exile, the individual agent comes to the fore, from individual responsibility (Jer 31:29–30) to "penitential" theology (Ezra 9; Nehemiah 9; Daniel 9). It was necessary for the ideal moral agent—even women—to be formed and improved. Our text presents a pious woman who separates herself from daily activities, remaining in a state of mourning longer than that required by Jewish law. Her prayer and ritual undressing and re-dressing (see chap. 9) are also similar to the more rending versions in Greek Esther 14:1–15:5 and Joseph

and Aseneth 10:9–17; 14:14–15, a type scene perhaps informed by dressing scenes in Greek epic and the Bible (see at 9:1–14).

What the women's prayer scenes in the novellas have in common is a narrative depiction of a ritualized act of ascetic discipline. The prayer scene, then, is not necessarily a feminist depiction, but it does raise questions of gender: why is the woman's detailed ritual of cleansing and transformation suddenly emphasized so strongly? Why is there a development of asceticism that places this ritual *at the center of multiple novellas*? If Judith is the very *model* of the new agency, along with Esther and Aseneth, then none of the three is really subversive. The scenes read like an ascetic ritual or a manual of transformation, from penitence to self-abnegation to a new agency. Judith's isolation chamber is also similar to Aseneth's more extreme one. The woman's scene of cleansing and re-dressing in these Jewish novellas focuses the locus of identity on the body, but on the *woman*'s body only; the novellas are female-gendered literature.[25]

Yet there are differences in the three Jewish novellas. In Greek Esther and Joseph and Aseneth there is, in the liminal state, a loss of bodily integrity for the heroine *based on her sin or impurity,* similar to what would later be postulated in full-blown ascetic practices. Judith, however, experiences no such loss of bodily integrity. Unlike Esther and Aseneth, Judith does not undergo a rending self-examination or self-abnegation but is convinced throughout of her own righteousness. As a result, there is no tension created around the protagonist's vulnerability, as there is in Esther, Aseneth, or Susanna, or even in the Greek novels.[26] True, there is a threat to the weak Bethulians and Judeans, but, without a true threat to the

---

23 LaCocque, *Feminine Unconventional*, 43, 44–45.

24 Shelly Matthews, *Perfect Martyr: The Stoning of Stephen and the Construction of Christian Identity* (Oxford: Oxford University Press, 2010).

25 Men's bodies are not often noted in this regard—compare the prayer of Esther in Greek Esther, for example, to that of Mordecai. See Stefan Schorch, "Genderising Piety: The Prayers of Mordecai and Esther in Comparison," in Géza G. Xeravits and József Zsengellér, eds., *Deuterocanonical Additions of the Old Testament Books: Selected Studies* (DCLS 5; Berlin: de Gruyter, 2010) 30–42. Similar to later female martyrs and ascetics, both Jewish and Chris-

tian, Judith is a model of heroic virtue for men and for women, as Jerome insisted (see §8 below).

26 See §7 below. As to lack of vulnerability, note that Judith 15:9–10 attributes to the heroine what is elsewhere only attributed to God; so Erich Zenger, "'Wir erkennen keinen anderen Gott an . . .' (Jdt 8,20). Programm und Relevanz des Buches Judit," *RHS* 39 (1996) 17–36, here 33. And whereas Elder ("Judith," 449) can say that Job 38 and Judith both attribute an omnipotence to God, Sawyer ("Gender Strategies," 19) reminds us that in Job it is God who speaks, while Judith speaks for God.

protagonist, is there really a *theme* of weak over strong? Is the theme not rather the trickster tale of reversal, that is, of strong over thinks-he's-strong? A triumphalism resides at the center of Judith, both for her personally and for the restored Israel. God is *already* on the side of Israel and does not have to be importuned, even though the Bethulians have wavered in their commitment to this notion. And even their wavering serves a function within the story frame. The Bethulians are stronger than other nations until their water runs out, at which point they begin to murmur. Yet they are reliving an "Israelite" moment: they are like Israel in the wilderness—very human but still Israel. Judith herself is now an idealized Moses, personified as "Jewish woman."[27]

Although Judith must guide her people in this moment of crisis, there is still a goodness about them. As weak-willed as the Bethulians at times appear, and as out of balance as their governance is *temporarily*—a woman tells the elders what to do—they are still described with functional social institutions, activated at a time of national crisis. They gather, fast, pray, and wear sackcloth as group penance—even if it is sometimes comical. These were crisis rituals in ancient Israel, and one may especially compare Ezra 9–10 and Nehemiah 9.[28] There is no stronger way to affirm the lordship of God and the recovered faith of Israel than to depict the people in stricken grief. Further, God's abode in Jerusalem, where the high priest is in firmer control, is really the center of interest.

---

27   Haag, *Studien*, 39; Moore, *Judith*, 62; van Henten, "Judith as an Alternative Leader"; Hellmann, *Judit*, 126, 137–38; Otzen, *Tobit and Judith*, 100–102.

28   See commentary on chaps. 4, 8–10; and cf. Saul

Olyan, *Biblical Mourning: Ritual and Social Dimensions* (Oxford: Oxford University Press, 2004) esp. 62–96, 137–40.

7. Genre and Literary Qualities of Judith; Humor, Irony, and Lying

To discuss the genre of an ancient text, one must ask four separate questions:

1. What are we choosing to call the genre?
2. Is this a native or a modern label? Would the ancient audience have understood this term?
3. Which texts are we including in the genre, and which are we excluding?
4. Would the ancient audience have perceived the same boundaries?

Questions 1 and 3 focus on modern perceptions, and 2 and 4 on ancient. Although historians must try to discern clear and distinct patterns of genres in the ancient world, social and artistic entities are generally called into existence and constructed by social usage—never inherent in the world of things-in-themselves; sometimes understood in a consistent way, sometimes not; sometimes conscious and named, sometimes not. Although Aristotle assumed that categories are real and clear, with clear names, and that an educated person would know them, since William of Ockham there has arisen a nominalist challenge: words have no clear and permanent relation to objects, and clearly defined categories do not exist in the real world. In the mid-twentieth century Ludwig Wittgenstein reintroduced this nominalist challenge, and the "linguistic turn" at the end of the twentieth century followed out the implications: there are no clear categories in the world, but through language people construct categories. Genres can be helpful categories by which to apprehend the world, but it is not clear that they name actually existing entities. Our treatment of the genre of Judith should recognize these ambiguities, and yet *it should be noted that the process is no more vexed here than it is for any other ancient genre, or for any modern one as well*. The ambiguity of Judith's genre is simply the ambiguity of *all* genres.

Previous Discussions of the Genre of Judith

When Judith was considered "Bible," or even "Apocrypha," the genre was not often discussed, and rare notations of genre seem confused. Jerome referred to Susanna, for instance, as a *historia* (*Preface to Daniel*), while Bel and the Dragon is a *fabula* (*Against Rufinus* 2.33), but the genre of Judith is not mentioned, and the text was simply analyzed with other biblical or deuterocanonical books. True, the early Christians may have perceived something of what we see in terms of genre, since Judith was placed with Esther and Tobit in the ancient Christian versions of the Old Testament and was later placed in the Syriac Book of Women with Ruth, Esther, Susanna, and Thecla.[1] Yet neither the genre of Judith nor that of the other texts was commented on. The historical questions about the text that were discussed, quite early on, were raised as problems relevant to a *biblical* narrative (see §2 above). It was not until Martin Luther that these difficulties—and perhaps difficulties in the moral aspects of the book—forced a reconsideration of the genre per se. Luther was the first to suggest that Judith was a fictitious text. A later Lutheran author, Cappellus, now opposing Catholic affirmations of the deuterocanonical books, was more negative: it is "a most silly fable invented by a most inept, injudicious, impudent, and clownish Hellenist."[2] The book of Judith became a lightning rod for Protestant–Catholic polemics, though surprisingly it was not always considered simply a "Catholic" text (see §8 below). Still, for centuries after there was little discussion of genre.

Historical-critical scholarship in the twentieth century took up anew the task of assigning genres to biblical texts, and various suggestions for Judith became popular.[3] Most of these provide some insight into the nature of the text, although in general they do not respond to all

---

1 Greg Goswell perceives subtle differences between Vaticanus, on the one hand, and Sinaiticus and Alexandrinus, on the other, in terms of the placement of the three novellas within the larger canon ("The Order of the Books in the Greek Old Testament, *JETS* 52 [2009] 449–66). In Vaticanus, they follow the wisdom texts, which contain many feminine images, while in Sinaiticus and Alexandrinus they are placed with historical books.

2 L. Cappellus, *Commentarii et notae criticae in Vet. Test.*, 575. Luther also referred to Tobit as a "very beautiful, wholesome, and useful fiction or drama by a gifted poet" (Carey A. Moore, *Tobit: A New Translation with Introduction and Commentary* [AB 40A; New York: Doubleday, 1996] 9–10 n. 7).

3 Surveys include Otzen, *Tobit and Judith*, 124–28; Helen Efthimiadis-Keith, *The Enemy Is Within: A Jungian Psychoanalytic Approach to the Book of Judith* (Biblical Interpretation Series 67; Boston: Brill Academic, 2004) 99–100; Gera, *Judith*, 5–6.

four of the questions above. Some of them, for instance, do not group the text with others—although is this not what genre means?—while others do not label our text in a way that would make sense in an ancient context. (This is not necessarily a problem; see below). Others drift over into theme rather than genre, but this may push us to consider theme as part of genre.

We begin with Anton Biolek's 1911 survey of ancient and modern opinions on the genre and historicity of Judith. He noted that, among his contemporaries, some still argued that Judith was history, even accurate history. Others, he said, held the book to be an allegory, historical novel, or an allegorical-prophetic or apocalyptic text.[4] More comparatively minded scholars labeled Judith as some sort of novel; so Ulrich von Wilamowitz, Ruth Stiehl and Franz Altheim, and Peter Weimar.[5] Similarly, Arthur E. Cowley saw it as historical fiction, and J. C. Dancy as a popular romance like Tobit and Esther. In 1975, Luis Alonso Schökel called it a short story, and in response Mary Coote, a folklorist, suggested "folk tale of rescue."[6]

Some scholars suggested more reflective categories. In 1963, Haag saw here a "tale of epic struggle" or a "paradigmatic history," and more recently Hans Jørgen Lundager Jensen looked to the odd refraction of history and geography in its pages and perceived a coded fiction or parable of history. He described the book as "universal history"—but in an unreal, parabolic sense—while the geography is "total geography, covering the whole world."[7] These latter terms, however, attempt to describe Judith's major theme and do not place it within a group of texts—again, a necessary step. Many scholars have connected Judith with Israelite wisdom, perceiving here a didactic short story similar to the Joseph story in Genesis 37–50, Ruth, Esther, Daniel, and Jonah. A subset of wisdom texts, the didactic short story is a narrative in which one could perceive the lessons of wisdom and virtue.[8]

Zenger recognized this didactic aspect, while still labeling it a *Roman,* or novel. Judith is a "romanhafte Erzählung mit didaktischer Absicht," or a "weisheitlicher Roman."[9] He relied, however, on modern definitions of a novel and short story: the novel has a world-encompassing or universal aspect, and Judith is universal history, based on the telescoping of the different time periods of Assyria, Babylon, the Restoration, and the Hasmonean period. Otzen, however, objected: it is more a short story than a novel, as it focuses on only one event and a few days before and after. He rightly asks, which is the true center of the reading experience, the novel time frame or the short story time frame? He then elaborates: Judith has a religious dimension and is therefore, like Tobit, also a legend, "a short story with a rather loose relation to history and reality but at the same time with its centre of gravity in religious edification."[10] Yet the genre category "legend" creates problems also. In folklore studies legend focuses on the belief of the audience; legends are stories

---

4   Biolek, "Die Ansicht," 335–68, where he lists scholars' names without references. Those who labeled it history were Roubion, Delattre, Brunengo, Rießler, Schöpfer, Schenz, Cornely, O. Wolff, Vigouroux, Steinmetzer, and Winckler (the last three found in the bibliography of this commentary). Those who said it was an allegory were J. Jahn, Fr. Lenormant, Luther, Movers, Schürer, and Gaster (on Luther, see above, and on the last two, see the bibliography). Those who judged it a historical novel were Erbt, Volkmar, Hilgenfeld, Lipsius, O. Fritzsche, and Klein (for all of these except Erbt, see bibliography). For allegorical-prophetic or apocalyptic text: A. Scholz (see bibliography).

5   Ulrich von Wilamowitz, *Die griechische und lateinische Literatur und Sprache* (3rd ed.; Leipzig: Teubner, 1912) 189; Stiehl and Altheim, *Die aramäische Sprache unter den Achaimeniden* (Frankfurt am Main: Vittorio Klostermann, 1963) 200–201; Peter Weimar, "Formen frühjüdischer Literatur," in Johann Maier and Joseph Schreiner, eds., *Literatur und Religion des Frühjudentums: Eine Einführung* (Würzburg: Echter Verlag, 1973) 123–62, here 130; Cowley, "Book of Judith," 242–67, here 246; Dancy, *Judith,* 127–31.

6   Alonso Schökel, *Narrative Structures,* 1, 21.

7   Haag, *Studien,* 16–18, 27 n. 104, 71–78; Milne uses similar terms ("What Shall We Do?," 48–55). See also Jensen, "Juditbogen," 153–89, summarized by Otzen, *Tobit and Judith,* 120–21.

8   Alonso Schökel, *Narrative Structures,* 1; Schmitz, *Gedeutete Geschichte,* 474–81; Otzen, *Tobit and Judith,* 106–7. G. Miller, "Femme Fatale," 226–27.

9   Zenger, "Judith/Judithbuch," 406; Zenger, "Der Juditroman," 65–80. Similar are Schmitz/Engel, *Judit,* 61: romanhafte theologische Lehrerzählung— yet does this judgment assume that the novella is earnest?

10 Otzen, *Tobit and Judith,* 125–26; also Hellmann, *Judit,* 52–62.

of revered figures that are believed by the audience to be true.[11] Indeed, the book of Judith was *later* believed to be true by Christian audiences, but probably not at the time of composition. Yet in Otzen's defense, he defines legend in terms of a seriousness of religious purpose and the goal of inculcating values, not in terms of the belief of the audience. He is correct about the goal of legends to edify and teach, which was perhaps true even for the satirical Judith, but the term *legend* should probably be limited to more earnest evocations of a figure to be imitated.

Scholars have also long recognized the relation of Judith to ancient Near Eastern novelistic texts, early Greek history, and the later Greek novels. Martin Braun asserted this in 1934, and Ruth Stiehl and Martin Hengel followed.[12] Recently Otzen has agreed:

> On the general level the Book of Judith was influenced by the Greek-Oriental or the Jewish-Hellenistic novel. Above all the erotic motifs—the counterpoise of eroticism and chastity—in the book of Judith are typical of this literature, and thus also an indication that the book belongs to this late time.[13]

I have argued this at length, and Deborah Gera's commentary of 2014 concluded as well that Judith was part of this broad, developing novelistic tradition.[14] Care must be taken, however, to distinguish the dates: the Greek and Roman novels were composed *after* our text. Another challenge, however, to these attempts to define Judith in terms of a single genre classification is that of Sara Raup Johnson. Rather than struggle to group certain *texts* that may or may not belong together, she argues for tracking a developing *fictional play* across different genres. In postexilic Judah, the origins of fiction are evident in the new obsession with imperial writings, edicts, and statecraft. There was an invasion of fictitious modes into more earnest Jewish genres. Whether Judith as a whole is fictional, she maintains, is not always clear, but many texts, even Ezra-Nehemiah, are spiced with moments of fictionality.[15] A history or a testament may indeed be angular or inventive concerning reality and yet not be quite fictional. Her challenge is valuable in pointing out a postexilic development in Jewish literature that cuts across genres, but as a result she is reluctant to assign a genre to Judith or other related texts.

Johnson's challenge does point up a problem concerning Jewish novellas, but it is also a problem for Greek novels, all novels, and indeed all genres. Even if she is correct that a fictional impulse cuts across genres, what precisely are those other "genres" that fiction cuts across? Their categories are as troubled as that of novella. It is illusory to think of Jewish novellas, or novels in general, as less precise a genre than others. It should surprise no one that Jewish novellas are difficult to pin down. It would be shocking if the boundaries of this genre *were* clear. Rather, as I have argued elsewhere,

> All *important* categories in culture are large, rambling, undefined around the boundaries, and have problematic names, while *unimportant* categories in culture are small, pristine, neatly defined around the boundaries, and have clear names. Conversely, if a category is large, rambling, undefined around the boundaries, and has a problematic name, this is *prima facie* evidence that it is important. If a category is small, pristine, neatly defined around the edges, and has a clear name, this is *prima facie* evidence that it is not important.[16]

---

11   Wills, *Jew in the Court*, 12–19.

12   Martin Braun, *Griechischer Roman und hellenistische Geschichtschreibung* (Frankfurter Studien zur Religion und Kultur der Antike 6; Frankfurt am Main: Klostermann, 1934); Ruth Stiehl, "Das Buch Esther," *Wiener Zeitschrift für die Kunde des Morgenlandes* 53 (1956) 4–22, here 6–9; Hengel, *Judaism and Hellenism*, 110–12, 203–4.

13   Otzen, *Tobit and Judith*, 80, 109.

14   Wills, *Jewish Novel*, passim, esp. 132–57; Gera, *Judith*, 27, 60. Below I prefer the term *novella* simply to acknowledge the difference in length from the Greek novels.

15   Johnson, *Historical Fictions*; and Johnson, "Novelistic Elements in Esther: Persian or Hellenistic, Jewish or Greek?" *CBQ* 67 (2005) 571–89. In *Wonders beyond Thule* by Antonius Diogenes, which ironically passed into Western tradition as a source of history, there are also many pseudo-authenticating documents and figures; see Gerald Sandy, "New Pages of Greek Fiction," in J. R. Morgan and Richard Stoneman, eds., *Greek Fiction: The Greek Novel in Context* (London: Routledge, 1994) 130–45, here 138.

16   Wills, "Jewish Novellas in a Greek and Roman Age: Fiction and Identity," *JSJ* 42 (2011) 141–65, here 147; see also Wills, *Jewish Novel*; Wills, "The Differ-

Genres also evolve so quickly and so organically that any attempt to freeze the development at one point to define the Platonic form will be misleading. Only in those cases where genres are defined and protected by elite authority structures—epic, lyric, and drama in classical Greece, for instance—can one even pretend that genres are precise. In this commentary, I assume that, although "Jewish novella" presents problems of definition, they are the same sorts of definitional problems that arise with almost all genres, at all times, in all places, and indeed, the problems are *part of what it means to be a genre.*

Precursors of the Jewish Novellas: Proximate History and Deep History

It is necessary to account for the background of Jewish novellas in two ways, a proximate history and a deep history. Although we may in part define the rise of the novelistic texts in terms of the proximate history of Hellenism (see below), some aspects of the novelistic impulse can be found much earlier, and we should not assume that these are too early to be relevant. Among the preserved texts of the ancient Near Eastern kingdoms are narratives that reveal an appreciation of certain literary techniques relevant to the novel. The moving Egyptian narratives of Sinuhe and Wenamun and the humor of The Two Brothers and the Eloquent Peasant surely cause the historian of the novel to take notice.[17] In Sumerian and Akkadian literature we find the Poor Man of Nippur, Three Ox Drivers of Adab, and The Old Man and the Young Girl.[18] These have been likened to trickster tales, which will be relevant below.

Through the reach of the Persian Empire, Aramaic became an international language for scribalism.[19] In this language we find a number of relevant fragments. A variation on the Two Brothers tale is preserved in Aramaic,[20] and above all, The Story of Ahikar. Known from a fifth-century BCE fragment from Elephantine in Egypt, it is probably an older, international story (see the excursus below in Judith 5). In Israel, the early oral narrative traditions of the Pentateuch and Deuteronomistic History provided many motifs found in the Jewish novellas (see §4 above) but in general did not exercise the same narrative approach. Still, the Joseph story in Genesis 37–50 exhibited the extension that we have come to associate with novelistic texts, along with the domestic focus. Much longer than the surrounding material in the Pentateuch, it also contains the rudiments of an introspective examination of emotions, and even that holy grail of the novel hunter, character development.[21] Niditch also asserts that between the early story of Tamar in Genesis 38 and the later books of Ruth and Jonah one can perceive novelistic growth: dialogue, inner thoughts, motivation, emotion, and interpersonal interaction.[22] In Greece, the histories of Herodotus, Ctesias, and Xenophon of Athens (espe-

entiation of History and Novel: Controlling the Past, Playing with the Past," in Ilaria Ramelli and Judith Perkins, eds., *Early Christian and Jewish Narrative: The Role of Religion in Shaping Narrative Forms* (WUNT 348; Tübingen: Mohr Siebeck, 2015) 13–30.

17 Even wisdom collections in Egypt, such as Any and Onkhsheshonq, include a powerful narrative frame. See Graham Anderson, *Ancient Fiction: The Novel in the Graeco-Roman World* (Totowa, NJ: Barnes & Noble, 1984); and Tawny L. Holm, *Of Courtiers and Kings: The Biblical Daniel Narratives and Ancient Story-Collections* (Winona Lake, IN: Eisenbrauns, 2013) 45–183 on Egyptian story traditions.

18 Keith Dickson, "Enki and Ninhursag: The Trickster in Paradise," *JNES* 66 (2007) 1–32.

19 Stephanie Dalley, "Assyrian Court Narratives in Aramaic and Egyptian: Historical Fiction," in T. Abusch et al., eds., *Proceedings of the XLVe Rencontre assyriologique internationale,* vol. 1: *Historiography in the Cuneiform World* (Bethesda: CDL, 2001) 149–62; Dalley, "Semiramis in History and Legend," in Erich S. Gruen, ed. *Cultural Borrowings and Ethnic Appropriations in Antiquity* (Oriens et occidens 8; Stuttgart: Franz Steiner, 2005) 11–22.

20 Richard C. Steiner and Charles F. Nims, "Ashurbanipal and Shamash-shum-ukin: A Tale of Two Brothers from the Aramaic Text in Demotic Script," *RB* 92 (1985) 60–81.

21 See Gen 42:24; 43:30–31; 45:1. Adelman, *Female Ruse,* 198–230; Wills, *Jewish Novel,* 93–131; Wills, *Jew in the Court,* 52–55.

22 Susan Niditch, *The Responsive Self: Personal Religion in Biblical Literature of the Neo-Babylonian and Persian Periods* (AYBRL; New Haven: Yale University Press, 2015) 120–33; cf. Crawford, "In the Steps of Jael," 7.

cially his *Cyropaedia*) also reflect an entertaining combination of eastern narrative traditions and stylized Greek storytelling.[23]

The transition of our genre from deep history to proximate history begins in the sixth century BCE. By encouraging Aramaic scribalism and the interdependence of peoples, the Persians could extend their control over much larger expanses than was the case with previous ancient Near Eastern kingdoms. The Persian restoration of a temple-state in Judah soon provided a larger context for the exercise of a Judean scribalism in both Aramaic and Hebrew, and Ezra-Nehemiah reflects this.[24] But it was the conquests of Alexander the Great in the fourth century that elevated these dreams of a large, interdependent empire to a new level. There emerged a common Hellenistic belief in the power of education, *paideia*, to transform people into new citizens of the *oikoumenē*, the entire civilized world. "'Hellene,'" said Isocrates (*Panegyricus* 4.50), "suggests no longer a race but an intelligence, and the title 'Hellenes' is applied rather to those who share our culture than to those who share a common blood."[25] Even provincials could become leading intellectuals; many heads of philosophical schools and universal historians were from the eastern ethnic groups, including Semitic peoples.[26] But despite Isocrates's high-minded gesture, this universalism, like modern Western universalism, ironically also defined a new particularism concerning the colonized. By becoming a means of access, this universalism imposed a visible boundary. And with that also arises a colonial universalism, the assertion by the colonized of a higher and truer universalism than that of the colonizer.[27] A triumphal vindication results: "You colonizers claim a universal perspective, but *we* are the authors of a true universalism."

The Jewish novellas thus arose in a colonized time and space in which domestic interiors become the settings for high-stakes dramas. Judith, like Esther and Susanna, is a domesticated woman forced out of her zone of domesticity. The later Greek novels did not likely borrow this deep structural element from Jewish novellas, but rather a broad range of literary experiments were moving along parallel lines, often at the margins of Greek hegemony. Some of these, which make the novel possible, can be traced. The focus on the individual has rightly been connected to the breakdown of the polis structure, as Bryan Reardon states:

> For in a world of large empires, essentially controlled from Alexandria or Antioch, there could not be the same intense interest in political matters as had characterized the classical city-state. The world had become bigger, and the individual . . . smaller in it—smaller, and more absorbed in himself, his private life.[28]

Israelite tribal structure, like classical Greek polis structure, had also been eroded, but in both Israel and Greece, what scholars call the "discovery of the individual" is more precisely the "discovery of the new moral agent." Hellenistic poetry, for instance, discovered a fuller expression of emotions, intentions, and a sense of the individual agent whose aspirations for self-realization must be taken seriously.[29] Many have commented on this change, from vastly different theoretical perspectives.

23 Lindsay Allen, "Le roi imaginaire: An Audience with the Achaemenid King," in Olivier Hekster and Richard Fowler, eds., *Imaginary Kings: Royal Images in Ancient Near East, Greece, and Rome* (Oriens et occidens 11; Stuttgart: Franz Steiner, 2005) 39–62; Stephanie West, "Croesus' Second Reprieve and Other Tales of the Persian Court," *ClQ* n.s. 53 (2003) 416–37.

24 Stiehl and Altheim, *Die aramäische Sprache*, 1:183–213.

25 Translation of James I. Porter, *Classical Pasts: The Classical Tradition of Greece and Rome* (Princeton, NJ: Princeton University Press, 2006) 384.

26 Of the universal historians of the first century BCE, Diodorus Siculus, Pompeius Trogus, and Strabo, the latter two hailed from the provinces; see Katherine Clarke, "Universal Perspectives in Historiography,"

in Christina Shuttleworth Kraus, ed., *The Limits of Historiography: Genre and Narrative in Ancient Historical Texts* (Mnemosyne Supplement 191; Leiden: Brill, 1999) 249–79.

27 The term was coined by Partha Chatterjee, *Nationalist Thought and the Colonial World: A Derivative Discourse?* (London: Zed; Totowa, NJ: Biblio Distribution Center, 1986), but in reference to the imposition of supposedly universal education by colonial rulers. Homi Bhabha saw a complex relation here, an affirmation by the colonized in a hybrid setting (*Location of Culture* [London: Routledge, 1994] esp. 85–92).

28 Bryan P. Reardon, "General Introduction," in Reardon, ed., *Collected Ancient Greek Novels* (Berkeley: University of California Press, 1989) 1–16, here 7.

29 For instance, Theocritus, *Idyll VI, XI*; see Sara Mack,

Michel Foucault, for instance, perceived here a transition from the philosopher in the polis to the high-level court scribe who is watched over by a distant, semidivine king.[30] Recent studies of imperial centers and colonies, ancient and modern, posit a creativity at the margins of an empire, or at the margins between two great world empires, or at the intersection of colonizer and colonized. Was it the local and colonized perceptions of worldwide empires that provoked the idea of novelistic play—prose that on the surface pretends to describe the *real* world, while constructing an *invented* world?

Differentiation of Novel and History and the Origins of the Novel

In Greece, prose was said to have been introduced by the philosopher Pherecydes of Syros (sixth century BCE). Called *Fachprosa,* technical prose, by German scholars, this new medium—prose rather than poetry—was used to create a new technical control in the areas of politics, law, science, rhetoric, medicine, theology, philosophy, history, and aesthetics. "Prose," says Simon Goldhill, "becomes the medium for authoritative expression, the expression of power."[31] History writing in Greece was a subset of *Fachprosa.* A significant characteristic of most of the Greek writings in the fields listed above is that they were attributed to known, real, named, elite, male authors. The named author controls *Fachprosa.* As with *Fachprosa* in general, the named, real author of history is the voice who controls the inquiry, controls the views of the past. In Herodotus, "the voice of the author as a personal, evaluating, reviewing presence is constantly being performed."[32] In Israel as well, an unadorned prose, a sort of *Fachprosa,* was being written by named, known, elite, male authors—Ezra and Nehemiah. The "I" of Ezra and the "I" of Nehemiah are as revolutionary as the "I" of Herodotus, and, although this is rarely noted, *they appear at about the same time.*[33]

It is often assumed that fiction follows history, but it is more complicated than that. Herodotus did not really *establish* history as a genre. It was not until after Herodotus, Thucydides, and Xenophon of Athens that *historia,* systematic inquiry, was first used as a name for the genre "history."[34] The earliest "histories" in Greece betray, rather, a combination of impulses, both historical and novelistic. Herodotus, later called both "father of history" and "father of lies," wrote a history that incorporated entertaining anecdotes. Xenophon of Athens created both history (*Anabasis*) and a more novelistic history (*Cyropaedia*). Ctesias, like Herodotus, produced histories of the East (Persia and India) that

---

"Acis and Galatea or Metamorphosis of Tradition," *Arion* 6 (1999) 51–67.

30 Michel Foucault, *Le gouvernement de soi et des autres* (Paris: Seuil, 2008); see also David Konstan, *Sexual Symmetry: Love in the Ancient Novel and Related Genres* (Princeton, NJ: Princeton University Press, 1994) 15–25.

31 Simon Goldhill, *The Invention of Prose* (Oxford: Oxford University Press, 2002) 5, 28. On *Fachprosa,* see Lars Rydbeck, *Fachprosa, vermeintliche Volksspruche und Neues Testament: Zur Beurteilung der sprachlichen Niveauunterschiede im nachklassischen Griechisch* (Acta Universitatis Upsaliensis: Studia Graeca Upsaliensia 5; Stockholm: Almqvist & Wiksell, 1967); Loveday Alexander, *The Preface to Luke's Gospel: Literary Convention and Social Context in Luke 1:1–4 and Acts 1:1* (SNTSMS 78; Cambridge: Cambridge University Press, 1993); and Harry Y. Gamble, *Books and Readers in the Early Church: A History of Early Christian Texts* (New Haven: Yale University Press, 1995) 33–34.

32 Goldhill, *Invention of Prose,* 28. Pamphile of Epidaurus (first century CE) was a rare female historian. Rosalind Thomas argues that the generic similarities of Herodotus are not to "history"—which did not yet exist!—but to natural philosophy and medicine—*Fachprosa* (*Herodotus in Context: Ethnography, Science, and the Art of Persuasion* [Cambridge: Cambridge University Press, 2000] 8–9).

33 This is true regardless of the origins of the Ezra Memoir and the Nehemiah Memoir, or of possible additions to them. See Tamara Cohn Eskenazi, *In an Age of Prose: A Literary Approach to Ezra-Nehemiah* (SBLMS 36; Atlanta: Scholars Press, 1988); Arnaldo Momigliano, *The Classical Foundations of Modern Historiography* (Berkeley: University of California Press, 1990) 5–28; G. W. Bowersock, "Momigliano's Quest for the Person," *History and Theory* 30 (1991) 27–36; and Morton Smith, *Palestinian Parties and Politics That Shaped the Old Testament* (Lectures on the History of Religions n.s. 9; New York: Columbia University Press, 1972) 122–25.

34 Aristotle, *Poetics* 1450a–1451b, 1459a; see Goldhill, *Invention of Prose,* 10–12. On Herodotus, see Rosalind Thomas, *Herodotus in Context.* On Xenophon, see John Marincola, "Genre, Convention, and Innovation in Greco-Roman Historiography," in Kraus, *Limits of Historiography,* 281–324.

were highly entertaining, with domestic court episodes. The later Greek novels may have even seemed superficially similar in taking real historical figures as their protagonists: Ninus, Sesonchosis, Nektanebos, and Hermocrates, the father of Chariton's heroine. Novellas, then, did not evolve neatly from histories; rather, both genres may have co-originated, co-differentiated, from the broader supergenre of *Fachprosa*. The same may indeed be true in the modern world: the modern novel may have evolved not from history but from a co-differentiating mitosis related to history and the new endeavor of journalism.[35]

From a modern perspective, it is difficult to imagine history and novel as anything but the purest of ideal forms. From our vantage point, ancient overlapping texts seem hybridized, even the bastardized offspring of these two. But Herodotus's *History*, the *Cyropaedia* of Xenophon of Athens, and Ctesias's *Persica* attest to an early novelistic tone in some histories. In Israel as well, the novelistic Joseph story (Genesis 37–50) and the entertaining stories of the judges are collected with the more historical texts. Even as late as the second–first centuries BCE, the Alexander Romance and Life of Aesop may be considered early experiments in the rise of the novel in Greece, one a popular history and one a popular biography (as *Cyropaedia* was also a popular biography).[36] The same may be said of Artapanus.

Yet, however we write the history of history and novel, and how they co-differentiated, we may still point to similarities and differences between the two. If history and novels are a contrasted pair, then history is the male-gendered member, novel the female. Female characters populate novels, performing virtuous or heroic deeds, what Massimo Fusillo calls a "phantasy of omnipotence."[37] This is true not only of Greek and modern European novels but of medieval Chinese and Japanese novels as well, and also of the Jewish novellas. For this reason it is often suggested that novels were written by or read by women, but in the ancient world the evidence is inconclusive. The preponderance of female characters, however, brings scholars back to this possibility again and again.[38] This much is still demonstrable: if history is a male-gendered discourse, with a known, named author who controls the discourse, novels cross-culturally are often anonymous or pseudonymous, and female-gendered, or at least bi-gendered.

In both Israel and Greece, then, by what process did novels and histories co-differentiate?[39] The ancient novel, like the early modern novel, was not openly recognized by elite commentators, and was rarely mentioned.[40]

35 Lennard Davis, *Factual Fictions: The Origins of the English Novel* (New York: Columbia University Press, 1983) 212; Michael McKeon, *The Origins of the English Novel, 1600–1740* (Baltimore: Johns Hopkins University Press, 1987); Jill Lepore, "Just the Facts, Ma'am," *The New Yorker*, March 24, 2008, 80–83. On the theoretical issues of what texts demand attribution to a particular author, see Michel Foucault, "What Is an Author?" in Paul Rabinow, ed., *The Foucault Reader* (New York: Pantheon, 1984) 101–19.

36 So Jouanno, "Novelistic Lives," 42–46.

37 Massimo Fusillo, "Modern Critical Theories and the Ancient Novel," in Gareth Schmeling, ed., *The Novel in the Ancient World* (rev. ed.; Boston: Brill Academic, 2003) 277–305, here 300; Michael Danahy, "Le roman est-il chose femelle?" *Poetique* 25 (1976) 85–106.

38 Arguing for a female audience are Brigitte Egger ("Looking at Chariton's Callirhoe," in Morgan and Stoneman, *Greek Fiction*, 31–48) and Jan M. Bremmer, "The Novel and the Apocryphal Acts," *Groningen Colloquia on the Novel* 9 (1998) 157–80.

More skeptical are Susan Stephens, "Who Read Ancient Novels?" and Ewen Bowie, "The Readership of Greek Novels in the Ancient World," both in James Tatum, ed., *The Search for the Ancient Novel* (Baltimore: Johns Hopkins University Press, 1994) 405–18, 435–59.

39 Since all genres have boundaries with many other genres, we might also trace the differentiation of novels from lyric, letters, and so on. For instance, Northrop Frye (*Anatomy of Criticism* [Princeton, NJ: Princeton University Press, 1957] 309–12) and Mikhail Bakhtin (*Rabelais*, 7–21), opposite voices in many ways, both suggest the Menippean satire as a precursor to the novel. Bakhtin especially likens the satire to the "carnivalesque," the temporary communal suspension of the community's rules that operates in Esther and Judith. Here, however, we limit our discussion to novel and history.

40 Leading authors could occasionally make passing references to novels and similar texts, but these were hardly indicative of sustained reflection. Sextus Empiricus said that *plasmata* described things that

There is, for instance, no clear or common ancient term for the genre, although *plasma, pathēma, fictio,* and *fabula* are sometimes applied to novelistic texts, as is the broad *mythos*. In Greece, there was some reflection on the nature of these different discourses. Rhetoricians and grammarians divided narrative into three types: (1) *historia*, true accounts of events that actually occurred; (2) *plasma* or *argumentum*, accounts narrating events that had not occurred but that are nevertheless like real events; and (3) *mythos* or *fabula*, narratives of events that have not occurred and are not similar to real events.[41] The second group, *plasma*, is most like the novels.[42] Words related to Latin *fictum* cover much the same range of meanings as well. The third category, *mythos*, was highly problematized in this rationalistic age, although it could still be used, even contemptuously, of good stories.

Ancient historians sometimes defended the first category, *historia*, by noting their own high standards of truthfulness, accusing lesser historians of incorporating *mythoi* and other cheap tricks. Yet historians varied on a scale in regard to how many "novelistic" elements they would include. Polybius criticized Phylarchus for introducing

tragic themes in history, but Dionysius of Halicarnassus would later embody a number of compromises. He included ancient myths and complained that Thucydides had omitted *to mythōdes*, while also chiding other predecessors for including figures such as monsters, *ta mythika plasmata*.[43] While the criticisms indicate that there was a perceived hierarchy of historical standards, a rigorous distinction between "history" and "novel" may still not have existed. It was not until a rationalistic history was more rigorously differentiated from this mass of entertaining history that a separate, wholly fictitious novel could also differentiate on the other side.

A similar process of co-differentiation of history and novel likely occurred in Israel as well. Stylized histories in epic style, with entertaining elements, existed in Israel and the ancient Near East at an early stage. In the larger and more diverse world of the Persian Empire, however, epic narrative receded as the dominant discourse. As noted above, a Hebrew *Fachprosa*, or unadorned, practical prose, can be discerned in Ezra-Nehemiah (fifth–fourth centuries BCE), in what Tamara Cohn Eskenazi rightly calls an "age of prose."[44] Thus "novel" may not

---

did not happen but might have happened—in a way that resembled what really happened—and Strabo and Julian denounced those who incorporated *mythoi* or *plasmata* as if they were *historia*; see Glenn W. Bowersock, *Fiction as History: Nero to Julian* (Sather Classical Lectures 58; Berkeley: University of California Press, 1994) 51; and see Strabo 1.2.35; Celsus insisted that the Gospels were wrong or fictitious, and Origen responded (*Contra Celsum* 1.42).

41 Pseudo-Cicero, *Ad Herrennium* 1.8.12–13, Quintilian 2.4.2; see David Konstan, "The Invention of Fiction," in Ronald F. Hock, J. Bradley Chance, and Judith Perkins, eds., *Ancient Fiction and Early Christian Narrative* (Symposium Series 6; Atlanta: Scholars Press, 1998) 3–18. In T. P. Wiseman and Christopher Gill, eds., *Lies and Fiction in the Ancient World* (Exeter: University of Exeter Press, 1993), see the following articles: Morgan, "Make-Believe and Make Believe: The Fictionality of the Greek Novels," 175–229; and T. P. Wiseman, "Lying Historians: Seven Types of Mendacity," 122–46, here 130. See also Niklas Holzberg, "Genre: Novels Proper and the Fringe," in Schmeling, *Novel in the Ancient World*, 11–28, here 17.

42 Indeed, in response to those who assert that there

is no ancient word for novel, *plasma* is often used in this way. Emperor Julian, for instance, cautioned that, while one should read histories about deeds that actually occurred, one should avoid "fictions [*plasmata*] . . . in the form of history, love subjects, and—in short—everything of that kind" (*Epistles* 89.301b; translation of Tomas Hägg, *The Novel in Antiquity* [Berkeley: University of California Press, 1991] 3). See Jan P. Stronk, *Ctesias' Persian History*: part 1: *Introduction, Text, and Translation* (Düsseldorf: Wellem, 2010) 47.

43 Dionysius 1.8.1, and see Jeff Jay, *The Tragic in Mark: A Literary-Historical Interpretation* (HUT 66; Tübingen: Mohr Siebeck, 2014) 62. Note Tacitus *Histories* 2.50.2, where myths and fiction (*ficta*) are rejected in history writing. However, R. Develin points out that Tacitus judges others' lies rigorously while demanding less of himself ("Tacitus and Techniques of Insidious Suggestion," *Antichthon* 17 [1983] 64–95, esp. 69, 94–95). Tacitus even uses the categories above that he rejects.

44 Eskenazi, *In an Age of Prose*. A kind of prose also arose in Egypt long before; see Miriam Lichtheim, *Ancient Egyptian Literature: A Book of Readings* (3 vols.; Berkeley: University of California Press,

have evolved out of "history," but, rather, history and novel may have co-differentiated from the supergenre of popular history. History and novel (or novella) existed as independent genres only once the operation to separate the conjoined twins was complete. If history *seems* to precede novel–Herodotus before *Cyropaedia,* the Deuteronomistic History before the Joseph story–that may be illusory, since Herodotus and the Deuteronomistic History were not truly "history" anyway, but proto-history.

The problem of finding an ancient genre name to apply to a truly separate novel can perhaps be addressed by utilizing a modern term, "free narrative," and taking Ctesias as an example. For Ctesias, "Writing history changes into a description of events in a more or less free interpretation of occurrences, perhaps occasionally even approaching a historical novel"–so Jan P. Stronk.[45] Yet why should we say that "history"–which does not exist yet–was changing into "historical novel"? Ctesias wrote before *historia* had become the name of a genre and was himself free to push narrative of the past into a storytelling zone. What if history evolved out of free narrative? "Free narrative," then, may be considered that great middle range of the spectrum that was only gradually dualized into history and fiction.

Even granting the separate methods of history and novel, there are still a range of texts in Greek, Roman, and Jewish literature that remain ambiguous in regard to genre, though now they are routinely included within the study of the novel. The novel and history lie on a continuum with many exempla. Here some selected texts can be arranged on a spectrum, from more historical to more novelistic:

History			Popular History	Novel	
1 Macc	2 Macc	Acts	Acts of Peter	Esther	Chariton
			Artapanus	Tobit	Heliodorus
			Ahikar	Judith	Longus
			Alexander Romance	Aesop	

In this arrangement, the genre categories do not register *qualitative* differences, but strictly *quantitative* ones. The middle area, however, the problem area for most analyses, should not be seen as a hybrid mix of two prior "clear" categories, history and novel. Was it the *earlier* category, in fact the more *typical* sort of text, from which both history and novel diverged?[46]

Rather than trying to adjudicate whether Jewish novellas "truly belonged" in the same genre category with the Greek novels, a more helpful line of inquiry would be to describe the *relation of earlier, eastern, colonized, "nationalistic," experimental prose fiction and the later ideal Greek novels.* What ecosystem can we perceive that contains all of these texts? The western authors

---

1975–1980) 1:10–11, 2:200–211, 3:126–38; Stephens and Winkler, *Ancient Greek Novels,* 12–13.

45 Stronk, *Ctesias' Persian History,* 39, 46–47, 79–80. Aristotle (*On Style,* 9.2) had suggested that the historian writes what happened, the poet what might happen. Ctesias, who was very popular in antiquity and was commented on both positively and negatively, was described by Demetrius (*On Style,* 215–16) as a poet because he included what might happen. Novelistic moments in *Cyropaedia* include: Panthea the Lady of Susa (5.1–7.3); King Croesus (7.2); Prince Gobryas (4.6–5.4); Gadatas the chieftain (5.3–4); see Llewellyn-Jones and Robson, *Ctesias' History,* 69–70; Gera, *Xenophon's Cyropaedia,* 209. Paradoxography also existed early: Palaephatus, *On Incredible Things;* Antigonus of Carystus, *Collection of Wonderful Tales;* Apollonius Paradoxographus, *Mirabilia;* and later as well: Phlegon of Tralles, *Book of Marvels;* Ps.-Aristotle, *On Marvelous Things Heard* (which may have contained early material). It is understandable

why Sylvie Honigman might reject the fact/fiction distinction in antiquity, since it was not commented on in clear terms (*The Septuagint and Homeric Scholarship in Alexandria: A Study of the Narrative of the Letter of Aristeas* [London: Routledge, 2003] 38–41, 65–91). But it is commented on in unclear terms.

46 Gerald Sandy also caricatures this assumption when he says, tongue in cheek, "ancient Greek fiction developed from a fusion of gradually diminishing doses of historiography and ever-increasing injections of love until at some measurable point the erotic novel was synthesized" ("New Pages of Greek Fiction," 139). The assumption that genres devolve from pure originals to derivative forms was long ago critiqued by Jacques Derrida ("La loi du genre," in his *Parages* [Paris: Galilee, 1986] 249–87) and René Wellek ("The Concept of Evolution in Literary History," in his *Concepts of Criticism* [New Haven: Yale University Press, 1963] 37–53).

are not following in the footsteps of the earlier eastern texts, but authors of both groups reflect new explorations appropriate to a mature Hellenistic world, perhaps reflecting opposite poles of a colonizer/colonized interface. Just as the protagonists in Greek novels descend into the barbarian and reemerge sharply distinguished, the Jewish author wants to reestablish the superior position of a new moral agent who possesses a God's-eye view of dignity and virtue.

The Differentiation of History and Novel

Despite a mixed origin for history and novel, distinctions between them did become pronounced enough to be perceived by an audience. The author of history, for instance, makes two assumptions: first, the events recounted really occurred; and, second, they occurred on the time line that continues down to the audience's day.[47] Poetry in Greece normally involved a resolution that allowed closure for the work of art, but most ancient histories avoided any such closure. Historians were explicit that their endings were arbitrary and *open:* history never ends. The named, known author controls the narrative and intervenes to stop the narrative arbitrarily, though the time line continues into the audience's present and will continue beyond.[48] The same openness is announced at the beginnings of histories: Greek and Roman historians inscribed themselves into their introductions by declaring their personae, and also by explicitly noting that they had *chosen* an *archē* on a continuous time line at which to begin.

These same patterns can be found in Jewish histories as well. The conclusions lack closure and provide an open ending:

Josephus, *Antiquities*

> With this I conclude my *Antiquities.* . . . I shall at some future time compose a running account of the war

and of the later events of our history up to the present day. . . . (20.11.3 §266–67)[49]

2 Maccabees

> This, then, is how matters turned out with Nicanor, and from that time the city has been in possession of the Hebrews. So I will here end my story. If it is well told and to the point, that is what I myself desired; if it is poorly done and mediocre, that was the best I could do. . . . And here will be the end. (15:37-39 NRSV)

The Jewish historians, like their Greek and Roman counterparts, also began by choosing an *archē* on the time line:

1 Maccabees

> After Alexander son of Philip, the Macedonian, who came from the land of Kittim, had defeated King Darius of the Persians and the Medes, he succeeded him as king. (1:1 NRSV)

Novelistic literature, however, both Jewish and Greek, differs from histories in regard to the two assumptions above. First, it is *not* assumed that the events recounted really occurred—although this is difficult for us to prove with certainty. But second, and more observable: novels do not place the narrative on the open time line that continues to the audience's own day. Novels may mimic history, playing with historical time lines, but it is *play:* neither the beginning nor the end of a novel really exists on the time line that continues to the present. Xenophon of Ephesus, for example, firmly closed his novel, *Ephesian Tale*, with no connection to the audience's present: "They lived happily ever after, the rest of their life together was one long festival." True, there is an artificial time line *within* novels—plot—and this is what makes novel prose look like historical prose. But the novel time line is unreal time, invented time, pretend time. The novel invents an artificial, domestic problem-in-time, and the audience is assured that the problem is resolved and closed.

---

47 In history, the exceptions to "events that really occurred" are often noted, such as Thucydides's invented speeches (*Hist.* 1.22) and digressions in Herodotus that he allows may not be true.

48 Deborah H. Roberts, Francis M. Dunn, and Don Fowler, eds., *Classical Closure: Reading the End in Greek and Latin Literature* (Princeton, NJ: Princeton University Press, 1997); John Marincola, "Closing

Narratives: How Histories End," public lecture, Harvard University, October 14, 1999. On the past, present, and future in Greek thought and its influence on Judith, see the excursus below at Jdt 8:35: "The Book of Judith and Greek Philosophy."

49 The translation is that of Louis H. Feldman (Loeb Classical Library; Cambridge, MA: Harvard University Press, 1965).

In the novel's introduction as well, a voice may announce himself (or herself?), but the voice is not that of a real, named author. The Greek novel authors' names are likely pseudonyms, and Jewish novellas either begin without an author's self-identification (Esther, Judith) or with a fictitious voice (Tobit). Novels may include an *archē*, but it is a pretend *archē*, and at both the beginning and the end the novel imposes a strict start and stop—closure. History places the train of the narrative on a track that theoretically began at the beginning of time and will end at the eschaton, while novel lays only enough track for the story to be told.

From this distinction, we may further refine a definition of history and of the novel. History need not be defined by its intellectual assumptions—by *historia* or reasoned investigation, by a theory of causality, or by any other reference to a rationalistic discourse, but simply by whether the author and audience assume that the events described really happened and by the assumption that the chosen *archē* of the narrative took place on a time line that began before that point and continues past the final words of the narrative and into the present of the audience. [50] History is extended, written prose narrative of a *chosen* segment of the continuous time line shared by the author and audience. The second part of the definition is this: events narrated are assumed by the author and audience to have really happened. In this definition of history, there is no distinction between good and bad history, first-register and second-register, theologically oriented history and rationalistic history, moral causality and historical causality. Nor is there a distinction between the history of the colonizer and that of the colonized. Novel, then, which was co-created with history, is extended written prose narrative of a chosen segment

of a time line that is *not* that of the author and audience, because it is unreal. Unlike the events in history, here the author and audience presume that the events did *not* happen, even if they are set in a real situation of the past.

The Greek and Roman Novel

Despite the fact that the Jewish novellas appeared one or two centuries before the Greek novels, there is an overwhelming tendency to take the high period of Greek and Roman novels as Platonic forms of the genre and to imagine the Jewish examples as lesser imitations. It requires an enormous act of will to treat the history of the genre in its actual order. Still, it was classicists who made great advances in the study of novels, and their conclusions can alert the scholar of the earlier Jewish texts to aspects that may constitute nascent novelistic developments. The fact that biblical scholars have often analyzed the Jewish novellas in relation to earlier biblical tradition only, and not in relation to non-Israelite texts, has also had a limiting effect on the study of Judith.

The advances in the study of the Greek and Roman novels can be rehearsed briefly. Classicists have long focused on a canon of five Greek and two Roman novels: Chariton, *Chaereas and Callirhoe;* Xenophon of Ephesus, *An Ephesian Tale;* Achilles Tatius, *Leucippe and Clitophon;* Heliodorus, *An Ethiopian Story;* Longus, *Daphnis and Chloe;* Apuleius, *Golden Ass,* and Petronius, *Satyricon.* The discussion has now expanded, however, to include earlier texts, marginal texts, newly discovered fragments, and ancient Near Eastern texts. [51] The more inclusive list now adds: Alexander Romance; Ninus Romance; Secundus; Pseudo-Lucius, *The Ass;* selections from Lucian and Dio Chrysostom; Life of Aesop; Phlegon of Tralles, *Book of Marvels;* Antonius

---

50 John Van Seters provides a similar definition: history reflects on the meaning of the past and defines the people of the present (*In Search of History: Historiography in the Ancient World and the Origins of Biblical History* [New Haven: Yale University Press, 1986] 2, 4–5, 354, 359). Cf. also Marc Z. Brettler, *The Creation of History in Ancient Israel* (London: Routledge, 1995) 12; and Baruch Halpern, *The First Historians: The Hebrew Bible and History* (San Francisco: Harper & Row, 1988) 8.

51 The fragments are collected and treated in Stephens and Winkler, *Ancient Greek Novels.* On mixed

texts, see also Christine Thomas, *The Acts of Peter, Gospel Literature, and the Ancient Novel: Rewriting the Past* (Oxford: Oxford University Press, 2003) 9–10, 74–79, 93–104; William F. Hansen, *Anthology of Ancient Greek Popular Literature* (Bloomington: Indiana University Press, 1998) xx–xxi; Paul Veyne, *Did the Greeks Believe in Their Myths? An Essay on the Constitutive Imagination* (Chicago: University of Chicago Press, 1988) esp. 21–22, 103–4; Wiseman and Gill, *Lies and Fiction;* Tomas Hägg, "*Callirhoe* and *Parthenope:* The Beginnings of the Historical Novel," *Classical Antiquity* 6 (1987) 184–204.

Diogenes, *The Wonders beyond Thule,* epistolary novels, the false histories of the Trojan War by Dictys and Dares, early Christian apocryphal Acts and Pseudo-Clementine literature. A relevant Egyptian narrative is Dream of Nectanebo (second century BCE). Less common are considerations of Parthenius, *Erotica Pathemata;* Aristaenetus, *Love Letters;* Alciphron, *Letters;* Aelian, *A Varied History;* and Polyaenus, *Stratagems.* Early stories like Aristides's *Milesiaka* are also seen as trial runs of the novel.

The main Greek novels feature young, beautiful, aristocratic protagonists who are either engaged or newly married, and who clearly deserve to experience nothing but the most perfect happiness. Forced out of their protected environment, they are kidnapped, dragged about the Mediterranean, and descend into the world of the "Other"—slavery, starvation, loneliness, imprisonment by barbarians, threat of rape, and death. They are finally reunited, entering into the blissful life of the aristocratic couple that they were promised. The Greek novels, according to Consuelo Ruiz-Montero, present a new heroic quest for utopia that ends right where the protagonists began, a social contract of the *oikos* based on love, an *erōtopolis:* "love is the overlord and the best [citizen] is the best lover."[52]

The depiction of chaos in the Greek novels might suggest that there is also a subversive element, a questioning of the values of elite domestic life. If the novels describe a movement east, yet do not mention Rome or the Greek mainland, and if the protagonists lose their protected, elite status and discover camaraderie with the lower classes, do we then perceive in the novels a critique of the imperial center? Perhaps. It must be noted—and is perhaps relevant for the study of Jewish novellas—that Heliodorus, Lucian, and Iamblichus were eastern (Phoenician or Syrian), and Apuleius describes himself as half-Numidian and half-Gaetulian (North African; *Apology* 24). His theme in *Golden Ass* is Egypt, Isis, and hybridity. Some have even perceived in the Greek novels the expression of an imagined, *primal* Greek identity, understood to be superior to the Roman wielders of power.[53] To be sure, there is ambiguity in the Greek novels' engagement with imperial values, but the descent into otherness may be liminal and temporary. The exhilaration, tension, even anxiety set off by the reading of a Greek novel results from the sense that aristocratic youths come to be treated exactly the way that poor people, slaves, and barbarians are treated every day all around them. The *eros* and fear is palpable, perhaps reflecting an ambivalence about the treatment of the Other. In the process, both Greek and non-Greek identity are interestingly stereotyped, referenced in a one-dimensional way.[54] Whatever buffeting the protagonists may experience, they return at the end

---

52 Consuelo Ruiz-Montero, "Rise of the Greek Novel," in Schmeling, *Novel in the Ancient World,* 29–85, here 41, 55–56, 80; Fusillo, "Modern Critical Theories," 277, 301–5; Holzberg, "Genre: Novels Proper and the Fringe," 20–21, 26.

53 Margaret Anne Doody, *The True Story of the Novel* (New Brunswick, NJ: Rutgers University Press, 1996) 15–32; Katharine Haynes, *Fashioning the Feminine in the Greek Novel* (London: Routledge, 2003) 156–62; Kathryn Chew, "'On Fire with Desire' (*puroumenē pothō*): Passion and Conversion in the Ancient Greek Novels and Early Christian Female Virgin Martyr Accounts," in Ramelli and Perkins, *Early Christian and Jewish Narrative,* 247–71, here at 250. Contrasting the accommodating novels and the antisocial perspective of Christian novellas are Judith Perkins, *The Suffering Self: Pain and Narrative Representation in the Early Christian Era* (London: Routledge, 1995) 26–28, 42–47, 67, 75, 116–17, 132–36; Michael E. Vines, *The Problem of Markan Genre: The Gospel of Mark and the Jewish Novel* (Academia Biblica 3;

Atlanta: Society of Biblical Literature, 2002) 20–21, 130; Eric Thurman, "Novel Men: Masculinity and Empire in Mark's Gospel and Xenophon's *An Ephesian Tale,*" in Todd Penner and Caroline Vander Stichele, eds., *Mapping Gender in Ancient Religious Discourses* (Biblical Interpretation Series 84; Leiden: Brill, 2007) 185–229; and Virginia Burrus, "Mimicking Virgins: Colonial Ambivalence and the Ancient Romance," *Arethusa* 38 (2005) 49–88.

54 On these issues, see Susan Stephens, "Cultural Identity," in Tim Whitmarsh, ed., *The Cambridge Companion to the Greek and Roman Novel* (Cambridge: Cambridge University Press, 2008) 56–71, here 61, 69; Simon Samuel, *A Postcolonial Reading of Mark's Story of Jesus* (LNTS 340; London: T&T Clark, 2007) 35–51; Perkins, *Roman Imperial Identities in the Early Christian Era* (Routledge Monographs in Classical Studies; London: Routledge, 2009) 62–89; Tim Whitmarsh, "Class," in Whitmarsh, ed., *Cambridge Companion,* 72–89, here 72, 84–86; Whitmarsh, *Greek Literature and the Roman Empire: The Politics of*

to a more secure status, away from the lower and foreign classes with whom they were mixing.

Where Greek novels were once viewed as déclassé, with a low literary quality, some are now held up as sophisticated literary productions. At the sophisticated end of the spectrum are Heliodorus, Longus, Petronius, and Apuleius, and we may now add Lollianos and Iolaus; at a mid-level are Achilles Tatius, Iamblichus, Aesop, and Ninus, and at a low level of technique are Apollonius King of Tyre, Sesonchosis, Alexander Romance, and the Christian acts and Pseudo-Clementine literature. An instructive case is the difference in literary qualities between Apuleius's *Metamorphoses* and his source text, *The Ass.* J. P. Sullivan notes in the latter an unsophisticated lack of variation in style: unnecessary connectives, participles, and the overuse of present tense.[55] Judith and other Jewish novellas might be considered roughly equivalent in terms of literary attainments, although the charges of ineptitude might also include the Semitizing effects of too few participles and the incessant use of *kai* and *kai egeneto*. But Judith and 3 Maccabees have the same novelistic habit of *Aesop*: simple sentence structure and a surprising variety of vocabulary items, even rare terms.[56]

A further cautionary tale on the issue of literary quality commands our attention. Xenophon's *Ephesian Tale* was long considered a lesser Greek novel, but David Konstan has pressed for a reassessment.[57] His colleagues, he suggests, missed some of the qualities of this novel. Xenophon creates a web of actions and relations that at the end serve to reestablish a well-ordered society. The ideal, young, elite couple is featured on one level, and less-elite or foreign characters on another. The elite protagonists suffer many threats and outrages, yet they respond in a passive way, by simply holding on to chastity, *sōphrosynē*, a protective wall of virtue erected against violence. Characters other than the two protagonists are depicted as brazen or active; we see, as a result, two different ways of relating to the world. It is not much of a leap from the protagonists' "lover's chastity" to the chastity in the Christian Apocryphal Acts. Yet *Ephesian Tale* is not quite Christian, because there is one arena in which the two protagonists are both *active,* even rivaling each other like athletes: in making love (1.9.9–10.1; cf. *erōtopolis* above). Christian novels would reject lovemaking in favor of permanent chastity, yet this novel does not affirm the Roman assumption that all love is hierarchical. Although some of the wordplay and sophistication of the other novels is not present in this text, a moral universe is deftly spun out. And so with Judith: do its simple narrative surfaces hide a more compelling literary experience?

Synchronic and Diachronic Considerations

There is a tension between diachronic investigations, which consider texts in their originary performance situations and separately in each subsequent period, and synchronic investigations, which telescope observations from different time frames, including the present, placing them in dialogue with each other. One must consider the advantages and disadvantages of applying the synchronic category of "novel," understood transhistorically and cross-culturally.[58] The word *novel* derives originally from *novella,* the diminutive of the Latin neuter plural of *novus,* new; *novella* means new things. But in continental Europe, *roman* and its cognates are used for the genre.[59] Novels may draw some of their narrative motifs from early epic or folk traditions, but the genre, properly

Imitation (Oxford: Oxford University Press, 2001) 17–20; Morales, "Challenging Some Orthodoxies: The Politics of Genre and the Ancient Greek Novel," in Karla, *Fiction on the Fringe,* 1–12, here 7.

55 Sullivan, "The Ass," in Reardon, ed., *Collected Ancient Greek Novels,* 589–618, here 591.

56 In terms of length, Holzberg classifies King of Tyre and True Histories as novels, texts only slightly longer than Judith ("Genre," 27).

57 Konstan, "Xenophon of Ephesus: Eros and Narrative in the Novel," in Morgan and Stoneman, *Greek Fiction,* 49–63; Konstan, *Sexual Symmetry,* 30–33;

Consuelo Ruiz-Montero, "Una interpretación del 'estilo KAI' de Jenofonte de Éfeso," *Emerita* 50 (1982) 305–23, here 318–21. Xenophon of Ephesus combines *apheleia* (simplicity) and *glykytēs* (sweetness) to imitate a traditional historical style of Ionic prose. Novel here also mimics an earlier *Fachprosa.*

58 John Frow affirms both diachronic and synchronic aspects as genre criteria (*Genre: The New Critical Idiom* [Oxford: Routledge, 2005] 74–76).

59 In the late twentieth century, there was a debate among English-speaking scholars over whether the Greek texts were novels or romances, a problem

speaking, arises only where written prose is the medium. Even if the texts functioned as readings for oral performance—say, in dinner entertainments—they arose only where there was an investment in the written medium. Novels have appeared in only a few historical contexts: in ancient Greece and Rome (and their eastern colonies), medieval China and Japan, and modern Europe and Russia.[60] A question of cultural anthropology remains to be resolved: why did novels appear in a few cultural contexts only, some of which could not have been influenced by the others? Yet in each case certain genre traits are characteristic: a dialogue of voices, the blending of traditional and new, real and unreal, restrained and indulgent, serious and entertaining, risqué and innocent. And finally: women.

In the twentieth century, some scholars addressed the role of the novel in Western culture, raising issues that apply to ancient Jewish novellas as well. While poetry and traditional forms, argued Claude Lévi-Strauss, communicated mythical beliefs, the novel deconstructed them; it was a form born from "the exhaustion of myth." Northrop Frye likewise despaired of the novel in relation to classical genres: the novel, confined as it is to everyday realism, cannot transcend everyday life as older forms had.[61] Champions of the novel were sure to arise, however. Erich Auerbach and Ian Watt raised up the European novel, with its modern, realistic worldview, as the appropriate art form for a new middle class.[62] Mikhail Bakhtin also countered Lévi-Strauss and Frye by insisting that the unity of vision of the older poetic forms was "monologic" only, and the novel affirms the dialogical, polyglot voices passing in and out of the text.[63] Each character acquires a zone in which to speak on his or her own; a polyphony of voices results. Bakhtin also posits another aspect of the novel that will be relevant for our discussion of Judith: there is a dialogic relation in the novel, not only among voices but also between a text and its predecessors in the tradition.

The origin of the novel, both modern and ancient, is thus explained in terms of its "borrowing" from history, biography, satire, poetry, and epic—although this judgment often assumes that other genres do not arise from the same sort of process. Still, while Levi-Strauss emphasized *bricolage* in culture, the borrowing and repackaging of motifs in new ways, it might be argued that the novel is different from other genres in being *all about bricolage*.[64] The novel author absorbs motifs from as many sources as possible, high and low traditions, while at the same time blithely exploding the classical orders. The mixed nature of the motifs and methods of the novel should not be seen as negative, nor as an embarrassment to the scholar. In §4 above, I stated that Judith is formed of Israelite and non-Israelite motifs thrown into a blender. Judith is a Bakhtinian orgy of the *joie de bricolage*. Motifs are broken off of their original settings and repurposed to tell a *different* story. There is a distinctly *new*—thus "novel"—vision that creates a fiction out of oppressive empires.

---

that would not have presented itself in European languages that use one word, *roman* (and related terms), for both.

60. Regarding very low literacy rates, consider here the Chinese, Japanese, or Russian novels.

61. Claude Lévi-Strauss, *The Origin of Table Manners* (Introduction to a Science of Mythology 3; London: Jonathan Cape, 1978) 129–31; Frye, *Anatomy of Criticism*, 250, 304–6; Frye, *The Secular Scripture: A Study of the Structure of Romance* (Charles Eliot Norton Lectures, 1974–1975; Cambridge, MA: Harvard University Press, 1976).

62. Erich Auerbach, *Mimesis: The Representation of Reality in Western Literature* (new ed.; Princeton, NJ: Princeton University Press, 2013); Ian Watt, *The Rise of the Novel: Studies in Defoe, Richardson and Fielding* (new ed.; Berkeley: University of California Press, 2001).

63. Bakhtin, *Dialogic Imagination*, esp. 89, 375; Bakhtin, *Problems of Dostoevsky's Poetics* (Minneapolis: University of Minnesota Press, 1984). My discussion is heavily indebted to McKeon, *Origins of the English Novel*, and Bruce D. MacQueen, *Myth, Rhetoric, and Fiction: A Reading of Longus's "Daphnis and Chloe"* (Lincoln: University of Nebraska Press, 1990).

64. On the *bricolage* of the novel, see Stephens and Winkler, "Introduction," in *Ancient Greek Novels*, 9. On the novel as an anti-genre, see Steve Nimis, "The Prosaics of the Ancient Novel," *Arethusa* 27 (1994) 387–411, here 398; and C. Thomas, *Acts of Peter*, 9–10.

As the modern novel was associated with popular culture and popular literature, so also the ancient.[65] But "popular literature" here does not refer to the number of readers, nor to the intellectual level of the text, but to the text's function. Popular literature is text that no one *has* to read. It functions as entertainment and is transmitted without any official sponsorship.[66] Popular art is often marked by theatricality and performativity, and indeed, Judith, Esther, Tobit, and 3 Maccabees may all have been associated with actual theatricality and performativity, if Judith, Esther, and 3 Maccabees (see 6:36, Josephus, *Against Apion* 2.55) were indeed read for festivals and Tobit for wedding celebrations.[67] Certain traits are associated with popular literature in general, and with novels as a subset: immediacy of impact; an indifference to elite conventions; repetition of common topoi and clichés; a surfeit of emotions and an elaboration of detail; schematic psychological characterizations established through simple parallels and dualistic contrasts; a snobbish setting in high society or a pastoral setting among innocents; sentimental themes; escapism; unequivocally happy endings; and, last—to adopt an oxymoron—a déclassé pretension. It is sometimes assumed that popular literature lacks complexity, but that is not, strictly speaking, true. The complexity in oral and popular narratives arises from the fears and yearnings evoked, not necessarily the characterizations presented.[68] Thus the novel, as popular literature, always looks like something else, often history. The military discussions and expeditions of the first half of Judith look like bad Greek history; the second half looks like bad Israelite history. But the genius of popular literature lies in not caring. This freedom—this studied, at times even *fake*

ineptitude—allows for an art form that survives by the criterion of entertainment alone.

Jewish Novellas

We circle back to the four questions with which we began:

1. What are we choosing to call this genre?
2. Is this a native or a modern label? Would the ancient audience have used or even understood this term?
3. Which texts are we including, and which are we excluding?
4. Would the ancient audience have perceived the same boundaries?

The questions are all important, and not easily resolved, but here we make some suggestions.

Around 200 BCE, or perhaps earlier in the case of Esther, entertaining texts arose among Jews that were characterized by imaginative, idealized, domestic settings; women characters; humor and irony; and happy endings.[69] Multiple stages of the Jewish texts can be discerned, and in some cases the order, relationships, and even dates can be known more precisely than is generally the case with popular literature. In addition, while the later Greek novels often *implicitly* engaged issues of center and periphery within the empire, the Jewish novellas appeared in a colonized situation and *explicitly* addressed the issues of indigenous people and empire. They thus provide a laboratory for the analysis of center and periphery, empire and colony.

The category of free narrative was introduced above, that broad range of texts that, from our point of view,

65 See Hansen, *Anthology*, i–xix; Pierre Bourdieu, *Distinction: A Social Critique of the Judgment of Taste* (Cambridge, MA: Harvard University Press, 1984) 32–35; Oswald Ducrot and Tzvetan Todorov, *Encyclopedic Dictionary of the Sciences of Language* (Baltimore: Johns Hopkins University Press, 1979) 151; Averil Cameron, *Christianity and the Rhetoric of Empire: The Development of Christian Discourse* (Sather Classical Lectures 55; Berkeley: University of California Press, 1991) 103–8.

66 We may rightly ask, of course, whether the Jewish novellas cease to be "popular literature" when they are canonized, but they may have continued on two levels, as Esther did for Jews.

67 On the last, see Wills, *Jewish Novel*, 68–92.

68 Adele Berlin argues that farce and carnival characters are necessarily two-dimensional type-characters (*Esther* אסתר: *The Traditional Hebrew Text with the New JPS Translation* [JPS Bible Commentary; Philadelphia: Jewish Publication Society, 2001] xvi–xxiii), but Adelman disagrees in the case of Esther (*Female Ruse*, 226).

69 Esther may have arisen as early as the fourth century BCE, and Tobit and parts of Daniel 1–6 may have been composed before 200 BCE.

seemed to partake of history *and* novel. Here I divide Jewish free narrative into three groups: (1) novellas, (2) popular histories, and (3) national hero romances.[70] The Jewish novellas include Esther and Daniel in both their Semitic and Greek forms; Judith; Tobit; and Joseph and Aseneth; in addition, some fragments of unidentified novellas have been found at Qumran.[71] Testament of Joseph, Testament of Abraham, and Testament of Job might also be included, but they, along with Joseph and Aseneth, may be later and Christian, a question that will not be treated here. The novellas take as protagonists unknown or marginal figures from the ancient past and include many women characters.[72] Likely read as fictions—at least at their early stages—they include wild and patently unbelievable royal figures: "Darius the Mede" (Darius was a famous Persian king), "Nebuchadnezzar king of the Assyrians" (Nebuchadnezzar was a famous Babylonian king) and "Esther queen of Persia" (there was no Jewish queen of Persia). Other novellas, 3 Maccabees and Testament of Abraham, mimicked familiar genres and were likely read as satirical.[73]

"Popular history" refers to those texts that, though probably treated as a kind of history, were nevertheless written in an engaging and entertaining manner. Second Maccabees and the Tobiad Romance and Royal Family of Adiabene from Josephus's *Antiquities* (12.4.1–11 §§154–236 and 20.2.1–20.4.3 §§17–96) may be considered popular history. Among the Greeks, it has been noted, there was an upper register of restrained, rationalistic histories—Herodotus, Thucydides, and Polybius—and a second register that exploited rhetorical means to manipulate emotion. These authors were accused of embellishing incidents, even inventing them, and may be similar to the Jewish popular histories.[74] The most respected historians complained about the low standards of texts such as these and assumed more discerning audiences for their own works.

The third category, national hero romance, included imaginative accounts of the exploits of the ancient heroes of a people: among Jews, Artapanus's *Moses Romance* (and related fragments), and among non-Jews, Story of Ahikar, Alexander Romance, Ninus, Sesonchosis, Petubastis, and

---

70   A similar division of Greek texts is put forward by Stephens, "Fragments of Lost Novels," in Schmeling, *Novel in the Ancient World*, 655–82: (1) ideal-romantic; (2) satirical novels; (3) indigenous national hero romance (such as Ninus and Sesonchosis); and (4) a mixed category including wonder tales such as Antonius Diogenes's *Wonders beyond Thule*. She separates ideal or earnest novels from satirical novels, which I consider to be two sides of the same coin. My category "popular histories" is not represented in Stephens's discussion, but she would perhaps consider them "second-register histories" (see below). There are no known ancient Jewish examples of wonder tales, although visionary traditions come to mind.

71   Sidnie White Crawford, "4QTales of the Persian Court (4Q550A–E) and Its Relation to Biblical Royal Courtier Tales, Especially Esther, Daniel, and Joseph," in Edward D. Herbert and Emanuel Tov, eds., *The Bible as Book: The Hebrew Bible and the Judaean Desert Discoveries* (London: Oak Knoll, 2002) 121–37. Some of these Qumran fragments were at first termed "pseudo-Esther," but it was later recognized that they simply partake of the same genre as Esther.

72   Note that the Greek novels do not depict their own times, but Latin novels do, satirizing and deconstructing their own society.

73   David Konstan and Robyn Walsh, "Civic and Subversive Biography in Antiquity," in Kristoffel Demoen and Koen De Temmerman, eds., *Writing Biography in Greece and Rome: Narrative Technique and Fictionalization* (Cambridge: Cambridge University Press, 2016) 3–24; and Konstan, "The *Testament of Abraham* and Greek Romance," in Ramelli and Perkins, *Early Christian and Jewish narrative*, 45–51, here 46, distinguish civic and subversive biography. The latter article depicts "the wit and cleverness of marginal or relatively powerless figures, who subtly criticized or undermined the dominant values of society." Testament of Abraham, Aesop and Life of Homer were examples of subversive biography, essentially a fictional version of biography. Judith is similar but parodies foreign powers, not Jewish powers. Only if we show that it deconstructs *the audience*'s treasured assumptions can we say that it is subversive biography; this has been proposed, but unconvincingly (see §6 above).

74   These three upper-register historians may not have been considered typical. See Emilio Gabba, "True History and False History in Classical Antiquity," *JRS* 71 (1981) 50–62, here 50; and Mendels, *Rise and Fall*, 35–37; T. P. Wiseman, *Clio's Cosmetics: Three Studies in Greco-Roman Literature* (Totowa, NJ: Rowman & Littlefield, 1979) x.

Setne Khamwas. Says Richard Stonemen regarding the Alexander Romance:

> The narrative and correspondence in the *Romance* seem alike to have been devised by authors familiar with Alexander's history but with no interest in using it other than as a starting-point for romance. The historical element, therefore, is often as fanciful as such Hollywood epics as *Spartacus*.[75]

The international theme of the Jewish national hero romances reflects an important trait of this eastern-based genre, and the relation of author and audience to a foreign empire must be noted.

The first category, then, Jewish novellas, were farcical deliverance texts: Esther, Judith, Tobit, 3 Maccabees, the early Daniel cycle.[76] There is some evidence, though meager, that the ancient audiences considered the Jewish novellas to be similar to one another. At Qumran, the novelistic texts were written on smaller scrolls, what one scholar refers to as the "'éditions de poche' de l'antiquité."[77] First Clement 55:3–6 holds up Esther and Judith as exemplars of *andreia*, courage (literally, manfulness), but is this a statement about the *text* genre, or simply about *heroines* of the faith? Perhaps both, for three centuries later Judith, Esther, and Tobit were placed together in the Christian Old Testament. A kinship was likely perceived here, but these texts were now also "Bible," and were perhaps viewed as history (see above).

These later pieces of evidence do not directly speak to the function of the texts when they were composed, about which we may only guess. However, festivals and celebrations are frame devices at the end of Esther, Judith, and 3 Maccabees (and perhaps hidden in Tobit), suggesting either that these texts were *Festlegenden* for actual festivals, or that this was the fictitious setting. The emphasis on the *mišteh*, drinking party, in Esther, the dinners in the Tobiad Romance, and the marriage in Tobit, which would have included a family celebration, all render "dinner entertainment" a possible performance situation, perhaps also true of the Greek and Roman novels. Greek dinners included performative aspects: the *pompē*, procession; the *theatron*, theater; and the *drama*.[78] Something like this was probably true for elite Jewish dinners as well.

Judith is a satire of the foreign rulers, but not a satire of the author's own institutions.[79] The book of Judith is propagandistic in that its target is external to its own society: Nebuchadnezzar and the Assyrians, who must be ciphers for the contemporary Syrians, the Seleucids. And the satire here can spill over into burlesque. Terms such as *burlesque*, *camp*, and *vamp* may apply to this text, as do modern popular culture concepts like performativity and theatricality.[80] The broad humor of Judith may have had a function in Judean society similar to what *grand guignol*, Yiddish theater, or vaudeville played in the twentieth century.

Judith exhibits parallels to ancient satire and trickster traditions. To be sure, trickster *tales*, as opposed to trickster novellas, often circulate in cycles. "The tale," notes Niditch, "does not end with unequivocal success, but [tricksters] survive to trick again."[81] But we saw above

---

75 Stoneman, *Alexander Romance*, 11.

76 Daniel 1–6, however, was evidently brought back from the edge of parody when it was combined with the apocalyptic visions of Daniel 7–12; see Wills, *Jew in the Court*, 75–152. On Tobit as comedy, see Anathea Portier-Young, "Alleviation of Suffering in the Book of Tobit: Comedy, Community, and Happy Endings," *CBQ* 63 (2004) 35–54, but opposing: J. R. C. Cousland, "Tobit: A Comedy in Error?" *CBQ* 65 (2004) 535–53.

77 J. T. Milik, "Les modèles araméens du livre d'Esther dans la grotte 4 de Qumrân," *RevQ* 59 (1992) 321–406, here 363–65.

78 Plutarch, *On Love of Wealth* 10 (*Moralia* 528B); cf. Petronius, *Satyrica* 26–78.

79 As Jonah is, and Job and Testament of Abraham may be; see Wills, *Jewish Novel*, 245–56; Konstan, "Testa-

ment of Abraham," 45–51; Jared Ludlow, *Abraham Meets Death: Narrative Humor in the Testament of Abraham* (JSPSup 41; London: Sheffield Academic Press, 2002). The distinction between satire and parody should not distract us from discerning the larger novelistic tendencies. Bakhtin saw all parody, satire, and so on as one intergeneric "immense novel" (*Dialogic Imagination*, 59–60).

80 One of the few Judith scholars to make such a modern comparison is Barbara Schmitz, who refers to Judith as a "vamp" ("Trickster, Schriftgelehrte oder *femme fatale*? Die Juditfigur zwischen biblischer Erzählung und kunstgeschichtlicher Rezeption," *Biblisches Forum* 1 [2004] 4–5).

81 Niditch, *Underdogs and Tricksters: A Prelude to Biblical Folklore* (San Francisco: Harper & Row, 1987) xi; see also Miller, "Femme Fatale," 231.

that committing a trickster story to writing seems to have been a common activity for ancient Near Eastern scribes. The written text of Judith, then, is different from the oral trickster tales in that it is not a cycle but a single story with a single arc, with a beginning, a middle, and an end. The resolution communicates closure, "they lived happily ever after." But the trickster tradition is still present, as it has influenced some of the other marginal novelistic texts, such as Artapanus, Tobiad Romance, Alexander Romance, and Life of Aesop. Corinne Jouanno argues that the early experimental forms of the novel—early "free narrative"?—constituted a "trickster genre." Invoking Carl Jung, she suggests that the trickster theme allows primitive instincts to surface: lying, cheating, stealing, committing adultery—all that the Ten Commandments forbid.[82] This is the shadow of the moral self, and where better than Judith? Further, the trickster is always sure of him- or herself and, by the convention of the trickster tradition, always succeeds.

Yet if Judith, Esther, Tobit, and parts of Daniel were novellas and were read as fiction, how did they *so quickly* come to be treated as scripture and history? It is not clear precisely how or when this occurred, but two pathways are possible. First, the *characters* Jonah, Daniel, Susanna, Esther, and Judith began in fiction and humor, but by the first century CE all of these personae were treated as models of faithfulness. Although it was likely the texts that

first popularized these virtuous personae, very quickly it was perhaps not so much the *texts* that come to be treated as historical but the *revered figures themselves,* the heroes and heroines, who now had a life outside of the texts, in a sort of secondary orality. The earliest known Christian art, admittedly several centuries later, depicted Susanna, Daniel, and Jonah as models, and the synagogue at Dura Europos depicted Esther.[83] Susanna, like Judith, was understood typologically as Christ, the church, Mary, chastity, or martyrdom. Thus, the line that led from fiction to history may have passed through hagiography and typology. Second, all biblical texts soon came to be understood as part of one universal history. Esther and Daniel, therefore, became required reading for both Jewish and Christian chronographers who needed these texts to fill in the gaps in God's time line.[84] Laying the track of history required the recruitment of more track!

Literary Qualities of Judith; Humor, Irony, and Lying

Any consideration of the book of Judith as a member of the genre novel or novella must include discussion of its literary qualities. The literary aspects are not in every case the same as those found in the Greek and Roman novels—nor should we expect that—but what is similar is an engagement with narrative entertainment.

---

82 Jouanno, "Novelistic Lives," 42–46. See also Radin, *Trickster,* 202–9. Although the trickster is usually driven by self-interest, Ehud's assassination of Eglon is an instance of the redeemer-trickster. On Artapanus, see Gruen, "The Twisted Tale of Artapanus: Biblical Rewritings as Novelistic Narrative," in Ramelli and Perkins, *Early Christian and Jewish Narrative,* 31–44.

83 Third Maccabees 6:6–8, though probably fictitious itself, indicates reverence for Jonah, Daniel, and his three companions; these figures also appear often in early Christian art, and Susanna appears arrayed with Abraham, Isaac, Moses, and others. See Annewies van den Hoek and John J. Herrmann, Jr., "Celsus' Competing Heroes: Jonah, Daniel, and Their Rivals," in Albert Frey and Rémi Gounelle, eds., *Poussières de christianisme et de judaïsme antiques: Études réunies en l'honneur de Jean-Daniel Kaestli et Éric Junod* (Publications de l'Institut romand des sciences bibliques 5; Lausanne: Éditions du Zèbre, 2007)

307–39, here 307–11; van den Hoek and Herrmann, "Thecla the Beast Fighter: A Female Emblem of Deliverance in Early Christian Popular Art," *Studia Philonica Annual* 13 (2001) 212–49; and Robin Jensen, *Understanding Early Christian Art* (London: Routledge, 2000) 25, 69. A glass bowl from Montenegro (fourth century CE) depicts Jonah, Daniel, the three companions, and Susanna. Irenaeus, Clement, and Tertullian mention some combination of Elijah, Enoch, Jonah, Daniel, and the three young men as examples of God's protection.

84 Cf. Josephus's *Antiquities* and the rabbinic chronology Seder Olam; see Wills, *Jewish Novel,* 221–22; and Chaim Milikowsky, "Midrash as Fiction and Midrash as History: What Did the Rabbis Mean?" in Jo-Ann A. Brant, Charles W. Hedrick, and Chris Shea, eds., *Ancient Fiction: The Matrix of Early Christian and Jewish Narrative* (SymS 32; Atlanta: Society of Biblical Literature, 2005) 117–27, here 122–23.

We begin at a basic level. Interesting examples of wordplay, humor, and irony have long been noted in Judith.[85] Words are often repeated to develop both theme and audience response—*kyrios* ("lord"), *ischys* ("strength"), *cheir* ("hand"), *phobos* ("fear" and synonyms), *apatē* ("deception"), *kallos* ("beauty"), *(ana)boaō* ("cry out"), and *dynamis* ("power")—a technique common in the Hebrew Bible.[86] Retardation and acceleration of plot, common in ancient storytelling, rise to extravagance in Judith. The entire first half of the book is retardation of plot, as the audience is treated to one military campaign—and discussion of it—after another, while, on the other hand, the famous beheading scene, the "acteme" that the audience would have been anticipating, is told in a few quick verses.[87] More experimental is the telescoping of historical epochs as an open advertisement of the text's fictionality. There are also highly developed structural patterns, a vast number of biblical and Greek allusions, and even occasional slapstick.[88] A delicious, balanced irony is created by Achior and Holofernes both unknowingly "prophesying" their own fates, one positively and one negatively (chaps. 5–6). Although it is not clear how intentional it was, there is an alternation of Semitizing biblical style in the narrative and Greek style in prayers and direct quotations. This distinction roughly parallels a further contrast, that between the self-willed nature of Judith's actions and the pious and dependent theme of her prayers, what I have likened in the commentary to the ironic distance found in some operas between music and libretto.[89] Finally, we should not overlook the literary and psychological qualities of the sheer effrontery of this author: the gleeful transgression of codes of decorum and, in the acteme, the intimate mixing of sex and violence.

Much of the irony of Judith, indeed, derives from the constant lying of the heroine. To be sure, some scholars formerly analyzed Judith's words closely to argue that, in a technical sense, she does not lie. She was deliberately imprecise, and allowed Holofernes to draw inaccurate conclusions, but it was held that she was not technically guilty of lying herself. In regard to some of her statements, this is possible, but the effort to absolve her on a technicality seemed strained. Moore's reading, however, is more typical: of the fifteen verses of her speech to Holofernes (11:5–19), only one contains a true statement: Achior did indeed speak before the Bethulian council (v. 9).[90] If Judith's attempt was to deceive, was an occasional defense by technicality significant? Ernst Haag provides a different defense.[91] The apparent *ethical* problem with Judith's deception is really *theological*: God is hardening the heart of Holofernes through the words of Judith, as he has elsewhere worked by the hand of Judith. But however much we might imagine here the figure of Pharaoh, the text says nothing about this. Holofernes seems rather to be a victim of his own stupidity *and Judith's manipulation,* not God's hardening of his heart.

The enjoyment of this farce depends on Judith's coming very close to actual violations of Jewish values, or even crossing over the usual lines, while being vindicated by her high-minded goal. Some of her words are deceiving in spirit even when they are not technically inaccurate. To complete the manipulation of Holofernes, for instance,

---

85   See the excursus "Literary Effects in the Acteme" at 13:9b–10a.

86   Zenger, *Das Buch Judit,* 433–34; Rakel, *Judit–Über Schönheit,* 88, 92; Gera, *Judith,* 86.

87   On the beheading as the "acteme" that the audience would have already known about and would expect, see Stocker, *Judith,* 11.

88   On the structural patterns, see Craven, *Artistry and Faith,* 47–112. On slapstick, see Ludlow, "Are Weeping and Falling Down Funny? Exaggerations in Ancient Novelistic Texts" and Angela Standhartinger, "Humor in Joseph and Aseneth," both presentations at Society of Biblical Literature Annual Meeting, Baltimore, Maryland, November 25, 2013.

89   Gera, "Speech in Judith," 413–23, speaks to these distinctions as well. On the distinction of Hebrew and Greek style, see Original Language. The self-willed aspect of Judith's persona is partially explained by the trickster theme.

90   Moore, *Judith,* 212.

91   Ernst Haag, "Judit und Holofernes: Zur theologisch-ethischen Problematik in Jdt 10–11," in Hans-Gerd Angel, Johannes Reiter, and Hans-Gerd Wirtz, eds., *Aus reichen Quellen leben: Ethische Fragen in Geschichte und Gegenwart; Helmut Weber zum 65. Geburtstag* (Trier: Paulinus-Verlag, 1995) 55–67.

Judith swears by what is holy to him—the name of Nebuchadnezzar—and praises the general shamelessly. In v. 7 Judith herself confesses Nebuchadnezzar as the divine power who gives life and abundance, not only to people, but adds that because of him "the animals and the cattle and the birds will live." Such things are said of Nebuchadnezzar also in Dan 2:37–38 and 4:12.[92] The mythology of kingship in the ancient Near East often attributed life-giving powers to the king, and Judith serves up this un-Israelite mythology without restraint. Holofernes will also believe every word of her false flattery:

> For we have heard of your wisdom [*sophia*] and the clever strategies of your heart [*panourgeumata tēs psychēs sou*]. It is proclaimed throughout the whole earth that you alone are best in the whole kingdom, able in experience and marvelous in military strategy [*dynatos en epistēmē kai thaumastos en strateumasin polemou*]. (11:8–9)

Judith's words here recall her own wisdom and intelligence, attested to in 8:29. But Judith here only *reports* the great things that *others* are saying; she does not affirm them herself—which Holofernes is too obtuse to notice.[93] The narcissist does not question adoration. A delicate touch of irony is that the words used are exaggerations, but the carefully chosen words may undermine his accomplishments. *Panourgeumata* can be either positive or negative, either clever or manipulative, crafty or sneaky (compare Sir 1:6; 42:18). *Thaumastos* resides mainly in the eye of the beholder; in the Platonic philosophical tradition, one would rather be *sophos* than *thaumastos*. Does the author here play on these ambiguities? Does Judith proffer ambivalent compliments that Holofernes chooses to understand too simply?

There have been comic and ironic elements in Judith before, but at this point they become the dominant discourse, continuing through chap. 12. Nearly every word out of Judith's mouth since arriving in the Assyrian camp

is a lie, and most of her words are highly ironic because of the double entendres. Judith is speaking on two levels, one level for the gullible Assyrians and another level for an aware audience. The irony is also presented as a type of discourse totally under her control and is as much her heroic attribute as is her sword.

From the time that Judith and her slave walk out of the gates of Bethulia until the time she returns and shouts for the gates to be opened (13:10b), three constant motifs can be noted:

1. Judith lies.
2. The Assyrians, overwhelmed by her beauty, stumble over themselves in order to cater to each successive wish.
3. She speaks in an extended series of comic and ironic utterances that involve double entendre.

In the Bakhtinian analysis of the zones created by characters in novels, this discourse defines Judith's zone.[94] It may be compared with the particular mode of discourse presented by such figures as Socrates (the *elenchus* and dialogue), Jesus (parables and *chreiai* in the Synoptic Gospels, revelation discourse in the Gospel of John), or Aesop (Cynic ridicule).

Both comedy and irony should be defined for this text. According to Henri Bergson, comedy functions by creating and then releasing tensions.[95] The book of Judith creates and sustains a host of tensions: a woman commands and upbraids the male elders; she lies; she flaunts her sexuality; she kills. In each of these ways Judith pushes to the edge and beyond of what would be permitted, creating and maintaining multisided tensions. All of these become sources of humor when they are spun out for chapters and then dissipated in a release of tension—the denouement initiated by Bagoas's discovery that Holofernes has lost his head. The book of Judith is the most extended use of comedy in the Bible and combines the physical comedy of Bagoas's discovery of the headless

---

92 Cf. also Jer 27:6–7, where God gives Nebuchadnezzar authority. See also the Babylonian affirmation of Nebuchadnezzar as savior of the world in the Wadi Brissa inscription in Stephen Langdon, *Building Inscriptions of the Neo-Babylonian Empire,* part 1 (Paris: Leroux, 1905) B. Col. VIII lines 17–35, 45–50; pp. 171–72, and see Wills, *Jew in the Court,* 104–9.

93 Steven Weitzman, "Literary Approaches," in Jonathan Klawans and Lawrence M. Wills, eds., *Jewish Annotated Apocrypha,* forthcoming.

94 See Bakhtin, *Dialogic Imagination,* passim; and Bakhtin, *Rabelais,* 7–21.

95 Henri Bergson, *Laughter: An Essay on the Meaning of the Comic* (Copenhagen: Green Integer, 1999).

corpse and the more intellectual comedy of irony and parody—even though the latter is also very broad.

Plato and Aristotle argued that humor in Greek drama followed from the audience's sense of superiority to a certain character: one could laugh at the incompetence of others (Plato, *Philebus* 49b–c; Aristotle, *Poetics* 1449a). In Greek New Comedy the chief character to be laughed at was the *alazōn,* the blustery figure who makes himself out to be something more than he is, usually undone by the *eirōn,* from which we derive the term "irony," who deceives by making himself out to be something less than he is. Sigmund Freud saw humor as a release of tension from suppressed fears and desires: repressed notions find relief in communal laughter.[96] Peter Berger argued that humor is a reaction to incongruity: the unexpected in life demands processing, and jokes and comedy highlight instances of incongruity and resolve them in laughter.[97] A more recent theory is helpful in regard to Judith. For A. P. McGraw and Caleb Warren, all forms of humor can be understood as "benign violations," a balancing of a violation of the usual order that is rendered benign through laughter or the "safe" personality of the comedian. The benign violation can be enjoyed communally.[98] If the violation is too great, the *communal* aspect of laughter cannot be maintained. But if the violation is too benign, there is no challenge of conventions. Humor exists, then, in a negotiated balance between benign and violation and allows for a communal processing of intentional, carefully manipulated violations. One may also consider the outrageous release in festivals such as Mardi Gras, Halloween, Indian Holi, and Purim; the book of Judith may indeed have been performed at a festival such as Nicanor's Day (b. Ta'an. 18b).

Irony, double entendre, and humor—Judith's "double-dealing"[99]—are her stock-in-trade, which draws the audience into the real attraction of the story, a series of flirtations with sexual transgression and a bloody decapi-tation, the "acteme" of the narrative. Many Bible stories of women feature humor and irony, and many feature sex and violence, but Judith combines humor, irony, sex, and violence more intimately than elsewhere in the Bible. To find a text with a higher combined index of sex and violence, one would have to pass over into pornography. It may be argued that the European painters of Judith sometimes did just that (see §8 below).

Judith is comic both in having a happy ending, which is never in doubt, and in the humorous skewering of the presumptuous enemy. In religious texts, irony can also be an intimation of providence. If the audience perceives a second or hidden meaning in a passage, that must reflect a God's-eye view of things rather than the human's-eye view of the surface level. The audience perceives what God intends, while many of the characters in the text do not. The lesson for the discerning reader is: the wise person can perceive God's role *behind* events. (This is treated explicitly in Wisdom 2–5, although without irony. The earnestness and explicit treatment take away the experience of irony.)

Most of the humor in Judith, then, comes through irony of two different sorts: the incongruity that results when an event has an unexpected outcome (situational irony), or the incongruity that results when a statement has both a surface meaning and a very different implied meaning (verbal irony). They are both related to the incongruity theory of humor above. A development of verbal irony is dramatic irony, when the incongruity is perceived by the audience, but not by one or more of the characters.[100] Cataloguing the examples of irony in Judith is almost as difficult as cataloguing the allusions to biblical texts. We may nevertheless register some of the most noted examples. Early on, for instance, the blustery tyrant Holofernes bellows at Achior, "You shall not see my face again from this day forth until I take my vengeance" (6:5). Yet the audience knows that when Achior does see Holofernes's

---

96   Sigmund Freud, "Humor," *International Journal of Psychoanalysis* 9 (1928) 1–6.

97   Peter Berger, *Redeeming Laughter: The Comic Dimension of Human Experience* (New York: de Gruyter, 1997) 22.

98   A. P. McGraw and Caleb Warren, "Benign Violations: Making Immoral Behavior Funny," *Psychological Science* 21 (2010) 1141–49. The edginess and danger of benign versus violation can be seen in the difference in the reception of Charlie Chaplin's tramp and his Hitler. For the latter, Chaplin was exiled from the United States to his native England.

99   Otzen, *Tobit and Judith,* 122.

100 Moore, *Judith,* 78–85; Alonso Schökel, *Narrative Structures,* 8–11; Rakel, *Judit–Über Schönheit,* 57–58.

face again, it will be severed from the rest of his body. In the present section, chaps. 10–12, the irony and humor are a constant, cascading literary effect; one ironic line follows upon another. Some play upon the double meaning of "lord" as both master and God in Israelite discourse:

I will say nothing false to my lord tonight! And if you follow closely the advice of your servant, God will accomplish a great deed through you, and my lord [Holofernes or God?] will not fail to achieve what he has prepared [having sex with Judith or destroying Holofernes?]. (11:5–6)

Who am I to refuse my lord [Holofernes or God?]? . . . I will do at once anything that pleases him; this will bring me joy till my dying day. (12:14)

I will indeed drink, my lord, . . . for my life today has been magnified for me more than ever, since I was born [because she will have sex with Holofernes, or behead him?]. (12:18)

Framing these instances of irony are the larger ironies that define the novella as a whole. An unreal history is boldly created for the setting of this novella, yet real history of Israel is interspersed as well (chap. 5). Achior, the weak agent, had told Holofernes that he would tell the truth (5:5), and does. Judith, the strong agent, said that she would tell the truth, but lies. Holofernes, however, rejects Achior's truth while believing Judith's lies. Foreign oppressors are shamed and reduced to mere foils. For Philip Esler the larger irony of the text is this: Assyrians operate in blind ignorance until it is revealed to them that they have been destroyed as a result. Steven Weitzman notes that Holofernes is "so beguiled by appearances that he cannot grasp what Judith is truly hinting at."[101] Lesser, though still significant, ironies are found in the unexpected relations of characters, summarized by Erich Gruen:

Achior, Gentile though he be, has a clearer vision of Jewish principles than Uzziah, the Judaean magistrate.

Achior also, warrior though he be, keels over at the sight of Holofernes' severed head. And Uzziah, chief magistrate though *he* be, gives Judith full authority to proceed with her plan—despite the fact that he had no idea what it was.[102]

A fascinating and erotic irony in Judith is that Holofernes tries to seduce our heroine by his power and actions, while she convinces him to drink more as she speaks to him. He comes no closer to having sex, but the erotic nature of her words leads him to count it all as foreplay. Yet it is Judith's foreplay. The pious Judith also misrepresents herself by swearing by Nebuchadnezzar (11:7) and finally simply lies, even though she has promised that she would not:

Death will descend upon them [the Israelites]. A sin has overtaken them. . . . They [the Bethulians] have even sent messengers to Jerusalem to ask permission [to violate the law]. . . . He [God] will tell me when they have committed their transgressions. (11:11, 14, 17)

Granted, there is a strong tradition of irony in the Hebrew Bible, continued as well by some early Christian texts, yet Judith is unusual in laying example upon example. The image above of cascading ironies seems appropriate. Gera rightly notes that the number of instances is higher than in other books of the Hebrew Bible (although Judges should be compared, and the Gospel of John likewise exhibits cascading ironies), and she notes as well the similar uses of irony in Greek tragedy.[103] In Aeschylus, *Agamemnon* 600–609, for instance, Clytemnestra speaks to her husband about his sweet return when she is about to kill him. Sophocles's *Oedipus the King* and Plato's *Apology* also play often on irony.

While all recognize that Judith is replete with irony and humor, can it really be compared to some of the great ironic texts of the ancient world—Judges, Greek drama, Plato, John? One might argue that the quantity of irony is very high, but not the quality. The irony is not really very profound, and the typical appeal of irony is

---

101 Esler, Sex, *Wives, and Warriors*, 292–94; Weitzman, "Literary Approaches"; Weitzman also provides an insightful analysis of Judith as a strategy for Hasmonean foreign policy (*Surviving Sacrilege*, 48–53).

102 Gruen, *Diaspora*, 170.

103 Gera, *Judith*, 57–58.

that it *suggests* profound underlying meanings. Our text supplies a sort of cheap irony, a low-level comedy that never rises to a higher-order message. One can hear the laughs of the audience, but never the gasp of a higher recognition.

Still, several observations are in order. First, the true theme of Judith is the brash juxtaposition of the empire's ineptitude and the resourcefulness of the colonized. Subtlety would be misplaced here. Second, the irony is indeed low-comedy humor, but, seen from one level remove, it is *her weapon*. Her wit, literally disarming, is seductive, and causes Holofernes to imbibe "more than he has ever drunk in his entire life." The irony is not the end, as in those other texts, but a means to *characterize* her. As he was undressing her with his eyes, she was undressing him with her words, which turn out to be more powerful. In a real world, her words would not distract a great general, but, with a willful suspension of disbelief, her words become her characteristic weapon. There is an irony-behind-the-irony, then, a separate vantage point that suggests that the liminal experience of transgression allows a different sort of moral victory.

Third, one should recall the nature of popular art and its unself-conscious goal of immediate impact, even carnivalesque enjoyment. If the text were subtler, or even noticeably profound, it would fail as popular art. If popular art were to be visibly raised in technique, it would not gain in artistry, but lose. One might argue the Shakespeare exception—popular art whose irony was as deep and subtle as Plato's—but that is an exception, and the comparison to Plato might have seemed ludicrous to Shakespeare's audience. The better comparison for Judith would be Life of Aesop.[104] One can look anywhere in Aesop and find the theme of the slave undoing the master class with his words, and a close parallel can be seen in the long episode in which the mouthy, disrespectful slave Aesop is commanded by his master

to serve the very best dish to his philosopher guests (Aesop 51–53). Aesop, of course, serves up tongue, accompanied by his own disquisitions on the power of the tongue. Simply put, Aesop is to slavery what Judith is to women's decorum.

Humor and irony, then, create a fictitious world, draw the audience in, destabilize the common cultural values, sometimes to the point where the values threaten to collapse. In parody, the deconstruction is not permanent; the original values are restored and the audience returns to the stable world whence they came. In satire, on the other hand, the deconstruction, the truer perspective, is more lasting, and the audience is changed. Which is Judith? Novelistic texts cross-culturally often employ humor and irony; it is a generic aspect. It is also sometimes assumed that such humorous texts are subversive, but, by depicting a *temporary* and *liminal* violation of social conventions, does a text such as Judith fundamentally call those conventions into question, or simply reinscribe them at the end as an aspect of the world as typically experienced? This is no easy determination. We might consider Jonah, on the one hand, as a satire that ends with a serious questioning of traditional assumptions, or Esther, on the other, a comedy of a woman's role that seems to leave gender roles intact. Yet Esther as a character also moves from meek and identityless in chaps. 1–3 to assertive and strategic in chaps. 4–10.[105] Many comedies, ancient and modern, remain ambiguous as to the final state of the audience—altered or returned to the original order? The generations of reception are also complex.

The Mode or Pleasures of Greek Novels and Judith

A genre may be defined by its motifs, themes, structure, frame, and so on, but can also be defined by its *mode*, the series of pleasures it evokes.[106] In addition to the humor

---

104 For a short introduction to Aesop, and also an English translation, see Wills, *Quest*. Aesop skewered his own society rather than outsiders, but that is precisely the difference between Jewish and Greek novelistic literature. Jewish literature did not have the luxury of passing over outside threats to focus on the ironies of domestic life. Is this the root of what

some classicists find wanting in Jewish novellas? In addition, Testament of Abraham is similar, or even Susanna, on which see Wills, *Jewish Novel*, 53–60, 245–55; and Ludlow, *Abraham Meets Death*.

105 Adelman, *Female Ruse*, 198–230.

106 Frederic Jameson, "Magical Narratives: Romance as a Genre," *New Literary History* 7 (1975) 135–63, here

and irony, other aspects of the mode or pleasures of the Greek novel are also found in Judith. Two overarching aspects are the moral arc and the commitment to virtue and chastity. In regard to the moral arc, it is often suggested that the Greek novel depicts the heroic quest in a post-heroic age. "Their characters," says Richard Stoneman, "are epic heroes newly clad in bourgeois dress and with their emotions tailored to fit a more domestic world."[107] This theme is discernible, though engaged differently, in the Jewish novellas. Some of the Jewish novellas retain "classical" aspects of the hero: the heroic activity, though now domestic, still serves to save others. Most of the Jewish novellas involve the salvation of Jews or Israel, and Judith's persona is often modeled on the Judges (see §4 above). The typical cross-cultural theme of the *essential* isolation and loneliness of the hero is still present in Judith, while reversed in the Greek: the protagonists begin in society, are *forced* into isolation, and are reintegrated into society at the end.[108] It is also ironic that the novel, a genre whose very existence is conditioned by entertainment, would play out themes of virtue, chastity,

and asceticism. The Greek novel, says Bakhtin, is a "test of the hero's integrity" in regard to chastity and faithfulness.[109] Love is here worth dying for; the protagonists strive to become citizens of an *erōtopolis*.

In addition, as noted above, ambiguity and complexity about the sexual themes are evident. Are the male and female protagonists in the Greek novels temporarily equal, the young woman becoming more active and "male," the man becoming more virginal and "female"? Or is this only a temporary and liminal state of affairs, with a return at the end to the hierarchy of male control? For all their thematizing of chastity, the Greek novels also provide a temporary escapism from the demands of *enkrateia* (self-control) as emotions overcome the protagonists.[110] In Heliodorus, *Ethiopian Tale* 4.9, for instance, *eros* is in tension with *enkrateia*:

> Charikleia now ceased to fight her passion [that is, her love-sickness], for struggle as she might mentally, her physical distress was too great, her body having

---

136–50. Simon Goldhill similarly refers to the *pleasures* of a genre ("Genre," in Whitmarsh, *Cambridge Companion*, 184–200, here 187); and see Wills, *Jewish Novel*, 21–23.

107 Stoneman, *Alexander Romance*, 18. Even cross-culturally, novels function as "post-classical" heroic quests. Lucien Goldmann posits a heroic quest at the core of the modern novel, an individual hero in a nontraditional world (*Towards a Sociology of the Novel* [New York: Tavistock, 1975]). Yet Jewish novellas are relentlessly *Israel* oriented; one wonders whether the themes that György Lukács perceived in some of the nineteenth-century European novels to affirm a new nation's identity in the workings of history might apply to ancient Jewish novellas and popular histories as well (*The Historical Novel* [Lincoln: University of Nebraska Press, 1983]).

108 Adele Reinhartz finds that the novella heroines Esther, Susanna, Sarah, and Judith are "pious, chaste, beautiful, and *unavailable*. . . . Despite their piety and chastity, however, all of these women have significant, perhaps even emotionally intimate, relationships with men other than their husbands" ("Chaste Betrayals: Women and Men in the Apocryphal Novels," in Lynn LiDonnici and Andrea Lieber, eds., *Heavenly Tablets: Interpretation, Identity, and Tradition in Ancient Judaism* [JSJSup 119; Leiden: Brill, 2007] 227–42, here 227; emphasis added).

109 Bakhtin, *Dialogical Imagination*, 106. The Roman novels, and various satirical novels, overturn the very notions of virtue and chastity but, by that, also bring the theme of virtue into sharper relief. Helen Morales has also wondered whether scholars' Foucauldian emphasis on the containment of sexuality and discipline of the self has had unforeseen effects on the field: "A less positive outcome [of the interest in sexuality] has been to privilege the 'erotic' novels over other works of imperial prose fiction, and thus to narrow our conception of the genre. Had biography or travel narrative driven the agenda as hard as the history of sexuality has, . . . what we commonly understand as 'the ancient novel' might look rather different" ("The History of Sexuality," in Whitmarsh, *Cambridge Companion*, 39–55, here 48).

110 One wonders at times whether scholars confuse what is *in* the novel with the effects that are assumed for *after* the novel. The novels coexist with the prevailing Stoic criticism of emotions as "irrational and unnatural movements in the soul" (Zeno in Diogenes Laertius, *Lives* 7.110). On Greek novels as a subversion of *enkrateia*, see Haynes, *Fashioning the Feminine*, 95, 99, although Judith Perkins sees the continuing value of *enkrateia* in the chastity and even philosophical passivity of the hero (*Suffering Self,* 91).

succumbed to the disease and being now too weak to resist the pain.[111]

The male protagonist, too, will be a bundle of emotions who does *not* face trials with equanimity. Yet all the demands of *enkrateia* will be reinstated at the end of the novel.

The Greek and Jewish novels have this in common: a woman, or a man and a woman, must respond to a threat, rise to the challenge, and discover within themselves a better, more courageous moral agent. The only thing unusual about Judith is that she *begins* as a brave moral agent and has nothing to discover, unlike Esther, Susanna, Aseneth, and the Greek heroines. The Jewish texts, like the Greek, draw the connection between self-discipline, chastity, and faithfulness, although in the Jewish it is more strongly emphasized that it is God, not love, that is worth dying for. The *erōtopolis* of the Greek novel becomes in the Jewish a *theopolis*, or a *diathēkopolis*–covenant city–or perhaps an *ethnopolis*. The attraction of asceticism and self-denial in this literature of entertainment serves the quest for identity. In the Jewish novellas, all of Jewish identity is at stake in the conflict between one pious person and the forces of empire. The book of Judith will depict this conflict in the most concentrated form imaginable: all of the surrounding nations, in alliance–Babylon *and* Assyria!–are bearing down on one mountain village–Bethulia means either "House of God" or "Virginity"–which will be defended by one person–named "Jewish woman." And this last, we note, is brought into sharper relief by other exemplars of the Jewish novella: the word we translate as "Jew"–*Yĕhûdî* in Hebrew, *Ioudaios* in Greek–surprisingly rare in Jewish texts until Josephus, is emphasized in the novellas of this period: Judith, Dan 3:8, Esther (often), Bel 28, Prayer of Nabonidus, Tales of the Persian Court. The tensions and resolutions of the Jewish novellas will indeed be paralleled in the Greek novels but are here viewed through *explicitly* colonized eyes, utilizing what may have been

a colonized identity term, "Jew."[112] If the tension in the Greek novel becomes how to *establish* the elite nuclear family, in part by reimposing a separation from the barbarian, the tension in the Jewish novella was how to affirm barbarian-ness without being erased.[113]

If these are the larger thematic structures of Judith—the heroic quest and the commitment to virtue and chastity—then what are the means that the author utilizes to develop these? Here we treat the alternating focalization, escapism, polypathy, and syllepsis. First, Judith focalizes or presents varying perspectives to the audience in the course of the novella. It begins with the third-person narrator's worldwide perspective of the first chapters. Nation after nation capitulates before the mighty expedition descending upon Jerusalem. The nations are listed in unreal series similar to what is found in the Alexander Romance; in neither text are they meant to be taken seriously.[114] The worldwide perspective is narrowed to a microscopic view when we approach Bethulia. Interesting effects have long been noted here, especially when, in a calm aside, the elders of Bethulia watch Judith and her slave descending the hill toward the enemy camp:

> Judith went out, together with her slave, and the men of the town continued watching her until she had descended the mountain and crossed the valley, and they could no longer see her. (10:10)

This literary effect has appropriately been called "cinematographic."[115] One thinks here also of Heliodorus's famous cinematographic opening scene in which the bandits' point of view introduces the story to the audience. In these cases, it is explicitly visual, but such an effect can also be broadened to include the way any situation is *understood*. Whose point of view is being reported to the audience? In regard to the Greek novel, Fusillo discussed the subtle shifts of focalization, as first one perspective and then another is highlighted.[116] The author of Judith also presents the audience with an array of varying focaliza-

111 Translation by J. R. Morgan in Reardon, *Collected Ancient Greek Novels*, 434.
112 Cf. also 2 Macc 6:6; 9:17; and see Wills, "Jew, Judean, Judaism."
113 Weitzman, *Surviving Sacrilege*, 48–53.
114 On the unreal lists of nations in the Greek novels, see Ken Dowden, "Pseudo-Callisthenes, *Alexander Romance*," in Reardon, *Collected Ancient Greek Novels*, 650–735, here 655.
115 Alonso Schökel, *Narrative Structures*, 7.
116 Fusillo, "Modern Critical Theories"; see also Morales, *Vision and Narrative in Achilles Tatius' Leucippe and Clitophon* (Cambridge Classical Studies; Cambridge: Cambridge University Press, 2005) 60.

tions. The voyeurism of the elders' perspective just noted is followed by the perspective of the first Assyrian soldiers who see Judith, and then by Holofernes's more explicitly erotic voyeurism of her body. The story's interest will a bit later hang on the *audience*'s voyeurism of *Holofernes*'s body, as the European artists well knew. When morning comes, and Judith's plan is realized, it is Bagoas's point of view that the audience enjoys. First he taps on Holofernes's tent; then (with a somewhat literal translation):

> When no one responded, he parted the curtain and went in to the bedchamber, and found him [Holofernes] sprawled over the footstool, dead, with his head taken from him! He [Bagoas] cried out with a loud voice, and screaming and wailing and a great cry, and tore his garments. . . . He rushed out to the people and cried, . . . "Look here! Holofernes is lying on the ground, and his head is missing!" (14:15–18)

The unexpectedly vibrant supporting characters—Bagoas and Achior—provide varied focalizations along the lines that Fusillo noted for the Greek novel.

One may question whether the author of Judith was really capable of exercising the same sort of sophisticated literary effects as those found in the Greek and Roman novels. In regard to the latter, for instance, Daniel Selden emphasizes the double perspectives that are often played upon: humor, satire, and irony. Events can be read in two ways at once, understood differently by Greek and barbarian, or upper and lower classes, even slaves.[117] He borrows the rhetorical term *syllepsis* to name this game of double perspectives. But is this rarefied sort of irony too highbrow for Jewish novellas? Perhaps, but on a fairly obvious level— too obvious for the higher art of the Greek novel?—there is in Judith the telescoping of a fictional "ancient" history and recent history. In 5:18, Achior explains the (later)

Babylonian captivity to the (earlier) "Assyrian" general of King "Nebuchadnezzar." Holofernes has a (later) Persian name, and even the term "Assyrians" is another (earlier) name for (later) Syrians (= Seleucids). This romp through history must have signaled a carnivalesque treat.

Further, Judith may play out a less sophisticated sort of syllepsis. Hans Jensen describes the large dualities of God and evil, Israel and the nations, but also piety and sin.[118] But, in tension with these pious trajectories, Judith herself skillfully skirts the boundary of piety and sin. She dresses and talks provocatively, even shamelessly, to "dazzle the eyes of as many men as might see her" (10:4) and yet publicly keeps her bathing and prayer practices, consuming only kosher food. She enters into a liminal danger zone, accomplishes her mission, and, upon returning, moves out of this liminal zone by reversing the symbols: she pulls the head—polluted by blood!—out of her Jewish food pouch and exhibits it to the townspeople while affirming: "he never committed a sin with me" (13:16).The reversal in the narrative is thus projected onto the reversal of the pouch: what was edible under Jewish law is turned into something unclean and never to be eaten. Eating and sexuality are symmetrical. The syllepsis here is of a more obvious kind, but no less sylleptic: one of the pleasures of the novel is the trying on of one sexual experiment after another, at the same time that chastity dominates the entire text. The novel in general is the safe—domestic!—space of erotic fantasy.

Another important mode or pleasure of Judith, and all the Jewish novellas, is the depiction of emotions. Cross-culturally, novels focus on emotions. Yet emotions are not simply presented seriatim; there is a surfeit of emotions, and they are often displayed together. As the narrator says in *Ephesian Tale* 3.7: "they felt a welter of emotions—grief, fear, and terror."[119] This trait has come

---

117 Daniel Selden, "Genre of Genre," in Tatum, *Search for the Ancient Novel*, 39–64; Hopkins, "Novel Evidence," 3–27; Stephens and Winkler, *Ancient Greek Novels*, 16, 315, the latter with regard to Lollianos. They also catalogued some of the rhetorical qualities of the Greek novels: occasionally ornate syntax, the use of clausulae, Attic vocabulary, the avoidance of hiatus, and ekphrases.

118 Otzen, *Tobit and Judith*, 121, summarizing Jensen, "Juditbogen," 177–78.

119 There is a rich vocabulary of emotions in tragedy as

well, but the spigots of different, even contradictory emotions are opened often and at the same time in novels. Cf. Xenophon, *Ephesian Tale* 4.2, 5.9, 13, and see Fusillo, "The Conflict of Emotions: A *Topos* in the Greek Erotic Novel," in Simon Swain, ed., *Oxford Readings in the Greek Novel* (Oxford: Oxford University Press, 1999) 60–82. Elder suggests that Judith's inner emotions contribute to complexity, or even the transcending of gender ("Judith," 460). Perhaps, but it is also part of the typical polypathy of novels. Cf. also the rending woman's scene of re-dressing in

to be called polypathy, the surfeit of emotions as the mode of the Greek novel. In the Jewish novellas, the emotions are often associated more with the female protagonist—contrast the prayer of Esther in Greek Esther with that of Mordecai—but in the Greek novels, just as the male protagonist is to remain chaste, he also explores the full world of emotions.

Propelling the polypathy of novels, generating multiple emotions, is also the constant dynamic of danger and escape. In regard to the Greek novels, Helen Morales sees in the threat of sex or rape a voyeuristic and pornographic interest. Anthia, for instance, in Xenophon's *Ephesian Tale* faces rape sixteen times: "The fantasy of the virgin/whore is a potent one in these novels."[120] Yet the male protagonist often comes in for the same treatment, to the extent that Konstan could argue that there is a sexual symmetry in the novels, a strategy of chastity and preparedness that both the male and female protagonists share in order to attain their goal of a successful love match.[121] A lively debate has followed concerning Konstan's thesis: do the lovers exist in a true symmetry, or in a slightly hierarchical, quasi, or temporary symmetry, since they return at the end to a hierarchical household? Yet, though they *return* to a socially acceptable hierarchy, the effect *of the reading experience* is to enjoy fully the liminal equality. And it is not difficult to discern another double perspective: in the novel, the couple is *generally* in symmetry, as part of the experience of their exile, while in particular ways the woman is unexpectedly *more* active. There is no reason to assume that only one view prevails. Rather, at the beginning the male is ascendant, they are dragged into an enforced symmetry, the woman often rises to a more active response to circumstances, and at the end the man's superiority is restored.

In both Jewish and Greek novels, and indeed in novelistic literature cross-culturally, the woman is *forced by circumstances to act*. She acts within the house if it is a palace, and if she is not part of the royal household, she is forced by circumstances out of the house into a zone unprotected by father or husband. The "feminism" of novelistic literature consists of this: women are forced to act, and they turn out to be quite capable in their extraordinary roles. Men and women alike admire their pluck, virtue, and dedication. The ode to the capable wife in Proverbs 31 may be indirectly related: a more straightforward, less narrative, less fictitious way of bringing out a certain enlistment of the woman in society-craft. In Greek novels, women dedicate their chastity to their fiancé or husband, and in Jewish novellas they dedicate themselves, which often includes their chastity, to God and their people.

In the newer studies of novels we should also not overlook the treatment of character. The idea of a complex character in fiction is generally defined by modern criteria, associated with modern psychology and the modern psychological novel. It is even argued that "character" in ancient literature was a repeatable type only, and not the individual character we discover in the modern novel.[122] Nebuchadnezzar and Holofernes indeed conform to the *alazōn* or braggart of Greek New Comedy (see irony in 10:14–19). Is the exuberant Judith also the *eiron*, ironic trickster? Is Bagoas a stock character, the sycophantic eunuch (see the excursus at 12:10–12: "Bagoas the Eunuch")? Is Achior an Israelite type, the righteous gentile (see commentary on chap. 5)?

Yet, while not denigrating the literary value of types, we should also consider the possibility of complex or individual characters in some Jewish texts. Several traits mark modern complex, individual characters:

- They are not purely good or evil, but are composed of good and bad qualities.
- They reflect on their own virtue, vice, worthiness, and unworthiness.
- Above all, they change over the course of the narrative.

We see aspects of these qualities, even character change, in Joseph and Esther, yet we may be disappointed to find

---

Greek Esther, Susanna, and Aseneth (see commentary at 9:1–14).
120 Morales, "History of Sexuality," 53.
121 Konstan, *Sexual Symmetry*. On the debate of symmetry versus hierarchical symmetry, see Morales, "History of Sexuality," 48.

122 Cornelis Bennema, *A Theory of Character in New Testament Narrative* (Minneapolis: Fortress Press, 2014); William M. Wright, "Greco-Roman Character Typing and the Presentation of Judas in the Fourth Gospel," *CBQ* 71 (2009) 544–59, here 558.

that none of these elements applies to Judith.[123] Judith, unlike Esther, Joseph, Susanna, or Tobit, does not change or grow as a character. Despite her prayers, she is fully committed to her actions from the first, endowed with a unique strength of conviction. In fact, Judith is barely a *character* in the modern sense; a perfect person cannot have personality. Gera points to the lack of attention to Judith's emotions:

> While the narrator sometimes describes the emotions and reactions of his other characters—we see an angry Nebuchadnezzar, a lascivious Holophernes, a distraught Bagoas—we are never privy to Judith's thoughts and feelings, and we must view her from the outside, examining both her words and deeds.[124]

This is especially noticeable by comparison to other Jewish novella heroines, Esther, Susanna, Sarah in Tobit, and Aseneth, and even more remarkable, the cascading emotions of the female and male protagonists of Greek novels, where their polypathy is a theme. The treatment of emotions in general in novelistic literature, both ancient and modern, communicates vulnerability and buffeting, two experiences that Judith does not have—no matter how later European artists compensated by projecting these aspects onto her. No male in the Bible is depicted with such imperturbability, nor is any female. To the extent that Judith is an opaque, perfect moral being, Holofernes becomes the more interesting, as Satan does in *Paradise Lost*. It may be best to compare her to some Greek philosophical legends of the sage who withstands all assaults on his equanimity, always ready with a wise word—or, alternatively, to the trickster, always in control. (See the excursus below at 8:35: "The Book of Judith and Greek Philosophy.")

Yet Judith is complex in other ways.[125] First, the distance between her given social role—pious, wealthy widow—and her role as phallic warrior is difficult to bridge. While her *character* is not composed of contradictory aspects, her *deed* is. Second, her persona provokes complex reactions in the audience. The fact that she is not bothered by her deed, as a typical complex character would be, does not detract from the fact that the *audience*'s experience is complex. The absence of complex elements—vulnerability, indecision, a mix of good and bad qualities—is precisely that which provokes a complex reaction in the audience. Judith also achieves a sort of complexity by being larger than life. Judith, like the developed Greek novels, presents the double perspective of transcendent virtue and salaciousness in the same scenes, in the same figure—with the important difference that Judith *wills* it. Still, art historians have discovered a syllepsis in European Judith: the audacious blending of contradictory, transgressive perspectives, which classicists and biblical scholars had earlier missed (see §8 below). The complexity in the modern reception of Judith, however, must be kept separate from discussions of the original performance situation.

Another sort of complexity can be detected in the reactions of modern audiences. Commentators on Judith often speak of her as a figure *behind* or *above* the text, as a heroine in the culture wars of antiquity, even as an imagined female "author" who *controls* the text *and its interpretation*. It is not quite the same as a finely wrought literary character (see §5 above). Why are scholars less likely to project Esther or Deborah as controlling figures *behind* the text, less likely to confuse them with the authors who composed the stories? Evidence for a complex reaction in the modern audience may perhaps be found in this distinction that obtains between Judith-as-character *within* a created text and Judith-as-imagined-figure *behind* the text, almost a mythical figure. This is not to suggest that Esther and Deborah lack complexity, or Joseph for that matter, but it is different; and scholars are less likely to imagine an Esther or a Deborah behind the text, or an Abraham, Moses, or David. There is no reason for scholars to pretend that this difference does not exist, or that they, alone in their guild, have risen above it. Rather, it seems to be a measurable aspect of Judith's complexity. Does this not force a reappraisal of "Judith as literature"? Is not one measure of art its ability to evoke alterna-

---

123 It is often claimed that character change does not exist in ancient literature, yet Joseph and Esther both show hints of real change; see Adelman, *Female Ruse*, 198–230; and Wills, *Jewish Novel*, 115.

124 Gera, *Judith*, 98.

125 Nutu, "Framing Judith," 117.

tive, even competing possibilities? The extent to which the text cannot be pinned down, the extent to which it pushes scholars to spin out reading options, the extent to which different eras have embraced vastly different and often troubling Judiths, is a direct measure of artistic worthiness.

Conclusion

In Greece and the ancient Near East there were many literary texts that could be considered novelistic, and Judith and the other Jewish novellas can be placed within this shared ocean of (written) story. Judith shares with the different sizes and subtypes of Greek, Roman, Egyptian, Christian, and other indigenous novelistic literature a common structure and reading experience—a common pleasure. If the canon of five Greek and two Roman novels constitutes a high point of the ancient history of the genre, Judith is still at home in the run-up to this moment, yet the teleological prioritizing of the later canon may obscure as much as it illuminates. At any rate, the Greek novel and Jewish novella alike depict heroic tests concerning anxiety and fortitude—enacted versions of the battle of virtue.

Whereas the Greek novels focus on sex hallowed at the end in a marriage—the nuclear couple as the house-ruling unit for the new Hellenistic order—Jewish novellas do not tie sex, marriage, and the domestic sphere *together*. All three are present, but strangely unrelated, even counter-related. While the Greek love novel follows the trials of the male and female protagonists in approximately equal measure, the Jewish texts move the woman into the starring role. Tobit is joined by Sarah and Edna, Susanna is added to the Daniel collection, Esther (in the Hebrew version) rivals Mordecai in dominance, and both Judith and Aseneth take the entire spotlight. They are not likely placed at the center of the drama for a predominantly female audience but provide a focalizing subjectivity for both men and women. They embody important virtues: courage and faithfulness (Hebrew Esther, Susanna), a vulnerable, rending penitence and renewal (Greek Esther, Aseneth), ascetic heroism (Judith).

We began this section on genre by asking these four questions:

1. What are we choosing to call the genre?
2. Is this a native or a modern label? Would the ancient audience have understood this term?
3. Which texts are we including in the genre, and which are we excluding?
4. Would the ancient audience have perceived the same boundaries?

These questions have been provisionally answered, although I have maintained that genre is always a complex matter. Here I have used the genre name *Jewish novella*. I have not used the term *novel* simply to recognize the difference in size between the Jewish texts and the Greek and Roman novels. The term is not a native one in either case, nor was there any known native term for this or most other genres. Although we may speak of the texts to be included as Jewish novellas—Esther and Daniel in different versions, Tobit, Tales of the Persian Court, and Joseph and Aseneth (if it is indeed Jewish)—we also emphasize that every genre relates at its boundaries to other genres, and thus one can speak of concentric circles of related texts—2 Maccabees, Tobiad Romance and Royal Family of Adiabene from Josephus's *Antiquities* (12.4.1–11 §§154–236 and 20.2.1–20.4.3 §§17–96) on the historical side, Artapanus as a national hero romance, and so on. In addition, other texts may simply be hard to pin down in such a taxonomy, such as 3 Maccabees and Testament of Abraham. The notion of genre-as-constellation or genre-as-attraction-zone seems helpful. Finally, as to whether ancient audiences would have perceived these divisions, we have some evidence that they did—the smaller size of novella scrolls at Qumran, the grouping of Esther, Judith, and Tobit together in the Christian Bible—but interestingly, Esther and Daniel were canonized in Jewish scripture, Judith and Tobit in the Christian Old Testament. At this point they seem to have been read, at least by some, as historically accurate—perhaps no longer novellas but second-order biblical history.

8. History of the Reception of Judith

The reception of Judith in Christian and Jewish tradition has passed through distinct phases. Contrary to the somewhat dismissive verdict on Judith in modern Protestant culture, historians of European art and literature know a Judith who was a towering figure. Says art historian Diane Apostolos-Cappadona, "The simple fact that the image of Judith has been a constant source of interest and inspiration for Western artists from the early Christian period into the present argues for the classic stature of Judith."[1] Judith got under the skin of Europe. At certain turns, Judith became one of the most compelling biblical heroines; later, she was treated as a threat or an embarrassment or was simply ignored. The most active theorizing about the ambivalences of Judith—Howell Chickering refers to it as an "exuberance of theory"[2]—has come from two groups of scholars: students of the Old English *Judith,* and of Renaissance and Baroque art. Biblical scholars, perhaps at first inhibited by the book's "biblical" status, finally came to import the questions posed by scholars of literature and art history.

We will have occasion here to distinguish diachronic and synchronic approaches to Judith. In the former, the differences of each time period are emphasized, while in the latter the resonances of Judith in different periods are considered together. Judith's story climaxes with a transgressive mixture of sex and violence—the purest admixture of sex and violence in respectable world literature—and this imprints on the imagination. Modern scholars often assume that the anxiety concerning gender issues that they perceive from post-1500 contexts must be present in the earlier periods as well, but this assumption will be tested. Yet synchronic approaches may alert us to issues in the ancient text that were not otherwise apparent.

There were several periods in history when the interpretation of Judith heated up dramatically, signaling significant shifts in interpretation:

1. About 400 CE: Jerome, Ambrose, Prudentius, Paulinus of Nola, and Augustine construct the classic Catholic view of Judith as a figure representing chastity, Mary, and the church.
2. 1000–1100: In England and Germany, on the one hand, and among eastern European Jews, on the other, Judith is taken up as a distinctly heroic figure.
3. 1350–1850: from the first rumblings of the Renaissance, and for five hundred years afterward, Judith becomes a powerful but ambivalent figure in European politics, visual art, music, and literature.
4. 1850–1920: Interest in Judith declines in a scientific age, yet in Germany and Austria there is a very negative turn as she becomes a femme fatale.
5. 1960–present: Feminist interest in biblical women, ancient discourse on gender, and the role of Judith in European art and culture revives academic appreciation of Judith, although she is little known outside the academy and museum.

Earliest References to Judith

There is no mention of Judith in Jewish tradition before the eleventh century. Philo and Josephus never refer to her, nor do the rabbis. Yet two early traces may be found. First, Greek Esther, Additions C and D may be influenced by Judith. Second, Pseudo-Philo's *Biblical Antiquities* 31.7 (first or second century CE) alters the description of Jael's deed in a way that reflects knowledge of our text.[3] But the earliest explicit reference to Judith is by Clement of Rome, near the end of the first century CE. Among Clement's many lists of biblical and other figures, he mentions Judith and Esther as examples of *andreia* ("manliness" or "courage"). The piety associated with Judith has shifted slightly from the LXX story: here she *asks permission* of the elders, rather than command them peremptorily, and it is stated that she exposed herself to *danger,* not sex. Further,

1 Diane Apostolos-Cappadona, "'The Lord Has Struck Him Down by the Hand of a Woman!' Images of Judith," in Diane Apostolos-Cappadona and Doug Adams, eds., *Art as Religious Studies* (New York: Crossroad, 1987) 81–97, here 97.

2 Howell Chickering, "Poetic Exuberance in Old English *Judith,*" *Studies in Philology* 106 (2009) 119–36, here 120–21.

3 Moore, *Judith,* 212–16; Jacobson, *Commentary on Pseudo-Philo,* 1:199–210, 226. This text is not to be confused with Pseudo-Philo, *Breviarium temporum;* see also Dubarle, *Judith,* 1:121–24, 2:180–81.

whereas the biblical book is negotiated between Judith's own agency and intervention by God, here it is the Lord alone who is given glory. Already one senses the reduction of Judith's willfulness that will characterize Jerome's Vulgate translation and the Western tradition in general.

It is possible that Clement of Rome was referencing the tradition about Judith and not the novella per se. The earliest evidence of the text of the book of Judith is found on an ostracon from the third century CE. It provides a fairly faithful witness to 15:1–7 (see §9 below). Many of the major figures of early patristic exegesis refer to Judith (see §2 above). Origen (*Letter to Africanus* 19) notes that Jews do not know of a version of Judith in Hebrew, but he also says that his Jewish informants do not know of a version of Tobit in Hebrew, while fragments of such a text have been found at Qumran. Origen is quite positive about Judith, connecting her name with Hebrew for praise (*On Prayer* 13.2–3), and he treats Judith also in *Homily on Jeremiah* 19.20. At the turn of the second to third centuries, Clement of Alexandria refers to Judith (*Paidagogos* 1.8; *Stromateis* 2.7, 4.19), as does Tertullian (*Against Marcion* 1.7, *On Monogamy* 17.1–3). In the Apostolic Constitutions (late fourth century) Judith is revered as a model of feminine piety, "sitting at home, singing and praying and reading and watching and fasting" (3.7)—compare Jerome below, separated by only a few decades. She is also honored as one of a group of female heroines of the faith, with Miriam, Huldah, Mary, Elizabeth, Anne, and the daughters of Philip (8.25).[4]

Judith as a Representative of Virtue and a Model Woman, 400 CE

In about 400 CE the interpretation of Judith takes a dramatic turn in Latin Christianity. Leading authors among the Latin fathers—Ambrose, Jerome, Prudentius, Paulinus of Nola, and Augustine—embraced her, and the classic Catholic ideal of Judith was established. Ambrose perceived her inner strength: how great is Judith's virtue if she takes command of the elders, how great her virtue to be certain of God's help. He also identified Judith with a number of virtues: *castitas, modestia, honestas, temperentia, humilitas, sapientia, prudentia,* and *fortitudo.* Holofernes represented *luxuria* and *superbia.* By this allegorization Ambrose reined in the transgressive sexualized woman of the Greek version. Her victory was now for chastity; her clothes, contrary to the text, were not seductive but emblems of her chastity. Her bloody act was not emphasized, but she simply "put forth her hand" and accomplished her goal.[5] Judith's continuing celibacy *after* the deed was emphasized more than her sexual cunning *during* the deed.

Judith's peculiar status—a widow as a result of the death of her husband but a celibate by choice—resonated even more with Jerome. Although he was concerned about the *text* of Judith because it was not in the Jewish canon and the available manuscripts varied so widely, he strongly affirmed the *figure* of Judith (see appendix). She was a true heroine of virtue who should be contemplated by women and men alike. In *Letter to Furia* 54 Jerome says:

> In the Book of Judith—if anyone is of the opinion that it should be received as canonical—we read of a widow wasted with fasting and wearing the somber garb of a mourner, whose outward squalor indicated not so much the regret which she felt for her dead husband as the temper in which she looked forward to the coming of the Bridegroom. I see her hand armed with the sword and stained with blood. I recognize the head of Holofernes which she has carried away from the camp of the enemy. Here a woman vanquishes men, and chastity beheads lust. Quickly changing her garb, she puts on once more, in the hour of victory, her own mean dress finer than all the splendors of the world.[6]

4   Biolek, "Die Ansicht," 335–68; see also Bogaert, "Judith," *RAC* 19 (2001) 245–58, esp. 254–55. Omitted by Biolek is Basil the Great, *On the Holy Spirit* 8.19. See also Dubarle, *Judith,* 1:110–19; Enslin, *Book of Judith,* 43–52; Lehtipuu, "Receive the Widow."

5   Tracey-Anne Cooper, "Judith in Late Anglo-Saxon England," in Kevin R. Brine, Elena Ciletti, and Henrike Lähnemann, eds., *The Sword of Judith: Judith Studies across the Disciplines* (Cambriege: OpenBook,

2010) 169–96, here 175–78. See Ambrose, *On Widows* 1.7.39–41, 2.4.24; *On the Offices of Ministers* 3.13.82–87, 14.88; *On Elijah and Fasting* 9; *Epistle* 1.62.29.

6   Translation from Cooper, "Judith," 174–75; see also Lydia Lange, *Die Juditfigur in der Vulgata: Eine theologische Studie zur lateinischen Bibel* (DCLS 36; Berlin: de Gruyter, 2016) 114–356.

The woman who is strong-in-action in the LXX has become strong-in-passivity in Jerome: "Now one who is weak is stronger" (*Letter to Eustochium* 22.21). A woman could now, like a man, attain strength through celibacy and virtue. By allegorizing the story, Judith's violence is reconfigured not as earthly violence inflicted on a man by a woman but as a cosmic battle. Judith was "a type for the Church, which cuts off the head of the devil" (*Letter to Salvina* 79). What was happening in church and society that would explain this dramatic shift? It should be noted that Jerome solicited the support of wealthy widows such as Furia, whose considerable wealth would fall under the control of more worldly men if they remarried. A more chaste view of Judith the widow would factor heavily in such a situation.[7]

Many scholars have wrongly assumed that Jerome's despair over the *manuscripts* of Judith carried over to his assessment of *her,* but this is not the case. We will also see that other supposed examples of anxiety about Judith before 1500 may be similar: a rigorous diachronic consideration indicates no discernible waves of anxiety concerning Judith's sexuality, mendacity, or violence. (See below on the possible exceptions, John Malalas and Geoffrey Chaucer.) To be sure, Jerome and others edited her narrative in a pious direction—as was done with all biblical figures—and this does reflect a sort of sanitizing of her sexual strategy; but no known author registers any explicit or extreme anxiety about Judith until about 1500. Despite the fact that the Latin fathers edited and channeled her energies, each progressively raised her status as a heroine of the faith.

There is, however, a small countercurrent to be noted. Although others distanced Judith from a mixing with sin, Paulinus of Nola appreciated the two sides of her story. Skating near the edge of sexual sin and deceit empowers her: "She remained inviolate in that lewd bed"; her "chaste cunning" saved her people (*Carmen* 26.159–65). She is, ironically, more virtuous *because* she courted sex and lies and used them for a virtuous end. But that difference aside, Paulinus is like Ambrose and Jerome in affirming that it is the weakness of Judith-as-woman, not her strength and agency, that allows her to find her truer, higher power. Associated with Paulinus (*Ep.* 32.10–16) is also the earliest mentioned artistic representation of Judith. On a basilica complex he erected at Nola, near Naples, in c. 404, frescoes (no longer extant) included Judith, Esther, Tobit's son Tobias, and Job.

Next in our series of Latin fathers is Prudentius, who created a handbook of moral psychology that would be extremely influential for centuries. His *Psychomachia,* or *The Battle within the Soul,* presented conflicts between personified, dualized virtues and vices, religious ethics dramatized for the philosophically oriented Christian. Prudentius continues the practice of distancing Judith from sin. She can wield a sword to decapitate Lust, a victory of virtue over vice. Lacking are the crass physical details associated with the LXX Judith—rolling the corpse onto the ground or hiding the head in a food bag. Prudentius takes away some of Judith's inherent willfulness and agency as well, promulgating instead a model for a devotional, disciplined self that is humble and weak. By that move, the new heroine is universalizable to all Christians' devotion and discipline: through virtue, anyone—man or woman—can become a "weak" hero of faith. For these Latin fathers her act of power prefigures the virgin birth. Judith prefigured Mary, though still "under the shade of the law" (line 66), and thus not as powerful to defeat vice as Mary-to-come. In Prudentius's handbook Judith also becomes a model of a Stoic agent capable of freely choosing moral actions. She is equated with the four classical virtues—fortitude, temperance, prudence, and justice—and Holofernes with the four vices—folly, venality, cowardice, and lust. The ideal reader is thus an aristocratic Roman Christian, whether male or female, formed by a combination of classical and Christian virtue education (see the excursus below at 8:35: "The Book of Judith and Greek Philosophy").

---

7   Marc Mastrangelo, "Typology and Agency in Prudentius's Treatment of the Judith Story," in Brine, Ciletti, and Lähnemann, *Sword of Judith,* 153–68, here 161, 167; Stefan Rebenich, *Jerome* (Early Church Fathers; London: Routledge, 2002) 28–39.

Augustine also referred to Ambrose's statements about Judith and repeated the identification of Judith with virtues, contrasted again with Holofernes's base vices; she was modesty and chastity to his libido, lust. She also prefigures Mary and the church, but her literal actions were de-emphasized as a result. Augustine was the first to connect Judith with Roman history as well as biblical salvation history. Lucretia, whose suicide initiated the overthrow of the last Roman king, was paired with Judith in a sort of Roman/Christian salvation history: a woman's act liberated both the Jews and the Romans (*City of God* 18.26).[8] Augustine added a cautionary principle for addressing the sexual level of this biblical text: "When that which is said figuratively is taken as though it were literal, it is understood carnally" (*Christian Doctrine* 3.5).[9]

In a period of just two or three decades, some of the greatest figures of the Latin church thoroughly reconfigured Judith. On the one hand, they promoted her to a very high position among the biblical figures, and, on the other, they reduced her sexuality and her willfulness to construct an icon of modesty, celibacy, and service. Mary Garrard has suggested that Judith "personified both the pulchritude that provoked Vice and the Virtue that defeated it."[10] But perhaps as a way of avoiding a too-obvious madonna and whore in one, the Latin fathers distanced Judith from illicit sex and deceit through allegory. They replaced much of her theatricality with sincerity.

Seventh–Tenth Centuries

Important aspects of the interpretation of Judith were thus established at the turn of the fifth century, and Jerome's new Vulgate translation provided a narrative in keeping with this new Judith. Later Latin theologians followed suit. At the turn of the seventh century Isadore of Seville (*Quaestiones in Vetus Testamentum*) linked Judith and Esther as representatives of *Ecclesia,* yet no Christian author had written a commentary on Judith. In the early ninth century, Hrabanus Maurus filled this gap with commentaries on Judith and Esther, dedicated to Judith, the second wife of Louis the Pious. Judith remains a prefiguration of the church, and risqué aspects are allegorized: the beautiful clothes are Faith, Hope, and Charity; her husband Manasseh becomes Jesus, bride of the church (the weakness of Manasseh is no problem).[11] The contributions of Isadore and Hrabanus concerning Judith, along with Jerome's preface to Judith, were incorporated into the *Glossa Ordinaria* of Walafrid Strabo (c. 806–849), which remained a standard reference through the seventeenth century. The book of Judith is a series of allegories understood mystically, with comments from many church theologians.[12]

There is some mention of Judith in the East as well. In a tone similar to that of the Latin fathers, the Syriac Book of Women (sixth century) recounts the stories of Ruth, Esther, Susanna, Judith, and Thecla as models of virtue. John Malalas, however, is quite different. He takes a singular turn—singular, that is, for the period before 1500—in that here Judith slept with Holofernes. His sixth-century *Chronographia* is a spirited and popular universal history, a section of which reads:

> So she came to him in secret, and when Holofernes beheld her beauty, he was consumed with desire for her. She said to him, "Do not allow anyone here to come near me, for my sake, because they will set upon me wanting to have sex with me [*porneusai me*]."

---

8 See also *On Christian Doctrine* 4.129–33; *City of God* 16.13; *Exposition on Psalm* 33; and *Sermons on Judith* 48–49, falsely attributed to Augustine.

9 Translation of D. W. Robertson Jr., *Saint Augustine, On Christian Doctrine* (New York: Liberal Arts, 1958) 84.

10 Mary Garrard, *Artemisia Gentileschi: The Image of the Female Hero in Italian Baroque Art* (Princeton, NJ: Princeton University Press, 1989) 556 n. 101; Mastrangelo, "Typology," 161, 167; and Elizabeth Bailey, "Judith, Jael, and Humilitas in the *Speculum Virginum*," in Brine, Ciletti, and Lähnemann, *Sword of Judith,* 275–90; Stocker, *Judith,* 24–25.

11 Hrabanus Maurus, *Expositio in librum Iudith,* chap. 8; see Susan Weingarten, "Food, Sex, and Redemption in *Megillat Yehudit* (the Scroll of Judith)," in Brine, Ciletti, and Lähnemann, *Sword of Judith,* 97–126, here 107–8; and, in the same volume, Sarah Blake McHam, "Donatello's *Judith* as the Emblem of God's Chosen People," 307–24, here 312.

12 Elena Ciletti and Henrike Lähnemann, "Judith in the Christian Tradition," in Brine, Ciletti, and Lähnemann, *Sword of Judith,* 41–65, here 49–50.

Persuaded by this, he spent time alone with her. She passed [*proskarterēsasa*] three days with him, and while she was sleeping [*katheudei*] with him at night she arose and chopped off his head. (6.159–160)[13]

Two ancient variants, however, read "while *he* was in bed," likely a censoring of the text, and a later copier, George Kedrenos (*Synopsis historiōn*) did likewise.[14] George le Moine (ninth century), perhaps influenced by Malalas, also wrote a universal history that included a summary of the Judith episode, set in the reign of Darius.[15]

The earliest preserved visual art of Judith comes from this period. At Santa Maria Antiqua in the Roman Forum there is a fresco (c. 705–707) that depicts the Assyrian camp with soldiers and a tent, a well-dressed Judith holding a head, and the wall of Bethulia; Uzziah greets the returning Judith, similar to the Siena Cathedral below. Judith is visually paired with Mary, and now the Bethulian elder Uzziah becomes a surrogate husband and authority figure for the unattached Judith. Indeed, placing Uzziah over Judith becomes a common way of domesticating her agency. (In the LXX, Uzziah is a weak figure.) Two ninth-century Bibles, the Bible of St. Paul's-Outside-the-Walls, Rome, and the Bible of Charles the Bald, include narrative cycles of the story.[16]

By the early Middle Ages Judith had found some currency in northern Europe. In England in the seventh century Aldhelm included Judith as a female model in his works on virginity (*Carmen de virginitate* and *Prosa de virginitate* 57). The conflict between Virtue and Vice reflects the influence of Prudentius, but a distinctively British move may be Aldhelm's depiction of Judith as a *soldier* of virginity. Virgins for Christ were "manly" women, martial virgins who fought against sin: "Aldhelm's Judith is simultaneously a masculine warrior hero and a feminine seductress," says Richard Abels.[17] Yet unlike male heroes, Judith's desire to wage war against sin is influenced by womanly compassion and affection for her struggling countrymen.

Eleventh-Century England and Germany

The second major development of the Judith tradition, after that of about 400 CE, occurs in the eleventh century in northern Europe, a development that evoked many important theoretical studies of the sex and violence inherent in the narrative. First, says Tracey-Anne Cooper, "Judith makes two spectacular appearances in the Old English corpus," the epic poem *Judith* and a homily by Ælfric. "Is she a courageous military hero, to be heralded at the 'mead-bench,' or is she a pious example of chastity to be meditated upon in the cloister?"[18] The Old English *Judith* was preserved in the Nowell Codex with the only surviving text of *Beowulf*, the two probably joined because they prominently featured heroic decapitations. What we now have of the *Judith* poem, however, is incomplete, covering Holofernes's feast, the beheading, and the return to Bethulia at the end of the narrative. The only individual characters who remain are Judith, Holofernes, and Judith's slave; the Assyrians and the Bethulians are present as groups.

---

13 Translation of Elizabeth Jeffreys, Michael Jeffreys, and Roger Scott, *The Chronicle of John Malalas* (Melbourne: Australian Association for Byzantine Studies, 1986) 84–85.

14 Dubarle, *Judith*, 1:117; Dubarle, "La mention de 'Judith' dans la littérature ancienne, juive et chrétienne," *RB* 66 (1959) 514–49, here 544; Jeffreys, Jeffreys, and Scott, *Chronicle of John Malalas*, 84–85. Malalas credits Hebrew Scriptures and Irenaeus as his sources, but he probably did not use Irenaeus at all, and he has altered the biblical record; so Elizabeth Jeffreys, "Malalas' Sources," in eadem, Brian Croke, Roger Scott, eds., *Studies in John Malalas* (Sydney: Australian Association for Byzantine Studies, 1990) 167–216, here 179.

15 Dubarle, *Judith*, 1:118–19; Greek text is at 2:179.

16 Bailey, "Judith," 281.

17 Richard Abels, "'Cowardice' and Duty in Anglo-Saxon England," *Journal of Medieval Military History* 4 (2006) 29–49, here 37–39.

18 Cooper, "Judith," 170; see also Patricia A. Belanoff, "Judith: Sacred and Secular Heroine," in Helen Damico and John Leyerle, eds., *Heroic Poetry in the Anglo-Saxon Period: Studies in Honor of Jess B. Bessinger, Jr.* (Studies in Medieval Culture 32; Kalamazoo, MI: Medieval Institute Publications, 1993) 247–64. On the Nowell Codex, see Mary Flavia Godfrey, "Beowulf and Judith: Thematizing Decapitation in Old English Poetry," *Texas Studies in Language and Literature* 35 (1993) 1–43, here 5–6.

Scholarly opinion has long affirmed the artistic achievement of the *Judith* poem. In 1967, Arthur G. Brodeur praised it thus:

> *Judith* exhibits an intensity of feeling and an eloquence in conveying it unmatched in any other Anglo-Saxon poem. Its author was incapable of detachment. . . . It is this complete emotional identification which gives his narrative its flaming vigor.[19]

The poem is surprisingly modern, even postmodern, in its appeal; the exuberance of the poem, says Howell Chickering, gives rise to an exuberance of critical perspectives.[20] "The heroic diction used throughout is conventional enough," says S. A. J. Bradley, "but when it is applied to the feminine and vulnerable Judith its effect is startling"; and Karma Lochrie adds: "the poem is unsettling because of the way in which it juxtaposes sexual violence and the politics of war."[21] The shocking combination, to be sure, is precisely that already found in the LXX version, although to be fair, the Vulgate translation had domesticated the presentation and perhaps created a milder expectation. Some scholars see a continuation of Prudentius's allegorical struggle between Virtue and Vice; historical interpretations perceive a call to action against Viking invaders; comparative literary analyses emphasize the parallels to *Beowulf* and the heroic tradition; and Freudian and Lacanian interpretations attempt to uncover hidden psychological and sexual meanings.

To what extent has the Judith of this Old English poem escaped the restrictions on women to become a self-actualized heroine? We may place recent interpretations on a spectrum. For Cooper, despite the heroic form of the epic poem, Judith does not escape from the role already assigned by Prudentius. Judith represents Virtue's defeat of Vice; she is not an independent heroine but can act only because she is empowered by God. As martial and concrete as the poem would like to be, the dualism of Holofernes and Judith means that she is "diminished as she is presented as an allegorical type in a contest between good and evil and she is portrayed very much as an instrument of God."[22] And while seeing Judith as a temporarily empowered servant of God, Cooper also perceives an insistently "feminine" weakness in the decapitation scene. Judith appears not so much as a competent warrior-maiden, but as someone struggling with a heavier inert body and unfamiliar weaponry, appropriate for a woman. Judith's bloody deed is all the more courageous precisely because it is physically difficult and emotionally harrowing for a woman unused to combat. The poem also protects Judith's modesty by taking away any real exposure to danger: "Heaven's Judge, Shepherd of the celestial multitude, would not consent [to Holofernes's intended rape of Judith] but rather He, the Lord, Ruler of the hosts, prevented him from the act."[23]

Others, however, argue that an allegorical duality of Virtue and Vice is not stated in the poem and that it is misleading to impose a Prudentian reading where none is present. Judith is less an ideal of church teaching than a heroic figure, the Germanic warrior woman or valkyrie. The poetry powerfully utilizes the *genre* of heroic action, and the images of Judith share the "lucency" of Nordic heroes: she is a "bright" and "shining" maiden.[24] Further, unlike the situation in the LXX, the Bethulians themselves are presented as a society that is martial-heroic, not priestly. On the one hand, we see an allegorical, dualistic church teaching and, on the other, a Germanic, heroic woman of action. There are indeed many elements of the pure Germanic hero found here, even if

---

19   Arthur G. Brodeur, "A Study of Diction and Style in Three Anglo-Saxon Narrative Poems," in Allen H. Orrick, ed., *Nordica et Anglica: Studies in Honor of Stefán Einarsson* (The Hague: Mouton, 1967) 98–114, here 109.

20   Chickering explicitly resists some of the more exuberant readings ("Poetic Exuberance," 120–21).

21   S. A. J. Bradley, *Anglo-Saxon Poetry* (London: Dent, 1995) 496; Karma Lochrie, "Gender, Sexual Violence, and the Politics of War in the Old English *Judith*," in Britton Harwood and Gillian Overing, eds., *Class and Gender in Early English Literature:*

Intersections (Bloomington: Indiana University Press, 1994) 5; Mark Griffith, ed., *Judith* (Exeter Medieval English Texts and Studies; Exeter: University of Exeter Press, 1997) 55–56.

22   Cooper, "Judith," 170, 180; see also Griffith, *Judith*, 93.

23   Bradley, *Anglo-Saxon Poetry*, 58–60.

24   Griffith, *Judith*, 79, 87–88; Ann W. Astell, "Holofernes's Head: *Tacen* and Teaching in the Old English *Judith*," *Anglo-Saxon England* 18 (1989) 117–33, here 120–21.

they are surprisingly applied to a woman. The images that describe Judith are usually reserved for male heroes.[25] Yet Judith is an *ambivalent* heroine, neither quite Christian (like Cynewulf's Juliana) nor Germanic-heroic (like Beowulf)—although a mixture of Christian and heroic tradition was typical in Old English poetry. Judith lacks the strength required of the Germanic hero—she is even weak, reflecting the Christianization of the tradition— and she also lacks a *comitatus*: she leads as a lone figure, through temporary charisma. She does not boast like a hero but is humble, even disturbed; and she asks for strength. At the time of battle, her exhortation to the Israelites is part command, part request.

Mary Dockray-Miller presents an even stronger criticism of the allegorical, dualistic reading of Judith and Holofernes: a dualism implies two, yet there are three individual characters, Judith, Holofernes, and Judith's slave. Judith and her slave share a near-equality of actions and interactions, and much of the vocabulary surprisingly describes them as a team.[26] Describing Judith with her companion emphasizes the heroic, not the virtuous, aspects; many epic heroes have a subordinate partner (see §3 above). The poem anticipates the paintings of Artemisia Gentileschi: an intimate portrait of two women of different classes bonded in the mistress's stratagem. In their guerrilla warfare, transgressing boundaries, they work in tandem. Holofernes represents a supermasculine threat to the woman, but the women acting together decapitate that threat—emasculate it—by relying on a bond between women. A distinction, of course, must be noted between the heroic action that the poet creates— one in which there is a harmony of agency between the two women—and the social realities of elites and slaves, where such an equality-in-action could not exist. Dockray-Miller notes some aspects of this disjuncture. For the poet, the bond of female agents is restricted to the liminal period when they are outside the walls of Bethu-

lia and in the valley of Holofernes. Once they return to Bethulia, even the vocabulary shifts to depict them as separate. Indeed, in quest narratives cross-culturally, the liminal equality of quest partners ends when the quest ends. Yet Helen Damico would even nuance their partnership within the liminal period. The two women are paired, but the slave *extends* and *enhances* the hero. The shared images "define the women as a character pairing, a characterization device whereby a minor figure is endowed with similar . . . traits belonging to the hero in an effort to enhance his person."[27] Judith's slave is a typical heroic-narrative helper, the Gunga Din or Passepartout.

Dockray-Miller, then, radicalizes *Judith*, while Cooper conventionalizes it. But the latter may reduce Judith's agency too far and perceive too static a characterization. The actual scene of the assassination, for example, presents a Judith who enters the court of male heroism. With less strength than a man and no training, she wills a successful decapitation:

> She seized then the heathen man firmly by his hair,
>   and with her hands dragged him towards her disdainfully the baleful one,
> skillfully laid down the loathsome man, as she the wretch most easily might control well.
> The curly-haired one struck down the fiend-foe with shining sword, the hostile one
> so that she half cut off then his neck, and he lay in a swoon drunk and wounded.
> He was not yet dead, entirely lifeless; she struck again earnestly the courageous virgin
> on the other side of the heathen hound, so that his head rolled forth on the floor.[28]

Is she merely an agent of God, or does she *find* her own agency? Has the woman become fully heroic and bloody? Like the biblical version, the poem *says* that

---

25 Jane Chance, *Woman as Hero in Old English Literature* (Syracuse, NY: Syracuse University Press, 1986) 40; Belanoff, "Judith," 252; Griffith, *Judith*, 62–63, 69.

26 Mary Dockray-Miller, "Female Community in the Old English *Judith*," *Studia Neophilologica* 70 (1998) 165–72.

27 Helen Damico, "The Valkyrie Reflex in Old English

Literature," in Helen Damico and Alexandra Hennessey Olsen, eds., *New Readings on Women in Old English Literature* (Bloomington: Indiana University Press, 1990) 176–90, here 185.

28 Cooper's translation ("Judith," 179, the structure compressed here).

Judith is empowered by God but *shows* her acting alone. We encounter again the discrepancy between the stated and enacted levels of narrative, the "libretto" (Judith's statements) and "music" (narrated events). Ironically, in both the LXX and the epic poem, it is the author's explicit words that may be lesser: actions speak louder than words.

These cross-cultural and diachronic comparisons also suggest synchronic, psychological interpretations. The very act at the center of the narrative, the acteme, has been read by scholars of the epic poem in both Freudian and Lacanian psychological terms, and also in terms of the resolution of opposites in heroic sacrifice. Interesting here is the relationship between *Judith* and *Beowulf*, placed together in the codex. Beowulf's relation to both Grendel and Grendel's mother expresses the theme of the hero's ambivalence toward the monster, who is both similar and Other, and terrifying because both similar and Other. In both *Beowulf* and *Judith* there is an intimacy of contact between hero and monster, and in the latter case even the danger that Holofernes will have sex with her. Jeffrey Jerome Cohen applies the theories of Lacan to argue that the monster exposes the "intimate alterity" of identity.[29] Beowulf displays an intimacy with Grendel in taking body parts and "becoming monster," just as Judith first "beds" Holofernes, takes his head—a sort of monstrous birth—and places it in her slave's womb-pouch, "rebirthing" it in Bethulia as a public talisman of her people's safety and solidarity.[30] The slaying of the monster by the hero resolves the tension of looking in the mirror of the Other, and thus Beowulf's slaying of Grendel and his mother and Judith's slaying of Holofernes has sacrificial aspects, analogous to those found in Greek and Roman hero cults (see commentary on 13:9b–10a). Not only are psychological tensions resolved on an individual level, but the sacrifice cements corporate or national identity. Kate Koppelman agrees: "Such becomings—becoming-hero, but also becoming-nation—cannot happen without physical and psychical intimacy."[31] What would have been problematic for a woman is processed through the sacrifice of the monster: "Good violence is split from bad."[32]

The other spectacular appearance of Judith in Old English literature is Ælfric's homily on Judith (c. 1000). The most famous churchman of the age, he addressed his sermon on Judith's chastity to nuns, although the audience likely included laypeople as well. His description of Judith is economical, with fewer prayers, images, and metaphors than the Old English poem.[33] Despite his audience of nuns, or perhaps because of it, Ælfric presents a flesh-and-blood figure. This may perhaps have been a response to the recent invasion of the Vikings (compare Vivaldi below, who celebrates a victory over the Turks). Ælfric emphasized Judith's true morality, softening her chiding speech to the elders and replacing it with a plea for faith in God. At the same time, although he allegorized elsewhere, he presents a less dualized account of good conquering evil. He allows for some ambiguity in Judith's character, a realistic heroine with human failings, "not at all the idealized sinless believer, but a more realistic and sympathetic Christian type, a sinner like the rest of us poor sinful wretches who will inevitably commit infractions but try their best to be righteous."[34] To correct some of the absurd historical facts of the story, he states that there were two Nebuchadnezzars, one of the exile and another, son of Cyrus, who invaded Israel after the Persian restoration.

29 Jeffrey Jerome Cohen, *Of Giants: Sex, Monsters, and the Middle Ages* (Medieval Cultures 17; Minneapolis: University of Minnesota Press, 1999) xviii; Jacques Lacan, *The Four Fundamental Concepts of Psycho-Analysis* (ed. Jacque-Alain Miller; New York: Norton, 1978) 208.

30 Kim, "Bloody Signs," 300–304.

31 Kate Koppelman, "Fearing the Neighbor: The Intimate Other in *Beowulf* and the Old English *Judith*," *Comitatus* 35 (2004) 1–21, here 1–2, 21.

32 Joyce Tally Lionarons, "Beowulf: Myth and Monsters," *English Studies* 1 (1996) 1–14, here 4.

33 Paul E. Szarmach, "Ælfric's *Judith*," in Michael Fox and Manish Sharma, eds., *Old English Literature and the Old Testament* (Toronto Anglo-Saxon Series 10; Toronto: University of Toronto Press, 2012) 64–88, here 69; Hugh Magennis, "Contrasting Narrative Emphases in the Old English Poem *Judith* and Ælfric's Paraphrase of the Book of Judith," *Neuphilologische Mitteilungen* 96 (1995) 61–66, here 61.

34 Cooper, "Judith," 175–76.

Mary Clayton notes the many ways in which Ælfric edits out controversial aspects of Judith's words and actions:

> Whereas martyrs resist temptation, Judith tempts, and while martyrs reject ornate clothing and all the trappings of sexual adornments, Judith adopts them in order to seduce Holofernes. Her dress and ornaments are reminiscent of what martyrs are tempted with. [35]

Even in the subtler aspects of negotiating Judith's deceit, Ælfric wants to assure his audience that Judith was acting in a moral way, as in this reflection:

> Judith had first promised that bloodthirsty leader
> That she would bring him within Bethulia to her
>   people.
> But it was by no means entirely a lie, what she
>   promised him,
> When she bore his head within the walls.[36]

The delicious irony, then, which audiences had long enjoyed—that Judith promises to "lead him through the city," meaning only his head—must be explained by Ælfric, lest it be viewed as a cunning deceit. Clayton attributes the entire effort to an inner conflict over Judith's role:

> In being unable to deal with such a figure, Ælfric understandably reveals a deep-seated anxiety with regard to women using their bodies in ways which had been firmly repressed by centuries of church prescriptions. . . . Ælfric is unable to think himself free of how such behaviour would normally be constructed in his own society. . . . [His editing reflects] a desire to make safe the text, to contain and defuse it.[37]

Clayton may be correct, but there is also a danger of over-psychologizing Ælfric, who is, after all, writing for nuns. Although "deep-seated anxiety" is a trait we may imagine with *every* interpretation of Judith, Ælfric may be doing what clerics have always done in applying biblical texts for a community: softening the edges of a very rough original.

We include here as well the German treatments of Judith in the eleventh century. Two Middle High German poems appear, the "ältere" and "*jüngere Judith.*" Popular ballads in the genre of the *Spielmann,* or minstrel, the ältere Judith was even referred to as "the only true example of a genuine minstrel-song." Edna Purdie contrasts this with the *jüngere*: "the uninspired versification of a biblical theme was not beyond the powers of the most mediocre practitioner."[38] The *ältere Judith* presents an active heroine, the *jüngere* a passive one, exhibiting beautiful dress and piety. This alternative between an active, heroic Judith and a passive, pious Judith, even an ascetic warrior, has been played out before and will be again. A heroic Judith reappears in a 1254 biblical history for Teutonic knights.[39]

At the end of the twelfth century, Hélinand of Froidmont, Belgium, composed a major sermon on Judith as a type of Mary and chose as the theme of the sermon Jdt 14:15, "One Hebrew woman has created confusion in the house of Nebuchadnezzar. Behold Holofernes lies on the ground, and his head is not on him."[40] In the commentary (on 14:18), I argue that this line is the narrative center of the text; Hélinand also exploited its vibrancy.

In England, Chaucer's *Canterbury Tales* (written 1387–1400) mention Judith several times: "Monk's Tale," 2.939–47, where Holofernes is discussed as an example

---

35 Mary Clayton, "Ælfric's *Judith:* Manipulative or Manipulated?" *Anglo-Saxon England* 23 (2009) 215–27, here 223.

36 The translation is from Chickering, "Poetic Exuberance," 128.

37 Clayton, "Ælfric's *Judith,*" 225.

38 Edna Purdie, *The Story of Judith in German and English Literature* (Bibliothèque de la Revue de littérature comparée; Paris: H. Champion, 1927) 35. See also Henrike Lähnemann, *Hystoria Judith: Deutsche Judithdichtungen vom 12. bis zum 16. Jahrhundert* (Scrinium Friburgense 20; Berlin: de Gruyter, 2006).

39 Purdie, *Story of Judith,* 38. Note also Hugh of St. Victor (twelfth century), *Sermons* 86–87: Judith is Humil-

ity and Nebuchadnezzar and Holofernes are guilty of hubris (see also his *Allegoriae in Vetus Testamentum* 11.3), and Heinrich von Meissen (Frauenlob), *Judith* (thirteenth–fourteenth century): the story portrays Nemesis and the fall of a man of high estate.

40 Anne T. Thayer, "Judith and Mary: Hélinand's Sermon for the Assumption," in Jacqueline Hamesse et al., eds., *Medieval Sermons and Society: Cloister, City, University; Proceedings of International Symposia at Kalamazoo and New York* (Textes et études du moyen âge 9; Louvain-la-Neuve: Fédération Internationale des Instituts d'études médiévales, 63 (1998–75).

of Nemesis; "Merchant's Tale," 2.1366–68; and "Tale of Meliboeus," or "Melibee," 1099, where Judith personifies Good Counsel. The characterization in the "Monk's Tale" has often been interpreted as a more negative depiction of Judith or, rather, more positive toward Holofernes. Chaucer does seem sympathetic here to Holofernes's temptation, and Garrard thought the villain "perilously close to being a tragic hero."[41] But he is perhaps elevated only by taking center stage. With attention placed on him, in an array with other major historical figures, he grows in stature, whether good or bad. Further, this discussion of Holofernes is in the voice of the misogynist Merchant; it is unclear whether Chaucer is expressing his own criticism of her.

Jewish Traditions of Judith

Although absent in Jewish literature for over a millennium, Judith resurfaces in the eleventh century in Jewish narrative and liturgical poems, acquiring some currency in Jewish tradition. Dubarle collected these retellings of the Judith story in prose and poetry and assigned them numbers, still the most common way of referring to them.[42] Referred to as midrashim, technically speaking they do not interpret Jewish biblical texts. At first glance they appear to be short summaries of the Judith story, but they are actually quite distinctive and surprisingly suggestive of new themes.

The titles of the midrashim are interesting in themselves: "Maaseh Yehudit," literally "Act of Judith" or "Story of Judith" (texts 1, 2, 4, 9); "Midrash le-Hanukkah," or "Midrash for Hanukkah" (text 3). One title clearly constructs the tale as a parallel to "Megillat Esther" and Purim: "Megillat Yehudit—To be Read at Hanukkah" (text 8). The most interesting may be text 5: "This is the Story of the House of Hasmoneus, Which Is Called Book of Judith, On the Subject of 'Woman.'" The conclusions to the narratives are interesting as well. They

may recount the mighty acts of God or intone an Amen or quote Isa 59:20: "As it is written, 'A redeemer shall come to Zion'" (text 3). Moses Gaster believed that the prose midrashim reflected the earliest traditions about Judith, earlier than and independent of the LXX, but this theory is no longer entertained.[43] Rather, the midrashim probably reflect the influence of the Christian tradition and do not predate the tenth or eleventh century.

The two most important differences between the medieval midrashim and the LXX are the addition of an episode *before* the feats of Judith and the shift of the setting to the period of the Maccabean Revolt. In most of these narratives there is an account of the deeds concerning Judah Maccabee and his sister, Hannah, a figure unknown in the ancient period (although the mother of 2 Maccabees 7 is given the name Hannah in both Jewish and Christian tradition). In the Hannah episode, the Seleucid king subjects Israel to the "law of the first night," known from European folklore as the *jus primae noctis* or *droit du seigneur*, and from Near Eastern folklore as well: when any man (here, any Jewish man) is married, the ruler first enjoys a marriage night with the bride, after which she is turned over to her new husband. In our texts, this practice had continued for three years until a marriage was arranged for Hannah, the sister of Judah Maccabee. She appears before her brothers naked, and when they react with outrage and threaten to burn her, she responds, "You say that I am dishonored now, yet you were going to subject me to the gentile king?" The ironic combination of Hannah's titillating exposure and moral superiority is similar to the story of Tamar and Judah (Genesis 38). The brothers are now inspired to plot the assassination of the governor. They arrange a wedding feast, but when the governor shows up to claim his night, they kill him and his generals. This prompts Holofernes, a Seleucid king and brother of the slain governor, to seek revenge. Now Judith enters the story.

41 Garrard, *Artemisia Gentileschi,* 291; see also Stocker, *Judith,* 15; but also Emerson Brown Jr., "Biblical Women in *Merchant's Tale,*" *Viator* 5 (1974) 387–412; L. O. Aranye Fradenburg, *Sacrifice Your Love: Psychoanalysis, Historicism, Chaucer* (Minneapolis: University of Minneapolis Press, 2002) 113–54.

42 Dubarle, *Judith;* see also Deborah Levine Gera, "The

Jewish Textual Traditions," in Brine, Ciletti, and Lähnemann, *Sword of Judith,* 23–40.

43 Gaster, "Unknown Hebrew Version," 156–63. His theory was countered by Carl Meyer, "Zur Entstehungsgeschichte des Buches Judith," *Bib* 3 (1922) 193–203.

The second half, the Judith episode, is set in the period of the Maccabean Revolt. The narrative focuses on her dialogues with the Jewish gatekeepers, the enemy soldiers, and the foreign king; her ruse of being in menses and her execution of Holofernes; her return through the gates; the binding of the king's counselor, deposited at the outskirts of Jerusalem; the discovery of the king's headless body and the victory of the Israelites; and the conversion of the counselor. We may outline the plot elements of the Judith segment:

1. Siege of Jerusalem and the reaction of Israel
2. Judith introduced
3. Dialogue between Judith and the gatekeepers
4. Dialogue between Judith and the enemy soldiers
5. Meeting of Judith and the king
6. Proposal of marriage by the king
7. Pretext of impurity
8. Request for a proclamation in the camp to allow Judith and her slave to go to spring unmolested
9. Banquet and drinking with the king
10. Withdrawal of those invited
11. Murder of the king
12. Return of Judith to Jerusalem
13. Dialogue between Judith and the gatekeepers
14. Remonstrances of the king by the importunate counselor
15. The counselor is bound near Jerusalem
16. Judith invokes counselor's testimony on her behalf
17. Joy of Israel, sortie of soldiers
18. The king is discovered by his soldiers assassinated
19. Massacre and pillage
20. Acts of thanksgiving of the Jews
21. Conversion of the importunate counselor
22. Decision to celebrate an anniversary feast
23. Doxological conclusion

The midrashim thus break with the LXX and the Vulgate in many ways. In the LXX, Judith's heroic passage through the gates into the danger zone is well marked as a rite of passage, part of the heroine's movement from culture to chaos in order to slay the monster. She commands the elders and gatekeepers as her lieutenants, and they watch her depart in awe. In the midrashim, however, this moment is thoroughly redrawn as an ordeal of innocence. The gatekeepers accuse her of leaving in order to seduce an enemy general into marrying her, or even colluding with the enemy to destroy Jerusalem. She convinces them otherwise and departs, but upon return, even though she has just saved her people, she is accused once again and must argue her innocence. In some of the midrashim she pulls out the head of Holofernes as proof, but in Midrash 8 this is not enough: the gatekeepers sarcastically point out that the head could belong to anyone.

Scholars have noted with surprise, even a sense of loss, what is different here. Greek Judith was a transgressive, assertive woman, but this midrashic Judith is a falsely accused pious damsel, not unlike Susanna. But cross-culturally, the hero often experiences an antagonism with his or her people.[44] A pious young woman—more sexually exposed because she is a marriageable young woman and not a widow—must face the sexual slander of the gatekeepers. Yet the narrator takes the side of the accused maiden: withstanding the ordeal of sexual slander is one of her heroic deeds. Achior has been moved quite awkwardly to just this position in the story in order to testify to her truthfulness. Whereas in the LXX Judith attested to Achior's trustworthiness, now he must attest to hers.

Just as Ambrose and Jerome had reined in a willful Judith, so have the midrashim. Judith is no longer a larger-than-life heroine but a more "typical," even dependent person who represents "woman."[45] In the LXX, Judith has a long genealogy, and her husband is said to be of *her* tribe and clan, unique in the Bible, while in the midrashim Judith depends on her family; her male relatives, prophets and priests, give her valid knowledge of God's intentions (contra LXX 11:16–17!). Most of the midrashim make no mention of her intelligence, a major element in the biblical versions. In the midrashim,

---

44 Nagy, *Best of the Achaeans*, esp. 303–8.
45 Gera, "Jewish Textual Traditions," 34; Gera, "Shorter Medieval Hebrew Tales of Judith," in Brine, Ciletti, and Lähnemann, *Sword of Judith*, 81–96, here 81, 84; Mira Friedman, "Metamorphoses of Judith," *Jewish Art* 12–13 (1986–1987) 225–46, here 225–32.

she gives no scolding speech to the men (as Hannah does) and no commands regarding military strategy. Her ironic, even transgressive, dominance-and-submission dialogue in the LXX characterized her as a boundary-smashing heroine, but here that is all gone. The spirit and willfulness of the LXX are found now not in Judith but in Hannah.

Interesting also is the fact that Judith deflects the king's advances by saying that she is in menses and must go to the spring each night for her purification. According to the LXX, the bathing purifies her (12:9; cf. 11:17; 12:7), but we are not told precisely what that means. A *mikveh* comes to mind, but in the LXX it is never stated that she has been in menses, and she bathes two nights in a row, which would not be typical of a postmenstrual *mikveh*. The LXX is evocative without being clear or realistic. Gera sees the change in the medieval stories as a loss for Judith's independent nature:

> The medieval [Jewish] authors apparently found this purification rite by a woman mystifying or possibly subversive: perhaps this independent, religious woman was too close to God for their taste. At any rate, it is easier for these storytellers to depict an impure, menstruating woman than to envision a holy woman of God, who immerses herself in water in a near-spiritual act of purification, common to men and women alike.[46]

Also noteworthy is the fact that some confusing passages in the midrashim can be explained as literate play on well-known biblical images. In text 12, for instance, it is surprisingly said that Judith *made* the sword that she would use, specifically, a two-edged sword that she hid in her sandal—an implausible detail. However, the biblical trickster Ehud (Judges 3) had also made a concealable, two-edged dagger in order to assassinate the king of Moab. In Midrash 8 biblical phrases are interwoven so thickly as to become a cultivated shrub of biblical pas-sages—over three hundred quotations and allusions in six pages of Hebrew text. The charged nature of the sexual motifs is played out in biblical phrases rather than in straightforward prose, creating at times an oddly indeter-minate reading.

Why a sudden interest in Judith among Jews, who had ignored her for a millennium? The Old English revival of Judith occurred at about the same time, but that text may have arisen as a response to the invasion of the Vikings. This would not apply to Jews five hundred miles to the east. Gera notes the Jewish rediscovery at this time of much nonrabbinic Jewish tradition, including the Apoc-rypha and related texts.[47] There may also be a deliberate anti-Christian polemic in Judith's change from widow to young woman. This resexualized her status, possibly in opposition to the Christian ascetic reading.[48] As Christian writings were often intended for priests and nuns, the Hanukkah context of the midrashim made them available for everyone, and the author's "audience were allowed, indeed encouraged, to enjoy food and sex in the right contexts."[49] But the fact that these midrashim arise spe-cifically in the eleventh century still requires explanation. Judith's association with Hanukkah proceeds in contrast to the Christian biblical tradition and may respond to the anti-Jewish pogroms at the time of the Crusades. The tone of the Judith narratives is assertive, polemical, and strongly identity oriented, like the stories of the Macca-bees, also being reasserted by Jews at this time.[50]

Other references to Judith in Jewish tradition, all post–eleventh century, have been culled by a number of scholars. Most of these references assume the narratives of the midrashim:[51]

- Rashi (1040–1105) comments on b. Shab. 23a ("Women are obligated to kindle lights on Hanukkah") by referring to the decree of the Greek governors to have the right of the first night of all Jewish marriages.

---

46 Gera, "Shorter Medieval Hebrew Tales," 87.

47 Gera, "Jewish Textual Traditions," 33, 36.

48 In one illustrated version (text 12), Hannah is pic-tured from the rear, seminude before her brothers; see Israel Adler, "A Chanukah Midrash," in Charles Berlin, ed., *Studies in Jewish Bibliography, History, and Literture in Honor of I. Edward Kiev* (New York: Ktav, 1971) i–viii, here v and vii.

49 Weingarten, "Food, Sex, and Redemption," 108.

50 Daniel Joslyn-Siematkoski, *Christian Memories of the Maccabean Martyrs* (London: Palgrave-Macmillan, 2009) 121–59.

51 Dubarle, *Judith*, 1:105–10; Gera, "Jewish Textual traditions"; Gera, "Shorter Medieval Hebrew Tales"; Friedman, "Metamorphoses."

- Rashbam (1086–1174), in *Tosafot Megillah* 4a: "Women are obligated to hear the reading of the story of Esther because they were also participants in a sign that came about through them: Purim through Esther and Hanukkah through Judith."
- Ramban (Nachmanides, 1194–c. 1270) quotes Jdt 1:7–11 from a Syriac "Susanna," probably the Syriac Women's Bible noted above.
- Rabbi Azariah de Rossi (c. 1550) and Rabbi Gedaliah ben Jechai (sixteenth century) rejected the connection between Judith and Hanukkah.[52]
- Rabbi Yosef Karo (1488–1575), *Shulchan Arukh* OH 570, 2: "There are those who say we should eat cheese on Hanukkah, because of the miracle over the milk which Judith fed the enemy."
- Judith was included in *Zemah David* (*Offspring of David*), an account of Jewish and non-Jewish history by David Gans (1592).
- R. Jehudah Arieh Modena (Rjam, 1571–1648), in his *Historia degli riti hebraici* (*History of Jewish Rites*) §9, written as an explanation of Judaism for Christians, connects Judith and Hanukkah.
- Menahem Azariah de Fano (1688) has an entry identifying Judith with Jael.

These references cover the medieval and early modern periods, but reference to Judith's relation to Hanukkah continued; Gera notes a *responsum* in 1996 that treats Judith.[53]

Hebrew and Yiddish translations of the Vulgate of Judith also circulated.[54] The earliest of these is dated by Dubarle to the twelfth century, and a Yiddish translation of Susanna and Judith was also published in Cracow in 1571 by Shalom bar Abraham. The introduction reads:

> I have published this little book in honor of all women: the story of pious Susanna, who did not want to lie with the judges but preferred to be put to death. Also, the story of Judith. . . . Therefore, you pious women, you should definitely buy this book. Then I

will print the whole Bible in Yiddish, and many other fine things.[55]

His text of Judith corresponds to the Vulgate version, but is not likely a direct translation from Latin and seems uninfluenced by the Hebrew translations above. Rather, it reflects the influence of Zwingli's German translation in Zurich.

Jewish depictions of Judith in the visual arts fall into two categories: textual illuminations and Hanukkah menorah and Torah shield decorations. Of the illuminated texts, the most impressive is the Rothschild Miscellany, an opulent collection of Jewish religious and secular texts. Commissioned by Moses ben Yakuthiel Hakohen in Italy in 1479, it included a *yozer,* or hymn, with images of Judah the Maccabee on the left and Judith on the right. Judah is the savior of his people, a shield before him and a sword in his raised right hand, while Judith is depicted as in Christian illuminated Bibles, in the tent of Holofernes, chopping off his head. Judah and Judith as parallel guardians of the people may be influenced by David and Judith in Christian Florence at this same time (see below). Another illuminated manuscript is the Prague Haggadah of 1526, where Judith is paired with Samson to illustrate the text "Pour out your wrath upon the nations" (Ps 79:6).

Judith, virtually the only woman to be depicted in Jewish ceremonial art, appeared mainly on Hanukkah menorahs, but also, surprisingly, on a Torah shield from Prague (1708). Notable are two Hanukkah menorahs from the sixteenth century from Italy. Judith stands at the top of one, with two subdued lions at the base. On an Augsburg menorah from 1759, Judith is again at the top, elegantly dressed in European lady's fashions, yet wielding an oversized sword. She was popular on menorahs in Holland and Germany as well. On some she is depicted with Moses, Aaron, and Judah. She sometimes appears with her slave, but at other times with an unidentifiable

52   Azariah de Rossi, *The Light of the Eyes* (ed. and trans. Joanna Weinberg; Yale Judaica Series 31; New Haven: Yale University Press, 2001) 636–39.

53   Gera, "Jewish Textual Traditions," 33.

54   Dubarle argued that they reflect traditions old enough to predate the LXX (*Judith*, 1:20–27, 33–37; 2:8–96), but scholars have generally disagreed and

treated the Hebrew texts as medieval adaptations of Christian sources.

55   Ruth von Bernuth and Michael Terry, "Shalom bar Abraham's Book of Judith in Yiddish," in Brine, Ciletti, and Lähnemann, *Sword of Judith,* 127–50, here 127.

woman holding a jug. Mira Friedman suggests that this may be a personification for Hanukkah–Rededication, a feminine word in Hebrew–the jug representing the miracle of the oil of Hanukkah.[56] A blessings miscellany for women from 1739, "A Seder for Grace after Meals" (*Seder Birkat Ha-Mazon*), was created with illuminations by Aaron Wolf Herlinger. Here Judith and her slave place the head of Holofernes in a pouch with a Hanukkah menorah in the background. Friedman also finds Judith on a Torah breastplate, perhaps a Torah to be used on Hanukkah.

Illustrations for Bibles and Other Books

If the Jewish midrashim reenlist Judith as a violent response to the Crusades, at about the same time a more violent image is found in Christian art as well, and remains throughout. Illustrated manuscripts of the Bible provided opportunities for depictions of Judith's deed. Since the Vulgate version began with A for Arphaxad, this shape lent itself to the depiction of the tent, the site of the acteme. Judith decapitating a passed-out Holofernes became a standard Bible illustration. Holofernes's lustful bed is emphasized, as is the just and ignominious punishment by a righteous Judith. Visible blood, absent from the LXX novella, is introduced for the first time, influenced perhaps by the increased emphasis on the expiatory theology of Christ's blood. Judith becomes a gleeful assassin, even flying with sword in hand over Holofernes, passed out in his bed. A carved tric-trac (backgammon) piece of the twelfth century, now in the Louvre, depicts such a brutal pleasure; Judith's left hand holds Holofernes's hair, as she slices off his head. The image itself stems from a long tradition of male conquerors, reaching back to the ancient world, sometimes slaying lions; compare also Claudius defeating Britannia at Aphrodisias. Yet the reversal of genders is powerful. By her phallic deed Judith dominates and humili-

ates Holofernes. She is not yet a particularly sexualized Judith–unless we consider the fact that she must enter his sexual domain–but rather a woman of action.

Typical are the twelfth-century Bible of Souvigny and Bible of Stephen Harding, and in c. 1310 we find the French Bible of Hainburg. In the fresco cycle in Padua attributed to Guariento di Arpo (c. 1350), the assassin for virtue could hardly be more beautiful. A jubilant, even provocative Judith is found in Diebold Lauber's illustration for a German Bible (c. 1445); the general's head is held aloft, with blood gushing. In the Cologne Bible of Heinrich Quentell (c. 1478), a headless corpse, spread like a dead animal, is spurting plentiful blood. Similar is that of Antoine Dufour (1505), or the woodcut of the Nuremberg Chronicle (1493). Some Bibles contained narrative registers of the stories. The Winchester Bible (c. 1170) presents the story in three registers. The top depicts Achior addressing Holofernes, and Achior tied to a tree; the middle features the general feasting with his men while Judith offers him a drink and Judith decapitating Holofernes as the slave looks on.[57] The lower register depicts Judith back in Bethulia, displaying the head of Holofernes, and the Israelites in battle. Significant here may be the first appearance of Achior in Christian representations, and the earliest depiction of Judith's slave acting beside her.

Nonbiblical texts as well contained important visual interpretations. Hartmann Schedel's depiction in the Nuremburg Chronicle (1493) presents a spirited Judith with the general's head lofted on a sword (compare Albrecht Altdorfer [c. 1520]). In Hortus Deliciarum (1188–1191), the decapitation represents Christ's human nature conquering the devil.[58] In Speculum Virginum (1100–1150) and De laudibus sanctae crucis (c. 1170) a theme from Prudentius is reintroduced: the decapitation represents Humilitas slaying Superbia. Two centuries later, the Speculum Humanae Salvationis depicted Old

---

56 Friedman, "Metamorphoses," 231–32.
57 The choice of scenes may have been influenced by Ælfric's homily; so Cooper, "Judith," 186. In the Bible of St. Paul's-Outside-the-Walls, Judith represents Humilitas defeating Superbia. The Sainte-Geneviève Bible delicately depicts Judith, her slave, and Holofernes in a beautiful bed frame, Judith in the act of slicing.

58 Ciletti, "Patriarchal Ideology," 53, 63; Bailey, "Judith," 281; and Richard Joseph Kubiak, "The Iconography of Judith in Italian Renaissance Art," master's dissertation, University of Wisconsin, Madison, 1965, 7–9.

Testament and classical figures arrayed with Mary conquering Satan: Jael slaying Sisera, Tomyris slaying Cyrus, and Judith slaying Holofernes. Judith raises a huge sword to deal the death blow.

In the thirteenth century, Chartres Cathedral introduced a vast new set of graceful biblical figures, Judith among them, prominent on the north porch, "a slender, lyrical lady whose feet rest on a dog, a symbol of fidelity to her dead husband Manasseh."[59] Five scenes from the story are arranged over her head. Also noteworthy are Judith's presence in the Amiens Cathedral (1230–1240) and Eriskirch Malereien Chor 42 (1410–1420). Simple yet beautiful stained glass windows decorate Sainte-Chapelle, Paris (1245).[60] In 1473, the biblical and classical figures on the floor of the Duomo Cathedral in Siena were expanded by the addition of a set of large narrative scenes, probably directed by Francesco di Giorgio Martini. Very prominent among them are narrative scenes from Judith. Says Bruno Santi, "The Siena Cathedral pavement is *the* synthesis—the most significant synthesis—of the Sienese school of art."[61] The privileged location of Judith in the cathedral floor came with a price; it is now nearly worn down by heavy foot traffic.

Renaissance and Baroque Art

The next developmental spurt in the interpretation of Judith came with the Renaissance. In the fourteenth century, Dante and Petrarch exploited the symbolic power of Judith in a new way: she was a political symbol of victory over tyranny—the triumph of the human spirit. Judith was good to think with, in a period when very clever people were doing a lot of thinking. In the early 1300s Dante saw Judith's slaying of Holofernes as the fall of *Superbia*,

Pride,[62] and associated Judith with the classical tyrant-slayer Tomyris, while in *Paradiso* 32.10 Judith is one of eight blessed members of the Old Covenant who surround Mary. A few years later, Petrarch wrote *Triumph of Chastity* and *Triumph of Fame*, in which he participated in the antityranny tradition then growing in Padua. Like Dante, he combined classical and biblical figures and Christian traditions of virtues. Minerva (Athena) is associated with Chastity and Judith, "wise and chaste and strong, . . . a widow who reft her foolish lover of his head."[63]

Both Dante and Petrarch were sensitive to, even obsessed with, the feminine and the symbolic. Beatrice, a woman of virtue and beauty whom Dante had admired from afar, guided him through heaven in *The Divine Comedy*. Petrarch also idealized female love and the woman of virtue, Laura, a distant creature who had spurned his attentions. Judith, a beautiful woman of virtue, was a natural persona for these two. But, significantly, this also marks the beginning of a process that released her from a static, eternal, iconic status and emphasized her narrative. She was now catapulted into a higher pantheon by those figures who chose to symbolize freedom as well as virtue. As a representation of the political aspirations of northern Italian cities, she quickly took her place next to David. When Cola di Rienzo revolted against nobles to create a republic, he invoked Judith to justify a tyrannicide, even the use of deceit: "Again by Judith is another Holofernes slain."[64] From this point forward Judith was given a commanding view of the Renaissance.

In Florence, monumental art constructed a Judith who was patroness of the city's freedom, now a virtual consort of David.[65] Lorenzo Ghiberti included her in the door panels of the baptistery that faced the Duomo

59   Kubiak, "Iconography," 8–9.

60   John Nassichuk, "The Prayer of Judith in Two Late-Fifteenth-Century French Mystery Plays," in Brine, Ciletti, and Lähnemann, *Sword of Judith*, 197–211, here 198–99.

61   Bruno Santi, *The Marble Pavement of the Cathedral of Siena* (Florence: Scala, 1982) 7, 16.

62   Dante, *Purgatory,* Canto 12.58-60. *Superbia* had actually been inserted into the Latin text of Judith by Jerome, where there was no equivalent in Greek; see appendix.

63   Petrarch, *Chastity,* 1340-44. In *Triumph of Fame*

Judith is arrayed with Tomyris, Cleopatra, and Zenobia; see Francesco Petrarca, *Triumphs* (Chicago: University of Chicago Press, 1962) 22, 45, 83; Ciletti, "Patriarchal Ideology," 58-60. In the Palazzo Pubblico of Siena, *Iustitia* was represented as Judith had been, holding a sword in one hand and the head of a tyrant in the other. The similarity of names in Italian—Giuditta and giustizia–contributed to this association.

64   See Kubiak, "Iconography," 19-21.

65   Mary Joan Leith notes that at Dura Europos, Esther and David are placed prominently on each side of

Cathedral (1452). Dubbed by Michelangelo the Gates of Paradise, they are often considered the first artistic production of the Renaissance. Judith was set very prominently among the scenes on the door, standing parallel to, yet larger than, David, and from here she was projected into the center of Florentine political life. She struck what came to be a new classic pose, somewhat similar to the Nike of Samothrace: she runs forward confidently in victory, sword raised in her right hand and the head of Holofernes in her left, her hips swayed slightly for balance.

The period 1450–1500 was marked by a dramatic increase in the size and visual power of the depictions of Judith. In 1455–1460 Donatello created a masterpiece, a bronze statue of Judith decapitating Holofernes (Fig. 1). Revolutionary, while yet embodying the "classic" pose, Judith is triumphant with her sword raised high, ready to finish the job of decapitation. Her garments hide her form, and thus she is hardly sexualized in the usual sense (compare Mantegna below), yet Holofernes is muscular and almost naked. More to the point, he is now human, problematic, even tragic, his face and position reminding one of Christ's in the popular *pietà*s. *This, indeed, may be the moment when the virtue of Judith and the vice of Holofernes begin to be problematized.* The turning, interconnected bodies of Judith and Holofernes also require the viewer to walk around the statue. There is a murkiness in the confused drapery of *Judith;* the only universal point, as Mary Jacobus notes, is her "ritually upraised sword [originally gilded!], which, visible from all sides, seems frozen—'petrified,' as it were—while Holofernes

dissolves beneath her."[66] And if Judith was no longer a timeless icon of virtue but a character in a realistic narrative, then she could be examined and evaluated like any woman. The more realistically Judith was depicted, the more she stepped outside of a protected realm of iconic Virtue, the more she became sexualized, and the more she and her slave could be portrayed not as destroyers of Vice but as colluding in the violent execution of . . . a real man?

Most likely sponsored by the Medicis, Donatello's statue of Judith stood in the garden of the Medici estate, accompanied by a civic plaque:

> Piero son of Cosimo Medici has dedicated this statue of a woman both to liberty and to fortitude, whereby the citizens with unvanquished and constant heart might return to the republic.[67]

Another plaque read:

> Kingdoms fall through licentiousness; cities rise through virtues. You see the proud neck severed by humility.[68]

The bronze statue, however, could not withstand the buffeting winds of political changes in Florence. After the Medici were swept out of power, it was moved in 1494 to its present location in the Piazza della Signoria with a further plaque, more pointedly antityrannical: "An example of public health to place before the city, 1495."[69]

When Michelangelo's David, however, was moved to the politically charged area of Palazzo della Signoria, a debate ensued as to whether the *Judith* should be exhib-

the Torah niche (personal communication). József Zsengellér draws attention to the fact that David was often painted as young and effeminate, Judith as manly and official, sometimes by the same artist ("Judith as a Female David," 201–2). Cf. paintings by Hans von Aachen (and also one formerly attributed to him at Middlebury College), Jacopo Amigoni, Giovanni Baglione, Valentin de Boulogne, Salomon de Bray, Giuseppe (Cavaliere d'Arpino) Cesari, Giorgio Vasari, and Pierfrancesco di Jacopo Foschi.

66 Jacobus, "Judith, Holofernes," 128; see also Bettina Uppenkamp, *Judith und Holofernes in der italienischen Malerei des Barock* (Berlin: Dietrich Reimer, 2004) 48–50; Laurie Schneider, "Donatello and Caravaggio: The Iconography of Decapitation," *American Imago* 33 (1976) 76–101; Alastair Fowler, *Renais-*

sance Realism: Narrative Images in Literature and Art (Oxford: Oxford University Press, 2003); Paola Tinagli, *Women in Italian Renaissance Art: Gender, Representation, Identity* (Manchester: Manchester University Press, 1997) 86.

67 *Salus Publica. Petrus Medices Cos. Fi. libertati simul et fortitudini hanc mulieris statuam quo civis invicto constantique animo ad rem pub. redderent dedicavit.* Translation from Nutu, "Framing Judith," 129.

68 *Regna cadunt luxu, surgent virtutibus urbes. Caesa vides humili colla superba manu.* On a possible twelfth-century model for Donatello, see Sarah Blake McHam, "Donatello's Bronze David and Judith as Metaphors of Medici Rule in Florence," *Art Bulletin* 83 (2001) 32–47; and Kubiak, "Iconography," 28–31.

69 *Exemplum salutis publicae cives posuere 1495.*

ited beside him, and a push was on to remove her. Said Francesco di Lorenzo Filarete,

> The *Judith* is an omen of evil, and no fit object where it stands. . . . It is not proper that the woman should kill the male; and above all, this statue was erected under an evil star, as things have gone from bad to worse since then.[70]

This is the first negative statement about Judith's act as a woman, referring to the first work of art that equivocates about her role. She was moved farther away, and David was placed on her pedestal, but she once again came to be visually paired with the copy of Michelangelo's *David*. Both in the Gates of Paradise and here, and also later in the Sistine Chapel, Judith was parallel to David, the female and male partners in the decapitation of tyrants and the protection of liberty.

Implicit in Judith's association with David was the notion that her goodness could vanquish the evils of repressive government and institutions. And what better symbol of the tyrant could be found than Holofernes? Her dominant pose over him replays the traditional depiction of her raised sword, and it also partakes of the tradition of the psychomachia of Prudentius, virtues conquering and standing over vices, mirroring also Cellini's *Perseus with the Head of Medusa*, placed in the Piazza in 1554.[71] But at the same time, the humanist and rationalist tradition was also "releasing" Judith from her previous association with Mary and unalloyed virtue. The more she was released from those protections, the more independent and threatening she became. "No longer must we believe that her strength was solely the miraculous gift of God," says Ciletti. "There is an unyielding angularity

about the statue which lends something of the inevitability of geometry to Judith's act."[72] But it is not just angularity. Judith's sword is raised high, ready to be released, all potential energy.

Donatello's *Judith* has been interpreted in wildly divergent ways: Sanctity over Lust or Humility over Pride; or as a political allegory, the victory of the Medici over their Florentine enemies, and then Florence over foreign foes, Florence over the Medicis and other tyrants deemed to be like Holofernes. "Despite, or perhaps because of, this iconographic density," says H. W. Janson, "the sculpture's symbolic power has readily been recognized and co-opted for various and sometimes opposing purposes."[73] Donatello's statue of Judith also represents a transition from unreservedly virtuous representations to a challenging mixture of virtuous and quite ambivalent Judiths.

The Explosion of Judith in the Renaissance and Baroque

From this point, Judith not only was featured in art and letters but became one of the most popular biblical women. Most of the major artists of the Renaissance and Baroque produced *Judith*s, many more than one. In addition to Donatello, there are important *Judith*s by Botticelli, Mantegna, Giorgione, Michelangelo, Titian, Tintoretto, Caravaggio, Lucas Cranach, Baglione, Orazio and Artemisia Gentileschi, Veronese, Rubens, Rembrandt, and myriad others. Sandro Botticelli painted Judith a number of times and included her in the backgrounds of two other paintings. In the earliest (c. 1470; Fig. 2), her pose was similar to the now-iconic version of the Gates of Paradise, though softened. Escaping the Assyrian camp after

---

70 Ciletti, "Patriarchal Ideology," 68; Garrard, *Artemisia Gentileschi*, 295; Bonnie A. Bennett and David G. Wilkins, *Donatello* (Mt. Kisko, NY: Moyer Bell, 1984) 82–90, 219–21; Andrea M. Sheaffer, "Judith versus Goliath? Visualizing David as Archetype," *Arts* 25 (2014) 5–14.

71 Cellini was indeed commissioned by the Medicis, on their return to power in 1545, to create a statue to mirror Judith and undercut her association with the republic; so McHam, "Donatello's *Judith*," 324.

72 Ciletti, "Patriarchal Ideology," 61.

73 H. W. Janson, *The Sculpture of Donatello* (Princeton, NJ: Princeton University Press, 1963) 200–204.

Janson argued that the sword was not realistically aimed at the neck of Holofernes, and Judith does not look at him, so the depiction is still iconic. The slow sweep of the sword is unmistakable, however; it is the beginnings of a narrative telling. See also Edgar Wind, "Donatello's *Judith*: A Symbol of 'Sanctimonia,'" *Journal of the Warburg and Courtauld Institutes* 1 (1937–38) 62–71; Hans von Erffa, "Judith—Virtus Virtutem—Maria," *Mitteilungen des Kunsthistorischen Institutes in Florenz* 14 (1970) 460–65; Jacobus, "Judith, Holofernes"; and Schneider, "Donatello and Caravaggio."

the beheading, she holds the sword in her right hand, but now lowered, rather than raised in triumph: "All pellucid beauty and mobile drapery," Stocker describes her, "unconscious of the sword in her hand."[74] But what does her face communicate? For Stocker, although she has a bloody sword in her right hand, she is at peace; the olive branch is the result of her acteme, the sword lowered because her act is over. Robert Knotts, however, sees in her face, as in that of Donatello's *Judith,* signs of remorse.[75] The scene as a whole may illuminate this. There is an engaged and beautiful slave, but a disengaged Judith; the slave suggests forward motion, Judith regret or passivity, melancholy. Also now emphasized in Botticelli's *Judith* is the slave as her ally. She holds the head of Holofernes on a platter perched on her head, an arrangement conducive to depicting the three faces close together.[76] The destinies of the three figures—one of high estate, one of middle estate, and one of low estate—are placed in dialogue in a number of ways. The viewer is led to a profound comparison and contrast of identities—the close, even sexual contact of the figures—irresistible to many artists who followed.

In 1875 the art critic John Ruskin, registering his extreme Judith-fatigue, championed Botticelli's *Judith* as a contrast:

Do you happen to know anything about Judith herself, except that she cut off Holofernes' head; and has been made the high light of about a million of vile pictures ever since, in which the painters thought they could surely attract the public to the double show of an execution, and a pretty woman—especially with the added pleasure of hinting at previously ignoble sin?[77]

To his relief, Botticelli's *Judith* "is not merely the Jewish Delilah to the Assyrian Samson, but the mightiest, purest, brightest type of high passion in severe womanhood offered to our human memory." She is "sweet, peaceful motion, while you read in her face only sweet solemnity of dreaming thought." Walter Pater objected: "Botticelli's *Judith* was free of religious and moral demands, feeling without reflection, a return from Hebraic moralizing to Hellenic aestheticism."[78] The serenity and grace of the painting belie the bloody narrative—even though the head of Holofernes sits on a platter inches from Judith's beatific face! Contrast as well Botticelli's own companion piece, the discovery of Holofernes's headless body, suffused in dark reds and earth tones. A *Judith* at the end of Botticelli's life also veers in a less-harmonious direction, a darker figure emerging after the grisly deed, head in hand. No longer oblivious to the severed head placed discreetly behind her, she is drained and world-weary, peering directly at it. There is just a hint of what will appear often in later paintings: a beautiful but distraught Judith, face-to-face with a horrific act.

By 1500, the painting of Judith in Florence had decreased, but she became a popular subject elsewhere.[79] Andrea Mantegna in Venice omitted the political overtones found in Florence and Siena, but new symbolism entered in. The materials, colors, and backgrounds of his *Judith*s all differed, but his central image remains. In his 1495 painting, Judith stands with her slave before the peach-pink tent of Holofernes, depositing the head into the slave's pouch. Judith is sturdy and dour; the slave mousy and subservient, only half the size of her mistress—a common way of depicting slaves. As with Donatello, Judith is unglamorous but dependable and heroic, a virtuous nun, a selfless warrior of virtue.[80] Yet sexual themes may be channeled elsewhere, away from Judith's body. Although the tent motif was popular from illuminated manuscripts—"A" was the first letter of the Latin text of

74 Margarita Stocker, "Biblical Story and the Heroine," in Martin Warner, ed., *The Bible as Rhetoric: Studies in Biblical Persuasion and Credibility* (Warwick Studies in Philosophy and Literature; New York: Routledge, 1990) 81–102, here 92.

75 Robert Knotts, "Judith in Florentine Renaissance Art, 1425–1512" (Ph.D. diss., Ohio State University, 1995) 336–37.

76 Paul Joannides, "Titian's *Judith* and Its Context: The Iconography of Decapitation," *Apollo* 135, no. 361 (March 1992) 163–70.

77 John Ruskin, *Mornings in Florence* (Kent: Allen, 1875) 65–66.

78 Walter Pater, *The Renaissance: Studies in Art and Poetry* (1873; repr. of 4th ed.; Berkeley: University of California Press, 1980) 50–53, 47; see Stocker, *Judith,* 174.

79 Knotts, "Judith in Florentine," 398.

80 Ciletti, "Patriarchal Ideology," 66; Apostolos-Cappadona, "Lord Has Struck," 333–34.

Judith and easily suggested the tent setting—it could also represent Holofernes's vagina, as it likely did in the LXX, which Judith penetrates to deflower him (see §5 above). Mantegna's tent suggests this as well.

In addition, the slave now holds open the pouch at womb height to receive Holofernes's head, as she would in many future paintings. In the visual medium, this reads as a reverse birth—the bloody head of Holofernes, about the size of a baby, placed into the slave's "womb." The subservience of the slave indicates Judith's instrumental control of her, and placing the head into her womb-pouch suggests the even greater power that Judith has over Holofernes. In addition, because of the presence of black African servants in Venice, Judith's slave here and in many subsequent Venetian paintings is depicted as African. In addition, Mantegna foregrounds Judith's thin arm crossing the very center of the frame. This communicates Judith's agency in putting Holofernes securely into the pouch, while looking away to the horizon of her escape.[81]

Donatello had introduced ambivalence in regard to Judith, Botticelli remorse, and Mantegna repression. It was now left to Giorgione to introduce a more open sexuality (c. 1504; Fig. 3). To be sure, compared with his fully nude *Sleeping Venus* (c. 1510), sexuality is here only suggested, but Venus was a classical, not a biblical, figure. The upper left of the painting is warm and light, the lower right dark, conveying danger and death. Judith's bare leg defines the boundary between the two zones. Referencing this erotic leg, Jan Białostocki could argue that Giorgione placed the "foot in the door" to the sexualizing of the heroine:[82]

[The sword's] cold, shiny blade rhymes visually with the warmth of the bared, slightly bent form of her leg; sensuality and weapons, *Eros* and *Thanatos* are joined in the new context of this painting. . . . Judith's left

leg, [is] bared to the thigh and almost caressing the severed head of the man.[83]

On the one hand, the same sort of calm and grace that is found in Botticelli's early Judith is seen here, but not only is Giorgione's Judith much stronger, there is something else as well:

[T]he whole painting is rife with a particularly perverse tension between . . . the dominant calm, collected, contemplative mood and . . . the motifs of death, like the severed head and the sharp, deadly weapon.[84]

Judith's foot resting on Holofernes's head resonates on several levels—Mary treading on the snake, but also dominance–submission as well. Many later paintings will copy this motif.

In Domenico di Pace Beccafumi's painting (c. 1510; Fig. 4), a steely Judith prowls the horizon, her oversized arm holding Holofernes's tiny head as a war trophy. She holds the phallic sword loosely over her right shoulder, with one of her breasts exposed. In many paintings Judith holds the head by the hair, suggesting power over and even abuse of the dead tyrant, but here the massive size of her body is remarkable. More important, she looks out toward the viewer, as if to ask, "Are you next?" A few decades earlier, Leonardo da Vinci had depicted a female subject looking directly at the viewer for the first time (*Ginevra*, 1480), but the present painting pushes the boundaries of what a biblical heroine can do. Judith can either be a woman warrior, like the valkyrie above, or no longer a heroine at all but a threat. From this point, we note a simple distinction in *Judith*s: if she looks up to heaven (as with Guido Reni, below), her deed appears to be God-directed; if at the audience, she often seems to have willfully stepped outside the bounds of what a woman should do; she engages the viewer with her eyes.[85]

81 In the Chapelle Notre-Dame de Puy, the altarpiece by Nicolas Blasset (1627) is influenced by Mantegna's presentation: Judith looks slightly upward, reaching an arm across to project the head out toward the viewer.

82 Jan Białostocki, "Judith: Story, Image, and Symbol: Giorgione's Painting in the Evolution of the Theme," in *The Message of Images: Studies in the History of Art* (Bibliotheca artibus et historiae; Vienna: Irsa, 1988) 124.

83 Białostocki, "Judith," 124, 131.

84 Białostocki, "Judith," 115. On the nude *Saint Catherine*, see 117.

85 Cf. also Matteo di Giovanni (c. 1491), a slightly earlier depiction of Judith looking at the viewer. See Uppenkamp, *Judith und Holofernes*, 123, 128–29; Helen Watanabe-O'Kelly, "The Figure of Judith in Works by German Women Writers between 1895 and 1921," in Claire Bielby and Anna Richards, eds., *Women and Death 3: Women's Representations of Death*

The ceiling of the Sistine Chapel (1508–1512) includes Judith, placed quite prominently. In the scalloped pendentives at the four corners are biblical figures who are transitional to the heavenly revelations in the highest ceiling. Michelangelo placed Judith on one of these pendentives (Fig. 5), parallel to David beheading Goliath in the facing corner—high praise for Judith! The act of David that is chosen, the decapitation of Goliath, is the deed that most closely matches Judith's. Yet Judith is running away, with her back to the viewer, obscuring her heroic act. She glances backward at the muscular, headless body of Holofernes. Michelangelo's friend Giorgio Vasari described her body language: "She shows by her attitude fear of the camp and terror at the sight of the dead body."[86] In her bulky garments, Judith is hardly dressed to allure; her slave is more impressive in blood-red and violet garments, and more visible to the viewer. Yet Judith is sturdy and athletic, as are many of Michelangelo's female figures. Retiring quickly from the beheading, past the sleeping guards, Judith and her slave form a sort of bridge of cooperation, acting in concert as in the later paintings of Artemisia Gentileschi (see below). Judith's evasion and concealment of her deed make perfect sense in the context of the biblical story, but are very unsettling visually. Charles de Tolnay suggested that "Judith horrified casts a furtive glance at the mutilated body of Holofernes as if to see the last tremblings of her victim,"[87] but is de Tolnay projecting his horror onto Judith? The rear view of Judith and her large, colorless garments create an anti-heroic presence. Indeed, Judith is the only figure in the Sistine Chapel to be viewed from the rear, her face not visible.

Contrasting sharply is Judith's partner in the facing pendentive, David slaying Goliath. Unlike other figures in the ceiling who exhibit torsion and potential energy, David enacts kinetic energy. He swings his sword at a hulking, helpless Goliath. The act is directly visible, even celebrated—as indeed Judith's had been in centuries past, and in the Bible. Holofernes's muscular body is also idealized like that of other male figures on the ceiling, notably Adam's. Michelangelo's friend Vasari would move in a different direction, painting a strong, muscular, male-heroic Judith holding a sword ready to fall—indeed, very like the Sistine David!

From this brief discussion of Renaissance and early Baroque art and letters, we begin to sense that many, but by no means all, depictions of Judith began to reflect ambivalence about Judith's character. She was formerly an unambiguous woman of virtue, tamed, to be sure, by Christian theology, as Holofernes was unambiguously a representative of lust or vice. But the visual medium of painting and the potentialities of Renaissance realism encouraged a full engagement with the *Eros/Thanatos* theme and, just as important, the disquieting effects of seeing a "real" woman seduce and decapitate/castrate. Beginning with Donatello, the viewer perceives a moral ambivalence concerning Judith, and later also a sexualizing of her, combined with a sympathy for Holofernes. The iconic Judith now becomes a boundary figure and a danger for the (male) viewer. The more realistically Judith was painted, the more she became sexualized, the more threatening she became, she and her slave sometimes colluding in a threatening act. In contrast to most other biblical women, Judith projects a moral ambiguity. Is she good or evil? One cannot tell. Art historians sometimes invoke notions of the dread of women and the Medusa effect to describe the paintings. Ciletti laments, "Once a sexual dimension is acknowledged for the female character, her identity as a legitimate, active heroine is simply not possible."[88] And yet there remained many positive, heroic *Judith*s.

in German Culture since 1500 (Rochester, NY: Camden House, 2010) 125–27; Mary Garrard, "Leonardo da Vinci: Female Portraits, Female Nature," in Mary Garrard and Norma Broude, *The Expanding Discourse: Feminism and Art History* (New York: Routledge, 1992) 58–86.

86 Quoted in Nanette Salomon, "Judging Artemisia: A Baroque Woman in Modern Art History," in Mieke Bal, ed., *The Artemisia Files: Artemisia Gentileschi for Feminists and Other Thinking People* (Chicago: University of Chicago Press, 2005) 33–61, here 53. See also Knotts, "Judith in Florentine," 378; Kim Butler, "The Immaculate Body in the Sistine Ceiling," *Art History* 32 (April 2009) 250–89.

87 Charles de Tolnay, *Michelangelo: Sculptor, Painter, Architect* (Princeton, NJ: Princeton University Press, 1975) 93.

88 Ciletti, "Patriarchal Ideology," 52; see also Ciletti's analysis of Ruskin's views, 37, 52, 56; and see Siegfried Kracauer, *Theory of Film: The Redemption of*

The acteme itself would seem, from the synchronic perspective, to provoke ambivalence, yet we should not interject our later judgments into the diachronic context of the early modern period. Still, we may explore some patterns that emerge between about 1500 and 1700. There is a psychosexual aspect in many of the post-1500 artworks and texts that seems inherent in the explosive sex and violence of the acteme. In the deed, and even in her clutch of the general's head, the thinnest possible film exists between clothed and naked, good and evil, *Eros* and *Thanatos*. Some tendencies of the change after 1500 are the following:

1. Judith is less obviously identified with virtue and more identified with seduction (both are emphasized in the biblical story). She is often highly eroticized, holding either the plainly phallic hilt of the sword, the phallic blade, caressing Holofernes's cheek, or clutching or fingering his hair.

2. Judith may subjugate the head, rendering it now as lifeless flesh, or physically dominate the body or head, in a way that can suggest bondage and discipline. About the size of a baby, the head is sometimes placed in the pouch, held at womb height by the slave, a reverse birth motif (Mantegna; see above). Judith can hold the head by gripping the hair and can lift it up high, exhibiting her triumph (like Perseus with the head of Medusa), or set it low and to the side, reminding us of the life that she took from him (Cranach). Judith can also care for the head, bearing it away, meditating on it, or even cradling it. She can even hold it to her breast in an erotic embrace (van Bossuit), or as if nursing it (Georg Pencz, 1531).

3. Judith's deed at Holofernes's bedside was the perfect zone for exploring the tensions of *Eros* and *Thanatos*, but it is even more accentuated here than with Jael and Sisera. From 1500 on, this only increases. Our story has more capability for exploring the simultaneous power of *Eros* and *Thanatos* because other figures are either too good or too evil.

4. In the male-dominated world of Renaissance and Baroque art, one generally assumes a male gaze and a male voyeurism. Judith's nudity is objectified, and the woman is sometimes reduced to a passive performer.[89] Formerly, in paintings only courtesans and prostitutes engaged the eye of the viewer, until Leonardo's *Ginevra* (1474). *Mona Lisa* followed.[90] Judith often looks directly at the viewer, which influences the dynamic of "gaze," even where it does not reverse it. Some *Judith*s who look out at the viewer seem brazen, threatening (Liss, c. 1625, Saraceni, c. 1615; compare also Simon Vouet c. 1630; Valentin de Boulogne, 1628; Peter Paul Rubens, c. 1616). Other artists register different effects. One of the first female artists to paint Judith was Lavinia Fontana, who provides a warmer effect; her Judith may be a portrait of herself or a patroness. Francesco del Cairo perhaps imagines the trauma of Judith. In Bernardo Cavallino's, Judith appears shell-shocked, her right hand gently caressing Holofernes's head. Are we to perceive trauma, regret, guilt, or even insanity? Contrast here the influential *Judith* by Guido Reni, where she is looking reverentially upward.

5. While Judith is now often threatening, Holofernes can be sympathetically portrayed. The splendid head of Holofernes by Il Sodoma (1510), for instance, is very similar to his Christs, and in Tintoretto's painting (c. 1579) Holofernes has the pose of a Christ brought down from the cross (compare Donatello above).[91]

6. Judith's facial expression is explored in many ways, often problematizing her virtuous or heroic status. Her beautiful, gracious, or virtuous face can be ironically contrasted with her deed (Caravaggio), or can reveal a range of emotions (Cavallino above).

Physical Reality (Princeton, NJ: Princeton University Press, 1997) 305–6; Tinagli, *Women*, 86; Fowler, *Renaissance Realism*, passim.

89 Laura Mulvey explores the types of "gaze" and notes that one should not assume strict gender norms of "male" and "female" gaze ("Visual Pleasure and Narrative Cinema," in Jessica Evans and Stuart Hall, eds., *Visual Culture: The Reader* [Thousand Oaks, CA: Sage, 1999] 381–89).

90 Garrard, "Leonardo da Vinci," 60–61; and Patricia Simons, "Women in Frames: The Gaze, the Eye, the Profile in Renaissance Portraiture," 38–57, both in Garrard and Norma Broude, *Expanding Discourse*.

91 Schmitz, "Trickster," 4–5, accessed at www.bibfor.de.

7. There is often a juxtaposition of two faces—Judith and Holofernes or Judith and her slave—or of all three faces in close proximity, forcing the viewer to reflect on the deeper relation of the figures, at times blurring the duality of Judith and Holofernes. Interestingly, under the influence of the Renaissance and Baroque paintings, we forget that in the LXX version the slave is not present in the inner chamber with Judith but is standing guard outside.

8. The character of the slave is often problematized, which then raises troubling issues about Judith's deed. The slave is often mousy, subservient, subhuman, instrumental. This registers very negatively for modern audiences, but in the historical context may have been perceived as an appropriate subordination of the servant. We should not assume that our reading of the slave matches that of the period. The slave may look like Judith, or alternatively like a crone, perhaps a *memento mori,* or a truer revelation of the character of Judith, which was hidden beneath the heroine's worldly beauty. The slave sometimes registers shock, horror, or condemnation at Judith's deed, or is her partner. The slave also often holds the pouch at womb height as Judith deposits the head—the reverse birthing noted above.

9. Although blood was conspicuously absent in the biblical version, it is depicted early in the artistic tradition, often spurting out. But while it had formerly seemed triumphant, after 1500 it registers as dangerous (Caravaggio). Even where it is subtle, restricted to a barely visible coating on the sword, it speaks of danger. A blood-red dress is also utilized to match Judith's deed (Ambrosius Benson, c. 1530–1533; Lorenzo Sabatini, c. 1562), or a background of red (Horace Vernet, c. 1830). The brutality of the deed is thus emphasized, as is the mortality of Holofernes's body. The exposed stump of the general's neck has a similar effect (Cranach), although this too had been featured for centuries, once triumphant but now gory. Above all, Judith's beauty is now "spliced" with the blood and gore, *Eros* and *Thanatos.* Judith comes to be visually associated with blood more than any other biblical woman, more so than Jael or Salome, and many of the painters of Judith do not stint on its effect. In the commentary on 13:9b–10a the question is also raised whether the biblical description of the beheading suggested sacrifice; regardless of the conclusion in that instance, the question of sacrifice has often been raised in regard to the European Judith traditions. The visual reality of decapitations and bloody punishments in Rome has been noted as a possible influence on Caravaggio, and an increased interest in visualizing blood, even a cult of Christ's blood, had earlier arisen in German culture. [92]

These traits of the depictions of Judith should be placed in the context of broader changes in European culture. In addition to the new realism in art, two other developments are relevant: first, nudity in art, and, second, new discussions on the power of women, stated both positively and negatively.

First, nudity. In the fifteenth century, certain figures were depicted nude for the first time since the classical period. Venus was the first classical figure and Adam and Eve the first biblical figures to be so depicted. The quasi-mythical nature of Adam and Eve, and the fact that they had been in Eden, allowed their appearance in the nude. Although the biblical text is absolutely emphatic that Judith did not disrobe for Holofernes, nor have sex with him, the nudity of both Holofernes and Judith, and even the slave, is sometimes depicted in Renaissance painting and sculpture. This in itself should not be over-interpreted as a femme-fatale motif; some of the Italian nude Judiths communicate a new *heroic* ideal analogous to the nude male heroic figures. "Within this climate of thought," says Paola Tinagli, "nudity functioned to transform the Old Testament widow into a heroine *all'antica* possessing the same active public virtues as men."[93] This representation of Judith engages a question of the period: could heroic women display virtue in the same way as men? It is answered in the affirmative.

92 Caroline Walker Bynum, *Wonderful Blood: Theology and Practice in Late Medieval Northern Germany and Beyond* (Middle Ages; Philadelphia: University of Pennsylvania Press, 2006) esp. 1–6.

93 Tinagli, *Women,* 86. See also Susan L. Smith, "A Nude Judith from Padua and the Reception of Donatello's Bronze David," *Comitatus* 25 (1994) 75–78.

Judith possesses the courage of a man and uses a man's weapon—the sword—and this is sometimes celebrated. Rosso Fiorentino painted the first fully nude Judith in Italy (1535–1540, though see below on earlier nude Judiths in the north), but surprisingly, both Judith *and her slave* are nude—the former beautiful and idealized, the latter old and haggard, perhaps a *memento mori*. The nudity of both may also communicate a classical distancing from a "contemporary" interpretation of a dangerous woman.[94] The head of Holofernes has all but disappeared into the pouch; he is not a presence.

The ideal nude woman was also changing. At the beginning of the sixteenth century nude women were painted with small, high, cone-shaped breasts, short waists, and rounded, pregnant-looking bellies. Large breasts were found on ugly women and witches. But by the middle of the sixteenth century women were often painted with larger breasts and small, chiseled waists and stomachs that mirrored the figure of the heroic male nudes (compare Hendrick Goltzius's *Judith*, c. 1585). Fleshier women soon followed, with larger, rounder breasts, culminating in the Rubensian woman. "In 1350," says Margaret Miles, "the breast was a religious symbol; by 1750, the breast was eroticized and medicalized, no longer usable . . . as a religious symbol."[95]

By the beginning of the sixteenth century, there were several nude *Judith*s that took up a heroic, classicizing mode. Other heroic women were depicted nude as well: Susanna, Lucretia, Mary Magdalene, Esther, Saint Catherine, but never Mary. At first it would seem misleading to suggest that the figure of Judith in particular was sexualized, or that artists and audiences suddenly indulged the voyeurism of seeing her nude. Rather, huge changes were proceeding in the representation of women in art, and Judith, who had already been prominent in art, was now enlisted. There also arose a growing canon of female villains depicted nude: Salome, Delilah, Phyllis, Tomyris, Dido, Cleopatra, Medea, Vashti, Lot's daughters, and witches. To which group, the saints or the sinners, did Judith belong? Here we address the development that begins about 1500 and continues to today: Judith alone, of all the biblical women, *moved between good and evil. She was a sexually transgressive woman who crossed moral boundaries.* Judith was depicted as exceedingly virtuous and exceedingly dangerous by different artists—and sometimes even by the same artist. None of the other women—not Mary Magdalene, Esther, Eve, Lucretia, Cleopatra, or Tomyris—could come close to the deeply conflicted engagements of artists with their *Judith*s. The tension in these paintings perhaps arises from her simultaneous virtue and sexuality and the close association of *Eros* and *Thanatos*. Across a large number of paintings, Judith also seems to be moving in and out of her clothes. They are a boundary that she is constantly crossing. The depiction of Judith *problematizes* her garments. Different from most biblical or classical women, she represents a "real woman" rather than a biblical or mythological figure, a woman emerging from her clothes, a woman stripping, a woman at the boundary, a woman in danger of escaping.

In regard to the depiction of nude women, we should also note the role of courtesans in Italian life. There was likely a relation between the Judiths who are depicted as courtesans and the real courtesans of Venice. There were many smart, powerful courtesans, and a line can be drawn between these courtesans, the painting of courtesans, and the painting of Judith as a courtesan. A salacious Judith appeared in courtesan art, but also a virtuous one in respectable bedrooms, and a romantic Judith for brides. Yet they were not quite separate: "There was an affinity between the Judith who decorated connubial interiors and the one who cavorted in brothels."[96]

---

94 Paul Crenshaw, personal communication. At first perplexing, the Master of the Mansi Magdalene painted a totally nude Judith (1525–1530) standing side by side with a nude baby Hercules holding a snake in each hand. But by this she becomes a "classical" rather than a "biblical" heroine; see Graeme J. Taylor, "Judith and the Infant Hercules: Its Iconography," *American Imago* 41 (1984) 101–15.

95 Margaret R. Miles, *A Complex Delight: The Secularization of the Breast, 1350–1750* (Berkeley: University of California Press, 2008) ix; see also Miles, *Carnal Knowing: Female Nakedness and Religious Meaning in the Christian West* (New York: Vintage, 1991) 62, 70; Anne Hollander, *Seeing through Clothes* (Berkeley: University of California Press, 1975) 98. Two nude *Judith*s may antedate some of the examples Miles provides: Luca Signorelli's frescoes in the San Brizio Chapel, Orvieto (1500–1503), and an engraving by Nicoletto da Modena (c. 1500).

96 Stocker, *Judith*, 40; see also 25–26, 37–43.

A second important development was the tradition of *la querelle des femmes,* the woman question, in almost every country of Europe during the fifteenth and sixteenth centuries. The new engagement with Judith's character could have been influenced by new roles for women in public life, whether as artists, writers, or benefactresses, even if the absolute numbers of such public women were not great. Jacob Burckhardt argued that this was the case, and although Joan Kelly has criticized his optimism on this issue, the noteworthy examples of women in public and artistic life may have been sufficient to occasion a backlash.[97] A similar reaction may have accompanied the partial emancipation of women in Germany in the late nineteenth century (see below).

From the fifteenth century on, male and female authors weighed in on the relative qualities of the sexes, the role of women argued both positively and negatively. In 1429, Christine de Pizan composed an early feminist advocacy text, *Le livre de la Cité des Dames.* In it she compared Joan of Arc to Esther, Judith, Deborah, and indeed all women. In the seventeenth century, Laura Cereta also advocated greater roles for women, citing Judith as one of her examples, while Johan van Beverwijck wrote an apology for the superiority of women to men. But in John Lydgate's *The Fall of Princes* (c. 1430), Judith was both a positive and negative example, and in his *Examples against Women* (c. 1440), she was a threat to men.[98] In Germany in 1486, Heinrich Kramer and Jacob Sprenger wrote *Malleus Maleficarum* on *Weibermacht,* the power of women. For them, women often consort with devils in insatiable lust.[99] Judith had attained sufficient status in the constellation of biblical women to be enlisted on both sides of the issue. Debates raged also about the role of the many queens ruling nations, the "gynecocratic controversy," which rarely omitted Judith as a positive or negative example.[100]

The topos of the "Power of Women" became common, with catalogues of shameful reversals, women getting the best of men. Philippe Galle created six such engravings in *Fatal Power of Women:* Adam and Eve, the seduction of Lot by his two daughters, Jael and Sisera, Judith and Holofernes, Samson and Delilah, and Solomon's idolatry at the instigation of the Queen of the South/Sheba. Judith and Jael were both rendered as negative examples along with these other women. Painters also produced "powerful, idiosyncratic treatments of subjects like Samson in Delilah's lap and Judith slaying Holofernes, in which it seems that every brushstroke imbues the image with a meaning that this artist has discovered in the story."[101] A partial emancipation of women had led to a backlash, and Judith was at the center of it.

But, as noted, some treatments of women were quite positive. Dirk Volkertsz Coornhert, in a plate from the *Power of Women* (1551), depicts a statuesque and muscular Judith slaying Holofernes. In 1647, Pierre Le Moyne dedicated *La gallerie des femmes fortes* to the French regent Anne of Austria. François Chauveau in 1645 produced *La femme héroique*: eight pairs of famous men and women of history, including Deborah, Tomyris, and Judith. Judith is paired with David, since both decapitated enemies. The illustrations of Jacques du Bosc produced one of the strongest equality texts: women possess the same virtues as men. Poulain de la Barre, *Égalité des deux sexes* (1673), theorized that equality was good for the state. He used the image of Minerva Pacifera, pacification of society through female rule.[102] On a more political level,

---

97 Jacob Burckhardt, *The Civilization of the Renaissance in Italy* (1860; repr., New York: Modern Library, 2002) 2:389–95; Joan Kelly-Gadol, "Did Women Have a Renaissance?," in Renate Bridenthal and Claudia Koonz, eds., *Becoming Visible: Women in European History* (Boston: Houghton Mifflin, 1977) 137–64. See also Garrard, *Artemisia Gentileschi,* 141–54; Poirier, *Judith: Echos,* 214.

98 Stocker, *Judith,* 47; Garrard, *Artemisia Gentileschi,* 143; Joan Kelly, *Women, History and Theory: The Essays of Joan Kelly* (Women in Culture and Society; Chicago: University of Chicago Press, 1984) 65–109; Ciletti, "Patriarchal Ideology," 60.

99 Stocker, *Judith,* 47.

100 Babette Bohn, "Death, Dispassion, and the Female Hero: Artemisia Gentileschi's *Jael and Sisera,*" in Bal, *Artemisia Files,* 107–28, here 123–24; Garrard, *Artemisia Gentileschi,* 157–65.

101 Smith, *The Power of Women: A* Topos *in Medieval Art and Literature* (Philadelphia: University of Pennsylvania Press, 1995) 202. Cf. also Lucas van Leyden (1511, 1516), and see Julia Nurse, "She-Devils, Harlots and Harridans in Northern Renaissance Prints," *History Today* 48 (1998) 41–48.

102 Bettina Baumgärtel, "Is the King Genderless? The Staging of the Female Regent as *Minerva Pacifera,*"

Judith became an important public identification for princesses, a political statement of their wisdom and the authority of their rule. Judith was also the subject of *tableaux vivants* at official entries of princesses.[103]

With this consideration of the trends in artistic representation in mind, we return to our sampling of some of the vast number of Renaissance and Baroque *Judith*s that so vexed Ruskin. Ultimately, it is very difficult to get a sense of which sorts of depictions represent the most common perception of Judith during the early modern period. Studies of Judith generally emphasize the countless images of an erotically charged heroine-villainess, placed seriatim to form a sort of zoetropic movie. But the impression that this is the dominant Judith may be an illusion that results from our synchronic selection of images. In the historical context, only elites would have seen a variety of images; most people would witness just a few Judith images in their lifetimes—church decorations and public sculptures. And only elites would have seen the more sexualized images of Judith. For the masses, Judith probably remained a heroine of virtue—although even the church sculptures could vary.[104]

We continue our tour in southern Europe. In one of Antonio da Correggio's earliest works (c. 1510), the face of Judith is thin and graceful, with beatific features, while that of her slave is broad, distorted, almost unfocused. The slave is African, partially explaining the different features, but the width of her face is quite exaggerated when compared to Judith's.[105] Lorenzo Lotto (1512) likewise juxtaposes the faces of Judith and her slave. They are very similar in hair, earrings, the bright colors of their draped garments, but, as in Correggio's painting, the slave's face contrasts with Judith's noble lines. Holofernes's deadened head, forced downward by the two women, is being swallowed by the pouch. A different pose is featured by Vincenzo Catena (c. 1520–1525;

Fig. 6), similar to what we will see in Cranach. Judith's unadorned white garment dominates the frame, her hair equally unadorned. Her calm, determined face looks directly at the viewer, perhaps in a heroic pose, her strong hand resting on the hilt of the sword held downward. Next to it is a dignified trophy head, facing away. Others, however, discover new ways to return to a heroine of virtue. Marco Palmezzano's 1525 *Judith* presents the three figures balanced in a horizontal frame: the beautiful Judith, the devoted maid, with the pallid Holofernes suspended over the pouch.

In c. 1562, Lorenzo Sabatini, a student of Vasari, painted a *Judith* with a placid, satisfied face looking straight into the eyes of the viewer, but does she seem shell-shocked? There will be other sad-eyed, shell-shocked, or trance-state *Judith*s. That of Agostino Caracci (c. 1595) and Francesco del Cairo (c. 1630) can be considered, but above all, that of Bernardo Cavallino (c. 1600).[106] He shows her slumping, with weary shoulders, patting Holofernes's head, as if she were in a dissociative state trying to bring a dead pet back to life. The sword is down, resting at her side; this is one of the few *Judith*s that depict her weary of holding it. She is dressed in drab colors, a shapeless dress and kerchief, with no jewelry whatsoever—how could she have seduced him?

Three famous Venetians rendered Judith as a beautiful lady who transcends her gruesome deed. Titian painted very different *Judith*s at the beginning and end of his life. His 1515 painting, once thought to be Salome, features the soft color tones of his early period. In his 1570 painting, the colors have disappeared, though Judith herself is well illuminated. In her slightly disheveled garments, she commands most of the frame.[107] New, however, is the way the head of Holofernes and her African slave have been pushed to the very bottom of the frame. They provide a stark constrast to the white of her skin

---

in Annette Dixon, ed., *Women Who Ruled: Queens, Goddesses, Amazons in Renaissance and Baroque Art* (London: Merrell, 2002) 97–111.

103 Barbara Wetzel, "Widowhood: Margaret of York and Margaret of Austria," in Dagmar Eichberger, ed., *Women of Distinction: Margaret of York/Margaret of Austria* (Davidsfonds: Brepols, 2005) 103–13.

104 Very commanding is Nicolas Blasset's statue in the Notre-Dame d'Amiens (early- to mid-seventeenth

century), a heroic and martial Judith, perhaps influenced by the sixteenth-century heroic, commanding Judith statue in the Hôtel d'Escoville, Caen.

105 Sheaffer, *Envisioning*, 78–79.

106 Compare also Charles Mellin's painting of the 1630s, in which Judith is not undone by her deed but seems coquettish.

107 Joannides, "Titian's *Judith*."

and garment. Tintoretto executed several *Judith*s, set in richly detailed interiors. In his 1579 painting (Fig. 7), the graceful Judith wears a beautiful lavender gown, and she and the slave work in tandem, hiding the blood and gore from the viewer all the while. It is sometimes suggested that Holofernes's nude, heroic body is arranged respectfully as on an altar, but Tintoretto's c. 1570 painting has an aspect of ghoulishness about it, as Judith passes the head, now at the very center of the painting, to the slave. Paolo Veronese (c. 1580) presents a Judith unsurpassed in elegance and beauty, contrasted with a smaller African slave in shadow.

Judith in the Northern Renaissance

The innovations in painting in northern Europe proceeded somewhat differently than in the south. The shift in the north from a virtuous Judith to a sexualized and dangerous woman seems to have occurred more quickly and more thoroughly than in Italy. Without the political symbolism of Florence and Siena, northern Europe also did not explore the strong positive endorsement of Judith. Rather, a sexualized, even dangerous Judith predominated. In regard to many of the northern European works—Hans Baldung Grien, Lucas Cranach the Elder, Jan Massys, Lucas van Leyden, the Beham brothers—"we have difficulty recognizing either the familiar Jewish patriot or the Virgin Mary prototype. . . . [W]e are explicitly asked to see the other side of the masculinist coin: a dangerous, erotic Judith."[108]

Conrad Meit's painted marble sculpture (c. 1510) presents a gentle, fully nude Judith depositing Holofernes's head on a trophy stand. Although the faces of Judith and Holofernes are not similar, her hair is visually likened to Holofernes's hair and beard. Her pregnant-seeming body and small breasts were typical of early nudes in the Renaissance. In 1525–1530, the Master of the Mansi Magdalen in Antwerp painted a totally nude Judith holding the head of Holofernes aloft in triumph, beside a nude baby Hercules with a snake in each hand (Fig. 8). The parallel pose indicates that her labors are like his. At this early stage, she is likened to a classical, not a biblical, heroine and thus can be depicted nude. Looking ahead to the engraving of Hendrick Goltzius (c. 1585), we find a fully athletic Judith, depicted in the manner of male heroes.[109] Her musculature is visually similar to Holofernes's powerful arm.

Lucas Cranach the Elder painted a large number of *Judith*s, generally very similar to his *Salome*s and portraits of aristocratic ladies. We take as examples two *Judith*s from 1530, now in Vienna and Berlin. Looking much like a wealthy, bored teenager, Judith holds the large sword lightly, as if it weighs nothing, and fingers Holofernes's head on the table before her. The exaggerated finery of her aristocratic attire, always in perfect place, is contrasted with the gory stump of Holofernes's severed neck, thrust out before the viewer. With his eyes rolled back and his mouth open, he seems to moan. In the Berlin version (Fig. 9), her more menacing look is matched by the "bondage-style accessories,"[110] and her spidery fingers seem to have caught the sword and the head in her web. How different from Cranach's portraits of others, both men and women, all substance and character!

The sexual aggressiveness of Hans Baldung Grien's nude *Judith* (1525; compare his 1530 painting) is striking, though still mild compared to his other works. She is fully nude, facing the viewer, with her eyes lowered and her lower legs strangely and even painfully crossed. In her right hand, she holds a small sword, really a knife, and in her left, held low is Holofernes's small head—almost an afterthought. Her sword is perhaps a mere knife because the Vulgate used the word *pugio* (13:8), but there is an undeniable visual irony here, in that at the center of the frame is her prominent, somewhat enlarged nude body, while at the top is her small face, at the side the small head of the general, and at the bottom her crossed legs. This irony tends to undercut her virtuous bearing; Garrard goes so far as to call her a "crafty nude with crossed

108 Ciletti, "Patriarchal Ideology," 46; Susan Smith and Larry Silver, "Carnal Knowledge: The Late Engravings of Lucas van Leyden," *Nederlands Kunsthistorisch Jaarboek* 29 (1978) 239–98.

109 See the discussion of Miles, *Complex Delight*, above.

110 Stocker, *Judith*, 29; see also Max J. Friedländer and

Jakob Rosenberg, *The Paintings of Lucas Cranach* (rev. ed.; London: Sotheby Parke Bernet, 1978) 214–15, 230–34, 358–59.

legs."[111] A similar visual irony may be seen in the *Judith* of Ambrosius Benson (c. 1530–1533). Judith faces the viewer, her blood-red garment falling to each side to expose her naked body. Holofernes's face seems to be world-weary, a sadder-but-wiser dead man. Yet do our contemporary viewings correctly gauge the irony that the original viewer might have seen?

Other artists greatly expanded the erotic potential. Three Germans should be considered together, known as the "godless painters," producers of engravings and paintings of Old Testament and other subjects often with a humorous or erotic element: Barthel Beham, his brother Hans Sebald Beham, and Georg Pencz.[112] For their efforts and their heretical views, they were charged in 1525 and banished temporarily from Nuremberg. In that same year, Barthel Beham produced an etching of a naked Judith astride Holofernes's naked body, her left hand holding the lifeless head. Quite contorted, she looks over her left shoulder to survey the horizon, a pugilistic look on her face. Her large, masculine right hand holds the sword forcefully, apparently implanted in Holofernes's groin. She dominates the body of Holofernes as she dominates the scene. She holds the head over the corpse in a way suggesting that it has been twisted and snapped backwards—as if she had wrung a chicken's neck. The position of the two figures suggests a sexual act, and also, as in many of Beham's engravings, dominance/submission and *Eros/Thanatos*. Further, the protections for Judith as a biblical heroine or type of Virtue are gone.

Yet, surprisingly, a later engraving by this artist shows Judith nude, reposing gracefully in an arch (1546). Now she contemplates the head lovingly, a different sort of *Eros/Thanatos*. She looks down at her trophy, the once-admired—beloved?—general now dead, a suggestion that will be realized in later renderings. In both of these, the gaze of Judith is central, magnified by the effect of the niche:

This emphasis on the eyes and the gaze reminds us that Judith's plan is based on ensnaring Holofernes through his eyes. The gaze represents his desire for her and it is this gaze that makes her murderous deed possible. The gaze is what the German artists, unlike their Italian counterparts, represent and which enables them to indicate the physical contact between Judith and the man she has killed. . . . [S]he gazes almost tenderly down at him. Judith and Holofernes are alone together in a separate space just as they were alone together in the tent.[113]

The *Judith* of Barthel Beham's older brother, Hans Sebald Beham, was very different (c. 1531). Judith is totally nude, but so is her maid (compare Rosso Fiorentino above). The nudity of both may suggest a classical distancing. Judith deposits the head into the bag held womb high by the slave.

The third of the godless painters, Georg Pencz, emphasizes Judith's nude body prominently in his 1531 painting. Her dress slips off her breast, where she holds Holofernes's head, his mouth open as if to take the nipple. She resembles *Maria lactans,* yet she looks away, with a melancholy expression.[114] A bolder painting by Pencz depicts her totally nude, striding forward with the head aloft. But among his engravings, *Judith Dining with Holofernes* (c. 1535) is interesting in showing Holofernes canoodling with Judith. Here we detect a bit of humor, which again draws attention to the fact that humor or irony might have been a common aspect of the viewing of Judith.

Jan van Hemessen's totally nude *Judith* (c. 1540; Fig. 10) boldly confronts the viewer. Judith twists uncomfortably to expose both her buttocks and her breasts simultaneously, her body parts seemingly assembled from different paintings. Her closer, right arm is small but muscular, holding aloft a large sword, more threat than triumph. Her left arm is farther from the viewer,

---

111 Garrard, *Artemisia Gentileschi,* 296.

112 Uppenkamp, *Judith und Holofernes,* 82–83. Cf. the similar, but massively clothed *Judith* of Jakob Binck (1528). Albrecht Altdorfer was also associated with the "godless painters"; his Judith engraving returns to the motif of the head hoisted on the sword.

113 Watanabe–O'Kelly, "Figure of Judith," 126–27.

114 Uppenkamp, *Judith und Holofernes,* 63–64. Cf. Francis van Bossuit (below).

yet larger and fleshier. Holofernes's head lies close to her naked buttocks. Burr Wallen, who says that van Hemessen was "by any standard the most bizarre" of the Antwerp Mannerists, seems to struggle to describe this artist:

> Challenging accepted norms of physical beauty, [van Hemessen] went to unheard-of extremes in the juxtaposition of mannered *grazia* and freakish distortion. The sublime, *artifizio* concept of *figura serpentinata* is expressed in his Judith . . . as an undulating giantess with fleshy hips and brazen muscles.[115]

Yet her beautiful face is at odds with all this.

> The idealized features of Judith—her V-shaped chin, large round eyes, elongated ears and broad forehead—follow the fashionable Mannerist standard of facial beauty established by Michelangelo's *Victory*.

Her face cannot be read easily for emotions, but one cannot help but think that it has been placed on the body of a wild, out-of-control avenger.

The new developments of Mannerism—for instance, the contortion of a body that fills the frame—partially explain the oddity of van Hemessen, yet quite different effects of Mannerism are explored by Pierfrancesco di Jacopo Foschi (c. 1540). He fills the frame even more fully to the corners, not by adding visual elements but by warping them. Judith's agency is shown by her sweeping motion with the sword (compare David in the Sistine Chapel), while the exposed, nude, limp body of Holofernes melts into the lower frame. Vasari's 1554 painting, already mentioned, also exhibits these attributes of Mannerism.

Jan Massys's nude *Judith*s exude sexuality yet retain a virtuous dimension. In his 1543 painting (Fig. 11), Judith is unsullied by the violent deed and blood, her serene face suggesting the triumph of innocence and virtue over tyranny. Because she is virtuous, she can turn to project her nude figure out to the viewer, creating intimacy—is it sensual but not sexualized? Respectfully holding the

head in her right hand, the exaggerated and graceful curves of the sword in her left hand follow and reflect the curves of her body. Her grip on Holofernes's hair is less clinched than in some, and her arms, neither muscled nor demure, seem relaxed, as do her whole figure and demeanor. Bolder and more heroic in tone is his painting now at the Palazzo Barberini in Rome.

Judith is sometimes piously presented, sometimes with great anxiety, but ironically, in an age of greater realism in art, few painters seem to present her simply as a strong, heroic woman of virtue. An interesting case, however, is that of Jan Cornelisz Vermeyen (1525–1530)—a painting formerly attributed to Barbalonga. This depiction was dedicated to Margaret of Austria, regent of Netherlands, which may explain the respectfulness for the subject.[116] She faces the viewer, but her gaze is somewhat arch, perhaps distancing herself from a direct engagement. She is calm, but one wonders whether tension may be channeled into her right hand, which grips the sword fiercely. (Vermeyen often emphasized the hands, usually in two contrasting, almost incompatible gestures.) Her left hand, however, strokes the dead general's hair, a gesture similar to the contemporary Cranach, but less macabre. Vermeyen is one of the few artists to depict a heroic Judith without sensationalizing her or subjecting her to male stereotypes, yet some ambiguity remains. With her eyes, Judith communicates her plan; with her grip, her execution of it.

Judith in the Italian Baroque

From northern Europe, we return to Italy to treat *Judith*s of the Baroque era. When the Council of Trent in 1545–1563 called on artists to create works that would communicate religious ideals for a broader public, paintings began to reveal more drama and emotion, and more concentration on character within the frame. Two paintings from c. 1600 by Jacopo Palma il Giovane combine the virtue of a heroic Judith with the gushing blood of Holofernes's dead body. Yet one of the most

---

115 Burr Wallen, *Jan van Hemessen: An Antwerp Painter between Reform and Counter-Reform* (Studies in Renaissance Art History 3; Ann Arbor, MI: UMI Research Press, 1983) 2, 107.

116 Maryan Ainsworth and Abbie Vandivere, "Judith with the Head of Holofernes: Jan Cornelisz Vermeyen's Earliest Signed Painting," *Journal of Historians of Netherlandish Art* 6 (2014) 1–23, DOI: 10.5092/jhna.2014.6.2.2.

influential *Judith*s of this period was that of Caravaggio (1599; Fig. 12). He famously jolted the tradition into terrifying new life by portraying the beheading *in progress*, Holofernes even awakening into screaming consciousness.[117] Holofernes suffers here, perhaps more so than in any other painting except for Artemisia Gentileschi's (below). We register both his shock and his sense of having been betrayed. He looks back up at Judith, or perhaps over her shoulder to see the crone-maid, or at the viewer. Garrard sees in this depiction of Judith a force that can reassert control over violent forces:

> [A] grotesque, shaggy Holofernes is brutally decapitated by an incongruously delicate and beautiful maiden; Judith is not so much a fearless heroine as she is a symbol of restraint and civility, refinement and good taste, who helps to contain the grosser impulses of the masculine sex by performing a violent, dreamlike act of psychic restraint, like the terrifying fairy tale that frightens a child into acceptable social behavior. In this guise, Judith is a thoroughly positive, though personally neutral, figure.[118]

Garrard also implies that Caravaggio, a male artist, could invest Holofernes with emotion while Judith remained a blank slate. Like many artists of his day, he inserted himself into some of his paintings, even as Goliath, put out of his misery by David (c. 1610). And indeed, Caravaggio, with some justification, may have seen himself here as an out-of-control Holofernes. Judith could conceivably represent a positive agent of order. Her arms create beams that keep the two main characters apart; she is in the process of cutting off his head at the same time that she holds him at a stiff arm's length.[119] Her delicate earrings frame a beautiful face, yet when viewed closely, she has a furrowed brow, suggesting doubt or fear as she grinds out the decapitation. Michael Fried finds here an allegory of the creative process of the painter: Judith is the artist, the sword her brush, the blood is paint, and the head is the masterpiece. The furrowed brow and frown depict the intensity of the artist.[120] Or do we rather see Caravaggio's view that a male Caliban requires a demure Judith (and a grizzled maid) to intervene and save the world from himself? Or again, does the painting project some warning about two women who collude too coolly against him?

The three faces are also arranged here in relation to each other. Since Botticelli, this had become common (compare Cohen above on "intimate alterity"), and the old woman is here nearly as prominent as the other two. In contrast to Judith's beauty and grace, her face perhaps represents the older version of Judith, what Judith will become, a *memento mori*. Catherine Puglisi suggests that the slave also expresses Judith's ambivalence, and while Jacobus saw in Judith's face a "severely resolute and purified image," the repressed emotions of her face are projected onto the slave, "all that Renaissance and seventeenth-century representations of a religious heroine could not admit."[121]

Cristofano Allori's *Judith*s are roughly contemporary with Caravaggio's. His 1613 painting in the Palazzo Pitti (Fig. 13) is "certainly [Allori's] best-known work and probably the most admired of all Florentine Seicento paintings."[122] Allori, like Caravaggio and many others, inserted himself as Holofernes in this *Judith*, but Judith resembles the lover who had jilted him, and the maid her mother. Judith looks out boldly at the viewer, from an elevated, dominant position.[123] Her grip on Holofernes's hair is as intense as in any painting, contrasting with the otherwise relaxed pose; all of her strength is channeled to her grip. Holofernes's gruesome head is suspended in

117　Ciletti and Lähnemann, "Judith in the Christian Tradition," 56.

118　Garrard, *Artemisia Gentileschi*, 291. See Bal, "Grounds of Comparison," in Bal, *Artemisia Files*, 129–68, here 135–36, on varying interpretations of Judith's icy composure here.

119　Uppenkamp, *Judith und Holofernes*, 61, 165, 183.

120　Michael Fried, *The Moment of Caravaggio* (Princeton, NJ: Princeton University Press, 2010) 154.

121　On varying interpretations of Judith's icy composure here, see Catherine Puglisi, *Caravaggio* (London: Phaidon, 1998) esp. 137–38; Jacobus, "Judith, Holofernes," 126–27; Stocker, *Judith*, 18; Garrard, *Artemisia Gentileschi*, 291; and Bal, "Grounds of Comparison," 135–36. The slave may also be derived from the procuress or chaperone; so Garrard, *Artemisia Gentileschi*, 298.

122　John Shearman, "Cristofano Allori's Judith," *The Burlington Magazine* 121 (1979) 2–10, here 3.

123　Uppenkamp, *Judith und Holofernes*, 140–41: "Fast trägt das Gemälde den Charakter eines Kultbildes."

midair, visually swimming in her golden gown. It is no longer possible to see Judith and Holofernes as representing virtue and vice; psychological themes and ambiguity dominate.[124] The tyrant is artist-as-martyr, and the moralistic resolution that the death of Holofernes should provide is lost. Contemporaries of Allori, however, interpreted the painting as the combination of the love and death of Holofernes, a theme that would develop in the nineteenth century as *la belle dame sans merci*. With Allori we must ask a question that has been bubbling up through the Renaissance and into the Baroque: has Judith passed over from heroine to villainess? Allori's Judith is the woman empowered, not by God,

> but by experience, her prowess not spiritual but rather sexual. . . . [S]he cannot be subjugated by the gaze of the viewer. . . . For Allori, Judith is the independent woman who dares to reject man's attentions, the phallic woman who escapes subjugation but instead subjects and thus emasculates, dephallicizes, man.[125]

While Caravaggio and Allori take Judith in a direction that accosts the male viewer, others continued the tradition of a heroic figure. In 1608, Giovanni Baglione executed a scene that balances Judith's beauty and eroticism, her heroic deed, and her agency with the slave at her side. Holofernes's over-sized face is contorted in defeat; there is no sympathy with the general, yet Judith looks back at his naked body and large legs and hand. Although Artemisia Gentileschi is more widely known today, her father Orazio also painted *Judith*s that created a zone of cooperation between the two women, visual themes realized in his daughter's works. In his 1621 *Judith*, folds of white fabric surround the maid's face, Judith's arms,

and the head of Holofernes. This suggests the purity and virtue of the deed. Yet the two women seem off balance as they respond to the dangers around them. The sword and the basket are held clumsily together, suggesting an unsure hold on both.[126]

The daughter, Artemisia, has recently eclipsed her father to become one of the most referenced interpreters of Judith. Although a victim of statutory rape, forcible rape, or both, and tortured during her testimony in the case, she later became the first female member of the Florentine Accademia del Disegno, befriended Galileo and Michelangelo's nephew, and continued to receive very important commissions.[127] Her *Judith*s were her most personal and powerful paintings. Here we will not explore the historical or psychological questions surrounding her life, but only her depictions of Judith.[128]

While Caravaggio and Allori inscribed themselves into their paintings in the visage of Holofernes, Artemisia entered into her paintings as Judith. Artemisia developed images of the freedom fighter that tower over the viewer, lacking many associations of the male-sanctioned tradition. In other paintings, the musculature of Holofernes is emphasized, whether heroic or mocked and satirized, but her Holofernes is neither muscled nor heroic, only large; he is not propped up by masculine myths, but is a demythologized leader. For other artists, the slave is almost always inferior or instrumental, serving merely to hold open the pouch, but for Artemisia the slave is a very active partner in the deed and may place the head in the pouch herself (c. 1625, Detroit).[129] In her 1620 Uffizi painting (Fig. 14), Artemisia followed Caravaggio in focusing unflinchingly on the very moment of decapitation, but whereas Caravaggio, against all

---

124 Uppenkamp, *Judith und Holofernes*, 146–50. This can be seen as an inevitable challenge to the dogmas of the Council of Trent, which had provided the original impetus to Baroque art.

125 Nutu, "Framing Judith," 140–41. Allori's subversion of the virtuous and heroic Judith was "corrected" by the Bavarian Art Institute of Munich stained glass window (1886–1891), now hanging at Saint Mary-of-the-Woods College, a Catholic women's college, in Terre Haute, Indiana. The influence of Allori's painting is unmistakable, though Judith's character is now rendered as pious!

126 Nutu, "Framing Judith," 137–38.

127 Bohn, "Death, Dispassion," 119.

128 On the nature of the rape and its importance in interpretation, see Griselda Pollock, "Feminist Dilemmas with the Art/Life Problem," in Bal, *Artemisia Files*, 169–81. Bettina Baumgärtel and Sylvia Neysters (*Die Galerie der Starken Frauen: Die Heldin in der französischen und italienischen Kunst des 17. Jahrhunderts* [Munich: Klinkhardt & Biermann, 1995] 246) question Garrard's projection of Artemisia's life issues onto the painting.

129 Concerning both Holofernes and the slave, see Sheaffer, *Envisioning*, 62, 132–33.

physical plausibility, depicted a slight Judith sawing through Holofernes's neck, Artemisia presents Judith and her slave pooling the strength in their arms to hold Holofernes down. The connection of decapitation and castration may be implied by the fact that his arms look like thighs, and thus his head can be seen as genitalia.[130] In no other *Judith* is the slave so central and so necessary to the completion of the act—she in fact dominates the scene by being above and absorbing Holofernes's resistance. Garrard suggested that in Artemisia's treatment Judith is

> beyond social or theological masculine control. . . . [I]t is not so much the male character who is acted upon, but the female character who acts, a lawless reality too horrible for men to contemplate.[131]

Jacobus, on the other hand, perceives an embeddedness of Artemisia in a larger context:

> Gentileschi's picture is significant not for representing decapitation from a feminine, still less a feminist, viewpoint (where castration is concerned there can be no other view than the boy's), but for its reinscription of the violent fiction.[132]

In the 1980s some feminist scholars affirmed the close relation of Judith and her slave—named Abra in the tradition, though this is simply the Greek word for favorite female slave (see §5 above, and the commentary at 8:11). Indeed, in Artemisia's 1613–1614 painting (Fig. 15), Judith and her slave are effortlessly in sync and communicate by gestures, not words, sharing a common agency. Yet this is Judith's agency, and more recent feminist scholarship has taken a nuanced perspective.[133] In the story, the slave never speaks, is put in harm's way with no choice of her own, and does not reap the benefits of a Jewish victory. Barely visible in the reproductions,

Judith's hand lies on the slave's shoulder, but it is Judith's direction, and we see only Judith's face, not the slave's. Artemisia thus succeeds in introducing an action-in-tandem between women of different classes, but the context remains hierarchical.

The revival of religious devotion that the Council of Trent hoped for was perhaps realized in a *Judith* by Guido Reni (c. 1625); it established a new iconic pose. Judith looks up to heaven, and her arms are open as in the *orante* posture, but their downward angle suggests action combined with prayer, as in the biblical text. Her look upward and the illumination from above protect Judith and redeem her actions. There is no blood depicted, and Holofernes's head is held over his naked body as if it were not severed. The shock of Judith's deed is thus minimized. This pose was copied often (compare Guido Cagnacci, c. 1650, and Simone Brentana, c. 1690; similar are several *Judith*s by Mattia Preti), and so when Francesco Podesti was commissioned to paint female figures on the ceiling of the Room of the Immaculate Conception in the Vatican (1854), Judith was one of the figures, her pose modeled on Reni's.

The wide variety of characterizations of Judith continued into the late Baroque. In c. 1640, Massimo Stanzione painted one of the most commanding and beautiful Judiths (Fig. 16), her pose modeled on the *Apollo Belvedere*.[134] Strong and resolute, she is neither eroticized nor masculinized; rather, she is a *female* heroine of virtue and strength. Above all, light falls evenly on a beautiful and virtuous Judith, and the head of Holofernes is turned downward where he cannot invade her zone; he is thoroughly under her control. Quite striking is the contrast between the illuminated, heroic face of Judith and the shadowy, weak presence of the slave. This slave is no sister but an older, weaker, worn individual in Judith's

---

130 Jacobus, "Judith, Holofernes," 133; Nutu, "Framing Judith," 124.

131 Garrard, *Artemisia Gentileschi*, 335–36.

132 Jacobus, "Judith, Holofernes," 132.

133 Elena Ciletti, "*Gran Macchina è Bellezza:* Looking at the Gentileschi *Judiths*," in Bal, *Artemisia Files*, 63–105. She also remarks on the differences. In the Detroit *Judith*, the maid's hands are bloody, but not Judith's. See also Bal, "Head Hunting: 'Judith' on the Cutting Edge of Knowledge," *JSOT* 63 (1994) 3–34, here 27; Nutu, "Framing Judith," 138–39; Stocker, *Judith*, 18. A common topos in slave-owning societies is the good slave who perfectly actualizes the will of the master.

134 Annette Dixon, *Women Who Ruled: Queens, Goddesses, Amazons in Renaissance and Baroque Art* (London: Merrell, 2002) 159.

shadow who waits with some trepidation for a command. The three faces betray no mutual interrelation.

Even these earnest *Judith*s, insists Garrard, are not endowed with the depth or complexity of the contemporaneous male figures, especially the reflective *David*s. She holds out one exception, the "pensive, monumental" *Judith* of Antiveduto Grammatica (1620–1625),

> whose queenly bearing and thoughtful absorption connect her at least superficially with Davids of the period. . . . Judith is not permitted to grow into a multi-dimensional character defined by psychological or philosophical complexity, because she could not be regarded by male artists as an heroic extension of themselves. Unlike David, she was not invested with the aspirations, doubts, and meditations of the dominant sex.[135]

This painting, and also his c. 1615 painting (in Stockholm), seem heroic in a traditional vein. Judith must obey women's rules in executing her plan, while David obeys men's, yet her face and her slave's as well communicate a virtuous engagement and pendulation in regard to the deed at hand. She is neither brazen nor demure. But in regard to Garrard's judgment, should Vermeyen's *Judith* (above) be admitted as another exception?

We turn next to seventeenth-century paintings; these suggest that speculations on the equality of women gave rise to a backlash. Carlo Saraceni paints Judith as a sweet farm-girl (c. 1615), but an unsettling shadow falls over her face. She manhandles Holofernes's head, which appears to be screaming, while the instrumental slave pulls the pouch open—with her mouth! Again, the contrast of the three faces could not be greater. Valentin de Boulogne copies Caravaggio's scene closely (c. 1626) but, according to Garrard, depicts Judith as a "cold-blooded executioner."[136] The pretty Judith possesses a look of determination as she saws the neck, an urgency surpassed only by that of the rough maid.

Peter Paul Rubens executed several *Judith*s. His bold drawing of 1609–1610 portrays a strong woman, positioned high and erect, about to bring the sword down upon Holofernes's exposed neck. Her subordination of Holofernes's body is extreme, and another Rubens, now lost but known through an engraving by Cornelis Galle, is similar. Here a heroic Holofernes is depicted, reminiscent of Michelangelo's Adam, but as fallen man—a powerful, sinewy Adam pulled down by Judith's soft, methodical grip. Colluding with Judith is the crone-maid, and contrasted with all are the overstated *putti* encircling them. But an even more unsettling tone pervades Peter Paul Rubens's c. 1616 painting (Fig. 17). The slave has a kindly face, but Judith offers a furtive smile directly to the viewer. Her large breasts are pushed up by her actions, visually rhyming with her muscular, oversized arms; her face, breasts, and arms dominate the frame. That would make her similar to other "Rubensian women," but her expression is not. According to Garrard, this is "perhaps the most unforgettable 'evil' Judith of art," and Mieke Bal is even more blunt: she is a "lewd provocative whore."[137] The maid also seems to smile as she helps support the head, satisfied by their actions.

Other scholars, however, have questioned this interpretation, an intrusion of the synchronic into the diachronic. While the Renaissance artists had expressed classical unities in the ideals of beauty and proportion, the artists of the Baroque preferred flawed characters, an overabundance of flesh and clothing, or a cascade of visual effects pouring out of the frame. How, then, to interpret paintings of Judith in this context? Does Rubens's portrait represent a sinister aspect of Judith or the conventions of the period? A comparison with Rubens's other women, however, even his *Salome,* would suggest that Judith is more threatening and more fundamentally alien to the male viewer. The difference between Judith and, say, Salome, may lie in this: Judith is *supposed* to be virtuous, one of us; but here, she is not.

A similar assessment applies to Johann Liss's c. 1625 painting (Fig. 18). Judith appears to be caught in the act of a gruesome decapitation. Her foregrounded body presents a partial barrier; she hides the head with her left

---

135 Garrard, *Artemisia Gentileschi*, 302.
136 Garrard, *Artemisia Gentileschi*, 296.
137 Garrard, *Artemisia Gentileschi*, 297; Bal, "Head Hunting," 30.

hand, the sword with the right. She cannot hide, however, the protruding body of Holofernes, his stump of a neck facing the viewer. The two bodies close together suggest an intimate, erotic mating of *Eros* and *Thanatos*. There is a bright light on Judith's bare shoulders, dress, face, and headscarf, but all else is in shadows. The slave's gaze from the shadows highlights her mistress's own agency and power. But Judith looks over her shoulder at the viewer, signaling an intimate and knowing partnership, the viewer as voyeur, privy to her astounding deed, and even complicit.[138] Is there a revulsion at Judith's attitude, or a mutual pleasure of the viewer and Judith in the sheer audacity? As in the case of the Rubens, is Judith's look over her shoulder part of the enjoyment of the period, the twisting of the body, with a simultaneous view of the front and back?[139] In c. 1640, Trophime Bigot also borrowed from Caravaggio to create a dark vision of Judith slicing down through Holofernes's neck. Merciless and relentless, Judith now places her second hand to apply added pressure to the blade. Unlike in Caravaggio's painting, here Holofernes is distant and not sympathetic. The focus on the act of sawing, as opposed to chopping, became common in the seventeenth century.[140] While it may have had a proximate source in Caravaggio's influential version, it was already a medieval motif, as seen in the illustration in Lorens of Orléans, *La somme le roi* (1295).

We note also two ivory sculptures. In Francis van Bossuit's sculpture (c. 1670), Judith is in a dreamlike state, holding the noble head of Holofernes to her breast, *Eros* in the grip of *Thanatos*.[141] Balthasar Griessmann's delicate ivory sculptures brought an unearthly transcendence to biblical scenes, yet his *Judith* bears a message seemingly at cross-purposes with the medium. She vaunts

over the dead Holofernes, invoking the pose of male conquerors.[142] The powerfully built Judith lays her sword across the buttocks of Holofernes's cowed body to suggest anal rape.

Contrasted with these is the understated presentation in Rembrandt's two drawings (1635, 1653) and a painting (1634) that affirm Judith as a virtuous figure. The warm colors of the painting, for instance, imbue the heroine with a harmonious aura, even though she is dining in Holofernes's tent, awaiting the chance to behead him. By portraying her at this moment in the story, however, Rembrandt avoids the more horrific details. His model was likely his wife, Saskia van Uylenburgh. The painting is similar to the *Judith* of Palma il Vecchio a century earlier (1528), and Palma had probably taken his daughter as subject. In both cases, the eroticism of Judith is replaced by a certain dignity and social consequence.

Women Painters of Judith

The sexualizing treatments of Judith, perhaps a backlash against gains by women in public life, can be compared to the paintings executed by women. These fall along a spectrum of approaches and do not consistently present a "feminist" Judith; some male artists saw in Judith a strong woman who broke clean through gender boundaries, while some women communicate an ambivalence.[143] Artemisia Gentileschi was treated above; here we note Lavinia Fontana, Fede Galizia, Virginia da Vezzo, Elisabetta Sirani, Giovanna Garzoni, and Giulia Lama.

Lavinia Fontana, the first major woman artist of the Renaissance, was presented by Vasari as a well-educated *dottoressa* of the University of Bologna. The artist inserted

138 Uppenkamp, *Judith und Holofernes,* 78–81; more negative is Stocker, *Judith,* 44–45.

139 Paul Crenshaw, personal communication.

140 Cf. Bartolomeo Manfredi (1626), Artemisia, Claudio Ridolfi (c. 1630), Nicola Vaccaro (c. 1680), Onorio Marinari (late 1600s), Francesco Rustici (il Rustichino), not to be confused with Giovanni Francesco Rustici.

141 Cf. Georg Pencz above, and Sigismondo Coccapani, 1620.

142 Cf. Claudius over the female Britannia at Aphrodisias, the Germania and Perseus and Medusa traditions, Rubens's *David* of 1616, and

Giambattista Zelotti's *The Triumph of Virtue over Vice* in Venice.

143 R. Ward Bissell also notes that women artists often chose a sexualizing interpretation (*Artemisia Gentileschi and the Authority of Art: Critical Reading and Catalogue Raisonné* [State College, PA: Pennsylvania State University Press, 2001] 43, 51–54), but Bohn insists that *Judith*s by Artemisia, Lavinia, and Sirani are less sexualized than men's ("Death, Dispassion"). See also Stocker, *Judith,* 39; Nutu, "Framing Judith," 120, 135–37.

herself as Judith in several of her paintings, which vary enormously.[144] In her paintings now in Krakow and Bologna, Judith looks directly at the viewer, yet she is somewhat static, while her Genoa Judith is very dynamic, a Giorgione in motion. Far from identifying Judith with her slave, in the latter there is a great distance between their characters; Judith is heroic and beautiful, her maid servile and asexual.

Stocker finds Fede Galizia's *Judith* (1596; Fig. 19) very suggestive. Noting the richness of her clothing and pearls, she remarks that Judith "may be yet another '*déshabillée* harlot,'"[145] but this seems an overreaction. Judith is calm and seems to communicate a self-satisfaction in her trophy, although this may be contrasted to the tension with which she grips the weapon. Although the sword is short—again, perhaps an influence of the Vulgate's choice of *pugio* in 13:8—it is steely and razor sharp, and her name is clearly inscribed on it. The blood has drained from Holofernes's face, now seen on the platter. Like Lavinia Fontana, Galizia emphasizes the distance between the heroine and her slave, who seems to be pondering her mistress's righteous deed.

Virginia da Vezzo's *Judith* (c. 1624) can be compared to that of her husband, Simon Vouet. One of her husband's paintings depicts a very strong Judith, while da Vezzo's looks down and away, suggesting uncertainty or ambivalence.[146] Here Judith uses a cloth, probably the tent curtain, and the sword to conceal Holofernes's head. Elisabetta Sirani, like Fontana, was active in progressive Bologna and founded a school of painting for women. Turning from the eroticism of others, Sirani imbued women like Portia, Timoclea, Cleopatra, and Judith with virtues usually associated with men.[147] In her triumphant *Judith* (1658), the heroine displays the head for the people of Bethulia. Judith commands the center of the brightly lit scene, which contributes to the celebratory tone. Giovanna Garzoni, an accomplished Italian painter of botanical still lifes, also painted a minor Judith, *Portrait of the Grand Duchess Vittoria della Rovere as Judith*. Like other Judiths of the period, it was commissioned to represent an aristocratic lady in the form of the biblical figure. In Giulia Lama's c. 1730 painting (Fig. 20), the well-muscled body of Holofernes is laid out before the viewer, unmarred at this point by the loss of his head. Judith is more recessed, as she looks up to heaven in prayer. Lama depicted the beheading of Saint Eurosia by a Moorish killer that is detailed and bloody, but here she protects Judith from the gruesomeness of the decapitation.

Literature, Drama, and Music in the Renaissance and Baroque Periods

Having surveyed the developments in artistic depictions of Judith from the Renaissance to the Baroque eras, we turn now to the renderings of Judith in literature, drama, and music covering the same time period. From the early moments of the Renaissance, mystery plays, epic poems, tragedies, and *paraphrastes* all featured Judith, in some cases reflecting strong affirmations of her deed, in others profound misgivings. Shifts in views of the acceptable roles for women are reflected. Although the public functions of women during the Renaissance have been debated, Merry E. Weisner has concluded that in France, more than in England or Italy, women did at times have a public voice.[148] Three French texts present a noble, pious, but more restrained Judith, each outdoing the previous in affirming a model for the church. Jean Molinet was probably the author of the theatrical drama *Le mystère de Judith et Holofernés* (c. 1500).[149] Judith exhibits an unshakable faith in an all-powerful God, prays for direct aid, and is pious and strong as a result. She is modest, nobly but not provocatively dressed. And yet she invites Holofernes to bed and kisses him onstage! The subsequent French versions will steer clear of this threat to her chastity.

---

144 Shearman, "Cristofano Allori's Judith," 9; Caroline Murphy, *Lavinia Fontana* (New Haven: Yale University Press, 2003) 41–43; see also Nutu, "Framing Judith," 120–22.

145 Stocker, *Judith*, 39, 141; Nutu, "Framing Judith," 136–37.

146 To be sure, Vouet painted two *Judiths*, the other very different.

147 Nutu, "Framing Judith," 132–33; Babette Bohn, "The Antique Heroines of Elisabetta Sirani," *Renaissance Studies* 16 (2003) 52–79.

148 Merry E. Weisner, *Women and Gender in Early Modern Europe* (Cambridge: Cambridge University Press, 1993) 129. Even if the number of elite women taking on public roles was small, the *perception* of women may have shifted.

149 On these three, see Kathleen M. Llewellyn, "The Example of Judith in Early Modern French Litera-

Still, God is her only true spouse, and, as in the days of Jerome, she is a model for widows who should give their inherited property to the church.

The goal in Guillaume de Salluste Du Bartas's epic poem *La Judit* (1574) was to imitate Homer and Virgil, although the author was aware of the discrepancy. The epic style suggests a traditional hero's saga, like the Old English *Judith*. Here Judith also has a quasi-divine "lucency" (1.141–44). Judith is sung in the opening lines, and the voice of the poet can be heard seeking a prophetic muse (3.239–50, 5.191–98). As in ancient epic, Du Bartas begins in medias res, but Robert Cummings suggests that Du Bartas gives too much attention to parallel or back stories: Achior's history of the Jews, Charmis's biography of Judith, Holofernes's history of Nebuchadnezzar.[150] Though the poem suffers from ponderousness and rhetorical flourish, Judith is emboldened: she lies, flatters, and seduces. The description of her beauty, detailed in twenty-five lines (339–63), from head to feet, comes under the male gaze. Judith is caressed by the general, whom she tells to wait in bed while she disrobes (6.59–62). Heightened in this poem is the humiliation of the general's body: the head is spat on, its beard pulled, eyes poked, tongue torn out, and then the trunk is dismembered, every part distributed among a mob. Yet Du Bartas softens one aspect of the original story: Judith is throughout respectful of Israelite men, even requesting permission of the priests to undertake her mission.

Du Bartas may be responding to his historical situation. Judith was often taken up by both Protestants and Catholics as a model of tyrannicide and religious freedom. She had already been the subject of a now-lost play performed for French Protestants. (The falling canonical status of Judith among Protestants did not disqualify her.) Du Bartas's French Protestant compatriots in Orléans were saved from a siege by the Catholic duke of Guise when the latter was assassinated. The increasing number of political assassinations and executions gave currency to the discussion of biblical models like Judith, Ehud, and Jael. Interestingly, Du Bartas's poem was dedicated to Protestants in the first edition, and later to the Catholic wife of Henry of Navarre in 1579. A Calvinist, Simon Goulart could also preface later editions by simply saying that it was an allegory of the victory of the church over its enemies. It is a testimony to the popularity of Du Bartas's poem that it was both commented on by Goulart and translated into English. Thomas Hudson dedicated his 1584 translation to James VI, king of Scotland.[151] Du Bartas's poem subsequently suffered a significant fall in its artistic estimation, exceeded only by that of Hudson's English translation: "While Thomas Hudson's *Historie of Judith* has usually been dismissed in a few contemptuous words," says James Craigie, its modern editor, "it is not wholly a contemptible piece of work."[152] Although both Du Bartas and the translation may seem fatuous to modern readers, they were popular in their day as a reverential reading of Judith.

Molinet and Du Bartas to some extent reversed the effects of Jerome's Vulgate and Catholic tradition in general, Judith now appearing as a sexualized woman— or, rather, a combination of sexualized, realistic, and political. A woman author and a widow, Gabrielle de Coignard, returned in c. 1580 to a more typical Catholic tradition, depicting a Judith more chaste than the two previous. While Du Bartas takes up a self-consciously epic style, Coignard writes in the *stilus humilis* or plain style of the day.[153] A heroine for a treatise on chastity for women,

---

ture," in Brine, Cilette, and Lähnemann, *Sword of Judith*, 213–25.

150 Robert Cummings, "The Aestheticization of Tyrannicide: Du Bartas's *La Judit*," in Brine, Ciletti, and Lähnemann, *Sword of Judith*, 227–38, here 233; Poirier, *Judith: Echos*, 217–20.

151 Cummings ("Aestheticization," 228) also notes that in 1614 the English poet Joshua Sylvester translated Du Bartas's poem to emphasize the ideal of the courtly lady.

152 James Craigie, *Thomas Hudson's* Historie of Judith (Edinburgh and London: Blackwood, 1941) xxii.

153 Coignard, *Imitation de la victoire de Judich*, published after her death in 1594. Her *Œuvres chrétiennes* is edited by Colette H. Winn (Geneva: Droz, 1995) and for English translation see: "Gabrielle de Coignard, *Imitation de la victoire de Judich* (1594)," translated by Colette H. Winn and Robert H. McDowell in *Writings by Pre-Revolutionary French Women*, ed. Anne R. Larsen and Colette H. Winn (New York: Garland, 2000) 171–211, here 172.

Judith here is frail and "une femmelette," a diminutive woman. Kathleen Llewellyn concludes that Judith is "less vigorous and independent" than the Judith of the other authors, and "closer to the ideal of her day."[154] The difference in Coignard's depiction is nowhere greater than in her description of Judith's beauty. While Du Bartas took the point of view of the Assyrian soldiers when first describing her beauty, lingering over an objectifying male gaze, for Coignard it is God who views Judith's beauty. Indeed, it is not Judith herself but her dress that is described, with characteristics that call to mind the high priest's garments in the Bible: varied colors and ornaments that represent earth, sea, sky, and cosmos. Not a sexual being at all, Judith is a creation of God's plan, a constructed servant of God, greater than most women, a true heroine. Femaleness has almost been transcended, as if she were a nun. Coignard reclaims a feminine ascetic warrior, one faithful to God, but one who does not so provocatively abandon the decorum of a lady. Men had long enjoyed a sexually provocative, deceitful, violent, and terrifying Judith, the exhilaration of outrageous burlesque. "That is *your* fantasy," Coignard seems to say, "our fantasy is to be faithful to God." Many of the women authors, like their Judith, interrupt the male gaze. But what of Holofernes? Though "a detestable prince," he is at times presented in a somewhat sympathetic way, overcome with a lovesickness that was typical of romance literature across the centuries.[155] Judith is not really threatened by rape, but the general longs for her in the tradition of chivalry. It is Holofernes's generals who lead him to drink too much, not Judith; she is not as exposed to his grasp (lines 1226–52).

Collette Winn and Robert McDowell contrast the "traditional representation of Judith as the castrating *femme fatale*"—although we will have occasion to question whether the femme fatale is the "traditional" view—with Coignard's substitution of the feminine virtues of humility, obedience, piety, chastity, "the very same qualities contemporary moralists celebrated in conduct books for women. . . . Coignard deliberately downplays the disturbing character of combative femininity."[156] This entire discourse must be seen in the context of humility as, ironically, a means to power, even absolutizing power. With Christ, Mary, and martyrs as models, Christian tradition affirmed that the weak, humble, persecuted person can experience a vindication that is dominating.[157] Coignard is not just a beneficiary of this tradition, she plays the theme very well. The humble will conquer their tormentors.

Yet, though she lacks full agency, Judith's actual deed and the attending blood are described fully, in keeping with the devotional revival of the last third of the sixteenth century. Say Winn and McDowell:

> The representation of Holofernes's violent decapitation is very much in the baroque style of the late sixteenth century. The reader is spared none of the gruesome details in the gestures or the background elements. Coignard dwells on the description of Judith's savage blow, Holofernes's severed neck, the hideous head with its spurting blood, and the canopies reddened and sprinkled with gore.[158]

Stunning, however, is the absence of honor to Judith at the end, or heroizing language at all; she has disappeared into God's saving act. Although the slaying of Holofernes is treated as a sacrifice, the heroine here is hardly honored, as would be the case in Beowulf or the Old English *Judith*.

German Song, Drama, and Literature

A parallel world to the northern paintings is found in popular German songs. With the invention of the printing press, broadsheets, often illustrated, became very popular for sermons, sensational news, and songs. In one song, Judith is clever (*klug*), and full of cunning (*list*), contrasted with the danger of pride for Holofernes.[159] Another song, c. 1560, is set to a popular military tune:

154 Llewellyn, "Example of Judith," 221–22.
155 Winn and McDowell, "Gabrielle de Coignard," 210 nn. 40, 49.
156 Winn and McDowell, "Gabrielle de Coignard," 174, 172.
157 Matthews, *Perfect Martyr*, 99–130; Wills, "Ascetic Theology"; Winn and McDowell, "Gabrielle de Coignard," 210 n. 41.
158 Winn and McDowell, "Gabrielle de Coignard," 172.
159 Lähnemann, "The Cunning of Judith in Late Medieval German Texts," in Brine, Ciletti, and Lähnemann, *Sword of Judith*, 239–58, here 239.

"Judith is my name, a free Jewess; I never did love any dalliance."[160] But does she protest too much? The illustration suggests a coquettish side: with sword in hand she hands her maid the head of Holofernes, but her posture also suggests she is dancing to the music. In the song, the "snare of his own eyes" from the Vulgate becomes a full-blown hunting motif. Judith sets the trap, hunts for three days, Holofernes comes to the banquet like an animal to bait, she kills him and takes his head as a trophy, hiding it in the bag so that no one can "get her scent." This is the only version of Judith to develop the hunting motif. Says Lähnemann:

> The broadsheet literally presents a double-sided Judith. In the inner story, as told from page two of the booklet onwards, all her actions are judged as being beyond reproach—by the other figures . . . , by the narrator, and by God himself. On the outer cover of the booklet, Judith is presented as a dangerous seductress.[161]

Lest we think that the scholar's extrapolation from Judith to Woman is a modern, synchronic imposition, the cunning of Judith in the first stanza is generalized to women in the last:

First stanza
Judith is my name, a free
    Jewess;
I never did love any dalliance
nor did I ever do it,
until I cleverly hacked off
    Holofernes's head
while he was asleep—
off I went safely.

Last stanza
Young women have such clever
    cunning;
no earthly man so strong, so
    wise,
so holy he may be:
if a woman reckons him with a
    glance,
soon she will have him in her
    coils;
but seldom he will get her.

The new fascination with Judith's brazen cunning and the generalization to all women indeed correspond to changes found throughout the visual arts.

In Germany, Catholics—and later Protestants as well—created and performed "academic drama" for the education of clergy and others, with priests-in-training as actors. Occasionally presented to larger audiences, these dramas rarely included women performers. In the twelfth to fourteenth centuries, Jesuit education was engaged with such *Schulkomödie* (*Komödie* at this time applied to all genres), combining drama and piety in *Theatrum asceticum*.[162] The subjects were sacred, at first in Latin, and by mid-eighteenth century in German as well. Given the clerical school context, any depiction of the bedroom scene was avoided. Choruses were later replaced by tourneys, dances, songs, or music alone. Epilogues and processions were added, sometimes with prizes; Judith and Esther were sometimes followed by procession through streets.

In the 1530s, Sixt Birck, a Protestant, composed an important German drama of Judith, subtitled "a useful history showing how to pray for help to the Lord God in times of war, especially when God's glory is challenged."[163] Didactic and virtuous, Birck dedicated the play to Augsburg, emphasizing the community of Bethulia, and other male leaders, as much as Judith. Judith was a model of a slayer of tyrants, but also of Turks. Birck's play, alone of early German dramas, exhibits an interest in psychological development. Edna Purdie suggests that Judith exhibits "religious trust and the faculty of self-surrender," and that Holofernes is now sympathetic, with a tragic fall—not evil so much as bound by the circumstances as the opposing general.[164] Yet Purdie's assessment also sacrifices Judith's agency and integrity to a twentieth-century ideal of "psychological development." Her analysis will become part of the Judith tradition itself, as reflected in her judgments about Hebbel (below). Helen Watanabe-O'Kelly provides a different interpretation: the sexual problem is solved by Judith's effectively becoming a man: "Judith acted like a man" (*Fraw Judith hat thon wie ain man*). The Bethulian women say she has a "body of a hero" (*helden*

160 Lähnemann, "Cunning of Judith," 48–246.
161 Lähnemann, "Cunning of Judith," 251.
162 Purdie, *Story of Judith*, 47, 56–60; Uppenkamp, *Judith und Holofernes*, 115, 131.
163 "Eine schön History in Spylsweiss für die Augen gestelt, wie man in Kriegsläuffen, besonders so man von wegen der Her Gottes angefochten würt, um hülff zu Gott dem Herrn flehend ruffen soll." English translation by Karin Schöpflin, "Judith on Stage: The Dramatic Career of a Biblical Heroine," in Xeravits, *Pious Seductress*, 198–213, here 199. Birck wrote two *Judiths*, and the second (1537 in Augsburg) alters the depiction: Judith is no longer manly, but it is God who has given her a strong arm; so Watanabe-O'Kelly, *Beauty or Beast?*, 117–18; see also Lähnemann, *Hystoria Judith*, 315–70.
164 Purdie, *Story of Judith*, 48–49.

leib) and "manliness" (*manlichkeit*), and the high priest Joachim says, "Judith is no woman, she is a man" (*Fraw Judith . . . ist kain fraw, sy ist ain man*).[165]

In the sixteenth to eighteenth centuries Judith became more popular in opera and drama. In 1536, Joachim Greff wrote the first German Protestant drama on Judith: God protects the people from Catholic tyranny. Martin Opitz's opera-drama *Judith* (1635), a translation of Andrea Salvadori's *Istoria di Iudit* (1626), begins in medias res on Judith's third day in the camp. Achior now eliminated, the focus turns to the encounter between Judith and Holofernes. Opitz opens with a love-plaint of Holofernes as romantic lover. He combines manliness and asceticism, as Judith presents "a man's heart in a woman's body" (*das Männliche Hertz in einem Weiblichen Leibe*); God can "make a woman into a man" (*der auch ein Weibesbild zum Manne machen kan*).[166] Opitz also incorporates the operatic technique of having minor characters singing what is happening or will happen; Abra sings that Judith is inside beheading![167] The off-stage beheading of Holofernes will be found in many subsequent operas and dramas (as in Martin Böhme, *Tragicomoedia vom Holoferne und der Judith*; 1618). In 1648, Christian Rose wrote another Lutheran drama, raising up, as Luther had, the vernacular language. His title, *Holofern*, indicates interest in the king, borrowed from the operas of Opitz and Andreas Tscherning.

Around the turn of the sixteenth century, Erasmus mentioned Judith in several passages. In "The Christian Widow," he champions Judith's heroic deed:

An illustrious female of manly strength who as a woman brought back a triumph over a foe unbeaten by men. Double was the triumph of Judith: a military victory, to be sure, which she produced for her country when it had lost hope, but also a victory for her chastity, which she preserved for herself unimpaired, for she killed a very brave man and made a mockery of a lewd one.[168]

He sums up what a devoted Christian should see in Judith: she is strong enough, like a man, to execute an enemy, but also strong enough to maintain her chastity. Far more important, however, for our discussion will be the case of Martin Luther. The Renaissance historical consciousness was not confined to Italy. Luther represented this new moment as well when he suggested that the Old Testament is no longer a set of timeless prefigurations of Christ but a *narrative*, set within its own time line, that prophesies future events fulfilled in the New Testament. Luther's preface to Judith in the 1534 German Bible gives clear voice to these new perspectives:

Judith hardly squares with the historical accounts of the Holy Scriptures, especially Jeremiah and Ezra. . . . Some people think that this is not an account of historical events but rather a beautiful religious fiction. . . . Such an interpretation strikes my fancy, and I think that the poet deliberately and painstakingly inserted the errors of time and name in order to remind the reader that the book should be taken and understood as that kind of a sacred, religious composition.[169]

---

165 Watanabe-O'Kelly, *Beauty or Beast?*, 116. The Birck quotations are from Manfred Brauneck, ed., *Sämtliche Dramen* (3 vols.; Berlin: de Gruyter, 1969–1980) 2:55–165, here 147, 154, 161; Watanabe-O'Kelly, "The Eroticization of Judith in Early Modern Art," in Mara R. Wade, ed., *Gender Matters: Discourses of Violence in Early Modern Literature and the Arts* (Internationale Forschungen zur allgemeinen und vergleichenden Literaturwissenschaft 169; Amsterdam and New York, Rodopi, 2014) 81–100. Marko Marulić, the chief figure of early Croatian literature, composed an epic poem in Croatian, *Judita*, in 1521. It champions the Croat people against the Ottoman Turks. Judith is an asexual and chaste heroine, somewhat in contrast to Birck's portrayal. See Gabrijela Mecky Zaragoza, "Virgo und Virago," *Daphnis* 31 (2002) 107–26.

166 Watanabe-O'Kelly, *Beauty or Beast?*, 118.

167 Purdie, *Story of Judith*, 78–79, 95; Mara Wade, "The Reception of Opitz's *Judith* during the Baroque," *Daphnis* 16 (1987) 147–65.

168 Erasmus, "De vidua christiana," in *Opera omnia*, 5:735; English: Erasmus, *Spiritualia* (ed. John W. O'Malley; 5 vols.; Collected Works of Erasmus 66–70; Toronto: University of Toronto Press, 1988–) 66:204. See Nassichuk, "Prayer of Judith," 200–201. Also see Erasmus, "Modus orandi Deum" ("On Praying to God"), *Opera Omnia*, 5.1:137.

169 *Luther's Works* (55 vols.; Philadelphia: Muhlenberg, 1960) 35:337–38. On Luther's historical consciousness, see James S. Preuss, *From Shadow to Promise: Old Testament Interpretation from Augustine to the Young Luther* (Cambridge, MA: Belknap Press of Harvard University Press, 1969).

A huge shift is reflected here: not simply ambivalence about the character, which was already common enough, but now there is a suggestion that the story is *fiction* (see §7 above). Yet he remained positive about Judith's persona. Like Jerome, he did not reverence the *book* of Judith as sacred but did affirm her image as a bearer of virtue.

Her perch had been lowered, however, and in 1689 a follower, Capellus called Judith an "almost silly fable, invented by a most inept, injudicious, impudent and clownish Hellenist" (*Comentarii et notae criticae in vetus testamentum*, 575). For Catholic Reformation figures, however, Judith remained a figure who vanquished Protestant heresy. Perhaps the most impressive example is found in the Lateran Palace, commissioned by Pope Sixtus V, where Judith was given pride of place in ceiling panels consisting of twenty-eight scenes from her story.[170]

Seventeenth to Eighteenth Centuries: Oratorios and Operas

In the seventeenth to eighteenth centuries, oratorios of Judith were composed by Alessandro Scarlatti, Wolfgang Amadeus Mozart, and Antonio Vivaldi. Scarlatti composed two Judith oratorios, in 1694 ("Naples") and 1697 ("Cambridge"). Like the Baroque paintings, the Cambridge focuses on Judith, her slave, and Holofernes, the relationship of the two women being especially emphasized.[171] When Wolfgang Mozart was only fifteen, he composed *La Betulia liberata* (1771). Although it is not highly regarded among his works, the young composer does explore a wide range of effects, perhaps to demonstrate

that he was up to the challenges of oratorio.[172] Here Judith's bloody deed occurs off-stage, and her singing communicates more anxiety about it than was the case before: "The severed trunk writhed on the blood-covered floor. I felt the half-alive head shiver beneath the hand which supported it." Such emotions were absent from the original story but were featured visually in many of the paintings.

We pause over the most significant and interesting of these, that of Vivaldi, a hauntingly beautiful and much undervalued composition. His only surviving oratorio, *Juditha triumphans* (1716), bore the title *Judith triumphant, Conqueror of the Barbaric Holofernes: A Sacred Military Oratorio Performed in Times of War by the Virgin Singers, to Be Sung in the Church of the Pietà*.[173] As the music director of a girls' school in Venice, most of Vivaldi's career was spent in composing and performing with female singers and musicians, mostly girls. Far from being subversive, it co-opts woman's agency in the traditional view of church belief and devotion. The oratorio celebrates the victory over the Turks at the island of Corfù. Not a monumental or large-stage operatic experience, Vivaldi's *Juditha* is characterized by an intimacy of vocal expression appropriate to its school context. "In maturity and sumptuousness, it fully equals the concertos, which by that time had already carried the fame of Vivaldi far and wide." Vivaldi had exploited an impressive range of musical instruments in his orchestrations and here "puts virtually the whole of the Pietà's arsenal of instruments on display."[174]

The allegorical meaning of the characters is given at the beginning of Giacomo Cassetti's libretto: Judith

---

170 It was designed by Giovanni Guerra and Cesare Nebbia in 1588–1589; see Ciletti, "Judith Imagery as Catholic Orthodoxy in Counter-Reformation Italy," in Brine, Ciletti, and Lähnemann, *Sword of Judith*, 345–68, here 345–46.

171 David Marsh, "Judith in Baroque Oratorio," in Brine, Ciletti, and Lähnemann, *Sword of Judith*, 385–96, here 390.

172 Neal Zaslaw, ed., *The Compleat Mozart: A Guide to the Musical Works of Wolfgang Amadeus Mozart* (New York: Mozart Bicentennial at Lincoln Center, 1990) 33. The libretto by Pietro Metastasio (1734) had already become a popular version, used by countless composers.

173 *Juditha triumphans devicta Holofernis barbarie; sacrum*

militare oratorium bisce belli temporibus a psalentium virginum choro in Templo Pietatis canendum. See Marsh, "Judith in Baroque Oratorio," 391–92; Howard E. Smither, *A History of the Oratorio* (4 vols.; Chapel Hill: University of North Carolina Press, 1977–2000) 1:350. For an earlier but somewhat analogous example in France, note François Fénelon, *De l'education des filles* (1687).

174 Marc Pincherle, *Vivaldi: Genius of the Baroque* (New York: Norton, 1957) 40; see also Michael Talbot, *The Sacred Vocal Music of Antonio Vivaldi* (Florence: Olschki, 1995) 409; Smither, *History of the Oratorio*, 1:348–55; Marsh, "Judith in Baroque Oratorio," 391–92.

stands for the Adriatic Sea, or Venice; Holofernes the Turkish commander; Bethulia is the church; Ozias represents Christians; and the slave Abra, interestingly, stands for Faith. It is Ozias—"Christians"—who prays for the fall of Holofernes, not Judith, as in other versions; and Abra, "Faith," says that she will be Judith's leader. Vivaldi's *Juditha* responds to the external threat from the Turks, but also to the heterodoxy, skepticism, deism, and Enlightenment thinking in Venice.[175] It affirmed a resurgent Catholicism—ironically, at a time that was Venice's last gasp.

Holofernes is a commanding and attractive, even sympathetic male figure who falls in love with Judith. He does not descend into the threat of rape but succumbs to lovesickness; he longs to be a courtly seducer. They sing a beautiful dialogue of separate but equally earnest paths to fulfillment, he through love and ardor, she through an abnegation of sexual desire. He worships Judith, but she insists that there is no image but the Creator. Rather than fanning the flames of his passion as she does in the Bible, she urges Holofernes to flee them. He fails to take the lesson, however, but pleads for her not to reject him. There are "moments of almost feminine sensuality in his words," says Paolo Bernardini; "[the oboe and organ] create a sophisticated, erotic atmosphere. Judith resists, but she seems very close to succumbing."[176] Judith compares Holofernes's deep sleep to the peace of one who rests in God—contrast here the Old English *Judith* or Coignard. Michael Talbot notes the extent to which the oratorio conjures empathy with Vagaus (Bagoas) and even the dead general: "Holofernes does not deserve to be assassinated in his sleep. . . . Vivaldi merely intensifies the contradiction by giving both Holofernes and Vagaus music of such great power and conviction."[177]

What goes through Judith's head when she decides to decapitate the general? The scene is oddly anticlimactic—musically, instrumentally, and structurally—and her words surprisingly restful:[178]

In somno profundo	While he lies
si jacet immersus	deep in slumber,
non amplius sit vigil	he whom you have cast into sleep
qui dormit in te.	cannot be watchful.
Quiescat exanguis,	Let the sleeper be drained of blood,
et sanguis	that I may glory
sic exeat	in that blood
superbus in me.	as it pours forth.

Judith *does* exhibit tremendous anxiety, however, but earlier, when Holofernes courts her. Her explosive agitation at being courted by him provides an ironic contrast to the more peaceful arias throughout. Soaring, valkyrie-like high strings accompany her frantic image of a swallow "tossed about by the fitful wind," longing for its nest:

Agitata infido flatu	Tossed about by the fitful wind
diu volatu	during its long flight,
vagabundo	the vagrant
maesta hirundo	swallow grieves,
it plorando	weeping as it flies
boni ignara.	for the good things it has never known.

The only other point in the oratorio where such agitation is displayed is when Vagaus (Bagoas) discovers the headless body and calls upon the Furies to avenge the Israelites: "Come forth from your blind, foul kingdom, you savage partners of raging frenzy!"

Judith, who in both libretto and score is no warrior, is nevertheless a model for girls, guided by faith—Abra—and patriotism. This oratorio plays to women's—or girls'—agency in affirming a traditional view of church belief and devotion. The girls would take the proper lesson from the oratorio: the *femme forte* serves the church and Venice. Despite the piety of this Judith, however, her extraordinary *Agitata* once again places her *at the boundary* between propriety and female eroticism.

175 Paolo Bernardini, "Judith in the Italian Unification Process, 1800–1900," in Brine, Ciletti, and Lähnemann, *Sword of Judith,* 397–409, here 400.

176 Bernardini, "Judith," 401–2; Talbot, *Sacred Vocal Music,* 437.

177 Talbot, *Sacred Vocal Music,* 437.

178 Translation of Talbot, *Vivaldi* (New York: Schirmer, 1992) 153.

Toward the Late Modern and the Postmodern

The richness of the Judith tradition in the fifteenth to seventeenth centuries could hardly be maintained. An interest in Judith remained, but she had perhaps been demoted.[179] Formerly Judith had been a heroic *individual,* and in the rise of nationalism, Europe now wanted to valorize *the people.*[180] Judith was often painted surrounded by the gathered Bethulians. Judith as individual, however, was given very different treatments. The visual motif of Judith forcing Holofernes down and sawing through his neck, observed from Caravaggio to Artemisia to Bigot, is continued in the nineteenth century. In Jose Maria Vázquez's 1810 painting, Judith has illuminated alabaster skin, yet a determination in her face; she looks squarely and unflinchingly at the neck as she slices through—yet angels watch. Her face is featured to reveal without question that she acts intentionally. She is not meeting any real resistance from Holofernes, as was the case in Artemisia's paintings, but there is no hesitation or self-doubt as in Caravaggio.

Francisco de Goya painted very intense *Judith*s that, despite first impressions, may not reflect misgivings about her persona. At the end of his life, thinking he was going insane, he executed his "black paintings," among them a powerful *Judith* (1820–1822; Fig. 21). Emblematic of the freedom and expressionism of the late modern period, it presents a very anxious vision. There may be a political message here, as the painting may express Goya's reaction to the restoration of the despised Fernando VII.[181] By contrast, in his 1824–1825 painting Judith is painted in quiet blues and whites. An ironic contrast yet remains: Holofernes is positioned down and off to the side, painted in an angry black. If Judith is viewed by herself, she is childlike and playful, yet her sword draws ribbons of red blood.

Orientalism in European art in the nineteenth century also found a ready subject in Judith. Orientalism was often joined to realism: the eastern subjects were rendered more "authentically." Many of the orientalized Judiths were "Judaized" as well. The most famous of these is by August Riedel (1840), but there were many others: Jean-Joseph Benjamin Constant (Fig. 22), Francesco Hayez, Jean-Jules-Antoine Lecomte du Nouÿ, and Francesco Paolo Michetti.[182] The cultural shift toward the emancipation of women was also anxiety producing. An engraving of Benjamin Constant's commanding Judith was published with a poem by Jean Lahor, which reads in part:

> Pale, she has stepped forward to stage her massacre—
> Her large eyes crazed with ecstasy and terror;
> And her voice, her dance, her lean, hypnotic body
> Have served the dark Assyrian as dread intoxicants.[183]

Viewed from the East—occidentalism?—the Western-trained Indian artist Raja Ravi Varma (1873) also painted an "orientalist" *Judith*.[184] (See below on his Kali.)

From Modern to Late Modern in German-Speaking Lands

We turn now to a disturbing, consistently demeaning trend in the interpretation of Judith in German-speaking countries. Any sense of Judith's heroic character is challenged. "From the nineteenth century on," says Watanabe-O'Kelly, "the sexual and erotic potential of the story becomes the main, sometimes the only, focus for male writers."[185] This development could hardly have been perceived in the French artist Horace Vernet's 1828 *Judith,* although that painting played a role. Judith here looks down at a sleeping Holofernes and prepares to raise her sword to put an end to him. Her face, though

---

179 Bernardini, "Judith," 397–401. With exceptions; see Alexandre Lhâa, "Marcello and Peri's *Giuditta* (1860)," in Brine, Ciletti, and Lähnemann, *Sword of Judith,* 411–30. See, for instance, the early eighteenth-century paintings of Francesco Solimena and Matthäus Guenther.

180 Bernardini, "Judith," 401.

181 Stocker, *Judith,* 115.

182 Madeleine Dobie, *Foreign Bodies: Gender, Language, and Culture in French Orientalism* (Stanford, CA: Stanford University Press, 2001).

183 Bram Dijkstra, *Idols of Perversity: Fantasies of Feminine Evil in Fin-de-Siècle Culture* (New York: Oxford University Press, 1986) 377–78, 400–401.

184 He was not the first easterner to do so; the Persian Muhammad Zaman was sent to Rome and converted to Catholicism, ending up in India, where in 1680 he painted a *Judith.*

185 Watanabe-O'Kelly, *Beauty or Beast?*, 102–3.

prominently at the center, is in shadow. The background is bright red, and the whole suffused in red. But what is most remarkable is how others viewed the narrative aspect of the painting. Heinrich Heine famously commented that her dress, falling from her shoulder, suggested to viewers that she had been naked and presumably ravished by Holofernes. She has quickly dressed, only to rise and kill him. Holofernes, it seems, has a postcoital smile on his face. "What an enviable end!" said Heine. "When I come to die, ye Gods, let me die like Holofernes!"[186] He was probably the first since John Malalas in the sixth century to suggest explicitly that Judith had had sex with Holofernes—although one might wonder about the undertones of many post-1500 paintings.

Influenced by Heine's interpretation of Vernet, the German Friedrich Hebbel wrote a play in 1840 that altered the biblical version greatly and became influential, reverberating through German culture.[187] First, Judith, though recently married, is still a virgin rather than a widow; her husband Manasses had been frightened into impotence by some terrible vision and had never consummated their marriage. (This motif is not totally absent from the original version; see §5 above.) In this play, Judith will later be deflowered *as a virgin,* and from this point forward this is a common motif in German versions. Second, Hebbel introduced the character Ephraim, who falls in love with Judith but, like Manasses, is impotent both sexually and militarily. In Hebbel's play, Holofernes is the only real man to be found. He rapes Judith—recall that this was the reading of Vernet's painting—creating a crisis in her psyche: she realizes she is just

a woman, and not a virgin soul dedicated to God's service. Judith is no longer maneuvering to save her people but is a sexually frustrated, self-willed young woman who will do anything to consummate a union with a real man.[188] She does, indeed, slay him, *but out of revenge for his rape,* not to save her people.

Hebbel's interpretation ushered in a period in which Judith is radically devalued as a sympathetic moral agent. After Hebbel, it became common to insist, with no basis in the biblical story, that Judith was a virgin even though she had been married to Manasses; indeed, she *must* be a virgin and *must* be raped and deflowered by Holofernes; she *must* seek revenge for the sexual assault by symbolically castrating and murdering him. This negative assessment is not to be assigned to Heine, who was associated with the *Jungdeutschen* liberals who advocated emancipation of women. But Hebbel, in his comments and even in his diary, provided ample justification to conclude that he was opposed to the emancipation of women. The earlier notorious case of Charlotte Corday, who had assassinated Jean-Paul Marat, a leader of the Reign of Terror in France, seemed a particular offense to Hebbel: "The Judith of the Bible is nothing more than a Charlotte Corday, a fanatical and cunning monster."[189]

Edna Purdie's 1927 analysis of Hebbel's drama becomes new data in itself on the influence of Hebbel, and indeed on a negotiation of diachronic and synchronic levels of analysis. She is typical of the positive response to Hebbel's psychologizing: his play reveals deeper, tragic conflicts and universalizing themes. The conflict between individuals has become "a fundamen-

186 "Welch ein beneidenswerdes Ende! Wenn ich einst sterben soll, ihr Götter, laßt mich sterben wie Holofernes!" (Heine, "Horace Vernet," in *"Ich bin Judith,"* in Hans Kaufman, ed., *Heinrich Heine: Werke und Briefe* [10 vols.; Berlin: Aufbau-Verlag, 1961–1964] 8:14–15. Here he equated Judith's hair in Vernet's painting to braids like snakes, suggesting Medusa, and foreshadowing Freud's interpretation below; see Jacobus, "Judith, Holofernes," 124; Sheaffer, *Envisioning,* 130–31.

187 For Hebbel's statements, see *Tagebücher,* in Marion Kobelt-Groch, *"Ich bin Judith": Texte und Bilder zur Rezeption eines mythischen Stoffes* (Leipzig: Leipziger Universitätsverlag, 2004) 245; Hebbel, *Mein Wort über das Drama! Eine Erwiderung an Professor Heiberg in Kopenhagen* (Hamburg: Hoffman & Campe, 1843), in *Deutsche Literatur,* vol. 1 of Digitale Bibliothek

(Berlin: Directmedia, 2005) 74250–302, here 74266. See also Linda Bennett Elder, "Virgins, Viragos and Virtuo(u)si among Judiths in Opera and Oratorio," *JSOT* 92 (2001) 91–118; Watanabe-O'Kelly, *Beauty or Beast?,* 132; Watanabe-O'Kelly, "Figure of Judith," here 103–4, 115.

188 Theodore Ziolkowski, "Re-Visions, Fictionalizations, and Postfigurations: The Myth of Judith in the Twentieth Century," *Modern Language Review* 104 (2009) 311–32.

189 "Der Judith der Bibel ist eben nichts, als eine Charlotte Corday, ein fanatisch-listiges Ungeheuer," in Hebbel, *Mein Wort über das Drama!,* 74266. Gabrijela Mecky Zaragoza, *"Da befiel sie Furcht und Angst . . .": Judith im Drama des 19. Jahrhunderts* (Munich: Iudicium, 2005); Jacobus, "Judith, Holofernes"; Schöpflin, "Judith on Stage," 205–7.

tal antagonism of God against Gods, of Judaism against paganism, of sex against sex, of the individual against the world-necessity. . . . Good conflicts with good, not good with evil, in the deepest tragic opposition."[190] All of the highest values of early twentieth-century modernist and humanist tradition are found by Purdie in this play. The characters transcend simple "types" to become complex and individualized; themes are "universalized." According to Purdie, Hebbel sees these conflicts as those that "ultimately condition human existence."[191] Once she champions Hebbel's drama, she also turns to condemning quite harshly any trickster Judith—a Judith closer, that is, to the biblical text. She says of Arnold Bennett's 1919 version,

> There is something repellent in Judith's efficiency in combining caressing flattery with murderous intent. . . . This Judith is no prey to nerves or to compunction; decisive, compelling, supremely competent in attaining her desires, she does not stir our sympathies.[192]

We are reminded of John Ruskin's reaction to *Judith*s above.

We note as well the Hebbelian development in Sigmund Freud. The latter saw in Hebbel's play a humiliated woman who was a "truer" Judith than the biblical version: "Judith is the woman who castrates the man who deflowered her."[193] For Freud, Judith's story also reflects the taboo of virginity because she is now the virgin who is violated. And of course, Freud found in Judith a symbol of penis envy. Hebbel and Freud saw themselves as explaining women's pathologies and restoring universal truth. Jacobus pondered the effects of these alterations of the story: Judith is no longer a strong female agent but a wild hysteric. Raped and psychologically driven by penis envy, she turns to decapitate and symbolically castrate her male tormentor.[194]

Just as the urge to biographize Artemisia Gentileschi is overwhelming, so also Hebbel. Dependent on women his entire life, his drama reads like compensatory masculinity. According to Watanabe-O'Kelly, "Men become more and more subordinate to women from play to play, [which] relates to Hebbel's biography and his marriage to Christine Enghaus, the strong self-possessed woman." And Barbra Hindinger states, "Masculinity is for Hebbel a fundamentally fragile thing, because it does not really exist. It only appears as a socially constructed behavior pattern."[195]

It is perhaps inevitable that, after the success of Hebbel's play, which indeed initiated an important trajectory (which continues below), two counterdevelopments would also appear: a savage satire of Hebbel, on the one hand, and a turn to the sado-masochistic, on the other. The satire of Hebbel by Johann Nestroy (1849) caused a sensation, although many condemned it.[196] Nestroy plays with gender roles by presenting a supermasculine Holofernes, while Judith's brother Joab—a new character—has taken her place, dressed as a woman. Holofernes, not to be out-tricked, presents a fake head for Joab to

---

190 Purdie, *Story of Judith*, 96.

191 Purdie, *Story of Judith*, 94–95.

192 Purdie, *Story of Judith*, 121. Purdie also denigrates Georg Kaiser's *Die jüdische Witwe: Biblische Komödie* (Berlin: S. Fischer, 1911) as the work of a more thoroughly "Freudian" author: Judith's sexual attraction to Holofernes is the *principal* interest.

193 In Freud's words, "Judith [ist] das Weib, das den Mann kastriert, von dem sie defloriert wurde," in "The Taboo of Virginity," in *The Standard Edition of the Complete Psychological Works* (24 vols.; London: Hogarth, 1953–1974) 11:207–8; 19:22. On decapitation as castration, see "Medusa's Head," 18:273.

194 Jacobus, "Judith, Holofernes," 117; Stocker, *Judith*, 160; Ciletti, "Patriarchal Ideology," 46.

195 "Mannlichkeit [ist] bei Hebbel etwas zutiefst Fragiles, weil sie nicht wirklich existiert. Sie ist nur vorhanden als soziokulturell konstruiertes Verhaltensmuster"

(Watanabe-O'Kelly, review of Barbara Hindinger, *Tragische Helden mit verletzten Seelen: Männerbilder in den Dramen Friedrich Hebbels* [Munich: Iudicium, 2004], *Modern Language Review* 102 [2007] 594–96, here 596). See also Mecky Zaragoza, *"Da befiel"*; Marion Kobelt-Groch, *Judith macht Geschichte: Zur Rezeption einer mythischen Gestalt vom 16. bis 19. Jahrhundert* (Munich: Fink, 2005).

196 An 1824 report of a satirical version notes hundreds of players; Judith beheads Holofernes and the head sings an aria: "Heinous hand, which has robbed me of the light of life!" (*Verruchte Hand, die mir das Lebenslicht geraubt!*); see Purdie, *Story of Judith*, 93–94. Cf. another notable parody, the 1871 musical by Telesforo Righi, *Giuditta*, with libretto by Attilio Catelli: Judith marries a journalist and kills her stalker Holofernes when he tries to rape her; see Bernardini, "Judith," 406.

chop off. Yet the tricking is not over. Joab takes the head, which he now knows is fake, and uses it to frighten the Assyrians, who are so stupid that they do not look for the real head. In this play Nestroy also skewered "Teutonism" and opposed a negative view of Judaism in the person of Judith.[197]

The sado-masochistic potentialites of the Judith narrative were taken up by Leopold von Sacher-Masoch, famous as the namesake for "masochist." Judith is a domina in his 1874 play, her weak husband humiliated by her.[198] The heroine is neither virgin nor widow, but a married woman, yet she does not seek her husband's permission. For von Sacher-Masoch, Judith's domination of her husband was not a condemnation or a satire but an erotic experience. The Belgian artist Arthur Greuell's monochromatic painting (c. 1920) is similar. Judith is a muscled dance-hall girl who subdues Holofernes by force, mimicking the pose of the boxer, popular at the time. Her shanks and stride also resemble a horse, and her arms, drawing the viewer's focus, are equally strong. In her tightly drawn corset, she seems to act out a scene of bondage and discipline.

In Georg Kaiser's *The Jewish Widow* (*Die jüdische Witwe*, 1904), Judith is a girl of twelve at the mercy of her family and others. She wants to be deflowered and does not intend to kill Holofernes, but does it by accident. She moves from man to man trying to have sex.[199] Manasses is an old, repulsive man, impotent but nevertheless exhibiting lecherous obsessions. A dark humor pervades this drama, ridiculing any integrity on Judith's part: she smothers to death her old, impotent husband offstage; she falls in love with Nebuchadnezzar and kills Holofernes to win him. Back in Bethulia, she is dragged to the temple, where she is raped in the holy of holies by the high priest. Sacher-Masoch thus presents a dominatrix, Kaiser a stupid girl who is at the mercy, first, of one Jewish patriarchal figure, then Nebuchadnezzar, and finally another Jewish patriarchal figure. Purdie suggests

that it is dark humor or a satire on what Hebbel might have made of it.[200]

Challenging, disturbing, even macabre effects continued to be explored in the visual art in German-speaking countries as well. Lovis Corinth's *Judith,* created for *Book of Judith* (published by Ernst Cassirer, 1910), is violent and vengeful. The seminude figure, with dark, shaded eyes, smiles to suggest sadism. Holofernes is down and helpless. In Léon Bakst's 1910 painting, Judith's face is obscured, but she holds up Holofernes's gruesome head by the hair. The Czech Josef Loukota presents a crazed and unbalanced Judith looking off to the side (1920). Walter Jakob extends this in an even more grotesque direction (1921). In the 1920s Franz von Stuck (Fig. 23) painted several openly sexualized *Judith*s that realized the image of femme fatale. Her fully naked body is juxtaposed with her oversized, phallic sword.[201] *Eros* and *Thanatos* are bluntly identified, her expression of self-satisfaction and control now an adolescent fantasy.

Yet there are interesting twists. At first glance, Gustav Klimt's two *Judith*s (1901, 1909; Fig. 24) appear to represent this prevailing view, yet all is not what it seems. The paintings are intentionally provocative, ironic, even satirical. The shimmering gold creates a two-level reality, a beautiful woman's body in a mythologized background: is she human or a sexualized goddess? By pushing the general's head gently down to her side, she exposes her naked body to the viewer. Schmitz notes the lascivious, lustful expression, as Judith massages the head of Holofernes, cradled near her vagina, and Bernardini says:

> Therefore, only with decadence, with "the pleasure of beheading" first rediscovered by Audrey Beardsley in his poignant *Salomé,* and by Oscar Wilde, is a new space opened for Judith, as Klimt's masterpiece of sensuality clearly testifies. Here, any political meaning is lost. . . . This artistic use of Judith is a signal of the strong detachment of the artist from the political world.[202]

197 Schöpflin, "Judith on Stage," 198–213.

198 Watanabe-O'Kelly, *Beauty or Beast?*, 124.

199 Watanabe-O'Kelly, *Beauty or Beast?*, 134.

200 Purdie, *Story of Judith*, 122–23.

201 Dijkstra, *Idols of Perversity,* 313. In 1908, Albert von Keller also produced a very popular painting of *Love,* a nude woman, holding her sword in a way very similar to von Stuck's, who looms over a decapitated body of a nude lover. The female figure looks Jewish, as is the case for many of the late modern Judiths. Is the image a combination of "Jew" and "Woman," in the form of a figure (Judith) whose name means "Jewish woman"?

202 Schmitz, "Trickster," 6; Bernardini, "Judith," 409. See also Ciletti, "Patriarchal Ideology"; Apostolos-Cappadona, "Lord Has Struck"; Stocker, *Judith,*

But the context must be carefully considered. Beardsley, Wilde, and Klimt all share an element of protest, a search for a personal meaning *outside* of politics. Identified with the so-called Decadent Movement, Klimt challenged the traditional renderings of female figures (as Artemisia had done in a very different way). In his second *Judith*, called *Judith II/Salome,* there is a deliberate deviance, indicated by the explicit blurring of Judith and Salome in the title.[203] His eroticism and orientalism evoked a combination realist/fantasy setting: a "real" nude, provocative woman swimming in a sea of gold and transcendent effects. Is Judith "merely" anxiety provoking, or the vehicle for a protest of social restraints? Klimt enlisted Judith as a boundary figure to distance himself from traditional themes. He released Judith to become the sexual being that the Christian tradition *supposedly* disallowed.[204]

Yet, as before, we note the danger of misinterpretation-by-selection. In every age, there have been positive engagements with Judith; how do we weigh the broad reception of Judith accurately? Contemporaneous with the many negative German compositions, some works by women writers de-eroticized Judith and attempted to restore her to a heroic status: Maria Janitschek, "Königin Judith" (1895); Anna Sartory, *Judith, die Heldin von Bethulia: Drama in vier Akten* (1907); Katharina Gondlach, *Judith: Eine Erzählung aus vorchristlicher Zeit* (1918); Rosemarie Menschick, *Judith: Ein biblisches Schauspiel in 4 Aufzügen mit nur weiblichen Rollen* (1921).[205] Watanabe-O'Kelly notes the surprising ways that these women authors valorize the heroine, sometimes removing the military themes and focusing on her moralizing influence on others. And yet:

> [T]hese women writers are just as troubled as male ones by the idea of Judith as a killer, as a warrior who efficiently slays a defenseless man with his own weapon and lives on to a ripe old age. . . . Even in the twentieth century, it seems women, like men, cannot regard the figure of Judith with anything other than unease.[206]

But to turn again to the reductive trend, one could hardly imagine that in the twentieth century anyone could devalue the character of Judith further than Hebbel and others had done, yet in Hamburg in 1966 Siegfried Matthus composed an opera inspired by Hebbel's play.[207] Judith is once again a helpless, pathetic non-agent, driven mad by inner conflicts. She insists that her prayer for her people is only for show; she is thinking of herself. Contemptuous of her brother for being unwilling to kill Holofernes, she seeks out the general as the only real man she has known but is raped by him. Her brother greets her, "Hail, whore of Israel!" and tears off her clothes; a series of symbolic degradations follow. One might psychologize by proposing that, after World War II, East Germans were susceptible to strange fantasies of redemptive violence, even a collective raping of a young girl whose name means "Jewess."[208] Yet the opera was also performed in Santa Fe, New Mexico, in 1990. Critics were dubious and noted the shifts from the ancient story. Stephanie Sundine, who played Judith, acrobati-

175–76; Watanabe-O'Kelly, "Figure of Judith," 103; Dijkstra, *Idols of Perversity,* vii–viii, 81, 280–81, 312–13, 374–75, 400–401. Tina Blondell reinterpreted Klimt's famous *Judith* in 1991, but it is unclear what this might suggest for the earlier painting; cf. Sarah Hinrich, "'Living on the Outside of Your Skin': Gustav Klimt and Tina Blondell Show Us Judith," in Robin Margaret Jensen and Kimberly J. Vrudny, eds., *Visual Theology: Performing and Transforming the Community through the Arts* (Collegeville, MN: Liturgical Press, 2009) 13–27. Roland Barthes sees a bond of *Eros/Thanatos* between Judith and Holofernes ("Deux Femmes/Two Women," in *Artemisia,* a volume of *Mot pour Mot/Word for Word* 2 [Paris: Yvon Lambert, 1979] 9), to which Griselda Pollock objects (*Differencing the Canon: Feminist Desire and the Writing of Art's Histories* [London and New York: Routledge,

1999] 116). Barthes was evidently influenced by the Hebbel-Freud interpretation.

203 There is a similarity to Salome in many *Judith*s, and yet it is Judith who is often more troubling. Salome, after all, was understood to be unambiguously bad, but Judith? Max J. Friedländer and Jakob Rosenberg compare the blurring of Judith and Salome in Cranach and Klimt (*Paintings of Lucas Cranach,* 214–15, 230–34, 358–59). Cf. also this ambiguity in paintings by Francesco Maffei and Simon Vouet.

204 Garrard, *Artemisia Gentileschi,* 300.

205 Watanabe-O'Kelly, *Beauty or Beast?,* 260; cf. Coignard above, and see Purdie, *Story of Judith,* 133–35, on Menschick.

206 Watanabe-O'Kelly, *Beauty or Beast?,* 264.

207 Elder, "Virgins, Virago," 112.

208 Cf. Dijkstra, *Idols of Perversity,* vii.

cally tried to defend it as an evocation and critique of male-dominated power. At any rate, the trajectory from Vernet to Hebbel to Freud to Kaiser to Corinth to Jakob to von Stuck is concluded in Matthus. Is Judith, the "Jewish woman" who transgresses boundaries, here finally punished?

Recent Developments in the Artistic Interpretation of Judith

Judith had long been a major ingredient in European popular culture. Punch and Judy likely displayed a Judith influence, visible as early as 1785 in Hamburg, and the playing-card image of the queen of hearts borrows from Judith. Judith continued in the twentieth century in both low art and high art (see §6 above). Jean-Jacques Henner had earlier painted two soft-focus *Judith*s as beautiful women (c. 1880), with only the sword to suggest her identity, and Jewish artist Isaac Grünewald (1924) and Frank Brangwyn (1948) produced *Judith*s that were also quite warm, despite the juxtaposition to the bloody deed.

Jean Cocteau painted two powerful Judith murals (1948, 1951). The Jewish artist Leonard Baskin treated Judith several times, one of which (1972) hangs in the Vatican. His earliest version, in fact (c. 1950), demands of the viewer an engagement with her violent deed. Judith's face dominates the frame, while Holofernes's face, held forward by the heroine, appears to be screaming. Superficially like the paintings of Corinth and Jakob (above), Baskin in contrast imbues Judith's act with a bluntness that seems to affirm her heroism. In his 1975 painting, a proud Judith presents the head in one hand, holding the sword prominently in the other to define the painting.

Some women artists register the macabre aspect while at the same time embracing the fact that Judith is wild and untamable; Cindy Sherman's *Judith* (1990) is such an example. In a 1996 paper-and-ink drawing, Irene Caesar depicts Judith nude, in the persona of a goddess, cradling the frightened, exaggerated head of Holofernes between her legs, all situated within a vagina made of her hair.[209] According to Efthimiadis-Keith, the once-powerful Holofernes appears to be sucked into the vagina by Judith. Is the *Judith* of Alex Savransky (2008) similar in this regard?

Dramatic and operatic productions quite expectedly continued to emphasize motives and yearnings, love complications, conflicted feelings, pleas, and sacrifices. In Thomas Bailey Aldrich's 1904 drama, *Judith of Bethulia: A Tragedy,* the heroine is overcome by Holofernes's heathen beauty, abandoning the hope of motherhood to kill him. Stricken and near suicide, she sacrifices herself like Oedipus. Uzziah is again raised up as a figure to take charge of her.[210] In Thomas Sturge Moore's 1911 one-act play *A Sicilian Idyll and Judith: A Conflict*, Judith, unsure of her resolve, speaks a monologue before her deed and behind the curtain weeps momentarily. She returns here to a model of ascetic warrior: only a widow, and one who is childless, could commit this antisocial act. "Her heart rebels," says Purdie, "at the cruelty which is so repugnant to her nature."[211] The dramatic conflict here is between a woman's sensibilities and the horror of the deed. Though Holofernes is not repellent in this play, Judith has no secret affection for him.

Interestingly, Judith is featured at the very birth of cinema. The new medium found the combination of sex and violence irresistible, especially, perhaps, because it was set within a biblical world. In 1907, Cines Roma produced a one-reel *Giuditta e Oloferne,* and two years later Louis Feuillade directed a one-reel *Judith et Holoferne.* In 1914 D. W. Griffith directed *Judith of Bethulia,* the first

209 Helen Efthimiadis-Keith, "Text and Interpretation: Gender and Violence in the Book of Judith, Scholarly Commentary and the Visual Arts from the Renaissance Onward," *Old Testament Essays* 15 (2002) 64–84.

210 Stocker, *Judith*, 184–86. Very well known at the time, Aldrich had also composed a poem in 1896, *Judith and Holofernes: A Poem.*

211 Purdie, *Story of Judith*, 118; see also 129. Other twentieth-century plays and operas include George W. Chadwick, *Judith: Lyric Drama* (1900); Sebas-

tian Wieser, 1918; Arnold Bennett, *Judith* (1919); Henry Bernstein, *Judit* (1922). Thompson Buchanan wrote a novel, *Judith Triumphant,* in 1910, and Jean Giraudoux the play *Judith: A Tragedy in Three Acts* in 1931. Paul Claudel, remarking on Judith in "Judith" (Œuvre poétique, 1935), objected to Giraudoux's blasphemy of an ambiguous Judith. He continues to develop an allegory of Holofernes as a series of Protestants and heretics and himself as Judith; see Poirier, *Judith: Echos,* 70–72.

full-length Hollywood film. Since the Italian film was released in the United States, it was doubtless known to Griffith.[212] Griffith's visual achievement at such an early point in film history is astonishing. Battle and city scenes are very stirring and remarkably convincing; there are numerous close-ups, orchestrated chaos, and a huge cast. Some gaps in the narrative are filled in by Griffith. At the beginning Judith walks about the city, unconcerned for a poor woman with a baby—because she herself has no child? The eunuch Bagoas is campy, a gay fop, with long hair and no beard, wearing effeminate clothes, almost cross-dressing (not unlike the ancient stereotype of the eunuch). Two Bethulian characters are introduced, Nathan and Naomi, providing a parallel plot line. When Naomi is captured by the Assyrians, Judith now becomes concerned for her people; we see filmed thought and growth in her face. Naomi and other women dance before Holofernes—an orientalist, odalisque vision. Other parts of the ancient story are omitted, however; there is, for instance, no upbraiding of the elders. The eroticism is also, straight out of the gate, pure Hollywood. When Holofernes sees Judith, he is smitten, at one point placing his hands on her bare shoulders. In being attracted to Holofernes, Judith feels conflicted; a title reads, "Again Judith faltered for the love of Holofernes—yet struggled to cast away her sinful passion." Her "Strengthen me" prayer is perhaps spoken to overcome love. There is still some reticence about depicting the decapitation. Judith pauses as she prepares to strike the general, but there is a cross-cut to the suffering Bethulians. She thinks of them and carries through. Both Judith and her slave are horrified but take the head in the bag. Griffith's would by no means be the last filmed *Judith*. In 1959 there was an Italian *Giuditta e Oloferne*, in 1969 a French *La Tête du tyran*, and televised versions of her story were aired in Germany and Yugoslavia.

At the end of the twentieth century important new interpretations were still being produced. The German playwright Rolf Hochhuth wrote *Judith*, first performed in 1984, as a commentary on violent acts committed in different contexts: in World War II, by the Red Army Faction, in Vietnam, and in the Cold War. Two Judiths intervene in modern situations: one in Minsk where a woman assassinates a Nazi-aligned official; the other in Washington, D.C., where she kills Reagan with nerve gas that he has just authorized. Hochhuth ultimately gives both Judiths moral bearing as warriors against tyrants, but he follows Hebbel in seeing Judith as driven by her attraction to "real men." Still, it affirms more at the end than the Hebbelian elements would suggest. In addition, the dissident Russian artists Vitaly Komar and Alexander Melamid created *Judith on Red Square* in 1999. Judith is a Russian girl, holding the large head of Stalin aloft—taken from a statue? The African American artist Kehinde Wiley created two paintings of *Judith and Holofernes* in 2012. In both, the black slave has chopped off the head of her mistress, Judith. There is a blandness to the white Judith—or what is left of her—and an exuberance in the slave's rebellion.

Finally, we may also ponder broad cross-cultural comparisons of Judith. Despite some similarities of Wonder Woman to Judith, it does not appear that her creators, William Moulton Marston and Harry G. Peter, drew conscious inspiration from Judith.[213] In ancient Greek religion, the epithet Brimo, "wild," was at times added to the names of some goddesses. Did that same aspect come to the surface in late modern Europe? We note as well the similar iconography of the Indian goddess Kali, although there is a great danger of misinterpretation. Kali is often depicted holding a demon's head while standing upon Siva's corpse, her mind frenzied as she projects her tongue to suck up blood.[214] Visually, she is

---

212 Many of the first short-reel films were biblical, e.g., *La Vie de Moïse;* see David J. Shepherd, *The Bible on Silent Film: Spectacle, Story, and Scripture in the Early Cinema* (Cambridge: Cambridge University Press, 2015) 44; and Adele Reinhartz, *Bible and Film: An Introduction* (New York: Routledge, 2013) 19.

213 Emma England, "Violent Superwomen: Super Heroes or Super Villains? Judith, Wonder Woman and Lynndie England," in Brenner-Idan and Efthimiadis-Keith, *Tobit and Judith*, 242–58; followed by England, "Second Thoughts on Female Terrorists and More: A Self-Response," 259–61. On p. 251 England includes an image from *Wonder Woman* #219 that is similar to the Judith visual tradition.

214 Roxanne Kamayani Gupta, "Kâlî Mâyî: Myth and Reality in a Banaras Ghetto," in Rachel Fell McDermott and Jeffrey J. Kripal, eds., *Encountering Kālī, in the Margins, at the Center, in the West* (Berkeley:

like a cross between Giorgione and Jakob. Indeed, one popular Indian depiction by Raja Ravi Varma (c. 1905) is influenced by Judith iconography (see his Judith above). Yet this extreme depiction of Kali is explicitly understood, even embraced, as the goddess's great cosmic actions, the triumph of good over evil.

Conclusion

There were relatively few commentaries on the biblical text of Judith, but to say that the figure Judith was a minor biblical personage would be incorrect. In terms of religious ideas, the book of Judith did not generate propositional theology, yet it possesses a high emotive and symbolic power that lends itself to popular, rather than scholarly, manifestations. Bathja Bayer has noted that "Judith has attracted more writers, artists and composers than any other figure in the Apocrypha"[215]—but why limit it to the Apocrypha? In art, music, drama, and imaginative literature she moved onto the stage with the most important men and women of the Bible. Many of the most important figures in arts and letters devoted great energies to her.

Our earliest known version, that of the Greek Bible, already places Judith in a liminal, parodic, burlesque position, at the boundary between taste and tastelessness, where her performative nature could explode expectations. She is a postmodern figure in a premodern age. The artistic reception of her tends toward the symbolic:

in Christian tradition, a personification of Courage, Virtue, Humility, Chastity, Temperance, Wisdom, Justice, Fortitude, and Sanctimonia; and in Jewish tradition associated with Hanukkah and an agent like Esther. And contrary to many summary statements found in scholarly treatments, Judith remained a fairly common subject for visual artists into the late twentieth and early twenty-first centuries, though her former dominance in Europe would never be recreated. A typical but incorrect view has been that there were negative depictions of Judith before the fifteenth century—for which there is no clear evidence—and that negative treatments of her dominated after 1600—which is an exaggeration—and that virtuous and affirming depictions virtually disappeared by 1900—also an exaggeration. Still, it became very common for Judith to be depicted in ways that robbed her of any female agency or virtue.

At different points in her history, Judith has moved between good and evil, iconically paired with Mary at the earliest stage and Salome later. Yet the extremes of her depiction—from every bit as good as Mary to every bit as evil as Salome—may not be the most interesting aspect of her moral ambiguity. What may be more significant is not her *radical* vacillation between the extremes of good and evil, but her *hovering* at the boundary, for in many of her incarnations she is not *clearly* good or evil. She has been a Rorschach test for Western culture and will not likely fade.

University of California Press, 2003) 124–42, here 127.

215 Bathja Bayer, "Judith: In the Arts," *EncJud* 11:567–69, here 567.

Figure 1
Donatello (ca. 1386–1466)
Judith and Holofernes
Piazza della Signoria
Photo Credit: Alinari / Art Resource, NY

Figure 2
Sandro Botticelli (1444–1510)
Judith with the Head of Holofernes, ca. 1472
Uffizi
Photo Credit: Alinari / Art Resource, NY

Figure 3
Giorgione (da Castelfranco) (1477–after 1510)
Judith (with the Head of Holofernes)
Hermitage
Photo Credit: Scala / Art Resource, NY

Figure 4
Domenico de Pace Beccafumi (1486–1551)
Judith with the Head of Holofernes
Wallace Collection
Photo Credit: By kind permission of the Trustees of
the Wallace Collection, London / Art Resource, NY

Figure 5
Michelangelo Buonarroti (1475–1564)
Spandrel with detail of Judith and her maid
carrying the head of Holofernes. Detail of the
Sistine ceiling.
Sistine Chapel, Vatican Palace
Photo Credit: Scala / Art Resource, NY

Figure 6
Vincenzo Catena (1470–1531)
Judith
Galleria Querini Stampalia
Photo Credit: Scala / Art Resource, NY

Figure 7
Jacopo Robusti Tintoretto (1518–1594)
Judith and Holofernes
Museo del Prado
Photo Credit: Erich Lessing / Art Resource, NY

Figure 8
Master of the Mansi Magdalene (fl. ca. 1515–1530)
Judith and the Infant Hercules, ca. 1525–1530
National Gallery
© National Gallery, London / Art Resource, NY

Figure 9
Lucas Cranach the Elder (1472–1553)
Judith with the Head of Holofernes
Kunsthistorisches Museum
Photo Credit: Erich Lessing / Art Resource, NY

Figure 10
Jan Sanders van Hemessen (c. 1504–c. 1566)
Judith, c. 1540
The Art Institute of Chicago
Photo Credit: The Art Institute of Chicago /
Art Resource, NY

Figure 11
Jan Massys (1472–1553)
Judith and Holofernes
Musée du Louvre
Photo Credit: Erich Lessing / Art Resource, NY

Figure 12
Michelangelo Merisi da Caravaggio
(1573–1610)
Judith and Holofernes, 1599
Palazzo Barberini.
Photo: Alessandro Vasari
Galleria Nazionale d'Arte Antica
Photo Credit: Alinari / Art
Resource, NY

Figure 13
Cristofano Allori (1597–1621)
Judith with the Head of Holofernes, ca. 1620
Musée du Galleria Palatina
Photo Credit: Scala / Art Resource, NY

Figure 14
Artemisia Gentileschi (1597–ca. 1651)
Judith and Holofernes, ca. 1620
Uffizi
Photo Credit: Scala / Art Resource, NY

Figure 15
Artemisia Gentileschi (1597–ca. 1651)
Judith and Her Maidservant
Galleria Palatina
Photo Credit: Alinari / Art Resource, NY

Figure 16
Massimo Stanzione (1597–ca. 1651)
Judith with the Head of Holofernes
The Metropolitan Museum of Art
Image copyright © The Metropolitan Museum of Art
Image source: Art Resource, NY

Figure 17
Peter Paul Rubens (1577–1640)
Judith and Holofernes
Herzog Anton Ulrich-Museum
Photo Credit: Scala / Art Resource, NY

Figure 18
Johann Liss (c. 1597–1629)
Judith and Holofernes
Kunsthistorisches Museum
Photo Credit: Erich Lessing / Art Resource, NY

Figure 19
Fede Galizia (1587–ca. 1630)
Judith with the Head of Holofernes
Galleria Borghese
Photo Credit: Scala/Ministero per i Beni e le
Attività culturali / Art Resource, NY

Figure 20
Giulia Lama (2nd half 18th century)
Judith and Holofernes
Gallerie dell'Accademia
Photo Credit: Cameraphoto Arte,
Venice / Art Resource, NY

Figure 21
Francisco de Goya (c. 1820)
Judith and Holofernes
Museo del Prado, Madrid
Photo Credit: HIP / Art Resource, NY

Figure 22
Jean Joseph Benjamin-Constant (1845–1902)
Judith
The Metropolitan Museum of Art
Image copyright © The Metropolitan Museum of
Art. Image source: Art Resource, NY

Figure 23
Franz von Stuck (1863–1928)
Judith and Holofernes, 1926
Staatliches Museum
Photo Credit: Erich Lessing / Art Resource, NY

Figure 24
Gustav Klimt (1862–1918)
Judith II
Galerie Vytvarneho Umeni
Photo Credit: Erich Lessing / Art Resource, NY

9. The Text of Judith and the Present Translation

Despite the fact that Judith is distinctly a specimen of popular tradition, the ancient text is relatively stable. Wildly different early versions of Daniel and Susanna, Esther and Tobit are found, but not of Judith (with the possible exception of the Vulgate; see the appendix).

The earliest text of Judith is reconstructed based on the following sources:

Principal Early Versions of the Christian Bible

B   Codex Vaticanus, fourth century
S   Codex Sinaiticus, fourth century
A   Codex Alexandrinus, fifth century
V   Codex Venetus (also called Basiliano-Vaticanus, or N), eighth century

Early Fragments Written in Uncial Letters

823   Damascus, Omajjaden-Moschee, Kubbet el-Hasne, no. IV, fifth–sixth century (contains only 2:19)
999   Cairo, Institut français d'archéologie orientale, ostracon no. 215, second half of third century (contains only 15:1-7)[1]

Later Greek Manuscripts Written in Cursive Letters (Minuscules)

Hanhart Siglum	Brooke-McLean Siglum	Description
19	b	Rome Bibl. Vat., Chigi R. VI.38, twelfth century
46	e	Paris Bibl. Nat., Coisl. 4, thirteenth–fourteenth c.
55	h	Rome Bibl. Vat., Regin. Gr. 1; tenth century
58	k	Rome Bibl. Vat., Regin. Gr. 10, eleventh century
64	c	Paris Bibl. Nat., Gr. 2; tenth century
71		Paris Bibl. Nat., Gr. 1, thirteenth century
71′		= 71-106-107
74		Florence, Bibl. Laur., S. Marco 700, thirteenth century
74′		= 74-76
98		Escorial, Real. Bibl., Sigma II-19; thirteenth century
106	p	Ferrara Bibl. Comun., Gr. 187.1
106′		= 106-107
107	d	Ferrara Bibl. Comun., Gr. 188.1
126	m	Moscow Syn.-Bibl., Gr. 19, dated 1475 (incomplete)
249	v	Rome, Bibl. Vat., Pii II gr. 1; twelfth century
249′		= 249-670
311	r	Moscow, ehem. Syn.-Bibl. Gr. 354; twelfth century
381		Escorial, Real Bibl., Omega-I-13; eleventh century
534	l	Paris Bibl. Nat., Coisl. 18, eleventh century
542	u	Paris Bibl. Gr. 10, ninth century
583	f	Paris Bibl Nat., Gr. 1087 fourteenth century
670		Rome, Bibl. Vat., Vat. Gr. 335, fourteenth century

Old Latin Texts (on Vulgate, see Appendix)

The sigla used here are those of Hanhart, but the sigla used by the Vetus Latina-Institut at Beuron Archabbey, Germany, are also provided.[2]

---

1   See Jacques Schwartz, "Un fragment grec du livre de Judith (sur ostracon)," *RB* 53 (1946) 534–37; and, on the text of Judith in general, Stephen D. Ryan, "The Ancient Versions of Judith and the Place of the Septuagint in the Catholic Church," in Xeravits, *Pious Seductress,* 1–21.

2   Pierre-Maurice Bogaert, "La version latine du livre de Judith dans la première Bible d'Alcala," *RBen* 78 (1968) 7–32, 181–212, here 12–13; Bogaert, "Recensions de la vielle version latine de Judith I. Aux origines de la vulgate hiéronymienne. Le 'Corbeiensis'; II. Le 'Monacensis'; III. La tradition allémanique; IV.

Hanhart Siglum (used here)	Beuron Institute Siglum	Description
B	153	Bern, Universitätbibl. 533, ninth century (86 [1976] 7–37)
C	151	Paris, Bibl. Nat., lat. 11549 (= Sabatier Corb. 7) twelfth century
G	7	Paris, Bibl. Nat., lat. 11553 (= Sabatier Sangerm. 15), ninth century
M	130	Munich, Bayer. Staatsbibl., Clm 6239, eighth–ninth century
N	152	Paris, Bibl. Nat., lat. 11563, seventeenth–eighteenth century
O	132	Oxford, Bodl Lib, Auct. E. infr. 1–2, twelfth century
P	150	Paris, Bibl. Nat., lat. 11505 (= Sabatier Sangerm. 4), written 822
Q	148	Paris, Bibl. Nat., lat. 93, ninth century (text see under P)
R	62	Paris, Bibl. Nat., lat. 6, tenth century (text under G)
S	131	Stuttgart, Württembergische Landesbibl., H. B. II Bibl. 35, eighth century (text under B)
X	109	Madrid, Bibl. Univers. Centr. 31, ninth century

The Old Latin textual tendencies result in the following groupings: SB often converge, as do QP; there are also many SBQP readings. MC diverge often from the preceding texts, and vary together; the same is true of GN. X varies the most radically from the Old Latin textual tradition. The edition of Pierre Sabatier of 1739–1749 was closest to G.[3]

Syriac and Other Languages

Hanhart concluded that the Syriac textual tradition was fairly stable and in agreement with the *O* recension. Others, however, now find more variation in the Syriac texts of Judith than Hanhart perceived.[4]

Medieval Hebrew Versions

The medieval Hebrew translations of the Vulgate version of Judith are interesting and important in themselves, as are the medieval Hebrew midrashic retellings of the Judith story, but although Dubarle thought they reflected very old textual traditions, predating even the LXX,[5] most scholars now agree that they are translations of the Vulgate.

The Reconstruction of the Earliest Text of Judith

In 1979, Hanhart provided a critical edition of Judith that has been adopted with minor changes by subsequent scholars.[6] The translation used in this commentary utilizes his edition with minor changes. Hanhart's reconstruction of the earliest recoverable textual form of Judith was based on the uncials B, A, V, and to a lesser extent, S, and the minuscules 55 (often in agreement with

Trois manuscrits et deux recensions; V. La tradition carolingienne," *RBen* 85 (1975) 7–37, 241–65; 86 (1976) 7–37, 182–217; 88 (1978) 7–44.

3   Bogaert, *Judith*, Fascicule 1: *Introduction* (Vetus Latina: Die Reste der altlateinischen Bibel 7.2; Freiburg im Breisgau: Herder, 2001) esp. 53–54, 69. The Sabatier edition is available in Pierre Sabatier, *Bibliorum sacrorum latinae versionis antiquae* (3 vols.; Reims: Reginaldum Florentain, 1743; repr., Turnhout: Brepols, 1976) 1:744–90.

4   Lucas van Rompay, "Two Syriac Manuscripts in the Special Collections Library of Duke University," in

Maria Doerfler, Emanuel Fiano, and Kyle Smith, eds., *Syriac Encounters: Papers from the Sixth North American Syriac Symposium, Duke University, 26–29 June 2011* (Eastern Christian Studies 20; Louvain: Peeters, 2015) 467–83. On Judith in the Slavonic versions, see also Francis Thomson, "The Slavonic Translation of the Old Testament," in J. Krasovec, ed., *Interpretation of the Bible* (Sheffield: Sheffield Academic Press, 1998) 605–920.

5   Dubarle, *Judith*, 1:33–37; 2:8–96.

6   Hanhart, *Iudith*; Hanhart, *Text und Textgeschichte*, 11, 46–60.

B), 249´ (= 249 and 670), 311, 318, 392, and 542 (often in agreement with A).

The minuscules were assigned by Hanhart to four recensional groups; in some cases they are closely related to particular versions. These four recensional groups are given italic sigla:

1. *O* Origenic/Hexaplaric[7]
2. *L* Lucianic[8]
3. *a*[9]
4. *b*[10]

Tendencies of Some Texts

The Greek, Old Latin, and Syriac texts of Judith are fairly stable. In terms of text criticism, "[t]he Book of Judith presents few if any special problems."[11] The Vulgate is an outlier, which will be discussed in the appendix. But, aside from the Vulgate, in the earliest textual evidence of Judith, a third-century ostracon (999) that contains parts or all of Jdt 15:1–7 (about sixty words over eighteen lines), there is no variation from Hanhart's text except for the spelling Batuloua.

Despite the stability of the text tradition, there are two tendencies observable in some texts: the tendency to reduce the text, presumably to improve it by pruning unnecessary or rambling elements, and the tendency of some Greek texts to correct to better Greek. At first it might appear that the habitual reducers are simply transmitting a shorter text tradition. The habitual reducers often omit the same clauses, although these clauses might have seemed expendable by any engaged editor. But, on closer inspection, the habitual reducers often eliminate different clauses; that is, aside from a few obvious deletions in common, the habitual reducers also have many minuses that are not the same. This is the case, for instance, in 8:14: the habitual reducers 71, 126, OL-M, and OL-C omit different parts of the verse. (But recall that *some* habitual reducers—71 and 106—are part of the same *a* recension.) Assuming, then, that the habitual reducers (with the exception of 71 and 106) are not part of the same textual tradition, we note as well that they reduce more in the "romance" narrative sections of chaps. 9–15 than in the "military" narrative of chaps. 1–7. The reducers also drop entire strophes in the parallel poetry of chap. 16, disrupting the parallelism.

The other tendency is to correct the Greek style. It has long been noted that *L* exhibits Atticizing tendencies. To a lesser extent, the Origenic tradition (*O* OL Sy) does as well.[12] Examples include correction of the first aorist endings on second aorist verbs (for instance, correcting *ēlthosan* to *ēlthon*) or the change from *eipen pros auton* to *eipen autō*. Less often noted is the fact that the Greek habitual reducers also correct to a higher standard of Greek, or that there is an occasional tendency in some manuscripts to eliminate Hebrew resumptive pronouns.[13] It is also possible that, as in the case of the Daniel tradition, some text variants arise from a re-oralizing performance.[14]

An interesting specimen of Greek correction is 126 (Moscow, Syn. Bibl. Gr. 19, dated 1475), perhaps characterized as "hyper-Lucianic." It corrects toward better Greek, reduces the text, and in general transmits a smoother, simpler text. It is very rare for a superfluous prefix to escape 126's razor. Yet 126 does not correct the

---

7 Includes 58, 583, and OL Sy. Many variants are found in *O* OL Sy but in no other branches of the textual tradition.

8 There is occasional agreement of *L* and S^c, OL-SBQP; so Hanhart, *Text und Textgeschichte*, 23–24.

9 Moore labels this Recension A (*Judith*, 92). It shares some readings with Venetus.

10 Moore labels this Recension B (*Judith*, 92). It shares some readings with Alexandrinus.

11 Alan E. Brooke, Norman McLean, and H. St. John Thackeray, eds., *Esther, Judith, Tobit* (The Old Testament in Greek, III, Part 1; Cambridge: Cambridge University Press, 1940) vii.

12 Hanhart, *Text und Textgeschichte*, 34–37, 44.

13 Hanhart notes the correction of reflexive pronouns in B, e.g., *heautou* for *autou* (check 8:5; 13:2, 4), but this is less significant in terms of a Semitizing Greek style.

14 Edgar Kellenberger, "Textvarianten in den Daniel-Legenden als Zeugnisse mündlicher Tradition," in Melvin K. H. Peeters, ed., *XIII Congress of the International Organization for Septuagint and Cognate Studies, Ljubljana, 2007* (SCS 55; Atlanta: Society of Biblical Literature, 2008) 207–23.

many first aorist endings found on second aorist verbs (e.g., *eipan* to *eipon*). And as in the case of Matthew's editing of Mark, 126 sometimes loses narrative detail and appeal (see 10:8-10).

The Present Translation

Elsewhere I have tried to provide a freer translation of Judith to capture more of the enjoyment of the text,[15] but here, for the purposes of scholarly comparison, I restrict myself to a more literal rendering. The translation here is intended to be simple, fairly literal, and "biblical" in that the text mimics biblical history books, even if they were not yet perceived as sacred literature. Although I lean toward the literal, I do not translate all the ubiquitous *kai*'s, and sometimes translate *kai* as "then," "but," or "when," as is often done for Hebrew *waw*, introducing some hypotaxis into a paratactic text. I also occasionally omit *kai egeneto* as superfluous. I did not, however, follow the example of *NETS* and try to reproduce the supposed equivalences created by a Greek scribe translating a Semitic original, for the simple reason that it is unclear to me whether our text was written in Greek or translated into Greek (see §2 above). Yet at points I still assume the influence of Semitic languages, even if the text was composed in Greek, as in 1:15 where I translate *heōs* as one would translate Hebrew *'ad*.

---

15   Wills, *Ancient Jewish Novels: An Anthology from the Greco-Roman Period* (New Milford, CT: Toby, 2007) 89–120.

Commentary

PART I

The book of Judith falls easily into two parts. The first, chaps. 1–7, describes a threat to the Israelites arising from the nonexistent king, "Nebuchadnezzar, king of the Assyrians," and his general Holofernes (see §4 above). To contextualize this dramatic threat, the book of Judith, like Tobit and Esther, and also the Gospels of Matthew and Luke, begins with antecedent action: the battle between two great empires, the Assyrians and the Medes. Nebuchadnezzar's defeat of Arphaxad,

king of the Medes, would not ordinarily concern Israel. In the process, however, Nebuchadnezzar called upon each of the nations to his west, including Israel, to ally with him, and when many refused, he quickly defeated Arphaxad and then turned to conquer the nations that had spurned him. A fear is thus cast over all the nations surrounding Israel that will rise to a climax at the end of chap. 7. At the same time, the focus of that fear is narrowed to tiny Bethulia, an Israelite mountain village where Judith, a wealthy widow, resides in seclusion.

1:1–16

1

Text		Textual Notes

1/ It was the twelfth[a] year of the reign of Nebuchadnezzar,[b] who ruled the Assyrians from Nineveh, the great city. In those days Arphaxad,[c] who ruled the Medes from Ecbatana,[d] **2/** erected walls around Ecbatana, made of hewn stones three cubits thick and six cubits long. He constructed the walls seventy cubits high and fifty cubits wide. **3/** At its gates he erected towers one hundred cubits high and laid a foundation for them sixty cubits wide. **4/** He made its gates seventy cubits high and forty cubits wide for the passage of the warriors of his armies[e] and the formed ranks of his infantry. **5/** And in those days King Nebuchadnezzar made war against King Arphaxad in the Great Plain, that is, the plain along the borders[f] of Ragau.[g] **6/** All of those who resided in the high country allied[h] with Nebuchadnezzar, as did all of those who resided along the Euphrates, the Tigris, and the Hydaspes, and in the plain of Arioch, king of the Elamites, a great many nations also arrayed their forces with the Cheleoudites.[i]

7/ Then Nebuchadnezzar, king of the Assyrians, sent word to all those who resided in Persia[j] and to all those residing in the west—those residing in Cilicia, Damascus, Lebanon, and Antilebanon, all those living along the coast, **8/** the peoples of Carmel and Gilead, Upper Galilee, and the great plain of Esdraelon, **9/** all those in Samaria and its cities, the region beyond the Jordan River as far as

a   For δωδεκατου: δεκατου 249; *decimo tertio* Sy-b.

b   One minuscule, 583, here and in v. 11 reads Cambyses, a Persian king no more historically plausible than Nebuchadnezzar. Eth reads Persians for Assyrians.

c   Arphaxad spelled Sarphaxar in 670 (see also 1:5), and Artaxeum in OL-X (Bogaert, "Version latine," 184).

d   On the awkward parenthesis and translation, see commentary and compare the beginning of the Ezra Memoir, Ezra 7:1–6.

e   For δυναμεων (preferred by Hanhart): δυναμεως B, 106´, 311, Sa, Ra, and Vg (preferred by *NETS*); των αρματων αθτων S*, some OL, Sy, which NAB prefers.

f   For οριοις: ορεσι 583. The similarity of the two words will cause variants each time they occur. Both terms will sound plausible, whether the geography is known or unknown. In 1:15 it is the mountains of Ragau, with only a few texts harmonizing it to this passage.

g   For Ragau: various spellings, and Sy has Dura'.

h   Συνηντησεν can mean both "allied with" and "met in opposition," that is, opposed him. Gera assumes that since συνηντησεν elsewhere (2:6; 10:11) is hostile, it must be here as well, but the word can mean either and could have been used for both meanings even in the same text. S corrector adds εις πολεμον.

i   For υιων χελεουδ: *cum chaldaeis* assumed by Sy, but this is weakly attested. The phrase could also read "a great many nations of the Cheleoudites also

Jerusalem, Bethany, Chelous, Kadesh, the river of Egypt; to Tahpanhes, Raamses, and the whole land of Goshen[k] 10/ even beyond Tanis and Memphis, and all those who resided in Egypt as far as the borders of Ethiopia.

11/ But all who resided in the whole region[l] showed contempt for the decree[m] of Nebuchadnezzar, king of the Assyrians, and did not ally with him for war; for they were not afraid of him, but regarded him as just one man. They sent back his messengers, shame-faced and empty-handed. 12/ Nebuchadnezzar then became enraged with this entire region and swore by his throne and his kingdom that[n] he would take vengeance on the whole territory of Cilicia, Damascus,[o] and Syria and destroy with his sword all those residing in the land of Moab, the Ammonites, all of Judea,[p] and all of those in Egypt as far as the coasts of the two seas.

13/ In the seventeenth year, he arrayed his armies against King Arphaxad and defeated him in battle, routing Arphaxad's entire army, all his cavalry and all his chariots. 14/ He took control of his cities and advanced as far as Ecbatana and seized the towers and plundered its streets, bringing its glory into disgrace. 15/ When Nebuchadnezzar overtook Arphaxad in the mountains of Ragau, he ran him through with his spears and destroyed him on that day.[q] 16/ He returned with them, along with all his mixed force, a vast host of troops, and there he and his army spent a period of rest and feasting that lasted a hundred and twenty days.

arrayed their forces with him." Note Chelous v. 9, and cf. 2:23.

j With Persia, Iamnia or Iamna added in S OL-SBQP; Bogaert, "Version latine," 185.

k The place-names vary in the manuscripts: E drops Cush; various spellings for Betane are attested, read as Ecbatana in some OL, an influence of 1:1; for Chelous: Thelos OL-G; Kades is spelled as in Gen 14:7 LXX (*Qadesh* in Hebrew); for του ποταμου, i.e., the Nile: τους χιμαρρους S; *flumina* OL; for Taphnas: Paphnas 583, Tachpis Sy, Tamne and Thampnas in some OL (see Bogaert, "Version latine," 185); for Raamses: Drames in OL-M; Gesem appears as in Gen 46:34 LXX for Goshen, omitted in some OL.

l Before την γην, πασαν is found in B A OL Sa Eth, rejected by Hanhart but read by Moore and *NETS*; cf., e.g., 2:11.

m For ρημα: ονομα 19.

n The phrase ει μην, an influence of the Hebrew idiom *kî im* for a solemn vow (cf. Gen 22:17), is omitted or altered in most OL.

o For Δαμασκηνης: Δαμασκου S L 71´ 74´ *b* OL Sa, a form found elsewhere in Judith.

p For Ιουδαιαν: Ιδουμαιαν B; see the excursus at 3:5-10 ("The 'Nations Roundabout'") and cf. 3:9.

q Even if Judith was composed in Greek, the usage here may reflect the Hebrew/Aramaic *'ad*, a broad preposition that can mean "until" or "at." *NETS* has "to this day," as does Gera; NRSV translates "once and for all."

Commentary

The function of chap. 1 is not simply to engage the audience with exciting action, although that is the stock-in-trade of popular narrative. Every adventure movie has a first engagement to establish the heroic opposition before the climactic engagement. The carefully orchestrated rising action dramatizes that Nebuchadnezzar seems to be invincible—even the great king Arphaxad of the Medes is easily defeated by him—and also that Nebuchadnezzar has now turned to move against all the nations to his west as part of a campaign of world domination. From this point, he will not stop his expansion until all the nations of the west are under his control.

■ 1:1

The book of Judith plunges the audience immediately into an exciting but unreal narrative. While Tobit mimics a wisdom court narrative and Greek Esther mimics an Ezekielian vision of the battle of cosmic forces, Judith uses the motifs of biblical history to create a broad historical-political canvas—a world conflagration. It will encompass more regions than any of the biblical books, although it is a similar geographical scope to Greek histories such as Herodotus and national romances such as the Alexander Romance.

The opening accomplishes a number of narrative goals in a few lines. First, it conjures a similarity with the authoritative biblical histories. The events of the narrative are dated by the year of the reign of a major king: "It was during the twelfth year of the reign of Nebuchadnezzar."[1] Joshua, Judges, 1 and 2 Samuel, Ruth, and Jonah open with a similar dating formula, and a similar usage can be found where a new segment of the historical narrative is introduced (1 Kgs 15:1; 16:15, 29; 2 Kgs 12:1; 13:1). In Greek, the use of the dative of the regnal year is also found (1 Kgdms 15:1; 16:28a; 2 Kgdms 12:1; 13:1). Contemporaneous histories (2 Esdr 1:1; 1 Macc 1:1) and faux-histories (both MT and Greek Esther; Dan 1:1; 2:1; 4:1; 5:1) are also similar. The first sentence is four verses long, 101 words in Greek. This is not unusual in Greek, and, as is often the case when such a Greek sentence is encountered, it is broken up in English translations into shorter sentences, five in the NRSV. Still, its breathless style plunges the audience into a world of kings and battles.

But the second goal of the opening, after invoking biblical history, is to establish the text not as history but as faux-history. Unlike long sentences in good Greek, there is no skillful hypotaxis, yet the ineptitude may be part of the artifice, a demonstration of the *absence* of Greek artistic pretension. Awkward, run-on clauses communicate chaos, excitement, and danger, as two legendary kings are brought together in combat. In just a few lines the author has plunged us into a dramatic world of the clash of nations and armies. The walls and towers seem impregnable—even though they will be captured in a few verses!—and the wide gates of Ecbatana (v. 4) evoke a vision of Arphaxad's armies marching out to war. There will be many visual images to come (see §7 above).

The clear marks of faux-history continue. Nebuchadnezzar was the famous king of the Babylonians, not the Assyrians. It was in reality Nebuchadnezzar's father Nabopolassar, in *alliance*, not *conflict*, with the Medians, who defeated the Assyrians. His persona was quite well known and vilified by Jews. The books of 2 Kings and Jeremiah had described the fall of Jerusalem to Nebuchadnezzar, and Daniel 1–4 had already processed the memory of Nebuchadnezzar in the winepress of fiction. Although other errors for famous rulers can be found in biblical texts, especially in the variant readings, there is no question that the author and audience would have seen "Nebuchanezzar, king of the Assyrians" as a humorous and fictitious mixing of evil empires.[2] Such flagrant historical blunders occur in other Jewish novellas as well—"Darius the Mede" in Dan 5:31, Esther as a Persian queen, "Xerxes the Mede" in Tobit 14:15—and appear to be a signal to the audience about the nature of the genre. In a more restrained manner, such known inaccuracies were found in Greek novels. While "Nebuchadnezzar, king of the Assyrians" is the greatest of the historical blunders in Judith, there will be many more. Just a few verses later, for instance (1:7), Persia will be listed as one of the world

---

1   The opening clause is a genitive of time-within-which, "It was in the twelfth year," which Grintz retroverts to *bishnat*, likening it to the beginnings of history and prophetic books in the Bible (*Book of Judith*, 69). The twelfth year of Nebuchadnezzar of Babylon was the year in which King Zedekiah of Judah went to Babylon to seek favor of the great king (Jer 51:59), but there does not seem to be any particular reference here to those events. The destruction of the Jerusalem temple occurred in the eighteenth year of the real Nebuchadnezzar of Babylon.

Daniel 3:1 Th and 4:1 OG also utilize a genitive of time-within-which for the formula, and Greek Esther begins with a genitive absolute that contains the regnal year. Dating by an event in an empire rather than a Judean regnal year is found in 2 Chr 1:1 and Ezra 1:1. Chariton mimics the openings of Herodotus and Thucydides; see Reardon, "Chariton: *Chaereas and Callirhoe*," in Reardon, *Collected Ancient Greek Novels*, 18–19.

2   See §2 above. Ezra 5:13 has "Cyrus king of Babylon" and Eupolemus (Eusebius, *Praep. ev.* 9.39) identified Nebuchadanezzar as an Assyrian king, but these instances likely associate kings with the empires they conquered and ruled; see also Priebatsch, "Das Buch Judith," 50–60. The royal fiction in Judith, by contrast, floats on a sea of historical and geographical absurdities, as noted below.

One should also not assume that Assyrians and Babylonians were considered *inherently* evil in Israel. In the earlier biblical texts, they were, like Egypt, considered *contingently* evil, depending on their relations with Israel. The Canaanites and related nations, on the other hand, were more likely to be considered inherently evil; see the excursus below at 3:5–10 ("The 'Nations Roundabout"). Cf. also Isa 10:12–14, 24–32, on Assyria, and the list of cities, different from the cities listed in Judith, through which Assyria passes before being stopped.

empires, even though it did not emerge until after Assyria was swallowed up by the Babylonians. The combination, then, of historical and fictional traits characterizes the entire book of Judith and other Jewish novellas.

The book of Judith is clear in its commitment to a fictional view of the events, but why specifically "Nebuchadnezzar, king of the Assyrians"? It is doubtless an amalgam of the two villainous empires of history who had conquered Israel: the Assyrians, under Sennacherib, had defeated the northern kingdom of Israel in 721 BCE, and Nebuchadnezzar and the Babylonians had defeated the southern kingdom, Judah, and destroyed the temple in 587 BCE. In both cases the leading citizens had been deported and resettled in various parts of the two empires. Yet these events would have been half a millennium in the past for the author of Judith. The Hellenistic rulers may also be pilloried in this fictitious king. The Seleucids founded Seleucia, a great fortress, as a capital, and occupied the same land as the Assyrians.[3] It was they who ruled Judea at the time of the Maccabean Revolt, and so the Assyrians could be equated with the Syrians, short for Assyrians, or the Seleucids. As Antiochus IV Epiphanes, the Syrian king, had been the villain during the Maccabean Revolt, this would suggest itself all the more. In the context of this novella, it is highly satisfying that this triple evil—Nebuchadnezzar, Assyria, and the Seleucids—can be merged into one figure, to be defeated by one woman whose name means "Jewish woman."

Nineveh was a great city and the capital of Assyria, famed for its huge walls. Although in reality likely eighty feet high and eighteen feet thick, the walls were enlarged by legend. Of Nineveh, founded by Ninus, the protagonist of a proto-novel (*Ninus Romance*), Ctesias says:

A city its equal, in respect to either the length of its circuit or the magnificence of its walls, was never founded by any man after his time. For the wall had a height of one hundred feet and its width was sufficient for three chariots abreast to drive upon; and the sum total of its towers was one thousand five hundred, and their height was two hundred feet.[4]

Nahum 2:6–11 prophesied against Nineveh while it was standing, calling it the embodiment of evil (3:1; cf. Zeph 2:13–15), but the historical Nineveh was destroyed by the Babylonians and Medes in 612 BCE. Its fall, and that of Assyria, was treated by all nations as a signal event in ancient Near Eastern history: "The very mention of Nineveh is perhaps an early hint of Nebuchadnezzar's ultimate defeat in our story."[5] After its fall, Nineveh also figures in two fictitious narratives in the Bible: Jonah and Tobit. Clearly, there is a satirical extravagance regarding Nineveh, since it is safely in the ancient past. The exaggerated scale of the buildings was part of the romanticized discourse on empire in fanciful histories and novels. The descriptions in Judith thus make no pretense of accuracy but simply represent the greatness of Nineveh: the Israelites will be engaging and defeating the legendary empires of old.

Despite the fame and importance of the Medes, scholars have generally assumed that the king Arphaxad was an invented figure. The name, however, may have evoked associations. One of the sons of Shem and an ancestor of Abraham, Arpachshad, is spelled Arphaxad in the LXX (Gen 10:22; cf. 11:10–12, Luke 3:36, and Genesis Apocryphon 12.10). The name thus might have resonated as a descendant of an eponymous ancestor,

---

3   The capital was moved to Antioch, which was less a fortress than an open city, but Seleucia remained important.

4   Diodorus Siculus 2.3.3; translation of C. H. Oldfather, *Diodorus of Sicily* (12 vols.; LCL; Cambridge, MA: Harvard University Press; London: Heinemann, 1968) 1:357. Semiramus, discussed in 2.7.3–4, was not to be outdone, and founded Babylon, huge in area, with great walls and towers. See Llewellyn-Jones and Robson, *Ctesias' History*, 115, 120. On the actual measurements of Nineveh's walls, see Eckart Frahm, "The Great City: Nineveh in the Age of Sennacherib," *Canadian Society for Mesopotamian Studies* 3 (2008) 13–20, here 17. One

may also compare Aristeas 84, where the Jerusalem temple's three walls were said to be seventy cubits high.

5   So Gera, *Judith*, 117. Jonah refers to Nineveh as "the great city" (1:2; 3:2, 3; 4:11), while Revelation refers to Babylon as the great city, understood as Rome (11:8; 14:8; 16:19; 17:18). Cf. also *megalopolis*, Pindar, *Pyth.* 2.1; 7.1. On the fall of Assyria, see Peter Machinist, "The Fall of Assyria in Comparative Ancient Perspective," in Simo Parpola and R. M. Whiting, eds., *Assyria 1995: Proceedings of the 10th Anniversary Symposium of the Neo-Assyrian Text Corpus Project* (Helsinki: The Project, 1997) 179–95.

another of Shem's offspring, but this is unlikely.[6] It is more likely that the name is related to Arbaces the Mede, known from Ctesias,[7] perhaps assimilated to the more biblical sounding Arphaxad. The accession of Arbaces was part of the gradual demise of Assyria and the beginning of the Median Empire, which lasted until Astyages the Mede was conquered by Cyrus in 550. This development would have been confined to the east, not affecting Israel or Judah; but in the Greek literary tradition, which was likely known to our author, Arbaces was said to be the founder and most noble of the Median kings.[8] Yet in our novella Arphaxad only serves as a foil for Nebuchadnezzar—a great king defeated by a greater. Arphaxad here is no villain but a secondary character; the only role of this great king is to demonstrate, in defeat, the greater greatness of Nebuchadnezzar. There is some narrative surprise and irony when his walled city is so quickly destroyed by Nebuchadnezzar (v. 14). The expectation that Arphaxad was a match for Nebuchadnezzar is quickly dashed, and thus the power of Nebuchadnezzar, our real antagonist, is dramatized. Ironically, in defeat Arphaxad attained a different sort of memory. As his name is the first word in the Vulgate translation, illustrated Bibles transformed the *A* in his name into a decorated representation of Holofernes's tent, the scene of the beheading (see §8 above).

Whatever the origin of the name Arphaxad, the Medes join the drama of nations at the beginning of this novella. They were not Semitic but related to the Iranians. As noted above, Cyaxares, king of the Medes, allied with Nebuchadnezzar's father to defeat the Assyrians in

612 BCE. The people in Israel had indeed hoped that the Medes would defeat the Babylonians (Isa 13:17; 21:2; Jer 25:25; 51:11, 28). Daniel 5:28; 9:1; and 11:1 adopt a prophecy originating in the East that preserves a memory of the eastern role of Medes in world kingdoms. The rise of Cyrus of Persia, however, put an end to the Medes' leading role. Although they would continue to appear in the pair Persians and Medes (Jdt 16:10), the former group had eclipsed the latter forever.

These verses thus establish that the story is set in a fictional past, but one that conveys some verisimilitude of the wars and empires known to the audience. We are not told until the next chapter what these two nations have to do with Israel, but the original audience likely knew where the narrative was heading. The description here proceeds quickly and with hyperbole to achieve a sense of menace—somewhat analogous to the faux-apocalypse at the beginning of Greek Esther—as two great kings to the north and east of Jerusalem are immersed in a world war. *Fear* and *power* will be recurrent terms in the first half of the book of Judith.[9]

■ **1:2–4**

A number of other details contribute to the tone of a historical-fiction setting among the famous empires of the past. Ecbatana, conquered by the Persians in 550 BCE, was known as a great city and the capital of the Median Empire, but how it would have been viewed by those in Judea in the second century BCE is unclear. The city figures accurately in Ezra 6:2, and in Tob 3:7 it is the home of Sarah, the woman who will marry Tobit's son.

---

6   In Genesis, Arphaxad is Elam's younger brother; it is conceivable but unlikely that he could be associated with the Elamites who were actually later in Persia, not in the Semitic orbit, and thus "Medes." Adolfo D. Roitman also notes that Arphaxad appears at Gen 11:10–26 as an ancestor of Israel! ("The Mystery of Arphaxad [Jdt 1]: A New Proposal," *Henoch* 17 [1995] 301–10). For Roitman, this expresses the notion that Judith wins back a triumph for Israel that Arphaxad had lost—speculative but possible. See also Jub. 9:4 and Josephus, *Ant.* 1.144.

7   Diodorus Siculus 2.24.1–28.8; Nicolaus of Damascus, *FGrH* 90 F66, 1. The name would originally have been Arbaku. Is Arphaxad's defeat on the great plain near Ragau understood as being similar

to Alexander the Great's defeat of Darius III at Gaugamela? It is possible, although Gaugamela is some five hundred miles east of Ragau. Nebuchadnezzar is not likened to Alexander the Great here as much as to Artaxerxes III Ochus or Antiochus IV Epiphanes.

8   Pfeiffer, who drew no connection between Arphaxad and Arbaces, noted how Judith's Arphaxad combines aspects of three other Median kings: Deioces, who fortified Ecbatana; Cyaxares, a contemporary of Nebuchadnezzar; and Astyages, the last king of Media before the rise of Cyrus (*History*, 295). Astyages also appears in Bel 1 and in variant readings of Dan 6:1 OG.

9   See Jdt 1:11; 2:28; 4:2; 16:25; Craven, *Artistry and Faith*, 60–62, 83–84; Schmitz/Engel, *Judit*, 414.

Ecbatana, renamed Epiphaneia, was also one of the capitals of the Seleucid Empire, and so it may well have been familiar as a Seleucid city and as an eastern home of diaspora Jews. Herodotus (1.98–99) said that the city had great walls, but one inside the other, the battlements of each painted in different colors. None of these specifics is mentioned in Judith. Polybius 10.27.5–13 describes a more open city with a great citadel and notes as well that exaggerated descriptions of the palace were common in sensationalist histories. In our text, the author describes walls as thick as those of Babylon (compare Herodotus 1.178) and towers nearly as high as those of Nineveh (compare Diodorus Siculus 2.3), but these comparative dimensions may also be exaggerated. The measurements are thus magnificent, but not beyond belief.[10] Yet we also note another literary function of these great walls: they provide a contrast to Judith's tent of seclusion; unlike Ecbatana, her tent will withstand Nebuchadnezzar's attack.

■ **1:5–6**

The Great Plain is likely the extensive plain to the northeast of Ecbatana, later called Irak Ajami. According to Judith, it extends to the borders of Ragau (also Ragae or Rages), but, because of the similarity of the Greek words for border and mountain, we encounter here for the first but not the last time the possibility that any reference to border could have been mountain, and vice versa. Ragau lay at the foot of the Zagros Mountains and therefore "mountains of Ragau" is possible here. Like Ecbatana, this city is important in the book of Tobit (1:14; 4:1) and highlights both Jewish interest in the eastern diaspora and also major cities that would become important on the Silk Road that would take Jewish merchants and traders, and later Christians, all the way to China.

The Tigris and Euphrates Rivers would refer to the area of the Assyrian and Babylonian Empires, but the Hydaspes is in India, perhaps significant here as the eastern extent of Alexander's expedition. Moore (125–26) notes that, since the Hydaspes, modern Jhelam River, Sanskrit Vitasta, was far off to the east, some

scholars conjectured that the text originally mentioned the Choaspes (modern Kerkheh; Herodotus 1.188; 5.49). Otto Fritzsche thought it unlikely that the Hydaspes should be taken as the eastern border of our story, so he chose the Syriac variant Ulai, a river near Susa (Dan 8:2), near the Elamites.[11] Whether Arioch is king of Elamites or Elymeans is also unclear. If the more likely Elamites, then it is interesting that Arioch and Elamites both appear in Abram's military campaign in Genesis 14 (see below).[12] The Cheleoudites are unknown; they could be linked with the Medes or with the Chaldeans and Nebuchadnezzar. It hardly matters; they are simply part of the local coloring of the narrative.

■ **1:7–10**

Excursus: The Sweep of Nations

The conflict between two great empires has spilled out onto the plains and will now engulf the small nations over the face of the earth, a world at war. At first, areas to the east ally with Nebuchadnezzar (v. 6), but the west resists him (v. 7). Would this represent the approximate situation of the Persian expeditionary force of 343 BCE, the force that also included a Holofernes and a Bagoas? This is not likely. The areas are listed by their historical, not contemporary, names; the list is more literary and imaginative, even cliché. Our text combines a wide variety of place-names—known, unknown, or misrepresented. A particularly inaccurate example is Holofernes's campaign in 2:21–28. Says Gera, "We are not meant to trace Holophernes' route carefully, map in hand, for the military march is intended rather to dazzle and impress readers with its sweep and success."[13] Yet why is the village of Bethulia, or even Jerusalem, not more at the center of the map of this narrative? The off-center location contributes to a notion that the story is part of a global drama. A similar eastward-looking perspective is found in Greek histories and will later be found in the Greek novels.

A close parallel to this opening is found, surprisingly, in the anomalous military campaign of Abram in Genesis 14: the eastern Elamite king Chedorlaomer—a sort of Nebuchadnezzar figure—gathers allies on the horizon, and the sweep of nations nar-

10   *Pace* Gruen, *Diaspora*, 163. On the comparison to Judith's tent of isolation, see §5 above.

11   Fritzsche, *Die Bücher Tobi und Judith*, 135–36.

12   Gera, *Judith*, 123. An Arioch also appears as one of Nebuchadnezzar's officials in Dan 2:14. There was

also an Elam, son of Shem, with Arphaxad in Gen 10:22. On Cheleoudites, see Haag, *Studien*, 12–13 n. 13; and Moore, *Judith*, 126. Fritzsche preferred Chaldeans (Syriac reading).

13   Gera, *Judith*, 28.

rows to Abram and his decisive victory. In addition, there is a common Israelite sense of the threat of the "nations roundabout" (see the excursus at 3:5–10, "The 'Nations Roundabout'"), and compare also the list in 1 Sam 14:47:

> When Saul had taken the kingship over Israel, he fought against all his enemies on every side—against Moab, the Ammonites, Edom, the kings of Zobah, and against the Philistines.

The sweep of nations here thus evokes biblical history, but also Greek literature as well. Ctesias had listed the conquests of Ninus, major nations first, although his listing of minor nations trails off as "many other lesser tribes" (Diodorus Siculus 2.2.3). The style of the Alexander Romance is even closer to Judith, with Darius similar to Nebuchadnezzar. From the point of view of the Greek Alexander, Darius of Persia makes an open claim of divinity, commanding all of the nations of the east to join his alliance. Darius, "the king of kings, the great god Darius and lord of all nations . . . wrote to all the subject nations, requiring them to join him with their troops" (1.40, 42). The list of nations coming against Nectanebo of Egypt sounds similar to the list from Judith: Indians, Nocimaeans, Oxydorcae, Iberians, Kauchones, Lelapes, Bosporoi, Bastranoi, Azanians, Chalybes, "and their massed army of countless armed men."[14] Diodorus's list of Pompey's conquered peoples is similar (40.4), as is Agrippa's report on the nations subdued by Rome, the Jews being the last to come under rule (Josephus, *Jewish War* 2.16.4 §§356–83).

The political background of the literary conceit is clear. The role of alliances and vassal states was crucial to all political history in the ancient Near East. An alliance of the Babylonians and Medes had resulted in the destruction of the historical Assyrian Empire, and treaties were typically drawn up that expressed a dominant relation of the great empires over the vassal states. The images of alliances are thus realistic, the very fabric of historical-political narrative. Israelite history had recorded the alliances of the great empires, but also the alliances of Israel or Judah with other empires, such as those of the Syro-Ephraimite War (2 Kings 16; Isaiah 7–8), and Herodotus often records the deliberations of cities in deciding whether to resist invading forces or sue for peace.

Some postexilic Jewish texts are also replete with both real and invented or heavily modified royal letters and decrees. Probably influenced by Persian administrative practices, Ezra-Nehemiah, Hebrew and Greek Esther, and Daniel reflect this discourse. The entire literary culture was formed by Persian dependence on court administration, letters and decrees, and even the very use of prose (see §7 above). The message here, however, is depicted more as an oral message than a written decretal.

But the sweep of nations is not just a biblical or historical tradition; it is also a second-century BCE political development. In the third century to mid-second century, Seleucids and Ptolemies had been strong enough to control small indigenous nations, as Persians had before them, but in the power vacuum of the mid-second century a number of indigenous nations reasserted their independence: Itureans, Nabateans, and independent city-states like Tyre, Sidon, and Ascalon.[15] A similar power vacuum of great empires had allowed David to found Israel at the same time that Ammon and Moab became independent kingdoms—and these nations are prominent in Judith as well (see the excursus "The 'Nations Roundabout'" at 3:5–10). In a more contemporary tradition, compare the neighboring peoples who threatened in 1 Maccabees 5: Idumaeans, Baeanites, Ammonites, and Jazerites.[16]

Unknown cities and sites are found in the somewhat earlier book of Jubilees—a sign of the "free narrative" aspect of both apocalypses and novellas—but it is not just the lists of known and invented nations that populate the story. The constant geographical interest in Judith is also seen in the many references to borders, mountains, plains, and rivers. Even numbers proliferate in our story; in chap. 1 alone: 12, 3, 6, 70, 50, 100, 60, 70, 40, 17, 120. These might be linked to an oral style, but they are actually too varied: they jump about too much for an oral telling. Like many of the popular texts of this period, the author combines typically oral motifs in a new way, in a written medium. The author is thus influenced by traditional or performance style, but the written medium—even if the text is performed aloud—allows for more and varied details, the very "evidence" of faux-historical knowledge. There is not likely the pretense of real knowledge here, but an excitable

---

14 Alexander 1.2; as in Judith, the list varies from text to text; text A has Scythians, Arabs, Oxydrakai, Iberians, Seres, Kaukones, Lapates, Bosporoi, Agroi, Zalboi, Chaldeans, Mesopotamians, Wild-game-eaters, Euonymitae; see Richard Stoneman's note, *Alexander Romance*, 36.

15 Schwartz, "Israel and the Nations," 16–38.

16 Gera notes that Judith uses the "biblical" gentilic of "sons of X" *more* than does the Hebrew Bible (*Judith*, 81).

yet effective storytelling technique. We look, for instance, at the nations mentioned in vv. 7–10:[17]

Persia	Bethany
Cilicia	Chelous
Damascus	Kadesh
Lebanon and	River of Egypt
Antilebanon	Tahpanhes
Carmel	Raamses
Gilead	Goshen
Upper Galilee	Tanis
Esdraelon	Memphis
Samaria	Egypt
Beyond the Jordan	Borders of Ethiopia
Jerusalem	

The nations are intentionally varied, with a certain pretense of a truly objective narrator's perspective, since in chap. 1 ancient enemies of Israel such as Moabites and Ammonites (1:12), neutral nations such as Cilicia or Ethiopia, Samaria (1:9), and Judea (1:12) are treated similarly, as if all part of "world history," not "Israelite history." Samaria and Jerusalem are introduced only as part of the sweep of nations, with Samaria first (on Samaria, see commentary on 4:4). This is not a historical pretense but a novelistic one; in an era when accurate history is advocated, the novelistic exploration of fiction will mirror history but derive fun from it at the same time.

Just as Greek novels later situate the protagonists in a fictionalized stage of "world history," just so here the author sets aside the Israel-centric assumption of biblical history and explores the perspective of the *oikoumenē*: what would it feel like to view the world from the colonizer's perspective? There is an aspect here of colonized audacity or "colonial universalism": the claim of the colonized to understand universalism better than the colonizer (see §7 above).

Aspects of some of these peoples and places are significant for our story. The plain of Esdraelon, Greek for Jezreel, lies between the highlands of Galilee to the north and those of Samaria and Judea to the south.[18] It was the site of many famous biblical battles (Judg 5:19–20; 1 Sam 29:1; 2 Kgs 23:29; Hos 1:4–5). Beyond the

Jordan calls to mind much of the dramatic discussion in Ezra-Nehemiah. Beyond the Jordan from the point of view of the eastern nations is intended, yet the author seems to slip in 1:12 and include Ammon and Moab, which are east of the Jordan.

The last sites mentioned are partly known and partly unknown, but they are equally places of the imagination. Kadesh is unclear. Friedrich Stummer thought that it must mean Kadesh Barnea, the base of the Israelites in the wilderness wanderings,[19] but in 5:13 Kadesh Barnea is referred to by that name—although inconsistency can hardly be ruled out. Earlier scholars, using great ingenuity, also sought to find the sites of Bethany, Chelous, and Kadesh.[20] The river of Egypt is likely the wadi of Egypt, Nachal Mizrayim (Num 34:5), also called Wadi el-Arish. It separates Egypt and Judah. Tahpanhes, Rameses, Tanis, and Memphis were major cities in the Nile Delta. Finally, Ethiopia is chosen as the southern boundary. The story world coincides with the eastern and southern extent of the Hellenistic *oikoumenē*.

■ 1:11–12

After presenting the sweep of nations, the narrative turns more to the psychological in terms of Nebuchadnezzar's character and the peoples' reactions to him (see also 2:2–3 and the excursus at 3:8: "Worship of Nebuchadnezzar and Danielic Motifs"). Nebuchadnezzar's revenge on the nations will be a theme of Judith; see also 6:5; 7:28; 8:27, 35; 9:2; 16:17, and plunder and revenge by Israelites will be recounted in 15:6–7. Several motifs should be noted:

• The nations to the west of Nebuchadnezzar are not afraid of him, for they consider him as "only one man."[21] Is this lack of fear of "only one man" to be contrasted with Israel's appropriate fear of one God? The language here may have resounded like a counter-Shema.

17   Cf. later texts: Acts 2, Philo, *Embassy to Gaius* 36.281–82, with a western orientation, Augustus, *Res Gestae Divi Augusti* 16–33 with a more eastern.

18   On the Greek form, see Hanhart, *Text und Textgeschichte*, 78–79.

19   Stummer, *Geographie*, 12–13.

20   See Gera's summary, *Judith*, 125–26.

21   This phrase is odd in Greek, and in addition to the Shema, may suggest Hebrew *kĕ'aḥad hā'dām*, "as an ordinary man," used of Samson (Judg 16:7, 11); so Gera, *Judith*, 127–28. The plain sense of Hanhart's text suggests, as the *NETS* translates, "in their eyes he was but one man," all alone against the world. This comports with the first half of the verse, the

- The lack of fear was probably understood ironically by the audience. They know that (a) the peoples *should* fear Nebuchadnezzar's power, and (b) the peoples, though now brazen, soon *will* fear him. They also know that (c) although Israelites *will also* fear him, (d) they should *not* fear him, and (e) a great victory will occur so that they will have release from fear. Fear in various forms is a leitmotif also in 2:28; 4:2; 5:23; 7:4; chap. 8; 10:16; 11:1; 15:2; 16:25.[22]
- The nations to Nebuchadnezzar's west shame his messengers, which will prove to be a miscalculation. The categories of honor and shame will be played on often in Judith (1:14; 4:12; 5:21; 8:22–23; 9:2).
- In his hubris and might he is set to defeat them all without allies. It captures Nebuchadnezzar's personality in a "Danielic" way.[23] He swells with rage in a way that is unlike a Greek philosopher but is surprisingly like the Israelite God.
- In the Bible, only God swears by himself (Num 14:21, 28; Isa 49:18; Jer 22:24). In Deut 32:40 God swears by himself to take vengeance, similar to Nebuchadnezzar here and in 2:12. Thus, Nebuchadnezzar arrogates images of God to himself.[24]

The audience knows that this passage is suggestive of what is coming; the peoples' perception will change. This short announcement only prefigures Nebuchadnezzar's broader, more threatening reactions in chaps. 2–3. Ancient Near Eastern texts often refer to the wrath of the king, and wisdom texts instruct the courtier to avoid incurring the king's anger (Prov 19:12; 20:2). Many Israelite and non-Israelite kings in the Bible are depicted as angry: David (2 Sam 12:25), Saul (1 Sam 20:30), Pharaoh (Gen 40:2), Ahasuerus (Esth 1:12). Anger is not treated as an inappropriate emotion for a king, or for

God (Exod 32:10). Greek tradition during the Hellenistic period became much more vocal that the king, like the philosopher, should be in control of his emotions. To be sure, Greek authors averred that eastern kings often lacked self-control (see the excursus at 8:35: "The Book of Judith and Greek Philosophy").

This is the first of a number of vows in Judith (2:12; 7:28; 11:7; 12:4; 13:16). Nebuchadnezzar's vow contributes to the plot and to his characterization, as is the case in the vows in other novellas. In Esther, the vows are classically "unbreakable," but here they merely extend both the plot and the dramatic emotions. The fact that Nebuchadnezzar vows "by his throne and kingdom" rather than by a deity contributes to the growing characterization of his hubris and pretensions to divinity.

Nebuchadnezzar wants revenge on "the whole territory of Cilicia, Damascus, and Syria," that is, Assyria! It would make some sense if Nebuchadnezzar were Babylonian. The real Nebuchadnezzar, king of Babylonia, and the fictional "Nebuchadnezzar, king of the Assyrians," are often merged in Judith. The fact that these nations do not correspond precisely to those listed in 1:7–10 only communicates the worldwide sweep of the drama. The breathless lists, inclusive as they are, cannot contain all the territory. Inconsistency only serves to reinforce the sense of the fullness of nations and the whimsy of the performance. Ammonites and Moabites, neighbors of Judea, but also, as the audience knows, perennial enemies are here threatened along with the other nations. This, however, will change; see commentary on 5:1–21.

The two seas are unclear. The Red Sea and the Mediterranean would make sense, or less likely the Red Sea and the Persian Gulf, but because the context is specifically Egypt, Moore prefers the White Nile and the Blue Nile, that is, the two branches of the Nile.[25]

---

contrast of all the world and Nebuchadnezzar by himself. The usage in Jdt 6:3 might suggest simply that he was weak, "only one man." Moore (*Judith*), noting Vaticanus *isos* and Grintz's reconstruction of the Hebrew (*Book of Judith*), translates "they regarded him as (only) an equal," that is, an ordinary man. The better witnesses argue against this. *Anēr heis* may also be an ironic allusion to *heis theos*.

22 Gera, *Judith*, 127; Schmitz/Engel, *Judit*, 414.

23 Cf. especially Daniel 3–5. Gera notes that the

expression "showed contempt for the decree" uses a biblical construction, *bāzâ dābār* (e.g., Num 15:31), which always refers to the word of God or his messengers (*Judith*, 127). Thus, Nebuchadnezzar's actions already suggest the hubris of considering himself to be a god.

24 Gera, "Judith," in Jonathan Klawans and Lawrence M. Wills, *Jewish Annotated Apocrypha* (Oxford: Oxford University Press, forthcoming).

25 Moore, *Judith*, 128.

■ 1:13–14

The seventeenth year may call to mind Jer 32:1, where Nebuchadnezzar captured Jerusalem in the eighteenth year. If in Judith Nebuchadnezzar moves across the land toward Jerusalem in his seventeenth year, his destruction of Jerusalem in the following year would be suggested (see 2:1). As in 1:12, the real and fictional Nebuchadnezzars are often merged. The defeat and death of Arphaxad and "all his cavalry and all his chariots" are told in very brief compass, indicating the ease with which Nebuchadnezzar could eliminate the great Arphaxad—after five years' preparation! The only detail comes in the subjugation of the Median kingdom: Nebuchadnezzar captured the cities, came to Ecbatana and captured its great towers, so commanding in 1:3, and plundered its markets. Completing this description is the humiliating result: the former glory is changed to disgrace. The theme of honor and shame was introduced just above, plays out here, and will return throughout.

■ 1:15

Arphaxad is run down and slain in the mountains, a quick end for a minor character. However, this scene also provides both context and a pivot for the book as a whole. The death of an opposing king in this fashion is a motif familiar from ancient Near Eastern conquest narratives,[26] developing further the tone of the entire book as a "typical," if fictitious, narrative set in the deep past—and indeed a rousing historical narrative. Arphaxad's ignominious death near Ecbatana may possibly call to mind the fact that Antiochus IV Epiphanes was said to have died there (2 Macc 9:3). Gera also notes that Darius I had defeated the Median king Fravartish at Ragae, and the Behistun inscription details how Darius had cut off the king's nose, ears, tongue, and eye, and then crucified him. The last Persian king, Darius III, was also run down near Ragae by Alexander the Great and was killed and mutilated by a Persian general.[27]

The plunder noted here returns as a leitmotif in Judith (2:7, 11, 23, 26–27; 4:1, 12; 7:27; 8:19, 21; 9:4; 15:6–7; 16:4); it will be reversed at the end when the Israelites enrich themselves with the plunder of the enemy camp. The destruction of Jerusalem by the actual Nebuchadnezzar is perhaps recalled (Lam 1:6–7), as well as the quick and ruthless victories like those of the Maccabean guerrilla leaders in 1 Macc 5:35, 51 and 2 Macc 12:16. The Assyrian kings were also famous for boasting of their plunder.[28]

■ 1:16

Structurally, we come to the end of the first act of our book, the historical action set chronologically before the main action of the story. Gera (115) captures the tone of the book's first movement: "Arphaxad is as colorless in death as he is in life, while in this chapter Nebuchadnezzar is the underdog, an angry king who is not properly feared by other nations." One might expect that Nebuchadnezzar would be sated by the victory and bloodletting, but this description has been but a preamble to the main campaign to come. Nebuchadnezzar has a "mixed force," even before the other nations capitulate and join him. Does this refer to the different kinds of soldiers, or to different peoples and mercenaries? If the latter, then this would be the first reference to the theme of the "nations roundabout" (see 2:28). We also encounter the first of a number of pauses in the narrative, where the enemy forces take their rest (see commentary on 2:28). The celebration at the defeat of Arphaxad is also near Hanukkah, and the celebration in 16:20 ends on the same day a year later; P.-M. Bogaert takes this as an intentional invocation of Hanukkah,[29] although this may be strained.

26   K. Lawson Younger, *Ancient Conquest Accounts: A Study in Ancient Near Eastern and Biblical History Writing* (JSOTSup 98; Sheffield: Sheffield Academic Press, 1990) 220–22.

27   Plutarch, *Alex.* 43.3; Curtius Rufus, 5.13.16; 7.5.40; 7.10.10. See Gera, *Judith*, 131; Robert Rollinger, "Altorientalisches im Buch Judith," in Mikko Luukko, Saana Svärd, and Raija Mattila, eds., *Of God(s), Trees, Kings, and Scholars: Neo-Assyrian and Related Studies in Honour of Simo Parpola* (Studia Orientalia 106; Helsinki: Finnish Oriental Society, 2009) 429–43.

28   Gera, *Judith*, 130–31; Younger, *Ancient Conquest Accounts*, passim; and see the excursus at 15:6: "Revenge, Vengeance, Vindication, and Plunder."

29   Bogaert, "Le calendrier," 67–72.

Text	Textual Notes

1/ And in the eighteenth year, on the twenty-second day of the first month,[a] there was discussion[b] in the palace of Nebuchadnezzar, king of the Assyrians, about taking revenge on the entire land, just as he had said. **2/** Summoning all his ministers and nobles, he placed before them his secret plan, and with his own lips he recounted all the wickedness of the land, **3/** and they resolved to destroy everyone who had not obeyed the command from his mouth.

4/ And when he had concluded his counsel,[c] Nebuchadnezzar, king of the Assyrians, summoned Holofernes, the commander-in-chief of his army and second in command after him, and said to him, **5/** "Thus says the Great King, lord of all the earth: Go forth from my presence and take with you men of proven strength, as many as[d] 120,000 infantry and a force of horses and riders numbering twelve thousand, **6/** and proceed against the entire country to the west, since they disobeyed the word of my mouth. **7/** Announce to them that they are to have earth and water available, for I am about to proceed out against them in my anger, and I will cover the entire face of the land with the feet of my army, and I will hand these people over to them to plunder. **8/** Those struck down shall fill their gullies, and every wadi and river shall overflow, filled with their dead.[e] **9/** I will lead them away in captivity to every corner of the earth. **10/** And you shall go out and seize every territory for me in advance. They shall surrender themselves to you, and you shall hold them for me to await the day of their punishment. **11/** And as for those who do not comply, your eye shall not spare them in handing them over to slaughter and pillage throughout your land.[f] **12/** For as I live and by the power of my rule, I have spoken and I will accomplish these things by my hand. **13/** As for you, do not transgress any of your lord's commands, but indeed you are to execute these orders as I have commanded you, and you shall not delay in doing them."

a The dating of events varies in the text tradition; Sy: "In the twenty-eighth year, on the twelfth day"; Vg: "In the thirteenth year on the twenty-second day"; 71 omits the day and month.

b For λογος, V has λογος κυριου.

c Or "confirmed his plan."

d For εις in this sense, see Smyth §1686c.

e For τους χειμαρρους, S O L 311 OL assume πας χειμαρρους as nominative singular, parallel to ποταμος; the latter noun still dictates the number of the participle. Moore and *NETS* adopt this reading, as I have here.

f Σου omitted by O L a 249 311 La Sy, but retained here as *lectio difficilior*.

Commentary

2:1–13

Attention shifts at this point to the main arc of the narrative, Nebuchadnezzar's marshaling of his western expeditionary forces. They are set to destroy those, such as the Israelites, who did not join him earlier. The plot pivots in this chapter toward Holofernes. Nebuchadnezzar holds a council, which will be followed by a council convened by Holofernes in chap. 5, a council in Bethulia chap. 6, a council of Judith with the elders in chap. 8 and upon her return, and a meeting with the town in chap. 13.

■ 2:1–3

Chapter 2 begins with an opening parallel to chap. 1, a dating of the next major event by the regnal year. The biblical histories also provided such dates for new developments in the narrative (1 Kgs 15:1; 16:15, 29; 2 Kgs 12:1, 13:1). The eighteenth year of the historical Nebuchadnezzar of Babylonia was 587 BCE, the year of Nebuchadnezzar's destruction of Jerusalem and the deportation of many of the elite citizens. This date was well known from Jer 32:1 and 52:29. Interestingly, in the LXX of Daniel 3 and 4, Nebuchadnezzar's construction of a golden tower, his attempt to burn Shadrach, Meshach, and Abednego, and Nebuchadnezzar's dream about his downfall are also dated to the eighteenth year. These stories, like Judith, were likely originally written and received as fiction; dating these revenge fantasies in that year was an act of revenge.[1] And, while the eighteenth year is associated with a disaster, the twenty-second day of the first month, Nisan, is good: it is the day after Passover when Pharaoh and his army were drowned.[2] At key points in Judith, parallels will be made to Exodus (see §4 above).

"There was discussion in the palace of Nebuchadnezzar" likely evoked an association for the audience. Deliberations between a king and his counselors are not common in the Hebrew Bible but do appear in the narratives of Jewish courtiers in foreign courts (Joseph, Daniel, Esther, Ezra-Nehemiah); "summoning all his ministers" is a typical motif in the Jewish court narratives (Dan 2:2–5; 3:2–9; 6:6–8; Esth 1:13). The phrase also conjures the atmosphere of the eastern court narratives such as those in Ctesias and the later Persian Shah Nameh. A Danielic motif is also discernible here that will culminate in 3:8. The court setting provides both the high stakes of the worldwide expanse and the promise of dramatic conflict among powerful personalities.[3] We are not disappointed here. Haag also notes that *egeneto logos* is always used in

the LXX for a pronouncement from God (translating *wayhî dābār*), and *kathōs elalēsen* is generally also used in regard to God.[4] Thus, Nebuchadnezzar is again using language associated with God (see the excursus at 3:8, "Worship of Nebuchadnezzar and Danielic Motifs").

While Thucydides and other Greek historians resorted to invented military speeches to enliven their battle narratives, highlighted here is the novelistic technique of utilizing direct and indirect quotation to get inside the mind of characters: "there was talk," "just as he had said," "set before them his secret plan," "recounted fully with his own lips," "they decided." Some of these phrases would be found in histories, but their use to create a court scene reflects the eastern court narrative tradition, and also the new emphases of novellas.

Somewhat odd here is "secret plan," literally, the "mystery of his plan" (*to mystērion tēs boulēs autou*). *Mystērion* is used in the LXX to translate *rāz;* in Dan 2:18 it refers to the knowledge of Nebuchadnezzar's dream, which concerns the cycle of kingdoms. In the New Testament *mystērion* is also used to refer to knowledge of the eschatological nature of events (Mark 4:11; Rom 11:25; 1 Cor 15:51; Rev 10:7). At Qumran, we also find the *raz nihyeh,* "the mystery that exists" or "is to be" (4Q417 2 i 10–11 and often; cf. 1Q27 1 i 3–4; 1QS 11.4). But outside of apocalyptic contexts, *mystērion* can simply mean "secret," as in 2 Macc 13:21. In Tob 12:7, it is used for the secret of a king, although a few verses later, 12:11, it could also be metaphorical for the secret plans of God that are yet to become clear. The word *boulē* is used in the LXX to translate *'ēṣâ* ("counsel") and is found also in 8:16, when Judith upbraids the Bethulians for trying to constrain "the designs of the Lord our God." In Judith, an apocalyptic sense or a secret plan of God is probably not intended, but the Danielic use might have granted the word a heightened, entertaining sense. At any rate, both Nebuchadnezzar and God have a *boulē.*

---

1   Wills, *Jew in the Court,* 83–120.

2   Haag, *Studien,* 15; Zenger, *Das Buch Judit,* 456; Otzen, *Tobit and Judith,* 79.

3   Wills, *Jew in the Court.* The royal "council scene" exists in Greek and Egyptian tradition as well (Gera, *Judith,* 135–36; Tawny Holm, *Of Courtiers and Kings: The Biblical Daniel Narratives and Ancient*

Story Collections (Explorations in Ancient Near-eastern Civilizations 1; Winona Lake, IN: Eisenbrauns, 2013), passim, but the Persian court narrative tradition was especially well developed and was described often in Greek histories.

4   Haag, *Studien,* 16.

■ 2:2 "With his own lips," repeated three times, emphasizes the speech-act of a king. In the ancient world, all words were believed to have real effects, but a king can create *basileia* ("kingship") through his words. God's power to create through speaking and to deliver words to prophets might also be suggested. The phrase "he recounted all the wickedness of the land," however, is uncertain. *Sunetelesen* usually translates *killāh* ("be complete"). It could mean recounted in the sense of tallied up, reckoned, made an account (1 Kgs 25:17). The same verb is used in Jdt 2:4; 10:1; and 15:4, with its usual meaning of "finish" or "complete."[5]

■ 2:3 "Everyone" is literally "all flesh," which may seem at first to be a typical biblical expression, but it is not common. It appears in regard to the destruction of Noah's flood (*kol bāśār*, Gen 6:17 and elsewhere). In these verses, then, Nebuchadnezzar has the hubris to play with God's language (see 1:11–12 and excursus at 3:8, "Worship of Nebuchadnezzar and Danielic Motifs").

■ **2:4–13**

Nebuchadnezzar appoints Holofernes as general over an army of huge proportions to attack each nation in turn. The tone of this section can be compared to the opening of the contemporaneous 2 Maccabees, which is virtually a history companion piece to our novella (see §4 above).

Excursus: Holofernes

Holofernes is introduced and leads the expeditionary force across the land, crushing nations in his path. His title, "commander-in-chief of the army," is also used of a messenger of God in Josh 5:13–15 and in the Testament of Abraham for the archangel Michael. Holofernes will prove to be a comic villain, but interesting nevertheless.[6] A structural contrast is introduced that will be played on throughout: Holofernes is the representative of Nebuchadnezzar, while Judith represents God.[7] Nebuchadnezzar and God will remain two lords outside of the immediate action, but their servants Holofernes and Judith will engage in heroic combat near Bethulia. Just as Holofernes will demand worship of Nebuchadnezzar (see 3:8), Judith will demand worship of God from the weak-willed Bethulians. The contrast is extended further: Holofernes has a faithful attendant in Bagoas and Judith in her female slave.

Other biblical antecedents come to mind. As Judith is a biblical Everywoman, says Gera, so Holofernes "is clearly a latter day Sisera, with touches of the royal officers Rabshakeh and Nebuzaradan, the frightening Goliath, uncomprehending Balak, and partying Haman."[8] Rabshakeh also delivered a speech denouncing God and raising up his own king, Nebuzaradan was a high official of Nebuchadnezzar, and Haman caused his own downfall by losing his judgment over Mordecai. Jeremy Corley compares also Shechem, the pharaoh of the exodus, Sennacherib, and Nicanor.[9] Friedrich Reiterer argues that Alexander's conquest, especially the siege of Tyre, is the model for Holofernes's path, which includes Tyre (2:28). Alexander as the Great King (cf. Jdt 2:5) may provide a model for the overreach motif of Nebuchadnezzar, and Alexander assumed the title of son of Zeus at Ammon (Plutarch, *Alex.* 27.5).[10] In the commentary on chap. 5 and in §4 above, I consider comparisons to Xerxes.

The name Holofernes, a Persian name, was common in historical works; it would be less expected, though not unheard of, for a general in the Assyrian or Babylonian armies. His name and that of his chief servant Bagoas (see excursus at 12:11) both appear for generals of the Persian king Artaxerxes

---

5   Fritzsche, *Die Bücher*, 140, instead proposes that *wyglh*, he recounted, was read for *wyklh*, he completed. Corley, "Septuagintalisms," 93, judges this to be unnecessary, as 1 Sam 25:17 *sunetelestai hē kakia* is similar, "the evil is reckoned," but Gera, *Judith*, 137–38, points out that in 1 Samuel the evil will be done by the king, while here it refers to the evil committed by the peoples. Gera argues that another verbal idea is assumed, such as finished recounting. See also Schmitz, *Gedeutete Geschichte*, 11–12.

6   As Helen Morales rightly insists in regard to Greek novels, we should not look for complex characters in ancient novels, but "embodiments of social and moral values" (*Vision and Narration*, 94). See §7 above.

7   See esp. Craven, *Artistry and Faith*, 30–31, 53–59.

8   Gera, *Judith*, 50–51.

9   Corley, "Imitation," 22–54.

10   Reiterer, "Religion und hellenistische Realpolitik," 29–54.

III Ochus, who invaded Asia Minor and Egypt in 350 and 343 BCE.[11] In Chariton's novel *Chaereas and Callirhoe,* the character Artaxerxes may also recall Artaxerxes III Ochus. The campaigns of Ochus took his armies through Judea as well, so these expeditions likely registered for Jews in the generations before the composition of Judith and may be a model for the faux-historical setting. A Holofernes was also associated with Demetrius I Soter, who commanded Nicanor to attack the Jews. Gera notes parallels between this Holofernes and our antagonist: the Holofernes at the time of Nicanor was known as a drunken figure who plundered temples (compare also Heliodorus in 2 Maccabees 3). His association with Nicanor suggests that our author may have collapsed the two figures together here.[12]

Holofernes is too comical to be invested with a tragic fall, while even the eastern kings in Herodotus who ignore the "tragic warner" have depth and strong qualities. But does Holofernes rise to the level of a Polyphemus figure? Polyphemus was not just an unfortunate opponent of Odysseus in *Odyssey* book 9 but also a character in Euripides's satyr play. Drunken and lustful, he was a semi-savage brute who violated the rules of society. The use of the Cyclops as an opposite to construct civilization is part of the larger Greek process of constructing Hellenism by contrast with the barbarian.[13] Finally, we recall that Greek novel protagonists encounter many brutes.

■ **2:5–6** Certain phrases here—"Thus says the Great King, lord of all the earth: Go forth from my presence"— are similar to Assyrian or Persian royal inscriptions. "Great King," for instance, is especially associated with the Persian monarch (Herodotus 1.188), although it can also be tied to the biblical messenger formulae.[14] It is thus both a typical elevated title for an eastern king and an exaggerated self-delusion on the part of Nebuchadnezzar, placing him once again in opposition to the God

of Israel. Such a title is similar to the Danielic depiction of Nebuchadnezzar and other Babylonian rulers (see also 2 Kgs 18:19 and the excursus at 3:8, "Worship of Nebuchadnezzar and Danielic Motifs"). "Lord" would carry a political meaning of "ruler," but here it also contrasts with *kyrios* for God. An ironic and comic level of misunderstanding will occur later when the arrogant Holofernes will mistake Judith's references to "my lord" as referring to himself and Nebuchadnezzar. "Lord of all the earth" is introduced here and will be used again, emphasizing the worldwide scale of the action; see 5:21; 6:4; 11:16, 21; 16:21. His pronouncement is introduced with "thus says"; compare the prophetic *kōh 'āmar* (Exod 4:22; 1 Sam 2:27). Royal inscriptions often utilize this formal introduction; cf. Cyrus in 2 Chr 36:23, and his own Behistun inscription.[15]

The assembling of the army is described with many details, providing more sweep and excitement. The formula *andras pepoithotas en ischui autōn* ("men of proven strength," or in the passive sense of the verb, "confirmed in their strength") calls to mind biblical expressions for a warrior: *'îš gibbôr,* or "man of valor," *gibbôr ḥayil.*[16] Gera, however, also proposes that this phrase anticipates the later opinions by Achior (5:15) and Judith (11:10) as to the source of the Israelites' strength, or, less theologically, the height of their mountain abode by the leaders of the Assyrian allies (7:8–9).[17]

Holofernes's expeditionary force consists of 120,000 infantry and 12,000 cavalry (see below on the auxiliary forces). Much is made of the cavalry here and in 7:2, but they disappear from the later battle scenes. The size of the army, like the dimensions of the walls of Ecbatana, is meant to awe the audience. The actual numbers of the most famous armies of the ancient world are diffi-

11   Diodorus 16.47.4; 31.19.2–3. On Chariton's reference, see Reardon, "Chariton," 18.

12   Gera, *Judith,* 139; see also Polybius 3.5.2; Justin 35.1; Diodorus 31.32; Appian, *Syrian Wars* 244–45.

13   François Hartog, *The Mirror of Herodotus: The Representation of the Other in the Writing of History* (New Historicism 5; Berkeley: University of California Press, 1988). On Polyphemus, see Paul Robertson, *The Cyclops and the Self* (forthcoming).

14   Josh 3:11, 13; Zech 4:14; 6:5; LXX Exod 8:18; LXX Ezra 5:11; Add Esth 13:1; 16:2; Tob 13:15. See A.

Miller, *Die Bücher Tobias,* 39; Otzen, *Tobit and Judith,* 100; Haag, *Studien,* 18; Zenger, *Das Buch Judit,* 458–60; Hellmann, *Judit,* 30–31.

15   Gera, *Judith,* 140; Amélie Kuhrt, *The Persian Empire: A Corpus of Sources from the Achaemenid Period* (London: Routledge, 2007) 141–51, 304, 491.

16   See also Grintz, *Book of Judith,* 84, 122: *'anashim botechiym becheylam.* Compare *aner dynatos* in 7:2 in regard to Assyrian troops.

17   Gera, *Judith,* 240.

cult to calculate, as there was a strong tendency toward exaggeration. Modern scholars place the size of Darius's army in the range of 50,000 to 100,000 total,[18] somewhat smaller than Judith's figures, but ancient historians often provided huge numbers: 800,000–1,000,000 infantry and 12,000–40,000 cavalry.[19] Ctesias also reports about Ninus's army: "The army . . . numbered . . . 1,700,000 foot soldiers, 210,000 cavalry, and slightly less than 10,600 scythe-bearing chariots" (Diodorus Siculus 2.5.4).[20] The Assyrian army in Judith is probably about the size of Xerxes's actual army, although the ancient tradition reported a much larger figure; Herodotus gives the size of the Persian army at Thermopylae, along with camp followers, as five million (7.186). Closer to our author's context, 1 Macc 15:13 reports the size of the army of Antiochus IV Epiphanes as 120,000 infantry and 8,000 cavalry—very close to that of Holofernes. Judith's figure is thus *not* an exaggeration by ancient assumptions of large armies.

In addition to the impressive size of the Assyrian army, there may be a numerological suggestion in the figures. Since an ancient myriad was 10,000, the two figures are easily discernible multiples of twelve; William Loader proposes that we find here the symbolic opponents of the twelve tribes,[21] but this seems an unlikely allusion. Gera notes that the "twelve thousand mounted archers," literally, "horses and riders," could conjure "horses and riders have drowned in the sea" (Exod 15:1), which will be alluded to clearly twice later (9:7; 16:2).[22]

■ **2:6** "The entire country" or "all the land" (*pasa gē*) is used eight times in the first two chapters and six times in chap. 11 in Judith's flattering dialogue with Holofernes. *Gē* in the LXX translates *'ereṣ*; both *gē* and *'ereṣ* share a range of meanings and are among the most common words in the Bible. In the context of Hasmonean restoration theology, the term is central to God's promise of land to Abraham (Genesis 12; 15; 17). Here "the entire country to the west" communicates the worldwide scope of the story, but it is not the more eastward-looking perspective of Herodotus and Ctesias; it is the westward-looking perspective as Judeans under Hasmonean rule would have recognized it. "Since they did not heed the word of my mouth" suggests that Nebuchadnezzar is an angry tyrant and makes demands concerning his commands that sound very close to God's (Deut 1:26; 9:23). While Cyrus of Persia and Alexander (and by extension Antiochus IV Epiphanes) had actually conquered lands that seemed to reach to the ends of the earth, there was already an admittedly unrealistic tradition of God ruling to the ends of the earth (Deut 28:64; 33:17; Isa 40:28; 42:10; 43:6; Jer 12:12).[23]

■ **2:7-8** "Have earth and water available" was a Persian symbol of surrender (Herodotus 6.48.2).[24] Since it is unknown outside of Herodotus and authors dependent on him, this phrase constitutes specific evidence that our author was influenced directly or indirectly by the Greek historian (see §4 above). "Cover the entire face of the land with the feet of my army" is yet another image of the size and diversity of the Assyrian army—an impending threat of destruction, again contrasting with Israelites covering the face of the earth (Exod 8:2; 10:5). As noted in §2 above, "I will hand you over to X" is completed with a large number of terms for death or destruction: *diarpagēn* ("plunder"), *phonon* ("murder"), *harpagēn* ("robbery" [by hooking]), *aphanismon* ("ruin"), *rhomphaion* ("sword"), *pronomēn* ("plunder"), *ekdikēsin*

18   Hans Delbrück (*History of the Art of War* [Lincoln: University of Nebraska Press, 1990]) and John Warry (*Warfare in the Classical World* [London: Salamander, 1998]) provide estimates of many of the great ancient armies.

19   Arrian 3.8, Diodorus Siculus 17.53, Plutarch, *Life of Alexander* 66. Judith 1:13 also notes Arphaxad's chariots, and ancient historians emphasize Darius's two hundred war chariots.

20   Translation of Oldfather, *Diodorus of Sicily* (LCL), 1:363.

21   Loader, *Pseudepigrapha*, 188 n. 193.

22   Gera, *Judith*, 142.

23   Gera, *Judith*, 144.

24   Amélie Kuhrt, "Earth and Water," in Kuhrt and H. Sancisi-Weerdenburg, eds., *Achaemenid History III: Method and Theory* (Leiden: Nederlands Instituut voor het Nabije Oosten, 1988) 87–99; Caponigro, "Judith, Holding," 49–53, Corley, "Imitation," 39–40.

("vengeance"), *aichmalōsian* ("captivity"), *katabrōma* ("food"), and *olethron* ("destruction").[25] More unrestrained threat language follows: their wounded will fill ravines, and the river will be filled with their dead.[26]

■ **2:9–11** Forced exile was the typical practice in ancient warfare, both to destabilize the native political organization and to create a class of workers in the new location. In addition to the threat of death and being dispossessed, the deportation would have loomed large as a destruction of both the ancestral control of land and tribe and family structures (see *klēronomia* in 4:12 and the commentary on 8:21–23). An Assyrian deportation here would also have reminded the audience of the defeat of northern Israel in 721 by Sargon II of Assyria, accompanied by a large deportation. Nebuchadnezzar the Babylonian king had defeated the south in 597 and 587 BCE and deported many of the elites. It was this deportation that put many Judeans in contact with the Persians who succeeded the Babylonians, and thus a Persian connection in the text of Judith would not be surprising.

■ **2:10** "To await the day of their punishment" has a dual function: on the one hand, it communicates the enormity of the stakes and Nebuchadnezzar's control of affairs, and, on the other, it suggests God's final judgment, a bit of faux-eschatology similar to the opening of Greek Esther. Nebuchadnezzar's words allow an option for each nation: surrender and join his alliance or face destruction. This creates a decision point for each that highlights a major theme of this and all of the Jewish novellas, the role of choice: choosing loyalty to God.

Although there is a strong Greek tradition of *prohairesis*, reasoned moral choice (see the excursus at 8:35, "The Book of Judith and Greek Philosophy"), what lies behind the novellas are passages such as Deut 30:19, "Choose life!" In our narrative, the nations are given a moment of decision, and most fail this test, although Israel—and Achior the Ammonite (see commenary on 5:5; 14:10)—will pass.[27]

■ **2:12–13** "I will accomplish . . . by my own hand" is recalled later when Judith refers to defeating Holofernes by the hand of a woman. This leitmotif is played on in 8:33; 9:9–10; 12:4; 13:4, 14–15; 15:10; 16:5 and echoes Moses's hand in Exodus.[28] It will be perceived as comical to the audience who knows the story; Nebuchadnezzar's fundamental error is in setting himself up as God-on-earth. He does not realize that God holds the actual power and can defeat Nebuchadnezzar by the hand of a woman (8:33; 12:4)—soon to come! "Do not transgress any of your lord's commands" also uses biblical phrases associated with God; see Num 14:41; 22:18; and Deut 1:43. There is a humorous play on the two references of "lord," and God's own demands on Israel. As in 1:12, Nebuchadnezzar swears by himself and his kingdom rather than by a deity. God swears by himself in Num 14:21; Isa 49:18; Jer 22:24; and Deut 32:40. God, like Nebuchadnezzar, also swears by himself to take vengeance.[29] A more subtle narrative irony is in evidence with the final phrase of this speech, "You shall not delay": Holofernes will successfully sweep through many nations quickly but will pause to lay siege to the tiny mountain village of Bethulia.

---

25 Gera, *Judith*, 86, 143.

26 Cf. Homer, *Iliad* 21.218–20 as well. Regarding the imagery of corpses filling streams, Schmitz points out the parallel with Ezek 32:5–6 (*Gedeutete Geschichte,* 37), and 35:8 in the LXX has similar wording. See also Holofernes's similar language in 6:4. The overflowing river, *epiklyzōn*, is rare but is used in regard to Egyptians drowning in Deut 11:4; 3 Macc 2:7.

27 The odd Greek phrase "Your eye shall not spare

them in handing them over" is doubtless influenced by Hebrew *lo' tachus 'ayineka*; so Grintz, *Book of Judith*, 85–86.

28 See Skehan, "Hand of Judith," and the excursus at 9:8–10, "Judith's Hand and Agency."

29 Gera, *Judith*, 144–45; and see the excursus at 3:5–10, "The 'Nations Roundabout.'" "I have spoken and I will accomplish these things" is also spoken by God in Ezek 17:24; 22:14 and elsewhere.

Text	Textual Notes

Text

14/ And Holofernes went out from the presence of his lord and summoned all the commanders, generals, and officers[a] of the Assyrian army, **15/** and counted and mustered the picked troops in battle formation as his lord had commanded, as many as[b] 120,000 infantry and 12,000 mounted archers, **16/** and he marshaled them as a great army is arrayed for war. **17/** He also assembled camels, asses, and mules to carry supplies—a vast number—as well as sheep, oxen, and goats for provisions—too many to count. **18/** A supply of food was provided for each man in abundance, as well as a large amount of gold and silver from the king's palace. **19/** He himself set out with his whole army to march out ahead of King Nebuchadnezzar to cover the entire face of the land toward the west with his chariots, cavalry, and picked infantry. **20/** A huge mixed collection of people also accompanied them, like a swarm of locusts or the sand of the earth,[c] a multitude too large to number. **21/** They marched from Nineveh three days to the edge of the plain of Bectileth[d] and made camp at a distance from Bectileth near the mountain north of upper Cilicia. **22/** He then took his entire army of infantry, cavalry, and chariots, and proceeded into the high country. **23/** He totally destroyed Put[e] and Lud and plundered all of the Rassisites[f] and the Ishmaelites[g] on the edge of the desert, to the south of the land of the Cheleans.[h] **24/** Following the Euphrates he proceeded through Mesopotamia, laying waste all the fortified[i] cities along the Wadi Abron[j] as far as the sea. **25/** He took control of the region of Cilicia, cutting down all those who resisted him, and then came as far as the border of Japheth which faces south toward Arabia, **26/** and surrounded all the Midianites, burned their tents, and plundered their sheepfolds. **27/** He went down into the plain of Damascus in the days of the wheat harvest and set fire to all their fields, the sheep and the cattle he gave over to destruction, their cities he plundered, and their plains he ravaged, striking all their young men with the mouth of the sword. **28/** Fear and trembling fell upon all those who lived along the coast at Sidon and Tyre, and on those residing in Sur, Ocina, all those residing in Jamnia, and those residing in Ashdod and Ashkelon[k] became deathly afraid of him.

Textual Notes

a S *L* add καὶ τοὺς σατραπας.

b Εἰς = "as many as"; see 2:5. So also *NETS*.

c For η αμμος της γης ("the sand of the earth"): η αμμος της θαλασσης ("the sand of the sea") 583 OL-MG; cf. Gen 32:12.

d Bectileth is spelled various ways as a result of itacism and the mistaking of *P* and *T*. Also occurring are Bekpelath *O*, Bet Qetiylath Sy, Bethialaat OL-R, Hetchilat OL-O, Paktalai A, Patale OL-O, and even variations on Bethulia S *L* OL 19 319. A placename with various spellings is sometimes inserted between ορους and επ' αριστερα: Galpatou 311, Αγγιου ου εστιν 58, Ange, etc. OL-QPMSCG; 'g'' or 'gn' Sy; see Bogaert, "Version latine," 188.

e Put is more varied in the tradition than Lud.

f Rassis is spelled various ways in the textual tradition because of itacism, but also found are Ramas Arm; Tharsis OL-MC Vg; also Thiras and Rasis (and similar) OL-SBQPGX Sy.

g For Ishmael, also found are Maek S, Mashaec OL-M.

h For Χελεων: Eleon Eth; Ebeleonis OL-SB; Chaldaiōn B 19 58 108 OL-X Sy; γης Χαλδαιων 583 OL-SBQP.

i Υψηλας could be understood as high cities, but in 3:6 they are along the coast. Based on Neh 9:25, it likely refers to fortified cities, yet Holofernes will garrison the cities in 3:6. Gera prefers "mighty" cities.

j For Abron: Naboraj Arm-te; Nabrona Arm-ap; Asrōna *a* (except 74´); Rasōna 74´; Chebron S *O* L; Cheurōn 19-108; Mambre OL-MC Vg; cf. Gen 13:18; Cedron OL-SB; Beccon OL-QPX; Yeboq Sy; see Bogaert, "Version latine," 188.

k Also added are Gaza S *O* 58 OL Sy, Gaia OL-X.

Commentary

2:14–28

Here begins a major section, 2:14–7:32, Holofernes's campaign leading him to Bethulia (see §3 above).

■ **2:14–16**

Superfluous language and repetition occur often in this section. There is an inherent folk humor in repetition and superfluity, especially in regard to the pretensions of the elite and powerful—how better to skewer the powerful than to amplify their pomp and pronouncements (see the commentary on 5:1–3 on *alazōn*)! Our novella accomplishes this exceedingly well. This technique also communicates color and atmosphere by reinforcing images before the eyes. The superfluity does not consist in the nouns alone, but in the actions, which the narrator underlines: "as his lord had commanded."

Nebuchadnezzar is depicted as both a present villain and an absent one. From the time he commissions Holofernes to carry out his *boulē*, he becomes physically absent. He will still be overshadowing the narrative throughout (see the excursus at 3:8, "Worship of Nebuchadnezzar and Danielic Motifs"), even though Holofernes is the main antagonist. "If Nebuchadnezzar opens our story," says Gera, "because his name is instantly recognizable as an arch-enemy and stereotyped evil king, having Judith seduce him and cut his head off would be too far-fetched to accept."[1] Focusing now on Holofernes also allows for the neat opposition of Judith and Holofernes as representatives of their two lords.

Holofernes "went out from the presence of his lord"; this language, which is understood as "Assyrian" court language, suggests as well a counter-reality of Israelites before the face of their Lord. His first actions are to carry out what Nebuchadnezzar had just commanded, as though Nebuchadnezzar's words make things happen. In 2:19 Holofernes's army will "cover the entire face of the land" as Nebuchadnezzar had commanded in 2:7.

The preparations for war are meant to overwhelm; the excitement of the story depends on this depiction of the great army. Holofernes summoned the "commanders, generals, and officers," overblown and repetitive. Yet this is precisely the aesthetic appropriate to the genre (cf. Dan 3:2; 6:7; and Esth 1:3). Orders and ranks are not only a technique of fiction; they can be used in earnest to describe the constitution of society, as in Ezra 2:70. The fatuousness of the language here and its charm and bravado are seen in the sentence's completion, "and he marshaled them as a great army is arrayed for war," a line that fairly shouts, "This is mock-history!"

Holofernes "counted" the troops, *ērithmēsen,* an unusual verb; normally Hebrew *pāqad*/Greek *episkeptō* is used (Num 1:3; Josh 8:10). Considering that, this verse may call to mind the difficulties caused when David *numbered* the people of Israel and Judah (2 Sam 24:1–10).[2] In addition to the enormity of troops, livestock, and so on, it is also emphasized that the troops are "picked troops" (*eklektous*), stated also in 2:19 and 3:6.[3] This is no citizen army—as are the Bethulians and other Israelites—but a trained expeditionary force of the most powerful kingdom in the world. And yet—we will see below that there is a mixed group, *epimiktos*, of camp followers.

■ **2:17–18**

Such expressions as "great army," "vast number," and "without number" occur throughout these verses, similar in literary effect to the "commanders, generals, and officers" above. The repetition-with-change conjures an image of a gathering storm of an expeditionary force. The effects also include listing the orders of animals: camels, donkeys, mules, sheep, oxen, goats. (Later the animals of Bethulia, in a simpler scene, will also be enlisted to wear sackcloth.) In addition to the animals there are rations, gold, and silver from the greatest royal palace in the world. With the camp followers mentioned in v. 20, it is clear that Holofernes's army is actually an entire nation on the move. It will become an even greater army when all the nations roundabout are added

---

1   Gera, *Judith,* 146.
2   Gera, *Judith,* 147. To be sure, numbering is not a negative process in Gen 14:14, but that is an anomalous tradition in the early epic material, while 2 Samuel is part of the Deuteronomistic

History, where numbering takes on a special but unexplained narrative role.

3   *Eklektos* could refer to "chosen men" of, e.g., 2 Sam 6:1, *kol-bāḥûr,* everyone who was chosen.

to it (see 2:28). At the end, this motif will be recalled when the Israelites plunder the enemy camp (15:6–7); the hyperbolic wealth will be lying on the ground for the taking.

■ 2:19–20

Aside from the numbers of soldiers, animals, and so on, the visual effect of the massive army is rendered here by the statement that the army will cover the whole face of the earth "with his chariots, cavalry, and picked infantry," repeating unnecessary terms to impress. Contrasted with the "picked troops" (*epilektois, eklektous*) are the "mixed group" (*epimiktos*) of camp followers (compare 2:28 and note at 1:16), evoking perhaps the biblical motif of the nations roundabout. The same word is used in the LXX of Exod 12:38; Num 11:4; and Neh 13:3. (See the excursus at 3:5–10, "The 'Nations Roundabout.'") We note the general sense of this motif and its emphasis in 1 and 2 Maccabees. A more specific biblical precedent is in Judg 6:5, where the Midianites and Amalekites, like the Assyrians, are oppressing the Israelites from the east,

> for they and their livestock would come up, and they would even bring their tents, as thick as locusts. Neither they nor their camels could be counted; so they wasted the land.

Ctesias (in Plutarch, *Artaxerxes* 11.9) also mentions the "poor men" who followed the great armies, and the Greek novels depict a virtual city that accompanied the Persian army:

> It is customary for the King himself and the Persian nobility, when they go off to war, to take along with them their wives and children and gold and silver and clothing and eunuchs and concubines and dogs and dining-room furniture and their costly treasures and luxuries. (Chariton 6.9)[4]

The enormity of the army, now on the move, is conveyed in a "cinematic" way—"like a swarm of locusts, like the sand of the earth" (see also the commentary on 10:10).

■ 2:21–28

The massing of troops and peoples is a prelude to the unleashing of this force on those nations, like Israel, who had refused to ally with Nebuchadnezzar. The geographical details help paint a vivid picture of nations, some major kingdoms, crushed in quick succession, indicating even more dramatically the seriousness of Holofernes's threat. How could Israel possibly resist? As many orders of the army have been mentioned, now many kinds of conquest are as well, a drumbeat to communicate the sense of a plague of locusts upon the land.

The superfluity of terms is the novella genre's stock-in-trade. Holofernes's actual campaign is not described as Thucydides or even 1 Kings would describe it, a series of military stratagems and maneuvers, but in the imaginative language of the oral or literary storyteller. The Alexander Romance will be a more natural comparison, as here, when Nectanebo perceives the threat of an army descending upon Egypt:

> It is not just one nation that is advancing upon us, but millions of people. Advancing on us are Indians, Nokimaians, Oxydrakai, Iberians, Kauchones, Lelapes, Bosporoi, Bastranoi, Azanoi, Chalybes, and all the other great nations of the East, armies of innumerable warriors advancing against Egypt. (1.2)[5]

Interesting to note is that the invasion referenced here is that of Artaxerxes III Ochus, the very same that may have provided the model for the invasion in Judith.

There are two series of peoples and places encountered here, a more distant set (vv. 21–27) and a closer set (v. 28). In the distant set are:

Nineveh
Plain of Bectileth
Cilicia
hill country
Put and Lud
Rassisites
Ishmaelites
Cheleon

---

4   Translation of B. P. Reardon in *Collected Ancient Greek Novels*, 100.

5   Translation of Stoneman, *Alexander Romance*, 36.

Euphrates
Mesopotamia
Wadi Abron
Cilicia
Japheth
Arabia
Midianites
plain of Damascus

Some of the sites are unknown or improbably presented. The plain of Bectileth is unknown, but here is located north of Upper Cilicia.[6] Rassisites are unknown, as are Cheleon and Wadi Abron.[7] Japheth, located near Arabia, is unknown in this context, although in Genesis 10 Japheth is the progenitor of Europeans. Put and Lud are uncertain sites, although in the primeval genealogies and table of nations in Genesis 10 Put is used for Libya (Gen 10:6), and Lud for a people of North Africa (Gen 10:13) or Lydia (Gen 10:22; also Isa 66:19). Put and Lud are mentioned together in Jer 46:9; Ezek 27:10; and 30:5. Ishmaelites and Midianites are archaizing but are mentioned together in Gen 37:28, 36. The plain of Damascus is difficult placed after Japheth, if the latter is near Arabia. The progression of the campaign is often as tortured as the fantasy place-names would suggest. Gruen sums up the problem thus:

> Holofernes' men must have trekked about three hundred miles from Nineveh to Cilicia in just three days, crossed and recrossed the Euphrates three times, entered Cilicia twice, and approached the Palestinian coast both by way of Damascus and through Arabia![8]

Why would the list include bygone and invented cities? Some scholars have labored to disentangle this jumble. Moore, for instance, corrects the itinerary by moving 2:25 to follow immediately after 2:21.[9] But such efforts seem to be missing the nature of the text. Like the *Alexander Romance*, the entertainment lives elsewhere than in a reasonable history of a military

engagement. "Nebuchadnezzar, king of the Assyrians" can be depicted sending his troops over the world in any arrangement the author and audience like. Yet one "*oikoumenē*-view" effect—viewing the campaign as though from an objective historical point of view—is to make the non-Israelite nations as sympathetic as Israel—temporarily! There is an assertion of fictionality in this, and it also presents pseudo-realistic local color. The effect is to conjure a list of bygone cities, the land as it would have been six hundred years earlier, at the same time that it mixes even earlier names. Mixing real historical cities and invented sites works perfectly to suggest this chronotope.

The quick and consistent repetition of Holofernes's acts of destruction is also carried largely in the action verbs: *destroyed* the cities, *seized* the territory, *killed* those who resisted, *burned* tents, *plundered* sheepfolds, *burned* fields, *destroyed* flocks and herds, *sacked* cities, *ravaged* lands, *killed* young men. This may be contrasted, for example, with the brevity of 2 Kgs 3:19, 25. In particular, in Judith *patassō* ("strike down") becomes a leitmotif (2:27; 5:12; 6:3; 9:3, 10; 16:6), as Israelites are struck and strike back. In all, there are twenty-one aorist indicatives in seven verses. The destruction carried out by Holofernes's army is also in keeping with the Israelite *ḥērem* and the theory of just war in the Hebrew Bible (see the excursus at 15:6–7: "Revenge, Vengeance, Vindication, and Plunder").

Holofernes's brutal treatment of other peoples and their gods and temples does not reflect the author's concern for their plight but merely demonstrates graphically what awaits Israel. A similar verbal effect will be deployed when Judith takes her revenge at the beheading of Holofernes (see the commentary on 13:6–10a). Gera notes the collection of verbs here as well and points out a possible influence on this description: Assyrian royal inscriptions. She quotes Sennacherib's First Campaign against Merodach-baladan, verbs in italics:

---

6   On the various spellings, see the textual notes.
7   But note Rossus, near Issus (Strabo 14.5.19), and for Cheleon, cf. Ruth 1:2, 5; 4:9. A textual variant is Chaldeans. See also C. J. Ball, "Judith," in Henry Wace, ed., *The Holy Bible: Apocrypha* (London: J. Murray, 1888), 241–360, here 276–77.
8   Gruen, *Diaspora*, 163.
9   Moore, *Judith*, 137–39; see also Stummer, *Geographie*, 23–27; and Otzen, *Tobit and Judith*, 88–89.

In my wrath, I *made* a fierce assault. . . . I *slaughtered* their warriors round about its wall like sheep and *took* the city. . . . I *raged* like a lion; I *stormed* like the flood. . . . I *defeated* them and *shattered* his forces. . . . With my own hands I *took* them alive as captives. I myself *seized* the chariots, wagons, horses, mules, asses, dromedaries. . . . I *besieged*, I *conquered*, I *plundered*.[10]

One can imagine that royal inscriptions similar to this would have fired the imaginations of the author and the audience of Judith, although the third-person description in Judith provides a more visual experience, again, from an objective narrative point of view. It is not the voice of a grandiose sovereign who speaks in Judith, but the entertaining narrator, turning faux-history into adventure. The images of conquest will also be indirectly referenced in 3:1–4, when the nations remaining turn over their people and property to the king.

This discourse conjures the Assyrian conquest of Israel as told in a poetic way by Isa 10:27–32, which lists what were likely at the time of Judith known and unknown towns. Just as peoples and places proliferate in the Isaiah passage, so also topographical categories, with a constantly changing range of topographical settings in this campaign—mountains, plains, and seacoasts.[11] To be sure, some of these would have reflected recent memories of campaigns. In summarizing the history of the battles between the Seleucids and Ptolemies, Paul Kosmin writes:

> Military contest between the Seleucid and Ptolemaic houses—the kings of the north and the kings of the south, in the cipher of Daniel 11—played out along the coastlands of Asia Minor and for control of the southern Levant. Even after the generation-long Wars of Succession that had broken up Alexander's empire, six Ptolemaic-Seleucid conflicts, collectively known as

the Syrian Wars, were fought between the 270s and 160s BCE, and inter-dynastic tensions continued to seek military resolution throughout the second and early first centuries BCE.[12]

The campaigns along the coast would indeed have scarred Judea's memory, but the imaginary aspects must also be noted, as when Bethulia is located at a mountain pass where none existed. Our text also often mentions the highlands (1:6; 2:22; 4:7; 5:1, 3, 5, 15, 19; 6:7, 11; 7:1, 18; 10:13; 11:2; 15:2–3, 5, 7), where the Maccabees had taken refuge during their guerrilla campaign, and so the combination of real and imagined campaigns and battlefields creates a "story land."[13]

The simple narrative of Holofernes crushing all the nations will be revised as we proceed. Holofernes slays by the sword, but he will famously die by the sword. Some nations will be raised up as collaborator nations—such as the Ammonites and Moabites, traditional enemies of Israel—and some will begin as opponents of Assyria but will fall away in weakness and join the alliance, effectively leaving only Israel to oppose him.

■ **2:28** Holofernes's progress stops at the seacoast, although in 1:9–10 the list of nations affected included Egypt. A new, closer set of cities is now listed, the coastal cities that lay near Judea. Five were well known in Israelite tradition: Sidon and Tyre, Jamnia (= Yavneh, or Yabneel in Josh 15:11), Azotus (= Ashdod), and Ascalon (= Ashkelon). Sur and Ocina are unknown.[14] The known cities would have been rough equivalents and even competitors with Judea, part of the traditional "nations roundabout." The motif of "nations roundabout" is, however, uniformly negative in Judith, contrasting as it does with the unity, clarity, and integrity of the Israelites, even those residing in Samaria! It is also used in Exod 12:38 and perhaps Num 11:4 in a more ironic way: even Israel of the exodus included a mixed crowd.[15] Sidon and

---

10 Gera, *Judith*, 153, quoting *COS*, 2:119A, lines 20–50. Gera also mentions the much shorter Esth 3:13 and 8:11.

11 Gera, *Judith*, 153.

12 Paul Kosmin, "Hellenistic Period," in Klawans and Wills, *Jewish Annotated Apocrypha*.

13 Ben-Eliyahu, *Between Borders*, chap. 4 on Judith and 1 Maccabees.

14 Sur may be another name for Tyre (so Stummer,

Geographie, 6, 28), but the latter was just mentioned; Moore rightly concludes that it is unknown (*Judith*, 39–44, 47). See also Sidnie White Crawford, "Ocina," *NIDB* 4:319.

15 "Mixed multitude" (*'ēreb rab*, Exod 12:38) is applied to Egyptians in Jer 25:20; to Chaldeans in Jer 50:37; Neh 13:3. Cf. also Judg 6:12; 7:12; Nah 3:15, 17; Joel 1:6; 2:4–5. Herodotus 7.55 uses a similar expression of the mixed ethnicities of Xerxes's army, but

Tyre, Phoenician cities, were descendants of the Canaanites. They could still be viewed with historical suspicion (Matt 11:21) but were sometimes viewed more neutrally (Neh 13:16, 20), while Ashdod could sometimes be treated like one of the historically despised nations (Neh 13:23–25). Outside nations were not depicted with consistency in Israel, despite modern assumptions on this issue.[16] It is important to note also that at the time of the writing of Judith, John Hyrcanus had likely expanded Israel to include Azotus and Jamnia, while Sidon, Tyre, and Ascalon remained independent.

"Fear and trembling" also fall on the people here, highlighted twice. It is a leitmotif of the book, building in the first half and finally resolved in 15:2, when Judith will cause "fear and trembling" to fall on the Assyrians, and also in the dramatic last line of the book: "No one was able to strike terror among the Israelites while Judith was alive, nor for a long time afterwards."[17] It is a biblical motif, specifically an exodus motif of the mighty acts of God.[18] It is also one of the ways that our author conjures the feel of Judges and Kings.

Verse 28 also functions as a sort of coda on the destruction arc of the story, probably connoting the completeness of the cities affected,[19] and it also provides one of the well-placed pauses in the first half of the book (see §3 above):

action	action	action	action	dialogue	action
pause	pause	pause	pause	pause	pause
1:16	2:28	3:10	4:13	6:21	7:32

---

it is not clear that it is meant negatively there as it sometimes is in the Bible. See Judith Lieu, "Not Hellenes but Philistines? The Maccabees and Josephus Defining the 'Other,'" *JJS* 53 (2002) 246–63. Moore rightly dismisses the theory that the absence of Gaza from the list suggests a dating after Alexander Jannaeus destroyed it in 96 CE (*Judith*, 139–41); that would be pressing the text to an overly specific set of references. That Jamnia and Azotus are not under Israelite control has suggested to some that our work should be dated before the conquest of those cities by Alexander Jannaeus, but this is also too specific; see §2 above.

16 Wills, *Not God's People*, 21–52.
17 Craven, *Artistry and Faith*, 54.
18 Exodus 15:15–16, recounted by Rahab in Josh 2:9; cf. also Gen 9:2; Deut 2:25.
19 Moore, *Judith*, 139–41.

Text	Textual Notes
1/ They sent envoys to him suing for peace, saying, **2/** "We, slaves of Nebuchadnezzar the great king, lie prostrate before you. Do with us as you please.ᵃ **3/** All our buildings, our entire region,ᵇ every wheat field, our flocks and herds, all the sheepfolds of our encampments lie before you; dispose of them as you please. **4/** Indeed, our cities and their inhabitants are your slaves. Come and deal with them as seems good in your eyes."	a Χρησαι . . . αρεστον lacking in S. b Και πας τοπος omitted by haplography in S, B, some minuscules. c For ανδρες: αγγελοι O OL Sy Arm. d For ορια, Sy reflects ιερα; Hanhart prefers ορια ("boundaries"), as *difficilior,* while Moore, *NETS,* NRSV, and Craven (*Artistry and Faith,* 77, 80–81) read shrines; cf. 4:1. e After αυτω: εν μυστεριω 58 OL-SB Sy; *ministerio* (from *misterio*) OL-QP; *in iuramentum* OL-G; *in sacramento* OL-R; *in sacra regis* OL-X. See Bogaert, "Version latine," 189. Since this aspect had not been mentioned before, "in secret" was perhaps understood as his added, private command.
5/ The menᶜ came before Holofernes and told him all this, **6/** and he and his army came down to the coast and stationed garrisons in all of the fortified cities, taking from them picked troops as auxiliaries. **7/** They and the entire surrounding areas welcomed him with garlands, dancing, and tambourines. **8/** He demolished all their shrinesᵈ and cut down their sacred groves, for heᵉ had been commissioned to destroy all of the gods of the land, so that every nation should worship Nebuchadnezzar alone, and all the languages and their tribes should call upon him as a god.ᶠ **9/** He then proceeded toward Esdraelon, near Dothan, which is opposite the great ridgeᵍ of Judea,ʰ **10/** and pitched camp between Gebaⁱ and Scythopolis. There they remained for a whole month in order to gather all of the supplies for his army.	f Οπως + subjunctive without αν occurs often in the LXX. g For πριων ("serrated ridge"), Fritzsche (*Die Bücher Tobi und Judith,* 143) perceives a misreading of Hebrew *myšwr* ("plain"); cf. Isa 10:15. Translations normally retain "ridge." Corley ("Septuagintalisms," 94) prefers the suggestion of Hanhart (66): πρεωνος was the original reading, from πρεων ("headland," or Mount Carmel), and was taken as πριονος by itacism. h For Ιουδαια: Idumea OL-MC; see the excursus at 3:5-10, "The 'Nations Roundabout'"; and cf. 2:12. i For Gaibai: Taiban A 542 Eth, by exchange of G and T (Hanhart, Praef 26); dictation of Gaibai kai Skythōn evidently also resulted in Libdaa Scitorum OL-M and Tabescestaran OL-X; also, *L* often changes names to known LXX traditions: Gebal; cf. Deut 11:29 (so Hanhart, *Text und Textgeschichte,* 50).

Commentary

3:1–10

Chapters 1–4 construct a large world stage on which many known and some unknown nations are swept up into world politics. The actions of the Assyrians and the nations who join or oppose them ultimately bring the focus "to the west,"[1] and the swirl of nations then gradually narrows to the region of Judea. Jerusalem was first mentioned in 1:9 and Judea in 1:12, mere footnotes to the blur of nations caught up in a world war. The author perpetuates this literary conceit by including Judea in the list of nations here at the end of the first stage of the campaign, as if an afterthought, while the audience knows it to be the true focus.

■ 3:1-4

Despite the rising narrative tension concerning the impending slaughter, the campaign occurs as a surprisingly quick takeover. The army of Assyria and its allies is so vast that no one resists. The nations sue for peace

---

1 The LXX assumes that the attack came from the north (4:6; 8:21; 11:14, 19), while the Vg assumes from the south; so Moore, *Judith,* 47, 141–42.

using the same images that were just described in Holofernes's scorched-earth campaign (2:26–27). Those surrendering present themselves now as slaves of Nebuchadnezzar. In classical Greek political theory, citizens are free, and there was suspicion of the elevated notion of kingship in the east, but in the east all could be called slaves of the great king. Only the king is a free man (Herodotus 7.103; Xenophon, *Anabasis* 1.9.29).[2] Even Holofernes (6:3) accepts his status as a slave of Nebuchadnezzar, and Judith, although dissembling (11:5), introduces herself as a slave of Holofernes.

The formulas of courtly submission here are not just literary coloring. They are, first, fairly typical expressions of fealty of a smaller nation to a greater; and, second, they contribute to the political theme of Judith.[3] Yet there is a comical overstatement found in the repetition, again, contrasted with the nations' former rashness in contemning Nebuchadnezzar. The categories of humiliation recall those listed in Holofernes's conquest above in 2:24–27.

■ **3:5–10**

Holofernes was bent on annihilation but is appeased for the moment by the new allies. It was not unknown for cities to welcome liberating armies, as many had welcomed Cyrus of Persia (see Isa 45:1–8), but here the acquiescence is not the celebration of a new liberator; rather, it is a desperate resignation to the power of Nebuchadnezzar. Coastal cities, which had been important sites in the Syrian Wars of the Ptolemies and Seleucids (see chap. 2), figure prominently here. Our author emphasizes that the other nations, many contemporary with Hasmonean Judea, capitulated and groveled. Although in 1:11 the peoples of the entire region blithely spurned Nebuchadnezzar's demands for an alliance, here in defeat they throw themselves on his mercy. Where they had formerly underestimated Nebuchadnezzar, here they overestimate him and capitulate with speed and determination, treating Nebuchadnezzar as the god that he will claim to be (3:8).

A contrast is drawn throughout between the weakness of other peoples and the humble strength of the Israelites (chaps. 4, 7). Although the Israelites were not smug when they earlier refused Nebuchadnezzar's demands, over the next chapters they will be unwilling to capitulate when the Assyrian army arrives. Israel's double response represents a form of wisdom in the face of great empires. In Greece, the Two Ways tradition—the easy path of vice versus the difficult path of virtue—was treated many times, for instance, in Hesiod, *Works and Days* 286–92, Prodicus on Heracles, and Life of Aesop 94.

The description here is also a characterization by means of contrast, the stock-in-trade of popular art (see §7 above). To be sure, the prophets had recorded both sorts of responses, the resistance of Isaiah 7 and the acquiescence of Jeremiah 29, and even the Bethulians, left to their own devices, will consider surrender (8:9–27). But even at that low point, they are depicted as stronger than the nations roundabout. We should note as well that "Israel" is represented not by the elders in Bethulia but by the high priest Joakim in Jerusalem (see the commentary on 4:6–7), who remains steadfast throughout.

Excursus: The "Nations Roundabout"

In 2:23–27 Holofernes destroyed the peoples who were at a distance from Judea, but closer neighbors are listed in 2:28: Sidon, Tyre, Sur, Ocina, Jamnia, Ashdod, and Ashkelon—mainly Phoenician cities along the eastern coast of the Mediterranean. After establishing garrisons in the fortified cities, Holofernes conscripts their "picked men," and "they and the entire surrounding areas welcomed him with garlands, dancing, and tambourines" (3:7). The Assyrian army, already huge, is now swelled further from these cooperating peoples. This corresponds to the traditional understanding in Israel that far-off nations were not necessarily viewed negatively, but the close neighbors, supposedly descended from the Canaanites and other nations on the land at the time of the conquest, were viewed as perpetual enemies. This expands the threat against Judea but also inserts other nations into the crucial deliberations of Holofernes that will arise in chap. 5. The literary effect should not be overlooked: Judea is threatened not only by a great foreign empire and its allies but also by the smaller nations roundabout. They are

---

2   Gera, *Judith*, 159.
3   So Reiterer, "Religion und hellenistische Realpolitik, " 37–38. Cf. the biblical phrase *kĕṯôb bĕ'ênêkā*.

perhaps even more to be condemned, because, while at first they acted haughtily in rejecting Nebuchadnezzar, now they capitulate readily and join the larger threat against Judea.

Just as the book of Judith idealizes an ancient Israel with its united boundaries, it also taps into a traditional view of the nations roundabout as Canaanites, whom the Israelites were commanded by God to exterminate, even though they did not complete the task (Deut 7:1–2; Judg 2:1–4). The phrase "the nations roundabout" (*haggôyîm missābîb,* Joel 4:12 and similar phrases) appears in different senses—sometimes neutral, sometimes negative, sometimes eschatological—but in Hasmonean political ideology it is generally negative: the surrounding small nations conspire against Israel in 1 Macc 5:1–2.[4] In Judith, the small nations roundabout nurse a particular animus against Israel and are increasingly limited to Ammon, Moab, and Edom, the main instigators against Israel, though this must come into focus slowly, as it would be too obvious a reference to Israelite enemies to focus on them from the beginning.[5] These nations are not just a part of Holofernes's army but want to lead the attack (Judith 5). They will be defeated in 15:3. Such an awareness of the threat of the neighboring peoples in some of the contemporaneous texts is reflected in the reference to those who would harass or oppress (ṣrr) Israel: Ezra 4:1 (compare Esth 7:4; 8:1; 9:10, 24).

Most modern readings of the biblical view of other nations assume a simple dualism of Israel and Other: all gentiles are equally suspect. But a variety of views are found, and we may note three types of outsiders:

1. Great empires such as Egypt, Assyria, or even Babylon, who were not considered *necessarily* evil but, rather, imperial "realities" on the horizon, with which Israel might be forced to engage either in warfare or alliance, or who might rule Israel temporarily. Babylon, a relative newcomer to ancient Near Eastern politics, became exceptional in that it remained a *symbol* of tyranny over Israel—Nebuchadnezzar is the enemy in our story—but it was theoretically just another empire, and the history of the relations could conceivably have been different.

2. Ancient peoples who were supposedly occupying the land that Israel was destined to occupy after the exodus: Canaanites and others, often in lists such as "Hittites, Girgashites, Amorites, Canaanites, Perizzites, Hivites, and Jebusites" (Deut 7:1; cf. Jdt 5:16). These smaller nations *in this land* were continually marked as perpetual enemies, unlike category 1, the great empires *not on the land*. By the time of the first temple, "Canaanites" was already an ancient name for the enemy nations on the land whom the Israelites supposedly defeated and expelled in the conquest. The names for these peoples were also anachronistic, or even legendary.[6]

3. Contemporaneous, real nations who were considered by Israel to be the *descendants* of those eternal enemies: Ammonites, Moabites, and Edomites, and the Phoenician cities. These were the contemporaneous nations roundabout for Israel, and in Judith they carry on the identity of the earlier evil nations.[7] At Qumran, the War Scroll refers to the army of Belial as composed of Edom, Moab, Ammon, Amalekites, Philistia, and the Kittim of Assur (1QM 1.1–3).

In the preexilic period, across the Jordan River from Israel were, north to south, Ammon, Moab, and Edom, small nations like Israel, in constant competition with it. According to Gen 19:37–38, Ammon and Moab were the offspring of Lot and his two daughters—born of incest. These nations were thus considered to have a polluted origin, and the relations with Israel remained combative. A stela erected by Mesha, king of Moab, in the ninth century depicts his battles with Israel and grants some perspective on the political and military struggles between Israel and the nations roundabout. Ammonites

---

4   S. Schwartz, "Israel and the Nations"; Daniel R. Schwartz, "The Other in 1 and 2 Maccabees," in Graham N. Stanton and Guy G. Stroumsa, eds., *Tolerance and Intolerance in Early Judaism and Christianity* (Cambridge: Cambridge University Press, 1998) 30–37.

5   The Phoenician (seacoast) cities were also—correctly—considered descendants of the Canaanites.

6   Wills, *Not God's People,* 21–51.

7   For Ammon and Moab see at 1:7–10, "The Sweep of Nations." Esau, the ancestor of Edomites, is first mentioned in 7:8. Despite the fact that these nations and the Phoenician cities are consistently seen as perpetual enemies, there are many passages in the Bible that describe political and economic, even alliance relations with these peoples—Deut 2:9; 1 Sam 22:3–4; 2 Samuel 10; 1 Kgs 11:7. Doron Mendels notes the mention in our novella of independent Moab, Ammon, Edomites, and argues for a date of composition for Judith of 140–134 BCE as a result (*Land of Israel,* 51–56), but this assumes too neat a relation between narrated events and the setting; the author of Judith archaizes and invents.

and Moabites threatened to invade Judah under Jehoshaphat (2 Chronicles 20), and the king's prayer perhaps influences Judith's in 9:11–14. Further, when the historical Nebuchadnezzar of Babylon attacked Judah, the Moabites and Ammonites were allied with him (2 Kgs 24:2).

Kosmin describes the difficult and competitive situation of small nations at the intersection of the Seleucid and Ptolemaic kingdoms:

> It was the great misfortune of Judea and its immediate Levantine neighbors—though, of course, a familiar one—to find itself on this geopolitical fault-line, under disputed Ptolemaic domination for most of the third century BCE, and tottering Seleucid rule for much of the second. The consequences included the militarization of the landscape, the amplifying of rivalries within and between indigenous communities, a politics of unprecedented unpredictability and consequence, and, alas, the full gamut of economic exploitation and personal suffering that accompanied ancient warfare.[8]

By the Hellenistic period, then, Ammon had been overrun by the Nabateans, or Arabs; some overlap of terminology for Ammonites and Nabateans is the result (1 Macc 5:6). Josephus seems to call this people both Ammonites and Arabs, reflecting the rule of Nabateans, or Arabs, over them (*Ant.* 1.11.5 §206; 14.1.4 §18). Although the Nabateans had at first allied with the Hasmoneans, they then opposed the Hasmoneans' encroachments and the annexations of Idumean/Nabatean lands.

Edomites were understood to be descendants of Esau, the child of Hagar. In Gen 25:22–33 Esau struggles with Jacob and ultimately loses his birthright; they part company but remain both near each other and mutually apprehensive. In 1 Esdr 4:45 the Edomites are particularly blamed for burning the temple (cf. Obad 11–14; Ps 137:7). The ancient animosity explains the history of conflict between Israel and the Edomites. In our period, they are known as Idumeans. To the east the Nabateans had swallowed them up, as well as the Ammonites and Moabites, to render the groups almost indistinguishable, even though the geographical designation "Ammon" continued in use. Within the boundaries of expanded Israel, they were forcibly converted by John Hyrcanus. After the period of the writing of Judith, Herod, whose father was an Idumean convert to Judaism, joined Rome in attacking the Nabateans. With Moab and Edom, therefore, our novella is utilizing older terms.

■ **3:7** The description of the reception of Holofernes might have seemed similar to Alexander's reception when he conquered Babylon (Curtius Rufus 5.1.17–23) or Cyrus's before him (Cyrus Cylinder). Gera notes the interesting distinction between the Cyrus Cylinder and this depiction of Nebuchadnezzar: Cyrus boasted of reestablishing local shrines, not destroying them.[9] The Assyrian and Babylonian kings had often destroyed the temples of subject peoples, while Cyrus's revolutionary policy was to rule through relative local autonomy. Alexander, like Cyrus, encouraged the continuation of local shrines, a policy his successors normally followed. It is important to note, however, how artificially this fictitious Nebuchadnezzar operates: his language is not that of former imperial practices but that of God's demands in the Hebrew Bible. For our story, the nature of the celebrations is also significant: garlands, dances, and tambourines will be part of the Israelite celebration at the end (see the commentary on 15:12–13). Such celebrations are common in the Hebrew Bible; note especially Exodus 15; Judg 11:34; 1 Sam 18:6–7; 1 Chr 13:8; and Ps 149:3.

■ **3:8** Aside from the bloodless change of empires described here (unlike 2:23–27), there is also a ritual marking of a new religious arrangement. Holofernes's only destruction in these cities is of religious institutions: he destroys the shrines and sacred groves. We may perceive here the Greek Two Ways tradition noted above: in trading their religious freedom for peace with Holofernes, the cities of the coast have chosen the easy road to slavery rather than the difficult path to freedom. Are the sacred groves simply a general reference to sacred outdoor precincts common throughout the Greek world, or does it also conjure up the condemnations found in the Hebrew Bible of the wooden poles used in the worship of Asherah (1 Kgs 14:15; 2 Kgs 18:4)? Here the author assumes an *oikoumenē*-wide view, a paternalistic but fair-minded sympathy for the polytheistic practices of the surrounding nations. Jews often engaged in

---

8   Kosmin, "Hellenistic Period."
9   Gera, *Judith*, 162; *COS* 2:124.

the Hellenistic anthropology of the period, sometimes expressing either a benevolent affirmation of others' religious institutions or, alternatively, a sense that Jewish practices were *viewed* as sectarian, divisive, even antisocial.[10] The threat to others' sacred precincts is here also perceived as a threat to the Jerusalem temple, clearer in the language in 4:1–4. The contemporaneous 2 Maccabees can also be described as "temple propaganda," motivated throughout by the theme of the protection of the Jerusalem temple.[11] The book of Judith assumes this perspective as well.

But we consider again the two-level view of history, one fanciful and one real. Holofernes is depicted as cruel and heartless, but Judith herself will later beam proudly about Israel's history of destroying offending altars (8:18–20). During a period roughly contemporaneous with the writing of Judith, the Hasmoneans under John Hyrcanus destroyed the Samaritan temple on Mount Gerizim. Although the removal of a rival temple was the motive here, the view may have prevailed that there was no suppression of the Samaritan way of life in general because they were Israelites (Josephus, *Antiquities* 13.9.1 §256). There were, however, probably destruction of sacred shrines and the introduction of

observant Jewish populations. This evidently occurred in the city of Gezer and in the area of Jerusalem known as the Akra (1 Macc 13:47–53). The Idumeans within the Hasmonean-controlled lands were defeated by Judah the Maccabee in 164 BCE and in about 120 were forced to convert under John Hyrcanus, and the Itureans were forced to convert in 103 under Aristobulus.[12] During hostilities, an ultimatum of convert or die was delivered to the residents of Hellenistic Pella (Josephus, *Antiquities* 13.15.4 §397). The immediate function of this passage, however, is rather that Holofernes's destruction of local sacred precincts will threaten Israel as well.

Excursus: Worship of Nebuchadnezzar and Danielic Motifs

The peoples have surrendered unconditionally to Holofernes, but he proceeds to destroy their shrines and sacred groves and demands that they worship Nebuchadnezzar as god, a demand that will later be repeated in the challenge, "What god is there except Nebuchadnezzar?" (6:2).[13] These steps were not specified by Nebuchadnezzar in 2:14–16 (see also the commentary on 1:11), but here we are told that he had ordered them to be carried out by his only-too-willing general.[14] For the author of Judith, Nebuchadnezzar's motives are not so much world

---

10 In general, see Gruen, *Diaspora*; John J. Collins, *Between Athens and Jerusalem: Jewish Identity in the Hellenistic Diaspora* (2nd ed.; Bible Resource Series; Grand Rapids: Eerdmans, 2000); Weitzman, *Surviving Sacrilege*; Malka Z. Simkovich, *The Making of Jewish Universalism: From Exile to Alexandria* (Lanham, MD: Lexington, 2017). On Jewish protection, and even founding, of polytheistic institutions, see Artapanus, *On Moses*; and also Aristeas. On the awareness of others' perception and condemnation of Jewish exceptionalism, cf. Esther and Greek Esther; and Josephus, *Against Apion* 2.29 §§209–10; 2.37 §§258–59 on *amixia*. Despite the biblical origin of the motif of the destruction of images, it is also attested for other cultures.

11 Robert Doran, *Temple Propaganda: The Purpose and Character of 2 Maccabees* (CBQMS 12; Washington, DC: Catholic Biblical Association of America, 1981).

12 There is some ambiguity about the forced conversions. Concerning the ultimatum of conversion, Josephus (*Antiquities* 13.15.4 §397) says that non-Jews could convert or be expelled; Strabo, *Geographica* 16.2.34 says Idumeans converted by

choice. See also *Antiquities* 15.7.9 §§253–58. See also §2 above on scholars who question the extent of the forced conversions.

13 Gera seems to say that Holofernes rebuffs the pleas of the humiliated peoples, since he conscripted able soldiers and destroyed their shrines (*Judith*, 160); however, it seems more accurate to say that he accepted their statements of loyalty while imposing the further stringent pacification. Yet note that Holofernes's actions here are described by *exolethreuō* ("destroy utterly"), a strong verb used in 1:15 and later in 5:15 in regard to Israel's defeat of the Amorites (see also 6:2). The promise to wipe a people from the face of the earth is elsewhere attributed only to God (Gen 6:7; Deut 6:15; 1 Kgs 9:7); see Gera, *Judith*, 222. Holofernes will also strike them, *patassō*, as Achior said that God struck the Egyptians (5:12).

14 That Holofernes derives so much of his identity from his devotion to his king is probably perceived as a weakness, an aspect of eastern court hierarchy treated negatively by Greeks and by Jews (see the excursus at 8:35, "The Book of Judith and Greek Philosophy").

domination as revenge: he does not seek *vindication* as Israel does (see 2:21–28), but *vengeance* as a result of being spurned.[15] He is also motivated by a divine pretension that is ridiculed by Jews.[16]

The outlawing of a religion, especially the religion of a recognized people, was very rare in the ancient world. Since polytheism assumed a harmony of the many gods of many peoples, religious persecution was not generally employed as a means of pacification. Killing a king and his sons and deporting the elite families was typical. Despite the brutal and destructive policies of the Assyrians and Babylonians, they did not require that conquered subjects worship their god, or worship the king as sole god, and neither did the Persians. By destroying other cults, Nebuchadnezzar establishes himself as an imperial Yahweh imitator: one world, one king, one god.[17] The king sets up a requirement for reverence to himself that is a threat to all faithful Jews. Ironically, the uniqueness of Nebuchadnezzar as god is even more "monotheistic" than Judith's later claim about the God of Israel, who is merely the *greatest* god.[18] It is also ironic that here Jews seem to be the protectors of others' shrines and religious cult (cf. Artapanus, *On Moses*).

In the Near East, from a very early period, there was a cult of kings as divine. Even the king of Israel was installed as the son of God (Ps 2:7). This continued under Greeks and Romans, but mainly as an *eastern* phenomenon; in the West, there was strong suspicion of that notion, which Herodotus commented on (1.204; 2.169; 7.10). By the Hellenistic period there often obtained a "hybrid iconography" of kings in the East rendered as gods; a king is something "resembling the divine" (*hoti theomimon enti pragma*, Stobaeus 4.7.61). Images were promulgated of Antiochus I of Commagene or Philip of Macedon, both considered *synthronos* with Olympian gods.[19] Yet in popular literature a differentiation of East and West was sometimes still imposed. A variant reading in Alexander Romance 1.26 (γ-text) has Darius threaten Alexander:

> The power of monarchy has been granted by god to Darius alone—and what god is there besides Darius, who has become lord of all that is below heaven by virtue of his limitless might?[20]

By the time of Judith's composition, Jews were more or less in agreement with traditional western Greek views that kings were not to be invested with divinity.[21]

The book of Judith introduces an interesting complexity in the depiction of Nebuchadnezzar. At the beginning, we saw him acting as a real king, enacting decisive battle plans. Afterward, however, he is replaced by Holofernes. The general describes his king with terms associated elsewhere with God, but Nebuchadnezzar himself "makes no direct claims to divinity and we do not see him actually usurping the power of God. . . . [I]t is his underling and chief commander Holofernes who demands that Nebuchad-

---

15 The Babylonian propaganda for Nebuchadnezzar's reign should not be overlooked. In the Wadi Brissa inscription, the tree of Babylon and the gathering of many nations are seen positively: "Under Babylon's everlasting shadow, I have gathered all the people in peace." See Langdon, *Building Inscriptions*, part 1, pp. 171–72, B. Col. VIII lines 17–35, 45–50.

16 Reiterer, "Religion und hellenistische Realpolitik," 39.

17 See also the commentary on 11:21–23, and see Otzen, *Tobit and Judith*, 120–21. Gera also notes that, although the religious persecution of Antiochus IV Epiphanes lies behind this narrative, there was a deeper background to the destruction of cult sites (*Judith*, 221). King Sennacherib of the Assyrians destroyed cult sites in Babylon in 682 BCE, hauling away the cult statue of Bel-Marduk. These actions of Sennacherib seem typical of the ancient Near Eastern struggle of empires, but note also the speeches of his general, Rabshakeh. His speech, as reported in 2 Kings 18 // Isaiah 36, is very similar to passages in Judith.

18 See Haag, *Studien*, 23–25; Voitila, "Deuteronomistic Heritage," 372–76.

19 Arthur Darby Nock noted that it is "impossible to know sometimes whether [the king] and the god in question were treated as separate entities" ("*Synnaos Theos*," HSCP 41 [1930] 1–62, here 12). See also Drew J. Strait, "The Wisdom of Solomon, Ruler Cults, and Paul's Polemic against Idols in the Areopagus Speech," *JBL* 106 (2017) 609–32; B. Schmidt-Dounas, "Statuen hellenistischer Könige als Synnaoi Theoi," *Egnatia* 4 (1993–1994) 71–141.

20 Translation of Stoneman, *Alexander Romance*, 165.

21 Biblical "monotheism" has traditionally been seen in Isa 45:5, although many now nuance this aspect; see Saul M. Olyan, "Is Isaiah 40–55 Really Monotheistic?" *JANES* 12 (2012) 190–201. Similar is opposition to foreign claims of kings-as-gods, e.g., Ezek 28:1–10.

nezzar be worshipped to the exclusion of all other deities."[22] By his separation from the story, Nebuchadnezzar becomes a king in absentia, a remote, semidivine figure, while Holofernes is very human. The author's earlier depiction of Nebuchadnezzar as a real king at war ensures that he will not be viewed as the equivalent of God. Holofernes may be foolish enough to elevate the king to semidivine status, but the audience knows better. But, although Nebuchadnezzar and God are both elevated above the plains of combat, they remain characters nevertheless.[23]

The view expressed here by Nebuchadnezzar and Holofernes can be traced to three sets of influences: (1) the Danielic depiction of kings; (2) a transformation of the demands of the God of Israel; and (3) the religious persecution of Antiochus IV Epiphanes, who outlawed the ritual practices of the worship of the God of Israel and presented himself as a god. Although other personae may have influenced the characterization of Nebuchadnezzar, his representation in Judith seems largely based on the book of Daniel.[24] In general, the blustery Babylonian kings in Daniel 1–5 provide the pattern for Judith's Nebuchadnezzar/Holofernes team. First, in Daniel 1, Nebuchadnezzar is matched but contrasted with God. In vv. 1–2 the Babylonian king is said to come to Jerusalem (bô') while God gave (nātan) the king of Judah into his hand.[25] Second, in Dan 2:38, Nebuchadnezzar is allowed by God—temporarily—to provide protection to the animals, a point that is repeated ironically by Judith in 11:17. In addition, in Daniel 3, Nebuchadnezzar requires worship of a golden statue, while in Daniel 6 the courtiers persuade Darius to declare an edict that no one may pray to anyone, human or divine, except the king. Not only is the king here placed in the role of a counter-Yahweh (by the other courtiers as much as by the king himself), but in both Judith and Daniel the various peoples and languages of the land are strongly emphasized (cf. Jdt 3:7; Dan 4:1; see §7 above). Might the audience have seen Judith as a *fictional* play on the *historical* situation in Daniel 1–6? Perhaps, although Daniel 1–6 was likely considered

fictional in its original performance situation, and only later, after being folded into the more serious historical references of Daniel 7–12, assimilated to "history."

Yet some significant differences can be observed in Daniel. First, the foreign king may require veneration, but there is no discussion of destroying other shrines (though cf. Dan 6:6–7). Second, the kings—even Nebuchadnezzar!—in Daniel 1–6 and Bel are less active in persecuting the Jewish religion than are the other courtiers. Third, at the same time that Daniel can depict the Babylonian king as a blustery tyrant, the latter also comes to confess Daniel's God (Dan 2:46–47; 3:28–29; 4:1–3, 34–37). Also different is the greater space that Judith allows for the issues to develop slowly and to be conducted through the personages of Nebuchadnezzar's general, Holofernes, and his eunuch, Bagoas.

The second influence on the characterization of Nebuchadnezzar is the historical memory of Alexander and Antiochus IV Epiphanes. First Maccabees, for instance, begins:

> After Alexander, son of Philip, the Macedonian, who came from the land of Kittim, had defeated Darius, king of the Persians and the Medes, he succeeded him as king. . . . Alexander fought many battles, conquered strongholds, and put to death the kings of the earth. He advanced to the ends of the earth, and plundered many nations. When the earth became quiet before him, he was exalted, and his heart was lifted up. He gathered a very strong army and ruled over countries, nations, and princes, and they became tributary to him. (1 Macc 1:1–4 NRSV modified)

First Maccabees 1:41–42 shares a similar view of Antiochus Epiphanes: "The king wrote to his whole kingdom that all should be one people and that all should give up their particular customs [*nomima*]" (NRSV).[26] Second Maccabees 5:21 and 9:8 attribute to Antiochius the pretension of thinking he could stride over the water and command the sea.[27]

---

22 Gera, *Judith*, 7.

23 Cf. 2:14–16, and 1:11–12 as a counter-Shema; and see Haag, *Studien*, 16; Gera, *Judith*, 146; Schmitz, *Gedeutete Geschichte*, 30–31; Voitila, "Deuteronomistic Heritage," 375–76.

24 Gera also perceives an influence of Pharaoh, Sennacherib, and the Babylonian Nebuchadnezzar of Jeremiah (*Judith*, 46–47, 296); see §4 above.

25 Carol A. Newsom, *Daniel: A Commentary* (OTL; Louisville: Westminster John Knox, 2014) 41.

26 Doron Mendels, *Memory in Jewish, Pagan and Christian Societies of the Graeco-Roman World* (LSTS 48; London: T&T Clark International, 2004) 44–53.

27 Cf. Job 26:11; Pss 18:16; 104:7; and see Debra Scoggins Ballentine, *The Conflict Myth and the Biblical Tradition* (New York: Oxford University Press, 2015) esp. 180–83.

Nebuchadnezzar's requirement in Judith thus finds a parallel in both the Seleucids' suppression of Jewish religion and in the Hasmoneans' program afterward of suppressing others' religious practices, including those of the Samarian Israelites. (This is one of the reasons for dating Judith to *late* second century rather than *mid*-century; see §1 above.)

The third influence on the characterization of Nebuchadnezzar is, as noted above at 1:11–12, the tradition of the demand for monolatry by the God of Israel. In Judith, the word *boulē* for "plan" (translating Hebrew *'ēṣâ*) is used only in regard to Nebuchadnezzar and God (2:2, 4; 8:16; see the commentary on 2:1–3). Nebuchadnezzar's commands to destroy sacred groves sound like God's similar demands concerning the centralization of worship in Israel, even the destruction of Israelite shrines (Exod 34:13–14; Deut 7:3; 12:3; 2 Kgs 23:14–15; Sir 36:5, 12 in Hebrew). They are surprisingly similar to God's demands in the covenantal passages in Deuteronomy (e.g., 6:1–3; cf. Josh 11:20), a comparison made even sharper in 6:2: "What God is there except Nebuchadnezzar?" In Judith 5, 8, and 9 Achior and Judith repeat the basic premises of Deuteronomic theology: if Israel obeys God's commandments, it will prosper; if it does not, it will fall. Nebuchadnezzar stands in the place of God in setting up a similar demand for a worldly kingdom. By drawing this parallel to satirize Nebuchadnezzar, the author of Judith inadvertently satirizes God for modern readers. And it is not only a modern sensibility; gnostic texts also took such statements by God as grounds to overturn reverence.

■ **3:9–10** Although many geographical entities are invented or incorrectly situated, some, especially those near Judea, are more accurately presented. The plain of Esdraelon (Greek for Jezreel) lies between the highlands of Galilee to the north and those of Samaria and Judea to the south (see commentary on 1:7–10). Geba, or Gaba, is likely Gilboa situated on the western end of the plain near the Mediterranean,[28] and Scythopolis is the Greek, and therefore anachronistic, name for Beth-shean on the eastern end near the Jordan River. Dothan (or Tel Dotha) lay to the south of the plain (Gen 37:17; 2 Kgs 6:13). Holofernes's army would have been amassed and waiting about forty miles north of Jerusalem, as he eyed the highland passes for a route to capture Jerusalem—even though the low hills are not a "great ridge," and hardly require a highland pass to transverse. It was also very near this spot that Jael was said to have slain Sisera, the closest biblical model for the actions of Judith.[29]

The size of the army is emphasized yet again by the need to gather the supply trains. The rest provides one of the regular pauses in the narrative (see 2:28). Highlands also figure prominently throughout our text, interestingly confused in the text tradition with borders because of the similarity of the Greek words.

---

28   Although Moore says it is unknown (*Judith*, 47).
29   Enslin, *Book of Judith*, 77.

4

Text

1/ When the Israelites living in Judea heard what Holofernes, the commander-in-chief of Nebuchadnezzar, king of the Assyrians, had done to the nations, and how he had plundered all their temples[a] and given them over to destruction, 2/ they were greatly terrified at his approach and very disturbed both for Jerusalem and for the temple of the Lord their God. 3/ They had indeed just returned from captivity; only recently had the people of Judea been gathered together again. Their sacred vessels, altar, and temple had just been consecrated after the profanation. 4/ So they sent word to every region of Samaria, Kona, Beth-horon, Belmain, and Jericho, to Choba, Aesora, and the valley of Salem,[b] 5/ and in advance of the attack[c] they took command of all the high hilltops, erecting fortifications around the villages on them. Their fields had just been harvested, so they stored away the crops as a preparation for war.

6/ Joakim,[d] the high priest, who was at that time in Jerusalem, wrote to the residents of Bethulia[e] and Betomesthaim,[f] which is near Esdraelon toward the plain near Dothan, 7/ and ordered them to take control of the passes into the high country, because entry into Judea was through them, and it would be easy to prevent any from passing through, since the approach was narrow, allowing only two men at a time to pass. 8/ The Israelites did as Joakim the high priest and the council of the entire people of Israel, in session in Jerusalem, had commanded.

9/ And every man of Israel cried out fervently to God, and humbled their souls with much fasting.[g] 10/ Then they and their wives, their young children, their cattle, and every resident alien, hired worker, and purchased slave all put sackcloth around their waists. 11/ And every man of Israel and every woman and the children residing in Jerusalem prostrated themselves before the temple and placed ashes on their heads and spread out their sackcloth before the Lord.[h] 12/ They even draped the altar with sackcloth, and all cried out fervently to the God of Israel with one voice not to give their babies over to capture nor their wives as plunder, nor to allow the cities of their inheritance[i] to be destroyed and the sanctuary profaned and disgraced, to become a laughingstock for the nations.

13/ So the Lord[j] heard their cry and had regard for their affliction. The people observed a fast for many days throughout Judea, and

a For ιερα: ορια A Eth minus, from 3:8; ειδωλα L; deos Sy.

b For variants of the place-names, see the commentary.

c Προκαταλαμβανω can mean "to occupy in advance as a military strategy," as in 2:10, but in the LXX it also translates *lākad* ("to seize or occupy"); cf. 7:1.

d For Iōakeim: Eliakeim O OL-MC Sy.

e The most likely original spelling is Βαιτυλουα, Baituloua, found in B. The English spelling derives from the Vg Bethulia. Minor variations include Baitoulia in S L OL, Betyloua in A V, Batyloua in 58 Arm, many arising from the lack of distinction in the vowel sounds. By comparison, Beth Horon in 4:4 is spelled Βαιθωρων, *Baithōrōn*. Batuloua was also attested in the third-century ostracon 999; see J. Schwartz, "Un fragment grec," 534–37. *Byt plō* in Sy reflects a sound similar to bapelua OL-X, but the latter could also result from misreading ΒΑΙΤΕΛΟΥΑ as ΒΑΠΕΛΟΥΑ; so Bogaert, "Version latine," 190.

f For Baitomesthaim: Bethomastel and similar OL-GROB; Bafobime OL-X; Bapomasal OL-C; *byt mštym* Sy. See also the commentary on 15:4–7.

g Εν εκτενεια μεγαλη is found in B A twice, which Moore, NRSV, and *NETS* attribute to dittography and follow S O L OL Sy Vg: εν νηστεια μεγαλη.

h For τον θεον: κυριον 71 OL; cf. 5:12; 7:30; 8:35.

i Της κληρονομιας is omitted by 55 126 Sy Vg, but is likely the reading; see the commentary.

j For κυριος: ο θεος b 534; κυριος ο θεος O.

k For των αγιων: των ηγιασμενων παρα O; phrase omitted by 126 249´.

also in Jerusalem before the sanctuary[k] **of the Lord Almighty. 14/ Joakim the high priest and all the priests who attended before the Lord and ministered to the Lord, with sackcloth around their loins, offered the daily burnt offering, votive offerings, and the freewill offerings of the people. 15/ With ashes on their turbans, they cried out to the Lord with all their might to look with favor on the whole house of Israel.**

Commentary

4:1–15

In chap. 3, the sweep of the military drama had shifted from the world at large to the cities "in the west," and now it shifts again when "the sons of Israel who reside in Judea" hear about all that had happened.[1] We begin to see the coordinated response of Judeans. Bethulia, to the north in Samaria and considered part of Judea, will be drawn into the defense. In 4:11, Joakim the high priest will coordinate the actions of "the Israelites living in Judea" and those of "every man of Israel and every woman and the children residing in Jerusalem."

It is important to note that it is at this point in the narrative—in the supposedly "disorganized" and "unnecessary" first half of the novella!—that many aspects of the identity construction of the people are introduced:

1. The first mention of the people as "the Israelites living in Judea."[2]
2. The more precise reporting of the interior psychological states of this people: "they were greatly terrified at his approach."
3. The specification that the fear concerns the threat to Jerusalem and the "temple of the Lord their God."
4. The contextualizing of identity in a historical narra-

tive: "they had indeed just returned from captivity; only recently had the people of Judea been gathered together again"; "the temple had just been consecrated."

5. The surrounding towns are included in the preparations for war, including the "region of Samaria," coming under the authority of "the Israelites living in Judea."

And all this in a few verses! This section is all the more effective because it is surreptitious: it is not on the surface about *Jewish* identity but about the swirling of *worldwide* forces, coming closer and closer to the small region of Judea, naming and arranging many different cities and groups. Rather, the identity of the audience is constructed by indirect, narrative means.

Concerning number 1, the phrase "Israelites living in Judea" (4:1) has evoked much discussion about identity. To Zeitlin, "Israelites living in Judea" implies a diaspora origin and perspective, looking at Judea from the outside.[3] David Goodblatt disagrees and avers, rather, that our text assumes that "Israel" is the main ethnonym of the people, as it was for most Jews throughout the ancient period. In Judith, for example, Israel appears fifty times, Hebrew three times, "people of Judea" two times, while *Ioudaios* never occurs.[4] Yet, considering that the name of the heroine is Judith, "Jewish woman," there is likely a conscious or unconscious juxtaposing

---

1   That the Israelites "heard" will also be echoed in 8:1, 9, when Judith "hears" about the developments in Bethulia; see Craven, *Artistry and Faith,* 81.

2   "Holofernes, the commander-in-chief of Nebuchadnezzar, king of the Assyrians," also seems repetitive at this point, an identity assertion about the enemy, and a similar unnecessary title appears in 5:1. Although a repeated epithet might suggest an oral

performance, it is more likely an attempt to mimic the style of biblical epic.

3   Zeitlin, *Book of Judith,* 31–32, entertained by Gruen, *Diaspora,* 321 n. 103.

4   See §1 above; and Goodblatt, "Israelites Who Reside," 74–89. Jan Willem van Henten argues that this text subtly subverts Hasmonean rule ("Judith as an Alternative Leader," 224–52), but this is

of the old, standard referent Israel and the new marker, Judeans, an identity marker that is common in the novellas and in 2 Maccabees.

Concerning number 2, the reporting of the interior psychological states of characters, we note first that the novel genre, ancient and modern, often communicates the buffeting of the protagonists through the more explicit and constant reporting of their fears and psychological states, what classicists sometimes refer to as *polypathy* (see §7 above). In this respect there is also a shift in the narrative here. The fear that has fallen on other peoples has already been mentioned, but only as part of the worldwide progress of the Assyrian army. Here the motif of fear comes home, so to speak, and is applied to the audience's people.

Concerning number 3, the book of Judith, while ostensibly about a northern rural town, is oriented toward Jerusalem and the temple. There are many affirmations of the temple and the role of the high priest. In this, Judith is, like the contemporaneous 2 Maccabees, concerned with protecting the sanctity of the temple. Judith and 2 Maccabees are both "temple propaganda."[5]

Concerning number 4, the contextualizing of identity in history, this is hardly information that the audience needs for the plot line—and is communicated in a parenthesis. It constitutes the author's version of a "historical credo" like Deut 26:5–9 and is not unlike what Achior the Ammonite will also report in chap. 5. It highlights the telescoping of three historical eras into one: the threat of Assyria in the eighth century BCE, the return from exile in the sixth century, and the rededication of the vessels in the second century BCE (see §2 above). This parenthesis has formerly been taken as evidence of a Persian-era dating for parts of Judith—if the Israelites had only *recently* returned—but such literalism does not comport with the carnivalesque nature of the text. Rather, the parenthesis accords with the experience of

the audience and the rededication at the time of the Maccabean Revolt (1 Macc 4:36–61; 2 Macc 10:1–8). Mock history, like serious history, is social history, defining the audience's social identity.

The use of the term *laos* ("people") is also important. In the Hebrew Bible, Israel can occasionally be a *gôy*, but *'am* is more often used for Israel, and *gôy* for other nations.[6] The LXX used *ethnē* for foreign nations, generally for *gôyîm* and occasionally *'ammîm,* and *laos* in the singular for Israel. *Laos* appears here in Judith for the first time, but forty-seven times in all. (But note also 7:1, where the newly formed mass of allies of the Assyrians is referred to as a *laos.*) The "ideal reader" in Judith (as opposed to the actual audience members) is not a person but a constructed people—which may be true for much of biblical literature and for other literature as well.

Concerning number 5, we find a different contextualizing of this newly regathered people. From the very centralized identity expressed in vv. 1–3, references are now made to the surrounding peoples. Yet they are not the "nations roundabout" that we have already heard about—Ammonites, Moabites, and Edomites—but Samarians and other towns presumably considered part of Israel.

Excursus: Samaria

Samaria was the name of a city (Shomron) and the region of the northern part of ancient Israel. When Samaria and Jerusalem were mentioned in 1:9, it was only as marginal entities in the sweep of nations. Now Samaria, along with surrounding cities that may have been considered separate in some real or fictitious historical past, brace for war *along with Judea.* This is fundamentally different from the way other nations have been described to this point. The history of the relations of Judah and Samaria must be kept in mind.

Within the region of Samaria was Shechem, the name of both an ancient Canaanite city and a leader who stands for the people of Shechem. In Genesis

---

probably incorrect. We note as well that Judith occasionally uses the term *Hebrew* as an ethnic marker (10:12; 12:11; 14:18), but as the appropriate outsider's designation? It is interestingly used quite affirmatively in 2 Macc 7:31; 11:13; and 15:37, but never in 1 Maccabees.

5   Doran, *Temple Propaganda.* The temple references argue against the Samarian origin that some schol-

ars have proposed for this text. Further, in 4:1 the author uses *ta hiera* for the foreign temples, but will use *ho naos, ho oikos,* and *ta hagia* for the Jerusalem temple.

6   E. A. Speiser, "'People' and 'Nation' of Israel," *JBL* 79 (1960) 157–63. Jerusalem is mentioned for the first time in 1:9, but for the second time in 4:6, where it becomes a central part of the story.

34, Shechem the leader rapes Jacob's daughter, Dinah, and is killed by her brothers Simeon and Levi. Judith will make much of Shechem's villainous act and the revenge on him (see the commentary on 9:2–14; compare Ben Sira's very negative language of Shechem, 50:25–26). When northern Israel was destroyed and the leading classes resettled by the Assyrians in 721 BCE, Samaria remained the principal city of the region. It was an administrative center under the Babylonians and, under the Persians, the capital of the province Beyond the River, that is, beyond the River Euphrates from the point of view of the Persians. This province included Judah and Jerusalem until Judeans were allowed by the Persians to return and rebuild the temple (as described in Ezra-Nehemiah), at which time the province Yehud was created.

Since the division of David and Solomon's kingdom into its two halves in the tenth century BCE, northern Israel had a tradition of more porous boundaries than the south in terms of religious practices. This continued to be a point of great friction when Judah was restored by the Persians in the fifth–fourth centuries BCE. Samarians, or Samaritans as they were later called, continued to exist both in their ancestral area and in the diaspora alongside Jews, but with a troubled relationship; the near-Other is often perceived as more of a threat than the far-Other.[7] In 107 BCE, John Hyrcanus destroyed the Samarian temple on Mount Gerizim and successfully reestablished the approximate historical boundaries of united Israel as a Hasmonean state. Josephus recounts the struggles between Jews and Samarians in the period leading up to and during the Jewish War of 66–70 CE, and the Gospels also reflect the problematic relations between these two groups in the first century CE (Luke 10:29–37; 17:11–19; John 4:9).

In the story-world of our text, the exact relation of these two entities, Samaria and Israel, is not described clearly, and the embattled relations of Judah and Samaria lie in the background. It is assumed that, in an earlier era, Samaria and Judah would have been two separate entities, and yet Bethulia is under the control of Jerusalem. Samaria, like many other entities, is not treated consistently. Moore suggests rightly that the control of Bethulia by Jerusalem is evidence that the book was written after the Hasmoneans' annexation of Samaria, rather than before, when the tensions with Samarians would likely have been depicted differently.[8] One almost senses that Judith was written and received *in celebration of* the annexation of Samaria, somewhat like the composition and performance of *Juditha triumphans* by Vivaldi after the victory of Venice over the Turks. This would explain the location of Bethulia in the area of Samaria.

The people of Samaria likely did not greet the annexation positively, and the text should be read not as harmonious but as triumphalist. The author may have also had a vision of a united Israel that was only coming into being. This idealization of the boundaries of old Israel was probably a strong, enduring phenomenon, arising in many places. It has been suggested, for instance, that the areas traversed by Jesus in Mark and Matthew may not represent an incorporation of gentile areas so much as a reconstitution of the Israel of David.[9] The book of Judith is a fictionalized and romanticized evocation of what John Hyrcanus had accomplished, or was looking to accomplish, militarily. Ultimately, "Israel" has smoothly come to include both Judea and Samaria, with Bethulia at the boundary. Despite the ambiguity in our text of the term *Israel*—real, idealized, or historical—it comes to include the brave residents of both Samaria and Judah, the old northern and southern kingdoms.

■ **4:4**

Judean and non-Judean sites are listed with Samaria. These cities all lay within Judea and Samaria, that is, historical Israel, and all are understood to be under the authority of Joakim the high priest. As before, the list is more for excitement than accuracy, yet some scholars have speculated on actual sites that may have disappeared as early as Hellenistic times.

7   See Wills, *Not God's People,* passim; Matthew Goff, "'The Foolish Nation That Dwells in Shechem': Ben Sira on Shechem and the Other Peoples in Palestine," in Daniel C. Harlow et al., eds., *The "Other" in Second Temple Judaism: Essays in Honor of John J. Collins* (Grand Rapids: Eerdmans, 2011) 173–87.

8   Moore, *Judith,* 67–70, 148–49; see also Ben-Eliyahu, *Between Borders,* chap. 4; Andrea Berlin, "Between Large Forces: Palestine in the Hellenistic Period," *BA* 60 (1997) 2–57, here 10–11. Ulrike Mittmann-Richert sees a different story function: stopping the foreign advance in Samaria demonstrates that the invasion did not come as far as the area of Jerusalem (*Einführung zu den jüdischen Schriften,* 82–96).

9   Seán Freyne, "Galilee, Jesus and the Contribution of Archaeology," *ExpT* 119 (2008) 573–81, esp. 577.

Kona: unknown, which gives rise to the textual variant of *kōma*, villages.[10]

Beth-horon: a northern Israelite city, about ten miles from Jerusalem. Judah the Maccabee won two important battles there, against Seron (1 Macc 3:16, 24) and Nicanor (1 Macc 7:39). In addition, the name may evoke in our story Sanballat the Horonite, governor of Samaria from Beth-horon, who opposed Nehemiah's reconstruction of the temple in Jerusalem.[11]

Belmain: unknown, but possibly to be identified with Abel-maim, about forty-five miles north of Jerusalem.[12] Cf. Belbaim (7:3) and Balamon (8:3); these unknown sites might originally have been understood to be one fictional city.

Jericho: a fortified city at the northeastern edge of historical Judah. The Hasmoneans took control in the Maccabean Revolt, and so in the author's day the city would have been Jewish controlled, with an ancient biblical past.

Choba: unknown, appearing only here and in Jdt 15:4, 5, spelled Chobai. Cf. also Choba in Gen 14:15 LXX.[13]

Aesora: unknown, though elsewhere it translates Hazor, the name of several sites in the Hebrew Bible (Josh 11:1; Judg 4:2; Neh 11:33).[14]

Salem: unknown, but from Gen 14:18, Salem is traditionally identified with Jerusalem; cf. also Salim near Aenon (John 3:23).

Some locations are well known—Samaria, Beth-horon, Jericho (only Samaria and Jericho are mentioned in the Vulgate)—but the others cannot all be identified clearly. If they could, they might have provided a clue as to the borders of Israel at the time of the writing, but that is not the case.[15] The cities are meant to be more evocative of the local color of the region (see also the commentary on 2:21–28).

■ 4:6–7

Immediately after the new center of identity is introduced in 4:1–5, we hear of "the high priest Joakim," who will lead the response from Jerusalem. In our story, there is no king in Judah but there is a high priest. A high priest Joakim (= Jehoiakim) is mentioned in Neh 12:26 serving with Zerubbabel; a different high priest by that name was said to serve in the period of Baruch (Bar 1:7).[16] Joakim in Greek was used for both Jehoiakim and Jehoiachin, two kings, father and son, who reigned 609–598 BCE. The son was exiled in 597 (2 Kgs 24:12, 15) and was associated with valiant resistance against Nebuchadnezzar and the hope of restoration.[17] Judith may

---

10   Fritzsche suggests it is an error for Kyamon (see 7:3) or Kola (15:4) (*Die Bücher Tobi und Judith*, 146–47); see also the textual notes and Miller, *Die Bücher Tobias*, 52; Zertal, "Reality," 161–75. Cf. also 15:4.

11   Wills, *Not God's People*, 52–86.

12   Aharoni and Avi-Yonah, *Macmillan Bible Atlas*, map 211. Stummer suggests Ibleam (Josh 17:11) as a real site for these names (*Geographie*, 7). For Belmain, Abelmaein and similar are found in S *L* OL.

13   F.-M. Abel, *Géographie de la Palestine* (2 vols.; Paris: Lecoffre, 1933–38) 2:299; Stummer, *Geographie*, 16. Some have tried to press an identification with Choabis, the same as el-Mekhubbi, between Tubas (biblical Thebez) and Besan; el-Marmaleh, thirty miles south of Scythopolis, three miles west of the Jordan River; or Hobah (Gen 15:14), north of Damascus (modern Tell el-Salihiye). The last seems particularly unlikely based on its location.

14   Aharoni and Avi-Yonah suggest Jazer in Gilead (*Macmillan Bible Atlas*, map 211).

15   See Moore, *Judith*, 148.

16   The name Joakim is also found as Alkimos and Iakim in Greek, Alcimus in Latin, and Eliachim in Latin and Syriac. Michael Chyutin notes that Joakim could conceivably call to mind Alkimos, the compromise high priest at the time of Judah Maccabee, appointed by the Seleucid king Demetrios (*Tendentious Hagiographies: Jewish Propagandist Fiction BCE* [LSTS 77; London: T&T Clark, 2011] 165). However, the high priest Joakim in Judith remains a heroic figure, strong in his defense of Judea. Chyutin avers that the book of Judith is not aligned with the Hasmonean dynasty, but that is hardly possible. Marie-Françoise Baslez also proposes the Alcimus connection ("Polémologie et histoire," 374–76), but Benedikt Eckhardt criticizes this ("Reclaiming Tradition," 246–47).

17   The husband of Susanna (v. 1), neither a priest nor a king, is also named Joakim.

once again be adopting one of these historical names for a fictional figure; this would be similar to the Greek novels. Although at the time of the historical Assyrians there would have been a king in Judah, our text once again merges historical time with the present of the text. Verse 3 has just told us that Israelites recently returned from exile and reconsecrated the temple, so this high priest is in charge of both political and military affairs.

Although Joakim might be considered a minor character, his role as high priest is important. He is the only character apart from Judith who remains consistently strong.[18] In preexilic Judah, the king and high priest coexisted, but in the postexilic period the high priest headed a temple-state, serving at the pleasure of the king of Persia or the Hellenistic kings. The Hasmoneans did not at first establish a separate kingdom of Judah, but rather an independent province of the Seleucid Empire. In 152 BCE, however, one of the Maccabee brothers, Jonathan, claimed the role of high priest, as did his successors (see 1 Macc 10:20; chap. 14).[19] In 141, when Simon Maccabee declared full independence, he claimed the title of high priest and assumed the role, but not the title, of king; his titles were, rather, *ethnarchēs* and *stratēgos* (1 Macc 14:47; *ethnarchēs* is not in Judith, *stratēgos* is used only for other nations). It was not until 104 BCE that Aristobulus I, the son of John Hyrcanus, officially became king and high priest. First Maccabees 14 gives a fulsome account of his coronation as high priest, which includes a hymn to his accomplishments not unlike Judith 16. (See §4 above.)

Despite the fact, then, that there is no king mentioned, the central leadership role of the high priest Joakim in Judith matches well the political theology of Hasmonean leaders in the second to first centuries BCE. The fact that there is a high priest and senate but no royal figure indicates that the period of restoration after the exile, as understood by the author, is being described, though verisimilitude is not a strong value. Joakim is thus a distant figure who nevertheless exer- cises authority over all of Judea, and, significantly, he is the only male figure who shows consistent strength and steadfastness. Alone among the men, he may be a stand- in for the Hasmonean political ideology.

In 1:7 and 3:1, messengers are the means of commu- nication; here it is letters, as Joakim wrote to all Israel- ites. One of the major innovations of the Persians was to greatly extend the distances that could be governed under one administration by the institution of relatively independent provinces or satrapies, and by the reliance on local and imperial court protocols, literacy, letters, and decrees. Ezra-Nehemiah is testimony to these great changes, as are the Jewish court narratives such as Esther and Daniel 1–6. Sara Raup Johnson highlights the letters as a motif common to both history and fic- tion; that is, letters provide a realism and an authorita- tive voice in both genres.[20] Even with the introduction of Hellenistic standards of education for the elite, letters probably still retained a bit of wonder about them, although they were being democratized. The description of Joakim's letters is similar to the narrative role that letters play in Esther; she and Mordecai send letters to all the Jews (Esth 9:29–32). But, though the *narrative* role is similar, there is an important difference. In Judith, Jerusalem is the center of the narrative world, and dias- pora Jews are never mentioned, while Esther is centered in Persia among diaspora Jews and Judah and Jerusalem are not mentioned—even though Mordecai is emphati- cally "Mordecai the Judean" throughout.

Joakim sends orders to two mountain towns, Bethulia and Betomesthaim, to fortify the mountain passes that allow access to Judah. This is the first mention of Bethu- lia, the fictional mountain town in Samarian territory where the main action will occur; it is next mentioned in 6:10–13 when Achior is taken there (see the excursus at 6:10–21, "Bethulia"). Betomesthaim, mentioned again in 15:4, is unknown. Torrey audaciously proposed that it suggested Bet-Mastema, house of animosity or even house of the devil, for Samaria, but that seems unlikely.[21]

---

18   See §5 above. He has a slightly expanded role in Vg Jdt 4:11–14 and in later Christian interpretations (on which see §8 above).

19   See Moore, *Judith*, 150.

20   Johnson, *Historical Fictions*; and Johnson, "Nov- elistic Elements," 571–89. See also §7 above. On Ezra-Nehemiah, see Eskanazi, *In an Age of Prose*; on the court narratives, see Wills, *Jew in the Court*.

21   Torrey, *Apocryphal Literature*, 92.

The obscurity of the villages is important: the protagonists' safety depends on two tiny, insignificant, fictitious villages. They are near Esdraelon, the Greek spelling of Jezreel, and the plain near Dothan. The hills surrounding the Jezreel valley are not so imposing as to require narrow passes to traverse, and so the plot device introduced (and explained!) here contradicts what the audience would likely have known about the terrain. (On the possibility that the text was composed in Egypt, see §1 above.) The narrative of the three hundred Spartans at the Battle of Thermopylae may well have been an inspiration for this element of our narrative (see §4 above).

■ 4:8–12

While the idealized nature of the audience's identity was established in 4:1–4, the political structure of the community is depicted here, literally: "The Israelites did as Joakim the high priest and the council of the entire peole of Israel, in session in Jerusalem, had commanded" (cf. also 15:8). Every word in this sentence is an important political term. A Hasmonean coin from the period of John Hyrcanus (from 128 BCE) reads "Jehohanan the High Priest and the council [wḥbr] of the Jews," although it is not clear whether ḥbr here means council (gerousia) or the entire congregation of Jews.[22] In Judith, the high priest gives military commands to all Israel, as ratified by the senate. Is the author trying to represent a time in the past when there was no king? That would not apply to the Assyrian period; further, the narrative has just described a time when the temple, but not the monarchy, was reestablished—say, the period of Haggai, Zechariah, or Ezra-Nehemiah. Judith does not use some of the explicit Greek political and ethical language that 2 Maccabees includes: politeia ("commonwealth," "way of life," 2 Macc 4:11; 8:17; 13:14) and ethismos ("custom," 4:11, 12:38).

■ 4:8

"Council of the entire people of Israel" is quite formal language. It conjures up the city body here as the idealized political leadership of Jerusalem. Just as there were many Jewish identity terms in vv. 1–4, here there are strong Hellenistic polis terms. Gerousia ("council") was a common term in the Hellenistic cities for the city council of aristocratic representatives. It was first used in the Hellenistic East in the charter of Antiochus III in about 200 BCE and continued until replaced by boulē in the Roman era. (Boulē occurs in Judith, but not in the political sense of a gathered body.) It seems here that the terminology belongs to the Hellenistic political sphere, although with some mixing and ambiguity. Would gerousia or boulē indicate Seleucid control and not Ptolemaic? Perhaps. Somewhat later, an inscription on the theater in Ephesus highlights Artemis, the emperor, and other leaders, and the boulē, gerousia, ephēbeia (institution for training young men), and dēmos of Ephesus, along with the six tribes of the city, and possibly others.[23]

The "whole people Israel" here is designated by pantos dēmou Israel. While dēmos in the LXX often translates mišpāḥâ ("clan"), here it conforms to the polis language of the Hellenistic East.[24] On the one hand, dēmos was the body of free citizens in a Greek polis. It is thus a collective noun and a constitutional term in Hellenistic politics, precisely what had been opposed in Jerusalem before the Maccabean Revolt—although the Hasmonean leaders came to model it as well. But the idea of the "whole people Israel" may also suggest the kol hā'ām, the whole people, from the Ezra Memoir section of Ezra-Nehemiah (Ezra 7–10; Nehemiah 8–10). There it is a term for the people gathered for a covenant renewal ceremony that reestablishes a restored Judah. (In the LXX of Nehemiah, however, laos is found rather than dēmos, e.g., Neh 8:1, 3, 5.) Our sentence thus mimics Hellenistic city terminology, while perhaps also evoking

22   Meshorer, *Treasury of Jewish Coins*, 35–36, treated in James C. VanderKam, *From Joshua to Caiaphas: High Priests after the Exile* (Minneapolis: Fortress, 2004) 307–8. On *gerousia*, see §2 above; on *hayĕhûdîm* on this coin, see §1 above. The Hasmonean coins of this period were sometimes stamped in Greek script, sometimes an archaizing Hebrew script, or both on opposite sides, which indicates dramatically the negotiation of Greek and Hebrew political assumptions that was taking place.

23   Elizabeth R. Gebhard, "The Theater and the City," in William J. Slater, ed., *Roman Theater and Society* (Ann Arbor, MI: University of Michigan Press, 1996) 121–22.

24   See the commentary on 8:18; also on 6:1, "the assembled foreigners." In 1 Macc 8:29; 12:6; and 14:20, *dēmos* carries the more typical Hellenistic political meaning of the constitutional body of citizens, but it is the *dēmos* of Jews, not of a city.

Ezra-Nehemiah. Elsewhere in Judith the term *laos* (for *'am*) predominates, used forty-seven times.[25] We may conclude, with Gera, that the varied terms for assemblies communicate a sense of the constant construction of political identities of both Assyrians and Israelites.[26] Judith is, among other things, a reflection on political identity.

Lacking in Judith is any reference to the Jerusalem Sanhedrin. Hebrew *sanhedryn* is a loan word from Greek *synedrion* ("council").[27] It is mentioned in the New Testament, Josephus, and rabbinic literature, but with important differences. In the New Testament and Josephus, it is the Jerusalem city council, headed by the high priest or ruler. Political and administrative control in Jerusalem thus rested in the Sanhedrin. In rabbinic sources, on the other hand, its power was limited to matters of religious observance. The former role applies in the period of our text's composition.

■ **4:9–12** The commands of Joakim are followed by the Israelites without question. The language evokes older biblical narrative: "And every man of Israel cried out fervently to God, and humbled their souls with much fasting." Crying out is a surprisingly common word in Judith; among the Apocrypha, *boaō* and *anaboaō* are disproportionately represented in our text. This emotional response dominates Judith, while weeping is more characteristic of Tobit.[28] In addition, the men of Israel "humbled their souls with much fasting." In the next verse this will be tied to the wearing of sackcloth and generalized to the other orders of society. Crying out, humbling oneself, fasting, and sackcloth must be viewed together. (Esther 4:15–16 commands fasting without mentioning prayer, likely an intentional omission in a text that omits God as well.)

Contrary to modern notions of internalized psychology, in ancient Israel it was assumed that one must make one's grief externally visible to an anthropomorphic God. A concern was often expressed that God would not know what grief one was experiencing internally in the absence of a striking, visible, externalized demonstration.[29] This is true not only of crying out but of humbling oneself as well—an *external* characteristic and not an *inner* virtue. (Matthew 6:16–18 is a pointed challenge to this view.) In the LXX the *tapein-* root translates the Hebrew *'ānah* ("afflict") and *šāpēl* ("be brought low") and related words, but the Hebrew words are not focused on the virtue of humility. Humility as a virtue barely makes an appearance in Judaism before the turn of the era (Sir 3:17–20; 35:16–26) and becomes a central virtue only in Christian usage (see the excursus at 9:11, "Reversal and Humility"). *Tapein-* in Jewish texts of our period thus generally means "to afflict," exhibiting the affliction in the body, including the clothes—sackcloth or ripped garments—visible signs that God cannot miss. Even *psychas* here does not refer to *inner* souls but to whole selves, both internal and external, equivalent to Hebrew *nepeš*.

Still, there is no hint here that Israel is repenting of past sins. This issue is broached in Judith, but it is insisted that Israel was *formerly* in a sinful state, *yet no longer* (8:8–9; cf. 5:19). The political ideology of the Hasmoneans can be seen in this surprising self-assessment. In addition, Judith herself will later exhibit not a hint of penitence for *her own sin,* nor does she repent on behalf of Israel. Unlike the similar scenes in Greek Esther or Joseph and Aseneth, Judith does not afflict herself over her sins or impurity. It is only the elders of Bethulia who come in for criticism from her (8:9–16), and this for their lack of fortitude, not their past sins.

■ **4:9–10** It is possible that only the men cry out and fast, but in the next emotional demonstration, that of wearing sackcloth, all of the dependent members of the

---

25 See esp. 8:11; 10:19; 15:10. Note in our present verse the variant reading *laos* for *dēmos.*

26 Gera, *Judith,* 219. She also notes that in the LXX *gerousia* often translates *ziqnê yiśrāʾēl,* although *presbyteroi Israel* is also found (p. 178). Cf. also 1 Macc 12:6; 2 Macc 1:10.

27 A quite general form of the word, *synedria,* meaning "meeting," is used in 6:1 for Holofernes's war council; also in 6:17; 11:9.

28 Ludlow, "Weeping and Falling Down."

29 Gary A. Anderson, *A Time to Mourn, a Time to Dance: The Expression of Grief and Joy in Israelite Religion* (University Park: Pennsylvania State University Press, 1991); David Lambert, "Fasting as a Penitential Rite: A Biblical Phenomenon?" *HTR* 96 (2003) 477–512; Olyan, *Biblical Mourning.*

household participate, including the cattle (see also the commentary on 7:23):

> Then they and their wives, their young children, their cattle, and every resident alien, hired laborer, and purchased slave all put sackcloth around their waists. (4:10)

Specifying the people as men, women, and children is common in the biblical scenes of communal supplication,[30] perhaps evoking the covenant renewal rituals of the Ezra Memoir noted just above. In Neh 8:1–3, the whole people, *kol-ha'am,* are assembled, "men and women." In Deut 31:12 as well, women are explicitly named as participants in the constitutional gathering of Israel (although in a similar passage in Exodus 19 they are not), and Jer 44:24 also mentioned "the people and all the women." These passages reflect a notion of the assembly of the people with women included as stakeholders. (Only in a modern context could the question be raised of whether this implies "equality"—which it does not—yet there is some sense of joint identity implied.) And even Judith's inclusion of children is not without precedent. In the Nehemiah Memoir (Neh 12:43), a celebration at the wall with sacrifices includes women and children.[31] Although the author of Judith is ostensibly simply describing a scene in which people are gathered, there is a constitutional aspect as well, "our people" in their orders.

Listed after the cattle are "every resident alien, hired worker, and purchased slave," *pas paroikos kai misthōtos kai argyrōnētos.* These terms are found in a number of biblical passages that relate to covenant inclusion or exclusion of slaves and other dependent classes, but the fact that three categories are mentioned together is unusual. It continues the theme of the completeness of the orders of society.[32]

■ **4:11–12a**

A repetitive and emotional style continues in v. 11. The temple is geographically and thematically central to this story; as noted above, the temple propaganda of 2 Maccabees finds its equivalent here. In 9:1 Judith will also time her prayers to coincide with the incense offerings in the temple.

The actions of the high priest and the *gerousia* in Jerusalem are coordinated with those of the Israelites in Bethulia and Betomesthaim. (See the commentary on 4:13–15, and compare MT Esth 9:29–32 on the coordinated celebrations of all the Jews in Persia.) Just as the people in Greater Israel pray, fast, and gird themselves with sackcloth, those living in Jerusalem perform these same acts before the temple. We are probably not meant to think of actual liturgical practices in every case, but rather of an idealized and unified image of Israel engaging in penitential prayer *together;* compare the *ekklēsia megalē* in 1 Macc 5:16. Still, the parallel practices of the Israelites in the north and those near the temple, especially the priests, resonate with the development of the *mišmārôt* and *ma'ămādôt,* local practices that were carried out in rotations to correspond with temple practices (see the commentary on 9:1). The emphasis on the profanation and desecration of the sanctuary would have been yet another telescoping of the ancient and contemporary historical situations, the latter being the desecration that precipitated the Maccabean Revolt.

The depiction of public wailing and tribulation is similar to narrative scenes in 2 Macc 3:14–21 and 3 Macc 1:16–21, although Judith emphasizes more the sackcloth and ashes, 2 Maccabees and 3 Maccabees the public display. Sackcloth is made of the hair of goats or camels rather than wool. Sackcloth and ashes were a common part of ancient Israelite and Jewish ritual (for ashes, see below). They were the signs of mourning and grief, but also of penitence and protest (Esth 4:1–2; 2 Macc

---

30   See 1 Sam 7:5; Esth 4:16; 2 Chr 20:4, 13; Joel 2:16; 1 Macc 3:44; also in regard to the petition of the Jewish community at Elephantine, *COS,* 3.51.

31   In Neh 5:1, also part of the Nehemiah Memoir, there is a great outcry of "the people and their wives (or women) against their Judean kinfolk."

32   See Gen 17:12–13, 23, 27; Exod 12:44–45; Lev 22:10; 25:6, 40; see Gera, *Judith,* 183.

3:19). In the Hebrew Bible, fasting was required on Yom Kippur (Lev 16:29–30), and it could also be an ad hoc preparation for war, as it is here. See also 8:5 and 9:1, where Judith's sackcloth is emphasized.

That the sackcloth is spread out and draped on the altar is unknown elsewhere, and what is also unusual is the placement of the sackcloth on the animals, although this also occurs in the satirical Jonah 3:8. Craven and Gruen rightly treat this in both texts as a humorous turn, yet Gera argues otherwise: "the context in both works is quite serious."[33] Both texts, however, find the satirical in the serious throughout. It is true that animals are sometimes included where modern readers would not expect it (Gen 43:18); cattle even sing, probably understood humorously, in b. ʿAboda Zara 24b. Zechariah 7:3–5, to be sure, likely expresses a critique of the show of fasting, as does Matt 6:16–18. But whereas the book of Judith can be ribald and irreverent, it is not critical of these practices; after all, the prayers of the Israelites are answered, and this because they have fasted (Jdt 4:13). Judith herself, we shall find, will be praised for her devotion and her supererogatory fasting, praying, and wearing of sackcloth. The book of Judith simply takes entertaining liberties, and the excesses of the villagers are likely a way of characterizing their earnestness.

■ **4:12b** They also cried out with one accord, *homothymadon*, idealizing the unity of the people's identity. Not common in the LXX (translating *yaḥad* or *yaḥdāw*), *homothymadon* functions similarly in Acts. The Greek oneness of *will* may or may not be emphasized as much as the notion in the Hebrew of acting *in unison* (but see other uses in, e.g., Jdt 15:2, 5, 9). This is a common problem in assessing the nuances of words in the LXX. No matter which language Judith was composed in (see §1 above), either Greek or Semitic meanings may be felt. The content of what they cried out for, both *homothymadon* and *ektenōs* ("fervently"), also involves the emotional, repetitive style: that God should not allow

their infants to be carried off, their women taken as plunder, the towns of their inheritance to be destroyed, and the sanctuary to be profaned and mocked for the gloating of the nations. The language of destruction is combined with the language of international shame, common in passages such as this.[34]

Gera perceives a developed rhetorical structure, first a chiasmus:[35]

A   B

Not to allow as <u>plunder</u> their <u>children</u>,

B´ A´

and their <u>wives</u> as <u>spoils</u>,

τοῦ μὴ δοῦναι εἰς διαρπαγὴν τὰ νήπια αὐτῶν
καὶ τὰς γυναῖκας εἰς προνομήν

Next, the cities of God's allotment and the temple receive greater attention. Terms are placed in a more climactic parallelism, with a culminating clause:

A   B

the <u>cities of their inheritance</u> for <u>destruction</u>

A´   B´

the <u>temple</u> for <u>profanation and disgrace</u>
—a laughingstock for the nations.[36]

τὰς πόλεις τῆς κληρονομίας αὐτῶν εἰς ἀφανισμὸν
καὶ τὰ ἅγια εἰς βεβήλωσιν καὶ ὀνειδισμὸν
ἐπίχαρμα τοῖς ἔθνεσιν.

■ **4:13–15**
The show of emotion of the Israelites under threat is repeated in these verses. One may ask why these verses are necessary, but the narrative is like an aria that cries out the emotions over and over. That "the Lord heard their cry" functions as a note to the audience from a narrator so omniscient as to know both human and divine intentions. Yet it is understated, in that this is the only place in Judith where God is said to act. Gera notes that the author of Susanna, like that of Judith, states that

---

33 Craven, *Artistry and Faith,* 115; Gruen, *Diaspora,* 164; Gera, *Judith,* 183. To be precise, Judith here *parodies* a solemn Israelite institution but *satirizes* the enemy; thus, it is not a *satire* of the excessive use of sackcloth or anything of the like.

34 See Nehemiah 4 for a graphic account of Jerusalem's shame before the northern Israelites. On

klēronomia ("inheritance"), see the commentary on 8:21–23.

35 Gera, *Judith,* 185.

36 Cf. 2 Macc 10:1–4. See 9:4 for Judith's use of these same motifs in terms of Simeon's revenge on Shechem.

God hears, even though the help will come only later in the form of a heroic deliverer (Sus 13:35, 44–45).[37]

In regard to narrative tension, why would the dramatic effect created by the threat to Israel be undercut by the assurance that God has heard? Does this lessen the artistry by dissipating narrative tension? At a distance of over two millennia, and addressing a popular genre tradition that was at this point so rudimentary, it is difficult to judge narrative techniques. We note first, however, that our text here takes up the paradigm of the judges of Israel; it is stated in Judg 2:18; 3:9, 15, and elsewhere that God heard the cries of the people and sent them deliverers.[38] Further, a similar forecasting of a happy end occurs in other novelistic literature of the period. In Tob 3:16–17, the comic predicament of Tobit is interrupted by the statement that "the prayers of Tobit and Sarah were heard in the glorious presence of God," and in the *Ephesian Tale* by Xenophon of Ephesus an oracle at the beginning (1.6.2) declares that the young lovers will be separated but then reunited. The author and audience in these texts may be invested less in *whether* the protagonists will be saved than in *how* they will be saved—and we recall that the audience likely knew the story well. The *how* is quite engaging in all three texts, in that it involves the protection of innocent people by the gods and, in Judith, the provocative and unexpected intervention of a sexual temptress. At any rate, that God

heeded their prayers and that their fast lasted over many days combine to create another pause in the narrative (see the commentary on 2:28).

Two different tones are expressed concerning the Bethulians' piety: this account of their heartfelt and unified demonstration (with God's response), and their later weakness (chaps. 7 and 8), to which God seems silent. The narrator, Andrea Sheaffer reminds us, has told the story's *audience* that God heard, but the *people* are left to doubt.[39] In addition, Judith the Stoic philosopher will later have her say (see the commentary on 8:35).

■ **4:14–15** The priestly ministrations are emphasized next, again with more repetition than is necessary. The offerings specified—"daily burnt offerings, votive offerings, freewill offerings of the people"—are not simply crisis offerings but evoke the continual piety of temple worship (Exod 29:38–42; Lev 7:11–17; Deut 27:7). There will be other references to the temple sacrifices (9:1; 16:18–19). The turban here is the *kidaris*, originally a Persian word for the linen headdress of the priests (Exod 44:18). Rituals of mourning for the dead are not permitted near the temple, on the assumption that the mourner has been in contact with a corpse, but petitionary mourning or mourning at the time of a national catastrophe does not render one impure and does not exclude one from temple practice.[40]

---

37   Gera, *Judith*, 188.

38   God's response to human crying out is found in different genres, e.g., Exod 3:7; 1 Sam 1:10; Ps 34:17; Isa 30:19.

39   Sheaffer, *Envisioning*, 85.

40   Olyan, *Biblical Mourning*, 62–96, 137–40.

5:1–21

Text	Textual Notes

Text

1/ And so it was reported to Holofernes, commander-in-chief of the Assyrian army, that the Israelites were preparing for war and had closed the mountain passes and fortified the top of every mountain, and had also laid traps[a] in the plains. 2/ Holofernes became violently enraged and summoned all of the leaders of Moab, the Ammonite commanders, and all the governors from along the coast[b] 3/ and said to them, "Tell me, you Canaanites, who is this people residing in the high country, and in what cities do they dwell?[c] How large is their army? In what does their power and strength consist? Who has arisen over them as king, leading their armies?[d] 4/ And why is it that they alone of all those residing in the west disdained to come out to meet me?"

5/ Then Achior, leader of all the Ammonites, said to him, "Let my lord hear the account from the mouth of your slave, and I will declare to you the truth concerning this people who reside in the high country near where you are. No lie shall issue from the mouth of your slave. 6/ This people are descendants of the Chaldeans. 7/ In former times they sojourned in Mesopotamia[e] because they did not want to follow the gods of their ancestors who were in the land of the Chaldeans.[f] 8/ They departed from the ways of their forebears, and worshiped the God of heaven, the god whom they had come to recognize. Their ancestors drove them out from the presence of their gods and they fled into Mesopotamia, where they sojourned for a long time. 9/ Their god commanded them to leave the land of their sojourn and proceed to the land of Canaan. There they settled and acquired great wealth in gold, silver, and very large herds.

10/ "And when a famine covered the land of Canaan, they went down into Egypt and sojourned there as long as they had food.[g] There they became a great multitude, a people so great that they could not be numbered. 11/ The king of Egypt,[h] however, turned against them, and exploited them and forced them into hard labor[i] making bricks. They oppressed them and made them into slaves. 12/ They called upon their god, who struck the entire land of Egypt with plagues for which there was no cure. The Egyptians then expelled them from their midst, 13/ but God dried up the Red Sea before them,[j] 14/ and led them by

Textual Notes

a For σκανδαλα, OL-GX has *tabernacula*, perhaps reading σκηνωματα (so Hanhart). Some translate as "barricades," but this hardly makes sense across a broad plain.

b Και παντας σατραπας της παραλιας omitted in S OL-M by haplography.

c For ας κατοικουσιν πολεις: αι πολεις ας κατοικουσι in *L* OL-X; αν ησαν αι πολεις 583 (= *O*).

d Ηγουμενος στρατιας αυτων lacking in S.

e After Mesopotamia, *Syriae* added in OL-SBQPM.

f For εν γη Χαλδαιων: ενδοξοι in 58 583 Sy OL-SBQP, and Augustine, *City* 16.13; see Moore; and Schmitz, *Gedeutete Geschichte*, 79 n. 150.

g Μεχρις ου here seems to mean "as long as" or "while," not "until" as it typically does, and as in 12:5, 9. As a result, some texts have διεστραφησαν ("until they returned") (248 122 392, cf. *contriti sunt* OL-C).

h The textual tradition varies here on the subject—king of Egypt or Egyptians?—and singular and plural verbs. Hanhart reads king as subject of the first verb and assumes "the Egyptians" as subject with a plural verb. Rahlfs takes Pharaoh as the subject of the second verb as well, in the singular. This reading is adopted here.

i For πονω, S *O* OL Sy have πελω ("in clay"), read by Vg, an influence of Exod 1:14. Modern translations differ, but Hanhart assumes that the text tradition has been assimilated to Exodus.

j Here and just below, God should perhaps be capitalized in modern translations. The first audience likely heard a slippage in Achior's usage, a sort of unconscious prophecy.

k For εις οδον του Σινα: εις το ορον το Σινα 46 58 64 126 *b* 249´ 381 534 OL-MC Sy; cf. Vg.

l Εσεβων in S A *b* OL-G, Sa, Aeth; Basanitas added in *O* OL-SBQPX.

m For την ορεινην: την γην V *a* 55 126 minus Arm.

n For Sychem: Aeueum OL-X, cf. Vg; Haueueos Sy; Achem 583.

o For ανεβησαν, V OL-QP read αναβοησαν, and OL-X has embellished: *clamaverunt in tribulatione et eruit illos deus ex captivitate*.

p For αγνοημα: αμαρτια in 126 and *iniquitas* in Vg, but both of these texts edit freely.

q *O* has the expected subjunctive αμαρτανωσιν, even though there is no εαν; see Hanhart, 45. The same is true for επισκειψομεθα, which is επισκειψωμεθα in *O* 71´ *b* 249´ 311. Note also that επισκειψομεθα could be either the continuation of the protasis or a Semitic apodosis, "then we will note," as in *NETS*.

r For αναβησομεθα: αναβησωμεθα 58; others: "let us set forth." The same is true for εκπολεμησομεν, which is read εκπολεμησωμεν in *O L* 106´ 249´ 311 542; cf. πολεμησομεν in *b* 126 534.

way of Sinai[k] and Kadesh-barnea. They then
drove out all those who lived in the desert,
15/ inhabited the land of the Amorites, and
utterly destroyed all the Heshbonites[l] by their
might. Crossing over the Jordan River, they
took possession of all the high country,[m]
16/ and drove out before them the Canaanite,
the Perizzite, the Jebusite, the Shechemite,[n]
and all the Girgashites, and dwelt in these
mountains for a long time. 17/ And as long
as they did not sin in the sight of their god,
things went well for them, because the God
who hates iniquity was with them. 18/ But
when they departed from the way that he had
set out for them, they were utterly defeated
in a great many wars, and led away captive
to a land not their own. The temple of their
god was also leveled to the ground, and their
cities were occupied by their enemies. 19/ But
now having turned back to their God, they
have returned[o] from the dispersion where
they were scattered, and have occupied
Jerusalem, where their sanctuary is located,
and settled in the high county, because it was
uninhabited. 20/ So now, my lord and master,
if there is any sin committed in ignorance[p]
among this people and they are sinning[q]
against their god, and we discover that they
have committed an offense, we can set forth[r]
and wage war against them. 21/ But if this
people has committed no wickedness, let
my lord pass them by, lest their lord and god
shield them and we become the laughingstock
of the whole world."

Commentary

5:1–21

This section centers on a longer dialogue, and thus provides a narrative break from the movements and battles
to this point. It reflects a shift of focus from the military
exploits of nations to the focalizing through the eyes of
a chosen individual. In addition to exploring Achior's
character, Gera notes that here we are first exposed to
Holofernes's character as an angry tyrant, as opposed
to his title and his deeds (see the commentary on 2:4–13
and 8:35).[1] It is in this chapter that we find the typically
novelistic investment in plot and character. Yet we note
that Holofernes begins by asking strategic questions of
information and only loses perspective—and reveals his
character—when he hears Achior's reply.

This chapter introduces an important figure, Achior
the Ammonite. The first of many ironies in this chapter
is that it is an *Ammonite* general who will become such
an important figure on the side of Israel, especially
since the Bethulian elders are so weak. His role must
be viewed in terms of two structuring arcs of the book.
The first half of this book, often criticized as too much
talk, actually constitutes the first panel of a diptych,
completed in the second half by Judith's actions. As
noted in the introduction, each panel of the diptych is
structured as an elaborate but neat chiasm. The center
of the chiasm of the first half is this chapter—the long
dialogue between Holofernes and Achior. He is one of
the characters who has a significant role in both halves:
he is both an eloquent spokesman here for the Israelite
view of God, history, and Deuteronomic theology, dem-

---

1   Gera, *Judith*, 196.

onstrating a higher degree of bravery for his faith than any of the men of Bethulia, and in the second half he will convert (14:10).

In a second structuring aspect, this chapter introduces a narrative arc parallel to Judith's: as the woman Judith will show courage in stepping up to lead the feckless men of Bethulia, so here the Ammonite Achior, who has no political motive to support the Israelites, shows *philosophical* courage, Greek *parrhēsia*, by speaking truth before the tyrant. The two arcs move at first in opposite directions. The Ammonite enemy is expelled from the Assyrian camp to Bethulia, and the Israelite patriot Judith boldly leaves Bethulia to enter the Assyrian camp. But the two figures end in the same place geographically and in terms of religious affiliation. Achior and Judith, two unlikely heroes of the faith, together vocally champion Deuteronomistic theology.[2] Both engage Holofernes in ironic dialogue, although only Judith is aware of it.

The parallel, coordinated stories of Achior and Judith may also tap into an ancient paradigm in Israelite tradition, that of paired figures: Abraham/Lot, Isaac/Ishmael, Jacob/Esau, Moses/Aaron, David/Jonathan, Zerubbabel/Jeshua, Ezra/Nehemiah. Such pairing continues as a literary technique in texts roughly contemporary to Judith: Mordecai/Esther, Hillel/Shammai, Jesus/John the Baptist, Peter/Paul in Acts. Paired gods or heroes can occasionally be found in Greek and Roman tradition—the Dioscuri, Romulus/Remus—but it seems to be a staple of Israelite folklore, taken over also by Christians. Yet, while Judith and Achior are paired in the LXX version, in much later Christian interpretation, Uzziah is reinterpreted as a stronger figure, supplanting Achior as the more honorable paired hero to Judith. Or,

alternatively, her slave rises in significance, now with the name Habra (often spelled Abra, which means slave), and she becomes Judith's Sancho Panza or Gunga Din figure, sometimes even a paired heroine (see §8 above).

■ **5:1–3**

The military actions depicted here are thrilling but quite absurd: the actual hills of the area were not sufficiently mountainous to limit access to the narrow passes, nor would fortifying the hilltops have been strategic, nor would traps constructed in the plains have been effective to stall the Assyrians' route to the passes.[3] Within this story-world, however, these preparations serve to sum up the dramatic actions of the previous narrative, and the traps in the plain succeed in forcing the Assyrian army to resort to a route via a mountain pass.

When Holofernes was introduced in 2:4, he was identified by his title, commander-in-chief (*archistratēgos*); this was repeated in 4:1 and again here. Holofernes's title contributes to his pompousness and his role as *alazōn* (see the commentary on 10:14–19 and 3:5–10). Holofernes's anger will also evoke the image of the *senex iratus*, blustery old man, a stock dramatic character similar to the *alazōn*. The listing of the Israelites' actions serves to bring their resistance to life—and since the ill-fated Arphaxad in chap. 1, they have been the only ones to continue standing up to the Assyrians. The book of Judith takes up the theme from 2 Maccabees that only Jews resisted—and in regard to the Maccabean Revolt scholars have often reinscribed this myth. Yet at the time of the Maccabean Revolt there were native rebellions in Egypt, Edom, and Tyre.[4] Still, we must recognize the successful myth building of the Hasmonean kingdom, evident here.

---

2   Sheaffer, *Envisioning*, 32–56; and Venter, "Function of the Ammonite," echoing Roitman, "Achior in the Book of Judith: His Role and Significance," in VanderKam, *"No One Spoke Ill,"* 31–45, here 33; see also the commentary on 8:18–20.

3   The actual course of an invading army would be to approach the Jordan River or the coastal valleys from the west. In the Vulgate, the invasion comes from the south. The *skandala* are likely traps rather than barricades as in some translations; barricades constructed across a plain would be even less plau-

sible than traps. Yet reality hardly intrudes in our narrative.

4   See Paul Kosmin, "Indigenous Revolts in *2 Maccabees*: The Persian Version," *CP* 111 (2016) 32–53. There was an uprising by Dionysius Petosiris in Egypt at the same time as the Maccabean Revolt; Antiochus IV was also a temple desecrator in Egypt (Polybius 30.26.9; P.Tebt. III 781); the Atargatis temple at Hierapolis-Bambyce was a site of resistance (Granius Licinus 28.6).

Aside from the great historical empires—the Assyrians, Medes, and Persians (16:12), the smaller near neighbors from Israelite history would have been the Ammonites, Moabites, Edomites, and also the Phoenicians and Philistines along the coast (see the excursus at 3:5–10, "The 'Nations Roundabout'").[5] The identity of the enemy nations here deliberating the demise of Israel is crucial: Moabite and Ammonite leaders, together with the leaders of the seacoast. The Moabites and Ammonites are the same peoples who began by opposing Nebuchadnezzar (1:12) but, like the seacoast cities, also capitulated quickly when first directly threatened (3:1–4). The seacoast cities are listed in 2:28 as Sidon, Tyre, Sur, Ocina, Jamnia, Azotus, and Ascalon. They are mostly Phoenician, the contemporary term equivalent to the ancient hated Canaanites. This corresponds to the traditional understanding in Israel that other nations were not necessarily viewed negatively, but the close neighbors, supposedly descended from the Canaanites and other nations on the land at the time of the conquest, were viewed with a particular animosity. The near other creates more anxiety than the far or exotic other.

Yet important shifts in alliances occur in Judith with little comment by the narrator, creating a narrative simplicity. As the worldwide sweep of nations moves toward Judah, the number of nations listed is reduced. Only the Assyrians, Moabites, Ammonites, and Canaanites are mentioned now as approaching Jerusalem, and the list of nations who were threatened has been reduced as well (Jdt 5:16 provides the *ancient* list of nations). Even Samaria, mentioned separately in 4:4, is now understood to be part of Israel, and Judea appears less often than Israel as well (only in 8:21; 11:19). The dramatic landscape has been simplified and reduced to Israel (including Samaria) and its ancient and eternal enemies.[6]

■ **5:3** Holofernes's inexorable progress has been impeded, and so he realizes that he must now gather information on who his opponents are, and why they have dared to act against him. He is elsewhere depicted in a Danielic way (see 3:8), and certain biblical passages come to mind, such as the questions put to Jonah (1:8–9) or those put to the spies sent out in Num 13:17–21. Achior also recalls the biblical figure of the righteous gentile (see below). Yet the leader's question to his generals and advisers is more similar to that of Xerxes to Demaratus in Herodotus 7.101–4. Among the similarities, Moses Hadas counts "the king's enormous wealth and power, his wrath at being crossed, his council, his long preparations which put the whole world in turmoil, and then the massive and seemingly irresistible movement of the huge armament."[7] Also similar in the two cases is the wise adviser's response: Demaratus says that the Spartans are motivated by their reverence for law and not by fear of the lash, an observation analogous to Achior's. To be sure, Spartan notions of law are not the same as Israel's. Greek political theory was ruled by the concept of reason, and even if there was a divine component to basic human laws, the authority of law must be derived by reason. Israel, on the other hand, may have possessed reasonable laws, but the authority for them was the reverence for God (*yir'at yhwh*).[8] Xerxes also asks fewer questions than does Holofernes and, when given an honest answer by Demaratus, responds with laughter rather than anger.

A military leader's question about the people he is encountering is a common motif elsewhere in Herodotus, but as Gera points out, it is "invariably ominous and signals their forthcoming defeat."[9] Holofernes's questions emphasize the terms *dynamis* ("power"), *kratos* ("might"), and *ischys* ("strength"). Although he is think-

5 Philistines disappeared as a people under Assyrian domination and thus would have been a "historical" people only; but the cities remained important, and Ashkelon is mentioned in 2:28.

6 On the "eternal Other" in Israel and elsewhere, see Wills, *Not God's People*, 14, 21–51, et passim; Mendels, *Rise and Fall*, 97–98.

7 Hadas, *Hellenistic Culture: Fusion and Diffusion* (New York: Columbia University Press, 1959) 168; Schmitz, "Zwischen Achikar," 31; Steinmann,

Lecture de Judith, 57; Caponigro, "Holding the Tale," 48. Regarding 2 Kings 18–19, see also the excursus at 6:10–21, "Bethulia."

8 Wills, "Jew, Judean, Judaism"; Christine Hayes, *What's Divine about Divine Law? Early Perspectives* (Princeton, NJ: Princeton University Press, 2015).

9 Gera, *Judith*, 64. Holofernes's questions are also similar to those asked by Atossa, queen of the Persians, in Aeschylus, *Persae* 230–45; it is thus a common Greek type scene.

ing of earthly powers, the audience knows that God supplies these for Israel. Herodotus can attribute both positive and negative aspects to other people's cultural differences, but the fact that an expeditionary leader *asks* this question is usually a prelude to fall. But, to be more specific, the Herodotus story about Demaratus, combined with the Lindos Chronicle, may have provided the idea for much of the narrative of the book of Judith. Indeed, the standoff at a mountain pass may derive from the story of the three hundred Spartans, the very context of the Xerxes/Demaratus dialogue (see §4 above).

While we may detect a "Greek" tone to Holofernes's questions, beneath the surface an Israelite response is pressing to get out. The general uses *laos,* the word the LXX uses for *'am,* the people of God, and not *ethnos,* the word normally used for the more neutral *gôy,* a distinction that the audience would likely have registered (see the commentary on 4:1–15). The questions also move in concentric circles from outer to inner layers of meaning. He begins on the military-strategic level—"Who is this people residing in the high country? How large is their army?"—but then moves inward, to a question that the audience would perceive on two levels—"In what does their power and strength consist?"[10] Gera finds a subtlety in the crafting of the questions and answers.[11] Holofernes asks the questions concerning military power and resolve in an open-ended way, while Achior fills in the gaps with profound theological truths about this people. Holofernes asks *en tini* does their might and strength lie, assuming the neuter, "in what?" But Achior speaks of their strength as lying in God, taking *en tini* as masculine.

The questions and answers thus converge on deeper layers of Israelite identity. Despite Holofernes's lack of awareness and his addressing the questions to "you Canaanites," his double-layered questions suggest the deepest themes of the book and the deepest core of Israelite identity: "Who has arisen over them as king? Why is it that they alone of all those residing in the west disdained to come out and meet me?" Holofernes assumes that he is asking about an opposing nation's military power, paltry as it may be, but the audience understands these questions as relating to Israel's special relation to God: God is king, and this fealty is absolute and will not allow for capitulation—all the more interesting that here this theme is suggested by *Holofernes*'s questions addressed to *Canaanites.* It also suggests the Israelite response to Nebuchadnezzar's insistence on being worshiped as god (3:8). Further, the ironic double layer sets the stage for the broader and more triumphant humor to follow. The irony of Holofernes's obtuseness would already be perceived to be humorous.

Yet we should not seek a neat distinction between Greek and Israelite modes of thought, since they are mixed throughout this novella. Whereas the discussion on Judah in chap. 4 had a biblical cast, the audience would perhaps detect here the Greek genre of *peri basileias* ("on kingship"). This genre arose in the Hellenistic period, with roots in Aristotle's discussion in *Politics* book 3. Numerous authors turned to the topic of kingship, for example, Philodemus, Plutarch, and Dio Chrysostom, but especially important for this discussion is the example already in a Jewish context, Letter of Aristeas. The Temple Scroll from Qumran even includes an "On Kingship" section.[12] The last two texts indicate the currency of the reflection on kingship for a Jewish audience. Here Achior the Ammonite responds to Holofernes's *peri basileias* questions by witnessing to the role of God, but the double level of references played upon throughout the book—earthly lords and heavenly Lord—is present as an irony here as well (see §7 above). It is only natural, of course, that a foreign general,

---

10 Cf. also 2 Kgs 19:20–21, the speech of Rabshakeh, "On whom do you rely?" Or the story of David against Goliath: "The Lord does not save by sword or spear" (1 Sam 17:47), or again in defeating the Arameans who thought that God was a god of the hills only and not the plain (1 Kgs 20:23–43).

11 Gera, *Judith,* 197–98.

12 Martin Hengel, "Polemical 'On Kingship' in 11QTemple," *JJS* 37 (1986) 28–38; Oswyn Murray,

"*Peri Basileias*: Studies in the Justification of Monarchic Power in the Hellenistic World" (D.Phil. thesis, Oxford University, 1971), and see the commentary on 8:35. In 5:23 the other members of the council use *dynamis* and *kratos* to argue that the Israelites have no power. Holofernes's questions are thus posed as the nations would articulate them and are answered by Achior, Judith, and others as Hasmonean Israel would express it.

understood anachronistically as a "Seleucid" or "Greek" general, would set the question in this way. The interest in kingship may seem superficial compared to *Aristeas*, but here we encounter a novelistic depiction more than a substantive presentation. In Bakhtin's terms, it defines Holofernes's zone (see §7 above). In addition, Achior the Ammonite's bold response will affirm one form of government, the Israelite, over the other, Hellenistic kingship, without appearing to do so explicitly.

Excursus: Achior the Ammonite

Achior the Ammonite is one of the pivotal characters in this novella. The Israelites' hearing of events in 4:1 brought the narrative around to Judea, and it will be the depositing of a bound Achior at Bethulia in 6:10–21 that brings the narrative to that village, a transition to the center of the story. Between these two points lies the long introduction of Achior.[13] His experiences are told in some detail. Mieke Bal and others speak of focalization in narratology—the restricting of information to the issues and perspectives of one character (or the narrator).[14] Here Achior's experiences and perspectives take over two chapters; he is the focalizing subject at the center of the chiasm of the first half.

In some ways Achior the Ammonite is like the biblical figure of the "righteous gentile." He recognizes God's true nature and power; compare Jethro (Exodus 18), Balaam (Numbers 22–24), Rahab (Joshua 2–6), Ruth, Naaman (2 Kings 5), and Darius (Daniel 6).[15] A somewhat later example would be the king and queen of Adiabene (Josephus, *Antiquities* 20.2.1–4.1 §§17–96). Like Balaam, Achior utters true words that place him in danger with a gentile king (see the commentary on 6:2). He is more courageous than the men of Bethulia; he speaks truth to Holofernes and is punished for it; and he ultimately converts to Judaism. He is thus a secondary model of faithfulness in this book. He will describe the God of Israel as a god who protects his people, and we may come to see that his transfer by Holofernes over to the Bethulians may be part of God's care for him. A male alter ego to Judith, he plays a role similar to Barak in the Deborah story.[16] Looking farther afield, Achior's role also calls to mind the tragic warners in Herodotus's accounts of eastern history (see §4 above), and, in Chariton, Dionysius exhibits the same combination of strength, weakness, and emotions that Achior does in Judith.

Yet more than any of these, the character Achior is probably based on the much-admired court adviser Ahikar.[17] In the Bible and cross-culturally there are two separate "wisdom" ideals, the earnest ideal of the wise and righteous person, especially a courtier, who bears witness to the demands of truth and uprightness and is often persecuted for it, and the clever, satirical, or trickster ideal, rarely a courtier but an independent agent who flouts convention and succeeds by his wits. In the biblical context, these two types may be called the Joseph and the Jacob ideals. Achior and Judith represent these two separate ideals perfectly. Ahikar had been the very model of the earnest yet persecuted wisdom ideal, and Achior—by necessity in this story, a general—also lives into the Joseph ideal.

Ahikar was originally a courtier of the Assyrian kings Sennacherib and Esarhaddon (eighth–seventh centuries BCE)—but perhaps himself a minority Aramean. His story was embellished often, and he appeared in many different ethnic identities with slightly different names. The Story of Ahikar, dating from the fifth century BCE, is the earliest known version, discovered, significantly, in the Jewish military colony at Elephantine. Like the later Alexander Romance, the Story of Ahikar enjoyed a very international appeal (see §7 above). An Israelite Ahikar appears in Tob 1:21–22; 2:10; 14:10. That "Ahikar" is an Israelite in Tobit and converts to Judaism in Judith suggests that the famous scribe Ahikar in the *Assyrian* court is now "ours." He is well known in Greek tradi-

---

13 Sheaffer, *Envisioning*, 85.

14 Bal, *Narratology: Introduction to the Theory of Narrative* (Toronto: University of Toronto Press, 1985) 60–71.

15 Balaam was a non-Israelite, perhaps an Ammonite? See Moore, *Judith*, 158, 166–67. Dubarle (*Judith*, 1:143–44) and Enslin (*Book of Judith*, 89) both perceive an even closer association of Judith and Rahab, because the latter is so impressed with God's history of deeds that she confesses his power (Josh 2:10–11), but she is really more similar to Achior.

16 On Achior/Barak, see White, "In the Steps of Jael," 10, 14; Levine, "Sacrifice and Salvation"; Gera, *Judith*, 105–6; and Gera, "Speech in Judith."

17 Henri A. Cazelles, "Le personnage d'Achior dans le livre de Judith," *RSR* 39 (1951) 125–37; Gera, *Judith*, 58–59; Wills, *Jew in the Court*, 44–49; West, "Croesus' Second Reprieve," 416–37; Stephanie Dalley, *Esther's Revenge at Susa: From Sennacherib to Ahasuerus* (Oxford: Oxford University Press, 2007) 112–36.

tion (e.g., Strabo, *Geography* 16.2.39), and part of his story is adapted to Aesop in the Greek Life of Aesop from the turn of the era. Like Ahikar, Aesop was a mobile, free-floating figure, and the Aesop/Ahikar persona is representative as well of the wise adviser and the tragic warner in Herodotus.[18] The fact that the Aesop tradition so freely incorporated the persona of Ahikar, and that the Croesus tradition may have as well, demonstrates how easy it would be for the author of Judith to do so also.[19] Ahikar would have been universally known as a wise courtier, the very paradigm of the brave adviser who told the truth before kings and suffered for it, and was later vindicated.

To be sure, some scholars are not convinced that Judith's Achior is based on Ahikar. André LaCocque argues against this connection, and proposes instead an association with Achan (LXX Achor) in Joshua 7, who is stoned to death in the Valley of Achor.[20] The parallel is vague, however, and Achan/Achor is a negative figure. LaCocque counters this argument by noting that Achior is meant as an "anti-Achan," but the association with the legendary Ahikar requires no such stretch; the latter's role as an international and very sympathetic counselor motivates the use of this obvious, even stereotyped name for a wise, pious, international figure. Achior's instinctive actions and Israelite sensibilities in witnessing to God express more of a path of wisdom than any other character except Judith and Joakim the high priest. The fact that Ahikar is known by Jews in a novelistic text at Elephantine should also be weighed. Further, the similar play on Ahikar in Tobit seals the argument. Other scholars have argued that Achior's name derives from Hebrew, My Brother Is Light,[21] but this also seems unlikely. It is possible, of course, that the name of the Assyrian courtier Ahikar is in Judith assimilated to a Hebrew-sounding name, as, for instance, Kong Fuzi was romanized as Confucius

and Jean Cauvin was anglicized as John Calvin. But why would an Ammonite have a Hebrew-sounding name? Still, in this text, anything is possible.

Ahikar would wind through many different national traditions, but the choice of Ammonite here is perhaps more noteworthy. As noted above at 5:2, Ammonites were a real neighbor and sometime enemy of Israel, supposedly descended from the dangerous nations on the land (such as Canaanites) at the time of the conquest. Biblical law is quite clear about Ammonites and Moabites: "No Ammonite or Moabite shall be admitted to the assembly of the Lord" (Deut 23:3). Like Ruth the Moabite, Achior the Ammonite becomes a surprising redemptive figure. That he is Ammonite rather than Moabite may be partially explained as an influence of 1 Samuel 11: Saul arises when Israel has promised to surrender within seven days to Nahash, king of the Ammonites. This Saul story may have been one model for Judith, and now the "king of the Ammonites" is co-opted. Achior's Ammonite identity may also serve to reassimilate the descendants or partisans of "Tobiah the Ammonite" of Neh 2:10. Tobiah's name was Yahwistic (Yah is my good), but Nehemiah had likely shamed his opponent by calling him Tobiah the Ammonite. The Tobiad family was centered in Ammon, and the descendants were involved in Jerusalem politics as well.[22] Judah the Maccabee also fought Timotheus, leader of the Ammonites (1 Macc 5:6), so Ammonites, a contemporaneous and not just historical people, are now assimilated, and perhaps the Jewish Tobiads from Ammon as well.

Achior plays key roles in the narrative. First, as central as he is to the first half of Judith, he also unites the two sections.[23] Judith and Achior exchange positions: Achior begins as a general in the Assyrian camp and moves to Bethulia, where he becomes a member of the people; Judith begins as a townsper-

---

18   On the tragic warner in Herodotus, see Richmond Lattimore, "The Wise Adviser in Herodotus," *CP* 34 (1939) 24–35.

19   Leslie Kurke, *Aesopic Conversations: Popular Tradition, Cultural Dialogue, and the Invention of Greek Prose* (Martin Classical Lectures; Princeton, NJ: Princeton University Press, 2011).

20   LaCocque, *Feminine Unconventional,* 31–48. Also rejecting the association with Ahikar is Otzen, *Tobit and Judith,* 108, but arguing in favor are Moore, *Judith,* 163; Haag, *Studien,* 32–33; Cazelles, "Le personnage d'Achior," 125–37; and Zenger, *Das Buch Judit,* 436.

21   Proposed by Enslin, *Book of Judith,* 86; Grintz, *Book of Judith,* 110; Reiterer, "'Meines Bruders Licht':

Untersuchungen zur Rolle des Achior," in Xeravits, *Pious Seductress,* 111–60, here 111–12. Reiterer presses further: Ammonite is a cipher for Samaritan, and Achior's conversion signals the return of the Samaritans to the proper worship of God.

22   Wills, *Jewish Novel,* 72, 187–93; Wills, *Not God's People,* 72–74.

23   See Roitman, "This People Are Descendants of Chaldeans (Judith 5,6): Its Literary Form and Historical Setting," *JBL* 113 (1994) 245–63. Achior moves from the farthest position to that of an adopted Israelite. Holofernes's rejection of Achior's advice in chap. 6 also finds a similar, if inverted, presentation in Judith's upbraiding of the elders in chap. 8; see below.

son in Bethulia and moves to become a general of sorts in the Assyrian camp. Physically, they cross over the same path in changing places. Both must pass through the same gates, and the gatekeepers mark their transition. In terms of theme, Achior presents an Israelite view of God's role in history as an earnest declaration; Judith will act it out in the context of a lie—Jacob trumps Joseph. Achior will describe Israel from an outsider's perspective that Judith will also say from an insider's. This is an assist to Judith; her lies are convincing because the table has been set by Achior. The narrative thus presents an exchange of focalizing protagonists, one male and one female, with the irony that the dominant one is female. Here Judith also orchestrates the irony; Achior more passively lives it out.

Pieter Venter also argues that Achior and Judith are both marginal figures and that, as a result, the text affirms more inclusive notions of Jewish identity, while at the same time advocating for a Hasmonean ideology.[24] One wonders, however, whether the characters push the audience to consider a more inclusive ideal or the text simply explores the transgressive challenge of a masculinized woman and a feminized man (see the commentary on 14:5–7). Yet Achior is a character who changes. At first he is bold and articulate; then he is silent and passive as he is moved about and taken in by the Bethulians. He remains passive when he faints upon seeing the head of Holofernes but steps up again and makes a life-changing conversion. In the process, he also grows as a character.[25] It is sometimes said that character growth does not exist in ancient literature but is rather an invention of modern novels, parallel to discoveries in modern psychology, but there is rudimentary character development in Esther and in the Joseph story. Achior's conversion is strangely not usually treated as character development, though perhaps it should be.

Aspects of hero legends cross-culturally may also be noted in regard to Achior. As the hero—in this case, Judith—leaves civilization and moves out toward nature, he or she is accompanied by a faithful "natural man," such as Enkidu or Chingachgook. The teaming of a hero and a man of nature continues into modern popular culture, with figures such as Tonto or the African American police partner. It is an ironic pairing; the hero cannot integrate into civilized society and must wander, while the natural man often acts in a way that is more civilized. They are both boundary crossers, who alone can understand each other. (See the commentary on 8:10 for Judith's relation to her female slave.) Judith is the heroine who leaves domesticity, and Achior is Judith's "natural man." Are we to understand "Ammonite" as "savage"? Perhaps, but Ammonite was also a real term for a contemporary people, which continued in use for centuries. "Philistine" was more likely the traditional term to inscribe the prejudice "savage."[26]

One overarching narrative role for Achior the Ammonite is certainly clear. An ideal observer, Achior seems to know, even from among the Ammonites or Assyrians, that the grounding in God is what sets Israel on a firm basis. He will exhibit the wisdom to live into this perspective and convert to belief in God in chap. 14.

■ **5:5–21**

Judith will deliver her major speech at 8:9–36; there we will note that F. W. Walbank found three types of speeches in Greek histories: debating speeches of politicians (*dēmēgoriai*), harangues of commanders (*paraklēseis*), and discourses of ambassadors (*presbyterikoi logoi*).[27] Judith's speech will be similar to the second

24 Pieter Venter traces an exclusivist trend in P, Chronicles, Ezra-Nehemiah, and Ezekiel and an inclusivist in Ruth, Jonah, Job, Ecclesiastes, Esther, Judith, and Tobit ("The Function of the Ammonite Achior in the Book of Judith," *HvTSt* 67[3] Art. #1101, 9 pages, http://dx.doi.org/10.4102/hts. v67i3.1101). This appears unlikely for Judith, but it must be acknowledged that Ruth the Moabite does seem to represent an inclusivist point of view. See also LaCocque, *Feminine Unconventional*, 41.

25 See the commentary on 6:1, and on his conversion at 14:5–10; Gera, *Judith,* 199. On character development in Esther and Joseph, see Wills, *Jewish Novel,* 114–15. Compare also Mordecai in Hebrew Esther as a character who is first active, then passive, then

active, and see Adelman, *Female Ruse,* 198–230, on Esther, Joseph, and character development.

26 Elizabeth Bloch-Smith, "Israelite Ethnicity in Iron I: Archaeology Preserves What Is Remembered and What Is Forgotten in Israel's History," *JBL* 122 (2003) 401–25; Mobley, *Samson;* Mobley, *The Empty Men: The Heroic Tradition of Ancient Israel* (ABRL; New York: Doubleday, 2005).

27 F. W. Walbank, "Speeches in Greek Historians," in Walbank, *Selected Papers: Studies in Greek and Roman History and Historiography* (Cambridge: Cambridge University Press, 1985) 242–61, here 253; Roger Tomes, "Heroism in 1 and 2 Maccabees," *BibInt* 15 (2007) 171–99, here 182 n 32.

type, while Achior's speech is a combination of the first and third. Achior's recitation of Israel's history is also in the tradition of the biblical "historical reviews," which often cover creation, patriarchs, exodus, journey through the desert, occupation of the land, exile, and return.[28] Achior's speech is organized along the lines of this historical review model, and, though it replays this schema effectively, it omits creation and the journey through the desert. He also makes no mention of Torah, nor does he echo any particular biblical passages, although perhaps that would have rung false in the mouth of a non-Israelite. There are also no Israelite kings, even though Holofernes has asked specifically about kings (5:3). Omitting the kings may seem odd in light of the Hasmonean independence, but there are ambiguities with regard to the title of king (see §2 above). Lacking also is any reference to the schism between north and south, but that would not generally be present in the historical summaries, and it is precisely the schism that the Hasmoneans thought to have resolved. (The schism is featured in the roughly contemporaneous Tob 1:2 and Sir 48:15.)

Moore finds Achior's speech general and imprecise, but Venter counters that this text constructs an Israelite identity *for the audience* and is not a real recitation of history *for Holofernes.*[29] Israel here is ruled by temple and God (5:18–19). The omission of the north–south schism may reflect the Hasmonean annexation of the territory of united Israel. Although Achior's recitation of Israelite history does not mention individual figures like Abraham, Moses, or David, it is the Israelites as a people who are the heroes of this story.[30] Perhaps this communal identity is the point here, although the author may simply be presenting a plausible account

from a foreigner's perspective, which the audience then knowingly fills in. But most important, assumed here is a nonspecific version of Deuteronomistic theology, the view that God rewards faithfulness and punishes sin, played out in the classic Deuteronomistic pattern of sin, punishment, penitence, and salvation. Achior does not begin by stating God's role in history but simply by recounting the history of this people, as it would be rendered by a very insightful neighboring leader—calling to mind Ahikar the famous court adviser. Achior's speech is a skeletal script that the audience mentally completes; that is the performative role of the audience. Gera confirms this by noting that at certain points (e.g., 5:12–14) Achior's speech prepares the audience to expect salvation from God.[31]

Holofernes will contemptuously refer to Achior's speech as prophecy (6:2), and indeed Achior's words are a combination of a wise reading of history and "unconscious prophecy," the literary motif of a foreigner or nonbeliever unconsciously delivering a prophecy of a god (see commentary on 6:2–4). The audience perceives the irony: the Assyrian general cannot see that the speech really is "prophetic." The truth is in the history, and, by representing it accurately, Achior in effect lives it. His conversion will confirm this. The transparency of history, and Achior's wisdom in seeing it, is sharply contrasted to that of the nations roundabout, who first cavalierly rejected Nebuchadnezzar (did they not know whom they were dealing with?) and then fecklessly prostrated themselves before his advancing army (did they not know that the path to freedom is difficult?).

■ **5:5** Achior's first words, seemingly innocuous, immediately establish certain speech patterns that will later be "ironized" by Judith (see the commentary on 10:14–19):

---

28   See Joshua 24 and Nehemiah 9; also Deut 26:5–9; 1 Sam 12:6–17; 2 Kings 17; Psalms 78, 105, 106, 135, 136; Ezra 9; Ezekiel 16; 20; parts of Daniel 2; 7; 9; Ben Sira 44–49; 1 Enoch 89:59–90:19; 93:1–10; Tob 14:4–7; parts of Damascus Document 1–6; Jub. 1:7–18; 23:13–21; Acts 7. Only one of these, Nehemiah 9, includes all of the themes. See Venter, "Function of the Ammonite Achior."

29   Moore, *Judith,* 162; Venter, "Function of the Ammonite Achior."

30   See also Friedrich V. Reiterer, "Meines Bruders

Licht: Untersuchung zur Rolle des Achior," in Xeravits, *Pious Seductress,* 111–60; Schmitz, *Gedeutete Geschichte,* 44–53; Schmitz, "Zwischen Ahikar"; Joosten, "Original Language," 171; and Caponigro, "Holding the Tale," 48. It is interesting to compare the eighteenth- to nineteenth-century artistic depictions of Judith, interacting with the gathered Bethulians, as a reflection of the nationalistic period in European history (see §8 above).

31   Gera, *Judith,* 210.

"Let my lord hear the account from the mouth of your slave, and I will declare to you the truth concerning this people." Although he uses "lord" for his superior in a way that is quite typical even in Jewish Greek, Judith will use "lord" to speak on two levels at once, referring to Holofernes and God (11:5–8). Achior couches his reply in courtly, deferential language, and emphasizes that "nothing false will come out of my mouth."[32]

The emphasis on truth in the court of the king or general is a Persian motif, found in both Persian inscriptions and Greek references to Persian court traditions (Herodotus 1.136, 138; 7.101; cf. 1 Esdras 3 on Persia). Israelite texts are more likely to mention wisdom or counsel.[33] Achior's promise to tell Holofernes the truth will be matched almost identically by Judith (11:5; cf. 6:9), but whereas Achior does speak the truth and is condemned for it, Judith lies in every line and is not only believed by Holofernes but praised by him as well. The audience likely knows the story well enough that, even at this point, these terms are recognized as motifs that Judith will later play on. They foreshadow and contrast with Judith's distinctive ironic dialogue with Holofernes. In addition, Achior refers to Israel as a *laos* rather than an *ethnos*, a distinction that a Jewish audience would likely have perceived (see the commentary on 4:1–15).

■ **5:6–16** Achior emphasizes three themes in his recitation of Israel's history: Israel was separated out by God for special, monolatric devotion; they were hounded as a people and expelled from Mesopotamia and Egypt; and, by appealing to their God, they ultimately succeeded in driving out the nations of the land and establishing their nation. "This people are descendants of the Chaldeans" (5:6) immediately establishes Achior's speech as a historical summary, the mighty acts of God (Deuteronomy 1–3; 26:5–10)—as told by a fictitious Ammonite outsider. Ironies abound. He notes, for instance, that Abraham had abandoned the Chaldean divinities, yet what would that suggest about Achior's Ammonite pantheon? The audience, however, would appreciate that Achior's account of Abraham provides a basis for his own conversion.[34] He is beginning to reveal the soul of an Israelite; does his double name, suggesting both Ahikar and, in Hebrew "My Brother Is Light," hint at his hidden potential?

■ **5:6–9** Technically, Genesis states that Abraham was an Aramean, not a Chaldean, but was resident in Ur of the Kasdim, translated in the LXX as Chaldeans (Genesis 11–12). It is not stated in Genesis that Abraham departs because he is a monotheist, although Jewish, Christian, and Muslim traditions later assumed that. Our passage is one of the earliest known statements of this view (cf. Jub. 11:16–17; 12:2, 6–7).[35] The Greek here is also precise: *paroikeō* ("sojourn," 5:7), for Hebrew *gwr*, and *katoikeō* ("dwell," 5:9) for the period in Canaan, for Hebrew *yšb*.[36] That Abraham was *expelled* from his homeland and that the Hebrews were *expelled* from Egypt (5:12) comport with some ancient gentile historians, a negative telling of Israelite history.[37] More to the point, in the competitive historiography of the day, the gentile historians often stigmatized the Jews by assuming that they had been expelled from Egypt; Achior might have been expected to take that perspective.

---

32 *Dē* might at first suggest the better Greek typical of the speeches in Judith, but it is not uncommon in the biblical history books. It does, however, contribute to the general sense of the courtly obsequiousness of the wise adviser, a style common in Daniel and Esther.

33 Gera, *Judith,* 203; Wills, *Jew in the Court*; 1 Kgs 22:16 features "truth," but highly ironically.

34 Roitman, "Achior"; Roitman, "This People," 259–61; Joosten, "Original Language," 173–74; Grintz, *Book of Judith,* 118; Schmitz, *Gedeutete Geschichte,* 76–78; Mercedes Navarro Puerto, "Reinterpreting the Past: Judith 5," in Nuria Calduch-Benages and Jan Liesen, eds., *History and Identity: How Israel's Later Authors Viewed Its Earlier History* (Deuterocanonical and Cognate Literature Yearbook 2006;

Berlin: de Gruyter, 2006) 115–39. That Hebrews were expelled was perceived as shameful, but, according to Judith, Israelites also expel others (5:14, 16); see the excursus at 9:11, "Reversal and Humility."

35 James L. Kugel, *The Bible as It Was* (Cambridge, MA: Belknap Press of Harvard University Press, 1997), 135–36; Roitman, "This People."

36 Engel, "Der HERR," 158; and Gera, *Judith,* 87; and see 4:1. God of heaven, on the other hand, was common in the Persian period and was likely Persian in origin; see Delcor, "Le livre de Judith," 151; Moore, *Judith,* 50.

37 John Gager, *The Origins of Anti-Semitism: Attitudes toward Judaism in Pagan and Christian Antiquity* (Oxford: Oxford University Press, 1983) 39–54.

■ **5:8** In "God of heaven," one senses an international, multireligious perspective, and this is probably accurate. It is used here by Achior, and also by Israelites (6:19) and Judith (11:17). It is not common in the Hebrew Bible (Gen 24:7; cf. 24:3) but appears at Elephantine addressed to Persian authorities (*COS* 3.51, 3.P116). It was likely a development in the Persian period, used in contexts with non-Israelites: a new international description used specifically to avoid the assumption that Yahweh was a local god (Jonah 1:9; Dan 4:34; Ezra 1:2; and others). "The title," says Gera, "conforms to the Jewish view of God as creator of heaven and earth, but also suits the 'Persian Zeus,' Ahura Mazda, who was located in, and co-extensive with, the heavens."[38]

■ **5:10–13** The exodus tradition is told quickly here but somewhat more fully in the Vulgate. Many terms have interesting resonances. "They became a great multitude" (*plēthos poly*) is taken from exodus references in the Bible (Deut 26:6), but Gera suggests that it also echoes the threatening *plēthos poly* of Holofernes's amassing army (Jdt 2:17; 7:2, 18; 15:7).[39] The same term applies to the innumerable people as well. *Patassō* ("strike or afflict") has been a leitmotif in Judith (2:27; 6:3; 9:3, 10; 16:6), as Israelites are struck and God and Israelites strike back. On oppressed, *tapein-*, see the excursus at 9:8–10, "Judith's Hand and Agency." "They called upon their god" echoes 4:12–13, where the Israelites at the time of Judith's story cried out against the Assyrians, so the exodus story can be expected to play out again. Finally, in 5:13, 17, does Achior slip into an Israelite usage of God, appropriately capitalized in English translations?

■ **5:14–16** Achior's account references some of the major events of the conquest (Num 21:21–31; Deut 2:24–37; Judg 11:19–28), some of which took place near Achior's native land of Ammon. Further, the high country mentioned here by Achior would have been the area of Bethulia.[40] Kadesh-barnea was the site of many of the important events of the wilderness wanderings, such as the sending out of the twelve spies, the first attempt to enter Canaan, Miriam's death and burial, and the striking of the rock by Moses (see Deut 1:46; Numbers 13–14; 20). It also marks the southern border of Israel (Num 34:4). Sihon, king of the Amorites, who was defeated by the Israelites, had his capital at Heshbon. Expelling those in the desert refers to Amalekites; see Exod 17:8–16. Historical reports such as Joshua 24 and Neh 9:22 reference some of these events.

The list of five nations driven out ("Canaanites, Perizzites, Jebusites, Schechemites, and Girgashites") corresponds partially to the stereotyped list of nations in the older biblical accounts (see the commentary on 5:1–3). In the biblical lists, however, there are usually six nations (Exod 3:8; Josh 9:1; Judg 3:5) or seven (Deut 7:1–2; Josh 3:10); Amorites and Heshbonites have also been mentioned to round out the seven. Unusual in the list is Shechemites, who would have been part of the Heshbonites; they are raised up to foreshadow Judith's focus on Shechem in chap. 9. Interesting here is the fact that Shechem as an *ancient* nation is treated as different from Samaria, now listed as a subservient partner to Israel (see commentary on 4:1–15). We should not assume a shocking ignorance on the part of the author or audience, but a playful manipulation of historical identities. It is precisely at this point, for example, that the audience of our book would be hearing the actual history of Nebuchadnezzar, king of the Babylonians, being explained to the general of "Nebuchadnezzar, king of the Assyrians"! However much it may have contradicted known historical facts, the story plays on several historical planes simultaneously and with abandon.

The narrative effect of a list of nations in all of these texts is to suggest the breadth of the conquest, the variety on the land—even "motley" or "bastard" peoples (see chap. 1), and the unique identity of Israel. By defeating these nations, they "took possession" or, more symbolically, "inherited" (*eklēronomēsan*) the land (see the commentary on 4:11–12); that is, they took possession of the land as an inheritance. Achior is evenhanded in his presentation, even positive about the Israelite victories, yet Israel had been commanded by God to wipe out the Ammonites along with the other nations on the land! According to Deut 2:9–19, the Ammonites, along with the Moabites, escaped the fate of the nations in the list, to become a perpetual thorn in the side of Israel.

---

38 Gera, *Judith*, 206.
39 Gera, *Judith*, 209–10.
40 Schmitz, *Gedeutete Geschichte*, 98–102.

■ **5:17–19** One of the themes of Judith, that true strength is based not on arms but on God, is expressed in many biblical texts, such as David to Goliath: "You come with sword and spear and javelin, but I come to you in the name of the Lord of hosts" (1 Sam 17:45), and in the contemporaneous 2 Maccabees as well (2 Macc 8:16–23; 13:13–15; 15:7–17). Achior's role as an ideal observer works well in the narrative. Israel's story sounds all the more compelling from his mouth, and now he even couches it in terms of Deuteronomistic theology: if Israel abides by God's laws, they will be blessed; if Israel disobeys, they will be cursed and punished.[41] Judith's later explanation to Holofernes in 11:9–15 as to why her people are being abandoned by God forms a bookend with Achior's speech here. For the audience, the truth of the Deuteronomistic theology must have seemed confirmed by historical events of the second century BCE, and an established Jewish philosophy of history could be played upon. The recitation of history concludes with the restoration of Israel and the renewal of the temple sacrifices (5:19). The people have returned to their God and reoccupied the land where their sanctuary lies. Like other statements above, this one will be repeated by Judith in 8:18–20. In addition, "they returned to their God," *epistrepsantes epi ton theon autōn,* takes up the biblical notion of *šwb* ("return"), as stated dramatically in Jeremiah 3.[42]

■ **5:20–21** Achior draws the lesson of his review of divine history and, though he is an Ammonite, draws a wise conclusion: If the people of Judea can be found to have sinned, then attack; you will be victorious. But if not, you will be defeated. It is unexpected that Achior should be so confident in God's control of history, but that is part of the "unconscious prophecy" by an outsider. Achior has also acted the part of Greek philosopher, not Israelite prophet, by presenting Holofernes with advice on two options.[43]

Surprising here is that the sin of the people is referred to as an *agnoēma,* a sin of ignorance or oversight. It seems to suggest that even a minor sin would be sufficient to bring them into danger, while in biblical tradition it was the serious sins that had caused Israel's downfall. (For the Stoic view that a minor sin is as grave as a major sin, see the commentary on 8:35.) Yet for the audience a point is reinforced: there has not been a significant national sin since the Hasmonean renewal. Further, Achior's statement prepares for Judith's later assertion to the same effect. That Achior expresses this in a neat *men . . . de* construction commends his observation to Holofernes and to the audience—it suggests the rhetorical ability of the wise courtier—and Gera notes the similarity to the speech of Croesus the wise adviser in Herodotus 1.207.[44] Achior's last clause, "lest their lord and god shield them and we become the laughing-stock of the whole world," is premonitory if not fully prophetic. Holofernes as lord and "their god" as lord are used closely together, highlighting an irony that will be played on to great delight in chap. 11.

---

41 See Deut 29:17–28; Judg 2:11–23; 2 Kgs 17:7–23; in the historical surveys: Deut 26:10; Josh 24:14–25; Neh 9:26–37; see Voitila, "Deuteronomistic Heritage," 380–82. The Deuteronomistic theology could also be stated in its converse; in 1 Macc 1:11 the assimilationist Jews supposedly proposed that separating from the nations had been *bad* for the nation: "In those days, lawless men came forth from Israel and misled many, saying, 'Let us go and make a covenant with the nations round about us, for since we separated from them many evils have come upon us.'"

42 The term *diaspora* appears here. In the LXX it appears in Deut 28:25; 30:4–5; and twelve times elsewhere; see J. Mélèze Modrzejewski, "How to

Be a Jew," in Shaye J. D. Cohen and Ernst Frerichs, eds., *Diasporas in Antiquity* (BJS 288; Providence, RI: Brown Judaic Studies, 1993) 65–71; and Tessa Rajak, *Tradition and Survival: The Greek Bible of the Ancient Jewish Diaspora* (Oxford: Oxford University Press, 2011) 100–101, 193–95.

43 Gera, *Judith,* 220.

44 Gera, "Speech in Judith," 421. On *agnoēma,* see also Daniela Scialabba, "What Does the Noun *agnoēma* Mean in Judith 5:20?," in Wolfgang Kraus, Michaël N. van der Meer, and Martin Meiser, eds., *XV Congress of the International Organization for Septuagint and Cognate Studies, Munich, 2013* (SCS 64; Atlanta: SBL Press, 2016) 393–400.

Text	Textual Notes

Text

5:22/ When Achior finished saying these things, all of the people standing around the tent began to complain. Holofernes's officers and all of the inhabitants of the seacoast and Moab called for Achior to be cut to pieces. **23/** "We have no fear of the Israelites! Indeed, they are a people with neither the power nor the might to mount a strong formation. **24/** Let us then proceed,[a] Lord Holofernes, and they will become fodder for your whole army!"

6:1/ When the disturbance of the men gathered around the council had subsided, Holofernes, commander-in-chief of the Assyrian army, said to Achior in the presence of all the assembled foreigners:[b] **2/** "Who are you, Achior and the mercenaries of Ephraim,[c] to prophesy among us as you have today, and tell us not to make war against the people of Israel[d] because their god will shield them? For what god is there[e] except Nebuchadnezzar?[f] He will send his forces to utterly destroy them from the face of the earth, and their god will not save them. **3/** But we, his slaves, will strike them down[g] as though they were one man, for they will not withstand the power[h] of our cavalry. **4/** With our cavalry we will wash[i] over them. Their mountains[j] will become drunk with their blood, and their fields will be filled with their dead. Not even their footprints will stand their ground before us, but they will be totally destroyed. Thus says King Nebuchadnezzar, lord of the entire world. For he has spoken, and not a word of his pronouncements[k] will be in vain.

5/ "But as for you, Achior, you Ammonite mercenary, who has uttered these words in a moment of perversity: you shall not see my face again from this day forth until I take my vengeance on this people out of Egypt. **6/** And when I return, the sword of my army and the spear[l] of my servants shall pierce your side, and you shall fall among their wounded. **7/** My slaves will now take you away to the high country and place you in one of the towns in the high passes, **8/** and you will not perish until you are utterly destroyed along with them. **9/** And if you still have hope in your heart that they will not be taken, then do not look downcast. But I have spoken, and not one of my words will fail to come true."

10/ Holofernes commanded the slaves who were waiting on him in his tent to seize Achior, take him to Bethulia, and hand him over to the Israelites. **11/** The slaves took him and led him out of the camp to the plain, and

Textual Notes

a   For αναβησομεθα: αναβησωμεθα 58 542, correcting a Semitizing future where a cohortative subjunctive is expected.

b   Moab is well attested in 5:22, but in 6:1, 2 the texts vary as to whether "the Moabites" are included. Moore omits them in 6:1, 2 as an influence of the previous verse, following B S V *O L b* 55 311 OL Sy Arm. The NRSV places "the Moabites" in a footnote as a variant. Added in 6:2 is ἐναντιον παντος του δημου αλλοφυλων και προς παντας υιους Μωαβ ("before all the foreigners and before all the people of Moab") S V *b* 55 Arm; προς παντας υιους Μωαβ ("before all the people of Moab") or similar in B *L O* 311 OL Sy; *mercennarius filiorum Ammon et Moab* ("mercenary of the sons of Ammon and Moab") OL-X, also as an influence of 5:22.

c   Και οι μισθωτοι του Εφραιμ: omitted by OL-MCGNX; cf. Vg. For Ephraim: Ammon *O L* OL-SBQP Sy 311. Cf. 6:5: μισθωτοι του Αμμων. Ephraim is *difficilior.*

d   For Israel: ιλημ *b*, as an abbreviation for Jerusalem.

e   For τις: ο θεος, *scito autem quoniam deus non est* ("I ask, moreover, for there is no god") in OL-X; cf. Vg.

f   After Nebuchadnezzar, *O* OL-SBQPGX Sy assume ο βασιλευς (*deus* OL-G) πασης της γης.

g   For παταξομεν: παταξωμεν 71; εξολοθρευσομεν or -σωμεν A *b* minus, cf. Hanhart, 36.

h   For το κρατος: τον αφρον 583 OL-SBQP (*spumam*).

i   For κατακλυσομεν: κατακλυσωμεν 71´; καταλυσομεν 311; κατακλασομεν 583; κατακαυσομεν (or -σωμεν) B S A V 58 542; καταπατησομεν *b* 249´ 534 670 Eth; Of the OL texts, only X (cf. also Sy-c) reads κατακαυσομεν; the others read the various Greek words above; see Bogaert, "Version latine," 193. Hanhart perhaps preferred κατακλυσομεν because it accounts better for the other readings, but Rahlfs and *NETS* prefer κατακαυσομεν ("incinerate"). See also Zimmermann, "Recovery," 68–69.

j   For ορη: ορια B 670 Sy; see Textual Note f on 1:5.

k   For τα ρηματα των λογων: τα ρηματα των στοματος S *L* OL-SBQPM Arm. The former is *difficilior.*

l   Hanhart and Rahlfs print ο λαος, but this is an exceedingly difficult reading, rejected by most. Λαος is evidently a misreading of λογχη, the conjecture of Fritsche, *Die Bücher Tobi und Judith,* 155; cf. *lancea* and similar in OL-SBQPG Sy; and cf. Vg.

m   Επι της κορυφης του ορους appears twice, the first omitted in *O* OL Sy. Moore omits the first occurrence, Enslin the second, while *NETS* keeps both.

n   For υποδυσαντες: *solverunt* (from υπολυσαντες?) *vinculum Achior* Aeth; αποχωρησαντες *O* Sy.

o   For Micah: Cheima A; Micel OL-X; Mirakos 126.

p   For Chabris: Gabris 583; Abris *a* 126; omitted

led him from the middle of the flatlands into the high country and arrived at the springs below Bethulia. 12/ **When the men of the town saw them,**[m] **they seized their weapons and ran out of the town to the mountain ridge. Every slinger threw stones at them and stopped their ascent. 13/ Finding shelter**[n] **below the mountain, they bound Achior and left him cast down at the base of the mountain, and returned to their lord.**

14/   **When the Israelites came down from their town and came upon him, they untied him and led him to Bethulia; there they placed him before the magistrates of their town, 15/ who were in those days Uzziah, son of Micah**[o] **of the tribe of Simeon, Chabris son of Gothoniel, and Charmis son of Melchiel.**[p] **16/ They then summoned all the elders of the town,**[q] **and all the young men and the women**[r] **rushed together to the assembly. They placed Achior in the middle of the whole people. Uzziah then asked him what had happened, 17/ and Achior responded and recounted to them what the parties had said in the council of Holofernes, and what he had said before the Assyrian leaders, and how Holofernes had boasted about what he would do to the house of Israel. 18/ The people fell down, prostrating themselves before God,**[s] **and cried out, 19/ "Lord God of heaven, behold their arrogance, and have mercy on account of the humiliation of our people. Look today upon the faces of those consecrated to you." 20/ They then reassured Achior, praising him warmly, 21/ and Uzziah took him from the town meeting to his home, and prepared a banquet with drinking for the elders. Throughout that night they called upon the God of Israel for help.**

q   OL-M; cf. Vg. For Charmis: Charmil 311; Chalmeis A; Chaob 126; Charu OL-C. Similar in the Hebrew Bible, and perhaps influencing our text, are Heber with Melchiel in Num 26:45, Gothoniel in LXX Josh 15:17, and Charmi in Gen 46:9; 1 Chr 4:1.

q   After πολεως, S has Israel.

r   After αι γυναικες: και τα παιδια αυτων in O OL Sy.

s   For θεω: κυριω 311 OL-MCN Sa Vg; κυριω θεω S OL-SBQPG.

Commentary

5:22–6:21

Holofernes's tent, mentioned for the first time here, becomes an important dramatic setting for the various councils of the generals and will later be the location of the interactions between Holofernes and Judith—and indeed the scene of the beheading. This dramaturgical focus on the tent worked well for later plays and operas of Judith. (Compare the similar dramaturgical use of the inside and outside of the praetorium in John 18–19.)

We have also just seen how the general's field tent, with its councils, counselors, and intrigues of a woman courtesan, comes to contain the same literary themes as the court in Herodotus or Ctesias (see §7 above). Because the first letter of Judith in the Vulgate was a capital A (for Arphaxad), in illuminated manuscripts the shape of this letter was easily adapted to a depiction of Holofernes's tent. This influenced many artists, such as Mantegna, who depicted Judith and her slave emerging from the mouth of the tent. (For the tent as a symbol of the vagina, see 13:1–10a and §8 above.)

The opposing generals murmur (*egongysen*) against Achior, calling to mind the Israelites' murmuring in the wilderness (Exod 17:3; Num 11:1; 14:27); compare the Israelites murmuring in Judith in 7:23–28; 8:12–13. It is easy to miss that Achior's peroration on God's role in Israelite history at first incenses not Holofernes but "all the people standing around," that is, "the inhabitants of the seacoast"—mainly Phoenicians—"and Moab," the nations roundabout who have now joined Nebuchadnezzar's cause. They reject Achior's view of the divine favor accorded the Israelites and insist to Holofernes, "they will become fodder for your whole army." Although these peoples were earlier under the threat of extermination by Holofernes (2:28), they now accept Nebuchadnezzar's lordship, and presumably his demand to be worshiped as a god. This forces them to reject Achior's assertion about the role of the God of Israel.

This narrative dynamic—the conspiracy of the other courtiers against the wise courtier—is similar to the court narrative tradition of Israel and the ancient Near East. Herodotus and Ctesias told such stories of the Eastern courts, and Jews took up this genre with enthusiasm: Daniel 1–6, Bel and the Dragon, Esther, and in an adapted form in Susanna. It may have first arisen in the Persian court, as it is strongly attested there as well.[1] A common element of this genre is that the king begins as neutral or even positively disposed to the courtier-protagonist, but is moved to persecute him *by the other courtiers,* generally representatives of another ethnic group. A slight difference in this case, however, is that we find generals, in a camp tent, acting as courtiers. It is an important arc of the book as a whole and should perhaps be considered another "Danielic" element, at the same time that it is "Herodotean."

■ **5:23–24**

Power and might become leitmotifs in Judith, here recalling Holofernes's question in 5:3 but also anticipating Judith's prayer in chap. 9, where power

motifs are emphasized, culminating in 9:14. "They will become fodder" is a particularly vivid image of destruction, both to be devoured but also to be reduced to the elements, to be consumed as though by animals. This image is repeated in 10:12. As above, there is a rhetorical heightening through the use of Greek particles; the speeches in Judith often use more elevated Greek than the narrative.[2]

■ **6:1–9**

As noted above, the wise Achior of chap. 5 is punished by Holofernes and appears thereafter as continually passive, moved about by the Assyrians and protected by the Bethulians. As Gera notes:

> Achior is moved in stages from the Assyrian camp to Bethulia and in the process is physically handled—and manhandled—by a series of people. He is given over to Holophernes' servants, taken up, led away, tied down, released by the Israelites, led to Bethulia, stood up in the assembly, and finally taken to Uzziah's home.[3]

■ **6:1** That Holofernes's meeting is considered a council is emphasized by the Greek term, *synedria,* as opposed to the term *gerousia,* which is used for the city council meeting convened by the high priest in Jerusalem (see the commentary on 4:8), or Nebuchadnezzar's *logos* or *boulē* (2:3–4), or the Bethulians' *ekklēsia* (6:16; 7:29; 14:6), or even the *dēmos* also in this verse. In Greek tradition, *synedrion* is used for war councils, both Greek and foreign, and also permanent ruling councils.[4] The term was adopted for the Sanhedrin in Jerusalem. The Sanhedrin in the New Testament and in Josephus is the Jerusalem city council, headed by the high priest.

Holofernes is now said to speak to Achior "in the presence of all the assembled foreigners" (*dēmou allophylōn*).[5] *Allophylos* is used often in the LXX; one might assume that it simply means foreigner, but it

1   Wills, *Jew in the Court,* 39–42; Gera, *Judith,* 61–64, 217.
2   Gera, *Judith,* 218.
3   Gera, *Judith,* 218–19.
4   Herodotus 8.56 and elsewhere; see Delcor, "Le livre de Judith," 158; cf. 2 Macc 14:5.
5   Moabites are noted in 5:22, and in some texts in 6:1, 2, probably an influence of 5:22; see the Textual Notes.

almost always translates Philistine. The more general term for foreigner in Jewish Greek is *allogenēs*, translating *zār* or *nēkār*.[6] In Jewish usage, *allophylos* was thus more charged—if Philistine was the coded meaning. The Philistines were early remembered in the ancient Near East as one of the marauding Sea Peoples. They had been defeated by David (Goliath was a Philistine) but remained independent, and were often referred to as "uncircumcised." Elizabeth Bloch-Smith argues that the Philistines functioned as *the* ethnic group against which Israelites defined their own identity: Israelites were circumcised, Philistines were not; Israelites abstained from pork, Philisitines ate pork; Israelites wore beards, Philistines were clean-shaven, and so on. A number of particular negative judgments were attached to Philistines that were not associated with Canaanites and others. Perhaps, says Moshe Weinfeld, the difference arises because the Philistines, *like Israel,* were considered to have migrated from outside the land, while the Canaanites, Ammonites, Moabites, Edomites, and others were understood to be the peoples on the land, or descended from them, when Israel entered.[7]

■ **6:2–9** Achior finds himself in trouble for no justifiable reason—Judith says the same thing to Holofernes in chap. 11 with no repercussions—and indeed no wise general would punish well-intentioned counsel. Holofernes's words are similar to Balak's to Balaam (Numbers 22–24) and King Ahab's to Micaiah (1 Kings 22) and characterize him also as the blustery tyrant of Greek tradition (see the commentary on 2:4–13). Further, the plot developments require that Achior be exiled among the Bethulians, and his suggestion that the God of Israel controls events challenges the divine pretensions of Nebuchadnezzar, although the audience knows that Achior is delivered to the Bethulians' care by the providence of God. By presenting to Holofernes a Deuteronomic view of Israel's history, Achior also prepares the way later for Judith to say that she left Bethulia because Israel was sinning.

Schmitz notes the similarities of Holofernes's speech here, Nebuchadnezzar's speech in 2:5–13, and Achior's speech in chap. 5.[8] In addition, Holofernes's speech upbraiding Achior bears some resemblance to Judith's upbraiding of the elders in 8:12–27. The similarities are more rhetorical than thematic, but we do note at the center of the speeches the contrast of "Who are you?" and the power of Nebuchadnezzar versus God:[9]

From 6:2–9	From 8:11–27
Who are you?	*Who are you?*
2 Who are you, Achior and the mercenaries of Ephraim, to prophesy among us as you have today, and tell us not to make war against the people of Israel because their god will shield them?	12 But who are you to test God today and set yourself in the place of God among human beings?
"God" is greater than you	*God is greater than you*
For what god is there except Nebuchadnezzar?	13 You are testing the Lord Almighty, but you will never understand anything! 14 You will not discover the depths of the human heart, nor comprehend a person's thoughts. How, then, would you search out God. . . .
	Military actions against Israel (past)
	19 And it was for this reason that our forebears were given over to sword and plunder, suffering a great fall before our enemies.

6   See also Schmitz/Engel, *Judit,* 165–66; Loader, *Pseudepigrapha.*

7   Bloch-Smith, "Israelite Ethnicity"; Moshe Weinfeld, *The Promise of the Land: The Inheritance of the Land of Canaan by the Israelites* (Taubman Lectures in Jewish Studies 3; Berkeley: University of California Press, 1993), 97; Wills, *Not God's People,* 35–37.

8   Schmitz, *Gedeutete Geschichte,* 124–25.

9   Cf. also Exod 5:2, where Pharaoh asks, "Who is the Lord that I should obey him and let Israel go?"

Military actions against Israel (future)	Military actions against Israel (future)
He will send his forces to utterly destroy them from the face of the earth, and their god will not save them. 3 But we, his slaves, will strike them down as though they were one man, for they will not withstand the power of our cavalry. 4 With our cavalry we will wash over them. Their mountains will become drunk with their blood, and their fields will be filled with their dead. Not even their footprints will stand their ground before us, but they will be totally destroyed.	20 We, however, do not recognize any God but him, and thus we hope that he will not disdain us or any of our nation. 21 For if we are taken, all of Judea will fall. The sanctuary will be plundered, and God will make us pay for its desecration with our blood. 22 The slaughter of our kindred, the captivity of the land (of Babylon), and the desolation of our inheritance he will bring upon our heads among the nations wherever we are enslaved, and we will become an offense and an object of shame among those who come to possess us. 23 Our slavery will not be turned into favor, but the Lord our God will account it as dishonor.

From the audience's point of view, the inherent truth of Achior's words affects Holofernes as well, as it places him at a decision point. Holofernes, however, demonstrates his folly by rejecting and even shaming Achior's advice. Achior's history lesson is viewed by Holofernes as audacity. Achior lives into the identity implied (to the audience) in his historical report by later converting, and Holofernes lives into his identity by deciding that Achior's truth stands in opposition to his own claims. Holofernes rules that Achior must die, but his arrogance even prevents him from doing that well. In order to subject Achior to the humiliation of witnessing him conquer Bethulia from within, he banishes him to the town, but the audience knows that this delay of execution, likely willed by God, eventuates in Achior living and Holofernes dying.

■ **6:2–4** The style of these verses is very "biblical," or per-

haps faux-biblical. Ironic here is the characterization of Nebuchadnezzar in a way similar to that of God in many biblical passages (see the excursus at 3:8, "The Worship of Nebuchadnezzar and Danielic Motifs"). "They will be totally destroyed" is more literally "by destruction they will be destroyed." The Hebrew construction of verb + infinitive absolute lies behind this, but Gera also notes that this same construction is used in Deut 4:26; 8:19; and 30:18 to express God's promise to destroy Israel if they worship other gods, and in Deut 12:2 it is a command to destroy foreign gods.[10] Holofernes again arrogates to himself biblical language of God's demands.

Somewhat unexpected, however, is Holofernes's insulting use of "Ephraim" for Achior.[11] Ephraim appears in some of the lists of the tribes of Israel and is often taken, *pars pro toto,* for northern Israel. Indeed, it sometimes appears with a similar negative connotation in southern Judahite sources: "O king, do not let the army of Israel go with you, for the Lord is not with Israel—all these sons of Ephraim!" (2 Chr 25:7). In Judith it could be taken in various ways. Is it *the character Holofernes* who associates Achior with Israel in general, that is, Achior is acting as if he is defending them, or does "mercenaries of Ephraim" also reflect *the audience*'s Judean, anti-northern perspective? If the latter, then Ephraim is considered *different from* and *worse than* the "good" Samarians above. To be sure, the audience may have heard "Ephraim" and "Samarian" as reflective of two different periods, ancient and recent, as an audience today might distinguish Anglo-Saxon and English. Ephraim may then be intentionally anachronistic. "Mercenaries of Ephraim" may also be interpreted in a way similar to "you Canaanites" in 5:3 and "this people out of Egypt" in 6:5; that is, Holofernes takes up ethnic terms more or less as they would be known to Jews.

Either way, the ethnonym is contemptuous, like the false ascription of Tobiah as "the Ammonite" in Neh 2:10.[12] The term mercenaries, *misthōtoi*, also means hired workers (see 6:5) and so may be contemptuous as well. Just as historical eras can be radically telescoped in the

10   Gera, *Judith,* 224.

11   Note the wide variations in the textual tradition, with Ephraim often lacking. Schmitz attempts to find meaning in the phrase in a mistranslation of Isa 28:1 LXX, where *škry 'prym* ("drunkards of

Ephraim") was misread as *śkyry 'prym* ("hired workers of Ephraim") (*Gedeutete Geschichte,* 126–27).

12   Michael Heltzer, *The Province Judah and the Jews in Persian Times (Some Connected Questions of the*

playful world of Judith, a merging of ethnic perspectives and class perspectives can be run together as well. In both cases, Holofernes is haughty, even contemptuous of the indigenous nations. Ultimately, Ephraim may simply constitute another example of an archaic term used to evoke the period of the narrative, when Judah would have asserted its control over northern Israel.

Holofernes also thunders, "Who are you to prophesy among us?" The audience understands the truth of the situation in a way that Holofernes does not. Achior's speech is in accord with Israelite prophecy, perhaps even unconscious prophecy, statements of a nonbeliever that unconsciously reveal God's plan (compare Balaam in Numbers 22–24 or the high priest Caiaphas in John 11:47–53). Holofernes continues, "What god is there except Nebuchadnezzar?" This expresses the great opposition in the book, the struggle between the claims of the foreign nations and foreign gods and that of the God of Israel (see §6 above). It is a Danielic moment, resonating with Daniel 3, but also with the posturing of Goliath in 1 Samuel 17. Holofernes also calls himself a "slave of Nebuchadnezzar," just as Judith will at times call herself a slave of Holofernes (11:5, 10, 16–17; 12:4), and at other points the audience will know that she is referring to herself as a slave of God. Holofernes is quite comfortable in the role of slave of Nebuchadnezzar as god; there is no restlessness of a man who would be king. In this narrative world, a sycophant is more loathsome than a tyrant.

Part of the dynamic of this book depends on the perfect balance of the dutiful soldier Holofernes and the dutiful Jewish woman Judith; they are both committed to the mission of their gods. To this end, Holofernes is truly a *false* prophet; or, more specifically, he is a true spokesperson for a false god, not a false spokesperson for a true god (cf. 1 Kgs 22:13–28; Jeremiah 28). He uses biblical idioms for prophecy concerning Nebuchadnezzar: "He has spoken," and "Not a word of his pronouncements will be in vain" (v. 4). He believes the words of his own prophecies and disbelieves Achior. In this ironic account, in which Holofernes accidentally announces true things, he denies that God will shield the Israelites, *hyperaspizō*. Gera suggests that this term echoes Gen 15:1, where God promises Abraham that he will shield him,[13] and Judith will use it in her prayer in 9:14.

■ **6:3–4** Holofernes insists that the Assyrians will destroy the Israelites "as one man," an image used in an interestingly ambiguous way in 1:11. "We, his slaves, will strike them down" utilizes the root *patassō*, as also in 2:27; 5:12; 9:3, 10; 13:8, 15; and 16:7, when Israelites are struck and strike back. The language of death and the piling up of corpses recalls Nebuchadnezzar's own words in 2:7–8, and the images here perhaps make a celluloid villain of both Assyrian leaders. Still, as the Assyrians claimed themselves—and were reputed by others—to employ particularly gruesome practices in their conquests, this imagery would ring true for Judith's audience.[14] An inscription of Shalmaneser III is particularly close: "I piled them in ditches and filled the extensive plain with the corpses of their warriors. Like wool, I dyed the mountain with their blood." The ultimate fall of Holofernes, and thus the repulse of Nebuchadnezzar's invasion, will make boasts like this verse seem foolish. That similar images are used of God's promise to destroy foreign nations—"Their slain shall be cast out, and the stench of their corpses shall rise; the mountains shall flow with their blood" (Isa 34:3)—indicates that Israel shared this imagery (see also Ezek 32:5–6; 35:8), as did Homer (*Iliad* 4.450-56). On "lord of the entire world," see the commentary on 2:5–6.

■ **6:5** Holofernes will take his revenge, *ekdikēsō*. This root was used often in regard to Nebuchadnezzar and the peoples of the West (1:12; 2:1), in regard to Simeon (9:2), and also with God as subject (7:28; 8:27, 35; 16:17).[15] Our author's broad humor is revealed here when Holofernes says to Achior, "You shall not see my face again from this day forth until I take vengeance on this people out of Egypt!"[16] The audience knows that the next time Achior will see Holofernes's face, it will be separated from the rest of his body. Holofernes's words have a way of com-

Persian Empire) (Tel Aviv: Archaeological Center Publications, 2008) 35–40.

13 Gera, *Judith*, 216.
14 *COS* 2.113A, i.41b–51a.

15 Schmitz/Engel, *Judit*, 275–76. See also 11:10.
16 For the use of the vow formula, see Gen 43:3.

ing true in a way that he does not intend. Presumably Holofernes chooses to delay Achior's execution so that the latter may witness the greater destruction as it happens, but from the audience's perspective, it is hubris on his part. (A similar exchange, with an ironic discrepancy between expectation and resolution, occurs between Moses and Pharaoh, Exod 10:28–29.) Like Achior's words in chap. 5, Holofernes's words seal his fate. With obvious sarcasm, Holofernes also refers to Israel as "this people out of Egypt," and it will be recalled that in Achior's account of history it was assumed that the Israelites were expelled from Egypt. This coheres with views of other indigenous peoples who competed with Israel within the empire and also, as a result, with some of the leading Greek and Roman historians (see the commentary on 5:6–9).

■ **6:9** Holofernes will conclude his judgment against Achior with two sentences that express deep irony. In the first, Holofernes mocks him using soft, emotionally sensitive language: "If you still have hope in your heart that they will not be taken, then do not look downcast." For the audience, it is ironic that his feigned concern actually expresses a hope that will come true—and hope is indeed a substantive and distinctive theological concept in Israel and in Judith (see the commentary on 9:11). We may expect here the audience to chime in, "Yes, Achior, do not be downcast!" In addition, Holofernes seals his unconscious prophecy when he says, "I have spoken, and not one of my words will fail to come true." Compare his words in 6:4, and recall that Achior and Judith also attest to their own truth before Holofernes (5:5; 11:5). Holofernes's words, however, suggest the prophetic idiom of one who speaks for the "god" Nebuchadnezzar. As one would expect with the *alazōn*, the depth of his folly is matched by the bombast of his claim.

■ **6:10–21**
This section may seem a mere transition in the narrative, moving Achior from the Assyrian camp to Bethulia, but it is excellent storytelling in a popular style, comparable to the style of the Ehud incident in Judges 3. At the same time that Achior's situation mirrors a previous section, it also anticipates a parallelism with the second half of the book: Achior will be moved *passively* from the camp to Bethulia; Judith will move *actively* from Bethulia to the camp. Achior will convert from polytheism to follow the one God of Israel; Judith will feign a betrayal of her people (and, implicitly, God) to join Holofernes's god, Nebuchadnezzar.[17] More verses are expended in regard to Achior's move here than to some of the previous important battles. Although Bethulia was first mentioned in 4:6 as part of the defense plans of Joakim, the high priest in Jerusalem, the story to that point was not focused on this mountain village. Now it is.

Excursus: Bethulia

Bethulia is an unknown and probably fictitious site. Since it is mentioned with the known sites of Esdraelon (Jezreel) and Dothan (3:9; 4:6; 7:3), some have sought an actual site among the towns south of them: Bethel, or lesser-known towns.[18] However, this is likely a pointless search. From the narrative, it is clear that the town lies in Samarian territory, but, as noted in the introduction, this probably does not imply a hidden Samarian origin or Samarian sympathy for our text. The location in Samarian territory actually has the opposite effect, to affirm Judean control over the regions of "greater Israel." The Jerusalem temple and Jerusalem authority, especially in the figure of Joakim the high priest, rule Israel (see the commentary on 4:4). The reason, in fact, that Bethulia is in Samaria may be that, for the Judean author, this is the site of the weak side of Israelite history and identity. As noted in §4 above, the exodus parallels condition this text; as a result, the elders and Bethulians represent weak-willed Israel, murmuring in the wilderness: "We will be slaves, but our lives will be spared" (7:27). The book of Judith then presents a triumph over Samaria that Ezra and Nehemiah had considered impossible. The fictitious Bethulia may also lie near Shechem, an important consideration in regard to Judith's retelling in chap. 9 of the Simeon/Shechem episode. That Bethulia lies at the edge of a mountain pass is also significant. The plot of our story—that a large foreign army must pause to confront a small number of opponents—requires a topographical barrier; the

---

17   Roitman, "Achior"; Steinmann, *Lecture de Judith*, 55–62.

18   Moore, *Judith*, 150–51; Stummer, *Geographie*, 6–10;

Carl Steuernagel, "Bethulia," *ZDPV* 66 (1943) 232–45. See also Zertal, "Reality," 161–75.

premise is perhaps inspired by the story of the three hundred Spartans (see §4 above and chap. 5).

One senses here the special story attraction of mountains, yet Israel and Greece did not have precisely the same associations. In Israel, mountains were generally places for separation and revelation. The first cult sites were called "high places" but were not universally in elevated places. The cultic aspects, however, do not seem to factor into our story. Rather, the Greek view of mountains seems more similar. Mountains are crucial in Greek discourse, but not simply defined by height; they are defined by what is opposite—cultivated plain and inhabited areas.[19] The mountain could be any uninhabited high area outside of the city: pasturage, an area for hunting or gathering raw materials, a site for battle, or a location for sanctuaries. There are three special aspects of mountains in Greek myth: (1) mountains are outside the domesticated area—marginal and wild; (2) they are primeval; and (3) they are sites for reversals and social transformations.

The spelling of Judith's village is usually *Baituloua* (Βαιτυλουα), Betuloua (Βετυλουα), or *Baitoulia* (Βαιτουλια).[20] In Latin, both OL and Vg, it is Bethulia, which provided the modern English spelling (see Textual Note e on 4:6).[21] The name of the village may suggest three possible Hebrew derivations:

1. *bĕtûlîm* ("virginity") or *bĕtûlâ* ("virgin")
2. *bêt-'ēl* or *bêt-'ĕlôha* ("House of God")
3. *bêt-'ălîyâ* ("House of Ascent")

1. *bĕtûlîm* ("virginity") or *bĕtûlâ* ("virgin")

Bethulia is often compared to Hebrew *bĕtûlâ* (*betulah*, "virgin") or *bĕtûlîm* (the tokens of "virginity"). The Latin spelling Bethulia is more similar than the Greek to Hebrew *bĕtûlâ*. It is conceivable that the Latin spelling is derived not from the Greek but from an independent Semitic version (see appendix), but this is not likely. As a result of itacism (the tendency in this period for some Greek vowels and diphthongs, including e and *ai*, to be pronounced as *iota*), the various spellings could equally have represented Semitic terms like *bĕtûlîm* or *bêt 'ēlâ*, and so on. Only Semitic speakers would have readily heard a connection to virgin, but it is possible that this was part of a reading tradition among Greek-speaking Jews.

Some biblical phrases might have suggested a comparison to virgin: "virgin Israel" (Jer 18:13; 31:4, 21), "virgin daughter Israel" (2 Kgs 19:21 = Isa 37:22; Lam 2:13); virgin daughter Judah (Jer 14:17; Lam 1:15).[22] Virgin daughter + city was a common personification for other peoples: Sidon (Isa 23:12), Babylon (Isa 47:1), Egypt (Jer 46:11). The virgin daughter Israel in 2 Kgs 18:13–19:37 (= Isaiah 36–37) is perhaps related to Judith. Our heroine is symbolically a perennial virgin (Judith's marriage to Manasseh seems unconsummated; see the commentary on 8:2–3), and Bethulia is thus equated with Judith. Yet a main argument for the virgin connection is thematic: Holofernes tried but failed to penetrate the town Bethulia.

2. *bêt-'ēl* or *bêt-'ĕlôha* or *bêt-'ĕlôah* ("House of God")

As "virgin" or "virginity" seemed a highly symbolic reading, some have sought a more typical derivation, such as *bêt-'ēl* or *bêt-'ĕlôha* ("house of God"). In the seventeenth century, Hugo Grotius suggested that it meant Bet-El-Yah, house of God. Following this, many modern scholars assumed *bêt-'ĕlôah* ("house of God"), that is, the temple.[23] The town would then be a fictitious Beth-El, a "high place" in the mountains (Gen 28:19). In the LXX, Beth El is spelled *Baithēl* (βαιθηλ), and in Latin Bethel. Bethel was a northern cult center for Israel, in fact, the southern boundary of the north, as Dan was the northern boundary. During the Maccabean Revolt, it

---

19 Richard Buxton, *Imaginary Greece: The Contexts of Mythology* (Cambridge: Cambridge University Press, 1994) 80–96. On the mountain in Israel, see Richard J. Clifford, *The Cosmic Mountain in Canaan and the Old Testament* (HSM 4; Cambridge, MA: Harvard University Press, 1972).

20 Βαιτυλουα in B; Βετυλουα in A V; Βατυλουα in 58 Arm; Βαιτουλια in S *L* OL.

21 Many variants arise from the lack of distinction in the vowel sounds. Cf. also Beth-horon in 4:4, spelled *Baithōrōn*. Most of the medieval Hebrew texts change Bethulia to Jerusalem, but those that keep the older tradition have בתול, Bethul (cf. Josh 19:14). This does not argue for a play on virginity, but it does not rule it out. The town Bethul in the inheritance of Simeon (Josh 19:4) was in the south, and so this name is not likely related.

22 See Amnon Shapira, "The City 'Bethulia' (Judith 4:6)—A Geographical Name or Literary Fiction?" *Studies of Judea and Samaria* 14 (2005) 67–76, here 74–75; Alonso-Schökel, *Narrative Structure*, 19; Christl M. Maier, *Daughter Zion, Mother Zion: Gender, Space, and the Sacred in Ancient Israel* (Minneapolis: Fortress Press, 2008) 60–93. Batuloua, one of the variants, would perhaps be "Daughter of Eloha"; see J. Schwartz, "Un fragment grec," 534–37. Martin Luther took Bethulia as Betul-Yah ("virgin of Yahweh"); so Otzen, *Tobit and Judith*, 89, 94.

23 Otzen, *Tobit and Judith*, 89, 94.

was occupied and fortified by the Seleucids. It might then resonate for the audience in the Hasmonean period.[24]

3. *bêt-ʿălîyâ* ("house of ascent")

Otzen discusses *bêt-ʿălîyâ* as "house of ascension," a village on the way of pilgrimage to Jerusalem, that is, Shechem or Bethel. He bases this on Charles Cutler Torrey's argument that Beth Aloa, "house of ascent" or "lofty abode," would suggest Shechem.[25] Torrey hypothesized a parallel etymology for Betomesthaim (mentioned with Bethulia in 4:6): Bet-Mastema ("home of the devil" or "place of enmity"), referring to Samaria. Neither of these suggestions, however, carries weight. House of Ascent might, however, suggest the mountain village of the story.

Regardless of the derivation of the name, and in apparent contradiction to its location at a mountain pass, Bethulia is sometimes presented as a city, with city walls, ramparts, and gates that figure importantly on several occasions. Here and elsewhere Bethulia is called a *polis* (although in 4:5 *kōmē* is used). As *ʿîr* can mean either city or town, one need not assume that in the LXX *polis* implies a Greek city, but the description represents another absurd mixing nevertheless.

While chaps. 5–6 are concerned mainly with the experiences and perspectives of Achior, the audience also recognizes here the point of view of the Bethulians. Their actions were first mentioned in 4:6–8, again in 6:12, and now they rise in importance. Narrative interest and tension are created in the details of the intervention of the Bethulians on behalf of Achior, even though they do not know who he is or why he is being left bound below their village. This section also provides a glimpse into activities in Bethulia, the villagers' fears, and the response that they are mounting.

■ **6:14–21** Nations have been swept up into a world war, but it is the nature of narrative, especially fiction, to find in the larger map of the drama a single encounter, the struggle between an Achilles and a Hector. That

moment is approaching as one of the antagonists moves toward the central moment. The point of view thus shifts to the residents of the tiny mountain village. Although Achior is hardly the master of his own fate, and the Bethulians' intervention is not strategic (since they do not know who he is), the actions of the two parties is a clear example of how the plot is moving people in God's chosen direction, the unconscious navigation toward a happy ending. How appropriate, then, that this section lies at the center of the chiasm of the first half of the text.[26] Within this section, it corresponds to and reverses the dialogue between Holofernes and Achior and the former's rejection of the wise counsel.

■ **6:14-15** Achior is placed before the *archontes tēs poleōs*, which in Greek usage would be the magistrates. In Judith, it seems to be equivalent to elders (8:10–11). This may be a hellenizing usage, since *archōn* is used for a number of Hebrew honorary offices: *nāśîʾ*, *śar*, *rōʾš*, but never *zāqēn* ("elder").[27] Since older Hebrew did not have a position of magistrate, the merging is not unexpected.

Uzziah is clearly the chief of the *archontes*. It is a common Israelite name—Yah is my strength—but ironic in that he proves to be a weak leader and bends to the circumstances.[28] He is also of the tribe of Simeon, which Judith valorizes in 9:2, but he does not act the part. In the European operatic and dramatic tradition, he was elevated to a position of strength and leadership, often commanding the weaker Judith, while Achior is diminished. But the ancient tradition knew nothing of this (see §8 above). The other town leaders are Chabris and Charmis, who are unknown outside of our text. On the comic effect of these two names, see the commentary on 8:10. Like Judith's slave, however, they remain silent throughout.

■ **6:16–19** Achior is brought before the assembly (*ekklēsia*)

---

24   Michael Chyutin assumes this connection but presents a speculative thesis that the text of Judith is then anti–Hasmonean (*Tendentious Hagiographies: Jewish Propagandist Fiction BCE* [LSTS 77; London: T&T Clark, 2011] 160-61). Zenger opts for House of God, either Jerusalem or the temple (*Das Buch Judit*, 435). Priebatsch suggests Beth El ("Das Buch Judith," 54–55); Stummer, Bethul or Bethuel in Simeon (Josh 19:14; 1 Chr 4:30) (*Geographie*, 8–9); see discussion in Otzen, *Tobit and Judith*, 89.

25   Otzen, *Tobit and Judith*, 94; Torrey, *Apocryphal Literature*, 91–92; Craven, *Artistry and Faith*, 73 n. 25.

26   See §3 above.

27   Grintz, *Book of Judith*, 133: *archōn* as *rōʾš*, and *presbyteroi* as *zĕqēnîm*.

28   See 8:10. He is somewhat similar to Barak, Aaron, and Saul; see notes on 7:30; 8:11, 30; 14:1-4; and Corley, "Imitation," 27–34.

of the people (*laos*: see the commentary on 4:1–15), which includes both men and women. (The council in 2:2 was a *boulē* and that in 6:1 a *synedria*.) The LXX of Ezra-Nehemiah uses *ekklēsia* for the *qāhāl*, congregation of Israel (Neh 5:7; 8:2; cf. 1 Macc 5:16), which also includes men and women (Neh 8:1–3). Jeremiah 44:24 also mentions "the people and all the women," and Deut 31:12 explicitly includes women, while Exodus 19 does not. The meetings of the Assyrians are called *boulē* (2:2) and *synedria* (6:1, 17). Achior is once again depicted as passive: "they stood him up."

The people as a whole, *laos*, fell and worshiped God and cried out, offering the first prayer of the book of Judith. Schmitz has rightly drawn more attention to the prayers in Judith as representative of its theological affirmations; see also 9:2–14; 13:4b–7, 17; and 16:13–17.[29] In this brief utterance, the Bethulians call upon God to witness the Assyrians' arrogance, to have pity on the Bethulians' humiliation, and to behold those consecrated (*hēgiasmenōn*) to him. As an unexpectedly large number of words were used to describe Achior's transition to Bethulia, an unexpectedly small number of words are used for the Bethulians' first prayer. This is transitional to their role later, but the author shows a keen sense of controlling the focalization of experience. Still, the prayer exhibits a strong and clear theological position, highlighting a few words (here in italics) that resonate as leitmotifs of the text as a whole:

> **Lord God of heaven,** behold their *arrogance,* and *have mercy* on account of the *humiliation* of our people. *Look* today *upon* the faces of those *consecrated* to you. (6:19)

> Κύριε ὁ θεὸς τοῦ οὐρανοῦ, κάτιδε ἐπὶ τὰς ὑπερηφανίας αὐτῶν καὶ ἐλέησον τὴν ταπείνωσιν τοῦ γένους ἡμῶν, καὶ ἐπίβλεψον ἐπὶ τὸ πρόσωπον τῶν ἡγιασμένων σοι ἐν τῇ ἡμέρᾳ ταύτῃ.

Some of these words will be intoned in Judith's prayer in chap. 9, and others, though quite important, will be used in slightly different ways.[30]

■ **6:21** Uzziah provides a *poton*, a banquet with drinking, for Achior and the elders, which is odd given that the town is under siege and will soon suffer from hunger and thirst. We might charitably note that the worst effects of lack of water are not mentioned until the end of chap. 7 (it will be more surprising that Judith bathes after the water crisis has begun!), although surely they might have been predicted. Or are we to see here the requirements of hospitality and what this means for the acceptance of Achior (cf. v. 20)? Hospitality is a much stronger cultural and narrative motif in premodern cultures, in novelistic texts as much as in others. The Bethulians must accept Achior ritually, honor him, and protect him. We need not require a strict logic of this text, but narratively it also provides another pause, a recurring literary structuring element of the first half (see the commentary on 2:28). There is one other consideration: is the banquet a "reading" experience that is paralleled by the real audience's performance experience *at a banquet*? That is, was the originary performance situation of Judith at the same kind of banquet as is described in the text? The literary motif of the drinking banquet is prominent in Esther, Daniel 1–6, Tobit, and 3 Maccabees—all similar in genre to Judith—and it balances the banquet to which Judith will be invited when she exchanges places with Achior in Holofernes's camp (12:10–20). The Israelites also call upon God (*epekalesanto*) in the same way that Holofernes had insisted that *all peoples* should call upon Nebuchadnezzar (*epikalesōntai*).[31] Is it somewhat taboo that a drinking banquet should be the scene of fervent prayer?

---

29   See also Pancratius C. Beentjes, "Bethulia Crying, Judith Praying: Context and Content of Prayers in the Book of Judith," in Renate Egger-Wenzel and Jeremy Corley, eds., *Prayer from Tobit to Qumran: Inaugural Conference of the ISDCL at Salzburg, Austria, 5–7 July 2003* (Deuterocanonical and Cognate Literature Yearbook 2004; Berlin: de Gruyter, 2004) 231–54, here 231–32.

30   See notes on *neaniskoi* in 7:23; in 7:20–29 on the clamor and suffering of the Bethulians; in 7:32 and 9:14 on humiliation.

31   Gera, *Judith*, 231.

Text

1/ On the next day Holofernes commanded his entire army, and all of the people who had come as part of his alliance, to break camp and set out for Bethulia to take control[a] of the passes into the high country and wage war against the Israelites. **2/** Every trained soldier thus set out that day, their army of warriors numbering 170,000 infantry[b] and 12,000, not counting the supply train and the foot soldiers assigned to it—a very great multitude. **3/** They set up camp beside a spring in the valley near Bethulia, spreading out in breadth over Dothan as far as Balbaim, and in length from Bethulia to Cyamon, which faces Esdraelon. **4/** When the Israelites beheld the size of the army, they became very distraught and said to one another, "They will now certainly lick clean the face of the entire land. Neither the high mountains nor the valleys nor the hills will bear their weight." **5/** Then each man took up his arms, kindled fires on the towers[c] and stood guard throughout the night.

6/ On the second day Holofernes led out his entire cavalry before the Israelites who were in Bethulia. **7/** He reconnoitered the passes that led to their town, inspected the springs and seized them, stationing at each of them a detachment of armed troops. Then he returned to his people. **8/** All of the leaders of the Edomites[d] and all of the rulers of the people of Moab and the generals from the coastal areas approached Holofernes and said, **9/** "Let our master listen to what we have to say, so that there be no losses for his armies. **10/** This people, the Israelites, do not place their trust in their spears, but in the height of the mountains on which they dwell, for it is not easy to approach the crests of their mountains. **11/** So, then, my lord, do not fight against them in battle formation, as it is normally done, and not a single man from your people will fall. **12/** Remain in your camp with your entire army in reserve, but allow your servants to take control of the spring that flows from the base of the mountain, **13/** for all those who live in Bethulia draw their water there. Thirst will destroy them and they will surrender their town. We and our people will ascend to the mountaintops nearby and set up camp upon them and will stand guard to ensure that not a single man leaves their town. **14/** They, their wives, and their

Textual Notes

a   See Textual Note c on 4:5.

b   For 170,000 infantry: $\rho o\beta$' (172,000) 583 OL-G Sy; $\rho\kappa$' (120,000) S-c OL-C Vg; $o\kappa\tau o$ (8,000) S*. For 12,000 cavalry: *viginti duo milia* (22,000) OL Sy Vg.

c   After $\pi\nu\rho\gamma o\nu\varsigma$: $\tau\omega\nu\ \tau\epsilon\iota\chi\epsilon\omega\nu$ added in *O* OL Sy.

d   Literally, sons of Esau, the eponymous ancestor of the Edomites.

e   For $\nu\iota\omega\nu\ A\mu\mu\omega\nu$: $\nu\iota\omega\nu\ M\omega\alpha\beta\ L$ OL-QPG Sy.

children will waste away from famine, and before the sword ever strikes them, they will be strewn about the streets of their settlement. 15/ In this way you will indeed exact a severe vengeance upon them for rebelling against you and not coming out to meet you in peace."

16/ Their words pleased Holofernes and all his ministers, and he gave orders to do as they said. 17/ The army of the Ammonites[e] set out with five thousand Assyrians and made camp in the valley; they seized the streams and wells belonging to the Israelites. 18/ Then the Edomites and the Ammonites went up and encamped in the high country opposite Dothan, and sent some of their troops to the southeast in the direction of Egrebeh, near Chusi on the Wadi Mochmur. The rest of the Assyrian army encamped in the plain, and covered the entire face of the earth. Their tents and supply train formed a huge encampment, for their multitude was great.

Commentary

7:1–18

Chapters 1–6 have prepared for this moment; the attack on the village of Bethulia begins here. The book of Judith has brought all the Near East's great empires together in war, and arrays the vast army to "make war on the Israelites." Gera calls attention to the clever storytelling techniques of this passage: movements of individuals and of armies, the fear and trembling of the Israelites, specific temporal notices and transitions and other fictitious details of time and space.[1]

The dramatic narrative to come is also prepared for by the notation that the camp—the setting for the central action of the novella—is in the plain below Bethulia, at the site of a spring that will play a role. The narrative presentation alternates between the point of view of the Assyrian forces and that of the Israelites of Bethulia. When the Israelites survey the enemy below they are greatly disturbed, *etarachthēsan sphodra* (7:4),

a common biblical expression for fear. The Israelites repeat the images of destruction that the Assyrians had used to threaten the peoples before them: "They will lick clean the face of the entire land . . . it will not bear their weight" (cf. 2:27; 6:2–4). Although the Bethulians will later wilt under the siege, they have so far been far braver than the other nations, and have responded with a simple courage by taking up their weapons, lighting fires, and remaining on guard throughout the night. Despite their understandable fear, the Bethulians' actions constitute the best military response they can offer.

The Edomites—"sons of Esau"—Moabites, Ammonites (see v. 18), and seacoast peoples offer a plan for Holofernes to capture the mountain village.[2] These are the nations roundabout, which, under one name or another, still existed at the time of the Hasmoneans, and are also understood as the descendants of the legendary peoples in the land when the Israelites conquered Canaan (see the excursus at 3:5–10, "The 'Nations Roundabout'"). And just as their speech occupied more

---

1   Gera, *Judith*, 235, 238.
2   The local color at this point includes Dothan (7:18; see the commentary on 8:2–3), a known site, but also Egrebeh, Chusi, and Wadi Mochmur, all unknown.

verses than one might have expected, so did the description of their actions. It is a narrator's trick to know when to slow down, relishing the talk and preparations for things to come. The amount of performance time taken to prepare for a climax is often more than the time it takes to resolve it. The narrator must build both interest and tension; release or resolution should not be precipitated quickly. The decapitation scene in chap. 13, for instance, will be told more economically than the tightening of the vise around Bethulia.

■ 7:1–7

After the multiethnic deliberations of chaps. 5 and 6, it is emphasized that the gathered forces, often mentioned separately, are also said to be constituent parts of the Assyrian army and all the peoples who had entered into alliance with them. Newly constituted allies of Assyrians, formerly a mixed mass, are now a *laos*. As in earlier chapters, the powers of the author are called upon to communicate the enormity of Holofernes's army. The language of warfare would suggest that Bethulia is a major opponent rather than a small mountain village. The size of the Assyrian army is given as 170,000 infantry, 12,000 cavalry, in addition to those handling the equipment and provisions (see the commentary on 2:5; the cavalry will conveniently disappear from the mountain siege and the later routing of the Assyrians). The immensity of the army is also rendered in expanse: "spreading out in breadth over Dothan as far as Balbaim, and in length from Bethulia to Cyamon, which faces Esdraelon."[3] The description is visual, told from the Bethulians' point of view. They look down from the mountain village at the expeditionary force in the plain, a gigantic stretch of armies, supplies, and camp-followers. The Bethulians will see and quiver in fear. Holofernes has marshaled his troops in formation to stir fright in the Israelites; he personally reconnoiters the approaches and springs of the mountain villages. As Holofernes marshals his troops and personally inspects the situation, the specific actions of military leadership are specified: he reconnoitered, inspected, seized, stationed, returned. All of the general's actions serve to frighten the Israelites. This will be contrasted with his later passive, sedentary role, as he waits wanly in his tent for Judith to act.[4] The ludicrousness of scale here—the great general of the expeditionary forces visiting and seizing the springs and then returning to his army— serves well the aesthetic goals of this text.

In addition to the awesome size of this army, the audience perceives the army's unwieldiness, its ineffectualness; it is a bloated cow waiting to be slaughtered. Still, Holofernes has arrayed his troops to terrify the Israelites, and he is not capable of perceiving the irony of his lumbering Goliath. The audience would have known that in 2 Kgs 19:35 the Assyrian king Sennacherib and his army of 185,000 men were defeated by God, and large armies were defeated by Israelites in Josh 11:4 and 1 Sam 13:5. More recently, the Hasmonean guerrilla forces had defeated large armies. Herodotus's description of Xerxes's Persian army (7.60) is also likely an influence.

■ 7:8–18

The Edomites, Moabites, and peoples of the coast (that is, Phoenicians, descended from Canaanites; see commentary on 1:7–10 and 5:1–3) suggest a stratagem and take the initiative in executing it. The list of peoples itself likely echoes the Song of the Sea; the leaders,

---

3   The area described is the Jezreel (= Esdraelon) valley. There were important biblical battles here: Gideon against the Midianites and Amalekites (Judg 6:3), and Saul's defeat by the Philistines (1 Sam 29:1–6). For Dothan, see 3:9; 4:6; 8:3. Cyamon, Greek Kyamōn, though similar to Jokneam or Jokmeam (1 Kgs 4:12) on the eastern slope of Mount Carmel (modern Tell Qeimon), is different enough to suggest that it is unrelated. It is thus unknown and mentioned only here in the Bible. The word means "bean field," and was likely

invented for the narrative. See Stummer, *Geographie*, 7; Denis Baly, *The Geography of the Bible* (rev. ed.; New York: Harper & Row, 1974) 144, 149–50; Yohanan Aharoni, *The Land of the Bible: A Historical Geography* (Philadelphia: Westminster, 1979) 313. Belbaim is similar to Belmain (4:4) and Balamon (8:3), but, despite the textual variants, there is no reason to identify any of these. Stummer (*Geographie*, 7) sees it as the *Yibleam* of Josh 17:11, but this is unlikely.

4   Gera, *Judith*, 238.

archontes, of the sons of Esau and the commanders, *hēgoumenoi,* of the people of Moab, and the generals of the coastland are very similar to the *hēgemones* of Edom, *archontes* of the Moabites, and residents of Canaan found in Exod 15:15 LXX (compare also Obad 1:1, 8). Specifically, these groups secure the mountaintops around Bethulia, a very visual and dramatic move, a storyteller's delight. The counsel of the opponents here is clever in the short term but does not see the nature of history that Achior has discerned. It may seem that Ammonites have fallen out because Achior has disgraced them, but they are the collective name for all the near nations in 7:17 (see the excursus at 3:5–10, "The 'Nations Roundabout'"). The text clearly uses the near neighbors as equivalents—the near neighbors that were independent kingdoms for centuries. In Hellenistic times called Idumeans, the Edomites remained as a people among the Hellenistic kingdoms. (The father of Herod the Great was an Idumean converted by the Hasmoneans.)

■ **7:8–10** More verses than expected are taken up with the speech. The tone is very similar to what Achior has said—endangering himself thereby—and what Judith will say in 11:9–10, but it is "naturalistic" and not "theistic": "This people do not place their trust in their spears, but in the height of the mountains" (7:10). The way to vanquish them is to lay siege and deprive them of water, not by observing their sin. Such a situation would be well known to the audience, and it is interesting that in Jerusalem there was a specially constructed tunnel for water to withstand a siege (2 Kgs 20:20), and the Siloam or Hezekiah's Tunnel had existed since the time of Sennacherib's siege in 701 BCE or even earlier. One should also not overlook the irony that guards can prevent even a single man from leaving Bethulia (7:13), but a single woman (and slave) will walk out and destroy them.[5]

■ **7:11–15** Unexpected, and unexpectedly acceptable to Holofernes, is the delay that this strategy will entail. Holofernes has styled himself an active leader, and so it seems strange when he agrees to bivouac his troops at the foot of the mountain of Bethulia to passively wait out the Israelites' surrender. Gruen draws our attention to the humor: the worldwide campaigns of Nebuchadnezzar and Holofernes cover extraordinary, even impossible, distances in record time, yet the field general is willing to pause at tiny Bethulia to wait for the inhabitants to succumb to thirst.[6] Kingdoms have fallen before him, but now he waits beneath this one village. Holofernes is not a wise general, and his reaction to good advice—he rejects Achior's—and bad advice—he accepts Judith's—indicates that he is destined to fail; accepting the advice here is in keeping with that. Further, his passivity and even feminization in the second half are anticipated here.[7] This, indeed, is the moment at which his character changes from active to passive. The leaders of his alliance counsel him, "Remain in your camp with your entire army in reserve" (7:12) and he agrees. He will sit in his tent until his head is taken away forcibly.

5   Gera, *Judith,* 57.
6   Gruen, *Diaspora,* 169.
7   Sheaffer, *Envisioning,* 119.

Text	Textual Notes

Text

19/ Their spirits flagging, the Israelites cried out to the Lord their God, for all their enemies surrounded them[a] and there was no means of escape from them. **20/** The entire assemblage[b] of Assyrians—infantry, chariots, and cavalry—surrounded them for thirty-four[c] days. All the jars of water gave out for all those who lived in Bethulia. **21/** Their cisterns were going dry, and on no day did they have enough water to drink, for they were rationing water to drink. **22/** Their babies grew listless, the women and young men fainted from thirst and were collapsing in the streets of the town and in the gateways; there was no longer any strength left in them.[d] **23/** All the people—young men, women, and children—gathered before Uzziah and the leaders of the town and cried out loudly and said before all the elders, **24/** "May God judge between you and us, for you have committed a grave injustice by not discussing terms of peace with the Assyrians. **25/** Now there is no one to help us, for God has sold us into their hands to be laid low before them in thirst and utter destruction. **26/** Therefore, call upon them and surrender the entire town as spoils to the people of Holofernes and his entire army. **27/** For it would be better for us to become their plunder;[e] we will be slaves,[f] but our lives will be spared,[g] and we will not witness the deaths of our babies before our eyes, nor our wives and children giving up their lives. **28/** We call as witness against you heaven and earth and our God and Lord[h] of our fathers, who punishes us for our sins and for the sins of our fathers: do today as we have spoken!"[i]

29/ With one accord, a loud lamentation rose up in the middle of the assembly of the whole people; they cried out to the Lord God with a loud voice, **30/** but Uzziah said to them, "Brothers and sisters, take courage! Let us hold out for five days more, during which time the Lord our God will turn his mercy toward us; for he will not forsake us completely. **31/** And if these days pass and help for us does not come, then I will do as you say." **32/** He then dismissed the people to their outposts, and they went off to the walls and towers of the city and they sent the women and children to their homes. They were in great misery in the city.

Textual Notes

a   After εκυκλωσαν· αυτους supplied by A *a* 126 542 La Sy Aeth Arm. This is likely a correction, but *NETS* adopts it.

b   Πασα συναγωγη Ασσουρ adopts both the archaizing use of Asshur and συναγωγη; the latter has no connection at this time with the early synagogue, but was, along with εκκλησια, the Greek term for *qāhāl*, the community of Israel.

c   For τριακοντα τεσσαρας: viginti in Vg; δεκατεσσαρας και μηνα ενα L; *diebus quattuor et mensibus duobus* OL-G Sy; *duos menses* OL-X.

d   Vg omits v. 22; see appendix.

e   Η αποθανειν εν διψη added in *L b* 534, which Moore includes.

f   Εσομεθα γαρ εις δουλους omitted by OL-MC; after δουλους: και δουλας added in *O* OL Sy.

g   In Greek, a collective singular: "our soul will live."

h   For τον θεον . . . και κυριον: κυριον τον θεον L OL-G Sy; Hanhart chooses the former as *difficilior,* and Moore notes that confusion could arise from *nomina sacra* abbreviations of κν for κυριον and θν for θεον.

i   Ινα μη ποιηση, found in B A S, is likely a Semitic oath formula, although Gera takes it more literally: "that *he* may not act according to these words." Some texts smooth it over: ινα ποιηση S V OL-G; *ut faciatis* OL; του ποιησαι 583 Sy; ποιησητε 311 534 Eth.

Commentary

7:19–32

The piety of the Israelites, both Judean and Samarian, was idealized in chap. 4, but here the tone changes to introduce the Bethulians' weakness of will. Our text distinguishes, whether intentionally or not, between the piety of "Israelites" in general, concentrated on those who are around the temple in Jerusalem (including the institutions of Jerusalem's theocracy), and the Bethulians, who are all-too-human and want to capitulate. Although the Jerusalemites are continually strong, those who are guarding the boundary, the Bethulians, must find their strength in a Jewish heroine. The lack of resolve of principal characters is a common biblical theme: the Israelites in the wilderness, Saul, the army in Deuteronomy, some kings and prophets. This theme is found as well among the followers of Jesus: Peter's denial and the disciples in Gethsemane. We see it also in the students of Socrates. The depiction of weak leaders may allow the audience to identify with their imperfection. The audience of our novella may have imagined themselves both as Bethulians and as Judith.

■ **7:19**

The siege lasts for thirty-four days, but Judith's action will last four days, and the military action some time after that. The period as a whole is sometimes said to last forty days, calculated from the beginning of Holofernes's campaign to his death,[1] but would the audience have discerned this? At any rate, the forty days, in addition to being a biblical number (Gen 7:4; 1 Sam 17:16), also corresponds to Judith's mourning for forty months and the forty years in the wilderness.

■ **7:20–22**

The description of the suffering of the Bethulians may strike modern readers as emotionalizing or melodra-matic, but it is typical of ancient accounts. While novelistic texts tended to grant free rein to the description of individual emotions and inner turmoil—the buffeting of the protagonists—historians, or at least historians of a more popular level, and rhetoricians made a studied art of recounting *public* anguish. Formerly, scholars supposed there was a subgenre of "tragic" or "pathetic history," and while there was probably no such recognized category, a quantitative distinction between more or less indulgent history did exist.[2] The corporate display of emotion and turmoil is also met in Ezra 9–10, where it is part of a quasi-constitutional renewal of the covenant, with a commitment of all the residents:

> While Ezra prayed and made confession, weeping and throwing himself down before the house of God, a very great assembly of men, women, and children gathered to him out of Israel. The people also wept bitterly. (Ezra 10:1)

Closer to the time and situation of our author, the description of the siege of Jerusalem in 2 Macc 3:18–21; 5:15–16 can also be compared.[3] To be sure, elite Greek and Roman historians would have criticized this as pandering to emotionalism. Polybius (2.56.7), for example, condemns the description of a siege by Phylarchus:

> In his eagerness to arouse the pity and attention of his readers he treats us to a picture of clinging women with their hair disheveled and their breasts bare or again of crowds of both sexes together with their children and aged parents weeping and lamenting as they are led away into slavery.[4]

But by the first century CE, the more open standard of Phylarchus had perhaps become accepted. The Roman rhetorician Quintilian instructs speakers on how to develop this audience experience:

---

1 Van Henten, "Judith as an Alternative Leader," 229–31.

2 Doran, *Temple Propaganda,* 86–87; and F. W. Walbank, "History and Tragedy," *Historia* 9 (1960) 216–34; and more recently Louis H. Feldman, *Josephus's Interpretation of the Bible* (HCS 27; Berkeley:

University of California Press, 1998), 13–14; and Mendels, *Rise and Fall,* 35–37.

3 See also the commentary on 4:9–10 and 7:23–32. For biblical parallels, see 2 Kgs 6:24–30; 25:3; Jer 19:6–10; Lam 2:11–12; 4:4–10.

4 Translation of Gera, *Judith,* 244.

We may move our hearers to tears by the picture of a captured town. For the mere statement that "the town was stormed," while no doubt embracing all that such a calamity involves, has all the curtness of a dispatch, and fails to penetrate to the emotions of the hearer. But if we expand all that the one word "stormed" includes, we shall see the flames pouring from house and temple, and hear the crash of falling roofs and one confused clamor blended of many cries; we shall behold some in doubt where to fly, others clinging to their nearest and dearest in one last embrace, while the wailing of women and children, and the laments of old men, that the cruelty of fate should have spared them to see that day, will strike upon the ears. Then will come the pillage of treasure sacred and profane, the hurrying to and fro of the plunderers as they carry off their booty or return to seek for more, the prisoners driven each before his own inhuman captor, the mother struggling to keep her child, and the victors fighting over the richest spoil. For though, as I have said, the sack of a city includes all these things, it is less effective to tell the whole news at once than to recount it detail by detail. (Quintilian, *Institutio oratoria* 8.3.67–70)

The description of the besieged Bethulians is thus effective, perhaps even told with relative restraint. At any rate, the description of Jewish suffering in 3 Maccabees 4 exhibits more pathos. What almost passes without notice, however, is that the lack of water is introduced here as a crucial factor, while in 10:3 Judith commences bathing. (The banquet for Achior in 6:21 could be understood as occurring *before* the effects of the siege were felt.) It is also ironic that "there was no longer any strength left in them," given that in the next verse they look to Uzziah, "Yahweh is my power," to make good on his name.

■ **7:23–28**

The people rebuke Uzziah for failing to negotiate a peace, even though it is not clear that they would have been granted any concessions from Holofernes. In fact,

in v. 26 they assume that they will have to "surrender the entire town as spoils"—contrast their brave determination to avoid this fate in 4:12. The Bethulians are not presented realistically, or even consistently. Compare, however, 1 Macc 13:43–47 for a case in which Simon the Maccabee did grant concessions to a city under siege (even though his occupation is still quite demanding).

The Bethulians murmur against Uzziah much as the Israelites had murmured against Moses during the wilderness wanderings on three different occasions (Exodus 15–17; Numbers 14, 20; Deut 6:16). The account of one of these occasions, Exod 17:1–7, is very similar to the Judith story. If the role of Uzziah here and the future role of Judith are combined, in both this text and Exodus there is: (a) a lack of water, (b) a complaint to the leader, (c) the assertion that it would have been better to be a slave, (d) a critique of the people's testing of God, (e) the leader calling upon God, (f) the leader delivering the people, and (g) an issue over the acclamation, "The Lord is with us!"[5] But the difference is also significant: in Judith, when the male leader is challenged, he cannot take the leadership role himself. Instead, a woman will step up to assume the mantle of leadership.

Despite Achior's earlier statement that Israel has now redeemed itself of past sins (5:19), and Judith's similar statement to come (8:18–20), here the people revert to the status of their ancestors wandering in the wilderness, and they attribute the danger to their sins *and those of their ancestors* (v. 28). They have no *boēthos* ("helper," v. 25), *'ēzer* in Hebrew. This is the essence of their problem: they have lost faith that God will help them, and they state that God has *already* sold them into slavery (cf. Isa 50:1–3).[6] *Boēthos* is a common motif in Judith (see 6:21; 7:31; 8:11, 17; 9:4, 11). Regarding the absence of hope, compare 9:11.

■ **7:23** The array of people here is the young men, the women, and the children. (See the commentary on 4:9–10 on the various orders of stakeholders in Israel, and on 2:14–28 for the orders of the Assyrian army in array.) The list of those present is not the orders of citizens but, as a narrative device, the orders of depen-

---

5   Van Henten, "Judith as an Alternative Leader," 235.
6   Sheaffer, *Envisioning*, 86; Moore, *Judith*, 175.

dents; the pathos of their situation is emphasized. As in 6:16, young men (*neaniskoi*) are featured. *Neaniskos* in the LXX can translate *naʿar, bāḥûr,* or *yeled.* There is not, as in Susanna OG, a thematic distinction between elders and *neaniskoi,* but perhaps a distinction between elders and free male citizens (not mentioned), on one hand, and their dependents, for whom they are responsible, on the other. It is possible, but less likely, that *neaniskoi* refers to warriors; cf. Judg 9:54; 1 Sam 14:1; 2 Sam 18:15. At any rate, in warfare, conquered young men are slaughtered to destroy a people and prevent a future uprising (Jdt 2:27; 10:9; 16:4, 6).

■ **7:24** "May God judge between you and us" normally assumes that God will judge favorably for the speaker against the other party (Gen 16:5; 31:53; Judg 11:27), but Gera notes the unexpected element here: in the next verse the Bethulians state that God has "sold us into their hands"—a very bitter judgment of the situation, exhibiting no trust in God.[7] This statement is also odd because the discussion in chap. 8 will turn on the extent to which God can be hemmed in by deadlines or importuned.

■ **7:29–32**

A great lamentation rose up *homothymadon,* of one will, and involved the entire *ekklēsia,* assembly (on which see the commentary on 6:16–19). Although Uzziah is somewhat more resolute than the other Bethulians, he sounds a benevolent tone. He responds to their words by saying "Take courage," and holds out hope of God's return (biblical *šûb*; see the commentary on 5:17–19). He also counters with a compromise position—waiting five days to see whether God will intercede—suggesting a default clause to be triggered if the deadline comes and God has not acted: "if no help comes, I will do as you say." In 8:11, however, Judith will condemn this compromise as weak. There will be reason to question whether Judith is too harsh; see the commentary on 8:10, 11, and 35. On God as helper of the oppressed, see the commentary on 9:11, and cf. Exod 15:2 LXX. The curtain falls on the first half of Judith with dramaturgical effectiveness: "They were in great misery in the city." The root for misery, *tapein-,* is used often in Judith (see the commentary on 9:8–10).

The actions of the first half of the book comprise a tremendous sweep of nations and battles, military threats, the intrigue of stratagems, Israel's demonstrations of humility before God, and the delivery of Israel's newfound ally, Achior, to the village of Bethulia. All of the issues of the first half come to bear on a single village in the mountains forty miles north of Jerusalem. The first half ends on a note of calm before the storm, with the people of Israel in despair, awaiting, as the audience knows, the appearance of Judith. It is the last of the narrative pauses of the first half of Judith (see the commentary on 2:28).

---

7   Gera, *Judith,* 246.

PART II

Judith is easily divided into two approximately equal acts, the second somewhat larger than the first. Each has a chiastic structure, on which see §3 above. Although the shift from worldwide perspective to Bethulia has occurred in chap. 6, the more important shift occurs here: from Bethulia we turn to its most heroic citizen— Judith. She dominates the second half of the book, not only as the principal character, center stage at all times, but also as a symbolic deliverer of Israel when none of the men would step forward.

The second act begins in a way similar to the first: a principal character is named; a long digression is introduced to describe a second, weaker character; the main narrative thread is resumed recounting the deeds of the main character as the lesser character falls away. In chap. 1 Nebuchadnezzar is introduced by a long sentence that quickly turns to a parenthesis on Arphaxad, with Nebuchadnezzar's accomplishments resumed in 1:5. Here, Judith is introduced with her genealogy; a description of her husband and his death then intervenes, after which her story is taken up again. The two qualities, good and evil, are thus distinguished from each other in high profile, but also distinguished from the run of humanity. And yet the second figure, Judith, arises not on the stage of world empires but humbly, in a mountain village.

8

8:1–8

Text

Textual Notes

1ᵃ/ **At this time**ᵇ **Judith,**ᶜ **daughter of Merari, son of Ox, son of Joseph, son of Oziel, son of Elkiah, son of Hananiah, son of Gideon, son of Rephaim, son of Ahitub, son of Elijah, son of Hilkiah, son of Eliab, son of Nathanael, son of Salamiel, son of Sarasadai,**ᵈ **son of Israel, heard about these things. 2/ Her husband was Manasseh, of her tribe and family. He had died during the barley harvest. 3/ He was overseeing those binding sheaves in the field when the searing heat came upon his head, and he collapsed on his bed and died in Bethulia, his town. They buried him with his ancestors in the field between Dothan and Balamon. 4/ Judith remained in her house as a widow for three years and four months. 5/ She erected a tent for herself on the roof of her house and wore sackcloth around her waist, and her clothes were widow's garments. 6/ She fasted all the days of her widowhood, except for the day of preparation for the Sabbath**ᵉ **and the Sabbath, the day of preparation for the new moon and the new moon, and the days of feasting and rejoicing of the house of Israel. 7/ She was beautiful in appearance, very lovely to behold,**ᶠ **and her husband Manasseh had left to her gold and silver, male and female slaves, livestock and fields; she remained over them. 8/ And no one raised a malicious word against her, for she feared God greatly.**

a At the head of this section, 583 adds αρχη Ιουδηθ, that is, the beginning of the Judith portion of the story.

b For και ηκουσεν: και ην εν τη πολει κατοικουσα *O* OL Sy.

c For spellings of Judith, see §1 above.

d Υιου Συμων read in V *O L* 311 OL Sy Vg. Many minor variants occur for the names; see Hanhart, 94; Moore, and the commentary below. After Manasseh, a genealogy is added in OL-SBQPG Fulg that is similar to Judith's in 8:1: Ioseph, Achitob, Melchis, Aelia, Nathanael, Sarisada, Simeon, Israel.

e Προσαββατων και omitted in *O* OL-MC Sy Vg.

f Και σοφη τη καρδια και αγαθη εν συνεσει και ην πλουσια a plus in *O* 58 OL Sy.

Commentary

8:1–8

Although many twentieth-century scholars opined that the first half of the book of Judith was too long and full of talk, Craven's structural analysis indicates the contribution of the first seven chapters to the narrative themes of the book. In the first half, tensions and threats are generated that require resolution, and from chap. 8 on, Judith will play the lead in a dizzying release of tension. "Once Judith takes the stage in chapter 8," says Craven, "she shares it with others but surrenders it to no one."[1] Second Maccabees as well does not turn to its main protagonist, Judah Maccabee, until chap. 8.[2] Even popular art knows enough to create and maintain tensions over time.

■ **8:1**

On Judith's name, see §1 above; we note briefly here that her name is the feminine form of Judah and likely connotes "Jewish woman." One ancient text of Judith (583) inserts a heading at this point in the book, *archē Ioudeth,* "Beginning of Judith's story." Even without that heading, the LXX text states, "Now in those days," a common transition to a new subplot in biblical narrative (Exod 2:11; Judg 19:1; 1 Sam 28:1; 1 Macc 1:11; cf. Jdt 1:2).

In 4:1–15 the Israelites living in Judea *heard* about the Assyrian armies marching across the face of the earth and were "very disturbed both for Jerusalem and for the temple." Here Judith's first act is to *hear*; it is the second word of the second half. Hearing will be picked up again in 8:9. The hearing marks the shift of the narrative first from the nations to Bethulia, and now from Bethulia to Judith.[3]

Before her hearing draws her into the main narrative (8:9), a long introduction is interposed. Meir Sternberg notes that biblical characters are often introduced with a "proleptic portrait" of characteristics, whether physical, social, singular (a name or genealogy), moral, or psychological. This proleptic portrait will later prove relevant in the story.[4] The singular traits of name and genealogy are prominent first. The other aspects of the proleptic portrait—physical (beauty), social (relation to Manasseh and his estate), moral (her virtue), psychological (her steely resolve)—are treated just after that. But while biblical narratives provide powerful but *minimal* information at the first mention of a character, novelistic literature often floods the audience with pieces of pseudo-realistic information, here dispensed *before any action.*[5]

A genealogy is provided for Judith but not for Manasseh. Genealogies are important in cultures that are structured by extended family—the relations and even marriageability of people depend on how the families are or are not related, and the integrity of the lineage. In addition, Jewish and Israelite identity was traced back to the patriarchs Abraham, Isaac, and Jacob. All Israelites understood themselves to be, not children of Abraham in some metaphorical sense, but actual descendants of Abraham. In texts of the period of Judith, genealogies also served to tie key figures back into the primal history (Jub. 4:1–33; Tob 1:1–2; Matt 1:1–17; Luke 3:23–38). The many genealogies in Ezra-Nehemiah and Chronicles indicate the assertion of the identity of lineages in the struggle for power in Judah. Christopher Gill has suggested that identity as revealed in genealogies was different in the ancient world, an "objective-participant" model (birth, social obligations, public persona) rather than the modern "subjective-individualist" model (individual and internal beliefs, desires, emotions, intentions).[6] The explorations of the nature of the self in ancient philosophy and of emotions

---

1 Craven, *Artistry and Faith*, 62.
2 Gera, *Judith*, 254.
3 See also Schmitz/Engel, *Judit,* 239; Craven, *Artistry and Faith*, 81–88, on the repeated motif of hearing in 8:1–9:12; and Gera, *Judith*, 270, on hearing propelling a plot shift in the Bible. On the importance of hearing in Deuteronomy, see Steven Weitzman, "Sensory Reform in Deuteronomy," in idem, David Brakke, and Michael Satlow, eds., *Religion and the Self in Antiquity* (Bloomington: Indiana University Press, 2005) 123–39.

4 Meir Sternberg, *The Poetics of Biblical Narrative: Ideological Literature and the Drama of Reading* (Indiana Literary Biblical Series; Bloomington: Indiana University Press, 1985) 326. See also Corley, "Unconventional Heroine," 72–73.
5 Gera, *Judith*, 254.
6 Christopher Gill, *The Structured Self in Hellenistic and Roman Thought* (Oxford: Oxford University Press, 2006).

in ancient novels both challenge this to some extent, and rather than anchor the hero in a past lineage, the work that genealogies usually do, here the irregular or even eccentric nature of the genealogy draws the audience to an appreciation of Judith's individuality.

Before she even appears or speaks, Judith's genealogy initiates her violations of typical behaviors for women. Her lineage upstages her husband Manasseh's, and he will be further demoted below. She is thus introduced as a woman without limits, as Nebuchadnezzar was introduced as a king without limits. Her genealogy, the only extended genealogy of a woman in the Bible,[7] is as muddled as the periods and places of the text. It is traced back sixteen generations to the patriarch Israel.[8] He is perhaps called Israel and not Jacob to emphasize that, as she is "Jewish woman," she is descended from "Israel."

The genealogy proceeds up the lineage, as in Luke 3 and 1 Enoch 37:1: Merari, Ox, Joseph, Oziel (or Uzziel), Elkiah, Ananias (= Hebrew Hananiah), Gideon, Rephaim, Ahitub, Elijah, Hilkiah, Eliab, Nathanael, Salamiel, Sarasadai, Israel. A number of scholars have suggested that the long genealogy is a comical exaggeration—"its very length warns the readers of its fictitiousness"[9]—or even mocks pretentious genealogies of elites. The practice here exhibits the same marriage of detail and comic invention found often in the book. Identifiable names as well as unidentifiable and fictive names are intermixed. Aside from the other absurdities,

the genealogy also contains a gap of hundreds of years between Sarasadai (= Zurishaddai) and Israel.[10] Van Henten emphasizes that the names go back to Jacob/Israel, yet the names are from different tribes. There is no plausible tribal genealogy here, but he perceives a different message: "Several of her forefathers' names—Gideon, Elijah, Joseph, and Merari—are identical with those of judges, prophets, ambassadors, and priests, all the various roles which Judith herself plays in the story. . . ."[11] It is perhaps an idealized past that is concocted, belonging to all the tribes and important roles in Israelite life. One thinks of the Hasmonean kings who claimed the three roles of king, priest, and prophet, but one cannot rule out a bit of simple, fantastic historical coloring.

It is tempting to look here for important figures from Israel's past, but some remain unclear:

Merari is descended from Levi and thus is connected to Aaron and Moses (Gen 46:11).

Ox is not Hebrew but may be a corruption of Hebrew Uz or Uzzi (Gen 22:21).

Oziel (or Uzziel) appears in Exod 6:18, identified only as a Levite.

Elkiah (Hilkiah) is an ancestor of Ezra (Ezra 7:1).[12]

Hananiah (Greek Ananias) was a common name.

Gideon was one of the most illustrious judges (Judges 6–8).

---

7   Some noncanonical genealogies include women: Pseudo-Philo, *Biblical Antiquities* 1:1–8; 4:12–14; Jub. 4:7–16; 8:5–9.

8   See Schmitz/Engel, *Judit,* 241; on variants, see Soubigou, *Judith,* 538. Matthew's genealogy of Jesus in Matthew 1 includes four women, but Jesus's genealogy is still through Joseph and not Mary. Note also the lengthy last will and testament of Rebekah in Jub. 35:18–27, which likens her to the patriarchs.

9   Gera, *Judith,* 256–57, also 27. Gera also notes that in the LXX Raphainis is used for the rephaim, the underworld dead, but here it is Greek for Rephaiah. On mocking elites, see Loader, *Pseudepigrapha,* 192; Moore, *Judith,* 187–88; Gruen, *Diaspora,* 165; Steinmann, *Lecture de Judith,* 72–74. Perhaps the last defender of a real genealogy here was Edgar J. Bruns, "The Genealogy of Judith," *CBQ* 13 (1956) 19–22.

10   Schmitz/Engel, *Judit,* 241.

11   Van Henten, "Judith as an Alternative Leader," 247–48. Joosten asks, "How did the tribe of Simeon end up near Samaria? One wonders whether the author may have derived this information simply from Gen. 34" ("Original Language," 170 n. 26). Dilys Naomi Patterson attempts to find an intentional connection of the names to ten of the twelve tribes, but many of the connections are weak and some of the names are probably not evocations of particular tribal ancestors ("Re-membering the Past," 121–23).

12   Arguing for reading the Syriac Elkana is Richard C. Steiner, "On the Dating of Hebrew Sound Changes (*H>H and *G>') and Greek Translations (2 Esdras and Judith)," *JBL* 124 (2005) 229–67.

Rephaim in the LXX is used for the *rĕpā'îm,* the under-
   world dead.[13]
Ahitub; compare 1 Sam 14:3.
Elijah, Greek *Ēliou* is used for both Elijah and Elihu
   (1 Sam 1:1).
Hilkiah; see Elkiah above.
Eliab and Nathanael are found as names for David's
   brothers (1 Chr 2:13–14) and as tribal leaders
   (Num 1:8–9).
Salamiel son of Sarasadai is similar to Shelumiel son
   of Zurishaddai, from the tribe of Simeon in Num
   1:6.[14]

Perhaps most intriguing, a number of ancient texts
(including Vg) also add "son of Simeon" at the end,
which Moore regards as the earliest reading—though
this is unlikely.[15] To be sure, in 9:2 Judith refers to "my
ancestor Simeon," but that is likely metaphorical (see the
commentary there).

■ **8:2–3**

After her genealogy we are told that her husband,
Manasseh, was of *her* tribe and family and that he had
died. It is quite remarkable that Manasseh is identified by reference to his wife's family.[16] In early Israel
the preferred marriage partner was not only from the
same tribe but also from the same clan (*mišpāḥâ*) (see
Numbers 36).[17] This relates to the meaning and importance of *klēronomia* ("inheritance"), below in 8:22; Tobit
reflects this marriage preference. Because Judith and
Manasseh are from the same *mišpāḥâ,* her distribution
of her wealth to both of their families is easily accomplished (16:24).

   There were several Manassehs in the Hebrew
Bible; the choice of this name could conceivably evoke

Manasseh, king of Judah, who came to be viewed as a
penitent (2 Chronicles 33; Prayer of Manasseh), but the
name may not be significant. What may be significant
are the sheaves and the timing at the barley harvest, as
these are narrative motifs in 2 Samuel 21 and Ruth 1.[18]
At first sight these may be viewed as stock elements of
Israelite storytelling, but Manasseh's death is unusually
told: as he stands overseeing those who were binding
sheaves, he suffers from sunstroke and dies in bed. This
appears to be an emasculated death, just as Holofernes
will die in an emasculated way. Similar to the emphases
in the death of Holofernes later, here the sun came upon
Manasseh's *head,* and he *fell* upon his *bed.* He dies just as
Holofernes will, passively.[19] And although Susanna is not
a widow, in her entire plight her wealthy husband Joakim
does not play a role. Rather, the young Daniel comes to
her defense much as Achior steps up in Judith.[20] In the
constant parallels and contrasts in Judith, it could be
argued that, while Holofernes has Bagoas as a eunuch,
Judith's "eunuch" is her dead husband. Still, Achior may
be a more telling equivalent to Bagoas (see the excursus
at 12:10–12, "Bagoas the Eunuch").

   Throughout, Judith is contrasted to the men around
her: first her husband, then Uzziah, Achior, and
Holofernes. She is active and aggressive, like a male
warrior, while they are weak and passive. The reversal
of gender roles that characterizes the book is given
quite a push here by the description of Manasseh.
The male protagonists of Greek novels are also often
passive in comparison with the female, but not nearly
so obviously as here. Gera reminds us, however, that a
number of weak husbands in the Bible are overshad-
owed by strong wives: Rebekah (Genesis 24–27), the
Shunammite woman (2 Kings 4), Manoah's wife (Judges
13), and Naomi (Ruth 1–4).[21]

13 Gera, *Judith,* 257.
14 The fact that both names in the best ancient texts
    are nearly identical to the two names in Numbers—
    concerning a person who was prominent in the
    tribe of Simeon—indicates that the latter names
    were originally meant; so Moore, *Judith,* 179.
15 Moore, *Judith,* 179.
16 See Di Lella, "Women in the Wisdom," 51. See also
    the commentary on 8:18.
17 The patriarchs married their first cousins, but this
    was a "primordial" practice; it was still assumed for

    the patriarchal period in Genesis Apocryphon 6.89
    and Jub. 4:9–28, but marrying within the *mišpāḥâ*
    was the ideal in Israel. The actual practice by the
    time of Judith is unclear.
18 Gera, *Judith,* 259–60; and see also Brian Britt,
    "Death, Social Conflict, and the Barley Harvest in
    the Hebrew Bible," *JHebS* 5 (2005) 1–28.
19 Levine, "Sacrifice and Salvation," 19.
20 Gera, *Judith,* 270.
21 Gera, *Judith,* 258.

Manasseh *should* be an exemplar of wisdom, virtue, and success. A pious, wealthy Israelite was understood to be a man of wisdom and virtue, and he should have enjoyed the earthly blessings of wisdom. (His burial with *his* ancestors, 8:3, is noted quite typically for an important male, even though the genealogy is for Judith and he is incorporated into it.[22]) We may even raise the question of whether the traditional wisdom of Israel is upended by the book of Judith (see §6 above). Yet Manasseh is finally buried with his ancestors, an honorable end (Gen 49:29; 1 Kgs 15:8; 16:6).

■ 8:4–6

The rich description of Judith turns now to her mourning regimen. Judith's behavior is indirectly related to typical mourning practices. In the Hebrew Bible mourning may include: removing festive clothes and putting on a sash of sackcloth next to the skin (Gen 37:34; 2 Kgs 6:30) or black garments (2 Sam 14:2; for a woman: Gen 38:14); exposing part of the body (Isa 20:2) or rending one's clothes (Gen 37:34); putting ashes, dust, or earth on one's head (2 Sam 13:19) or shaving one's head or pulling one's hair or beard (Lev 10:6); lying down (Gen 23:3), fasting (2 Sam 1:12), or cutting one's body (Jer 16:6–7). It often involves group mourning (Gen 50:3; Jer 16:7–8). Gera also lists other reasons for wearing sackcloth: distress (1 Kgs 20:31) or confession (1 Kgs 21:27; Neh 9:1, here combined with fasting).[23] Fasting, sackcloth, and ashes are combined also in Isa 58:5; Jonah 3:6–8; Esth 4:3; Dan 9:3; cf. 1 Macc 3:47; 2 Macc 10:25.

The initial period of mourning in the Bible is generally seven days (Gen 50:10) as the most intense period, and sometimes a mourning period of thirty days is mentioned (Deut 34:8). The Bible does not contain a clear reference to mourning beyond that period, although Gen 38:12–14 implies that Tamar wears mourning garments *after* Judah has concluded his period of mourning, and 2 Sam 14:2 suggests that a woman could

continue dressing in mourning garments for a time. In rabbinic sources (b. Moʿed Q. 27b, b. Ket. 103b) we find reference to continuing mourning for a parent for a full year. Nowhere do we find reference to Judith's extended mourning, and excessive displays of mourning were also criticized (Deut 14:1–2; Lev 19:27–28). Some of the typical elements of mourning are found here, but, as noted, for Judith they are not an ad hoc display of grief—as is usually the case in the Bible, with much wailing and expressions of grief—but a continuing and very controlled discipline (see the excursus below, "Asceticism"). Throughout it should be noted that ritual elements are not just reported but *narrativized*; they carry some story significance, if we can discern it.

At any rate, Judith continued as a widow (present participle *chēreuousa*) for a period beyond that prescribed in Jewish law. The three years and four months, or forty months, perhaps suggests the forty years in the wilderness wanderings, the forty days of the flood (Gen 7:17), the spies in the land of Israel (Num 13:25), the forty days of fasting (Exod 34:28; 1 Kgs 19:7–8), and even Bethulia under siege for forty days (7:1, 20, 30; 8:9, 15). Alternatively, is forty simply a common story number? Moore notes that the resonance with forty in biblical narratives is not likely relevant because the author says "three years and four months."[24] An association with forty is thus not implausible, but what is clearer is the extension beyond the usual period of mourning. We compare here the more fantastic reference in Jub. 4:7 to Adam and Eve mourning Abel for twenty-eight years.

Commentators on this text have also pondered why our heroine is a widow and not a virgin or a married woman.[25] Widowhood would normally have reduced her status in a patriarchal structure (1 Kgs 17:17–24; 2 Kgs 4:1–7; Luke 7:11–17). The vulnerable status of widows was often linked to that of orphans and sojourners (Exod 22:20–23; Deut 24:17–21; Isa 1:17), and, as a result, God affords them special protection, which Israelites

---

22 Dothan is one of the few real sites in the book; see 3:9; 4:6. Joseph's first misadventure was in Dothan (Gen 37:17), and, according to Tal Ilan, Judith's "exploits are in some sense designed to set straight the record of Joseph's misfortunes" (*Integrating Women*, 147). Balamon is unknown, but compare Belmain (4:4) and Belbaim (7:3), and see the commentary on 4:4. In Jdt 16:23 we will learn that the burial site is a cave, similar to Machpelah (Gen 23:17–19); see Schmitz/Engel, *Judit,* 242.

23 Gera, *Judith,* 184.

24 Moore, *Judith,* 181.

25 Moore, *Judith,* 180.

are called upon to emulate (Deut 10:18; 14:29; Ps 146:9; cf. Jdt 9:4, 9). Israel's plight is also sometimes likened to widowhood (Lam 1:1; Isa 54:4–8).[26] Perhaps for all these reasons, the widow becomes a stock figure in biblical narratives, whether wealthy, on one hand, or poor and vulnerable, on the other. "Both conditions," says Karel van der Toorn, "could signal a state of grace."[27] It is also true, as Gera notes, that a widow would have been experienced in sexual relations, which is indeed part of her *sophia* and *synesis* (see the commentary on 8:28–31).[28] The cleverness of the trickster consists in an intuitive knowledge of human nature and how it can be manipulated. That is not stated here, but it will become clear (see also 14:1–5).

By examining both Greek and biblical notions of the widow, Gera forces a reconsideration of Judith's widowhood. The widow in biblical tradition is understood as a defenseless and desperate figure whom the *gô'ēl* or extended-family redeemer is obligated to protect. Widows in Greek tradition are not to be trifled with. Says Gera:

Widows who do not remarry have been recognized as liminal or anomalous figures—masculine, dangerous, and powerful—and this is manifestly true of the [widow queens of *Tractatus de mulieribus*]. . . . None of the widows in [this] work seems interested in remarrying. In several instances, . . . the widow queens . . . are much more famous than their spouses.[29]

Indeed, because Judith is wealthy, her widowhood is not presented as a status of weakness. Still, as we proceed, it is necessary to recall, first, that the warrior widow from the Greek perspective was a type of the *barbarian*, and, second, that the warrior widow is probably interesting in the histories *because* of the shock and transgression. Mary Lefkowitz also observes that Greek women act independently only when it is for the public good and only in times of emergency, acting for a husband or male relative; they then return to private life.[30] This is true of Judith's return to privacy as well, but Gera also notes that the barbarian women are more often motivated by power and enjoy a long tenure as queen.

In our story world, a widow is vulnerable but also freer to act. True, Judith is already wealthy, but the widow-figure is still one that is unattached, and there is less danger that a respectable man will be shamed by her actions. The fact that she is a widow becomes a necessity of the story. Ruth and Tamar, for instance, are also widows, but both search out husband and kinsman relations. The narrative *point* of Ruth, for example, is that a poor, vulnerable widow finds a *gô'ēl*, a redeemer. It is also significant that, at the end of our novella, Judith *chooses* to remain a widow even though there are many suitors, which sequesters Judith from social relations going forward. Margarita Stocker suggests that Judith is symbolically married to God: "This is why . . . no one ever manages to sleep with Judith."[31] Yet here we see a trait of heroes cross-culturally: the hero cannot reinte-

26 Dombkowski Hopkins, "Judith," 282; Enslin, *Book of Judith,* 180–81; Moore, *Judith,* 180–81.

27 Van der Toorn, "The Public Image of the Widow in Ancient Israel," in Jan Bremmer and Lourens van den Bosch, eds., *Between Poverty and the Pyre: Moments in the History of Widowhood* (London: Routledge, 1995) 19–30, here 23. See also §5 above. Although there was a mixed view of agency for real women in rabbinic Judaism—so Judith Romney Wegner, *Chattel or Person? The Status of Women in the Mishnah* (Oxford: Oxford University Press, 1988); and cf. m. Qidd. 1:1—Judith is an imaginary woman, even more difficult to contextualize.

28 Gera, *Judith,* 262.

29 Gera, *Warrior Women,* 13. On the view of emancipated widows in the ancient world, see also M. Buitelaar, "Widows' Worlds: Representations and Realities," in Bremmer and van den Bosch, eds., *Between Poverty,* 1–18; P. Walcot, "On Widows and

their Reputation in Antiquity," *Symbolae Osloenses* 66 (1991) 5–26.

30 Mary R. Lefkowitz, *Women in Greek Myth* (Baltimore: Johns Hopkins University Press, 1986) 80–94. In Plutarch, *Virtues* 255e–257e, Aretaphilia frees the city from a tyrant, rejects pleas to join in the government, and returns home to women's quarters, spending the rest of her life weaving. (Cf. also Penelope's desire at the end of the *Odyssey.*) Gera (*Warrior Women,* 17) chose not to include the Amazons in her study because they were mythical, but she notes that, although they were positive early on, they became negative in later valuations, e.g., Hellanicus, *FGrH* 4 F167c.

31 Stocker, *Judith,* 7; see also Di Lella, "Women in the Wisdom," 51. For a widow remarrying, see Abigail (1 Sam 25:39, 42), Bathsheba (2 Sam 11:27), and Ruth.

grate into society and must either die or depart from society again.

Although as a widow, Judith would have shamed Manasseh's family and his memory by her actions in the Assyrian camp, there would have been even more prohibitive problems in casting Judith as a virgin or a wife. A virgin would be under the control of her father, and her behavior and decorum would be guarded by him; any transgression of decorum would reflect on him and shame him. The ancient audience could never have accepted a woman who would so shame a *living* husband.[32] To be sure, a widow might be in the charge of a *gô'ēl*, or redeemer-guardian, perhaps a patriarchal *'ab-bayit*, but that did not involve the exposure to great shame that would have been entailed by a virgin daughter or a wife exposing herself. The most likely reason, then, that Judith is a widow is that violations of the rules of decorum would be impossible for a virgin or a married woman.

Judith is also never faulted for being childless, which would normally be seen as a great problem to be resolved. She would be vulnerable because she lacked sons who could support her, or who would continue the memory of her husband. The three rewards of being wise in Israel, for both men and women, were wealth, old age, and children, and the wise Judith has two of these but not the third. If she had had children, however, she would have been limited in her ability to act aggressively and shamelessly.[33]

Excursus: Asceticism

Judith is engaged in an unusually demanding set of practices: she mourns for a period beyond that pre-scribed by Jewish law; she lives secluded in a tent on her rooftop; she wears sackcloth beneath her widow's garments; and she fasts on *all* days, not just fasting days, except those holidays on which fasting was prohibited. There is a relation between Judith's dis-cipline and Jewish asceticism, which was developing somewhat in this period. Megillat Ta'anit lists thirty-five days on which fasting is not permitted (see also y. Ta'an. 2.8, 66a). Judith's list also includes the eve of the Sabbath (a rare term, but cf. Mark 15:42) and the eve of the new moon, not found in the restrictions in rabbinic literature. That Judith does not fast on the Sabbath or on certain festival days is a detail that sug-gests to Gera that this sort of asceticism was indeed practiced but had to be limited.[34] What is perhaps more likely, however, is that what we witness here is a literary creation only, not reflecting actual practices.

Mourning and grief (sackcloth, ashes, and fasting) in the Hebrew Bible is an ad hoc display to demon-strate one's grief to others and to God (Lev 16:29, 31; 23:27; Num 29:7; Judg 20:26; 1 Kgs 21:9; Jer 36:9; Jonah 3:5). It was believed that visible, external afflic-tions were necessary for others to see one's internal grief, and even for God to be able to perceive human grief,[35] which applies precisely to what the Bethu-lians do in chaps. 4 and 7 (see also the commentary on 9:1–14). In the postexilic period, however, the role of fasting in Jewish spirituality was evidently greatly increased—a correlative in practice perhaps corresponding to the earlier so-called penitential theology. (See below, and compare Ezra 8:21, 23; Ezra 10, in the context of defining the *ḥārēdîm*, those who tremble before God; more contemporary are 1 Macc 3:44–48; Esther 4.) Judith's practice, indeed, becomes a continuous discipline of the self, related to the beginning of asceticism if we take the latter term in a broad sense.[36] There is a transition here from occasional, ad hoc practices of asceticism, generally assumed to fall upon all Israelites equally, to disciplinary practices of a special practitioner. Her

---

32   On the anxiety of a male head of household controlling his wife and daughters, see Michael Satlow, "'Try to be a Man': The Rabbinic Construc-tion of Masculinity," *HTR* 89 (1996) 19–40, here 23–25; and see Sir 4:17; 9:1–9; 18:30; 19:2–3; 22:3–6; 25:16–26; 26:1–18; 31:25; 36:21–25; 37:27–31; 42:9–14. Concerning the wife of a living husband, there is a folk motif of a wife dressing as a man to save her husband (Alonso-Schökel, *Narrative Structure*, 21–29), but that concerns a wife coming to where her husband is held, not leaving her hus-band behind to seduce a general. It is also a *folktale*, breathing the freedom of that genre. Note also the modern alterations of the story in which Manasseh is a living but impotent character; see §8 above.

33   Montague registers the typical Israelite view (*Esther and Judith*, 11).

34   Gera, *Judith*, 265–66.

35   David Lambert, "Fasting as a Penitential Rite: A Biblical Phenomenon?" *HTR* 96 (2003) 477–512. Matt 6:16–18 is a deliberate and deviant excep-tion. Communal confession and prayer in Judith is similar to 2 Chr 20:3–13, Jehoshaphat perceiving a foreign army on the horizon; cf. also Joel 1–2; and more contemporaneously at 1 Macc 3:42–54, 3 Macc 1:17–29, Pseudo-Philo, *Biblical Antiquities* 30:4–5.

36   Wills, "Ascetic Theology;" idem, *Jewish Novel*, 15, 123, 139, 228–44.

practices may also be compared to the special rites she observes in Holofernes's camp (see the excursus at 12:5b–9: "Bathing and Related Issues"), and by her seclusion and her relinquishing of her wealth at the end. The book of Judith may be depicting not real practices but a fictitious ascetic ideal. Nevertheless, this passage in Judith is perhaps the earliest Jewish text to suggest a discipline—what Michel Foucault referred to as a discipline of the self—that sees fasting and wearing sackcloth as a process *to perfect oneself* and not simply an ad hoc communication *outside oneself.*[37]

Indeed, as ascetic practices were only in the process of being developed, an isolated proto-ascetic engagement such as this might conceivably arise anywhere. Gera supplies a surprising example concerning Adad-Guppi, the queen-mother of Nabonidus, king of Babylon (sixth century BCE):

> In order to appease the heart of my god and my goddess, I did not put on a garment of excellent wool, silver, gold, a fresh garment; I did not allow perfumes or fine oil to touch my body. I was clothed in a torn garment. My fabric was sackcloth. I proclaimed their praises.[38]

This parallel is also significant because it is a woman who engages the discipline of the self. And what was the motive for her practices? "The fame of my god and goddess were set firmly in my heart."[39]

Yet Judith's practices are not as isolated and correspond to developed forms that arise in later Judaism and Christianity—that is, they are likely part of a trajectory. Childlessness is presented as a desirable state in Wis 3:13; 4:1, and the new discourse at Qumran introduces stricter asceticism. Among the Therapeutae and Therapeutrides, the women fast, except on the Sabbath, and wear simple clothing (Philo, *On the Contemplative Life* 34–38). Pharisees fast on Monday and Thursday, and, according to T. Jos. 3:4, Joseph fasted while resisting Potiphar's wife.

Rabbinic texts, however, often register a resistance to increased asceticism (y. Ḥag. 2:2, 77d). In Judith's time, however, there is no apparent reservation about her becoming a heroine of virtue; her isolation was similar to the more extreme version depicted later in Joseph and Aseneth (see §7 above). The first followers of Jesus also negotiated demands of celibacy and asceticism (1 Corinthians 7; 1 Tim 5:14; and cf. Matt 19:12).

In addition to her mourning and fasting, other parts of her regimen are also relevant. First, she lives secluded in a tent on the roof of her house. The tent figures as a special, reclusive environment for the heroine. It is the combination of tent and rooftop that is significant, and atypical. The booth is set apart, and its very simplicity and self-denial will be contrasted below with the indulgence and sensuality of Holofernes's tent. From Aristeas through rabbinic literature the holiness root, *qādaš*, as "set apart," gives rise to metaphors of set-apartness: laws "fenced us around" (Aristeas 139) and "God hedged us round" (142); in m. Abot 3:14 there is a "fence around the Torah." Joan Branham elaborates:

> Halakhic and purity concerns, masquerading as architectural metaphors, also become regular motifs . . . . [T]hese symbolic barriers materialize in the physical form of actual chancel screens in front of Torah shrines in fifth- to seventh-century synagogues.[40]

Yet, while the tent seems to figure symbolically, much dramatic action occurs on rooftops in the Hebrew Bible. The rooftop is *not* private space, as is the interior of the house, but open and visible.[41] It could be a functional part of an ancient Near Eastern house: as a secluded area for some household meetings and activities (Josh 2:4–14; 1 Sam 9:25; Ps 102:7–8; Acts 10:9), even for erotic meetings (2 Sam 16:22), and David sees Bathsheba from a roof (2 Sam 11:2). In biblical narrative, women are often

37 Michel Foucault, *The Order of Things: An Archaeology of the Human Sciences* (New York: Pantheon, 1971); Foucault, *The History of Sexuality*, vol. 3: *Care of the Self* (New York: Pantheon, 1986); Foucault, "Technologies of the Self," in *Ethics: Subjectivity and Truth*, vol. 1 of *Essential Works of Foucault, 1954–1984* (3 vols.; New York: New Press, 1997) 223–51; Wills, "Ascetic Theology."

38 Gera, *Judith*, 264, quoting *COS* 1.147, col. 1.

39 Gera, *Judith*, 264, quoting *COS* 1.147, col. 1.

40 Joan Branham, "Penetrating the Sacred: Breaches and Barriers in the Jerusalem Temple," in Sharon E. J. Gerstel, ed., *Thresholds of the Sacred: Architectural, Art Historical, Liturgical, and Theological Perspectives on Religious Screens, East and West* (Washington, DC: Dumbarton Oaks Research Library and Collection; distributed by Harvard University Press, 2006) 6–24, here 10.

41 Schmitz/Engel, *Judit*, 243; Grintz, *Book of Judith*, 131.

depicted at the window or on the roof. They are often passive or oppressed (Judg 5:28), while men are not (Gen 26:8), but here Judith takes on a special power. "Judith's spatial position on the roof," says Gera, "symbolizes her elevated role and she uses her superior perspective in order to rescue her people from disaster."[42] Judith indeed summons the elders to meet her on her roof. The biblical motif of the strong woman character as a "watcher at the window"— Sisera's mother, Michal, and Jezebel—is suggestive,[43] but Judith is intriguingly different in being *withdrawn by choice*. Gera likens Judith to these other characters because of her gaze, but our heroine seems to be different, to have chosen to withdraw so as not to gaze. When she reengages, it is because of what she *hears*. Judith partakes more of the cross-cultural hero/heroine who begins in a withdrawn state than the typical female character in the Bible.

Judith's tent also suggests a special autonomy and piety. The book began with a description of the exaggerated walls of Ecbatana, and Adele Reinhartz suggests that the audience may come to contrast that with Judith's tent; the thick walls do not protect Ecbatana, yet the tent is ironically much stronger. In addition, it "demonstrates her independence of male control and protection"[44] and is part of her discipline to exercise control over her life (see the commentary on 8:35). And as the tent recalls the earlier walls of Ecbatana, Judith's pious and simple tent will later be perceived as similar to but contrasted with Holofernes's rich and luxurious tent.

Judith's tent may call to mind some specific biblical associations. In the LXX the Greek word *skēnē* is used to translate *miškān,* and in fact the two words derive from the same eastern Mediterranean loanword (Hebrew *š-k-n,* compare *šĕkînâ*). In the Bible the word can refer to any tent or makeshift booth, but it sometimes comes to have a particular significance. The tent in the wilderness wanderings was in Greek also a *skēnē,* though known in English tradition as the tabernacle. The tabernacle, or tent of meeting in Exodus 25–26, was a rough prototype of the temple, a makeshift holy place for the presence of God while Israel was in the wilderness. Judith, we are told, times her prayers to coincide with the temple sacrifices in Jerusalem, and so the tabernacle parallel is strong. Does her tent call to mind Sukkot, the Festival of Booths? As part of the Jerusalem restoration in Ezra

3:4–5, Sukkot is observed with the offerings also mentioned in Jdt 4:14: daily burnt offerings, regular burnt offerings, new moon and festival offerings, freewill offerings (see Lev 23:33–38). Indeed, the booths of Sukkot could be constructed on roofs (Neh 8:13–18), which reflects a transformation of a harvest field observance into a city practice. But the tabernacle or Sukkot connection seems unlikely. The possibility of a proto-synagogue here would at first also seem unrealistic, given the date of Judith, but our text may presage the synagogue as it does Christian asceticism; see the commentary on 9:1. Here, however, her practices are solitary.

The other Jewish novellas also find significance in upper-chamber settings. Sarah in the book of Tobit has a room in an upper chamber (Tob 3:17); Aseneth lives her young life in a tower (Joseph and Aseneth 2), and in the Vulgate Judith resides in a similar cloistered situation (Vg Jdt 8:5). Aseneth's tower is perhaps the most interesting. Judith, like Aseneth, does not come into contact with any male, only with a female slave. The Aseneth novella likely dates from a later period, a possible aftereffect of Judith's narrative rather than an influence, yet it may indicate some of the ascetic and spiritual resonances of the secluded chamber.

Finally, Judith's sackcloth should be noted. She apparently wears sackcloth around her waist or loins (cf. Gen. 37:34; 2 Sam 3:31; Lam 2:10), over which she wears her widow's garments. She will uncover the sack in 9:1 (see also 10:3), presumably to exhibit her mental state to God. The Bethulians engaged in a public, communal, ritualized grief (4:10), while Judith is private and continuous in her observance beyond the requirements of mourning, not even responding at first to the serious external threats.

The individual aspects of Judith's discipline, then, are already known in Israel, but the combination and the peculiar emphasis on them are remarkable. Her dressing and preparation in chap. 10 and practices within the Assyrian camp in chap. 12 will also look like extensions of this discipline. Within the Judaism of the period, then, a new ascetic discipline is being explored, at least in literary contexts. While rabbinic Judaism curtailed this form of spirituality, Christians would expand upon this tendency.

42 Gera, *Judith*, 263.

43 Don Seeman, "The Watcher at the Window: Cultural Poetics of a Biblical Motif," *Prooftexts* 24 (2004) 1–50. Cf. also 2 Macc 3:19 and 3 Macc 1:18.

44 Reinhartz, "Better Homes," 327; Levine, "Sacrifice and Salvation," 22.

■ **8:7–8**

Above it was noted that biblical descriptions often begin with elements of a person's appearance or character that provide a proleptic portrait. We arrive at the only *physical* aspect of Judith's proleptic portrait: her beauty. (Her wealth will be noted just below, but her wisdom and intelligence will not be noted until v. 29.) The hero or heroine can have physical characteristics that are positive or negative or serve simply to individuate the hero.[45] In Judith's case, however, her beauty is an absolute requirement of her mission, along with her trickster's cleverness, the greatest weapon in her arsenal. "Beautiful in appearance, very lovely to behold" (Greek), is nearly identical to the description of Rachel (Gen 29:17) and similar to that of Sara (Gen 12:11) and Esther (2:7), but also Joseph (Gen 39:6). Just as the descriptions of the Greek novel heroines are very stereotyped, so also to some extent are the descriptions of these women (and man) in the Israelite tradition.[46]

In comparison to some of the other beautiful protagonists, the initial description of Judith is still restrained—a mere ten words in Greek. The *reaction* of men in the narrative, however, will communicate her beauty, and this is perhaps a novelistic development of a folktale motif. Her beauty is frequently referenced hereafter: 10:7, 14, 19, 23; 11:21, 23; 12:13; 16:6, 9. Different words are used; in 11:23 it is *asteia,* used also of Susanna (OG 7). From *astu,* ("city"), this word may connote sophistication, ironic for a mountain village.[47] One may wonder how Judith could maintain her beauty while fasting continuously for so long; but, first, she is understood as an extraordinary person, a heroine of a novella, and, second, we find that the righteous often remained healthy and beautiful even while fasting (Dan 1:4–15; T. Jos. 3:4).[48]

The fact that she is wealthy is as necessary an element of her role as her beauty or her intelligence. Proverbial wisdom in Israel assumed that the rewards for a wise person were to live a long life, to have many children, and to be wealthy (compare Gen 13:2 and Jdt 5:9). Judith's husband failed to attain the first reward, he and Judith have both failed in the second, but they succeeded in the third. Wealth is symbolic as well as real; it is a proof of the favor of God and a foundation for high status within the community. It is physical honor. In the Jewish novellas, Susanna is beautiful and wealthy, Esther is beautiful and promoted to wealth and royal status, Sarah in Tobit is beautiful and a woman of means, and Aseneth is beautiful and nobly born.

The description of Manasseh's and Judith's wealth is more involved than the description of her beauty. It is a catalogue of categories, similar to the hyperbolic descriptions of Holofernes's armies: gold and silver (see 2:18), male and female slaves (2:20), livestock (2:17), and fields (3:3). "She remained over them" after Manasseh's death, which communicates the matter simply. Just as the great general Holofernes manages his armies, so Judith also administers her own estate. The story requires that Judith remain an unmarried, childless widow, and levirate marriage is not raised as an issue (see Deut 25:5–10); no brother or kinsman of Manasseh is mentioned.

That Judith inherits and manages an estate as a wealthy widow is unusual in comparison with earlier Israelite custom, but not totally at odds. Without remarks in the literature, certain biblical women appear to be both wealthy and widows, exercising control over their wealth, for example, Micah's mother (Judg 17:1–4), Abigail (1 Sam 25:42), and the Shunammite woman (2 Kgs 4:8–9; 8:1–6).[49] Judith's inheritance of her dead husband's estate would be a difficulty in rabbinic literature, but there were accommodations: it could be bequeathed by the husband or part of a

---

45   Mobley, *Empty Men,* passim.

46   See Adelman, *Female Ruse,* 203. See also the extended treatments of Sarah's beauty in Genesis Apocryphon 20.1–8, a novelistic Jewish text. Judith's fasting does not diminish her beauty, and T. Jos. 3:4 avers that fasting for God's sake, as Joseph did, increases his beauty. In Daniel 1, Daniel and his companions likewise become fatter for all their abstention from the king's meats.

47   See Schmitz/Engel, *Judit,* 245.

48   Gera, *Judith,* 267.

49   Gera, *Judith,* 268. See also the commentary on 16:24. Gera lists daughters as well who inherit. See also Bezalel Porten, *Archives from Elephantine: The Life of an Ancient Jewish Military Colony* (Berkeley: University of California Press, 1968) 237–40; Sarah Pomeroy, *Goddesses, Whores, Wives and Slaves: Women in Classical Antiquity* (New York: Schocken, 1995) 190–204; Claudia V. Camp, *Wisdom and the Feminine in the Book of Proverbs* (Bible and Litera-

ketubbah.[50] For a widow to inherit was evidently also known in Greece and late Second Temple Judaism; 2 Macc 3:10 mentions widow's deposits in the temple treasury. This is even clearer in Roman law.[51] A final touch to the story remains intriguing. Although Judith and not Manasseh was favored in the first mention of Judith above, including the genealogy, in 16:24 she distributes her wealth to *both* sides of the family—his first.

What a fictional character gave to another fictional character, however, as part of the back-story of our present narrative is hypothetical, although it is true that the language suggests a real-world variance from Jewish law, however acceptable that variance may have become. To be sure, a general verb is used here, *hypeleipeto* (Manasseh "left" his property), rather than the technical language of bequeathing (*klēronomeō*, *klērodoteō*, for Hebrew roots *yrš* and *nḥl*). More significant for the characterization of the protagonist as an isolated heroine, however, in 16:21 the Bethulians return to their *klēronomia*, but Judith to her property, *hyparxis*.[52]

Judith's administration of the estate also calls to mind the *'ēšet ḥayil* of Prov 31:10–31. Usually translated "woman of valor" or "substance," it is, rather, "woman of strength," parallel to the *'iš ḥayil*, strong man or even heroic man. In Proverbs' paean to admirable womanhood, the matriarch of a household (and evidently an extensive estate is assumed) is accomplished not only in domestic crafts and maintaining a pious household but also in acquiring fields and planting vineyards. Like Judith, "she opens her mouth with wisdom," and teaches others (31:26). But this woman is not described as beautiful or sexualized in any way; she remains perfectly contained within a male-controlled hierarchy (31:23).

The anxieties of Ben Sira concerning the sexual wanderings of wives and daughters (noted above) indicate how the sexuality of the *'ēšet ḥayil* must be repressed. Judith's unnamed slave, who administers her estate while Judith is in seclusion (8:10), is likely regarded not as an *'ēšet ḥayil* but as an extension of her mistress.

The fact, then, that the heroine is both exceedingly beautiful and exceedingly wealthy is common in folktales but was exploited as a motif in novels as well. The large combination of traits, however, is unusual in Israelite tradition. Says Gera, "Her piety, asceticism, beauty, wealth, and good reputation are all mentioned together in these verses and these qualities are, unusually, linked."[53] This combination is perhaps more common for the female protagonists of the Greek novels, but those texts arose only after Judith, and the earlier Greek novelistic traditions, such as Semiramis and Aesop, do not play on all of these motifs. In addition, Judith's role *in Bethulia* is *not* primarily that of a woman famed throughout the land for her beauty, but—as we will learn in a subsequent scene—as a woman of wisdom, integrity, and command. It is, ironically or understandably, *this* kind of woman who will explode all decorum.

■ **8:8** "No one spoke ill of her," literally, no one "raised a malicious word against her," *epēnenken autē rhēma ponēron*. Might the audience have understood this as "cast an evil word against her," in the sense of a magical spell? This seems unlikely, given the various common senses of *epipherō* (usually translating *šālaḥ*). In the LXX, *ponēros* is equivalent to Hebrew *ra'*, a quite broad term for bad, evil, or wicked; and note especially LXX Num 14:36: "The men Moses sent to spy out the land

ture Series 11; Sheffield: Almond, 1985) 85–86. The complexities of the system of inheritance and widowhood are laid out by Naomi Steinberg, "Romancing the Widow: The Economic Distinctions between the *'almānâ*, the *'iššâ-'almānâ* and the *'ēšet-hammēt*," in Rolf P. Knierim et al., eds., *God's Word for Our World: Theological and Cultural Studies in Honor of Simon John De Vries* (2 vols.; London: T&T Clark International, 2004) 1:327–46.

50   Ilan, *Jewish Women*, 167–72; Joosten, "Original Language," 173–74; Michael L. Satlow, *Jewish Marriage in Antiquity* (Princeton, NJ: Princeton University Press, 2001) 93–100, 204–9; Elder, "Judith,"

456–59; and Wegner, *Chattel*, 143, on rich widows in the Mishnah. See Num 27:8–11, but cf. Sir 22:4; 25:21–22; T. Job 46–52; Joseph and Aseneth 24:5; 6:1–4; 12:15; m. B. Batra 8:1.

51   Sawyer, "Gender Strategies," 17–18.

52   Gera, *Judith*, 268. On *klēronomia*, see the commentary on 8:21–23. Grintz proposes that the special language of our text indicates that Manasseh had granted Judith ownership of all of his property before his death, and so typical Jewish inheritance laws did not apply (*Book of Judith*, 188–89).

53   Gera, *Judith*, 261.

. . . brought back a bad report [*rhēmata ponēra*] about it," and also the *ponēra* words spoken against Uzziah in the next verse.[54] Several aspects of this should be considered. First, in a culture emphasizing honor and shame, Judith is honored by her townspeople and not shamed with derogatory language. In such a cultural context, words were perceived as powerful and could actually "do things"; words could build up or tear down. Gossip could affect a person's social honor, and the audience is told that Judith enjoyed a blameless public reputation. Was gossip concerning her sexuality the issue, or envy for her wealth and privilege, or both? Ultimately, Judith is not a typical woman, nor a realistically rendered woman. The text romanticizes her persona, protecting her both from the resentments to which a real woman might have been subject, and the narrative also builds a prophylactic fence around her virtue, so that her actions to come would not endanger her social standing. Throughout, Judith is protected from censure.

The verse continues, "for she feared (or revered) God greatly," *ephobeito ton theon sphodra.* Schmitz/Engel note that she demonstrates little fear or anxiety,[55] but fearing God is more an Israelite expression for revering and committing to God (*yarē*'; cf. Greek Esth 2:20). It is still markedly different from the Greek emphasis on reason and the preferred Greek concept *eusebēs,* used of Judith in 8:31; she is also devout, *theosebēs,* in 11:17. For Greeks, reason is the arbiter of true *eusebeia,* and they criticized fear as *deisidaimonia,* an excessive and irrational fear of gods, often translated as superstition (see excursus below; and Wills, "Jew, Judean, Judaism"). It is ironic, then, that the "fear of gods," negative for Greeks, is so similar to "fear of God" as a positive relation in Israel. But fear of God in Israel referred to an intensity of feeling for a *particular* deity and is related to the increasing use among Jews of *'aman* in Hebrew and *pist-* in Greek. Words in these groups are usually translated "trust" or "believe," but they are really about holding God as a patron (see the commentary on 14:10). It was specifically in the period of Judith's composition that a Jewish negotiation of this difference between Jewish and Greek understandings became so noticeable.

---

54 The Greek novel heroines are similarly virtuous, sometimes more than the male protagonists. Although the word virtue, *aretē,* does not occur in Judith and is rare in the LXX of the early biblical books, it is interesting that it is found in Wisdom of Solomon and 2, 3, and 4 Maccabees.

55 Schmitz/Engel, *Judit,* 248; also Wills, "Jew, Judean, Judaism." For Schmitz/Engel, *Judit,* 254–55, Judith is arguing from the sovereignty of God, which is true, but the mode owes something to Stoic philosophy in addition to the Israelite fear of God; see the commentary on 8:35. Here *phobeō* is in the middle voice, while in 2:28 and 4:2 people fear Nebuchadnezzar greatly using the passive with *sphodra.* Fear of God was an ideal for male figures in the Bible—Abraham (Gen 22:12), David (1 Chr 13:12), Joseph (Gen 42:18)—and women as well: the Egyptian midwives (Exod 1:15–21) and Esther in the LXX (Esth 2:20).

Text	Textual Notes

Text

Textual Notes

9/ When Judith heard the malicious words that the people had spoken against the magistrate—for they were fainthearted from the lack of water—and she also heard all the words that Uzziah had said to them, how he had[a] sworn an oath to them that he would surrender the town to the Assyrians after five days, 10/ she sent her favorite slave, who was in charge of all her possessions, to summon Uzziah,[b] Chabris, and Charmis, the elders of the town. 11/ When they had come to her, she said to them, "Listen to me, magistrates of those who reside in Bethulia! The word that you addressed to the people today was not right. You have made this oath, pronounced between God and yourselves, and have stated that you will hand over the town to our enemies unless the Lord turns to provide us[c] help during these days. 12/ But indeed, who are you to test God today and set yourself in the place of God among human beings? 13/ You are testing the Lord Almighty, but you will never understand anything! 14/ You will not discover the depths of the human heart, nor comprehend a person's thoughts. How, then, would you search out God, who created these things, and understand his mind or follow his reasoning? No, my brothers, do not provoke the Lord our God to anger! 15/ If he does not choose to help us within these five days, he has the power to protect us in whatever number of days he wishes, or even[d] to destroy us in the face of our enemies. 16/ Do not extract a pledge on the designs of the Lord our God, for God is not like a man, to be threatened, nor like a son of man, whose help is demanded.[e] 17/ Therefore, while waiting patiently for deliverance by his hand, let us call upon him for aid. He will heed our voice, if it pleases him.

18/ "Indeed, there has not arisen in our generation, nor is there today, either a tribe or family or body of citizens or town among us who worships gods made with hands, as was done in former days. 19/ And it was for this reason that our forebears were given over to sword and plunder, suffering a great fall before our enemies. 20/ We, however, do not recognize any God but him, and thus we hope that he will not disdain us[f] or any of our nation. 21/ For if we are taken, all of Judea will fall.[g] The sanctuary will be plundered, and God will make us pay for

Textual Notes

a Ενωτισατο και a plus in *O* OL Sy.

b Οζιαν και lacking in B S A *L* and other manuscripts, but Hanhart retained it with little textual support because it appears to be assumed in 8:28.

c For ημιν: υμιν B S A Sa some minuscules Vg; *NETS*, Moore, and Rahlfs prefer υμιν.

d Ἠ και can simply mean "or," as *NETS* translates (Smyth, 2862; but cf. 2888a), but can also be more emphatic, translated "or even" by NRSV.

e On this difficult reading, see the commentary and Hanhart, *Text und Textgeschichte,* 84–85; Bogaert, "Recensions," *RBen* 85 (1975) 31. Διαιτεω is rare; διαρτηθεναι/-τιθεναι is found in V 19 107 311 583 others; cf. Num 23:19.

f After ουδε, αποστησει το σωτεριον ελεος αυτου or similar appears in *O* 311 583 OL. Moore adopts this, translating "remove his mercy and his salvation" rather than (as in a Hebrew construct state) "remove his saving mercy."

g For κλιθησεται: κληθησεται V 106´ 126 some minuscules *b* by itacism; cf. eradicabitur Sa for κλιθησεται. Καθησεται is found in B S A 311* 542 Eth; κανθησεται in 249 311-c; ληφθησεται in *O* 318 Sy. Agreeing with Hanhart and the present reading are *NETS* and Gera; see also Hanhart, *Text und Textgeschichte,* 62. By conjecture, Rahlfs reads και λημφθησεται. Moore (following Zimmermann, "Recovery," 72) argues that all variants go back to a confusion of two Hebrew roots, *yāšab* ("to sit") and *šābāh* ("to carry off"). However, Corley ("Septuagintalisms," 88–89) finds no warrant for the Hebrew explanation; καθησεται ("will be situated thus") makes sense as a difficult original with later Greek clarifications, not alternative readings of Hebrew roots. Yet here I retain Hanhart's reading.

h For αιματος: στοματος 46 64 107 534 Eth, which Hanhart and Gera prefer as *difficilior.* Αιματος is found in B S A V 583 *L* 55 542 OL Sy Sa Vg, and NRSV, *NETS,* and Moore prefer this reading.

i Land of αιχμαλωσια is always the land to which Israelites were deported, e.g., Neh 3:36; so Schmitz/Engel, *Judit,* 238.

j Κατευθυνω, "act as carpenter's line, straighten, direct"; in the LXX it often translates צלח or כון.

k For επιδειξωμεθα: αποδεχωμεθα 583 OL Sy; cf. 1 Esdr 9:14, 2 Macc 2:26, 3 Macc 6:26, Sir 50:21. The NRSV breaks up the clauses: "let us serve as an example for our kin. Their survival. . . ."

l *NETS:* "On account of all these things. . . ."

m For ποιμαινοντι B *O L* and others, some texts (V S 64 107) read ποιμαινοντος, which Hanhart prefers (*Text und Textgeschichte,* 15–16).

its desecration with our blood.[h] 22/ The slaughter of our kindred, the captivity of the land,[i] and the desolation of our inheritance he will bring upon our heads among the nations wherever we are enslaved, and we will become an offense and an object of shame among those who come to possess us. 23/ Our slavery will not be turned into[j] favor, but the Lord our God will account it as dishonor.

24/ "So now, my kinsmen, let us set an example for our kindred,[k] for their survival depends on us. The sanctuary, the temple, and the altar depend on us. 25/ Despite all these things, let us give thanks to our Lord God,[l] who tests us just as he did our ancestors. 26/ Remember the things he did for Abraham, and the ways he tested Isaac, and the things that happened to Jacob in Mesopotamia of Syria as he was tending the sheep of Laban, the brother of his mother.[m] 27/ For he has not tried us by fire, as he did them[n] as a test of their hearts, and he has not taken his revenge upon us, but the Lord scourges those who approach him in order to admonish them."

28/ Uzziah said to her, "Everything that you have said was spoken with a good heart. No one can contradict your words. 29/ Your wisdom did not appear in a day,[o] but from your youth all the people have recognized your understanding, for the inclination of your heart is good. 30/ But the people have become very thirsty and have forced us to act in accordance with what we said to them, and to bind ourselves with an oath that we cannot violate. 31/ Therefore, pray for us,[p] for you are a pious[q] woman, and the Lord will send enough rain to fill our cisterns, and we will no longer be faint."

32/ Judith said to them, "Listen to me, for I am about to do a deed[r] that will reach to generations upon generations of our people. 33/ Stand by the gate tonight, and I will go out with my slave, and within the days after which you said you would surrender the town to our enemies, the Lord will deliver Israel by my hand.[s] 34/ Do not inquire[t] about what I am doing, for I will not tell you until I have completed my task."

35/ Uzziah and the town magistrates said to her, "Go in peace, and may the Lord God go before you to take vengeance on our enemies." 36/ And withdrawing from her tent, they proceeded to their posts.

n   For $ου$ $καθως$: $ως$ O Sy; $καθως$ OL Sa. For $επυρωσεν$: $επει$-$ρωσεν$/-$ασεν$ 71′ 583 OL-M Sy Sa Eth Arm, which Moore evidently prefers.

o   For $ουκ$ $εν$ $τη$ $σημερον$: $ουκ$ $εν$ $τη$ $ση$ $μεριμνη$ S*, which gives rise to *sollicitudo* OL-CX (see Bogaert, "Version latine," 197).

p $Και$ $ταχα$ $εισακουσεται$ $ο$ $θεος$ $ημων$ added by O OL Sy. See Beentjes, "Bethulia Crying," 239 n. 32.

q   For $ευσεβης$: $θεοσεβης$ O, perhaps reflected in Sy Eth Vg; *sancta* OL.

r   After $πραγμα$, O OL Sy also read $σοφιας$.

s $Καθοτι$ $εγω$ $πεποιθα$ read in O OL Sy.

t   For $εξερευνησετε$ and similar: $ερω$ B V a 55 126 311; $απαγγελω$ O and some minuscules.

Commentary

8:9–36

Judith's speech in chap. 8 and her prayer in chap. 9 lie at the approximate midpoint of the novella, and, according to Schmitz, they define both the theology and the story. In §3 above, I noted that the novella as a whole may be said to have two arcs, a sort of libretto and music, or explicit speech and narrated action, with two different centers. But it is certainly the case that the center of the prayers, the theological arc or "libretto," lies in chaps. 8 and 9.

■ **8:9–10**
As noted above, the introduction of Judith in 8:1 was interrupted by a long descriptive aside with a number of parentheses, just as in 1:1 the introduction of Nebuchadnezzar is interrupted by a parenthesis on Arphaxad. The introduction of Judith is now continued with her *hearing*: she *hears* about the "wicked words" of the Bethulians' protest against their ruler. (The phrase, *ta rhēmata . . . ta ponēra,* calls to mind the previous verse, where none spoke *rhēmata ponēra* against Judith.) Why had Judith not heard before? Linda Day suggests that the late involvement is viewed negatively, and Loader concludes that Judith must live at a distance.[1] From the point of view of the story, however, the tension must be developed before she is introduced. The Bethulians are bereft until she finally emerges. Mentioning her or her hearing earlier would simply be bad storytelling. Further, it is typical of hero legends that the protagonist is called out of isolation by a desperate people. Judith's late entry, if anything, heroizes her.

The awkward parentheses of 8:1–8 are followed by different sorts of parenthetical statements at 8:9–10, here analyzed into clauses:

When Judith *heard*	the malicious *words* that the people had spoken against the magistrate,	for they were fainthearted[2] from the lack of water,
and when Judith *heard*	all the *words* that Uzziah had said to them,	how he had sworn an oath to them that he would surrender the town to the Assyrians after five days

Her double hearing is stated in a parallel way in this construction, as are the two actions of the Bethulians—the people spoke wicked words, and Uzziah swore an oath to surrender in five days. But it will become clear that Judith is more exercised by the second part. The sentence structure throughout this section seems at first turgid and overdone—recall that the introduction of Nebuchadnezzar and Arphaxad in chap. 1 was also executed through long, awkward parentheses. Still, Xeravits and others argue that the architecture is an artful construction (see below). At any rate, we now hear of Uzziah's oath, and indeed various words for oaths are found in Judith (8:11, 30; 11:7; 12:4; 13:16), by Nebuchadnezzar as well (1:12, 2:12).

■ **8:10** Judith does not come out of seclusion at first but responds to what she has heard by sending her favorite slave (see the excursus below) to summon Uzziah, Chabris, and Charmis. The three elders together represent the city leadership. Their gathering is somewhat parallel to Holofernes's war councils of the first half. In what may be a comic touch, Chabris and Charmis, with their similar-sounding names, always appear together. Compare the comical Shadrach, Meshach, and Abednego in Daniel 3, whose names are admittedly more assonant than rhyming, or even Rosencrantz and Guildenstern in *Hamlet.*

In the Bible, strong women sometimes summon men—Rebekah (Gen 27:42), Tamar (Gen 38:25), Rahab (Josh 2:21), Bathsheba (2 Sam 11:5), and the wise woman of Abel Beth-maacah (2 Sam 20:16)—as do some wicked women as well—Delilah (Judg 16:18) and Jezebel (1 Kgs 19:2). Later, however, the rabbis were critical of Deborah for summoning Barak (Judg 4:6; see also b. Meg. 14b).[3] The three elders appear immediately without questioning, since the slave carries the authority of the master.

1   Linda Day, "Faith, Character, and Perspective in Judith," *JSOT* 95 (2001) 71–93, here 76; Loader, *Pseudepigrapha,* 191.

2   The word *oligopsycheō* occurs also in Exod 6:9 and Num 21:4 in regard to the Israelites disbelieving Moses.

This has been taken to demonstrate Judith's authority, and indeed it does; she is a wealthy and respected figure. It might also be suggested that a proper lady would not appear in public before the elders, but this may be an imported assumption. She will later transgress all rules of decorum, but at this point it is not clear whether her reason for remaining isolated is ascetic practice or modesty. Aseneth was depicted at first as even more isolated, although it is taken to a symbolic extreme. Isolation of unmarried girls was not assumed in the Greek novels, where the female protagonist is often seen and marveled at in religious processions. But the fact that Judith is a widow and not a wife or daughter is likely relevant.

■ 8:11

Part of the novelistic development of this text is to emphasize dialogue as the dominant mode of discourse in both halves. Ironically, oral storytelling emphasizes plot and short speeches, and only assumes or reports speech, while written novelistic literature often relies on dialogue and long speeches. The words of the people against the ruler, Uzziah, were *ponēra*, harsh, even wicked, in direct contrast to the *ponēra* words that were *not* spoken against Judith in the previous verse. But Judith's condemnation will be harsh as well.

Achior had said that the Israelites' power was in God, and it is ironic that Uzziah's name means Yahweh is my power, yet he disappoints (see also 6:14–15). He is another of the weak figures in Judith, although in the modern European tradition he is often granted a stronger role, sometimes that of a father figure who controls Judith.[4] Here, however, her authority to criticize Uzziah is that of the prophet who speaks for God. Judith transgresses the typical social order by rebuking the elders,[5] as Esther does to Mordecai in Esther 4, and as the young upstart Daniel does in Susanna. Judith, Esther, and the young Daniel share a brash disregard of elders. This is partly comic hutzpah, but they are also wise agents. Not coincidentally, all three examples are in novellas.

Technically, Uzziah had not sworn an oath (7:30–31), but rather the Bethulians had (7:28); Uzziah, however, recognizes and reaffirms the oath that the people have sworn (8:30). Oaths were considered very important in the maintenance of social order, but, like oracles and unalterable laws, they have a literary function as well. In imaginative literature, oaths often propel people down a path that, if not reversed, will lead to destruction. Compare the story of Jephthah's daughter, where a vow is followed to its destructive end, and Esther, where the unalterable law of the Persians is finally replaced by another. The motif of a leader coerced by his people into unwise actions occurs also in Daniel 6 and Bel.

Excursus: Judith's Slave, Habra/Abra

No sooner do we encounter the wealthy widow who is in charge of a major estate than we also meet the person who keeps it all running while Judith remains in her tent: her female slave, "in charge of all her possessions" (v. 10). A male owner of an estate would have his *oikonomos*, but the term for this slave in Judith is *habra* (later also *abra*), derived from the adjective *habros, -a, -on* ("delicate," "pretty," "dainty," "soft," or "luxurious"). It is the standard Greek term for a favorite female slave, as opposed to the more general *paidiskē, doulē*, or *korasion*.[6]

This slave is never given a name in Judith, but in later tradition the noun is treated as a name; she is called Habra or Abra, as Lazarus's "rich man" in Luke 16:19–31 was later given the name Dives, Latin for "rich man." A *habra* or favorite female slave appears in the Greek novels and in Greek drama, often a go-between or confidante who sometimes even outwits her mistress.[7] In Judith, however, she says nothing and plays no role as a confidante, yet her continuing presence and status at the end may indicate a Greek influence.

---

3   See Gera, *Judith*, 273; Tikva Frymer-Kensky, *Reading the Women of the Bible: A New Interpretation of Their Stories* (New York: Schocken, 2002) 149, 397 n. 149.

4   See also Sheaffer, *Envisioning*, 30–39, on the changing role of Uzziah in the history of Judith.

5   Stocker, *Judith*, 6.

6   Used for *'āmâ* and *na'ărâ*, but not for *šipḥâ*. In the Vulgate, we find the transliterated *abra*, but also *ancilla* and *puella*. The term *habra* appears a number of times in the LXX but almost always in the plural, the maidservants of matriarchs or wealthy women (e.g., Gen 24:61; Exod 2:5; Greek Esth 2:9; 4:4; Joseph and Aseneth 10:4; singular only in Exod 2:5).

7   Gera, *Judith*, 71, 75–76, 272; Gera, *Xenophon's Cyropaedia*, 242 n. 173; Ben Akrigg and Rob Tordoff, eds., *Slaves and Slavery in Ancient Greek Comic*

Judith's slave is introduced as an incidental character and performs the typical symbolic function of the slave-in-literature.[8] She administers Judith's estate, is constantly at Judith's side when they face danger in the Assyrian camp, and is freed at the end. She serves as Judith's lieutenant, much as the very audible Bagoas will serve as Holofernes's second. A principal function may be to carry away the bloody, impure head in a pouch. After everything else, it still might have been too much to imagine Judith carrying a severed head across the valley. The slave's role—as is every slave's role—is to act as a barrier between the master and the negative aspects of life. In European art, she is sometimes depicted as a visual counterpart or partner to Judith, but at other times as a disempowered, even animalized instrument of her mistress (see §8 above).

There were multiple layers to the practice of slavery in our period that apply to the depiction of Judith's slave. In some cases, there was tremendous economic and political power placed in the hand of slaves by the master. Slaves were often educated, powerful, and refined. This is perhaps assumed by the depictions of Judith's slave. On the other hand, the duality of free and slave assumed the strongest possible symbolic and even ritualized distinction between them. Both aspects, the powerful administrator and the abject nonhuman, can be observed here, as also, for example, in another Jewish novella, the Tobiad Romance from Josephus, *Antiquities* book 12.[9] In addition, in folklore and popular stories there is often a "Gunga Din" motif, the creation of an idealized story-relationship between a master and slave.

Slaves often appear in the Hebrew Bible, although they sometimes blend into the context. Abraham's slave Eliezer had authority over his property (Gen 24:2), as Joseph was over Potiphar's house (Gen 39:4). Israelite women owned slaves as well; Sarah owned Hagar (Gen 16) and Abigail owned five female slaves (1 Sam 25:42). Speaking female slaves are encountered in Judg 19:9; 1 Sam 9:3–10, 14:1–15; and 2 Kgs 5:2–3. Proceeding later to the novelistic literature, strictly instrumental female slaves are depicted in Greek Esth 15:2–3; a bitter female slave challenges Sarah for beating her in Tob 3:7–9, as also in T. Job 7:1–12; and a more "positive" female slave is seen in Aseneth 10:6–7. The protagonist of Life of Aesop is a slave, which is played upon ironically. He is constantly cursed for being a worthless slave and is even beaten for comic effect. Yet the audience perceives that Aesop is the real protagonist and philosopher, and his pretentious and blustery owner is a comic foil because he cannot assert mastery over him.

In her early analysis, Craven raised up the slave's role and her relationship with Judith, and the discovery of Artemisia Gentileschi's *Judith*s contributed to an affirmation of the relationship between Judith and her slave. Some have rightly questioned this interpretation. "Unlike Bagoas," says Gera, "Judith's maid is a nameless, drab, and silent figure who weaves in and out of the story according to the needs of the plot."[10] To be sure, Robin Branch and Pierre Jordaan are more positive about the slave's role, cataloguing the slave's attributes: obedience, silence, anonymity, competency, trustworthiness, humility, companionship, and love for Judith. "She willingly risks her life," they assert, "for Judith and her fellow Israelites."[11] But Jennifer Glancy rightly objects to their attribution of agency to her. The slave never speaks or makes a decision and has no agency *in what is depicted,* only in the back-story of her management of Judith's estate. Even if high-placed slaves could administer estates in the ancient world, *they did so as slaves.* Sheaffer resists romanticizing Judith's relationship with her slave, though she does remind us that the slave is not an insignificant character.[12] Here as well, a multilevel understanding of her narrative function is called for. Branch and Jordaan, and also Sheaffer, assume that if a slave has an overseer role, then that communicates a high regard for the figure. In the Tobiad Romance, however, the high-placed *oikonomos* is ridiculed. At any rate, it is not an unusual role for a slave in ancient literature, though perhaps it is for a female slave.

Drama (Cambridge: Cambridge University Press, 2013).

8   Sheaffer, *Envisioning,* 57–80.

9   Wills, *Jewish Novel,* 185–211; Wills, "The Depiction of Slavery in the Ancient Novel," *Semeia* 81 (2000) 113–32; Wills, *Quest,* 23–50; Camp, *Wisdom and the Feminine,* 85–86, on women managing estates.

10   Gera, *Judith,* 75; Craven, *Artistry and Faith,* 121; Wills, *Jewish Novel,* 151.

11   Robin Branch and Pierre Jordaan, "The Signifi-cance of Secondary Characters in Susanna, Judith, and the Additions to Esther in the Septuagint," *Acta Patristica et Byzantina* 20 (2009) 389–416, here 407; Glancy, "The Mistress–Slave Dialectic: Paradoxes of Slavery in Three LXX Narratives," *JSOT* 72 (1996) 71–87, here 82; see Wills, "Depiction of Slavery," especially on the Tobiad Romance.

12   Sheaffer, *Envisioning,* 21. See the nuanced discussion of Gera, *Judith,* 106, and her notes on 8:6, 7, 8; 10:5; 12:1–4; 16:23, 24.

Judith's slave acts out the virtues of Judith herself; she is resolute, courageous, and implacable. She is a contrast to Bagoas, who is talkative, gullible, and openly sycophantic—one mirrors the other. Further, though it would be possible for a wealthy Jewish woman to have a non-Jewish slave, the slave is presumably Jewish.[13] However, during the journey to Holofernes's camp, Judith sits on a lambskin and bathes, while the slave does not. The slave's food is also not mentioned, although it is possible that she eats the acceptable food that she brought for Judith. In the author's day, it was certainly possible to grant the slave a name, spoken words, or complexity. However liminal and ultimately restricted it may have been, in Greek comedy slaves were depicted with a broad range of roles, and the Aesop tradition takes a slave as the protagonist—although even here there is a brutal exploitation of Aesop as a comic figure. As slaves in ancient literature served a dramatic purpose to further the elite themes of the works, so also in Judith: this shadow extension of Judith serves to characterize her mistress as an agent in absolute control. There is no banter or manipulation by the clever slave here.

The crude instrumentality of Judith's slave has been mollified in Christian tradition in two ways. First, English translations of the Bible typically translate all words for slave as "servant," which obscures the actual relationship and reduces the modern reader's discomfort with the slave status. Second, because the less common term *abra* is used for slave, the Vulgate retained it as a loanword, and, as noted, this word came to be treated as this slave's name. For centuries, then, audiences unaware of the meaning of the word have assumed that Judith's slave had a name, and they have at times accorded to her human agency and subjectivity that at first may not have been a typical audience response.

In the end, Judith manumits her slave (16:23). The freeing of a slave was probably not uncommon and was viewed as praiseworthy, although our direct evidence of Samaria in the Hasmonean period is limited. The benevolent manumission of this slave is depicted *as a reward* for her, not as a redress of the limitations on slaves in general. "The maidservant's

emancipation is a cunning literary effect," says Stocker, "designed to reassure us that Judith's own bondage is freedom."[14] At the most basic level, we must ask: would the slave have been worse off under the Assyrians? Would the slave have been justified in lopping off Judith's head? This eventuality is depicted by the African-American artist Kehinde Wiley (see §8 above)

■ **8:11–27**

Judith chides the elders for accepting the idea of a deadline for God to act which the Bethulians demanded. In their desperation, the people have assumed that if rain does not come, they will have to surrender to avoid the worst possible fate. Judith's strictures on prayer have seemed unfeeling to some, and far stricter than earlier biblical narratives. Gera observes the unexpected similarity between Judith's note to the beleaguered Bethulians and God's to Job in Job 38.[15] Is it not rather Judith who is putting herself in the place of God? And one interpretation of Job at this point is that God is being too rigid.

Schmitz's focus on the speeches and prayers in Judith is well justified, and Gera comments that Judith's speech to the elders is "the longest and richest theological discussion in our book."[16] I will examine the structure and rhetoric first, followed by the themes and theological arguments.

The speech falls into two parts, vv. 11–17 and 18–27:

8:11–17: Judith rebukes the leaders for setting a deadline on God's response

8:18–27: Judith sets out the dangers of surrender and suggests a better view of God's role, since Israel has not sinned: God is testing Israel as he did the patriarchs

The first section is marked by more dependence on second person plural; the second, on first person

---

13   If she is Jewish, according to Deut 15:12 the period of servitude would be six years. Glancy raises the question of her ethnic identity ("Mistress–Slave Dialectic," 82–86). Ilan notes that rabbinic law distinguished Hebrew and "Canaanite" (= foreign) slaves (*Jewish Women*, 205). A common false assumption is that male and female slaves were

foreign, but rabbinic references indicate that many were Jewish.

14   Stocker, *Judith*, 9; see also Ilan, *Jewish Women*, 207–08.

15   Gera, *Judith*, 278.

16   Gera, *Judith*, 274; Schmitz, *Gedeutete Geschichte*, passim.

plural.[17] Note that v. 17 is an exhortation that follows upon the previous verses, but it also functions as a transition to the next argument; as a result, it could be placed in either section. The use of exhortations to end one rhetorical section and begin another is common in Jewish and Christian rhetoric.[18]

There is a mixing of discourses throughout. Terms from Israelite wisdom appear, but by form the speech is closer to Greek rhetoric and contains less Semitic, Septuagintal style.[19] Greek rhetorical aspects include, first, Judith's more formal address to her audience ("Listen to me, magistrates of those who reside in Bethulia!"); second, her exposition of her different arguments, very much in the deliberative style of Greek rhetoric; and, third, her gathering up of the arguments to that point with a conclusion followed by an exhortation (vv. 17, 24, 25):[20]

	Conclusion	Exhortation
17	Therefore, while waiting patiently for deliverance,	let us call upon him
24	So now,	let us set an example
25	Despite all these things,	let us give thanks

The very verb "let us set an example," *epideixōmetha,* for instance, was a staple in Greek-influenced Jewish and Christian rhetoric; a Hebrew verbal equivalent is lacking. Last, we note that there is less use of Semitic paratactic *kai* in this speech.

This style of hortatory-paraenetic address was evidently given a name in Greek-influenced Jewish and Christian rhetoric, *logos paraklēseōs,* hortatory address

(1 Macc 10:24; 2 Macc 7:24; 15:11; Heb 13:22; Acts 13:14–41).[21] As generic as the speech may seem to modern readers, this style of deliberative rhetoric is rare in the Hebrew Bible. Indeed, it now *seems* generic precisely because it was established as a staple of Greek rhetoric. The similarity to a speech before a gathered *dēmos* or *boulē* is unlike the patriarchal-tribal, prophetic, or royal model of rhetoric in Israel.[22] As a possible influence on Judith, we note the "military harangues" Thucydides places in the mouths of military leaders, often to rally the troops (e.g., 2.11), and in the mouths of civic leaders as well (e.g., 1.86). Other Jewish examples include Susanna (OG ending), Epistle of Jeremiah, T. Reub. 5:1–5; 4 Macc 16:16–22; and Josephus, *Jewish War* 5.9.3–4 §§362–415, 7.8.7 §§341–379.

The fact that a woman is delivering this Greek address is also significant. In Greece, women were limited in public speaking or leadership. "Public speech was a—if not *the*—defining attribute of maleness."[23] To be sure, Judith is technically speaking not in public at this point, but she speaks *as if* she were in public, and she will later speak in public. Mary Beard points out that, when Penelope, like Judith, comes down from private quarters into the great hall to reprimand the bards, her son Telemachus insists, "Mother, go back into your quarters, and take up your own work, the loom and the distaff. . . . Speech will be the business of men." For Beard, this is "Western literature's . . . first recorded example of a man telling a woman to 'shut up'; telling her that her voice was not to be heard in public."[24]

But, although questions will remain about whether women could occasionally speak, act, or lead in public,

17 Schmitz, *Gedeutete Geschichte,* 160; Haag, *Studien,* 40–43; Hellmann, *Judit,* 121–26.

18 Wills, "The Form of the Sermon in Hellenistic Judaism and Early Christianity," *HTR* 77 (1984) 277–99.

19 Gera, *Judith,* 274–75, 286; Gera, "Speech in Judith." On wisdom motifs, see Dubarle, *Judith,* 1:170–71. On Judith as a *Kriegstheologin* who channels Israelite calls to war, see Fischer and Obermayer, "Die Kriegstheologie," 227–42.

20 Wills, "Form of the Sermon."

21 Wills, "Form of the Sermon." Walbank discerned three kinds of speeches in Greek histories: debating speeches of politicians (*dēmēgoriai*), harangues

of commanders (*paraklēseis*), and discourses of ambassadors (*presbyterikoi logoi*). Judith's speech here matches the second, and Achior's speech in chap. 5, a combination of the first and third. See also Tomes, "Heroism," 182 n. 32.

22 2 Chronicles 15:2–7 can be compared, but is short, not ordered in the same way, and lacks a clear rhetorical ending. See also 2 Chr 32:7–8; Ezekiel 20; and occasionally in Deuteronomy.

23 Gera, *Judith,* 382–83.

24 Beard, "The Public Voice of Women," *London Review of Books,* February 14, 2014, http://www.lrb.co.uk/2014/02/14/mary-beard/the-public-voice-of-women.

there was yet a *literary* tradition of women carrying out public speaking and leadership roles. In *Menexenus*, a dialogue attributed to Plato, Aspasia was a foreign woman who became a famous rhetorician, but, as noted in the introduction (see §5), Judith does what in Greece only *foreign* women could do. If Judith in her *parrhēsia* (the Greek value of boldness of speech) "stood for" other Jewish women, this might be viewed as a sort of colonial critique—but she may be as exotic as Aspasia.

We turn now from rhetoric and the structuring of Judith's speech to an analysis of the themes. In the background of Judith's address to the elders lies Deuteronomistic theology (see also chap. 9): sin leads to punishment, which leads to repentance, which leads to salvation; Israel sins but, by turning, can receive God's mercy. This is expressed fully in Deuteronomy 28–32, and in the postexilic period there developed so-called penitential theology in Ezra 9, Nehemiah 9, Daniel 9, and Baruch 1. This theology may have arisen as a response to the destruction of the exile (Zech 7:3–5).[25] The scenes of communal confession take on aspects of mourning, and fasting is also enjoined (Neh 1:4; 9:1; Dan 9:3; see the commentary on 4:8–12 on fasting).

Judith's points range widely in a few verses, summarized here:

1. By setting a deadline you are testing God, and assuming God's role in deciding.
2. You cannot understand God.
3. God has power—and freedom—to protect or destroy us.
4. God is not like a human being, to be threatened or affected by pleading.
5. He will hear our voice, if it pleases him.

Judith imposes a demanding, even unrealistic expectation upon the people. "The word that you addressed to the people today is not right" (v. 11), she says, using the most general terms possible, *ouk euthēs,* which in the LXX translates *yāšar.* More specific reasoning follows.[26] "You have made this oath [*horkon*], pronounced between God and yourselves." Technically speaking, Uzziah did not enact an oath but merely promised the people to surrender if God did not intervene within five days. It is they who used oath language (7:28).[27] But both parties are in collusion on this issue, and as will be noted below at 8:35, it may be Stoic principles that inform Judith's condemnation. The high standards of correct prayer in Judith correspond to the Greek value of self-mastery found elsewhere in Judith.

The testing of God is key to Judith's theology in this chapter. The idea of testing in the Bible is sometimes used of God testing Israel (Gen 22:1; Exod 16:4; 20:20; Deut 8:5; 13:4; Pss 26:2; 94:12; Tob 12:13 Sinaiticus; Wis 3:5; T. Jos. 2:6–7) and also Israel testing God (Exod 17:2; Num 14:22; Wis 1:2).[28] More relevant to Judith, God uses an attack by Sennacherib of Assyria, one of the models of Judith's Nebuchadnezzar, to test the good king Hezekiah (2 Chr 32:31). In Ben Sira the trustworthy slave of God is tested by proving his loyalty to the commandments; a similar theme is found in the testament of Mattathias, the patriarch of the Hasmoneans (1 Macc 2:52).[29]

When Judith sounds the theme of testing God, she evokes the murmuring in the wilderness but strangely continues in v. 18 with her reassurance to the people that Israel is now righteous: "We do not recognize any God but him, and thus we hope that he will not disdain us or any of our nation" (v. 20). This is possible because there is an unacknowledged distinction between the Bethulians, who murmur as the Israelites had done, and the more recent Hasmoneans, who restored Jerusalem. The latter are represented in the story by the high priest Joakim. Two different pictures of Israel are telescoped

25 Rodney Alan Werline, *Penitential Prayer in Second Temple Judaism: The Development of a Religious Institution* (EJL 13; Atlanta: Scholars Press, 1998). See also Angela Kim Harkins, "The Function of Prayers of Ritual Mourning in the Second Temple Period," in Mika S. Pajunen and J. Penner, eds., *Functions of Psalms and Prayers in the Late Second Temple Period* (BZAW 486; Berlin: de Gruyter, 2017) 80–101.

26 Cf. this root in 13:20, and its opposite in 5:8, 18; also see 2 Sam 19:19; 1 Kgs 11:33; and Schmitz/Engel, *Judit,* 249–50.

27 Gera, *Judith,* 276. *Estēsate ton horkon touton = hēqîm šĕbûʿâ* (Gen 26:3).

28 Schmitz/Engel, *Judit,* 236, 250–51; Kugel, *Bible as It Was,* 167–68.

29 Ben Sira 2:1; 27:5, 7; 33:1; 44:20. See Giovanni B. Bazzana, *Kingdom of Bureaucracy: The Political Theology of Village Scribes in the Sayings Gospel Q* (BETL 274; Leuven: Peeters, 2015) 194–95.

here: the "ancient" motif of murmuring in the wilderness—which allows Judith to be a second Moses—and the contemporary Hasmonean pride at the time of composition.

The second of the two arguments above, the inability to comprehend God, can be viewed in more detail both in rhetorical and theological dimensions. "How will you search out God who created all things?" is a plea for intellectual humility before God, a theme found in Isa 40:12–14; Job 38:4; and Prov 30:2–4.[30] A careful parallelism is found here: four similarly structured clauses, each concluding with a second person plural verb, and a strong concluding prohibition in the present tense (vv. 14):

For the depth of the heart of a human	you have not found
And thoughts of his (human's) mind	you have not grasped
And how then, God, who created all things,	will you discover?
And his mind	will you know?
And his reasoning	will you perceive?

In no way, then, my brothers, should you continue to anger the Lord our God.

ὅτι βάθος καρδίας ἀνθρώπου	οὐχ εὑρήσετε
καὶ λόγους τῆς διανοίας αὐτοῦ	οὐ διαλήμψεσθε.
Καὶ πῶς τὸν θεόν, ὃς ἐποίησεν πάντα ταῦτα,	ἐρευνήσετε;
Καὶ τὸν νοῦν αὐτοῦ	ἐπιγνώσεσθε;
Καὶ τὸν λογισμὸν αὐτοῦ	κατανοήσετε;
Μηδαμῶς, ἀδελφοί, μὴ παροργίζετε κύριον τὸν θεὸν ἡμῶν.	

The three searchings of God reflect an inappropriate comparison of human abilities with God's (see also 8:34). By setting a deadline, the Bethulians were attempting to negotiate an arrangement with God, placing themselves on God's level. Further, by *limiting* God's freedom by a deadline, they deny the very premise of God's sovereignty: God *chooses* when and if to act.

Judith's assurance that follows regarding Israel's newfound obedience is also not unique. Even within Ezra-Nehemiah, with its deep confession and recommitment (Ezra 9; Nehemiah 9), we also find Neh 1:8–9, which assumes a sense of justification before God.[31] In regard to chap. 9 we will see that Judith, the one who prays, speaks for the people but does not have a sense of her own sins. In fictional narratives, it was also possible to find perfect righteousness—not only Daniel in Daniel 1–6, but his three companions as well. It was left to the LXX to add to Daniel the Prayer of Azariah, raising penitential issues and the confession of sins. The Vulgate also includes a plus at 8:14 in which Judith would join the elders in penitence (see appendix). We note as well the absence of penitential tradition in Hasmonean ideology.[32]

Scholars have expressed some disquiet over aspects of this speech. It contains a set of themes that, *if pressed*, would result in inconsistencies or at least difficulties, here listed as A and B:

A. Just as Nebuchadnezzar had taken on God's prerogatives, so now the elders have done so by holding God to a deadline.

B. Yet Uzziah's desire to wait to see whether God would act might more charitably be viewed as a very human response, even faithfulness.

Further:

A. The Bethulians' testing of God is a sin.

B. Yet Israel has not recently sinned.

Or, stated differently:

A. God is free to save his people *if he wishes*.

B. God will *surely* save Israel because "we have not sinned."

Or again:

---

30 On the depth of a person's heart, cf. Job 11:7; Jer 17:9–10; Wis 9:13; Schmitz/Engel, *Judit*, 250, 252.

31 Wills notes that in the rise of asceticism there are both self-accusing and self-assured texts, perhaps both read by the same practitioners ("Ascetic Theology").

32 Eyal Regev, *The Hasmoneans: Ideology, Archaeology, Identity* (JAJSup 10; Göttingen: Vandenhoeck & Ruprecht, 2013).

33 Judith's words are similar to those of Daniel's three friends in Dan 3:17–18, although Judith imposes an unexpected stringency about *petitioning* God.

A. God is free to act *whenever* he chooses or *not at all* (8:15).[33]

B. Within the time of five days God *will rescue* Israel *by my hand* (8:33).

One can imagine a logic that could harmonize these points to some extent.[34] For instance, God is indeed free to save Israel or not, but God's word is good, and covenant history and theology reassure Israel that God will save them. Or, since Israel has been good, the threat of Assyria is not *punishment*, as is usual in Deuteronomistic theology, but a *test* of Israel, as the patriarchs were tested. Yet the inconsistencies are not clearly resolved; they may indeed arise from the mixture of Israelite and Greek ways of thinking (see excursus below at 8:35).

Some scholars simply affirm Judith's hard stance here and are not concerned about the apparent inconsistencies: her condemnation is just, and the townspeople lack her faithfulness or insight into God's ways.[35] Helen Efthimiadis-Keith, however, perceives Judith's words on two levels. Deuteronomy 28 and Deuteronomic theology provide the theological context of Judith, but our author *counters* this theology (see §6 above). God has absolute freedom to act, and, besides, Israel has not recently sinned gravely.[36] The only sin now lies in imposing a deadline on God. But Judith's claim of the absolute sovereignty of God—a sovereignty with which one dare not negotiate—seems different in tone from the exodus narrative. When the Israelites murmured against Moses (Numbers 14), he turned to God, reminded the deity what he promised, and pointed out that if God kills them in the wilderness, the nations will think God *unable* to bring the people into Canaan. Judith does not, strictly speaking, reject the notion of a petition to God (8:17), but the tone is different from the very human dialogue between Moses and God. Judith ultimately

insists that not rain, but more strength of character, is called for.

Yet there is another way of looking at this problem. When Judith criticizes the imposition of a deadline for surrender as a testing of God, her discussion turns to *theological* arguments, but the *audience* may simply perceive a contrast between weak Bethulians and strong Judith. It is a *narrative* point, not a *theological* one. In the centuries following, the theological question rose in importance only because it was believed that a biblical book must be theological. In the original performance situation, however, the audience also registered the distinction of strong and weak. Judith's able rhetoric does in fact drive her point home, but even so, does the investment in rhetorical structure function to affirm the theology of Judith, or simply to characterize the heroine as powerful in word as well as deed? Still, her words demonstrate a commitment on another level, the discipline of one who exercises self-control.

■ **8:11–17** In addition to these large-stroke observations, some details should also be noted. Judith's sharp, imperious tone—"Listen to me!"—is also used by Deborah to Barak (Judg 4:6–9) and the wise woman of Abel Bethmaacah to Joab (2 Sam 20:17). Her harsh "Who are you?" recalls Holofernes's "Who are you?" addressed to Achior (6:2). In the Bible, "who?" questions are often used to communicate an absolute incomparability with God; the answer is always "No one" (Job 38–39; Isa 40:12–14). *Kyrios pantokratōr* translates *yhwh* or *ʾĕlōhê ṣĕbāʾôt*. It is not common in the LXX, but appears five times in Judith, reflecting a sense of omnipotence: it is folly to pretend to God's powers or likeness, but the proper human response is recognition. Judith often uses forms of *ginōskō*, esp. *epiginōskō*, for knowledge of God; see esp.

---

34   See Gera, *Judith*, 274, 292; and compare Schmitz/ Engel, *Judit*, 254–55, regarding 8:15: "So ist es kein Widerspruch, sondern gehört gerade zusammen, dass Judit in ihrer Rede in Jdt 8, 15 betont, dass Gott weder zur Hilfe [*boētheō*] noch zum Schutz [*skepazō*] verpflichtet werden kann, gleichzeitig ihn aber im Gebet in Jdt 9, 11 als *boēthos* 'Helfer' (im Unterschied zur Klage des Volkes in Jdt 7, 25) und als *skepastēs* 'Beschützer' anruft." Judith assumes a general notion of God's protection and the relation of act and consequence in Israel. In addition, how-

ever, she imposes a strict sense of how one would *petition* God—and this was a Greek philosophical concern. On act/consequence, see Samuel L. Adams, *Wisdom in Transition: Act and Consequence in Second Temple Instructions* (JSJSup 125; Leiden: Brill, 2008).

35   Zenger, *Das Buch Judit*, 491.

36   Efthimiadis-Keith, "Genealogy," 873–75. On Deuteronomistic theology in Judith, see also Voitila, "Deuteronomistic Heritage," 378–81.

9:14, but also 5:8; 8:20; 11:16; 14:5. The entire narrative suggests that Judith does have knowledge of God.

Judith's phrase—to "set oneself up in the place of God" (*hyper tou theou*, 8:12)—is indeed ambiguous: it could also mean "above God" or "on God's behalf." The king and high priest in Jerusalem stand "for God," but at the time of composition they were Hasmoneans. Do elders of this town have no right, while Hasmoneans do? Only someone named "female Judah" can put it right, and she makes all the right sacrifices in Jerusalem afterward.

Among other details in the use of language: God has the *exousia* ("power"), perhaps a term from discussions of Hellenistic kingship (God has handed authority over to worldly leaders, Sir 10:4), but it is also found in apocalypticism (Dan 7:12, 14; cf. Dan 4:31, 32). "Do not extract a pledge," *enechyrazete* (v. 16), is a strong, graphic metaphor, the imperative strengthened by the inclusion of the subject.[37] *Diaitēthēnai* ("to be cajoled") is the *lectio difficilior;* see excursus below. It is influenced by Balaam's words in Num 23:19 LXX: "God is not indecisive as a man is, nor to be threatened as is a mere mortal."[38] On counsels or designs of the Lord, *boulas kyriou,* compare Wis 6:4; 9:13; LXX Ps 106:11; but *boulē* is also used for the secret or mystery of Nebuchadnezzar's plan in 2:2.

■ **8:18–27** Judith devotes significant space here to the present threat to Israel: not simply death but a loss of freedom and independence, the preservation of the temple, and humiliation among the nations. While deportation was the common practice in the ancient Near East (see 2:9), in Greece and Rome conquered peoples were more often enslaved (although deportation and enslavement are not mutually exclusive). In Greece and Rome, a discourse grew up of freedom as the opposite of slavery, both for individuals and for city-states. Greek texts often speak of the inherent dignity of being independent, of not being enslaved cities.[39] This is enshrined in Greek philosophical language as well, even on the popular level, for instance in Aesop's fable of the two ways that

lie ahead (Life of Aesop 94): the rough, stony, and difficult path that leads to freedom and the smooth, level, pleasant path that leads to slavery. At the time of the Persian War, Greek texts speak of liberating the Greek colonies of Asia Minor from the Persians. Our text is often influenced by the Greek tradition, but relevant as well is Isaiah's call for national independence that allows for loyalty to God (Isa 10:24–27; 30:1–7). Independence, then, is valued not as an end in itself but as a precondition for dependence on God.

■ **8:18** Moore points out that the affirmation that "there has been no idolatry in our generation" is made three times: here, in Achior's speech in chap. 5, and before Holofernes in 11:10.[40] It is a central affirmation of the author, and it reflects Hasmonean political propaganda. There is even a bit of irony about her chiding of the elders. She seems to say "We are strong because we have not sinned" *and* "Your prayer is sinful before God." We may extrapolate: "Your prayer will thus cause us to fall."

"Tribe," "family," and "body of citizens" are categories traditional in Israel, although the Greek terms can be translated various ways. Do they also have Hellenistic political meanings? In the LXX, these Greek terms usually translate the following:

Greek	Hebrew
phylē	*maṭṭeh, mišpāḥâ,* and *šēbeṭ*
patria	*'āb* and *mišpāḥâ*
dēmos	*mišpāḥâ* and occasionally *'am* (see also at 4:8; 6:1)
polis	*'îr*

The LXX usage is not consistent, and more common are three orders, *phylē* (=*maṭṭeh*), *patria* (=*mišpāḥâ*), *polis* (= *'îr*), while in Josh 19:16, 23 LXX we find four orders, *phylē, dēmos, polis, kōmē*–tribe, clan, city, and village. The last might have seemed more appropriate for Bethulia. As the orders of Israel are often priests, Levites, and "all Israel," this list is understood to cover the orders of "all Israel," that is, minus the priests and Levites. As

---

37   Gera, *Judith,* 279.

38   Gera prefers *diartēthēnai,* arguing that "God is not to be misled" makes more sense than "God is not to be entreated," since prayer is affirmed in the next verse (*Judith,* 279–80). Neither, however, seems perfectly logical, and the author's point in 8:17 may be

more that prayer should not involve a *self-interested* petition.

39   Orlando Patterson, *Freedom* (New York: Basic Books, 1992).

40   Moore, *Judith,* 182.

Schmitz/Engel suggest, *dēmos* and *polis* are thus not understood in specifically Hellenistic terms (but compare Jdt 4:8 and 6:1, which is more general).[41]

"Gods made with hands" (*theois cheiropoiētois*) was a relatively recent term in Israel's critique of idolatry, but compare the earlier "works of human hands" in Deut 4:28; 2 Kgs 19:18; and the postexilic parody of idols (Isa 40:18–20; 41:5–14; 44:6–22; Jer 10:1–16; Wisdom 13–15; Bel; Baruch). It normally translates *ĕlîl* ("weak") but is particularly dramatic in the roughly contemporaneous LXX of Dan 5:4, 23; 6:28, and Bel 5 (Th), and compare Mark 14:58; Acts 7:48; 17:24; Heb 9:11, 24.[42] Earlier in Judith (3:8), Nebuchadnezzar was also characterized as a sort of idol. The great fall experienced by Israel must be the destruction of the First Temple and the exile, again telescoped with an imagined "Assyrian" period.

■ **8:20** Does "we do not recognize any God but him" imply monotheism, or only monolatry, Israel's allegiance to one god only? See 9:14.[43] Earlier biblical statements of Israel's steadfast allegiance to one God (Exod 8:6; Deut 3:24; 1 Kgs 8:23) can also be compared to passages that appear to deny the existence of other gods (Deut 4:35, 39; 2 Sam 7:22; 1 Kgs 8:60; 2 Kgs 19:19; Neh 9:6), but these passages, and even Isa 45:5, may not be truly monotheistic. Technically speaking, Judith does not insist that Israel is monotheistic, but it shows allegiance to God over other figures such as Nebuchadnezzar, who doubtless stands for other divinities and divinized kings.

■ **8:21–23** "The sanctuary will be plundered" reflects ancient Near Eastern practices and the fictional scenario of Jdt 3:8, but historical memories of the actions of Antiochus IV Epiphanes motivate this. For *hagia* as "temple," here and in 8:24, see also at 4:13; 9:8; 16:20. This term is a strong leitmotif in Judith.

See 2 Kgs 21:14 for similar language of the loss of the inheritance to plunder and spoils. The inheritance, *klēronomia*, is a powerful biblical motif, whose significance is often missed by modern readers. It translates Heb. *naḥălâ* and *môrāšâ/yĕrûšâ*. *Klēronomia* is often rendered in English as "heritage" as well as "inheritance,"

but it would be wrong to understand this as an abstract cultural transmission and not as concrete inheritance, specifically land rights. With the conquest of Canaan, the land as a whole becomes the inheritance for Israel as a promise from God (Exod 15:17; Deut 26:1; Josh 11:23; Greek Esth 13:15–17; 14:5; Sir 46:8; 1 Macc 15:33, 34; see also Jdt 4:12; 5:15; 9:12; 13:5; 16:21). Inheritance is also a central feature of the historical surveys in Josh 24:8; Neh 9:15; Ps 105:44; 135:12; and Greek Esth 13:15. This is the macro-level of *naḥălâ*; at the micro-level, it is also the plot of land of the *bêt 'āb*, "house of the father," or the patriarchal father and his extended family, understood as a historical gift from God. Inheritance is understood to apply to family or clan first, and to the individual only as a member within that unit.

The emotional and extended-family importance of this may be seen in the emphasis on the location of the bones of the deceased and of the ancestors, together with the tribal *naḥălâ:*

> [T]he ancestral plot constitutes the location wherein the living (in their tents), the dead ancestors (in their tombs), and the tribal deity (via the familial altar) form an integral whole of considerable importance to the welfare of all.[44]

And we may add, perhaps even welfare for the dead. In Joseph and Aseneth the *klēronomia* becomes a mystical and inexplicable symbol that Aseneth and others may join through conversion. In all of this rhetoric, the author presses a strong notion of an ideal Israel.

■ **8:24–27** The end of Judith's speech continues the theme of testing begun above, but with a difference: whereas before it was negative, Israel testing God, now it is positive, God testing Israel (see Deut 8:5; Ps 94:12; Prov 3:11–12; Sir 2:1–6; Wis 3:4–6; Tob 4:20–23; 11:14; 13:2, 6; 2 Macc 3:34; Ps. Sol. 10:1–2; Heb 12:5–6; James 1; 1 Clement 56). A strong theme in Israelite wisdom is God's teaching or discipline of the wise, Heb. *mûsār* or Gk. *paideia* (see below). The souls of the righteous are

41   Schmitz/Engel, *Judit*, 237.
42   Wills, *Jew in the Court*, 121–27.
43   Voitila, "Deuteronomistic Heritage," 373–75; Olyan, "Isaiah 40–55," 190–201.
44   Lightstone, *Commerce of the Sacred*, 46–47. See also Schmitz/Engel, *Judit*, 412; Voitila, "Deuteronomistic Heritage," 382–84.

also tested (Wis 3:5–6). Accepting God's testing is not passive, but an occasion for Judith's bold action.[45] Gera notes that Judith looks back on the very different situation of the patriarchs and their history. "In the Bible," says Gera, "testing is reserved for inexplicable and momentous divine occasions."[46] This is the perspective of early epic cross-culturally, when there was a special and open relationship between gods and heroes; gods intervene in particular historical moments and heroes respond and engage. The author of Judith is part of a new development of testing that is not epic but assumes that the philosophical agent is tested regularly in order to become a perfect citizen. A historical passage such as 2 Chr 32:31 on the testing of Hezekiah lies between early heroic epic and the more philosophical testing of Judith.

A number of verbs are used here regarding God's testing, understood in a larger sense: *peirazei, epyrōsen eis etasmon, exedikēsen, nouthetēsin, mastigoi*.[47] It is a concentrated and intense collocation of verbs, fitting for Judith's righteous, even overwrought style. There is a strong Jewish tradition about the testing of Abraham (Sir 44:19–21; Jub. 17:17–18; 1 Macc 2:51–52; m. 'Abot 5:3; cf. Rom 4:1–8; Heb 11:8–12), but in Judith the word *peirazō* is associated more with Isaac (although the Vulgate alters this, 8:22–23). The testing of Isaac is not as common in the tradition, but compare 4 Macc 7:14; 13:12; 16:20; Targum Neofiti 1 (Exod 12:42).[48] It is probably the general life story of Isaac that is in view, with many trials, rather than specifically the binding of Isaac (Genesis 22). Testing is not used with Jacob, but there is somewhat more detail. Gera provides a possible, but not provable reason: "Judith identifies with the dissimulating Jacob. . . . She also alludes to Jacob's partner in deceit, his mother Rebecca."[49] The lists of paradigmatic figures is often longer, but the effect of this short list is to invoke the theme without actually exploiting it; here it is more a literary, not a truly didactic device. The varieties of "test" words may be more significant.

■ 8:28–31

Uzziah will respond to her positively, acceding to her point of view, but with some ambiguity. He will affirm her wisdom (*sophia*) and understanding (*synesis*), which throughout her life all the people have recognized. *Synesis* appears often in Ben Sira and in lists of Stoic virtues (Diogenes Laertius, *Lives* 7.116). Compare the very didactic ending of Susanna OG concerning the *epistēmē* and *synesis* of young men like Daniel, and also the Babylonian queen mother's words about Daniel (5:11). Contrast, indeed, the less philosophical terms that Judith will use in 11:8 to flatter and befuddle Holofernes. Uzziah further states that her heart's disposition is right, as Holofernes and his slaves will also recognize (11:20–21).

Despite the size and importance of the biblical wisdom texts, in the narrative books there are only eight people who are called wise, five men and three women: Joseph (Gen 41:33), Joshua (Deut 34:9), David (1 Sam 16:18), Jonadab (2 Sam 13:3), Solomon (1 Kgs 2:9), Abigail (1 Sam 25:3), the woman from Tekoa (2 Sam 14:2), and the woman from Abel Beth-maacah (2 Sam 20:16). We note that the last two women, though members of a select club, remain unnamed in the texts! Gera perceives important connections between Judith and these women:

> All three of the wise biblical women manage to avert a crisis or bloodshed by means of their eloquence and persuasive powers, manipulating the powerful men whom they address and deflecting their anger. They

45   Schmitz/Engel, *Judit*, 261–65. Also, "Let us give thanks" (*eucharistēsōmen*) lacks a Hebrew equivalent in the MT. The Hebrew Bible tends to use "bless" for this dynamic relationship, but development of a Hellenistic notion of the reciprocity of giving thanks to the gods may be in evidence, arising in the Christian Eucharist as well.

46   Gera, *Judith*, 285–86.

47   Compare, among others, Gen 12:17; Exod 5:14, 16; Deut 8:5; 25:2, 3; Prov 2:2; Isa 1:25; Zech 13:9; Jer 6:27–30; 9:6; Sir 2:5; Wis 3:5–6; 11:9–10; 12:2; 16:6;

2 Macc 3:26; 7:37; Ps. Sol. 13:6–10; Heb 12:7–11. God does not take revenge, but *ekdik-* appears in Judith in regard to Nebuchadnezzar and Simeon, and sometimes with God as the subject: 1:12; 2:1; 6:5; 7:28; 8:35; 9:2; 11:10; 16:17; see Schmitz/Engel, *Judit*, 275–76.

48   Kugel, *Bible as It Was*, 173–77; Moore, *Judith*, 183; Schmitz/Engel, *Judit*, 263–64.

49   Gera, *Judith*, 286–87, referencing also Navarro Puerto, "Reinterpreting," 127.

reprove the men with whom they converse and cast their arguments at least partially in theological terms, just as Judith does here. . . . [Judith] possesses the beauty and seductive powers of Abigail, the disguise and deceptive tongue of the woman of Tekoa, and the ability to rescue the city by decapitating an enemy, just as the woman of Abel does.[50]

Other women who are not specifically called wise are also similar in regard to courtly intervention, such as Esther. Deborah is not called wise but is possessed of prophetic qualities; still she, like Judith, knows how to wield military violence (see also §5 above). Whether Judith received a formal education, as Elder supposes,[51] is unknown, but the approximately contemporaneous story Susanna recounts her instruction by her parents in the law of Moses (Dan 13:3 LXX).

What seems apparent is that, just as Nebuchadnezzar and Holofernes do *not* have self-mastery, neither do the elders of Bethulia, which Uzziah seems to concede: "The people have become very thirsty and have forced (*ēnankasan*) us to act in accordance with what we said to them" (v. 30). Further, Uzziah and the other elders passively accede to the previous oath: "an oath we cannot violate," which the people forced on them. Uzziah is characterized as malleable, now accepting Judith's leadership but closing with an excuse as well. The oath that cannot be rescinded is a common storytelling device,[52] but this principle is not explicitly invoked. At any rate, in the modern period Uzziah was often treated as a more authoritative leader than Judith (see §§5 and 8 above).

Uzziah also says that Judith has a "good heart" (*agathē kardia*), which elsewhere in the LXX translates *ṭôb lēb*, meaning joyful (Deut 28:47). Uzziah adds, "the inclination [*plasma*] of your heart is good." *Plasma* translates *yēṣer*, the molding of a person, or inclination, whether

for good or evil (Gen 8:21; Ps 103:14; T. Asher 1:3–9, the Qumran Community Rule 1QS 3.13–4.26). Later Jewish texts developed this notion and the balancing within the person of the good and evil inclinations.[53] Our text likely predates this treatment, but may show some relation.

Uzziah provides a weak excuse for his ill-conceived oath: the leaders were forced by the people, who were driven by thirst. But his excuse mongering is very biblical: Aaron in Exod 32:22 and Saul in 1 Sam 15:20–24 speak similarly.[54] Uzziah's request that Judith pray for rain is also passive and ineffectual: it puts the entire onus on God to act, and it does not remove the threat of the Assyrians. Judith will ignore this request entirely and move to a direct attack on the enemy. Her own prayer in chap. 9 will also invoke Simeon as a model of an aggressive and violent response.

For Judith as a pious woman, *gynē eusebēs*, compare *theosebēs* in 11:17, and see below. Is this more like the Greek notion than like its Hebrew equivalent *ṣaddîq* and *yārē'*, fearful or reverent? The term *eusebēs* is found in the LXX, but never about a woman; women are described, rather, as fearing God (see 8:8). (Compare Deborah in Pseudo-Philo, *Biblical Antiquities* 33:6.) The *euseb-* word group would soon become central in Jewish and Christian ethical discourse, as it had in Greek. Fourth Maccabees 16:14, for instance, commends the mother of the seven martyr brothers as a "soldier of piety" (*di'eusebeian theou stratiōti*), who thus conquered a tyrant and is stronger than a man in word and deed—precisely Judith's persona.[55]

■ 8:32–33

"Listen to me" continues her command to the elders and also the motif of hearing. "I am about to do a deed" ignores Uzziah's more traditional requests and establishes Judith's own agency separate from the elders and

---

50 Gera, *Judith*, 288.

51 Linda Bennett Elder, "Judith's *Sophia* and *Synesis*: Educated Jewish Women in the Late Second Temple Period," in eadem, David L. Barr, and Elizabeth Struthers Malbon, eds., *Biblical and Humane: A Festschrift for John F. Priest* (Atlanta, GA: Scholars Press, 1996) 53–70.

52 See Gen 27:34–38; Lev 5:1–4; Judg 11:35; Ps 15:4; Esth 3:12–14.

53 See Gen. Rab. 9:7; Satlow, "Be a Man," 23–28, 32; Ishay Rosen-Zvi, *Demonic Desires: Yetzer Hara and the Problem of Evil in Late Antiquity* (Divinations; Philadelphia: University of Pennsylvania Press, 2011).

54 Moore, *Judith,* 184; Gera, *Judith,* 289.

55 See Gera, *Judith,* 290.

even relatively independent of God (see §5 above). She herself speaks as the agent in charge. A prophet often claims personal weakness or confusion but bears the authority of God; a prophet is indeed the slave of God. This comes through to some extent in Judith's references to her hand (8:33; 9:9, 10; 13:15; 16:5; cf. 12:4; 13:14; 15:10; and see also on Judg 4:9 below).

Judith also provides her own advance publicity—possible, perhaps, in this audacious novella—by stating that her deed will become part of Israel's heroic tradition.[56] "I am about to do a deed" would normally be said by God to a patriarchal figure, but Judith speaks for God, and not as a prophet would. True, in the next verse Judith says, "*The Lord* will deliver Israel by my hand," but it is still presented as *her* plan (cf. 9:9). It could be argued that Judith presents herself more as a free agent in relation to the Bethulians, and more a petitioning servant in her prayers to God. Yet the plan and the actions will be hers.

"Stand by the gate" introduces a dramatic transition of the narrative, the heroine's crossing of the boundary from society into the zone of chaos and danger. This is both a powerful biblical motif and also a heroic narrative motif (see chap. 9). One of the ways that the Bible creates the motif of strong women is to depict them "going out" by their own agency: Rebekah (Gen 24:15), Leah (Gen 30:16), Dinah (Gen 34:1), Tamar (Gen 38:25), Miriam and other women (Exod 15:20), Jael (Judg 4:18), Jephthah's daughter (Judg 11:34), Michal (2 Sam 6:20), the Shunammite woman (2 Kgs 4:21), and Naomi (Ruth 1:7). Judith's independence should not be viewed as *sui generis* in Israelite narrative; rather, she is being likened to figures from an earlier, golden age.

On "by my hand," see the excursus at 9:8–10, "Judith's Hand and Agency."

■ 8:34

"Do not inquire about what I am doing [*praxin*]"—Just as Judith imposed a boundary above on asking about God's designs, she demands an independence from being examined also. It characterizes our heroine, although

to pause here would also interrupt the story and force a premature revelation of her plan; it would be bad storytelling.

■ 8:35

The language here conjures Deborah's commission of Barak in Judg 4:14, although the gender roles are reversed. It also serves to bring Judith's perspective and the elders' perspective—which have been expressed somewhat differently—into harmony and common cause. Moore considers psychologically plausible explanations as to why the elders would accept her plan and allow her to leave Bethulia to go to the enemy's camp, but he grants that the original audience probably did not demand a neat logic.[57] The elders acquiesce and do not inquire about her plan, but that is in keeping with her power in this relationship.

Excursus: The Book of Judith and Greek Philosophy

In 8:8 it was said that Judith "feared God greatly," and below she is explicitly described as having wisdom and understanding; her inclination (*yēṣer* in Hebrew) is good. All these terms are readily associated with Israelite tradition. As noted in the introduction, however, this level of explicit statement is what we may call, borrowing terms from opera, the "libretto," an explicit level of spoken statements in our text, as opposed to the "music," the narrated events, which often move in a different direction. What Judith embodies in her actions, as opposed to her prayer language, often has similarities to Greek philosophy.

Although one would not expect to find philosophical concepts treated in works of narrative fiction, it has been shown that the Greek novels incorporate aspects of philosophical discourse. Ironically, they assume an ideal of self-mastery yet derive much of their interest by stripping the protagonists of their protections and exposing them to a temporary, liminal descent into hyper-emotionalism. The protagonists face temptations and sometimes succumb to their own irrational decisions. At the end, however, they are returned to the safe haven of a controlled estate.[58]

---

56 Moore, *Judith*, 185: it is the opposite of Esther (4:4–17), who reacts to Mordecai's demands. In Esther's defense, it is precisely at this point where *she* first speaks and takes command, giving orders to all, including Mordecai, and he is no longer depicted as

speaking; see Wills, *Jewish Novel*, 114–15; Adelman, *Female Ruse*, 198–230.

57 Moore, *Judith*, 184, 186.

58 See §7 above, and also Konstan, *Sexual Symmetry*, 30–33, here 31; J. Perkins, *Suffering Self*, 77–103,

In the case of Judith, the influences of Greek philosophy may be perceived in five related ways:

1. Judith's determination suggests the Greek virtue of *enkrateia,* self-mastery.
2. The characterization of the blustery tyrants Nebuchadnezzar and Holofernes mirrors Greek philosophical critiques of the angry tyrant who exhibits the opposite of *enkrateia–akrasia,* the lack of self-mastery.
3. Judith exhibits *parrhēsia,* or frank speech, in addressing the elders.
4. Judith's division of time into past, present, and future reflects Greek philosophical notions of time.
5. Judith's critique of the Bethulians' prayer is similar to Greek philosophical reflections on rational prayer.

Although no single one of these aspects of Greek discourse is unambiguously present in Judith, the combination justifies the conclusion that Greek philosophy influenced the depiction of the character of Judith.

By the second century BCE, Greek philosophy was already clearly felt among Jews in Alexandria. Demetrius the Chronographer and Aristobulus partake of Greek thought and philosophical terms. For Aristeas, there is a parallel between how a good king acts and how God acts. The king, like God, entertains petitions of all kinds if they are just and not intended to respond to one's own needs (192–94). Wisdom 12:18 sounds even more Stoic: God is free to act whenever he chooses. Even in Jerusalem, the "laws of Noah" in Jub. 7:20 are similar to Greek unwritten laws, and Ben Sira reveals some negotiation with Greek philosophy as well. While narrative parallels with Greek tradition were noted in the introduction, here we focus on philosophical developments.

The First Aspect of Greek Philosophy: *Enkrateia*

Enkrateia, self-mastery, held a central position in Greek philosophy. The philosopher has equanimity of soul, is happy regardless of circumstances, is self-sufficient, independent, and not disturbed by external circumstances. While prior to Plato *enkrateia* was understood to be the mastery *of something or someone else* (as it also was in Ben Sira), Plato himself elevated it as an abstract virtue, including it as one the four virtues (*Republic* 427e, 435b). A technical term was thus created in philosophy that would remain: *enkrateia* is control *of oneself.*[59] With this change, *enkrateia* became central to Greek philosophy for centuries afterward. Aristotle accepted the basis of Plato's view and investigated the role of *enkrateia* in checking its opposite, *akrasia*. Stoics also gave self-mastery a central role. Assuming a unified psyche over Plato's divided soul, they turned attention to the psychological processes within the soul, especially *prohairesis,* reasoned choice, and the *hēgemonikon,* controlling reason.[60] A strong emphasis on the discipline of the self arose from this. The true sage lives in the details: a minor misstep is as serious as a major one.[61]

Judith throughout exhibits a remarkable degree of *enkrateia*. An unrealistic novelistic heroine, she takes matters into her own hands in a remarkable show of personal agency. She does not betray any doubt or temptation, as do Esther, Susanna, Aseneth, and the heroines of the Greek novels. She is a heroine of virtue. A Jewish asceticism began to be explored, and, although it influenced Christian asceticism, it was, for the most part, suppressed or co-opted in the rabbinic turn in Judaism.[62] In line with the Stoic doctrine that small sins are as grievous as major sins, Judith rejects all special pleading about mitigating circumstances (8:30).

esp. 80–85; John R. Morgan, "The Representation of Philosophers in Greek Fiction," and Ken Dowden, "Novel Ways of Being Philosophical or a Tale of Two Dogs and a Phoenix," both in Morgan and Meriel Jones, eds., *Philosophical Presences in the Ancient Novel* (Ancient Narrative: Supplementum 10; Eelde: Barkhuis; Groningen: Groningen University Library, 2007) 23–52, here 40–42, and 137–49, here 148, respectively.

59 Xenophon of Athens argued that "genuine freedom consists in dominating one's pleasures, while the worst slavery is to be subjected to them" (*Memorabilia* 1.5; cf. 2.1; 3.9; 4.5–6). Xenophon also affirmed Socrates as a model of *enkrateia.*

60 Gretchen Reydams-Schils, *The Roman Stoics: Self, Responsibility, and Affection* (Chicago: University of Chicago Press, 2005) 15–26; Troels Engberg-Pedersen, "Stoic Philosophy and the Concept of the Person," in Christopher Gill, ed., *The Person and the Human Mind: Issues in Ancient and Modern Philosophy* (Oxford: Clarendon; New York: Oxford University Press, 1990) 109–35; Gill, *Structured Self*; Foucault, *Care of the Self*, 39–68; Wills, "Ascetic Theology"; Wills, "Jewish Novellas."

61 See Stobaeus, *Eclogae* 2.113.18–23, Diogenes Laertius, *Vitae* 7.101, 120. Fourth Maccabees 5:20–21 later expresses this Stoic principle, and, on Matthew, see Nathaniel DesRosiers, "Matthew's Charity: Righteousness, Almsgiving, and the Greek World" (unpublished manuscript, 3).

62 See Wills, *Jewish Novel*, esp. 1–39, 224–32; Wills, "Ascetic Theology"; Satlow, "Be a Man." Note,

It may be countered that Judith appears to exercise self-mastery because she has placed herself in God's hands; her prayers will articulate this. Yet in ironic narratives, there is often a distinction between what is stated by the characters, or even by the narrator—the libretto—and what actually occurs—the music. What *happens* is prioritized over what is *said;* what people *do* is truer than their *words.* While Judith prays to God and twice asks for strength (9:9–10; 13:7; compare 8:35), she has already embarked on her own plan of action, where she did not express any need for God's help: "Listen to me, for I am about to do a deed that will reach to generations upon generations of our people" (8:32), and later: "Now command that they open the town gates for me, and I will go forth to accomplish all the things you spoke of with me" (10:9). Although later art would discover a buffeted Judith, in the LXX Judith always exhibits self-mastery.

The Second Aspect of Greek Philosophy:
Akrasia of Foreign Leaders

As Judith is characterized by *enkrateia,* Nebuchadnezzar and Holofernes are associated with its opposite, *akrasia.* The figure of the angry tyrant was a common topos in Greek tradition, for example, Sophocles on Creon and Herodotus on the Persian kings.[63] To be sure, Israel also transmitted a condemnation of the bad king, from the suspicion of Saul and the limitation of the king in Deuteronomy 17 to the skewering of Babylonian kings in Daniel 1–5. Yet the depiction of Nebuchadnezzar and Holofernes cannot be explained from the biblical tradition alone. In the Hellenistic period, the role of the Greek kings gave rise to a more philosophical discourse on monarchy. There were deliberations about kingship, both good and bad. The bad king seems to borrow from the dramatic type of the *senex iratus,* or blustery old man, of Greek New Comedy.[64] Nebuchadnezzar, then, exhibited hubris by becoming enraged at the whole world and arrogating to himself aspects of a god. Holofernes becomes a slave to his passions. His sexual excitement breaks out of its bounds, and he proceeds to drink without restraint, "more than he had ever drunk in one day" (12:20).

The Third Aspect of Greek Philosophy:
Parrhēsia, Frank Speech

Judith speaks to the Bethulians like a philosopher, exercising *parrhēsia,* free and open expression (though the word does not occur in Judith and is rare in the LXX; compare also Achior in Judith 5). The word *parrhēsia* had indeed evolved, from the freedom of speech of the Athenian citizen to the freedom of the Cynic philosopher to upbraid others, to provoke and teach.[65] The young Daniel had also spoken with *parrhēsia* in denouncing the wicked elders in Susanna (compare Wis 5:1). When one looks at the qualities that the founder of Cynicism, Antisthenes, bequeathed to Diogenes, they look exactly like the traits of Judith: *sophia, autarkeia, alētheia, parrhēsia,* and *eleutheria.* It is not likely that the author subscribed to the Cynic school of philosophy (though the roughly contemporary Greek text Life of Aesop might very well have been a "Cynic" novel), but rather, at the colonized level, certain indigenous authors were internalizing—and perhaps in their minds perfecting—Greek ideals (§7 above on "colonial universalism").

however, that in Jdt 9:8 she invokes the Israelite and very un-Stoic notion of God's righteous anger.

63 Plato, *Republic* 579c. See Benjamin G. Wright, "Ben Sira on Kings and Kingship," and Tessa Rajak, "Angry Tyrant," both in Rajak, et al., eds., *Jewish Perspectives on Hellenistic Rulers* (S. Mark Taper Foundation Imprint in Jewish Studies; HCS 50; Berkeley: University of California Press, 2007) 45–62 and 76–91, respectively; Barbara Schmitz, "Judith and Holofernes: An Analysis of the Emotions in the Killing Scene (Jdt 12:10–13:9)," in Stefan C. Reif and Renate Egger-Wenzel, eds., *Ancient Jewish Prayers and Emotions: Emotions Associated with Jewish Prayer in and around the Second Temple Period* (DCLS 26; Berlin: de Gruyter, 2015) 177–91; Edith Hall, *Inventing the Barbarian: Greek Self-Definition through Tragedy* (Oxford Classical Monographs; Oxford: Oxford University Press, 1989) 157; Gera,

Xenophon's Cyropaedia, 254–59, on Greek suspicions of the emotional eunuchs.

64 Hector Avalos, personal communication. Holofernes's indulgence in wine is contrasted with Judith's fasting; so L. Lange, *Die Juditfigur,* 368–69; Corley, "Imitation," 46–50. In addition, the panic of the retreating Assyrians is told in 15:1–3 with psychological interest. Ahasuerus in the book of Esther could be added to the list of bad kings, but it may have predated Greek control. On good kingship and the *peri basileias* tradition, see Aristeas; and cf. also 3 Maccabees.

65 Heinrich Schlier, "παρρησία, κτλ," *TDNT* 5:871–77, here 874; Abraham J. Malherbe, "'Gentle as a Nurse': The Cynic Background to I Thess ii," *NovT* 12 (1970) 203–17; see Dio Chrysostom, *Oration* 32.11; Plutarch, *How to Tell a Flatterer from a Friend* 65F–74E.

The Fourth Aspect of Greek Philosophy: Time in Past, Present, and Future

Judith divides time into past, present, and future, which may reflect Greek notions. A literal translation of 9:5–6 reads:

> For you have done the things prior to those things, and those things, and the things that follow upon them. Both the things that are now and those that are to come you designed. What you conceived of came to pass, and the things you decided on presented themselves and said, "Behold, here we are!" For all your ways are prepared, and your judgment is with foreknowledge.

As natural as it may seem to modern readers to think of time in past, present, and future, time was not divided in this way in ancient Israel (nor in many other cultures). Yet consider Plato's *Timaeus:*

> The "was" and "will be" are forms of time that have come into being, although we do not notice that we wrongly apply them to the eternal [i.e., present] being. For we say that "it was," "it is," or "it will be," but in true speech "is" alone is the appropriate term; "was" and "will be" are properly said to be coming to be in time. (38a)[66]

The Stoics also reflected on the causal relations of events from past to present to future (Cicero, *On Divination* 1.126).

There were, to be sure, Hebrew and Aramaic words for past, present, and future, but they were not used together as here to express the extension of time in three phases.[67] In the Hebrew Bible, past or present used with the future suggests prophecy and future fulfillment, not a historical relationship of past, present, and future. Hebrew even lacks a present tense, but there is more at stake here than simply the insertion of a present tense.[68] The balanced, philosophical description of time at this point in Judith suggests the Greek and Roman partition of time. For Plato, the present was the eternal and "superior" tense, while for Second Isaiah the present is a lesser mode, caught between past prophecy and future realization. (On the past as determining the present, see also Deut 5:2–3; 29:14–15.) To be sure, the past-and-future perspective of biblical prophecy is still found in Judith's prayer, and Judith, like biblical prophets, speaks of *events,* not *abstract time per se.* In addition, it is specifically the God of Israel who is lord of past, present, and future. But Judith brings something new to Israel, a reflection on the role of God as lord of past, present, and future.[69] The *events* of past, present, and future coexist *on a time line* as a category of God's management. Even though it is stated awkwardly, even naively, indeed in a "colonized" manner, in tone it is an engagement with Greek past, present, and future.

---

66   See Michael Papazian, "Stoic Ontology and the Reality of Time," *Ancient Philosophy* 19 (1999) 105–19 (his translation). Aristotle discusses past and present (*Physics* 219b2).

67   Earlier comparisons of time in Israel and Greece have been criticized, but more recent scholarship has rearticulated certain distinctions; see Simon De Vries, *Yesterday, Today, and Tomorrow: Time and History in the Old Testament* (Grand Rapids: Eerdmans, 1975); Sacha Stern, *Time and Process in Ancient Judaism* (Littman Library of Jewish Civilization; Portland, OR: Littman Library of Jewish Civilization, 2003) 90–124; and Gershon Brin, *The Concept of Time in the Bible and the Dead Sea Scrolls* (STDJ 39; Leiden: Brill, 2001) 177–88; Paul Kosmin, *Time and Its Adversaries in the Seleucid Empire* (Cambridge, MA: Belknap Press of Harvard University Press, 2018). Philo can express the Greek terms (*On the Creation* 26, *On the Eternity* 4, 52–54), but Ben Sira rarely comes close to Judith's scope (but note 18:1, 10; 24:9; 42:19). Wisdom of Solomon 7:18, "the beginning and end and middle of times," at first sounds similar, but it is really referencing a cosmic

knowledge of beginnings (that is, origins), of the end (eschatology), and the "middle" of time where our worldly life takes place. See also §7 above; and Wills, "The Differentiation of History and Novel: Controlling the Past, Playing with the Past," in Ramelli and Perkins, *Early Christian and Jewish Narrative*, 13–30.

68   Which, interestingly, Judith does not use here, and which Hebrew might later discover in the *raz nihyeh* at Qumran. Grintz retroverts Judith's words into Hebrew, borrowing expressions from Isa 41:22–23; 42:9; 43:9; 44:7; and 46:9–10 (*Book of Judith,* 142).

69   The closest two parallels are Ezekiel the Tragedian, influenced by Greek culture, who says that Moses received knowledge of past, present, and future (Eusebius, *Preparation for the Gospel* 9.29), and Rev 1:8; 4:8; 17:8; 22:13. For Judith, were "past things" Simeon's revenge, or were they generalized to the mighty acts of God in history? Likely the latter; cf. 9:12 for God as creator of all. Judith includes a term not in Isaiah, *ta nyn,* the present things. The retroversion of Grintz is *hhwywt,* and for *ta*

The Fifth Aspect of Greek Philosophy: Strict Requirements of Rational Prayer

Judith's harsh criticism of the imperfect prayer of the Bethulians resonates with Greek philosophical critiques of the prayer of common people. For all schools of Greek philosophy, there was a high standard for rational prayer. One should not pray for any specific thing but only for that which is good. Stoic prayers existed, but they were of a high-minded sort—prayers not for boons but for moral change and virtue, a faint shadow of "prayer."[70] There is a concern not only about what it is proper to pray for but also about whether the gods would even be moved by pleading—note Judith's dismissal of pleading. The freedom of the gods was essential to the Greeks, which Judith also emphasizes. Plutarch asserts that the *deisidaimōn,* one ruled by fear of the gods, expects bad things from the gods, while the *eusebēs,* pious person, expects that the gods will grant good things (*On Superstition* 11 [2.170d–e], 4 [2.167e]). Petitionary prayers were seen by the Stoics to restrict the gods' freedom, and this was difficult to reconcile with a Stoic doctrine of fate. Condemned as well was praying for things that reflect either worldly desires or *adiaphora,* things about which the sage should be indifferent.

Judith's strict requirements on prayer in 8:12–17 are similar to Greek strictures on rational prayer. Her words can be noted carefully:

Who are you to test God today and set yourself in the place of God among human beings? . . . How, then, would you search out God . . . and understand his mind or follow his reasoning? . . . If he does not choose to help us within these five days, he has power to protect us in whatever number of days he wishes, or even to destroy us in the face of our enemies. Do not extract a pledge on the designs of the Lord our God, for God is not like a man, to be threatened, or like a son of man, whose help is demanded. Therefore, while waiting patiently for deliverance by his hand, let us call upon him for aid. He will heed our voice, if it pleases him.

By focusing on putting God to the test, Judith also evokes the tradition of the Israelites in the wilderness—"Do not put God to the test as you did at Massah" (Deut 6:16)—and also the dynamic of Judith as Moses and the Bethulians as murmuring Israelites. Yet the sense of testing is quite different.[71] In ancient Israel the placing of a deadline on God's actions would not have been considered as serious a breakdown in faithfulness as the murmuring in the wilderness, but Judith equates the two and perhaps even presses more strongly on the deadline.

Indeed, Judith's judgment does not seem to correspond to the notions of prayer found in the Hebrew Bible. There Israelites are free to utter almost any sort of prayer that they choose. Abraham may call God back to a "humane" standard (Gen 18:20–33), and Isaiah insists that Ahaz should set aside his reservations and ask God for any sign he chooses (Isa 7:10–16). In Judg 6:36–40, Gideon tests God twice by asking for signs, and in Isa 7:10–16 Ahaz at first refuses to test God by asking for a sign, but Isaiah insists that he should set aside his scruples and ask for any sign he wishes. First Samuel 11:1–11 also seems to address the same challenge as in Judith—during a siege Israelites set a time limit by which they hope to be rescued—but there is no condemnation of the people for doing so. Rather, Saul saves the Israelites of Jabesh Gilead without chiding them as Judith does. In 2 Chr 20:3, Jehoshaphat can show fear in praying, and it is seen positively.

Judith's reaction, then, seems unsympathetic, overly stringent, even self-righteous—hardly what one finds either in Gen 18:20–33 *or* in the Greek Lindos

---

eperchomena, the niphal of *hyh, hnhywt* (cf. also 1QS 3:15–16; Sir 42:18–19).

70   Jon Mikalson, *Greek Popular Religion in Greek Philosophy* (Oxford: Oxford University Press, 2010) 18; see Seneca, *Natural Questions* 2.35. Yet would Greeks and Romans in general, aside from the philosophers, have felt such restrictions? See §4 above on the Lindos Chronicle, a close Greek parallel to Judith, in which Greeks under siege pray for rain and also impose a five-day deadline.

71   One could argue that Judith is saying that setting a deadline is *intruding* on God's absolute sovereignty in managing events. Yet in a later text, m. Ta'an.

1:1–8, when praying for rain, Jews enact a fast every three days, each more stringent than the last. By Judith's standard, they test God by raising the intensity. See also 1 Macc 4:30–34; 2 Macc 3:15–24; 3 Maccabees 2; and see James L. Crenshaw, "The Restraint of Reason, the Humility of Prayer," in *Urgent Advice and Probing Questions: Collected Writings on Old Testament Wisdom* (Macon, GA: Mercer University Press, 1995) 206–21, here 207–8, 214, 221; Josef Haspecker, *Gottesfurcht bei Jesus Sirach: Ihre religiöse Struktur und ihre literarische und doktrinäre Bedeutung* (AnBib 30; Rome: Päpstliches Bibelinstitut, 1967) 339.

Chronicle.[72] Judith asserts a Greek philosopher's sense of how one may rationally pray to God. She does allow, finally, for an actual petition—"let us call upon him to help us"—but it is conditioned on a philosophical understanding of prayer: "God is not like a man, to be threatened, nor like a son of man, whose help is demanded."

To be sure, at times a distinction can be discerned between her words and Stoic prayer. In 9:8 she will call forth the *wrath* of God, and she herself *fears* God (8:8). She also asks for something tangible for herself and others, rather than simply a general good, such as virtue. Yet she has gone a long way toward holding the community to the standards of a Stoic sage. Although she does conclude by urging the Bethulians to "call upon God to help us," she adds: "He will heed our voice, if it pleases him."

One question remains. How does Judith embody the attributes of the Greek sage while violating every rule of female decorum? Part of the literary achievement of this novella is to present a great mixing. Judith can unleash dangerous social forces because she controls them. The Greek novels, coming somewhat later, also presented a mixing: they assumed the values of *enkrateia*, while allowing the protagonists, particularly the male protagonist, the liminal space to dissolve into fear and tears. But like the hero cross-culturally, Judith has the power and control to move through boundaries and yet maintain her mastery of herself and others.

---

72 Wills, "Greek Philosophical Discourse in the Book of Judith?," *JBL* 134 (2015) 753–73.

Text

1/ Falling upon her face, Judith placed ashes on her head and[a] uncovered the sackcloth[b] she was wearing. At precisely the time that the evening's incense was being offered in the house of God in Jerusalem, Judith uttered a loud cry to the Lord and said, 2/ "O Lord, God of my ancestor Simeon, in whose hand you gave a sword for vengeance against those foreigners who exposed[c] the womb of a virgin to defile her, who uncovered her thighs to shame her, and who profaned her womb to disgrace her. For you said, 'This shall not be done,' yet they did it. 3/ For this reason, you handed over their leaders for slaughter, and their bed, which was shamed by their deceit,[d] was in turn deceived and stained with blood. You struck dead the slaves with their princes, and the princes upon their thrones.[e] 4/ You gave their wives over to plunder and their daughters to captivity; all their spoils were divided among your beloved sons, who were zealously devoted to you and abhorred the pollution of their blood, and called upon you for help. O God, my God, heed now the plea of a widow! 5/ For you accomplished what happened before those things, what happened then, and the things that came afterward. You have designed the things that are now, and those that follow upon them, and what you have conceived has come about. 6/ All the things that you have willed to be have presented themselves and said, 'Here we are!' All your ways are prepared beforehand; your judgment is based on foreknowledge.

7/ "And now the Assyrians have grown into a huge army, exalted in their horses and riders, and have prided themselves in the strength of their infantry. They have placed their hope in the shield and the javelin, the bow and the sling, but they have not recognized that you are the Lord who crushes wars. 8/ The Lord is your name! With your power, break their strength, and with your wrath cast down their might. For they have resolved to profane your sanctuary, to defile the tabernacle in which the name of your glory finds its rest, and to break off the horns of your altar with a sword. 9/ Behold their arrogance! Send your wrath down upon their heads and place in my hand—the hand of a widow!—the strength to do what I conceived. 10/ By the deceit of my lips, strike the slave with his ruler and the ruler with his servant! Crush their arrogance by a female hand! 11/ For your strength lies not in numbers, nor is your power found

a Και διερρηξε τον χιτωνα αυτης added by *O* OL Sy.

b OL-QP: *vestivit se cilicium*.

c For ελυσαν: ελυμηναντο *L* (*maculaberant* OL-X); ελυπησαν 311*; *violaverunt* OL Vg; see commentary.

d A difficult and awkwardly personified reading, with variants. Moore takes the subject of απατηθεισαν as Dinah, not the bed; that is, the bed is ashamed for the deceived Dinah. Hanhart's text, however, retained here, assumes that the bed is also deceived and stained by blood. For ηδεσατο: εδεχατο *O* 311 OL Sy. For την απατην αυτων απατηθεισαν: την αγαπην αυτων την απατηθεισαν 583; την αγαπηθεισαν 58, which gives rise to dilectam and delictam in OL; see Bogaert, "Version latine," 198.

e Based on 9:10, the NAB conjectures θεραπουσιν, "princes together with their servants."

f For λογον: δολον *O* OL Sy.

g Singular "house" could refer to the house that the children possess, that is, their homes (so NAB), or to the temple, repeated from before. For οικου κατασχεσεως: οικου κατασκηνωσεως V *a* 126 Eth.

h Rather than "all your nation," that is, Israel, *O* OL Sy omit σου and so read every nation; Moore and *NETS* prefer this reading because Judith already assumes that Israel knows that God protects the nation (8:18, 20); but the hyperbole of prayer could allow for the present reading.

among the strong, but you are the God of
the lowly, a helper of the weak, protector of
the forsaken, guardian of those in despair,
deliverer of those without hope. 12/ Yes,
yes! O God of my father and God of the
inheritance of Israel, ruler of heaven and
earth, creator of the waters, king of your
whole creation, hear my prayer! 13/ Grant
that my deceptive speech[f] wound and maim
those who plotted cruel things against
your covenant, your sacred house, Mount
Zion, and the house of your children's
possession.[g] 14/ Let your entire nation[h] and
every tribe know and understand that you
are the God of all power and might and that
there is no one other than you who shields
the people Israel."

Commentary

9:1–14

At the end of chap. 8, Judith had announced that she would perform a deed (*pragma*) that would be known to generations; the elders have now departed, allowing her freedom to execute it. Chapter 9 transitions to a series of scenes with highly charged symbols and ritual markers that remain unclear. There is a freedom of invention at work here that might be associated with the Freudian interpretation of dreams or the symbolism of myth.[1] Popular narrative can present a rich forest of symbols that often overrides the demands of verisimilitude. Even if "fiction" was an unclear category for the ancient world (see §7 above), we can speak of texts on a spectrum of "free narrative," from more historical (1 Maccabees), to an imaginative retelling of biblical narrative (Genesis Apocryphon), to unconstrained narrative (Judith and the novellas). The freer the narrative, the more that symbols could be introduced without regard to a specified narrative meaning.

Judith prays to God, timing her prayer to coincide with the evening incense in the Jerusalem temple.

The prayer has received a great deal of attention in recent scholarship, but before we turn to its text, we must consider her preparations. Whereas European tradition focused on the "acteme" of the decapitation scene, the ancient text spends far more time on Judith's preparations—admittedly, a build-up to the acteme. She has extended her mourning period longer than that required by Jewish law (8:4), remaining in seclusion, but she will now undress, bathe, and reclothe herself in garments appropriate to her mission. Her prayer is contained within this ritual of undressing and redressing that is continued in chap. 10.

The content of Judith's prayer is treated below; here we consider its role in chap. 9. Biblical prayers were often short, but in postbiblical Jewish literature prayers were expanded and often "scripturalized."[2] Even if "scripture" is a concept only beginning to come into focus in this period, the intertextual play on authoritative texts was a perceptible phenomenon. Although Hannah is the only woman to pray in the Hebrew Bible (1 Sam 1:11), in postbiblical texts there are many others: Sarah (Tob 3:11–15), Susanna, Rebecca (Jub. 25:11–23), Jael and Elumah (Bib. Antiq. 31:5, 7; 42:2), Job's daughters (T. Job 48:3–50:3), and Aseneth

---

1   Weitzman, "Literary Approaches."
2   Judith Newman, *Praying by the Book: The Scripturalization of Prayer in Second Temple Judaism* (EJL 14; Atlanta: Society of Biblical Literature, 1999); Steven Weitzman, *Song and Story in Biblical Narrative: The History of a Literary Convention in Ancient Israel* (Indiana Studies in Biblical Literature; Bloomington: Indiana University Press, 1997); Toni Craven, "'From Where Will my Help Come?' Women and Prayer in the Apocryphal/Deuterocanonical Books," in M. Patrick Graham et al., eds., *Worship and the Hebrew Bible: Essays in Honour of John T. Willis* (JSOTSup 284; Sheffield: Sheffield Academic Press, 1999) 95–109.

(Aseneth 12–13). And while in MT Esther the heroine commands all the Jews of Susa to *fast* (4:16), in the Greek version full prayers for both Esther and Mordecai are included (14:1–9). Esther's prayer in the LXX is more personal and confessional. It registers more fear than Judith's, and Esther is less confident in her own plan. She petitions God to "rescue us by *your* hand" (14:14), as opposed to Judith's "*my* hand" (9:9), and is very aware of her own vulnerability: "Lord, protect me from my fears!" (14:19)—hardly a prayer that Judith would utter, although we do note that it sounds like a Greek novel heroine.

■ 9:1

Judith's name is stated twice here, framing the verse. A pious tone is established for her prayer. She prostrates herself to begin the complex ritual to come; her bow when she sets out on her mission in 10:8 will form an *inclusio*.[3] In between lies her long and involved preparation and dressing for combat. She puts ashes on her head while exposing the sackcloth she was wearing beneath her widow's garments, practices that are traditionally associated with grief and mourning.[4] Rituals of mourning also expressed outrage and protest (see the excursus at 8:4–6, "Asceticism").

Judith's prayer ritual, unlike that of Esther or Aseneth, is explicitly timed to coincide with the evening incense offering in the temple.[5] This emphasizes the correlated world of the temple, and in Judith the role of the high priest is affirmed—he is the only Israelite character apart from Judith who is depicted as strong. It is not clear why the prayer is at the time of the evening incense and not the morning incense, or why it is not coordinated with the *tamid* (daily offering), since the latter was mentioned in 4:14 in the context of the distress of all Israel.[6] The *tamid*, an offering of a lamb twice a day, might be considered the most important of the regular offerings (Exod 29:38–42; Num 28:6; Ezra 3:5; m. Yoma 4:4). Yet the burning of incense was not a minor offering; the rabbis later expressed the ideal of praying at the time of the evening incense.[7]

An important postexilic development is the organization of priests and Levites into orders (1 Chronicles 24–26; cf. Neh 12:45–46). These *mišmārôt* evidently involved a rotation, in which each tribe would make provisions for the temple service, and the delegations of priests and Levites resident in that area would go up to Jerusalem to "stand by" (*ma'ămādôt*) at the temple service. More important for our text, during this period of service, the tribal towns held services accompanied by fasting ritu-

---

3   Falling on one's face before God or a superior is common in the Bible: see Gen 17:3; Num 17:10; Ruth 2:10. Cf. Tamar in severe distress in 2 Sam 13:19, and Judah at Mizpah, 1 Macc 3:47; 4:39. In 10:23 Judith will prostrate herself again before Holofernes. On this section, see also Grintz, *Book of Judith,* 139–40; Gera, *Judith,* 302–3; Schmitz, *Gedeutete Geschichte,* 230–31; Beentjes, "Bethulia Crying," 249.

4   In some biblical cases sackcloth is put on; in others it is exposed by taking off the outer garments. In 2 Kgs 6:30, the king of Israel, in grief and horror, exposes sackcloth. Schmitz considers the possibility that sackcloth *is* Judith's widow's garment, and that she takes off her garment and prays nude (*Gedeutete Geschichte,* 224–25). This is unlikely, but note below on the Soṭah ritual and Christian baptism in the nude, and the development of ascetic practices. In some manuscripts Judith tears her outer garments, as was typical in scenes of distress (e.g., 2 Sam 13:19; Ezra 9:3–5; cf. Dan 9:3; Esth 4:16; T. Jos. 4:3). Schmitz/Engel state, probably

correctly, that the sack was worn beneath her dress and was exposed, partially as an expression visible to God (*Judit,* 273). See further Lambert, "Fasting."

5   See Exod 30:7–8; 40:5; Lev 4:7; 16:12–13; Ezra 9:5; Dan 9:20–22; 1 Kgs 18:36; Luke 1:10; Rev 8:3. Praying three times a day is mentioned in Dan 6:11 and Ps 55:17–18 and was a common practice by the mishnaic period (m. Ber. 4:5).

6   Luke 1:10 and Rev 8:3 also time prayer to coincide with the incense offering. Praying at evening is also mentioned in Jdt 6:21; 11:17; and 12:7–8. Ezra (9:5) and Daniel (9:21) are said to pray at the time of the evening sacrifice; these prayers are both in the confessional prayer section of the two books. Note also 1 Kgs 18:36, prayer at the time of the meal offering. Orienting toward Jerusalem while praying is noted in 1 Kgs 8:38 and Dan 6:11; praying near a window or in an upstairs room occurs in Tob 3:10–11 (cf. 2:9) and Aseneth 10:4.

7   T. Ber. 3:1, b. Ber. 26b; b. Yoma 44a. These traditions likely derive from the period after the destruction of the temple.

als, that is, a local service with fasting to coincide with the tribe's offerings in the temple.[8] This form of local worship in the town squares may have been the principal means of communal worship in the tribal areas away from the temple, before the synagogue services came to play a strong local role in worship. The local town-square services may have even contributed to the development of the synagogue liturgy. The Pharisees' practice of praying and fasting on Monday and Thursday may also be an outgrowth of the *mišmārôt/ maʿămādôt*. The references to these practices are mainly later than our text but likely reflect the practices of the period in question. There may have been a relation, then, between Judith's fanciful practices and the local tribal observances, Pharisaic practices, and the beginnings of the synagogue liturgy.

■ **9:2–14**

The content of Judith's prayer is similar to Esther's in Greek Esther, but whether this suggests a common source is unclear.[9] Judith's prayer also differs from that of the Bethulians, whom she has criticized. According to Moore, the themes of Judith's prayer are "retributive justice, God's omnipotence and omniscience, the true basis of might and power, the central importance of Jerusalem and its Temple, and God's universality."[10] He judged Judith's prayer to be inferior to Esther's, but three factors should be considered. Judith's prayer and speeches sometimes reflect Greek rhetoric, which may seem more studied but less biblical, and therefore less sincere to modern ears.[11] But, second, Moore's judgment may miss the nature of the artifice. Judith is less humble than Esther; her prayer may represent a highly rhetorical style and a stridency of verbs and motifs, reflecting what reads as a lack of earnestness on the author's part. It is not clear, for instance, whether the prayer is an earnest expression of the author's theology or Judith's speech-in-character as a transgressive trickster, presented ironically by the author. And, third, Judith's prayer may

---

8   In Isa 1:13, Sabbaths as a weekly holiday and new moon as a monthly holiday seem to be associated, away from the temple, with gatherings or at least meals (cf. 1 Sam 20:18; 1 Macc 10:34; Jub. 1:14). References later than Judith include m. Sukk. 5:6–7, m. Taʿan. 2:6–7; 4:2, T. Taʿan. 2:1; 4:2; Josephus, *Antiquities* 7.14.7 §§363–67. A reference nearer in time is War Scroll (1QM) 2.2–4; 4QMishmarot; Tertullian, *On Fasting* 16. See Eliezer Diamond, *Holy Men and Hunger Artists: Fasting and Asceticism in Rabbinic Culture* (Oxford: Oxford University Press, 2004) 17, 102–4; S. Lowy, "Motivation of Fasting in Talmudic Literature," *JJS* 9 (1958) 19–38; Sidney Hoenig, "Historical Inquiries: I. *Hebir Ir;* II. City-Square," *JQR* 48 (1957) 123–39; Hoenig, "The Ancient City-Square: The Forerunner of the Synagogue," *ANRW* 2.19.1 (1979) 448–76; Esther Eshel and Hanan Eshel, "4Q471 Fragment 1 and *Maʿamadot* in the War Scroll," in Julio Trebolle Barrera and Luis Vegas Montaner, eds., *The Madrid Qumran Congress: Proceedings of the International Congress on the Dead Sea Scrolls, Madrid 18–21 March, 1991* (2 vols.; STDJ 11; Leiden: Brill, 1992) 2:611–20; Lee I. Levine, *The Ancient Synagogue: The First Thousand Years* (New Haven: Yale University Press, 2000) 19–41.

9   Charl Pretorius Van der Walt assumes that the scene and prayer in Greek Esther are based on Judith, just as Judith responds to the earlier MT Esther ("The Prayers of Esther [LXX] and Judith against their Social Backgrounds: Evidence of a

Possible Common 'Grundschrift'?," *JSem* 17 [2008] 194–206). Gera (*Judith,* 299–300) follows Van der Walt in this, though the relation of the texts is uncertain. Cf. also Jer 32:16–25; Ezra 9; Nehemiah 9; Greek Esther 13–14; 2 Macc 8:14–15; 15:21–24; 3 Macc 3:44–54; 4:30–33; 7:40–42. See also Schmitz, *Gedeutete Geschichte,* 236–37; Johannes Marböck, "Das Gebet der Ester: Zur Bedeutung des Gebetes im griechischen Esterbuch," and Jeremy Corley, "Divine Sovereignty and Power in the High-Priestly Prayer of 3 Macc 2:1–20," both in Renate Egger-Wenzel and Jeremy Corley, eds., *Prayer from Tobit to Qumran: Inaugural Conference of the ISDCL at Salzburg, Austria, 5–9 July 2003* (Deuterocanonical and Cognate Literature Yearbook 2004; Berlin: de Gruyter, 2004) 73–94, 359–86, respectively; Gert J. Steyn, "'Beautiful but Tough': A Comparison of LXX Esther, Judith and Susanna," *JSem* 17 (2008) 156–81.

10   Moore, *Judith,* 195, followed Norman Burrows Johnson, *Prayer in the Apocrypha and Pseudepigrapha: A Study of the Jewish Concept of God* (JBLMS 2; Philadelphia: Society of Biblical Literature and Exegesis, 1948) 67–77.

11   Gera, "Speech in Judith." Greek Esther displays Greek rhetorical flourish in the two royal edicts, Additions B and E, but not in the prayer.

actually be more comparable to *Mordecai*'s prayer in Greek Esther rather than Esther's. If Esther's prayer is gendered female and Mordecai's is gendered male, then Judith's prayer may be more "male."[12]

The prayer has many repeated terms for God—not unexpected in a hymnic prayer—but also many other repeated or coordinated words and motifs. Such repetitions include hand, woman/widow/virgin/daughter, mentally conceive (*bouleuō, dianoeō*), give, know/recognize, power (*kratos, dyna-, ischy-*), lowly/weak, deceit (*apat-*), pollute (*mia-*), number, hear, strike, ancestor, leader/ruler/slave, and lord. The repeated terms and the parallelism and rhetorical flourishes listed below have brought some scholars to a more positive assessment of the literary qualities of the prayer. Schmitz and others perceive intricate rhetorical patterns, and Xeravits "an artfully arranged prayer."[13] It contains the elements of psalms of lament:

address (9:2a)
God's mighty acts in the past (9:2b–4a)
introductory petition (9:4b)
confession of trust (9:5–6)
lament (9:7)
petition (9:8–10)
vow of praise (9:14)

But, as noted, the patterns may also represent an intentional excess, a different sort of artistic achievement: a counteraesthetic, an aesthetic of excess, or even bombast as entertainment. Gera perceives by turns rhetorical sophistication but also overstatement. Is there an irony in Judith's unladylike verbiage? Should allowance be made for the extravagance of popular literature? Indeed, while Claude Levi-Strauss and Northrop Frye had maintained that the rise of the novelistic impulse killed off the elegance of the poetic, Mikhail Bakhtin welcomed the celebration of the multiplicity of voices and styles in the novel and found value in precisely this type of excess (see §7 above).

At first, the prayer appears to work within the standards of biblical style: simple parallel lines with inserted explanatory notices. Yet there is no single rhetorical pattern that continues for more than a few lines. Explanatory notices, often insistent, break up what might have amounted to rhythm. In Greek rhetorical lists, there is often a deliberate growth from simple to increasingly complex clauses, culminating in a longer capstone clause, and this can be found in Jewish and Christian texts. Paul, for example, in 2 Cor 4:8–10 constructs a rhetorically pleasing list that moves from simple to complex, while in 2 Cor 11:22–29 he upends a smooth development as a form of self-satire.[14] And so we draw two conclusions here: there is an unsettling variety of simple lists, shifting in complexity to be sure, but not an artful or elegant growth, and this is matched by a strident use of words. The two effects go together.

The opening of Judith's prayer may seem at odds with her earnest preparation. In a coupling of virtue and rhetorical excess that is typical of the entire book, it affirms a collusion between Judith and the violent Simeon rather than a humble channeling of the will of God. The language of biblical prayer is found not just in words like "hear" (*eisakouson*, 9:4) but also in requests for aid or vindication: "break," "bring down," "send your wrath," "strike down," "crush" (*raxon, kataxon, aposteilon tēn orgēn sou, pataxon, thrauson*). Schmitz/Engel note that wrath is an important theme in the entire book (the *thymo-* and *org-* roots are found in Exodus 15 as well; see below).[15] Judith's violent language poses challenges to modern readers, and perhaps to ancient ones as well; her petition—which admittedly has been prepared for by her mourning and self-affliction—should not be romanticized. Judith's prayer does not petition God to bring down his wrath directly, but to empower her to exercise wrath. The wrath, whether God's or Judith's, also balances that of Nebuchadnezzar, who threatened violence against the Israelites (4:12).

---

12   See also Schorch, "Genderising Piety," 30–42.

13   Xeravits, "Supplication," 161; Corley, "Divine Sovereignty," 365; Larry Perkins, "Lord Is a Warrior," 121–33.

14   See also Gera, *Judith*, 299; Gera, "Speech in Judith"; Xeravits, "Supplication."

15   Schmitz/Engel, *Judit*, 292–93; cf. Jdt 1:12; 2:7; 5:2; 8:14; 9:8, 9; 11:11. Note also 8:14: the Bethulians' actions may bring on the wrath of God.

JUDITH'S PRAYER: STRUCTURE

The prayer exhibits a mixed and complex structure, evoking a number of biblical phrases and motifs:[16]

Part 1	9:2–4	Simeon's revenge for the rape of Dinah	Genesis 34
Part 2	9:5–6	God as lord of past, present, and future	Second Isaiah
Part 3	9:7–11	Song of the Sea	Exodus 15
Part 4	9:12–14	Prayer of the national leader as intermediary	various

Prayer Part 1: 9:2–4, Simeon's Revenge for the Rape of Dinah (Genesis 34)

The first part of the prayer is made up of "compressed and difficult verses" according to Gera.[17] A fairly clear rhetorical pattern, however, is maintained in v. 2: aorist verbs (here underlined), followed by objects that produce an assonance (*mētran/mēron/mētran*), each followed by *eis* + a strong negative term (*miasma/aischynēn/oneidos*). At the end is an insistent summary statement.

O Lord, God of my ancestor Simeon,
　　in whose hand you gave a sword
　　　　for [*eis*] vengeance against those foreigners
　　who exposed the *mētran* (womb)[18] of a virgin
　　　　as [*eis*] a *miasma* (to defile her),
　　who <u>uncovered</u> her *mēron* (thighs)
　　　　as [*eis*] an *aischynēn* (to shame her),
　　and who <u>profaned</u> her *mētran* (womb)
　　　　as [*eis*] a disgrace.
For you said: 'This shall not be done'—yet they did it!

Κύριε ὁ θεὸς τοῦ πατρός μου Συμεών,
　ᾧ <u>ἔδωκας</u> ἐν χειρὶ ῥομφαίαν
　　εἰς ἐκδίκησιν ἀλλογενῶν,
　οἳ <u>ἔλυσαν</u> μήτραν παρθένου
　　εἰς μίασμα
　καὶ <u>ἐγύμνωσαν</u> μηρὸν
　　εἰς αἰσχύνην
　καὶ <u>ἐβεβήλωσαν</u> μήτραν
　　εἰς ὄνειδος.
<u>Εἶπας</u> γὰρ Οὐχ οὕτως ἔσται, καὶ <u>ἐποίησαν</u>.

It is not uncommon in Jewish prayers of this period to take up, in a time of trial, a single biblical episode as an exemplary story.[19] Verse 2 invokes Simeon's revenge on Shechem for the rape of Dinah. Although Simeon is mentioned by name, Dinah is not, and neither is Simeon's coavenger, Levi: "Dina wird unsichtbar gemacht und tritt hinter dem mit Namen genannten Simeon völlig zurück" (Schmitz/Engel, *Judit*, 276–77). Judith even refers to Simeon as "my ancestor [*patros*] Simeon," which has caused confusion.[20] Simeon is not mentioned in her genealogy (though see the Textual Notes), and so this statement should be taken as metaphorical: Simeon is her metaphorical ancestor in redeeming others through deceit and violence. Judith too "will use tricky, deceitful words to lull her enemy and she too will kill her foe when he is weak and off guard."[21]

According to Matthew Thiessen, the memory of Shechem and his rape of Dinah is invoked to illustrate the threat of gentile outsiders: "Genesis 34 depicts graphically the potential danger posed by gentile bodies. When gentiles enter where they should not, the result

---

16　Schmitz/Engel collapse parts 2 and 3 together (*Judit*, 272). They also place v. 4e with part 2. See also Xeravits, "Supplication," 171–74.

17　Gera, *Judith*, 303.

18　Xeravits, "Supplication," 165, and see the Textual Notes on variants. Some modern translations conjecture *mitran* for *mētran* by itacism: a girdle, headdress, or tiara. Moore adds that to open the womb in Hebrew means to overcome barrenness and have a first child (*Judith*, 191), but he rightly keeps the unanimous Greek witness of *mētran*. Still, the conjecture should be considered; *mitran lyein* is used in Hellenistic poetry for the undoing of a virgin's belt to rape her (Apollonius of Rhodes,

Argonautica 1.288; so Gera, *Judith*, 306). In 10:3 and 16:8 Judith also adorns herself with a *mitra*.

19　Cf. Tob 8:4–8; 1 Macc 4:30–33; 7:40–42; cf. also Jdt 16:4–5; see Newman, *Praying by the Book*, 150–54.

20　Joosten, "Original Language," 170 n. 26. Moore argues that Simeon must have been in the original genealogy, since that is assumed in Judith's claim here (*Judith*, 179–80). Yet a metaphorical ancestry is more likely.

21　Gera, *Judith*, 303. To pray for God's wrath is not common, but it can be found in the Bible: Pss 40:15–16; 137:9; Isa 47:1–3; Jeremiah 50–51. In 1 Macc 2:26, Mattathias, the father of the Maccabee brothers, was likened to Pinchas (Phineas) because

is the pollution and disgrace of Israel."[22] Note, however, that Genesis 34 is written *as if* Shechem is *on* ancestral land and Israel is the one entering. Still, Judith is clear: Simeon took revenge on a *foreigner* who raped Dinah. Thiessen continues, "Judith sees in the Assyrian army both a threat to her body and a threat to the Jerusalem temple, the invasion of which will lead to Israel's defilement, profanation, shame, and humiliation." Judith seems to identify the historical threat to Dinah's body with the threat to her body, and the threat to the temple as well. The profanations of all three tend to merge. But Thiessen also hypothesizes that Judith "appears to provoke the very scenario that will force God's hand to rescue her."[23] Judith's act forces God's hand in taking vengeance anew.

In Gen 34:30 and 40:5–7, Jacob condemns the revenge of Simeon and Levi, not as an ethical violation but because it endangers the tribes.[24] Judith, however, affirms the revenge, and this is central to her prayer. Given the constant incorporation of biblical motifs in Judith, it is remarkable that Jacob's condemnation of Simeon is ignored. Further, according to Judith, it is not just that Simeon has acted heroically, but God was behind the revenge and shared the brothers' outrage.[25] Judith was not the only ancient source to valorize this deed. Jubilees 30 and Testament of Levi 2–6 betray no ambivalence about the revenge, and Joseph and Aseneth 23:13 mentions Simeon's violent nature without condemning it.[26] Judith here shows no restraint, certainly no "feminine" decorum in describing Simeon's slaughter of the males, the taking of the women and their daughters as booty, the plundering of the spoils. It is all part of God's righteous vindication, the execution of the just war.[27]

Judith thus invokes the memory of the virgin Dinah who was raped by Shechem without mentioning her name.[28] In the Second Temple period, Dinah became

of the latter's zeal for executing idolators (Num 25:6–15); see Gera, *Judith,* 310. Navarro Puerto detects here anxiety over underlying issues, including rape as a metaphor for the former subjugation of Israel ("Reinterpreting the Past," 130–31); see also Stocker, *Judith,* 8.

22 Thiessen, "Protecting the Holy Race," 167. The parallel treatment of defiling the body and defiling the temple had already been noted by Newman (*Praying by the Book,* 124) and Gera (*Judith,* 321, 406), but Thiessen presses this further. He also notes that, while Judith says that God helped Simeon, Genesis 34 does not mention the brothers asking God for help, and does not mention God. Jacob will later condemn the revenge (34:30), although it is treated as reckless and not an offense against God.

23 Thiessen, "Protecting the Holy Race," 183.

24 Genesis records *Jacob's* criticism, not necessarily God's. Regarding "For you said, 'This shall not be so,' yet they did it," our text also calls to mind the similar wording of Gen 34:7 LXX; so Newman, *Praying by the Book,* 123–38. In Genesis, however, it is not explicitly God's judgment against Shechem, but the brothers'. Was divine law also presumed to lie behind the narration of Genesis? See James Kugel, *Traditions of the Bible: A Guide to the Bible As It Was at the Beginning of the Common Era* (Cambridge, MA: Harvard Uiversity Press, 1999) 411–12. The author of Judith probably perceived a divine voice at work. Cf. also 2 Sam 13:12.

25 Schmitz/Engel, *Judit,* 275–76. God has placed the sword, *rhomphaia,* in Simeon's hand and is therefore the author of the deed. The sword that Judith will use is Holofernes's "Persian" *akinakēs,* and elsewhere in Judith *rhomphaia* is the sword of the enemy (1:12; 2:27; 7:14; 8:19; 11:10; 16:4). See also James Kugel, "The Story of Dinah in the Testament of Levi," *HTR* 85 (1995) 1–34.

26 See also Epic of Theodotus fr. 7. Simeon and Levi, treated equally in Genesis, are differentiated somewhat in the tradition. Simeon is featured in Judith and Theodotus, Levi in Jubilees 30 and T. Levi 5:3; 8:2. Schmitz/Engel note that *ekdikēsis* and *allogenēs* are not found in Genesis 34, but *ekdik-* occurs in regard to Nebuchadnezzar and the peoples of the West in Jdt 1:12; 2:1; 6:5; in 9:2 in regard to Simeon, and also with God as subject, 7:28; 8:27; 16:17 (*Judit,* 275–76).

27 Benedikt Eberhardt explains our text as an intentional remaking of Hasmonean state making ("Reclaiming Tradition: The Book of Judith and Hasmonean Politics," *JSP* 18 [2009] 243–63, here 249–55). In T. Levi the Shechemites are identified as ancestors of the Samaritans, which would resonate in Hasmonean political ideology. Is there an evocation of Simon Maccabee here, just as Judah Maccabee may be suggested by the name Judith? The language of zeal is also similar to that applied to Pinchas (Phinehas) in Numbers 25. It was he who served as a model for Mattathias, the father of the Hasmonean brothers (1 Macc 2:24–27).

28 The word for virgin in Hebrew is *bĕtûlâ,* possibly

a symbol of Israel and the temple violated by gentiles.[29] By repetition, Judith emphasizes the outrage committed against the virgin but does not explicitly express sympathy *for the woman*. Rather, the repeated statements take the point of view of the wronged people, perhaps even the wronged *males*: "your beloved sons . . . were zealously devoted to you and abhorred the pollution of *their* blood" (9:4)—that is, the pollution of the brothers' family line, not the blood of Dinah. Judith, indeed, explicitly identifies with "my ancestor Simeon" and not Dinah (9:12). In the patriarchal extended families and clans of ancient Israel, the *gōʾēl* was the male patriarchal figure on whom fell the duty to avenge an attack on any family member. Judith takes on the role of the *gōʾēl*. Such ancient patterns of the extended family may not have remained intact into the Hellenistic period, but our text can still invoke them as romanticized forms of vindication. Through this prayer, Judith establishes that she is like the *gōʾēl haddām*, the avenger of blood or murder (Num 35:19), even though Dinah was not murdered.

The single enemy Shechem becomes a cipher for all "foreigners" (*allogenōn*). Despite the large number of foreigners in the book, this is the only use of the term.[30] In Genesis, Shechem, son of the Hivite Hamor, was a near-Other, a more dangerous figure than a distant, exotic Other.[31] Shechem, then, is the historic near-Other who will stand as a model of the present nations roundabout (see the excursus at 3:5–10, "The Nations 'Roundabout'"). And since Shechem lay very near the capital of Samaria, the name may represent the contemporary

Samarians. Ben Sira 50:25–26, for instance, says, "Three nations I abhor, Seir [= Idumeans], Philistines, and Shechem." While Shechem is thoroughly negative in our text, we saw in the excursus at 4:1–15 ("Samaria") that Samaria is an ambiguous entity. At any rate, the replaying of the rape of Dinah in graphic images and the violent revenge on Shechem in equally graphic images serve as a prelude to the sexual seduction and violent, symbolic castration of Holofernes.

Although Judith identifies more with Simeon than with Dinah, she still perceives *miasma* ("pollution") and *aischynē* ("shame") in Dinah's situation as a threat to herself as well (13:16).[32] The protection of virgins may be considered a novelistic theme cross-culturally, present not only in Greek novels but also in the first novels in the English language, Samuel Richardson's *Pamela* and *Clarissa*. Does the novel genre arise out of anxiety for the family and a concern for the protection of the family's women? Compare the roughly contemporary Ben Sira and the protection of wives and daughters.[33]

■ **9:3–4** The prayer continues, utilizing rough parallelism:

So you gave over
> their leaders for slaughter,
> and their bed, which was shamed by their deceit,
was in turn deceived and stained with blood,

You struck dead
> the slaves with their princes,
> and the princes upon their thrones.[34]

---

the point of the name of the village Bethulia; see the excursus at 6:10–21, "Bethulia."

29 Eszter Balassa, "The Consequences of Dinah's Rape," in Xeravits, *Pious Seductress*, 188–97; see also Kugel, *Bible as It Was*, 403–35.

30 Gera, *Judith*, 305. The term contrasts with the *genos* Israel at the end of the prayer, 9:14; so Schmitz/Engel, *Judit*, 276. In the LXX *allophyllos* specifically translates Philistine, while *allogenēs* is more general (Heb. *zûr* and *nēkār*); see Loader, *Pseudepigrapha*, 199; Bloch-Smith, "Israelite Ethnicity."

31 Wills, *Not God's People*, 13, 36–37. On the import of Shechem at the beginning of the Hasmonean period as a Samarian enclave and the site of the Mount Gerizim sanctuary, see Berlin, "Between Large Forces," 10–11.

32 The noun *aischynē* and its cognate verb are quite

common in the Bible (Hebrew *bôš*), although in the Pentateuch it only occurs in Gen 2:26, where it is negated: Adam and Eve were not ashamed in Eden. Dinah here is also a *parthenos* ("a virgin"), a detail not stated in Genesis 34, which resonates with the common Israelite trope of Jerusalem as a woman or a virgin, whether prostitute/adulterous woman (Jer 13:22–26; Ezek 16:37–39; Hos 2:4–15) or a raped woman (a reversal of Isa 47:3; Nah 3:5; cf. below); see Newman, *Praying by the Book*, 135; Kugel, *Bible as It Was*, 233–44; Mary Anna Bader, *Tracing the Evidence: Dinah in Post-Hebrew Bible Literature* (New York: Peter Lang, 2008) 115–37.

33 Ibolya Balla, *Ben Sira on Family, Gender, and Sexuality* (Göttingen: De Gruyter, 2011) 153, 230.

34 What appears to be melodramatic overkill in regard to the Shechemites ("you struck down slaves

You gave

    their wives over   to [*eis*] plunder

    and their daughters   to [*eis*] captivity;

    all their spoils[35]   to [*eis*] a division

        among your beloved sons,

           who were zealously devoted to you

           and abhorred the pollution [*miasma*]

               of their blood

           and called upon you for help.

O God, my God, heed now the plea of a widow!

ἔδωκας

    ἄρχοντας αὐτῶν εἰς φόνον

    καὶ τὴν στρωμνὴν αὐτῶν, ἣ ᾐδέσατο τὴν ἀπάτην

    αὐτῶν, ἀπατηθεῖσαν εἰς αἷμα

καὶ ἐπάταξας

    δούλους ἐπὶ δυνάσταις,

    καὶ δυνάστας ἐπὶ θρόνους αὐτῶν.

καὶ ἔδωκας

    γυναῖκας αὐτῶν εἰς προνομὴν

    καὶ θυγατέρας αὐτῶν εἰς αἰχμαλωσίαν

    καὶ πάντα τὰ σκῦλα αὐτῶν εἰς διαίρεσιν υἱῶν

        ἠγαπημένων ὑπὸ σοῦ,

          οἳ καὶ ἐζήλωσαν τὸν ζῆλόν σου

          καὶ ἐβδελύξαντο μίασμα αἵματος αὐτῶν

          καὶ ἐπεκαλέσαντό σε εἰς βοηθόν.

ὁ θεὸς ὁ θεὸς ὁ ἐμος, καὶ εἰσάκουσον ἐμοῦ τῆς χήρας.

A rhetorical balance can be discerned here. In v. 2 God *gave* (*edōkas*) a sword to Simeon, and here God *gives over* (*edōkas*) the wives, daughters, and booty. That God gave a sword to Simeon is not in keeping with Gen 34:25 but is similar to Judith's assertion in vv. 9–10 that now God

is acting through a "female hand" (see the excursus below). In addition, the list of male enemies killed in v. 3 is completed in v. 4, where the women are also included. Victory is complete, mirroring what happened to Dinah. The "cure," indeed, for the rape of Dinah is the raping of all the Shechemite women (see also the commentary on 13:9b–10a).

The scale of revenge is also asymmetrical. The background of the Hasmonean Revolt may be in mind; that is, the rape of Dinah is now a cipher for Seleucid imperialism. In addition, we note the exaggerated revenge in Esther, although there the revenge was not asymmetrical *in numbers,* since Haman and his partisans wanted to destroy the Jews, but it was asymmetrical in that an *actual* revenge was carried out for an assault that was *intended* but never carried out.

A number of terms stand out strongly in these verses, as they are prominent elsewhere in the novella. The deceit of the Shechemites is referenced, but *apataō* ("deceive") is often part of Judith's positive strategy (Jdt 9:10, 13; 10:4; 12:16; 13:16; 16:8; and cf. Sus OG 56; 4 Macc 18:8).[36] "Strike" (*patassō*) is also a recurring leitmotif (2:27; 5:12; 6:3; 9:3, 10; 16:6). Bed and blood will be prominent later in Judith's plan and are highlighted here. Xeravits suggests that the odd personification of the bed being ashamed of the treachery occurring upon it is an example of *Spiegelstrafe,* punishment mirroring the crime, as in the hanging of Haman's sons on the gallows he constructed for Mordecai (Esth 7:9–10).[37] "Hear me, a widow" will also resonate just below in 9:9–10.

The themes of *miasma* and *aischynē* from v. 2 continue in vv. 3–4. The outrage committed against Dinah is

---

35   "Spoils" here recalls the booty of Holofernes (4:12; 7:26; cf. 16:4), but also the Shechemite women, both wives and virgins, who became booty for Simeon and the Israelites. The moral view assumed here, and indeed throughout the ancient Near East, is that the victor will take the spoils in goods, women, and slaves. Cf. Num 31:7–11; Deut 20:10–15; and Gera, *Judith,* 309, who draws our attention to *Iliad* 9.590–594, 22.58–71.

36   There are many positive tricksters in the Bible—

with their princes and princes on their thrones") more likely reflects the merging of the revenge on Shechem with the Exodus, the latter referenced at vss. 7–10.

Jacob, Ehud, Rebekah, even David at times—but Simeon, who is not ordinarily a "trickster," also uses deceit in his revenge on Shechem. Other terms in v. 10 resonate with biblical passages. "Strike" (*patassō*), a leitmotif throughout, is first associated with the Assyrian assault (2:27; 6:3). It calls to mind biblical *nkh* regarding the plagues in Egypt (Exod 3:20) and also God's striking of the Egyptians (Jdt 5:12); likewise *thrauō* ("shatter [their pride]") is found in the Song of the Sea (Exod 15:6); see also Jdt 7:9; 13:14.

37   Xeravits, "Supplication," 167. See also Gera, *Judith,* 308–9.

interpreted in language of pollution. (Recall from above that in Greek Esther her prayer confesses the *sins* of Jews in general, but her own sexual pollution in particular.) The noun *miasma* appears three times in this section and once in 13:6, while the verb *miainō* appears just below in 9:8: what Shechem did to Dinah, the Assyrians threaten to do to the temple. As a female *gô'ēl,* Judith symbolically defends both Dinah and the temple—both can be raped. While the verb *miainō* is common in the LXX, generally translating forms of *ṭāmē'*—thus the ritual impurity of rape more than the violence perpetrated on a woman—the nouns *miasma* and *miasmos,* translating Hebrew *beṣa', piggûl,* or *šiqqûṣ,* are rare. They occur only six times, not including this passage.[38] In Judith the noun and verb are both used, and with a similar meaning: outrage and moral and ritual impurity run together.

Miasma is such an important concept in Greece that we should consider whether Greek influences are perceptible here in the use of this rare noun. A general difference between the two traditions can be discerned: *miasma* in Greek culture is a pollution, often resulting from a moral sin, that requires sacrifice for purification. The Israelite system distinguishes ritual impurity and moral impurity, and *ṭāmē'* applies to the former.[39] Gera notes that *ṭāmē'* "is not normally used of the rape of virgins in the Bible, and is generally reserved for illicit sexual relations with married women" (as in Lev 18:20, Num 5:13–14, Deut 24:4)—that is, not outrage but impure relations.[40] Still, *ṭāmē'* occurs three times in the Bible in regard to Dinah (Gen 34:5, 13, 27), and *miasma* is found in T. Levi 7:3 and Aseneth 23:13. So, although rape of virgins is not *typically* perceived as a pollution, it can be, and especially in Genesis 34. The author of Judith perceives the rape of Dinah as an outrage but also as a pollution of the family ("the pollution of their blood," 9:4). Whether or not one ascribes this to a Greek influence in the LXX, a *similarity* to Greek cultural views seems evident.

Prayer Part 2: 9:5–6, God as Lord of History (related to Second Isaiah)

A literal translation of this section reveals a rhetorical pattern:

Division 1:

> For you <u>created</u>
> > the things prior to those things,
> > and those things,
> > and the things that followed;
> > and the present things
> > and those that are to come
> you have <u>designed</u>.

Division 2:

> And have happened   the things you had in
> >   mind.
> And presented themselves   the things you decided on,
> > and they said, "Here we are!"

Summary:

> For all your ways are prepared,
> And your judgment is with foreknowledge.

Division 1:

> Σὺ γὰρ ἐποίησας
> > τὰ πρότερα ἐκείνων
> > καὶ ἐκεῖνα
> > καὶ τὰ μετέπειτα
> > καὶ τὰ νῦν
> > καὶ τὰ ἐπερχόμενα
> διενοήθης,

---

38   The Hebrew words that *miasma* translates seem mixed between moral and ritual violations—*beṣa'* is unjust plunder; *piggûl* is unclean sacrificial meat; and *šiqqûṣ* is a detestable thing; but the verb *miainō* almost always translates forms of *ṭāmē'*. In Genesis, Dinah has also been "defiled" (Gen 34:5, 13, 27; forms of Hebrew *ṭāmē',* Greek *miainō*), but here this is understood as the pollution of the brothers and the family, which they detest, *ebdēluxanto;* see

Newman, *Praying by the Book,* 129; Gera, *Judith,* 310. In Greek Esther the heroine uses the same verb concerning her detestation of the marriage bed with the uncircumcised Ahasuerus, a "menstrual rag" (a motif that is not stated in MT Esther).

39   Jonathan Klawans, *Impurity and Sin in Ancient Judaism* (Oxford: Oxford University Press, 2004); see further the commentary on 12:5b–9.

40   Gera, *Judith,* 307.

Division 2:

καὶ ἐγενήθησαν ἃ ἐνενοήθης,
καὶ παρέστησαν ἃ ἐβουλεύσω
καὶ εἶπαν Ἰδοὺ πάρεσμεν.

Summary:

πᾶσαι γὰρ αἱ ὁδοί σου ἕτοιμοι,
καὶ ἡ κρίσις σου ἐν προγνώσει.

While the other parts of Judith's prayer are more clearly based on particular biblical passages, this section is a reflection on God's command of creation and history—as God commands the cosmos, so Judith will control events as well. This stanza begins with God's cosmic, eternal deeds (*poieō*), contrasted with the previous worldly and destructive deeds (*poieō*, 9:2) of Israel's enemies. It is composed of two sections, with a summary of the previous verses.[41]

The divisions have different structures. The first throws clauses together suggestively but haphazardly, introducing the notion of past, present, and future. Past, present, and future are never treated together in ancient Israelite literature, although partial parallels are found in Isa 40:3; 41:22–23; 42:9; 43:9; 44:7; and 46:9–10. Is our verse a Greek philosophical topic rudely executed?[42] Judith's abstraction of time to past, present, and future may be said to be halfway between Second Isaiah and Greek philosophy (see the excursus at 8:35, "The Book of Judith and Greek Philosophy").

"Created" (*epoiēsas*) at the beginning and "designed" (*enenoēthēs*) at the end create a chiasm. The second division utilizes synonymous parallelism, interrupted by the dramatic declaration of the events themselves. In wisdom texts, we sometimes find a similar notion concerning God's control of natural phenomena and historical events (Wisdom 10–19). That they say, "Here we are!" is similar to the lightning in Job 38:35 and the stars in Bar 3:34. (Compare also Psalm 148 and Song of the Three Young Men; as background, see Exod 20:11; Neh 9:6; Pr Man 1–2.) If the things created here are understood to be cosmic phenomena, this passage may reflect a response to Babylonian and Phoenician astronomy and astrology, which attributed divinization to the stars. Jewish apologists raised up Near Eastern astrology in order to counter it, emphasizing that the stars were God's creation and not divine in themselves.

Here and in 9:9, Judith uses the verb *dianoeō* ("to have in mind"), a verb found in late texts in the LXX (although the noun *dianoia* for *lēbāb*, "mind," "will," or "heart," is found early). The Hebrew Bible tends to externalize discourse on human beings into words and deeds, less often internalizing thoughts and conceptions as later Greek philosophy did.[43] Along with this more Greek use of *dianoeō*, we also find *prognōsis*, "foreknowledge." (In 11:19, Judith herself, as part of her ruse, boasts to Holofernes of her *prognōsis*!) *Prognōsis* also occurs in 11:19, but it is found elsewhere in the LXX only in Wis 6:13; 8:8, concerning the foreknowledge of Wisdom (compare Wis 18:6). The lack of a Hebrew term for foreknowledge is invoked by Engel as evidence for a Greek original,[44] but Grintz proposed *mēʿôlām*.[45] That God's ways are prepared in advance and that God has *prognosis* has also been likened to the moderate predestination of the Pharisees (Josephus, *Jewish War* 2.8.14 §163). Despite the reflections of the author, and parallels with Greek thought on the nature of time, this passage retains a doctrine of the transcendence of God throughout, never the idea of immanence. Ben Sira 39:17–27 is similar in this regard.

---

41 Cf. Sus 35a OG/42–43 Th, "God, who knows all things before they come into being. . . ." Ezra 9 and Nehemiah 9 give thanks for the *kosmokratōr*, and the creator is not unusual in prayers (2 Kgs 19:15; Jer 32:17; Neh 9:6; 2 Chr 2:11; Greek Esth 13:10; 2 Macc 1:24; 3 Macc 2:3; Pr Man 2–3). On this section, see Xeravits, "Supplication," 168; he begins it with the last clause of v. 4, as do Schmitz/Engel, *Judit*, 272.

42 See Cleanthes, *Hymn to Zeus* esp. 11–21. On the Isaiah parallels, see Grintz, *Book of Judith*, 142.

43 Exceptions include God's thoughts and intentions in Isa 14:24; 25:1; Jer 23:20; 49:20.

44 Engel, "Der HERR," 158.

45 Grintz, *Book of Judith*, 142; see also Moore, *Judith*, 192.

Prayer Part 3: 9:7–11 and Song of the Sea

These verses constitute the center of the prayer. The created cosmos in v. 6 had said "*Idou,* here we are," and God is now called upon to look at the Assyrians, "*Idou gar.*" The enemy is then described with aorist verbs in five parallel lines, followed by a confession:

> The Assyrians <u>grew</u> into a huge force,
>> <u>prided</u> themselves in their horses and riders,
>> <u>boasted</u> in the might of their infantry,
>> <u>trusted</u> in their shield and spear, in bow and sling,
>> and <u>did not know</u> that you are the Lord who crushes wars.
>
> The Lord is your name!

> Ἀσσύριοι ἐπληθύνθησαν ἐν δυνάμει αὐτῶν,
>> ὑψώθησαν ἐφ' ἵππῳ καὶ ἀναβάτῃ,
>> ἐγαυρίασαν ἐν βραχίονι πεζῶν,
>> ἤλπισαν ἐν ἀσπίδι καὶ ἐν γαίσῳ καὶ τόξῳ καὶ σφενδόνῃ
>> καὶ οὐκ ἔγνωσαν ὅτι σὺ εἶ κύριος συντρίβων πολέμους.
>
> Κύριος ὄνομά σοι.

The first four verbs recount the Assyrians' false trust in their military strength, while the fifth verbal line, a negative, presents the truth of the matter, their ignorance of God's coming role. By priding themselves in their horses and riders—likening themselves to the Egyptians of the Song of the Sea (further referenced in v. 11)—the Assyrians unconsciously prophesy their own demise.[46] God's providence may be seen here as well.

Excursus: Quoting the Song of the Sea

Simeon has been Judith's explicit inspiration, but she concludes this section of her prayer by quoting from the LXX of Moses's victory song, the Song of the Sea (Exod 15:3): "You are the Lord who crushes wars. The Lord is your name!" Aside from the quotation of a single line from Exodus 15, there are many other resonances as well. The five titles of God in Jdt 9:11 are paralleled in Exod 15, in addition to *ta hagia* ("the sanctuary") and *klēronomia* ("inheritance"). Schmitz/Engel append a long list of words from

Song of the Sea that are featured here in Judith: *hypsoō* ("to lift up"), *hydōr* ("water"), *skyla* ("spoils"), *akouō* ("to hear"), *hetoimos* ("ready"), *brachiōn* ("arm"), *dynamis* ("power"), *plēthos* ("multitude"), *harmata* ("chariots").[47] There are other terms as well that appear elsewhere in Judith. The whole suggests that the author in this chapter, if not in the whole, plays on the Song of the Sea.

Exodus was considered God's central act in saving his people (Josh 24:5–7; Neh 9:9–11) and remained a popular theme in Judaism at the time of the composition of Judith (Greek Esth 13:16; 1 Macc 4:9; 3 Macc 2:6; 6:4). The connection of Jdt 9:7–8 and Exod 15:3 LXX is identified by Schmitz/Engel as a core confession of the book. Van Henten convincingly argues that our text presents Judith as a new Moses, a theme even more visible in the Song of Judith, where she will also incorporate this verse in her own victory song in 16:2.

The LXX of Exod 15:3 differs from the MT, and the quotation in Judith follows the LXX:

MT:
The Lᴏʀᴅ is a man of war; the Lord is his name.
יהוה איש מלחמה יהוה שמו

LXX:
The Lord shatters wars; the Lord is his name.
Κύριος συντρίβων πολέμους, κύριος ὄνομα αὐτῷ.

Judith:
"You are the Lord who crushes wars. The Lord is your name!
σὺ εἶ κύριος συντρίβων πολέμους. κύριος ὄνομά σοι.

In the MT version, the affirmation for Israel resides in the protection that was brought about by God's anger (Exod 15:7). Elsewhere in the Bible, God crushes wars by crushing the enemy, even if the metaphor is at one remove: after defeating all enemies, God can crush the weapons of war (Isa 2:4; Hos 2:18; Pss 46:9; 76:3).

Much has been made of the difference between the MT and LXX of Exod 15:3. In the MT God is presented as a warrior, while in the LXX God brings peace by crushing war. The LXX translator may have avoided the affirmation of God as warrior rather than a military figure who through might can contain wars. The Greeks had a tradition of the wrath of the gods, but by the Hellenistic period

---

46   Cf. Xeravits, "Supplication," 171, for whom the five lines are a tricolon and a bicolon. Note also in 9:7–8 the repeated *en* and *eph'* in parallel.

47   Schmitz/Engel, *Judit,* 298–300.

this was spurned among the philosophers as divine *akrasia* (see the excursus at 8:35, "The Book of Judith and Greek Philosophy"). It is possible that the LXX tradent simply wanted to avoid the anthropomorphism of the MT statement. In the context of Judith, however, the "Lord who crushes wars" has been taken by some scholars as a critique of war: Judith seeks revenge against *warriors*—surely a reading that ignores Judith's endorsement of Simeon's revenge (despite Jacob's condemnation), or the gleeful slaughter at the end of our text—a military action. Philip S. Nolte and Pierre J. Jordaan do not perceive a significant difference from the MT affirmation. The intertextual background (despite the change in LXX Exodus) is still to a tradition of God waging war triumphantly on Israel's behalf: "We believe that God is pictured in Judith as a God of war."[48]

As noted, it is not just Exod 15:3 that is relevant for Judith; Exodus 15 as a whole is a thematic spur of the narrative.[49] Other parallels between Exodus 15 LXX and both Judith 9 and 16 include:

> The enemy's intentions (Exod 15:9; Jdt 9:7–8; 16:4)
> The enemy's cavalry (Exod 15:1, 4; Jdt 9:7; 16:3)
> The hand of the savior (Exod 15:6, 12; Jdt 9:9–10; 16:5)

Judith 9 (but not Judith 16) also exhibits the following parallels with Exodus 15 LXX:

> The temple and holy places (Exod 15:13, 17; Jdt 9:8, 13)
> The land inherited by Israel (Exod 15:17; Jdt 9:12)

God as helper and defender (Exod 15:2 LXX; Jdt 9:11)
God sending forth his anger (Exod 15:7; Jdt 9:9).

■ **9:8–10** Seven imperative petitions are found in these verses, here in italics, with an explanatory aside inserted at one point:

> *Break* their strength with your might,
> And *bring down* their power with your anger!
>> for they intend to profane your sanctuary,
>> and to defile the tabernacle
>>> where your glorious name[50] resides,
>> and to break off the horns of your altar with the sword.[51]
> *Look* at their arrogance,[52]
> *Send* your wrath upon their heads,
> *Place* in my hand—the hand of a widow!—
>> the strength to do what I have conceived.
> *Strike* the slave—by the deceit of my lips—
>> with the prince and the prince with his servant!
> *Crush* their arrogance with a female hand!

> σὺ ῥάξον αὐτῶν τὴν ἰσχὺν ἐν δυνάμει σου
> καὶ κάταξον τὸ κράτος αὐτῶν ἐν τῷ θυμῷ σου,
>> ἐβουλεύσαντο γὰρ βεβηλῶσαι τὰ ἅγιά σου,
>> μιᾶναι τὸ σκήνωμα
>>> τῆς καταπαύσεως τοῦ ὀνόματος τῆς δόξης σου,
>> καταβαλεῖν σιδήρῳ κέρας θυσιαστηρίου σου.

---

48   Nolte and Jordaan, "Ideology and Intertextuality," 7. See also Otzen, *Tobit and Judith,* 98–99; Schmitz distinguishes Judith's act from a military strategy ("War, Violence and Tyrannicide," 103–19). As we also note just below, Judith's prayer has in general retained the revenge motif of the Song of the Sea: "Send your wrath" (v. 9) alludes to Exod 15:7 "you sent out your wrath." See also Otzen, *Tobit and Judith,* 99; Joosten, "Original Language," 165–66; L. Perkins, "Lord Is a Warrior," 135; Lang, "Lord Who Crushes," 179–87; Gera, *Judith,* 315.

49   Schmitz/Engel, *Judit,* 282–85, although there are some key differences. See also Gera, *Judith,* 313; Moore, *Judith,* 192–93; Schmitz, "Wer ist Dir gleich unten den Göttern? (Ex 15,11 LXX): Das Gottesbild in Ex 15 (LXX) und seine Rezeption im Buch Judit," International Congress of the International Organization for Septuagint and Cognate Studies, Munich, August 1, 2013.

50   Literally, tent of the repose of the name of your

glory. Do four genitives together suggest the overstatement of popular literature? From Exod 3:13–15 on, God's name is a metonym for God, but it also becomes an actual extension of God. Cf. Ps 25(26):8; 73(74):7; Neh 9:5. The temple is thus the home for God's holiness and *kābôd* ("glory"), but also for his name (Deut 12:5; Jer 7:12; 3 Macc 2:9). Lacking in the biblical references is repose, *katapausis.*

51   The threat here that the horns will be cut off *with iron* is also significant, since the altar is not to be touched by iron (Deut 27:5).

52   *Hyperēphania* ("arrogance") was used in contemporaneous texts for Antiochus IV Epiphanes (1 Macc 1:21–24; 2 Macc 5:21; 9:4–11)—especially regarding acts similar to those condemned here—and also cf. Nicanor in 1 Macc 7:34–37; Sennacherib in Sir 48:18; and Pharaoh in Neh 9:10.

βλέψον εἰς ὑπερηφανίαν αὐτῶν,
ἀπόστειλον τὴν ὀργήν σου εἰς κεφαλὰς αὐτῶν,
δὸς ἐν χειρί μου τῆς χήρας
ὃ διενοήθην κράτος.
πάταξον δοῦλον ἐκ χειλέων ἀπάτης μου
ἐπ᾽ ἄρχοντι καὶ ἄρχοντα ἐπὶ θεράποντι αὐτοῦ,
θραῦσον αὐτῶν τὸ ἀνάστημα ἐν χειρὶ θηλείας.

These verses constitute the central petition of her prayer, which is for God to intervene *by means of her deed* to destroy the enemy, and it is clear that Judith has already conceived her plan. As noted above in 9:2, the Assyrians intend to do to the temple what Shechem did to Dinah: pollute (*bebēlōsai*) and defile it (*mianai*; cf. also 4:3, 12; 8:21; 9:8).[53] The decrees of Antiochus IV (1 Macc 1:44–47; 2:12; 4:38; 2 Macc 5:16) also contained these terms. In the author's period, the pollution of the temple and its reconsecration defined the age. Emphasized in 9:8 are God's *ischys, dynamis,* and *kratos,* "strength," "power," and "might." These roots, very common in Judith (*isch-* 14x, *dyna-* 37x, and *krat-* 20x), are also found in Exodus 15. In Jdt 5:3, 23, they are also combined in the mouths of the enemy, an ironic foreshadowing of this prayer, and there is an afterthought in 13:11, when Judith turns to celebration.[54]

As Gera notes, Judith's concern is here directly with the temple, although in 9:11, 13, she will include the threat to the people.[55] The temple orientation of Judith is very strong, evident in her regard for the high

priest, the offerings of the temple, and the altar. The defilement of the temple building here suggests not only a sexual penetration but also emasculation by the breaking of the phallic horns of the altar. Below Judith reverses this image by penetrating the tent of Holofernes and emasculating him.

Schmitz/Engel's argument that vv. 9c–10 constitute the theological center of the book is corroborated by the structure.[56] This subunit begins with Judith's plea for God to act through the "hand of me, a widow" (recalling the sword placed in Simeon's hand in 9:2 and her plea as a widow in 9:4). It ends with a plea to "crush their arrogance by a female hand." Seeing that Judith's agency is the theme of the book, her hand at the beginning and end of these verses is significant.

Excursus: Judith's Hand and Agency[57]

Four motifs, concentrated in two verses here, resonate throughout Judith: hand, deceit, reversal, widow. Patrick Skehan focused on the use of hand.[58] In the exodus story, God's mighty hand and outstretched arm are associated with Moses's hand and arm. In Judith, hand occurs often as a very pointed leitmotif (8:33; 9:2, 9, 10; 12:4; 13:4, 14, 15; 14:6; 15:10, 12; 16:3, 6), also contrasted with Nebuchadnezzar's hand in 2:12. Judith's many references to hand thus call to mind God and Moses, while at the same time they rhetorically overpower Nebuchadnezzar's hand. Moreover, Judith refers to a *female* hand (*thēleias*) in v. 10, as in 16:5, rather than the hand of a *woman* (*gynaikos*).[59] *Thēleia,* usually translat-

---

53 The combination of the *bebēl-* root and the *mia-* root (for Heb. *ḥālāl* and *ṭāmē᾽*) is also used in Lev 20:3 and Ezek 23:38 in regard to the defiling of religious sites. *Bebēloō* is used with *ta hagia* in Zeph 3:4; Mal 2:11; and Ezek 24:21, and *miainō* with *skēn-* in Lev 15:31; Num 19:13; see Newman, *Praying by the Book,* 135; Otzen, *Tobit and Judith,* 133–34.

54 Cf. 2 Sam 22:3; Pss 18:3; 144:2.

55 Gera, *Judith,* 316.

56 Schmitz/Engel, *Judit,* 106–8, 296–97; see also Xeravits, "Supplication," 170.

57 See also the commentary on 13:3–5.

58 Skehan, "Hand of Judith." For Moses and hand, see Deut 5:15; Exod 3:19, 20; 4:2; 6:1; 10:21–22; 13:9; 14:21–27, 31. Note also that God's providential hand will lead to a happy ending (Greek Esth 10:9–12; cf. Ben Sira 33:1–13a; 36:16b–22). There is also the shameful hand of a woman in Judges 4–5; 9:53–54; 2 Sam 11:21. In Judg 16:28, 30, Samson

prays for strength for his hand and his plan; this also relates to revenge and is less than noble. On 1 Macc 3:6 and other biblical passages, see Gera, "Judah and Judith," 37. The importance of the status of widow has been addressed above regarding chap. 8.

59 See also Jdt 13:15, and cf. Judg 4:9 regarding Jael. Note that the human is created *male* and *female* (Gen 1:27), not *man* and *woman* (cf. Gen 5:2). Cf. the use of "male" and "female" in Gal 3:28; and see Hans Dieter Betz, *Galatians: A Commentary on Paul's Letter to the Churches in Galatia* (Hermeneia; Philadelphia: Fortress Press, 1979) 193. Bernadette Brooten notes that both Paul in Rom 1:28–29 and *Sentences of Phocylides* 175–227 use male/female (*Love between Women: Early Christian Responses to Female Homoeroticism* [Chicago: University of Chicago Press, 1998] 64).

ing Hebrew *nĕqēbâ,* applies to the female gender across species, and not woman per se. As a result, it is seen by some[60] as being a rhetorically weaker image, female not woman. Claudia Rakel counters, however, that this terminology emphasizes gender, even gender abstracted.[61] Just as Judith's name may emphasize "Jewish woman," so her hand is emphatically a "female hand."

By focusing on Judith's hand, we also bring to the surface the question of her agency, and whether she is dependent on God or independent. Lest one suggest that acting on one's own initiative would be an unthinkable suggestion in a Jewish book of this period, we should recall that 1 Maccabees, unlike 2 Maccabees, consistently downplays the role of God and the role of pietists who rely on God's intervention. Judith indeed invokes her humble status as servant of God's mission—"Give to me, a widow, a strong hand"—but she continues, "*to do what I have conceived.*" Is this the same plan that God conceived in 9:5? Whose plan is it? Judith's own initiative is emphasized in 9:9; 15:10, and her role as God's instrument in 8:33; 12:4; 13:14–15; 16:5. This is in contrast to the Song of the Sea.[62]

Schmitz/Engel rightly emphasize the double causation:

Nach Jdt 9, 9 und 13, 4 ist es unmissverständlich, dass es Judit ist, die die Tat begeht und zu verantworten hat, während die anderen Stellen die Tat Judits als Tat Gottes *deuten.* Judit ist es, die Holofernes tötet, in der theologishen Reflexion der Tat aber ist es Gott, der durch Judits Hand handelt.[63]

Gera also comments:

Our text regularly moves between these two poles of human initiative and divine assistance, underlining at times the part played by Judith, the courageous heroine, and stressing at other times God's role as savior.[64]

The same theme of double causation can be seen in other novelistic protagonists such as Esther, Susanna, and Joseph, where it may read as a premise of "wisdom theology": God's control is perceptible in the actions of wise protagonists. Judith's prayers make this explicit, which is unusual. In our novella, then,

both modes, independent agency and dependence on God, seem to be expressed. There is yet another possibility, though it requires a more complex interpretation: Judith's own strong plan is to *choose* to live into *God's* strong plan of vindicating the weak over the strong (cf. v. 11).

Yet the possibility of double causation is raised often and in different ways in biblical narrative. Abraham, for example, is generally presented as surprisingly passive, even vulnerable; faithful, to be sure, but only moved to action when directed by God to fulfill his role as patriarch. Yet in Genesis 14 we encounter a different tradition: "Abram the Hebrew" (14:13), an active, independent warrior. There is also a tension between God as agent and Moses as agent in the exodus narrative,[65] and two originally separate traditions about Gideon have now been joined in Judges: a brash, self-made agent, and an instrument of God's miraculous interventions (Judg 7:24–8:28 and 6:1–7:23, respectively). David is not as verbally brash as Judith, although that may simply reflect the difference between early oral tradition and the development of the novelistic genre. It is also in the nature of wisdom narratives in the Bible—Joseph, Esther, and Susanna—that God takes a hidden role, while the wise protagonist who senses God's hidden reality succeeds by adhering to a wisdom lifestyle. The case of Judith, however, is quantitatively but not qualitatively different from Joseph, Esther, and Susanna: she is never buffeted.

Greek historians also at times play on the distinction between God's actions and human agents. In some narratives, the gods intervene to save the sites that have been dedicated to them, while in other narratives human agents engage in clever stratagems to effect the same result. But the Greeks evidently distinguished between two kinds of circumstances: "our" gods miraculously appear to repel those who would violate their temples, but the temples of "their" gods are saved by trickster-priests. From the Greek point of view, Judith would fall into the latter category. She does something for *her* people that in Greece was ascribed only to *barbarians.* The temple is saved, but not by an epiphany of God as in 2 Maccabees 3–4; it is saved by a sort of "trickster-priest." But Rakel sees the Hellenistic influences as the

---

60   E.g., Moore, *Judith,* 193, 232.
61   Rakel, *Judit–Über Schönheit,* 120–24. On Aristotle, see Brooten, *Love between Women,* 15.
62   Exod 15:6, 12, 17, 19; cf. Jdt 9:11; 13:4.
63   Schmitz/Engel, *Judit,* 297.
64   Gera, *Judith,* 318.

65   Howard Jacobson, *The Exagoge of Ezekiel* (Cambridge: Cambridge University Press, 1983) 142–44. See also Judg 3:9, 15; 4:14–15; 1 Sam 19:5; 2 Sam 23:10, 12; and, regarding Judah Maccabee, 1 Macc 2:66; 3:3–9; 9:21; cf. 4:11; 16:3.

source of a double causation.[66] As a result of Greek transcendentalizing of divinity, Judith may be both an independent agent *and* God's agent on earth. Yet here Rakel may not be giving full recognition to the biblical treatments of double causation.

Finally, as an intriguing point of comparison, Karen King traces the question of agency and double causation to the case of female Christian martyrs. A distinction can be made between the modern notion of agency—an individual acting for him or herself—and a more common ancient notion of an individual acting for his or her group. The female martyrs were depicted as acting alone, but explicitly to fulfill their duty to their group:

> The Christian scripting of martyrdom gave Christians the roles of God's representatives: they are the tools through whom he brings about his will. This kind of instrumental agency gave God a predominant role in the drama. . . . [A]gency [is] not something that belongs to individuals, but to situations.[67]

Yet King's period is later, and her task is different from the present one. She searches for an explanation of how passively dying can constitute agency for social change, while our task is determining how a woman can be piously devoted to God and also a strong warrior who actively cuts her own path.

Scholars have thus presented varying interpretations of Judith's agency. For Pamela Milne, God is the chief protagonist, not Judith. The emphasis on a "female hand" is, as noted above, an ironic element only, which serves to shame the dead villain, as it does in numerous biblical narratives.[68] And while Judith is often compared to David or Moses, Gera presses a reading of Judith's "perfection" that ironically works against her: Judith is, on the one hand, without human flaw, and, on the other, she is a self-appointed agent of God: "While there is no explicit indication in our text that God has chosen, guided, or aided her in any way, Judith presents herself as God's emissary."[69] The lack of a tragic flaw—and most great heroes have tragic flaws—causes her own agency to disappear into her service of God, something not true for Moses or David. Despite the

apparent independence of Judith's actions, then, Gera concludes that she "is little more than an instrument, a tool used by God to save his people." However, the placement of this woman warrior in the context of Israelite religion may press us to a false view of the earnest servant of Yahweh. Judith does indeed say all the right things in regard to God's sovereignty. But she is also a woman warrior in the mold of Fa Mulan, Semiramus, and others: she makes her own luck, even her own grace (see §5 above). All of that, however, may serve only to reinscribe women's subservient roles in Judean society. As in the case of the female protagonist of the Greek novels, there is only a liminal escape before the heroine is returned to the patriarchal household.

■ **9:10** Judith here invokes the biblical theme of the reversal of the humble and mighty, as also in 16:11–12. Holofernes relies on his army, in contrast to Israel and its reliance on God (see Achior's speech in chap. 5). Evoking Simeon's wrath from 9:3, Judith utilizes a stylized chiasm (Gera, *Judith*, 309):

A	B
Strike the slave . . . /	with [*epi*] the prince

B´	A´
and the prince /	with [*epi*] his servant

The chiasm of slave/prince//prince/servant, as well as the merism of naming the orders, communicates the completion of social transformation: the top-to-bottom includes everyone.[70] It echoes God's judgment in passages such as Isa 24:2. Women sometimes announce reversal (Song of Hannah in 1 Sam 2:1–10, Magnificat in Luke 1:46–55), but it is unusual, though not unknown, for a woman to act as avenger (Judges 4–5). Still, in the Bible and in Greek tradition, the active or avenging woman is often foreign, and it is for this reason that she can act in such a singular way (Jael, Tamar in Genesis 38; see §5 above). Indeed, this is not simply a tale of a heroine rising to defend her people; it also casts

---

66 Rakel, *Judit–Über Schönheit*, 120–24; Rakel, "I Will Sing," 42–44.

67 Karen King, "Willing to Die for God: Individuation and Instrumental Agency in Ancient Christian Martyr Literature," in Jörg Rüpke, ed., *The Individual in the Religions of the Ancient Mediterranean* (Oxford: Oxford University Press, 2013) 342–84, here 379.

68 Milne, "What Shall We Do?," 48–55. Cf. Judg 9:53; 2 Sam 11:21; see also van Henten, "Female Moses."

69 Gera, *Judith*, 7, 99.

70 Moore, *Judith*, 193.

shame on Holofernes. Just as Abimelech is shamed by being slain by a woman (Judg 9:53; 2 Sam 11:21), so also Holofernes. The motif of sexual reversal becomes very graphic, even pornographic in some later art (see §8 above).

Here and in 9:13 Judith prays for the power of deceit, but in the service of a righteous cause.[71] She freely states that her weapon of choice will be "the deceit of my lips." She will not simply find herself in a difficult situation and *resort* to lying; it will be the very *basis* of her plan from the beginning. She asks for God's help in advance, and *prays* to God for heroic competence in lying. A lying tongue occupied a central place in the wisdom teachings of the period, always as a very negative attribute.[72] For women, it was condemned categorically. Specifically, we may note that the strange or foreign woman (*'ēšet zārâ* in Proverbs 1–9) seduces the young man *with her words* (Prov 1:11–14; 5:3–6). Indeed, the male-centered perspective of Proverbs 1–9 assumes that the male has agency to choose, but the wicked woman seduces him with her dangerous words.[73] We should consider as well the influence of *mētis* ("cleverness") in Greek culture, in addition to *ḥokmâ* in Israelite culture, although both cultures know tricksters. And while it was Judith's sexuality that exercised later Christian figures, her deceit is mentioned numerous times, and it is likely that her lying and her temerity with the elders were originally as great a transgression of decorum as her sexuality.

Nevertheless, every hero has associated attributes, and Judith's deceit is part of her heroic memory. Of the many women in the Bible who use deceit to save their people, Judith is the only one to pray fervently for it.[74] The theme of Judith's deceit is woven with a beautiful irony: the *spoken* deceit of her *lips* here is parallel to her *beauty*, which *visually* deceives or leads astray in 10:4. As

Schmitz/Engel say, "Diese Gleichzeitigkeit von betörender Schönheit, die täuscht, und täuschender Rede, die betört, bewirkt den Erfolg Judits."[75] Quite different from this is Greek Esther C 24, where Esther prays for persuasive speech rather than deceptive speech, and in the Vulgate of Judith the vice is attributed more to Holofernes, and the virtue to Judith: "Let him be caught in the net *of his own eyes;* strike him by the gracious words of my lips. Grant me constancy and fortitude."

■ **9:11** The final verse of this section, taken by some as the first verse of the next section, begins with a chiasm:

$$
\begin{array}{cc}
\text{A} & \text{B} \\
\end{array}
$$
For not in numbers is your power,
$$
\begin{array}{cc}
\text{B}' & \text{A}' \\
\end{array}
$$
nor your might in strong men

οὐ γὰρ ἐν πλήθει τὸ κράτος σου,
οὐδὲ ἡ δυναστεία σου ἐν ἰσχύουσιν

That Israel's strength does not consist in numbers echoes David to Goliath (2 Sam 17:45–47) and God to Gideon (Judg 7:2). It is a heroic motif, present also in the Greek tradition of the three hundred Spartans, and would also resonate with the Hasmonean memory of the Maccabean Revolt (1 Macc 3:17–19).

The negative assertion of v. 11a is followed by a positive one in v. 11b, again balanced. It utilizes the second-person singular of *eimi*, followed by five nouns with genitives:

But	you are [*ei*]	the God of the lowly,[76]
	you are [*ei*]	the helper of the weak,
		Protector of the forsaken,
		Guardian of those in despair,
		Deliverer of those without hope![77]

71 The *apata-* root is also used in 9:3; 10:4; 12:16; 13:16; 16:8; and compare the deceit of a woman in Judg 4:8–9.

72 E.g., Pss 17:1; 34:14; Prov 6:17; 12:22; Lev 19:11. Yet an unexpected and ironic valuation of deceit is seen in 1 Kings 22, where God sends forth a lying spirit of prophecy.

73 Gale A. Yee, "'I Have Perfumed My Bed with Myrrh': The Foreign Woman (*'isha zarah*) in Proverbs 1–9," *JSOT* 43 (1989) 53–68, here 66. Note,

however, that Proverbs 31 may return some of a woman's agency to her.

74 Toni Craven, "Women Who Lied for the Faith," in Douglas A. Knight and Peter J. Paris, eds., *Justice and the Holy: Essays in Honor of Walter Harrelson* (Scholars Press Homage Series 12; Atlanta: Scholars Press, 1989) 35–49, here 45.

75 Schmitz/Engel, *Judit,* 278–79.

76 *Tapeinos* here is contrasted with *hyperēphania* in 9:9.

77 *Apēlpismenoi* is not common but is found also in

ἀλλὰ   ταπεινῶν εἶ θεός,
        ἐλαττόνων εἶ βοηθός,
                ἀντιλήμπτωρ ἀσθενούντων,
                ἀπεγνωσμένων σκεπαστής,
                ἀπηλπισμένων σωτήρ.

This half-verse emphasizes God as *sōtēr*.[78] Just as Judith quoted Song of the Sea (Exod 15:3) in 9:7, here as well she uses several terms—helper, protector, savior (*boēthos, skepastēs, sōtēr*)—that also occur in Exod 15:2 in the same order. The Vulgate, making the exodus connection explicit, pauses to name some of the events of the exodus.[79] In addition, there are two instances of alliteration in this passage, *alla* and *elattonōn, apegnōsmenōn* and *apēlpismenōn*. The rhetorical flourishes suggest that Greek was the original language, at least for the prayers and speeches in Judith (see §2 above). A genitive cannot precede the noun it is related to in Hebrew, although it is conceivable that a clever translator also introduced a Greek style.[80]

While in Greece *elpis* communicates a weaker and more limited sense ("expect, wish for"), in Hebrew *bāṭah* also has the meaning of confidence or assurance, with God as its object. Hope can be theocentric, potentially certain, and even efficacious. The *elpid-* root occurs in Jdt 6:9; 8:17, 20; 9:7, 11; 13:19; 9:11, often with the *sōtēr* root—a theology of hope.[81] We also find in 9:11 reference to those whose hope had been stripped from them, the *apēlpismenōn*, parallel here to *tapeinōn*.

Excursus: Reversal and Humility

The reversal of fortunes in Judith is often compared to biblical precedents, but this theme is a universal feature of folk narrative, the definitive justice that

lies at the heart of "story." The biblical background is certainly felt, but it is not the sole source. Among the proverbs of the fifth-century BCE Ahikar, it is stated that God humbles the lofty person and exalts the lowly (10.149–50). In Greek culture *nemesis* (from *nemō*, "to distribute what is due") is a primeval concept of righting the balance of society. In our period, it is associated with *Tychē*, Fortune. Nemesis is a goddess sometimes associated with other female divine figures and sometimes called Adrasteia, "one from whom there is no running." She punishes humans' hubris in regard to the gods, as in the story of Narcissus, and this notion could connect to Nebuchadnezzar. That she is at times depicted with instruments such as sword, whip, dagger, or scourge suggests Judith's iconography. (Compare the iconographic similarity to the Indian goddess Kali in §8 above.) In regard to reversal per se, one might compare Euripides, *Troades* 612–13 and Horace, *Carmina* 1.34, but perhaps closest to our text is the slave-philosopher Aesop. When Aesop was asked what Zeus was up to, he replied, "He is lowering what is high, and exalting what is low" (Diogenes Laertius, *Lives*, Chilo 2).

Still, reversal in Israel is a very central theological theme. Both Exodus and Isa 41:11–16 emphasize it.[82] The Song of Hannah (1 Samuel 2; see Ps 113:7–9) expresses it on a personal level, although references to monarchy suggest that it probably refers to triumph over a greater enemy. The centrality of this concept in Israel may result from the cultural memory of a small nation besieged all around by great empires—"Remember that you were slaves in Egypt" (Deut 5:15). Later Jewish texts also emphasize reversal (Philo, *On Dreams* 1.155), and m. 'Erub. 13b will remind one of the Aesop quotation above: "He who humbles himself the Holy One, blessed be He, raises up, and he who exalts himself the Holy One, blessed be He, humbles."

The theme of reversal also evokes the theme of humility; but the history of humility is complex, and modern notions should not be assumed. Humility

---

Esth C 30 (4:17z) at the end of her prayer, and in Isa 29:19; see Schmitz/Engel, *Judit,* 271; and note similar senses in Isa 27:13; Ezek 37:11; Lev 26:38.

78 Judith is here taking up a traditional Israelite and Greek notion of *sōtēr* without registering the new Hellenistic developments of this term, either as a political savior or a cosmic savior. Based on such observations, however, Schmitz/Engel wrongly distance Judith from Hellenistic uses in general (*Judit,* 300). See also Wills, "Wisdom and Word among the Hellenistic Saviors: The Function of Literacy," *JSP* 24 (2014) 118–48.

79 Craven, *Artistry and Faith,* 91; Moore, *Judith,* 193.

80 Gera, *Judith,* 299, 321. She also notes sophisticated

stylistic effects of rhyme and rhythm (9:8, 11–12; 4:9–15), and alliteration and assonance (5:19; 8:32). See also Engel, "Der HERR," 158; Joosten, "Original Language," 161.

81 See Boyd-Taylor, "Semantics," 41–57; also Ryan, "Judith's Deed," 10–14: they suggest that Judith understands *elpizō* with God as object, automatically granting it more certainty? See also 8:17 *anamenō* ("wait for") with *sōteria* ("deliverance"). Judith's uses are also paralleled in a Greek plus in Job 2:9a: *anamenō, prosdechomai* ("wait for"), *elpis, sōtēria.*

82 Schmitz/Engel, *Judit,* 299.

was not considered a universally positive quality in ancient Israel or Greece. In the LXX, the *tapein-* root generally translated *'ānāh* and related forms, "to afflict, humble, do violence to." It is used in regard to the rapes of both Dinah and Tamar (Gen 34:2; 2 Sam 13:12, 14). In Israelite tradition, humility enters in at times in connection with the hope for deliverance and restoration, for the people as a whole or for the individual Israelite before God. "For you deliver a humble (or oppressed?) people," says Ps 18:27, "but the haughty eyes you bring down."[83] David is described as humble and not *endoxos* ("honored," 1 Sam 18:23 LXX, translating *qālāl niphal*, "humble oneself"), and Song of Hannah (1 Sam 2:1–10) and Isaiah of the exile, as noted, celebrate the reversal of the oppressed and mighty. Humility as a positive virtue is occasionally met in Proverbs (11:2; 15:33; 18:12; 22:4) and is more consistently lauded as a virtue in Ben Sira (3:17–24), although in both cases it is often understood as humility *before God*.

In the Greek world as well, *tapeinos* suggests lowly or even ignobly born and is not, in general, the positive virtue that it came to be in Christianity. It was conceived of as humiliation and shame, not the honor of the sage's discipline or the wisdom of the poor. In Judith, for instance, *tapein-* appears in the typical ignoble sense, combined with slavery, in Jdt 5:11; see also 7:32. Although elite Greek authors had difficulty seeing any positive valuation of humility, there was an occasional, perhaps Cynic, admission that truth could sometimes be found among those who lacked elite pretensions and safeguards. One can perhaps find humility romanticized in the Greek novelistic tradition, for example, in the pastoral scenes in *Daphnis and Chloe* or *Hunters of Euboea*; the Aesop tradition presents Cynic philosophy in the sharp-tongued sayings of a lowly slave. Yet the fascination with non-elites should not be mistaken for true empathy.

Reversal, then, as a theme does not necessarily affirm either humility or equality. Rather, the reversal of the arrogant and the lowly may affirm a sense of divine justice, even a vindication ("Now *we* are mighty! Now *we* are vindicated!"). Early Christians also affirmed the expected justice of the reversal of the high and low (see Luke 6, noted above) and would later transform the negative associations of *tapeinos* as lowly and ignoble into a positive virtue, *tapeinophrosynē*

(1 Clem. 13.3; 56.1). Even within pre-Christian Judaism there can be discerned the beginnings of asceticism and a discipline of the self that was perhaps a forerunner of the Christian doctrine of humility (see the commentry on 8:4–6). In our period, however, what lies behind Judith's prayer is the political ideology of the Maccabean Revolt: reversal and vindication, the victory of God's small nation against the worldwide Greek empire, symbolized here by the Assyrian alliance of the nations roundabout.

Despite such considerations, some have still sought a theology of humility in Judith's remarks in this prayer.[84] In 16:11 as well, Judith refers to Israelites as "my humiliated people . . . my weak people." Any humility, however, must be compared to her audacity in the narrative. She *stands* for the humble, but she is herself assertive and aggressive. For Gera, God of the humble "is perhaps the strongest acknowledgement by Judith of her powerlessness and dependence on God, but she uses only general plural terms."[85] Judith herself is more the *protector* of the humble—like God!—and her invocation of humility, like her sinlessness, can inoculate her from condemnation. Christian tradition would later also forge a theology that combines humility and power, the lamb that conquers (Revelation 5). In Acts, Stephen claims the righteous position of the martyr, but this contributes to a theological program of triumphalism.[86]

In the composition of Judith, then, is humility thoroughly integrated into her bold assertiveness? Are her prayer and Song in chap. 16 simply at odds with the narrative? Does Judith, like Stephen, exhibit "humility" that provides a stage in the construction of triumphalism? Moore may have sensed this problem in his search for theology in Judith: "If most, or at least many, of the important ideas of Judaism exist in Judith, that is all they really do, that is, they do not seem alive and vibrant."[87] What is expressed in Judith is not really a fully engaged theology of humility but an incorporation of an Israelite motif of God's protection of the oppressed—as they await the reversal that will return them to power. Our novella is about shame and reclaimed honor, reversal and the humiliation of the enemy, not the affirmation of humility as a virtue. The Christian doctrine of humility could at times become very similar: humility as a discipline of the self that will bring about power and triumph.

---

83   See also Pss 10:18; 138:6; 146:7–9; Mic 6:8.
84   Brian McNeil, "Reflections on the Book of Judith," *Downside Review* 96 (1978) 199–207, here 200; LaCocque, *Feminine Unconventional,* 41; see §6 above.
85   Gera, *Judith,* 321–22. The Vulgate adds to the theme of humility in 9:16: "the prayer of the hum-

ble and the meek has always pleased thee." Gera also notes the difference between this and Esther's focus on *her own* vulnerability (Greek Esth 14:3).
86   Matthews, *Perfect Martyr.*
87   Moore, *Judith,* 195.

Prayer Part 4, 9:12–14: Prayers of Israelite National Leaders as Intermediators[88]

The most salient structuring feature of our novella is the telescoping of a number of historical moments in Israel's history into one new narrative arc—history in play, or free narrative (see §7 above). Simeon and the rape of Dinah, themes from Isaiah, and Song of the Sea have just been played upon, and Jael and Sisera will provide the background for Judith's decapitation of Holofernes. In this section, we find motifs that are common in prayers of national leaders as intermediators—the uniqueness of God, the creation of the universe, and the call for retribution—Moses (Deut 3:23–25), David (2 Sam 7:22–24), Solomon (1 Kgs 8:23), and Jeremiah (Jer 32:17–23).[89] Gera, Newman, and Schmitz/Engel note the similarities to King Hezekiah's prayer when Sennacherib the Assyrian was repelled, found in nearly identical forms in 2 Kgs 19:15–19 and Isa 37:16–20.[90] Similar to Judith in both motifs and tone is also Jehoshaphat's prayer as the Moabites and Ammonites gathered to besiege Israel (2 Chr 20:5–12).

The narrative contexts of 2 Kgs 19:15–19//Isa 37:16–20 and 2 Chronicles 20 also indicate the way that the book of Judith mimics history writing. As Nebuchadnezzar in Judith is an "Assyrian," so in 2 Kings the actual Assyrian Sennacherib was attacking Jerusalem. In 2 Kings the Assyrian Rabshakeh is a field commander similar to Holofernes, and his contempt for God is similar to Nebuchadnezzar's in our text. Judith can here be likened to King Hezekiah, who was viewed very favorably in Israelite tradition, a second David who rebelled against the Assyrian kings (2 Kgs 18:3). Northern Israel,

or Samaria, fell to the Assyrians at the time that Hezekiah was king of Judah, and the story of Judith reincorporates the north, where Bethulia is located. Other similarities can be noted. In 2 Kings 18–19, the king of Assyria had conquered all the lands, "destroying them utterly" (19:11). The lists of peoples conquered in 2 Kgs 19:11–13, though shorter, is similar to the real and fictitious cities and lands conquered in Judith. The dialogue between the Assyrian and Judahite counselors (18:19–37) is similar to conversations in Judith: the Rabshakeh asks about the source of the Judahites' strength, just as Holofernes does in Judith 5, and Hezekiah asserts that the Judahites should rely on the Lord (18:30).[91]

Likewise, Jehoshaphat in 2 Chronicles 20 prays for God's aid against the Moabite and Ammonite invasion—the nations roundabout who are featured in Judith's narrative (see the commentary on 2:28)—and his prayer contains many similarities to Judith's (God of our ancestors, God of heaven, power and might, sanctuary for your name, inheritance). Hezekiah and Jehoshaphat are recognized as righteous kings in Israel, and appropriate models for Judith's leadership.

■ **9:12** As the previous section had ended with five titles for God that emphasize the God of the humble, so this one begins with five titles that emphasize power and sovereignty. The sovereign of the universe here may be contrasted with the weaker view of God that Uzziah affirms in chap. 8:

Yes, yes![92]

O God of my father
and God of the inheritance[93] of Israel,

---

88 In the structural analysis of Judith's prayer, v. 11 could conceivably be taken with the previous section, with a new rhetorical move beginning in v. 12; so Xeravits "Supplication."

89 Moshe Weinfeld, *Deuteronomy and the Deuteronomic School* (Oxford: Oxford University Press, 1972) 32–43.

90 Gera, *Judith*, 298, 322; Newman, *Praying by the Book*, 139–45; Schmitz/Engel, *Judit*, 298–99.

91 In 2 Kgs 19:21, Jerusalem is called "Virgin daughter Zion," *bĕtûlat bat ṣiyyôn*, which might have suggested the name Bethulia for Judith's village; see commentary on 6:10–21.

92 The prayer in Judith begins "*Nai, nai*," usually

translated "Please, please." This suggests a rending entreaty, similar to Esther's prayer (but not Mordecai's!) in Greek Esther. However, *nai nai* may mean, more literally and more accurately, "Yes! Yes!" or "Yes, indeed!"—not pleading, but emphasizing conviction. Schmitz/Engel also have "Ja, ja!" (*Judit*, 269–70, 300) and cf. the "Amen, Amen" of the Gospel of John. Some Latin manuscripts read *etiam* or *itaque*. "Nai, nai" is found in Matt 5:33–37; Jas 5:12; and 2 Enoch 49:1–2 (long recension) in lieu of an oath, not exactly the same as this context, but perhaps indirectly related.

93 Modern translators have difficulty with *klēronomia*. It translates Hebrew *naḥălâ* and *môrāšâ* and is a key

Ruler of heaven and earth,
Creator of the waters,
King of all your whole creation,
Hear my prayer!

ναὶ ναὶ
    ὁ θεὸς τοῦ πατρός μου
    καὶ θεὸς κληρονομίας Ἰσραήλ,
    δέσποτα τῶν οὐρανῶν καὶ τῆς γῆς,
    κτίστα τῶν ὑδάτων,
    βασιλεῦ πάσης κτίσεώς σου,
    σὺ εἰσάκουσον τῆς δεήσεώς μου.

Gera observes that Judith presents a better-structured invocation here than in v. 11, naming God in outwardly moving concentric circles: God of my father, God of the inheritance of Israel, ruler of heaven and earth, creator of the waters, king of your whole creation—from a single father, out to all of creation, for all time.[94] As noted above, some of the prayers of national leaders are similar, such as that of Judah Maccabee (1 Macc 4:30–33) and David's farewell prayer (1 Chr 29:10–19).[95] In the biblical tradition, God the creator was also God the vanquisher of Sea or sea monsters (Ps 74:12–17; Isa 51:9–10), which would mythologize further Judith's slaying of a larger-than-life enemy (see above). The motif of the conqueror is not mentioned in this verse, but it is present in the context and will be found below in regard to Judith's venturing out.[96]

"My father" may refer (1) to Simeon, as in 9:2, either as a real or metaphorical progenitor; (2) to Judith's own father, invoking her family's place in the tradition of worshiping God; or (3) to the patriarchs Jacob or Abraham. Moore argues for the first; there is a rhetorical expansion from the most specific (God of my father) to the people Israel (God of the inheritance of Israel) to the cosmic (king of all your creation).[97] Schmitz/Engel, however, place father and inheritance of Israel in parallel; God of my father is a reference to the ancestry of the people. In addition,

> Die Sorge um den Erbbesitz (Jdt 4, 12; 8, 22) geht mit der Bitte an Gott einher, sich für seinen Erbbesitz einzusetzen (Jdt 13, 5). . . . Die Rückkehr eines jeden auf seinen Erbbesitz . . . (16, 21) ist daher ein ersehntes Ziel.[98]

Their reading appears more likely. The complex but plausible arrangement of Xeravits would support this. Of the five cola in this verse, he sees the first two, God of my father and God of the inheritance of Israel, as parallel and nearly identical—God as sole deity of Israel. The last two, creator of the waters and king of all creation, are also parallel—God as creator.[99] At the center lies an affirmation of universal Lordship: *despota* of heaven and earth. This *despota* harks back to and contrasts with Holofernes as *despota* (5:20, 24; 7:9, 11; 11:10) and Nebuchadnezzar as lord and king of whole earth (6:4; 11:1).[100]

Several of the phrases are not found elsewhere in the Bible in these precise forms—God of the inheritance of Israel, ruler of heaven and earth, and creator of the

---

term in many texts, including Jdt 4:12; 5:15; 8:22; 13:5; 16:21. It is sometimes translated as "heritage" but that loses the patriarchal family content of the term. God's own "inheritance" becomes the inheritance for Israel and the tribes. All personal inheritance in Israel is understood as part of the tribal, or more locally, extended family ownership of the *bêt 'āb*. Even when this notion is reconstituted, as in Ezra-Nehemiah, what is negotiated is the inherited lands of the ancestors, with intense scrutiny of genealogies.

94 Gera, *Judith,* 314; and Gera, "Speech in Judith," 417–18. The Song of the Sea also presents titles of God, but the multiplication of titles for God is common in prayers in this period, both Jewish and Greek; cf. 2 Macc 1:24–25; 3 Macc 2:2–3; 6:2; Cleanthes, *Hymn to Zeus.* See Corley, "Divine Sovereignty," 371–72.

95 On the former, see Gera, "Judah and Judith," 36.

96 Gera, *Judith,* 322.

97 Moore, *Judith,* 193–94.

98 Schmitz/Engel, *Judit,* 300–301.

99 Xeravits, "Supplication," 175. For God as king, see Exod 15:18; 3 Macc 2:2. *Basileus* is often used for earthly kings in Judith, for God only here.

100 Gera notes that *despotēs* for God became more common in later LXX works, e.g., in the prayer in Jonah 4:3; Tob 8:17; Dan 9:8, 15–17, and others. Cf. the creator in Ezra 9 and Nehemiah 9.

waters, and, as noted in the excursus at 8:35 ("The Book of Judith and Greek Philosophy"), there is some innovation in this prayer in terms of theological ideas; the lord of heaven and earth is the God who controls past, present, and future in v. 5. The creator of waters could resonate with the lack of water in the story (see also 16:15),[101] but this is not necessary; it suggests power over Yamm, Sea.

■ **9:13–14** While v. 12 repeats names for God and concludes with a petition, v. 13 begins with a petition and repeats the evil intentions of the enemy:

> Grant me persuasive speech and deception
> > For the wounding and bruising[102] of them,
> > > Those who,
> > > > Against your covenant[103]
> > > > And your sacred house,
> > > > The hill[104] of Zion,
> > > And the house your children have inherited
> Plotted cruel things[105]

δός λόγον μου καὶ ἀπάτην
εἰς τραῦμα καὶ μώλωπα αὐτῶν,
    οἳ

κατὰ τῆς διαθήκης	σου	A
καὶ οἴκου ἡγιασμένου	σου	B
καὶ κορυφῆς	Σιὼν	A′
καὶ οἴκου κατασχέσεως υἱῶν	σου	B′

ἐβουλεύσαντο σκληρά.

Judith asks for *logon* and *apatēn*—reasoned or persuasive speech and deception—an odd, perhaps oxymoronic, ironic, and humorous combination. Xeravits takes it as hendiadys to mean deceitful discourse.[106] Be that as it may, it is similar to Judith's *sophia* and *synesis* in 8:29, but now openly transgressive.[107] Pertinent also is the connection to Judith's *logoi* in chap. 11, full of deception! The verse enumerates the threats of the Assyrians. Elsewhere Israel as a whole is threatened, but here the focus is on the temple (see also Jdt 4:12; 6:19; 8:21, 24; 9:8), Judith's interest all along, as in 2 Maccabees. A rough structural parallelism is noted.

In v. 14 this emphasis is also broadened to "your whole nation [*ethnos*] and every tribe [*phylē*]." Textual variants allow for two possible meanings here: the whole nation (*pan to ethnos*) recognizes God, or every nation (*pantos ethnous*) recognizes God. This would represent quite a difference in eschatology. Most commentators have chosen the former variant, which recognizes the parallelism of the clauses, but some, including Enslin, have argued for the latter.[108] The former is better attested textually, and the universalistic focus of the latter does not match the context. The verse does not depict an idealized or eschatological vision of every nation recognizing God (as in Hezekiah's prayer, 2 Kgs 19:19 = Isa 37:20), but a prayer for all Israel to come together in unity—this is the focus of Judith. Judith asks, therefore, that God intervene so that all Israel—other nations are not mentioned at this point—may know fully God's transcendent power.

---

101 Schmitz/Engel, *Judit*, 301.
102 "Wound and bruise" may seem an odd, understated vindication against the brutal Assyrians, but it is a stock phrase in Hebrew (Gen 4:23; Exod 21:25; Isa 1:6).
103 Covenant is found only here in Judith, but *kataschesis* (translating Heb. *'ăḥuzzâ*) refers to the land of Israel granted by God as an eternal possession (Gen 17:8), roughly equivalent to *kleronomia* (9:12).
104 Zion here is the unusual *koryphē* ("hill"); elsewhere in Judith this term refers to the fortified hilltops in which the Israelites place their security (4:5; 5:1; 7:10).
105 Cf. the events of Exod 1:14, 6:9.
106 Xeravits, "Supplication," 177.
107 Gera, *Judith*, 323; Schmitz/Engel, *Judit*, 302; and see 9:10. Xeravits also sees *logos* as recalling the speech-act of Gen 1:1 ("Supplication," 176), but that is not likely. Still, the identity of the repeating verb "said" of God's acts in Genesis and the noun "word," assumed by first-century CE writers (Philo and John 1:1), may have been introduced into Jewish thought by the first century BCE; see Daniel Boyarin, "The Gospel of the Memra: Jewish Binitarianism and the Prologue to John," *HTR* 94 (2001) 243–84.
108 See discussion in Schmitz/Engel, 312–13. Gera follows that judgment here but also suggests that the phrase "all the tribes," rather than being a repetition in parallel with nation, means all the tribes of the world (*Judith*, 324). This is possible, but unlikely. Cf. 2 Macc 10:8: *panti tō tōn ioudaiōn ethnei*, "in the entire nation of Jews."

The prayer ends with phrases that are contrasted with the pretensions of Nebuchadnezzar (2:5, 12; 6:2): "You are God," "there is no other who shields . . . but you alone," "power and might." "No other god protects Israel" probably does not assume that no other god exists, as one might assume from the statements of Nebuchadnezzar in 3:8.[109] Power and might here are similar to their occurrence in 2 Chr 20:6, but see also Jdt 5:23, recalling Holofernes's question in 5:3.

---

109 Voitila, "Deuteronomistic Heritage," 373–75. "Give recognition to know" (translated as "let . . . know and understand" above) is also odd in Greek and is not easily explained as a mistranslation of Hebrew. The *gnō-* root is played upon often in Judith (5:8; 8:13–14, 20; 11:16; 14:5). In the phrase "God of all power," the word *dynameōs* can translate *ṣĕbā'ôt,* usually in the form *dynameōn*; see also 13:4; *pantokratōr* is also found in Jdt 4:13; 8:13; 15:10; 16:5, 17.

Text	Textual Notes

Text

1/ When Judith had ceased crying out to the God of Israel and had concluded all of these words, **2/** she arose from where she lay prostrate and, summoning her slave, went down into her house where she spent Sabbaths and feast days. **3/** She removed the sackcloth she had been wearing and took off her widow's garments, and bathed her entire body in water and anointed herself with rich ointment, combed[a] her hair, placed a tiara[b] on her head, and dressed in her festive garments, those that she wore in the days when her husband Manasses was alive. **4/** She put sandals on her feet, and put on anklets, bracelets, rings, earrings, and all her other beautifications; thus she made herself very beautiful, to dazzle the eyes of as many men as might see her. **5/** She gave her slave a small wineskin full of wine, a flask of oil, and filled a pouch with a barley loaf, a cake of figs, andfine bread.[c] She wrapped[d] all her vessels, and placed them in her maid's pouch as well. **6/** They then went out[e] to the gate of the town of Bethulia and found waiting there Uzziah and the elders of the town, Chabris and Charmis.[f] **7/** When they beheld her, her face transformed and her garments now changed, they were quite astounded at her beauty, and said to her, **8/** "May the God of our ancestors give you favor to complete your plans for the greater glory of the Israelites and the exaltation of Jerusalem." And she bowed to God.[g]

9/ She said to them, "Now command that they open the town gates for me, and I will go forth to accomplish all the things you spoke of with me."[h] They ordered the young men to open the gates as she had said, **10/** and they did so. Judith went out, together with her slave, and the men of the town continued watching her until she had descended the mountain and crossed the valley, and they could no longer see her.

Textual Notes

a   According to Corley ("Septuagintalisms," 89), S shows the original reading of the rare word διεξανε ("combed," although it actually means to card wool), which B and A replace with διεταξεν. If Corley is correct, there is no need for the complicated hypothetical reconstructions of Zimmermann that Moore follows; see also §2 above.

b   Perhaps a diadem or headband with jewels.

c   Αρτων καθαρων could be pure in quality or clean in terms of Jewish food laws; cf. Ezek 4:14–15. It is not "showbread" or bread of the presence; see Moore. Dubarle (*Judith*, 1:166) conjectures that it is a misreading of αρτων και τυρου, bread and cheese. O OL L Sy Vg include τυρον here. Medieval Jewish versions also include cheese, associated with Hanukkah; see §8 above.

d   Περιδιπλοω is a *hapax legomenon*.

e   Αι δυο και αμα και επορευθησαν also read in O OL Sy.

f   Chabris and Charmis lacking in 71´ OL-CNX Vg.

g   A difficult passage textually. While many texts read προσεκυνησεν (B S A O L 249´ 311 OL Sy Sa Eth Vg), V reads προσεκυνησαν, and OL-C *adoraverunt illam*. Moore conjectures a confusion in Hebrew: she bowed down to them—אליהם was read as she bowed down to God לאלהים. Alternatives are thus "they bowed to God," and "they bowed to her (as God)." See also Corley, "Septuagintalisms," 95.

h   The Greek is somewhat ambiguous in terms of agency. It could mean "the things you said to me"—providing more authority to the elders—or "the things you spoke of with me"—simply referring back to their conversation.

Commentary

10:1–10

Joseph Campbell describes the central element of the heroic quest as passing over the threshold between the known world and the unknown, from civilization to the wilderness realm where the monster resides.[1] Judith's journey begins at night, the period of vulnerability to dangerous forces. Like the redressing scene, this arc can also be likened to a rite of passage, the liminal state being her sojourn in a dangerous land. The gates are

---

1   Joseph Campbell, *The Hero with a Thousand Faces* (New York: Pantheon, 1949) 90–91. The gates and Judith's two passages through them were played up in the medieval Jewish versions of the story; see §8 above. The cross-cultural nature of the plot of Judith is now accepted by many critics, a process

the portal, the literal *limen*—threshold—through which she passes to move into the valley and slay the monster. Judith's commands mark the transitions: she ordered the gate of the town to be opened (10:9); upon her return, she shouts, "Open, open the gate!" (13:11).

In moving across the boundary into the wild zone of danger, Judith will utilize uncivilized practices normally forbidden to women. She will be sexually provocative and verbally suggestive, deceitful, treacherous, and murderous. She will abuse the dead body of an enemy. While she is in this zone of conflict with the monster, every word out of her mouth will be provocative, flattering, manipulative, and deceitful. This is her heroic identity. Other biblical women use deceit and sex, and even violence, but on the spectrum of women's brazen acts in the Bible, Judith occupies the extreme edge. Clearly, the excesses derive from a genre based in fantasy. The actions of Tamar and Jael might seem much more challenging, committed in narratives that retain a claim on plausibility; but it is perhaps also possible for them because they are not Israelite.

■ 10:1–4

Judith, her prayer concluded, resumes her ritual actions of dressing and preparing for battle (see the commentary on 8:4–6). There is a marking of time and space, with ritualized actions, and the prayers coincide with the sacred schedule of the temple. Especially noteworthy is that each of the following actions—"she went down into her house," "removed the sackcloth," "bathed her entire body in water," and "dressed in her festive garments"—bears some similarity to the high priest's actions on Yom Kippur. The sacred is never very far from the actions in Greek novels or Jewish and Christian novellas. According to Timothy Beal, if texts reflect relations with multiple previous texts and cultural influences, then every text "suggests an indeterminate *surplus* of meaningful

possibilities."[2] But it is novelistic texts in particular that evoke many different associations without restraint.

The fact that Judith is a woman does not render an association with the priesthood an unlikely or even a necessarily "subversive" association. In folklore or popular tradition, the enjoyment of narratives of women in men's roles is quite common, often explored in unrealistic story lines. In Acts of Paul and Thecla 34, for instance, Thecla baptizes herself. Although here one might argue that her general role and her self-baptism are radical challenges to established gender roles, in other folk or popular narratives women sometimes embody roles that are forbidden to them in real life. The *khoja*, or priestess girl, in Turkish folktales is such an example.[3]

Also in keeping with the antic disposition of popular novellas, the connection that Judith establishes with the temple is recounted even though she does not adhere precisely to biblical law in more realistic aspects. For instance, she does not enter into a levirate marriage, and her period of mourning exceeds that required by biblical law. Remarriage would indeed be a realistic path for her. In the world of free narrative, however, Judith follows the dictates of her own discipline and piety and is a prototype of the heroine of virtue found in the Jewish Therapeutae/Therapeutrides and in Christian asceticism. It is a characteristic of the ancient novellas—Greek, Jewish, and Christian—that the protagonists give vibrant expression to the spirit of the law while not always conforming to the letter. By their romantic inspiration, they are in some sense above the law.

Judith is here in the third stage of an initiation ritual: incorporation back into society in a new status (see the commentary on 9:1). The text carefully notes how previous ritual actions are undone: "When Judith *had ceased crying out* to God, and had *concluded* all these words, she

---

made easier by "canonization" of the plot in literary handbooks: see, e.g., Christopher Booker, describing the seven basic plots, places Overcoming the Monster as the first plot (*The Seven Basic Plots: Why We Tell Stories* [London and New York: Crossroad, 2004]). To be sure, Holofernes is pathetic, one-dimensional as a chaos monster, but this is a farcical text.

2 Timothy K. Beal, "Ideology and Intertextuality: Surplus of Meaning and Controlling the Means of Production," in Danna Nolan Fewell, ed., *Reading between Texts: Intertextuality and the Hebrew Bible* (Literary Currents in Biblical Interpretation; Louisville: Westminster John Knox, 1992) 27–39, here 31.

3 See §5 above.

arose from where she had lain." Each part of this third stage is related carefully, with some detail:

- She called her slave.

  Her favorite slave is her assistant or second in a quest to slay the beast. The fact that she calls her may indicate that the latter is only at her side when she is below in her house, that is, not when she is in her isolation tent. Esther and Aseneth are also alone in their liminal phase. Vulgate 8:4 may include a Christian alteration: Judith prays together with her female slaves.

- She went down into her house.

  Typically, she isolated herself in the tent on the roof and engaged in fasting practices, but on Sabbaths and festival days, days on which it is not permitted to mourn or fast, she would descend to the house. Although not "sacred" space, the tent is "marked" space, a refuge where deeper mourning and a more private relation to God could be explored. From the narrative point of view, marked space, even ascetic space, is similar to sacred space. But Judith's ritual redressing, similar to priestly practices, occurs in the house and not in the tent.

- She removed the sackcloth she had been wearing, and took off her widow's garments.

  Judith had worn sackcloth under her mourning garments (8:4–6). Her undressing may call to mind the Soṭah ritual (Numbers 5 and m. Soṭah), in which the suspected adulteress is stripped and tested.[4] This ritual, or perhaps the *idea* of this ritual, played an important role in this period; when Queen Helena of Adiabene converted to Judaism, her lavish donations to Jerusalem included a public inscription of the Numbers 5 Soṭah passage.

- She bathed her entire body in water.

  See the excursus at 12:5b–9, "Bathing and Related Issues."

- She anointed herself with rich ointment.

- She combed her hair.

  In the Greek tradition, disheveled hair could be viewed as both wild and frenzied, an association with the Maenads of the Bacchae. In Israelite tradition, there is also some attention to women's hair (perhaps reflected in 1 Corinthians 11).

- She put on a tiara.

  NETS translates it "turban," but Greek *mitra* may perhaps be a diadem or headband with jewels. In other contexts, it could be a sash, but here it is an adornment for her hair.

- She dressed herself in the festive garments that she used to wear when her husband was alive.

  Her clothes are the same garments that she formerly wore as a respectable wealthy lady and wife of Manasseh,[5] yet her entire presentation at the "court" of Holofernes will be as a courtesan awaiting elevation to Nebuchadnezzar's harem. The Vulgate interrupts to assure the audience that her increased beauty proceeded from virtue:

  > And the Lord conferred even more beauty upon her, because all this adornment did not proceed from lust but from virtue, and so the Lord increased her beauty so that she appeared incomparably lovely to everyone's eyes. (10:4 Vg)

Judith's redressing in the LXX is a kind of performativity or theatricality. Did the original text assume an almost magical "drift" from the persona of a local wealthy matron, known for her wisdom and probity, to a captivating woman who can bewitch the eyes of any man, the sort of transformation typical of popular narratives? Yet an overzealous questioning on our part will interfere with the pleasures of free narratives. The double level of voyeurism, viewing the heroine as both virtuous and erotic, will also later be found in the Greek novels.[6]

---

4   See also Ishay Rosen-Zvi, *The Mishnaic Sotah Ritual: Temple, Gender and Midrash* (JSJSup 160; Leiden: Brill, 2012). On Queen Helena, see Wills, *Jewish Novel*, 206–11.

5   Loader, 193; see also 200–201.

6   Morales, *Vision and Narrative*, 38, 186.

- She put sandals on her feet, put on her anklets, brace-lets, rings, earrings, and all her other jewelry.

Judith's redressing is told with attention to detail, allowing for as much eroticism as the Jewish genre would allow. (Tobit 8:1–9, for example, recounts the consummation of a honeymoon without mention-ing sex, while Xenophon's *Ephesian Tale* 1.9 provides details of a sexual encounter.) Every conceivable part of Judith's accessorizing is mentioned to address the voyeurism of the audience: ointment, combing of hair, tiara, festive attire, sandals, anklets, bracelets, rings, earrings, and "all her other jewelry." There is no veil, but it is not clear whether in Jerusalem at the turn of the first century BCE a veil would be consid-ered necessary for a woman in public.[7] The tiara does not likely cover her hair but adorns it. The items that Judith puts on are nearly identical to those that Esther condemns in Greek Esther 14. In Isa 3:16–24 the wealthy daughters of Zion are also castigated for wearing similar cosmetics, but this should not be taken as a universal Israelite rule.

The part-by-part description of her beautification is vaguely similar to the *wasf* genre, Near Eastern love poetry that stylistically treats each part of a woman's beauty in turn.[8] But though her beautification is listed, the description does not attain the detail nor the stylized extravagance of the *wasf*.

Excursus: Undressing and Redressing

By taking off her mourning clothes, Judith is not committing an unusual or highly charged act. On the surface level, this scene communicates a simple transition from mourning, evidenced by the change of clothing.[9] Saul M. Olyan finds four types of mourning-like behavior in ancient Israel: at death, in petitionary contexts, at times of national catas-trophe, and in response to skin disease—although we might also ask whether they are all part of some larger umbrella category, self-abjection or the like.

This, however, is a broader question, and it is clear that Judith has been or will be participating in three of these actions: mourning her husband, preparing to petition God, and responding to national disaster. We may ask as well whether a fifth is being added in Jewish practice, ascetic discipline of the self (see above at 8:4–6). We also note that in a text such as Judith, ritual elements are not simply described but may be invested with symbolic significance revealed by the themes of the novella. Our author may go beyond the simple details of ritual—if we are able to discern it.

In addition to the change from mourning clothes, the author has invested the scene with many potential symbolic layers. First, Judith changes from mourning clothes into her most beautiful clothes and adornments. This could also be perceived simply as a transition from the clothes of mourning to those of rejoicing, yet her *stated* motive in redressing is strate-gic, to "dazzle the eyes of as many men as might see her" (10:4). Her beautification may suggest the attire of a courtesan—what the Assyrians will see—though we must improbably reconcile that with the fact that her clothes and jewelry are actually her own, those of a wealthy Israelite woman in a mountain village. Elsewhere in Israel, her jewelry might have been viewed as a sign of excess (Isa 3:18–21), but here it is seen as *both* her own jewelry from her previous life *and also* her accoutrements to bewitch the eyes of the Assyrians. The fact that she ritually bathes during a life-threatening water shortage also indicates the free-narrative aspect of the story.[10]

In a provocatively but helpfully entitled article, "Clothing Seduces: Did You Think It Was Naked Flesh That Did It?," Athalya Brenner-Idan notes that in the Hebrew Bible, nudity is not described eroti-cally but is usually mentioned as a social shame. It is dressing up that is the means for a woman to seduce. Women who dress up as temptresses in the Hebrew Bible include Esther, Tamar, Ruth, and Judith. (The exceptions, Bathsheba and Susanna bathing, are notable because it is not *the woman*'s act that is the focus but that of the voyeuristic men.) There are a number of common elements to the women dressing:

7   Brenner-Idan, "Clothing Seduces."

8   Compare Song of Songs 4–7, 1QapGen 20.1–8. In Esther's prayer in Greek Esther 14, she humbles every part of her body that had formerly been adorned, a sort of negative *wasf*; Wills, *Jewish Novel*, 122; Wills, "Ascetic Theology."

9   Olyan, *Biblical Mourning*, 62–96, 137–40; Gary A.

Anderson, *A Time to Mourn, A Time to Dance: The Expression of Grief and Joy in Israelite Religion* (Uni-versity Park: Pennsylvania State University Press, 1991). The transition from mourning is played upon ironically by David in 2 Samuel 12, where he transitions surprisingly early in the process.

10   Gera, *Judith*, 331.

1. They are women in mourning, either for their husbands or their parents.
2. They dress for a new role or mission.
3. They are generally beautiful, but not always—and men's beauty is often described in more detail.
4. They change clothes.
5. The lack of bodily description is compensated for by details of clothing and adornments.
6. The lack of bodily description is also compensated for by the woman's rhetorical ability, loquaciousness, or cleverness.
7. Surprisingly, the women's honor remains intact, "thus also saving the honour of the readerly viewer."[11]

For a "biblical" woman—although Judith was not "biblical" at the time of composition—we have more notations of her beauty, even her *asteia* ("graciousness," 11:23), but often focalized through the voyeuristic eyes of the men—both Israelite and Assyrian.

It is, of course, not just these women whose transformations are signaled by changes of clothing. God dresses Jerusalem as his bride and queen (Ezek 16:9-13). In the novelistic Joseph story of Genesis, each of his transitions is marked by the putting off of his former garments and redressing in different garments. His changes are not as explicitly marked as psychological transformations as are the women's, but over the course of the story, one can discern character development.[12] In Deut 21:10-14 the captive non-Israelite women must also shave their hair, cut their nails, remove their former clothing, and mourn their former family identity before being received by their new Israelite husband. Somewhat later than Judith and probably influenced by it, the Protevangelium of James contains a Judith, a slave who upbraids her mistress Anna for being barren. Immediately after Judith's words, Anna "put off her mourning garments, cleansed her head, and put on her bridal garments" (2:4).

The Judith example, then, begins with a change from mourning clothes into garments of rejoicing, but that is only the beginning of the symbol making. In addition to the motif of seduction, other resonances can be suggested. In heroic narrative cross-culturally, the protagonist often begins withdrawn from society and emerges in response to a threat to the people, dressing for war. In Greek literature, one also finds a type scene of the woman dressing in beautiful or seductive clothing.[13] The book of Judith seems to combine them. Judith takes off her mourning garments and transitions back to her wealthy woman's clothes—a typical end to mourning—but she is also dressing for war, even girding for war, using the best weapons at her disposal: adorned beauty, courage, and her ability to manipulate others by speech.[14] The hero's dressing scenes also often involve a faithful servant as an assistant; Judith's favorite slave—an *abra*, not a *doulē*—plays this role. Another accompanying feature cross-culturally is a blessing of the hero by an elderly figure of authority.[15] This function is performed by Uzziah, an elder of Bethulia (8:35).

There is a central undressing and redressing scene in Greek Esther and Aseneth that is very similar, also invested with symbolic levels beyond simply mourning/rejoicing—or alternatively, one might say that the transition from mourning to rejoicing becomes a canvas on which many layers of meaning can be painted. The three women are changing

11   Athalya Brenner-Idan, "Clothing Seduces: Did You Think It Was Naked Flesh That Did It?" in Brenner-Idan and Efthimiadis-Keith, *Tobit and Judith*, 212-25, here 224; see also Bach, *Women, Seduction*, 201-3.

12   Adelman, *Female Ruse*, 198-230.

13   N. Forsyth, "The Allurement Scene: A Typical Pattern in Greek Oral Epic," *California Studies in Classical Antiquity* 12 (1979) 107-20. There are three instances in the *Iliad* (Helen with the old Trojans and with Paris, Hera with Zeus), and four in the *Odyssey* (Penelope in books 1, 18, and 21, and Nausicaa in book 6). Cf. Aphrodite and Aeneas in the Hymn to Aphrodite, and Pandora in Hesiod's *Works and Days*. Cf. also the arming scene of Goliath, 1 Sam 17:4-7, 34-35, where the young David ironically forgoes an arming scene (1 Sam 17:38-40).

14   Judith and 2 Maccabees (more than 1 Maccabees) contain gestures, prostration, and kneeling in common. Judith's putting on jewels is similar to Judah's dream of a great sword (2 Macc 15:15-16). In the Talmud as well a woman's clothes are likened to men's weapons (b. 'Abod. Zar. 25b, b. Yeb. 115a; so Malka Simkovich, "Book of Judith." Nancy Tan helpfully compares Judith's bathing and dressing to Exek 16:9-14, where beautification is to impress foreigners ("Judith's Embodiment," 25-26). Yet it is not clear whether our text borrows *specifically* from Ezekiel; they may both partake of dressing scenes in general.

15   On the hero's servant, see Mark W. Edwards, "Homer and Oral Tradition: The Type-Scene," *Oral Tradition* 7 (1992) 284-330. On the blessing, see C. M. Bowra, *Heroic Poetry* (London: Macmillan, 1952) 184-86.

out of unattractive clothes and dressing to enter into a zone of attraction to men and to complete an important mission. The scenes in Greek Esther and Aseneth are more typical of the woman's literary dressing scene than that of the military hero, yet Judith will be more martial. Still, they all function to reveal the inner emotional world of the female protagonist. Judith is taken out of one status, undergoes a ritual transformation, and reemerges in a new status, from pious recluse to worldly soldier.[16]

The scene itself can be analyzed as a rite of passage, divisible into three stages: separation from society, a liminal period of being "betwixt and between," and incorporation back into society in a new status.[17] The process of separation occurs when the individual steps out of mundane space and time, the former status in society now deconstructed. The use of ashes or dung serves to deconstruct the former personality; the person becomes earth. Disrobing or changing clothing is often a part, as is washing or other purification rituals. One enters the liminal stage, in which former status markers of social order, class, gender, and so on, either disappear or are reversed; the person is temporarily isolated from society as a whole. In this liminal stage, space and time are not regulated by mundane markers, and there may be an element of danger and exposure to cosmic forces. Communication with the divine is direct, unmediated, even prophetic, mystical, or shamanic. Judith's prayer will occur in this liminal phase. The final stage is incorporation; the individual moves out of the unmarked time and space and back into marked time and space, now with a new status or mission.[18]

The narrative pattern of the heroine redressing can also be compared with Near Eastern myths of goddesses. The Akkadian goddess Ishtar removes her crown, her jewels, and her dress when she descends to the underworld. In this liminal and dangerous passage, she loses all her power and faces death—a return to nature and earth. These same items are restored to her as she reemerges and regains her powers.[19] The Sumerian equivalent of Ishtar, Inana, dies when she is stripped of her clothing in the underworld but is later brought back to life.[20] Inana also bathes, anoints herself with oil, and puts on a queen's robe and jewelry to seduce the mortal Dumuzi. In the Ugaritic Aqhat epic, his sister Paghat bathes, puts on cosmetics, dons a woman's dress over warrior's garments, and with knife and sword in hand avenges her brother's death. As Gera notes in reference to our story, "she used both conventionally female and . . . male weapons."[21] Paghat also enters into the enemy's tent where they both drink.[22]

In Greek myth, Hera prepares in a similar way to seduce Zeus (Iliad 14.166–86, 214–17). Says Gera, "Hera turns to Aphrodite for her special embroidered sash which contains intimacy, desire, and deceptive persuasion, while Judith has prayed to God for the power of persuasion and deception (9:10, 13)."[23] Thus the preparation of the heroine is found in ancient literature, especially concerning the freer acts and hyper-agency of goddesses: Judith is as free as a goddess. Further, just as it is conjectured that the personae of Semiramis and Ninus, on one hand, and Esther and Mordecai, on the other, are based partially on Ishtar and Marduk, so also Judith may owe something of her authority to these goddesses.[24]

---

16   Wills, *Jewish Novel,* 224–32; Wills, "Ascetic Theology."

17   Arnold van Gennep, *The Rites of Passage* (Chicago: University of Chicago Press, 1960); Victor W. Turner, "Betwixt and Between: The Liminal Period in *Rites de Passage,*" in Turner, *The Forest of Symbols: Aspects of Ndembu Ritual* (Ithaca, NY: Cornell University Press, 1970) 93–111; Wills, *Jewish Novel,* 224–32.

18   As free narrative, our text seems to assume a *series* of rites of passage, even in concentric circles. It is not unusual, even in actual rituals as opposed to narratives, for the three-part rites of passage to be repeated or contained one inside another; so Martin Pehal and Markéta Preininger Svobodová, "Death and the Right Fluids: Perspectives from Egyptology and Anthropology," *Journal of Ancient Egyptian Interconnections* 17 (2018) 114–36, here 125.

19   *COS* 1.108; Hugo Winckler, "Zum Buche Judit," in *Altorientalische Forschungen* (Leipzig: Eduard Pfeiffer, 1899) 2, II, 266–76; Aage Bentzen, "Der Hedammu–Mythus, das Juditbuch, und ähnliches," *Archiv Orientální* 18 (1950) 1–2.

20   *Electronic Text Corpus of Sumerian Literature* t.1.4.1, http://etcsl.orinst.ox.ac.uk; ANET, 639.

21   Gera, *Judith,* 329; Carole Fontaine, "The Deceptive Goddess in Ancient Near Eastern Myth: Inanna and Inaras," *Semeia* 42 (1988) 84–102; Jacqueline Vayntrub, "Transmission and Mortal Anxiety in the Tale of Aqhat," forthcoming.

22   The conclusion is missing; *COS* 1.103.

23   Gera, *Judith,* 328.

24   Gera, *Judith,* 59–60, 72–74. Quite interesting is the wearing of sackcloth—and the accompanying self-affliction—by the queen mother of Nabonidus (*COS* 1.147, col. 1), on which see the excursus at 8:4–6, "Asceticism."

As noted above, Greek Esth 14:1–15:5 and Aseneth 10:9–17, 14:14–15 also present a highly stylized undressing and redressing scene, in the latter case lasting for seven days. The type scenes in Judith and these other Jewish novellas exhibit a balanced V-pattern with a prayer at the center, presented as a spontaneous, heartfelt communication:

```
       rends self *                          * emerges for mission
 takes off beautiful garments*              * puts on beautiful garments
    puts on mourning garments*             * takes off mourning garmentss
         puts ashes on head *            * bathes
                              *
                            prays
Narrative: ─────────────────────────────────────────────────►
```

The separate actions are quite precise and ritualized. Judith's scene, the earliest, may have established a model for the others.[25] There is a balanced downward and upward movement. All three involve a private audience before God, all involve mourning garments and ashes on the head (Esther adds dung as well). Prayer lies at the center of each—the liminal moment when communication between the realms occurs more directly—and Judith and Aseneth ritually bathe before reintegrating. At the end of each scene the heroine proceeds to her mission.

Slight differences between Judith's prayer and those of Esther and Aseneth can also be observed. First, Judith's prayer is more martial; she is a warrior. In addition, while Esther has organized the Jews of Persia to fast with her (4:16), Judith the warrior fasts alone on her roof (though her timing does correspond to the incense offering in the temple).[26] Esther's actions are new for her, and ad hoc, while Judith's are an intensification of her existing semiascetic regimen. Judith has simply added ashes, although this is also known from mourning rituals.

Postexilic confessional theology (Ezra 9; Nehemiah 9; Daniel 9; and Bar 1:15–3:8) likely influenced these scenes of women disrobing and rerobing, but several caveats must be noted. First, there is a tendency to read the tradition backward, retrojecting a Christian interest in *penitential* theology back into the Second Temple period. Second, even confining ourselves to the earlier period, we often make certain assumptions. Are confessions of sin an externalizing and wiping away of sin, or do they reflect an interior self-examination, remorse, a change of heart, and a renewed commitment to God? It has been argued that the biblical notions of fasting, prayer, and confession are not, strictly speaking, *penitential* in the manner of later theology.[27] Even the Second Temple texts mentioned above that depict rending may not be as penitential as once assumed. Esther's prayer in Greek Esther 14 registers her difficult situation but does not explicitly focus on *interior* change. Esther specifically notes her sexual impurity but not her "sins" per se. Prayer of Azariah 16 may be the lone exception. This is an important question for placing Judith in a theological tradition. Does our text continue in a confessional tradition, or does it map out a more deviant or satirical path? It is also possible that Judith lies at the cusp of changes in confession and interiorizing theology. Indeed, if Judith engages in a proto-ascetic discipline, we are surprised that she calls to mind the rich biblical tradition of confession yet betrays no awareness of her own sins.[28] We may even say that she takes up the *genre* of confession but mentions only the outrages of the Assyrians. The Bethulians' weakness, condemned in chap. 8, is not noted here in her prayer.

Although the postexilic "penitential" theology is usually understood in relation to Deuteronomic theology, Angela Kim Harkins also turns to the figure who prays, the ritual enacted, and the social context. In this confessional tradition, the (male) figure who prays enacts

---

25 Cf. the very similar diagram for the disrobing, cleansing and reclothing of Christian baptism in Wayne A. Meeks, *The First Urban Christians: The Social World of the Apostle Paul* (New Haven: Yale University Press, 1983) 156.

26 Gera, *Judith*, 301.

27 David A. Lambert, *How Repentance Became Biblical: Judaism, Christianity, and the Interpretation of Scripture* (New York: Oxford University Press, 2016); Olyan, *Biblical Mourning*, 62–95.

28 Wills, "Ascetic Theology."

practices of self-diminishment: fasting, sackcloth, ashes, depilatory acts, anguished weeping, collapsing, and hands opened in supplication. The prayers themselves also contribute to the diminishment of the pray-er through the enactment of petitions, confession of sinfulness, and confession of God's greatness.[29]

Yet although the outward context of Judith's redressing scene is like that in Greek Esther and Joseph and Aseneth, there are important differences. First, there is a connection between Judith's prayer in chap. 9 and the other prayers in her text (6:18–19; 13:4b–7; 13:17; 16:13–17), and other direct speech as well. Schmitz traced a common theology in the speeches and prayers in Judith, and others followed.[30] Gera also discerns a difference in style in the narrative sections of Judith, on the one hand, and the speeches and prayers, on the other. The narrative betrays a strong Semitic style; the direct speech, Greek syntax. In Judith's speeches there are connectives, particles, and syntactic constructions not found in narrative sections. The prayer in chap. 9 utilizes chiastic poetic constructions, internal rhyme, and varying order of genitive and nominative. Not only is this typical of elevated Greek style, but in Hebrew the genitive cannot come first. In addition, "The speech sections of Judith are . . . less constrained by biblical precedent."[31]

Second, Judith expresses a sinlessness in her prayers and speeches, even a sense of self-righteousness in relation to the imperfect Bethulians. This is very different from Esther and Aseneth. Judith does not confess her own sins. Yet Harkins reminds us

that, in the penitential tradition, the man who prays for Israel does not register *his own sins*. The elevated male mediator—Moses in Exod 34:9, Ezra in Ezra 9, Nehemiah in Nehemiah 9, Daniel in Daniel 9—confesses the *community's* sins, not his own.[32] An external ritual process is depicted, creating an emotional experience, even a covenant-renewal experience, above all for the *text's* audience. Judith's sinlessness is therefore not unusual in this tradition, except for three aspects: first, she is a woman; second, she seems less sympathetic to the Bethulians' weakness; and, third, she certifies that Israel as a whole has been virtually sinless regarding idolatry (8:18).

Yet, in each of the three women's scenes, there is still a question of what the woman's new, "truer" identity is. In Greek Esther, the protagonist's beautified self is a false identity—"Oh Lord, you know that I despised the veneration I received from the lawless and loathed the bed of the uncircumcised or of any foreigner" (14:15). In Aseneth, her emerging identity is a conversion or even mystical identity—"She put on her new linen robe and placed around her the double sash of virginity, one sash around her waist and the other around her breasts" (14.8). But what is the "true" identity for Judith, the vamp who deceives? Is it to emerge as a harlot? We think here of Tamar (Gen 38:14–15). For Jerome, however, Judith's true identity comes when she puts her mourning garments back on at the end of the story and returns to seclusion:

We see here a woman vanquishing men, and chastity beheading lust. She quickly changes her garments, and in the hour of victory puts on once again her plain dress, finer than all the splen-

29 Harkins, "Function of Prayers," 80. The question of whether this tradition is penitential is raised by Olyan (*Biblical Mourning*, 65–70) and Lambert (*Repentance*, passim).

30 Schmitz, *Gedeutete Geschichte*; Gera, *Judith*, 296; Beentjes, "Bethulia Crying," 231–54; van den Eynde, "Crying to God," 217–31; Xeravits, "The Supplication of Judith (Judith 9:2–14)," in Xeravits, *Pious Seductress*, 161–78.

31 Gera, "Speech in Judith," 413, 417–18. We raise again the possibility that the direct speech and the narrative were composed by different hands, although this is unlikely.

32 Angela Kim Harkins, "A Phenomenological Study of Penitential Elements and Their Strategic Arousal of Emotion in the Qumran Hodayot (1QH cols. 1[?]–8)," in Renate Egger-Wenzel and Stefan Reif, eds., *Ancient Jewish Prayers and Emotions: Emotions Associated with Jewish Prayer in and around the Second*

Temple Period (DCLS 26; Berlin: de Gruyter, 2015), 297–316, here 303. In addition, a minor exception to Harkins's observation about the sinlessness of the one who prays may be Ezra 9:6–7. See also Eve Levavi Feinstein, *Sexual Pollution in the Hebrew Bible* (Oxford: Oxford University Press, 2014) 68. In Wills, "Ascetic Theology," a distinction is made between the stricken penitent—Esther, Aseneth, Qumran Hodayot, and most Christian asceticism—and the confident ascetic—Judith and Testament of Job. This distinction plays out in an interesting way in Paul, where it was formerly assumed, based on Romans 7, that he was a stricken penitent, although Krister Stendahl demonstrated that Paul exhibited a "robust" rather than an "introspective" conscience ("Paul and the Introspective Conscience of the West," in *Paul among Jews and Gentiles, and Other Essays* [Philadelphia: Fortress, 1976] 78–96).

dors of the world. (*Letter to Furia, Ep.* 54.16; my translation).

The inner identity of this trickster masters any performance. Judith the vamp can wear a courtesan's clothes with no risk of losing her identity. The three women thus go through similar processes, but emerge with very different missions. An idealization of this transformation scene is affirmed by some scholars. Says Esther Menn concerning Greek Esther,

> The almost voyeuristic scenes in Hellenistic Jewish literature depicting these women's radical alteration of their clothing, appearance, and comportment dramatize their protest and rejection of the values held dear by the foreign political worlds in which they move and occupy exalted positions, and their rightful alignment and devotion to the one true God. . . . The queen's body becomes the tangible means of her embrace of membership in an alternative community of those who similarly owe their exclusive allegiance to the one God.[33]

True, the women are transformed in regard to typical dress, to embrace an identity that is understood as God-against-empire. But if the scene is also similar to the redressing of warriors or ancient Near Eastern goddesses, is it as countercultural as it claims?

Aseneth's transformation scene is presented as a conversion, and this, along with the similarities to the *mikveh* in the later Jewish conversion ceremony (b. Ker. 8b), raises the question of whether Judith's actions are influenced by the conversion ritual.[34] One may object that Judith is not *converting* to anything and not really being *internally* transformed as Esther and Aseneth are. Her character is set; she is merely preparing for battle. It is possible, however, that all of

these scenes have in common an affirmation of a new *missional* identity in a colonized setting: the women go through the stages of mourning and emerge wearing beautiful, "public" clothes to effect their own or others' salvation. The new, beautified self sets out on a mission in the context of a voyeuristic empire. Free narrative introduces a set of coded obstacles—adultery, idolatry, foreign rule—and a strategy for opposing them—transforming the self.

■ 10:5

Judith gave her slave "a wineskin full of wine, a flask of oil, and filled a pouch with a barley loaf, a cake of figs, and fine bread."[35] Were these simply staple foodstuffs of the period, or do they signify something else? The fact that they are specified is suggestive. All but the fig cakes are associated with tithing and offerings in the temple. The roughly contemporary Temple Scroll 19–22 from Qumran extends the observances of food offerings beyond the list in Leviticus 23 and consists of barley, wheat, wine, oil, and also recounts a wood festival.[36] Judith also wraps up and packs her dishes, presumably to have separate dishes in the camp. In this period, a higher concern for the purity of dishes is indicated by the number of hewn stone vessels discovered; hewn stone, as opposed to clay pottery, was not considered susceptible to impurity.[37]

Excursus: Judith's Special Foods

Judith's transition from regular fasts to packing her food is somewhat similar to her transition from mourning garments to festive attire, yet the foods are everyday foodstuffs, not lavish or celebratory. Packing them along allows her to observe Jewish food

33   Esther Menn, "Prayer of the Queen: Esther's Religious Self in the Septuagint," in David Brakke et al., eds., *Religion and the Self in Antiquity* (Bloomington: Indiana University Press, 2005) 70–90, here 84.

34   Wills ("Ascetic Theology") references Michel Foucault and Geoffrey Harpham on developments in ascetic discipline and suggests how these developments appeared earlier than most have assumed. See also Satlow, "Be a Man."

35   Some texts add "and cheese"; see Moore, *Judith*, 201. From the eleventh century CE on, this became part of the Jewish tradition of Judith and was sometimes associated with Hanukkah. See §8 above.

36   Oil, however, is mentioned vaguely as a tithe in Num 18:12, as is "must," freshly pressed grape juice. See also Jdt 11:12–13 on Judith's ruse of the sin of the Bethulians to consume all the parts of the cattle, the firstfruits of wheat, and the tithes of wine and oil.

37   Roland Deines, *Jüdische Steingefässe und pharisäische Frömmigkeit: Ein archäologisch-historischer Beitrag zum Verständnis von Joh 2.6 und der jüdischen Reinheitshalacha zur Zeit Jesu* (WUNT 2/52; Tübingen: Mohr, 1993) 268–74; see also below on developments in purity practices.

laws while in the enemy camp, but it is unclear how these laws would have been observed in this period. First, it should be noted that the terms *kosher* and *kashrut* appear only later as standard terms for food laws; rabbinic and later Jewish practices, such as the prohibition of eating meat and milk together, should not be assumed. Biblical categories of dietary laws are not extensive. Leviticus 11 and Deuteronomy 14 provide lists of prohibited categories, which include animals that are "disgusting" to God (*šeqeṣ*) and thus prohibited. A different set of eating restrictions applies to blood, fat, and certain parts of the sacrificial animals, plants grown together in fields, or meat sacrificed to idols.

In particular, Judith is making preparations for eating while among gentiles. As early as Hos 9:3–4 and Ezek 4:13, there is a concern voiced that among gentiles one might be eating impure food, yet Jehoiachin dined at the Babylonian king's table (2 Kgs 25:29–30), and Nehemiah was the wine bearer for the Persian king (Neh 1:1). Carol Newsom suggests that in the Hellenistic period there was an increasing discussion of food-as-marker, but it was not consistent.[38] Daniel, for instance, resolved not to defile himself (*gā'al*, 1:8) with royal food and also wine, even though wine would not likely have been an issue until later (m. 'Abod. Zar. 2:3; 4:8–12; 5:1–12). It may, however, have been perceived as wine of libation for a Babylonian observance. The problem of observing Jewish food laws while in foreign lands was not even raised in MT Esther, although Greek Esther 14:17 emphasizes that Esther has observed the food laws. The avoidance of meat was a common strategy while away from home; there is a surprising universalizing of Daniel's observant practices in Josephus, *Antiquities* 10.10.2 §§190–194. Two centuries later, Christians who observed Jewish law also avoided eating meat for this reason (Clementine Homilies 12).

We are perhaps to perceive in Judith's dietary practices a *general* concern for the protection of Jewish identity, as referenced in Aristeas 139, 142, 145–56, and 3 Macc 3:2–4. To the extent that the book of Judith tells the story of a heroic quest, the food, her bathing, and the lambskin on which she sits are almost like magical protections for her while she is in the wilderness. The food, bathing, and lambskin together protect her, even though, like her extended mourning period, they may lie outside normal halakic restrictions.

Even though our text is quite vague about the specific concerns of food laws, in her deceitful speech to Holofernes in 11:11–15 Judith will be much more specific about the supposed grievous sins of the residents of Jerusalem that provoked her to abandon them: they will consume all the parts of their cattle, including those parts forbidden by God, and eat the firstfruits of wheat and the tithes of wine and oil, which were reserved for priests. These are not general food laws but laws pertaining to temple offerings, a point that Judith emphasizes strongly. The text once again reflects a temple-centered perspective.

Judith also bathes as part of her preparation and redressing. In their redressing scenes, Esther does not bathe, while Aseneth does. Moore suggests vaguely that the immersion is a preparatory ritual for prayer, but he does not explain the background of the practice.[39] Judith will also bathe while she is in the Assyrian camp (see 12:5b–9). Are the two bathing actions equivalent? Is the bathing here a ritual cleansing, part of a cosmetic process, or something else? Bathing for hygienic or cosmetic purposes was not typical in the ancient world, but there is a sexual association of wealthy ladies at leisure and bathing: for example, Bathsheba (2 Samuel 11), or Susanna. For Judith, the bathing may indeed be sexual, cosmetic, *and* ritually purifying for the woman's mission for God.

■ 10:6–10

The previous section depicted Judith's prayer and preparations; this section continues the narrative arc by describing her departure, accompanied by her slave. She crosses the threshold of the gate of Bethulia from known, safe space to unsafe space. This will be balanced in 13:10–14 by her marked return across the threshold back to Bethulia.

The actions of the two women are drawn out by the last-minute interactions with the elders. Important novelistic techniques are explored here. Retardation and acceleration of action are often related, used in an alternating fashion. In this passage we find retardation, while

38 Newsom, *Daniel*, 47–48. Cf. Ezek 4:13; Tob 1:10–11; Greek Esth 14:17; 1 Macc 1:62–63; 2 Macc 5:27; 3 Macc 3:4; Aristeas 139, 142, 145–46; Aseneth 7:1, 8:5; Jub. 22:16; and Josephus, *Life* 3.14.

39 Moore, *Judith*, 219.

in the central scene of the beheading, the action will be accelerated. Everything the audience has been prepared for, partly by the slow observation of action here, will take place there—surprisingly—in just a few verses. Dialogue is also used here in tandem with ritual actions. The verbal and physical exchanges become almost ceremonial as the two women first find the elders, receive Uzziah's blessing, bow down, ask the elders to open the gate, wait for them to have the order executed, and depart the city. Uzziah and two elders, Chabris and Charmis, have a certain authority in fictitious Bethulia, but in addition, Uzziah functions to provide a blessing of the gods on the heroine.[40] The narrator does not need to state directly that Judith is now beautiful; rather, the audience is told that Uzziah, Chabris, and Charmis are "greatly astounded at her beauty." The male voyeurism is focalized through their eyes and will continue just below, as her departure is seen from their point of view. The words of the three elders celebrate her mission and are almost liturgical, as they pray that "the God of our ancestors" fulfill her plan "for the glory of Israelites and the exaltation of Jerusalem." Jerusalem is always at the center of the political theology of Judith.

■ **10:8** As for the statement "she bowed down to God," the text is uncertain. Many good witnesses have this reading. Her bowing is a last pious gesture before departing, a conclusion of the ceremonial dressing and mission. Judith's heroic preparation (9:1—10:5) both begins and closes with her bowing to God, an *inclusio* as she readies for combat. Moore, however, conjectures a misreading in Hebrew and emends the text to "she bowed down to *them,*" that is, to the men.[41] For Moore, this fits the narrative better; she makes a similar bow when she first comes before Holofernes (10:23; compare also 14:7, where Achior does obeisance to Judith). Her bow to the elders would then communicate her dutiful respect for their position. The two bows, in that case,

provide a contrast with her commanding personality. But would she act deferentially before the elders? The bow is more likely to God, corresponding to the bow in 9:1, and provides another pious inoculation for her transgressive plan.

■ **10:9–10** Judith instructs them, "Now command that they open the town gates for me." In 1:3–4 we saw the military aspect of city gates: they must be opened for the expeditionary forces to exit the walled city. A mountain village would not have gates to speak of—yards and sheepfolds might have small wooden gates to restrain animals, but no city gates. As noted in 6:10–21, Bethulia, a mountain village, is treated as a city.

Just as there is an *inclusio* at the beginning and end of her preparation for combat, the opening of the gates here for her departure and also for her return in 13:11 constitutes an *inclusio.* In her structural analysis of Judith, Craven also registered the narrative importance of the going and coming through the gate. These actions correspond to each other in the chiastic arrangement of the second half of Judith, coming before her journey into the valley.[42] In 13:11 she will call out poetically, but here in prose. Her power over others is communicated also by the transitive property of authority: she can provide a prime cause for a string of actions, here noted in italics:

> Then she said to them, "Now *command* that they open the town gates for me, and *I will go forth* to *accomplish* all the things you spoke of with me." *They ordered* the young men to open the gates as *she had said,* and *they did so.* Judith *went out,* together with her slave, and *the men of the town continued watching her* until she had descended the mountain and crossed the valley and *they could no longer see her.*

40   Bowra, *Heroic Poetry,* 184–86. Chabris and Charmis were first mentioned, in the same auxiliary role, in 6:15; see there for the comic aspects.

41   Moore conjectures that she bowed to them, *'lyhm* for *l'lhym* (*Judith,* 201–2), while Corley ("Septuagintalisms," 95) avers that the text as it is—bowed to God—makes sense. Yet bowing to a heroine as an epiphany of a deity occurs in Aseneth 18:11 and

Greek novels; see Meredith Warren, "A Robe Like Lightning: Clothing Changes and Identification in *Joseph and Aseneth,*" in Kristi Upson-Saia, et al., eds., *Dressing Judeans and Christians in Antiquity* (Oxford: Taylor and Francis, 2016) 137–55, here 138.

42   Craven, *Artistry and Faith,* 62–63; see §3 above.

"Open the gates" may resonate as part of the call in the Divine Warrior myth, in which the young god such as Ba'l proceeds out to battle. The Divine Warrior can be observed in Exodus 15, an important source for Judith, and in many other passages as well.[43] Related to this is the victory shout of the people (Ps 89:15), which may also resound in Judith 16. The image of opening gates also occurs in texts such as Ps 118:19–20, a psalm well known from the Passover celebration (see also Psalm 24). But Judith's command is to open the gates for a journey into the zone of danger. In Judges 3, Ehud also moves out into a dangerous zone to slay an enemy.[44]

■ **10:10** The fact that the departure of Judith and her slave and their encounter with the Assyrians occurs at night is not often noted. Why at night? One may suggest that there was a full moon or that she took a lamp or torch, but this matters little. The liminal state of her passing is perhaps underscored, or the element of exposure or danger, although the text offers no answer.

Alonso-Schökel rightly described her departure as "cinematographic," and Mieke Bal calls our text a "story of vision," because the cinematic and voyeuristic effects are constant.[45] In the case of Judith, her now-magnified beauty has just been described, so the men's perspective is both cinematographic and voyeuristic. The male point of view of the elders is reproduced for the audience. The transitional observation in 10:10, "they could no longer see her," also uses this cinematographic view of the elders to mark the limit of where the men are willing to go. The danger, however, will be perceived only for Judith, not for her slave. And since the Assyrians will also view Judith lustfully, there will soon be more voyeurism. Several centuries later, "cinematographic" scenes will be found in the Greek novels, most notably the opening of Heliodorus's *Ethiopian Tale*.[46] A different cinematographic scene is found in Achilles Tatius, *Leukippe and Cleitophon* 3.15, that is quite relevant here: the protagonist, describing ritual sacrifice, says that everyone looked away while he continued to watch in shock. The audience wants lurid details and watches through the character's eyes.

---

43   Deuteronomy 33; Judges 5; 2 Samuel 22; Isaiah 24; 42; 51; 60; 64; Ezekiel 38–39; Hab 3:3–6, Zechariah 9; Job 38; Psalms 29, 46, 48, 68, 77, 89, 99, 104, 114, 148. Postbiblical Jewish and Christian texts also included the Divine Warrior; see 1 En. 1:3–8; 102:1–3; Jub. 31:18–20; Sir 43:9–26; Wis 5:17–23; 4 Ezra 11; 13; Ps.-Philo, *Biblical Antiquities* 11; 5; 2 Bar

59:2–3; T. Levi 18:2–4; Revelation 12. See most recently Ballentine, *Conflict Myth*.

44   Mobley, *Empty Men*, 81–85.

45   Alonso-Schökel, *Narrative Structure*, 7; Bal, "Head Hunting," 277.

46   Tomas Hägg, *The Novel in Antiquity* (Berkeley: University of California Press, 1983) 55–56.

Text

11/ As Judith and her slave were passing[a] straight through the valley, an Assyrian patrol met her. 12/ They placed her under guard and began to question her: "To what people do you belong? Where do you come from? Where are you going?" She said, "I am a daughter of the Hebrews, but I am fleeing from them because they are about to be handed over to you to be devoured. 13/ I am now on my way to meet Holofernes, commander-in-chief of your army, to give him a true report. I will show him a way by which he can advance and take control of all the high country without losing a single man, captured or killed."

14/ As the men listened to her speaking and gazed upon her face, she seemed marvelously beautiful to behold. They said to her, 15/ "By hurrying down to meet our lord, you have saved your life. Now go to his tent; some of us will escort you and hand you over to him. 16/ When you stand before him, have no fear in your heart, but tell him what you have told us and he will treat you well." 17/ They chose a hundred men and arranged them alongside her and her slave, and they led them to the tent of Holofernes.

18/ A commotion spread throughout the encampment, as news of her arrival was announced from tent to tent. Soldiers came and gathered around her as she stood outside Holofernes's tent, waiting until they informed him about her. 19/ They marveled at her beauty,[b] and marveled at the Israelites as well on her account, saying to one another, "Who could despise this people that has women such as this among them? It would not be good to allow a single man of them to live; those released would be able to outwit[c] the whole world."

20/ Holofernes's guards[d] and all of his attendants came out and brought her into the tent. 21/ Holofernes was reclining on his bed behind a canopy interwoven with purple, gold, emeralds, and other precious stones. 22/ They informed him about her, and he came out into the forechamber of the tent, with silver lamps going before him. 23/ When Judith came before him and his attendants, they all marveled at the beauty of her face. She fell down and knelt before him, but his slaves raised her up.

a   For ἐπορεύοντο: ἐπορεύετο O 534 OL Sy Sa Eth; the singular ignores the slave's presence. The text is also singular in the next clause.

b   Also read in 58 OL Sy: και παρεδεχοντο τους λογους αυτης οτι ησαν αγαθοι σφοδρα, "they accepted her words because they were very good."

c   The playful verb here provoked some textual variants; for κατασοφισασθαι, κατασοφισαι 71, σοφισασθαι 126, καταψηφισασθαι 542.

d   Παρακαθευδοντες, "those who sleep beside"; the verb can be used for a sleeping dog or guards on duty at night. Other texts read παρακαθεζοντες 106´; παρεστωτες 126; παντες οι παρεδρευοντες O OL Sy.

Commentary

10:11–23

As noted in the introduction, the second half of the novella is structured by a chiasm, simplified here:

A Introduction of Judith (8:1–8)
  B Judith with the Bethulians (8:9–10:9a)
    C Judith and her slave depart (10:9b–10)
      D Judith engages Holofernes (10:11–13:10a)
    C´ Judith and her slave depart (13:10b–11)
  B´ Judith with the Bethulians (13:12–16:20)
A´ Conclusion about Judith (16:21–25)

The present section begins the central moment in the chiasm of the second half. We move to the much-anticipated meeting of Israelite and Assyrian. It has been delayed for nine chapters, but as Judith and her slave are challenged by Assyrian guards, the story will begin to move more quickly. The retardation of plot in the preceding scene is followed by acceleration, communicated by more urgent words: the women "were passing straight through the valley," "I am now on my way to meet Holofernes," "Now go to his tent." Judith's plan, which has been anticipated but not described, is also beginning to be realized. The audience doubtless knew where the story was heading—it is a common aspect of popular narrative performance that the audience knows the stories well—but they would take delight in hearing the story performed.

Judith is now seen by men four times in quick succession, 10:7, 13, 14, 18. "The structure of the text," says Rakel, "is the same each time, repeating itself to the point of monotony and thus exposing the male gaze to ridicule."[1] Rakel suggests that by repeating the male gaze, the author satirizes it, although this may reflect a postmodern sensibility and not the typical reception of the ancient audience, whether male or female. At

any rate, Judith actively establishes herself in the role of object of male voyeurism—not her real identity but a temporary and strategic performativity. By worldly standards, the Assyrian soldiers would have the upper hand, but the audience takes pleasure in seeing the manipulative Judith at work.

This scene also exhibits an increased use of novelistic dialogue, which continues through chap. 12. There was direct quotation before in Judith and dialogue as well—the council meeting of Holofernes and his advisors, the dialogue of Holofernes and Achior, and Judith's exchange with the elders—but from this point on dialogue becomes more central to the text performance. The exploitation of novelistic dialogue is not a minor accomplishment; it is the stock-in-trade of the novel genre.[2] Dialogue, as we shall see, is also an apt medium for irony. Oral narratives rely less on dialogue, presumably because back-and-forth speech is difficult for one performer to create. If, as suggested in the introduction, ancient novels—Jewish, Greek, Roman, and Christian—may have been performed aloud as dinner, festival, or liturgical entertainments, we would still distinguish between oral storytelling and the reading of novelistic entertainments. At any rate, in novelistic literature cross-culturally, dialogue is more highly developed to create multiple characters' zones and to communicate their viewpoints and enduring character traits.

■ **10:12–13**

When Judith enters the Assyrian camp, she introduces herself as a "daughter of the Hebrews." There are not many identity terms for Israelites in Judith, but Hebrews is also used by the Assyrians (12:11; 14:18). The narrator also refers to the people as Israelites, as do the surrounding enemy nations (5:23; see the commentary on 4:1–15). The origin of the term "Hebrew" will not be addressed here, but its continued use to express identity in an international context is noted.[3] In the Apocrypha,

---

1   Rakel, "Judith: About a Beauty," 523; see also Wright and Edwards, "She Undid Him," 73–108; and §5 above.

2   We find moments of dialogue in the Joseph story—which is itself proto-novelistic—and elsewhere in the Hebrew Bible (1 Kings 22), and even between patriarchs and God (Gen 18:16–33). Dialogue is

also explored at times in Herodotus and Ctesias. Plato's "dialogues" are highly stylized philosophical discussions and occasionally include novelistic dialogue, especially in *Symposium*.

3   See Gen 14:13; Exod 1:15; Josh 24:2; and esp. Gen 39:14 and Jonah 1:9. In Gen 10:21, "Hebrew" may possibly be understood as referring to descendants

the term appears only in Judith (10:12; 12:11; 14:18) and in 2 Macc 7:31; 11:13; and 15:37 in very loaded identity affirmations. It is later found in Paul (Phil 3:5), in the title of the Epistle to the Hebrews, in Aseneth 1:4–5, and in the law-observant Christian Pseudo-Clementine literature. Is "Hebrew" perceived here as a more ancient and formal term, appropriate for converse with the great empires? It may be used to contribute to historical coloring or perhaps was perceived as the common term used in discourse with foreigners (compare at 14:18).

Judith's presence, with only a slave, would have caused suspicion, but her explanation to the soldiers justifies her presence and starts her full plan in motion. She provides them with a reason for her coming to the camp, which the book's audience would perceive as a ruse. She will repeat it in more detail to Holofernes in 11:5–19. Judith says that she is bringing to Holofernes a true report, *rhēmata alētheias*, but the audience will learn—and probably already knows from the tradition—that what she will say is as far from the truth as one can imagine. This is the first marker of a new zone in the narrative. She is already lying, and she knows that the most effective lie is the one that people want to hear. Now that she is in the Assyrian camp, every word out of her mouth will be deceitful, and every action will be deceitful, sexually provocative, or murderous.

■ 10:14–19

The long section dominated by comic dialogue and irony begins not with Judith or Holofernes or even Bagoas, but with the Assyrian soldiers, who discover the beautiful lady and her slave wandering in a field and escort them to Holofernes's quarters. The narrative exposition continues the male voyeurism, in that all is described from the soldiers' point of view: the men gazed upon (*katenoēsan*) her face.[4] The voyeurism will be a constant in the last half of Judith, commented on more explicitly in 10:19, but it is not only sexual. Judith's appearance also brings out a patronizing protectiveness in the Assyrian soldiers: "Have no fear in your heart. . . . Holofernes will treat you well." Choosing a hundred men to escort her is also surely a comic exaggeration, maximizing the effect that she has had on the soldiers. Judith is hosted as a visiting celebrity, because in the Assyrians' eyes her beauty will earn her a role as Holofernes's courtesan, and then also Nebuchadnezzar's.

Based on her example, the Assyrian soldiers draw conclusions about Israelite women in general: "Who could despise this people that has women such as this?" This trope is found also in Aseneth 1:4–5:

> [Aseneth was] tall and comely, and more beautiful than any young woman on earth. Indeed, she bore little resemblance at all to Egyptian women, but was in every way more like the women of the Hebrews: as tall as Sarah, as comely as Rebecca, as beautiful as Rachel.[5]

Comparable also is 1QapGen 20.2–6 concerning Sarah. In the Greek novels, it is assumed that the beauty of the protagonists is evidence of the superiority of Greeks.

The broad humor reminds the modern reader of a screwball comedy, but it brings with it a different narrative foreshadowing: the more the soldiers think they have taken charge of her, the more she is conducting them to their doom.[6] Their pomp and show are matched only by their obtuseness. At the same time that they remark on the danger of her power over men, she is working it on them. Her agency, indeed her power over others, extends to the fact that the Assyrian soldiers are drawn into her language game. The depiction of these mighty Assyrian soldiers will approach slapstick again in chap. 15 when, in their panic, they trip over each other to escape the overwhelming force of . . . highland villagers!

The soldiers' words also provide an overture to the extended irony that is coming, in which many lines can be understood in two ways, depending on whether the

---

of Eber. The Maccabee references are 2 Macc 7:31; 11:13; 15:37; 4 Macc 4:11; 5:2, 4; 8:2; 9:6, 18; 17:9.

4   On the multiple layers of voyeurism in Judith, see §5 above and the excursus below at 14:14–18, "Judith 14:18 as Peripety and the Theme of the Book."

5   Translation of Wills, *Ancient Jewish Novels,* 124.

6   See also Esler, *Sex, Wives, and Warriors,* 293.

word "lord" (*kyrios*) is understood to refer to Holofernes or to God: "You have saved your life by hurrying down to meet our lord. . . . Some of us will escort you and hand you over to him." The audience would have caught the double references. One can imagine an audience game of discerning each occurrence, and many will follow.

Novelistic description is expanded here beyond what one would find in early Israelite prose. It is more like the Greek novels, where the beautiful hero and heroine often cause astonishment among those who meet them. This propels the plot by endangering both the hero and the heroine, who are lusted after time and time again. In Judith, the same effect is created for our heroine, even though it is she who has created the situation and manipulates it. Judith *controls* the lust, thus differentiating our text from both the Jewish and Greek novels. (See also §7 above.)

■ 10:20–23

We first encounter Holofernes in his tent, which is symbolically parallel to Judith's tent of isolation. Judith's tent in Bethulia was a retreat from the world, even a temple in miniature, while his is a palace in miniature. Very active in the first half, Holofernes is now "resting on his bed," and will remain stationary, isolated, and even passive, while his officers and Judith come to him in his tent. In the Greek texts on the East—Herodotus and Ctesias—the courtesans have their place in the inner bedrooms of the palace, and the kings move in and out. Here it is Holofernes who rests on his bed languorously. While on her mission, Judith is very active and dynamic, moving constantly and with remarkable freedom into the camp, about the camp, and ultimately out of the camp; cross-culturally, the hero is a boundary-crosser.

In Chariton we encounter a similar interaction of a great military leader and a beautiful woman in a camp, although the leader in this case—the king of Babylon—equips himself with far more philosophical restraint than does Holofernes. As he leads an army out to battle,

the King had by no means forgotten Callirhoe; the recollection of her beauty came back to him even in that indescribable confusion. But he was too embarrassed to mention her; he did not want to be thought altogether adolescent, thinking of a pretty girl in the middle of a war like that. He did not say anything to the Queen herself, or even to the eunuch who knew about his love; but he devised the following plan. It is customary for the King himself and the Persian nobility, when they go off to war, to take along with them their wives and children and gold and silver and clothing and eunuchs and concubines and dogs and dining-room furniture and their costly treasures and luxuries. So he summoned the man in charge of this. After much preliminary talk, . . . he ended up by mentioning Callirhoe with a well-counterfeited expression meant to convey that it did not matter to him. "Oh," he said, "that foreign girl whose case I undertook to judge—she can come along with the other women." (*Chaereas and Callirhoe* 6.9)[7]

This later text could not have influenced Judith, but both may reflect traditions such as Ctesias and the Alexander Romance.

The decorations of Holofernes's tent are rendered in detail, revealing sumptuous royal field quarters. There is a novelistic aspect to the dramatic scene-setting. Compare also the bridal chamber in Xenophon of Ephesis 1.8:

The wedding chamber had been prepared: a golden couch had been spread with purple sheets, and above it hung an awning with an embroidered Babylonian tapestry. . . . Under this canopy they brought Anthia to Habrocomes and put her to bed, then shut the doors.[8]

Holofernes sits "behind a canopy"—likely a mosquito net (*kōnōpion*)—"interwoven with purple, gold, emeralds, and other precious stones." Schmitz notes that *kōnōpion*

7   Translation of B. P. Reardon in *Collected Ancient Greek Novels*, 100.
8   Translation of Graham Anderson in Reardon, *Collected Ancient Greek Novels*, 132–33.

is not attested in the Bible, Greek texts, ancient Near Eastern texts, or archaeology until the first century BCE, after the usual date of Judith.[9] There it occurs as a loanword in Latin, *conopium*. Horace and Propertius use it in regard to Cleopatra, and Varro in regard to an aristocratic Roman woman. In all three cases, it is a negative image of effeminacy and luxury. The indulgence of his curtain and tent, of course, are contrasted with the spare self-denial represented by Judith's tent of isolation.

Crucial to the plot is the fact that the mosquito-net-as-curtain creates an inner and outer chamber. Textiles are described often in ancient literature and can increase a sense of mystery: "[C]oncealment is also the opportunity for a performative theatricality of ostentation."[10] There is a resemblance to the Jerusalem temple, with an inner chamber (the holy of holies) and an outer chamber, separated by the highly symbolic temple curtain. Some of the colors are the same (Exod 26:31).[11] We hear from Pliny the Elder (*Natural History* 8.196) that "weaving different colors into a pattern was made fashionable in Babylon, from which it derives its name." Exorbitantly expensive, Arrian says that Babylonian cloth, representing opulence and luxury, covered the tomb of Cyrus (*Anabasis* 6.29). At Chariton, *Chaereas* 8.4, a special royal tent is set up on a ship, "with its sides made of purple, gold-stitched Babylonian cloth." The "Babylonian weave" was perhaps even associated with the Jerusalem temple curtain; according to Josephus (*Jewish War* 5.5.4 §212), the curtain in the temple was similar to the Babylonian

tapestry of the cosmos. Yet, while such fabrics are appropriate for the temple curtain, the strange woman of Prov 7:16–17 entices with furnishings, "colored spreads of Egyptian linen."

Gold and silver have already been used in our text as evidence of status for Nebuchadnezzar (2:18), for Israelites (5:9), and even for Judith in her previous life (8:7). Some ancient authors aver that gold, silver, and stone as symbols of gods serve as an appropriate way of theologizing about gods and kings.[12] This was critiqued, however, by other Greek philosophers, the Jewish idol parody narratives (Isa 44:9–20; Wis 13:10–15:17), and Acts 17:29. Tacitus (*Historiae* 5.5.4) noted specifically how Jews, because of their aniconic beliefs, lacked this way for appropriately honoring gods and kings.

Evident here is an element of contempt for eastern court luxury and perhaps also the belief that such luxury is not appropriate in Israel. The sumptuous court decorations of the Persian king are perhaps mildly satirized in Esth 1:6–7. In Greek tradition, the luxury of the eastern court was viewed with fascination, but also with condemnation and the belief that luxury would destroy military resolve.[13] Alexander Romance 2.14 describes Darius's robes in a way very similar to Holofernes's tent: "his crown set with precious stones, his silk robes woven with gold thread in the Babylonian style, his cloak of royal purple, and his golden shoes studded with gems which covered his shins." Greek depictions of Persians in general focused on luxury, military equipment, freedom

9   Barbara Schmitz, "Holofernes's Canopy in the Septuagint," in Brine, Ciletti, and Lähnemann, *Sword of Judith*, 71–80, here 77. Crawford notes the similarity to Jael's *śĕmîkâ* in Judg 4:18, likely a skin used as a rug or covering ("In the Steps of Jael," 9). However, both the net here and the sheepskins below do not seem to be similar in narrative function to Jael's rug.

10   Jaś Elsner, "Relic, Icon, and Architecture: The Material Articulation of the Holy in East Christian Art," in C. Hahn and H. Klein, eds., *Saints and Sacred Matter: The Cult of Relics in Byzantium and Beyond* (Washington, DC: Dumbarton Oaks Publications, 2015) 13–40, here 17; see also the commentary below on 13:9b–10a and the remarks of Branham, "Penetrating the Sacred."

11   The colors of the Jerusalem temple curtain are played upon in a symbolic way in Aseneth; so Cyn-

thia Baker, personal communication. On the Greek references, see Morgan, "Representation of Philosophers," 29. See Arrian, *Anabasis* 6.29; Chariton, *Chaereas* 8.4.7; Josephus, *Antiquities* 3.6.4 §124; 7.7 §183; Philo, *On Mating* 117; *Laws* 1.84, 3.33; *On Flight and Finding* 110; *Life of Moses* 2.17.84–85; 3.6; *Questions on Exodus* 2.85.

12   Pliny, *Natural History* 33.54; Dio Chrysostom, *Orations* 12.44. The philosophical critique is found in Plato, *Republic* 416e–417a; Plutarch, *On Superstition* 167E, 170E; Suetonius, *Caligula* 21–22; see Strait, "Wisdom of Solomon," 609–32.

13   Yoshinori Sano, "The Representations of the Persian Empire," in Johannes Unsok Ro, ed., *From Judah to Judaea: Persian Period: Socio-economic Structures and Processes in the Persian Period* (Hebrew Bible Monographs 43; Sheffield: Sheffield Phoenix, 2012) 197–204; Enslin, *Book of Judith*, 133–34.

versus slavery, and in particular Darius as a representative of hubris. All of these relate to Judith.

According to 1 Macc 1:22, Antiochus IV Epiphanes had confiscated the temple curtain in Jerusalem. Holofernes's multivalent netting, then, in part representing his "temple curtain," will be taken to Jerusalem as a plunder offering (16:19). Given the gender reversals in Judith, the effeminacy of Holofernes's role, and Judith's penetration of his tent, the tent canopy may also symbolically represent Holofernes's effeminacy and even his hymen.[14]

■ **10:23** In 9:1 Judith prostrated herself before God; here she shows equal humility before Holofernes as part of her ruse; she will even refer to herself as his slave (11:5). Judith can be as strategically obsequious to Holofernes as she is imperious to the elders of Bethulia (8:11). The trickster-hero can change modes effortlessly.

Despite some similarities of motif between Judith's entrance and the scene in Greek Esther in which the heroine comes before Ahasuerus, the tone of the two could not be more different. Greek Esther 15:6–7:

She came before the presence of the king, as he sat upon his royal throne, dressed in the awesome radiance of his majesty and covered with gold and precious jewels—a formidable sight! He lifted his face, flush with the power of his bearing, and glared at her in anger. The queen suddenly swooned, turned pale and faint, and collapsed upon the slave at her side.[15]

Even though Ahasuerus is a foreign king, the Esther novella paints a picture of an awesome, authoritative king of a great empire—and God will soften his disposition. The author of Judith, however, demythologizes the power of Holofernes's jewel-encrusted camp tent and, in a subtle move, insists that Holofernes and his attendants all marveled at the beauty of *her* face. *She* is the one who is radiant as the sun. She does, to be sure, bow humbly before him, but the attendants, unbidden by Holofernes, instinctively raise her up. A common motif in the Greek novels is that the heroine is recognized by others, including barbarians, as being too beautiful to be a slave. A similar effect is communicated here: they sense, without being commanded, that she is to be treated with respect. Still, the quotation from Esther does call to mind another scene in Judith: when Achior is feminized by fainting upon seeing the head of Holofernes (14:6).

14 See Schmitz, "Holofernes's Canopy," 77; and for the canopy as his hymen, see §5 above.
15 Translation of Wills, *Ancient Jewish Novels*, 40.

Text

1/ Holofernes said to her, "Take courage, woman, and have no fear in your heart, for I have never harmed anyone who chose[a] to serve Nebuchadnezzar, king of all the earth. 2/ But as for your people who reside in the high country, if they had not slighted me, I would never have raised my spear against them. Now they have brought this upon themselves. 3/ But tell me, why have you fled from them and come to us? For you have saved yourself. Take courage; you will live tonight and hereafter. 4/ There is no one who will harm you, but one who will treat you well, as it happens for all of the slaves of my lord, King Nebuchadnezzar."

5/ Judith said to him, "Heed the words of your slave, and allow your servant to speak before you. I will say nothing false to my lord tonight! 6/ And if you follow closely the advice of your servant, God will accomplish a great deed through you, and my lord will not fail to achieve what he has prepared. 7/ For as Nebuchadnezzar, king of the whole earth lives, and as his power lives, who sent you to bring order for every living being, not only do people serve him on account of you, but even the beasts of the field and the cattle and the birds of the air will live through your might on account of Nebuchadnezzar and his entire household.[b] 8/ For we have heard of your wisdom and the clever strategies of your heart.[c] It is proclaimed throughout the whole earth that you alone are best in the whole kingdom, able in experience and marvelous in military strategy. 9/ But as for the speech that Achior gave in your council, we have heard his words, since the men of Bethulia spared him, and he recounted to them all that he had uttered in your presence. 10/ Therefore, my lord and master, do not disregard his speech, but take it to heart, for it is true. Indeed, our people will not punished,[d] nor does a sword have power over them unless they sin against their God. 11/ But now, so that my lord not be frustrated and fail to achieve his goal, death will descend upon them. A sin has overtaken them by which they are about to provoke their God to fury, at whatever time they commit their misdeed. 12/ When their food had run out and all their water was scarce, they decided to turn to their cattle,[e] and resolved to consume all the parts that God had commanded them in his laws not to eat. 13/ Also they have

a   For ηρετικεν: ηκεν S; ηθελησε 534.

b   Επι plus accusative is ambiguous, and translations vary. The NEB notes the problem and translates, "will owe their lives to your power as long as Nebuchadnezzar and his dynasty reign," but includes the alternative, "will live at the disposal of Nebuchadnezzar and his household."

c   Πανουργευματα can be either positive—"great accomplishments"—or negative—"crafty deeds"—with irony.

d   See Enslin, *Book of Judith,* 138 n. 10.

e   Vg 11:11 simplifies the infraction, but adds "and drink their blood"; see Moore.

f   Rahlfs prefers the future participle μετακομισοντας ("those who will take the message") found in some minuscules, while Hanhart reads an aorist participle, μετακομισαντας ("those who have taken the message"), found in B A. The latter makes no sense in this context.

g   For διφρον (which Moore translates as "chariot seat"): θρονον V *a* 126 311. NAB translates "judgment seat."

decided to consume entirely the firstfruits of wheat and the tithes of wine and oil that they have consecrated and reserved for the priests who serve in the presence of our God in Jerusalem, things that those of the laity are not to touch with the hands. 14/ They have even sent messengers[f] to Jerusalem to ask permission from the council, because they who dwell there have done the same things. 15/ And so when they send word to them and they act upon it, on that day they will be given over to you for destruction. 16/ Thus, when I, your servant, found out that these things had occurred, I fled from them, and God sent me to you to accomplish deeds about which the whole world, as many as hear about it, will be astounded, 17/ because your slave is pious and serves the God of heaven night and day. And now I will remain with you, my lord, and your slave will go out by night to the valley and pray to God; he will tell me when they have committed their transgressions. 18/ I will then return and report to you, so that you may go out with your entire army, and there will be no one among them who will oppose you. 19/ I will lead you through the middle of Judea until you arrive at Jerusalem, where I will set your seat[g] in its midst. You will lead them like sheep for whom there is no shepherd, and no dog will so much as growl in your presence. All of this was proclaimed to me as foreknowledge and announced to me, and I was sent to announce these things to you."

20/ Her words pleased Holofernes and all his attendants, and they marveled at her wisdom and said, 21/ "There is not a woman like her from one end of the world to the other for beauty of face and intelligence of speech."

22/ Holofernes said to her: "God has done well in sending you before your people so that control may fall into our hands, while there will be destruction for those who despised my lord. 23/ You are both elegant in your appearance and refined in speech; if you do as you say, your god shall be my god, and you shall sit in the house of King Nebuchadnezzar and be famous throughout the world."

Commentary

11:1–23

At the first meeting of Holofernes and Judith, he is a powerful general, she servile and flattering. They both play their parts, but she is laying the groundwork for a great reversal, at which point he will be weak and passive. Holofernes has grandiose designs on Judith, both for himself and for Nebuchadnezzar, but it is actually Judith who has effective designs: she is in complete control of the situation and manipulates Holofernes and everyone else to her own ends. Holofernes's words here indirectly characterize Nebuchadnezzar, and the audience would see this as a Danielic theme, even though other biblical examples could be cited, for example, Ahasuerus in MT Esther (not quite the same in LXX); King Eglon in Judges 3; Ahab in 1 Kings 21–22. Holofernes

318

also conforms to the Greek negative model of the blustery tyrant (see §4 above; and the commentary on 8:35).

Holofernes entertains his beautiful visitor very graciously. This might be seen as a sort of expediency on his part, as he realizes he can deliver her unharmed to Nebuchadnezzar as a prized courtesan. But, as in the Greek novels, extraordinary protagonists come before monarchs, generals, and elites and are treated with awe and respect (see 10:23). Judith's own courtly respect for her host, however, is part of a web of deceit; there is a continuing irony and humor derived from the fact that her obsequious lines have two meanings depending on whether "lord" refers to Holofernes (and sometimes Nebuchadnezzar) or God: "I will say nothing false to my lord tonight," "my lord will not fail to achieve what he has prepared" (see irony at 10:14–19). It is her beauty and ability to manipulate through lying that will propel her plan forward. Holofernes's words as well resonate on two levels: "You will live tonight and hereafter!" (11:3), which signifies for the audience her heroic memory.

■ 11:1–4
Holofernes begins by saying "Have no fear," similar to what the divinity says in an ancient Near Eastern theophany, but this form may also reflect the supposed language of a king at court (see also Greek Esth 15:12). Holofernes's questions sound similar to his questions about the Israelites at the beginning of chap. 5. There, however, when Achior responded with excellent information and advice, the general reacted as a blustery tyrant and banished his wise adviser. Here Holofernes is fawning and reassuring: he will protect Judith from all harm. It could be argued that Holofernes himself views his different tone here as strategic—Judith is a prize to be turned over to Nebuchadnezzar—but the audience likely perceived his words as evidence that he is blinded by her beauty and acts foolishly, and this will be confirmed.

■ 11:5–8
Judith claims to speak the truth, but lies in almost every line. Her first words are also couched in the courtly

modes of address of an inferior to a superior. Courtly wisdom and language were well known in Israel as a literary trope. It was the basis of the Jewish court narratives; Esther and Daniel were indeed very good at it. Judith also speaks at times in parallel lines, which mimics biblical poetry:

> Heed the words of your slave,
>> and allow your servant to speak before you.

> God will accomplish a great deed through you,
>> and my lord will not fail to achieve what he has prepared.

> δέξαι τὰ ῥήματα τῆς δούλης σου,
>> καὶ λαλησάτω ἡ παιδίσκη σου κατὰ πρόσωπόν σου.

> τελείως πρᾶγμα ποιήσει μετὰ σοῦ ὁ θεός,
>> καὶ οὐκ ἀποπεσεῖται κύριός μου τῶν ἐπιτηδευμάτων αὐτοῦ.

Judith's speech, by this technique, is perhaps connected to a prophetic channeling of God's will, but it more likely depicts Judith treating Holofernes with a ceremonial and exaggerated respect. There is even here a charming use of archaizing and poetic style. Holofernes's preceding lines occasionally reflect two-part statements connected by *kai*, but they are not in poetic pairs. They mimic instead the language of ordinary speech.[1]

■ **11:7** Nebuchadnezzar's protection of animals reminds the audience of Dan 2:38, the imperial rule that God has temporarily bequeathed to him (see the excursus at 3:8, "Nebuchadnezzar and Danielic Motifs"). Judith swears by Nebuchadnezzar, as he had sworn by himself in 1:12 and 2:12, but Judith slyly references God as well. Is Nebuchadnezzar's correction, *katorthōsis*, an ironic contrast to God's? (See §7 above.)

■ 11:9–18
Judith explains to Holofernes why her people are about to be abandoned by God, which recalls Achior's speech in 5:5–21. The situations of Judith and Achior are often quite parallel (see excursus at 5:3, "Achior the Ammo-

---

1   Holofernes's words are still stylized, but not in biblical parallelism. Verse 1 ("Take courage . . . serve Nebuchadnezzar") forms an *inclusio* with vv. 3b–4 ("Take courage. . . . servants of Nebuchadnezzar").

nite"). There Achior the Ammonite had served as an unexpectedly fair-minded commentator. Here also Achior has been an unintentional partner of Judith in that his account of God's role in Israelite history has prepared Holofernes to hear and accept Judith's similar explanation: If Israel has sinned, then their God will not protect them and they will surely fall.

Achior's and Judith's speeches are equally accurate in the audience's eyes, the former speech demonstrating its supporting role—one might even say its providential role—in the novella. But there are two important differences. The first has to do with truth-telling. Achior said that "nothing false will come out of my mouth," and it is truly and sincerely uttered, as opposed to Judith's similar declaration in 11:5, a bald lie. The overly earnest Achior had spoken only the truth—and had gotten himself severely punished for it—while Judith will use this view of history as the basis for a great lie: now Israel is about to sin and will easily fall. The second difference is Holofernes's reaction.

The polytheistic religions of the ancient Near East would generally accept that a people's strength in war was a function of the strength of their gods. Israel struggled to counter this, however, by asserting that its military setbacks resulted not because God was weak but because God, though stronger than the other gods and nations, had chosen to punish Israel. It is God, then, who will inform Judith when the violation has occurred and, according to Judith's ruse, it is God who will *allow* the foreign nations to destroy Israel. This would hardly be an acceptable divine explanation to the Assyrians, and in fact such a view had angered Holofernes when Achior the Ammonite had uttered it. Yet Holofernes accepts this view from Judith's mouth quite gladly. Is he seduced by her beauty, and then won over by her theology of history, or does he simply sense an easy victory over her and her people and sees no need to contradict her? The text does not say at this point, but over the course of the next chapter the general will seem to believe everything she says.

■ **11:12-15** Judith must also explain to Holofernes precisely what the sin consists of that will provoke God to abandon Israel. Otzen notes that, despite the theme of devotion to God in Judith, this verse contains the only use of the word *nomos*.[2] Although the question is often raised about a less law-oriented Jewish identity in Hellenistic Judaism, it is likely the case that our text is fully nomistic. The audience is also aware that there was an *actual* sin of the Bethulians—they were weak-willed and feckless and put a deadline on God's intervention—but this would not suffice for Judith at this point in the story. For the Jewish audience of the novella, although not for any foreign general, her ruse requires a sin involving Jewish boundary markers. Judith offers up a showcase example, a distinctive marker of Judaism, unlike the essentially Greek philosophical moral failing contained in her earlier rebuke of the elders (see excursus at 8:35, "The Book of Judith and Greek Philosophy"). The narrative logic demands that Holofernes would see it as some special law that binds Israel to God—what Israel would call covenant—and at no point does he doubt or question her account as he did Achior's. (Later he will readily allow her Jewish diet and lustrations as well.) A case has been chosen that requires a complicated description involving practices that could be understood only in the context of the Israelite laws of temple sacrifices. The example highlights the centrality of priestly practices, a theme, no doubt, about which the Hasmonean leaders would have wanted to make assurances. While in Jewish law compromise provisions had been entertained in times of danger—one such occurs in 1 Macc 2:32–41 regarding the Maccabean Revolt—Judith states here that God would not overlook the particular violation at hand. On the story level, it is part of Judith's deception of Holofernes, and it works well within this farcical narrative.

Geoffrey Miller has interestingly argued that Judith does not *need* to lie at this point in regard to the sin of Israel,[3] but from the literary point of view it helps her gambit. She must weave a web to entrap Holofernes, but, more to the point, this description is *for the audience,* not Holofernes. The playing out of the sin of Israel contrasts with the piety that the author elsewhere assumes for the Hasmonean rulers. Miller notes further that Judith need

2   Otzen, *Tobit and Judith*, 104.
3   Miller, "Femme Fatale," 231–32.

not say she is going out to pray in order to find out from God when the sin has occurred, but this is likewise also part of a design to reel Holofernes in and is intended for the audience, not for our befuddled general.

Because the list of violations is intended for the audience, some details are supplied that would be insignificant for Holofernes. As their food and water have become exhausted, the Bethulians are prepared to "kill their livestock" and "to consume all the parts that God had commanded them in his laws not to eat." This may refer to slaughtering their animals without draining the blood properly, as Lev 17:10–14 stipulates and as Acts 15:20 references. (The Vulgate understood it in this way, but this may be a Christian interpretation; see also the excursus at 10:5, "Judith's Special Foods".) Certain parts of the slaughtered animals should be restricted to the priests. Further, out of desperation the Bethulians will now consume the firstfruits of grain and the tithes of wine and oil that were reserved for temple offerings. Judith's tale of the fall from civilized practices almost reads like the cannibalism that arises in the Greek novels. Yet it is a highly representative and symbolic list of the main categories of temple sacrifice. These are precisely the same offerings that Maccabee rebels had made in an alternative temple service at Mizpeh just before they captured and rededicated the Jerusalem temple (1 Macc 3:49). More to the point, if the book of Judith was a Jerusalem writing, the audience would recognize the temple sacrifices as the heart of the city's renewed sacred economy.

Now her ruse will involve not just the Bethulians but the Jerusalem authorities as well. The special status of the temple priests and the rules associated with the tithing come into play: non-priests could not so much as touch the offerings once they had been consecrated. The Jerusalem council, so she says, has allowed the citizens to eat these offerings and is about to extend permission to Bethulians to follow suit. Bethulia is awaiting messengers from Jerusalem bearing this permission. Judith tells Holofernes that she must pray to learn the exact time that the transgression has occurred, but the audience would perceive the similarity between this deadline and the deadline that the Bethulians had earlier placed upon themselves. The emphasis on tithing here also comports in a general way with the Pharisees' emphasis on proper tithing—but not so precisely as to offer evidence for the Pharisaic connection that some scholars have seen in Judith.[4] In the excursus on Greek philosophy (8:35) it was noted that Judith imposed on the Bethulians a stricter standard of prayer than was the case earlier in Israel. Even in her false narrative, her strictness about what could or could not be done in a crisis was perhaps greater than earlier practices. In 1 Sam 21:2–7, David and his companions, suffering from hunger, eat the consecrated bread (referenced also at Matt 12:1–4). Finally, Judith continues with an ironic double-entendre: "God has sent me to accomplish with you things that will astonish the world."

■ **11:17** Judith presents herself as a very righteous (*theosebēs*) Israelite, serving God night and day, which the audience knows to be true, yet even this is folded into her false narrative: it is *because* she is devoted to Israel's God that she will inform *against Israel*. That Holofernes would not question this is absurd, but plausibility means little here. In addition, her stated *theosebeia* provides her with the pretext for her last demand on Holofernes's hospitality: Judith and her slave must go out each night to pray to God, during which time God will communicate when he has made his judgment against Israel.

■ **11:19–23**

Judith's statements here are sometimes half-true, when one understands how the story will resolve. Her statement "I will lead you through the middle of Judea, until you arrive at Jerusalem" is true, although it will be in defeat: Holofernes's head will be taken to Bethulia, and many of his possessions to Jerusalem as plunder offerings. Judith also continues her strategy of assimilating Nebuchadnezzar and Holofernes to ancient Near Eastern as well as biblical theological themes. Her words are like an "oracle of salvation" from Second Isaiah (e.g., 40:3–4); when she says, "There I will set your seat (throne)," she attributes to her adversaries aspects of the throne theology, the city as the throne of God. This

---

4   See §2 above: grain, wine, and oil were to be tithed; see Deut 12:17; 14:23; 18:4; Neh 10:40; and cf. Tob 1:6–7, and see also the commentary on 10:5.

is similar to God's promise to David (2 Sam 7:13; cf. Jer 3:17). She continues by saying, "You will lead them like sheep for whom there is no shepherd," a common image of the importance of leaders in Israel.[5]

The audacity of Judith's words concerning her role is only increased by her assumption of prophetic inspiration (*prognōsis;* see 9:6 on God's *prognōsis*). It is ironic on many levels: she is prophesying while addressing a foreign general, an enemy of Israel, but she is lying, which, surprisingly, makes it acceptable.[6] She is a lying prophet, although even this is not unique in Israel. But, unlike the false spirit of prophecy that God was said to have sent in 1 Kings 22, Judith is *knowingly* propounding a false prophecy—in fact, words that are not really a prophecy at all—in order to save Israel. In the Deuteronomistic histories, God works through imperfect people, but a common theme in Judith is that she is virtually perfect, and it is she who wills a deceptive stratagem and effects its success. Both Achior (5:21; 6:2) and Nebuchadnezzar (6:3) also had moments when they seemed to prophesy; so Judith as well. When Achior had spoken by "prophecy," Holofernes condemned him to death, but here he and the entire Assyrian command are struck by her words (vv. 20–21). Although it is her *wisdom* that is celebrated here by the Assyrians, the audience knows it is her *cleverness* that allows her to deceive them. Here she enacts the Jacob ideal, not the Joseph ideal.

■ **11:21–23** Holofernes confirms Judith's ironic statements by accidentally speaking again in an ironic double-entendre: "God has done well in sending you . . . while there will be destruction for those who despised my lord." As Judith's zone in this narrative is to speak cleverly and deceptively, Holofernes's zone is to speak as a self-deluding fool or *alazōn*. He happily talks his way into a decapitation.

Excursus: "Your God Shall Be My God"

Captivated by Judith, Holofernes willingly makes statements that reverence the God of Israel: "Your god shall be my god," recalling Ruth 1:16; 3:1–2. He subordinates himself to Judith without realizing it, and in the eyes of the audience, he is taking up the speech of a famous woman.[7] He is also at least giving lip service to the workings of the God of Israel. There is some background to this in our novella. Otzen points out the irony that in 3:8 the Assyrians assumed a "monotheistic" stance about Nebuchadnezzar, but Judith later insisted (8:20) that it is Israel who knows only one God.[8] In addition, it could be hyperbole when Holofernes says, "Who is god except Nebuchadnezzar?" (6:2), or an ironic contrast that Holofernes *thinks* he has found his one true god. Yet here, when the general is impressed by Judith, has he transferred over from the influence of Nebuchadnezzar to the influence of Judith?

"Your god shall be my god" must also be seen in its ancient Near Eastern context. In polytheistic systems, kings could embrace the gods of other peoples as a way of soliciting alliances or even as advance propaganda for defeating them. Cyrus claimed that his defeat of the Babylonians was ordained by *their* god Bel. And in Israel there appears to have been monotheistic negotiation with this motif, as foreign leaders were depicted as becoming convinced of the Israelite God's powers (Dan 2:47; 3:28–29; 4:34–37; 2 Maccabees 3; cf. 2 Kgs 5:17). Holofernes is perhaps even more effusive than Nebuchanezzar in Daniel, but he also sees sex in his future. And we cannot rule out that Holofernes assumes that Judith will adopt *his* god, especially if she becomes a courtesan of Nebuchadnezzar. Hans J. L. Jensen argues that Holofernes's confession pulls the Israelite God down into the world of Nebuchadnezzar; that is, the confession assimilates God by treating this deity like the other conquered peoples' gods.[9] Perhaps, but the audience enjoys the irony of the general's *attempt* to impose a benevolent superiority when he is so thoroughly lacking in strategic skills.

There is yet another possibility: Holofernes may be speaking a deeper truth without knowing it. Judith's God will be his God in judgment. This may be the audience's understanding. To complete Holofernes's ironic pronouncement of doom on his own head, he concludes that Judith "will be renowned throughout the whole world," which she will, holding his head in her upraised

---

5   Cf. Num 27:17; 1 Kgs 22:17; Isa 40:11; Ezek 34:8; Zech 10:2; 13:7; Matt 9:36; also: Jdt 11:19 (dogs that will not growl); and Isa 56:10–11.

6   Vague, but only vague, parallels may be seen to the foreign prophet Balaam counseling King Balak of Moab in Numbers 22–24; 31:16.

7   Sheaffer, *Envisioning*, 121–22.

8   Otzen, *Tobit and Judith*, 101.

9   Jensen summarized by Otzen, *Tobit and Judith*, 121.

hand. Again moving to the audience's perspective, Holofernes's confession of loyalty to Judith and her God is a parodic contrast to Ruth's—parodic, in that Holofernes believes that Judith will come to the palace of Nebuchadnezzar, Israel to Assyria and not Moab to Israel. Compare here Holofernes's earlier contrapositive: if he fails she will ridicule him. His self-elevation here, then, is as marked as his earlier fear of being shamed. For a weak leader, the public assertion of strength and the secret fear of weakness go together. Schmitz sees this dynamic as the explanation for how a woman could kill a man,[10] if such an explanation is needed.

---

10   Schmitz, "Holofernes's Canopy," 80. See Sheaffer, *Envisioning*, 121–22.

Text	Textual Notes

Text

1/ He then commanded that she be brought into the place where his silver vessels were laid out, and commanded that she be served some of his delicacies and some of his wine to drink. 2/ But Judith said, "I cannot partake of these, lest it be an offense, but my food will be provided from the things brought with me."

3/ "But if what you have with you runs out," said Holofernes to her, "from where shall we provide food of a similar kind for you, as there is no one among us of your people?"

4/ Judith said to him, "(I swear) as you live, my lord, your slave will not use up what she has with her before the lord accomplishes by my hand what he has planned."

5/ Holofernes's attendants then led her to her tent, where she slept until the middle of the night. Just before the morning watch she arose 6/ and sent word to Holofernes saying, "Let my lord issue a command to allow your slave to go out for prayer." 7/ Holofernes then instructed his bodyguards not to hinder her. She remained in the camp three days, and each night she proceeded out to the valley of Bethulia and bathed in the spring in the camp.[a] 8/ When she came out of the water, she prayed to the Lord God of Israel to direct her path for the triumph of his[b] people. 9/ Thus purified, she entered camp and remained in her tent until she brought forth her food toward evening.

10/ On the fourth day, Holofernes gave a feast for his slaves alone and did not invite any of his officers. 11/ He said to Bagoas, the eunuch who was in charge of all his affairs, "Go now and persuade the Hebrew woman in your charge to come join us to eat and drink. 12/ We would have to hide our faces in shame if we pass by a woman such as this without having intercourse with her. If we cannot seduce her, she will ridicule us."

13/ Taking leave of Holofernes, Bagoas entered Judith's tent and said, "Such a fair young woman as you should have no hesitation in coming before my lord to be honored in his presence and joining us in wine and merriment. Today you can become like one of the Assyrian women who serve in Nebuchadnezzar's palace."

14/ "Indeed, who am I to refuse my lord?" Judith said to him. "I will do at once anything that pleases him; this will bring me joy till my dying day."

Textual Notes

a Εν τη παρεμβολη is found twice in the sentence. Moore adopts the conjecture of C. F. Movers ("Über die Ursprache der deuterokanonischen Bücher des A.T.," *Zeitschrift für Philosophie und katholische Theologie*, Part 13 [1835] 31–41) that מהנדה ("from the uncleanness") was read as במחנה ("in the camp"), but this is speculative. Corley ("Septuagintalisms," 93–94) argues that it is dittography, but I have chosen to retain both.

b Hanhart reads αυτης (*O* V), but αυτου is well represented in B S A *L* and minuscules. Moore follows Hanhart.

c Moore (following Zimmermann) suggests a complex series of misunderstandings of a Hebrew original, but Corley ("Septuagintalisms," 89–90) sees no need for this: the text was ετηρει καιρου του απατησαι, "he was observing a time to seduce her." Later Christian scribes preferred εζητει καιρον του απαντησαι, "he was seeking a time to meet her." Εζητει is read by *O* OL Sy Arm.

15/ She arose and beautified herself with garments and every feminine adornment. Her slave then proceeded and laid out lambskins on the ground before Holofernes, which she had received from Bagoas for her daily practice, to recline on while eating. 16/ Judith then entered and reclined upon them, and Holofernes's heart leapt from him on account of her. He was aroused with passion, enflamed with the desire to lie with her. From the day he saw her he had been waiting for an opportunity to seduce her.ᶜ 17/ "Drink up," Holofernes said to her, "and join us in revelry."

18/ "Yes, I will indeed drink, my lord," said Judith, "for my life today has been magnified for me more than ever since I was born."

19/ She then took what her slave had prepared for her, and ate and drank with him. 20/ Holofernes was delighted with her, and drank vast amounts of wine, more than he had ever drunk in one day since he had been born.

Commentary

12:1–20

In this chapter Judith finally engages her enemy, but not on the actual battlefield; rather, as is appropriate for a novelistic text, the action takes place in a domestic setting. This encounter between Judith and Holofernes, especially their dialogue, suggests a "harem intrigue" like those in Ctesias's courtly narratives of the East, which had also influenced Esther. Judith's ironic exchanges with Holofernes are also similar to those found in Greek tragedies, but here irony is in the service of comedy, not tragedy (see the commentary on 10:14–19).

Although we saw above that Judith's sharp upbraiding of the elders (8:11–17) violated cultural standards—to a degree greater than modern readers register—Judith's outright violations of sexual ethics and truthfulness all occur in the liminal period of her sojourn in the zone of danger, between the time that she exits the gates of Bethulia and the time she returns through them. This is the zone in which her most important actions occur, the acts that cause her to be sung as a heroine, even if she is understood as a fictitious heroine. Judith had prayed in 9:10 for a deceitful tongue. She now displays it, although we are not told explicitly whether it is God's gift or her own native talent.[1]

■ 12:1–5a

Holofernes's speech throughout this chapter reflects both desire and the delay of gratification. There is a tension present that the audience would experience erotically through the voyeurism of Holofernes, and the asides of Holofernes to Bagoas indicate that he has lost his self-mastery. He is descending into *akrasia* (see the excursus at 8:35, "The Book of Judith and Greek Philosophy"). Judith, on the other hand, remains in total

---

1 See excursus at 9:8–10, "Judith's Hand and Agency"; the Vulgate also ascribed her increase of beauty to God's intervention; see the appendix below. On the question of whether Judith's actions might be seen as encouraging others, or indeed as feminist, see §5 above.

control and communicates to Holofernes a reciprocity and a different kind of excitement on her part. This serves to arouse Holofernes further; the mouse is torturing the cat. Judith creates a feedback loop to manipulate the general into losing his restraint. This will not happen immediately; his actions in chap. 13 will complete it, and the soldiers will follow his model. The layers of desire, tension, and manipulation that exercised European artists and audiences are present in the original text. And indeed Judith *is* apparently excited, but for a hidden reason.

With courtly manners, Holofernes entertains Judith, providing as many luxurious accommodations as the battlefield will allow. His tent is furnished with all of the luxuries of a palace: silver dinnerware, delicacies, an embroidered curtain. The tent of the representative of an eastern monarch requires a palace-in-miniature; the king is present wherever his representative sets his tent. (In *Chaereas* 8.4.7, the special royal tent is set up on a ship.) Are we to take these furnishings as the typical accoutrements of command in the field, or as the sort of excessive luxury associated with eastern potentates that was criticized in many Greek histories? In Herodotus the overindulgence in luxury is a theme of the downfall of Xerxes, who may have been a model. Demaratus had warned Xerxes just as Achior had warned Holofernes; there is a "Xerxizing" of Holofernes.[2] At the end of his life, Xerxes was also drawn into harem intrigues and was considered to be at the mercy of a queen.

Judith's statement of her dietary needs is similar to Dan 1:8–16, a century or two older (see excursus at 10:5, "Judith's Special Foods"). Surprising is Holofernes's graciousness in responding to her dietary restrictions and her special prayer needs. He understands her requirements immediately as a Jewish boundary practice, even if it is partly fictitious and contrived. He has vowed to destroy nations; here he is a magnanimous facilitator of Jewish particularism. He sees her *precisely* as she wants to be seen, and her manipulation is total. This is ironic, of course, because her requests stem partly from piety and partly from treachery, a combination that the audience would have enjoyed. He gladly accedes to her requirements out of deference to her position, even showing added concern that she may not have enough food. His solicitousness almost suggests a discourse of equals, not quite the treatment of the courtesan. The Greek novels will later depict beautiful heroines who are sometimes treated graciously by potentates. In those cases, as in Esther, the vulnerability of the heroine remains in play, but in our text Judith is not vulnerable—she is, rather, circling for the kill. A wonderfully ironic touch is Judith's oath in 12:4, "as you live, my lord;" she *swears* by the assurance of his long life, when she is about to end it!

■ **12:5a** We are expressly told that Judith slept in her own tent. It serves as a narrative pause, similar to those pauses in the first half (see at 2:28 and §3 above), but it functions more as an assurance to the audience that she did not sleep with Holofernes, a fact she will emphasize upon her return to Bethulia (13:16). It was only in the modern period that artists began to suggest that she actually had sex with Holofernes, although in the sixth century the historian John Malalas seems to suggest that she slept with the general (see §8 above).

■ **12:5b–9**

Why does Judith spend three days in the camp (v. 7)? In terms of storytelling, this would provide an appropriate amount of time for her to enact her stratagem—she must establish a pattern of going out to pray—but in addition, the vow of the Bethulians had imagined God acting within five days. If she leaves Bethulia on one day and passes three days in the camp, the next day, the day of the battle, would be the fifth day. "Toward evening" (v. 9) also recalls her prayer at the time of the evening incense in 9:1, and many of the biblical washings noted above stipulated that the waiting period of purification extended till evening.[3] She is perhaps viewed as fulfilling the time requirement to be cleansed, and eats her

---

2   Although Xenophon of Athens had argued that rugged and austere living strengthened the wise leader Cyrus of Persia (Xenophon, *Cyropaedia* 1.3.4–7; 1.6.8; 1.6.17; 4.2.40–47; 4.5.1–4, 7, 54; 5.1.1–8), the more typical Greek view was that luxury had weakened the eastern kings; see also §4 above.

3   In regard to bathing, the Hebrew term *rāḥaṣ* was used in the Bible for both general and ritual bathing (e.g., Lev 14:9). It is not usually immersion,

acceptable food only when the waiting period is over. (On parallels to Pharisaic practice, see §2 above.)

She arranges to go out each day to bathe and pray at a spring outside the camp, establishing a pattern that will allow her to escape unhindered on her final day. All of her actions, then, though they may be devotional, contribute to her greater plan to deceive the enemy. Moving daily outside the camp may call to mind the temple motif of conducting certain ritual actions outside the camp, despite the fact that some ancient texts of Judith locate the spring "in the camp" (v. 7; cf. 7:3: the camp was *epi tēs pēgēs*). It is in the valley of Bethulia, so it is likely to be understood as outside the camp proper but close enough to serve as its water source.

Although the text does not explicitly label the actions as "outside the camp," the ritual, priestly, and temple motifs in the book all taken together may suggest this resonance. The pentateuchal legislation was enjoined on Israel while the people were wandering in the wilderness; in those texts the camp prefigures the later temple compound. When the ark was being transported, many potentially impure functions, especially elimination-of-impurity rituals, were enacted "outside the camp" to protect the purity of the camp (Num 5:1–4).[4] In the red heifer ritual, the priest's washing occurs outside the camp, and the man who burns the remnants of the sin offerings must do so outside the camp. The one suffering from scales ("leprosy") must also live outside the camp while unclean. Whereas the biblical legislation is concerned with maintaining the purity of the tabernacle *within* the camp, Judith ironically moves outside the camp to bathe and pray, thus avoiding the impurity of Holofernes's tent—a mock-temple within the camp? The reversal, even confusion, of the narrative's satiric act and the biblical referent may be part of the farcical, Purim-like experience of the text.

That the "outside-the-camp" motif could be taken up and yet reversed is indicated by Heb 13:11–12. There it is emphasized that, when the bodies of animals offered for sin are burned outside the camp, the high priest brings the blood inside the sanctuary (Exod 29:14; Lev 4:11–12, 21). The author of Hebrews draws from this that Jesus is the opposite, going outside the camp to bear his reproach, in the zone where potentially impure parts were eliminated and burned. Jesus is also crucified outside the camp so that his blood might sanctify the people; his blood moves in the opposite direction of the priests' administration of blood. But the book of Judith does not explain its understanding; we are simply left to wonder whether there may be a satirical meaning to her reversal: she is taking her pure observance outside of Holofernes's impure "temple" compound, in a way opposite of the priestly practices of "outside the camp."

Excursus: Bathing and Related Issues

In addition to Judith's bathing in her dressing scene in chap. 10, her daily regimen while in the Assyrian camp includes bathing each day in a spring—an unbelievable practice in the presence of 182,000 foreign soldiers! However, a beautiful woman bathing is almost as common in ancient Israelite literature (Bathsheba, Susanna) as in Hollywood westerns, though strangely absent in Greek novels.[5] Does she bathe as a prelude to prayer, to purify herself, as an erotic scene, or all of these? As in chaps. 9 and 10, the motivations of her ritual actions are not explained. The text couples her bathing with her prayer: "When she came out of the water, she prayed to the Lord God of Israel to direct her path for the triumph of his people." Perhaps for this reason, Moore suggests that her bathing is a preparation for prayer.[6] But v. 9 adds that "she returned (from the bathing) purified" (*eisporeuomenē kathara*), which reminds us that both

---

even if it removes *ṭum'â*, ritual impurity. Where the early biblical texts assumed total immersion, *ṭābal* is used (e.g., 2 Kgs 5:14), and similarly in rabbinic usage *ṭābal* ("dip") became the technical term for ritual bathing. The rabbis assumed total immersion, rather than the washing of parts, from Lev 22:6–7 (Sifra Emor 4:7), and where *rāḥaṣ* appeared, it was now taken to mean full immersion, and was replaced by *ṭābal*. But this may have already begun in the Second Temple period, indicated by the use of *baptizō* (as opposed to *louō*) in Sir 34:25; see

Yonatan Adler, "The Hellenistic Origins of Jewish Ritual Immersion," *JJS* 69 (2018) 1–21.

4 See esp. David P. Wright, *Disposal of Impurity: Elimination Rites in the Bible and in Hittite and Mesopotamian Literature* (SBLDS 101; Atlanta: Society of Biblical Literature, 1996).

5 Bathsheba, 2 Sam 11:2; Susanna, Dan Th 13:15–21; cf. Gen 35:22; 49:4. Note also Jub. 33:2; 39:1–9; T. Reub. 3:11; and *Shepherd of Hermas* 1.1.1–9.

6 Moore, *Judith*, 219.

purity and preparation for prayer are relevant. (Compare *ekatharisthē ho laos* in 16:18.)

Her preparations in the camp and the decapitation of Holofernes seem to mimic highly stylized Jewish ritual processes. Though they do not comport *precisely* with what we know of Jewish rituals, they resonate as a sort of idealized, even fictitious Jewish observance. The following actions should be noted:

1. Judith bathes and prays each night outside the camp, and eats afterwards.
2. Her only food is that which she has brought with her.[7] Her slave bears it in a pouch, and this same pouch will later be used to carry Holofernes's head back to Bethulia.
3. While in the enemy camp, Judith sits on a lambskin.

Now, it is possible that her bathing while in the Assyrian camp has only the most general association with piety and purity and should not be overinterpreted. Yet the possibility that there are other, more particular resonances with her ritual acts must at least be entertained. If the similar scenes in Greek Esther and Aseneth are also noted, the comparisons become even more compelling. It is also unwise, however, to assume that any later development must be present *in nuce* in Judith.

In 10:3 Judith had bathed before praying *and dressing*, which is similar to the high priest's bathing before dressing at Yom Kippur. Here Judith bathes before praying *and eating*, similar to the case of the priest who has incurred impurity and must bathe before eating (Lev 22:6).[8] This law evidently loomed large as a salient principle of priestly practice, and if Judith were to be symbolically likened to a priest—an open question—then this ideal would lie behind her pious discipline: she bathes before eating her special food on her own dishes (10:5).

Modern readers will likely associate Judith's bathing with the *mikveh*, but, as was noted at 10:3, this association would be much less obvious at the time of composition of the book. *Mikvaot* had a long background in biblical religion. They were, for instance, constructed for pilgrims approaching the temple and were thus not originally related to women's purity.[9] In the late Second Temple period, there were important developments that expanded the use of *mikvaot*. Following the Maccabean Revolt evidence can be found not only of a nativist revival—an archaizing Hebrew script and distinctive Judean Herodian lamps—but also a broad increase in purity concerns: ritual bathing and washing of hands, and a greater reliance on hewn stone vessels thought not to be susceptible to impurity.[10] Andrea Berlin speaks of the rise of "household Judaism" throughout Judea in this period, which includes *mikvaot*:

7   Judith has also brought along her own dishes. The food in her bag consists of wine, oil, roasted grain, fig cakes, and bread, similar to Abigail's food for David (1 Sam 25:18; cf. 1 Chr 12:41), but Abigail's food also includes meat. Gera suggests that Judith's lack of meat indicates "asceticism" (*Judith*, 333), on which see below. Does Judith have "pure" loaves? Cf. "pure loaves of bread" in Ezek 4:9–15; Tob 1:10–11; m. 'Abod. Zar. 2:6; and see Grintz, *Book of Judith*, 147–48; and Randall D. Chesnutt, "Perceptions of Oil in Early Judaism and the Meal Formula in Joseph and Aseneth," *JSP* 14 (2005) 113–32, here 129. Cheese, also included in the Vulgate and in textual variants, was emphasized in the medieval Jewish texts; see §8 above; and Pierre-Maurice Bogaert, "La halakha alimentaire dans le livre de Judith," in Michel Quesnel, et al., eds., *Nourriture et repas dans les milieux juifs et chrétiens de l'antiquité: Mélanges offerts au professeur Charles Perrot* (Paris: Cerf, 1999) 25–40, here 30–34.

8   Judith's former isolation tent might have suggested the *liškat parhedrîn* or *palhedrîn*, the apartment within the temple where the high priest resided for the seven days prior to Yom Kippur (m. Yoma 1:1–2). The high priest's isolation was to ensure that he would not be exposed to his wife's menstrual impurity or the impurity associated with sexual intercourse. On the relation of Judith's supererogatory mourning and Jewish and later Christian ascetic practices, see the commentary on 8:4–6.

9   Aristeas 106. See Ronny Reich, "The Synagogue and the *Miqweh* in Eretz-Israel in the Second Temple, Mishnaic and Talmudic Periods," in Dan Urman and Paul V. M. Flesher, eds., *Ancient Synagogues: Historical Analysis and Archaeological Discoveries* (2 vols.; SPB 47; Leiden: Brill, 1995) 1:289–97; Jodi Magness, *The Archaeology of Qumran and the Dead Sea Scrolls* (Grand Rapids: Eerdmans, 2002) 145–50. That Judith bathes in a spring may be significant as well. In rabbinic law (m. Miqw. 2-7) "drawn water"—collected through human agency—was forbidden for a *mikveh*.

10   On stone vessels, see Deines, *Jüdische Steingefässe*, 71–115, 268–74; and Ofra Guri-Rimon, et al., *"Purity Broke Out in Israel" (Tractate Shabbat, 13b): Stone Vessels in the Late Second Temple Period* [in Hebrew] (Haifa: University of Haifa, 1994), and see m. Ohalot 5:5.

Mikva'ot allow individuals to purify themselves in connection with household-based events. . . . [B]oth the installations and the practice they allow advertise ethnic identity and proclaim cultural separation.[11]

The bathing structures under discussion have been unearthed dating from the mid-second century BCE, but there is debate about whether some may simply be Roman-influenced baths.[12] Even in that case, however, the emphasis on purity should not be discounted. It is not impossible, then, that the combination of a rise in purity concerns and the increase of either Roman-influenced baths or *mikvaot* gave rise to a romanticized depiction of our heroine's practices—and this even if women's post-menstrual ritual bathing did not become widespread until later.

Yet Judith's actions differ from practices associated with *mikvaot*. In biblical and rabbinic law, a woman is to bathe at the end of her menstrual period or after an irregular genital discharge, and in either case only once (Lev 15:19–24). Judith, however, bathes each day she is in the Assyrian camp, and

there is no suggestion that she had been in menses or had a genital discharge.[13] The usual associations of *mikvaot,* then, do not appear to be suggested here. In rabbinic Judaism, ritual immersion was a required part of proselyte initiation, but as in the case of the *mikveh,* there is no evidence for this practice as early as Judith, and indeed ritual bathing is not required of Achior (14:10).

Aside from the *mikvaot,* however, ritual bathing was known in many different contexts in Israel, more often for men than for women. The Israelites as a whole are to wash their clothes as part of their consecration in anticipation of God's descent on Mount Sinai (Exod 19:10–11; cf. 29:4). The men who release the scapegoat and burn the remains of the sin offerings outside the camp bathe before reentering (Lev 16:26–28), and in the ritual of the red heifer the priest washes his clothes and also bathes outside the camp (Num 19:7). On Yom Kippur the high priest bathes and puts on special linen garments to perform the liturgy,[14] but in a manner that seems the opposite of Judith's, he changes from splendidly embroidered garments to plain linen—liminal

---

11 Andrea Berlin, "Manifest Identity: From *Ioudaios* to Jew," in Rainer Albertz, ed., *Between Cooperation and Hostility: Multiple Identities in Ancient Judaism and the Interaction with Foreign Powers* (JAJSup 11; Göttingen: Vandenhoeck & Ruprecht, 2013) 151–75, here 169. See also Jonathan D. Lawrence, *Washing in Water: Trajectories of Ritual Bathing in the Hebrew Bible and Second Temple Literature* (Academia Biblica 23; Atlanta: Society of Biblical Literature, 2006); Adler, "Between Priestly Cult and Common Culture: The Material Evidence of Ritual Purity Observance in Early Roman Jerusalem Reassessed," *JAJ* 7 (2016) 228–48.

12 Ronny Reich tends to interpret all pools as *mikvaot* ("*Miqva'ot* [Jewish Ritual Baths] in the Second Temple Period and the Period of the Mishnah and Talmud" [in Hebrew; Ph.D. diss., Hebrew University of Jerusalem, 1990; Reich, "The Bath-House [Balneum], the *Miqweh* and the Jewish Community in the Second Temple Period," *JJS* 39 [1988] 102–7). More cautious are Katharina Galor, "Qumran's Plastered Pools: A New Perspective," in Jean-Baptiste Humbert and Jan Hunneweg, eds., *Science and Archaeometry at Khirbet Qumran and 'Ain Feshkha: Studies in Archaeology and Anthropology,* vol. 2 (Fribourg: Presses Universitaires de Fribourg, 2003) 169–98; Benjamin G. Wright III, "Jewish Ritual Baths—Interpreting the Digs and the Texts: Some Issues in the Social History of Second Temple Judaism," in Neil Asher Silber-

man and David Small, eds., *The Archaeology of Israel: Constructing the Past, Interpreting the Present* (JSOTSup 237; Sheffield: Sheffield Academic Press, 1997) 190–214; Hanan Eshel, "The Pools of Sepphoris—Ritual Baths or Bathtubs? They're Not Ritual Baths," *BAR* 26 (2000) 42–45, 49; and Lawrence, *Washing in Water.* A more comprehensive corpus of archaeological evidence is now available in Yonatan Adler, "The Archaeology of Purity: Archaeological Evidence for the Observance of Ritual Purity in Erez–Israel from the Hasmonean Period until the End of the Talmudic Era (164 BCE–400 CE)" (Ph.D. diss., Bar-Ilan University, 2011).

13 The medieval Jewish tales of Judith assume that she is in menses, but why then bathe three days? According to Gera , this indicates a lack of imagination on the storyteller's part concerning a woman's ritual outside of menstruation (*Judith,* 373).

14 Lev 16:4, 24; cf. 8:6. Mishnah Yoma 1 provides more details concerning the ablutions: the high priest bathes his whole body five times, and his hands and feet ten times. The mishnaic text is perhaps simply a more thorough cataloguing of what had been the common practice, or it may reflect the increased purity concerns of the period. Other references to bathing include: 2 Kgs 5:1–19; Tob 2:9; Aristeas 304b–306; 2 Macc 12:38; Aseneth 14:12–15; Philo, *Special Laws* 1.119, 191; Josephus, *Antiquities* 3.11.1 §258; 6.11.9 §235.

clothes. Still, it is possible, although not likely, that in a parodic rereading Judith's dressing ceremony and special garments for her mission are likened to the same process for the high priest.[15]

We note, then, that there are many associations with bathing in ancient Israel, some broad, some quite specific. Other examples include the bathing that is commanded as a ritual cleansing for those healed of scales or ṣāra'at (wrongly translated as "leprosy," noted above), for men and women after genital emissions (Lev 14:8, 47; 15:5), or immersion after touching a corpse (Ben Sira 34:30).[16] More general examples might include the ironic case of David bathing, anointing himself, and putting on his garments during the period when he should be mourning his son, or the vague purification before the Sabbath in 2 Macc 12:38, probably the bathing that is enjoined after warfare.

Nicole Ruane has investigated the rich symbolic world of bathing, laundering, and changing garments in the Bible, and has reached the following conclusions:[17]

1. Although bathing rituals in biblical law sometimes mark community and belonging (Exodus 19), they also register distinctions. They are applied differently for high priests and other priests, priests in general and Levites, Levites and all Israel, and men and women. They also distinguish Israel from outsiders.

2. Bathing and laundering of garments often take place in conjunction with anointing, sacrifice, and elimination rites.

3. Even though the *precise* function of bathing is often unclear, it generally serves to prepare one for cultic service. Yet women, with the exception of bathing after sex,[18] are not commanded to bathe for reasons of impurity, presumably because they cannot approach the cultic act of sacrifice as closely as the approach permitted even for a lay man. Menstruation regulations connected with the *mikveh* arise later.

4. Carefully distinguished are bathing *before* a cultic ritual and *after* incurring impurity. (Judith bathes *before* she decapitates Holofernes but does *not* bathe *after* she has handled a corpse!) The most common bathing in biblical law is that enjoined on all men when they have encountered impurity. On first view these laws seem gender-neutral, but important differences can be discerned. Bathing for women is not mentioned, for example, in Lev 15:19, 28. Some scholars have argued that it was simply assumed here, but Ruane follows those who accept the text as it stands. Since there was no occasion for women to approach the temple for cultic purposes, bathing was not viewed as necessary.[19]

As helpful as these conclusions are regarding the gendered nature of washing rituals, they do not provide all the information necessary regarding Judith's bathing. Gera looks to the theory of Gedaliah Alon: contact with gentiles in general, and not just sex, was considered a source of ritual impurity.[20] Judith's bathing, therefore, must represent an attempt to render her purified from this contact. Jonathan Klawans,

---

15 After the sacrifice, the high priest will change back, but Judith's hasty escape from the camp would preclude a second change. Plain linen was also distinguished from mourning garments such as sackcloth; plain linen suggested purity, sackcloth a return to undifferentiated earth and nature.

16 It was bathing after genital emissions that gave rise to the *mikveh* practices; see below. Treatment of ṣāra'at on clothing (that is, mold, fungus, or mildew) also involved washing (Lev 13:47–58). The possibility of "extra-purification" by bathing was hypothesized by Eyal Regev, "The Ritual Baths near the Temple Mount and Extra-Purification before Entering the Temple Courts," *IEJ* 55 (2005) 194–204, but now see Yonatan Adler, "The Ritual Baths near the Temple Mount and Extra-Purification before Entering the Temple Courts: A Reply to Eyal Regev," *IEJ* 56 (2006) 209–15.

17 Nicole Ruane, "Bathing, Status and Gender in Priestly Ritual," in Deborah W. Rooke, ed., *A Question of Sex? Gender and Difference in the Hebrew Bible*

and Beyond (Hebrew Bible Monographs; Sheffield: Sheffield Phoenix, 2007) 66–81.

18 Ruane argues that, in the case of bathing after sex, a woman is raised to the higher standard of a man's regulations. The biblical period gives more attention to men's discharges, but rabbinic discussions of ritual impurity are often focused more on women's discharges.

19 Supporting Ruane's position is the fact that the ritual for taking a captured foreign woman as wife, which involves shaving the woman's head, paring her nails, and discarding her old garments, does not include bathing (Deut 21:10–14).

20 Gera, *Judith,* 372–73; Alon, *The Jews in Their Land in the Talmudic Age, 70–640 C.E.* (Cambridge, MA: Harvard University Press, 1989) 152–57, 201–3. See also Hellmann, *Judit,* 128. Gera also considers the rabbinic ritual of washing hands before prayer (on which see below), yet Judith bathes her whole body.

Christine Hayes, and others, however, reject Alon's theory that all contact with gentiles was thought to communicate ritual impurity. Rather, gentiles were deemed a danger in terms of idolatry, not in terms of contact or ritual impurity.[21] The evidence varies, however, and certain passages seem to assume—perhaps in an idealizing way—that sexual contact with gentiles, or perhaps other contact as well, is defiling in some sense (Aristeas 139–46; Greek Esth 14:15–16).

The *generalized* threat of impurity may thus lie behind our text. (See the remarks of Thiessen at 9:2–4.) Although Judith does not have sex with Holofernes, she is in fact circling the parameters of illicit sexual intercourse with a gentile. The problem of Esther sharing a bed with a gentile king is not raised in MT Esther but is cause for confession in the prayer scene of Greek Esth 14:16–17. Might the imaginative and unreal world of the novellas have allowed for the view that sexual contact with gentiles communicated impurity? On an imaginative plane, Alon's view may have been correct; Esther bemoans her gentile crown, "like a menstruous rag." In Judith, the audience knows that she will not consummate this relationship, yet an erotic tension motivates the narrative—and tension is the basis of all comedy (see the commentary on 10:14–19 and §7 above). The fact that she actively insinuates herself into Holofernes's bedroom and into his thoughts may pose a threat to her sexual purity. This aspect is not remarked on in the passage, and we recall that she also bathed while still in her house (10:3). Yet bathing more than once in succession may suggest a need for continual cleansing. Indeed, Judith's acceptable food, her bath-

ing, and her lambskin may together be understood as magical protections while she is in a zone of danger and exposure.

We look as well at evidence from shortly after the period of Judith, which derives from several contexts. The Pharisaic practice of washing hands before meals has been offered as a comparison to our text.[22] The law of Lev 22:6 noted above—that any priest who, at any time, contracts ritual impurity must bathe before eating of the offerings in the temple—may have been the basis for the Pharisees' transferal of priestly purity to the table fellowship of all Jews. Yet Judith does not wash her hands but rather bathes, and this outside the camp. Ritual immersion also became very important at Qumran as a continuing ritual cleansing, followed by communal meals. Yet even at Qumran, with its elaborate system of water channels and *mikvaot*, immersion is not often mentioned; *rāḥaṣ*, not *ṭābal*, is almost always the verb. One exception, however, is relevant:

> Whatever comes in contact with semen, whether a person or any vessel, shall be immersed; and whoever bears it shall immerse; and the garment upon which it [the semen] is, as well as the vessel that bears it, is to be immersed in water. (4QToharot [4Q274] 2 i 4–6)

Josephus also describes the Essene morning ritual of dressing in linen cloths and bathing (*apolouontai*) in cold water; the priest prays and they eat, now *katharoi* ("clean").[23] Josephus also notes a continuous bathing practice in regard to the Jewish ascetic Ban-

---

21 Klawans, *Impurity and Sin*, 48; Christine Elizabeth Hayes, *Gentile Impurities and Jewish Identities: Intermarriage and Conversion from the Bible to the Talmud* (Oxford and New York: Oxford University Press, 2002) 49. T. M. Lemos ("Where There Is Dirt, There Is System? Revisiting Biblical Purity Constructions," *JSOT* 37 [2013] 265–94) disagrees with Klawans and assumes that Judith incurs impurity simply by spending time in the Assyrian camp. Judith bathes daily to wash away that impurity. But the texts that she and others must refer to are ambiguous. Nehemiah throws "Tobiah the Ammonite" out of the temple precincts and cleanses it (13:4–9). But despite Nehemiah's name for him, Tobiah is likely a Judean resident in the Tobiad family estate in Ammon. Nehemiah, then, is not actually expelling a gentile, but he does "Ammonite" him, creating a symbol world in which he cleanses the temple of "gentile" associations. It

is possible that Judith also conjures up a symbolic sense of impurity by contact.

22 On earlier scholars who compared Judith to Pharisaic concerns, see §2 above. Our text's strong Hasmonean leanings may argue against it, although a Pharisaic connection cannot be ruled out. On a concern for halakic issues in general in Judith, see Shmuel Safrai, "Halakha," in Safrai, ed., *Literature of the Sages: First Part* (Philadelphia: Fortress Press, 1987) 121–210, here 136–37.

23 Josephus, *Jewish War* 2.8.5 §129; see also 1QS VI.20. See Adler, "Jewish Ritual Immersion," where the origin of ritual immersion is assigned to the early first century BCE or a bit earlier, an influence of the Hellenistic hip bath. On Bannus, see Josephus, *Life* 2 §11: Bannus "bathed himself in cold water frequently, both night and day, to purify himself." The Mandaeans, who claimed John the Baptist as

nus. These actions are both concerned with purity, and the ascetic discipline of continuously washing away impurities may be instructive. Judith's repeated bathing, though earlier, is thus similar to these.

What would these practices have connoted for the first audience? Many connections may be posited, but one must beware the photographic fallacy, the temptation to see a text as a photograph of social practices, each element corresponding to what people actually did. Free narratives may refract contemporary concerns in indirect or even fanciful ways. The arts also give expression to longings or idealizations that are only later enacted more concretely. Our text may present an idealized, fictionalized, and unreal notion of purification, probably heightened by the danger of Judith's proximity to Holofernes's bed. Her acts could presage a higher discipline that is purity oriented and related to the rise of asceticism.[24] It was probably the most general bathing law—that all priests who at any time contract ritual impurity must wash before eating the food offerings in the temple—which provided the impetus for expanding the ideals and practices of ritual cleansing. If in beheading Holofernes Judith does indeed play the role of a (parodied) sacrificing priest (see below), then these priestly associations would have an even stronger connection.

■ 12:10–12

Holofernes is passive and remains in his tent while Judith is active and moves about the camp at will. He even excludes his officers from attending his seduction banquet; only his slaves are present. In chaps. 1–7, Holofernes was at home among his generals, but with Judith's arrival he has been isolated from his military entourage. This scene may call to mind a Persian harem intrigue rather than an expeditionary council as the Alexander Romance might have depicted it. The fact that it is on the fourth day indicates to the audience that it is Judith's own clock that is ticking down (see 12:7); the audience knows what is coming, when, and why. On

Holofernes referring to Judith as a "Hebrew woman," see 10:12; 14:18.

Mikhail Bakhtin proposed that every character in a novel occupies, even constructs, his or her zone (see §7 above). In this novella, Holofernes's zone is the world of the great general, satirized. His libido and bravado—both ludicrous—run together. Reflected here is the mind of a man who, on the one hand, thinks he will soon have sex with Judith, whether she agrees or not, yet, on the other, waits patiently on her every word and has yet to say no to a single one of her strange demands. The agency of Judith throughout is thus contrasted with the absurd passivity of Holofernes. (To a lesser extent, compare Daniel 6 and Bel.) Each clause of his statement to Bagoas reveals weakness, rendered more ironic by the fact that he broadcasts his impotence. Note the italicized words:

> Go now and *persuade* [her] to *come join us* to eat and drink. We would have to *hide our faces in shame if we pass by* a woman such as this *without having intercourse* with her. If *we cannot seduce her,* she will *ridicule* us.
>
> πεῖσον δὴ πορευθεὶς . . . τοῦ ἐλθεῖν πρὸς ἡμᾶς καὶ φαγεῖν καὶ πιεῖν. . . . ἰδοὺ γὰρ αἰσχρὸν τῷ προσώπῳ ἡμῶν εἰ γυναῖκα τοιαύτην παρήσομεν οὐχ ὁμιλήσαντες αὐτῇ. ὅτι ἐὰν ταύτην μὴ ἐπισπασώμεθα, καταγελάσεται ἡμῶν.

Holofernes talks as if he will seduce Judith to gain power over her body, yet he states it as a pathetic fear of shame, barely even a desire. He is only effectual in preparing a trap for himself![25] He shares with his eunuch a series of declarations of what he is about to do to this woman, a language of seduction, yet the gap between his view of what is about to happen and the reality of the situation is opening into a wider, more farcical chasm. Holofernes is a fool by Greek philosophical standards

a founder, emphasized continuous water purifications.

24 Wills, "Ascetic Theology." The distinction between acted rituals and descriptions is addressed also by Jonathan Z. Smith, "The Domestication of Sacrifice," in Robert Hamerton-Kelly, ed., *Violent Origins: Walter Burkert, René Girard, and Jonathan Z. Smith on Ritual Killing and Cultural Formation* (Stan-

ford, CA: Stanford University Press, 1987) 191–238, here 210.

25 Gruen, *Diaspora,* 167. Loader insists that the text does not state all this outright (*Pseudepigrapha,* 204), but here Gruen is justified in his interpretive leap. What good would irony be if it were spelled out?

(see the excursus at 8:35, "The Book of Judith and Greek Philosophy"), and a comic fool (*alazōn*) by Greek dramatic standards. A comparison with ancient Near Eastern wisdom can also be made: the wise courtier knows more than he speaks, speaks at the right time, and acquires favor when he does. The wise courtier is understated and carefully measures his words. The fool blathers on, and does not even know that he is talking his way into his own destruction.

Excursus: Bagoas the Eunuch

Bagoas is first mentioned as the "eunuch who was in charge of all [Holofernes's] affairs" (12:11). The last reference to him will be at the peripety of the narrative (14:14–18; see excursus there, "Peripety and the Theme of the Book"). Both his status as eunuch and his name are important. The word translated as "eunuch" in Hebrew is *sārîs*, from Akkadian, in Greek *eunouchos*. Castrating men for service at the highest levels was a Near Eastern practice. Some eunuchs had been captured in war, or were sons of slaves; some were castrated at birth, while those designated as pleasure-boys were castrated nearer to puberty.[26] Originally designating a castrated servant who oversaw the king's harem, the term "eunuch" was generalized to mean also a counselor in the king's court and even a military leader. Others around Holofernes, for instance, may also have been eunuchs.

Eunuchs were valued for their dependency and loyalty. Although it should not be assumed that every figure called a eunuch was castrated, in general these individuals were, and this related to their social and political function. Castrated eunuchs could not produce offspring and thus could not create dynastic intrigue or family alliances; they were viewed as safer and time-limited. They performed both courtly and military functions and occupied a zone between the king and others. Like slaves, they demonstrated the separation, elevation, and isolation of the king, and as a result eunuchs had access others did not have. The eunuch became a symbol of the intermediary figure who could be trusted in the palace and would carry out the will of the king who was separated from the world.[27] Herodotus 8.105 tells the story of a trusted eunuch of Xerxes, and the eastern histories of Ctesias were replete with court eunuchs like Bagoas, who provided much intrigue. In particular, Ctesias tells of Stryangaeus and his dependence on a eunuch to explore his interest in Zarinaea.[28] Eunuchs were depicted as sycophants, but also as devious and treacherous. Eunuchs were often excitable; they mourned and wailed for their dead masters, or killed themselves as well.

The role of the eunuch was originally unknown in Greece, but the term *eunouchos* was created from *eunē* and *echō*, "guardian of the bed." Castrated devotees in religious orders also became known in the West, mainly in Asia Minor, during the Hellenistic period. The Greek tradition of the eunuch as both a castrated servant and a court official may have been reinforced by the similarity of *eunouchos* and *oinochoos* ("cupbearer"), as reflected also in the text history of Neh 1:11 in Greek.[29] Greek suspicions of the emotional eunuch were registered; the eunuch could be depicted as the foil to the self-control of the good king.[30] The Greek novels reflect a point of view that may be compared to our text. In *Chaereas* 5.2–4 (compare 6.4), a Persian court eunuch tries to force himself upon the beautiful heroine Callirhoe. "Indeed," says the narrator, "he was thinking like a eunuch, a slave, a barbarian. He did not know the spirit of a wellborn Greek."[31]

---

26 Peter Guyot, *Eunuchen als Sklaven und Freigelassene in der griechisch-römischen Antike* (Stuttgart: Klett-Cotta, 1980) 28–45. The term may not have originally assumed castration; see Jürgen Ebach, *Genesis 37–50* (HThKAT; Freiburg: Herder, 2007) 163–64. The following discussion is based partly on this resource and Helena M. Bolle and Stephen R. Llewelyn, "Intersectionality, Gender Liminality and Ben Sira's Attitude to the Eunuch," *VT* 67 (2017) 546–69.

27 According to Diodorus Siculus 2.20.1, 21.2, Semiramis gave her rule over to her son, who subsequently became withdrawn, seen only by his concubines and eunuchs; see Llewellyn-Jones and Robson, *Ctesias' History*, 130–31.

28 Gera, *Judith*, 72–73; and see §4 above.

29 Joseph Blenkinsopp rejects this possibility (*Ezra-Nehemiah: A Commentary* [OTL; Philadelphia: Westminster, 1988] 213). See also Lloyd Llewellyn-Jones, "Eunuchs and the Royal Harem in Achaemenid Persia (559–331 B.C.)," in Shaun Tougher, ed., *Eunuchs in Antiquity and Beyond* (London: Duckworth, 2002) 19–49, here 24.

30 Hall, *Inventing the Barbarian*, 157; Gera, *Xenophon's Cyropaedia*, 254–59.

31 Ruiz-Montero, "Rise of the Greek Novel," 29–85, here 70.

In the Hebrew Bible, the term *sārîs* is used both for castrated officials and for military leaders or officials who were evidently not castrated (Gen 39:1; 2 Kgs 25:19).[32] A negative view of eunuchs is generally evident here. The exclusion of the eunuch likely lies behind Deut 23:1–2: "No one whose testicles are crushed or whose penis is cut off shall be admitted to the assembly of the Lord." Isaiah 56:3–5 overturns this, but the joining of eunuch and foreigner communicates a symbolic eschatological reversal rather than a halakic revolution.[33] The book of Esther presents the courtly world of the eunuch that is found in Ctesias. She is under the devoted care of the Persian eunuch Hegai (chap. 2), and there are other eunuchs in Esther (2:21–23; 6:2; 7:9). It is also possible that Nehemiah, Daniel and his friends, and Mordecai were eunuchs. Josephus reports that the three chamberlains in Herod's court were eunuchs (*Jewish War* 1.24.7 §488).

Ben Sira and Wisdom of Solomon are particularly interesting for their depictions of eunuchs. As the author of a training book for scribes, Ben Sira seems at times to respond to the competition between (non-Jewish?) eunuchs and the Jewish scribe-courtier. As a third gender, eunuchs are met with an ambivalence about their sexuality. The eunuch is an unsexed servant who protects the harem, and yet as a boundary crosser he can also be a traitor. Eunuchs were sometimes depicted as both the objects and the agents of lust. Ben Sira very cruelly derides and shames the eunuch—making light especially of the eunuch who tries, but cannot, copulate (20:4; 30:20). The ridicule of the eunuch serves to reinscribe traditional husband–wife roles.[34] Wisdom of Solomon, on the other hand, may be composing a secretive defense of the wise eunuch who cannot have children (Wis 2:3–4; 3:13–15; 4:1, 6–7, 19). Wisdom 3:14 may indeed affirm the spiritual life of eunuchs in Israel, hidden as it is.

We turn now to the name Bagoas. Like the name Achior/Ahikar, it suggests a well-known type. Bagoas was so common as a name for a highly placed Persian eunuch that Pliny the Elder took it to be the Persian word for eunuch (*Natural History* 13.41). Several eunuchs with this name are prominent in Persian history:

1. A Persian Bagoas was governor of Jerusalem at the end of the fourth century.[35]
2. An Egyptian Bagoas was a powerful court figure under Artaxerxes III Ochus; he assassinated Ochus and arranged for Darius III to succeed to the throne.
3. Bagoas was also a powerful vizier under Darius III in about 340–336, and was the latter's favored male companion, *eromenos;* after Darius's death he was given to Alexander the Great.

Of particular relevance for Judith is the second of these. In the Persian expeditionary army of Artaxerxes III Ochus, which invaded the West (including the area of Judea) in 350 and 343 BCE, the general was named Holofernes and Bagoas was his officer.[36] These two invasions may have provided the model for the invasion in Judith (see §2 above). The name evidently remained common. In 4QTales of the Persian Court (4Q550a–d) from Qumran, a court narrative set in the court of Darius, two courtiers are Bagoshi, a non-Jew (4Q550d 2.5), and Bagasro, a Jew (2.6). The name of the former, the antagonist, is likely a variation of Bagoas, the latter perhaps also. Heliodorus includes a Persian eunuch named Bagoas, a high-strung eunuch (*Aethiopica* 8.6) who is also wise (8.13) and a military leader throughout.

In the case of Judith, then, because Bagoas plays the role of the go-between, the audience likely assumed that Bagoas was castrated. Further, Holofernes's impotence, revealed gradually in the story, would in this case be mirrored by Bagoas's

32 See also Gen 40:2, 7; 1 Sam 8:15; 1 Kgs 22:9; 2 Kgs 9:32; 20:18; 23:11; 24:12, 15; 25:19; Isa 56:3–4; Jer 29:2; 34:19; 38:7–13; 52:25; 2 Chr 18:8; Esth 1:10; 2:3, 21; Dan 1:3; cf. also Matt 19:12; Acts 8:26–40.

33 Leszek Ruszkowski, *Volk und Gemeinde im Wandel: Eine Untersuchung zu Jesaja 56–66* (FRLANT 191; Göttingen: Vandenhoeck & Ruprecht, 2000) 136; Raymond de Hoop, "The Interpretation of Isaiah 56:1–9," *JBL* 127 (2008) 671–95.

34 Guyot, *Eunuchen*, 63; Bolle and Llewelyn, "Intersectionality"; Ibolya Balla, *Ben Sira on Family, Gender, and Sexuality* (DCLS 8; Berlin: de Gruyter, 2011) 153, 230.

35 The references are Elephantine A4.7, A4.8 = EP 30,31 (Jews in Elephantine complain to Bagohi "governor of Judah," *paḥat yĕhûdāh*); Ernst Badian,

"The Eunuch Bagoas: A Study in Method," *ClQ* 3 (1958) 144–57; Pierre Briant, *From Cyrus to Alexander: A History of the Persian Empire* (Winona Lake, IN: Eisenbrauns, 2002) 269–70; A. K. Grayson, *Baylonian Historical-Literary Texts* (Toronto: University of Toronto Press, 1975) 28–36; Curtius Rufus 6.5.28 (Arrian has a different tradition). See also Louis Crompton, *Homosexuality and Civilization* (Cambridge, MA: Belknap Press of Harvard University Press, 2003) 76; Sheaffer, *Envisioning*, 109; Llewellyn-Jones, "Eunuchs," 35.

36 Diodorus Siculus 16.47.4; 17.5.3–5; 31.19.2–3; see the excursus at 2:4–13, "Holofernes"; and Gera, *Judith*, 36. On 4QTales of the Persian Court, see Crawford, "4QTales of the Persian Court," 121–37.

castrated status.[37] Other structural patterns can be discerned. Both Bagoas and Judith's slave act as instruments to achieve their masters' ends, but Bagoas, with a famous name, is talkative, emotive, and foolish, and the maid, unnamed, is silent and appears at first to have no visible personality. She is, nevertheless, cool, dependable, and wise in that she administers Judith's affairs and ultimately, when freed, takes ownership of the household.[38] Judith's slave is a functional helpmate in the stratagem, while Bagoas will only provide comic comment on Holofernes's foolish decisions. Given the tradition of the jealousy and court intrigue of eunuchs, it is interesting that there is no explicit jealousy or competition between Bagoas and Judith; rather, he is as thoroughly subordinated to Holofernes's foolish wishes as the female slave is to Judith's wise ones. Bagoas is a dysfunctional enabler of Holofernes's dysfunctional strategy.

It is also significant that the last we see of Bagoas (14:18) is when he channels the audience's point of view at the first sight of Holofernes's headless body. His comic line is at the recognition and peripety of the drama and provides the transition to the cascading denouement:

> These slaves have deceived us! One woman of the Hebrews has shamed the house of King Nebuchadnezzar! Look here! Holofernes is lying on the ground, and his head is missing![39]

> ἠθέτησαν οἱ δοῦλοι, ἐποίησεν αἰσχύνην μία γυνὴ τῶν Ἑβραίων εἰς τὸν οἶκον τοῦ βασιλέως Ναβουχοδονοσόρ. ὅτι ἰδοὺ Ὀλοφέρνης χαμαί, καὶ ἡ κεφαλὴ οὐκ ἔστιν ἐπ᾽ αὐτῷ.

Bagoas's line here may even constitute the theme of the entire book. It captures not only the main action of the novella but also the radical reversal that is played for release and humor. The view of Schmitz and Rakel that the interpretation of Exod 15:3 in Jdt 9:7 and 16:2 (see above and §6) is the theological center of our text highlights an interpretive problem: the book proceeds on different levels, what I have referred to as music (narrative arc) and libretto (prayers and speeches). This utterance by Bagoas

states the narrative theme of Judith; the interpretation of Exod 15:3 in Jdt 9:7, the prayer theme. We witness a similar phenomenon contributing to the peripety in Esther when Haman's wife Zeresh states, "If Mordecai, before whom your fall has begun, is of the Jewish people, you will not prevail against him, but will surely fall before him" (6:13).

■ 12:10–20

A dinner invitation, delivered by Bagoas, moves the plot toward the resolution of the tensions, just as in Esth 5:4–8.[40] Holofernes's treatment of Judith anticipates his view of what her life will be like as Nebuchadnezzar's courtesan (12:13). His discourse with Judith is suggestive, yet he remains respectful; she must be treated with the dignity that the power of her beauty requires. In the Greek novels, the extraordinary beauty of the female and male protagonists makes it obvious to those who encounter them that they must be highborn. Similar here is the fact that Bagoas and Holofernes treat Judith almost as visiting royalty, although there is also a rational explanation: they perceive in Judith an ornament in Nebuchadnezzar's harem, and for the moment she can be an ornament in Holofernes's as well. There is a great chasm between the way she is treated and the way a conquered woman, or slave or prostitute, would be treated.[41]

Bagoas compliments her by graciously inviting her to become like the Assyrian courtesans, but in Israelite eyes this threatens her with gross sexual impurity (Greek Esther 14). Still, while in the Greek novels and in other Jewish novellas, female protagonists are buffeted as they are dragged into threatening situations, Judith is not buffeted; rather, she controls the situation. She *would* feel threatened, of course, if she were not confident that she can control others, and for the audience the experience of threat is present, even exhilarating, although they share her confidence about the ending. The tension created by this threat to her purity is thus not as keenly

---

37 Stocker, *Judith*, 7.

38 Sheaffer, *Envisioning*, 114. Does Achior's fainting at the sight of Holofernes's head indicate that he is a histrionic counterpart to Bagoas?

39 Cf. the denouement of the Ehud/Eglon story in Judg 3:25.

40 Sheaffer, *Envisioning*, 103. The exact nuance of *paidiskē hē kalē hautē* is not clear. *Paidiskē* can

mean young woman, girl, or prostitute; see Moore, *Judith*, 224; Schmitz/Engel, *Judit*, 348. "Fair young woman" here is an attempt at a general term.

41 See the discussion of the treatment of female slaves and prostitutes in Jennifer A. Glancy, *Slavery in Early Christianity* (Minneapolis: Fortress Press, 2006) 50–57. On conquered women in Israel, see Deut 21:10–14.

felt as it would be in the Greek novels; it is humorous and parodic, but not deeply challenging to the audience. Indeed, Judith can even arouse Holofernes further by answering in a way that is suggestive on one level, though heard differently by the audience:

> Who am I to refuse "my lord"? . . . I will do at once anything that pleases "him"; this will bring me joy till my dying day.

"Who am I" here contrasts with Holofernes's "who are you" to Achior (6:2) and Judith's "who are you" to the Bethulians (8:12).[42] Her joy will be the satisfaction of having decapitated Holofernes. Her arch reply extricates herself from a harem intrigue and places her in charge in a military way; the audience knows that she will slice her way out. Judith's dressing for her engagement with the enemy is also repeated—"She arose and beautified herself with garments and every feminine adornment"—a mere summary of her dressing scene in chap. 10, but still significant in the course of the story.

■ **12:15–16** Judith's use of the lambskin has yet to be fully explained. We begin by noting that the lambskins (plural) had been provided for her by Bagoas. It is possible that this reflects a solicitousness on Bagoas's part for her comfort. In addition, carpets and rugs placed on the ground were viewed as an eastern luxury. Sheepskins draped over the stools at the Eleusinian mysteries is also suggestive.[43] From the audience's point of view, perhaps the lambskins serve to protect Judith from the dangers of contact impurity. Lambskin does not have a prescribed role in menstrual or genital discharge impurity, but, practically speaking, lambskin came to have a recognized role for men or women to sit on, to avoid communicating impurity to surfaces. If a man or a woman has a genital discharge, not only is that person ritually impure but every bed or surface on which that person has sat is impure as well:

> All who touch anything that was under him shall be unclean until evening, and . . . shall wash their clothes and bathe in water, and be unclean until evening. . . . Any earthen vessel that the one with the discharge touches shall be broken; and every vessel of wood shall be rinsed in water. (Lev 15:10, 12)

According to Lev 15:20–23, a woman can communicate menstrual impurity to beds and mats. Judith, as an especially pious and careful woman, is perhaps depicted as employing a means at hand to prevent incurring pollution.

The audience, however, may register not so much that she *sits on* a lambskin as that she *does not sit* on couches or beds. The lambskin is a safe alternative to the contact impurity of sitting on the general's furnishings. The biblical prescriptions for menstrual impurity, then, are indeed vaguely similar, but Judith's actions do not suggest an impurity on *her* part. Rather, they suggest a protection from impurity *from Holofernes* and his quarters, and the bathing before eating (vv. 7–9) suggests the same generalized protection.

Yet the offer by Bagoas may take on a different meaning for Judith and her audience: a lambskin can have an erotic association as a site of intercourse. Indeed, when Judith sits on the lambskins, Holofernes becomes excited:

> Judith then entered and reclined (upon them), and Holofernes's heart leapt from him on account of her. He was aroused with passion, enflamed with the desire to lie with her. From the day he saw her he had been seeking an opportunity to seduce her. (12:16)

κα\ εἰσελθοῦσα ἀνέπεσεν Ἰουδίθ, καὶ ἐξέστη ἡ καρδία Ὀλοφέρνου ἐπ' αὐτήν, καὶ ἐσαλεύθη ἡ ψυχὴ αὐτοῦ, καὶ ἦν κατεπίθυμος σφόδρα τοῦ συγγενέσθαι μετ' αὐτῆς. καὶ ἐτήρει καιρὸν τοῦ ἀπατῆσαι αὐτὴν ἀφ' ἧς ἡμέρας εἶδεν αὐτήν.

The words are strong words: his heart *exestē*, his *psychē esaleuthē*, he was *katepithymos sphodra* to lie with her.

---

42   Gera, *Judith*, 277.
43   Lewis Richard Farnell, *The Cults of the Greek States* (5 vols.; Oxford: Oxford University Press, 1907) 3:237–42; see also Gera, *Judith*, 385; Xenophon, *Cyropaedia* 5.2.15, and *Hellenica* 4.1.30. Sitting on the floor was also a typical eating position, but here it appears to be marked as a special practice by Judith.

There is a fullness of expression, even rhetorical overkill here, appropriate to Holofernes's own lack of control.

The verb *anepesen* is ambiguous. It could mean she "lay down"—a more suggestive reading—but the word often means recline at a meal. In the Greek and Roman world, and likely among wealthy Jews as well, it was accepted for wealthy women to participate in dinners. This act in itself would not have been unusual, but Judith is the sole guest, and the narrative is in a heightened erotic state.

■ **12:20** Holofernes is *ēuphranthē ap' autēs*, gladdened or made merry *by her*—a stronger yet more passive sense than merely charmed or pleased *with her* (the more common *ep' autēs*). A common story motif in this period involves a brash and clever protagonist who works his or her way into the good graces of a powerful superior. As a result of Judith's gladdening him, he—in better Greek—"drank vast amounts of wine, more than he had ever drunk in one day since he had been born."

Wine was generally treated in a positive way in Greece and Israel. In Euripides, *Bacchae* 282–83, Dionysus bestows the gift of good sleep through wine. Drinking too much wine, or unmixed wine, was often considered a violation of proper celebration and led to a loss of self-mastery. Eubulus, *Semele or Dionysus*, frg. 93 (c. 375 BCE), states that in a symposium three kraters of wine is an appropriate amount, while more leads to disastrous effects. In Ctesias, when generals are arguing at a symposium, one of them says, with some irony, "As the Greeks say, there is truth in wine" (Plutarch, *Artaxerxes* 15.4). In Plato's *Symposium* there is much drinking, and many of the guests fall asleep, yet it is Socrates who remains unaffected by wine, who keeps his wits and does not fall asleep (214a, 223b–c). Judith's self-mastery is indeed similar to Socrates's.

Wine is a key element in many biblical stories (e.g., Gen 9:20–27; 19:30–38; Esth 1:7–8; Dan 5:1–4; 1 Macc 16:15–16), with a sense of the danger of the loss of judgment. The wisdom texts are sometimes positive about wine (Sir 31:25–31) but provide warnings as well (Prov 23:29–35; Tob 4:15; 1 Esdr 3:17–24; and cf. T. Judah

14:1–8). Especially relevant here is the powerful leader, whether in Greek or Israelite tradition, who loses control or falls asleep after drinking too much wine. The cyclops Polyphemus (in both *Odyssey* 9 and in Euripides's satyr play *Cyclops* 557–59, 583–89) descends into a self-destructive spiral by drinking too much wine.[44] Finally, we note the book of Esther, where Ahasuerus is likely perceived as far too indulgent in wine.

The structure of vv. 18 and 20 also place Holofernes's drinking at the center of the plot element. The words form a parallelism, abbreviated here:[45]

18 I will indeed drink . . .
    more than the days of my life (*geneseōs*).

20 He drank a quantity of wine . . .
    since the day he was born (*egennēthē*).

Verses 18 and 20 indulge the typical overstated emotions of popular literature, although Judith and Holofernes adopt different speech strategies. Judith's "my life has been magnified for me" can be compared to the later Magnificat of Luke 1:46–55, but behind both are the Song of Hannah (1 Sam 2:1, using different words) and psalmic language such as Ps 34:2–3. There are interesting differences as well. Judith does not mention God; the latter is more part of her hidden plan, as the ironic use of the word "lord" implies. And while Hannah and Mary are extremely pious and earnest, Judith is using the language duplicitously. Her inflated language is designed to fool Holofernes and place him off his guard, and it works.

Between vv. 18 and 20, v. 19 provides the narrator's contrasting remark, also in passable Greek: "She then took what her slave had prepared for her, and ate and drank with him." The stylized dialogue of vv. 18 and 20 is contrasted to the simple action of v. 19—the expansive words of Judith and Holofernes, on the one hand, and the narrator's own description of her precise, careful observance of self-mastery, on the other.[46] The audience would perceive here the contrast of the two charac-

---

44   Paul Robertson, "The Cyclops and the Self," unpublished manuscript.

45   Craven, *Artistry and Faith,* 89.

46   Moore, *Judith,* 225.

izations. Although one is provided by dialogue and the other by narration, in a Bakhtinian reading the author of the book has created the two zones. The contrast between an exaggerated clause regarding appearances and a simple clause to express the underlying reality may have been known to the author from Plato, *Apology* 21c. Our passage, then, despite its charming simplicity, moves to a surprising artistry in the very techniques that would become the stock-in-trade of novelists: narrative description; suggestive, revealing dialogue; and irony.

Text	Textual Notes

1/ When evening came, his slaves quickly withdrew. Bagoas closed the tent from the outside and dismissed those who attended his lord. They went off to their beds, all of them weary because the drinking party had gone on so long. **2/** Judith was left alone in the tent, with Holofernes collapsed headlong on his bed, the wine flowing over him. **3/** Judith ordered her slave to stand outside the bedchamber[a] and await her departure, as was her daily custom. For she had said that she would go out for her prayers, and she had spoken in this way to Bagoas. **4/** Everyone, therefore, had now departed, and no one, from lowly to great, was left in the bedchamber. Standing beside his bed, Judith said in her heart, "O Lord, God of all power, at this time look upon the work of my hands for the exaltation of Jerusalem. **5/** Now there is an opportunity for you to come to the aid of your inheritance and to accomplish my plan to crush the enemies who have risen up against us." **6/** Stepping up to the bedpost, near the head of Holofernes, she took down his sword, **7/** and coming near the bed, grasped him by the hair of his head and said, "Give me strength today, O Lord God of Israel!" **8/** Then she struck him twice in the neck with all her strength,[b] severing his head from him. **9/** She then rolled his body off the bed and pulled down the curtain from its poles. She quickly went out and handed the head of Holofernes to her slave, **10/** and she placed it in her food pouch. The two of them then proceeded out together as was their custom at the time of prayer.

a   Most manuscripts include αυτης, "her bedchamber"; see commentary.

b   For ισχυι αυτης: παραξιφιδι 58 583 Sy.

Commentary

13:1–10a

In the chiastic structure of the second half (see §3 above), the beheading scene—or acteme, as Margarita Stocker has labeled it[1]—constitutes the climax and center. As the novella has featured two opposing "gods"—Nebuchadnezzar and God—and their two representatives—Holofernes and Judith—this scene is the moment when the two proxies become most closely engaged, coming indeed into intimate contact.[2] The scenario of intimacy planned by one of the proxies—Holofernes—will be supplanted by the counter-scenario of "intimacy" planned by the other—Judith. Holofernes's tent is similar to Judith's tent of isolation above her house. She has very

---

1   Stocker, *Judith*, 11.
2   Craven, *Artistry and Faith*, passim; Gera, *Judith*, 7–8.

dramatically emerged from seclusion to play an active role, but Holofernes remains in his tent, reclusive and passive, not the field general that he was formerly. The European artistic tradition established this setting as the domain of Judith: the tent "becomes, in art, Judith's own and only realm."[3]

While chap. 12 featured a flurry of dialogue and preparatory action, chap. 13, which contains the climactic beheading scene, begins with a sense of repose. In narrative, the preparation for important or climactic events often takes longer to develop than the events themselves. The narrator must first build both interest and tension; release or resolution can then be precipitated quickly. But the power of the decapitation scene derives in part from the fact that it is, on one hand, told quickly in just a few lines, while, on the other, each of the motions is precisely listed and ritualized. Taking a departure from the previous scene, this section adopts a hushed, simple style as a way of ironically building tension in anticipation of the beheading that the audience knows is imminent.

In vv. 1–2 alone, a sort of dramaturgy can be perceived in the quiet and orderly actions, indeed, actions-on-tiptoe:

- The slaves quickly withdraw.
- Bagoas closes up the tent from the outside.
- He dismisses the attendants.
- They go off to their beds, all weary from the long banquet.
- Judith is left alone inside.
- Holofernes is stretched out on his bed—the wine "flowing over him."[4]

These actions quickly and deftly define a zone for her actions. While in the first half of the novella, sweeping movements of armies over hundreds of miles could be recounted in a single verse, we now see that the dramatic actions of individual characters within and without the bedchamber become the *telos* toward which all of those

nations were converging. The tiny actions are sometimes even repeated, as the voyeuristic audience looks on at the central deed. (See also above at 10:21.)

Playful narrative elements are also found here. Bagoas performs an instrumental role by dismissing others while allowing Judith alone to remain. He assumes the role of a master manipulator, but there is a deep gap between how he and the audience perceive his role. Judith has actually manipulated the access to Holofernes's private space as if she were an officiating priest. (This will be emphasized in v. 4: "Everyone, therefore, had now departed, and no one, from lowly to great, was left in the bedchamber."[5]) The careful narration emphasizes this, even delectates in it. In addition, Holofernes is now also seen for the first time at his full nadir. At the end of chap. 12 he was drinking heavily; now he is passed out, the text saying literally, "the wine had been poured [*perikechymenos*] over him."[6] The translations often normalize this expression to something like "he was dead drunk" (NRSV), but it is important to note the stylized, even magical realism of the transformation. In Greek the wine has a causative role; as in Esther, it is almost a separate character, but here acting at Judith's command. The trickster understands people and things; one thinks of Ehud hiding his sword in Judg 3:16, or Daniel as trickster feeding the dragon in Bel 27.

■ 13:3–5

Judith arranges for her slave to stand outside to be ready to depart quickly, but is it outside Holofernes's tent or her own? Although it may seem more plausible that the slave waits just outside Holofernes's inner chamber, or outside his tent as a whole, the literal sense of the text would place the slave outside "her tent," that is, Judith's, *exō tou koitōnos autēs*. Some translations, as here, drop the possessive *autēs* to read "outside the bedchamber," that is, outside Holofernes' tent. The text remains ambiguous. The European artistic tradition, at any rate, included the slave in the inner chamber with Judith.

---

3   Garrard, *Artemisia Gentileschi*, 295.

4   The wine flowing over him might suggest a foreshadowing of his flowing blood, but the latter is conspicuously absent in the LXX version. It does, however, appear in quantity in the artistic tradition; see §8 above.

5   Sheaffer calls attention to the Hebrew merism "neither small nor great" (*Envisioning*, 104).

6   Here Gruen suggests, "wine had virtually overflowed all about him" (*Diaspora*, 167).

For much of the interpretive tradition, the two women are linked in a single, salutary act. In the original story Judith acted as a lone agent, her slave waiting patiently outside.

Verse 3b interrupts the point-by-point details of the actions-on-tiptoe with a reminder to the audience that preparations had already been laid: ". . . as was her daily custom. For she had said that she would go out for her prayers, and she had spoken in this way to Bagoas." Even though the audience likely knew the story, they had not been openly informed that her nightly regimen was staged for a purpose. Verse 4 returns to the events by restating that Judith was alone in the tent, providing a more definitive summary of the calm before the storm.

It is emphasized here that she stands beside his bed and speaks "in her heart." Standing beside his bed likely increases the sexual tension. The European paintings quite often highlight the bed and Judith's intimacy with it, even her "mastery" of the bed; early paintings depict her flying down at the bed, much as ancient kings were depicted slaying lions, or Claudius subduing Britannia in the Aphrodisias Sebasteion. Her violent act of decapitation—symbolic castration—occurs at the site of sexual intercourse.[7] Although Judith's act of decapitation is most often likened to Jael cradling Sisera before driving a spike through his head (Judges 4–5), there are wider parallels as well. Judith's circling of the bed might have conjured images of Odysseus's bed and the killing of the suitors, or (in some versions) Clytemnestra inviting Agamemnon to their marital bed where, once he is drunk, she kills him by wielding an axe or hitting him on the head.[8]

Judith intones her second prayer silently (see 9:2–14; 13:17; 16:13–17), presumably so as not to wake the general. Partly serving to retard the plot, the prayer is expressed in two parts, perhaps corresponding to the fact that his head will be severed in two blows. The first part repeats previous elements. Judith calls upon God to "look upon the work of my hands." Many artists fixated on her hands and how they represented her act, and indeed this corresponds to the emphasis on her hand throughout (see the commentary on 9:8–10). From a novelistic point of view, the prayer communicates the dramatic nature of the moment and provides a divine warrant, protecting her piety as she engages in an action that no woman should have to do. The close proximity of praying and assassination is indeed unusual.

There are further challenging elements as well. In a manner now seen as quite characteristic, she prays for aid from God but does not express any actual need. Her words are more a confirmation of her own plan, or even a field command directed to God to carry out *his* role:

> *Look* . . . upon the work of *my* hands. . . . *Now there is an opportunity for you* to come to the aid of your inheritance and to accomplish *my plan* to crush the enemies.[9]

> ἐπίβλειψον . . . ἐπὶ τὰ ἔργα τῶν χειρῶν μου. . . . ὅτι νῦν καιρὸς ἀντιλαβέσθαι τῆς κληρονομίας σου καὶ ποιῆσαι τὸ ἐπιτήδευμά μου εἰς θραῦσμα ἐχθρῶν.

Contrast 2 Macc 15:24, where the male general Judah Maccabee prays for the actions of *God*'s hand: "By the might of *your* arm may these blasphemers who come against your holy people be struck down." Greek Esther 14 also reveals a more rending dependence on God. To be sure, at the final moment Judith also asks for aid: "Give me strength today, O Lord, God of Israel!" Yet, *in the next line*, God's strength is matched by Judith's (*en tē ischui autēs*).

Her deed will also redound "for the exaltation of Jerusalem,"[10] and central is God's inheritance (*klēronomia*; Heb. *naḥălâ*), that is, Israel understood as God's land, historically bequeathed to the twelve tribes (see at 8:22). Israel as God's inheritance is also featured in the somewhat similar prayers in Greek Esth 13:15–17; 14:5.

---

7   Alan Dundes, "Response," in Alonso-Schökel, *Narrative Structure*, 28–29; Levine, "Sacrifice and Salvation;" Jacobus, "Judith, Holofernes," 110–36; Stocker, *Judith*, 3–23.

8   Robertson, "Cyclops and the Self."

9   See Sawyer, "Gender Strategies," 19–20.

10   On the Jerusalem-centered nature of the text and the exaltation of Jerusalem, see §2 above.

Because of the association of the bed with Holofernes's intended sexual triumph, the vertical bedpost is suggestively phallic and, hanging on it, the even more phallic sword. Holofernes's head is said to lie near the bedpost, but because he is drunk, he is robbed of the virility that would normally be attached to his personal symbols. One might assume that the pictorial tradition was forced to emphasize the visual aspects of Judith looming over Holofernes, while the literary tradition might emphasize her prayer or internal monologue, but her debasing of the body is strongly thematized in the original text. As in the European paintings, the LXX text also focuses on her agency, her manipulation of his body, her rude debasing of his head and body, her ritualistic shaming and dehumanizing of him, and her disempowering of the corpse. She ritually demythologizes the *numen* that should reside in a great general.

It is noted specifically that Judith grasps Holofernes by his hair. For a woman to manhandle the general's head by grasping his hair would represent a shocking act. Warriors from Samson to Alexander the Great were often identified by their hair; Absalom had voluminous hair (2 Sam 14:25–26), and in Herodotus 7.208 it is said that the Spartans combed their hair before going into battle. When Artaxerxes II exhibits the head of the rebel Cyrus the Younger, Ctesias recounts, "Seizing the hair, which was long and shaggy, he showed it to those [of the rebels] who were wavering and deserting" (Plutarch, *Artaxerxes* 13.2). Grasping his head by the hair suggests a phallic control on Judith's part, more typical of a general's triumph. Since she chooses *not* to have sex with the general, this clutch of his hair is the closest physical contact they will have; it is *her* version of the embrace that Holofernes has fantasized. (See Beowulf and Grendel in §8 above.) This detail as much as anything else communicates the Eros/Thanatos aspect of the beheading. And as Amy-Jill Levine notes, the focus on Holofernes's head,

both here and in chap. 14, was strangely anticipated in the "searing heat" that came upon the head of Judith's husband Manasseh in 8:3, and in Holofernes's statement to Achior in 6:5.

For Holofernes's all-important sword hanging on his bedpost, the LXX uses a Persian loanword, *akinakēs,* a short, straight Persian sword. Hebrew *ḥereb* is in Greek normally *machaira,* a small sword (Gen 34:25–26), but sometimes *rhomphaia,* a large sword (as in Simeon's sword in Jdt 9:2). An *akinakēs* seems a small sword to behead a general, even in two strokes, but it was seen as a characteristically eastern weapon. On one Persian coin of the period, a Persian king kills a Greek soldier; like Judith, he holds the soldier by his hair in his left hand and an *akinakēs* in his right.[11] Similar also is the account of an Assyrian general's wife Panthea in Xenophon's *Cyropaedia* (7.3.14; see §4 above). She, also like Judith, speaks in ambiguous words, asking Cyrus permission to mourn over her dead husband's body. But when alone with the body, she pulls out an *akinakēs* and kills herself.

■ 13:8–9a Stocker's characterization of this scene as an acteme is supported by the minute ticking off of very resilient details, details that have become attributes of Judith through hundreds of iterations. Just as her prayer above was in two parts, the text emphasizes that she struck twice to sever Holofernes's head. (*Patassō* recalls Simeon and Shechem, 9:3.) The dual strike is surprisingly retained in many European paintings, demonstrated visually when Judith raises an already bloody sword to strike a second blow. Why the persistence of this detail? It may communicate that, as a woman, she is still frail, requiring two strokes—the first a hesitation stroke. This would problematize Judith's agency and suggest her dependence on God. In that case the text would seem to rein her in—contrast David's slaying of Goliath, both in 1 Samuel 17 and in the Sistine Chapel, where there is a swift, decisive dispatching of the Philistine.[12] But the text of Judith says that she struck "with all her

---

11 M. Rahim Shayegan, *Arsacids and Sasanians: Political Ideology in Post-Hellenistic and Late Antique Persia* (Cambridge and New York: Cambridge University Press, 2011) 169–72. For *akinakēs,* see Herodotus 3.118; Ctesias apud Plutarch, *Artaxerxes* 15.2; also Jdt 16:9; Delcor, "Le livre de Judith," 151. A variant is *paraxiphidion* ("dagger"; cf. 2 Kgdms 5:8), and note Vg *pugio* ("dagger"). Some European artists,

for example, Il Sodoma, depicted the *pugio* as a small weapon, and indeed the Vulgate suggests this. Cf. also Let Jer 15 *encheiridion.*

12 Sawyer notes that Judith required two strokes, but David one, as a sort of rank ordering ("Gender Strategies," 21). But David is still "just a boy" (1 Sam 17:33), so in that story as well the weak is used as a means for God to triumph. Cf. also Moses

strength." The two blows may not demonstrate weakness, but they slow the very action itself to emphasize Judith's intentionality: she is determined to carry the act through, not turning back after the first stroke. It is also possible, but not likely, that since a "good" sacrifice must be rendered in one stroke, the two blows may represent a satire of sacrifice (see below).

What is interestingly omitted is the blood that would spurt over Judith as well. Is the text restrained, decorous? Does it respond to purity concerns? This is not a realistic text, and indeed in violent films blood is often abundant or absent by the director's choice. Judith will carry away the bloody head, so purity does not seem to be the concern. The bloodlessness may empower Judith and humiliate the victim; blood would suggest chaos, and she controls even the blood. The depiction may be somewhat similar to Bel and Dragon, where the "dragon" turns out to be not powerful but a mortal, defenseless beast whose bursting is also bloodless. Yet in 9:3 the slaughter of Shechem was marked by blood.

Judith continues to shame Holofernes even after the beheading, enacting every symbol of contempt. After removing his head, she rudely rolls his carcass onto the floor. If the name Bethulia means virginity—the Jewish certification of virginity based on an examination of the hymen is called *betulim* (see 6:12; 10:21; 16:19)—and Holofernes intended to penetrate both the town and Judith, then his intent has been reversed: Judith has penetrated his vagina—his inner chamber—pulled down his symbolic hymen—the canopy—raped and deflowered him, and taken his symbolic hymen as a spoils offering for the temple in Jerusalem. Earlier scholars had rejected the sexual associations in this scene, but many now readily accept the imagery of castration and inverted rape, and Susan Kim also registers the curtain as a symbolic hymen.[13]

■ **13:9b–10a** In contrast to the retardation of plot at the beginning of the scene, the acteme is told very briskly. Judith's dramatic act allows for, indeed necessitates, a quick release of tension. The two women exit together, according to their custom, for prayer—darkly ironic, since it is Judith's prayer practice that has provided the cover for a quick escape after a violent act. Judith and her slave, with the head in hand, retrace their steps instantaneously—again, at night—back up the mountain to the walls of Bethulia. The two women are most united while in their transit, first from Bethulia to the camp, and now back to Bethulia. (Recall that, although in paintings they are depicted together in the act of decapitation, in the text the slave was outside.) The denouement of the novella must flow quickly at this point.

As suggested above at 13:3, *met' oligon* here is odd after the steady *kai*'s, unless we understand Judith's slave as stationed outside *Judith*'s tent. Merely standing outside the inner chamber, or outside Holofernes's tent, would not require this temporal transition. At any rate, all of the actions are quick and calculated, confirming that all parts of Judith's plan have come off as she had intended. Nothing here is left to chance.

Judith's pouch, which had been significant before as the means of carrying her special food—a visible, portable Jewish identity for a woman named "Jew"—is now significant for a very different, macabre reason. She is able to secrete the head of Holofernes and take it out of the camp in her pouch because she has so carefully broadcast to everyone that she carried her own food in the pouch. It will now contain a bloody, impure head and will become a trophy pouch as well, since the head and the curtain are in it. The transfer of head to pouch also connects Judith with her slave in an act of treachery. European paintings often depicted the slave as holding the pouch in front of her—never in front of Judith—as

---

striking the rock twice, along with other parallels listed in van Henten, "Judith as an Alternative Leader," 232–38. Gruen also suggests that the phrase "she took his head from him" implies a mock delicacy (*Diaspora*, 167). The precise comic tone of the verbs, however, is difficult to register with certainty.

13   Kim, "Bloody Signs," 286, 292–93, 300–304; Wills, *Jewish Novel*, 148–51. Cf. Bruce Rosenstock, "David's Play: Fertility Rituals and the Glory of

God in 2 Sam 6," *JSOT* 31 (2006) 63–80. On the older view, see Moore, *Judith*, 72–73, 240. The fact that Judith steals and uses Holofernes's own sword to decapitate him can be seen as further emasculating him. It is a motif found in the narrative of David and Goliath, but not the same as Jael, who uses a more domestic tent peg—emasculating in a different way. On decapitation as castration, cf. also the cutting off of the horns of the altar in Jdt 9:8; Amos 3:14–15; Exod 27:2; 1 Kgs 1:50.

a visual womb.[14] Judith then places Holofernes's head, about the size of a baby, into the pouch as if the slave-surrogate is reverse-birthing him. Though little of this is perceptible in the ancient text, Judith's powerful agency is still seen in her use of the instrumental slave and the ironic pouch. The perfectly instrumental slave, indeed, is a common motif cross-culturally in slave-owning societies.

Excursus: Literary Effects in the Acteme

The actions occurring in Holofernes's bedchamber characterize him as impotent and unmanned, the beheading often viewed as a symbolic castration. The book of Judith is the story of a brazen woman, but it also focuses on a weak, passive man who lacks self-mastery (see the commentary on 8:35). The oft-noted voyeurism here becomes triple voyeurism—the audience first viewing Judith's provocative body, then Holofernes's headless corpse, and later Bagoas's own viewing of the corpse. It contributes to the sense that Judith has reversed the voyeurism and raped Holofernes, first with her words and then with his sword, and forced Bagoas to witness the result.

Popular literature often employs literary techniques that are meant to go unnoticed. What may indeed seem natural or typical of this and related texts may, however, reflect studied effects. The structure, for instance, can be analyzed in different ways, perhaps all valid in terms of audience reception.

1. Though the acteme is told quickly, the combination of a quick pace (paratactic clauses connected by *kai*) and many individual steps has the paradoxical effect of both accelerating and retarding the plot at the same time. Many short sentences with active verbs are used in roughly parallel structure, and the meticulous observation of each action shows quasi-liturgical care. Just as Holofernes's successful campaign was described with quickly repeated aorist indicatives (see 2:21–28), here Judith's actions, as if in response, are similar:

She *went up* to the bedpost near Holofernes's head, and *took down* his sword which hung there. She *came close* to his bed, *took hold* of the hair of his head, and *said*, "Give me strength today, O Lord God of Israel." Then she *struck his neck twice*

with all her might, and *cut off* his head. Next she *rolled* his body off the bed and *pulled down* the canopy from the posts. She quickly *went out* and *gave* Holofernes' head to her slave, who *placed it in* her food bag. (13:6–10)

καὶ προσελθοῦσα τῷ κανόνι τῆς κλίνης, ὅς ἦν πρὸς κεφαλῆς Ὀλοφέρνου, καθεῖλεν τὸν ἀκινάκην αὐτοῦ ἀπ᾽ αὐτοῦ καὶ ἐγγίσασα τῆς κλίνης ἐδράξατο τῆς κόμης τῆς κεφαλῆς αὐτοῦ καὶ εἶπεν Κραταίωσόν με, κύριε ὁ θεὸς Ἰσραήλ, ἐν τῇ ἡμέρᾳ ταύτῃ. καὶ ἐπάταξεν εἰς τὸν τράχηλον αὐτοῦ δὶς ἐν τῇ ἰσχύι αὐτῆς καὶ ἀφεῖλεν τὴν κεφαλὴν αὐτοῦ ἀπ᾽ αὐτοῦ. καὶ ἀπεκύλισεν τὸ σῶμα αὐτοῦ ἀπὸ τῆς στρωμνῆς καὶ ἀφεῖλεν τὸ κωνώπιον ἀπὸ τῶν στύλων. καὶ μετ᾽ ὀλίγον ἐξῆλθεν καὶ παρέδωκεν τῇ ἄβρᾳ αὐτῆς τὴν κεφαλὴν Ὀλοφέρνου, καὶ ἐνέβαλεν αὐτὴν εἰς τὴν πήραν τῶν βρωμάτων αὐτῆς.

2. In addition to this structure, a second literary pattern comprises five references to Holofernes's bed, the most common motif in the section (*klinē* and *strōmnē*). Each reference brings Judith into a more intimate relationship with the bed, building a tension of sex and violence. Like the wine, the bed is a character in the narrative, drawing Judith—and the audience—voyeuristically to it:

V. 2 Holofernes was collapsed upon his bed.
V. 4 Judith was standing beside the bed.
V. 6 She approached the post of the bed, which was at Holofernes's head.
V. 7 She took down his sword.
V. 8 She came near the bed and grasped the hair of his head.
V. 9 She rolled his body off the bed.

The audience's view is focused in each case more closely and intensely on the bed, each action more sexually charged, at the same time that each is more debasing and violent. On one hand, it is like a sexual act satirized, or perhaps like a sacrifice satirized, but Judith is also like a hawk, gliding in ever-tightening circles before diving at the prey.

3. This scene can also be compared with the equivalent scenes in Ehud's killing of Eglon, Jael's killing of Sisera, and David's killing of Goliath:

---

14 It is perhaps not coincidental that the slave as instrumental womb appears at about the same time in art that nude women are depicted as fleshy in the midriff, as though pregnant (§8 above).

Ehud Judg 3:20–23 LXX	Jael Judg 4:21 LXX	David 1 Reigns 17:48–51
Ehud came to him, while he was sitting alone in his cool roof chamber, and said, "I have a message from God for you." So he rose from his seat and came near him.		And Goliath came to meet David,
And it happened when he arose that Ehud reached with his left hand, took the sword from his right thigh,	Jael wife of Heber took a tent peg and took a hammer in her hand, and went softly to him	And David stretched out his hand into the bag and took from it one stone
and thrust it into Eglon's belly.	and drove the peg into his temple (jaw?), and it went down into the ground— he was writhing between her knees, and weary— and he breathed his last and died.	and slung it and struck him on his forehead, and the stone went through the helmet into his forehead, and he fell on his face on the ground. And David ran and stood over him and took Goliath's sword and killed him and cut off his head.
The hilt also went in after the blade, and the fat closed over the blade, for he did not draw the sword out of his belly; (MT includes: and the filth came out.)		
Then Ehud went out into the vestibule and closed the doors of the roof chamber on him, and locked them.		

Ehud's slaying of Eglon ("Calf") and Judith's of Holofernes are alike in that both involve the trickster's deception of a foreign leader, the phallic penetration of his private quarters, the ritual humiliation, and the humorous and ironic tone.[15] Jael's slaying of Sisera is on the surface a more obvious

comparison, yet it features fewer parallels of motif. Nevertheless, it involves a phallic blow to the head by a woman, with an ironic contrast at the center: "She went softly to him and drove the peg into his temple." The irony is further "driven home": "and the peg went down into the ground." David's slaying of Goliath, though shorter, is similar in that David uses Goliath's own sword, and similarly beheads the villain. The Hellenistic context of Judith perhaps accounts for the fact that it is more novelistic, more like real time, with visual, cinematic steps (see also the commentary on 10:10).

Excursus: A Satire of Sacrifice in the Acteme

Although modern readers often assimilate Judith to women's roles and rituals, it is possible that she acts as a sort of officiating priest, or rather, in killing Holofernes she performs a mock sacrifice, complete with its own inverted ritual. Yet to consider this possibility, one must first determine the definition of sacrifice. We will consider sacrifice in both a general and an Israel-specific sense. We pause to provide a broad definition of sacrifice for the present discussion. Sacrifice is generally the ritualized killing, burning, or pouring out of something of value: a cultivated animal or plant; wine, oil, or incense; an object of value; a valued person, such as a king, general, soldier, hero, or child. It is a practice of reciprocity between human culture and the culture of the gods, in which something of value from the human realm is offered to the gods. An underlying assumption, sometimes unspoken, is that the human society (defined by the sacrificial participation) will receive some boon from the gods—growth, release from a disease or war, life with the gods. Yet some sacrifices involve the symbolic expulsion not of a cultivated item of value but of something despised: waste, the scapegoat that carries away sins, a "lesser" human, such as a criminal or someone with a disability. Just as the offering to the gods of a valued commodity maintains the peace of a society, the expulsion of a detested person or thing outside of society does as well. If nature and culture are understood as a binary, then sacrifice is primarily an offering of human-cultivated objects to the super-culture of the gods, while expulsion is a processing of human-despised objects *outward* to nature and wilderness.

Some argue that expulsion rites are not really sacrifice—since the victim is not killed—but only a

---

15   Gera notes that the Ehud and the Jael stories both depend on an inner room or tent, and it is conceivable that Ehud's assassination of Eglon in the

inner chamber evokes the temple precincts (*Judith*, 388–89).

metaphor for sacrifice. Yet some examples speak against this. It is true that in Leviticus 16 the scapegoat is not killed, but in m. Yoma 6:6 it is. And even in Leviticus, the second goat *is* sacrificed. The *pharmakos* ("scapegoat") in Greece embodies a similar dynamic, although the tradition is unclear about whether the marked person is killed or expelled.[16] The salient characteristic of these rituals may in fact be the *ambiguity* of death: is the individual expelled or killed? Is expelling something into the wilderness the same as killing it? In both cases, the subject is removed *from culture,* either to the superculture of the gods or to the wilderness. Some Roman examples exhibit this ambiguity. The Roman *homo sacer* embodies two meanings of the term *sacer,* "sanctified" and "desanctified." The *homo sacer* is a cursed man, expelled for a crime, who has no rights or protection; anyone can kill him with impunity. The Greek *anathema* (two spellings with slightly different meanings, *anathema* and *anathēma*) came to translate *ḥērem* in the LXX, communicating a similar ambiguity among Jews: a zone of power and danger that can connote either an offering to the gods or desanctification by deconstructing something to its natural elements. And even if some examples should turn out to be literary only, such as Carabas (Philo, *Against Flaccus* 6.36–39), they still possessed a powerful figural role in society and could have influenced the narrative performance of Judith.

The general sense of a sacrificial act in regard to the Judith acteme was raised by Hans Jørgen Lundager Jensen. Nebuchadnezzar's plan had been a de-differentiation, reducing all to sameness. The solution to the crisis comes with the rise of a hero and a "sacrifice":

> [A] select person—the priest or the hero—acts on behalf of the collective, saving it by sacrifice or by murder. . . . The priest and the hero . . . move out of the "room" of the collective, either into the "room of the holy," or out into "the room of the enemy."[17]

In the fields of medieval literature—French, English, and Arabic—there have been attempts to see Judith's act as a sort of sacrifice understood in this general way: Judith achieves a kind of resolution of opposite realms, or removal of a threatening realm, by ritually killing the beast.[18]

---

16 Daniel Ullucci, "Sacrifice in the Ancient Mediterranean: Recent and Current Research," *CurBR* 13 (2015) 388–439, esp. 407. Ullucci rightly avoids a notion of sacrifice as a separate, disembedded, cross-cultural phenomenon and sees it instead as an embedded phenomenon that can vary tremendously in different cultural contexts. Still, in eastern Mediterranean societies there are similar sorts of actions and discourses that may reflect the assumptions of Judith's audience. In addition, in place of actual ritualized behavior we are here analyzing a fictitious text. Ullucci grants that a text is different, referencing Jonathan Z. Smith, "The Domestication of Sacrifice," in Smith, *Relating Religion: Essays in the Study of Religion* (Chicago: University of Chicago Press, 2004) 145–59. See also Kathryn McClymond, "Sacrifice and Violence," in Andrew R. Murphy, ed., *The Blackwell Companion to Religion and Violence* (Oxford: Wiley-Blackwell, 2011) 320–30, here 326–28.

While Ullucci argues for a limited definition of sacrifice—and excludes much of what others discuss as part of this category, Kathryn McClymond proffers a broader and more inclusive definition (*Beyond Sacred Violence: A Comparative Study of Sacrifice* [Baltimore: Johns Hopkins University Press, 2008]). On *pharmakos,* see Gregory Nagy, *Best of the Achaeans: Concepts of the Hero in Archaic Greek Poetry* (Baltimore: Johns Hopkins University Press, 1979) 251–316; Walter Burkert, *Greek Religion* (Oxford: Blackwell, 1984) 82; Burkert, *Structure and History in Greek Myth and Ritual* (Sather Classical Lectures 47; Berkeley: University of California Press, 1982) 59–64; James B. Rives, "Magic, Religion, and Law: The Case of the *Lex Cornelia de sicariis et veneficiis,*" in Clifford Ando and Jörg Rüpke, eds., *Religion and Law in Classical and Christian Rome* (Potsdamer altertumswissenschaftliche Beiträge 15; Stuttgart: Steiner, 2006) 47–67, here 56–57; Wright, *Disposal of Impurity;* Jan Bremmer, "Scapegoat Rituals in Ancient Greece," *HSCP* 87 (1983) 299–320. K. M. Coleman notes that the victim was sometimes humiliated before death in mythological reenactments, as in the case of Carabas ("Fatal Charades: Roman Executions Staged as Mythological Enactments," *JRS* 80 [1990] 44–73). On Paul's similar use of *peripsēma* ("dirt") and *perikatharmata* ("refuse") in 1 Cor 4:13, see C. K. Barrett, *A Commentary on the First Epistle to the Corinthians* (London: A. & C. Black, 1968) 112–13; and see Photius, *Lexicon,* s.v. *peripsēma.* In Israel, note Prov 21:18.

17 Otzen, *Tobit and Judith,* 120–21, summarizing Jensen, "Juditbogen," 174–75.

18 Note LaCocque, *Feminine Unconventional,* 48; Kate Koppelman, "Fearing the Neighbor," 1–2, 21; and see Weststeijn, "Wine, Women"; and §8 above.

There are many resonances of sacrifice and ritual killing in the ancient Mediterranean. Suzanne Pinckney Stetkevych analyzes the vendetta in pre-Islamic poetry and treats it as a form of sacrifice. Interesting for our discussion, she draws attention to the connection with women's purification: "Men's cleansing themselves of the pollution of unavenged blood is equated with women's washing and perfuming themselves after menstruation."[19] The curtain, with Holofernes's head in it, would have taken on some of his blood, like the bloodstained cloth of the wedding chamber (see below). The revenge tradition is also like an inverted sacrifice and meal. Normally, the sacrifice of an animal would provide a meal for one's kin, but the killing of a perpetrator in revenge devitalizes *the enemy's kin* and is understood *to feed the avenger's kin.* In other revenge tales of women warriors, says Johan Weststeijn, "the victim is treated by the avenger as if he were food and drink."[20]

A satire of Israelite priestly sacrifice? We turn to more particular associations with Israelite sacrifice. Judith's ritualized scene of redressing (chap. 10) and her daily purifications (12:5–9) call to mind priestly preparation.[21] For a female to be portrayed with a male persona is not unknown in the fantasy world of folktales. A genre of Turkish folktales concerns the *khoja* priestess-girl (a category that does not exist in Islam), in China the girl Hua Mulan disguises herself as a man and becomes a great warrior, and in Europe a woman disguised as a man becomes pope.[22] To be sure, Judith does not take on the outward appearances of a man as these female figures do; rather, dressed as a woman, she performs male actions.

The art of storytelling in the acteme creates a rich symbol field, much of which could be associated with the temple or priestly practices. First, Holofernes's tent may suggest the Jerusalem temple, or perhaps the earlier tent of meeting. Crucial to this compari-

son is the fact that Holofernes's tent has an inner and an outer chamber, separated by a curtain. The Jerusalem temple was also constructed with an inner chamber—the holy of holies—and an outer chamber, separated by the temple curtain. Even some of the colors of Holofernes's net appear on the temple curtain (Exod 26:31).[23] In Judith, the symbolic and dramatic zones are created by filmy fabrics—a field tent and an inner mosquito net—but the fact that the net is so gauzy does not preclude a temple image. In 8:4–6 it was noted that Judith's own tent of seclusion may evoke a personal temple, and Joan R. Branham explores what might be called the "velvet rope effect" of lattices, thin fences, veils, and low barriers to construct *marked* spaces, even sacred versus profane space, without establishing a hard barrier. This even applies to the "impenetrable" Jerusalem temple, where the *soreg* or lattice fence in the temple court provided a symbolic barrier, signaling an unbreachable divide without precluding a view within. Says Branham,

> Just as fences, parapets, gates, and veils acted primarily to generate and establish gradational sanctity in the Temple, so the defilement and destruction of the Temple are defined by foreign penetration of these same barriers.[24]

The inner chamber of Holofernes's tent, with its mosquito net, and the outer flap of the tent may then become *marked* areas out of proportion to the thin material.

The violation of the Jerusalem temple by Antiochus IV Epiphanes (1 Macc 1:20–21; Josephus, *Antiquities* 12.5.4 §250) might have influenced our author; the Seleucid king took the curtain "made of fine linen and scarlet." Later Jewish reflections on the violation of the Jerusalem temple by the Roman gen-

---

19 Suzanne Pinckney Stetkevych, *The Mute Immortals Speak: Pre-Islamic Poetry and the Poetics of Ritual* (Myth and Poetics; Ithaca, NY: Cornell University Press, 1993) 173; see also 65, 72.

20 Weststeijn, "Wine, Women," 112; Stetkevych, *Mute Immortals,* 73.

21 The motif of "outside the camp," for instance (see 12:5b–9), is part of this reversal: rather than eliminating impure substances "outside the camp," as was typical in the temple cult, she removes *herself* from the potentially defiling quarters *inside* the camp.

22 On *Khoja,* see Walker and Uysal, *Tales Alive,* 260; on Mulan, see Yee, "Hand of a Woman," 101–16.

See also Motif K1837, Disguise of woman in man's clothes; K1961.2.1, Woman in disguise becomes pope, both in Thompson, *Motif-Index.*

23 The colors of the Jerusalem temple curtain are also commented on by Philo and Josephus, and played upon in an indirect way in *Aseneth;* see above at 10:20–23. In 10:21 it was noted that the curtain conjured images of opulent Babylonian curtains, but that would not preclude an association with the temple also. Note, however, that Judith uses *kōnōpion,* an Egyptian mosquito net placed over a couch, rather than *katapetasma,* the word used in the LXX for the temple curtain.

24 Branham, "Penetrating the Sacred," 22.

eral Titus are also suggestive for our earlier period. According to b. Giṭṭin 56b:

> Titus took a harlot by the hand and entered the Holy of Holies and spread out a scroll of the Law and committed a sin on it. He then took a sword and slashed the curtain. Miraculously, blood spurted out. . . . Titus further took the curtain and shaped it like a basket and brought all the vessels of the Sanctuary and put them in it, and then put them on board ship to go and process in triumph with them in his city.[25]

For Branham, this talmudic passage

> associates spatial, foreign, and sexual penetration with the desecration of the veil. . . . This remarkable text ironically posits Titus in a mimetic relationship to the high priest, while simultaneously reversing the elements that characterize the sanctity of Yom Kippur. . . . [The miraculous blood] recalls sacrificial blood of atonement the high priest brings in from the altar. . . . Titus is not simply a foreign violator of space but is a metonymy for the high priest, realizing sacrality through the violent parody of it.[26]

This "mimetic relationship to the high priest" and the satire of elements may apply in the case of Judith as well. Judith's cleansing and preparation are similar to priestly cleansing rituals, and the audience perhaps sees in Judith's decapitation, drawn in some detail, a satire of a sacrifice. Following are the relevant motifs with short notes:

1. Judith has bathed each evening in preparation, explicitly "purifying" herself (12:8–9).
   Judith bathes regularly *before* her bloody act, but not afterward, even though she has handled a dead body and a bloody head! This suggests more a sacrificial process, which requires purification ahead of time, than an impurity ritual, which requires a cleansing after the fact.

2. She moves through the curtain to Holofernes's inner sanctum, his "holy of holies," to kill him.
   In 9:8 the Assyrians also threatened to penetrate the Jerusalem temple and "emasculate" the altar by breaking off the horns. Although sacrifice at the Jerusalem temple occurred on the altar outside and not in the holy of holies, a satirical similarity may still be suggested.

3. She approaches the bed.
   Does the bed suggest an altar?

4. She pauses to utter a prayer.

5. She takes down Holofernes's sword.
   Does the sword, a Persian *akinakēs,* suggest a special priest's implement?

6. She grasps his head by the hair.
   This detail, though powerful, does not in itself suggest sacrifice, since the sacrificial victim would be well treated. Rather, it is a shaming motif.

7. She severs his head in two strokes.
   Sacrificial practice in both Greece and Israel required one clean cut or blow to kill an animal; two strokes would have constituted a botched sacrifice. The motif of two strokes is extremely stable in the Judith tradition. Thus, her grasping his head by the hair and her two strokes both diverge from a sacrificial scenario, although they may constitute the very substance of a *satire* of sacrifice: the decapitation is carried out like a bad sacrifice.
   The absence of blood in the Judith narrative might be taken as counterevidence for a sacrificial connection, yet this fact would not likely be relevant in any case. Sacrifice in Greece is *depicted* as orderly, bloodless, and humane, while irregular sacrifice, such as human sacrifice, is marked as bloody and disordered.[27] We also recall the danger posited above of the "photographic fallacy," the assumption that every motif of a fanciful narrative could or should correspond to real actions in the world. From the medieval period on, Judith's deed is often depicted with blood spurting uncontrollably, or with the bloody stump of Holofernes's neck viewed centrally. In medieval paintings, the blood appears to be celebrated, while in the Renaissance it begins to register as dangerous (see §8). It is

25 Translation of Branham, "Penetrating the Sacred," 23–24.

26 Branham, "Penetrating the Sacred," 23–24.

27 Jean-Pierre Vernant, "A General Theory of Sacrifice and the Slaying of the Victim in the Greek *Thusia*," in Vernant, *Mortals and Immortals: Collected Essays* (Princeton, NT: Princeton University Press, 1991) 290–302, here 295; see also Jan Bremmer, "Myth and Ritual in Greek Human Sacrifice: Lykaon, Polyxena and the Case of the Rhodian Criminal," in Bremmer, ed., *The Strange World of Human Sacrifice* (Studies in the History and Anthropology of Religion 1; Leuven: Peeters, 2007) 55–79, here 61.

possible that the LXX version omits the blood because it would be an impurity, but it can hardly be ignored, and the irony of Judith handling the head to place it in her kosher pouch calls attention to it.

8. She rolls the headless corpse onto a footstool.

It might be suggested, though it is speculative, that the footstool, mentioned in 14:15 but not here, suggests a ground altar. The ambiguous term *chelōnis* means raised mound, but in Hos 12:11 *chelōnē* is associated with ground altars.[28] In Israel, sacrificing animals on the ground was not acceptable even at the ancient high places; a stone was required to drain blood, which could become an altar stone (1 Sam 14:31–35). In Greece, however, the chthonic cults required a ground altar, although nothing points to that connection here. Is animal slaughter rather than sacrifice suggested? The more likely explanation is that Judith rolls the headless body onto the footstool as a means of abusing the corpse.[29]

9. She deposits the head in what had been a pouch for acceptable Jewish food.

10. She takes down the inner curtain of the tent, a decorated mosquito net. She will later deposit this as a plunder offering in the Jerusalem temple.

In addition to Holofernes's hymen, does the inner curtain suggest the temple curtain? The fact that the Jerusalem temple curtain was later taken by Titus is to be noted, although it is possible that the curtain taken by Judith is simply a plunder offering and not in any way associated with the temple curtain.

Johan Weststeijn draws out relevant motifs here.[30] The Near Eastern woman warrior Jalila,

in order to avoid sleeping with the tyrant, engages in a ruse: she says she will be impure from her menstrual period for eighty days. When the tyrant is killed, a white piece of cloth is used to soak up his blood, which is then raised as a flag of triumph. In traditional Muslim weddings the bloodstained cloth of the wedding chamber is shown to the guests as proof of the bride's virginity, and she retains this cloth as a sign as well. Another Near Eastern warrior woman, Zenobia, captures a drop of the tyrant's blood in a piece of cotton and keeps it among her perfumes.

11. When she returns to Bethulia, she will exhibit the head to the Bethulians, which causes Achior to faint.

There is a numinous power in both sacred and polluting substances. Does the head have talismanic power? (See below.)

12. The head will be displayed on the wall of Bethulia to rally the citizens.

These motifs may suggest temple architecture and practices, although at some points they are at variance. It may be a deliberate and satirical variance, or the motifs may bear no relation to the temple and sacrifice at all. The association remains intriguing yet ambiguous at every turn.

Human sacrifice. And what of *human* sacrifice? In the realm of actual practice, it probably did not occur during our period in the ancient Mediterranean except in Canaanite-Phoenician tradition, but it lived in literature as a charge projected onto foreign peoples, and a common plot point in Greek and Roman novels.[31] Romans commented on human sacrifice as barbarous and foreign, or a grotesque practice of groups like Bacchics and Christians.[32] The killing of

---

28 Johan Lust, Erik Eynikel, and Katrin Hauspie, eds., *Greek-English Lexicon of the Septuagint* (rev. ed.; Stuttgart: Deutsche Bibelgesellschaft, 2003), s.v. χελωνίς, and T. Muraoka, *A Greek-English Lexicon of the Septuagint* (Louvain: Peeters, 2009), s.v. χελωνίς, both note that the word is a neologism and suggest "threshold." *LSJ*, reading Hesychius, assumes that it means threshold in this passage as well. Gera draws the parallel to the god Dagon falling on the threshold in 1 Sam 5:2–5 and opts for "threshold" (*Judith*, 428). Although they are merely judging from context, "threshold" would not make sense if Bagoas has to enter to see him lying on it. The other meanings of the word, "mound" or even "tortoise shell,"

allow for the translation "footstool" here in 14:15, as Moore (*Judith*, 240), Schmitz/Engel (*Judit*, 364, 385), and *NETS* agree. In 4 Kgdms 23:17 *skopelon* refers to a mound that is a grave.

29 The verb is *apekylise*; cf. Hebrew *gālal* in Gen 29:3. In Sus OG 62 "they hurled [*erripsan*] the elders into a chasm."

30 Weststeijn, "Wine, Women"; see §4 above.

31 Warren, *My Flesh Is Meat*, passim.

32 James Rives, "Human Sacrifice among Pagans and Christians," *JRS* 85 (1995) 65–86. On the linking of foreign atrocities and those of internal Others, see Wills, *Not God's People*, esp. 13–14. See also Zsuzsanna Várhelyi, "Political Murder and

humans in Greece and Rome was also often treated as metaphorical sacrifice. The killing of a woman in Greek tragedy always has an expiatory aspect. In Rome, political murders of one's own partisans were also treated as sacrifices. The fact that blood is not mentioned in Judith might argue against *human* sacrifice, in that the latter is associated with chaos and barbaric practice. Yet some of these metaphorical associations with sacrifice, even human sacrifice, may have accrued to the beheading of Holofernes.

Degradation rites. Associations with sacrifice or priestly practice remain speculative, however, although the elimination rites noted above may be more suggestive, as Judith deconstructs Holofernes's body and exhibits the head. In addition, degradation rites should be considered in regard to Judith's deed. In the ancient world, the shaming and mutilation of the enemy may seem to be a reverse sacrifice, but it has also been analyzed as a ritual humiliation lacking any sacrificial aspect. The ritual degradation and shaming of an enemy's head and body are found in the Hebrew Bible, and are a common motif cross-culturally.[33] Degrading the enemy body—dishonoring it by deconstructing the elements back to a natural state—is a way of establishing control, torturing the

dead, a process of desacralization and reclassification. The *numen* of a great leader is symbolically reclassified into its earthly elements, now powerless. Cutting off and separating the body parts denies integrity to the person and, most important, denies the opportunity for the living to bury the victim. David, for instance, in the battle with Goliath and the Philistines says:

> I shall cut off your head! I shall give your corpse and the corpses of the Philistine camp to the birds of the sky and the wild animals of the land! Then all the earth will know that there is a God in Israel. (1 Sam 17:46)

The reuniting of body parts and the release of the body to the mourners then symbolizes a restitution. It demonstrates that the prior deconstitution of the body was to make mourning impossible, although now burial can occur.[34]

Other cases in Israelite tradition and elsewhere are instructive. When the head of Ishbaal is brought to David, he responds by ordering that the two who bore it be hanged, with their hands and feet cut off and separated from them (2 Sam 4:5–12). A dialogue of body dismemberment results: the head of Ishbaal

Sacrifice: From Roman Republic to Empire," in Várhelyi and Jennifer Wright Knust, eds., *Ancient Mediterranean Sacrifice* (Oxford: Oxford University Press, 2011) 124–41; Nicole Loraux, *Tragic Ways of Killing a Woman* (Cambridge, MA: Harvard University Press, 1987) 4; Bremmer, "Myth and Ritual."

33   See Saul Olyan, "Jehoiakim's Dehumanizing Interment as a Ritual Act of Reclassification," *JBL* 133 (2014) 271–79; Olyan, "The Instrumental Dimensions of Ritual Violence against Corpses in Biblical Texts," in Olyan, ed., *Ritual Violence in the Hebrew Bible: New Perspectives* (Oxford: Oxford University Press, 2015) 125–36. See also T. M. Lemos, "Shame and Mutilation of Enemies in the Hebrew Bible," *JBL* 125 (2006) 225–41; and see Gen 40:19; 2 Sam 16:9, 21:12–14; 2 Kgs 10:7; Jer 8:1–2; 1 Macc 11:17; 2 Macc 1:16. But see Volker Mergenthaler, *Medusa Meets Holofernes: Poetologische, semiologische und intertextuelle Diskursivierung von Enthauptung* (Bern: P. Lang, 1997): in general, decapitation was mandated for the killing of a king, a deity, or a respected opponent, while lesser opponents were subjected to hanging, drowning, strangling, quartering, or burning. It may be advisable to divide the biblical cases accordingly. See the shaming of a foreign deity in 1 Sam 5:1–5: when the statue of the god Dagon falls, his head and hands are broken

off. Xerxes removed hands of a Marduk statue to demonstrate his power, and the Meröe head of Augustus, now in the British Museum, was actually preserved because a statue of Augustus had been beheaded by the King of Meröe, the head buried in the lintel of a building so that all who entered would trample the head of Augustus. Statue beheadings are common cross-culturally.

34   Olyan, "Family Religion in Israel and the Wider Levant of the First Millennium BCE," in Olyan and John Bodel, eds., *Household and Family Religion in Antiquity* (Malden, MA: Blackwell, 2008) 113–26. Cf. also the actions of Hanun, who shows his contempt for David's messengers by shaving half of their beards and exposing their buttocks (2 Sam 10:4). According to Olyan, these shaming acts violently reverse voluntary mourning customs of shaving or pulling out hair or exposing oneself ("Theorizing Violence in Biblical Ritual Contexts: The Case of Mourning Rites," in Olyan, ed., *Social Theory and the Study of Israelite Religion: Essays in Retrospect and Prospect* [Atlanta: Society of Biblical Literature, 2012] 169–80, here 173–74). The odd detail of Judith grasping the head by the hair, one of the most stable motifs in the artistic tradition, could also be seen as a satirical reversal of the mourning act of pulling out one's hair.

is removed and debased; then those who perpetrated this are debased; and then the head of Ishbaal *is returned* and treated respectfully.[35] The head of the rebel Sheba is given to Joab, who hangs it from the city wall (2 Sam 20:14–22); in the LXX version, it is a woman who decapitates him. Jezebel's body is exposed to be eaten by dogs. Only her skull, feet, and hands remain, which is quite ironic; the small pieces left are visible signs that her "whole" is gone: "The corpse of Jezebel shall be like dung on the field, . . . so that no one can say, 'This is Jezebel'" (2 Kgs 9:30–37). Somewhat equivalent is the burning of bodies and bones on an altar to pollute it in 2 Kgs 23:15–20. We may even make comparisons here to the "parody of idols" motif in Israelite tradition (e.g., Isa 44:9–20; Wisdom 13–15; Letter of Jeremiah): to deconstruct an image of a "god" back to its constituent natural elements—renaturalizing it—is analogous to deconstructing a powerful human being back to constituent elements.

This phenomenon appears outside Israel as well. In *Iliad* 24, Achilles begins to reduce Hector's body by dragging it around the tomb of the former's fallen friend Patroclus, but perhaps because Hector is a hero, this is not allowed to continue. Apollo protects the corpse from decay and scavengers and turns to Zeus to force Achilles to allow the body to be ransomed.[36] The Behistun inscription details how Darius had cut off the Median king Fravartish's nose,

ears, tongue, and eye, and then crucified him, and after Darius III was defeated by Alexander the Great, he was also mutilated by a Persian general (Plutarch, *Alex.* 43.3; Curtius Rufus 5.13.16; 7.5.40; 7.10.10). When Cyrus the Younger was killed in battle, his head and right hand were cut off "in accordance with Persian custom;" the parts were later recovered and buried (Ctesias *apud* Plutarch, *Artaxerxes* 13.2).

In Israel and in the ancient Near East, this cutting up of the enemy's body appears to be an accepted part of warfare always carried out by men (except in Judith).[37] It is never explicitly interpreted sacrificially, although it has a relation to ritualized aspects of mourning, especially since burial is denied or even reversed. The Greeks, however, vocally condemned the degrading of the enemy's body after death, viewing it as barbarian; Sophocles's *Antigone* problematizes this strongly held belief. Herodotus 4.103 tells of the barbarian Scythians placing the heads of their enemy on stakes to guard the victors' houses, and after-death effects of their processed bodies are specifically mentioned. Herodotus reports on beheadings by other barbarians as well, Persians and Taurians.[38] In addition, "a city's enemy may turn out to be not only beneficent after death but actually a hero . . ." and a bearer of boons.[39] And if there are post-death boons of the body parts, is that prima facie evidence that the process was indeed a sacrifice?

35   Debra Scoggins Ballentine, "What Ends Might Ritual Violence Accomplish? The Case of Rechab and Baanah in 2 Samuel 4," in Olyan, *Ritual Violence*, 9–26. Saul Olyan notes the role of clearly demarcated categories and reversal in ritual and points out that ritual reversal can be punitive: exhumation and spreading or exposure of body parts is one of the most extreme examples ("Ritual Inversion in Biblical Representations of Punitive Rites," in John J. Collins, T. M. Lemos, and Olyan, eds., *Worship, Women, and War: Essays in Honor of Susan Niditch* [BJS 357; Providence, RI: Brown Judaic Studies, 2015] 135–43).

36   Robertson, "Cyclops and the Self." Another example of the abuse of a dead body is the anti-sacrifice contained in the *sparagmos* and *homophagia* of the Dionysiac Pentheus, the tearing of the flesh of an animal or Pentheus and eating it raw. Eating raw flesh and blood is in itself a return to nature.

37   But, as noted above, a fatal blow to the head by a woman is found a number of times in the Hebrew Bible, although this motif may have had currency precisely because of the surprise and irony—a "man undone by a woman." Assyrian reliefs showed

beheadings of the enemy, and, in one, Ashurbanipal basks under the distorted head of the king of Susa; see Stephanie Dalley, *Esther's Revenge at Susa: From Sennacherib to Ahasuerus* (Oxford: Oxford University Press, 2007) 51–52.

38   Herodotus 3.79; 7.238; 9.78–79; see Gera, *Judith*, 66–67, 397. There are other significant parallels with Tomyris, including culture-specific food prohibitions; see §4 above. But just as Greeks condemned barbarian abuse of a dead body, the Greek stories are specifically told of *barbarian* women. One may also compare the symbolic sacrifices of characters in the Greek novels; as they are in the realm of fantasy, a combination of motifs is possible. Some of the "sacrifice" motifs in the Greek novels are also degradation rituals; see Warren, *My Flesh Is Meat*, passim.

39   Margaret Visser, "Worship Your Enemy: Aspects of the Cult of Heroes in Ancient Greece," *HTR* 75 (1982) 403–28, here 403. Yet, as much as the Greeks might have claimed to oppose human sacrifice or the abuse of the bodies of the dead, this may cover over a repressed attraction; inter-Greek examples are known.

David Frankfurter's cross-cultural reflection on this dynamic is very instructive:

> How does one "process" the body . . . to extract sacred material *or else* to obliterate what that body represents? . . . The resemblance to "sacrifice" might lie only in structure and technique; yet it points to an important convergence in ritual attention: how does one get a body from one state to its extreme?[40]

In death, the body parts of saints and martyrs could provide power, and in lynchings of African Americans in the Unites States, body parts were kept to display continuing power—not power *from* the relics of those lynched but power *over* their bodies. Renaturalizing the bodies rendered them powerless. But can "dis-empowering" the potent figure ironically result in body parts that still channel the dead person's power? The *body* may in fact be dis-empowered and returned to nature at the same time that the *head* is charged, channeling power. The headless, lifeless body of Holofernes, for instance, may be contrasted with the power of his talisman-like head in 14:6.[41]

Modern readers register a distaste for the abuse of the dead, but it lies as a repressed impulse just beneath the surface of modern society as well. In addition to Frankfurter's example of the processing of African American bodies, only a few decades earlier the same treatment had been visited by European Americans on the bodies of Native Americans. In the Sand Creek Massacre of 1864, the hands and fingers of Native Americans were cut off to plunder their jewelry; the genitalia of men, women, and children were cut off; and body parts were hauled away to Denver to be displayed.[42] In Europe as well, the destruction of Jews and others in World War II included the abuse and renaturalization of their bodies. Between 1850 and 1950 white people of European descent engaged in a campaign to dehumanize and naturalize the body of the Other.

With these cross-cultural examples in mind, we return now to several examples closer in time and place to the writing of our text, where we find similar treatments of an enemy's head. Zabdiel, king of Saba, defeated Alexander Balas, king of the Seleucids, and sent his head back to Ptolemy. A bit later than Judith, the Jewish rebel Theudas was defeated, captured, and decapitated by the Romans, his head taken back to Jerusalem (Josephus, *Antiquities* 20.5.1 §§97–99). We reintroduce the closest parallel to our text, 2 Maccabees 15: Nicanor is defeated by Judith's "consort," Judah Maccabee, and his tongue is cut out and his head and right arm are cut off and exhibited on the citadel opposite the temple (2 Macc 15:30–36; cf. 1 Macc 7:47–49). The treatment of Holofernes's head is probably modeled on this.

Conclusions

We are left with little clarity on the precise interpretation of Judith's deed. The surface arc in Judith concerns the sexual control and degradation of the enemy general's body, and the use of the head to rally Bethulians (see 14:18). A powerful subtext is also the ethnic and cultural reversal, the revenge of the colonized: the woman whose name is "Jewish Woman" reprocesses the "Assyrian" (read: Syrian or Seleucid) general, reducing him from an imperial height down to nature. In the surface narrative, and in the biblical examples as well, the remains of the dead may simply be exhibited, and not *explicitly* invested with any post-death power. Yet the degradation motif may function as another kind of channeling of power: channeling power *outward* to nature rather than *handed upward* to the superculture of the gods. Was dividing and exposing Holofernes's body a way of *processing* the body ritually, attaining some post-death desired end, and not merely draining the life out of it? Does Judith channel the power of the newly signified head and redirect its power, first to convert Achior, and then back at the enemy, like Medusa's head, a talisman that now protects?[43]

40 David Frankfurter, "On Sacrifice and Residues: Processing the Potent Body," in Brigitte Luchesi and Kocku von Stuckrad, eds., *Religion im kulturellen Diskurs: Festschrift für Hans G. Kippenberg zu seinem 65. Geburtstag* (Religionsgeschichtliche Versuche und Vorarbeiten 52; Berlin: de Gruyter, 2004) 511–33, here 531.

41 On human bones as binding or cursing, see Christopher Faraone, "Necromancy Goes Underground: The Disguise of Skull- and Corpse-Divination in the Paris Magical Papyri (*PGM* IV 1928–2144)"

Mantikē, 155 (2005) 255–82; Dan Levene, "*Calvariae Magicae:* The Berlin, Philadelphia, and Mousaieff Skulls," *Orientalia* 75 (2006) 359–79. See also Visser's observations above.

42 Glenn Frankel, *The Searchers: The Making of an American Legend* (New York: Bloomsbury, 2013) 31–32.

43 Bettina Uppenkamp, indeed, compares the head of Holofernes in art to that of Medusa (*Judith und Holofernes,* 65). It is similar to the depictions of the head of Goliath as well, which may also have power.

But a warning must also be sounded. Some scholars rightly question the overly broad use of the word *sacrifice* for the ancient West, and indeed, some of the typical ritual elements of sacrifice are lacking in Judith. Although there is a prayer and cleansing beforehand, there is no explicit reciprocity concerning the body between the human and divine realms, nor exchange of one death for life or boons, no *explicit* reclassification of a being from one kind to another, no purification effected, no expiation of sins or appeasing of the gods. Indeed, God has not demanded the slaying of Holofernes in any way.[44] In addition, since Israelite sacrifice took place not in the inner chamber of the holy of holies but at the altar at the door of the temple, the location of the killing in Judith is not quite the same. In Israelite sacrifice the head is also not removed at the time of the blow, and so the decapitation on the surface might suggest abuse of the body and not sacrifice. Judith's grasping of the hair is also not found in sacrifice, since the animal is well treated.

Yet one must still note the deliberateness and ritualized precision of the actions, the rich symbol field produced, the importance evidently placed on them by the narrator, and the interplay of these actions with the prayer language of the heroine. If we pursue the notion of a satirical reading, Judith's purification and dressing may suggest a priest's preparations for sacrifice. And if one takes in the Greek, Roman, and other evidence, the signification of abused bodies could also be understood as a kind of sacrificial *analogy,* whether "positive" or "negative," "upward" or "outward," "constituting" or "deconstituting," "sacralizing" or "desacralizing." Perhaps a valid reading also allows for myriad possibilities—which are in fact not mutually exclusive—without ruling out any of them. Judith moves beyond the boundary of the city into the wild area, where she can do many things that were not permitted for Israelite women. In all these ways, the farcical nature of the narrative may allow for an ironic depiction of Judith as a high priest—bathing, dressing, praying, and finally sacrificing a wicked enemy—just as Ehud "sacrificed" Eglon the Calf.

The French epic tradition of Judith by Du Bartas also magnified the degradation. Says Robert Cummings ("Aestheticization of Tyrannicide," 236):

What even the most inattentive reader would not miss is the mutilation of Holofernes's corpse, first the head spat on, its beard pulled, its eyes poked, its tongue torn out, and then the trunk, its every part distributed among a mob.

44 Sidnie White Crawford, personal communication. One could argue that there is a cult of memory at the end of Judith typical of Greek sacrifices to heroes, but the festival is a victory celebration, not a cultic celebration *of her.* It is said to result from her heroism and the victory, not her *slaying* of Holofernes per se; yet is this merely the surface level? In Jdt 16:19 the canopy is also treated with some attention as an *anathema,* votive offering, yet the head is not taken to Jerusalem; cf. the head of Goliath, taken to Jerusalem (1 Sam 17:51, 54), but as an exhibit or an offering?

Text

10b/ Passing through the camp they went
around the valley, then climbed the
mountain of Bethulia and came to its
gates. 11/ Judith called out from afar
to the sentries at the gate, "Open, open
the gate! God, our God is with us, who
still shows his strength in Israel[a] and his
power against his enemies, as he has
done today!"

12/ When the men of her town heard her
voice, they rushed down to the town
gate and summoned the town elders.
13/ All came running, from lowly to great,
for it seemed unbelievable that she had
returned, and they opened up the gate to
receive them. They kindled a fire for light,
and gathered around. 14/ Judith cried
out to them in a loud voice, "Praise God!
Give praise! Praise the God who has not
withdrawn his mercy from the house of
Israel, but this very night has crushed our
enemies by my hand!" 15/ Then drawing
the head out of the pouch, she showed
it to them and said, "This is the head of
Holofernes, commander-in-chief of the
Assyrian army! And here is the curtain,
behind which he lay in a drunken stupor!
The Lord struck him down by a female
hand! 16/ (I swear) as the Lord lives, who
protected me as I proceeded on my way,
it was my face that seduced him and
led to his destruction, and yet he never
committed a sin with me to defile or
shame me."[b]

17/ All the people were astounded, and bowing
down in worship to God, said with one
voice, "Blessed are you, our God, who on
this day put to shame the enemies of your
people!"

18/ And Uzziah said to her, "My daughter,
you are blessed by the Most High God
above all women on earth, and blessed be
the Lord God, who created the heavens
and the earth, who guided your path
to strike the head of the leader of our
enemies! 19/ Till the end of time your
hope[c] will never desert the hearts of
those who remember the power of God.
20/ May God do these things for you as a
perpetual honor, and visit blessings upon
you, because you did not hesitate to risk
your own life when you saw your people
humiliated, but when we were brought
low you set forth and proceeded along a
straight path in the presence of our God."
And all the people responded, "Amen,
amen!"

a For Israel: ιλεμ for Ierusalem as *nomen sacrum* 583.

b For μασμα και αισχυνην: *quoinquinationis confusionem* OL-SB.

c For η ελπις: ο επαινος O OL Sy Eth Vg. Moore, follows Zimmerman in arguing that the translator of the Hebrew misread תהלתך ("your praise") for תחלתך ("your hope") and concludes that Zimmerman "has ended all debate on the LXX's ambiguous reading." Corley ("Septuagintalisms," 90–91), however, prefers ελπις by noting Prov 23:18b. Proverbs 23:15–21 LXX exhibits a number of parallels with Judith. Ἡ ελπις could also be a scribal error for ο επαινος, and so Zimmerman's Semitic key is hardly necessary. Hanhart, Rahlfs, and Brooke-McLean all prefer ελπις.

Commentary

13:10b–20

Narrative does not depict continuous time but only key moments, connected by transitions; v. 10b is such a transition. After the beheading, Judith and her slave move quickly across the valley and up the mountain to Bethulia. At that point (v. 11), the next key moment of the story is treated, Judith's hailing of her fellow Bethulians. "Open, open the gates" corresponds to 10:9, where she called for the gates to be opened for her to leave. All of the intervening time constituted her liminal sojourn in the wilderness and her encounter with the beast. The heroine now returns to her own society, although Bethulia's task is not complete.

The words "open, open the gates" will also strike the audience as an enthronement motif, as in Ps 24:7:

Lift up your heads, O gates!
Be lifted up, O ancient doors, that the king of glory may come in![1]

The mountain village of Bethulia is constantly depicted as a city, with walls and gates, but in the psalms the gates are the gates of the temple. Judith adds as she approaches, "God, our God is with us," which is similar to this psalm, and her words in v. 14, "Praise God, who has not withdrawn his mercy from the house of Israel," resound like a victory ode. Chapter 16 will be similar.

■ **13:12–16**

Judith's dramatic action is met with the unified response of the Bethulians, but there is an order in terms of the people's participation: the *andres* first, presumably the men on watch ready for battle; the elders, whom they have summoned; and then all, "from lowly to great," who come running. This corresponds to a similar order when Judith first entered the enemy camp. The Bethulians are amazed because of the *paradoxon*, an unbelievable event that is the stuff of novelistic stories. The fact that a woman has gone out into the enemy camp and returned would have contributed to the paradoxography.

Once back among her fellow Bethulians, her first act is to produce both the head of Holofernes and the canopy of his bed. European paintings of the fifteenth to seventeenth centuries focused on the person of Judith, positively or negatively, but in the eighteenth to nineteenth century many paintings enlarged the subject to depict this scene of Judith's return before the gathered Bethulians. This reflects the rise of European national consciousness, emphasizing the *Volk* over individual heroism (see §8 above).

Judith once again says that God had shattered the enemy by her hand, recalling precisely her earlier prayer; compare also her final victory ode (see 9:10; 16:5). As always, the text of Judith is visual; here one cannot help but connect "my face that seduced him and led to his destruction" (v. 16) with the face of Holofernes, which she is holding aloft. Artists often chose to place in close proximity the faces of Judith and Holofernes, and often her slave as well, and this literary text suggests it. The fact that the head does not have any visible effect at this point may argue against taking it as a talisman.

There are a number of grisly recognition scenes that involve the head of a dead figure. From Herodotus, Tomyris placing Cyrus's head in a vat of blood—thereby "quenching" his thirst for blood—would likely have been known to the author (see §4 above), but closer in time and culture would be the display of the head of the enemy general Nicanor (2 Macc 15:28–36), and somewhat later would be the story of Salome with the head of John the Baptist (Mark 6). Judith is in some ways the grisliest in the traditional sense, for the simple reason that here a woman was the direct agent who severed and now exhibits the head.

Judith is surprisingly forthright that "it was my face that seduced him and led to his destruction," clarifying it immediately, however, by saying that Holofernes had not defiled her. She herself raises the specter of *miasma* and *aischynē* in her situation, echoing the same words she had used in regard to Dinah in 9:2.[2] She

---

1 Other enthronement psalms are 47, 93, 96–99, and especially cf. 93, 96, 97 on the destruction of adversaries; see Alonso-Schökel, *Narrative Structure*, 12.

2 Mary Anna Bader, *Tracing the Evidence: Dinah in Post-Hebrew Bible Literature* (Studies in Biblical Literature 102; New York: P. Lang, 2008) 115–37.

has skirted close to scandalous actions in her brazen dialogue with Holofernes, and it may have seemed hard to believe that she had gotten close enough to clutch his head, while still evading the clutch of his hands. In the ancient text, she is fully in control of her situation, and no one doubts her story. The European Judith tradition, however, explored the possibility that she had had a sexual encounter. In the medieval Jewish tradition, she is doubted and shamed; the townspeople even point out that the head could be anyone's. Yet in the LXX she remains undefiled, and her townspeople believe her. In regard to her assurance, one may also compare passages near the end of two Greek novels: in Achilles Tatius, *Leucippe and Clitophon* 8.13–14, the heroine passes a virginity test, and in Xenophon of Ephesus, *Ethiopian Story* 5.14.1-2, Anthia affirms that she returned chaste.

■ **13:17–20**
"All the people" respond to Judith. It is a gathering of the whole town, a sort of corporate personality, which acclaims Judith's actions, repeated in v. 20. This may suggest a constitutional moment, sealed in v. 20 and also in 14:6. Uzziah blesses Judith in language very similar to the blessing of Jael after killing Sisera in the Song of Deborah (Judg 5:24), and also similar to the blessing of Mary in Luke 1:42: all three are "the most blessed of women." Melchizedek's blessing of Abram (Gen 14:19–20) can also be compared: "Blessed be Abram by God Most High, maker of heaven and earth; and blessed be God Most High, who has delivered your enemies into your hand!" In both there is a double blessing, of the individual and of God, and in both are expressed the themes of creation and deliverance over enemies. Uzziah emphasizes several times that God has guided Judith, assuring the audience that her actions should not be suspect. Uzziah and the Bethulians attribute the deed to both Judith and God, as she herself had insisted, and Uzziah further exclaims that the memory of her deed will live forever (see 16:21–25). In Christian tradition, there is a strong identification of Judith and Mary (see §8 above), and Uzziah's praise is used in Catholic liturgy regarding Mary (see the commentary on 15:8–13).

■ **13:19–20** In v. 19, the word *elpis* may refer to a vague hope—the Greek sense—or a sure trust in God—Hebrew *beṭāḥ*. The same question arose in 9:11–14. Some commentators emphasize the latter idea and translate *elpis* here as trust, as in the present translation (see also Textual Note c). This section is concluded with an "*Amen, amen,*" the gathered people's quasi-liturgical affirmation of Uzziah's blessing. Judith's return to Bethulia indeed reestablishes a social order, in that the murmuring and the disorder are now put to rest. Judith fulfills a Mosaic paradigm, although in this novelistic romance the Bethulians are more quickly and easily brought around than were the Israelites in the wilderness.[3] Finally, it is unusual for a person to be exalted, but see the Song of Hannah, 1 Sam 2:1. Here, however, there is also a contrast with the former state of the people, who were brought low. Exaltation and reversal are common biblical motifs, in Judith as well: exaltation of the Assyrians (9:7), of Jerusalem (10:8; 13:4), of Israel (15:9; see also the commentary on 9:11).

---

3   Van Henten, "Female Moses."

Text

1/ Judith said to them, "Now listen to me, my brothers and sisters. Take this head and hang it on the parapet of your wall. 2/ When dawn breaks and the sun rises over the earth, let each of you take up his battle gear and let every warrior proceed outside the town. Station a commander before you, as though you were about to march down upon the plain to attack the guards of the Assyrians, but do not go down. 3/ They will then seize their armor and go to their camp and rouse the Assyrian generals. When they rush together to Holofernes's tent, they will not find him there. Fear will fall upon them and they will flee before you. 4/ All of you and all of those who live in the entire territory of Israel will then pursue them and cut them down in their tracks. 5/ But before you do these things, summon for me Achior the Ammonite, so that he may see and recognize the one who despised the house of Israel and sent him to us as though to his death."

6/ They summoned Achior from the house of Uzziah, and when he came and saw the head of Holofernes, held in the hand of one of the men in the assembly of the people, he fell on his face and his spirit left him. 7/ When they raised him up,[a] he threw himself down before Judith and did obeisance to her. "Blessed are you," he said, "in every tent of Judah. In every nation, whoever hears your name will be disturbed! 8/ But now tell me what you did during these past days." And in the midst of the whole people Judith recounted to him everything that she had done, from the time she had left until the moment she began speaking to them. 9/ When she stopped speaking, the people raised a great shout and made a joyful noise in their town. 10/ When Achior saw all that the God of Israel had accomplished, he came to believe fervently in God. He was circumcised[b] in the flesh of his foreskin and was added to the house of Israel, as he is today.

a   For αναλαβον: αναλαβεν αυτον A V OL Sa 55, or εαυτον 542c; Moore chose the latter and translated, "recovered himself."

b   Περιετεμετο in the middle is to circumcise oneself, as in Vg and Gen 17:24 LXX; NAB translates, "He had the flesh of his foreskin circumcised." Περιετεμε is found in 534, and also περιετμηθη a 126; περιετεμνετο 98.

Commentary

14:1–10

Here Judith follows through on her plan by producing the head of Holofernes before the Bethulians. She com-

mands them to place it on the parapet and lays plans for the Israelite charge. This section, like some of the passages of prayer and dialogue, uses slightly better Greek constructions, although not consistently. Judith's heroism and cleverness do not consist simply in decapitating the enemy general but also in the continuation of her stratagem—or, more precisely, her clever actions give rise to a series of cascading results. Presumably, she has planned it in exactly this way (8:32–34; 10:8). The cleverness of the trickster, in fact, lies in the intuitive grasp of human nature and ways to predict and manipulate it. But "predict" seems too weak a word; she describes to the Bethulians precisely what will happen. Judith's control and agency are the center of this story, although her power and agency are *not* assumed in some later European versions of the story, both Jewish and Christian (see §8 above).

After the meticulous narration of individual movements and actions in chap. 13, we are now treated to a quick denouement, expressed through Judith's commands and action verbs:

Listen to me
Take this head, *hang* it on the parapet
Take up your weapons and *proceed outside*
Station a captain
but *do not go down*
When their panic sets in
pursue them, *cut* them down
But before you *do* all this, *bring* Achior so that he may see

Whereas her decapitation of Holofernes required a woman's attributes to seduce him, now her leadership follows more traditionally male roles, like the cross-cultural "strong women" (see §4 above). She is in complete command of the Bethulians, all those who live within the borders of Israel, and, indirectly, the Assyrians. Judith's prediction (v. 3) of what will happen when the Assyrians discovery the headless body of Holofernes not only demonstrates her self-mastery and the Assyrians' lack of it (see 8:35), but also how she has carefully manipulated them to achieve maximum panic.

■ 14:2–4

Pas anēr ischyōn conjures the heroic tradition and the historiography of Israel; cf. 1 Sam 14:52:

There was hard fighting against the Philistines all the days of Saul, and when Saul saw any strong man

or valiant warrior [*andra dynaton* and *andra huion dynameōs,* translating *'îš gibbōr* and *ben-ḥayil*), he took him into his service."[1]

"Fear will fall upon them" is also a narrative motif in Israelite historiography (Josh 2:9, Exod 15:16). *Pan horion Israel* (Jdt 14:4) has been translated "entire territory of Israel" or "within the borders of Israel." The former may be more accurate to emphasize the nationalist concept of the Hasmoneans.

■ 14:5–6

After commanding a unified attack, Judith pauses to complete the important subplot of Achior's inclusion into Israel. She has commanded that Achior be brought in order that he may recognize (*epignō*) the head of Holofernes. Is it to confirm that the head is really that of Holofernes—only Achior would know—as the medieval Jewish versions take it, or to demonstrate its power when Achior faints (see the excursus at 13:9b–10a, "A Satire of Sacrifice in the Acteme")? The motif appears to play on both levels: the former is the surface-level reason, the latter the deeper narrative logic. Judith's words suggest that a reversal of shame is necessary: Holofernes had "despised the house of Israel and sent Achior to us as though to his death." Achior's fainting ironically confirms Holofernes's earlier prediction to him: "You shall not see my face again from this day until I take revenge on this people" (6:5).

It is ironic that it is Achior who faints, because Judith has shown no squeamishness in chopping off Holofernes's head or in handling it roughly.[2] Achior's sensibilities render him less "manly" than Judith. Esther, depicted as a demure maiden in that novella, faints and leans on her female slaves when the king first looks at her (Greek Esth 15:7). "Esther fainting," a motif not in Hebrew Esther, became a common subject in European art, perhaps as a contrast to Judith (see §8 above). The Bethulians in general were fainthearted, and the only Israelite male who escapes the charge of weakness is the high priest Joakim in Jerusalem.

As Judith is more masculine, Achior is more feminine. Novels cross-culturally are characterized by

---

1   Noted by Grintz, *Book of Judith,* 166.
2   Moore, *Judith,* 235.

polypathy, a surfeit of varied emotions (see §7 above). In this context, men are often "feminized" in that they display more delicate sensibilities and emotions. Compare *Chaereas* 3.9: "Dionysius fainted when he heard that; darkness spread over his eyes." Modern English novels also projected feminine sensibilities onto the male protagonists. In the case of the book of Judith, however, we are in a novella whose main virtue is self-mastery, and whose main narrative theme is the reversal of typical male and female roles.

It may also be significant that in v. 6 the head is held aloft by one of the men in the assembly of the people (*ekklēsia tou laou*), not by Judith or even Uzziah. Judith 13:12-20 had prepared for this. In the LXX, *ekklēsia* translates *qāhāl*, and this may suggest a constitutional notion—the people of Bethulia, representing also the people of Israel. It is similar to the political narrative of Neh 8:2, where a constitutional moment is evoked.

■ **14:7**

Achior once again plays the role of the author's spokesman within the text, recognizing Judith for her military accomplishment: "In every nation, whoever hears your name will be disturbed."[3] The reference to the nations and the verb *tarassō* seem to convey the disturbance caused by the Divine Warrior, so "tremble" would not be strong enough (see the commentary on 10:9-10). Judith is heroic not simply in this one setting, but, as the ending will signify, she is like the judges of old, whose heroism is capable of striking fear into the hearts of enemies for a long time to come. The form of Achior's blessing may be unexpected for an Ammonite—"Blessed are you in every tent of Judah"—but that is in keeping with his perspective and the process of conversion. These blessings also anticipate the long round of blessings near the end of Judith, part of the general celebration. The book of Tobit contains many more blessings, an exaggeration for comic effect.

■ **14:10**

"He was added to the house of Israel, as he is today" would seem to imply that he is still alive—unlikely, since the book ends with Judith's death at a very old age. It may suggest that his family lineage is still a part of Israel, or, more likely, it is simply another fanciful detail.

Excursus: Achior's Conversion

A central plot point in the novella, related *before* the final denouement, is the conversion of Achior. His conversion was prepared for by his speech to Holofernes in chap. 5. There we noted that the name Achior is probably derived from Ahikar, a legendary Aramean scribe in the Assyrian court, a popular tradition of wisdom narratives. In Tobit, Ahikar is an Israelite courtier, and so Tobit and Judith, two roughly contemporary novellas, shared in appropriating this famous Ahikar as one of their own. In an age that began to reflect more on conversion, there is a colonized audacity in claiming this famous Aramean for Israel. No greater prize could be imagined.

A number of important issues arise in this one verse. We begin with the two halakic matters that exercise modern scholars: first, that an Ammonite would be accepted as a convert, and, second, that the conversion would not include a bathing ritual. Deuteronomy 23:3-6 specifically excludes Ammonites and Moabites from "entry into the assembly," along with their descendants, "even to the tenth generation." Ammon and Moab, the progenitors of the Ammonites and Moabites, were offspring of Lot's incestuous relations with his two daughters (Gen 19:36-38). That would presumably disqualify Achior from converting.[4] Nevertheless, here he is circumcised and allowed to convert. We also hear in the book of Ruth that she was accepted within Israel even

---

3 *Tarachthēsontai*; in Matt 2:3 Herod is also *etarachthē*; cf. also Matt 14:26; Luke 24:38. Cf. the laden use of *ekplēssō* as well (Nathaniel DesRosiers, "*Eklēssō* in Mark," unpublished paper).

4 In Neh 2:10, Tobiah is called "the Ammonite," and from this one might infer that Ammonites were indeed more accepted by at least some in Jerusalem—though not by Nehemiah. Tobiah, however, is likely Jewish and is probably called "the Ammonite" by Nehemiah in order to disgrace him. See Wills, *Not God's People,* 70–74. Achior could

conceivably escape this exclusion by being past the tenth generation. On the exclusion or inclusion of Ammonites, see Saul Olyan, *Rites and Rank: Hierarchy in Biblical Representations of Cult* (Princeton, NJ: Princeton University Press, 2000) 68–69, 72–80. Shaye J. D. Cohen argues that, unlike the rabbinic interpretation, Deut 23:3 does not forbid intermarrying, but rather entering the temple ("The Prohibition of Intermarriage: From the Bible to the Talmud," *Hebrew Annual Review* 7 [1983] 23–39, here 32–33). 4QFlorilegium is similar on this score.

though she was a Moabite. Although the exclusion of Ammonites in Deut 23:3–6 was seconded by Ezra 9:1–2, 12 and Neh 9:2, 13:1–3, a counter-tendency of acceptance of foreigners is found in Isa 56:3, 7, Ruth, and Jonah. One may wonder whether Judith falls into the latter trajectory.

In both Judith and Ruth, there may also appear a sort of novelistic exception, a common cross-cultural phenomenon: women, foreigners, slaves, people with disabilities—in other words, the full catalog of the Other—often enjoy very fully realized, heroic roles and acceptance in popular literature. The master class reserves some room in popular fantasy for the acceptance of the occasional Other.[5] Implausibility, or even impossibility, is no barrier to full enjoyment: the same novella that introduces a "Nebuchadnezzar, king of the Assyrians" could also affirm an "Achior the Ammonite" who joins Israel.

The other surprising halakic question is why ritual bathing was not part of the ceremony, a fact at variance with later rabbinic requirements for conversion. Although the city was under siege and the citizens were dying of thirst, Harry M. Orlinsky was certain that the omission of bathing was what prevented this book from being canonized. However, Cohen notes that bathing may only later have become a requirement of the conversion process.[6] As noted in the excursus at 12:5b–9 ("Bathing and Related Issues"), water rituals in Judaism were evolving during this period.

There are other literary and theological issues as well. First, what specifically prompted the conver-sion? Sheaffer asserts that Achior converts when he sees Judith present the head of Holofernes (14:6),[7] but, although his conversion does come after this, the text says that it occurred when Achior "saw all that the God of Israel had done." This answers nicely to Achior's description of God and the protection of Israel in chap. 5. It is also similar to the confessions of the power of God by foreign leaders in Daniel and especially in 2 Macc 3:30–40, even though those, strikingly, do not seem to lead to "real" conversions.

Further, what precisely is meant by the prob-lematic term "conversion"? Our text does not use forms of *metanoeō* (which may not necessarily mean "convert" in the modern sense).[8] The verbs of the text are significant:

- He "came to believe fervently in God" (*episteuse sphodra*)
- He "circumcised himself" or "had himself circum-cised" (*perietemeto*)[9]
- He was "added to the house of Israel, as he is today."

The idea of "conversion" became central in Christian discourse but should not be read back into the pre-Christian period. The earliest references to joining Israel are ambiguous. The account of Abram called out of Aram to worship God (Genesis 12) was not conceived of as a conversion, nor was it described as a turn from polytheism to monotheism as is often assumed. Rather, this was the account of the creation of a new family responding to God's desires. Ruth enters Israel when she confesses her loyalty to Nao-mi's God and people.[10] Is this an early conversion,

---

At the time that Judith was composed, the author might have been unaware of a *conversion* problem for an Ammonite, as long as he did not enter the temple.

5   In 8:11, I referred to this as the "Gunga Din motif." Yet, although Ruth *may* have been composed as a fanciful text, it was utilized in Jewish tradition as if it were history. The rabbis take it up regarding the issue of Ruth's conversion and solve the Moabite problem by noting that Deuteronomy excludes "Moabites" but says nothing about "Moabitesses"! See Ruth Rabbah 4:1 and Cynthia M. Baker, *Jew* (Key Words in Jewish Studies 8; New Brunswick, NJ: Rutgers University Press, 2017) 32.

6   Orlinsky, *Essays in Biblical Culture*, 281; Shaye J. D. Cohen, *From the Maccabees to the Mishnah* (2nd ed.; Louisville: Westminster John Knox, 1989), 51.

7   Sheaffer, *Envisioning*, 42–43.

8   *Prosēlytos*, often translated Hebrew *gēr*, yet the latter may suggest not a conversion but the status as a resident alien, although it is not a clear concept and

changed over centuries. Joel Kaminsky suggests that the use of *prosēlytos* to translate *gēr* misleads us into considering the conversion aspect ("A Light to the Nations: Was There Mission and or Conversion in the Hebrew Bible?," *Jewish Studies Quarterly* 16 [2009] 6–22, here 6–8). The *gēr* will not be consid-ered here as part of the landscape of conversion; see Wills, *Not God's People*, 40–50.

9   For meaning and variants of *perietemeto*, see Textual Note b.

10   There is no ritual described for Ruth. The purifica-tion ritual for the taking of foreign wives (Deut 21:10–14) comes to mind, but it describes forced incorporation. Ruth's change of status is sometimes seen as an ethnic change only, or simply incorpo-ration into a family, because she continues to be called "Ruth the Moabite"; see Cohen, *Beginnings of Jewishness*, 122 n. 36. That, however, may simply be a storytelling device, much like "Mordecai the Jew" in Esther; the text is unclear. Interestingly, Cynthia Baker denies that the situation of Ruth is

an imaginative and romanticized, idyllic conversion, or not a "conversion" at all? On the surface, Ruth's confession is more oriented toward her mother-in-law Naomi and her "people" than to any embrace of the peculiar traits of the God of Israel: "Where you go, I will go. . . . Your people shall be my people, and your God my God" (Ruth 1:16). But that may simply reflect an earlier time period, much like the movement of Abram, the creation or incorporation in a different family structure. We should not consider Ruth's change "lesser" if it met the expected norms of status change of the day.

Israelite literature contains other accounts of people who ally with Israel in some way: Jethro (Exodus 18), Naaman (2 Kings 5), and Rahab (Joshua 2). Other passages express the eschatological prediction that nations will stream to Jerusalem to worship God or join Israel: Isa 2:2–4; Zech 2:10–17; 4:14; 6:5; 8:22–23.[11] Closer to the period of Judith, the book of Daniel and its Additions depict kings of great empires—Nebuchadnezzar, Darius the Mede, and Cyrus of Persia—confessing the God of Israel (Dan 2:46–47; 4:1–3 [3:31–33 MT]; 4:39 [4:37 MT]; 6:25–28; and Bel 41). A fanciful notion may be reflected in these novelistic texts, as also in the novelistic history 2 Macc 3:30–40, yet there is also the decree of Cyrus in Ezra 1:2–4 (which may have been altered).

Roughly contemporaneous texts differed greatly on the conversion of gentiles, so greatly as to suggest that there were two very different party positions on the issue. A number of texts contemporary with Judith assume a hope of a general gentile conversion (1 Enoch 10:21; 90:38; 91:14; Tob 14:6; Sibylline Oracle 3), while Qumran texts are opposed (Damascus Document [CD] 14.3–6; Pesher Nahum [4Q169] 3–4 ii 9, 4QFlorilegium [4Q174] 1.3–4). The Letter of Aristeas in general is also quite positive about the hope for gentiles, while Jubilees is negative. Although we do not know the numbers of converts, the *idea* of conversion was vibrant.[12]

Other accounts are comparable, but also problematic because of the novelistic elements. In Esth 8:17 many are forced to "take on the practices of the Jews" (*mityahădîm*), which perhaps evokes forced conversion. The dating of Esther cannot be determined, but the Greek translation clarifies the passage: they were circumcised (Greek Esth 8:17). Certainly, by the time of the so-called Royal Family of Adiabene in Josephus, *Antiquities* 20.2.1–4 §§17–96, written in first century CE, clearer references to conversion can be found.

Yet the conversion of Achior, though a novelistic treatment, is the first *unambiguous* reference to male conversion. And here we pause over another aspect

---

different because the book was written centuries earlier; rather, the difference is simply that Ruth is a woman, and male and female converts were understood differently (*Jew*, 29–33). Yet one difference in no way denies the other: the text is earlier, *and* she is a woman. Still, Baker continues, for the rabbis there was less ambiguity: Ruth was truly a convert. Jill Hicks-Keeton (*Arguing with Aseneth: Gentile Access to Israel's "Living God" in Jewish Antiquity* [Oxford: Oxford University Press, 2018] 118–20) rightly compares the conversion of Achior to that of Aseneth, and, like Baker, attributes the differences to their genders. Thiessen assimilates the seven-day conversion of Aseneth more to the eighth-day circumcision of boys and the consecration of priests ("Aseneth's Eight-Day Transformation as Scriptural Justification for Conversion 1," *JSJ* 45 [2014] 229–49, here 241–47). Regarding Antiochus (2 Macc 9:12-17) and Achior as subjects of conversion, see Seth Schwartz, "How Many Judaisms Were There?," *JAJ* 2 (2011) 208–38, here 233; Ross Shepard Kraemer, *Unreliable Witnesses: Religion, Gender, and History in the Greco-Roman Mediterranean* (Oxford and New York: Oxford University Press, 2011) 194.

11   Tobit will end with a similar eschatological vision.

12   Some scholars emphasize different models of conversion, although this remains constroversial. Moshe Greenberg distinguishes those who join themselves *to God,* and those who join themselves *to Israel* ("A House of Prayer for All Peoples," in Alviero Niccacci, ed., *Jerusalem: House of Prayer for All Peoples in Three Monotheistic Religions; Proceedings of a Symposium Held in Jerusalem, February 17–18, 1997* [SBFA 52; Jerusalem: Franciscan Printing Press, 2001] 31–37). Yet our text, though fictitious, provides insights into both: "he came to believe fervently in God" and "was added to the house of Israel." Thiessen's "Aseneth's Eight-Day Transformation" is a well-documented study but nevertheless tends to minimize the importance of conversion by simply arguing that it was not recognized *by all Jews.* That it was an embattled concept perhaps renders it more significant for historical study.

See Simkovich, *Jewish Universalism,* 70–73; Cohen, *Beginnings of Jewishness;* Martin Goodman, *Mission and Conversion: Proselytizing in the Religious History of the Roman Empire* (Oxford: Clarendon, 1994) 90; Scot McKnight, *A Light among the Gentiles: Jewish Missionary Activity in the Second Temple Period* (Minneapolis: Fortress Press, 1991) 30–45.

of his reported experience. Achior's conversion is marked by *believing* (*episteusen sphodra*). After the exile, the motif of faith and believing—the Hebrew root *'mn* and Greek root *pist-* are used both for the noun "faith" and the verb "to believe"—became increasingly common as a way of prioritizing the person's commitment to God.[13] Because of the centrality of faith/believing in later Christianity, this development in pre-Christian Judaism often goes unnoticed. To be sure, there was no contrast of faith and law in a Pauline sense; rather, faith/believe indicated a commitment to God's law, perhaps even a "colonized" interpretation of the patron–client relationship to God. The use of *pisteuō* in our passage may also be matched conceptually in 8:8 by the older term for commitment, the fear of God (*yir'â/phobos*): "No one spoke ill of her, because she feared (or revered) God exceedingly [*ephobeito ton theon sphodra*]."

If Achior's conversion is the earliest unambiguous male conversion, however fictitious it may be, it is significant that it is ritually marked by circumcision, in conformity with later rabbinic tradition.[14] Even if not universally endorsed, circumcision was well known as a sign of conversion in ancient Judaism, to the extent that the roughly contemporaneous Epic of Theodotus (frg. 6) could insist that Simeon and Levi must have carried out their slaughter *before* the Shechemites had been circumcised; otherwise, the latter would have been Jews and would not have been slaughtered. Still, Jewish identity without circumcision was sometimes referenced. Philo (*Migration of Abraham* 89–93) speaks of philosophically oriented Jews who have forgone circumcision and other basic observances, and the first Jewish missionary to the king and queen of Adiabene does not press circum-

cision as a requirement—although it is conceivable that this missionary is merely a foil invented for the "truer" missionary who does require circumcision. But most surprisingly, in b. Yeb. 46b circumcision is not required as part of a conversion.[15]

At any rate, in Judith circumcision is presumed without question as the marker of conversion. There are possible theological implications of this passage, as well as political. First, covenant renewal in Israel can almost be seen as a kind of conversion, a reaffirmation of devotion to God (compare esp. Ezra 8–9; Nehemiah 9). For the audience of Judith, the conversion of a gentile might in fact have been experienced less as a story of the incorporation of a noble gentile than as an inner-group reaffirmation of God's agency in history. Even the Ammonite with the famous name can see that the God of Israel is lord of history.

Second, Pieter Venter has pointed to a theological theme concerning Achior's conversion.[16] Judith, as a woman and a widow, is an outsider figure who courageously rises up to save her people. Achior is likewise an outsider, and according to Deut 23:3, would be excluded from access and conversion. Judith and Achior together, then, provide a more inclusive ideal of identity in this otherwise quite nationalistic text. Ruth the Moabite, in a less satirical text, may also be opening a door for inclusion, in opposition to Deuteronomy, Ezra-Nehemiah, and Jubilees. One may question, however, whether "inclusive" and "nationalistic" are as simply contrasted as Venter assumes.

Yet this brings us to the possible political implications of the text. The centrality of this episode, and the clear role of circumcision, may have been read as justification for the Hasmonean policy of the conversion of Idumeans and others. ("Ammonites" would

---

13 Greek examples are similar but mainly later, yet note Emma J. Edelstein and Ludwig Edelstein, *Asclepius: Collection and Interpretation of the Testimonies* (Baltimore: Johns Hopkins University Press, 1998), nos. 423.3 and 4, 1.222, 230; no. 423.9, 1.223, 231–32. See Wills, "Jew, Judean, Judaism," 190–91. It is not only a matter of the increasing number of uses of *'mn/pisteuō*, but an increased importance in their rhetorical uses, from *'āmēn* ("believe it!") in liturgy to the "faith covenant" in Neh 9:38/10:1. By the turn of the Common Era we encounter the *ně'ĕmānîm* ("faithful ones") of the Pharisees. See also *pistis* matched with *haplotēs* in Wis 1:1–2, and Philo (*On Abraham* 46.268–74) extols the importance of Abraham's faith in God. In the Jewish Amidah prayer God also maintains his *'ĕmûnâ* to those asleep in the dust by reviving the dead and is a "faithful healer." At Qumran,

11QPs[a] 19.13–16 speaks of a "spirit of faith and knowledge." See Teresa Morgan, *Roman Faith and Christian Faith: Pistis and Fides in the Early Roman Empire and Early Churches* (Oxford: Oxford University Press, 2015).

14 See b. Šabb. 135a; b. Yeb. 46a–b; m. Gerim 1:6, 2:2.

15 Simkovich, *Jewish Universalism*, passim and 63 n. 35; Cohen, *Beginnings of Jewishness*, 158, 198–238; Moshe Lavee, "The 'Tractate' of Conversion—BT Yeb. 46–48 and the Evolution of Conversion Procedure," *European Journal of Jewish Studies* 4 (2010) 169–72. In m. Yad. 4:4, women can convert because Deut 13:9 says sons and not daughters, but the case of Judah (!) an Ammonite is given confusing justification.

16 Venter, "Function of the Ammonite," 67(3) Art. #1101, 9 pages, http://dx.doi.org/10.4102/hts. v67i3.1101

have likely been understood as an ancient term for the contemporary peoples roundabout; see 2:28.)[17] Whether the program of Hasmonean conversions, or the Jewish mission in general, involved many converts or a few is not pressing here. Achior's circumcision may have been a narrativized and idealized correlative to the Hasmonean policy of subsuming peoples.

There may be other resonances as well, not all mutually exclusive. Erich Gruen suggests that the conversion of an Ammonite is simply deliberate humor, and Terence L. Donaldson perceives an ideal-izing but unreal irony, perhaps similar to Isa 56:3 on the acceptance of foreigners and eunuchs.[18] Granting the many ambiguities noted here, some might minimize the significance of this scene as "conversion." To the contrary, however, the many rough edges of this passage would suggest that it speaks to a major cultural concern of Jews in this period, a cultural concern that might have been in transition. The central place that it holds just before the resolution of the story confirms this judgment.

17 The Idumeans had been incorporated into the Judean state by Hyrcanus (135–104 BCE), and the Itureans by Aristobulus (104–103 BCE), but see Cohen, *Beginnings of Jewishness,* 109–39. On the numbers of those converted by force or in a broad voluntary Jewish mission, see Louis H. Feldman, *Jew and Gentile in the Ancient World* (Princeton, NJ: Princeton University Press, 1993) 288–341 (arguing for high numbers), and Seth Schwartz, *Imperialism and Jewish Society, 200 B.C.E. to 640 C.E.* (Jews, Christians, and Muslims from the Ancient to the Modern World; Princeton, NJ: Princeton University Press, 2001) 19–48 (arguing for low numbers);

Michael E. Fuller, *The Restoration of Israel: Israel's Regathering and the Fate of the Nations in Early Jewish Literature and Luke-Acts* (BZNW 138; Berlin: de Gruyter, 2006) 127 n. 87 (low numbers).

18 Gruen, *Diaspora,* 168; Terence L. Donaldson, *Judaism and the Gentiles: Jewish Patterns of Universalism (to 135 CE)* (Waco, TX: Baylor University Press, 2007) 62. At the same time, the motif may be "novelistic" even if not "humorous." At the end of Xenophon of Ephesus's *Ephesian Tale,* the protagoninsts' comrade Hippothous decides to live in Ephesus. No change of citizenship is noted, but cf. also the end of *Chaereas* and Greeks enrolled as citizens.

Text

Textual Notes

11/ When morning came, they hung the head of Holofernes on the wall. Every man took up his weapons, and they all marched out in companies to the mountain passes. 12/ When the Assyrians saw them, they sent word to their officers, who went to their generals, commanders, and all their leaders. 13/ When they came to Holofernes's tent, they said to the steward in charge of all his affairs, "Wake our lord, for the slaves[a] have dared to come down against us in battle, so that they might be totally destroyed!"

14/ Bagoas entered and knocked at the entrance[b] of the tent, for he supposed that Holofernes was asleep with Judith. 15/ When no one responded, he parted the curtain and went in to the bedchamber[c] and found him sprawled over the footstool,[c] dead,[d] his head taken from him! 16/ He cried out with a loud voice, with screaming and wailing and a great cry, and tore his garments. 17/ Then he entered the tent that Judith had occupied but did not find her. He rushed out to the people and cried,[e] 18/ "These slaves have deceived us! One woman of the Hebrews has shamed the house of King Nebuchadnezzar! Look here! Holofernes is lying on the ground, and his head is missing!" 19/ When the officers of the Assyrian army heard this, they tore their garments, and their souls were seized with panic as their wailing and crying filled the camp. 15:1/ When those who were in their tents heard this, they were shocked by what had happened. 2/ Fear and trembling overcame them and not a single man held rank, but to a man they poured out and fled[f] over every path of the plain and the high country. 3/ Those encamped in the high country around Bethulia were also thrown into flight. And then the Israelites—every soldier among them—streamed down upon them.

4/ Uzziah sent messengers to Betomasthaim, Choba, Kola,[g] and to every territory of Israel to proclaim everything that had happened, so that everyone would rush out against the enemy and destroy them. 5/ When the Israelites heard, with one accord they all fell upon them and cut them down as far as Choba. Similarly, those from Jerusalem and from all the high country also arrived, for people had informed them about what had happened in the camp of their enemies. Those in Gilead and Galilee struck at their flanks with a great blow,[h] going even beyond

a   For οι δουλοι: *Iudaei* OL—QP Sa; *filii Israel* OL-QP. Moore follows Movers ("Über die Ursprache," 31–41) in positing here a misreading in the Hebrew: העבדים ("slaves") was read for העברים ("Hebrews"). This could conceivably have given rise to OL *Iudaei* and *filii Israel*. Vg has "mice," which might have been a misreading of העכברים, as in the medieval Hebrew texts.

b   Judith has taken the inner net (13:9), so perhaps Bagoas, who is said to have entered, knocks on a partition between the sections (Gera, *Judith*). Alternatively, Bagoas may have entered the marked area before the entrance of the general's large tent and knocks upon a tent pole at the entrance to the front section of the tent. A *b* read την αυλην. For εκρουσεν την αυλαιαν: εκροτησε or εκρωτισεν τη χειρι εν τη αυλαια *L* OL-C Vg, "clapped his hands in front of the curtain."

c   Hesychius notes this usage as "threshold" (LSJ), but is that possible if Bagoas has entered the inner chamber?

d   For νεκρον, 58 OL-SBQPGN Sy Arm 583 read γυμνον, an embarrassment for Judith, but a motif in many European paintings.

e   For κραζων in B; λεγων S 126 OL-M; και ειπεν V *O L a* 55 OL-M Sy Vg; και εβοησεν A *b* minus Sa.

f   For εφυγον: εφευγον B S A.

g   Other texts add Bebai.

h   For υπερεκερασαν, there are many variants. Gera (*Judith*, 55) notes that in LXX this word is used only here and in 1 Macc 7:46 in regard to the defeat of Nicanor.

i   Πολεις is read in most texts, but επαυλεις, the more difficult reading, is found in B *a* and some minuscules.

Damascus and its territories. 6/ The remainder of those who lived in Bethulia descended upon the Assyrian camp and plundered them, taking away great riches. 7/ When the Israelites returned from their slaughter, they seized what was left, and those from the villages and towns[i] in the high country and the plain also seized a large share of booty, for there was a vast quantity.

Commentary

14:11—15:7

The Bethulians make the necessary preparations that Judith has commanded: they have exhibited the head of Holofernes to rally their people (the enemy will not see the head, and only Bagoas will see the headless corpse in the Assyrian camp). With weapons in hand, they have gone out in companies to the mountain passes to wait for the strategic moment. On the Assyrian side, the news that the Israelites had taken the field against them in 14:11—much like the news that a beautiful Hebrew woman had entered the camp in 10:11–23—moves up the chain of command until it reached Bagoas. The Assyrians declare they will destroy "the slaves." This term emphasizes the shame that these soldiers wish to inflict.

The narrative of the book to this point has been told slowly by biblical standards: fourteen chapters to arrive at the denouement. The beheading was told quickly and bloodlessly, and now, after Judith has initiated the next stage of her stratagem, the narrative resolves in a few verses. In popular-literature fashion, the description shifts almost visually from the appearance of the Bethulians on the horizon (14:11), to the reaction in the Assyrian camp (14:12–15:3), and back again to the Bethulians and other Israelites (15:4–7). As before, the comic effect of the denouement is achieved by both plot retardation and acceleration at the same time. Retardation of plot allows the audience to delectate over the irony, reversal,

and comic panic that all know will come when the headless body of Holofernes is discovered.

The audience knows that the Assyrians are about to discover the headless body of Holofernes, but it will be experienced through the eyes of Bagoas, one of the most voluble characters in the novella. Bakhtin asserted that point of view in a novel is not simply restricted to that of the main protagonist or the ideal narrator; point of view is subdivided among many characters as "focalization."[1] The novel is capable of creating zones for each character, with focalizations for each, or even different focalizations of the same character at different points in the narrative. In our novella, the audience perceives the world through Bagoas's eyes, but now we see that there are two Bagoases, the self-satisfied sycophant that we first met, and the weak and exposed figure who now speaks for the Assyrian characters. Such multiple perspectives create *syllepsis,* or perception of multiple levels simultaneously, a trait found also in the later Greek novels as well (see §7 above).

Irony sometimes consists in the contrast in scales, here the exaggerated difference between Bagoas's assumptions about his general and the depths to which the general has actually fallen; it is not a subtle irony. The same ironic distance between assumptions and fall is found masterfully developed in Judg 5:28–30. But for Judith's audience, there is also a measure of the salacious enjoyment of popular literature: the text projects *both* a scandalous and erotic scene of a powerful general who thinks that he will enjoy a night of ecstasy with his odalisque, *and* a virtuous and pious Jewish woman who,

---

1   Gérard Genette (*Figures, essais* [3 vols.; Paris: Seuil, 1968–72] 3:206–23) and Bal (*Narratology*) also nuanced this discussion.

like David, can slice an enemy general's head off to save her people. The audience has its cake and eats it too.

■ 14:14–18

The energy of the raised expectations of the audience sets the stage for the description of Bagoas's crucial actions. From his point of view, the enemy, pitiful as it is, is on the horizon. He knocks or taps decorously, presumably on a wooden tent pole, to awaken Holofernes. Here we compare part of the LXX narration of the stories of Ehud (Judg 3:25) and Jael (4:22):

Ehud Judg 3:25 LXX	Jael Judg 4:22 LXX	Judith Jdt 14:15, 18
They waited until they felt ashamed, and behold, when no one opened the doors of the upper room, they took the key and opened them, and behold, there was their lord, having fallen dead [*peptōkōs . . . tethnēkōs*] on the floor.	Barak went into her, and behold, Sisera was cast down dead [*rherimmenos nekros*], and the tent peg was in his temple.	When no one responded, he parted the curtain and went in to the bedchamber, and found him sprawled [*errimmenon nekron*] over the footstool, dead, his head taken from him. . . . Bagoas cried out with a loud voice, with screaming and wailing and a great cry, and tore his garments.
(No reaction.)	(No reaction.)	"Look here! Holofernes is lying on the ground, and his head is missing!"

Not paralleled in Judges 3 or 4 is Bagoas's uncontrolled reaction in 14:16. Sheaffer asks whether Bagoas is stricken at realizing that he contributed to his master's downfall, but it seems unlikely given his scream, "The slaves have deceived us!" (v. 18).[2] For the audience to perceive a sense of guilt in Bagoas would be one step too deep in terms of psychological complexity. In oral and popular written literature, complexity of this type is rarely explored in characterization; rather, stories portray universal human fears and yearnings.

The reversal of honor and shame, anticipated in 14:13, culminates in the broad humor of the last remarks we will hear from the entertaining Bagoas. The story is told deftly in that, first, in 14:15 the omniscient narrator tells us what Bagoas sees. Then we hear Bagoas's own description. The wording is oddly humorous, even macabre. The literal translation used here, often rounded off somewhat in modern translations, is intended to get at imagery that is brusque and contemptuous: "Look here! Holofernes is lying on the ground, and his head is missing!" His head is not "missing," it is "cut off," as if it were still there somewhere, or should be there somewhere.[3] Through Bagoas's eyes, we are looking into a void—"Look here!"—and his stunned utterance seems unable to communicate exactly what has happened.

Excursus: Judith 14:18 as Peripety and Theme of the Book

It has been argued, and perhaps rightly, that the main theme of the book of Judith is expressed in her prayer to God in 9:9c–10:

> Place in my hand—the hand of a widow!—the strength to do what I conceived. By the deceit of my lips, strike the slave with his ruler and the ruler with his servant! Crush their arrogance by a female hand![4]

---

2   Sheaffer, *Envisioning*, 194–5.

3   Gera, *Judith*, 181. See at 4:9 for the leitmotif of crying out; here Bagoas and the Assyrians cry out. Gruen, *Diaspora*, 168, notes the "consciously coy language" of "his head had been taken from him." Perhaps the language is coy in that, beneath the "serious" military developments, it communicates a satirical perspective to the audience. By the same token, *errimenos* may mean thrown or tossed, but can also mean prostrate, as a drunk person (Polybius 5.48) or as a corpse (Plutarch, *Galb.*, 28). Is *errimenos*, then, happening *now*, or is it a *resultative* expression?

4   Schmitz/Engel, *Judit*, 106–8, 296–97; Xeravits, "Supplication," 170.

δὸς ἐν χειρί μου τῆς χήρας ὃ διενοήθην κράτος.
πάταξον δοῦλον ἐκ χειλέων ἀπάτης μου ἐπ᾽ ἄρχοντι
καὶ ἄρχοντα ἐπὶ θεράποντι αὐτοῦ, θραῦσον αὐτῶν τὸ
ἀνάστημα ἐν χειρὶ θηλείας.

But our novella is constructed of two arcs, a narrative arc and a theological arc. Although it is possible that they are created by different authors, this is unlikely. Rather, they may play out in different rhythms and functions over the course of the book. Taking opera as a metaphor, there is a "music" arc and a "libretto" arc. In this metaphor, the outrageous narrative is the music and the pious theology—the theology that protects Judith from charges of gross sin, and which might even be "cover theology"—is the libretto. The main theme of the theology arc is indeed found in chap. 9, but the main theme of the narrative arc is located here in 14:18:

> These slaves have deceived us! One woman of the Hebrews has shamed the house of King Nebuchadnezzar! Look here! Holofernes is lying on the ground, and his head is missing![5]

> ἠθέτησαν οἱ δοῦλοι, ἐποίησεν αἰσχύνην μία γυνὴ τῶν Ἑβραίων εἰς τὸν οἶκον τοῦ βασιλέως Ναβουχοδονόσορ. ὅτι ἰδοὺ Ὀλοφέρνης χαμαί, καὶ ἡ κεφαλὴ οὐκ ἔστιν ἐπ᾽ αὐτῷ.

The thematic nature of this verse is emphasized in the ethnic label itself: "One woman of the Hebrews has shamed the house of King Nebuchadnezzar!" The "woman of the Hebrews" is contrasted with the noble-sounding "house of King Nebuchadnezzar"; the former has defeated and shamed the latter. Recall that in 10:12 Judith introduced herself to Holofernes as "a daughter of the Hebrews."

It may be countered that 14:14–18 represents not the thematic statement of the narrative but the peripety only, the reversal of fortunes that brings a narrative from tension to resolution. Aristotle suggested that, at its best, peripety occurred at the point of *anagnōrisis,* discovery or recognition, which occurs here upon Bagoas's entry into the tent.[6] True enough, but, in addition to discovery and peripety, we find that the heroic and trickster themes of the book are expressed not in Judith's pious utterances in chaps. 8 and 9 but in the mouth of the excit-

able Bagoas. (Likewise in Esther, there is a sort of peripety stated by a minor character in 6:13: Haman's wife and friends say, "Since Mordecai, before whom your downfall has begun, is of Jewish origin, you cannot stand against him.") The climactic moment is absurdly constructed. Modern translations often find ways to improve the language of this crucial recognition scene, but the original audience may have heard a contrived set of verbs emitted by a sputtering Bagoas, culminating in "his head is missing!" The courtier has lost the art of articulation. In addition, this is the moment of truth-stating that reveals to the world the irony and deception of Judith's stratagem. From this point on, truth no longer lies beneath the surface but is revealed to all. The fact that many code words are used here—"these slaves have deceived us, one Hebrew woman has shamed the house of Nebuchadnezzar"—contributes to the sense that the peripety is also the statement of theme, the revenge of the colonized.

■ 14:19–15:3

Upon learning that Holofernes has lost his head, the Assyrians lose theirs as well. Chaos results; their vaunted army flees in panic. Any semblance of military organization disintegrates as soon as the panic has hit. The Assyrians react exactly as Judith had planned. Bagoas's eruption of emotions opens the floodgates of others' panic, first the Assyrian leaders (14:19), then "those in the tents" (15:1), and lastly those stationed in the mountains (15:3). The Assyrian leaders cry out and tear their garments in much the same way as Bagoas had. They do not question whether Bagoas is correct or wait to see the body for themselves.[7] The bumbling Bagoas has become the mouthpiece of Assyrian panic. Their display of emotion mirrors his, but for soldiers this is unthinkable cowardice; they are not facing defeat with fortitude. Judith has thus demonstrated *enkrateia,* while the Assyrians its opposite, *akrasia* (see the excursus at 8:35, "The Book of Judith and Greek Philosophy").

The panic and flight of the enemy—retreat is too posi-

---

5   The medieval monk Hélinand took this passage as the theme of a major sermon on Judith and Mary; see Thayer, "Judith and Mary," 63–75.

6   Aristotle, *Poetics* 1452a. Esler similarly argues that the true moment of definition is Bagoas's

anagnōrisis in 14:16–15:2 (*Sex, Wives, and Warriors,* 294–95).

7   Moore, *Judith,* 234.

tive a term—are similar to the scenes in 2 Macc 3:14–21 and 3 Macc 1:16–29. In our novella, the panic does not result from the appearance of an angel, but solely from Judith's stratagem. (The Vulgate will add the appearance of an angel.) In the description, nearly every relevant term in the LXX vocabulary is used:

14:16: ἐβόησεν φωνῇ μεγάλῃ . . . κλαυθμοῦ . . . στεναγμοῦ . . . βοῆς ἰσχυρᾶς . . . διέρρηξεν
he cried out with a great voice . . . screaming . . . wailing . . . a great cry . . . he tore

14:17: κράζων
cried

14:19: διέρρηξαν . . . ἐταράχθη . . . κραυγή . . . βοὴ μεγάλη
they tore . . . panic . . . wailing . . . a great cry

15:1–2: ἐξέστησαν . . . φόβος . . . τρόμος . . . ἐκχυθέντες ὁμοθυμαδόν . . . ἔφυγον
they were shocked . . . fear . . . trembling . . . they poured out together . . . fled

15:3: ἐτράπησαν εἰς φυγήν
they were thrown into flight

The author strains to find new and alternative terms. What possible aspect of emotional disintegration have the Assyrians not exhibited? One can imagine how this cascade of terms would have resounded in a performance of Judith.

The routing of the Moabites after Ehud's assassination of Eglon, and of the Philistines after the slaying of Goliath, may very well have served as influences.[8] The account in these two cases is shorter and more realistic in each detail. The slaughter of ten thousand in Judges 3 was probably an exaggeration in its day, yet realistic by the standards of Judith. The exaggerated resolution in Esther—the slaying of seventy-five thousand enemies of the Jews on one day (Esth 9:16)—is similar to Judith. The distance of the pursuit in 1 Samuel is somewhat less than in Judith. Gath and Ekron were Philistine cities not far from the setting of the battle. In Judith, the chasing

down of the enemy extends to Damascus, about a hundred miles. Yet one wonders whether the unknown cities of the Judith text increase the sense of a spread of the soldiers to far corners, while Damascus would by Judith's day be associated with the contemporary Seleucids.

Other differences between our novella and David's routing of the Philistines may be considered. First Samuel references external actions only; internal states are communicated only indirectly, for example, "with a shout." All emotions are to be inferred from what can be seen or heard. Judith, on the other hand, in addition to the descriptions of flight, contains psychological referents that refer to the lack of self-control: "were greatly dismayed," "amazed," "overcome with fear and trembling," "with one impulse." A gratuitous detail should not be overlooked: the flight of the enemy who had been stationed in the mountains (15:3). These need hardly have been mentioned, but the notice recalls the moment in 7:13 when the Edomites and Moabites volunteered to take up stations in the mountains around Bethulia. Although not specifically labeled as Edomites and Moabites, the audience would have likely recalled their identity.

One may also compare the more contemporaneous 3 Macc 1:16–29, the general grief of Jerusalem when Ptolemy threatens to enter the temple, but the actions of panic and abandon are found mainly among the women (1:18–20). In addition, the priests and all the citizens, men and women, remain steadfast in their defense of the temple and do not desert. Here the vaunted Assyrian soldiers are acting like women, lacking in philosophical restraint.

■ 15:4–7

In contrast to the Assyrian armies, the Bethulians, though citizen-soldiers, have kept their discipline under the command of Judith. Uzziah, the chief elder of Bethulia, now executes her plan by sending out to nearby towns a summons to attack. Deborah had prophesied but not commanded, allowing Barak to lead the attack; Judith has prophesied and commanded, but now the battle will be carried out by men. The Bethulian citizen-

---

8   Some details also evoke Abraham's (Abram's) anomalous military hero story in Genesis 14, where he pursues the captors of Lot. In the LXX of that story, Choba and Damascus also appear.

soldiers embody a highly romanticized notion. How could there actually be more than a few hundred adult males, not well armed or in fighting shape, against the mightiest army in the world?

The Bethulians are not alone in carrying out the vengeance on the Assyrians; the villages of Israel also attacked the flanks of the fleeing soldiers. The village names mentioned first are unknown—Betomasthaim, Choba, Kola—but the regions of Gilead and Galilee also participate.[9] The rout of the enemy includes towns in the reverse order of the Assyrian conquest in chaps. 1 and 2. The account thus shifts from defending a narrow pass—a three-hundred-Spartans motif (even though that rearguard action involved many more troops than the three hundred)—to an offensive routing involving all of Israel. The Assyrian casualties mount up until the invaders are outside the boundaries of Israel.

While a variety of terms for panicked reaction were used in 14:16–15:3, we find the opposite here, a more typical Hebraic style, which generally makes use of a small, repeated vocabulary describing concrete acts connected by *waw*. In this climactic routing scene, this technique is utilized specifically to communicate that the panicked actions of the Assyrians are matched by organized, aggressive actions of the Israelites. The rush of the Israelites after the fleeing Assyrians here and in 15:3 employs the same verb (*ekchyō*) used to describe the pouring of the enemy out over the land (15:2). Further, as the Assyrians had run "with one impulse" (*homothymadon*) so also the Israelites have now been rallied, in accordance with Judith's plan, to attack them *homothymadon* (15:5).[10] As fear and trembling fell upon (*epepesen*) the Assyrians, so the Israelites fell upon (*epepeson*) the enemy. There is perhaps an artificiality or archaism to the description of the routing scene, calling forth the memory of past patriarchs, judges, and kings, in contrast to the proliferation of panic terms associated with the Assyrians. Indeed, this victory is probably understood as a reconquest of Canaan. It serves as a sort of expulsion narrative, eliminating the offending people.

Further, just as the Assyrian armies are described in orders—Bagoas, Assyrian leaders, those in camp (the tents), and those stationed in the mountains—so also the Israelites: Uzziah, the Bethulians, those from surrounding towns, those from all the borders of Israel, and more specifically, those in Jerusalem and the hill country, those in Gilead and Galilee. "All the frontiers of Israel" is significant here in the concluding action; the boundaries of David's Israel were probably being intentionally restored at this time by the Hasmonean expansion.[11] Yet it is interesting that the author would use invented towns—Betomasthaim, Choba, and Kola, and that the routing of the enemy would go as far as Damascus and beyond. Damascus was the ancient capital of Syria but had declined as a power center by the Hellenistic period. The Seleucids had made Antioch their capital, and Seleucia on Tigris the eastern capital, but in the civil wars of the Seleucid empire of the second century—the period just before the composition of Judith—Damascus was temporarily the capital of one of the pretenders, Demetrius II Nicator, who ruled from 145 to 140 BCE. It was likely viewed as the ancient and symbolic capital of the Seleucid forebears.

■ **15:6–7** The slaughter here is described without blood; only the poetic account in 16:12 mentions blood. There is, however, much looting. There is an order in those who loot the Assyrians: Bethulians first, then Israelites, then the villages in the hill country and the plain. Bethulians thus remain at center stage in the story, though the vast amount of plunder—enough for all—is also emphasized. On one hand, this motif might seem to be a typical folk motif of this kind of story—the blunt justice of folktales cross-culturally—but in Israel it would also have been viewed as an expected consequence of being favored by God. Wealth was in general a confirmation of a powerful God; in Third Isaiah, the wealth of nations will flow into Jerusalem (Isa 60:5, 11; 61:6; 66:12). The motif evokes as well the Israelite plundering of Egyptians during the exodus (Exod 12:35–36; cf. Judg 8:24–26). Plundering was viewed as a legitimate part of

9   First Maccabees 7:44–47 may be relevant here: the enemy troops are attacked on both flanks by surrounding villagers. *Hyperkeraō* in the LXX is only used here and in Judith; so Gera, *Judith*, 55.

10   This adverb is used six times in Judith, ten times in Acts of the Apostles, and rarely elsewhere.

11   So Ben-Eliyahu, *Between Borders*, 175–93.

warfare in this period, even of economic restoration. The shifts of the fortunes of war in this region between the time of Alexander and the writing of Judith—two hundred years—would have been extraordinary. The struggles among the successors of Alexander and among the rival claimants of the Seleucid kingdom, and then also the expansion of the Hasmonean state, would have meant a constant process of warfare and plundering.[12]

In Esth 9:10, 15–16, the Jews do not touch the plunder of those whom they kill. The two alternative policies have a background in the *ḥērem*, the holy war or ban, common in the ancient Near East and in Israel. In the Bible, there are two types of *ḥērem*. The total ban applies to the conquest of the land that would become Israel. Israelites are instructed by God to destroy the cities entirely, including all women, children, and slaves, in addition to all property and livestock (Deut 7:1–2; 20:16–18; Josh 6:19, 24). The partial ban applies to conquered cities outside Israel: all males are to be killed, but women and children should be taken as slaves, and the plunder is to be kept (Deut 20:10–15). It is possible that the total ban was never enacted. It seems unlikely that Israelites would forgo women, children, slaves, and plunder; it is more likely an invented motif of a later period to create a romanticized notion of the purifying of the land imposed by God.[13] Be that as it may, the viewpoint in Judith corresponds to the partial ban. Plunder falls to the victor and is a confirmation of God's favor in war. Yet Judith will present all of *her* items at the temple (16:19).

Excursus: Revenge, Vengeance, Vindication, and Plunder

The moral objection to the revenge motif in the Bible has a long history. Martin Luther devalued Esther in comparison with other biblical texts partially on the basis of the nationalistic revenge motif (though, contrary to common assumptions, he did not wish to displace Esther from the canon; he only subordinated it to other texts). The modern critique of the just war also condemned excessive revenge. Vengeance, vindication, and plunder all overlap but are not the same thing and can be introduced separately. Vengeance,

for example, is one party's satisfaction in punishing those who have wronged that party (see the commentary on 13:9b–10a). Vindication is not precisely vengeance on a perpetrator-nation, but re-righting a previous imbalance, placing the correct people—Israel under Yahweh—back in a position of freedom from external control. Vindication is the restoration of justice and balance after it has been disturbed. Vengeance can be masked within vindication, but the ideal of vindication is that it restores justice, and this is generally what is treated in the ancient texts.

Vindication does have an unacknowledged self-interested aspect, however. The outrage reported in Judith is not that violence occurred but that another nation did it *to Israel* (Deut 7:1–2; 20:1–20). Achior's account of Israelite history in 5:14–16 expresses the author's own sense of the justice of the scorched earth when God, not Nebuchadnezzar, commands it. Yet we should not assume hypocrisy on the author's part; rather, in a different world of honor and shame, the author simply asserts, in agreement with other peoples, that times were accounted good when the gods led one's own army in triumph, and bad when the gods allowed a defeat. "Peace" was a time not of ebb but of flow. Was there ever a sense that a general peace for all was ethically preferable to a period of victory? Passages such as Isa 19:24–25 suggest this (see Jdt 9:7; 16:2, 17).[14]

In the modern critique of biblical vengeance, it is thus important to understand this theme within the culture of the ancient Near East. Greek *ekdikēsis* and Hebrew *nāqām* should often be translated as "vindication" rather than "vengeance," because the action is presented as a restitution of justice and *šālôm*—not peace as the absence of violence but the balance and proper wholeness of the parts. Deuteronomy 32:35 and Isa 34:8, for instance, both place *nāqām* and *šālôm* together. Vindication produces wholeness and integrity. Within Israel, the day of judgment is actually a day of vindication, *yôm nāqām*, Isa 34:8.

Several questions remain, however, in regard to Judith. In early twentieth-century scholarship on Judith, it was at times suggested that the book of Judith may be pointing toward a notion of eschatological judgment, but Morton Enslin rightly rejected this. In the Song of Judith (e.g., 16:17), the author may reference eschatological motifs, but in a noneschatological sense.[15] Verse 17 may use some of the language of Isaiah 66, and may even evoke the

12   Kosmin, *Land of the Elephant Kings.*
13   Wills, *Not God's People,* 28–31; Susan Niditch, *War in the Hebrew Bible: A Study in the Ethics of Violence* (Oxford: Oxford University Press, 1995).
14   See also Simkovitch, *Jewish Universalism.*
15   Enslin, *Book of Judith,* 175 n. 17. The only other passage in Judith that approaches this possibility is 9:4–5. Worms as a fitting end to the arrogant per-

urgency of apocalyptic judgment, but it stands alone in the book of Judith. The doctrine of judgment in Enslin's mind evoked comparisons to Pharisaic judgment, but this is too specific. Still, we note that novelistic literature can borrow the motifs and sensibilities of other genres, often for a temporary or superficial effect, as when Greek Esther is introduced with mock apocalypticism.[16] The book of Judith uses this language to condemn those who would rise up "against my people."

In addition, since shame is often involved in the injustice, the retrieval of honor and the infliction of shame reside in the gray area between vindication and vengeance. Further, who determines which national ideal of boundaries and allegiance is the just and balanced one? And what is obscured when the injustice is described as "opposing God"? With modern recourse to international perspectives, economic rebuilding, and the remaking of nations, the concept of vengeance becomes repugnant and is often seen as opposed to the hope of peace. The modern sensibilities also assume universalizable ethical principles, as opposed to ancient values of in-group loyalty.[17]

Genre is also a particular concern when interpreting Judith. Unlike Deuteronomy, which is part of an epic history, Judith, Esther, and 3 Maccabees are fictions, even farces. These texts create one-dimensional characters representing good and evil, which then call forth one-dimensional solutions to the problem of revenge: the enemy is so deserving of annihilation, and the protagonist so pure, that the revenge becomes a narrative necessity. This is a staple of much popular narrative; the original Grimm's fairy tales resolved conflicts with brutal justice, toned down in each later edition. It is also a narrative requirement that a further advance by the Assyrians will not occur (see 16:25); the ending is at least temporarily happily ever after.

Does the "generic defense" extricate the author from a moral condemnation? Is the text then merely high camp? Excessive revenge is tolerated in modern popular entertainments on the grounds that the genres are unreal, but neither in the ancient nor the modern period does this address what effect that might exercise on the audience's view of others. What positive and negative identities are constructed by these popular genres that can then be projected out onto a conflicted world, where it may be seen as totally justified to kill certain kinds of people?[18]

---

son are also found in Isa 14:11; Sir 7:17; Acts 12:23; and T. Job 20, but in Jdt 16:17, we may also see an allusion to the death of Antiochus IV Epiphanes, as found in 2 Macc 9:9.

16   Tobit 14, likely an addition to that book, may be more sincerely eschatological, and Pss. Sol. 15:12 certainly so.

17   Analogous is the condemnation of Judith's deceit. Esler reminds us that in the ancient world deceit would not have been viewed as a vice if it was plied against outsiders (*Sex, Wives, and Warriors*, 288).

18   Wills, *Not God's People*, passim.

Text

8/ **Then Joakim the high priest and the council of the Israelites who lived in Jerusalem came to witness**ᵃ **the good things that the Lord had done for Israel, and to see Judith and wish her peace. 9/ When they came in before her, they all blessed her with one voice and said to her, "You are the exaltation of Jerusalem! You are a great glory for Israel! You are the proud boast of our people! 10/ You have done all these things by your own hand! You have bestowed great benefits upon Israel, and God is greatly pleased with these things. May you be blessed by the Almighty Lord forever!"**
And all the people said, "Amen."

11/ **For thirty days the whole people plundered the Assyrian camp. They gave Judith the tent of Holofernes, along with his silver vessels, his couches, his basins, and all his furnishings, which she took and loaded upon her mules**ᵇ **and she harnessed her wagons and heaped these things upon them. 12/ Every Israelite woman came running to see her; they blessed her, while some performed a dance in her honor. She took garlanded wands in her hands and handed them out to the women with her, 13/ and she and those with her crowned themselves with the olive branches.**
Then she led the dance of all the people, leading all the women, with every man of Israel coming behind fully armed, wearing garlands, a song of praise on their lips.

a   For θεασασθαι: θεμελιωσαι *b* 534.

b   106ʹ reads την ημιονα, which Hanhart prefers as the more difficult reading, while τας ημιονους is found in *O L* OL. *NETS* follows Hanhart, but the singular is hard to reconcile with the text, unless we take the loading on a mule to be partial or transitional to the next clause, loading on carts.

Commentary

15:8–13

Jerusalem and the temple have been at the symbolic center of this book from the beginning, and here the connections are emphasized. The high priest Joakim and the elders of the "Israelites who lived in Jerusalem" have now arrived as the representatives of the institutions of Israel (see also 4:8). It is noticeable that the high priest comes to find Judith even though she will soon be at the temple. The entourage from Jerusalem evidently meets her in her home and blesses her profusely.

The end of this novella, like the end of many others, is a series of blessings, processions, rituals, and piously intoned words that are almost liturgical: "exaltation of Jerusalem, great glory for Israel, proud boast of our people," "you have bestowed great benefits upon Israel," "God is greatly pleased with these things."[1] Judith is blessed again (v. 10b), and the people affirm,

---

1   Gera provides some particulars: Uzziah and then Achior bless Judith with lines similar to Judg 5:24—Uzziah similar to Gen 14:19, and Achior similar to Num 24:5 (*Judith,* 49). Note also that *hypsōma* can be pride, as with the Assyrians in 9:7, or glorification in a good sense, as of God in Exod 15:2. It is unusual for a person to be exalted (13:20), or stand for the exaltation of Israel (15:9), but here also are the exaltation of the enemy (9:7) and of Jerusalem (10:8; 13:4). In the Fourth Glorious Mystery of the Roman Catholic Rosary, v. 9 is associated with the Virgin Mary.

"Amen!" This provides a celebratory end to the text's performance. Popular narrative cross-culturally often concludes with an acclamation scene, the visible chorus of the representatives of governing institutions—priests, governors, judges, police, citizens. This conclusion not only acclaims the hero's achievement but also confirms that the threat of chaos has been removed and order restored to the polis. This is as true of modern films and television as it is of ancient literature.

Tobit and Greek Esther also end with celebrations, but not as broad as Judith's. Tobit emphasizes "blessings," but on a lower scale. The celebration is of a happy marriage, and indeed the text may have been written for a wedding celebration of the Tobiad family.[2] Greek Esther expands on MT Esther to include:

> The Lord has saved his people; the Lord has rescued us from all these evils. God has done great signs and wonders, wonders that have never happened among the nations. . . . And God remembered his people and vindicated his inheritance. (Greek Esth 10:9b, 12)

■ 15:10

Those acclaiming Judith here attribute all glory to her and have no reservation in acclaiming *her* actions by *her* hand. This stands somewhat at odds with Judith's prayers, where she shared agency with God (see 8:32–33; 9:9–10). The people attribute to Judith here what is elsewhere only appropriate for God. They trust her completely when she says that she did not have sex with Holofernes (cf. 13:16), although in some Christian and Jewish retellings the Bethulians express doubt about her sexual purity (see §8 above). In LXX, however, Judith's total control of the situation allows no opening whatsoever for others to second-guess her.

■ 15:11

The celebration continues with "all the people" plundering the enemy camp for thirty more days. One of the pauses in Holofernes's campaign (3:10) also lasted thirty days, so this is a point of some irony. Judith does not plunder the camp—was plundering restricted to men?—but she was given Holofernes's tent, silver vessels, couches, dishes, and furnishings. Judith thus inherits Holofernes's bed, "a memento of her deed and a further symbol of what is denied her," since she returns to cloistered widowhood.[3] As one who is in control of her own desires and has restricted them drastically, she will turn all the plunder over to the temple (16:19). It may be significant that she loads these riches onto carts pulled by mules (*tas hēmionous*), not asses. This may be a further shaming motif, or it may have a proto-ascetic implication: mules, hybrid crosses between horses and asses, are infertile.

■ 15:12–13

Just as the high priest and elders from Jerusalem have arrived to bless her, so also the women of Israel gather for the same. "Every woman of Israel," *pasa gynē Israel*, appears only here in the entire LXX, a feminine equivalent of *pas anēr Israel*.[4] Their dance not only celebrates the victory, it is "for her." Women in Israel performed victory dances and songs; the brief renditions in Exod 15:20–21, Judg 11:34, and 1 Sam 18:6–7 are given fuller treatment in the Song of Deborah (Judges 5) and here. The women are here said to gather with tambourines, mentioned in 16:2 (see Judg 11:34).

The appearance in Judith of "ivy-wreathed wands" (*thyrsous*) and olive wreaths is different from the Hebrew Bible examples, but this originally Greek practice occurs also in 2 Macc 10:7; 3 Macc 7:16; Wis 2:8; and Jub. 16:30–31 at Sukkot; it had been adopted by Jews.[5] It is specified that Judith takes the garlands "in her hands." This unnecessary detail recalls the leitmotif of her hand (see the excursus at 9:8–10, "Judith's Hand and Agency"); no longer a woman of war, she uses her hands in the more typical woman's role of the victory celebration. Is this indeed a ritual shifting of her identity back to respectable women's activities? Finally, the order of the dance is specified: Judith leads the dancing, women first and then men.

---

2   Wills, *Jewish Novel*, 68–92.
3   Nutu, "Framing Judith," 142.
4   Gera, "Speech in Judith," 416.
5   Contrast as well, however, 3 Macc 2:29, and also Jdt 3:7, where it is the Assyrian allies who celebrate Holofernes with "garlands and dances and tambourines." It is also possible that *thyrsoi* refers to *lulavim*.

Text

14/ Judith took up this thanksgiving before all of Israel, as the whole people also jubilantly sang this hymn of praise:

16:1/ And Judith said:
Begin a song to my God with tambourines,
Sing to my Lord with cymbals.
Compose for him a new song;[a]
Exalt him, and call upon his name.

2/ For the Lord is a God who crushes war.
For into his camp,[b] in the midst of the people,
He has snatched me from the hands of my persecutors.

3/ The Assyrian came out of the northern mountains.
He came with an army of thousands,
Its size so great that it clogged the wadis,
Their horses covered the hills.

4/ He threatened to burn my lands[c]
And to destroy my young men by the sword,
To cast my nursing babes to the ground,
To hand over my infants for booty,
And my virgins as spoils.

5/ But the Lord Almighty has thwarted them
By the hand of a female.[d]

6/ For their leader was not brought low by young men,
Nor did sons of the Titans[e] strike him,
Nor mighty giants set upon him;
But Judith, daughter of Merari,
Undid him with the beauty of her face.

7/ She stripped off her widow's garments
To lift up those struggling in Israel,
She anointed her face with precious oils,

8/ And fastened her hair[f] with a tiara.
She chose out her linen garment in order to seduce him.

9/ Her sandal bewitched his eye;
Her beauty took his soul captive.
The sword sliced through his neck!

10/ Persians shuddered at her daring,
Medes quaked at her courage.

11/ Then my humiliated people raised a war cry,[g]
My weak people shouted out[h] and the enemy trembled,[i]
They[j] lifted up their voices and my enemies were turned back.

12/ The sons of slave-girls ran them through,[k]
And wounded them like children of fugitives.
They perished before the ranks of the Lord my God.[l]

13/ I will sing to my God a new song:[m]
O Lord,[n] you are great and glorious,

Textual Notes

a Καινον A V *a* OL Sy Vg, but Hanhart prefers και αινον as *difficilior*. Either could be a misreading of the other. Cf. 16:13.

b Hanhart's reading is retained, but it is a difficult line, with many variants; see Bogaert, "Version latine," 208; "Recensions," 85 (1975): 34, 263.

c For ορια, B has ορη; cf. 1:5.

d After θελειας, κατεσχυνεν αυτους *O L* OL PsSin PsTh Sy. Parallelism would argue for this, but the text as is is the more difficult reading.

e For τιανων: γιγαντων 46 381 534 OL-R.

f For τας τριχας: τους βοστρυχους 583 Sy Vg (*cincinnos* OL, *scingillos* PsSin).

g Schmitz/Engel (*Judit*) note that this is onomatopoeia in Greek: to shout the αλαλη, war cry.

h Hanhart reads εβοησαν from V. Εφοβηθησαν is found in B S A OL-MCG Eth some minuscules. Schmitz/Engel (*Judit*) prefer εβοησαν because it does not require a change of subject, and Moore finds εφοβηθησαν inappropriate with the preceding clause. For Corley, however ("Septuagintalisms," 95), εφοβηθησαν makes adequate sense as fear of God.

i For επτοηθησαν: επτοησαν S*; εποιηθησαν 583; ηττηθησαν V *L* some minuscules Arm; *ceciderunt* OL-G Sy. See Corley, "Septuagintalisms," 91.

j The unstated subject could also be the enemy.

k A difficult line, with many variants. A difficult passage in the MT of 1 Sam 20:30 was translated in LXX as υιε κορασιων αυτομολουντων, "son of traitorous girls," and may influence this passage. Haag (*Studien,* 58) and Zenger (*Das Buch Judit,* 519) both accept ως υιους κορασιων (comparing with object) 583 OL-MCG; *sicut puellas* Sy. Schmitz/Engel (*Judit,* 366, 403) prefer the nominative υιοι and keep the parallelism. See also Gera, *Judith,* 463–64, but also at 53. For αυτομολουντων: αυτομολουντας 583 *L* OL PsTh Sy Vg, *ultraneos* PsSin.

l Hanhart reads κυριου θεου μου, but this may be dittography with the next line; Rahlfs reads κυριου μου.

m For καινον: και αινον in some minuscules; cf. 16:1.

n For κυριε: αδωναι κυριος *O* OL Vg.

o For ωκοδομησεν: ωκοδομηθησαν S OL Eth Arm some minuscules, *constituta sunt* Sy, *renovata sunt* OL-MG PsSin PsTh, *creata sunt* Vg; cf. Ps 103(104):30.

p For συν υδασιν, Moore, following Joüon, suggests that כמים was read as במים. Corley, however ("Septuagintalisms," 91–92), questions this, since ב would normally become εν; his reading is adopted here. He also points out the similarity to Pss 23(24):2, 135(136):6, and esp. 17:8(18:7); cf. 76(77):20, 103(104):3.

q For επι: ετι B S A 311 542, which Rahlfs prefers.

r Some texts read καυθησονται or καυσονται.

Marvelous and invincible in your strength.
14/ **Let all creation serve you,**
For you spoke, and they came into being.
You sent forth your spirit, and it built them up.[o]
There is no one who can resist your voice.
15/ **For the mountains shall be shaken from their foundations to the seas;[p]**
Before you, rocks shall be melted like wax.
Yet for those who fear you,[q]
You shall show mercy.
16/ **For every sacrifice conducted for a fragrant smell is a small thing,**
And all the fat burned for the whole burnt offerings is a trifle to you.
But the one who fears the Lord is great forever.
17/ **Woe to the nations who oppose my people!**
The Lord Almighty will punish them on the day of judgment.
He will place fire and worms in their flesh.
They will weep[r] in pain forever.

Commentary

15:14–16:17

Judith and Tobit both conclude their narratives with a hymn of thanksgiving. Greek tradition rarely combines poetry and prose, but it is a common practice in the Hebrew Bible and Judaism.[1] Judith's song is referred to as *exomologēsin* in Greek, which in the LXX usually translates *tôdâ* ("thanksgiving") and is parallel here to *ainesin,* "hymn of praise." However, the word can also mean "confession," and the increasing interest in faith and confession among Jews in this period, long before the rise of Christianity, is significant.[2]

The "Song of Judith" bears strong similarities to two other biblical women's songs, the Song of Moses (Exodus 15), probably originally a "Song of Miriam," and the Song of Deborah in Judges 5; cf. also the Song to Simon in 1 Macc 14:4–15. The Song of Judith is an example of the woman's victory song, common to both ancient Israel and Greece.[3] As Schmitz emphasizes, Jdt 16:2 and 9:7–8 both quote Exod 15:3 according to the LXX, but the hymn here also references Exod 15:1–18 as a whole. The Song of Moses, then, provides a theological springboard for the story of Judith.[4] Rakel finds a similar structure in Judith 16 and Exodus 15:

	Judith	Exodus
Introduction: God makes an end to wars	16:1–2	15:1–3
Description of the enemy and his plans	16:3–4	15:9
Reaction to God's intervention	16:10–12	15:14–16

1 Cf. Exodus 15, Judges 5, Deuteronomy 32–33, 2 Samuel 22, Jonah 2, Prayer of Azariah and Song of the Three Jews, and cf. Luke 1:46–55, 67–79. See Weitzman, *Song and Story.*

2 See §6 above; and Wills, "Jew, Judean, Judaism."

3 See above at 15:12–13; cf. also 1 Sam 18:6–7. On the role of ode and song in cults and processions, including ruler cults, see Andrew Bell, *Spectacular Power in the Greek and Roman City* (Oxford: Oxford University Press, 2006) 100–105.

4 Schmitz, *Gedeutete Geschichte*, passim. The similarity in structure to Exodus 15 had also been argued by Craven, *Artistry and Faith,* 105–12. The one clear reference to Exod 15:3 cannot be dismissed, but

The call to sing at the beginning is similar in each case, and many terms are the same or similar: quoting the enemy general; announcing the enemy's plans; the enemy as pursuer; sword, spoils, shuddering, and dread of the enemy; the nations trembling. In addition, the same roots are used in both songs to say that God is *megas* ("great"), *endoxos* ("glorious"), and *thaumastos* ("wonderful").

Whereas Anne E. Gardner argued that the parallels to the Song of Deborah are stronger than those to the Song of Moses, the influences of the latter are more pervasive.[5] And, unlike the case of Judges 5, Exod 15:3 is clearly quoted in Jdt 16:2, a God who "crushes wars," *syntribōn polemous*. Rakel concludes,

> As a synecdoche this quotation calls to mind the entire exodus tradition, which is for Israel not only a historical event but also a token of remembrance [*Erinnerungsfigur*]. . . . The theology of the hymn thus becomes the theology of the exodus.[6]

Judith also restores the woman's role to the victory song that Miriam lost when her song was ascribed to Moses.[7] Finally, unlike the prose narrative of Judith 1–15, here Judith adopts the persona of the Mother of Israel: it is "my" territory, men, infants, children, and virgins.[8] It may seem in some lines as though the Song wants to return the agency to God, after Judith has acted more on her own in the prose story, but the audacity of Judith remains here as well. As Rakel notes, the hand of God at Exod 15:6, for instance, becomes the hand of Judith at Jdt 16:6.[9]

As is often the case, it is emphasized that Judith has acted for "all Israel," despite the fact that Bethulia is located in Samaria. The region of Samaria is here part of ideal Israel, or the newly reunited Israel, with Jerusalem at its center (see the excursus at 4:1–15, "Samaria"). The communal confession of "all the people" is similar to that in Ezra 10 and Nehemiah 8–9, which are covenant renewal scenes. Both of these are in the "Ezra Memoir" section of Ezra-Nehemiah, which develops a very strong sense of the new constitution of "all the people," *kol hā'ām*. Though the people were historically broken apart, they are now whole again.[10] The context of Judith 16 is not, strictly speaking, a covenant renewal ceremony but rather a celebration of a great military victory. No actual festival is established, as there is in Esther and 3 Maccabees (but see 16:20), yet the strong affirmation of identity has resonances with covenant renewal. As noted above (see the excursus at 14:10, "Achior's Conversion"), the covenant renewal theme may perhaps be sensed in the conversion of Achior.

Although it is most often assumed that the author of Judith penned this hymn as a concluding celebration, it is conceivable that it was composed by a separate author, perhaps even at an earlier stage, and appended to the prose story.[11] This would be analogous to the relation of the Song of Deborah (Judges 5) to the prose version

---

the literary parallels between the Song of Judith and the Song of the Sea are often found as well in enthronement psalms, and cf. Psalm 46. Is the ultimate model, then, Exodus 15 or the enthronement psalms genre more generally?

5   Gardner, "Song of Praise," *HeyJ* 29 (1988) 413–22, here 418. On parallels to the Song of Moses, see also Skehan, "Hand of Judith," 96–98; Fokkelien van Dijk-Hemmes, "Traces of Women's Texts in the Hebrew Bible," in Athalya Brenner-Idan and Fokkelien van Dijk-Hemmes, eds., *On Gendering Texts: Female and Male Voices in the Hebrew Bible* (Biblical Interpretation Series 1; Leiden: Brill, 1993) 17–109, here 40–44; Zenger, "Der Juditroman," 72–74; Dubarle, *Judith*, 1:142–43; Moore, *Judith*, 247–57; Craven, *Artistry and Faith*, 111.

6   Rakel, *Judit–Über Schönheit*, 40, 44–45.

7   Note also 4Q365 (4QReworked Pentateuch[c]) from Qumran, which restores the ascription to Miriam.

8   Daniel J. Harrington, *Invitation to the Apocrypha* (Grand Rapids: Eerdmans, 1999) 41.

9   Rakel, *Judit–Über Schönheit*, 42.

10 Wills, *Not God's People*, 64–70, 77–80; Katherine E. Southwood, *Ethnicity and the Mixed Marriage Crisis in Ezra 9–10: An Anthropological Approach* (Oxford: Oxford University Press, 2012).

11 Gardner, "Song of Praise"; H. Ludin Jansen, "La composition du chant de Judith," *Acta Orientalia* 15 (1936) 63–71; A. Deprez, "Le livre de Judith," *Évangile* 47 (1962) 5–69; Zenger, *Das Buch Judit*, 516; Moore, *Judith*, 255–57. Jansen still granted that the *present* hymn is a literary composition that functions as a capstone to the book. If there were an independent oral tradition, then the later Near Eastern tradition of Jalila might be considered a

(Judges 4). We note as well that only some sections of the hymn mention plot elements that are found in the book as a whole. However, the separate authorship of chap. 16 is unlikely, as the chapter seems to be a "novelistic" poem, written for its present role. Below we will see that its rhetorical excess would work better in a novelistic performance than in oral-tradition poetry.

A number of different structural divisions have been proposed. H. Ludin Jansen divided the hymn into three parts:[12]

1. vv. 1–4   Introduction to a thanksgiving psalm
2. vv. 5–12   Story of Judith
3. vv. 13–17   Enthronement hymn

It was Jansen's observation that the three sections reflected different themes—only the middle section referring to the Judith narrative—that spurred scholars to speculate that some parts may have predated the present work. Craven counters that there is more unity among the sections, and she sees no reason to entertain separate authorship.[13] She still, however, grants structural breaks:

1. vv. 1–2   Hymnic introduction
2. vv. 3–12   Narration of the story
3. vv. 13–17   Hymnic response

A somewhat more refined structural division was proposed by Rakel and Pancratius C. Beentjius, who point to a pattern of singing that alternates between Judith and the people, suggested already in the introduction of the song (15:14):[14]

1. vv. 1–2   Judith calls the people to worship God
2. vv. 3–4   Judith describes the Assyrian threat
3. vv. 5–10   The people describe Judith's response
4. vv. 11–12   Judith recounts the actions of the people
5. vv. 13–17   Judith continues praising God

Parts 2, 3, and 4 include motifs found also in the narrative, with part 3, the people's role, lying at the center.

This antiphonal arrangement of the singing of Judith and the people, as Rakel has noted, is similar to that of Deborah and Barak in Judges 5, although the parallel sections are not in the same order:[15]

	Judith	Judges
1. Hymn introduction	16:1–2	5:2–3
2. Narrative of epic event	16:3–12	5:6–30
3. Praise of God as Lord of nature	16:13–15b	5:4–5
4. Plea to God for Continual justice	16:15c–17	5:31

As a result of this antiphonal arrangement, Judith moves from first person to third person in v. 6, and back to first person in v. 11. Judges 5 provides a model for this as well, shifting from first person to second person (addressing Deborah?) in 5:12, and eventually to third person.

Rakel also finds differences between Judith and Judges: Judith begins by focusing on the enemy, Judges on the sufferings caused by the chaotic situation in Israel;[16] Judith's triumph is mentioned at the beginning, Judges builds to the women's victory; Judith's enemies are thrown into panic, while the text of Judges turns instead to the deep irony of Sisera's mother imagining her son's triumph; Judith 16 mentions the death of the antagonist briefly, leaving Judith's role unclear, while Judges 5 describes the act in detail, with a pathetic death.

Although such structural divisions based on content seem plausible, the first half of the hymn exhibits a lack of regularity in the parallelism, and unusual rhetorical patterns result. The song begins clearly enough, with two strong connections to the biblical tradition. Raising a new song (v. 1) evokes Isa 42:10–13, and v. 2 quotes Exod 15:3 LXX (see also at Jdt 9:7–8). We discern here a typical pattern of parallel lines, AABB (recurring sense-terms italicized):

Begin (a *song*) to my God with *tambourines*,
Sing to my Lord with *cymbals*.

further development. The European Jewish tradition of Judith is likely derived from the Vulgate version and thus does not reflect an independent hymnic tradition; see §8 above.

12 Jansen, "La composition."
13 Craven, *Artistry and Faith*, 105–12.
14 Rakel, *Judit–Über Schönheit*, 33–35; Beentjes, "Bethulia Crying," 248–49.

15 Rakel, *Judit–Über Schönheit*, 33–35; Gardner also provided similar suggestions ("Song of Praise," 419–20); see also Crawford, "In the Steps of Jael," 11.
16 This is an editorial theme of Judges, which Judith eliminates in favor of her emphasis that "we do not recognize any God but him" (8:20).

Compose to him a new *song;*
  Exalt him, and *call upon* his name.

ἐξάρχετε τῷ θεῷ μου ἐν τυμπάνοις,
  ᾄσατε τῷ κυρίῳ μου ἐν κυμβάλοις,
  ἐναρμόσασθε αὐτῷ ψαλμὸν καινόν,
  ὑψοῦτε καὶ ἐπικαλεῖσθε τὸ ὄνομα αὐτοῦ.

Yet, unlike the Song of the Sea, which continues to exhibit a similar parallelism in each bicolon, next we encounter here wide variations of insistent parallelism that rise to a level of tension, relieved finally by a simple, strong asseveration. Similar strident patterns were discerned in chap. 9. Judith 16:22 consists of three roughly parallel lines, AAA; v. 3 returns to the AABB of v. 1, but v. 4 extends to a much more insistent AAAAA pattern. These differences are then resolved with a strong exclamation in v. 5: "But the Lord Almighty has thwarted them by the hand of a female!" Verse 5 is normally counted as the first line of the following section, but it serves as well to release the tension created by v. 4.

Following this is a similar pattern of extended, repetitive parallel members that build tension, subsequently broken by a simple declaration: v. 6 creates a rising tension with an AAA pattern, followed by "but Judith . . . undid him with the beauty of her face." Verses 7–9a then develop an even more insistent AAAAAA pattern; Judith's decisive deeds punctuate each of the run-on lines.[17] This climaxes in v. 9b with the resounding "and the sword sliced through his neck!" The rhetorical effect thus noted in vv. 2–9 runs counter to the content divisions that were first introduced but suggests a sort of "sprung rhythm" that we may take as indicative of a popular, less "classical," less oral-traditional poetry. But even this pattern, or lack of a pattern, does not continue consistently. The song in the first half has been insistent, even overwrought, but in vv. 13–16 it is more beautiful—yet capped off again by the strident v. 17.

■ **16:1**
Exalting God is more than simply praising God. In the polytheistic context of the ancient Near East, it was believed that worshiping a deity actually magnified that deity among the gods. Just as honor and shame worked to magnify or diminish people on the human plane, so also honor and shame of gods magnified or reduced their power in heaven. Even in monolatrous Israel, this common view likely prevailed and rendered it possible to magnify God by praise and liturgy. Exalting God is also contrasted with kings who exalt themselves: Dan 4:19(22) LXX; Tob 13:4, 6, 7. For Israel, a small province or buffer state in a world of great empires, God is returned to a status towering over these empires as they had towered over Israel.

■ **16:2**
On the alteration of Exod 15:3 MT to "a god who crushes war," see the excursus at 9:7–11, "Judith 9:7–11 and Song of the Sea." "Camp" is a recurrent motif in Judith; *parembolē/paremballō* are found twenty-one times. But this is God's "camp," his habitation in Israel. See also 12:5b–9 on the motif of "outside the camp." Rakel also argues that traces of women's perspective can be attributed to an ancient text if it varies from male-ordered victory, and she finds this in the fact that Judith was not raped but rather, "[God] snatched me from the hands of my persecutors."[18] However, this should perhaps be attributed to the unreal nature of this tale—the tale of a female trickster (see §5 above).

■ **16:3–4**
The idea of Assyrians coming out of the northern mountains corresponds to the narrative of Judith, but it also sounds a biblical note, the "enemy out of the north" (Jer 1:13–15; Ezek 39:2–5).[19] The threats to Israel refer back to Holofernes's destruction of the nations in his path in 2:27 and use many of the same images.

■ **16:5–10**
Regarding the hand of a woman and the humility of Judith (16:5–6), see the discussion at 9:4, 11, and below at 16:11–12. One difference between chaps. 9 and 16 is that in chap. 9 Judith will act by *deceit,* while here she

---

17   The next bicolon (v. 10) begins a new section in some analyses; in others it completes the previous verses. I take it with the next section, though the motif of the "Persians and Medes" seems added in any case; see below.

18   Schmitz/Engel, *Judit,* 399–400.

19   Schmitz/Engel, *Judit,* 398.

conquers Holofernes by her *beauty*. Alternatively, in 13:2 it is the *wine* that undoes Holofernes. Clearly, all three are necessary—deceit, beauty, and wine—and we may add wisdom (or cunning) and courage. Yet it is interesting to note what is specified at the different points. If the Song of Judith was ever a separate tradition, which is not likely, it is possible that it emphasized her beauty over her deceit.

■ 16:6

Titans and giants are further examples of the super-abundance of references in Judith. Our heroine can, first, be seen as an "anti-Goliath,"[20] but Titans here is a specifically Greek reference. The term giants, *gigantes*, may be a reference to either Israelite or non-Israelite mythological tradition.[21] That the sons of the Titans did not *epataxan* ("strike") Holofernes recalls the use of this leitmotif in 2:27; 5:12; 6:3; 9:3, 10.

■ 16:7–9

In 9:9–10, 13, Judith had asked for strength and speech, but here her beauty, cosmetics, clothes, and jewelry are noted—along with her violent deed. It is possible, but not likely, that the hymn here reflects a separate source focused more on sex and violence. Either way, her dressing scene now moves more into the center of the hymn (see the commentary on 9:1–14), and not her deceit or wine. As her traits are told in succession, it is a bit closer to the *wasf*, the ancient Near Eastern genre of love poetry that recounts a woman's beautiful traits in order;

this genre has likely influenced Song of Songs. But here the examples of Judith's beautification are ironically contrasted with the culminating act, "the sword sliced through his neck!" It is this provocative marriage of sex and violence that propels the entire book, summarized in the hymn.[22]

■ 16:10–12

Verse 10 can be taken either with the previous verses or with the following. The structural divisions of Rakel and Beentjes above reflect this ambiguity, and modern translations differ. In favor of taking v. 10 with what precedes, the Persians and Medes can act as a conclusion to the references to international conflict. In favor of taking it with what follows, "the sword sliced through his neck!" (v. 9) could conclude the previous building of images, and the trembling of the enemy is played upon in vv. 10–11. In addition, vv. 10–12 together emphasize not her dressing, as in v. 7–9, but the victory of the humble, oppressed people and the lowly sons of slaves over the haughty.[23] This was also a motif in Judith's prayer in 9:11. A biblical theme, it is present also in various forms in Greek culture (see the commentary on 9:11). The humble/haughty tradition looks for a reversal: God will protect the humble and bring justice by correcting the imbalance. Judith's victory, however, is also military, and she and the Bethulians—not God directly—reverse the honor and shame of the parties: "sons of slave-girls ran them through." This will be accompanied by vengeance motifs in v. 17.

---

20   Gera, "Judah and Judith," 36.

21   For Israelite tradition, see Gen 6:1–10; 14:5; 15:20; Num 13:32–33; Deut 2:10–21; 1 Sam 17:4–7; 2 Sam 21:16–22; 1 Enoch 7:2; 15:8–12; Jub. 4–5; 3 Macc 2:4–5; Sir 16:7–8; Philo, *On the Giants*. Hesiod (*Theogony* 185) refers to Erinyes, or Meliades; cf. also *Odyssey* 7.59, 206. Indeed, in the Hellenistic period the battle of the Titans with the Olympian gods was sometimes confused with the battle of the giants and Olympians (Callimachus, *Hymn 4 (to Delos)* 173–76). The Greek terms here are not necessarily evidence that the book was composed in Greek; the translator might have introduced the Greek terms; see Cameron Boyd-Taylor, "Judith," in *NETS*, 442. Gera (*Judith*, 460) assumes that the Greek words would have been widely known, and Moore (*Judith*, 248) assumed a translation of

Hebrew terms like *rp'ym* Gen 14:5 or *nplym* Gen 6:4. See also Benjamin G. Wright III, "Hellenization and Jewish Identity in the Deuterocanonical Literature," in Géza G. Xeravits, József Zsengellér, and Xavér Szabó, eds., *Canonicity, Setting, Wisdom in the Deuterocanonicals: Papers of the Jubilee Meeting of the International Conference on the Deuterocanonical Books* (DCLS 22; Berlin: de Gruyter, 2014) 29–68, here 41–43.

22   She puts on a linen dress for the purpose of deception, *apatēn*, which picks up 9:10, 13; 12:16; and 13:16. LaCocque suggests improbably that the sandal in v. 9 conjures up the sandal of Ruth's relative in Ruth 4:7–8 (*Feminine Unconventional*, 37).

23   Yet the break remains ambiguous, in that v. 10, with vv. 7–9, focus on *her*, while vv. 11–12 feature *the people*.

Grouping v. 10 with vv. 11–12 is suggested also by the similarity of this section to a part of the Song of Moses, Exod 15:14–15:

The nations will hear and tremble;
    anguish will grip the people of Philistia.
The chiefs of Edom will be terrified,
    the leaders of Moab will be seized with trembling.
The people of Canaan will melt away;
    terror and dread will fall upon them.

In Exodus 15 there are more references to specific nations, while in Judith it is generalized: only Persians and Medes are mentioned, which would elicit some surprise—if this were a history book. These two nations entered into Israel's history *after* the Assyrians and Babylonians, so reference to them is anachronistic. In this version of history, however, the Medes are mentioned as victims of Nebuchadnezzar in chap. 1, and the Persians in 1:7 as respondents to Nebuchadnezzar's charges. Persians and Medes enter into this historical fiction as a stock literary element. They appear together in Ezra 6:2; Esth 1:19; 10:2; Dan 5:26–28; 6:7, 15; and are probably two of the nations referred to in the four-nation cycle that was common in Near Eastern eschatological histories and in Daniel 2 and 7. Recall also that there are a number of parallels in our text to the historical invasion of the Persian king Artaxerxes III Ochus (see §2 above), and one of the Seleucid kings took on the title "king of the Medes."[24] In our narrative, Arphaxad as king of the Medes was likely perceived as fictitious, and Persian terms are found in our narrative (*akinakēs*, 13:6; 16:9; *kidaris*, 4:15; "prepare earth and water" 2:7; the names Holofernes and Bagoas; see §4 above). We may also perceive Divine Warrior motifs in Jdt 16:10: the Persians trembled and the Medes were daunted. (On the Divine Warrior in Judith, see 10:9–10). Translations often rationalize the mythical language of 16:10.

■ **16:11–12** The verb *alalazō* means shout *alalē*, originally the trilling sound of a war cry in Greek, although in the LXX it is more the language of joyful noise in the Psalms (Pss 46[47]:1; 65[66]:1; Josh 6:19 [20]; compare *euphrosynē*, "joy," in Pss 15[16]:11; 104[105]:43; 105[106]:5). It is onomatopoeic, and perhaps analogous to Hebrew *ḥālal* ("shout"), the root of *hallelujah*.[25] The text in v. 12 is challenging at this point. Translations generally choose between "sons of young women" and "children of deserters." Our text echoes 1 Sam 20:30, and the choice here reflects problems in that text (see Textual Notes).

■ **16:13–17**

Several aspects of these verses have suggested to scholars that the Song of Judith was not all composed by the same author: v. 13 introduces a "new song"; there is no mention here of the narrative motifs of Judith; and the structure differs from the previous verses. To be sure, Craven finds connections here to the rest of the book: the two references to the fear of God (vv. 15–16) register as a culminating theme to the Song and the book as a whole.[26] The lordship of God here also provides an *inclusio* with the beginning of Judith, where Nebuchadnezzar asserts that he is the "lord of all the earth" (2:5). This is possible within the large chiastic structure of Judith, but the fear of God and the lordship of God are so common in biblical confessions that their presence here is not probative. We leave the question unresolved.

The "new song" in v. 13 is a common motif in the psalms (Pss 33:3; 96:1; 144:9; 149:1).[27] Thus, while it may appear ironic to modern readers to call this a "new song," it is a new song in that it announces rescue: celebration is a recovered experience. Moore finds in vv. 13–17 a pastiche of biblical motifs, not very effective in its rhetoric and beauty.[28] Craven, however, was more positive: vv. 1–12 provide the causes for singing; vv. 13–17 constitute the song. It is somewhat similar to Jdt 9:12 and expresses final resolution. "Now," says

---

24 Kosmin, *Land of the Elephant Kings*, 256. See also the prophecy of Jer 51:11 that Medes will destroy Babylon, and see 1:1–6.

25 Schmitz/Engel, *Judit*, 402:

26 Craven, *Artistry and Faith*, 109–10.

27 Weitzman, *Song and Story*, 73. Skehan also notes

the less precise parallel to Judg 5:3 ("Hand of Judith," 95). This section, 16:15–21 in the Vulgate, is included in the Roman Breviary for *feria quarta ad Laudes I.*

28 Moore, *Judith*, 255.

Craven, "the people know that Yahweh, not Nebuchadnezzar, is the true 'king of all the earth.'"[29] Yet, while Jdt 9:12 also exhibited the strident, heavily laden style that we saw just above, this section exhibits a fairly consistent and pleasing structure. Beentjes, in fact, pulls this section of chap. 16 out as a "prayer of Judith," to be treated with her other four prayers, 6:18–19; 9:2–14; 13:4b–7; and 13:17.[30] (The distinction, however, between song and prayer should be kept in mind.)

The introductory call to sing a new song is followed by two lines in parallelism, establishing a pattern repeated in the lines that follow—that is, a strong hymnic line followed by two parallel lines. This pattern does not extend to v. 17, which results in a short poem of some beauty, here with a more literal translation (parallel terms in italics):

> I will sing to my God a new song:
>> O Lord, you are *great and glorious,*
>> *wonderful in strength,* invincible.
>
> Let all your creatures serve you,
>> for you *spoke,* and they *were made.*
>> You *sent forth your breath* and it *formed* them.
>
> There is none that can resist your voice.[31]
>> For the *mountains* with the seas shall be *shaken*
>>> from their foundations;
>> before you, *rocks* shall be *melted* like wax.
>
> But to those who fear you, you show mercy.
>> For every *sacrifice as a fragrant offering* is a *small thing,*
>> and the *fat of all whole burnt offerings* is a very *little thing;*
>
> But whoever fears the Lord is great forever.

> ὑμνήσω τῷ θεῷ μου ὕμνον καινόν·
>> κύριε, μέγας εἶ καὶ ἔνδοξος,
>> θαυμαστὸς ἐν ἰσχύι, ἀνυπέρβλητος.

> σοὶ δουλευσάτω πᾶσα ἡ κτίσις σου,
>> ὅτι εἶπας, καὶ ἐγενήθησαν,
>> ἀπέστειλας τὸ πνεῦμά σου, καὶ ᾠκοδόμησεν.

> καὶ οὐκ ἔστιν ὃς ἀντιστήσεται τῇ φωνῇ σου.
>> ὄρη γὰρ ἐκ θεμελίων σὺν ὕδασιν σαλευθήσεται,
>> πέτραι δὲ ἀπὸ προσώπου σου ὡς κηρὸς τακήσονται.

> ἐπὶ δὲ τοῖς φοβουμένοις σε, σὺ εὐιλατεύσεις αὐτοῖς.
>> ὅτι μικρὸν πᾶσα θυσία εἰς ὀσμὴν εὐωδίας,
>> καὶ ἐλάχιστον πᾶν στέαρ εἰς ὁλοκαύτωμά σοι.

> ὁ δὲ φοβούμενος τὸν κύριον μέγας διὰ παντός.

The individual motifs of this section echo many Psalms, some of which should be noted. The first two verses are similar to Psalm 33:[32]

Judith 16:13–17	Psalm 33:3, 9, 6, 8
13 I will sing to my God a new song: O Lord, you are great and glorious, Marvelous and invincible in your strength.	3 Sing to (the LORD) a new song: Play skillfully on the strings, With loud shouts.
14 Let all creation serve you, For you spoke, and they came into being.	9 For he spoke, and it came to be; 6 By the word of the Lord the heavens were made, And all their host by the breath of his mouth.
You sent forth your breath, and it built them up.	
There is none who can resist your voice.	8 Let all the earth fear the Lord; let all the inhabitants of the world stand in awe of him.

The hymn fragment found in Isa 42:10 is also similar.[33] Yet note, with Schmitz/Engel, that although our text alludes to theophany traditions, there is, technically speaking, no actual appearance of God.[34] Rather, the

---

29 Craven, *Artistry and Faith,* 109–10.

30 Beentjes, "Bethulia Crying," 231–32.

31 This line begins with *kai* and therefore could be read as a continuation of the previous line. Still, it reads well as the beginning of the new thought.

32 Above at 9:5–6 it was also noted that there may be reflected the influence of Stoicism as well, e.g. Cleanthes *Hymn to Zeus,* esp. 11–21.

33 See also John R. Levison, "Judith 16:14 and the Creation of Woman," *JBL* 114 (1995): 467–69.

34 Schmitz/Engel, *Judit,* 408.

phenomena of nature are in the service of God (cf. Jdt 9:5–6), and indeed the act of rescue has been executed by Judith. Yet in her song of thanks, "Judit stellt . . . nicht sich selbst, sondern Gott in den Mittelpunkt, den Schöpfer von allem und Herrn der Geschichte."

Verse 15 is influenced by the Divine Warrior tradition (on which see the commentary on 9:1–14 and above in 16:10), as in Ps 18:7:

Judith 16:15	Psalm 18:7
For the mountains shall be shaken from their foundations to the seas;[35] Before you, rocks shall be melted like wax.	Then the earth reeled and rocked. The foundations of the mountains trembled and quaked, because he was angry.

Judith's defeat of enemies on earth is likened to God's defeat of enemies in heaven.

■ **16:16** A common biblical motif is found here: sacrifices in the temple, reduced to their physicality, are not the only obligation of the Israelite. Other obligations are also affirmed, be they acting justly, loving mercy, and walking humbly as in Mic 6:7–8, or exhibiting mercy and the knowledge of God in Hos 6:6, or as here, fearing the Lord. Sometimes considered a prophetic theme, it is found in passages such as Ps 40:6 as well: "Sacrifice and offering you do not desire, but you have given me an open ear." Only in the Christian rejection of Jewish law could the rhetorical trope of "*x* is greater than *y*" be interpreted as a rejection of *y*. Certainly not here, when Judith and the Bethulians are about to rush to the temple to offer very physical sacrifices.[36] This motif is, rather, a way of affirming the many commitments of an Israelite before God, and especially the subjective side. Similar ideas are expressed in Pss 40:6 and 50:8–15, and so Jdt 16:13–16 may derive from an older psalm, or at least breathe this genre. It is not an isolated desire of the author to warn the audience away from insincere sacrifice.

Whoever fears the Lord is also "great forever." This is not a reference to Pharisaic resurrection or the immortality of Wisdom of Solomon. The fear of the Lord provides a boon, but it is not personal immortality. Psalm 33:18–19 expresses a general sense of well-being, the psalmist's hope:

> Truly the eye of the LORD is on those who fear him,
> > on those who hope in his steadfast love,
> to deliver their soul from death,
> > and to keep them alive in famine.

So then, the one who fears the Lord will be great forever, but precisely how will our heroine be great forever? The text will indicate that she is not storing up credits for a resurrection judgment or immortality, she will be *memorialized* as a protector of her people (16:21–25), even if she is only a fictional heroine! It is a *faux*-memorial.

■ **16:17** The distinctive, effective structural pattern in vv. 13–16 is not continued into v. 17. Judith's phrases, "placing fire and worms in their flesh" and "they will weep in pain forever," seem inspired by the prophetic poetry of the last line of Isaiah (66:24):

> They will go out and look upon the dead bodies
> > of those
> > who rebelled against me.
> The worms that devour them will not die,
> > the fire that burns them will never go out,
> And they will be loathsome to all humanity.

Psalm 149, which begins, "Sing to the LORD a new song," also ends with a similar call to carry out God's vindication:

> Let the faithful . . . have two-edged swords in their
> > hands
> To execute vengeance [*nĕqāmâ, ekdikēsin*] on the
> > nations
> > And punishment on the peoples.

35   See Susan Niditch, *Oral World and Written Word: Ancient Israelite Literature* (Library of Ancient Israel; Louisville: Westminster John Knox, 1996) 21–24. The motifs "mountains shake" and "rocks melt" are found also in Judg 5:4–5: the mountains quake when Yahweh marches forth from Seir.

36   Schmitz/Engel, *Judit*, 409.

To bind their kings with fetters
    And their nobles with chains of iron.

Vindication is God's to exact in some biblical texts (Deut 32:35) and is assigned to a combination of divine and human agency in others (2 Sam 22:32–43 = Ps 18:31–42; on vindication, vengeance, and eschatological vindica-tion, see the excursus at 15:6–7, "Revenge, Vengeance, Vindication, and Plunder"). The *ekdik-* root occurs in this verse of Judith and in regard to Nebuchadnezzar and the peoples of the West in Jdt 1:12; 2:1; 6:5; 9:2; and in regard to Simeon, also with God as the subject, in 7:28; 8:27; 16:17; cf. 8:35; 11:10.[37]

---

37   Schmitz/Engel, *Judit*, 275–76.

Text	Textual Notes

Text

18/ When they arrived at Jerusalem they worshiped God,[a] and when the people were purified, they brought forth their whole burnt offerings and their freewill offerings and gifts. 19/ Judith dedicated to God[b] all of the furnishings from Holofernes's tent that the people had given to her and deposited the curtain she had taken from his bed as a votive offering to God. 20/ For three months, the people continued their celebration before the sanctuary in Jerusalem, and Judith remained with them.

21/ After this, the people set out, each to his family land,[c] and Judith went back to Bethulia and remained on her estate. For the rest of her life she was honored throughout the land. 22/ While many men desired her, none knew her for as long as she lived, from the time her husband Manasseh had died and was gathered to his ancestors. 23/ Her reputation continued to grow, and she grew old in her husband's house, reaching the age of a hundred and five. She gave her slave her freedom. She died in Bethulia, and they buried her in the cave of her husband Manasseh. 24/ The house of Israel mourned her for seven days. Before she died she divided her wealth among all the close kindred of Manasseh her husband and to all her own next of kin.

25/ And no one was able to strike terror among the Israelites while Judith was alive, nor for a long time afterwards.

Textual Notes

a   For θεω: κυριω *a* some minuscules OL Sy Vg.

b   For θεω: κυριω S A *O L b* some minuscules OL Sy Sa.

c   For εις την κληρονομιαν: εις τα σκηνωματα *O* OL Sy.

Commentary

16:18–25

The conclusion to the book is composed with a charming simplicity, yet it is still a jumble of statements with no clear order. It is possible that some were added, disrupting the flow. The Vulgate, for instance, registers what appears to be an addition: "The day of the celebration of this victory is counted by the Hebrews in the number of holy days, and has been observed by the Jews from that time until the present day." Some of the statements in the LXX could equally have been inserted, although it is possible that there was a deliberate attempt to provide a cascade of references to the happy circumstances of the

Israelites, the jumbled effect contributing to the unreal sense and also to the celebration.

A popular novella, like popular narratives across time and culture, must resolve with a totalizing sense of well-being. Judith is similar in this respect to the Greek novels, but also to countless modern movies, novels, and television shows. The celebratory public festival is also a powerful literary and political motif, part of the metaphysical underpinnings of kingship. Political systems, both ancient and modern, often affirm that the king or judge, acting as a benefactor, can command a celebration and cessation of labor. He takes the side of the poor, provides forgiveness of debts, release, or amnesty, and occasionally acts as the agent of redistribution for the weakest subjects. The festival motif in Judith, Esther, and

3 Maccabees assumes that the king—or in this fictional case, the high priest—acts constitutionally to bestow a festival on the people with all of its abundance, blessings, cessation of labor, and liminal equality.[1]

■ 16:18–20

These verses treat the harmony of the *laos* ("people") with their God (*laos* in the LXX translates *'am*, while *ethnos* translates *gôy;* see 4:1–15). Those from Bethulia come to Jerusalem to worship God and make thanksgiving offerings. The author pauses to note that the people purified themselves in preparation for offerings at the temple, as required in biblical law. In a literary exaggeration, the celebration continues for three months, in the presence of the temple. Judith remains with them in their festivities for this period.[2]

The offerings here are nearly identical to those brought by the high priest Joakim in 4:14 in response to the crisis, although Joakim's votive offerings, *euchas,* are not included here. Their absence reflects the particular nature of votive offerings as petitions before the fact, rather than thank-offerings after the fact. Under the conditions of the *ḥērem* or ban, the property of a defeated people is to be presented to God (Josh 6:19, 24). The transmission of plunder offerings is noted here: Judith offers up the possessions of Holofernes, which the people had given her after the routing of the enemy. Judith had herself collected the curtain, and just as David had offered Goliath's sword (1 Sam 21:9), Judith provides as an *anathema* or *ḥērem* offering the canopy that marked off Holofernes's inner sanctum. This canopy may have represented Holofernes's hymen in a reversal of gender roles and sexual penetration (see §5 above).

■ 16:21–25

The pious celebrations of vv. 18–20 are now concluded, but the aftereffects are no less pious. After the festivities, "each set out to his family land," a phrase resonating from Judg 2:6; 21:24. Inheritance here (*klēronomia*) recalls the use of this term in 4:12; 5:15; 8:22; 9:12; and 13:5 (see the commentary on 8:21–23). Each person returns to live peacefully on the land allotted to his or her clan or *mišpāḥâ* in the tribal history of Israel. There is a nod both to the restoration specific to Israel and to the golden-age peace that comes at the end of all romance.

As noted, these verses are a hodgepodge of items that memorialize Judith; we note some of the crowded motifs. Verse 22 states that many men desired her—is this sexually or as suitors who desired to marry her? Modern translations vary, but this may not have been distinguished in the original setting. At any rate, this novella, which focuses so often on sexual voyeurism, surely registers that she was still desired sexually; the verb *epithymeō* was used also in Susanna (OG 8) for the erotic desire of the two elders. The fact that the *epithym-* root is more generalized in Stoicism and elsewhere does not gainsay its erotic sense here and in Susanna; in fact, the Stoic use of *epithym-* likely influences the popular understanding in Judiasm and Christianity.

Mary Lefkowitz also notes that Greek women act independently only when it is for the public good and only in times of emergency, acting for a husband or male relative; they then return to private life.[3] One example from Plutarch (*Virtues* 255e–257e) is noteworthy. After Aretaphilia frees the city from a tyrant, she rejects pleas to join in the government, returning home instead to the women's quarters, where she spends the rest of her life weaving.

■ 16:23

Living to the age of 105 years was surely exceptional in the ancient world, a sign that Judith was favored by God. Enslin points out that the Hasmonean kingdom lasted for 105 years, from 168–63 BCE,[4] but the text was not likely written this late. Moore, however,

---

1   Carl Schmitt, *Politische Theologie: Vier Kapitel zur Lehre von der Souveränität* (Munich: Duncker & Humblot, 1934) 49; Jan Assmann, *Politische Theologie zwischen Ägypten und Israel* (Munich: Carl Friedrich von Siemens Stiftung, 1992) 54, 62–63.

2   Bogaert suggests that, since the feast at the defeat of Arphaxad in 1:16 is near Hanukkah, and the celebration here ends on the same day a year later, the book expresses a hidden Hanukkah theme ("Le calendrier," 67–72). Although this would make sense in light of the Hasmonean shadow over Judith, it is quite speculative.

3   Lefkowitz, *Women in Greek Myth*, 80–94.

4   Enslin, *Book of Judith*, 181.

notes that it could be an insertion.[5] (Compare Manasseh in 8:3.)

Freeing her slave is another benefaction for Judith's household. The text does not say whether the slave remains as *oikonomos,* the person in charge of a large household or estate, usually a slave. A different sort of narrative of the slave in charge of an estate is found in the Jewish novella Tobiad Romance.[6] The wealthy young son struggles with his father's *oikonomos* until the son finally puts the slave in his place. In Judith's time, manumission could often expose the slave to a harsh life but more often placed the former slave in the continuing position of client. At any rate, the realities of manumission are not so much of interest here as the literary topos, an act of public benevolence.

Modern readers may connect the burial of Judith at her husband's family tomb with the burial of members of Abraham's descendants, especially Rebekah and Leah, at the family burial site that Abraham had acquired at Machpelah (Gen 49:29–32). The practice was quite established and traditional, however, so the ancient audience might not have associated it in this way. The emphasis on her burial in the tomb of her husband may be a symbol of her being returned to patriarchal authority.

■ **16:24** After her death and burial are reported, the text returns—an addition?—to specify that before she died she disposed of her estate. She distributes her wealth, first, to her dead husband's family, and, second, to her own family. Biblical laws of inheritance generally assume that there are sons to inherit. Where there were no sons, the inheritance could pass to a daughter, but in that case she would be required to marry within the tribe. If there were no heirs (as in the case of levirate marriage), there was an assumption that the property would remain within the clan or *mišpāḥâ:* "you shall assign the deceased's property to his nearest relative in his own clan" (Num 27:11). Inheritance in general is not understood as falling to individuals as much as specified relations within the clan; extended households and clans thus retain the inheritance. Later Jewish reflection (Sifre to Deut 15:7) also affirms the concentric circles of charity: one should be concerned for a kinsperson on the father's side before one on the mother's side. Judith's distribution to her kin is not in keeping with biblical law, but as she was of the same tribe and clan as Manasseh (8:2), it is not far outside of the spirit of the law.[7] Her property, then, remains within her and her husband's families, as would be expected.

Is her distribution of the estate perceived as simply bequeathing it before her death, or as an act of charity? We may distinguish here Jewish inheritance, almsgiving, and public benefaction (see also 8:7–8). Almsgiving was a Jewish form of charity.[8] Many Hebrew Bible passages mandate giving to the poor (Deut 24:13–22; Amos 2:6; Pss 85:12; 89:15; Prov 10:2; 19:17; Tob 4:5–7; Sir 7:29–36), as did the rabbis (t. Pe'a 4:19; Lev. Rab. 3:1). Yet giving *all* of one's possessions was not viewed as positive in these passages. A person's obligations for one's own clan and inheritance would preclude such large-scale charity. But in Roman culture almsgiving was not valued as much as public works, a form of patronage. Although Judith's act seems technically to be an administration of inheritance, the fact that she grants part to her own family and also manumits her slave imbues it with an air of benefaction.

There is a temptation to read in Judith's act a disbursement of all of her possessions. Perhaps, and it may find parallels in later Christian notions of heroic, sacrificial giving. Some New Testament texts promote a higher level of giving (Acts 2:43–47; 4:32–5:11; 2 Corinthians 8; 9; Jas 2:1–7), and this is expanded as a supererogatory virtue in Christianity. Later Christians perceived ascetic almsgiving as a payment for sins, yet there is no precedent for Jewish charity at this level. A closer inspection of some texts, however, indicates that Judith is not totally unique.[9] Though Tobit's virtue is perhaps seen as supercilious, and there is a satiric aspect as

---

5 Moore, *Judith,* 260.

6 From Josephus, *Antiquties* 12.4.1–11 §§154–236. See Wills, *Jewish Novel,* 187–93; Wills, "Depiction of Slavery."

7 Gera, *Judith,* 106; and see her notes on 8:6, 7, 8; 10:5; 12:1–4; 16:23, 24; Schmitz/Engel, *Judit,* 241.

8 Gary A. Anderson, *Sin: A History* (New Haven: Yale University Press, 2010) 10–11. Job, who was not

necessarily Israelite, was depicted as a patron of the poor, a benefactor, but he never willingly gave away enough of his wealth to jeopardize his economic superiority to the poor—until God took it away.

9 Wills, "Ascetic Theology."

well, his almsgiving and care for the bodies of fallen Israelites also testify to his character, much as it had for Job. Does the ending of Judith push the edges of these notions to develop a doctrine of a higher righteousness, later to evolve into central parts of the ascetic life? Or later challenged by the domestic piety of rabbinic Judaism? Judith's heroic charity may be seen as similar to her heroic self-control earlier, and roughly analogous to the heroic abstinence of Daniel and his three friends (Daniel 1).

Although, as a typical heroine, Judith herself is not precisely reintegrated into society, her benefactions establish that she is the patroness for both her husband's extended family and her own. She is a new category, a female redeemer; no feminine form of *gôʾēl* appears in the Bible or ancient Judaism, but Judith is such a figure. She has given away her wealth but at the same time dispenses patronage and has received an enormous store of honor. If she has shown independence of spirit and agency, she is finally safely buried in her husband's burial cave. She remained a wealthy woman on her estate and was honored by Israel both in life and in death.

■ **16:25** The final line turns to Judith and the bestowal on her of a heroic memory: no one could spread terror in Israel during her lifetime, or for a long time after her death. This coda is the typical ending for the accounts of the judges, or heroes, who arose before the foundation of Israel (Judg 3:11, 30; 5:31; 8:28; 16:25; and see §4 above), and it is also comparable to hero legends cross-culturally. Schmitz draws attention especially to the Greek cult of memory that is associated with the tyrannicide of Harmodius and Aristogeiton, which established democracy in Athens.[10] It is also similar to, but somewhat longer than Tob 14:2, the heroic coda that probably originally concluded the book of Tobit. Judith 16:25 also closes the chiastic structure of the second half of the book by echoing the line from 8:8: "No one raised a malicious word against her, for she feared God greatly." The *phob-* root is thus a leitmotif in Judith.[11] It builds up in the first half and is finally resolved in 15:2

when Judith will cause "dread and fear" to fall on the Assyrians. Now the fear has been laid to rest.

We may compare two Maccabean passages. After the death of Nicanor in 1 Macc 7:50, there was rest for a few days. This is a more "historical" and realistic reference than Judith or Judges. In the romanticized narrative of 2 Macc 15:37, however, we hear of a longer peace: "From that time the city has been in the possession of the Hebrews." Third Maccabees 7:21 is similar: "The Jews possessed greater prestige among their enemies, being held in honor and awe; and they were not subject at all to confiscation of their belongings by anyone." In Esth 10:2–3, Esther and Mordecai are parallel benefactors of their people, but there is no reference to their deaths.

Greek and Roman culture exhibited a much richer tradition of heroes and heroines than did Israel, with a particular terminology, more explicit reverencing of the dead figures, and belief in the boons that they provided for the living. Yet within Israelite tradition many of the same aspects of hero tradition can be found from time to time and figure to figure, from Moses and the patriarchs, to the prophets, judges, sages, seers, and even figures like Ezra and Nehemiah and high priests such as Simon in Ben Sira 50 (see §3 above). It is likely that the religious life of the people included a reverence for heroes even though the literary tradition has not preserved it in its full extent.

In Greek and Roman as well as Israelite heroic tradition, there is what may be called a cult of remembrance, that is, not necessarily an actual cult as at a gravesite but a literary or cultural tradition that remembers and honors the hero—a literary monument. Aesop may have had such a function within Greek society, with no physical hero cult, and Jeremiah, Enoch, Ezra, and Nehemiah may have attracted this sort of reverence in Israel. Yet the book of Judith may have played on this with a fanciful and fictitious memory, not a true memory of a heroine. And from the time that her story became authoritative, as early as the end of the first century CE for Christians (1 Clem. 55), her memory was real and effective. In the collective memory of Israel—and later of

---

10   Herodotus 5.55–57, among other passages; see Schmitz, "War, Violence and Tyrannicide," 103–19.
11   Schmitz/Engel, *Judit*, 414. See also the commentary on 1:11–12 and 2:28; Craven, *Artistry and Faith*, 54.

Christians—Judith, though a fictional character, became larger than life and was, as a result, remembered as a historical figure.

Excursus: Judith's Status at the End

What is the status of our heroine at the end? She returns to her estate and remains a widow, presumably in seclusion, although this is not stated. For Amy-Jill Levine, after Judith's sojourn as a wildly independent woman, she returns to patriarchal norms.[12] By comparison, Esther, *alongside Mordecai*, at the end of that novella retains a high authority as a writer of edicts. Susanna is returned to the control of her parents and husband at the end of the Theodotionic version but not at the end of the OG. Judith, however, does exercise a high degree of agency in giving away her wealth, freeing her slave, and in deciding not to remarry. Yet for Tal Ilan,

> What the story lacks, in my opinion, is a "happy end" in which the righteous heroine marries a righteous hero; the hero is present—the proselyte Achior the Ammonite—only the marriage is missing, to the sorrow and surprise of the reader.[13]

Yet Ilan may have the wrong genre in mind, perhaps the Greek novel. It is common in hero narratives for the male hero, at the end of his story, to be unable to integrate as a husband or father in the society he has just saved. This is the cross-cultural motif of the loneliness of the male hero, now applied to a woman.

Ilan goes on to say, "We can assume that the first Christian widows aspired to the same ideal." Here Ilan may perceive an important connection. From a later perspective, Judith's return to her estate would seem to be a foreshadowing of celibacy and asceticism, and even the Jewish examples of Qumran, the Therapeutae/Therapeutrides, and Josephus's description of the Jewish hermit Bannus fill out a picture of Jewish ascetic experiments dated only a bit after our novella.[14] And is there a parallel across the centuries? It was noted in §5 in the introduction that the early French proto-novel *Princesse de Cleves* ended with the female protagonist finally able to marry her lover but refusing to out of duty, living part of each year in a convent. And as noted above, the Greek female redeemer Aretaphilia ended her life by returning to weaving.

Gera sees Judith's decision to remain a widow as a choice for continuing independence; remarrying would involve a loss of independence.[15] Perhaps, but how would "independence" of anyone, especially a woman, read in this period? Outi Lehtipuu points out that "early Christian writers did not see Judith's decision as an enactment of autonomy but of chastity."[16] Still, chastity for the early Christians, especially for women, may have also been a channel for independence and agency. At any rate, Judith's many practices indicate a set of probably fanciful proto-ascetic ideals at a time when this was beginning to be explored.

By the standards of ancient Jewish wisdom, is our heroine happy? One of the benefits of righteousness was a long life (Prov 16:31), and Judith does live to be 105 years old. Jon Levenson also argues that in ancient Israel the rough equivalent or analog for personal immortality was having children and a continuous family lineage. But Judith refuses marriage. She forgoes remarriage and children, or indeed any direct involvement in the family structure, apart from distributing her wealth. What Judith acquires is a memory, the equivalent of Greek *kleos*. In ancient Greece, the memory of the hero was understood as the compensation for his loss of life or the living out of a normal life.[17] Hebrew *zākar* is a similarly strong notion, but not generally tied to the memory of *hero*. Rather, it is used of the *people's* memory of the mighty acts of God that lie at the foundation of the covenant. Yet, noted above, there is also a memorializing in Israel of many leading figures, not quite as systematized as in Greece and Rome but still quite strong. Judith is depicted as enjoying a heroine's memory.

12   Levine, "Sacrifice and Salvation," 27–28; see also §5 above.
13   Ilan, *Jewish Women*, 149 n. 38.
14   Wills, "Ascetic Theology."
15   Gera, *Judith*, 473.
16   Lehtipuu, "Receive the Widow," 42.
17   Oedipus in Pindar, *Olympian Ode* 7.77; *Nemean Ode* 1.69–72; Euripides, *Hippolytus* 1423; see Nagy, *Best of the Achaeans*, passim; Robert Parker, *Miasma: Pollution and Purification in Early Greek Religion* (Oxford: Clarendon, 1996) 320–21.

Appendix

Jerome's Vulgate and Septuagint Compared

(See English synopsis of Vulgate and
Septuagint at end of this section)

On first inspection, the salient characteristic of the text history of Judith is that it is not interesting. The other novelistic texts of the Christian Bible—Tobit, Esther, Daniel—exist in wildly different recensions, a phenomenon of novelistic texts also noted by Christine Thomas in regard to Christian Apocryphal Acts. From the earliest period, other novelistic texts, *even within the Greek Bible tradition,* were transmitted in versions that were vastly different in order, wording, theme, and so on. The same is true of nonbiblical novelistic texts like Joseph and Aseneth and Testament of Abraham, non-Jewish novelistic texts like The Story of Ahikar, Life of Aesop, and the Alexander Romance, as well as the Apocryphal Acts.[1] Judith, on the other hand, circulated in the Greek tradition in textual versions that were as fixed as most of the proto-canonical books—much more fixed, indeed, than Jeremiah or Proverbs. Unfixed textual traditions are typical for novelistic texts in the ancient world, so why should Judith be so uninteresting? Why was this textual tradition so fixed at an early stage? Often consid-

ered the least pious of any of these texts, why should it enjoy a greater textual fixity?

The question takes a turn, however, at the time of Jerome. In taking up the great translation project of the Vulgate, he resisted including those texts of the Septuagint and Old Latin Bibles that were not part of the Jewish Bible. He referred to the texts of the Jewish Scriptures as *hebraica veritas,* and it was he who coined the term "apocrypha" with a decidedly negative connotation for the books not found there. When, late in the process of translation (about 400 CE), he turned to Tobit and Judith, he sought out Semitic texts as witnesses to the *hebraica veritas* and deemed these preferable to the LXX and Old Latin.[2] But he was not positive about including these and dismissively says that he translated Tobit in one day, Judith in an evening, although this is likely rhetorical exaggeration.[3] Jerome's preface to Judith reads:

Among the Jews the book of Judith is counted among the apocrypha,[4] but the authoritative weight of this for affirming those [i.e., the apocryphal texts] which have come into dispute is judged to be less than sufficient. Yet because it was written in the Chaldean language [Aramaic], it is counted among history

---

1   See Thomas, *Acts of Peter*. The differences in the versions of Tobit, Esther, and Daniel are so great that the alternative traditions are often presented in parallel columns. They have also provoked a number of book-length studies and a host of articles about the contexts of the various recensions. Although Edwin Edgar Voigt rightly contends that there was not one Old Latin textual tradition of Judith but several, he is actually referring to very minor differences, nothing like what we have for other biblical books (*The Latin Versions of Judith* (Leipzig: Drugulin, 1925).

2   The text used here for the Vg is Robert Weber, ed., *Biblia sacra: Iuxta Vulgatam versionem* (5th ed.; Stuttgart: Württemburgische Bibelanstalt, 2007).

3   Patrick W. Skehan, "St. Jerome and the Canon of the Holy Scriptures," in Francis X. Murphy, ed., *A Monument to Saint Jerome: Essays on Some Aspects of His Life, Works and Influence* (New York: Sheed & Ward, 1952) 259–87, here 287 n. 26; in agreement and in the same volume, Louis N. Hartmann, "St. Jerome as Exegete," 65–75, here 71–72.

4   The word *agiografa* was used by Jerome for both

apocrypha and for the Writings or Ketuvim (see also his preface to Daniel), so "among the Hagiographa" could conceivably mean "among the Ketuvim;" so Voigt, *Latin Versions,* 46; and Johann Gamberoni, *Die Auslegung des Buches Tobias in der griechisch-lateinischen Kirche der Antike und der Christenheit des Westens bis zum 1600* (Munich: Kösel, 1969) 78. But Vincent T. M. Skemp rightly concludes that in regard to Tobit and Judith *agiografa* means apocrypha (*The Vulgate of Tobit Compared with Other Ancient Witnesses* [SBLDS 180; Atlanta: Society of Biblical Literature, 2000], 17), as indicated by the preface to Tobit (see below). Still, Jerome utilizes Christian categories to characterize Jewish texts. See also Barbara Schmitz, "ΙΟΥΔΙΘ and *Iudith*: Überlegungen zum Verhältnis der Judit-Erzählung in der LXX und der Vulgata," in Johann Cook and Hermann-Josef Stipp, eds., *Text-Critical and Hermeneutical Studies in the Septuagint* (VTSup 157; Leiden: Brill, 2012) 359–79.

389

books.[5] But since the Council of Nicaea is judged to have counted this book in the numbers of the Sacred Writings, I have acquiesced to your request,[6] indeed your demand; and after my occupations were laid aside—from which I was forcibly restrained—I gave one short night's work to it, translating not word for word but more from sense to sense. I have pruned away the wide variety of the many manuscripts,[7] and have expressed in Latin only those readings that I could find expressed coherently in Aramaic. Receive, then, the widow Judith, example of chastity, and in triumphal praise acclaim her with perpetual public celebration. For the one who rewards chastity has provided her as a model not only for women, but for men as well, and has bestowed such heroic virtue that she conquered the one who was invincible to all humanity, and she surpassed the unsurpassable.

Apud Hebraeos liber Iudith inter Agiografa legitur; cuius auctoritas ad roboranda illa quae in contentione veniunt, minus idonea iudicatur. Chaldeo tamen sermone conscriptus inter historias conputatur. Sed quia hunc librum sinodus nicena in numero Sanctarum Scripturarum legitur conputasse, adquievi postulationi vestrae, immo exactioni, et sepositis occupationibus quibus vehementer artabar, huic unam lucubratiunculam dedi, magis sensum e sensu quam ex verbo verbum transferens. Multorum codicum varietatem vitiosissimam amputavi; sola ea quae intelligentia integra in verbis chaldeis invenire putui, latinis expressi. Accipite Iudith viduam, castitatis exemplum, et triumphali laude perpetuis eam praeconiis declarate. Hanc enim non solum feminis, sed et viris imitabilem dedit, qui, castitatis eius remu-

nerator, virtutem talem tribuit, ut invictum omnibus hominibus vinceret, insuperabilem superaret.

Among the points to be noted are the following:

- Jerome is skeptical about those texts not in the Jewish Scriptures, but he grudgingly agrees to translate them.
- He says he has eliminated dubious variants—of the LXX and Old Latin, or of Aramaic texts?—and translated only what was coherent in the Aramaic.
- As uneasy as he is about the canonicity of the *text* of Judith, he strongly affirms the *figure* of Judith as one deserving perpetual praise.

This last observation raises a crucial issue: we should not assume that Jerome harbored reservations about the book of Judith, since he fully affirms the figure of Judith at the end of his preface, and his attitude toward the canonicity of Tobit seems identical (see below). He may, however, have harbored some ambivalence about the novelistic aspect of the *text*. Jerome calls Susanna a *historia* (Preface to Daniel, though later he calls it a *fabula*) but Bel and the Dragon a *fabula*. In §7 above, I argue that for most Christians the progression of these texts from fiction to history could occur because the *figures* were *first* revered in a hagiographic tradition; the line from fiction to history may run through oral hagiography.[8] Jonah, Daniel, Susanna, Esther, and Judith began in fiction and sometimes in humor, but by the first century CE were all treated as historical figures and models of faithfulness, sometimes in both Jewish and Christian contexts. While other Christians, then, were accepting Susanna as a fully

---

5   Does Jerome mean "considered by Jews to be a noncanonical history book," or "placed by Christians with the histories in the Bible"? Probably the former.

6   That is, the request of his fellow bishops Chromatius and Heliodorus, to whom he had dedicated the translation of Tobit.

7   I am told by Giovanni Bazzana that when Jerome uses *vitiosissimam,* he likely means simply the wide variety of OL variants.

8   The hagiographical tradition is treated by Annewies van den Hoek and John J. Hermann, Jr.,

"Celsus' Competing Heroes: Jonah, Daniel, and Their Rivals," in Albert Frey and Rémi Gounelle, eds., *Poussières de christianisme et de judaïsme antiques: Études réunies en l'honneur de Jean–Daniel Kaestli et Éric Junod* (Publications de l'Institut romand des sciences bibliques 5; Lausanne: Zèbre, 2007) 307–11. Josephus already utilizes the Daniel and Esther novellas as "historical" texts (*Antiquities* 10.11.6-7 §§254–81); see Wills, *Jewish Novel,* 222–24. Later Jewish tradition, however, may have allowed for a fictional Esther.

historical text, Jerome may have remained uncertain because of its language.

But be that as it may, since the Vulgate version of Judith is shorter than both the LXX and the Old Latin (which is based on LXX), it is often assumed that, out of disdain for what he perceived to be a deuterocanonical text, Jerome summarized and shortened the text. This common assumption, however, may not be what the preface implies. First, Jerome often defended his translation as *sensum e sensu* rather than *ex verbo verbum,* so his practice here was not necessarily different.[9] Jerome held to a notion of "Hebrew truth," which could include biblical texts in Aramaic as well, and he may have privileged a shorter Aramaic text over longer Greek witnesses. The "sense" for Jerome also does not likely mean a summary or paraphrase; rather, he may intend here simply to differentiate his translation style from the hyperliteral practice of LXX translation practiced by Theodotion, Aquila, and others. Jerome's earlier statements in defense of his use of Hebrew texts, the *Prologus galeatus,* or "Helmeted Preface," to his translation of Samuel and Kings (392 CE), would seem to reject the possibility of a loose paraphrase:

> First read, therefore, my Samuel and Kings—mine, I say, mine. For whatever by diligent translation and zealous emendation we have learned and now hold, is ours. And when you understand something of which you were formerly ignorant, either consider me a translator, if you are grateful, or a paraphrast (παραφραστην) if you are ungrateful, although I am

not in the least aware of having veered in any way from the Hebrew truth.

> Lege ergo primum Samuhel et Malachim meum; meum, inquam, meum: quicquid enim crebrius vertendo et emendando sollicitius et didicimus et tenemus, nostrum est. Et cum intellexeris quod antea nesciebas, vel interpretem me aestimato, si gratus es, vel παραφραστην, si ingratus, quamquam mihi omnino conscius non sim mutasse me quippiam de hebraica veritate.

Still, paraphrase and editing may have entered in. It is sometimes suggested that Jerome provided looser translations in the later years of his project. In addition, Jerome did not know Aramaic well. As his preface to Tobit states, his process of translation with Aramaic texts was to engage in a simultaneous translation process, or *viva voce*: a qualified assistant would translate Aramaic aloud into Hebrew, which Jerome translated into Latin. This raises the possibility that more than the usual amount of paraphrasing could have entered into the process without Jerome's awareness.[10]

Rediscovering Jerome's Aramaic Source?

Some scholars note in passing that there are significant pluses and minuses in the Vulgate of Judith, but their very language suggests that their only goal is the reconstruction of the LXX Greek.[11] The Vulgate version is dismissed as secondary or inferior. According to Joosten,

---

9   Skemp (*Vulgate of Tobit,* 21) notes that the Vulgate of Esther is paraphrased, yet Jerome says that he translated *verbum e verbo.* Thus we must take note not only of what he says, but also what he does. Jerome's famous comments about the avoidance of overly literal translation are evidently influenced by Horace, *Ars poetica* 133.

10   Pierre Nautin, "Hieronymus," *Theologische Realenzyklopädie,*15:309–10, concludes that Jerome was not as knowledgeable in Hebrew as he made himself out to be, and used informants and notations in the Hexapla to render his translations, but Adam Kamesar, *Jerome, Greek Scholarship, and the Hebrew Bible: A Study of the* Quaestiones Hebraicae in Genesim (Oxford: Clarendon, 1993) 97, insists that

Jerome was indeed an able Hebrew translator. See also Benjamin Kedar-Kopfstein, "The Latin Translations," in Martin Jan Mulder and Harry Sysling, eds., *Mikra: Text, Translation, Reading and Interpretation of the Hebrew Bible in Ancient Judaism and Early Christianity* (Assen: Van Gorcum/Minneapolis: Fortress, 1990) 308–27; Dennis Brown, *Vir Trilinguis: A Study in the Biblical Exegesis of Saint Jerome* (Kampen, The Netherlands: Kok Pharos, 1992) 82–85; and in general, Megan Hale Williams, *The Monk and the Book: Jerome and the Making of Christian Scholarship* (Chicago: University of Chicago Press, 2006).

11   E.g., Moore, *Judith,* 95–103.

What is not subject to doubt is that Jerome's translation is vastly inferior to the Greek text. In hardly any passage does the Vulgate appear to offer a better text than the Greek manuscripts, and in many places the Latin clearly goes back to the Septuagint.[12]

Vulgate Judith is considered an aberration, and yet, ironically, it has been *the* edition of Judith for more people than any other version.[13] It could just as easily be considered the base text for which LXX is an eccentric precursor. Indeed, Lydia Lange points to a significant theological development in Jerome's translation: "The Book of Judith is . . . more than a simple translation. It is part of a program to construct the Christian-ascetic ideal."[14]

The differences between the two versions are thematically interesting and stylistically significant, reflecting two possible early notions of what "Judith" is all about. It is usually assumed that Jerome, in paraphrasing, introduced many changes into the text, but it is possible that he utilized an Aramaic version of Judith that was independent of the LXX text, perhaps a witness to an earlier tradition.[15] We may also consider a middle alternative: the version underlying the Vulgate

of Judith may not have derived directly from an early Jewish story, whether Aramaic or Greek, but a Christian version that had circulated independently before Jerome.[16] For instance, had a Christian ascetic interest influenced this branch of the Judith tradition before Jerome took it up?

To be sure, in response to these suggestions it could be argued that it is prima facie more likely that the LXX text type predates the Vulgate textual tradition: the LXX can be assumed as a textual version several centuries before Jerome. Yet Jerome chose the Aramaic text because he assumed the Semitic tradition was more authentic, and it could have represented an early, eastern textual family. Further, discussion should not be limited to a debate about which text reflects the older tradition. In textual criticism, the Vulgate has often been considered useless if it does not aid in the restoration of LXX, but recent scholarship in textual criticism emphasizes that every textual variant is an interpretation and should be investigated as a new turn in the tradition.[17] So here as well, the Vulgate represents either Jerome's interpretation—or perhaps a Christian interpretive tradition at the time of the translation, both of

12   Joosten, "Original Language," 167–68.

13   We should not as a result assume that the Old Latin of Judith, based on LXX, faded from use. I am told by Bazzana that the Old Latin continued in use throughout Europe.

14   Lange, *Die Juditfigur,* 383: "Das Buch Judith ist . . . mehr als eine einfache Übersetzung. Es ist Teil eines Kampfes für die christlich-asketischen Ideale."

15   On the differences between the Vg and LXX versions of Judith in general, see Dubarle, *Judith,* 1:48–74; Voigt, *Latin Versions,* 48–49. Arguing that the differences should be attributed to Jerome are Pierre-Maurice Bogaert, "Judith dans la première Bible d'Alcala (Complutensis 1) et dans la version hiéronymienne (Vulgate)," in Roger Gryson, ed., *Philologia sacra: Biblische und patristische Studien für Hermann J. Frede und Walter Thiele zu ihrem siebzigsten Geburtstag* (2 vols.; Aus der Geschichte der lateinischen Bibel 24; Freiburg: Herder, 1993) 1:116–30; Bogaert, *Judith,* Fascicule 1, 58, 64; Vincent T. M. Skemp, "Learning by Example: *Exempla* in Jerome's Translations and Revisions of Biblical Books," *VC* 65 (2011) 257–84, here 263; Ryan, "Ancient

Versions," 1–21; Lange, *Die Juditfigur,* 387; Edmond L. Gallagher, "Why Did Jerome Translate Tobit and Judith?," *HTR* 108 (2015) 356–75, here 361. Suggesting that Jewish traditions may have influenced Jerome are Robert Hayward, "Saint Jerome and the Aramaic Targumim," *JSS* 32 (1987) 105–23; Benjamin Kedar-Kopfstein, "Jewish Traditions in the Writings of Jerome," in D. G. R. Beattie and M. J. McNamara, eds., *The Aramaic Bible: Targums in Their Historical Context* (JSOTSup 166; Sheffield: JSOT Press, 1994) 420–30.

16   J. N. D. Kelly suggests that Jerome's divergences may reflect previous developments in Christian tradition (*Jerome: His Life, Writings, and Controversies* [London: Duckworth, 1975] 285).

17   David Parker, *The Living Text of the Gospels* (Cambridge: Cambridge University Press, 1997); Eldon Jay Epp, *Perspectives on New Testament Text Criticism: Collected Essays, 1962–2004* (NovTSup 116; Leiden: Brill, 2005). I have learned much on this topic from Epp and Jennifer Knust.

which would be interesting—or that of a Semitic Judith tradition, however old that may be.[18] It may not be possible to make a definitive judgment about which differences in Vg Judith can be attributed to source and which to redaction, but probabilities can be discussed.

Comparison of the Vulgate and the LXX

We may begin a comparison of the Vulgate and the LXX versions of Judith by examining the military campaigns at the beginning, where the differences are among the most striking. The LXX here is over twice as long as the Vulgate. The LXX famously begins with an impossible villain, "Nebuchadnezzer, king of the Assyrians" (Nebuchadnezzar was king of the Babylonians). This historical blunder was likely intentional as a way of signaling the carnivalesque tone of the text that follows; other Jewish novelistic texts of this period contain similar, evidently intentional blunders (see §2 above). Judith in the LXX contains more violations of historical decorum than the other Jewish novellas, but it will become clear that the Vulgate exhibits fewer; it is less parodic. True, a few verses later the Vulgate also includes "Nebuchadnezzar, king of the Assyrians," but it does not lead with this fictitious figure, and the sheer number of impossible elements is reduced. In LXX 2:21, for instance, it is said that Holofernes's mighty army marched from Nineveh to northern Cilicia, a distance of three hundred miles, in just three days. This geographical absurdity is often highlighted as evidence of the cavalier nature of the text, but the Vulgate lacks this reference. The Vulgate introduction is also neater. Rather than moving from Nebuchadnezzar to his first opponent, Arphaxad, back again to Nebuchadnezzar, then to the general Holofernes, the Vulgate begins with Arphaxad and proceeds in a clearer order—Arphaxad-Nebuchadnezzar-Holofernes. The awkwardness of the LXX introduction may have resulted from a desire to heighten the parody by placing "Nebu-

chadnezzar king the Assyrians" in the opening clause. Jerome may have decided to smooth over the beginning, but an Aramaic source may have opened with a neater introduction.

The historical pretension of the chronicles-style dating in the opening of the LXX ("In the twelfth year of the reign . . .) can also be contrasted with the Vulgate's opening, which does not mimic historical style. As a result, Nebuchadnezzar is more foregrounded in the LXX. He does not vanquish Arphaxad quickly as in the Vulgate, but the conflict is drawn out until 1:13–15 LXX, when Nebuchadnezzar finally runs Arphaxad through. Further, in the LXX the forced alliances with the formerly rebellious nations are emphasized more strongly. In LXX 2:5–13 Nebuchadnezzar's orders to Holofernes are much longer, practically a Thucydidean oration, while in the Vulgate they are very simple and in biblical style. Further, Nebuchadnezzar ends with a warning not to transgress any of the king's commandments—a Nebuchadnezzar/ God duality that is more typical of the LXX and is not found in the Vulgate. The general Holofernes's punitive expedition in the LXX also includes revenge on the whole territory of Cilicia, Damascus, Syria, Moab, Ammon, Judea, and Egypt—with the exception of Cilicia all "biblical lands." In the LXX, therefore, Judith is responsible for saving all the biblical lands, while the Vulgate describes the campaign as a more typical revenge motif (1:12).

The Vulgate is in general less marked by such novelistic techniques and is more similar to a typical oral, martial tradition. The LXX is wordier than the Vulgate, and at times this could be read as a novelistic expansion of the Vulgate's more typically oral style.[19] In each point, then, we must ask: would Jerome have likely introduced the changes in the Vulgate? Would he, for instance, have dropped literary flourishes to return the narrative to the style of an oral, martial romance? Perhaps so, especially if he did engage in a brief and very loose translation process.

---

18 At one point, it might have been assumed that a Hebrew or Aramaic text arose from a Jewish community, but Jerome was in contact with Jewish converts, and recent research on observant Christians would caution us to allow for a Christian Semitic text as well, perhaps in Syriac; see Joosten, "Original Language," 167–68.

19 Note the dialogue in LXX 7:13–15, and the longer

description in LXX 7:18–20. In Vg 3:1 some of the place-names from before are repeated, a common oral technique. Semitic parallelism is found in Vg 8:15, but in the LXX only in Judith's Song at the end of the book.

Some military motifs, to be sure, are treated in a similar way. The marshaling of Holofernes's army that follows is almost identical in the two versions (2:14–18 LXX, 2:7–10 Vg). The same situation obtains elsewhere: passages that are very different are found side by side with passages that are virtually identical. There is greater attention given in the LXX to the Assyrians' plot to take the springs of Bethulia and the effects of the lack of water (LXX 7:8–22). Still, the wording of the people's demand to negotiate terms of surrender is nearly the same (LXX 7:19–24; Vg 7:12–17). LXX 2:1–4 and 14–18 are virtually identical with their Vulgate equivalent, yet between these two parallel blocks, LXX 2:5–13 is much longer, filled out by Nebuchadnezzar's rant and his "Yah-wistic" pretensions. Here we must judge it unlikely that Jerome simply chose to drop Nebuchadnezzar's speech and the Nebuchadnezzar/God duality.

Style and Theme in the LXX and the Vulgate

The LXX of Judith is characterized by excess, irony, and the carnivalesque transgression of norms. The transgression and deviance are greater in LXX Judith than in the Vulgate. If the Vulgate version of Judith were read in isolation, without any knowledge of the LXX, would the style seem parodic or transgressive? The irony and double-meanings are found more often in the LXX, especially in regard to the double sense of "lord" as both Nebuchadnezzar and God: (The comparisons of the LXX and Vg of Judith that follow utilize a more literal English translation than that of the commentary in order to facilitate a closer comparison of the texts.)

LXX 11:5–6, 22	Vg 11:4
[5]"I will not speak falsely to *my lord* tonight. [6]And if you follow the advice of your servant, God will accomplish a great deed through you; *my lord* will not fail in his plan." [22]Holofernes said to her, . . . "Death will be the lot of those who ridicule *my lord*."	[4]"Take heed to the words of your handmaiden, for if you follow the words of your handmaiden, *the Lord* will do a perfect thing through you."

We are left to wonder whether Jerome would have eliminated the humor and irony in order to clarify that only God is "lord," although in his theological vision, this sort of change is possible. One of the most memorable cases of ironic excess in the LXX is Holofernes's unconscious prophecy to Achior in 6:5: "You shall not see my face again until I take my revenge!" The audience knows from the popular tradition that Achior *will* see Holofernes's face again when Judith delivers his head to Bethulia, but this humorous line is lacking in the Vulgate. Would Jerome have suppressed it? Perhaps, if we consider that the Vulgate at this point highlights instead the conversion of Achior as a representative gentile: "From this hour you shall be one of their people!"

A number of other comic elements are also more strongly exploited in the LXX. An outrageous comic moment occurs in the LXX when the community, in abject penance, places sackcloth on the cattle (4:10; compare Jonah 3:8, 10). This humorous moment is lacking in Vulgate. When Judith and her maid first approach the Assyrian camp, the description of the reaction and the infatuation of the troops are more emphasized in LXX 10:17–19: the sentries fall over themselves to escort Judith to Holofernes. Yet at one point the Vulgate contains more comic detail—when the Assyrians discover Holofernes's headless body. In this case, the retardation of the plot and the soldiers' bumbling reluctance to disturb Holofernes in his postcoital slumber render this scene more comical in the Vulgate. Would Jerome have eliminated humorous motifs in a number of passages and yet have added one in another? It might be argued that it is more likely that two separate traditions already differed in terms of their comic portrayals.

At one point in the narrative the Ammonite Achior delivers a précis of the history of the Israelites. It begins very similarly in the two versions, but the LXX strangely truncates the exodus miracle at the Red Sea, while the Vulgate, equally strangely, omits the destruction of the temple (LXX 5:13; Vg 5:22). Again in 9:7–8, the LXX merely alludes to the Red Sea miracle but the Vulgate explicitly compares the contemporary situation to the destruction of the Egyptian armies. Is it likely that Jerome added the exodus or deleted the destruction of the temple? Elsewhere the situation seems reversed. In the LXX, the women's celebration at the end evokes the Song of Miriam (Exodus 15, esp. 15:20), but this association is lacking in the Vulgate:

LXX 15:12–13	Vg 15:15
[12]All the Israelite women came running to see her; they blessed her, while some performed a dance for her. She took garlanded wands in her hands and distributed them to the women with her, [13]and they crowned themselves with the olive branches, she and those with her. Then she led a procession of all the people, the women in front, every man of Israel behind and fully armed, wearing garlands and a song of praise on their lips.	[15]And all the people rejoiced, including the women, young girls, and young men, playing on instruments and harps.

It would be surprising if Jerome increased the references to Exodus in some passages and decreased them in others, yet such a free translation is possible.

We turn now to an issue that goes beyond mere motifs. In the first half of the LXX version, transition points in the narrative are facilitated by a rest from the action, for example, 1:16 LXX: "Nebuchadnezzar and all the mixed peoples arrayed with him . . . then returned, and he and his army began a period of rest and celebration which lasted a hundred and twenty days." Such pauses, alternating with rousing military action, occur in the following regular pattern in the LXX, but not in the Vulgate:

action	action	action	action	dialogue	action
pause	pause	pause	pause	pause	pause
1:16	2:28	3:10	4:13–15	6:21	7:32

It would be surprising if Jerome eliminated these pauses in the process of translation.

Throughout, the LXX also provides fictitious local color by peppering the narrative with more references to cities, nations, and places that are often invented or wildly incorrect (1:10; 7:16–19). In the victory scene at the end as well, the LXX traces the path of the Israelite revenge on the fleeing Assyrians by including many place-names, now reversing the course of the Assyrians in chaps. 1 and 2. The names in both cases are much reduced in the Vulgate. The Vulgate is clearly not opposed to false names in principle—recall that it includes Nebuchadnezzar king of the Assyrians—but it provides fictitious local color less often. Indeed, this suggests an interesting challenge: without the LXX as reference, would the place-names in the Vulgate appear as humorous?

Edwin Voigt argues that the Vulgate contains more Semitisms,[20] and I add to his observation by noting the greater Semitic parallelism in the Vulgate version of Judith's first speech:

LXX 8:14–17	Vg 8:12–17

[14]My brothers, do not in any way provoke the Lord our God!	[12]This is not a prayer that will provoke mercy,
	    but rather will excite anger
	      and bring down wrath.
	[13]You have set a schedule for
	    the mercy of the Lord,
	    by your own reckoning have
	      appointed him a day.

[15]If he does not choose to aid us in these five days, he has the authority—in whatever number of days he wishes—to come to our defense, or to destroy us in the very presence of our enemies. [16]Do not attempt to extract a pledge on the designs of the Lord our God,	[14]But since the Lord is patient,
	    let us be penitent
	    concerning this as well,
	    and with tears beg his
	    pardon.

for God is not like a man,
    to be threatened,
    or like a son of man
      to be bargained with.
[17]Therefore, while waiting patiently for deliverance by his hand, let us call on him for aid.
	[15]For God does not threaten
	    thus
	    like a man,
	      nor is he inflamed to anger
	    like a son of man.
	[16]So, therefore, let us humble
	    our souls,
	    and serve him with a
	      continually humbled spirit.
	[17]Let us ask the Lord in tears that he show mercy to us according to his will, so that as our heart is disturbed by their pride, so also we may glory in our humility.

---

20   Voigt, *Latin Versions*, 48–49.

The Vulgate scans much more easily into parallel lines, but note also that Vg v. 17, which is not found in the LXX and which does not scan into parallel lines, contains a number of terms that are characteristic of Jerome: tears, mercy, pride, humility (more on this below). This might suggest that the parallelism does not derive from Jerome's editing, while v. 17 does.

Yet Lange discerns a number of differences in the Vulgate that can plausibly be attributed to Jerome's own interests, as indicated partly from comments found in his letters to widows, especially *Epistle* 54:

> I see her hand armed with the sword and stained with blood. I recognize the head of Holofernes which she has carried away. . . . Here a woman vanquishes men, and chastity beheads lust. (*Epistle* 54)[21]

In the Vulgate, Judith's beauty is described in two passages (chaps. 8 and 10). In the first she is *elegans,* and in the second God increases her beauty. (The LXX had attributed her beautification to her agency.) Distinctive pluses in the Vulgate include Judith's chastity,[22] her prayer discipline in a *cubiculum* with female slaves, her presentation as *humilitas*. Likewise, Holofernes is now marked by *libido, ebrietas,* luxury, excess, and arrogance. Judith and Holofernes are more clearly contrasted as virtue and vice, humility and arrogance.

The LXX version of Judith is dated by many scholars to about 125–75 BCE in the reconstruction after the Maccabean Revolt, and there are many references to the Hasmonean restoration in both the LXX and the Vulgate. Both versions read the Maccabean triumph back into the early postexilic setting of the story. It is a Hanukkah text and has retained some currency in Jewish tradition in that context. But in the LXX version we find more references to Hasmonean ideology:

> For they had only recently returned from the captivity, and all the people of Judea were newly gathered together, and the sacred vessels and the altar and the temple had been consecrated after their profanation. (4:3)

This line is lacking in the Vulgate. The motif of the reconstitution of the temple in the LXX is also accompanied by more references to temple offerings than in the Vulgate (LXX 4:14; 8:21, 24). In LXX 9:1, but not in the Vulgate, Judith times her prayers to coincide with the offering of the evening incense in Jerusalem. The Jewish dietary issues are also expressed differently in the two texts. In LXX 11:12–13 the Jews' supposed sin, which Judith invents to give her a pretext with Holofernes to betray her people, is that starvation will force the people to eat the parts of the offerings reserved for the altar, and also eat the priests' portions. In the Vulgate, the sin is that the people will drink the blood of the sacrificial animals and, in addition, consume the crops reserved for offerings. Here as well, the differences in the Vg might reasonably be attributed to Jerome's redaction. The drinking of blood is taken up also in Acts 15, as part of the nonnegotiable core of Jewish law and, despite its antiquity, may also be typical of a Christian interpretation of Jewish law. Likewise, it is conceivable that Jerome would minimize references to temple sacrifices. Another interesting difference between the two occurs in their conclusions. The LXX and the Vulgate are nearly identical in the "heroic coda" at the end, but the Vulgate follows the heroic coda with a "festival coda," lacking in LXX: "The day of the celebration of this victory is counted by the Hebrews in the number of holy days, and has been observed by the Jews from that time until the present day" (16:31). Jerome is perhaps asserting for our text a status in Jewish practice.

Character Traits of Judith

One stream of modern discourse analysis is relevant for our comparison. It addresses the narrative depiction of a character's agency: Is a character depicted with strong

---

21   Lange, *Die Juditfigur,* 357–87, esp. 365–66; see also Schmitz, "ΙΟΥΔΙΘ und Judith," 376–77.

22   In Vg 15:11 Judith has loved chastity, *castitas*. In 16:26 it is said that "chastity was joined to her virtue, so that she knew no man all the days of her life." The LXX merely says that "many desired to marry her, but she remained a widow all the days of her life." See Schmitz, "ΙΟΥΔΙΘ and Judith," 375–76.

or weak agency? Is a character active or passive? Does a character impose her or his will on others or is she or he rather affected by others? It is not just a question of who is the subject of active verbs, although it can include that, but rather, whose will lies at the beginning of a chain of actions? For whom are actions performed? (See §5 above.) Arphaxad, Nebuchadnezzar, and Holofernes are all depicted at first as having strong agency, although Arphaxad's strong agency is cut short by Nebuchad-nezzar, which in turn redounds to the latter's stronger agency. Even Israel has strong agency in this text as Holofernes's long list of questions (5:3–4 in both the LXX and the Vulgate) concerning Israel implies that it is somehow different. Holofernes here also becomes the strong agent working for Nebuchadnezzar, as Judith is the strong agent working for God. Yet we note that Judith is depicted with stronger agency in the LXX than in the Vulgate.

Judith's entire speech in LXX chap. 8, for example, communicates stronger agency. She intervenes more directly: "Listen to me!" (8:32). Compare also these two passages:

LXX 8:32	Vg 8:30–31
I am about to do something that will live in the memory of our people for many generations to come.	Indeed, then, if you recognize the words I say as God's words, judge for yourselves whether the deed I mean to do is of God's ordaining; and pray to him to bring my design to effect.

In the LXX, Judith is ultimately tougher and will press, with no concession to human nature, the sterner demand that she will place upon the people: "If we are captured, all Judea and our sanctuary will fall, and God will demand from us the reason for its destruction" (8:21). In the Vulgate, however, there is encouragement (8:20).[23] In the LXX she is wordier in regard to the elders' ill-conceived oath, and the words are sharper, while the Vulgate offers only these words regarding a communal petition: "While we wait for his deliverance, let us call upon him to help us, and he will hear our voice, if it pleases him" (8:17). Judith's longer prayer in

the LXX ultimately emphasizes a God of power more than a God of mercy who responds to tears. Judith's invocation of Simeon's revenge in LXX chap. 9 is also longer and more bellicose, and the declarations are sometimes rather clumsily piled on top of each other:

LXX 9:11–12	Vg 9:16–17
You are a God of the lowly, a helper of the poor, protector of the weak, guardian of those in despair, deliverer of those without hope.	From the beginning, the proud have been unacceptable to thee, but the prayer of the humble and the meek have always pleased thee.
Indeed, O God of my father and God of the inheritance of Israel, ruler of heaven and earth, creator of all the waters, king of your whole creation! Listen to my plea!	O God of the heavens, creator of the waters, and Lord of the whole creation, hear me, a poor wretch.

The beheading scene at first appears to be almost identical in the two versions, but if one compares closely the wording of Judith's prayer, a difference in agency emerges:

LXX 13:4–5	Vg 13:7
[4]O Lord, God of all power, look now upon the actions of my hands	[7]Give me strength, O Lord God of Israel, and at this moment look upon the works of my hands,
for the exaltation of Jerusalem. [5]Now is the time for the rescue of your inheritance and the accomplishment of my plan to destroy the enemies who have risen up against us.	so that as you have promised, you may raise up your city Jerusalem
	and that what I have conceived I may bring to pass,
	though I believe that it could only be done through you.

In the LXX, Judith presumes to exercise God's power of attorney; in the Vulgate, she attributes all to God. An angel is also inserted to protect her in Vg 13:20. Another passage in chap. 8 corroborates this view:

---

23   Vulgate 7:18–23 adds a penitential prayer for the Bethulians; this changes the nature of their charac-ter here, from a negative murmuring to a *peccator* status, with a discipline of penitence.

LXX 8:33	Vg 8:32
During that period after which you vowed to surrender the town to our enemies, the Lord will preserve Israel by my hand.	*Pray* that as you have said, in five days the Lord may look down upon his people Israel. . . . *Pray for me to the Lord.*

To be sure, in LXX 13:6 Judith does pray for greater strength, but we are not sure that she actually needs it. Another difference in detail remains quizzical. While the LXX—and the iconography of Judith paintings generally—depict her as utilizing Holofernes's *sword* to chop off his head (rather, a Persian *akinakēs*, a small sword), the Vulgate describes her as taking up the general's *dagger* (*pugio*, 13:8). This raises the question of plausibility: is it possible to chop off a man's head in two strokes using a dagger? Does this render Judith as more dainty? At any rate, some European paintings put a small sword or dagger in her hand, likely a result of the Vulgate reading.

Stronger agency in the LXX is also demonstrated by her transgression of norms. The "unbreakable" oath of the people, mentioned above, is effectively canceled by Judith, but in addition, the strong, charismatic woman strides across social boundaries; the mission and personal charisma justify the freedom from rules. In LXX 12:13, Judith is explicitly invited by Bagoas to become a courtesan, not just to dine with Holofernes, an extra insinuation not found in the Vulgate. She transgresses boundaries and taboos on her own in the LXX without the *explicit* mention of God's protection until 13:4–7, 16. Indirectly, her strong agency in the LXX is highlighted also by comparison to the weak agency of others. The LXX adds the excuse of the elders noted above, which underscores their weak agency: "the people were thirsty and made us swear an unbreakable oath" (8:30), lacking in the Vulgate. Achior as well is acted upon and buffeted more in the LXX and finally faints at the sight of Holofernes's head, which Judith and her maid have been spiriting about with abandon. (We will see below that Achior in general is stronger in the Vulgate.)

The way Judith is viewed by others also communicates strong agency in the LXX, for instance, as she departs from Bethulia for the Assyrian camp (words of strong agency in italics):

LXX 10:9–10	Vg 10:10
"Now *command* that the town gates be opened for me," she said to them, "and *I shall go forth* to *accomplish* all the things about which we spoke." *They ordered* the gatekeepers to open the gates *as she had said, and they did so.* Judith *went out,* together with her maid, and *the men of the town watched her closely* until she had descended the mountain and crossed the valley, and *they could no longer see her.*	Judith, praying to the Lord, *passed through* the gates, she and her maid.

There is a chain of obedience, which the LXX emphasizes: she orders them, and they order others. (The relationship of Judith and her slave is roughly the same in the two versions.) The last line of the LXX here has also appropriately been called cinematic in its utilization of point of view and visual effects, but one can also see that it focuses the audience's gaze quite literally on the presence and absence of Judith. Since the audience knows that the Assyrians will soon gaze lustfully at Judith, this perspective of the men of Bethulia is also voyeuristic—another social restraint crossed.

To be sure, some of the differences in the depiction of Judith's agency in the Vulgate may be attributed to Jerome's interests as seen in his other writings. Consider these passages, which at first seem very similar:

LXX 9:9–10	Vg 9:12–15
[9]Behold their arrogance! Bring your wrath down upon their heads and give into my hand—the hand of a widow!—the strength that my plan requires. [10]By the guile of my lips strike the slave with his ruler and the ruler with his slave! Crush their arrogance by a female hand!	[12]Bring to pass, O Lord, that his pride may be cut off with his own sword. [13]Let me be the cause for him to be caught by the snare of his own eyes, and strike him by the beauty of my lips. [14]Give resolve to my mind, so that I may despise him, and power, in order that I may overthrow him. [15]For this will be a memorial for your name when you cast him down by the hand of a woman!

Certain details in the Vulgate do not likely derive from a source. Not only was pride, *superbia,* found in the Vulgate, a common vice in Christian discourse, but the snare of his own eyes focuses on the sin of lust. This can be seen also in a Vg plus in 10:17: "Holofernes was the captive of his own eyes."[24] In these cases, the language of the Vulgate may be Jerome's, although we should not rule out the influence of an anonymous Christian predecessor. That Judith did not act in lust probably emanates from Jerome's hand:[25]

LXX 10:4	Vg 10:4
She was now fully adorned in order to lead astray the eyes of as many men as might see her.	The Lord gave her more beauty because all this dressing up did not proceed from lust, but from virtue, and therefore the Lord increased her beauty, so that she appeared to all men's eyes incomparably lovely.

As we note Judith's greater agency in the LXX, partly derived from the unmanning of Achior, we note in the Vulgate a stronger role for Achior. While the LXX (6:14–17) folds Achior's account of how he had been treated by Holofernes into the general alarm, the Vulgate version (6:10–13; 6:15–21) foregrounds Achior's report. Similarly, Achior's meeting with Judith near the end is longer in Vg 13:27–31 and is not in the same sequence as the LXX. Achior's conversion is also longer in the Vulgate. Judith's presence is increased in the LXX over the Vulgate; Achior's is increased in the Vulgate over the LXX. In the Renaissance and after, the role of one of the town elders, Uzziah, will also be dramatically increased, a male surrogate or symbolic husband to the dangerously independent Judith. In the Vulgate, Achior seems to be groomed for that role.

A Comparison with Tobit

Jerome translated Tobit just before he translated Judith; his preface reads:

Jerome to the Bishops in the Lord, Chromatius and Heliodorus, greetings. I do not cease to wonder at the urgency of your demand. For you demand that I translate into Latin a book written in the Aramaic language—to wit, the book of Tobit—which the Jews exclude from the collection of Divine Scriptures, since they pay careful attention to those texts which they have placed in the category of Apocrypha.[26] I have satisfied your desire, but not the requirements of my own study. For the studies of the Jews accuse us and find fault with us, when we translate for Latin ears these texts that are outside of their canon. But it is preferable to decide to cause displeasure to the decision of the Pharisees and to be devoted to the commands of bishops. I have persisted as I have been able, and because the Aramaic language is very similar to Hebrew, I found a speaker very skilled in both languages, and I took up the work for one day; whatever he expressed to me in Hebrew words, I dictated in Latin words to a note-taker I had summoned.

Cromatio et Heliodoro episcopis Hieronymus in Domino salutem. Mirari non desino exactionis vestrae instantiam. Exigitis enim, ut librum chaldeo sermone conscriptum ad latinum stilum traham, librum utique Tobiae, quem Hebraei de catalogo divinarum Scripturarum secantes, his quae Agiografa memorant manciparunt. Feci satis desiderio vestro, non tamen meo studio. Arguunt enim nos Hebraeorum studia et inputant nobis, contra suum canonem latinis auribus ista transferre. Sed melius esse iudicans Pharisaeorum displicere iudicio et episcoporum iussionibus deservire, institi ut potui, et quia vicina est Chaldeorum lingua sermoni hebraico, utriusque linguae peritissimum loquacem repperiens, unius diei laborem arripui et quicquid ille mihi hebraicis verbis expressit, haec ego accito notario, sermonibus latinis exposui.

---

24 Leslie Abend Callahan, "Ambiguity and Appropriation: The Story of Judith in Medieval Narrative and Iconographic Traditions," in Francesca Canadé Sautman, Diana Conchado, and Giuseppe di Scipio, eds., *Telling Tales: Medieval Narratives and the Folk Tradition* (New York: St. Martin's, 1998) 79–99, here 82.

25 Callahan, "Ambiguity and Appropriation," 82.

26 *Agiografa*. It is not likely that by the year 400 Jews would still consider the Ketuvim, or Writings, to be a secondary part of the canon that could also include texts like an Aramaic Tobit.

As noted above, Jerome's translation of Tobit involved the same issues as those regarding the translation of Judith: he rejected the LXX and Old Latin tradition in favor of an Aramaic text, and the resulting Vulgate translation is also shorter and quite different from the LXX and Old Latin, and different from the Qumran Tobit fragments as well. Vincent Skemp investigated the differences between the Vulgate and LXX of Tobit, but, like most text critics, concentrated more on the small differences where the text was roughly parallel, what we might call micro-differences, and did not devote as much attention to the larger, thematic differences where the texts diverged widely.[27] It may be possible, however, through a comparison with Jerome's translation of Tobit, to discover tendencies that might illuminate the situation of Judith. If a difference found in the Vulgate of Judith is also found in the Vulgate of Tobit, then the difference would be somewhat more likely to have arisen from Jerome's editing. Conversely, if a tendency found in the Vulgate of Judith is not found in the Vulgate of Tobit, then the tendency would be somewhat less likely to have arisen from Jerome's editing and more likely to have derived from a source. Such observations are not definitive, however, since Jerome might have proceeded differently in the two cases, even though he translated the two texts at about the same time.

The Vulgate version of Tobit, also said by Jerome—probably by hyperbole—to have been translated in one day from an Aramaic original, does not differ from the LXX/Old Latin as much as Judith does. Still, the differences are far greater than for most biblical books, and are significant. A number of scholars, in fact, have concluded that the Vulgate of Tobit is based on an Ara-maic source quite different from LXX/Old Latin.[28] We note, for example, the following items in regard to the versions of Tobit:

- The Vulgate has a clearer narrative logic.[29]
- The figure of Ahikar is almost totally lacking in the Vulgate (see only 11:20).
- There is less dialogue in the Vulgate.[30] (Ironically, dialogue is indicative not of oral narrative but of written novelistic tradition; oral stories rely much more heavily on narration and monologue.) Apparently, Jerome summarized and shortened dialogue with phrases such as "by these and other such words."
- Vg Tobit omits some details of narrative interest.
- Elements of a heroic narrative are increased in the Vulgate. It lists Tobit's boyhood virtue (1:4, 8); the plaints and negativity of Tobit are reduced (5:13); the ending heroic coda, where Tobit is "registered" as a hero, is stronger (14:17).
- The LXX emphasized the *horizontal* extension of family—the extended family relations of Tobit across borders, likely a Jewish diaspora issue or even a Tobiad family theme—while the Vg emphasizes *vertical* family—the progeny of Tobit (Vg 6:13–14; 9:11–12; 10:11; 14:15–17).[31]
- There is a greater emphasis on the rejection of lust in the Vulgate (3:16–18; 6:16–22), and on body/soul dualism (4:3), likely ascetic themes.[32]
- The Vulgate increases fasting, prayer, and tears.[33]
- The Jerusalem hymn at the end is fuller in LXX Tobit, while eschatological fulfillment is much more positive in the Vulgate (Vg 14:6–8).

27 Skemp, *Vulgate of Tobit*. Although he discussed the distinction between Jerome's source for Tobit and his editing, he did not clearly delineate his own criteria for distinguishing them.

28 Skemp rehearses the question and allows that some differences must originate in the source (*Vulgate of Tobit*, 465–66); see also Romualdo Galdos, *Commentarius in librum Tobit* (Paris: Lethielleux, 1930) 39–40 (I have not seen this source).

29 Gamberoni, *Die Auslegung des Buches Tobias*, 85 n. 313. The Vulgate, for instance, does not change from first-person to third-person narration as the LXX does.

30 Vg 5:10; 6:10–11; 7:1; 10:7; 12:4–6; see Skemp, *Vulgate of Tobit*, 458.

31 Skemp, *Vulgate of Tobit*, 460. Granted, LXX 1:1 plots Tobit's genealogy back to one of the twelve tribes, Naphtali, seemingly a "vertical" issue, but this defines his *extended* family. The Vulgate minimizes this and refers often to Tobit's progeny.

32 Vg 3:16–17; 6:17–20, but note LXX 8:7. See also Gamberoni, *Die Auslegung des Buches Tobias*, 86.

33 Skemp, *Vulgate of Tobit*, 463: likely a Hieronymian emphasis.

- Vg 1:6, 7; 5:19 exhibit less interest in the temple cult in Jerusalem.

The following similar elements in Tobit and Judith are somewhat more likely to result from Jerome's editing:

- The Vulgate of Tobit and Judith both improve the narrative order.
- The Vulgate of Tobit and Judith both have fewer examples of narrative interest and color.
- The Vulgate of Tobit and Judith both highlight ascetic engagement and lust as a vice.
- The Vulgate of Tobit and Judith both exhibit an emphasis on fasting, prayer, and tears.
- The Vulgate of Tobit and Judith both reduce the references to temple cult.

The treatment of Achior in Judith and Ahikar in Tobit, however, raises an interesting question. The Assyrian courtier Ahikar, famous from the popular international novella Story of Ahikar, provides the background for both. In Judith, his name is changed slightly and he is an Ammonite general who converts to Judaism. In Tobit, as in the legendary tradition, he is a counselor to the Assyrian kings, though now an Israelite. The Vulgate translations of Judith and Tobit modify the Ahikar character in opposite directions. The Vulgate of Judith increases the role of Achior while the Vulgate of Tobit eliminates the figure of Ahikar almost entirely. By our criteria, this would indicate that neither interpretation of Achior/Ahikar results from Jerome's editing. Still, it is conceivable that, in the case of the Book of Judith, Jerome wanted to affirm the importance of the gentile who converts, while in Tobit he chose to minimize any confusion with the famous pagan courtier Ahikar. This explanation assumes, however, that Jerome did not accept Tobit's characterization of Ahikar as an Israelite. It is possible that, regarding Achior/Ahikar, the divergences from the LXX in one or both of the texts derive from the Aramaic sources.

Conclusion

Regarding both Judith and Tobit, the differences between the Vulgate and the LXX are many and intriguing, both stylistically and theologically. But in neither case can the differences be clearly ascribed to either source or redaction. We either have before us insights into Jerome's bold new turn in the interpretation of Judith and Tobit, or a window into an independent, eastern Semitic narrative tradition. However, after choosing Aramaic texts and imposing his own text-critical criteria, it is unlikely that Jerome would have thoroughly recast the stories. The sheer number and extent of the differences in Vulgate Judith are such that it is unlikely that Jerome is responsible for all or even most of them. We note that the differences in Judith, and even in Tobit, are far greater than for those translations that are sometimes mentioned as more "paraphrastic." Each alteration would involve an editorial decision, and in some cases a rearrangement of the order of the text. In addition, Jerome would not likely have omitted the literary structure of alternating action and rest found in the first half. A number of Danielic echoes, as well as some of the comic elements, are also found *at different places* in the two versions.[34] Would Jerome have omitted certain motifs in one passage, only to add similar motifs in another? Though some of the differences reflect his interests known from elsewhere, many likely reflect the discrepancies in the textual tradition. The difference in the two Judiths highlighted by this comparison is quite remarkable, and certain aspects of the difference may be attributed with some likelihood either to Jerome or to his source, but other differences cannot be so easily adjudicated at this time. The discussion of differences should continue, even as the uncertainty of the situation is recognized.

---

34   For some of the Danielic motifs, see LXX 1:11; 2:5–13; 3:8; Vg 5:29; on the comic elements, see above. From the synopsis one can note that a number of other details are found in slightly different positions.

Synopsis of LXX and Vulgate Judith

The following English synopsis of Judith in the LXX and Vulgate versions utilizes a more literal English translation than that of the commentary in order to facilitate a closer comparison with my somewhat literal translation of the Vulgate, based on Robert Weber, ed., *Biblia sacra: Iuxta Vulgatam versionem* (5th ed.; Stuttgart: Württembergische Bibelanstalt, 2007).

LXX	Vulgate

Chapter 1 LXX

[1]It was the twelfth year of the reign of Nebuchadnezzar, who ruled the Assyrians from Nineveh, the great city. In those days Arphaxad, who ruled over the Medes from Ecbatana, [2]erected walls around Ecbatana, made of hewn stones three cubits thick and six cubits long, and made the height of the walls seventy cubits and its width fifty cubits. [3]At its gates he erected towers one hundred cubits high and laid their foundation sixty cubits wide. [4]He raised its gates seventy cubits high and forty cubits wide so that the officers of his army could march forth in battle with his infantry in full formation.

Chapter 1 Vulgate

[1]Now Arphaxad king of the Medes had brought many peoples under his rule, and built a very strong city which he called Ecbatana. [2]He made its walls of squared and cut stones, and constructed its walls seventy cubits high and thirty cubits thick;

he also erected towers one hundred cubits high. [3]The width of each of the towers measured twenty feet on each side, and he placed gates at them as tall as the towers.

[4]And he exalted himself as a mighty one in the power of his army and in the renown of his chariots.

[5]And in those days King Nebuchadnezzar made war against King Arphaxad

in the great plain, that is, the plain along the border of Ragau. [6]All of those who resided in the high country allied with Nebuchadnezzar, as did all of those who resided along the Euphrates, the Tigris, and the Hydaspes, and in the plain, Arioch, king of the Elamites; a great many peoples of the Cheleoudites also arrayed their forces with him.

[5]And in the twelfth year of his reign, Nebuchadnezzar king of the Assyrians, who reigned in Nineveh the great city, fought against Arphaxad and overcame him [6]in the great plain which is called Ragau

in the area of the Euphrates, the Tigris, and the Hyadas, in the plain of Erioch king of the Elicians.

[7]King Nebuchadnezzar of the Assyrians summoned all those who resided in Persia and to all those residing to the west—those residing in Cilicia, Damascus, Lebanon, and Antilebanon, all

[7]The kingdom of Nebuchadnezzar was then exalted and his heart was elevated. And he sent to all who lived in

Cilicia, Damascus, and Lebanon, [8]and to

those living along the coast, [8]the peoples of Carmel and Gilead, Upper Galilee, and the great plain of Esdraelon, [9]all the residents of Samaria and its cities, the region beyond the Jordan River, as far as Jerusalem, Bethany, Chelous, Kadesh, the river of Egypt, Tahpanhes, Raamses, and the whole land of Goshen [10]till one comes to the north of Tanis and Memphis, and all those who resided in Egypt as far as the region of Ethiopia.

[11]But all who resided in the whole land showed contempt for the decree of Nebuchadnezzar, king of the Assyrians, and did not ally with him in his campaign; for they were not afraid of him, but to them he was only one man. They sent his messengers away empty-handed and dishonored.

[12]Then Nebuchadnezzar became enraged with this entire land and swore by his throne and his kingdom that he would take vengeance on the whole territory of Cilicia, Damascus, and Syria and destroy them with his sword, as well as those residing in Moab, the Ammonites, all of Judea, and all of those in Egypt until one comes to the coasts of the two seas.

[13]In the seventeenth year, he arrayed his armies against King Arphaxad and was victorious in the battle. He routed Arphaxad's entire army, all his cavalry and all his chariots. [14]He conquered his cities, advancing as far as Ecbatana, and seized the towers and plundered the city's markets, bringing its former glory into disgrace. [15]And he overtook Arphaxad in the mountains of Ragau, and ran him through with his spears, and destroyed him on that day. [16]He and all the mixed peoples arrayed with him—a mighty host of warriors!—then returned, and he and his army began a period of rest and celebration which lasted a hundred and twenty days.

Chapter 2 LXX

[1]And in the eighteenth year, on the twenty-second day of the first month, the decree was announced in the palace of Nebuchadnezzar, king of the Assyrians, to exact revenge on the entire region, just as he had said.

[2]Summoning all his ministers and nobles, he placed before them his secret plan.

all the peoples who are in Carmel, Kedar, and to the inhabitants of Galilee in the great plain of Esdraelon, [9]and to all who were in Samaria, and beyond the Jordan River all the way to Jerusalem,

and all the land of Jesse until one reaches the mountains of Ethiopia.

[10]To all of these Nebuchadnezzar king of the Assyrians sent messengers, [11]who all with one mind refused him

and sent them back empty-handed; they dismissed them and shamed them.

[12]Then Nebuchadnezzar the king was angry at the entire land, and swore by his kingdom and his throne that he would avenge himself against all those regions.

Chapter 2 Vulgate

[1]In Nebuchadnezzar the king's thirteenth year, on the twenty-second day of the first month, it was announced in the house of Nebuchadnezzar king of the Assyrians that he would avenge himself.

[2]He called for all the nobles and all his generals and placed before them the secret elements of his plan.

From his own lips he recounted every evil of the land.
³And they decided to destroy everyone who had not obeyed the decree of his mouth.
⁴And when he had thus concluded his council, Nebuchadnezzar, king of the Assyrians, called in Holofernes, the commander-in-chief of his army and his second in command, and said to him,
⁵"Thus says the Great King, lord of all the earth: Go out now from my presence,

[See LXX 2:6 below.]

[See LXX 2:11 below.]

and taking an army of tested and seasoned troops, consisting of one hundred and twenty thousand infantry and twelve thousand cavalry,
⁶proceed against the entire country to the west, since they have disobeyed the decree of my mouth.
⁷Proclaim to them that they are to prepare an offering of earth and water, for I am about to descend upon them in my anger, I will cover the entire face of the earth with the feet of my army, and I will hand these people over to my soldiers as plunder. ⁸Their wounded shall fill the gullies and wadis. Every river shall swell to overflowing, choked with their corpses. ⁹I will lead them in captivity to every corner of the earth. ¹⁰But you shall go out before me to seize every territory for me in advance. They will surrender themselves to you, and you shall hold them for me to await the day of their punishment. ¹¹But as for those who resist, your eye shall show them no restraint, but give them over to slaughter and pillage throughout the land. ¹²For as I live, by the power of my rule, what I have promised I will do with my own hand. ¹³As for you, you shall not transgress any of your lord's commands, but execute these orders as I have commanded you without delay."
¹⁴Taking leave of his lord, Holofernes summoned all the commanders, generals, and officers of the armies of Assur, ¹⁵and mustered his army of chosen troops in battle formation as his lord had commanded, 120,000 infantry and twelve thousand

³He said that his plan consisted in this: that he would bring the entire earth under his rule.
⁴When this word had pleased them all, Nebuchadnezzar the king called for Holofernes, his commander-general,
⁵and said to him,

"Go out against all the kingdoms of the west, and especially against those which showed contempt for my rule. ⁶My eye will not spare any kingdom, and you will bring every fortified city under my rule." ⁷Then Holofernes called the generals and commanders of the Assyrian army and mustered men for the expedition as the king had commanded him, one hundred and twenty thousand infantry and twelve thousand mounted archers.

[See Vg 1:5.]

[See Vg 2:6 above.]

mounted archers. [16]He arrayed them as a great army is arrayed for a campaign.

[17]He commandeered in addition a vast multitude of camels, asses, and mules to carry supplies; sheep, oxen, and goats for their provisions, of which there was no number; a plentiful supply of food for each man;

and from the king's palace a very large amount of gold and silver.

[19]He set out with his whole army to march out ahead of King Nebuchadnezzar and toward the western regions, covering the entire face of the earth with his chariots, cavalry, and chosen infantry.

[20]Accompanying them also was a motley throng of people, a multitude too large to number, like locusts or the dust of the earth.

[21]They marched from Nineveh three days to the edge of the plain of Bectileth, making camp a slight distance from Bectileth at the mountain north of Upper Cilicia.

[22]Holofernes then set out with his entire army of infantry, cavalry, and chariots, and proceeded into the high country.

[23]He totally destroyed Put and Lud, plundered all of the people of Rassis and the Ishmaelites on the border of the desert, south of the land of the Cheleans.

[24]Following the Euphrates, he proceeded through Mesopotamia, laying waste all the fortified towns along the Wadi Abron until one comes to the sea,

[25]and captured the regions of Cilicia, cutting down all those who resisted him. Next he came to the southern border of Japheth, facing Arabia,

[26]and surrounded all the Midianites, burned their tents, and plundered their sheep.

[27]He descended into the plain of Damascus during the wheat harvest and burned all their crops, and slaughtered their flocks and herds, destroyed their cities, stripped their fields, and struck down their young men with the edge of the sword.

[See LXX 2:27 above.]

[8]He commanded that an entire train go before him, with an innumerable multitude of camels, along with the livestock to supply his armies bounteously, herds of oxen and flocks of sheep too numerous to count. [9]He arranged for a supply of wheat from all Syria for his passage.

[10]He also requisitioned a vast amount of gold and silver from the royal treasury.

[11]He himself then set out with all his armies,

with the chariots, cavalry, and archers,

who covered the face of the earth like locusts.

[12]When he had passed through the borders of the Assyrians he came to the great mountains of Ange which are to the north of Cilicia, and went up to all their fortresses and took all their garrisons.

[13]Then he stormed the famed city of Meluthos and pillaged all the people of Tharsis, and the Ishmaelites who lived at the edge of the desert and on the south of the land of Celeon.

[14]He crossed the Euphrates and came to Mesopotamia and stormed all the mighty cities which were there, from the falls of Mambre till one comes to the sea.

[15]He occupied all these borders, from Cilicia to the frontiers of Japhet on the south.

[16]He deported all the Midianites and plundered all their wealth;

[See Vg 2:17 below.]

all who resisted he slew with the edge of the sword.

[17]After these things he went down into the plains of Damascus in the days of the harvest and set fire

²⁸Fear and dread of him fell upon all those who lived along the coast at Tyre and Sidon, and on those residing in Sur, Ocina, those residing in Jamnia, and those residing in Azotus and Ashkelon became deathly afraid of him.

Chapter 3 LXX

¹They sent envoys to him suing for peace, saying, ²"Now we, servants of Nebuchadnezzar the great king, lie prostrate before you to do with as you please.

³Indeed, all our buildings, our land, every wheat field, our flocks and herds, all the sheepfolds of our encampments are yours to dispose as you wish. ⁴Indeed, our cities and their inhabitants are your slaves; come and deal with them as seems good in your eyes."

⁵The envoys came to Holofernes and proclaimed these words to him,
⁶whereupon he and his army came down to the coast and garrisoned all of the fortified cities,

taking from them the chosen men as allies.
⁷They and the entire surrounding areas

welcomed him with garlands, dancing, and tambourines.

⁸He demolished all their shrines and cut down their sacred groves, for he had been commissioned to destroy all of the gods of the land, so that every people should worship Nebuchadnezzar alone, and every tongue and every tribe should invoke him as god.

to all the crops, and ordered that all the trees and vineyards be cut down.
¹⁸Fear of them fell upon all the inhabitants of the land.

Chapter 3 Vulgate

¹Then the kings and princes of all the cities and provinces of Syria, Mesopotamia, Syria Sobal, Libya, and Cilicia sent their ambassadors, who came to Holofernes and said, ²"May your anger against us cease! It is indeed better for us to live and serve Nebuchadnezzar the great king, and be your subject, than to die from slaughter or suffer the punishments of our bondage.
³All our cities and property, all our hills and mountains and fields, all our herds of oxen, flocks of sheep and goats, horses and camels—all that we have and our families—are now under your control. ⁴Let these all be subject to your law; ⁵we and our children are your slaves. ⁶Come to us as a peaceable lord, and use our servitude as it pleases you."

⁷Then he came down from the mountains with cavalry and a great army and took control of every city and all the inhabitants of the land.
⁸From every city he conscripted as allied troops brave warriors chosen for war, ⁹and so great a fear lay upon those provinces that the inhabitants of all those cities—the princes and nobles as well as the people—went out to meet him,
¹⁰welcoming him with garlands and processions by torchlight, leading dances with flutes and timbrels.
¹¹And yet, though they did all these things, they could not mitigate the ferocity within his breast.
¹²Indeed, he both destroyed their cities and cut down their sacred groves, ¹³for Nebuchadnezzar the king had commanded him to destroy all the gods of the land so that he alone might be called god by those nations which could be subjugated by the power of Holofernes.
¹⁴And after passing through Syria Sobal and all

[9]He then advanced toward Esdraelon, near Dothan, which faces the great ridge of Judea, and pitched camp between Geba and Scythopolis. There the Assyrians remained for one month in order to gather together all of the supplies for his army.

Chapter 4 LXX

[1]When the Israelites living in Judea heard what Holofernes, the commander-in-chief of Nebuchadnezzar, king of the Assyrians, had done to all the peoples, and how he had plundered all their temples and given them over to destruction, they were terrified before his advance,

[2]and were disturbed both for the fate of Jerusalem and for the temple of the Lord their God.

[3]Indeed, they themselves had just returned from captivity; only recently had the entire people of Judea been gathered together again. Their sacred vessels, altar, and temple had just been reconsecrated after the profanation.
[4]So they sent into every region of Samaria, Kona, Beth-horon, Belmain, Jericho; into Choba, Aesora, and the valley of Salem
[5]and occupied all the mountaintops, erecting fortifications around the villages on them. They stored away the crops as a preparation for war, because their fields had just been harvested.
[6]Joakim, the high priest, who was in those days in Jerusalem, wrote to the residents of Bethulia and Betomesthaim, which lie opposite of Esdraelon toward the plain near Dothan, [7]and told them to take control of the mountain passes, because access to Judea was possible through them, and it would be easy to prevent the Assyrians from passing through, since there was room for no more than two men to pass at a time.
[8]The Israelites did as Joakim the high priest and the Council of the Israelites who resided in Jerusalem had commanded.
[9]Every man of Israel then very fervently called upon God, and they all very fervently humbled their souls.
[10]Then they, their wives, their infants, their cattle,

Apamea and Mesopotamia, he came to the Idumeans in the land of Geba. [15]He took possession of their cities and remained there for thirty days, during which he commanded that all of his military force be united into one body.

Chapter 4 Vulgate

[1]When the Israelites who inhabited the land of Judah heard these things,

they became exceedingly afraid before his advance. [2]Dread and horror seized their minds, out of fear that he would do to Jerusalem and to the temple of the Lord what he had done to other cities and their temples.

[3]And so they sent word around all Samaria as far as Jericho,

and occupied all the mountaintops.
[4]They encircled their towns with walls and gathered their crops in preparation for war.

[5]Eliachim the priest also wrote to all those who resided opposite Esdraelon, facing the great plain near Dothan, and to all those who lived where passage through the land was possible [6]that they should occupy the mountain passes through which access to Jerusalem was possible and to guard the narrow passages by which it was possible to pass through the mountains.

[7]The Israelites did as Eliachim, the priest of the Lord, had commanded them.

[8]All the people cried out urgently to the Lord, and both they and their wives humbled their souls with fasts.
[9]The priests put on sackcloth

407

and every alien, hired worker, and slave put sack-cloth around their waists.

¹¹Every man, woman, and child of Israel residing in Jerusalem prostrated themselves before the temple and placed ashes on their heads and draped their sackcloth before the Lord.

¹²They even draped the altar with sackcloth, as they all cried out fervently to the Lord with one voice not to give their babies over to capture nor their wives as plunder, nor to allow their ancestral cities to be destroyed and the sanctuary profaned, to become a laughing-stock for the gentiles.

¹³When the Lord heard their voice, he took note of their affliction, as the people continued fasting for many days over all of Judea, and also in Jerusalem before the temple of the Lord Almighty.

¹⁴Joakim the high priest and all the priests who stood before the Lord and served him with sack-cloth around their waists offered the continual burnt offerings, votive offerings, and the freewill offerings of the people. ¹⁵They placed ashes on their headdresses and cried out to the Lord with all their might to look kindly on the whole house of Israel.

Chapter 5 LXX

¹And so it was reported to Holofernes, com-mander-in-chief of the Assyrian army, that the Isra-elites had been preparing for war by closing the mountain passes and fortifying the top of every mountain, and also by laying traps in the plains. ²Enraged, Holofernes summoned all of the leaders of Moab, the Ammonite commanders, and the governors from along the coast, ³and said to them, "Tell me, you Canaanites, who is this people situ-ated in the high country, and in what cities do they

and the children
lay prostrate before the
temple of the Lord,

and they covered the altar of the Lord with sack-cloth. ¹⁰They cried out with one voice to the God of Israel that their children might not be given over to plunder, that their wives not be taken as spoil, that their cities not be destroyed, that their holy places not be profaned.

¹¹Then Eliachim the high priest of the Lord went about all Israel exhorting them, ¹²saying, "Know that the Lord has heard your prayers, if you continue steadfastly in fasting and prayers

in the presence of the Lord.
¹³Remember that Moses the servant of the Lord defeated Amalek—who trusted in his strength and in his power and in his army and in his shields and in his chariots and in his cavalry—not by fighting with the sword but by praying holy prayers. ¹⁴So will it be for all the enemies of Israel if you perse-vere in this work that you have begun."
¹⁵Thus as a result of his exhortation, they prayed to the Lord and continued in the presence of the Lord, ¹⁶so that even they who offered the whole burnt offerings to the Lord offered them to the Lord dressed in sackcloth and there were ashes upon their heads. ¹⁷And they all prayed to God with all their heart that he would come to his people Israel.

Chapter 5 Vulgate

¹And it was told to Holofernes, general of the army of the Assyrians, that the Israelites were preparing themselves to resist and had closed the mountain passes.

²He was inflamed with a violent rage and great indignation, and called all the chiefs of Moab and the generals of Ammon ³and said to them, "Tell me, who is this people who have occupied the mountains? What are their cities, of what sort, and

dwell? How big is their army? What is the source of their power, and what king has arisen to lead their armies? [4]And why is it that they alone of all those residing in the west have not seen fit to come out to greet me?" [5]Then Achior, leader of all the Ammonites, answered him, "Let my lord hear the account from the mouth of his slave, and I shall tell you the truth concerning this people who resides in the high country near where you reside; no lie will issue from the mouth of your slave.
[6]This people are descendants of the Chaldeans, [7]and migrated first to Mesopotamia because they resolved not to follow the gods of their ancestors who came from the land of the Chaldeans. [8]Departing from the ways of their forebears,

they began to worship the God of heaven, a god whom they had come to know. They drove them out from before their gods and they fled into Mesopotamia, where they sojourned for a long time.
[9]Their god commanded them to leave the land of their sojourn and proceed to Canaan. There they dwelt and acquired great wealth in gold, silver, and livestock.
[10]When a famine covered the land of Canaan, they went down into Egypt where there was food and sojourned there. There they multiplied until they became a great people, beyond number.
[11]The king of Egypt, however, turned on them and forced them into hard labor, where they worked as slaves to make bricks. [12]They called upon their god, who struck the entire land of Egypt with plagues from which there was no cure.
The Egyptians then expelled them from their midst,

[13]but God dried up the Red Sea before them,

[14]and led them on to Sinai and Kadesh-barnea.

how great? And what is their power? How many are they? Who is the king over their army? [4]And why have they, above all who inhabit the east, despised us and have not come out to greet us so that they might receive us in peace?" [5]Then Achior, general of all the Ammonites, answered, "If you will hear me out, my lord, I will speak the truth in your presence concerning this people who inhabit the mountains, and a false word will not come out of my mouth.
[6]This people is descended from the Chaldeans, [7]and lived first in Mesopotamia because they did not want to follow the gods of their fathers who were in the land of the Chaldeans. [8]Forsaking, therefore, the observances of their fathers, which consisted in the worship of many gods, [9]they worshiped one God of heaven,

who also commanded them to depart from there and to dwell in Haran.

When a famine had covered the entire land, they went down into Egypt, and there for four hundred years became so numerous that the army of them could not be numbered.
[10]When the king of Egypt oppressed them and made slaves of them to make mud and bricks for the building of his cities, they cried out to their God, and he struck the entire land of Egypt with various plagues.
[11]When the Egyptians had cast them out from them and the plagues had ceased from them, they once again determined to capture them and return them to slavery. [12]The God of heaven opened up the sea as they fled, so that the waters stood firm as a wall on either side, and they passed along the bottom of the sea walking with dry feet. [13]And in the same place, when an innumerable army of Egyptians pursued them, it was overwhelmed by the waters, so that there was not a single man left who could recount to posterity what had happened. [14]Once they came out of the Red Sea, they came to the desert region of Mount Sinai, where

They in turn cast out all those who lived in the desert and, [15]in a show of strength, utterly destroyed all the Heshbonites, and inhabited the land of the Amorites. Crossing over the Jordan River, they took possession of the high country, [16]and drove out before them as they went the Canaanites, the Perizzites, the Jebusites, the Shechemites, and all the Girgashites. They dwelt in that land for many years.

[17]And as long as they did not sin before their god, things went well for them, because the god who hates iniquity was with them.

[18]But when they strayed from the path that had been set for them, they were destroyed by many wars for a long time, and exiled into a land not their own. The temple of their god was also leveled to the ground, and their cities were captured by their enemies.

no man could dwell, nor son of man find rest. [15]But there the brackish springs produced sweet water for their drinking, and for forty years they received provision from heaven.

[16]Wherever they entered the land without bow and arrow, without shield and sword, their God fought for them and conquered.

[See Vg 5:20–21 below.]

[17]There was no one who could belittle this people, except when they departed from the worship of the Lord their God. [18]But as often as they worshiped another god beside their own God, they were given over to capture and to the sword and to shame. [19]But as often as they repented for departing from the worship of their God, the God of heaven gave them the power to resist. [20]As a result, they overthrew the king of the Canaanites, and of the Jebusites, and of the Perizzites, and of the Hittites, and of the Hivites, and of the Amorites, and all the leaders of Heshbon, and they possessed their lands and cities. [21]As long as they did not sin in the sight of God, it went well for them, for their God hates iniquity. [22]And it indeed happened some years ago, when they had departed from the path in which God had given them to walk that they were destroyed in battles with many nations and many of them were led away as captives to a land not their own.

[19]But now turning to their god, they have returned from the dispersion where they had been taken, and have occupied Jerusalem, where their holy place is located, and settled in the high county, because it was uninhabited.

[20]So now, my lord and master,
if this people have committed any misdeed out of ignorance or sinned against their god, and we discover that they are guilty of such an offense,

[23]But recently, returning to their God from the widespread areas where they were dispersed, they are united and have gone up into all these mountains, and have once again occupied Jerusalem, where their sacred precincts are.

[24]Therefore, my lord, now inquire whether there is any iniquity of theirs in the presence of their God.

410

we should set forth and wage war against them.

²¹But if there is no sin in this people, let my lord pass them by, lest their lord and god protect them with his shield, and we become a laughingstock over the entire land."

²²When Achior finished saying these things, all of the people standing around the tent began to object. Holofernes's officers and all of the inhabitants of the seacoast and Moab called for Achior to be cut to pieces.

²³"We have no fear of the Israelites!" they said. "Indeed, they are a people with no power or military strength.

²⁴Let us then proceed, lord Holofernes, and they will become fodder for your whole army!"

Chapter 6 LXX

¹When the disturbance of those gathered in the council had subsided, Holofernes, commander-in-chief of the Assyrian army, said to Achior in the presence of the whole council of foreigners and all the Moabites:

²"Who are you, Achior, and the mercenaries of Ephraim, to prophesy among us as you have today, and tell us not to make war against the people of Israel because their god will shield them? For who is god except Nebuchadnezzar? He will send his army to wipe them off the face of the earth, and their god will not save them. ³But we, his slaves, will strike them down as though they were one man, for they will not resist the power of our cavalry. ⁴We will pile them on top of each other; their mountains will become drunk with their blood, and their fields will be filled with their dead. Not even their footprints will remain in the wake of our attack, but they will be totally

Let us go up against them, for their God will surely deliver them over to you, and they will be subjugated to the yoke of your power.

²⁵But if there is no offense of this people before their God, we cannot resist them, for their God will defend them and we will be an object of shame to the whole earth."

²⁶But it happened that when Achior had finished speaking these words, all the leaders of Holofernes were angry and wanted to kill him,

saying to each other, ²⁷"Who is this who says that the Israelites are able to resist King Nebuchadnezzar and his armies even though they are without weapons, without military might, and without training in the art of war?

²⁸So that Achior may know that he is a liar, let us go up into the mountains, and when their leaders are captured, then shall he be run through with a sword along with them, ²⁹so that every people may know that Nebuchadnezzar is god of the earth, and beside him there is no other."

Chapter 6 Vulgate

¹And it happened when they finished speaking that Holofernes, exceedingly angry, said to Achior,

²"Because you have prophesied to us, saying that the people of Israel are defended by your God, in order to show you that

there is no god but Nebuchadnezzar,

³when we slay them all as one man, then you as well shall perish by the sword of these Assyrians, and all Israel shall perish with you.

destroyed. Thus says King Nebuchadnezzar, lord of the entire world. For he has spoken, and not a word of his pronouncements will be in vain.

[See LXX 6:6 below.]

⁵As for you, Achior, you Ammonite mercenary, uttering these words in a moment of treachery,
[See LXX 6:9 below.]

you shall not see my face again from this day forth until I take my vengeance on this people who came out of Egypt. ⁶And upon my return, the sword of my army and the spear of my servants shall run you through, and you shall fall among their dead.

⁷My slaves will now take you into custody and deliver you to the high country, and place you in one of the towns in the high passes, ⁸and you will not perish until you are wiped out along with them. ⁹And if you believe in your heart that they will not be taken, you will not become despondent. But I have spoken, and not one of my words will fail to come true."

¹⁰Holofernes commanded the slaves who were serving him in his tent to take Achior to Bethulia and hand him over to the Israelites. ¹¹The slaves took him and led him out of the camp to the plain, and took him up into the high country to the springs below Bethulia.
¹²When the men of the town saw them at the mountain ridge, they seized their weapons and ran out of the town to the mountain ridge.
All the slingers retained control of the pass by pelting them with stones. ¹³Finding shelter below the mountain, they bound Achior and left him lying

⁴You shall learn that Nebuchadnezzar is lord of the whole earth and then the sword of my soldiers shall pass through your side, and you shall fall, pierced through, among the wounded of Israel and you shall not draw another breath until you have been destroyed with them.
⁵But if, on the other hand, you think your prophecy is true,
let your countenance not sink and let the pallor that has come over your face depart from you,

if you suppose that my words cannot be accomplished.
⁶And so that you may know that you will experience these things together with them, behold, from this hour you shall be one of their people so that when they experience the punishment they deserve from my sword, at the same time you will also be subject to the same vengeance.

⁷Then Holofernes commanded his servants to take Achior and lead him to Bethulia and deliver him into the hands of the Israelites. ⁸The servants of Holofernes took him and set out across the plain, but when they came near the mountains,

the slingers came out against them. ⁹The servants then turned aside at the edge of the mountain and there at the base of the mountain, and returned to their lord.

[14]When the Israelites came down from their town and came upon him, they untied him and led him to Bethulia; there they presented him to the magistrates of their town,

[15]who were in those days Uzziah, son of Micah of the tribe of Simeon, Chabris son of Gothoniel, and Charmis son of Melchiel. [16]They then summoned all the elders of the town, and all the young men and the women rushed together to the town meeting,

and they placed Achior in the middle of the whole citizenry. Uzziah then asked him what had happened, and [17]Achior informed them of the council of Holofernes and what he had said before the Assyrian leaders, and how Holofernes had boasted about what he would do to the house of Israel.

[18]The townsfolk fell down, prostrating themselves before God,

and cried out, [19]"Lord God of heaven, behold their arrogance, and have mercy on account of the humility of our people. Look today upon the face of those sanctified to you."

[20]They then comforted Achior, praising him warmly,

tied Achior hand and foot to a tree, and so left him tied with ropes and returned to their lord.

[10]But the Israelites came down from Bethulia to him, and releasing him brought him to Bethulia, and standing him in the midst of the people asked him what the reason was that the Assyrians had left him bound.

[11]In those days the leaders there were Uzziah, son of Micah of the tribe of Simeon, and Charmis, also known as Gothoniel.

[12]In the middle of the elders and in the presence of all the people
Achior recounted all the things he had said when interrogated by Holofernes

and how the people of Holofernes had wanted to kill him on account of his words, [13]and how Holofernes himself became angry and for this reason commanded him to be turned over to the Israelites, and that when he conquered the Israelites, at that time he would command that Achior also perish by various torments for having said, "The God of heaven is their defender."
[14]When Achior had recounted all these things, all the people fell upon their faces, praising the Lord, and all together poured out their prayers to God in communal lamentation and weeping, [15]saying, "O Lord God of heaven and earth, behold their pride and take note of our humility; look upon the faces of your holy ones,

and show that those who put their faith in you are not forsaken and that you humbled those who put faith in themselves and glory in their own power." [16]When their weeping had ended, and the prayer of the people, which had continued all day long, was completed,
they comforted Achior, [17]saying, "God of our fathers, whose power you, Achior, have expounded, will reverse your situation, so that you shall rather see their destruction. [18]And indeed, when the Lord our God shall give this freedom to

and Uzziah took him from the town meeting to his home, and prepared a feast for the elders.

Throughout that night they called upon the God of Israel for help.

Chapter 7 LXX

¹On the next day Holofernes commanded his entire army and all of the people who had joined forces with him to break camp and set out for Bethulia to capture the passes into the high country and to wage war against the Israelites. ²Every valiant soldier thus set out that day, the army of seasoned troops numbering 170,000 infantry and twelve thousand cavalry, not counting the retinue of the supply train and their guard—a very great multitude. ³They set up camp beside a spring in the valley near Bethulia.

The encampment spread in the direction of Dothan all the way to Belbaim, and in the other direction from Bethulia to Cyamon, near Esdraelon. ⁴When the Israelites beheld the size of the army, they were very troubled and said to each other, "These men will certainly devour the whole countryside. Neither the high mountains nor the valleys nor the hills can withstand their weight."

⁵Then each man took up his arms, lit the fires on the towers,
and stood guard throughout the night.

⁶On the second day Holofernes led out his entire cavalry before the Israelites who were in Bethulia. ⁷He reconnoitered the passes that led to their town, and surveyed the springs and assigned to

his servants, may God be with you in our midst, and if it pleases you, may you and all your family convert." ¹⁹Then Uzziah, after the assembly was concluded, took him into his home, and prepared a great banquet. ²⁰All of the elders were also invited, and revived themselves now that their fast was over. ²¹Afterwards, the entire populace was called together,
and they prayed all night long in their assembly, praying for help from the God of Israel.

Chapter 7 Vulgate

¹On the next day Holofernes gave orders to his army

to go up against Bethulia.

²There were 120,000 foot soldiers and twenty-two thousand horsemen, in addition to the preparations of those men whom bondage had taken, and who, of all the youth in the cities and provinces, had been taken away. ³They all prepared together for war against the Israelites, and they came from the base of the mountain to the top that looked toward Dothain, from the place which is called Belma, as far as Chelmon, opposite Esdraelon.

⁴But the Israelites, when they saw their vast numbers,

prostrated themselves upon the ground, placing ashes upon their heads praying with one voice that the God of Israel would show his mercy for his people. ⁵Taking up their weapons of war, they took up their posts at the narrow passes that led directly through the mountains, and stood guard day and night. ⁶But Holofernes, scouting about, discovered that the spring that supplied their water ran by a channel outside the city to the south; he commanded that this channel be cut off.

414

each of them camps of armed troops. Then he returned to his people.

⁷There were at the same time other springs not far from the walls, from which the children of Israel were seen drawing water secretly, more to refresh themselves than to meet all their needs for water. ⁸But the Ammonites and Moabites

⁸All of the leaders of the Edomites and all of the rulers of the people of Moab and the generals from the coastal areas approached Holofernes and said, ⁹"Let our master heed our advice, and his armies will suffer no losses.

approached Holofernes and said,

¹⁰This people, the Israelites, do not place their trust in their spears, but in the height of the mountains on which they dwell, for it is no easy task to make a way through the crests of these mountains. ¹¹So, then, my lord, do not make war against them in full formation, as it is normally done, and not a single man from your people will fall. ¹²Remain in your camp with your entire army in reserve, but allow your servants to take control of the spring that flows from the base of the mountain,

"The Israelites do not place their trust in spears, nor arrows, but their mountains defend them and the high hills provide fortifications for them and they are protected by the steep inclines. ⁹Therefore, so that you may overcome them without engaging them in battle, place guards at the springs so that they may not draw water from them, and you can destroy them without sword, or else once they are wearied they will hand over their city, which, they suppose, because of its position in the mountains, is impregnable."

¹³for all those who live in Bethulia draw their water from this source. Thirst will destroy them and they will hand over their town. We and our people shall ascend to the mountaintops near their town and set up camp upon them and shall stand guard to ensure that not a single person leaves their town. ¹⁴They, their wives, and their children will waste away from famine, and before the sword ever strikes them, they will be strewn about the streets of their settlement. ¹⁵In this way you shall indeed exact a severe vengeance upon them for rebelling against you and not coming out to meet you in peace."
¹⁶Their counsel pleased Holofernes and all his ministers, and he gave orders to do as they said.
¹⁷The army of the Ammonites set out with five thousand Assyrians and pitched camp in the valley; they seized the streams and wells belonging to the Israelites.
¹⁸Then the Edomites and the Ammonites went up and pitched camp in the high country oppo-

¹⁰These words were pleasing to Holofernes and his entire staff,

and he placed a hundred men to guard each spring round about.

site Dothan, and sent some of their troops to the southeast in the direction of Egrebeh, near Chusi on the Wadi Mochmur. The rest of the Assyrian army encamped in the plain, covering the face of the earth. Their tents and supply train formed a great mass of people, for their multitude was great. [19]The Israelites, their spirits flagging, cried out to the Lord their God because their bitter enemies surrounded them and there was no means of escape from them. [20]The entire Assyrian force—infantry, chariots, and cavalry—remained all around them for thirty-four days.

[21]The cisterns that the residents of Bethulia possessed gave out; their cisterns were going dry, and even though they rationed water each day, there was not enough to drink.

[22]Their babies grew listless, the women and young men fainted from thirst and were collapsing in the streets and gates of the town; there was no longer any strength left in them.

[23]All the people—young men, women, and children—gathered before Uzziah and the leaders of the town and cried out loudly and said before all the elders, [24]"May God judge between you and us, for you have committed a grave injustice by not seeking peace with the Assyrians.

[25]Now there is no hope, for God has sold us into their hands to be destroyed before them by thirst and a great destruction.

[26]Therefore, sue for peace and offer to hand over the entire town as spoils to the people of Holofernes and his entire army; [27]it would be better to be plundered by them and become their slaves, for at least our lives would be spared, and we would not witness the deaths of our babies before our eyes, nor our wives and children giving up their lives. [28]We call heaven and earth to witness against you, and our God the Lord of our fathers who punishes us for our sins and the sins of our fathers that you not do today as you have said!"

[11]When this watch had continued for twenty days, the cisterns and supplies of water were depleted for all the inhabitants of Bethulia, so that within the city there was not enough to satisfy them for one day, for a daily ration had been given out to the people.

[12]Then all the men and women, young people, and children gathered together around Uzziah and in one voice
[13]said, "Let God judge between you and us, for you have done evil against us, because you did not want to seek peace with the Assyrians, and for this reason God has sold us into their hands.
[14]Therefore, there is no one to help us, when we are cast down before their eyes in thirst and great destruction.

[15]So now assemble all those who are in the city so that we may all, of our own accord, hand ourselves over to the people of Holofernes.
[16]For it is better that, though captive, we should live and bless God, than that we should die and be an object of shame to all flesh after seeing our wives and our infants die before our eyes.
[17]We call heaven and earth as witness this day, and the God of our fathers, who punishes us according to our sins, that you are to hand over the city into the hand of the army of Holofernes, and that our end should come quickly at the edge of the sword, which is only made longer by the want from thirst."

²⁹A loud lamentation rose up at once in the middle of the assembly of the people; they raised a mighty cry to the Lord God,

³⁰but Uzziah said to them, "Brothers, take courage! Let us hold out for just five days more during which time the Lord our God will turn his mercy on us; in the end he will not forsake us. ³¹And if these days pass and there is no help, then I shall do as you say."
³²He then dismissed the people to their outposts, and they went to walls and towers and the women and children to their homes. They remained throughout the town in a wretched state.

Chapter 8 LXX

¹At this time Judith, daughter of Merari, son of Ox, son of Joseph, son of Oziel, son of Helkiah, son of Hananiah, son of Gideon, son of Rephaim, son of Ahitub, son of Elijah, son of Hilkiah, son of Eliab, son of Nathaniel, son of Salamiel, son of Sarasadai, son of Israel, heard about these things.

²Her husband was Manasseh, of her own tribe and family. He had died during the barley harvest. ³He was overseeing those binding sheaves in the field when the burning sun shone on his head, and he collapsed upon his bed and died in Bethulia, his town. They buried him with his ancestors in the field between Dothan and Balamon.
⁴Judith remained in her house as a widow for three years and four months. ⁵On the roof of her house she erected a tent,

and wore sackcloth and widow's garments. ⁶Every day of her mourning period she fasted, except for

¹⁸And when they had said these things, there was great weeping and lamentation of everyone in the assembly, and for many hours with one voice they cried out to God,
saying, ¹⁹"We have sinned along with our fathers, acted unjustly, committed iniquity. ²⁰Because you are holy, have mercy on us, or else punish our iniquities by your own scourges and do not choose to deliver those who trust in you to a people who do not know you, ²¹that they may not say among the gentiles, 'Where is their God?'" ²²And when, wearied by these cries and this weeping, they had become silent,
²³Uzziah stood up, welling with tears, and said, "Brothers, be steady, and let us wait five days for God's mercy, ²⁴for it is possible that he will relent from his anger and give glory to his name. ²⁵And if five days have passed and no aid has come, we will do the things which you have said."

Chapter 8 Vulgate

¹And so it happened that when Judith, a widow, heard these things—she was the daughter of Merari, the son of Idox, the son of Joseph, the son of Ozias, the son of Eli, the son of Jamnor, the son of Gideon, the son of Raphaim, the son of Ahitub, the son of Melchias, the son of Enan, the son of Nathanias, the son of Salathiel, the son of Simeon, the son of Reuben,
²and her husband was Manasseh, who died in the days of the barley harvest. ³For he was standing over those who were binding sheaves in the field when the heat came upon his head, and he died in Bethulia his city, and was buried there with his fathers.

⁴Judith had remained a widow for three years and six months. ⁵In the upper part of her house she had made a private chamber in which she lived shut in with her maids.
⁶She wore sackcloth upon her loins, and fasted

the Sabbath and the day of preparation, the day of the new moon and the day before, and the days of feasting and joy at the temple in Israel.
[7]She was exceedingly beautiful, and her husband Manasseh left to her gold and silver, male and female slaves, livestock and fields. She continued in charge of his estate,
[8]and no one spoke ill of her, because she feared God greatly.

[9]When Judith heard the distressing words that the people had spoken against the magistrate—the result of faintheartedness brought on by thirst— and also heard all that Uzziah had said to them in response sworn to them, that he had sworn an oath to surrender the town to the Assyrians after five days,
[10]she sent her favorite maid, who was in charge of all her possessions,
to summon Uzziah, Chabris, and Charmis, the elders of the town. [11]When they arrived, she said to them,
"Hear my words, magistrates of all the citizens of Bethulia, because you were wrong to speak to the people as you did today.
You have made a vow between God and yourselves and have promised to hand over the town to our enemies unless the Lord comes to our rescue during these days. [12]But who are you to test God today and set yourself in the place of God among the people? [13]You are testing the Lord Almighty, but you will remain ignorant forever! [14]Indeed, you will not discover the depths of the human heart, nor comprehend a person's thoughts. How then could you possibly search out God, who created these things, and understand his mind or follow his reasoning?
My brothers, do not in any way provoke the Lord our God! [15]If he does not choose to aid us in these five days, he has the authority—in whatever number of days he wishes—to come to our defense, or to destroy us in the very presence of our enemies.
[16]Do not attempt to extract a pledge on the designs of the Lord our God, for God is not like a man, to be threatened, or like a son of man to be bargained with.

every day of her life, except for Sabbaths, new moons, and the feasts of the house of Israel.

[7]She was very beautiful in appearance, and her husband had left her great riches and many servants and large possessions of herds of oxen and flocks of sheep.
[8]She was highly reputed to all, because she feared the Lord very much;
there was no one who spoke a bad word about her.
[9]When, therefore, she heard

that Uzziah had promised that he would deliver over the city after five days,

she sent for the elders Chabri and Carmi. [10]They came to her and she said to them,

"What is this report that Uzziah has consented

to deliver up the city to the Assyrians if within five days no aid comes for us?
[11]And who are you to test the Lord?

[12]This is not a prayer that will call forth mercy, but rather will excite anger and kindle wrath. [13]You have set a schedule for the mercy of the Lord, and by your own reckoning have appointed him a day. [14]But since the Lord is patient, let us be penitent concerning this as well, and with tears beg his pardon. [15]For God does not threaten thus like a man, nor is he inflamed to anger like a son of man. [16]So, therefore, let us humble our souls, and serve

[17]Therefore, while waiting patiently for deliverance by his hand, let us call on him for aid.

He will heed our voice, if it pleases him. [18]Indeed, there has not arisen in our generations, nor is there today, either a tribe or family or body of citizens or town among our people who worships gods made with hands, as was done in former days. [19]And it was for this reason that our forebears were given over to sword and plunder, suffering a terrible defeat before our enemies. [20]We, however, do not recognize any God but him, and thus we hope that he will not ignore us or any of our people. [21]For when we fall, all of Judea will follow. The sanctuary will be ransacked, and God will demand from us the reason for its desecration. [22]The slaughter of our brothers and sisters, the captivity of the land, and the desolation of our inheritance he will bring upon our heads among the nations wherever we are enslaved, and we shall become an object of derision and shame among those who possess us. [23]Our slavery will never be replaced by gladness, but the Lord our God will reckon it to our shame.

[24]So now, my brothers, let us serve as an example for all our other brothers and sisters. Their survival depends on us; the sanctuary, the temple and the altar depend on us. [25]Let us give thanks for all these things to our Lord God, who tests us just as he did our fathers. [26]Remember all he did for Abraham,

and the many ways he tested Isaac, and what happened to Jacob in Mesopotamia of Syria as Laban, the brother of his mother, was herding sheep.

him with a continually humbled spirit. [17]Let us ask the Lord in tears that he show mercy to us according to his will, so that as our heart is disturbed by their pride, so also we may glory in our humility.

[18]For we have not followed the sins of our fathers who abandoned their God and worshiped strange gods.

[19]For this offense they were given over to their enemies, and to the sword, to rape, and to chaos, but we know no other God but him.

[20]Let us humbly await his consolation, and the Lord our God will seek recompense for our blood in the afflictions of our enemies and he will humble all the peoples who have risen up against us and bring them to shame.

[21]And now, brothers, since you are elders among the people of God, and on you depends their very souls, encourage their hearts with your words, so that they may be mindful of how our fathers were tested so as to be proven to be true worshipers of their God. [22]They must be mindful how our father Abraham was tempted and through many tribulations was proved worthy so that he was made a friend of God. [23]Just so Isaac, and Jacob, and Moses and all those who pleased God passed through many tribulations and were faithful. [24]But those who did not undergo testing with the fear of the Lord and endurance but brought on

27For he is not testing our hearts by fire as he did them, nor has he taken his revenge upon us, but the Lord scourges those who would approach him in order to admonish them."

28Uzziah said to her, "Everything that you have said was spoken with a good heart. No one can contradict your words.

29Your wisdom did not appear in a day, but from your youth all the people have recognized your understanding, for the inclination of your heart is good. 30But the people have become very thirsty and have forced us to speak to them as we did, and take upon ourselves an oath that we cannot violate. 31Pray for us, therefore, for you are a pious woman, and the Lord will send enough rain to fill our cisterns, and will no longer grow faint."

32"Listen to me," Judith said to them, "for I am about to do something that will live in the memory of our people for many generations to come.

33Stand by the gate tonight, and I shall go out with my maidservant, and during that period after which you vowed to surrender the town to our enemies, the Lord will preserve Israel by my hand. 34Do not ask any questions about what I am going to do—I shall say nothing more to you until I have completed my task."

35"Go in peace," replied Uzziah and the town magistrates, "and may the Lord God go before you to take vengeance on our enemies." 36And leaving her tent, they returned once more to their posts.

Chapter 9 LXX

1Falling upon her face, Judith smeared ashes over her head and uncovered the sackcloth she was wearing.

At the same moment that the evening's incense offering was being brought into the house of God in Jerusalem,

themselves the shame of their murmuring against the Lord 25were destroyed by the destroyer and perished from the serpents. 26Let us, therefore, not avenge ourselves for these things that we suffer, 27but considering these punishments to be more minor than our sins,

let us believe that these scourges of the Lord, with which like servants we are chastened, occur for our correction and not for our destruction."

28And Uzziah and the elders said to her, "All the things you have said are true, and there is nothing in your discourse that can be contradicted.

29Now, therefore, pray for us, for you are a holy woman who fears God."

30And Judith said to them, "Just as you know that what I have been able to say is from God, 31test also whether what I intend to do is from God, and pray that God should strengthen my plan. 32Stand at the gate tonight and I will go out with my maidservant. Pray that, as you have said, in five days the Lord will bring relief for his people Israel. 33But I do not want you to inquire into what I am doing, and until I bring you word, let nothing else be done except prayer for me to the Lord our God."

34And Uzziah, the leader of Judah said to her, "Go in peace, and may the Lord be with you in the vengeance on our enemies." They took their leave and went back.

Chapter 9 Vulgate

When they were gone, Judith went into her prayer room and putting on sackcloth, placed ashes on her head, and prostrating herself before the Lord,

Judith uttered a loud cry to the Lord and said,
²"O Lord, God of my forefather Simeon, in whose hand you placed a sword for vengeance on foreigners who defiled the womb of a virgin.
They uncovered her thighs to shame her, and disgraced her by polluting her womb, and even though you had said, 'This shall not be done,' yet they did it.
³For this reason you handed over their leaders for slaughter, and their bed, which was shamed by their treachery, you allowed to be stained with blood. You struck dead the slaves with their princes, and the princes upon their thrones.
⁴You gave their wives over to plunder, and their daughters were led away to captivity; all their spoils were divided by the sons whom you loved, who were zealously devoted to you and abhorred the pollution of their blood, and called upon you for help.
O God, my God, heed now the plea of a widow!
⁵For you are the one who is responsible for all that happened before those things, for what happened then, for the present events, and what is to come. Everything has come about as you have planned.
⁶All the things that you have willed to be have stood forth and said, 'Here we are!' All your ways have already been prepared; your judgment is based on foreknowledge.
⁷And now the Assyrians have grown into a huge army, priding themselves in their horses and riders, and glorying in the might of their infantry.

They have placed their faith in the shield and the javelin, the bow and the sling,
but they have not recognized that you are a Lord

who crushes wars—the Lord is your name! ⁸Break through their battle lines and bring low their might in your wrath.
They intended to pollute your sanctuary, defiling

cried to the Lord and said,
²"Lord God of my father Simeon, who gave him a sword for vengeance against foreigners,
violators conspicuous by their uncleanness,
and uncovered the thigh of a virgin in an outrage,

³you gave their wives for plunder and their daughters into captivity, and all their spoils to be divided by your servants, who were zealous with your zeal.

Come to me, a widow, I pray to you, Lord, my God.
⁴For you have done great things before, and you have conceived deeds upon deeds, and what you have willed has come to pass.

⁵All your ways have been prepared beforehand, and your justice you have brought about by providence.

⁶Look now on the camp of the Assyrians, just as you saw fit to take note of the camp of the Egyptians, when they, fully armed, pursued your servants, placing their faith in their chariots and in their cavalry and in the size of their army. ⁷But you looked over their camp, and shadows overcame them. ⁸The deep took hold of their feet, and the waters flowed over them. ⁹Thus may it be with these, Lord,
who place their faith in their great numbers, and in their chariots, their lances, their arrows, and glory in their lances,
¹⁰and they do not know that you yourself are our God, who from the beginning has crushed wars—the Lord is your name! ¹¹Lift up your arm as from the beginning and crush their might with your might. Let their might fall by your wrath, those who promise to violate your sanctuary and

the tabernacle in which the name of your glory finds its rest, and sever the horns of your altar with a sword.

⁹Behold their arrogance! Bring your wrath down upon their heads and give into my hand—the hand of a widow!—the strength that my plan requires. ¹⁰By the guile of my lips strike the slave with his ruler and the ruler with his slave!

Crush their arrogance by a female hand!

¹¹For your power lies not in numbers, nor is your strength found among the strong,

but you are a God of the lowly, a helper of the poor, protector of the weak, guardian of those in despair, deliverer of those without hope.

¹²Indeed, O God of my father and God of the inheritance of Israel, ruler of heaven and earth, creator of all the waters, king of your whole creation! Listen to my plea!

¹³Grant, I pray, that my speech and my deception wound and maim those who have plotted evil against your covenant, your sacred house, Mount Zion, and the house of your children's possession. ¹⁴Cause all the nations and every tribe to recognize that you are the God of all power and might and that there is none other but you who shields the people Israel."

Chapter 10 LXX

¹When Judith had ceased crying out to the God of Israel and had concluded all of these words, ²she arose from where she had lain, and, summoning her maid, went down into her house where she spent Sabbaths and feast days. ³Removing her sackcloth in which she was clothed, and her widow's garments, she bathed her body in water and anointed herself with costly ointment, braided her hair, placed a tiara on her head, and dressed in festive garments,

those that she had worn in those days when her husband Manasseh was alive.

pollute the tabernacle of your honor and to cast down the horn of your altar with their sword.

¹²Bring to pass, O Lord, that his pride may be cut off with his own sword.

¹³Let me be the cause for him to be caught by the snare of his own eyes, and strike him by my gracious lips. ¹⁴Give resolve to my mind, so that I may despise him, and power, in order that I may overthrow him. ¹⁵For this will be a memorial for your name when you cast him down by the hand of a woman!

¹⁶For your power, O Lord, lies not in numbers nor does your will favor the number of horsemen, nor from the beginning have the proud pleased you, but the prayer of the humble and the meek have always pleased you.

¹⁷O God of the heavens, creator of the waters and Lord of all creation, hear me, a poor wretch who is praying to you and placing faith in your mercy. ¹⁸Remember, O Lord, your covenant and place words in my mouth, and strengthen the resolve of my heart so that your house may continue in your holiness,

¹⁹and all the peoples may acknowledge that you are God and there is no other beside you."

Chapter 10 Vulgate

¹And so, when she had ceased crying out to the Lord, she arose from the place where she had lain prostrate before the Lord. ²She called her maidservant, and, going down into her household quarters, she took off her sackcloth and laid aside her widow's garments.

³She washed her body and applied the finest myrrh, braided her hair,

and placed a tiara on her head. She put on her festive garments,

⁴She then put sandals on her feet, which she also adorned with anklets, and put on her bracelets, rings, and earrings, in addition to all her other beautifications, and was now fully adorned in order to lead astray the eyes of as many men as might see her.

put sandals upon her feet and taking up her bracelets, lilies, earrings, and rings, she adorned herself with all her jewelry.

⁴And the Lord conferred even more beauty upon her, because all this adornment did not proceed from lust but from virtue, and so the Lord increased her beauty so that she appeared incomparably lovely to everyone's eyes.

⁵She gave her maid a small wineskin full of wine, a flask of oil, and filled a pouch with a barley loaf, a cake of figs, fine bread, and, wrapping her dishes, she placed them also in her maid's pouch.

⁵She gave her maid a skin of wine, a vessel of oil, parched grain, dried figs, bread, and cheese, and went out.

⁶They then went out to the gate of the town of Bethulia and found waiting there Uzziah and the elders of the town, Chabris and Charmis.

⁶When she came to the gates of the city they found Uzziah waiting there with the elders of the city.

⁷When they beheld her, her face and her garments transformed, they were very amazed at her beauty,

⁷When they saw her they were astonished at her great beauty.

⁸Yet they asked her no question, but let her pass, saying, "May the God of our fathers give you grace, and may he strengthen all the designs of your heart with his power, so that Jerusalem may be glorified in you, and your name may be found among the number of the holy and just." ⁹And those present said with one voice, "Amen, amen."

and said to her, ⁸"May the God of our fathers give you favor to complete your plans for the greater glory of Jerusalem and the Israelites."

And she bowed to God.
⁹"Now command that the town gates be opened for me," she said to them, "and I shall go forth to accomplish all the things about which we spoke." They ordered the gatekeepers to open the gates as she had said, ¹⁰and they did so.
Judith went out, together with her maid, and the men of the town watched her closely until she had descended the mountain and crossed the valley, and they could no longer see her.

¹⁰And Judith, with a prayer to God, went out of the gates, with her maid with her.

¹¹As Judith and her maid were passing through the valley without incident, they were met by an Assyrian patrol. ¹²Placing her under guard they began to question her: "To what people do you belong? Where do you come from and where are you going?"
"I am a Hebrew, but I am fleeing from them because they are about to be devoured by you.

¹¹And it happened when she went down the mountain, about daybreak, that the scouts of the Assyrians met her
and detained her, saying,
"Where are you coming from and where are you going?"
¹²She answered, "I am a daughter of the Hebrews, and have fled from their presence because I knew they would be given over to you for plunder

¹³I am now on my way to meet Holofernes, commander-in-chief of your army, to give him reliable information. I shall show him a path by which he can take control of all the high country without losing a single life."
¹⁴As they listened to her,

they were struck by her remarkable beauty and said to her, ¹⁵"By coming down now to meet our lord, you have saved your life. Now you may go to his tent; some of our men will escort you and present you to him.
¹⁶When you stand before him, do not be afraid, but tell him what you have told us and he will treat you well."

¹⁷They assigned a hundred men to escort her and her maid to the tent of Holofernes. ¹⁸A commotion spread throughout the encampment, as news of her arrival was announced from tent to tent. Soldiers came and gathered round her as she stood outside Holofernes's tent waiting to be announced. ¹⁹They marveled at her beauty, but marveled at the Israelites as well on her account, saying to one another, "Who could despise a people who has women such as this among them? It would be better not to allow a single man of them to live; those left standing would surely be able to beguile the whole world."

²⁰All of those who sat in council with Holofernes and all of his servants came out to meet her and escorted her into the tent.

[See LXX 10:19 above.]

²¹There Holofernes was reclining on his bed behind a curtain interwoven with purple, gold, emeralds, and other precious stones.
²²They informed him of Judith's presence, and he

because they despised you and refused to surrender themselves to you in order to find mercy in your sight.
¹³Because of this I reasoned with myself, 'I shall go before the leader Holofernes that I may tell him their secrets and show him how he may find a means of access to take them without losing a single man of his army.'"
¹⁴As the men listened to her words they beheld her face and their eyes were astounded, for they were astonished at her beauty.

¹⁵They said to her, "You have saved your life in that you have thus taken up this plan to come down to our lord.

¹⁶And be assured of this, that when you stand before him it will go well for you, and you will be most agreeable to his heart."

[See Vg 10:18 below.]

So they brought her to the tent of Holofernes and announced her.

¹⁷When she had entered before him, immediately Holofernes was the captive of his own eyes. ¹⁸His officers said to him, "Who can despise the people of the Hebrews who have such beautiful women, and ought we not with good cause fight against them for such women?"
¹⁹Judith saw Holofernes sitting behind a canopy woven with purple and gold, emeralds and precious stones,

424

came from behind the curtain into the forechamber of the tent, with silver lamps going before him. [23]When Judith came before him and his attendants, they were all stunned by the beauty of her face.

She fell down and kneeled before him,
and his servants helped her to her feet.

[20]and when she looked on his face, she bowed down to him, prostrating herself on the ground. The servants of Holofernes, at their lord's bidding, lifted her up.

Chapter 11 LXX

[1]"Woman, take heart and do not be afraid," Holofernes said to her. "I have never harmed anyone who chose to serve Nebuchadnezzar, king of all the earth. [2]But as for your people who reside in the high country, if they had not slighted me, I would never have raised my spear against them. Now they have brought this upon themselves. [3]But tell me, why have you fled from them and come to us? By doing so, you have saved yourself. Have courage—you will live tonight and hereafter. [4]There is no one who will harm you, but you will be treated well, as are all of the slaves of my lord, King Nebuchadnezzar."

[5]"Heed, then, the words of your slave," Judith said to him, "and allow your servant to speak before you. I will not speak falsely to my lord tonight. [6]And if you follow the advice of your servant, God will accomplish a great deed through you; my lord will not fail in his plan.

[7]For as Nebuchadnezzar, king of the whole earth lives, and as his power lives, who sent you to order all people, not only do all people serve him on account of you, but even the beasts of the field and the cattle and the birds of the air live through your might for the greater glory of Nebuchadnezzar and all of his household.

[8]For we have heard of your wisdom and the clever strategies you have conceived. It is proclaimed throughout the whole earth that you alone in the whole kingdom are worthy and intelligent, and marvelous in military strategy.

[9]But we have now also heard what Achior told you in council, since the men of Bethulia spared him, and he recounted to them all that he had uttered in your presence. [10]Therefore, do not disregard his

Chapter 11 Vulgate

[1]Then Holofernes said to her, "Let your soul be steady, and do not fear in your heart, for I have never harmed a man who chose to serve Nebuchadnezzar the king. [2]And if your people had not despised me, I would not have lifted my spear against them.

[3]But now tell me, why have you left them and why has it pleased you to come to us?"

[4]Judith said to him, "Take heed to the words of your handmaiden,

for if you follow the words of your handmaiden, the Lord will do a perfect thing through you.

[5]May Nebuchadnezzar king of the earth live, and his power live which is in you for the chastising of wayward souls. For not only human beings serve him through you, but even the beasts of the field obey him.

[6]Indeed, the diligence of your mind is spoken of by all peoples, and it is recounted throughout the whole world that you alone are good and powerful in all his kingdom, and your training is praised in every province.

[7]It is no secret what Achior said, nor is it unknown what you commanded to be done to him.

advice, my lord and master, but take it to heart, for it is true.

Our people cannot be avenged nor can a sword overpower them unless they sin against their God. [11]But now, in order that my lord not be frustrated and fail to achieve his goal, death will descend upon them. A sin is overtaking them that will provoke their God to fury, as soon as they commit their sacrilege.

[12]When their food and water were depleted, they decided to turn to their cattle, consuming them entirely—even those portions that God had commanded them in his laws not to eat; [13]likewise the firstfruits of wheat and the tithes of wine and oil, which they have sanctified and reserved for the priests who serve in the presence of our God in Jerusalem.

They have decided to consume entirely even things that are not to be touched by anyone of the laity.

[14]They have even sent messengers to Jerusalem to ask permission from the Council, because they who dwell there have done the same things. [15]And so when they return word to them and they act upon it, on that very day they will be given over to you for destruction.

[16]Thus, when I, your servant, found out that these things had occurred, I ran away from them, and God sent me to you to accomplish something so great that whoever hears about it the world over will be astounded, [17]because your servant is indeed pious and serves the God of heaven night and day. For now, I shall remain with you, my lord, and your servant will go out by night to the valley to pray to God; he will tell me when they have committed this sin. [18]I shall then return and report to you, and at that time you should march forth with your entire army, and none of them will oppose you. [19]I shall also lead you through the middle of Judea until you arrive at Jerusalem, where I shall set your seat in the midst of the town. You will lead them away like sheep without a shepherd, and no dog

[8]Indeed, it is certain that our God is so offended by sins that he has commanded the people through his prophets that he will deliver them up for their sins, [9]and because the children of Israel know that they have offended their God, fear of you is upon them.

[10]In addition, a famine has come upon them, and as a result of the lack of water they are already counted among the dead.

[11]And so now they have a plan to kill their cattle and drink their blood, [12]and the portions of grain, wine, and oil consecrated to their Lord which God forbade them to touch they have now planned to dispense, and intend to consume the things which they should not touch with their hands.

Therefore, because they are doing these things, it is certain that they will be handed over to destruction.

[13]And I, your maidservant, aware of this, have fled from them, and the Lord has sent me to tell you these very things.

[14]For I, your maidservant, worship God even now

while I am with you, and your maidservant will go out and I shall pray to God,

[15]and he will tell me when he will requite them for their sin. Then coming to you, I will tell you so that

I may bring you through the middle of Jerusalem,

and you will have all the people of Israel, like sheep that have no shepherd, and not so much as will so much as growl as you pass. All of this was proclaimed ahead of time and revealed to me, and

I have been sent to announce these things to you." [20]These words pleased Holofernes and all his attendants, and marveling at her wisdom,
they said, [21]"There is not another woman like her from one end of the world to the other for beauty of face and intelligence of counsel."
[22]Holofernes said to her: "God has done well in sending you from your people so that control may fall into our hands, for death will be the lot of those who ridicule my lord. [23]You are both elegant in your appearance and refined in speech; if you do as you say, your god shall be my god, and you shall sit in the house of King Nebuchadnezzar and be famous throughout the world."

Chapter 12 LXX
[1]He then commanded that she be brought into where his silver vessels were laid out, and commanded that she be served some of his delicacies and wine.
[2]But Judith said, "I cannot eat from these, lest it be an offense, but I shall eat from the things which I brought with me."

[3]"But if your provisions fail," Holofernes said to her, "where shall we find food of a similar kind for you, as there is no one among us of your race." [4]"As you live, my lord," Judith said to him, "your servant will not use up what she has with her before the Lord accomplishes by my hand what he has planned."
[5]Holofernes's servants then led her to her tent, where she slept until the middle of the night. Just before the morning watch she arose [6]and sent word to Holofernes, "Command, I pray you, my lord, that your servant be allowed to go out for morning prayer."
[7]Holofernes then instructed his bodyguards to give her freedom to come and go as she pleased. In this way she passed three days in the camp. Each night she made her way into the valley of Bethulia and bathed in the spring at the edge of camp.

one dog will bark at you—[16]for these things are told to me through the providence of God,
[17]and because God is angry with them,
I have been sent to say these very things to you."
[18]All these words were pleasing to Holofernes and his servants, and they marveled at her wisdom and said to each other, [19]"There is no other woman on the entire earth like her in appearance, in beauty, and in the sensibility of her speech."
[20]Holofernes said to her, "God has done well in sending you before the people that you may give them into our hands. [21]Because your promise is good,
if your God will do this for me,
he will also be my God and you will be great in the house of Nebuchadnezzar, and your name will be renowned over the entire world."

Chapter 12 Vulgate
[1]Then he commanded that she should go into the tent where his treasures were stored, and commanded that she stay there, and appointed what should be given to her from his own table.
[2]But Judith responded to him, "Indeed, I shall not be able to eat of these things which you have commanded to be given to me, lest some sin come upon me; rather, I will eat from these things which I brought."
[3]Holofernes said to her, "If these things which you have brought with you run out, what shall we do for you?"
[4]And Judith said, "As your soul lives, my lord, your maid will not use up all these things until God does by my hand what I have planned."

And his servants brought her into the tent that he had appointed. [5]And as she was going in, she asked that an opportunity be granted to her to go out at night and before dawn to pray and make petitions to the Lord.

[6]And he commanded his attendants that for three days she be allowed to go out and in as it pleased her to pray to her God.
[7]And she went out each night into the valley of Bethulia and washed herself in a spring of water.

8When she came out of the water, she called upon the Lord God of Israel to direct her path for the victory of her people. 9Thus cleansed, she entered camp and remained in her tent until she brought forth her food for the evening meal.

10On the fourth day, Holofernes gave a feast for his servants alone, and did not invite any of the soldiers on duty. 11He said to Bagoas, the eunuch who was in charge of all his affairs, "Go now and persuade the Hebrew woman in your charge to come join us to eat and drink.

12We would have to hide our faces in shame if we allowed a woman such as this to pass through without enjoying her company. If we cannot win her favors, she will surely ridicule us."

13Taking leave of Holofernes, Bagoas entered Judith's tent and said, "Such a fair young woman as you should have no hesitation in coming before my lord to be honored in his presence and join us in wine and merriment. Today you can become like one of the Assyrian women who serve in Nebuchadnezzar's palace."

14"Indeed, who am I to refuse my lord?" Judith said to him. "I am anxious to do anything that pleases him; this will bring me joy till my dying day."

15She arose and arrayed herself in her garments, making herself up with every feminine charm. Her maid then went ahead of her and laid out lambskins on the ground before Holofernes, which Bagoas had given her for her daily practice, to recline on while eating.

16Judith then entered and reclined upon them, and Holofernes, upon seeing her, was beside himself. He began to tremble with excitement, enflamed with the desire to lie with her. From the first moment he saw her he had been waiting for just such an opportunity to seduce her.

17"Drink up," Holofernes said to her, "and join us in revelry." 18"Yes, I shall drink, my lord," said Judith, "**for** my life today has been magnified beyond all the days of my existence."

19She then took what her maid had prepared for her, and ate and drank with him. 20Holofernes was overjoyed, and began downing his wine, consum-

8And as she came up she prayed to the Lord the God of Israel to guide her way for the liberation of her people. 9And entering again into her tent, she remained there pure until she took her own meal in the evening.

10And on the fourth day, Holofernes made a dinner for his servants
and said to Bagoas his eunuch,
"Go and persuade that Hebrew woman to agree of her own accord to come and stay with me."

11For it is a mark of abject shame among the Assyrians if a woman mocks a man and after doing so gets away from him unharmed.

12Then Bagoas went in to Judith and said, "Let my fair young lady not be afraid to enter in to my lord and be honored before his face, eat with him, and drink wine and enjoy herself."

13To whom Judith answered, "Who am I to contradict my lord? 14All that is good and best before his eyes I will do, and whatever would please him will be best to me all the days of my life."

15She arose and dressed herself in her beautiful garments, and entering she stood before his face.

16The heart of Holofernes was struck hard, for he was burning with desire for her.

17And Holofernes said to her, "Drink now, sit down and be merry, for you have found favor with me."

18And Judith said, "I will drink, my lord, because my soul is magnified today above all my days."

19She took and ate and drank before him what her maid had prepared for her. 20And Holofernes was delighted with her company, and drank a great deal, more than he had ever drunk in his life.

ing more in one day than he had ever drunk before since he had been born.

Chapter 13 LXX

[1]When evening came, his servants quickly retired; Bagoas closed the tent from the outside, and dismissed the servants of his lord who went straight off to bed, for they were wearied because the drinking party had gone on so long.
[2]Judith alone remained in the tent, as Holofernes lay on his bed, his head now swimming in wine.
[3]Judith ordered her maid to stand outside the curtain and wait for her to emerge
as she had done each day.
She had said that she would go out for prayer, and she had spoken to Bagoas about this arrangement.
[4]Everyone, therefore, had now departed, and no one, whether lowly or powerful, remained.
Standing beside the bed, Judith said in her heart,

"O Lord, God of all power,
look now upon the actions of my hands

for the exaltation of Jerusalem.
[5]Now is the time for the rescue of your inheritance and the accomplishment of my plan to destroy the enemies who have risen up against us."

[6]Stepping up to the bedpost that was beside his head, she took down the sword, [7]and approaching the bed, lifted his head by the hair

and said, "Give me strength tonight, O Lord God of Israel!" [8]Then she struck him twice in the neck with all her might, severing his head from him.
[9]She then rolled his body off the bed and pulled down the curtain from its poles. A moment later she stepped outside and handed the head of Holofernes to her maid, [10]who placed it in her food pouch.
The two of them then proceeded out together as was their practice at the time of prayer. They passed through the camp and circled the edge of

Chapter 13 Vulgate

[1]And when it was late his servants hurried back to their tents, and Bagoas closed the entrance of his inner chamber and withdrew. [2]They were all drowsy from the wine.

[3]Judith was alone in the inner chamber, [4]while Holofernes lay sprawled on his bed, quite drunk and fast asleep. [5]Judith spoke to her maidservant to stand outside the inner chamber and keep watch.

[6]Judith stood before the bed praying with tears, her lips moving in silence, [7]saying,
"Give me strength, O Lord God of Israel,
and at this moment look upon the works of my hands, so that as you have promised,
you may raise up your city Jerusalem
and so that what I have conceived I may bring to pass,

though I believe that it could only be done through you."
[8]And when she had said this
she stepped to the pole at the head of his bed and loosed his sword that was hung tied upon it. [9]When she had drawn it out, she took hold of the hair of his head,
and said, "Give me strength, O Lord God of Israel, in this moment." [10]She struck him twice in his neck, and cut off his head.
She pulled down his canopy from the poles and rolled away his headless trunk. [11]A moment later she went out and gave the head of Holofernes to her maidservant and told her to place it in her pouch.
[12]And the two of them went out, as was their custom, as though to pray, and passed through the

the valley, then climbed the mountain of Bethulia and came to its gates.

¹⁰From a distance Judith called out to the gate-keepers, "Open, open the gates! Our God is with us, who manifests his strength for Israel and his might against his enemies, as he has done today!" ¹²When the men of the town heard her voice, they rushed down to the town gates and called together the elders. ¹³All came running, from lowly to powerful, astounded that she had returned, and opened up the town gates to receive them. They kindled a fire to see them, and everyone gathered round.

¹⁴"Praise God! Give praise!" Judith cried out to them. "Praise the God who has not withheld his mercy from the house of Israel, but has destroyed our enemies tonight by my hand!"

¹⁵Drawing the head out of the pouch, she showed it to them and said, "This is the head of Holofernes, commander-in-chief of the Assyrian army! And here is the curtain, behind which he lay in a drunken stupor! The Lord struck him down by a female hand! ¹⁶As the Lord lives, who protected me on my path, as I proceeded it was my face that seduced him and led to his destruction, and yet,

he never committed a sin with me to defile or shame me."

¹⁷The people were all astounded and bowed down and worshiped God, crying out with one voice, "Blessed are you, O God, who on this day humiliated the enemies of our people!" ¹⁸"My daughter," Uzziah said to her, "you are blessed by the Most High God above all women on earth, and blessed be the Lord God who created the heavens and the earth, who

camp, and circling the valley came to the gate of the city.

¹³From afar Judith said to the guards on the walls, "Open the gates, for God is with us, who has done a powerful thing in Israel!"

¹⁴When the men heard her voice they called the city elders.

¹⁵All, from the least to the greatest, ran to meet her, for they had held out no hope that she would ever return. ¹⁶They lit torches and all gathered around her, while she stepped up to a higher place and commanded that there be silence, and when all became quiet ¹⁷Judith said, "Praise the Lord our God, who has not deserted those who hope in him. ¹⁸Through me, his maidservant, he has fulfilled his mercy, which he promised to the house of Israel. By my hand, on this night he has killed the enemy of his people." ¹⁹Then she brought the head of Holofernes out of the pouch and showed it to them, saying, "Behold the head of Holofernes, general of the army of the Assyrians, and behold this canopy in which he lay in his drunkenness, and where the Lord our God struck him down by the hand of a woman. ²⁰And indeed this very Lord lives, for his angel has guarded over me—while going from here, while staying there, and while coming back—and the Lord did not allow me, his maidservant, to be defiled, but has brought me back to you without pollution of sin, rejoicing in his victory, in my escape, and in your liberation. ²¹Let us all confess him, because he is good and his mercy endures forever."

²²And so all of them, revering the Lord, said to her, "The Lord has blessed you by his power, for through you he has reduced our enemies to naught."

²³And Uzziah, the leader of the people of Israel, said to her, "Blessed are you, O daughter, by the Lord the most high God, above all the women of the earth. ²⁴Blessed is the Lord who created heaven and earth, and who led you to strike a blow against

guided your way to strike the head of the leader of our enemies!

[19]Your hope will never fade from the hearts of those who remember God's strength. [20]May God grant that this be an eternal honor to you, and may he shower you with blessings, because you did not hesitate to risk your own life when you saw your people humiliated, but during our humiliation stepped forward and walked a straight path before our God."

And all the people responded, "Amen, amen!"

[See LXX 14:6–7 below.]

the head of the general of our enemies, [25]for he has so magnified your name today that praise of you will not cease from the mouths of people who will be mindful of the power of the Lord forever, for which things you have not spared your life because of the distress and tribulation of your people, but you have saved us from ruin in the presence of our God."

[26]And all the people said, "Amen, amen."
[27]Then Achior was called and came forward, and Judith said to him, "The God of Israel, concerning whom you have given testimony that he avenges himself against his enemies, this night he himself, by my hand, has cut off the head of all those who do not believe in him. [28]And so that you might confirm that it is true, behold the head of Holofernes who in the contempt born of his pride despised the God of Israel, and threatened destruction for you, saying, "When the people of Israel is taken captive, I shall command that your sides be pierced by a sword." [29]And when Achior saw the head of Holofernes, seized with a great fear he fell on his face upon the earth and his soul was disturbed. [30]But afterward, his spirit recovered, he regained composure and fell down at her feet and revered her and said, [31]"Blessed are you by your God in every tent of Jacob, for among every people that hears your name the God of Israel will be magnified on account of you."

Chapter 14 LXX

[1]"Now listen to me, my brothers and sisters," Judith said to them, "Take this head and hang it on the parapet of your walls. [2]When morning comes and the sun has risen over the earth, let each warrior among you take up his weapons and assemble outside the town. Station a commander before you, as if you were going to charge down upon the plain into the ranks of the Assyrians, but do not go down. [3]They will then seize their weapons and go to their camp, where they will rouse the Assyrian generals.

When they rush together to Holofernes's tent,

Chapter 14 Vulgate

[1]Judith said to all the people, "Hear me, my brothers and sisters, hang this head upon our walls, [2]and when the sun rises,
let every man take up his weapons,

and rush out, not as though marching down but charging forward.

[3]Then it will be necessary for the scouts to run back to rouse the general for battle.
[4]When their leaders run to the tent of Holofernes

they will not find him there. A panic will overcome them and they will flee before us.

⁴All of you and all of those who live in every territory of Israel will then cut them down in their path.

⁵But before you do this, bring to me Achior the Ammonite, so that he can identify the one who despised the house of Israel and threatened him as well by sending him to us as though to his death."

[See LXX 14:10 below.]

⁶They summoned Achior from the house of Uzziah, and when he came and saw the head of Holofernes, held aloft by one of the people gathered around, he fell faint before them. ⁷When they helped him to his feet, he threw himself down before Judith and did obeisance before her. "Blessed are you," he said, "in every tent of Judah, and among every people! When they hear your name, they will tremble! ⁸But tell me, what did you do during these past days?" In the presence of the whole people Judith recounted to him everything that she had done, from the time she had left until the moment she was speaking with them. ⁹When she stopped speaking, the people cried aloud with a great voice, filling their town with sounds of joy. ¹⁰Seeing all that the God of Israel had accomplished, Achior also came to believe in God with all his heart. He was circumcised in the flesh of his foreskin and was added to the house of Israel, as he is today.

¹¹When morning came, they hung the head of Holofernes from the wall, and every man took up his weapons, and they all marched out to the mountain passes.

¹²When the Assyrians saw them, they sent word to their officers; they, in turn, informed their commanders, generals, and all the other officers.

and find him a headless body wallowing in his own blood, fear will fall upon them.

⁵And when you see that they are fleeing, go after them knowing that the Lord will destroy them under your feet.

⁶When Achior saw the power that the God of Israel had manifested, he forsook the religion of the gentiles and believed in God, and he circumcised the flesh of his foreskin and he was joined to the people of Israel, along with the progeny of his family to the present day.

[See Vg 13:29–31 above.]

[See Vg 14:6 above.]

⁷And as soon as it was daybreak, they hung the head of Holofernes on the walls and every man took up his weapons and went out with a loud clamor and shouting. ⁸When the scouts saw this, they ran to Holofernes's tent.

⁹Those who were in the tent came to the entrance of the inner chamber and made a noise to create a stir so that Holofernes might awaken from his sleep, but not by their rousing him. ¹⁰For no man

¹³When they came to Holofernes's tent, they said to his officer,

"Rouse our lord, for these slaves have dared to come down against us! Now they will be wiped out, once and for all!"

¹⁴Bagoas entered and tapped on the inner curtain of the tent, for he supposed that he was sleeping with Judith.

¹⁵When no one responded,

he parted the curtain and went in to the bed-chamber, and found him tossed on the floor dead, with his head missing! ¹⁶Bagoas cried out with a loud voice, and screaming and wailing and crying mightily, he tore his garments.

¹⁷He entered the tent where Judith had stayed but did not find her there. He then rushed out of the tent and cried, ¹⁸"These slaves have deceived us! One woman of the Hebrews has shamed the house of King Nebuchadnezzar! For behold, Holofernes is on the ground, and his head is not on him!"

¹⁹When the Assyrian generals heard this, they tore their garments and their souls were seized with panic, as wailing and a great cry filled the camp.

Chapter 15 LXX

¹Those who were in their tents were dumbfounded when they heard what had happened. ²Fear and trembling overcame them and not a single man remained with his fellow, but to a man they poured out over every path of the plain and over the high country. ³Those encamped in the high country around Bethulia were thrown into flight.

And then the Israelites—every soldier among them—streamed down upon them.

---

of the army of the Assyrians dared open by knocking and entering.

¹¹But when his generals and captains and all the officers of the army of the Assyrians arrived, they said to the attendants,

¹²"Enter and rouse him, for these mice have come out of their holes and are spoiling for a fight!"

¹³Then Bagoas went into the tent and standing before the curtain, made a clapping sound with his hands, for he assumed that Holofernes was sleeping with Judith.

¹⁴But when he listened carefully and heard no motion of one lying inside, he approached the curtain and, lifting it up, saw the body of Holofernes, lying on the ground—without a head!—weltering in his own blood. He cried out with a loud voice, weeping and rending his garments.

¹⁵He went into Judith's tent, where he did not find her, and ran out to the people ¹⁶and said, "One Hebrew woman has brought chaos to the house of King Nebuchadnezzar! For behold, Holofernes is lying on the ground, and his head is not on him!"

¹⁷When the generals of the army of the Assyrians heard this, they all rent their garments, and an unbearable fear and dread fell upon them, and their minds were greatly disturbed.

¹⁸A tremendous cry rose from the middle of their camp.

Chapter 15 Vulgate

¹When the entire army heard that Holofernes was beheaded, sense and good counsel fled from them, and seized by fear and trembling they thought only of taking refuge in flight, ²so that not one man spoke to his comrade, but with heads bent forward and leaving all others behind, they ran away from the Hebrews who, they heard, were coming down upon them armed, and they fled by the roads in the plains and the paths of the hills.

³When the Israelites saw them fleeing, they descended upon them, sounding trumpets and shouting after them. ⁴The Assyrians, now in

⁴Uzziah sent messengers to Betomasthaim, Bebai, Choba, Kola, and to every territory of Israel to proclaim everything that had happened, and to urge everyone to stream out against the enemy and destroy them. ⁵When the Israelites heard, they all attacked at once, fell upon them, and cut down their ranks as far as Choba. Similarly, those from Jerusalem and from all the high country also joined them, for people had informed them about what had happened in the camp of their enemies. Those in Gilead and Galilee, by outmaneuvering them, struck a decisive blow and drove them back beyond the borders of Damascus.

⁶The remainder of those who lived in Bethulia descended upon the Assyrian camp and plundered it, taking away great riches.

⁷When the Israelites returned from their slaughter, they seized what was left, and those from the villages and towns in the high country and the plain took possession of a large share of booty, for there was a great deal.

⁸Then Joakim the high priest and the Council of the Israelites who lived in Jerusalem came to witness what the Lord had done for Israel, and to see Judith and celebrate with her.

⁹When they came to her, they all blessed her with one voice and said to her, "You are the exaltation of Jerusalem! You are a great glory for Israel! You are the great pride of our people! ¹⁰You have done these great things by your own hand! You have done great things for Israel, and God is greatly pleased with them. May you be blessed by the Almighty Lord forever!"

And all the people said, "Amen."

¹¹For thirty days all the people plundered the Assyrian camp.

disorder, went helter-skelter in their flight, but the Israelites followed in one body and overpowered all they could find.

⁵Uzziah sent messengers throughout all the cities and regions of Israel.

⁶Every region and every city sent their chosen young men armed for war after them,

and they pursued them with the edge of the sword until they came to the limits of their borders.

⁷The rest who were in Bethulia entered the camp of the Assyrians and took away the spoils which the Assyrians had left behind when they fled, for they enriched themselves greatly. ⁸Those who returned as conquerors to Bethulia brought with them all that they had acquired so that their cattle, draft-animals, and other spoils could not be counted. From the least to the greatest all became rich from the spoils. ⁹Joachim the high priest came from Jerusalem to Bethulia with all his elders to see Judith.

¹⁰When she came out to him, they all blessed her with one voice saying, "You are the glory of Jerusalem! You are the joy of Israel! You are the honor of our people!

¹¹You have acted manfully, and your heart has been strengthened, because you have loved chastity, and after your husband you have not known another. Indeed, the hand of the Lord strengthened you and therefore you will be blessed forever."

¹²And all the people said, "Amen, amen."

¹³Thirty days were scarcely enough for the spoils of the Assyrians to be collected by the people of Israel.

They gave to Judith the tent of Holofernes, along with his silver vessels, his beds, his basins, and all his furnishings, which she loaded upon her mule and she harnessed her wagons and heaped these things upon them.

¹²All the Israelite women came running to see her; they blessed her, while some performed a dance for her. She took garlanded wands in her hands and distributed them to the women with her, ¹³and they crowned themselves with the olive branches, she and those with her. Then she led a procession of all the people, the women in front, every man of Israel behind and fully armed, wearing garlands and a song of praise on their lips.

¹⁴Judith took up this confession before all of Israel, as the whole people jubilantly sang this hymn with her:

¹⁴But all those things that were confirmed to be the personal property of Holofernes were given to Judith. The gold, silver, vestments, and jewels, and furnishings of all kinds were all given to her by the people.

¹⁵And all the people rejoiced, including the women, young girls, and young men, playing on instruments and harps.

[See Vg 16:1 below.]

Chapter 16 LXX

¹And Judith said:
Raise up a song to my God with tambourines.
  Sing to the Lord with cymbals.
Compose for him a psalm of praise,
  Exalt and invoke his name.
²For the Lord is a God who crushes war.

  Into his camps in the midst of the people
  He plucked me out of the hands of those
    who pursued me.

³Assur came out of the northern mountain.
  He came with thousands in his might.
Its size so great that it clogged the torrents,
  Their horses covered the hills.
⁴He gave command to burn all my lands

And destroy my young men by the sword.
My nursing babes he commanded to cast
    to the ground,
  To give over my infants for spoils,
  And to defile my young women.
⁵But the almighty Lord foiled them
  By a female hand.

⁶Indeed, their mighty one was not undone

Chapter 16 Vulgate

¹Then Judith sang this song to the Lord:
² Begin a song to God with timbrels,
  Sing to the Lord with cymbals,
Count out to him a new psalm,
  Exalt and invoke his name.
³The Lord crushes wars;
  The Lord is his name.
⁴Who has set his camp in the middle of his people
  To snatch us out of the hand of all our
    enemies.

⁵Assur came out of the mountains from the north
  With the multitudes of his might.
His great numbers clogged the torrents
  And their horses covered the valleys.
⁶He said that he would set my borders on fire

And kill my young men with the sword,
He would give my infants over to booty

  And my virgins to captivity.
⁷But the almighty Lord has harmed him,
  And has delivered him into the hands
    of a woman

And has brought chaos upon him.

by young men,
 Nor did sons of the Titans strike him,
 Nor mighty giants set upon him;

But Judith, daughter of Merari,
 Led him astray with the beauty of her face.
[7]She stripped off her widow's garments.

 To lift up those struggling in Israel,

She made up her face with precious oils,
[8]And fastened her hair with a tiara.
 She chose out her linen garments in
  order to seduce him.
[9]Her sandal ravished his eye,
 Her beauty took his soul captive—
 Her sword sliced through his neck!

[10]Persians quivered at her daring,
 Medes shuddered at her courage.

[11]My humiliated people shouted in triumph,
 My weak people raised a cry and the
  enemy trembled,
 They lifted up their voices and my
  enemies were turned to flight.

[12]The sons of handmaids ran them through,
 And beat them like runaway slaves.
 They were broken by the battle line of
  my Lord.

[13]I will sing to my God a new song:

 O Lord, you are great and glorious,
 Marvelous and invincible in your strength.

[14]Let all creation serve you,
 For you spoke, and they came into being.

You sent forth your spirit
 and it built them up.
There is no one who can withstand your voice.

[15]For the mountains and the seas
 shall be shaken from their foundations
  by the waters.

[8]For their powerful one did not fall by young men,
 Nor did the sons of Titan strike him,
 Nor mighty giants set themselves against him,

But Judith the daughter of Merari
 destroyed him by the beauty of her face.
[9]She took off her garments of widowhood
 And put on the garments of festivity
 So that the children of Israel might rejoice.

[10]She put makeup on her face,
 And fastened her locks with a tiara

 in order to deceive him.
[11]Her sandals ravished his eyes,
 Her beauty took his soul captive,
 And with a sword she sliced through his neck!

[12]The Persians quaked at her strength,
 The Medes at her boldness.
[13]Then the camp of the Assyrians howled
 When my lowly ones appeared,
 Parched with thirst.

[14]The sons of the young girls ran them through,
 And have killed them like fleeing children.
 They perished in battle before the face
  of my Lord.

[15]Let us sing a hymn to the Lord,
 Let us sing a new hymn to our God.
[16]Adonai, Lord, you are great
 And glorious in your power
 Which no one can overcome!
[17]Let all your creatures serve you,
 Because you spoke and they were made.

You sent forth your spirit
 and they were created.
There is no one who can resist your voice.

[18]Mountains will be moved from their
 foundations by the waters.

Before you rocks shall be melted like wax.
Yet for those who fear you,
    You shall show mercy.
¹⁶For every sacrifice of a fragrant
        offering is a small thing,
    And all fat for the burnt offering is a trifle
        to you.
    But the one who fears the Lord is great forever.

¹⁷Woe to the nations who oppose my people!

The Lord Almighty will take vengeance
    upon them on the day of judgment.

He will place fire and worms in their flesh,
    causing them to scream in torment forever.

¹⁸When they came to Jerusalem they bowed to
God, and when the people were purified, they
brought forth their whole burnt offerings and their
free-will offerings and gifts.
¹⁹Judith offered to God all of the furnishings from
Holofernes's tent which the people had given to
her, and deposited the curtain she had taken from
his bed and gave it to God as a votive offering.
²⁰For three months, the people continued their
celebration before the sanctuary in Jerusalem, and
Judith remained there with them.
²¹After this, the people returned each to the family
lands, and Judith went back to Bethulia to reside
on her estate. In her day she became famous
throughout the land.
²²While many men desired her, none knew her for
as long as she lived, from the time her husband
Manasseh had died and was gathered to his ancestors.
²³Her reputation continued to grow,
and she grew old in her husband's house, reaching
the age of a hundred and five. She gave her maid
her freedom,
dividing her wealth among all the close relatives of
Manasseh her husband and to all her relatives.
She then died in Bethulia, and was buried in the
tomb of her husband Manasseh. ²⁴The house of
Israel mourned her for seven days.

Rocks will melt like wax before your face.
¹⁹But those who fear you will be great
    in your eyes in all things.

²⁰Woe to the people that rises up against
        my people,
For the Lord almighty will take vengeance
        upon them
In the day of judgment he will visit them.
²¹For he will place fire and worms in their flesh
    that they may burn and suffer forever.

²²And so it happened that after the victory all the
people came to Jerusalem to worship the Lord,
and as soon as they were purified they all offered
whole burnt offerings, free-will offerings and their
vows. ²³Judith offered as an anathema of oblivion
all the weapons of Holofernes that the people
had given her and the curtain which she herself
had taken away. ²⁴The people were joyful in the
presence of the sanctuary, and for three months
the festivities of this victory were celebrated with
Judith.
²⁵After those days all returned to their own home,
and Judith was revered in Bethulia, and she was
famous in the whole land of Israel.

²⁶Chastity was added to her virtue,
for she did not know any man all the days of her
life after the death of Manasseh her husband.
²⁷And on festival days she came forth with great
glory.
²⁸She lived in her husband's house a hundred and
five years and set her handmaid free;

she died and was buried with her husband in
Bethulia, ²⁹and all the people mourned for seven
days.

²⁵And no one was able to strike terror among the Israelites while Judith was alive, nor for a long time afterwards.

³⁰In all the days of her life there was no one who troubled Israel, nor for many years after her death.

³¹The day of the celebration of this victory is counted by the Hebrews in the number of holy days, and has been observed by the Jews from that time until the present day.

Bibliography

1. Ancient Versions and Languages

Abbey of S. Girolamo
Libri Ezrae, Tobiae, Iudith (Biblia Sacra iuxta Latinam Vulgatam versionem ad codicum fidem 8; Rome: Typsis Polyglottis Vaticanis, 1950).

Arzt, Peter, Michael Ernst, Wilhelm Niklas, and Josef Falzberger
Sprachlicher Schlüssel zu Judit: Mit dem Text der Göttinger Septuaginta (Robert Hanhart) (Sprachlicher Schlüssel zu den deuterokanonischen Schriften [Apokryphen] des Alten Testaments 2; Salzburg: Institut für neutestamentliche Bibelwissenschaft, 1997).

Bogaert, Pierre–Maurice
"La Bible latine des origines au moyen âge: Aperçu historique, état des questions," *RTL* 19 (1988) 137–59.

Idem
"La halakha alimentaire dans le livre de Judith," in Michel Quesnel, Yves-Marie Blanchard, and Claude Tassin, eds., *Nourriture et repas dans les milieu juifs et chrétiens de l'antiquité: Mélanges offerts au professeur Charles Perrot* (LD 178; Paris: Cerf, 1999) 25–40.

Idem
"Judith," *RAC* 19 (2001) 245–58.

Idem
Judith, Fascicule 1: *Introduction* (Vetus Latina: Die Reste der altlateinischen Bibel 7.2; Freiburg: Herder, 2001).

Idem
"Judith dans la première Bible d'Alcala (Complutensis 1) et dans la version hiéronymienne (Vulgata)," in Roger Gryson, ed., *Philologia Sacra: Biblische und Patristische Studien für Hermann J. Frede und Walter Thiele zu ihrem siebzigsten Geburtstag* (2 vols.; Aus der Geschichte der lateinischen Bibel 24; Freiburg: Herder, 1993) 1:116–30.

Idem
"Un manuscrit de Lérins: Contributions à l'histoire de la vieille version latine de livre de Judith," *RBen* 84 (1974) 301–12.

Idem
"Recensions de la vieille version latine de Judith: I. Aux origines de la vulgate hiéronymienne. Le 'Corbeiensis'; II. Le 'Monacensis'; III. La tradition allémanique; IV. Trois manuscrits et deux recensions; V. La tradition caroligienne, *RBen* 85 (1975) 7–37, 241–65; 86 (1976) 7–37, 182–217; 88 (1978) 7–44.

Idem
"La version latine du livre de Judith dans la première Bible d'Alcala," *RBen* 78 (1968) 7–32, 181–212.

Idem
"La vieille version latine de Judith dans 1a Bible d'Oxford, Bodléienne, Auct Einfra 1–2," in F. L. Cross, ed., *Papers Presented to the Fifth International Conference on Patristic Studies Held in Oxford*, 1967 (Studia patristica 10; Berlin: Akademie-Verlag, 1970) 208–14.

Bons, Eberhard, and Jan Joosten, eds.
Septuagint Vocabulary: Pre-History, Usage, Reception (SCS 58; Atlanta: Society of Biblical Literature, 2011).

Boyd-Taylor, Cameron
"Judith," in Albert Pietersma and Benjamin G. Wright, eds., *A New English Translation of the Septuagint, and the Other Greek Translations Traditionally Included under That Title* (New York and Oxford: Oxford University Press, 2007).

Brooke, Alan E., Norman McLean, and H. St. John Thackeray, eds.
The Old Testament in Greek according to the Text of Codex Vaticanus, vol. 3.1: *Esther, Judith, Tobit* (Cambridge: Cambridge University Press, 1940).

Corley, Jeremy
"Septuagintalisms, Semitic Interference, and the Original Language of the Book of Judith," in Jeremy Corley and Vincent Skemp, eds., *Studies in the Greek Bible: Essays in Honor of Francis T. Gignac, S.J.* (CBQMS 44; Washington, DC: Catholic Biblical Association of America, 2008) 65–96.

Gaster, Moses
"An Unknown Hebrew Version of the History of Judith," *PSBA* 16 (1893–94) 156–63.

Hanhart, Robert, ed.
Iudith (Septuaginta: Vetus Testamentum graecum 8.4; Göttingen: Vandenhoeck & Ruprecht, 1979).

Idem
Sprachlicher Schlüssel zu Judith [Text] (Sprachlicher Schlüssel zu den deuterokanonischen Schriften [Apokryphen] des Alten Testaments 2; Salzburg: Institut für neutestamentliche Bibelwissenschaft, 1997.

Idem, ed.
Text und Textgeschichte des Buches Judith (Mitteilungen des Septuaginta-Unternehmens 14; Göttingen: Vandenhoeck & Ruprecht, 1979).

Lust, Johan, Erik Eynikel, and Katrin Hauspie
Greek-English Lexicon of the Septuagint (rev. ed.; Stuttgart: Deutsche Bibelgesellschaft, 2003).

Martin, Raymond A.
"Some Syntactical Criteria of Translation Greek," *VT* 10 (1960) 295–310.

Idem
"Syntactical Evidence of Aramaic Sources in Acts I–XV," *NTS* 10 (1964) 38–59.

Idem

Syntactical Evidence of Semitic Sources in Greek Documents (SCS 3; Cambridge, MA: Society of Biblical Literature, 1974).

Idem

"Syntax Criticism of Baruch," in Claude E. Cox, ed., VII Congress of the International Organization for Septuagint and Cognate Studies (Leuven, 1989) (SCS 31; Atlanta: Scholars Press, 1991) 361–71.

Idem

"Syntax Criticism of the LXX Additions to the Book of Esther," JBL 94 (1975) 65–72.

Muraoka, T.

A Greek-English Lexicon of the Septuagint (Leuven: Peeters, 2009).

Nestle, Eberhard

"Das Buch Judit in der syrischen Hexapla," in idem, Marginalien und Materialien (Tübingen: Hecknhauer, 1893) 43–48.

Ploeg, J. P. M. van der

The Book of Judith (Daughter of Merari): Syriac Text with Translation and Footnotes (Kottayam, Kerala: St. Ephrem Ecumenical Rsearch Institute, 1991).

Idem

"Some Remarks on a Newly Found Syriac Text of the Book of Judith," in F. García Martínez, A. Hilhorst, and C. J. Labuschagne, eds., The Scriptures and the Scrolls: Studies in Honour of A. S. van der Woude on the Occasion of His 65th Birthday (VTSup 49; Leiden: Brill, 1992) 125–34.

Rahlfs, Alfred

Ioudith: Septuaginta, id est Vetus Testamentum graece iuxta LXX interpretes (5th ed.; Stuttgart: Württembergische Bibelanstalt, 1952) 973–1002.

Sabatier, Pierre

"Judith," in Bibliorum sacrorum latinae versiones antiquae (3 vols.; Reims: Apud Reginaldum Florentain, 1743) 1:744–90.

Schleusner, Johann Friedrich

Novus thesaurus philologico-criticus sive lexicon in LXX et reliquos interpretes Graecos ac scriptores apocryphos Veteris Testamenti (3 vols.; Leipzig: Weidmann, 1820–21).

Schwartz, Jacques

"Un fragment grec du Livre de Judith (sur ostracon)," RB 53 (1946) 534–37.

Steiner, Richard C.

"On the Dating of Hebrew Sound Changes (*H>H and *G>‘) and Greek Translations (2 Esdras and Judith)," JBL 124 (2005) 229–67.

Swete, Henry Barclay, ed.

Ioudeith: The Old Testament in Greek according to the Septuagint (4th ed.; 3 vols.; Cambridge: Cambridge University Press, 1907–12) 2:781–814.

Thomson, Francis

"The Slavonic Translation of the Old Testament," in Joze Krasovec, ed., The Interpretation of the Bible: The International Symposium in Slovenia (Sheffield: Sheffield Academic Press, 1998) 605–920.

Thompson, H. F., ed.

A Coptic Palimpsest in the British Museum Containing Joshua, Judges, Ruth, Judith, and Esther in the Sahidic Dialect (London: Oxford University Press, 1911).

Van Rompay, Lucas

"'No Evil Word about Her': The Two Syriac Versions of the Book of Judith," in W. Th. Van Peursen and R. B. Ter Haar Romeny, eds., Text, Translation, and Tradition: Studies on the Peshitta and Its Use in the Syriac Tradition Presented to Konrad D. Jenner on the Occasion of His Sixty-Fifth Birthday (Monographs of the Peshitta Institute Leiden 14; Leiden: Brill, 2006) 205–30.

Idem

"Two Syriac Manuscripts in the Special Collections Library of Duke University," in Maria Doerfler, Emanuel Fiano, and Kyle Smith, eds., Syriac Encounters: Papers from the Sixth North American Syriac Symposium Duke University, 26–29 June 2011 (Eastern Christian Studies 20; Louvain: Peeters, 2015) 467–83.

Voigt, Edwin Edgar

The Latin Versions of Judith (Leipzig: Drugulin, 1925).

Weber, Robert

Biblia sacra: Iuxta Vulgatam versionem (5th ed.; Stuttgart: Württembergische Bibelanstalt, 2007).

2. Commentaries on Judith (listed in order of their publication)

Fritzsche, Otto Fridolin

Die Bücher Tobi und Judith (Kurzgefasstes exegetisches Handbuch zu den Apokryphen des Alten Testamentes 2; Leipzig: Hirzel, 1853).

Thielmann, Philipp

Beiträge zur Textkritik der Vulgata, insbesondere des Buches Judith (Speier: Gilardon, 1883).

Bissell, Edwin Cone

The Book of Judith (The Apocrypha of the Old Testament; New York: Charles Scribner's Sons, 1886).

Ball, Charles James

"Judith," in Henry Wace, ed., The Holy Bible: According to the Authorised Version (A.D. 1611); Apocrypha I (London: J. Murray, 1888) 241–360.

Zöckler, Otto

Judith (Die Apokryphen des Alten Testamentes. Kurzgefasstes Kommentar zu den Heiligen Schriften des Alten und Neuen Testamentes sowie zu den Apokryphen 1; Munich: Oskar Beck, 1891) 185–213.

Scholz, Anton

Commentar über das Buch "Judith" und über "Bel und Drache" (2nd ed.; Leipzig: Leo Wörl, 1898).

Cowley, Arthur E.

"The Book of Judith," in APOT 1:242–67.

Dimmler, Emil
  Tobias, Judith, Esther, Makkabäer (Munich: Gladback, 1922).

Miller, Athanasius
  Die Bücher Tobias, Judith und Esther (Die Heilige Schrift des Alten Testaments 4.3; Bonn: Peter Hanstein, 1940).

Soubigou, Louis
  "Judith: Traduit et commenté," in Louis Pirot and Albert Clamer, *La Sainte Bible* (Paris: Letouzey et Ané, 1952) 481–575.

Steinmann, Jean
  Lecture de Judith (Paris: Gabalda, 1953).

Bückers, Hermann
  Esdras, Nehemias, Tobias, Judith und Esther übersetzt und erklärt (Herders Bibelkommentar 4; Freiburg im Breisgau: Herder, 1954).

Grintz, Jehoshua M.
  The Book of Judith: A Reconstruction of the Original Hebrew Text with Introduction, Commentary, Appendices, and Indices (in Hebrew with English summary; Jerusalem: Bialik Institute, 1957).

Barucq, André
  Judith, Esther (2nd ed.; La Sainte Bible de Jerusalem 14; Paris: Cerf, 1959).

Priero, Giuseppe
  Giuditta (La Sacra Bibbia; Turin: Marietti, 1959).

Grzybek, Stanislaw, and Sylvester Baksik
  Ksiega Tobiasza; Ksiega Judyty; Ksiega Estery (Pismo Swiete Starego Testamentu 6; Lublin, 1963).

Stummer, Friedrich
  Tobias, Judith, Esther (Die Heilige Schrift des Alten Testaments in deutscher Übersetzung [Echter Bibel] 2; Würzburg: Echter Verlag, 1956; 4th ed. updated by Heinrich Groß, 1967).

Dumm, Demetrius R.
  "Tobit, Judith, Esther," in Raymond E. Brown, Joseph A. Fitzmyer, and Roland E. Murphy, eds., *The Jerome Biblical Commentary* (Englewood Cliffs, NJ: Prentice-Hall, 1968) 620–32.

Arenhoevel, D., A. Deissler, and A. Vögtle
  "Das Buch Judit," in *Jerusalemer Bibel* (Freiburg: Herder, 1969) 626–42.

Dancy, J. C.
  Judith (The Shorter Books of the Apocrypha; Cambridge: Cambridge University Press, 1972).

Enslin, Morton S., and Solomon Zeitlin
  The Book of Judith (Jewish Apocryphal Literature 7; Leiden: Brill, 1972).

Lamparter, Helmut
  "Das Buch Judith," in Helmut Lamparter, *Die Apokryphen* (2 vols.; Die Botschaft des Alten Testaments 25; Stuttgart: Calwer, 1972) 2:135–82.

Alonso Schökel, Luis
  Rut, Tobias, Judith, Ester (Los Libros Sagrados 8; Madrid: Ediciones Cristiandad, 1973).

Montague, George T.
  The Books of Esther and Judith (Pamphlet Bible Series 21; New York: Paulist Press, 1973).

Zenger, Erich
  "Das Buch Judit," in *Historische and legendärische Erzählungen* (JSHRZ 1.6; Gütersloh: Mohn, 1981).

Craghan, John
  Esther, Judith, Tobit, Jonah, Ruth (Old Testament Message 16; Wilmington, DE: Michael Glazier, 1982).

Moore, Carey A.
  Judith: A New Translation with Introduction and Commentary (AB 40B; Garden City, NY: Doubleday, 1985).

Nowell, Irene
  Jonah, Tobit, Judith (Collegeville Bible Commentary: Old Testament 25; Collegeville, MN: Liturgical Press, 1986).

Groß, Heinrich
  Tobit, Judit (Die Neue Echter Bibel: Altes Testament 19; Würzburg: Echter Verlag, 1987).

Haag, Ernst
  Das Buch Judit (Geistliche Schriftlesung 15; Dusseldorf: Patmos, 1995).

Lehnardt, Andreas
  "Das Buch Judit," in Andreas Lehnardt, *Bibliographie zu den Jüdischen Schriften aus hellenistisch-römischer Zeit* (JSHRZ 6.2; Gütersloh: Gütersloher Verlagshaus, 1999) 143–52.

Wills, Lawrence M.
  "Judith," in Leander E. Keck, ed., *The New Interpreter's Bible* (12 vols.; Nashville: Abingdon, 1999) 3:1073–1183.

Alonso Schökel, Luis
  "Judith," in James Luther Mays et al., eds., *The HarperCollins Bible Commentary* (San Francisco: HarperCollins, 2000) 732–41.

Vílchez Líndez, José
  Tobías y Judit (Nueva Biblia Española; Estella: Verbo Divino, 2000).

Otzen, Benedikt
  Tobit and Judith (Guides to the Apocrypha and Pseuepigrapha 11; Sheffield: Sheffield Academic Press, 2001).

Wolfe, Lisa M.
  Ruth, Esther, Song of Songs, and Judith (Eugene, OR: Cascade, 2011).

Gera, Deborah Levine
  Judith (Commentaries on Early Jewish Literature; Boston: de Gruyter, 2014).

Schmitz, Barbara, and Helmut Engel
  Judit (Herders theologischer Kommentar zum Alten Testament; Freiburg: Herder, 2014).

3. Books, Monographs and Articles
(Alphabetically by author and title)

[For a list of German works on Judith, see Edna Purdie, *The Story of Judith in German and English Literature* (Paris: Librairie Ancienne Honore Champien, 1927).]

Adelman, Rachel
> *The Female Ruse: Women's Deception and Divine Sanction in the Hebrew Bible* (Sheffield: Sheffield Phoenix, 2017).

Adler, Yonatan
> "Between Priestly Cult and Common Culture: The Material Evidence of Ritual Purity Observance in Early Roman Jerusalem Reassessed," *JAJ* 7 (2016) 228–48.

Idem
> "The Hellenistic Origins of Jewish Ritual Immersion," *JJS* 69 (2018) 1–21.

Aharoni, Yohanan, and Michael Avi-Yonah
> *Macmillan Bible Atlas* (New York: Macmillan, 1968).

Alonso Schökel, Luis
> *Narrative Structures in the Book of Judith* (Protocol of the Colloquies, Center for Hermeneutical Studies in Hellenistic and Modern Culture 12.17, March 1974; Berkeley: Center for Hermeneutical Studies, 1975).

Altheim, Franz, and Ruth Stiehl
> "Esther, Judith, und Daniel," in Franz Altheim and Ruth Stiehl, *Die aramäische Sprache unter den Achaemeniden* (2 vols.; Frankfurt am Main: Vittorio Kostermann, 1963) 1:195–213.

Anderson, Gary A.
> *A Time to Mourn, a Time to Dance: The Expression of Grief and Joy in Israelite Religion* (University Park: Pennsylvania State University Press, 1991).

Anderson, Jaynie
> "The Head-Hunter and the Head-Huntress in Italian Religious Portraiture," in Wendy James and Douglas H. Johnson, eds., *Vernacular Christianity: Essays in the Social Anthropology of Religion Presented to Godfrey Lienhardt* (New York: Lilian Barber Press, 1988) 60–69.

Eadem
> *Judith* (Paris: Regard, 1997).

Apostolos-Cappadona, Diane
> "'The Lord Has Struck Him Down by the Hand of a Woman!' Images of Judith," in Diane Apostolos-Cappadona and Doug Adams, eds., *Art as Religious Studies* (New York: Crossroad, 1987) 81–97.

Eadem
> *Martha Graham and the Quest for the Feminine in Eve, Lilith, and Judith: Dance as Religious Studies* (New York: Crossroad, 1990).

Archer, Léonie J.
> *Her Price Is Beyond Rubies: The Jewish Woman in Graeco-Roman Palestine* (JSOTSup 60; Sheffield: Sheffield Academic Press, 1990).

Astell, Ann W.
> "Holofernes's Head: *Tacen* and Teaching in the Old English *Judith*," *Anglo-Saxon England* 18 (1989) 117–33.

Auneau, Joseph
> "Le livre de Judith," in Joseph Auneau, *Les Psaumes et les autres écrits* (Paris: Desclée, 1990) 367–79.

Bach, Alice
> *Women, Seduction, and Betrayal in Biblical Narrative* (New York: Cambridge University Press, 1997).

Baïche, André, ed.
> *La Judit* (Toulouse: Association des publications de la faculté des lettres et sciences humaines de Toulouse, 1971).

Bailey, Elizabeth
> "Judith, Jael, and Humilitas in the *Speculum Virginum*," in Kevin R. Brine, Elena Ciletti, and Henriki Lähnemann, eds., *The Sword of Judith: Judith Studies across the Disciplines* (Cambridge: OpenBook, 2010) 275–90.

Baker, Cynthia M.
> *Jew* (Key Words in Jewish Studies 8; New Brunswick, NJ: Rutgers University Press, 2017).

Bakhtin, Mikhail
> *The Dialogic Imagination: Four Essays* (University of Texas Press Slavic Series 1; Austin: University of Texas Press, 1981).

Idem
> *Rabelais and His World* (Cambridge, MA: MIT Press, 1968).

Bal, Mieke, ed.
> *The Artemisia Files: Artemisia Gentileschi for Feminists and Other Thinking People* (Chicago: University of Chicago Press, 2005).

Eadem
> *Death and Dissymmetry: The Politics of Coherence in the Book of Judges* (Chicago: University of Chicago Press, 1988).

Eadem
> "Head Hunting: 'Judith' on the Cutting Edge of Knowledge," *JSOT* 63 (1994) 3–34.

Eadem
> *Narratology: Introduction to the Theory of Narrative* (Toronto: University of Toronto Press, 1985).

Eadem
> *On Story-Telling: Essays in Narratology* (Foundations and Facets: Literary Facets; Sonoma, CA: Polebridge, 1991).

Eadem
> *Quoting Caravaggio: Contemporary Art, Preposterous History* (Chicago: University of Chicago Press, 1999).

Ballentine, Debra Scoggins
> *The Conflict Myth and the Biblical Tradition* (New York: Oxford University Press, 2015).

Baltzer, Otto
> *Judith in der deutschen Literatur* (Berlin and Leipzig: de Gruyter, 1930).

Barag, Dan
> "Jdt 12,11: A Coin of Bagoas with a Representation of God as a Winged Wheel" [Hebrew], *Qadmoniot* 25 (1992) 97–100.

Baslez, Marie-Françoise
> "Polémologie et histoire dan le livre de Judith," *RB* 111 (2004) 362–76.

442

Bayer, B.

"The Book of Judith in the Arts," *Encyclopedia Judaica* (16 vols.; New York: Macmillan, 1971–72) 10:451–59.

Beentjes, Pancratius C.

"Bethulia Crying, Judith Praying: Context and Content of Prayers in the Book of Judith," in Renate Egger-Wenzel and Jeremy Corley, eds., *Prayer from Tobit to Qumran: Inaugural Conference of the ISDCL at Salzburg, Austria, 5–9 July 2003* (Deuterocanonical and Cognate Literature Yearbook 2004; Berlin: de Gruyter, 2004) 231–54.

Belanoff, Patricia A.

"Judith: Sacred and Secular Heroine," in Helen Damico and John Leyerle, eds., *Heroic Poetry in the Anglo-Saxon Period: Studies in Honor of Jess B. Bessinger Jr.* (Studies in Medieval Culture 32; Kalamazoo, MI: Medieval Institute Publications, 1993) 247–64.

Bellis, Alice Ogden

Helpmates, Harlots, and Heroines: Women's Stories in the Hebrew Bible (Louisville: Westminster John Knox, 1994).

Ben-Eliyahu, Eyal

Between Borders: The Boundaries of Eretz-Israel in the Consciousness of the Jewish People in the Time of the Second Temple and in the Mishnah and Talmud Period [Hebrew] (Jerusalem: Yad Ben-Zvi, 2013).

Bentzen, Aage

"Der Hedammu-Mythus, das Juditbuch, und ähnliches," *Archiv Orientální* 18 (1950) 1–2.

Berlin, Andrea

"Between Large Forces: Palestine in the Hellenistic Period," *BA* 60 (1997) 2–57.

Eadem

"Manifest Identity: From *Ioudaios* to Jew," in Rainer Albertz, ed., *Between Cooperation and Hostility: Multiple Identities in Ancient Judaism and the Interaction with Foreign Powers* (JAJSup 11; Göttingen: Vandenhoeck & Ruprecht, 2013) 151–75.

Bernardini, Paolo

"Judith in the Italian Unification Process, 1800–1900," in Kevin R. Brine, Elena Ciletti, and Henriki Lähnemann, eds., *The Sword of Judith: Judith Studies across the Disciplines* (Cambridge: OpenBook, 2010) 397–409.

Berthelot, Katell

"Hellenization and Jewish Identity in the Deuterocanonical Literature: A Response to Ben Wright," in Géza G. Xeravits, József Zsengellér, and Xavér Szabó, eds., *Canonicity, Setting, Wisdom in the Deuterocanonicals: Papers of the Jubilee Meeting of the International Conference on the Deuterocanonical Books* (DCLS 22; Berlin: de Gruyter, 2014) 69–88.

Białostocki, Jan

"Judith: Story, Image, and Symbol: Giorgione's Painting in the Evolution of the Theme," in *The Message of Images: Studies in the History of Art* (Bibliotheca artibus et historiae; Vienna: Irsa, 1988).

Biolek, Anton

"Die Ansicht des christlichen Altertums über dem literarischen Charakter des Buches Judith," *Weidenauer Studien* 4 (1911) 335–68.

Bird, Michael F.

"'Waiting for His Deliverance': The Story of Salvation in Judith," in Daniel M. Gurtner, ed., *This World and the World to Come: Soteriology in Early Judaism* (LSTS 74; London: Bloomsbury T&T Clark, 2011).

Birnbaum, Elisabeth

"Dimensionen des Juditbuches und ihre Bedeutung für die neuzeitliche Rezeption," in Irmtraud Fischer, ed., *Macht–Gewalt–Krieg im Alten Testament: Gesellschaftliche Problematik und das Problem ihrer Präsentation* (Basel: Herder, 2013) 198–224.

Eadem

Das Juditbuch im Wien des 17. und 18. Jahrhunderts: Exegese–Predigt–Musik–Theater–Bildende Kunst (Frankfurt am Main: Lang, 2009).

Bloch-Smith, Elizabeth

"Israelite Ethnicity in Iron I: Archaeology Preserves What Is Remembered and What Is Forgotten in Israel's History," *JBL* 122 (2003) 401–25.

Bogaert, Pierre-Maurice

"Le calendrier du livre de Judith et la fête de Hanukka," *RTL* 15 (1984) 67–72.

Idem

"Un emprunt au judaisme dans la tradition médiévale de l'histoire de Judith en langue d'oil," *RTL* 31 (2000) 344–61.

Idem

"Le 'rouleau' de Judith: Hanukka et le vingt-quatre du mois d'Ab," in P. Gignoux, ed., *La commémoration* (Louvain and Paris: Peeters, 1988) 163–71.

Idem

"Tobie, Esther et Judith dans la stichométrie de Mommsen," in Pierre Cockshaw, Monique-Cécile Garand, and Pierre Jodogne, eds., *Miscellanea codicologica F. Masai: dicata MCMLXXIX* (2 vols.; Publications de Scriptorium 8; Ghent: E. Story-Scientia, 1979) 2:545–50.

Bohn, Babette

"Death, Dispassion, and the Female Hero: Artemisia Gentileschi's *Jael and Sisera*," in Mieke Bal, ed., *The Artemisia Files: Artemisia Gentileschi for Feminists and Other Thinking People* (Chicago: University of Chicago Press, 2005) 107–28.

Bolle, Helena M., and Stephen R. Llewelyn

"Intersectionality, Gender Liminality and Ben Sira's Attitude to the Eunuch," *VT* 67 (2017) 546–69.

Bons, Eberhard
"The Meanings of the Noun *skandalon* in the Book of Judith," in Wolfgang Kraus, Michaël van der Meer, and Martin Meiser, eds., *XV Congress of the International Organization for Septuagint and Cognate Studies* (SCS 64; Atlanta: SBL Press, 2016) 473–81.

Börner-Klein, Dagmar
Gefährdete Braut und schöne Witwe: Hebräische Judit-Geschichten (Wiesbaden: Marix Verlag, 2007).

Boyd-Taylor, Cameron
"The Semantics of Biblical Language Redux," in Robert J. Hiebert, ed., *"Translation Is Required": The Septuagint in Retrospect and Prospect* (SCS 56; Atlanta: Society of Biblical Literature, 2010).

Bowra, C. M.
Heroic Poetry (London: Macmillan, 1952).

Bradley, S. A. J.
Anglo-Saxon Poetry (London: Dent, 1995).

Branch, Robin, and Pierre Jordaan
"The Significance of Secondary Characters in Susanna, Judith, and the Additions to Esther in the Septuagint," *Acta Patristica et Byzantina* 20 (2009) 389–416.

Branham, Joan
"Penetrating the Sacred: Breaches and Barriers in the Jerusalem Temple," in Sharon E. J. Gerstel, ed., *Thresholds of the Sacred: Architectural, Art Historical, Liturgical, and Theological Perspectives on Religious Screens, East and West* (Washington, DC: Dumbarton Oaks Research Library; distributed by Harvard University Press, 2006) 6–24.

Braun, Martin
History and Romance in Graeco-Oriental Literature (New York: Garland, 1987).

Bremer, M.
Judit: La refundacion del pueblo desde un Dios casero (Quito, Ecuador: Parroquia 'Cristo Resucitado', 1992).

Bremmer, Jan
"Myth and Ritual in Greek Human Sacrifice: Lykaon, Polyxena and the Case of the Rhodian Criminal," in Jan Bremmer, ed., *The Strange World of Human Sacrifice* (Studies in the History and Anthropology of Religion 1; Leuven: Peeters, 2007) 55–79.

Bremmer, Jan, and Lourens van den Bosch, eds.
Between Poverty and the Pyre: Moments in the History of Widowhood (London: Routledge, 1995).

Brenner, Athalya, ed.
A Feminist Companion to Esther–Judith–Susanna (Feminist Companion to the Bible 7; Sheffield: Sheffield Academic Press, 1995).

Brenner-Idan, Athalya
"Clothing Seduces: Did You Think It Was Naked Flesh That Did It?," in Athalya Brenner-Idan and Helen Efthimiadis-Keith, eds., *A Feminist Companion to Tobit and Judith* (Feminist Companion to the

Bible [Second Series]; London: Bloomsbury T&T Clark, 2015) 212–25.

Brenner-Idan, Athalya, and Helen Efthimiadis-Keith, eds.
A Feminist Companion to Tobit and Judith (Feminist Companion to the Bible [Second Series]; London: Bloomsbury T&T Clark, 2015).

Brenner-Idan, Athalya, and Fokkelien van Dijk-Hemmes
On Gendering Texts: Female and Male Voices in the Hebrew Bible (Biblical Interpretation Series 1; Leiden: Brill, 1993).

Brighton, Mark
"A Comparison of Literary Conventions in Judith with the Ancient Greek Novels," in Dean O. Wenthe, Paul L. Schrieber, and Lee A. Maxwell, eds., *"Hear the Word of Yahweh": Essays on Scripture and Archaeology in Honor of Horace D. Hummel* (Saint Louis: Concordia, 2002) 163–71.

Brine, Kevin R., Elena Ciletti, and Henrike Lähnemann, eds.
The Sword of Judith: Judith Studies across the Disciplines (Cambridge: OpenBook, 2010).

Brooten, Bernadette J.
Love between Women: Early Christian Responses to Female Homoeroticism (Chicago Series on Sexuality, History, and Society; Chicago: University of Chicago Press, 1996).

Brunner, Gottfried
Der Nabuchodonosor des Buches Judith: Beitrag zur Geschichte Israels nach dem Exil und der ersten Regierungsjahres Darius I (2nd ed.; Berlin: Rudolph Pfau, 1959).

Bruns, Edgar J.
"The Genealogy of Judith," *CBQ* 18 (1956) 19–22.

Idem
"Judith or Jael?," *CBQ* 16 (1954) 12–14.

Burstein, Stanley M.
"Cleitarchus in Jerusalem: A Note on the *Book of Judith*," in Frances B. Tichenor and Richard F. Morton Jr., eds., *The Eye Expanded: Life and the Arts in Greco-Roman Antiquity* (Berkeley: Unversity of California Press, 1999) 105–12.

Callaghan, Leslie Abend
"Ambiguity and Appropriation: The Story of Judith in Medieval Narrative and Iconographic Tradition," in Francesca Canadé Sautman, Diana Conchado, and Giuseppe di Scipio, eds., *Telling Tales: Medieval Narratives and the Folk Tradition* (New York: St. Martin's, 1998) 79–99.

Calmet, Augustin
Commentaire littéral sur tous les livres de l'Ancien et du Nouveau Testament, vol. 8: *Les deux livres d'Esdras, Tobie, Judith et Ésther* (Paris: Emery, 1722).

Idem
Commentarius literalis in omnes libros Veteris Testamenti, vol. 4 (Wirceburgi: Riener, 1789–93).

Camp, Claudia V.
Wisdom and the Feminine in the Book of Proverbs (Bible and Literature Series 11; Sheffield: Almond, 1985).

Caponigro, Mark Stephen
"Judith, Holding the Tale of Herodotus," in James C. VanderKam, ed., *"No One Spoke Ill of Her": Essays on Judith* (EJL 2; Atlanta: Scholars Press, 1992) 47–59.

Carpanè, Lorenzo
Da Giuditta a Giuditta: L'epopea dell'eroina sacra nel Barocco (Alessandria: Edizioni dell'Orso, 2006).

Carroll, Michael P.
"Myth, Methodology and Transformation in the Old Testament: The Stories of Esther, Judith, and Susanna," *Studies in Religion* 12 (1983) 301–12.

Cartusiani, D. Dionysii [Denis the Carthusian]
"Enarratio in Librum Judith," in Cartusiani, *Opera Omnia* (Monstrolii: Cartusiae Sanctae Mariae de Pratis, 1898).

Cazelles, Henri A. "Le personnage d'Achior dans le livre de Judith," *RSR* 39 (1951) 125–37, 324–27.

Chesnutt, Randall D., and Judith Newman
"Prayers in the Apocrypha and Pseudepigrapha," in Mark C. Kiley, ed., *Prayer from Alexander to Constantine: A Critical Anthology* (London and New York: Routledge, 1997) 38–42.

Chickering, Howell
"Poetic Exuberance in Old English *Judith*," *Studies in Philology* 106 (2009) 119–36.

Christiansen, Ellen Juhl
"Judith: Defender of Israel—Preserver of the Temple," in Géza Xeravits, ed., *A Pious Seductress: Studies in the Book of Judith* (DCLS 14; Berlin: de Gruyter, 2012) 70–84.

Christiansen, Keith, and Judith W. Mann
Orazio and Artemisia Gentileschi (New Haven: Yale University Press, 2001).

Chyutin, Michael
Tendentious Hagiographies: Jewish Propagandist Fiction BCE (LSTS 77; London: T&T Clark, 2011).

Ciletti, Elena
"Patriarchal Ideology in the Renaissance Iconography of Judith," in Marilyn Migiel and Juliana Schiesari, eds., *Refiguring Woman: Perspectives on Gender and the Italian Renaissance* (Ithaca, NY: Cornell University Press, 1991) 35–70.

Ciletti, Elena, and Henrike Lähnemann
"Judith in the Christian Tradition," in Kevin R. Brine, Elena Ciletti, and Henriki Lähnemann, eds., *The Sword of Judith: Judith Studies across the Disciplines* (Cambridge: OpenBook, 2010) 41–65.

Clanton, Dan W., Jr.
Daring, Disreputable and Devout: Interpreting the Hebrew Bible's Women in the Arts and Music (New York: T&T Clark, 2009).

Clayton, Mary
"Ælfric's *Judith:* Manipulative or Manipulated?" *Anglo-Saxon England* 23 (1994) 215–27.

Coats, Catharine Randall
"Holofernes' Textual Impotence: Discourse vs. Representation in Du Bartas' 'La Judit,'" in Raymond-Jean Frontain and Jan Wojcik, eds., *Old Testament Women in Western Literature* (Conway, AR: University of Central Arkansas Press, 1991) 108–26.

Coffin, Tristram Potter
The Female Hero in Folklore and Legend (New York: Seabury Press, 1975).

Cohen, Shaye J. D.
The Beginnings of Jewishness: Boundaries, Varieties, Uncertainties (HCS 31; Berkeley: University of California Press, 1999).

Colunga, Albert L.
"El género literario de Judit," *Ciencia Tomista* 74 (1948) 94–126.

Condamin, Albert
"Un Pseudonyme de Samarie dans le livre de Judith," *RSR* 14 (1910) 570–71.

Cooper, Tracey-Anne
"Judith in Late Anglo-Saxon England," in Kevin R. Brine, Elena Ciletti, and Henrike Lähnemann, eds., *The Sword of Judith: Judith Studies across the Disciplines* (Cambridge: OpenBook, 2010) 169–96.

Corley, Jeremy
"Divine Sovereignty and Power in the High-Priestly Prayer of 3 Macc 2:1–20," in Renate Egger-Wenzel and Jeremy Corley, eds., *Prayer from Tobit to Qumran: Inaugural Conference of the ISDCL at Salzburg, Austria, 5–9 July 2003* (Deuterocanonical and Cognate Literature Yearbook 2004; Berlin: de Gruyter, 2004) 359–86.

Idem
"Imitation of Septuagintal Narrative and Greek Historiography in the Portrait of Holofernes," in Géza Xeravits, ed., *A Pious Seductress: Studies in the Book of Judith* (DCLS 14; Berlin: de Gruyter, 2012) 27–34.

Idem
"Judith," in James K. Aitken, ed., *T&T Clark Companion to the Septuagint* (London and New York: T&T Clark, 2015) 222–36.

Idem
"Judith: An Unconventional Heroine," *Scripture Bulletin* 31 (2001) 70–85.

Cornelius, E. M.
"An Interpretation of the Rhetorical Power of the Dual Character of Judith," *Theologia Viatorum: Journal for Theology and Religion in Africa* 33 (2009) 242–60.

Craghan, John F.
"Esther, Judith, and Ruth: Paradigms for Human Liberation," *BTB* 12 (1982) 11–19.

Idem
"Judith Revisited," *BTB* 12 (1982) 50–53.

Craven, Toni
Artistry and Faith in the Book of Judith (SBLDS 70; Chico, CA: Scholars Press, 1983).

Eadem
"Artistry and Faith in the Book of Judith," *Semeia* 8 (1977) 75–101.

Eadem
"The Book of Judith in the Context of Twentieth-Century Studies of the Apocryphal/Deutero-canonical Books," *CurBR* 1 (2003) 187–229.

Eadem
"Convention and Tradition in the Book of Judith," *Semeia* 28 (1983) 49–61.

Eadem
"'From Where Will My Help Come?' Women and Prayer in the Apocryphal/Deuterocanoni-cal Books," in M. Patrick Graham et al., eds., *Worship and the Hebrew Bible: Essays in Honor of John T. Willis* (JSOTSup 284; Sheffield: Sheffield Academic Press, 1999) 95–109.

Eadem
"Is That Fearfully Funny? Some Instances from the Apocryphal/Deuteronocanical Books," in Athalya Brenner, ed., *Are We Amused? Humour about Women in the Biblical Worlds* (JSOTSup 383; New York: T&T Clark International, 2003) 65–78.

Eadem
"Judith," in B. W. Anderson, ed., *The Books of the Bible*, vol. 2 (New York: Charles Scribner's Sons, 1989) 43–49.

Eadem
"Judith," in Raymond E. Brown, Joseph A. Fitzmyer, and Roland E. Murphy, eds., *The New Jerome Biblical Commentary* (Englewood Cliffs, NJ: Prentice-Hall, 1990) 572–75.

Eadem
"Judith," in G. Chapman, ed., *The New Jerome Bible Handbook* (London: Cassell, Petter, Galpin, 1992) 188–90.

Eadem
"Judith 2" and "Jdt 4.10–12," etc., in Toni Craven, Carol Meyers, and Ross Kraemer, eds., *Women in Scripture: A Dictionary of Named and Unnamed Women in the Hebrew Bible, the Apocryphal/Deuterocanonical Books, and the New Testament* (Grand Rapids: Eerdmans, 2001) 104–6, 360–64.

Eadem
"Judith Prays for Help: Judith 9.1–14," in Mark C. Kiley, ed., *Prayer from Alexander to Constantine: A Critical Anthology* (London and New York: Routledge, 1997) 59–64.

Eadem
"Tradition and Convention in the Book of Judith," *Semeia* 28 (1983) 49–61.

Eadem
"Women as Teachers of Torah," in Lamontte M. Luker, ed., *Passion, Vitality, and Foment: The Dynamics of Second Temple Judaism* (Harrisburg, PA: Trinity Press International, 2001) 275–89.

Eadem
"Women Who Lied for the Faith," in Douglas A. Knight and Peter J. Paris, eds., *Justice and the Holy:*

Essays in Honor of Walter Harrelson (Scholars Press Homage Series 12; Atlanta: Scholars Press, 1989) 35–49.

Crawford, Sidnie White
"4QTales of the Persian Court (4Q550A–E) and Its Relation to Biblical Royal Courtier Tales, Especially Esther, Daniel, and Joseph," in Edward D. Herbert and Emanuel Tov, eds., *The Bible as Book: The Hebrew Bible and the Judaean Desert Discoveries* (London: Oak Knoll, 2002) 121–37.

Eadem
"Esther and Judith: Contrasts in Character," in Sidnie White Crawford and Leonard J. Greenspoon, eds., *The Book of Esther in Modern Research* (JSOTSup 380; London: T&T Clark, 2003) 60–76.

Eadem
"Esther Not Judith: Why One Made It and the Other Didn't," *Bible Review* 18 (2002) 22–31, 45.

Eadem [as Sidnie Ann White]
"In the Steps of Jael and Deborah: Judith as Heroine," in James C. VanderKam, ed., *"No One Spoke Ill of Her": Essays on Judith* (EJL 2; Atlanta: Scholars Press, 1992) 5–16.

Cummings, Robert
"The Aestheticization of Tyrannicide: Du Bartas's *La Judit*," in Kevin R. Brine, Elena Ciletti, and Henrike Lähnemann, eds., *The Sword of Judith: Judith Studies across the Disciplines* (Cambridge: OpenBook, 2010) 227–38.

Dahbany-Miraglia, Dina
"Was Judith an *Eshet-Chayil*?," *Women in Judaism* 6 (2009) 1–10.

Dalley, Stephanie
Esther's Revenge at Susa: From Sennacherib to Ahasu-erus (Oxford: Oxford University Press, 2007).

Daube, David
"Judith," in Calum M. Carmichael, ed., *Essays on Law and Religion: The Berkeley and Oxford Symposia in Honour of David Daube* (Studies in Comparative Legal History; Berkeley: University of California Press, 1993) 31–63.

Day, Linda
"Faith, Character and Perspective in Judith," *JSOT* 95 (2001) 71–93.

Eadem
"Power, Otherness, and Gender in the Biblical Short Stories," *Horizons in Biblical Theology* 20 (1998) 109–27.

Deines, Roland
Jüdische Steingefässe und pharisäische Frömmigkeit: Ein archäologisch-historischer Beitrag zum Verständnis von Joh 2.6 und der jüdischen Reinheitshalacha zur Zeit Jesu (WUNT 2/52; Tübingen: Mohr, 1993).

De Jong, Mary
"God's Women: Victorian American Readings of Old Testament Heroines," in Raymond-Jean Frontain and Jan Wojcik, eds., *Old Testament*

Women in Western Literature (Conway, AR: University of Central Arkansas Press, 1991) 238–60.

Delcor, Mathias
"Le livre de Judith et l'époque grecque," *Klio* 49 (1967) 151–79.

DelSignore, Gabriella
"Giuditta e Achior: Il future nelle mani dei deboli," *Horeb* 7 (1998) 36–42.

Dennis the Carthusian. *See* Cartusiani, D. Dionysii

Deprez, A.
"Le livre de Judith," *Évangile* 47 (1962) 5–69.

deSilva, David A.
"'Hear Me Also, a Widow,'" in David A. deSilva, ed., *Introducing the Apocrypha: Message, Context, and Significance* (Grand Rapids: Baker, 2002) 85–109.

Idem
"Judith the Heroine? Lies, Seduction, and Murder in Cultural Perspective," *BTB* 36 (2006) 55–61.

Dijkstra, Bram
Idols of Perversity: Fantasies of Feminine Evil in Fin-de-Siècle Culture (New York: Oxford University Press, 1986).

Di Lella, Alexander A.
"Women in the Wisdom of Ben Sira and the Book of Judith: A Study in Contrasts and Reversals," in J. A. Emerton, ed., *Congress Volume: Paris 1992* (VTSup 61; Leiden: Brill, 1995) 39–52.

Dimant, Devorah
"Use and Interpretation of Mikra in the Apocrypha and Pseudepigrapha," in Martin Jan Mulder and Harry Sysling, eds., *Mikra: Text, Translation, Reading, and Interpretation of the Hebrew Bible in Ancient Judaism and Early Christianity* (Philadelphia: Fortress, 1990) 379–419.

Dixon, Annette, ed.
Women Who Ruled: Queens, Goddesses, Amazons in Renaissance and Baroque Art (London: Merrell, 2002).

Dombkowski Hopkins, Denise
"Judith," in Carole A. Newsom and Sharon H. Ringe, eds., *Women's Bible Commentary* (expanded ed.; Louisville: Westminster John Knox, 1998) 279–85.

Doran, Robert
"Judith," in Robert A. Kraft and George W. E. Nickelsburg, eds., *Early Judaism and Its Modern Interpreters* (2 vols.; Bible and Its Modern Interpreters 2; Atlanta: Scholars Press, 1986) 2:302–5.

Idem
Temple Propaganda: The Purpose and Character of 2 Maccabees (CBQMS 12; Washington, DC: Catholic Biblical Association of America, 1981).

Dreißen, Joseph
"Das Buch Judith in heilsgeschichtlicher Schau," *Katechetische Blätter* 77 (1957) 324–327.

Dubarle, A.-M.
"L'Authenticité des textes hébreux de Judith," *Bib* 50 (1969) 187–211.

Idem
Judith: Formes et sens des diverses traditions (2 vols.; AnBib 24; Rome: Institut biblique pontifical, 1966).

Idem "La mention de 'Judith' dans la littérature ancienne, juive et chrétienne," *RB* 66 (1959): 514–549.

Idem
"Rectification: Sur un texte hébreu de Judith," *VT* 11 (1961) 86–87.

Idem
"Les textes divers du livre du Judith : A propos d'un ouvrage recent," *VT* 8 (1958) 344–73.

Idem
"Les textes hébreux de Judith: Un nouveau signe d'originalité," *Bib* 56 (1975) 503–11.

Idem
"Les textes hébreux de Judith et les étapes da la formation du livre," *Bib* 70 (1989) 255–66.

Dube, Musa
"Jumping the Fire with Judith: Postcolonial Feminist Hermeneutics of Liberation," in Silvia Schroer and Sophia Bietenhard, eds., *Feminist Interpretation of the Bible and the Hermeneutics of Liberation* (JSOTSup 374; London: Sheffield Academic Press, 2003) 60–76.

Eadem
"Rahab Says Hello to Judith: A Decolonizing Feminist Reading," in Fernando F. Segovia, ed., *Toward a New Heaven and a New Earth: Essays in Honor of Elisabeth Schüssler Fiorenza* (Maryknoll, NY: Orbis Books, 2003) 54–72.

Eadem
"Rehabilitating Judith," in R. S. Sugirtharajah, ed., *The Postcolonial Bible Reader* (Malden, MA: Blackwell, 2006) 142–58.

Duncan, James A.
"A Hebrew Political Romance," *Biblical World* n.s. 3 (1894) 429–34.

Duran, Nicole
"Having Men for Dinner: Deadly Banquets and Biblical Women," *BTB* 35 (2005) 117–24.

Durzak, Manfred
"Hebbels 'Judith': Deutungsprobleme und Deutung," *Hebbel Jahrbuch* 32 (1971–72) 36–62.

Eckhardt, Benedikt
"Reclaiming Tradition: The Book of Judith and Hasmonean Politics," *JSP* 18 (2009) 243–63.

Efthimiadis-Keith, Helen
"The Dream of Judith: A Jungian Perspective," *Journal of Northwest Semitic Languages* 25 (1999) 153–71.

Eadem
The Enemy Is Within: A Jungian Psychoanalytic Approach to the Book of Judith (Biblical Interpretation Series 67; Boston: Brill, 2004).

Eadem

"Genealogy, Retribution and Identity: Re-Interpreting the Cause of Suffering in the Book of Judith," *Old Testament Essays* 27 (2014) 860–78.

Eadem

"Judith: Lorena Bobit of Yesteryear? A Psychoanalytic Perspective on the Book of Judith according to the Castration Complex," *Scriptura* 70 (1999) 211–28.

Eadem

"Judith, Feminist Ethics and Feminist Biblical/Old Testament Interpretation," *Journal of Theology for Southern Africa* 138 (2010) 91–111.

Eadem

"Text and Interpretation: Gender and Violence in the Book of Judith; Scholarly Commentary and the Visual Arts from the Renaissance Onward," *Old Testament Essays* 15 (2002) 64–84.

Egger, Brigitte Maria

"Women in the Greek Novel: Constructing the Feminine" (Ph.D. diss., University of California, Irvine, 1990).

Egger-Wenzel, Renate

"Judith's Path from Grief to Joy—From Sackcloth to Festive Attire," in Renate Egger-Wenzel and Jeremy Corley, eds., *Emotions from Ben Sira to Paul* (Deuterocanonical and Cognate Literature Yearbook 2011; Berlin: de Gruyter, 2012) 189–224.

Eadem

"Judits weise Klugheit zur Rettung Betulias," in Renate Egger-Wenzel, Karin Schöpflin, and Johannes Friedrich Diehl, eds., *Weisheit als Lebensgrundlage: Festschrift für Friedrich V. Reiterer zum 65. Geburtstag* (DCLS 15; Berlin: de Gruyter, 2013) 65–94.

Eadem

"Mirjam, Debora und Judit: Eine Prophetinnentradition?," in Hermann Lichtenberger und Ulrike Mittmann-Richert, eds., *Biblical Figures in Deuterocanonical and Cognate Literature* (Deuterocanonical and Cognate Literature Yearbook 2008; Berlin: de Gruyter, 2009) 95–122.

Eichhorn, Johann Gottfried

"Ueber das Buch Judith," in Johann Gottfried Eichhorn, *Einleitung in die Apokryphischen Schriften des Alten Testaments* (Leipzig: Weidmann, 1795) 291–334.

Elder, Linda Bennett

"Judith," in Elisabeth Schüssler-Fiorenza, ed., *Searching the Scriptures*, vol. 2: *A Feminist Commentary* (New York: Crossroad, 1997) 455–69.

Eadem

"Judith's *Sophia* and *Synesis*: Educated Jewish Women in the Late Second Temple Period," in Linda Bennett Elder, David L. Barr, and Elizabeth Struthers Malbon, eds., *Biblical and Humane: A Festschrift for John F. Priest* (Scholars Press Homage Series 20; Atlanta: Scholars Press, 1996) 53–70.

Eadem

"Virgins, Viragos and Virtuo(u)si Among Judiths in Opera and Oratorio," *JSOT* 92 (2001): 91–119.

Engel, Helmut

"Das Buch Judith," in Erich Zenger, ed., *Einleitung in das Alte Testament* (Stuttgart: Kohlhammer, 1998) 256–66.

Idem

"'Der HERR ist ein Gott, der die Kriege zerschlächt': Zur Frage der griechischen Originalsprache und der Struktur des Buches Judit," in Klaus-Dietrich Schunk and Matthias Augustin, eds., *Goldene Äpfel in silbernen Schalen: Collected Communications to the XIIIth Congress of the International Organization for the Study of the Old Testament, Leuven 1989* (BEATAJ 20; Frankfurt am Main: Lang, 1992) 155–68.

England, Emma

"Violent Superwomen: Super Heroes or Super Villains? Judith, Wonder Woman and Lynndie England," in Athalya Brenner-Idan and Helen Efthimiadis-Keith, eds., *A Feminist Companion to Tobit and Judith* (Feminist Companion to the Bible [Second Series]; London: Bloomsbury T&T Clark, 2015) 242–58.

Eskenazi, Tamara Cohn

In an Age of Prose: A Literary Approach to Ezra-Nehemiah (SBLMS 36; Atlanta: Scholars Press, 1988).

Eadem

"Out from the Shadows: Biblical Women in the Postexilic Era," *JSOT* 54 (1992) 25–43.

Esler, Philip F.

"'By the Hand of a Woman': Culture, Story and Theology in the Book of Judith," in John J. Pilch, ed., *Social Scientific Models for Interpreting the Bible: Essays by the Context Group in Honor of Bruce J. Malina* (Biblical Interpretation Series 53; Leiden: Brill, 2001) 34–44.

Idem

"Ludic History in the Book of Judith: The Reinvention of Israelite Identity?," *BibInt* 10 (2002) 107–43.

Idem

Sex, Wives, and Warriors: Reading Biblical Narrative with Its Ancient Audience (Eugene, OR: Wipf & Stock, 2011).

Exum, J. Cheryl, and Ela Nutu, eds.

Between the Text and the Canvas: The Bible and Art in Dialogue (Bible in the Modern World 13; Sheffield: Sheffield Phoenix, 2007).

Eynde, Sabine van den

"Crying to God: Prayer and Plot in the Book of Judith," *Bib* 85 (2004) 217–31.

Fischer, Henry

Nur Mut Judit: Biblische Zumutungen (Hildesheim: Bernward, 1985).

Fischer, Irmtraud
"Gestalten als politische Programme in der europäischen Malerei und Plastik," in Erich Zenger, ed., *Lebendige Welt der Bibel: Entdeckungsreise in das Alte Testament* (Freiburg: Herder, 1997) 34–44.

Fischer, Irmtraud, and Bernd Obermayer
"Die Kriegstheologie des Juditbuches als Kondensat alttestamentlicher Sichtweisen des Krieges," in Ulrich Dahmen and Johannes Schnocks, eds., *Juda und Jerusalem in der Seleukidenzeit: Herrschaft, Widerstand, Identität; Festschrift für Heinz-Josef Fabry* (BBB 159; Göttingen: V&R Unipress, 2010) 227–42.

Fitz-Gerald, J. D.
"La historia de Judit y Holofernes en la literatura espanola," *Hispania* 14 (1931) 193–96.

Flesher, LeAnn Snow
"The Use of Female Imagery and Lamentation in the Book of Judith: Penitential Prayer or Petition for Obligatory Action?," in Mark J. Boda, Daniel K. Falk, and Rodney A. Werline, eds., *Seeking the Favor of God*, vol. 2: *The Development of Penitential Prayer in Second Temple Judaism* (EJL 22; Atlanta: Society of Biblical Literature, 2007) 83–104.

Foucault, Michel
The History of Sexuality, vol. 3: *Care of the Self* (New York: Pantheon, 1986).

Fowler, Alastair
Renaissance Realism: Narrative Images in Literature and Art (Oxford: Oxford University Press, 2003).

Friedländer, Max J., and Jakob Rosenberg
The Paintings of Lucas Carnach (rev. ed.; London: Southeby Parke Bernet, 1978).

Friedman, Mira
"Metamorphoses of Judith," *Jewish Art* 12–13 (1986–87) 225–46.

Fritzsche, Otto F.
"Judith," in Daniel Schenkel, ed., *Bibel-Lexikon* (5 vols.; Leipzig: Brockhaus, 1869–75) 3:445–52.

Frye, Northrop
Anatomy of Criticism (Princeton, NJ: Princeton University Press, 1957).

Fuchsberger, Franziska
Die "De-Mut" Judits: Eine Frau zwischen Gottesfurcht und Eigenständigkeit im Wandel der Epochen (Saarbrücken: AV Akademikerverlag, 2012).

Fusillo, Massimo
"Modern Critical Theories and the Ancient Novel," in Gareth Schmeling, ed., *Novel in the Ancient World* (rev. ed.; Boston: Brill Academic, 2003) 277–305.

Gallagher, Edmond L.
"Why Did Jerome Translate Tobit and Judith?," *HTR* 108 (2015) 356–75.

Gamberoni, Johann
Die Auslegung des Buches Tobias in der griechisch-lateinischen Kirche der Antike und der Christenheit des Westens bis zum 1600 (Munich: Kösel, 1969).

Gardner, Anne E.
"The Song of Praise in Judith 16:2–17 (LXX 16:1–17)," *HeyJ* 29 (1989) 413–22.

Garrard, Mary
Artemisia Gentileschi: The Image of the Female Hero in Italian Baroque Art (Princeton, NJ: Princeton University Press, 1989).

Eadem
"Leonardo da Vinci: Female Portraits, Female Nature," in Mary Garrard and Norma Broude, *The Expanding Discourse: Feminism and Art History* (New York: Routledge, 1992) 58–86.

Garrard, Mary, and Norma Broude
The Expanding Discourse: Feminism and Art History (New York: Routledge, 1992).

Gaster, Moses
"Judith, The Book of," in T. K. Cheyne and J. Sutherland Black, eds., *Encyclopaedia Biblica* (New York: Macmillan, 1901) 3:2642–46.

Georgen, Helga Theresa
"Die Kopfjägerin Judith—Männerphantasie oder Emanzipationsmodell?," in Cordula Bischoff, Brigette Dinger, Irene Ewinkel, and Ulla Merle, eds., *Frauen, Kunst, Geschichte: Zur Korrektur des herrschenden Blicks* (Gießen: Anabas, 1984) 111–24.

Gera, Deborah Levine
"The Jewish Textual Traditions," in Kevin R. Brine, Elena Ciletti, and Henriki Lähnemann, eds., *The Sword of Judith: Judith Studies across the Disciplines* (Cambridge: OpenBook, 2010) 23–40.

Eadem
"Judah and Judith" [in Hebrew], in Joseph Geiger, Hannah M. Cotton, and Guy D. Stiebel, eds., *Israel's Land: Papers Presented to Israel Shatzman on His Jubilee* (Ra'anana, Israel: Open University, 2009) 29–38.

Eadem
"Judith," in Jonathan Klawans and Lawrence M. Wills, eds., *Jewish Annotated Apocrypha* (New York: Oxford University Press, forthcoming).

Eadem
"Shorter Medieval Hebrew Tales of Judith," in Kevin R. Brine, Elena Ciletti, and Henriki Lähnemann, eds., *The Sword of Judith: Judith Studies across the Disciplines* (Cambridge: OpenBook, 2010) 275–90.

Eadem
"Speech in Judith," in Melvin K. H. Peters, ed., *XIV Congress of the IOSCS, Helsinki, 2010* (SCS 59; Atlanta: Society of Biblical Literature, 2013) 413–23.

Eadem
Warrior Women: The Anonymous Tractatus de mulieribus (Mnemosyne Supplement 162; Leiden: Brill, 1997).

Eadem
    Xenophon's Cyropaedia: Style, Genre, and Literary Technique (Oxford Classical Monographs; Oxford: Clarendon, 1993).

Gershenson, Daniel E.
    "Baitomesthaim in the Book of Judith," *Henoch* 20 (1996) 51–55.

Gierlinger-Czerny, Elisabeth
    Judits Tat: Die Aufkündigung des Geschlechtervertrages (Vienna: Promedia, 2000).

Gil, Roger
    "Judith 5:5–21 ou le récit d'Achior: Les mémoires dan la construction de l'identité narrative du peuple d'Israël," *VT* 64 (2014) 573–87.

Gill, Christopher
    The Structured Self in Hellenistic and Roman Thought (Oxford: Oxford University Press, 2006).

Gillet, Gustave
    Tobie, Judith et Esther: Introduction critique (Paris: Lethielleux, 1879).

Glancy, Jennifer A.
    "The Mistress–Slave Dialectic: Paradoxes of Slavery in Three LXX Narratives," *JSOT* 72 (1996) 71–87.

Goldhill, Simon
    The Invention of Prose (Oxford: Oxford University Press, 2002).

Goodblatt, David
    "'The Israelites Who Reside in Judah' (Judith 4:1): On the Conflicted Identities of the Hasmonean State," in Lee I. Levine and Daniel R. Schwartz, eds., *Jewish Identities in Antiquity: Studies in Memory of Menahem Stern* (TSAJ 130; Tübingen: Mohr Siebeck, 2009) 74–89.

Graham, Helen R.
    "Hand of Yahweh, Hand of a Woman: A Study of Judith's Song of Victory (Jdt 16:1b-17)," *MST Review: A Journal of Theological and Cultural Studies* 5 (2003) 86–128.

Grassmann, Irina
    "Judit—Heldin, Dämonin oder jungfräulicher Marientyp?," *Religionspädagogische Beiträge* 43 (1999) 167–76.

Greenfield, Jonas C.
    "Nebuchadnezzar's Campaign in the Book of Judith" [in Hebrew], *Yediot* 28 (1964) 204–8.

Griffith, Mark, ed.
    Judith (Exeter Medieval English Texts and Studies; Exeter: University of Exeter Press, 1997).

Grintz, Jehoshua M.
    "Judith, Book of," *Encyclopedia Judaica* (16 vols.; New York: Macmillan, 1971–72) 10:451–59.

Idem
    "On the Source of the Basic Motif in the Book of Judith" [in Hebrew], *Malad* 17 (1959) 564–66.

Gros Louis, Delores
    "Narrative Art in the Book of Judith," in K. R. R. Gros Luis, ed., *Literary Interpretations of Biblical Narratives* (2 vols.; Nashville: Abingdon, 1974–82) 2:259–72.

Gruen, Erich
    Diaspora: Jews Amidst Greeks and Romans (Cambridge, MA: Harvard University Press, 2002).

Idem
    Heritage and Hellenism: The Reinvention of Jewish Tradition (HCS 30; Berkeley: University of California Press, 1998).

Guyot, Peter
    Eunuchen als Sklaven und Freigelassene in der griechisch-römischen Antike (Stuttgart: Klett-Cotta, 1980).

Haag, Ernst
    "Die besondere literarische Art des Buches Judith und seine theologische Bedeutung," *Trierer Theologische Zeitschrift* 71 (1962) 288–301.

Idem
    "Judit und Holofernes: Zur theologisch-ethischen Problematik in Jdt 10–11," in H.-G. Angel, ed., *Aus reichen Quellen leben: Ethische Fragen in Geschichte und Gegenwart; Helmut Weber zum 65. Geburtstag* (Trier: Paulinus-Verlag, 1995) 55–67.

Idem
    Studien zum Buche Judith: Seine theologische Bedeutung und literarische Eigenart (Triere theologische Studien 16; Trier: Paulinus-Verlag, 1963).

Idem
    "Der Widersacher Gottes nach dem Buch Judith," *Bibel und Kirche* 19 (1964) 38–42.

Hägg, Tomas
    The Novel in Antiquity (Berkeley: University of California Press, 1991).

Haider, Peter W.
    "Judith—Eine zeitgenössische Antwort auf Kleopatra III. als Beschützerin der Juden?," *Grazer Beiträge* 22 (1998) 117–28.

Hall, Edith
    Inventing the Barbarian: Greek Self-Definition through Tragedy (Oxford Classical Monographs; Oxford: Oxford University Press, 1989).

Hall, T. O., Jr.
    "Judith," in Watson E. Mills and Richard F. Wilson, eds., *Mercer Commentary on the Bible* (Macon, GA: Mercer University Press, 1995) 811–18.

Hammer-Tugendhat, Daniela
    "Judith und ihre Schwestern: Konstanz und Veränderung von Weiblichkeitsbildern," in Annette Kuhn and Bea Lundt, eds., *Lustgarten und Dämonenpein: Konzepte von Weiblichkeit in Mittelalter und früher Neuzeit* (Dortmund: Ebesbach, 1997) 343–85.

Harkins, Angela Kim
    "The Function of Prayers of Ritual Mourning in the Second Temple Period," in Mika S. Pajunen and Jeremy Penner, eds., *Functions of Psalms and Prayers in the Late Second Temple Period* (BZAW 486; Berlin: de Gruyter, 2017) 80–101.

Harris, Rendel
"A Quotation from Judith in the Pauline Epistles,"
ExpT 27 (1915–16) 13–15.

Haynes, Katharine
Fashioning the Feminine in the Greek Novel (London:
Routledge, 2003).

Hein, Jürgen
"Aktualisierungen des Judith-Stoffes von Hebbel
bis Brecht," *Hebbel Jahrbuch* 32 (1971–72) 63–92.

Hellmann, Monika
*Judit–eine Frau im Spanngsfeld von Autonomie und
göttlicher Führung: Studie über eine Frauengestalt des
Alten Testaments* (Frankfurt am Main: Lang, 1992).

Heltzer, Michael
"Akko-'Okiyá in the Book of Judith and the Ques-
tion of Its Original Language," in D. Barag, G.
Foerster, and A. Negev, eds., *Michael Avi-Yonah
Memorial Volume* (Jerusalem: Israel Exploration
Society/Hebrew University Institute of Archaeol-
ogy, 1987) 246–47.

Idem
"Eine neue Quelle zur Bestimmung der Abfassungszeit des Judithbuches," *ZAW* 92 (1980) 437.

Idem
"Μισθωτός im Buch Judith," in Michael Wisse-
mann, ed., *Roma Renascens: Beiträge zur Spätantike
und Rezeptionsgeschichte; Ilona Opelt von ihren Freun-
den und Shülern zum 9.7.1988 in Verehrung gewidmet*
(Franfurt am Main: Lang, 1998) 118–24.

Idem
"The Persepolis Documents: The Lindos Chronicles and the Book of Judith," *La Parola del Passato*
32 (1989) 81–101.

Hengel, Martin
*Judaism and Hellenism: Studies in Their Encounter in
Palestine during the Early Hellenistic Period* (Phila-
delphia: Fortress Press, 1974).

Henten, Jan Willem van
"Judith as an Alternative Leader: A Rereading of
Judith 7–13," in Athalya Brenner, ed., *A Feminist
Companion to Esther–Judith–Susanna* (Feminist
Companion to the Bible 7; Sheffield: Sheffield
Academic Press, 1995) 224–52.

Idem
"Judith as a Female Moses: Judith 7–13 in Light
of Exodus 17, Numbers 20, and Deuteronomy
33:8–11," in Fokkelien van Dijk-Hemmes and
Athalya Brenner, eds., *Reflections on Theology and
Gender* (Kampen: Kok Pharos, 1994) 33–48.

Herrmann, Wolfram
"Jüdische Selbstbehauptung: Anmerkungen zum
Buche Judit," in Herrmann, *Jüdische Glaubensfun-
damente* (Frankfurt am Main: Lang, 1994) 9–92.

Hicks, E. L.
"Judith and Holofernes," *Journal of Hellenic Studies*
6 (1885) 261–74.

Hilgenfeld, A.
"Die Bücher Judith und Tobit und Baruch und die
neue Ansicht von Hitzig und Volkmar über die

Apokryphen des Alten Testaments," *Zeitschrift für
wissenschaftliche Theologie* 4 (1861) 335–85.

Idem
"Volkmar's chronologische Entdeckungen über
die Apokalypse des Esra und das Buch Judith, die
Briefe des römischen Clemens und des Barnabas,
2: Die Entstehung des Buches Judith," *Zeitschrift
für wissenschaftliche Theologie* 1 (1858) 270–81.

Hobyane, Risimati
"Clashing Deities in the Book of Judith: A
Greimassian Perspective," *HvTSt* 71 (2015) 1–8.

Holzberg, Niklas
"Genre: Novels Proper and the Fringe," in Gareth
Schmeling, ed., *The Novel in the Ancient World* (rev.
ed.; Boston: Brill Academic, 2003) 11–28.

Hopkins, Keith
"Novel Evidence for Roman Slavery," *Past and
Present* 138 (1993) 3–27.

Hughes, H. Maldwyn
The Ethics of Jewish Apocryphal Literature (London:
R. Culley, 1910).

Ilan, Tal
Integrating Women into Second Temple History (TSAJ
76; Tübingen: Mohr Siebeck, 1999).

Eadem
*Jewish Women in Greco-Roman Palestine: An Inquiry
into Image and Status* (TSAJ 44; Tübingen: Mohr
Siebeck, 1995).

Eadem
*Silencing the Queen: The Literary Histories of
Shelamzion and Other Jewish Women* (TSAJ 115;
Tübingen: Mohr Siebeck, 2006).

Jacobson, Howard
*A Commentary on Pseudo-Philo's Liber antiquitatum
biblicarum: With Latin Text and English Translation*
(2 vols.; AGJU 31; Leiden: Brill, 1996).

Jacobus, Mary
"Judith, Holofernes, and the Phallic Woman," in
Mary Jacobus, *Reading Women: Essays in Feminist
Criticism* (New York: Columbia University Press,
1986) 110–36.

James, Montague R.
Judith (reprinted from Revised Version of the
Apocrypha; London: Haymarket Press, 1928).

Jansen, Andreas
"Das Gebet der Judith," *Theologie und Glaube* 2
(1910) 441–49.

Idem
"Der verschollene Verfasser des Buches Judith,"
Theologie und Glaube 4 (1912) 269–77.

Jansen, H. Ludin
"La composition du chant de Judith," *Acta Orientalia* 15 (1936) 63–71.

Jeffreys, Elizabeth, Michael Jeffreys, and Roger Scott
The Chronicle of John Malalas (Melbourne: Australian Association for Byzantine Studies, 1986).

Jellinek, Adolph
    Bet ha-Midrasch: Sammlung kleiner Midraschim und vermischter Abhandlungen aus der ältern jüdischen Literatur (3rd ed.; 2 vols.; Jerusalem: Wahrmann, 1967).

Jensen, Hans Jørgen Lundager
    "Family, Fertility and Foul Smell: Tobit and Judith," in Mark Bredin, ed., *Studies in the Book of Tobit: A Multidisciplinary Approach* (LSTS 55; London: T&T Clark, 2006).

Idem
    "Juditbogen," in Troels Engberg-Pedersen and Niels Peter Lemche, eds., *Tradition og nybrud. Jødedommen i hellenistik tid* (Forum for bibelsk eksegese 2; Copenhagen: Museum Tusculanum, 1990) 153–89.

Joannides, Paul
    "Titian's *Judith* and Its Context: The Iconography of Decapitation," *Apollo* 135, no. 361 (March 1992) 163–70.

Johnson, Norman Burrows
    Prayer in the Apocrypha and Pseudepigrapha: A Study of the Jewish Concept of God (JBLMS 2; Philadelphia: Society of Biblical Literature and Exegesis, 1948).

Johnson, Sara Raup
    Historical Fictions and Hellenistic Jewish Identity: Third Maccabees in Its Cultural Identity (HCS 43; Berkeley: University of California Press, 2004).

Eadem
    "Novelistic Elements in Esther: Persian or Hellenistic, Jewish or Greek?," *CBQ* 67 (2005) 571–89.

Joosten, Jan
    "The Original Language and Historical Milieu of the Book of Judith," in Moshe Bar-Asher and Emanuel Tov, eds., *Meghillot: Studies in the Dead Sea Scrolls V–VI: A Festschrift for Devorah Dimant* (Jerusalem: Bialik Institute; Haifa: University of Haifa, 2007) 159–76.

Jordaan, Pierre Johan
    "Reading Judith as Therapeutic Narrative," in Johann Cook, ed., *Septuagint and Reception: Essays Prepared for the Association for the Study of the Septuagint in South Africa* (VTSup 127; Leiden: Brill, 2009) 335–46.

Jouanno, Corinne
    "Novelistic Lives and Historical Biographies: The *Life of Aesop* and the *Alexander Romance* as Fringe Novels," in Grammatiki A. Karla, ed., *Fiction on the Fringe: Novelistic Writing in the Post-Classical Age* (Mnemosyne Supplement 310; Leiden: Brill, 2009) 33–48.

Joüon, Paul
    "Judith 16,15 (Vg. 18)," *Bib* 4 (1923) 112.

Kalmonofsky, Amy
    Dangerous Sisters of the Hebrew Bible (Minneapolis: Fortress, 2014).

Karla, Grammatiki A.
    Fiction on the Fringe: Novelistic Writing in the Post-Classical Age (Mnemosyne Supplement 310; Leiden: Brill, 2009).

Kehr, Wolfgang
    "Bilder von Judit und Salome," *Kunst und Unterricht* 117 (1987) 17–26.

Keil, C .F.
    "Das Buch Judith," in C. F. Keil, *Lehrbuch der historisch-kritischen Einleitung in die kanonischen und apokryphischen Schriften des Alten Testaments* (3rd ed.; Frankfurt am Main, 1873) 724–30.

Kim, Susan
    "Bloody Signs: Circumcision and Pregnancy in the Old English Judith," *Exemplaria* 11 (1999) 285–307.

Klawans, Jonathan
    Impurity and Sin in Ancient Judaism (Oxford: Oxford University Press, 2004).

Klawans, Jonathan, and Lawrence M. Wills, eds.
    Jewish Annotated Apocrypha (New York: Oxford University Press, forthcoming).

Klein, Gottlieb
    Über das Buch Judith (Leiden: Brill, 1893).

Knotts, Robert
    "Judith in Florentine Renaissance Art, 1425–1512" (Ph.D. diss., Ohio State University, 1995).

Kobelt-Groch, Marion
    "Ich bin Judith": Zur Rezeption eines mythischen Stoffes (Leipzig: Uni-Vlg, 2003).

Eadem
    Judith macht Geschichte: Zur Rezeption einer mythischen Gestalt vom 16. bis 19. Jahrhundert (Munich: Wilhelm Fink, 2005).

Koebner, Thomas
    "Zum Weiterleben des Judith-Typus in der Filmgeschichte," in J. Blänsdorf, ed., *Die femme fatale im Drama: Heroinen – Verführerinnen – Todesengel* (Tübingen: Francke, 1999) 141–58.

Konstan, David
    Sexual Symmetry: Love in the Ancient Novel and Related Genres (Princeton, NJ: Princeton University Press, 1994).

Idem
    "The *Testament of Abraham* and Greek Romance," in Ilaria Ramelli and Judith Perkins, eds., *Early Christian and Jewish Narrative: The Role of Religion in Shaping Narrative Forms* (WUNT 348; Tübingen: Mohr Siebeck, 2015) 45–51.

Koppelman, Kate
    "Fearing the Neighbor: The Intimate Other in *Beowulf* and the Old English *Judith*," *Comitatus* 35 (2004) 1–21.

Kosmin, Paul J.
    "Hellenistic Period," in Jonathan Klawans and Lawrence M. Wills, *Jewish Annotated Apocrypha* (New York: Oxford University Press, forthcoming).

Idem
    The Land of the Elephant Kings: Space, Territory, and Ideology in the Seleucid Empire (Cambridge, MA: Harvard University Press, 2014).

Kraus, Christina Shuttleworth, ed.
The Limits of Historiography: Genre and Narrative in Ancient Historical Texts (Mnemosyne Supplement 191; Leiden: Brill, 1999).

Kreuzer, H.
"Die Jungfrau in Waffen: Hebbels Judith und ihre Geschwister von Schiller bis Sartre," in Wolfgang Dorst and Christian W. Thomsen, eds., *Aufklärung über Literatur*, II: *Autoren und Texte* (Heidelberg: Winter, 1993) 92–111.

Kubiak, Joseph
"The Iconography of Judith in Italian Renaissance Art" (master's dissertation, University of Wisconsin, Madison, 1965).

Kugel, James L.
The Bible as It Was (Cambridge, MA: Belknap Press of Harvard University Press, 1997).

Kuhrt, Amélie
"Earth and Water," in Amélie Kuhrt and Heleen Sancisi-Weerdenburg, eds., *Method and Theory: Proceedings of the London 1985 Achaemenid History Workshop* (Achaemenid History 3; Leiden: Nederlands Instituut voor het Nabije Oosten, 1988).

Labourie, Guy
Judith, Espérance d'Israel: Une femme contre le totalitarisme (Paris: Centurion, 1991).

Lachs, Samuel T.
"Two Difficult Readings in the Book of Judith (1,11; 3,4)," *JQR* 74 (1984) 298–300.

LaCocque, André
The Feminine Unconventional: Four Subversive Figures in Israel's Tradition (OBT; Minneapolis: Fortress, 1990).

Lähnemann, Henrike
"The Cunning of Judith in Late Medieval German Texts," in Kevin R. Brine, Elena Ciletti, and Henriki Lähnemann, eds., *The Sword of Judith: Judith Studies across the Disciplines* (Cambridge: OpenBook, 2010) 275–90.

Idem
Hystoria Judith: Deutsche Judithdichtungen vom 12. bis zum 16. Jahrhundert (Berlin: de Gruyter, 2006).

Lambert, David
"Fasting as a Penitential Rite: A Biblical Phenomenon?," *HTR* 96 (2003) 477–512.

Idem
How Repentance Became Biblical: Judaism, Christianity, and the Interpretation of Scripture (Oxford: Oxford University Press, 2015).

Lamparter, Helmut
Das Buch Judith (Stuttgart: Calwer, 1972).

Lang, Judith
"'The Lord Who Crushes Wars': Studies on Judith 9:7, Judith 16:2, and Exodus 15:3," in Géza G. Xeravits, ed., *A Pious Seductress: Studies in the Book of Judith* (DCLS 14; Berlin: de Gruyter, 2012) 179–87.

Langdon, Stephen
Building Inscriptions of the Neo-Babylonian Empire, part 1 (Paris: Leroux, 1905).

Lange, Lydia
Die Juditfigur in der Vulgata: Eine theologische Studie zur lateinischen Bibel (DCLS 36; Berlin: de Gruyter, 2016).

Lange, Nicholas de
"Judith and Holofernes," in Nicholas de Lange, *Apocrypha: Jewish Literature of the Hellenistic Age* (New York: Viking, 1978).

Lapide, Cornelius A. S. J.
Commentarius in Esdram, Nehemiam, Tobiam, Judith, Esther et Machabaeos (Antwerp: Ioannem & Iacobum Meursios, 1645).

Lawrence, Jonathan D.
Washing in Water: Trajectories of Ritual Bathing in the Hebrew Bible and Second Temple Literature (Academia Biblica 23; Atlanta: Society of Biblical Literature, 2006).

Lefèvre, A.
"Judith, Livre de," in L. Pirot and A. Robert, eds., *Dictionnaire de la Bible: Supplément* (5 vols.; Paris: Letouzey et Ané, 1949) 4:1315–19.

Lefkovitz, Lori Hope
In Scripture: The First Stories of Jewish Sexual Identities (Lanham, MD: Rowman & Littlefield, 2010).

Lefkowitz, Mary R.
Women in Greek Myth (Baltimore: Johns Hopkins University Press, 1986).

Lehtipuu, Outi
"'Receive the Widow Judith, Example of Chastity': The Figure of Judith as a Model Christian in Patristic Interpretations," in Agnethe Siquans, ed., *Biblical Women in Patristic Reception/Biblische Frauen in patristischer Rezeption* (JAJSup 25; Göttingen: Vandenhoeck & Ruprecht, 2017) 186–218.

Lemos, T. M.
"'They Have Become Women': Judean Diaspora and Postcolonial Theories of Gender and Migration," in Saul M. Olyan, ed., *Social Theory and the Study of Israelite Religion: Essays in Retrospect and Prospect* (Resources for Biblical Study 71; Atlanta: Society of Biblical Literature, 2012) 81–109.

Levine, Amy-Jill
"Apocryphal Women: From Fiction to (Arti) Fact," in William G. Dever and Seymour Gitin, eds., *Symbiosis, Symbolism, and the Power of the Past: Canaan, Ancient Israel, and Their Neighbors from the Late Bronze Age through Roman Palaestina* (Winona Lake, IN: Eisenbrauns, 2003) 501–9.

Eadem
"Character Construction and Community Formation in the Book of Judith," in David Lull, ed., *Society of Biblical Literature Seminar Papers* 29 (Atlanta: Scholars Press, 1989) 561–69.

Eadem

"Sacrifice and Salvation: Otherness and Domestication in the Book of Judith, in Athalya Brenner,
ed., *A Feminist Companion to Esther–Judith–Susanna*
(Feminist Companion to the Bible 7; Sheffield:
Sheffield Academic Press, 1995) 208–33.

Levison, John R.

"Judith 16:14 and the Creation of Woman," *JBL*
114 (1995) 467–69.

Lewy, Julius

"Enthält Judith I–IV Trümmer einer Chronik zur
Geschichte Nebukadnezars und seiner Feldzüge
von 591 und 597?," *ZDMG* 81 (1927) lii–liv.

Ley, Klaus

"Typologie und Bewußtseinsgeschichte: 'La Judith
moderne' im historischen Roman bei Vigny,
Mérimée, Balzac, Hugo und Flaubert," in F. Link,
ed., *Paradeigmata: Literarische Typologie des Alten
Testaments*, vol. 1, *Von den Anfängen bis zum 19.
Jahrhundert* (Berlin: Duncker & Humblot, 1989)
393–409.

Licht, Jacob

"The Book of Judith, as a Work of Literature," in
M. Z. Kaddari, A. Saltman, and M. Schwarcz, eds.
Baruch Kurzweil Memorial Volume [in Hebrew] (Tel
Aviv: Shoken, 1975) 169–83.

Idem

*Testing in the Hebrew Scriptures and in Post-Biblical
Judaism* [in Hebrew] (Jerusalem: Hotsa'at Sefarim
'al Shem Y. L. Magnes, 1973).

Lightstone, Jack N.

*The Commerce of the Sacred: Mediation of the Divine
among Jews in the Greco-Roman World* (New York:
Columbia University Press, 2006).

Lindez, J. V.

"Sobre el género litarario del libro Judit," *Estudios
Bíblicos* 57 (1999) 759–75.

Lipsius, R. A.

"Jüdische Quellen zur Judithsage," *Zeitschrift für
wissenschaftliche Theologie* 10 (1867) 337–66.

Idem

"Ueber das Buch Judith und seinen neuesten
Dollmetscher," *Zeitschrift für wissenschaftliche
Theologie* 2 (1859) 39–121.

Llewellyn, Kathleen M.

"The Example of Judith in Early Modern French
Literature," in Kevin R. Brine, Elena Ciletti, and
Henriki Lähnemann, eds., *The Sword of Judith:
Judith Studies across the Disciplines* (Cambridge:
OpenBook, 2010) 213–25.

Eadem

Representing Judith in Early Modern French Literature
(Farnham, Surrey/Burlington, VT: Ashgate, 2014).

Llewellyn-Jones, Lloyd

"Eunuchs and the Royal Harem in Achaemenid
Persia (559–331 B.C.)," in Shaun Tougher, ed.,
Eunuchs in Antiquity and Beyond (London: Duck-
worth, 2002).

Llewellyn-Jones, Lloyd, and James Robson

Ctesias' History of Persia: Tales of the Orient (London:
Routledge, 2010).

Loader, William R. G.

*The Pseudepigrapha on Sexuality: Attitudes towards
Sexuality in Apocalypses, Testaments, Legends,
Wisdom, and Related Literature* (Attitudes towards
Sexuality in Judaism and Christianity in the
Hellenistic Greco-Roman Era; Grand Rapids:
Eerdmans, 2011).

Loretz, Oswld

"Roman und Kurzgeschichte in Israel," in Josef
Schreiner, ed., *Wort und Botschaft: Eine theologische und kritische Einführung in die Probleme des
Alten Testaments* (Würzberg: Echter-Verlag, 1967)
290–307.

Ludlow, Jared

*Abraham Meets Death: Narrative Humor in the Testa-
ment of Abraham* (JSPSup 41; London: Sheffield
Academic Press, 2002).

Idem

"Are Weeping and Falling Down Funny? Exaggerations in Ancient Novelistic Texts" (paper
presented at the Society of Biblical Literature
Annual Meeting, Baltimore, Maryland, November
25, 2013).

Magennis, Hugh

"Contrasting Narrative Emphases in the Old
English Poem *Judith* and Ælfric's Paraphrase of
the Book of Judith," *Neuphilologische Mitteilungen*
96 (1995) 61–66.

Marsh, David

"Judith in Baroque Oratorio," in Kevin R. Brine,
Elena Ciletti, and Henriki Lähnemann, eds., *The
Sword of Judith: Judith Studies across the Disciplines*
(Cambridge: OpenBook, 2010) 385–96.

Mastrangelo, Marc

"Typology and Agency in Prudentius's Treatment
of the Judith Story," in Kevin R. Brine, Elena
Ciletti, and Henriki Lähnemann, eds., *The Sword
of Judith: Judith Studies across the Disciplines* (Cambridge: OpenBook, 2010) 153–68.

Matthews, Shelly

*Perfect Martyr: The Stoning of Stephen and the
Construction of Christian Identity* (Oxford: Oxford
University Press, 2010).

McCarthy, Carmel, and William Riley

*The Old Testament Short Story: Explorations into
Narrative Spirituality* (Wilmington, DE: Michael
Glazier, 1986).

McDowell, Markus

*Prayers of Jewish Women: Studies of Patterns of Prayer
in the Second Temple Period* (WUNT 2/211; Tübingen: Mohr Siebeck, 2006).

McHam, Sarah Blake

"Donatello's *Judith* as the Emblem of God's
Chosen People," in Kevin R. Brine, Elena Ciletti,
and Henriki Lähnemann, eds., *The Sword of Judith:*

Judith Studies across the Disciplines (Cambridge: OpenBook, 2010) 275–90.

McKeon, Michael

The Origins of the English Novel, 1600–1740 (Baltimore: Johns Hopkins University Press, 1987).

McNeil, Brian

"Reflections on the Book of Judith," *Downside Review* 96 (1978) 199–207.

Mecky Zaragoza, Gabrijela

"Da befiel sie Furcht und Angst . . .": Judith im Drama des 19. Jahrhunderts (Munich: Iudicium, 2005).

Eadem

"Virgo und Virago," *Daphnis* 31 (2002) 107–26.

Mehlman, Bernard H., and Daniel F. Polish

"Ma'aseh Yehudit: A Chanukkah Midrash," *Journal of Reform Judaism* 26 (1979) 73–91.

Menchú, Rigoberta

"The Bible and Self-Defense: The Examples of Judith, Moses, and David," in Ursula King, ed., *Feminist Theology from the Third World: A Reader* (Maryknoll, NY: Orbis, 1994) 183–188.

Mendels, Doron

The Land of Israel as a Political Concept in Hasmonean Literature: Recourse to History in Second Century B.C. Claims to the Holy Land (TSAJ 15; Tübingen: Mohr, 1987).

Idem

The Rise and Fall of Jewish Nationalism (ABRL; New York: Doubleday, 1992).

Mensing, Roman

"Die biblischen Bücher Rut, Ester und Judit im Religionsunterricht," *Ein Arbeitsbericht* 39 (1996) 37–46.

Merideth, Betsy

"Desire and Danger: The Drama of Betrayal in Judges and Judith," in Mieke Bal, ed., *Anti-Covenant: Counter-Reading Women's Lives in the Hebrew Bible* (Sheffield: Almond Press, 1989) 63–78.

Metzger, Bruce M.

"Judith," in Bruce M. Metzger, *The Apocrypha of the Old Testament* (New York and Oxford: Oxford University Press, 1977) 76–95.

Meyer, Carl

"Utrum Judith laudanda an reprehenda sit?" *Verbum Domini* 3 (1923) 173–79.

Idem

"Zur Enstehungsgeschichte des Buches Judith," *Bib* 3 (1922) 193–203.

Miller, Athanasius

Die Bücher Tobias, Judith und Esther (3 vols. in 1; Die Heilige Schrift des Alten Testamentes 4.3; Bonn: P. Hanstein, 1940–41).

Idem

"Der Nabuchodonosor des Buches Judith," *Bib* 23 (1942) 95–100.

Miller, Geoffrey D.

"A Femme Fatale of Whom 'No One Spoke Ill':

Judith's Moral Muddle and Her Personification of Yahweh," *JSOT* 39 (2014) 223–45.

Milne, Pamela J.

"What Shall We Do with Judith? A Feminist Reassessment of a Biblical 'Heroine,'" *Semeia* 62 (1993) 37–58.

Misiak, Anna Maja

Judit: Gestalt ohne Grenzen (Bielefeld: Aisthesis, 2010).

Mittmann-Richert, Ulrike

Einführung zu den jüdischen Schriften aus hellenistisch-römischer Zeit: Historische und legendarishe Erzählungen (JSHRZ Supplement 6.1.1; Gütersloh: Gütersloher Verlagshaus, 2000) 82–96.

Mobley, Gregory

The Empty Men: The Heroic Tradition of Ancient Israel (ABRL; New York: Doubleday, 2005).

Idem

Samson and the Liminal Hero in the Ancient Near East (LHBOTS 453; New York: T&T Clark, 2006).

Moda, Aldo

"Libro di Giuditta," *Biblica et Orientalia* 32 (1990) 21–26.

Momigliano, Arnaldo

"Biblical Studies and Classical Studies: Simple Reflections about Historical Method," *BA* 45 (1982) 224–28.

Idem

"Eastern Elements in Post-Exilic Jewish, and Greek, Historiography," in *Essays in Ancient and Modern Historiography* (Middletown, CT: Wesleyan University Press, 1977) 25–35.

Montley, Patricia

"Judith in the Fine Arts: The Appeal of the Archetypal Androgyne," *Anima* 4 (1978) 37–42.

Moore, Carey A.

"Judith (Book of)," *ABD* 3:1117–25.

Idem

"Judith: The Case of the Pious Killer," *BR* 6 (1990) 26–36.

Morales, Helen

"The History of Sexuality," in Tim Whitmarsh, ed., *The Cambridge Companion to the Greek and Roman Novel* (Cambridge: Cambridge University Press, 2008) 39–55.

Eadem

Vision and Narrative in Achilles Tatius' Leucippe and Clitophon (Cambridge Classical Studies; Cambridge: Cambridge University Press, 2005).

Moraud, Yves

Judith ou l'impossible liberté (Paris: Minard, 1971).

Morgan, John R.

"The Representation of Philosophers in Greek Fiction," in John R. Morgan and Meriel Jones, eds., *Philosophical Presences in the Ancient Novel* (Ancient Narrative: Supplementum 10; Eelde: Barkhuis; Groningen: Groningen University Library, 2007) 23–52.

Morgan, John R., and Richard Stoneman, eds.
Greek Fiction: The Greek Novel in Context (London: Routledge, 1994).

Motté, Magda
Esthers Tränen, Judiths Tapferkeit: Biblische Frauen in der Literatur des 20. Jahrhunderts (Darmstadt: Wissenschaftliche Buchgesellschaft, 2003).

Müllner, Ilse
"Der Gott Israels verwandelt Schwäche in Stärke: Das Gebet der Judit in Kapitel 9," *Bibel Heute* 110 (1992) 128–31.

Eadem
"Mit den Waffen einer Frau? Stärke und Schönheit im Buch Judit," *Katechetische Blätter* 118 (1993) 399–406.

Musschoot, Anne Marie
Het Judith-thema in de Nederlandse letterkunde (Gent: Secretariaat van de Koninklijke Academie voor Nederlandse Taal en Letterkunde, 1972).

Nagy, Gregory
The Best of the Achaeans: Concepts of the Hero in Archaic Greek Poetry (Baltimore: Johns Hopkins University Press, 1979).

Narito, Zonia C.
"The Book of Judith," in Oo Chung Lee, Choi Man Ja, Sun Ai Lee-Park, Elli Kim, Mirza Rodriguez and Debra Goodsir, eds., *Women of Courage: Asian Women Reading the Bible* (Seoul, Korea: SaDang Publishing House, 1992) 53–62.

Nassichuk, John
"The Prayer of Judith in Two Late-Fifteenth-Century French Mystery Plays," in Kevin R. Brine, Elena Ciletti, and Henriki Lähnemann, eds., *The Sword of Judith: Judith Studies across the Disciplines* (Cambridge: OpenBook, 2010) 197–211.

Navarro Puerto, Mercedes
"Narraciones biblicas," in J. M. Sánchez Caro, ed., *Historia, narrativa, apocaliptica* (Estella: Verbo Divino, 2000) 379–478.

Eadem
"Reinterpreting the Past: Judith 5," in Núria Calduch-Benages and Jan Liesen, eds., *History and Identity: How Israel's Later Authors Viewed Its Earlier History* (Berlin and New York: de Gruyter, 2006) 115–39.

Navè Levinson, Pnina
"Judith und wir Juden," *Bibel Heute* 110 (1992) 124–25.

Nelson, Marie
Judith, Juliana, and Elene: Three Fighting Saints (New York: Peter Lang, 1991).

Neteler, Bernhard
Untersuchung der geschichtlichen und der kanonischen Geltung des Buches Judith (Münster: Theissing, 1866).

Newman, Judith H.
Praying by the Book: The Scripturalization of Prayer in Second Temple Judaism (EJL 14; Atlanta: Society of Biblical Literature, 1999).

Newsom, Carol A.
Daniel: A Commentary (OTL; Louisville: Westminster John Knox, 2014).

Nickelsburg, George W. E.
Jewish Literature between the Bible and the Mishnah: A Historical and Literary Introduction (2nd ed.; Philadelphia: Fortress Press, 2005).

Niditch, Susan
"Eroticism and Death in the Tale of Jael," in Peggy Day, ed., *Gender and Difference in Ancient Israel* (Minneapolis: Fortress Press, 1989) 43–57.

Nolte, S. Philip, and Pierre J. Jordaan
"Ideology and Intertextuality: Intertextual Allusions in Judith 16," *HvTSt* 67 (2011) 1–9.

Noorda, S. J.
Judit (Haarlem: Nederlands Bijbelgenootschap, 1998).

Nowell, Irene
"Judith: A Question of Power," *The Bible Today* 24 (1986) 12–17.

Nutu, Ela
"Framing Judith: Whose Text, Whose Gaze, Whose Language?," in Ela Nutu and J. Cheryl Exum, eds., *Between the Text and the Canvas: The Bible and Art in Dialogue* (Bible in the Modern World 13; Sheffield: Sheffield Phoenix, 2007) 117–44.

Oesterley, W. O. E.
The Books of the Apocrypha (New York: Ravel, 1914).

Idem
An Introduction to the Books of the Apocrypha (London: SPCK, 1935).

O'Kane, Martin, ed.
Borders, Boundaries and the Bible (JSOTSup 313; London: Sheffield Academic Press, 2002).

Olyan, Saul
Biblical Mourning: Ritual and Social Dimensions (Oxford: Oxford University Press, 2004).

Idem
"Is Isaiah 40–55 Really Monotheistic?," *JANES* 12 (2012) 199–201.

Idem, ed.
Ritual Violence in the Hebrew Bible: New Perspectives (Oxford: Oxford University Press, 2015).

Orlinsky, Harry M.
Essays in Biblical Culture and Biblical Translation (New York: Ktav, 1974).

Patterson, Dilys Naomi
"Re-membering the Past: The Purpose of Historical Discourse in the Book of Judith," in Patricia G. Kirkpatrick and Timothy D. Goltz, eds., *The Function of Ancient Historiography in Biblical and Cognate Studies* (New York: T&T Clark International, 2008) 111–23.

Perkins, Judith
The Suffering Self: Pain and Narrative Representation in the Early Christian Era (London: Routledge, 1995).

Perkins, Larry
"'The Lord Is a Warrior,' 'The Lord Who Crushes Wars,' Exodus 15:3 and Judith 9:7; 16:2," *BIOSCS* 40 (2007) 121–33.

Pervo, Richard I.
"Aseneth and Her Sisters: Women in Jewish Narrative and in the Greek Novels," in Amy-Jill Levine, ed., *"Women Like This:" New Perspectives on Jewish Women in the Greco-Roman World* (EJL 1; Atlanta: Scholars Press, 1991) 145–60.

Peters, Renate
"The Metamorphoses of Judith in Literature and Art: War by Other Means," in Aránzazu Usandizaga and Andrew Monnickendam, eds., *Dressing Up for War: Transformations of Gender and Genre in the Discourse and Literature of War* (New York: Rodopi, 2001).

Peus, Gabriele
Untersuchungen zum Stoff des Biblischen Buches "Judith" in der französischen Literatur (Münster: n.p., 1973).

Pfeiffer, Robert H.
History of the New Testament Times, with an Introduction to the Apocrypha (New York: Harper, 1949).

Philpot, Elizabeth
"Judith and Holofernes: Changing Images in the History of Art," in David Jaspar, ed., *Translating Religious Texts: Translation, Transgression, and Interpretation* (New York: St. Martin's Press, 1993) 80–97.

Eadem
Old Testament Apocryphal Images in European Art (Göteborg, Sweden: University of Gothenburg, 2009).

Poirier, Jacques
Judith: Echos d'un mythe biblique dans la littérature française (Rennes: Presses universitaires de Rennes, 2004).

Preuss, Samuel L.
From Shadow to Promise: Old Testament Interpretation from Augustine to the Young Luther (Cambridge, MA: Belknap Press of Harvard University Press, 1969).

Priebatsch, Hans J.
"Das Buch Judith und seine hellenistischen Quellen," *ZDPV* 90 (1974) 50–60.

Pringle, Ian
"Judith: The Homily and the Poem," *Traditio* 31 (1975) 83–97.

Prouser, Ora Horn
"The Truth about Women and Lying," *JSOT* 61 (1994) 15–28.

Purdie, Edna
The Story of Judith in German and English Literature (Paris: Librairie Ancienne Honore Champien, 1927).

Raboisson, Pierre A.
Judith: La véracité du livre de ce nom devant les documents cunéiformes et les histoires d'Hérodote (Rome: Polyglotte, 1898).

Radavich, David A.
"A Catalogue of Works Based on the Apocryphal Book of Judith, from the Medieval Period to the Present," *Bulletin of Bibliography* 44 (1987) 89–92.

Radin, Paul
The Trickster: A Study in American Indian Mythology (New York: Schocken, 1972).

Rakel, Claudia
"'I Will Sing a New Song to My God': Some Remarks on the Intertextuality of Judith 16.1–17," in Athalya Brenner, ed., *Judges: A Feminist Companion to the Bible* (Second Series; Sheffield: Sheffield Academic Press, 1999) 27–47.

Eadem
"Judith: About a Beauty Who Is Not What She Pretends to Be," in Louise Schottroff, ed., *Feminist Biblical Interpretation: A Compendium of Critical Commentary on the Books of the Bible and Related Literature* (Grand Rapids: Eerdmans, 2012) 515–30; originally published as "Das Buch Judit: Über eine Schönheit, die nicht ist, was sie zu sein vorgibt," in Louise Schottroff und Marie-Theres Wacker, eds., *Kompendium Feministischer Bibelauslegung* Gütersloh: Gütersloher Verlagshaus, 1998) 410–21.

Eadem
Judit–Über Schönheit, Macht, und Widerstand im Krieg: Eine feministisch-intertextuelle Lektüre (BZAW 334; Berlin: de Gruyter, 2003).

Eadem
"Männermordend und rettend: Bibelarbeit zu Judit," in G. Theuer, ed., *Frauenstärke* (Stuttgart: Katholisches Bibelwerk, 2001) 26–31.

Ramelli, Ilaria, and Judith Perkins, eds.
Early Christian and Jewish Narrative: The Role of Religion in Shaping Narrative Forms (WUNT 348; Tübingen: Mohr Siebeck, 2015).

Reardon, Bryan P.
"Chariton: *Chaereas and Callirhoe*," in Bryan P. Reardon, ed., *Collected Ancient Greek Novels* (Berkeley: University of California Press, 1989).

Idem, ed.
Collected Ancient Greek Novels (Berkeley: University of California Press, 1989).

Reinhartz, Adele
"Better Homes and Gardens: Women and Domestic Space in the Books of Judith and Susanna," in Stephen G. Wilson and Michel Desjardins, eds., *Text and Artifact in the Religions of Mediterranean Antiquity: Essays in Honour of Peter Richardson* (Studies in Christianity and Judaism 9; Waterloo, ON: Wilfrid Laurier University Press, 2000) 325–39.

Eadem
"Chaste Betrayals: Women and Men in the Apocryphal Novels," in Lynn LiDonnici and Andrea Lieber, ed., *Heavenly Tablets: Interpretation, Identity and Tradition in Ancient Judaism* (JSJSup 119; Leiden: Brill, 2007) 227–42.

Reiterer, Friedrich V.

"Meines Bruders Licht: Untersuchung zur Rolle des Achior," in Géza Xeravits, ed., *A Pious Seductress: Studies in the Book of Judith* (DCLS 14; Berlin: de Gruyter, 2012) 111–60.

Idem

"Religion und hellenistische Realpolitik im Buch Judit," in Friedrich V. Reiterer, Renate Egger-Wenzel, and Thomas R. Elßner, eds., *Gesellschaft und Religion in der spätbiblischen und deuterokanonischen Literatur* (DCLS 20; Berlin: de Gruyter, 2014) 29–54.

Renaud, Bernard

"Une femme juive dans le combat politique: Judith; Une figure historique ou réprésentation symbolique?," in Edmond Lévy, ed., *La Femme dans les sociétés antiques: Actes des colloques de Strasbourg mai 1980 et mars 1981* (Contributions et travaux de l'Institut d'histoire romaine 2; Strasbourg: AECR, 1983) 125–38.

Rizzante Gallazzi, Ana Maria

"La mujer sitiada: Lectura de Judit a partir de Dina," *Revista de interpretação biblica latino-americana* 15 (1993) 47–58.

Robertson, Paul

The Cyclops and the Self (forthcoming)

Rocca, Samuele

"The Book of Judith, Queen Sholomzion and King Tigranes of Armenia: A Sadducee Appraisal," *Materia Giudaica* 10 (2005) 85–98.

Roddy, Nicolae

"The Way It Wasn't: The Book of Judith as Anti-Hasmonean Propaganda," *Studia Hebraica* 8 (2008) 269–77.

Roitman, Adolfo D.

"Achior in the Book of Judith: His Role and Significance," in James C. VanderKam, ed., *"No One Spoke Ill of Her": Essays on Judith* (EJL 2; Atlanta: Scholars Press, 1992) 31–45.

Idem

"The Mystery of Arphaxad (Jdt 1): A New Proposal," *Henoch* 17 (1995) 301–10.

Idem

"'This People Are Descendants of Chaldeans' (Judith 5,6): Its Literary Form and Historical Setting," *JBL* 113 (1994) 245–63.

Idem

"The Traditions about Abraham's Early Life in the Book of Judith (5:6–9)," in Esther G. Chazon, David Satran, and Ruth A. Clements, eds., *Things Revealed: Studies in Early Jewish and Christian Literature in Honor of Michael E. Stone* (JSJSup 89; Leiden: Brill, 2004) 73–87.

Roitman, Adolfo D., and Amnon Shapira

"The Book of Judith as a 'Reflection Story' of the Book of Esther" [in Hebrew], *Beit Mikra* 49 (2004) 127–43.

Rollinger, Robert

"Altorientalisches im Buch Judith," in Mikko Luukko, Saana Svärd, and Raija Mattila, eds., *Of God(s), Trees, Kings, and Scholars: Neo-Assyrian and Related Studies in Honour of Simo Parpola* (Studia Orientalia 106; Helsinki: Finnish Oriental Society, 2009) 429–43.

Ruiz-Montero, Consuelo

"Rise of the Greek Novel," in Gareth Schmeling, ed., *The Novel in the Ancient World* (rev. ed.; Boston: Brill Academic, 2003) 29–85.

Russell, H. Diane

Eva/Ave: Women in Renaissance and Baroque Prints (Washington: National Gallery of Art, 1990).

Ryan, Stephen D.

"The Ancient Versions of Judith and the Place of the Septuagint in the Catholic Church," in Géza Xeravits, ed., *A Pious Seductress: Studies in the Book of Judith* (DCLS 14; Berlin: de Gruyter, 2012) 1–21.

Idem

"Judith's Deed of Hope and Hope in the Book of Judith" (unpublished paper) 10–11.

Safrai, Ze'ev

"The Land of Israel according to the Book of Judith" [in Hebrew], in Ze'ev Erlich, ed., *Samaria and Benjamin* (Ofra: Ha-Hevrah la-Haganat ha-Teva, 1987) 163–72.

Sandy, Gerald

"New Pages of Greek Fiction," in J. R. Morgan and Richard Stoneman, eds., *Greek Fiction: The Greek Novel in Context* (London: Routledge, 1994) 130–45.

Satlow, Michael

"'Try to be a Man': The Rabbinic Construction of Masculinity," *HTR* 89 (1996) 19–40.

Sawyer, Deborah F.

"Dressing Up/Dressing Down: Power, Performance, and Identity in the Book of Judith," *Theology and Sexuality* 8 (2001) 23–31.

Eadem

"Gender Strategies in Antiquity: Judith's Performance," *Feminist Theology* 28 (2001) 9–26.

Eadem

God, Gender and the Bible (Biblical Limits; London and New York: Routledge, 2002).

Schedl, Claus

"Nabuchodonosor, Arpaksad, und Darius," *ZDMG* 115 (1965) 242–54.

Schmeling, Gareth, ed.

The Novel in the Ancient World (rev. ed.; Boston: Brill Academic, 2003).

Schmitt, Carl

Politische Theologie: Vier Kapitel zur Lehre von der Souveränität (Munich: Duncker & Humblot, 1934).

Schmitz, Barbara

"'Achior aber glaubte aus ganzem Herzen an Gott' (Jdt 14,10): Der Ammoniter Achior im Buch Judit (3)," *Bibel und Liturgie* 78 (2005) 215–19.

Eadem

"Casting Judith: The Construction of Role Patterns in the Book of Judith," in Hermann Lichtenberger and Ulrike Mittmann-Richert, eds., *Biblical Figures in Deuterocanonical and Cognate Literature: International Conference of the ISDCL at Tübingen* (Deuterocanonical and Cognate Literature Yearbook 2008; Berlin: de Gruyter, 2009) 77–94.

Eadem

". . . Denn mit ihnen ist ein Gott, der das Unrecht hasst' (Jdt 5,17): Das Gottes-Porträt im Buch Judit (4)," *Bibel und Liturgie* 78 (2005) 263–66.

Eadem

"'Dir soll Deine ganze Schöpfung dienen': Schöpfungstheologie im Buch Judit," in Tobias Niklas and Korinna Zamfir, eds., *Theologies of Creation in Early Judaism and Ancient Christianity: In Honour of Hans Klein* (DCLS 6; Berlin and New York: de Gruyter, 2010) 51–60.

Eadem

"Durch die Hand einer Frau: Das Buch Judit," *Bibel Heute* 159 (2004) 4–7.

Eadem

"Freiheitsheldin oder *femme fatale?*," *Bibel Heute* 159 (2004) 22–23.

Eadem

"The Function of the Speeches and Prayers in the Books [*sic*] of Judith," in Athalya Brenner-Idan and Helen Efthimiadis-Keith, eds., *A Feminist Companion to Tobit and Judith* (Feminist Companion to the Bible [Second Series]; London: Bloomsbury T&T Clark, 2015) 164–74.

Eadem

Gedeutete Geschichte: Die Funktion der Reden und Gebete im Buch Judit (HBS 40; Freiburg im Breisgau: Herder, 2004).

Eadem

"Holofernes's Canopy in the Septuagint," in Kevin R. Brine, Elena Ciletti, and Henriki Lähnemann, eds., *The Sword of Judith: Judith Studies across the Disciplines* (Cambridge: OpenBook, 2010) 71–80.

Eadem

"'Hört mir zu!' (Jdt 8,11): Einleitendes zum Buch Judit (1)," *Bibel und Liturgie* 78 (2005) 37–42.

Eadem

"ΙΟΥΔΙΘ and *Iudith:* Überlegungen zum Verhältnis der Judit-Erzählung in der LXX und der Vulgata," in Johann Cook and Hermann-Josef Stipp, eds., *Text-Critical and Hermeneutical Studies in the Septuagint* (VTSup 157; Leiden: Brill, 2012) 359–79.

Eadem

"Die Juditfigur als Modell diakonischen Handelns," in Adelheid M. von Hauff, ed., *Frauen gestalten Diakonie,* vol. 1: *Von der biblischen Zeit bis zum Pietismus* (Stuttgart: Kohlhammer, 2007) 81–92.

Eadem

"Judith and Holofernes: An Analysis of the Emotions in the Killing Scene (Jdt 12:10–13:9)," in Stefan C. Reif and Renate Egger-Wenzel, eds., *Ancient Jewish Prayers and Emotions: Emotions Associated with Jewish Prayer in and around the Second Temple Period* (DCLS 26; Berlin: de Gruyter, 2015) 177–91.

Eadem

"Männlichkeit im Mückennetz: Gendering und Crossgendering der Holofernesfigur in der Juditerzählung," *Forschungsforum Bamberg 2003: Berichte aus der Otto-Friedrich-Universität* 11 (2003) 21–26.

Eadem

"Dem Rad in die Speichen fallen: Zivilcourage im Buch Judit," *Bibel Heute* 159 (2004) 14–16.

Eadem

"Trickster, Schriftgelehrte oder *femme fatale*? Die Juditfigur zwischen biblischer Erzählung und kunstgeschichtlicher Rezeption," *Biblisches Forum* 2004, www.bibfor.de (ISSN: 1437-9341).

Eadem

"Vor-Denken und Nach-Denken: Die Funktion der Reden und Gebete im Buch Judit," in Renate Egger-Wenzel and Jeremy Corley, eds., *Prayer from Tobit to Qumran: Inaugural Conference of the ISDCL at Salzburg, Austria, 5–9 July 2003* (Deuterocanonical and Cognate Literature Yearbook 2004; Berlin: de Gruyter, 2004) 221–29.

Eadem

"War, Violence and Tyrannicide in the Book of Judith," in Jan Lisen and Pancratius Beentjes, eds., *Visions of Peace and Tales of War* (Deuterocanonical and Cognate Literature Yearbook 2010; Berlin and New York: de Gruyter, 2010) 103–19.

Eadem

"'Wer kann dieses Volk verachten, das solche Frauen in seiner Mitte hat?' (Jdt 10,19): Judit – die Frau, die dem Buch seinen Namen gibt (2)," *Bibel und Liturgie* 78 (2005) 139–43.

Eadem

"Zwischen Achikar und Demaratos—die Bedeutung Achiors in der Juditerzählung," *BZ* 48 (2004) 19–38.

Schmitz, Barbara, and Lydia Lange

"Judith: Beautiful Wisdom Teacher or Pious Woman? Reflections on the Book of Judith," in Eileen Schuller and Marie-Theres Wacker, eds., *Early Jewish Writings* (Bible and Women 3.1; Atlanta: SBL Press, 2017) 29–48.

Schneider, Laurie

"Donatello and Caravaggio: The Iconography of Decapitation," *American Imago* 33 (1976) 76–101.

Scholz, Anton

Das Buch Judith – eine Prophetie (Würzburg and Vienna: Leo Woerl, 1885).

Schöpflin, Karin

"Judith on Stage: The Dramatic Career of a Biblical Heroine," in Géza Xeravits, ed., *A Pious Seductress: Studies in the Book of Judith* (DCLS 14; Berlin: de Gruyter, 2012) 198–213.

Schorch, Stefan

"Genderising Piety: The Prayers of Mordecai and Esther in Comparison," in Géza G. Xeravits and József Zsengellér, eds., *Deuterocanonical Additions of the Old Testament Books: Selected Studies* (DCLS 5; Berlin: de Gruyter, 2010) 30–42.

Schroer, Silvia

"Zerschlage ihren Stolz durch die Hand einer Frau!," *Bibel heute* 110 (1992) 126–27.

Schubert, K.

"Makkabäer- und Judithmotive in der jüdischen Buchmalerei," *Aachener Kunstblätter* 60 (1994) 230–37.

Schuller, Eileen M.

"Introduction to the Apocrypha," in Carol A. Newsom and Sharon H. Ringe, eds., *Women's Bible Commentary* (expanded ed.; Louisville: Westminster John Knox, 1998) 263–65.

Schürer, Emil

"Das Buch Judith," in Emil Schürer, *Geschichte des jüdischen Volkes im Zeitalter Jesu Christi* (3 vols.; Leipzig: Hinrichs, 1898) 3:167–74.

Schwartz, Seth

"Israel and the Nations Roundabout: 1 Maccabees and the Hasmonean Expansion," *JJS* 42 (1991) 16–38.

Scialabba, Daniela

"What Does the Noun *agnoēma* Mean in Judith 5:20?," in Wolfgang Kraus, Michaël van der Meer, and Martin Meiser, eds., *XV Congress of the International Organization for Septuagint and Cognate Studies* (SCS 64; Atlanta: SBL Press, 2016) 393–400.

Shapira, Amnon

"The City 'Bethulia' (Judith 4:6)—A Geographical Name or Literary Fiction?" [in Hebrew], *Studies of Judea and Samaria* 14 (2005) 67–76.

Sheaffer, Andrea M.

"Judith versus Goliath? Visualizing David as Archetype," *Arts* 25 (2014) 5–14.

Eadem

Envisioning the Book of Judith: How Art Illuminates Minor Characters (Bible in the Modern World; Sheffield: Sheffield Phoenix, 2014).

Shearman, John

"Cristofano Allori's Judith," *Burlington Magazine* 121 (1979) 2–10.

Sheldon, Rose Mary

"Spy Tales," *Bible Review* 19 (2003) 12–19, 41–42.

Shemesh, Yael

"The Stories of Women in a Man's World: The Books of Ruth, Esther, and Judith," in Susanne Scholz, ed., *Feminist Interpretation of the Hebrew Bible in Retrospect*, vol. 1, *Biblical Books* (Recent Research in Biblical Studies 5; Sheffield: Sheffield Phoenix, 2013) 248–67.

Eadem

"'Yet He Committed No Act of Sin with Me, to Defile and Shame Me' (Judith 13:16): The Narra-

tive of Judith as a Corrective to the Narrative of Yael and Sisera" [in Hebrew], *Shnaton: An Annual for Biblical and Ancient Near Eastern Studies* 16 (2006) 159–77.

Simkovich, Malka

"The Book of Judith: A Fantasy Alternative Narrative to 2 Maccabees" (unpublished paper, 2013).

Eadem

The Making of Jewish Universalism: From Exile to Alexandria (Lanham, MD: Lexington, 2017).

Siquans, Agnethe

"Die Macht der Rezeption: Eckpunkte der patristischen Juditinterpretation," in Irmtraud Fischer, ed., *Macht – Gewalt – Krieg im Alten Testament: Gesellschaftliche Problematik und das Problem ihrer Präsentation* (Basel: Herder, 2013) 171–97.

Skehan, Patrick W.

"The Hand of Judith," *CBQ* 25 (1963) 94–110.

Idem

"Why Leave Out Judith?," *CBQ* 24 (1962) 147–54.

Skemp, Vincent T. M.

"Learning by Example: *Exempla* in Jerome's Translations and Revisions of Biblical Books," *VC* 65 (2011) 257–84.

Idem

The Vulgate of Tobit Compared with Other Ancient Witnesses [SBLDS 180; Atlanta: Society of Biblical Literature, 2000).

Smith, Jonathan Z.

"The Domestication of Sacrifice," in Robert Hamerton-Kelly, ed., *Violent Origins: Walter Burkert, René Girard, and Jonathan Z. Smith on Ritual Killing and Cultural Formation* (Stanford, CA: Stanford University Press, 1987) 191–238.

Smither, Howard E.

A History of the Oratorio (4 vols.; Chapel Hill: University of North Carolina Press, 1977–2000).

Sölle, Dorothée, Joe H. Kirchberger, and Anne-Marie Schnieper-Müller, eds.

Great Women of the Bible in Art and Literature (Grand Rapids: Eerdmans, 1993).

Sommerfeld, Martin

Judith-Dramen des 16./17. Jahrhunderts nebst Luthers Vorrede zum Buch Judith (Berlin: Junker & Dünnhaupt, 1933).

Steinmann, Jean

Lecture de Judith (Paris: Gabalda, 1953).

Steinmetzer, Franz

Neue Untersuchung über die Geschichtlichkeit der Juditherzählung: Ein Beitrag zur Erklärung des Buches Judith (Leipzig: Rudolf Haupt, 1907).

Stemberger, Günther

"La festa di Hanukkah, il libro di *Giuditta* e *midrašim* connessi," in G. Busi, ed., *We-Zo't le-Angelo: Raccolta di studi giudaici in memoria di Angelo Vivian* (Bologna: Associazione Italiana per lo Studio del Giudaismo, 1993) 527–45.

Stephens, Susan A., and John J. Winkler
  Ancient Greek Novels: The Fragments; Introduction, Text, Translation, and Commentary (Princeton, NJ: Princeton University Press, 1995).

Stern, Hildegard
  Friedrich Hebbels "Judith" auf der deutschen Bühne (Berlin: Behr; Leipzig: Feddersen, 1927).

Stetkevych, Suzanne Pinckney
  The Mute Immortals Speak: Pre-Islamic Poetry and the Poetics of Ritual (Myth and Poetics; Ithaca, NY: Cornell University Press, 1993).

Steuernagel, Carl
  "Bethulia," *ZDPV* 66 (1943) 232–45.

Steyn, Gert J.
  "'Beautiful but Tough: A Comparison of LXX Esther, Judith and Susanna," *JSem* 17 (2008) 156–81.

Stiehl, Ruth, and Franz Altheim
  Die aramäische Sprache unter den Achaimeniden (Frankfurt am Main: Vittorio Klostermann, 1963).

Stocker, Margarita
  "Biblical Story and the Heroine," in Martin Warner, ed., *The Bible as Rhetoric: Studies in Biblical Persuasion and Credibility* (Warwick Studies in Philosophy and Literature; New York: Routledge, 1990) 81–102.

Eadem
  Judith: Sexual Warrior Women and Power in Western Culture (New Haven: Yale University Press, 1998).

Eadem
  "On the Frontier: Judith and Esther in the Myth of America," in Martin O'Kane, ed., *Borders, Boundaries and the Bible* (JSOTSup 313; Sheffield: Sheffield Academic Press, 2002) 229–53.

Stolte, Heinz
  "'Judith': Die Geburt der modernen Tragödie," in I. Koller-Andorf, ed., *Hebbel: Mensch und Dichter im Werk; Wegweiser zu neuem Humanismus* (Vienna: VWGÖ, 1987) 25–38.

Stoneman, Richard
  The Greek Alexander Romance (London: Penguin, 1991).

Stowe, Harriet Elisabeth Beecher
  Woman in Sacred History (New York: J. B. Ford, 1873).

Strait, Drew J.
  "The Wisdom of Solomon, Ruler Cults, and Paul's Polemic against Idols in the Areopagus Speech," *JBL* 106 (2017) 609–32.

Straten, Adelheid
  Das Judith-Thema in Deutschland im 16. Jahrhundert: Studien zur Ikonographie–Materielen und Beiträge (Munich: Minerva, 1983).

Stronk, Jan P.
  Ctesias' Persian History, part 1: *Introduction, Text, and Translation* (Düsseldorf: Wellem, 2010).

Stummer, Friedrich
  Geographie des Buches Judith (Bibelwissenschaftliche Reihe 3; Stuttgart: Katholisches Bibelwerk, 1947).

Swidler, Leonard
  Biblical Affirmations of Women (Philadelphia: Westminster, 1979).

Szarmach, Paul E.
  "Ælfric's *Judith,*" in Michael Fox and Manish Sharma, eds., *Old English Literature and the Old Testament* (Toronto: University of Toronto Press, 2012) 64–88.

Talbot, Michael
  The Sacred Vocal Music of Antonio Vivaldi (Florence: Olschki, 1995).

Tamber-Rosenau, Caryn
  "Biblical Bathing Beauties and the Manipulation of the Male Gaze: What Judith Can Tell Us about Bathsheba and Susanna," *Journal of Feminist Studies in Religion* 33 (2017) 55–72.

Tan, Nancy
  "Judith's Embodiment as a Reversal of the Unfaithful Wife of Yʜwʜ in Ezekiel 16," *JSP* 21 (2011) 21–35.

Tatum, James, ed.
  The Search for the Ancient Novel (Baltimore: Johns Hopkins University Press, 1994).

Thayer, Anne T.
  "Judith and Mary: Hélinand's Sermon for the Assumption," in Jacqueline Hamesse et al., eds., *Medieval Sermons and Society: Cloister, City, University; Proceedings of International Symposia at Kalamazoo and New York* (Textes et études du moyen âge 9; Louvain-la-Neuve: Fédération Internationale des Instituts d'études médiévales, 1998) 63–75.

Thiel, Inari
  "Judith: A Jewish Identity," *Lutheran Theological Journal* 31 (1997) 69–75.

Thiem, Annika
  "No Gendered Bodies without Queer Desires: Judith Butler and Biblical Gender Trouble," *Old Testament Essays* 20 (2007) 456–70.

Thiessen, Matthew
  "Aseneth's Eight-Day Transformation as Scriptural Justification for Conversion 1," *JSJ* 45 (2014) 229–49.

Idem
  "Protecting the Holy Race and Holy Space: Judith's Reenactment of the Slaughter of Shechem," *JAJ* 49 (2018) 165–88.

Thomas, Christine
  The Acts of Peter, Gospel Literature, and the Ancient Novel: Rewriting the Past (Oxford: Oxford University Press, 2003).

Thomas, Rosalind
  Herodotus in Context: Ethnography, Science, and the Art of Persuasion (Cambridge: Cambridge University Press, 2000).

Thompson, Stith
  Motif-Index of Folk-Literature (rev. and enl. ed.; 6 vols.; Bloomington: Indiana University Press, 1955–58).

Tilford, Nicole
"Judith and Her Interpreters," in Carol A. Newsom and Sharon H. Ringe, eds., *Women's Bible Commentary* (3rd. ed.; Philadelphia: Westminster John Knox, 2012) 391–95.

Tinagli, Paola
Women in Italian Renaissance Art: Gender, Representation, Identity (Manchester: Manchester University Press, 1997).

Tolley, Kim
"Xena, Warrior Princess, or Judith, Sexual Warrior? The Search for a Liberating Image of Women's Power in Popular Culture," *History of Education Quarterly* 39 (1999) 337–42.

Tomes, Roger
"Heroism in 1 and 2 Maccabees," *BibInt* 15 (2007) 171–99.

Torrey, Charles Cutler
Apocryphal Literature: A Brief Introduction (New Haven: Yale University Press, 1945).

Idem
"Judith, Book of," in *The Jewish Encyclopaedia* (12 vols.; New York: Funk & Wagnalls, 1901–6) 7.388–90.

Idem
"The Site of Bethulia," *JAOS* 20 (1899) 160–72.

Uppenkamp, Bettina
Judith und Holofernes in der italienischen Malerei des Barock (Berlin: Dietrich Reimer, 2004).

Vaccari, Alberto
"Note critiche ed esegetiche, Giuditta xvi:11," *Bib* 28 (1947) 401–4.

Van der Walt, Charl Pretorius
"The Prayers of Esther (LXX) and Judith against Their Social Backgrounds: Evidence of a Possible Common 'Grundschrift'?," *JSem* 17 (2008) 194–206.

VanderKam, James C., ed.
"No One Spoke Ill of Her": Essays on Judith (EJL 2; Atlanta: Scholars Press, 1992).

Venter, Pieter
"The Function of the Ammonite Achior in the Book of Judith," *HvTSt* 67(3) Art. #1101, 9 pages, http://dx.doi.org/10.4102/hts.v67i3.1101.

Vigouroux, Fulcran
"Judith," in *La Sainte Bible polyglotte: Les Paralipomènes; Esdras; Néhémie; Tobie; Judith; Esther; Job* (Paris: Roger et Chemoviz, 1902) 524–603.

Vílchez Líndez, José
"Sobre el género literario del libro de Judit," *Estudios bíblicos* 57 (1999) 769–75.

Voitila, Anssi
"Judith and Deuteronomistic Heritage," in Hanne von Weissenberg, Juha Pakkala, and Marko Marttila, eds., *Changes in Scripture: Rewriting and Interpreting Authoritative Traditions in the Second Temple Period* (BZAW 419; Berlin: de Gruyter, 2011) 369–88.

Volkmar, Gustav
"Die Composition des Buches Judith," *Theologische Quartalshrift* 16 (1857) 441–98.

Vollmer, Ulrike
"Auf Leinwand Gebannt: Judith im (Miss-)Verständnis von Malerei und Film," *BibInt* 14 (2006) 76–93.

Walbank, F. W.
"Speeches in Greek Historians," in F. W. Walbank, *Selected Papers: Studies in Greek and Roman History and Historiography* (Cambridge: Cambridge University Press, 1985) 242–61.

Walker, Warren S., and Ahmet E. Uysal
Tales Alive in Turkey (Cambridge, MA: Harvard University Press, 1966).

Warren, Meredith J. C.
My Flesh Is Meat Indeed: A Non-Sacramental Reading of John 6:51–58 (Minneapolis: Fortress Press, 2015).

Watanabe-O'Kelly, Helen
Beauty or Beast? The Woman Warrior in the German Imagination from the Renaissance to the Present (Oxford: Oxford University Press, 2010).

Eadem
"The Eroticization of Judith in Early Modern Art," in Mara R. Wade, ed., *Gender Matters: Discourses of Violence in Early Modern Literature and the Arts* (Internationale Forschungen zur allgemeinen und vergleichenden Literaturwissenschaft 169; Amsterdam and New York: Rodopi, 2014).

Eadem
"The Figure of Judith in Works by German Women Writers between 1895 and 1921," in Claire Bielby and Anna Richards, eds., *Women and Death 3: Women's Representations of Death in German Culture since 1950* (Rochester, NY: Camden House, 2010) 101–16.

Wegner, Judith Romney
Chattel or Person? The Status of Women in the Mishnah (Oxford: Oxford University Press, 1988).

Weimar, Peter
"Formen frühjüdischer Literatur," in Johann Maier and Joseph Schreiner, eds., *Literatur und Religion des Frühjudentums: Eine Einführung* (Würzburg: Echter Verlag; Gütersloh: Gerd Mohn, 1973) 123–62.

Weinberger, Leon J.
"Notes on the Translation of the Judith Legend for Chanuka," *Journal of Reform Judaism* 32 (1985) 44–48.

Weingarten, Susan
"Food, Sex, and Redemption in *Megillat Yehudit* (the Scroll of Judith)," in Kevin R. Brine, Elena Ciletti, and Henriki Lähnemann, eds., *The Sword of Judith: Judith Studies across the Disciplines* (Cambridge: OpenBook, 2010) 97–126.

Weitzman, Steven
"Literary Approaches," in Jonathan Klawans and Lawrence M. Wills, eds., *Jewish Annotated Apocry-*

pha (New York: Oxford University Press, forthcoming).

Idem

"Sensory Reform in Deuteronomy," in Steven Weitzman, David Brakke, and Michael Satlow, eds., *Religion and the Self in Antiquity* (Bloomington: Indiana University Press, 2005) 123–39.

Idem

Song and Story in Biblical Narrative: The History of a Literary Convention in Ancient Israel (Indiana Studies in Biblical Literature; Bloomington: Indiana University Press, 1997).

Idem

Surviving Sacrilege: Cultural Persistence in Jewish Antiquity (Cambridge, MA: Harvard University Press, 2005).

West, Stephanie

"Croesus' Second Reprieve and Other Tales of the Persian Court," *ClQ* n.s. 53 (2003) 416–37.

Weststeijn, Johan

"Wine, Women, and Revenge in Near Eastern Historiography: The Tales of Tomyris, Judith, Zenobia, and Jalila," *JNES* 75 (2016) 91–107.

Wetter, Anne-Mareike

"On Her Account:" Reconfiguring Israel in Ruth, Esther, and Judith (LHBOTS 623; London: Bloomsbury T&T Clark, 2015).

White, Sidnie Ann: see Sidnie White Crawford.

Whitmarsh, Tim, ed.

The Cambridge Companion to the Greek and Roman Novel (Cambridge: Cambridge University Press, 2008).

Wills, Lawrence M.

Ancient Jewish Novels: An Anthology from the Greco-Roman Period (New Milford, CT: Toby, 2007).

Idem

"Ascetic Theology before Asceticism? Jewish Narratives and the Decentering of the Self," *JAAR* 74 (2006) 902–25.

Idem

"The Death of the Hero and the Violent Death of Jesus," in Jonathan Klawans and David A. Bernat, eds., *Religion and Violence: The Biblical Heritage* (Recent Research in Biblical Studies 2; Sheffield: Sheffield Phoenix, 2007) 79–99.

Idem

"The Depiction of Slavery in the Ancient Novel," *Semeia* 81 (2000) 113–32.

Idem

"The Differentiation of History and Novel: Controlling the Past, Playing with the Past," in Ilaria Ramelli and Judith Perkins, eds., *Early Christian and Jewish Narrative: The Role of Religion in Shaping Narrative Forms* (WUNT 348; Tübingen: Mohr Siebeck, 2015) 13–30.

Idem

"The Form of the Sermon in Hellenistic Judaism and Early Christianity, *HTR* 77 (1984) 277–99.

Idem

"Greek Philosophical Discourse in the Book of Judith?," *JBL* 134 (2015) 753–73.

Idem

"Jew, Judean, Judaism in the Ancient Period: An Alternative Argument," *JAJ* 7 (2016) 169–93.

Idem

The Jew in the Court of the Foreign King: Ancient Jewish Court Legends (Minneapolis: Augsburg Fortress, 1990).

Idem

The Jewish Novel in the Ancient World (Myth and Poetics; Ithaca, NY: Cornell University Press, 1995).

Idem

"The Jewish Novellas," in J. R. Morgan and Richard Stoneman, eds., *Greek Fiction: The Greek Novel in Context* (London and New York: Routledge, 1994) 223–38.

Idem

Not God's People: Insiders and Outsiders in the Biblical World (Religion in the Modern World; Lanham, MD: Rowman & Littlefield, 2008).

Idem

"Jewish Novellas in a Greek and Roman Age: Fiction and Identity," *JSJ* 42 (2011) 141–65.

Idem

The Quest of the Historical Gospel: Mark, John, and the Origins of the Gospel Genre (London: Routledge, 1997).

Wilson, Brittany E.

"Pugnacious Precursors and the Bearer of Peace: Jael, Judith, and Mary in Luke 1:42," *CBQ* 68 (2006) 436–56.

Winckler, Hugo

"Zum Buch Judith," in *Altorientalische Forschungen* (3 vols.; Leipzig: Eduard Pfeiffer, 1893–1905) 2:266–67.

Wojcik, Jan

"The Recovery of Gender," in Raymond-Jean Frontain and Jan Wojcik, eds., *Old Testament Women in Western Literature* (Conway, AR: University of Central Arkansas Press, 1991) 283–90.

Wright, Benjamin G., III

"Hellenization and Jewish Identity in the Deuterocanonical Literature," in Géza G. Xeravits, József Zsengellér, and Xavér Szabó, eds., *Canonicity, Setting, Wisdom in the Deuterocanonicals: Papers of the Jubilee Meeting of the International Conference on the Deuterocanonical Books* (DCLS 22; Berlin: de Gruyter, 2014) 29–68.

Wright, Benjamin G., and Suzanne M. Edwards

"'She Undid Him with the Beauty of Her Face' (Jdt 16.6): Reading Women's Bodies in Early Jewish Literature," in Géza G. Xeravits, ed., *Religion and Female Body in Ancient Judaism and Its Environments* (DCLS 28; Berlin: de Gruyter, 2015) 73–108.

Wright, David P.
Disposal of Impurity: Elimination Rites in the Bible and in Hittite and Mesopotamian Literature (SBLDS 101; Atlanta: Society of Biblical Literature, 1996).

Wright, G. R. H.
"The Head Huntress of the Highlands," in Tomis Kapitan, ed., *Archaeology, History and Culture in Palestine and the Near East: Essays in Memory of Albert E. Glock* (ASOR Books 3; Atlanta: Scholars Press, 1999) 203–34.

Xeravits, Géza, ed.
A Pious Seductress: Studies in the Book of Judith (DCLS 14; Berlin: de Gruyter, 2012).

Idem, ed.
Religion and Female Body in Ancient Judaism and Its Environments (DCLS 28; Berlin: de Gruyter, 2015).

Xeravits, Géza G., and József Zsengellér, eds.
Deuterocanonical Additions of the Old Testament Books: Selected Studies (DCLS 5; Berlin: de Gruyter, 2010).

Yee, Gale A.
"'By the Hand of a Woman': The Biblical Metaphor of the Woman Warrior," *Semeia* 61 (1993) 99–132.

Zeitlin, Solomon
"Jewish Apocryphal Literature," *JQR* 40 (1949–1950) 223–50.

Zenger, Erich
"Judith/Judithbuch," in *TRE* 17:404–8.

Idem
"Der Juditroman als Traditionsmodell des Jahweglaubens," *TTZ* 83 (1974) 65–80.

Idem
"'Wir erkennen keinen anderen Gott an . . . .' (Jdt 8,20): Programm und Relevanz des Buches Judit," *Religionsunterricht an höheren Schulen* 39 (1996) 17–36.

Zertal, Adam
"The Reality of the Book of Judith," *Eretz-Israel* 29 (2009) 161–75.

Zimmermann, Frank
"Aids for the Recovery of the Hebrew Original of Judith," *JBL* 57 (1938) 67–74.

Zocchi, Anita Christina
"Eine schöpferische Auseinandersetzung mit dem Buche Judit," *Dielheimer Blätter zum Alten Testament* 28 (1992–1993) 172–85.

Zorell, F.
"Canticum Judith, Vg 16, 1–2," *Verbum Domini* 5 (1925) 329–32.

Zsengellér, József
"A Bible's Digest—The Book of Judith as a Hermeneutical Composition," in Renate Egger-Wenzel, Karin Schöpflin, and Johannes Friedrich Diehl, eds., *Weisheit als Lebensgrundlage: Festschrift für Friedrich V. Reiterer zum 65. Geburtstag* (DCLS 15; Berlin: de Gruyter, 2013) 451–86.

Idem
"Judith as a Female David," in Géza G. Xeravits, ed., *Religion and Female Body in Ancient Judaism and Its Environment* (DCLS 28; Berlin: de Gruyter, 2015) 186–211.

477

In the design of the visual aspects of *Hermeneia*, consideration has been given to relating the form to the content by symbolic means.

The letters of the logotype *Hermeneia* are a fusion of forms alluding simultaneously to Hebrew (dotted vowel markings) and Greek (geometric round shapes) letter forms. In their modern treatment they remind us of the electronic age as well, the vantage point from which this investigation of the past begins. The Lion of Judah used as visual identification for the series is based on the Seal of Shema. The version for *Hermeneia* is again a fusion of Hebrew calligraphic forms, especially the legs of the lion, and Greek elements characterized by the geometric. In the sequence of arcs, which can be understood as scroll-like images, the first is the lion's mouth. It is reasserted and accelerated in the whorl and returns in the aggressively arched tail: tradition is passed from one age to the next, rediscovered and re-formed.

"Who is worthy to open the scroll and break its seals. . . ."
Then one of the elders said to me
"weep not; lo, the Lion of the tribe of David,
the Root of David, has conquered,
so that he can open the scroll and its seven seals."
Rev. 5:2, 5

To celebrate the signal achievement in biblical scholarship which *Hermeneia* represents, the entire series will by its color constitute a signal on the theologian's bookshelf: the Old Testament will be bound in yellow and the New Testament in red, traceable to a commonly used color coding for synagogue and church in medieval painting; in pure color terms, varying degrees of intensity of the warm segment of the color spectrum. The colors interpenetrate when the binding color for the Old Testament is used to imprint volumes from the New and vice versa.

Wherever possible, a photograph of the oldest extant manuscript, or a historically significant document pertaining to the biblical sources, will be displayed on the end papers of each volume to give a feel for the tangible reality and beauty of the source material.

The title-page motifs are expressive derivations from the *Hermeneia* logotype, repeated seven times to form a matrix and debossed on the cover of each volume. These sifted-out elements will be seen to be in their exact positions within the parent matrix.

Horizontal markings at gradated levels on the spine will assist in grouping the volumes according to these conventional categories.

The type has been set with unjustified right margins so as to preserve the internal consistency of word spacing. This is a major factor in both legibility and aesthetic quality; the resultant uneven line endings are only slight impairments to legibility by comparison. In this respect the type resembles the handwritten manuscripts where the quality of the calligraphic writing is dependent on establishing and holding to integral spacing patterns.

All of the typefaces in common use today have been designed between AD 1500 and the present. For the biblical text a face was chosen which does not arbitrarily date the text, but rather one which is uncompromisingly modern and unembellished so that its feel is of the universal. The type style is Univers 65 by Adrian Frutiger.

The expository texts and footnotes are set in Baskerville, chosen for its compatibility with the many brief Greek and Hebrew insertions. The double-column format and the shorter line length facilitate speed reading and the wide margins to the left of footnotes provide for the scholar's own notations.

Kenneth Hiebert

Category of biblical writing,
key symbolic characteristic,
and volumes so identified.

1
Law
(boundaries described)
  Genesis
  Exodus
  Leviticus
  Numbers
  Deuteronomy

2
History
(trek through time and space)
  Joshua
  Judges
  Ruth
  1 Samuel
  2 Samuel
  1 Kings
  2 Kings
  1 Chronicles
  2 Chronicles
  Ezra
  Nehemiah
  Esther

3
Poetry
(lyric emotional expression)
  Job
  Psalms
  Proverbs
  Ecclesiastes
  Song of Songs

4
Prophets
(inspired seers)
  Isaiah
  Jeremiah
  Lamentations
  Ezekiel
  Daniel
  Hosea
  Joel
  Amos
  Obadiah
  Jonah
  Micah
  Nahum
  Habakkuk
  Zephaniah
  Haggai
  Zechariah
  Malachi

5
New Testament Narrative
(focus on One)
  Matthew
  Mark
  Luke
  John
  Acts

6
Epistles
(directed instruction)
  Romans
  1 Corinthians
  2 Corinthians
  Galatians
  Ephesians
  Philippians
  Colossians
  1 Thessalonians
  2 Thessalonians
  1 Timothy
  2 Timothy
  Titus
  Philemon
  Hebrews
  James
  1 Peter
  2 Peter
  1 John
  2 John
  3 John
  Jude

7
Apocalypse
(vision of the future)
  Revelation

8
Extracanonical Writings
(peripheral records)